A Manual of
European Languages
for Librarians

A Manual of
European Languages
for Librarians

C. G. ALLEN
Formerly Superintendent of Readers' Services
British Library of Political and Economic Science

BOWKER
LONDON & NEW YORK
in association with the London School of Economics

Catalog Room A

✓

Published in the United Kingdom by the Bowker
Publishing Company, and in the United States of
America by R. R. Bowker Inc., New York

Set by Santype International Limited,
Salisbury, and printed in Great Britain
by Robert MacLehose & Co. Ltd., Glasgow

PREFACE

I have seen prefaces that are simply entitled 'Thanks', and so could this one be. Thus I owe a good deal to the interest and encouragement of friends and colleagues, and have been overwhelmed at times by the generosity of busy experts; but I shall shelter behind the example of Dr Johnson and not mention them by name, for I too 'would be loath to leave any out in the enumeration'.

Among institutions first place is due to the London School of Economics and the British Library of Political and Economic Science. It was the multilingual collections in the library and the problems connected with them that first suggested the idea of the book, two periods of sabbatical leave enabled it to be begun—and finished, and the imprint testifies to the School's continued interest. During my absences I was a nuisance to other libraries, which often gave more than I asked for, producing specialist typists as well as specialised books and expert advice and criticism: the libraries of the School of Slavonic and East European Studies and of the School of Oriental and African Studies; the Scandinavian and Celtic library at University College London; the University of London Library; the Burrows Library, University of London King's College; the British Library; the Metropolitan Special Collection on languages at the Central Reference Library, Kensington; the Royal Library in Malta.

Nor is it to libraries alone that I am indebted. The British Council through its representatives in Toulouse and Malta provided valuable contacts and arranged supplies of periodicals, the secretary of the Musée Basque and the editor of *Anaitasuna* not only supplied copies of periodicals but answered detailed questions about the language, the Basque delegation in London supplied expert critics, and the British Broadcasting Corporation (Overseas Broadcasts) gave a variety of help, especially in connexion with Maltese. To all these I am grateful, but they must not be blamed for my shortcomings.

Finally, to return to individuals, much of the donkey work in connexion with the glossaries, most of the indexing and a good deal of the typing were ably carried out by my son Peter.

CONTENTS

ARRANGEMENT OF SECTIONS

Unless otherwise stated, this applies to all languages. The headings given here are generalised and do not agree in detail with those used in some chapters. Where no details are given, further subdivision, if any, varies from language to language.

The scheme does not apply to subsections 1–6 of the Turkish verb or at all to the Basque verb.

ABBREVIATIONS AND SYMBOLS

A	accusative; see also below
Ab	ablative
B	broad (Irish); the third root consonant (Maltese)
BM	(Department of Printed Books), British Museum, now British Library
BS	British Standard
C	common gender; comparative; complement; any consonant; and see below
D	Danish (Norwegian); dative; demotic (Modern Greek); and see below
F	feminine
G	Geg (Albanian); genitive; gerund; Guipuzcoan (Basque)
I	indirect; infinitive; instrumental; see also below
Il	illative (Estonian)
ISO	International Standards Organization
K	kathareuousa (Modern Greek); the first root consonant (Maltese)
L	Labourdin (Basque); locative; the fourth consonant of a quadriliteral root (Maltese)
LC	Library of Congress
M	masculine
N	neuter; nominative
O	object (O_d direct, O_i indirect); see also below
P	participle; partitive; person; plural; pluraliser (Basque); present
R	reflexive
S	singular; slender (Irish); strong stem (Estonian, Finnish); superlative
SVOC	subject, verb, object, complement
T	Tosk (Albanian); the second root consonant (Maltese)
U	see below
V	verb; any vowel
W	weak stem (Estonian, Finnish)

A, C, D, I, O, U: In Finnish, Hungarian and Turkish the vowel of an ending may vary in accordance with vowel harmony; in Turkish the initial consonant of an ending may vary according to what it follows. These variable sounds are represented by capital letters, details being given under the language concerned at 2.5 for consonants and 2.6 for vowels.

The abbreviations for languages are usually the first two letters of the vernacular name given in the table of contents. If not, the abbreviation follows. (The names of the languages are sometimes different from the corresponding adjectives, e.g. Euskara, *Basque*, adjective **Euskal**.)

*   soft mutation (Irish, Welsh); palatalisation (Slavonic and Baltic languages); postulated form

†   spirant mutation (Welsh)

§   nasal mutation (Welsh); eclipsis (Irish)

>   produces, becomes

<   results from

[ ]   encloses phonetic representations in the International Phonetic Alphabet

/ /   encloses phonemes

GENERALISED RULES FOR WORD-DIVISION

1. Compounds are divided according to sense, e.g. loop-hole.

2. Prefixes are kept intact, provided they are recognised as such, e.g. trans-act, com-plex; but not necessarily per-use.

3. Suffixes are kept intact, e.g. keep-ing.

4. A consonant between two vowels is taken over to the following syllable, e.g. ta-ken.

5. Of two consonants:
   (a) the second is taken over, e.g. es-cape, en-ter;
   (b) both are taken over if they may begin a word, e.g. e-scape; otherwise the second, e.g. en-ter.

6. Of three or more consonants:
   (a) the last is taken over, e.g. nost-rum;
   (b) as many are taken over, after the first, as may begin a word, e.g. nos-trum;
   (c) as many are taken over as may begin a word, e.g. no-strum, mon-ster;
   (d) any number may be taken over, provided they may begin a word, e.g. no-strum, nos-trum or nost-rum.

7. (a) A division may be made between vowels provided they do not form a single sound, diphthong or triphthong, e.g. na-ïve but not fa-ilure.
   (b) All division between vowels is avoided.

8. A single letter may not stand (a) at the beginning or (b) at the end of a line.

INTRODUCTION

SCOPE

It is doubtless a mark of prudence not to attempt either to order or to catalogue books in languages with which one is not thoroughly familiar, and to refuse to answer any enquiries concerning them. A critical study, in the company of the appropriate experts, of international bibliographies or the catalogues of wide-ranging libraries would convince the doubtful that any other course is certain to lead to the perpetration of those linguistic howlers whose existence is of no practical importance, but whose belated discovery is a source of unreasonable mortification. But there must be many libraries where such prudence is out of the question: even without the necessary expert knowledge one must accept and deal with the books for the sake of completeness, and risk the errors. It is with the hope of minimising these errors and making the adventure somewhat less hazardous that this manual is written.

TYPES OF LANGUAGE

There are many ways of classifying languages; but for one who is trying to puzzle out a passage in a language that he does not know, two distinctions are of practical importance. The first concerns the degree of inflexion. Most English verbs, for instance, have four different forms (*love*, *loves*, *loving*, *loved*), one in the dictionary and three others whose exact meaning depends on the ending: at the other extreme a Basque verb has hundreds, and what are parts of the verb in Basque will be separate words in languages like English. Similarly with nouns, whose relations can be indicated either by prepositions or by endings. Some languages by the use of endings can dispense with conjunctions also. If you wish to make out the sense of a passage in a language of the English type, you can usually look up the words in the dictionary first and then see what more you need to know; but if the language is highly inflected, you may not know what to look for until you have sorted out the endings. Languages of the English type will be described as analytical, those of the opposite type as synthetic, while for those in between the degree and nature of the mixture will be indicated so far as is practicable. (Linguists should note that the treatment is deliberately naïve. A word is a word.)

ORDER OF WORDS

The second matter of practical importance is the order of words. In some languages qualifying words and phrases precede the words they qualify, in others they follow; in most some do one and some the other. Thus in French and other Romance languages adjectives, prepositional phrases, adverbs and noun objects generally follow the noun or verb that they limit, e.g.

1

La Direction[1.1] / du Dépôt[1.1.1] / des Imprimés et des Estampes / du Ministère[1.1.1.1] / de l'Éducation[1.1.1.1.1] /
a entrepris[2.1] / la préparation[2.1.1] / de la Bibliographie / de la Turquie[2.1.1.1] / depuis[2.2] / l'an[2.2.1] / 1934[2.2.1.1] /;
but in the original Turkish 1934[2.2.1.1] / yılından[2.2.1] / beri[2.2] / Türkiye[2.1.1.1] / Bibliyografyasının[2.1.1]
hazırlanması[2.1] / Maarif[1.1.1.1.1] / Vekâleti[1.1.1.1] / Basma Yazı ve Resimleri[1.1.1] / Derleme[1.1] / Müdürlüğüne[1.1] /
ait idi[2]

almost in reverse order. The figures indicate the equivalent expressions and the stage of qualification: 1.1 qualifies 1; 1.1.1 qualifies 1.1 and so on. (It will be noted also that there is no word in Turkish corresponding to the **de** of the French; the idea is expressed, appropriately enough, by endings.) Much the same holds of Finnish and Hungarian. In many respects English resembles the Romance languages, and the translation of languages like Turkish is best begun at the end; but where clusters of nouns are permissible, e.g. *University College Physics Laboratory*, the English order agrees with the Turkish. The characteristic order of the various parts of speech or of the sentence is briefly indicated hereafter by such phrases and symbols as: Qualifiers precede, Adjectives follow, SVO (i.e. subject, verb, object) and so on.

LAY-OUT

The articles on individual languages have the following pattern: a specimen passage followed by general remarks on the language; a detailed analysis of the use of the language on title-pages, dealing systematically with authors' names, the form of titles, numeration, the indication of editions, with imprints, series and periodicals, and with the various grammatical points, traps and snags which occur in connexion with all these; a short systematic grammar, designed to help in manipulating title-pages and understanding prefaces; a glossary and indexes of words and endings. Some notes on older forms and spellings are given, though not for all languages; but the number of books in less known languages that will be acquired by any but specialists is few. In any case, sufficient unto the day .... There are three short excursuses on topics common to several languages. The lay-out, basically the same for all languages, is set out on page ix.

METHOD OF USE

I realise that this treatment will not provide easy answers, but easy answers are often half-truths and are only made possible by severely limiting the number of problems dealt with. Two ways of using the manual are possible: to read the section dealing with the part of the book in question—statement of authorship, imprint, etc.— and follow up the references to the grammar; or to consult the index of endings. As one may not know where the ending begins, they are indexed from the end backwards (-a, -aa . . . -taa . . . -ba . . . -da . . . -nda . . . -za, -b, etc.), so that all the possibilities are present at one glance. Having found the appropriate paragraph, one should read all that is said about the form in question. Thus on a Latin title-page one may meet **digessit**. The only endings that fit are **-t** (8.2.1, 8.5.1, 8.7.1) and **-it** (8.4.1): 8.2.1 presupposes **digesso**, which does not exist, and 8.5.1 and 8.7.1 turn out to be irrelevant. By 8.4.1 **digessit** is perfect tense, but one must read 8.4.2 to see that the -s- is part of the perfect stem and has ousted the **-r-** of the dictionary form **digero**, *I edit*. Similarly with internal changes such as **redegit** from **redigo**. Such changes are mentioned wherever they occur, with a reference to the general treatment in 2.5 and 2.6; and so with other languages.

THE NOTION OF CASE

In dealing with nouns the notion of case, in the sense of the systematic modification of form to indicate the function of the noun in the sentence, has been introduced wherever convenient; but the invariable suffixes sometimes called cases in Finnish, Estonian and Hungarian have been excluded. The cases regularly used are:

> nominative: the case of the subject
> accusative: the case of the object
> genitive: that of the possessor or source (*of*)
> partitive: that of the whole of which something is part
> dative: that of the recipient (*to, for*)
> ablative: that of removal (*from*)
> instrumental: that of means or accompaniment (*with*)
> locative: that of place where (*in, at, on*)

The vocative, which rarely occurs in titles and has usually the same form as the nominative, has been ignored.

The labels attached to these cases, and particularly the equivalent English prepositions, are intended as identifications rather than definitions. Cases have a wide variety of uses, and as no modern language possesses all of them, the allocation of these uses among the remaining cases differs from language to language. The particular uses of the cases will accordingly be dealt with very summarily under the language in question.

LIMITATIONS

It must also be clearly understood that the purpose of the grammatical notes is a limited one. It is assumed, for instance, that readers will often need to know the nominative of a noun, given the genitive, but not vice versa, and the tables are grouped accordingly. Others besides librarians may find the grammatical sections useful, but they should use them with due caution.

The book makes no pretence to absolute uniformity of treatment, but it is hoped there are no serious inconsistencies in the text. Those in the examples (cf. German 1.3.3) are inherent in the language itself, and it should always be borne in mind that the examples are examples, drawn in some cases from a long span of time, and not models of contemporary practice.

GERMANIC LANGUAGES

General note
Dutch
Afrikaans: a note
German
Danish
Norwegian
Swedish
Icelandic

GENERAL NOTE: GERMANIC LANGUAGES

1 FAMILY LIKENESS

1.1 The Germanic languages—English, Dutch, German, Danish, Norwegian, Swedish and Icelandic—have common characteristics and family relationships, which, provided too blind a reliance is not placed upon them, can assist the transition from one to another. Some of these characteristics are shared in some measure by English and others not; and phonetics apart, German may be taken as the typical Germanic language. Within the whole the Scandinavian languages form a compact sub-group.

1.2 One consequence of a common origin is a common stock of words—words not identical in the various languages, but showing phonetic correspondences. Both consonants and vowels may correspond, but so many factors affect vowels that the consonants are more reliable.

English	Dutch	German	Danish	Norwegian	Swedish	Icelandic
book	boek	Buch	bog	bok	bok	bók
come	komen	kommen	komme	komme	komma	koma
drink	drinken	trinken	drikke	drikke	drikka	drekka
father	vader	Vater	fader	far	fader	faðir
find	vinden	finden	finde	finne	finna	finna
fowl [*bird*]	vogel	Vogel	fugel	fugel	fågel	fugl
give	geven	geben	give	gi(ve)	giva	gefa
hope	hopen	hoffen	håbe	håpe	hoppa	[vona]
house	huis	Haus	hus	hus	hus	hús
lay	leggen	legen	lægge	legge	lägge	leggja
milk	melk	Milch	mælk	mjølk	mjölk	mjólk
night	nacht	Nacht	nat	natt	natt	nótt, nátt
pipe	pijp	Pfeife	pibe	pipe	pipa	pípa
red	rood	rot	rød	rød, rau	röd	rauður
shoot	schieten	schiessen	skyde	skyte	skyta	skjóta
sit	zitten	sitzen	sidde	sitte	sitta	sitja
snow	sneeuw	Schnee	sne	snø	snö	snjor
that	dat	das	det	det	det	það
thick	dik	dick	tyk	tykk, tjukk	tjock	þykkur
which	welk	welch	hvilken	hvilken	vilken	hvílíkur
wind	wind	Wind	vind	vind	vind	vindur
word	woord	Wort	ord	ord	ord	orð
young	jong	jung	ung	ung	ung	ungur

But words can change their meaning as well as their form. German **Zimmer** corresponds to *timber* but means *room*; Icelandic **tima** means *time*, but **time** and **timma** in the other Scandinavian languages mean *hour* and the words for *time* in most of the Germanic languages, viz. **tijd, Zeit, tid**, correspond to *tide*.

1.3 All the above examples are short and simple words. When it comes to learned words, it will be found that while English derives most of these from Greek or Latin, directly or via French, the other Germanic languages, especially German and Icelandic, tend to form them from native roots, e.g.

English	Dutch	German	Danish	Norwegian	Swedish	Icelandic
agriculture	landbouw	Landwirt-schaft	landbrug	jordbruk	jordbruk	jarðraekt
compassion	medelijden	Mitleid	medlidenhed	medlidenhet	medlidande	meðaumkvun
edition	uitgave	Ausgabe	udgave	utgave	utgivande	útgafa
		Auflage	oplag	opplag	upplaga	upplag
reason	rede	Vernunft	fornuft	fornuft	förnuft	vit
future	toekomst	Zukunft	fremtid	framtid	framtid	framtið
success	succes	Erfolg	succes	súksess framgang	framgång	hepni
to place	*plaatsen*	anlegen	*placere*	*plassere*	*placera*	leggja
credit	*krediet*	*Kredit*	*kredit*	*kreditt*	*kredit*	útlán

Many of these words correspond in form to the classically derived English words, e.g. *com-passion*, **mede-lijden** (suffering with); *e-dition*, **uit-gave** (giving out): in such cases a rational guess can be made at their meaning.

2   WORD-FORMATION

2.1   Though often complex, the words in the last list correspond to simple English words; but many single words in Germanic languages correspond to phrases in English, e.g. **De Gesamtausgabe**, *collected edition*; Da **rettskrivningskomité**, *committee on orthography*. This facility in forming compounds is characteristic of Germanic languages but survives in English chiefly in 'nexus compounds' such as *income tax*, which become single words only when further compounded, as in *income-tax return* (**De Einkommensteuererklärung**). If a pair of words joined by *and* enters into a nexus compound, the connexion of the first is not formally indicated in English but is deduced from the context, e.g. *gas and electricity works*. In the other languages the connexion is made clear by a pendent hyphen, viz. **Gas- und Elektrizitätswerke**. (Note that this expression could equally well mean *gas-and-electricity works*, if such things exist.) With an adjectival ending, e.g. **innen- und aussenpolitisch**, English usually resorts to a more roundabout phrase, viz. *relating to domestic and foreign affairs*.

2.2   Apart from whole words there are also formative elements that are alike in the various Germanic languages, e.g. -*dom* and -*tum*; -*hood*, -*head*, -*heid*, hed, -*het* and so on. Nevertheless, **Eigentum**, ejendom and the like must still be translated *property*, not *owndom*.

3 MORPHOLOGY

3.1 As is obvious from the first table, English has shed a good many endings such as other Germanic languages have retained. In English only the pronouns have distinct forms for subject, object and possession, and much the same is true of Dutch, Danish, Norwegian and Swedish. Icelandic on the other hand has nouns with a total of seven different forms and adjectives with fourteen; German, with the same number of cases, has up to five and six different forms respectively. Most English verbs, like those of Danish, Norwegian and present-day Swedish, have four or five different simple forms, Dutch has eight, German twelve and Icelandic twenty.

3.2 The pattern of English speech is therefore bound to be different from that of the other Germanic languages; but there remain some fundamental similarities. English, as to a lesser extent Dutch and German, has developed the plural in -s, but the (e)n and -er plurals and changes of vowel common in the other languages have left their mark, e.g. *child*, (*childer*), *children; ox, oxen; man, men:* cf. **Kind(er)**; **Ochs(en)**; **mand, maend**; but also **Buch, Bücher**; **bok, bøker**, *book(s)*; **Lippe(n)**, *lip(s)*.

3.3 The old-fashioned *whereof, thereon* is normal in German (e.g. **darauf**, *on it*; **wovon**, *of which*) and Dutch (**daarop, waarvan**) and possible in Danish (**hvoraf**) and Swedish, but all the Scandinavian languages prefer constructions like *the number (that) you first thought of.*

3.4 The division of verbs into strong (all of them old verbs) and weak is common to all the Germanic languages, though there are differences of detail.

En	*give*	*gave*	*given*	*hear*	*heard*	*heard*
Ne	geven	gaf	gegeven	hooren	hoorde	gehoord
De	geben	gab	gegeben	hören	hörte	gehört
Da	give	gav	given	høre	hørte	hørt
No	gi(ve)	ga(v)	gitt	høre	hørte	hørt
Sv	giva	gav	given	höra	hörde	hörd
Is	gefa	gaf	gefinn	heyra	heyrði	heyrður

and even peculiarities like *sell, sold; bring, brought* have their counterparts.

3.5 Again, the Germanic languages dispose of a stock of auxiliaries similar to our *shall, will, may, must, can* and so on, to meet similar linguistic situations, though they do not make identical use of them.

3.6 There are of course divergences. The -*est* and -*eth* of the Bible prepare one somewhat for the present tense in German and Dutch but not for the single ending in -r of Danish, Norwegian and latterly Swedish. Nor have the other languages any direct equivalent of the English continuous tenses in -*ing* except Icelandic, which can say **eg er** (**var**, etc.) **að fara**, *I am* (*was*, etc.) *going*. The Scandinavian languages have developed a peculiar passive in -s(t), as well as appending the definite article to the noun.

4 ORDER OF WORDS

The order of words is basically that of older English before the auxiliary *do* became usual in question and negation; but inversion of the subject and the main verb is not confined to a few phrases such as *Thus saith the Lord*, but occurs whenever any word, phrase or clause precedes the subject. In Dutch, German and Icelandic dislocation of the normal order occurs in some or all subordinate sentences. (For details see those languages.)

DUTCH

SPECIMENS

Contemporary

In deze druk zijn verschillende kleinere en grotere veranderingen aangebracht. Achterin is een lijst van belangrijke boeken en tijdschriftartikelen opgenomen, die geraadpleegd kunnen worden als men van een bepaald taalverschijnsel een dieper gaande studie wenst te maken.

In this edition various smaller and greater changes have been made. At the end a list of important books and periodical articles has been included, which can be consulted if one wishes to make a more thoroughgoing study of a particular linguistic phenomenon.

Nineteenth-century

Ten slotte moge hier de mededeeling een plaats vinden dat het Tweede Deel reeds voor meer dan de helft is afgewerkt en dus na niet al te langen tijd zal volgen. Intusschen houde men in het oog dat de tijd, welke aan het bewerken van dezen catalogus besteed kan worden, tegenwoordig zeer beperkt is.

Current forms: **mededeling, lange, intussen**

Seventeenth-century

Post-brieven, soo uyt Vranckrijck, Duytslandt ende Italien, waer in verhaelt wert van de aencomste der vloot-scheepen, soo die tot Venetia aenghecomen zijn.

Current forms: **zo, uit, Frankrijk, Duitsland, waarin, verhaald, werd, aankomst, -schepen, aangekomen**

0 GENERAL CHARACTERISTICS

0.0 INTRODUCTORY

While we speak of *Dutch*, the Dutch themselves and those Belgians whose native language it is use the more general term **Nederlands**. As an official language of Belgium it is sometimes called Flemish, but the use of two terms for one language is confusing, and not to be generally recommended.

0.1 DEGREE OF INFLEXION

Though somewhat more open to Romance influences than German, it is still noticeably Germanic. As now written it is predominantly analytical, especially as regards the noun. Genitives of words denoting kin precede the noun, and so do adjectives and participial phrases; other genitives and prepositional phrases follow, e.g. **mijn vaders** huis, *my father's house*; een dieper gaande studie (specimen 1); de geschiedenis des Nederlandsen handels, *the history of Dutch trade*; de oorzaken van het verval, *the causes of the decline*.

0.2 ORDER OF WORDS

The simple sentence order SVO is often modified: where another clause, or anything but the subject, comes first, the verb is brought forward. There are several examples in the specimens. Verbs dependent on conjunctions or other verbs are postponed, e.g. Toen hij groter was, *When he was bigger*. When two or three verbs thus come together at the end their order is fluid, but the finite verb is not put at the end of more than two, cf. specimen 1: geraadpleegd kunnen worden. Phrases which qualify participles or infinitives often precede them (cf. 1.2.2).

0.3 HISTORICAL

Formerly Dutch had three distinct genders and four cases, NAGD, but first the dative, and in the twentieth century the accusative also ceased to be distinguished, except in stereotyped phrases, while the genitive has been largely replaced by van, e.g. De geschiedenis van het kapitalisme, *The history of capitalism*. As for gender, there is now scarcely any grammatical difference between M and F.

1 BIBLIOLINGUISTICS

1.1 NAMES

1.1.1 Dutch and Flemish names today consist of Christian name and surname in the common fashion. A good many of them incorporate van or some other preposition, or the definite article in the form de or 't, or a combination of van with the article—van der, van den, van 't, ver. Except for ver these prefixes are ignored by the Dutch in filing but the Belgians file under Van.

1.1.2 As van means *of* or *from*, it may in medieval names simply denote origin and not be part of a surname. Equally so de (*the*).

1.1.3 Up to the 17th century patronymics are still common in their original function and have not decayed into surnames. They may or may not be accompanied by a surname, so that the same name may appear as Bruyn Harmansz., Bruyn Schinkel or Bruyn Harmansz. Schinkel. They appear most often in abbreviated form as above, but may be given in full, e.g. Adriaen Lenertsz. or Leenaerdtszoon; Jansz., Janssen or Janszoon; and they are more susceptible than surnames to alterations in other languages. Thus Albrecht Heyndricsz(oon) appears as Albert Henry and Albertus Henrici. The words of Molhuysen and Blok on their treatment are worth pondering: 'Names like Jan de Backer, Willem van Hulst (cf. 1.1.2), Claes Pietersz. we put under Backer, Hulst, Pietersz. In the absence of a family name it seemed to us more rational and convenient to take as a substitute not the Christian name but the nickname, which later became a surname.'

1.1.4 Names are rarely affected nowadays by grammatical relationships, but in earlier Dutch one occasionally finds the genitive -s (1.2.4).

1.2 NAMES OF AUTHORS, EDITORS, ETC.

1.2.1 Authorship may be indicated simply by putting the name at the head of the title-page. If it follows the title it will usually be preceded by door, or occasionally van.

1.2.2 The simple door may indicate an editor or compiler, but usually there will be some participle such as **samengesteld**, *put together*; **verzameld**, *collected*; **bewerkt**, *worked over*; **uitgegeven**, *edited*, especially in an old text; or of course (**uit het Engels**) **vertaald**, *translated (from the English)*.

1.2.3 An alternative to the above is the use of a noun of action, e.g. **onder redactie van**, *under the editorship of*, a phrase naturally common in collective works; **Nederlandse vertaling van**, *Dutch translation by*; **onder medewerking van**, *with the collaboration of*. In none of these cases does the preposition have any effect upon the name.

1.2.4 The genitive is rare today, but it is found occasionally in old titles such as **Reinier Telles Tweede vrede-sang, Samuel Costers Iphigenia**; and more often with the name Latinised, e.g. **Het achste sermoen Henrici Bullingerii**. There was some reluctance to leave Latinised forms in the nominative after prepositions: **door** usually takes the accusative and **bij** shows a slight preference for it, but **van** prefers the nominative or the genitive, which is not unknown with the other two.

1.2.5 *Corporate authors*

Bodies responsible for the preparation of a book are shown in much the same way as individual authors, though the appearance of the name of a body at the top of a title-page may merely indicate sponsorship, and detailed information about authorship may be contained in the preface. Subordinate units may follow the main one, in which case the phrases are grammatically independent, or precede it, the main body being in the genitive or joined by **van**, e.g. **Het Studie- en Documentatiecentrum van het Ministerie van Justitie**. In this example separation of the elements involves no changes, but a genitive **-s** would have to be removed, and the omission of **het** before an adjective may make adjustments necessary, e.g. **het sociale** to **sociaal** (5.2.2). Changes of spelling (2.7) may occur in names of institutions of long standing.

1.3 TITLES

1.3.1 Apart from fiction and 'praeadviezen', Dutch titles consist largely of nouns, adjectives and prepositions, e.g. **Verhandeling over de oorzaken van het verval des Nederlandschen handels en de middelen tot herstel of uitbreiding van denzelve, ter beantwoording eener vrage van de Hollandsche Maatschappij der Wetenschappen te Haarlem**, *Essay on the causes of the decline of Dutch trade and the means of restoring or expanding the same, in answer to a question by the Holland Society of Sciences at Haarlem*. Praeadviezen usually quote verbatim a complicated question, which in view of the order of words (0.2) needs careful disentangling before being abbreviated. Fiction and popular writing produce more varied titles, e.g. **Ik ontwikkel en vergroot mijn foto's zelf**, *I develop and enlarge my photos myself*.

1.3.2 The indefinite article, which is ignored in filing, has the same form as the numeral and pronoun *one*, which are not, e.g. **Eén wereld of geen wereld**, *One world or no world*; **De één of de ander**, *One or the other*, both filed under **één**; but the numeral and pronoun have the accent.

1.4 VOLUMES AND PARTS

1.4.1 The usual word for volume is **deel**, literally *part*, which may be divided by **stuk** (*piece*). **Band** (*volume*) is far less common but is useful if **deel** is wanted for *part*.

1.4.2 Numeration is most often by a preceding ordinal number, e.g. **tweede deel**, but **deel II**, read **twee**, is also possible. Older books may produce numeration at the beginning of the title, e.g. **Het 2de deel van 't Nootwendigh teghen-vertoogh**.

1.5 EDITIONS

1.5.1 The Dutch equivalent of *edition* is **uitgave**, but the word **druk** (*'impression'*) also occurs in the numeration of editions. It is sometimes explicitly contrasted with **uitgave**, but mostly it is neutral. The **tweede druk** may be an obvious reprint and the third a really new edition, **een werkelijke 3de druk**, with the **bewerking en bijwerking** that this entails. The words for revision are as likely to occur with **druk** as with **uitgave**.

1.5.2 Numeration, as indicated above, is by a preceding ordinal number, in words or figures, with a word for *revised* if necessary, e.g. **verbeterde**, *improved*; **vermeerderde**, *enlarged*; **(geheel opnieuw) bewerkte, omgewerkte, herziene**, (*completely*) *revised*.

1.5.3 A *reprint* is indicated by **herdruk**, emphasised by **onveranderde**, *unaltered*. *Offprints* are **overdrukken** or **overdrukjes** (**overgedrukt uit**, *reprinted from*).

1.6 IMPRINTS

1.6.1 Modern imprints cause little difficulty, consisting for the most part of the name of the place and the press in that order. Of the place-names, which may be preceded by **te** (*at*), **'s Gravenhage** should be noted for its small **'s** and the space before **G**. It also appears as **den Haag**, with **den** even in the nominative and a capital only at the beginning of the sentence. Some places in Belgium, known in English by their French names, have different forms in Dutch, e.g. **Liège, Luik**.

1.6.2 The names of publishers may be personal names or names like **De Sikkel** or **Het Wereldvenster** given to the press itself. Minor complications are **Gebr(oeder)**, *Brothers*; **M(aatschapp)ij**, *Co(mpany)*; **N.V.**, *and Co.*, as in **N.V. Drukkerij en Uit-geverij J. H. de Bussy**. Note the combination of printing and publishing.

1.6.3 Older imprints are often those of printers, explicitly so in the form **g(h)e-dru(c)kt bij**. Some printers stick to one type of imprint, some alternate between **gedrukt (geprent) bij** and plain **bij**. Printers were also frequently publishers, which presumably explains the occasional alternation of the **bij** of the printer with the **voor** of the publisher; but for the most part the names found after **bij** are a different set from those found after **voor**.

1.7 SERIES

1.7.1 The titles of series may be plural, **Mededelingen van** . . . (*Proceedings of* . . .), **Studiën over** . . . (*Studies in* . . .), or collective, **Verzameling bouwstudies, Anne-Marie Serie**.

They may appear at the top of the title-page, on a special title-page, or overleaf. Sub-series are indicated by **reeks**.

1.7.2 Numeration is usually given by **nummer**.

1.7.3 One special difficulty of Dutch series is that long series span the historical changes in the language (0.3). Thus one may have the body changing **Nederlandsche** to **Nederlandse** in its name and **Mededeelingen** to **Mededelingen** in the title.

1.8 PERIODICALS

1.8.1 The titles of periodicals are for the most part straightforward combinations of nouns and adjectives, e.g. **Nieuwe Theologische studiën, Kroniek van kunst en kultuur**, or more laconically **De Economist, De Gids** (*The Leader*). The word itself (**tijdschrift**) appears in the titles of a number of them. Naturally enough some, like **Merlyn**, are enigmatic.

1.8.2 Titles may include the name of an institution, or it may form part of the sub-title, e.g. **Officiaal orgaan van de Dialektcentrales van Gent, Leuven en Amsterdam**.

(Here, in fact, the three centres have individual names given elsewhere.) As with series the spelling both of the title and of the body may change.

1.8.3 There is a great variety of words referring to editing. The simplest, **geredigeerd van,** *edited by,* perhaps in conjunction with (**in samenwerking met**) one or more assistants, is the least common. Nouns are the usual mode of expression, a **redactieraad** or **redactiecommissie,** *editorial committee,* or just plain **redactie,** which comes to the same thing, with various grades of editor from **eereredacteur,** who is concerned only with policy, through the **hoofdredacteur** or *editor-in-chief,* to the **redacteur** or **redacteur-secretaris.** Behind all may be a **commissie van bijstand,** intellectual backers, or a body of collaborators, **medewekers,** but these are usually contributors. Distinct from all these is the **administrateur** or *business-manager.*

A third form of expression uses nouns of action such as **onder leiding (redactie) van,** *under the direction (editorship) of.*

Long-established periodicals may give as much prominence to the **aanvanklijke redacteur,** the *original editor,* by whom the periodical was founded (**opgericht**) as the present one (**tegenwoordige**).

Uitgegeven and **uitgave** refer to the publisher.

1.8.4 Numeration is almost invariably by **jaargang** (annual run), occasionally **deel** (*part*), subdivided by **nummer** or **aflevering.** The numbers may be in either order, e.g. **deel XXII, no. 4** (read as cardinals) or **drieëntwintigste jaargang.** There may be more than one series (**reeks**) of numeration.

1.8.5 Periodicity may be implicit in the title, or more likely the sub-title, e.g. **maandblad, tweemaandelijks tijdschrift,** *monthly, bi-monthly periodical;* but more often there is a complete statement beginning with **verschijnt,** *appears,* or if the title is plural, **verschijnen,** e.g. **verschijnt maandelijks, elke maand, viermaal per jaar, per jaar in vier afleveringen,** *appears monthly, every month, four times a year, in four issues a year,* or putting it another way round, **een jaargang telt 6 nummers,** *one volume counts 6 numbers.*

1.8.6 Subscription (**abonnement**) is most often stated in some such form as **de abonnementsprijs bedraagt,** *subscription amounts to,* or there may be a quotation for **algemeen jaarabonnement,** *ordinary annual subscription* alternatively called **de prijs per jaargang.** As opposed to the ordinary subscription there may be special rates such as **docentenabonnement** for university teachers or **steunabonnement** for supporters. Single numbers (**losse nummers**) are usually obtainable (**verkrijgbaar**), **de prijs per nummer** being quoted. Alternatively we are told: **dit nummer kost,** *this number costs.* Internal and external rates (**binnenland** and **buitenland**) are naturally different.

1.8.7 Addresses usually distinguish various activities, though they may group some or all together in various ways. Thus we may have a **redactie- en administratieadres,** *editorial and business address* or **uitgever, correspondentie en administratie** may be distinguished from **abonnement.** More elaborately **Publicaties ter recensie gelieve men te zenden aan . . . , Overige voor de redactie aan . . . , Abonnementen en advertenties . . . ,** *Please send publications for review to . . . , Other editorial matter to . . . , Subscriptions and advertisements to . . . .* Alternatively directions may take the form: **wendt men zich tot,** i.e. *apply to.*

2 ALPHABET, PHONETICS, SPELLING

2.1 ALPHABET

2.1.1 The alphabet is the same as in English. The letters **q** and **y** are now used in foreign words only.

2.1.2 Dutch words formerly spelt with y are now spelt ij (a typographical development of ÿ) and arranged in dictionaries among the i's, viz. **bigot, bij, bik**. Some names, however, may retain the y, e.g. **Dijk** or **Dyck**, and the same person's name may be variously spelt. To secure one alphabetical sequence names in ij are arranged in encyclopaedias, biographical dictionaries, bibliographies and catalogues as if they were spelt with y. Thus in ENSIE we find the sequence **Xylose, IJ, Yak, IJken, Ylang**, only **Ijar**, where i and j are historically separate, being put among the i's. Most Dutch printers have a single fount for **IJ, ij**; but if none is available the capital should be IJ not Ij.

2.1.3 An acute accent is used occasionally to distinguish, e.g. **voor**, *for*; **vóór**, *before*; a grave accent is used to indicate unusual stress.

2.2 CAPITALISATION

2.2.1 Capitals are used for proper names, national adjectives and the pronoun U and its derivatives, but not nowadays for months, days of the week, or points of the compass.

2.2.2 In names of corporate bodies, and other compound names, all words are capitalised except prepositions and articles. So often are the titles of books and periodicals, but official bibliographies follow the usual practice of dispensing with them unless the word is one that would normally be spelt with a capital in any case.

2.2.3 Titles of office preceded by the article begin with a small letter, but not as a rule when the article is absent. The abbreviations **Dr., Ir. (Ingenieur)** usually have capitals.

2.2.4 Common nouns attached to geographical names do not have initial capitals in expressions of the form **de rivier de Maas**, *the River Maas*; but **Zuider Zee**. In **den Haag** the article is spelt with a capital only at the beginning of a sentence.

2.2.5 **'k, 'n, 's, 't** are written small even at the beginning of a sentence, and the next word has a capital.

2.3 DIVISION OF WORDS

2.3.1 Rules 1, 2, 4, 5a, 6c, 7a (p. xiii) apply subject to the provisos below.

2.3.2 Suffixes beginning with a consonant are kept intact; hence, **paar-tje** but **kaart-je**. Suffixes beginning with a vowel, with the exception of **-aard(ig)** and **-achtig**, take with them the preceding consonant, e.g. **boe-ken**.

2.3.3 Ch and sch are not divided, but **ng** is, and so are **dj, sj, tj** if **j** begins a suffix, though all these are single sounds. Rule 5a does not apply to words like **pro-bleem** and **pro-gram**.

2.3.4 On rule 7 note that **aai, eeu, ieu, oei, ooi** are diphthongs.

2.4 PUNCTUATION AND ABBREVIATIONS

2.4.1 Punctuation presents few surprises. When two compound words sharing the same final (or less commonly initial) element follow one another, the first ends with a hyphen (or the second begins with one as the case may be), e.g. **redactie- en administratieadres** for **redactieadres en administratieadres**; **electriciteitsvoorziening en -verbruik**, *electricity supply and consumption*.

2.4.2 It is apparently correct to put a full stop after abbreviations like **dr.** for **doctor**, as well as after ones like **d.i., d.w.z.** for **dat is, dat wil zeggen** (*i.e.*), or **enz.** for **en zoo voorts** (*etc.*) or **bijv.** for **bij voorbeeld** (*e.g.*). But many writers leave out the stop when the last letter is included.

2.7 PHONETICS AND SPELLING

2.7.1 A single vowel in a closed syllable is short, a single vowel in an open syllable, a double vowel or a diphthong is long. Final consonants are unvoiced, but this is reflected in the spelling only in the case of **z** > **s** and **v** > **f**. When endings are added, vowel quality is usually preserved and the spelling may be altered, e.g. **stuk, stukken; deel, delen**; s and f after **l, m, n, r**, long vowels and diphthongs are usually changed to **z** and **v**.

2.7.2 In the course of the last fifty years spelling has been simplified, chiefly by the elimination of double vowels in open syllables, e.g. **delen** not **deelen**, and by the substitution of **-s(e)** for **-sch(e)**, **t** for **th**, **f** for **ph**. In using older dictionaries, however, one should remember that some long vowels in open syllables, e.g. **geven**, have always been single.

2.7.3 Earlier still spelling is much more variable. **Aa** appears as **ae**; **d** as **dt** or **t**, where, as for instance in **Holland(sch)**, it is so pronounced; **g** is frequently spelt **gh**, or at the end of a syllable **ch**; **i** may appear as **y**; **k** as **c** or **ck**; **ks** as **x**; **z** as **s**.

3 ARTICLES

There are three genders: masculine, feminine and neuter, inanimate objects being of any gender. The neuter always shared some forms with the masculine, and with the obsolescence of some cases the distinction between M and F is often irrelevant.

3.1 DEFINITE

	M	*N*	*F*	*P*
N	de	het	de	de
[*A*	den	het	de	de]
G	des, 's	des, 's	der	der
[*D*	den	den	der	den]

Nowadays only the nominative and to some extent the genitive are used.

3.2 INDEFINITE

	M	*N*	*F*
N	een	een	een(e)
[*A*	een(en)	een	eene]
G	een(e)s	een(e)s	e(e)ner
[*D*	eenen	eenen	eener]

Only een and the genitive survive today.

4 NOUNS

4.1 SINGULAR

4.1.1 M and N nouns add **-s** in the genitive. F nouns do so only when the genitive comes first, e.g. **mijn moeders huis**, *my mother's house*. For use see **4.6.1**.

4.1.2 The dative, where it survives, ends in -e.

4.2 PLURAL

4.2.1 The plural is invariable and ends in -en (4.2.2, 4.2.5), -eren (4.2.3) or -s (4.2.4, 4.2.5).

4.2.2 Changes of consonant (2.7.1) may take place. A single consonant following a short vowel is not always doubled, in other words the vowel is long in the plural. So stuk-ken, but weg-en; and with change of vowel, stad, steden; schip, schepen; -heid, -heden.

4.2.3 Some neuters, e.g. lam, kind, add -eren.

4.2.4 Diminutives, words like foto, and most words in -el, -em, -en, -er, -aar, -aard as well as vader and other nouns denoting kin, add -s.

4.2.5 Nouns in -ie (unstressed) and those in -eur, -ier, -or which denote occupations may have -s or -en, e.g. studies or studiën. The plural in -en is more academic.

4.2.6 In older works a dative ending in -en may be found when the normal plural is -s.

4.2.7 Words of Latin form may have Latin plurals, e.g. catalogus, -gi.

4.6 NOTES ON THE CASES

4.6.1 The genitive, besides indicating possession, is used adverbially in such expressions as 's nachts, *at night*.

4.6.2 The dative survives only in a dwindling number of stereotyped expressions such as ten (= te den) behoeve, *on behalf of*, and in names in van den and van der.

5 ADJECTIVES

5.2 ENDINGS

5.2.1 Before M and F nouns, expressed or understood, most adjectives have the ending -e always, with changes as in 2.7.1.

5.2.2 Before N nouns they add -e after het and in the plural, e.g. het politieke leven, but politiek leven, met een warm hart.

5.2.3 Used as nouns they add -e in the singular and -en in the plural.

5.2.4 Long comparatives, rechter and linker, adjectives in -en, and local adjectives such as Roterdammer never take -e. Other long adjectives are often used loosely, e.g. het koloniaal kapitalisme (1902) for koloniale.

5.2.5 The ending -en is found for some cases in older writers, and -s and -er (cf. 3.1) survive in stereotyped expressions.

5.3 COMPARISON

Comparative -er (2.7.1); superlative -st.

Note wijs, wijzer, wijst; geschikt, geschikst.

5.4 POSSESSIVES

Mijn, uwe, zijn, haar (*her* and *their*); onze, hun (*their*) may be declined like een with plural -e, -er, -en; but the endings are now little used. With the article they behave as in 5.2.3.

6 NUMERALS

6.1 CARDINAL

1 een	11 elf	60 zestig
2 twee	12 twaalf	70 zeventig
3 drie	13 dertien	80 tachtig
4 vier	14 veertien	90 negentig
5 vijf	15, etc. vijftien, etc.	100 honderd
6 zes	20 twintig	102 honderd (en) twee
7 zeven	21 eenentwintig	1000 duizend
8 acht	30 dertig	2000 tweeduizend
9 negen	40 veertig	2968 tweeduizend negen-
10 tien	50 vijftig	honderd achtenzestig

6.2 ORDINAL

1 eerste	6 zesde	11 elfde
2 tweede	7 zevende	12 twaalfde
3 derde	8 achtste	13, etc. dertiende, etc.
4 vierde	9 negende	20, etc. twintigste, etc.
5 vijfde	10 tiende	100 honderdste

521st vijfhonderd eenentwintigste

6.3 FIGURES

Cardinals are represented by plain arabic figures, ordinals add **-de** or **-ste**. Roman figures are used as in English, e.g. **Karel I, Karel de Eerste.**

6.4 DATES

The months are:

**januari, februari, maart, april, mei, juni,
juli, augustus, september, october, november; december**

6 juni 1962 is read **zes juni negentienhonderdtweeenzestig.**

7 PRONOUNS

7.1/7.2 DEMONSTRATIVE, INTERROGATIVE, RELATIVE, ETC.

7.1.1 These are declined either like **een** or like adjectives, with plural endings **-e**, **-er, -en.** The endings are now little used.

7.1.2 Die, dat (*that, who, which*) and **wie, wat** (*who, which, what*) make **dien, diens, dier,** etc. In familiar language **die z(ij)n, die d(e)r** are substituted for **wiens, wier.**

7.3 PERSONAL

7.3.1 The forms in the subject and object are as follows:

	S	*P*
1	(i)k; mij, me	wij, we; ons
2	jij, je; jou, je	jullie; je(lui)
	U, gij; U	U, gij; U
3*m*	hij; hem	hen, hun
f	zij; haar	zij, ze; haar ⎬ ze
n	het	

B

7.3.2 Those of the 1st and 2nd person have also a reflexive meaning. For *himself, herself, themselves* there is a special pronoun **zich**.

7.3.3 There are also antiquated genitives: **mijner, zijner** (*of him*), **harer, onzer, uwer, hunner, harer**.

7.3.4 **Er** (*there*) is used in many ways. In the sentence: **Er is besloten nog vier delen uit te geven; er zijn er twee reeds uitgegeven, en wij zullen er voor zorgen dat de andere spoedig uitkomen** (*It has been decided to publish four more volumes; two have already been published and we shall see to it that the others appear shortly*) the first is impersonal (*it*), the second anticipates the subject (*there*), the third (*of them*) is omitted in translation, the fourth (*to it*) anticipates the object-clause. Like the English *there* it is combined with prepositions, e.g. **ervan, er . . . van**, *of it, thereof.*

8 VERBS

8.1 STRUCTURE
The Dutch verb is very like the English but has a few more endings. It is listed in the dictionaries under the infinitive, which ends in **-en**, e.g. **gev-en**.

8.2 PRESENT
8.2.1 The endings are:

     -, -/-t, -t; -en, -t/-en, -en

8.2.2 The **-t** of the third person is omitted after **-t-** and optionally **-d-** of the stem, and changes of spelling are found, e.g. **kost-en; vind(t); trek(t), trekken; geef(t), geven.**

8.3 PAST
8.3.1 Weak verbs (the majority) add **-de(n), -te(n)**, e.g. **brandde(n), lachte(n)**.

8.3.2 There are some changes of stem, nearly all with parallels in English, e.g. **bracht** (sic) from **brengen; dacht, denken; docht, dunken; deed, doen; kocht, kopen; lei; leggen; moest, moeten; wist, weten; zei(den), zeggen; zocht, zoeken.**

8.3.3 Strong verbs have endings:

     -, -/-t, -; -en, -t/-en, -en

and change the vowel of the stem. The changes, viz.

Past	Infinitive
a	e, i
e(e)	ij
i(e)	a, e, o, oe
o	e, i
o(o)	ie, ui
oe	a, e

are the same in principle as those in English verbs but the actual changes are different, and many verbs are still strong in Dutch which are weak in English, e.g. **begon, beginnen; but reed, rijden; hielp, helpen** (Eng. *rode, helped*). It is advisable to use a dictionary which gives the parts of the verb. Note **ging** < **gaan, hield** < **houden, werd** < **worden.**

8.3.4 The past sometimes has a conditional meaning.

8.10 COMPOUND TENSES

The perfect, pluperfect and future perfect are expressed by the present (past, future) of **hebben** (8.17.1) or **zijn** (8.17.2) followed by the past participle, e.g. **ik heb gegeven, ik ben gevallen**. It is often used instead of the simple past.

8.12 PARTICIPLES

8.12.1 The present ends in **-end(e)**.

8.12.2 Past, weak: **(ge)—d**, **(ge)—t**, e.g. **gevolgd, gemaakt, betaald** (from **volgen, maken, betalen**).

8.12.3 Past, strong: **(ge)—en**, usually with change of vowel, viz.

Participle	Infinitive
-a-	-a-, -e-
-e-	-e-, -i-, -ij-
-o-	-e-, -ie-, -o-, -ui-
-oe-	-oe-

8.12.4 Weak past participles usually go with weak pasts, strong with strong.

8.15 PASSIVE

8.15.1 The present, past, future and conditional are expressed by the corresponding tense of **worden** (8.3.3) followed by the past participle, e.g. **het wordt (werd) uitgegeven**, *it is (was) being published*.

8.15.2 The perfect, pluperfect and future perfect are expressed by the present, past and future of **zijn** (8.17.2) followed by the past participle, e.g. **het is (was) uitgegeven**, *it has (had) been published*.

8.15.3 Alternatively the passive may be expressed by **men** (*one*) and the active, e.g. **men wendt zich tot**, *application is made to*.

8.17 AUXILIARIES

8.17.1 **hebben**, *to have*
Present: **heb, hebt, heeft; hebben, hebt, hebben**
Past: **had; hadden, hadt, hadden**
Past participle: **gehad**

8.17.2 **zijn**, *to be*
Present: **ben, bent, is; zijn, zijt, zijn**
Past: **was; waren, waart, waren**
Past participle: **geweest**

8.17.3 **kunnen**, *can*
Present: **kan, kunt/kan, kan; kunnen, kunt, kunnen**
Past: **kon; konden, kondt, konden**
Past participle: **gekund, kunnen**

8.17.4 **moeten**, *must*
Present: **moet; moeten, moet, moeten**
Past: **moest; moesten, moest, moesten**
Past participle: **(ge)moeten**

8.17.5 mogen, *may*
Present: **mag, moegt/mag**, mag; mogen, moogt, **mogen**
Past: **mocht;** mochten, mocht, mochten
Past participle: **gemoogd,** mogen

8.17.6 willen, *will*
   Present: wil, wil(t), wil; willen, wilt, willen
   Past: wilde/wou; wilden, wildt, wilden
   Past participle: gewild, willen

8.17.7 zullen, *shall, will*
   Present: zal, zult/zal, zal; zullen, zult, zullen
   Past: zou; zouden, zoudt, zouden
   Past participle: zullen

8.17.8 The plural forms in -t, now rare, are used with gij.

8.23 SEPARABLE VERBS

8.23.1 In the sentences Ik geef het boek aan mijn broeder (*I give the book to my brother*) and Ik geef het boek uit (*I publish the book*) corresponding places in the sentence are occupied by aan mijn broeder and uit. With other orders we have:

Ik heb het b. aan m. b. gegeven	Ik heb het b. uitgegeven
Ik zal het b. aan m. b. geven	Ik zal het b. uitgeven
Als ik het b. aan m. b. gaf	Als ik het b. uitgaf

Whereas aan mijn broeder remains a separate element, uit is joined to the verb when it precedes it; and it is under the form uitgeven that it appears in the dictionary. Words like aan, af, in, op, uit all behave like this, and in certain verbs goed, geluk, lief, vast, vrij, waar and so forth.

8.23.2 Inseparable prefixes like be- and ver- present no difficulty: the verbs behave like any other except that the past participle has no ge-. But door, mis, om, onder, over, voor are sometimes detached and sometimes not, and the meaning varies accordingly. Het is voorgekomen (sep.) means *It has appeared*; Het is voorkomen (insep.), *It has been prevented*. The infinitive is in both cases voorkomen; one should look therefore for the notes (sep.) and (insep.) in the dictionary.

8.24 MISCELLANEOUS POINTS OF SYNTAX

8.24.1 Note Ik heb hem horen lachen, *I heard him laugh*; not gehoord. Similarly with other verbs.

8.24.2 The infinitive corresponds to the verbal noun in -*ing* as well as to the infinitive. Note especially such expressions as die er niet aan konden wennen, niets te zijn, *who could not get used to being nobodies.*

9 ADVERBS

Most adjectives serve also as adverbs.

GLOSSARY

aanhangsel, *appendix*
aantekening, *note*
aanvulling, *supplement*
abonnement, *subscription*
afdeling, *section, division*
aflevering, *issue* (1.8.4)
afzonderlijk, *single, separate*
auteursrecht, *copyright*

band, *volume* (1.4.1)
beeld, *picture, portrait*
bestellen, *order*
bewerkt, *revised* (1.5.2)
bibliotecaris, *librarian*
biblioteek, *librarian*
bijdrage, *contribution*
bijgewerkt, *revised*

bijlage, *appendix, supplement*
bijvoegsel, *supplement*
bladwijzer, *index*
bladzijde, *page*
boekhandel, *bookshop*
boekhandelaar, *bookseller*
brief, *letter*
brochure, *pamphlet*
buitenland, *abroad*

deel, *volume, part* (1.4.1)
driemaandelijks, *quarterly*
druk, *edition, impression* (1.5.1)
drukkerij, *printer's* (1.6.2)

exemplaar, *copy*

gebonden, *bound*
gedicht, *poem*
genootschap, *society*
geredigeerd, *edited* (1.8.3)
geschiedenis, *history*
gestorven, *died*

halfjaarlijks, *half-yearly*
handelingen, *proceedings*
handschrift, *manuscript*
herdruk, *reprint* (1.5.3)
herzien, *revised* (1.5.2)

inleiding, *introduction*
ter inzage, *on approval*

jaar, *year*
jaarboek, *yearbook*
jaargang, *volume, year* (1.8.4)
jaarlijks, *annual*

korting, *discount*
kwartaalblad, *quarterly*

lid, *member*
losse nummers, *single numbers*

maandblad, *monthly publication*
maandelijks, *monthly*
maatschappij, *company, society*
mededeling, *communication*
medewerker, *contributor, collaborator*
medewerking, *collaboration*

omgewerkt, *revised* (1.5.2)
onderzoek, *research*
ongedrukt, *unpublished*
oplaag, *edition*
oud nummer, *back number*
overdruk(je), *offprint* (1.5.3)
overzetting, *translation*

pers, *press*
ter perse, *in the press*
prijs, *price* (1.8.6)

redacteur, *editor* (1.8.3)
redactie, *editing* (1.2.3, 1.8.3),
    editorial office (1.8.7)
rede, *speech*
reeks, *series* (1.7.1)
register, *index*
rekening, *bill*
ruil(ing), *exchange*

samengebracht, samengesteld,
    compiled (1.2.2)
samenvatting, *summary*
stuk, *part* (1.4.1)

tabel, *table*
tijdschrift, *periodical*
toegevoegd, *added*
tooneelstuk, *play*

uitgave, *edition* (1.5.1)
uitgebreid, *enlarged* (1.5.2)
uitgegeven, *edited* (1.2.2), *published*
    (1.8.3)
uitgekozen, *selected*
uitgeverij, *publishing house* (1.6.2)
uitkomen, *come out*
uitlegging, *commentary*
uitverkocht, *out of print*

veertiendaags, *fortnightly*
verbeterd, *corrected, improved* (1.5.2)
vereniging, *society*
verhaal, *story*
verhandelingen, *proceedings*
verklaring, *commentary*
vermeerderd, *enlarged* (1.5.2)

verschijnen, *appear*
vertaling, *translation* (1.2.2)
vertelling, *story*
verzameld, *collected* (1.2.2)
verzameling, *collection, series* (1.7.1)
verzending, *dispatch*
vlugschrift, *pamphlet*
voorbereiding, *preparation*

voorbericht, voorrede, voorwoord,
  preface

wekelijks, *weekly*
woord vooraf, *preface*
woordenboek, *dictionary*
word vervolgd, *to be continued*

zelfde, *same*

GRAMMATICAL INDEX: WORDS

ben(t), 8.17.2

dat, 7.1.2
den, 3.1
der, 3.1
des, 3.1
die d(e)r, 7.1.2
die z(ij)n, 7.1.2
dien(s), dier, 7.1.2

een-, etc., 3.2
ener, 3.2
er, 7.3.4

gehad, 8.17.1
gekund, 8.17.3
gemoeten, 8.17.4
gemoogd, 8.17.5
geschikst, 5.3
geweest, 8.17.2
gewild, 8.17.6
ging(en), 8.3.3

haar(-), 5.4, 7.3.1
had(t), 8.17.1
hadden, 8.17.1

harer, 7.3.3
heb(t), 8.17.1
hebben, 8.10, 8.17.1
heeft, 8.17.1
hem, hen, 7.3.1
het, 3.1
hield(en), 8.3.3
hun(-), 5.4, 7.3.1, 7.3.3

is, 8.17.2

je, 7.3.1
jelui, 7.3.1
jou, 7.3.1

kan, kon(den), kondt,
  kunnen, kunt, 8.17.3

mag, 8.17.4
me, 7.3.1
men, 8.15.3
mij, 7.3.1
mijn(-), 5.4, 7.3.3
mocht(en), moogt, mogen,
  moogt, 8.17.5

moest(en), moet(en), 8.17.4

ons, 7.3.1
onze(-), 5.4, 7.3.3

's, 3.1

ten, 4.6.2

uwe(-), 5.4, 7.3.3

waart, waren, was, 8.17.2
wat, 7.1.2
werd(en), 8.3.3, 8.15.1
wien(s), wier, 7.1.2
wijst, wijzer, 5.3
wilde(n), wildt, wil(t),
  willen, wou, 8.17.6

zal, 8.17.7
zijn(-), 5.4, 7.2.3, 8.5,
  8.15.2, 8.17.2
zijt, 8.17.2
zou, zouden, zoudt,
  zullen, zult, 8.17.7

GRAMMATICAL INDEX: ENDINGS

- (no ending), 8.2.1, 8.3.3

-d, 8.12.2
-end, 8.12.1

-e, 4.1.2, 5.2.1, 5.2.3, 5.4,
  7.1.1
-de, 8.3.1
-ende, 8.12.1

-te, 8.3.1

-en, 4.2.1, 4.2.2, 4.2,5,
  4.2.6, 5.2.3, 5.2.5, 5.4,
  7.1.1, 8.1, 8.2.1, 8.3.3,
  8.12.3
-den, 8.3.1
-eren, 4.2.1, 4.2.3
-ten, 8.3.1

-er, 5.2.5, 5.3, 5.4, 7.1.1

-s, 1.1.4, 4.1.1, 4.2.1,
  4.2.4, 4.2.5, 5.2.5, 5.4,
  7.1.1
-es, 5.4, 7.1.1

-t, 8.2.1, 8.3.3, 8.12.2
-st, 5.3

AFRIKAANS: A NOTE

SPECIMEN

Die hele gebied van die maatskaplike werk is deur die Komitee in sy vernaamste onderdele verdeel, bv. gevallewerk, groepwerk en gemeenskapsorganisasie. Die gebiede soos ingedeel, is aan dié medewerkers toegewys wat die beste in staat was om 'n bydrae op daardie terrein te lewer. Die skrywers van verhandelings en proefskrifte wat handel oor die maatskaplike werk is ook versoek om terme en definisies in te stuur. Die Komitee-klerk het vakwoordeboeke en handboeke self deurgewerk en stof versamel.

The whole field of social work was sorted out by the Committee into its principal divisions, e.g. case work, group work and community organisation. The fields thus divided up were assigned to those collaborators who were in the best position to make a contribution in that sphere. The writers of dissertations and theses dealing with social work were also asked to send in terms and definitions. The Committee Clerk worked through technical dictionaries and handbooks himself and collected material.

1 GENERAL

1.1 Afrikaans is an independent development of the language brought to South Africa by the 17th-century Dutch settlers. It is marked, like English, by the wearing away of endings, as well as by the loss of some consonants between vowels and changes in the quality of some vowels and consonants, e.g.

Dutch	Afrikaans
zeven	sewe
bemerken	bemerk
klagen	kla
vragen	vrae
aanleggen	aanlê
bladen	blaaie
scheiden	skei
uitgeven	uitgee
zwijgen	swyg
denken	dink

1.2 Accents are used in principle as in Dutch; but one also meets the circumflex, e.g. **hê**, *to have*; **môre**, *tomorrow*. The diaeresis is more common, e.g. Ne **regen** Af **reën**. (Note also Ne **zeeën** Af **seën**.)

2 INFLEXIONS

2.1 Nearly all parts of speech have been simplified. The articles are **die** and **'n** (pronounced by many like the English *a*), all distinctions of number and gender having been lost.

25

2.2 Nouns have no cases, the possessive being marked by a separately written **se** after the noun. The plural is much the same as in Dutch except that **-en** has become **-e**, and consonants are lost between vowels (**blaaie** and **vrae** above are the plurals of **blad** and **vraag**. In some cases phonetic loss has led to complications, e.g. **produk**, **hoof**: P **produkte**, **hoofde**.

2.3 Most adjectives add **-e** when used before nouns. Complications akin to those in nouns may occur, e.g. **nuut/nuwe**, **oud/ou**, **lank/lang**, **reg/regte**, **goed/goeie**.

2.4 Verbs are very much simplified, each tense having only one form, e.g. **ek is** (*I am*), **hy is** (*he is*); **ek**, **hy**, **skryf** (*I write, he writes*), while **ek het geskryf** means both *I have written* and *I wrote*. Strong verbs have ceased to exist, though some strong past participles survive as adjectives or adverbs: Ne **binden, gebonden**; Af **bind, gebind**, with adjective **gebonde**, *forced*.

3 POINTS OF USAGE

3.1 Numerals and months differ only slightly from those used in Dutch, e.g., Ne **acht**, Af **ag(t)**; Ne **Juni**, Af **Junie**. Dates are expressed in the same way.

3.2 The pronoun **dié** (note the accent) now coincides with the article; hence the substitutes **hierdie** and **daardie**.

3.3 The infinitive with **te** is nearly always preceded by **om**, e.g. **hy leer (om te) lees**, *he learns to read*, but Ne **hij leert (te) lezen**.

3.4 If a negative sentence does not already have the negative word at the end, **nie** is added, except where the negative is **nog. . .nog** (*neither. . .nor*). If the final negative is other than **nie**, **nie** may be added, e.g. **dit het nog nie uitgekom nie**, *it has not yet come out*; **ek doen dit nooit (nie)**, *I never do that*.

GLOSSARY

aanhangsel, *appendix*
aanmerking, *note*
abonnement, *subscription*
afgerol, *duplicated*
aflewering, *issue*
afslag, *discount, reduction*
afstuur, *dispatch*
auteursreg, *copyright*

beknop(te), *abridged*
beperk, *limited*
bestel, *order*
bewerk, *edit*
biblioteek, *library*
bibliotekaris, *librarian*
bladsy, *page*
boek, *book*
boekhandelaar, *bookseller*
boekwinkel, *bookshop*
brief, *letter*
buiteland, *abroad*

bydrae, *contribution*
byvoegsel, *supplement*

deel, *part, volume*
druk, *edition, impression*
drukker, *printer*

eksemplaar, *copy*
enkel-, *single*

faktuur, *invoice*

gebore, *born*
gebrosjeerd, *sewn* (paperback)
gedigte, *poetry*
gekose, *selected*
genootskap, *society*
gereed, *ready*
geselskap, *society*
geskiedenis, *history*
gestaak, *ceased*

gesterf, *died*

halfjaarliks, *half-yearly*
herdruk, *reprint, offprint*
hersien, *revised*

inleiding, *introduction*
intekening, *subscription*

jaar, *year*
jaarboek, *yearbook*
jaarliks, *annual*

te koop, *on sale*
kopiereg, *copyright*

lid(maat), *member*

maandblad, *monthly publication*
maandeliks, *monthly*
maatskappy, *company*
me(d)edeling, *communication*
me(d)ewerking, *cooperation*
monster, *sample*

navorsing, *research*
novelle, *short story*

onuitgegee, *unpublished*
oordruk, *offprint*
oplaag, *impression, circulation*
opstel, *essay*

redaksie, *editing, editorial office*
redakteur, *editor*
reeks, *series*
register, *index*
roman, *novel*
ruil, *exchange*

saamgestel, *compiled*
selfde, *same*
separaat, *offprint*
op sig, *on approval*
slapband, *limp cover*
stuur, *send*

tabel, *table, list, index*
toespraak, *speech*
toevoeging, *addition*
toneelstuk, *play*
tydskrif, *periodical*

uitgawe, *edition*
uitgebrei(de), *enlarged*
uitgegee, *published*
uitgewer, *publisher*
uitkom, *come out*
uittrek, *taken from*

verbeterd, *corrected, improved*
vereniging, *association, society*
verkort, *abridged*
vermeerderde, *enlarged*
versameling, *collection*
verslae, *report*
vertaling, *translation*
vervang, *supersedes*
vervolg, *continuation*
verwerk, *edit*
vlugskrif, *pamphlet*
voorbereiding, *preparation*
voortgesit, *continued*
voortsetting, *continuation*
voorwoord, *preface*
vry, *free*

woordeboek, *dictionary*

GERMAN

SPECIMENS

Contemporary

Diesem Zeitraum ist die vorliegende Sammlung gewidmet, die sich die Aufgabe stellt, dem deutschen Leser ein Bild der polnischen Gegenwartsprosa zu vermitteln — freilich mit gewissen Einschränkungen. Romanfragmente sowie Arbeiten, die aus den Randgebieten der Epik stammen, wurden grundsätzlich nicht aufgenommen; größere Erzählungen, die den durch den Charakter der Edition bedingten Umfang sprengen würden, mußten ebenfalls unberücksichtigt bleiben. Geboten werden also Novellen und Kurzgeschichten.

It is to this period that the present collection is devoted. It sets itself the task of providing the German reader with a picture of contemporary Polish prose—admittedly with some limitations. Fragments of novels, as well as works which come from the borderlands of epic, have been excluded on principle; lengthy narratives, which would exceed the bounds which the character of this edition imposes, had likewise to be left out of consideration. What are offered, therefore, are short stories and brief narratives.

Eighteenth-century

Doch, da es in diesem philosophischen und critischen Zeitalter schwerlich mit jenem Empirism Ernst seyn kann, und er vermuthlich nur zur Uebung der Urtheilskraft, und um durch den Contrast die Nothwendigkeit rationaler Principien a priori in ein helleres Licht zu setzen, aufgestellet wird: so kann man es denen doch Dank wissen, die sich mit dieser sonst eben nicht belehrenden Arbeit bemühen wollen.

Modern spellings: kritischen, sein, vermutlich, Übung, Urteil-, Kontrast, Notwendigkeit, Prinzipien, aufgestellt.

Sixteenth-century

Eyn warhafftig erschröcklich Histori von der Bewrischen uffrur, so sich durch M. Luthers leer inn Teutscher nation anno 1525 erhebt und leyder noch nit erloschen ist.

Modern spellings: eine, wahrhaftig, erschreckliche, Historie, bäuerischen, Aufruhr, Lehre, in, deutscher, leider, nicht.

0 GENERAL CHARACTERISTICS

0.1 DEGREE OF INFLEXION

German is in practice a fairly analytical language, for though nouns have four cases, so that *of* and *to* can be expressed by endings, not by prepositions, the forms of the verb are not so differentiated as to obviate the need for subject pronouns.

0.2 ORDER OF WORDS

0.2.1 Adjectives precede the noun they qualify, and this applies even to long adjectival phrases (see specimen). A genitive without the article may precede, but most genitives follow.

0.2.2 Sentence order is in some ways freer than in English, but is subject to certain rigid laws. If the basic order SVOC is varied, as it often is, the variants can only be OVSC or CVSO, e.g. **ich legte das Buch auf den Tisch** (*I put the book on the table*) or **das Buch legte ich auf den Tisch** or **auf den Tisch legte ich das Buch.** This same reversal takes place if a subordinate clause precedes the main clause, e.g. **da ich das Buch gefunden hatte, legte ich es auf den Tisch.**

0.2.3 The last example illustrates the effect of subordination, the verb being transferred to the end. As a past participle or dependent infinitive is in any case relegated to the end, three verb forms may come together, but this clutter is usually avoided, e.g. **die Bände, die später werden herausgegeben werden,** *the volumes which will be published later*, not **herausgegeben werden werden.**

0.3 DEVELOPMENT OF UNIFIED GERMAN

The movement towards a unified German, associated with the name of Luther, begins in the 15th century and spreads first in the Protestant north, at the expense of Low German. In Catholic Bavaria there was opposition to 'Lutheran' German even in the 18th century. One therefore finds much more diversity, according to locality, in German texts of the earlier period than is the case with most European languages.

0.4 RELATION TO OTHER LANGUAGES

For the relation of German to English and other members of the Germanic family of languages see the General note on the Germanic languages.

0.5 WORD-FORMATION

As is mentioned in the General note on the Germanic languages (q.v.), German makes compounds freely, so freely that they will not all be found in the dictionary; and when they are, they tend to be entered under the first member, e.g. **tal|wärts** before **Talent.**

1 BIBLIOLINGUISTICS

1.1 NAMES

1.1.1 German names today follow the common western pattern of Christian name followed by surname, sometimes with a linking **von** (**vom, von der, von den**). Although some writers have dropped the 'aristocratic' **von**, as a rule the presence or absence of **von** would differentiate otherwise identical names. In the Middle Ages, however, **von** (*of, from*) usually indicates origin, and names are entered under the Christian names with the **von** element regarded as an epithet. Hence, in the genitive, **Johann Wolfgang von Goethes** but **Wolframs von Eschenbach.**

1.1.2 Noble names frequently appear in the form **Hieronymus Karl Friedrich, Freiherr von Münchhausen** (*Baron Munchausen*). Nevertheless most of them would be entered under the title as surname.

1.1.3 During the Renaissance a number of German surnames were given Greco-Latin dress, such as **Faber** for **Schmied, Ökolampadius** for **Hausschein, Melanchthon** for **Schwarzert** and even **Hylacomylus** for **Waltzemüller.** Some of these, as well as forms like **Andreä, Henrici,** have persisted since.

1.1.4 Conversely classical names are often modified, rather more so than in English, e.g. **Catull** for **Catullus**, **Ovid(ius)**, **Tibull(us)**, **Terenz(-tius)**; **Herodot(os)**; and sometimes Italian names, e.g. **Ariost(o)**, **Tizian(o)**.

1.1.5 Christian names are affected by changes of spelling. Thus **Carl** and other names beginning with **Ca, Co, Cu** are now usually spelt with a **K**, and this modernisation is often applied to names of earlier writers, though they were never so spelt in their own lifetimes. (Conversely the British Museum Catalogue used to spell both ancient and modern with a **C**.) Practice with **th** is less uniform: **Walther** may keep its **h** (which is etymological) or lose it according to taste, **Bert(h)a** has lost it, **Mathilde** kept it. In native names such as **Adolf ph** has given way to **f**.

1.1.6 There are a few compound Christian names such as **Lieselotte, Janheinz**, which may also be written with a hyphen, or, of course, as two separate words.

1.2 NAMES OF AUTHORS, EDITORS, ETC.

1.2.1 Names are very little affected by title-page relationships. If they stand at the head of the page or are preceded by prepositions such as **von** and **durch** this has no effect on them today, but in earlier works one meets **geschrieben durch Benjamin Leubern** (N Leuber). (See 4.3.5.)

1.2.2 Complete works, correspondence, diaries and the like, and reprints of classics are liable to produce names ending in the genitive **-s**, e.g. **Schillers sämtliche Werke, Jozef Filsers Briefwechsel, Goethes Faust**. Forms in **-ens** are probably from names in **-en**, but **-ens** could be an ending (4.3.5).

1.2.3 Names of corporate authors may present peculiar difficulties. They are much more likely to be in the genitive (4.3), preceded by some such word as **Bericht** (*report*) or **im Auftrage** (*by order*), and if the body is a subordinate one this may be followed by another genitive or by a phrase involving a preposition, e.g. **Studienkonferenz-Schriften der wissenschaftlichen Tagungen der Deutschen Bundesbahn,** *Study-Conference Papers of the Scientific Meetings of German Railways.*

If the name begins with an adjective, as in the above example, there is a further complication. The adjectives here are in the weak form (5.2.2), but in a catalogue heading there will be no articles, so that the strong forms (5.2.1) must be used, in the nominative: viz. **Deutsche Bundesbahn. Wissenschaftliche Tagungen. Studienkonferenz-Schriften**. Note the process of separating the main and the subordinate body. The above is not the only possible arrangement: in **bearbeitet im Kaiserlichen Statistischen Amt, Abteilung für Arbeiterstatistik (Kaiserliches Statistisches Amt)**, the subordinate body simply follows. In **Bericht der vom Bundesminister eingesetzten Parteienrechts-kommission,** *Report of the Commission on the Law relating to Parties appointed by the Federal Minister,* the relation is more complicated.

1.3 TITLES

1.3.1 Most titles consist of nouns (including infinitives) and adjectives (including participles) in various cases with or without prepositions, e.g. **Das Trinken in mehr als 500 Gleichnissen und Redensarten,** *Drinking in over 500 similes and locutions*; **Die Schäden der deutschen Zeitungen, ihre Ursachen und ihre Heilung,** *The defects of German newspapers, their cause and cure.* Works of fiction and the literature of persuasion show a wider variety, e.g. **Wie der Türke auf der Karlsbrücke um seinen Säbel kam,** *How the Turk on the Charles Bridge lost his scimitar*; **Dein Garten wächst mit dir,** *Your garden grows with you*; **Kommt und seht!,** *Come and see.*

1.3.2 British-Museum-style title entries require the recognition of oblique cases and the restoration of the nominative, though probably the first noun will be in the nominative already. Translating headings containing proper adjectives may require courage, as when **Brandenbürgische Landbücher** produces *Brandenburg Terriers*. With title entries under Anglo-American rules, as with titles generally, the ignoring of articles must be done with circumspection. Some forms of the definite article are identical with the demonstrative (7.1.2). So **Der Vogel im Baum** (*The bird in the tree*) is filed as **Vogel**; **Der Vogel, scheint mir, hat Humor** (*That bird, it seems to me, has a sense of humour*) as **Der**; **Das ist die Freiheit** (*That is freedom*), **Den die Götter lieben** (*Whom the gods love*) as **Das** and **Den**.

Most forms of the indefinite article are identical with those of the numeral *one* and easily confused with those of the pronoun **einer** (7.1.1). Hence **Ein Buch der Rose** (*A book of the rose*) is filed as **Buch** but **Einer gegen alle** (*One against all*) as **Einer**. Oblique cases of the article are ignored: **Des Knaben Wunderhorn** is filed as **Knaben**.

1.3.3 Titles in context normally obey the grammar of the sentence they occur in, e.g. **in Schillers Räubern**, *in Schiller's 'Räuber'*; **in der „Natürlichen Tochter"**, *in 'Die natürliche Tochter'*; but there are many occasions when such treatment is not felt to be appropriate and it is avoided by devices like the following: **in der Schrift:** *Die deutschen Volksstämme und Landschaften*. Here **die Schrift** is declined while the title remains unaltered. (See also 1.8.1.) As the examples indicate, German does not always differentiate the title typographically.

1.4 VOLUMES AND PARTS

1.4.1 It might be expected that **Band** (P **Bände**), *volume*, and **Teil-e**, *part(s)*, would stand in a hierarchical relationship to each other. Sometimes they do, but more often **Band** and **Teil** are used indifferently for *volume*. As a subdivision of **Band** only **Halbband** is at all common, while below **Teil** one finds **Abteilung**. Confusingly enough, however, both **Teil** and **Abteilung** are used for major divisions in a work, comprising several volumes, so that one finds **Vierter Teil (Vierte Abteilung), Erster Band**, *Section 4, volume 1*, as well as **Vierter Teil, Erste Abteilung**—presumably *Volume 4, part 1*, but the **Abteilung** can be still further subdivided into **Halbbände**! Nor is this the worst: I have seen **Vierter Teil, II. Teil, II. Hälfte, 1. Band**. At the same time **Teil**, like **Buch**, is quite common for the internal, non-bibliographical, divisions of a work, like *part* in English.

1.4.2 Besides the numeration illustrated above, in figures **4. Teil, 1. Abteilung**, the reverse, **Band I (eins)**, is quite common. Occasionally the two are grammatically linked, e.g. **Zweiten Bandes erster Theil**, *First part of the second volume*.

Sometimes the first volume bears no numeration, even though the preface may contain phrases like **ich hoffe, den zweiten Teil in absehbarer Zeit vorlegen zu können**, *I hope to be able to produce the second volume in the foreseeable future*, or **soll zwei Bände einnehmen**, *is to comprise two volumes*.

1.4.3 In older books the numeration, instead of following, may precede the title and be connected with it grammatically, e.g. **Ander Theil des Tractats von der Müntze**, *Second part of the treatise on coinage*.

1.5 EDITIONS

1.5.1 There are two words for *edition*: **die Ausgabe**, which is restricted in use, and **die Auflage**, which is ambiguous. **Ausgabe** refers rather to a mode of publication than to a body of copies, and is commonest in compounds like **Gesamtausgabe**, *complete* *edition*; **Volksausgabe**, *popular edition*. **Auflage**, the word for successive editions, can also mean *impression*; indeed **dritte und vierte Auflage** is very like our *third and fourth thousands*. A less equivocal word for *impression* is **Druck**.

1.5.2 **Auflage** will usually be preceded by an ordinal number or by some word indicating revision, such as **neue, neu bearbeitete, durchgesehene, revidierte, erweitete** (*enlarged*) and so forth. On the other hand **unveränderte Auflage** indicates a straight reprint. An *offprint* is usually **Sonderdruck.**

1.6 IMPRINTS

1.6.1 Modern imprints are usually those of the publisher, though one may meet **Verlag und Druck von**, i.e. *published and printed by*. The word **Verlag** can mean *publication* but is most common in the sense *publishing firm*, and enters into the name of many publishers. Sometimes it is an essential part, e.g. **Insel-Verlag**, sometimes, as in **Paul Klett Verlag**, it is dispensable.

The same root is found in the phrase formerly common: **in Verlegung**, equivalent to *published by*, but followed by the genitive.

The root **-druck-** also appears in various forms, such as **gedruckt bei/von**, *printed by*; **Buchdruckerei**, *press*. As appears above, the printer might also be the publisher. Apart from names one meets with **Gebrüder** (*brothers*), **Nachfolger** (successors), **Witwe** (*widow*), **Söhne** (*sons*).

1.6.2 The place may stand alone or be preceded by a preposition such as **in** or **zu**. These have no effect on the name, but the spelling and form of place-names change in the course of time, e.g. **Hall in Sachsen, gedruckt bey Peter Schmieden, in Verlegung Salomon Gruners, Buchhändlers in Jehna (1624) (Halle, Jena).**

1.7 SERIES

1.7.1 The names of series, to be found either at the head of the title-page or on the preceding page, are for the most part simply descriptive of the series as a whole or of the individual members, e.g. **Sammlung außerdeutscher Strafgesetzbücher**, *Collection of non-German penal codes*; **Dokumente und Berichte des Europa-Archivs**, *Documents and reports of Europa-Archiv*, and innumerable **Schriften** and **Veröffentlichungen** of institutions. The names of more popular series are freer, e.g. **Insel-Bücherei**.

Sometimes the names of the series includes that of the institution which publishes it, or of a periodical, e.g. **Schriften des Vereins für Sozialpolitik, Beihefte zur Deutschen Rechts-Zeitschrift** (entries under Verein, etc., and **Deutsche Rechts-Zeitschrift**).

1.7.2 Numeration is usually by **N(umme)r** or **Band**, less commonly by **Heft**. (One series has changed its numeration from **Sonderhefte, Nr. 66** to **Sonderheft 88**.) **Neue Folge**, *new series*, is fairly common, division into simultaneous series, **Reihe A, Reihe B**, etc., less so.

1.8 PERIODICALS

1.8.1 There is little difference between the language of periodical titles and those of books and series (1.7.1), e.g. **Raumforschung und Raumordnung, Zeitschrift für Geschichtswissenschaft**, though some of them are more allusive, e.g. **Akzente** (a literary periodical). The title of a periodical should conform to the grammar of the sentence, e.g. **die „Akzente" erscheinen** (Akzente is plural); but one meets **in „Neue Literatur" for Neuer** (cf. 1.3.3).

1.8.2 The title or sub-title may include the name of an institution, e.g. **Unternehmensforschung: Organ der Deutschen Gesellschaft für Unternehmensforschung.** (On the adjective **Deutschen** see 1.2.3.) In the case of **Mitteilungen** (*Communications*), **Verhandlungen** (*Transactions*) and the like many libraries will enter the periodical under the institution.

1.8.3 The persons concerned with the editing are variously indicated. A common form is exemplified by **herausgegeben von Walter Dirks und Eugen Kogon**, *edited by W. D. and E. K.* In this case the same two are listed as **Mitglieder der Schriftleitung** (*members of the editorial staff*) together with a third described as **verantwortlicher Redakteur** (*responsible editor*). Elsewhere the two sets of names are different, or the **Herausgeber** may be supported by the **Redaktion**, presumably much the same as the **Schriftleitung**, and **Ständige Mitarbeiter** (*regular collaborators*). In other periodicals again we find a **Chefredakteur** assisted by a **Redaktionskollegium**, or a **Redaktionskollegium**, **Chefredakteur** and **Redaktion**. **Verantwortlich** is typically a legal concept, but this does not prevent the person so described from being the real editor. Finally, here as elsewhere, **herausgeben** is ambiguous, for it means both *to edit* and *to publish*. (The latter is less equivocally indicated by **Verlag**.)

1.8.4 Numeration is usually by **Jahrgang** (*annual volume*) or **Band**, subdivided by **Nummer (Nr.)** or **Heft**. As with books, numbers may precede as ordinals or follow as cardinals. The numeration may run into more than one series (**Folge**).

1.8.5 Periodicity may be implicit in the title, e.g. **Vierteljahrsschrift, Vierteljahrsberichte** (*quarterly, quarterly reports*), **Wirtschaftswoche** (*Commercial Week*); but **Schmollers Jahrbuch** is quarterly. More often an adverb is used, e.g. **erscheint monatlich** (or **zwölfmal jährlich**), **sechsmal jährlich**, **(einmal) vierteljährlich**, *comes out monthly*, etc., or the number of parts per annual volume is stated, e.g. **jährlich erscheinen vier Hefte**, *four parts come out every year*, **der Band umfaßt 3 Hefte**, *the volume comprises three parts*.

1.8.6 Subscriptions are stated in terms of **Abonnement(spreis)** or **Bezugspreis, pro Jahr** or **pro Band**, alternatively **des Heftes**, the price of an odd part being **Einzelpreis, Preis des Einzelheftes** or **für das Einzelheft**. Alternatively the **Jahresabonnement, Halbjahresabonnement** and **Quartalsabonnement** are quoted. Occasionally no fixed price is quoted for parts: **Einzelhefte werden nach Umfang berechnet**, *Single numbers are priced by the number of pages*. Some periodicals quote a special rate (**Vorzugspreis**) for members.

2 ALPHABET, PHONETICS, SPELLING

2.1 ALPHABET

2.1.1 The alphabet in its Roman form is identical with the English alphabet except for the digraph ß, for which see below. The now obsolete Gothic form (**Fraktur**) is as follows:

𝕬 𝕭 𝕮 𝕯 𝕰 𝕱 𝕲 𝕳 𝕴 𝕵 𝕶 𝕷 𝕸 𝕹 𝕺 𝕻 𝕼
a b c d e f g h i j k l m n o p q

𝕽 𝕾 𝕿 𝖀 𝖁 𝖂 𝖃 𝖄 𝖅
r ſ s ß t u v w x y z

At least, those are the standard modern shapes. Not all founts distinguish between capital **i** (𝕴) and **j** (𝕵). On the title-pages of earlier books the capital letters may appear in elaborated forms that can be very troublesome. In older books **j** is found initially for **i**, e.g. **jhm**, but not in all words, while initial **u** regularly appears as **v**.

The form ẞ is used at the end of a word or syllable. For the purpose of alphabetical order ẞ(ß) is equivalent to ss, and like the English ss represents a single sound. As both ß and ſſ are possible in the middle of a word, ß has been added to the Roman alphabet. Where it is not available, ss should be used for ß as well as for ſſ and ßſ. Although sz is found in some books and is recommended by *Duden* in special cases, one must disregard this in catalogue headings and stick to ss. In any case sz too is ambiguous, since a genuine sz (ſʒ) is found in words like **Transzendenz.**

2.1.2 The umlaut, found on **a, o** and **u,** consists of two dots or two short vertical strokes, and modifies the pronunciation. It is of grammatical and semantic importance, e.g. **Fuße,** *to the foot*; **Füße,** *feet*; **Bar,** *bar*; **Bär,** *bear*. In earlier books it is printed as a small superscript e, and until the early years of this century was not used on capitals: **Über** was spelt out as **Ueber.**

The same spelling out is found in many names, e.g. **Goethe,** and most English catalogues make a practice of expanding all modified letters and filing accordingly. This has given rise to a legend that German works of reference normally file ä for instance as if it were ae. Some do, notably the *Deutsche Bibliographie,* and *Neue deutsche Biographie,* but the *Allgemeine deutsche Biographie* files names in general without reference to the umlaut, separating those which differ only in this respect into two sequences, so that **Büsch** follows **Busch** but both precede **Buscher;** and *Brockhaus* and the majority of dictionaries simply ignore the umlaut, as *Duden* recommends, even to the extent of filing **Goethe** after **Gotha.** (*Neue Österreichische Biographie* has **Boroevic** before **Bösendorfer** but **Högelmüller** before **Hoffmann.** Caveat lector!)

2.1.3 The apostrophe most commonly indicates an omission, e.g. **'raus** for **heraus, mach'** for **mache, g'ring** for **gering;** also **ich hab's** for **ich habe es.** It was standard until recently in adjectives formed by adding **-sch** to personal names, e.g. **die Kant'sche Kritik,** *the Kantian critical method* (now **Kantsche**) and is used to form the genitive of names ending in **-s, -sch, -ß, -x** or **-z,** e.g. **Die Bulle Innozenz' VIII,** *the bull of Innocent VIII.*

2.1.4 An acute accent is found on a few words of French origin such as **Komité** (standard form **Komitee**).

2.2 CAPITALISATION

2.2.1 All nouns, and words used as nouns, have an initial capital. This is simple enough in most cases, but note **ein paar** (*a few*) as distinct from **ein Paar** (*a pair*); expressions like **anfangs** (*in the beginning*), the genitive of **Anfang, dank** (*thanks to*), used as adverbs; and conversely **nichts Neues** (*nothing new*), **das Entweder-Oder,** *the either-or.* (Before 1650 practice is less uniform.)

2.2.2 Most proper adjectives have a small initial, e.g. **römisch,** *Roman,* except those formed by adding **-er** to a place-name, e.g. **Berliner.** Those formed from personal names have a small initial only when used in a general sense, e.g. **platonische Liebe,** *Platonic love.*

2.2.3 Proper names and titles consisting of several words have an initial capital for the first word and follow the general rule for the rest, e.g. **das Rote Meer,** *the Red Sea;* **die Vereinigten Staaten,** *the United States;* **Außerordentlicher Gesandter und bevollmächtigter Minister,** *Envoy Extraordinary and Minister Plenipotentiary.* Likewise generic names such **as die Gefleckte Hyäne,** *the spotted hyena.*

2.3 DIVISION OF WORDS

2.3.1 Rules **1, 2, 4, 5a, 6a, 7a, 8** (p.xiii) apply, with the provisos set out below.

2.3.2 In connexion with rule 1 note that although there are a vast number of words whose combining form ends in -s, there are others which are joined directly; so one has **Recht-sprechung** as against **Rechts-spruch** and **Rechts-pflege**.

2.3.3 In connexion with rule 2 the following prefixes ending in a consonant should be noted: **ab-, an-, auf-, aus-, dar-, durch-, ein-, ent-, er-, erz-, fort-, her-, herab-**, etc., **hin-, hinab-**, etc., **mit-, nach-, un-, unter-, ur-, ver-, vor-, zer-, zurück-, zusammen-**. Conversely **be-, ge-, zu-**.

2.3.4 Rules 5 and 6 have a number of real or more often apparent exceptions, some only in foreign words, or the treatment of the division may be peculiar. The combinations of letters involved and the paragraphs dealing with them are:

bl, br	2.3.7	**ph**	2.3.5
ch	2.3.5	**pl, pr**	2.3.7
ck	2.3.6	**ss**	2.3.5, 2.3.6
dr	2.3.7	**sch**	2.3.5
ff	2.3.6	**st**	2.3.5
kl, kr	2.3.7	**th**	2.3.5
ll	2.3.6	**tr**	2.3.7
mm	2.3.6	**tt**	2.3.6
nn	2.3.6		

2.3.5 Certain combinations represent single sounds and cannot therefore be divided, others are ambiguous. Thus **ch** is never divided, nor are ſch and ß (ß), e.g. **Bü-cher**, ſri-ſchen, gro-ße, but in the Roman alphabet **sch** is ambiguous, and if **ß** is not used, so is **ss**: **fri-schen** but with the diminutive ending -chen, **Häus-chen** (Häuschen), **Schlöss-chen** (Schlößchen); likewise compounds such as **Volks-charakter**; **gro-ssen** but **Was-ser**.

ph and **th** are ambiguous: **ph** in words like **Telephon** represents the sound **f** and must not be divided, but **pph**, except in the name **Sap-pho**, is divided as in **Knapp-heit**; **th** in words of Greek origin such as **or-thodox** is indivisible, but is divisible in compounds like **Rat-haus**. Unfortunately, up to the early years of this century many native words were spelt with the digraph **th** which now are spelt with **t**, e.g. **nö-thig**.

st 'is not divided', except in compounds like **Wachs-tum, Diens-tag**; hence **ge-stern, sech-ste** (*sixth*).

2.3.6 **ck** when divided becomes **kk**, e.g. **drücken** > **drük-ken**. The reverse is not invariably true, since two k's come together in words like **Funkkanal**.

The ambiguity of **ss** is dealt with in 2.3.5. It is possible in a word like **Esssaal** (i.e. **Eßsaal**) for three s's to come together. Other letters are reduced to two, e.g. **Schiffahrt** (*navigation*), **stillegen** (*to shut down*). The original structure, **Schiff-fahrt, still-legen**, is restored when such words are divided. But note on the one hand the division of words like **Hof-fart** (*pride*), **stil-los** (*without style*) where the first element ends in a single letter, and of words like **den-noch** (denn + noch), which are no longer thought of as compounds; and on the other the triplication in words like **Auspufffflamme**, where the second element begins with two consonants.

2.3.7 The division of consonants in words derived from foreign languages differs slightly. Thus **l** and **r** are not separated from a preceding stop, e.g. **Pro-blem**, nor are **gn** and **sz** separated, e.g. **Ma-gnet, fa-szinieren**. The natural division of compound words is followed, but not pedantically, e.g. **Atmo-sphäre, Inter-essant**; but **ab-stract** is allowed as well as **abs-tract**.

2.3.8 Instances of division **between** vowels are found where there is an obvious break, e.g. **Muse-um**, especially if it is structural, e.g. **Anschau-ung, unge-ahnte**. Otherwise such division is avoided.

2.3.9 Rules apart, one should avoid divisions which go against the grain of the word, e.g. **Literaturge-schichte** for **Literatur-geschichte**.

2.4 PUNCTUATION

2.4.1 The full stop is absent after series of initials such as **BGB** (abbreviation for **Bürgerliches Gesetzbuch**) and after **m** for **Meter** and similar abbreviations. On the other hand **Dr.** for **Doktor** has a stop.

2.4.2 The comma is more common in German than in English, being obligatory before a variety of subordinate clauses, e.g. **ich weiß, daß** . . ., *I know that* . . .; **besser, als ich war**, *better than I was*.

2.4.3 The great majority of words whose English counterparts require a hyphen are written as one in German, but there are some hyphenated words. As the distinction between say **Schillertheater** and **Schiller-Museum** is not easily grasped, one should be on the look-out if such words are divided between two lines. The **M** of **Museum** would show that the hyphen is an integral part of the word.

If successive compounds end (or less commonly begin) with the same element, this common element is replaced in the first (or second) word by a hyphen, e.g. **Innen- und Außenpolitik**, *domestic and foreign policy*; **Arbeitgeber und -nehmer**, *employers and employees*. At one time this applied even to words of like formation such as **männ- und weiblich**, *male and female*, instead of **männlich und weiblich**.

2.5 VARIATION OF CONSONANT

2.5.1 There is very little consonant change in the course of inflexion. Occasionally a consonant is doubled to indicate the shortening of a vowel, e.g. **ich nehme, er nimmt**; and in a few irregular verbs there is a complete change, e.g. **stehen, stand**; **bringen, brachte**. (See 8.3.1 and 8.3.2.)

2.5.2 The **d-** of the definite article vanishes after certain prepositions, e.g. **am = an dem** (10.2.2).

2.6 VARIATION OF VOWEL

2.6.1 Change of vowel is quite common. Changes of the *man/men, mouse/mice* type are more frequent in German than in English (see 4.3.3), and occur also in the derivation of adjectives, e.g. **Maß, mäßig**.

2.6.2 In verbs changes parallel to the English *sing/sang* are found (8.3.2), as well as others such as **geben/gibt** (8.2.3), **brennen/brannte** (8.3.1), **gab/gäbe** (8.7.2), which have no parallel.

2.6.3 Unaccented **-e-** disappears before an ending, e.g. **teuer, teure**.

2.7 SPELLING

2.7.1 The differences between the text of a 15th or 16th-century composition and one of today are not wholly matters of spelling, but to some extent of linguistic history (0.3). One finds on the one hand **warhait/Wahrheit, zů/zu, new/neu, zwychen/zwischen, dyser/dieser, verschrybung/Verschreibung, erwelt/erwählt, unnd/und**; and on the other **nennet/nennt, diss/dies, buech/Buch, Rich/Reich, gulden/golden, verpündtnus/Bündnis, küniglich/königlich, gethon/getan, gegenwürd/Gegenwart, uff auf**—to take a few random examples.

2.7.2 By the late 18th century the forms are substantially modern and the principal differences of spelling (which lasted until the early years of this century) are the following:

(a) Long vowels in monosyllables and open syllables, indicated by doubling or **h**, are now in some instances reduced to a single vowel, e.g. **Maaß** > **Maß**;

(b) **ie** replaces **i** in the suffix **-ieren**, and conversely **i** replaces **ie** in **gibt**;

(c) **ey** becomes **ei**;

(d) **e** is now omitted in some words, e.g. **t(h)eil(e)te, Arz(e)nei**; and the distinction between **e** and **ä** is sometimes reversed, e.g. **nemlich, ächt**, now **nämlich, echt**;

(e) **c** becomes **k** or **z** except in the combination **ch**, e.g. **das practische Princip**, now **das praktische Prinzip**;

(f) **d** is omitted in words like **todt**, but **Stadt**, which has a short vowel, keeps it;

(g) **f** replaces **ph** in native words. In words derived from Greek the change has only taken place recently in a few common words, e.g. **Foto** (but **Photographie**), **Telephon** or **Telefon**;

(h) **-niß** becomes **-nis**;

(i) **th** becomes **t** except in words of Greek origin and in some proper names, e.g. **Wert(h), nöt(h)ig, T(h)eil**;

(j) French words which had retained their native spelling, e.g. **Volontaire**, are respelt according to German phonetics: **Volontär**. This is a continuing process; many French words have still not been Germanised.

3 ARTICLES

3.1 DEFINITE

3.1.1 The article has three genders and varies according to case as follows:

	M	*N*	*F*	*P*
N	der	das	die	die
A	den	das	die	die
G	des		der	der
D	dem		der	den

3.1.2 The principal difference in the use of the definite article is that in German it is used with abstract and general nouns and with many proper names where English omits it, e.g. **die Vernunft**, *reason*; **der Mensch**, *man*(*kind*); **die Schweiz**, *Switzerland*, and sometimes where English has a possessive, e.g. **er hat das Glas in die Finger genommen**, *he took the glass in his fingers*.

3.1.3 Note that most of the forms of the definite article can also be demonstrative (7.1.2) and relative (7.2.1).

3.2 INDEFINITE

3.2.1 The forms are:

	M	*N*	*F*
N	ein	ein	eine
A	einen	ein	eine
G	eines		einer
D	einem		einer

Similarly **kein**, *no, not any*, with plural NA **keine**, G **keiner**, D **keinen**.

4 NOUNS

4.1 GENDER AND FORM

The three genders have little relation to the meaning: the neuter gender can refer to persons, and things may be of any gender. Nor is form much guide in simple nouns, e.g. **der Band, das Land, die Hand.** Formative suffixes, however are tied to gender, viz. M: -er (agent), -ling; N: -chen, -lein, -nis (or F), -tum; F: -de, -ei, -heit, -keit, -ie, -in, -ion, -schaft, -tät, -ung.

Most nouns that begin with the prefix **Ge-** are neuter.

4.3 CASE ENDINGS

4.3.1 Case endings fall into two types, called weak and strong. In weak masculines all cases except NS end in -(e)n; in weak feminines (of which there are many) the singular, as is invariably the case with feminine nouns, remains unchanged, the plural takes -(e)n. **Herr** (*lord, gentleman, Mr.*) takes **-n** in the singular, **-en** in the plural.

4.3.2 *Strong nouns*, other than feminine ones (4.3.1), are characterised by GS -(e)s, DS -e/-.

4.3.3 Various endings mark the plural of strong nouns:

	1	*2*	*3*
NAG	no change, or modified vowel	¨er	-e or ¨e
D	-n is added to NAG		

Type 1: Nouns in -el, -en, -er, -lein; neuters in -e with prefix Ge-, e.g. **Apfel, Äpfel**
Type 2: About half the neuter and a few masculine monosyllables, and words in -tum, e.g. **das Buch, die Bücher; Männer, Irrtümer**
Type 3: All the rest, e.g. **der Band, die Bände; die Hand, die Hände; der Monat, die Monate; die Kenntnis, -nisse**

4.3.4 Some nouns are strong in the singular and weak in the plural, e.g. **Doktor, Doktors, Doktoren; Studium-s, Studien,** and some nouns which used to end in -en, e.g. **Name, Schmerz,** have GS -ens, the rest -en.

4.3.5 GS -ens is sometimes found (instead of the apostrophe, 2.1.3) with personal names ending in a sibilant, and in former times AS and DS -(e)n, e.g. **mit Hume'n, bey Pieter Schmieden** (cf. 1.2.1).

4.3.6 For adjectives used as nouns see 5.1.2.

4.3.7 *Foreign nouns*

English and French nouns make the plural by adding -s, e.g. **Cowboy(s), Chagrin(s),** and so do short forms like **Auto, Foto,** and some family names, e.g. **Buddenbrook(s).**

A few Latin plurals may be encountered e.g. **Modi,** *moods,* from **Modus, Tempora,** *tenses,* from **Tempus,** and **Christus** keeps its entire declension, viz. A -um, G -i, D -o. Formerly such Latinisms were much commoner, e.g., **des Autoris, vierley Fundamenta, Herrn Antonio Heinrichen, durch Andream Aperger, mit andern Constitutionibus.** Nowadays S -um usually has P -en, e.g. **Museen, Spektren** (or -ra), **Daten.**

4.6 USE OF CASES

4.6.1 Proper names, which nowadays take only GS -s, dispense with that too if the case is already clear, e.g. **eines Alexander II., des Kardinals Corsini** (contrast **Papst Pauls II.,** where the title dispenses with the -s). Similarly **die Mörder Galeazzos,** *the murderers of Galeazzo,* but **die Mörder Galeazzo Sforzas.**

4.6.2 The cases do not cause much difficulty in translation: the genitive will not always require *of* in English, especially with verbs, and the dative with verbs denoting removing will be translated *from* not *to*. The adverbial genitive, e.g. **meines Erachtens,** *in my opinion*, requires a variety of translations.

5 ADJECTIVES

5.1 FORMS

5.1.1 Adjectives have distinctive forms for different genders and cases (5.2.1), but if these are already sufficiently indicated by the article, or by a demonstrative, possessive or the like, the ending of the adjective becomes neutral or weak (5.2.2). When used as predicates or in apposition, they have no ending, e.g. **guter Wein,** but **der Wein ist gut.**

5.1.2 Adjectives used as nouns have adjectival endings, so that one has **der Gesandte, ein Gesandter,** *the (an) ambassador*, and so on. Hence dictionary entries like **Gesandte(r).**

5.1.3 **Hoch** has stem **hoh-.**

5.2 ENDINGS

5.2.1 The strong forms, used when there is no other indication of gender and case, are as follows:

	M	N	F	P
N	-er	-es	-e	-e
A	-en	-es	-e	-e
G	-en (-es)		-e	-er
D	-em		-er	-en

The GS **-en** is imported from the weak declension. The proper **-es** is still found in some set expressions such as **gutes Muts sein,** *to be of good cheer*.

5.2.2 The weak forms (5.1.1) are: NS, ASN, ASF **-e**; all others **-en**.

5.3 COMPARISON

5.3.1 The comparative ends in **-er**, with irregular comparatives like **besser**, as in English. A good many monosyllabic adjectives modify the stem vowel, e.g. **alt, älter**. Where they do not, there is no difference between the strong form of the positive and the bare comparative, e.g. **ein kleiner Band,** *a small volume*; **dieser Band ist kleiner als jener**, *this volume is smaller than that one*; **ein kleinerer Band,** *a smaller volume*.

5.3.2 The superlative ends in **-(e)st**, sometimes with, sometimes without modification. Note **nächst** (*nearest, next*) from **nah**. The bare form of the superlative is not used as a predicate (5.1.1): either the article or **am** is added, e.g. **das beste,** *the best*; **am besten**, *best*. For emphasis **aller-** (*of all*) can be prefixed to any superlative.

5.4 POSSESSIVES

5.4.1 The possessive adjectives, e.g. **mein,** *my*; **sein,** *his*; **Ihr,** *your* are declined like **ein** (3.2.1).

5.4.2 Used as pronouns they have strong endings (5.2.1).

6 NUMERALS

6.1 CARDINAL

6.1.1

1 ein(s)	11 elf	21 einundzwanzig	101 hundert (und) eins
2 zwei	12 zwölf	22 zweiundzwanzig	200 zwei hundert
3 drei	13 dreizehn	30 dreißig	1000 tausend
4 vier	14 vierzehn	40 vierzig	2000 zweitausend
5 fünf	15 fünfzehn	50 fünfzig	
6 sechs	16 sechzehn	60 sechzig	
7 sieben	17 siebzehn	70 siebzig	
8 acht	18 achtzehn	80 achtzig	
9 neun	19 neunzehn	90 neunzig	
10 zehn	20 zwanzig	100 hundert	

6.1.2 **Ein** is declined like the indefinite article (3.2.1), the form **eins** being used in counting and telling the time. **Zwei** and **drei** have G -er and D -en, but they are only used to avoid ambiguity. The others may have D -en when used without a noun, e.g. **auf allen Vieren,** *on all fours*.

6.1.3 The numerals from 2 upwards are followed by the plural, except in the case of nouns of quantity, e.g. **zwei Mark, vier Stück Papier,** *four pieces of paper*.

6.1.4 When spelt with initial capitals **Hundert** and **Tausend** are nouns (2.2.1).

6.2 ORDINAL

6.2.1

1 erste	6 sechste	20 zwanzigste	
2 zweite	7 siebente	21 einundzwanzigste	
3 dritte	8 achte	30 dreißigste	
4 vierte	9 neunte	100 hundertste	
5 fünfte	10 zehnte	1000 tausendste	

6.2.2 The ordinals, being used mostly with the definite article, naturally appear as weak adjectives (5.2.2).

6.3 FIGURES

6.3.1 Plain figures are used for cardinals, ordinals being indicated by a full stop or, less frequently nowadays, by the addition of the ordinal ending, e.g. **Vorwort zur 3. (3ten) Auflage,** *preface to the third edition*. Roman figures may represent either, e.g. **Heinrich IV (der Vierte), Teil II (zwei), XIX. Band (neunzehnter).**

6.3.2 The decimal point is represented by a comma, and thousands and millions are marked by a space or stop on the line.

6.4 DATES

6.4.1 The months are:

Januar, Februar, März, April, Mai, Juni,
Juli, August, September, Oktober, November, Dezember

6.4.2   Dates are expressed as follows:

(*On*) *the 21st of March 1972*, den (am) **einundzwanzigsten März neunzehn hundert zweiundsiebzig**

In 1848, (**im Jahre**) **1848**

The years have no case endings.

7   PRONOUNS

7.1   DEMONSTRATIVE, INDEFINITE

7.1.1   All these pronouns have strong adjectival endings, with GS -es not -en (5.2.1). Special points are dealt with in the following paragraphs.

7.1.2   **Der, das, die** (3.1.1) is also a demonstrative. As a pronoun it has the following distinctive forms: GS **dessen, deren**; GP **deren/derer**, DP **denen**. Adverbs in **da(r)**- are substituted for forms with prepositions, e.g. **damit**, *with it* (*therewith*); **daran**, *on it*.

7.1.3   **Dieser**, *this*, has a neuter form **dies**.

7.1.4   **Derjenige**, *that one*; **derselbe**, *the same*, are complex, the second part being a weak adjective (5.2.2). Both parts are declined.

7.1.5   Demonstratives are often used where English would use a third person pronoun, and the cautions as to gender set out in 7.3.3 apply here also.

7.2   RELATIVE, INTERROGATIVE

7.2.1   The relative **der**, etc., is declined like the demonstrative (7.1.2).

7.2.2   **Wer**, *who*(*ever*), both relative and interrogative, has A **wen**, G **wessen**, D **wem**. **Was**, *what*, is also used as a relative after **all**, *all*. **Was für**, *what* (*sort of*) *a*, behaves as an indeclinable adjective.

7.2.3   Forms in **wo(r)**- translate relatives and interrogatives with prepositions, e.g. **wonach**, *after which*; **worauf**, *on what?*, *on which*.

7.2.4   In early books one finds an indeclinable relative **so**, *which*.

7.3   PERSONAL

7.3.1

	S					S & P	P		
	1	2	3*m*	3*n*	3*f*	3*r*	1	2	3
N	ich	du	er	es	sie		wir	ihr	sie
A	mich	dich	ihn	es	sie	sich	uns	euch	sie
G	mein(er)	dein(er)	sein(er)		ihrer		uns(r)er	eu(r)er	ihrer
D	mir	dir	ihm		ihr	sich	uns	euch	ihnen

7.3.2   The forms in the last column, spelt with an initial capital, are the polite forms for the second person, singular and plural, and **Sich** is used for *yourself* (-*ves*).

7.3.3   The pronouns **er, es, sie**, in the absence of indications to the contrary, mean *he, it, she*; but as nouns denoting inanimate objects may be of any gender, they can all mean *it*, while in reference to a neuter noun like **Mädchen**, *girl*; **Kind**, *child*, es can mean *she* or *he*.

8   VERBS

8.1   STRUCTURE

8.1.1   The German verb is very much like the **English** verb, even more like the English verb as it used to be, with the same distinction of **strong verbs** (*sing, sang*) and weak ones (*love*, *-d*), much the same uses of the infinitive, with and without **zu** (*to*), but with a subjunctive still very much alive. Verbs are listed under the infinitive.

8.1.2 The number of distinct forms is greater than in English, but is not enough to enable subject pronouns to be dispensed with. The proper forms of the second person are familiar, those of the 3PP being substituted in more formal contexts (cf. 7.3.2).

8.2 PRESENT

8.2.1 *Endings*

> **-e, -(e)st, -(e)t; -en, -(e)t, -en**

8.2.2 The presence or absence of **e** is a matter of euphony: **er sagt** but **er findet**. Verbs like **handeln** have **ich handle**, **er handelt**, etc. Some strong verbs whose stem ends in **-t** have no ending in the 3PS but simply change the vowel (8.2.3).

8.2.3 The vowel is changed in 2 and 3PS in some strong verbs, the changes being **a/ä, e/i(e), au/äu**, e.g. **fahren/fährt**; also **(er)löschen/(er)lischt**. Note **nehmen/nimmt**.

8.2.4 There is no special form for the continuous present: *I am coming* is **ich komme**. As in English, but more freely, the tense can refer to the future. Sometimes it must be translated by the English perfect, e.g. **es ist seit lange vergriffen**, *it has been out of print for a long time*.

8.3 PAST

8.3.1 The majority of verbs add **-te** to the stem, the resultant endings being:

> **-te, -test, -te; -ten, -tet, -ten**

In a few verbs there is a change of vowel from **e** to **a**, e.g. **kennen/kannte**, and **bringen** and **denken** make **brachte** and **dachte** (En *brought, thought*).

8.3.2 As in English, many old verbs make the past by changing the vowel, the endings being:

> **-, -est, -; -en, -et, -en**

The principal changes of vowel are:

Past tense	Infinitive
-a-	**-e-, -i-, -ie-**
-i-, -ie-	**-a-, -ei-**
-o-	**-e-, -ie-, -o-**
-u-	**-a-** usually; but **-u-** is sometimes a variant of **-o-** or **-a-**

but there are some irregularities, such as **kam/kommen; ging/gehen; rief/rufen**. Most dictionaries have lists of such verbs.

8.3.3 The tense mainly corresponds to the English past or imperfect, e.g. **ging**, *went* or *was going*, sometimes to the pluperfect (cf. 8.2.4). Occasionally the appropriate translation will be the perfect (cf. 8.15.1).

8.7 SUBJUNCTIVE

8.7.1 The present has the following endings:

> **-e, -est, -e; -en, -et, -en**

It coincides to a great extent with the indicative, but the vowel changes mentioned in 8.2.3 do not occur.

8.7.2 The past subjunctive is either identical with the indicative or differs only by modifying the vowel (2.1.2), or, in the case of the strong verbs, modifies the vowel and adds the same endings as the present, e.g. I **sah,** S **sähe,** etc.

8.7.3 Some uses of the subjunctive have English parallels such as *Long live the king!, if I were you,* but are much more extensive, e.g. **wenn er käme,** *if he came*; **es wäre besser,** *it would (might) be better.* It is frequent in such polite softenings as **ich möchte,** *I should like*; **nicht daß ich wüßte,** *not that I know.*

8.7.4 The subjunctive is used in clauses expressing purpose, wish or command, in-introduced by **daß,** *that,* and **damit,** *in order that,* but its commonest use is after verbs of saying, thinking, and the like, e.g. **Der Knabe antwortete: seine Mutter wohne in der Stadt, aber er sähe sie fast nie, er dürfe nicht hin,** *The boy answered: His mother lived in the town, but he used hardly ever to see her, he dared not go there.* The use is so characteristic that even without the introductory verb it implies indirect speech.

8.10 COMPOUND TENSES

8.10.1 The future is formed by combining the present of **werden,** *to become,* with the infinitive. **Werden** (8.19.3) is irregular. The future sometimes expresses conjecture.

8.10.2 The conditional is formed by combining the past subjunctive of **werden** (8.19.3) with the infinitive, e.g. **man wußte nicht, was er tun würde,** *they did not know what he would do.*

8.10.3 The perfect (pluperfect, future perfect) is formed of the present (imperfect, future) of **haben** or **sein** with the past participle, e.g. **er hat gefunden,** *he (has) found*; **sie war ausgegangen,** *she had gone out.* The perfect tense quite often corresponds to an English simple past.

8.11 INFINITIVE

8.11.1 The infinitive, which except for the word **tun,** *to do,* ends in -en, corresponds to the English infinitive, to the gerund and also to abstract nouns, e.g. **ich möchte wissen,** *I should like to know*; **das Parken,** *parking*; **das Erscheinen der letzten Nummer,** *the publication of the last number.*

8.11.2 It follows verbs, like the English infinitive, sometimes with, sometimes without **zu,** and also prepositions, e.g. **ohne etwas zu sagen,** *without saying anything.* Most prepositions, however, require a prop, e.g. **ich bestehe darauf** (7.1.2), **es zu wissen,** *I insist on knowing it.* Note also **er glaubt, Kenner zu sein,** *he thinks he is an expert.*

8.12 PARTICIPLES

8.12.1 The present participle ends in -end corresponding to the infinitive -en. It is commonest as an adjective (5.1), e.g. **die vorliegende Sammlung,** *the present collection,* or the equivalent of an adjectival clause, e.g. **aus dem 19. Jahrhundert stammende Vorurteile,** *prejudices dating from the 19th century.* Occasionally it corresponds to an adverbial clause, e.g. **jeweils der unmittelbaren Gegenwart dienend,** *while it occasionally serves the immediate present.* In this use it has no endings.

Preceded by **zu** it expresses -*able,* e.g. **ein nicht zu vergessendes Ereignis,** *an unforgettable event.*

8.12.2 The past participle has in most cases the prefix ge- and the ending -t. Strong verbs (cf. 8.3.2) have the ending **-en** and may change the vowel, e.g. **genommen** from **nehmen**. The principal vowel correspondences are:

Participle	Infinitive
a	a
au	au
i(e)	ei
o	e, i, ei, o
u	i, u

Some common verbs have different vowel correspondences or show changes of consonant, notably **gegangen** from **gehen**. The dictionary should be consulted. Note **getan** from **tun**, *to do*.

Some verbs omit **ge-** (cf. 8.23.2) and in what are known as separable verbs (8.23.1) it is inserted after the prefix, e.g. **aufgenommen**.

8.12.3 The commonest uses of the past participle are as an adjective and as a component of the perfect tenses (8.10.3). Its adjectival use is freer than in English, e.g. **die in diese Sammlung aufgenommenen Arbeiten**, *the works which have been included in this collection*; **seine Gestorbenen**, *his friends who have died*. Absolute uses, such as **die Augen geschlossen**, *with eyes closed*, are also found.

8.14 REFLEXIVE VERBS

8.14.1 These result from the use, as direct or indirect object, of the pronoun of the same person as the subject, or in the third person, of the special reflexive pronoun **sich**, e.g. **ich bemühe mich**, *I concern myself*.

8.14.2 The reflexive has various other uses: reciprocal, **sie umarmten sich**, *they embraced each other*; intransitive, **die sich dem Realismus widersetzen**, *who are opposed to realism*; passive: **beschränken sich nicht**, *are not confined*. Many uses are idiomatic, e.g. **es handelt sich um**, *it is a question of*.

8.15 PASSIVE

8.15.1 The passive form consists of the verb **werden** (8.19.3) with the past participle (contrast 8.10.1), e.g. **die Umlaute wurden nicht aufgelöst**, *umlauts have not been* (8.3.3) *spelt out*. The future and the perfect are a little tricky, e.g. **es wird getan werden**, *it will be done*; **es ist getan worden**, *it has been done*.

8.16 IMPERSONAL

8.16.1 A few verbs, e.g. **mich dünkt**, *I think* ('*methinks*') are used only in the 3PS; a great many ordinary verbs have impersonal uses, e.g. **es tut mir leid**, *I am sorry*; **es gibt**, *there is (are)*; **es gelang uns**, *we succeeded*; **es klopfte**, *there was a knock*; **es sei gedankt**, *thanks are due*.

8.17 MODAL AUXILIARIES

8.17.1 These auxiliaries, the equivalents of *can, may, must*, etc., are peculiar in their conjugation; and their various meanings, in view of their formal similarity to English, need watching. Only pointers are given here. In the present they have the same pattern as the past of strong verbs (8.3.2) but have a different vowel in the plural.

8.17.2 **dürfen**, *may* (*to be allowed*)
  Present: **darf . . . dürfen**

Past: durfte
Past subjunctive: dürfte

8.17.3 können, *can*
Present: **kann . . . können**
Past: **konnte**
Past subjunctive: **könnte**

8.17.4 mögen, *may* (possibility), *to like to*
Present: **mag . . . mögen**
Past: **mochte**
Past subjunctive: **möchte**
Ich möchte, *I should like*

8.17.5 müssen, *must, to be obliged to*
Present: **muß . . . müssen**
Past: **mußte**
Past subjunctive: **müßte**

8.17.6 sollen, *ought, shall*
Present: **soll(en)**
Past: (indicative and subjunctive) **sollte**

Diese Sammlung soll ein Bild der polnischen Gegenwartsprosa vermitteln, *this collection is intended to supply a picture of contemporary Polish prose.*

8.17.7 wollen, *will, wish to*
Present: **will . . . wollen**
Past: (indicative and subjunctive) **wollte**

Wer lernen will, *a man who wants to learn.* Neither **wollen** nor **sollen** is a simple future (8.10.1).

8.17.8 All these verbs have a weak past participle which matches the past tense, e.g. **gekonnt,** but it is rarely met with, for whenever the participle follows an infinitive a form identical with the infinitive is used instead, e.g. **er hätte das nicht tun sollen,** *he ought not to have done that.*

8.19 IRREGULAR VERBS

8.19.1 haben, *to have*
Present: **habe, hast, hat; haben,** etc.
Past: **hatte,** *subjunctive:* **hätte**

8.19.2 sein, *to be*
Present: **bin, bist, ist; sind, seid, sind**
Past: **war** (8.3.2)
Subjunctive, present: **sei,** *past:* **wäre**
Past participle: **gewesen**

8.19.3 werden, *to become*
Present: **werde, wirst, wird; werden,** etc.
Past: **wurde/ward**
Past subjunctive: **würde**
Past participle: **(ge)worden**

8.19.4 wissen, *to know*
Present: **weiß . . . wissen**
Past: **wußte**
Past subjunctive: **wüßte**
Past participle: **gewußt**

8.23 SEPARABLE VERBS

8.23.1 Owing to the rules of order (0.2) the adverbial complement of the verb occupies various positions in relation to the verb: **ich gehe nach Hause, dann gehe ich nach Hause, als ich nach Hause ging, ich werde nach Hause gehen, ohne nach Hause zu gehen, ich bin nach Hause gegangen.** If for **nach Hause**, *home*, we substitute **zurück**, *back*, we get **ich gehe zurück, dann gehe ich zurück, . . . zurückging, . . . zurückgehen, . . . zurückzugehen, . . . zurückgegangen.** Whenever **zurück** immediately precedes a part of the verb, the two are joined together. There are many such verbs in German, which from this habit of joining up are called 'separable'. They must be looked for in the dictionary in the joined-up form. The elements involved are mostly adverbs of position such as **ab, auf, aus, ein, unter, vor,** and their derivatives **herab, hinab, darauf,** and so on, but there are some other words, for instance **fest,** which behave in the same way. It is impossible to list them all but they will easily be found in the dictionary once one is aware of their existence.

8.23.2 With **durch, über, um** and **unter** we get pairs of verbs, one separable and the other not, some of whose written forms will be identical, e.g. **ich setze über,** *I ferry over*; **ich übersetze,** *I translate*; **übergesetzt,** *ferried over*; **übersetzt,** *translated*; but **wenn ich übersetze** and the infinitive **übersetzen** may be from either. Some dictionaries mark the verbs sep. or insep. as the case may be, but some rely on the fact that separable verbs have the stress on the prefix and inseparable verbs have it on the root, and simply give ˈübersetzen, *to ferry over*; überˈsetzen, *to translate*.

9 ADVERBS

9.1 FORMATION

Adverbs derived from adjectives have no termination. Distinguish therefore **ein gut gebundenes Buch,** *a well bound book*, from **ein gutes, gebundenes Buch,** *a good, bound book*.

9.2 COMPARISON

The same as for adjectives.

9.3 MISCELLANEOUS

The negative **nicht** usually comes after the object and adverbial complements, though it precedes the predicate, the past participles and dependent infinitives. When it occupies another position it qualifies the word which it precedes, e.g. **Die Prediger lieben dieses Wort nicht, auch Luther gebraucht es nicht oft,** *The preachers do not like this word, and Luther too uses it infrequently*.

10 PREPOSITIONS

10.2 SIMPLE PREPOSITIONS, FORMS AND SYNTAX

10.2.1 Prepositions govern particular cases. The local prepositions govern the accusative when motion is indicated, the dative when rest, e.g. **ins Haus,** *into the house*; **im Hause,** *in the house*. **Über** with the accusative also means *about* of subject matter.

10.2.2 A number of prepositions combine with the article. Thus **an, in, von,** with **dem** make **am, im, vom**; **bei** and **zu** make **beim** and **zum**. **Zu** also combines with **der** to make **zur**. **An das** gives **ans**, and other prepositions behave in the same way.

10.4 SECONDARY PREPOSITIONS
Besides the simple prepositions there are a large number of words, originally nouns, adjectives, adverbs and participles, which are used in the same way. Many of them, such as **anstatt**, *instead of*, correspond to phrases in English.

10.5 MEANING
In view of their similarity to English prepositions one should beware of traps in translating German ones. Thus **zu** is more likely to mean *at* than *to*, the commoner word for *to* being **nach**, which also means *after*.

11 CONJUNCTIONS

11.1 COORDINATING
Apart from the simple conjunctions like **und, aber, oder**, sentences are joined by a large number of other words which cause inversion of verb and subject (0.2.2). Of the words for *but* **aber** (which also means *however*) is the commonest; **sondern** is used in contexts of the *not this but that* type. *So* is frequently used simply to indicate the main clause and is not separately translated. (In old German **so** is often a relative (7.2.4).)

11.2 AMBIGUOUS FORMS
Some conjunctions, like **da**, may be either coordinating conjunctions, causing inversion, or subordinating ones, with the verb at the end of the clause (0.2.3), e.g. **Er trug sie dem Slowaken hin, da tauchte plötzlich Lorenz auf**, *He was taking them to the Slovak, when suddenly up popped Lorenz*; but (more commonly) **da diese Erzählung im Exil geschrieben wurde**, *as this tale was written in exile*.

11.3 MEANING
The meanings of some of the conjunctions may be deceptive, especially if one relies on similarity to English. Thus **als** is as likely to mean *when* as *as*; **da** (besides being an adverb meaning *there*) means *as, when, while, because*, or *since*; **weil** means *because* not *while*; **wenn** means *if* or *whenever*. Note also the use of **auch** (*also*) to add the nuance *-ever* to pronouns and conjunctions, e.g. **was es auch sei**, *whatever it may be*.

GLOSSARY

Abdruck, *copy, offprint*
Abhandlung, *essay*
Abonnement(spreis), *subscription* (1.8.6)
Abteilung, *part* (1.4.1)
Abzug, *discount*
alte Nummer, *back number*
Anhang, *addition, appendix*
Anschrift, *address*
Ansichtssendung, *dispatch on approval*
Arbeit, *work*
aufgelegt, *published*
Auflage, *edition, impression* (1.5.1)
Aufsatz, *essay, study*
Ausgabe, *edition* (1.5.1)

ausgewählt(e), *selected*
Ausland, *abroad*
Ausschuß, *committee*

Band, *number* (1.7.3); *volume* (1.4.1
Bändchen, *pamphlet*
bearbeitet, *revised* (1.5.2)
bearbeitet von, *edited by, compiled by*
Beiblatt, *supplement*
Beifügung, *addition*
Beiheft, *supplement*
Beilage, *appendix, supplement*
Beitrag, *contribution*
Berichtigung, *correction*

besorgt, *edited*
Bestellung, *order* (sb.)
Bezugspreis, *subscription* (1.8.6)
Bibliothek, *library*
Bibliothekar, *librarian*
Brief, *letter*
Briefwechsel, *correspondence*
broschiert, *sewn* (*paperback*)
Broschüre, *pamphlet*
Buch, *book* (1.2.2)
Buchdrucker(ei), *printer, press*
Buchhändler, *bookseller*
Buchhandlung, *bookshop*

Chefredakteur, *chief editor* (1.8.3)

Dichtung, *poetry, fiction*
Druck, *impression* (1.5.1)
Drucker(ei), *printer, press*
durchgearbeitet, *revised*
durchgesehen, *revised* (1.5.2)

Einleitung, *introduction*
Eintragung, *note*
Einzelheft, *single issue* (1.8.6)
englisch broschiert, *cased*
Ergänzung, *supplement*
erscheinen, *come out* (1.8.5)
erschienen, *published* (already)
erweitert, *enlarged* (1.5.2)
Erzählung, *short story*
Exemplar, *copy*

Flugschrift, *pamphlet*
Folge, *series* (1.7.3, 1.8.4)
Forschung, *research*
fortgesetzt, *continued*

geboren, *born*
gebunden, *bound*
geheftet, *sewn, stitched*
Gesellschaft, *society*
Geschichte, *history*
gestorben, *dead*

Halbband, *part* (half volume) (1.4.1)
halbjährlich, *half-yearly*
halbmonatlich, *semi-monthly*

Halbmonatsheft, -schrift, *semi-monthly publication*
Handschrift, *manuscript*
Heft, *number* (1.7.2); *part*
Herausgeber, *editor* (1.8.3)
herausgegeben von, *edited by* (1.8.3)

im Druck, *in the press*

Jahr, *year*
Jahrbuch, *yearbook*
Jahrgang, *volume* (1.4.1)
jährlich, *annual*

kartoniert, *in boards*
korrigiert, *corrected*
kostenlos, *free*

Leseexemplar, *sample*
Lieferung, *issue, number, part; delivery*

Mitglied, *member*
Mitteilung, *communication*
monatlich, *monthly*
Monatsheft, -schrift, *monthly publication*

Nachtrag, *appendix*
neu, *new* (1.5.2)
Neuausgabe, *reprint*
Neudruck, *reprint* (1.5.2)
Novelle, *long short story*
Nummer, *number* (1.7.2)

Platte, *plate*
Probeexemplar, *sample, specimen copy*

Rabatt, *discount*
Rechnung, *bill*
Redakteur, *editor* (1.8.3)
Redaktion, *editing*
Redaktionskollegium, *editorial board*
Rede, *speech*
redigiert, *edited*
Register, *index*
Reihe, *series* (1.7.2)
revidiert, *revised* (1.5.2)
Roman, *novel*
Rundschau, *review*

Sammlung, *collection* (1.7.1)
Schriftleitung, *editorial staff* (1.8.3)
Schauspiel, *play*
Seite, *page*
selbe, *same*
Sitzungsberichte, *proceedings*
Sonder(ab)druck, *offprint* (1.5.2)
Sonderheft, *supplement* (to a periodical)
(1.7.2)

Tabelle, *table*
Tafel, *plate*
Tagungsberichte, *proceedings*
Teil, *part, volume* (1.4.1)

überarbeitet, *revised*
Übersetzung, Übertragung, *translation*
umgearbeitet, *revised*
ungedruckt, *unpublished* (not printed)
unveröffentlicht, *unpublished*
Urheberrecht, *copyright*

verändert, *revised*
verantwortlich, *responsible* (1.8.3)

verbessert, *improved*
Verein(igung), *society, association*
vergriffen, *out of print*
Verhandlungen, *proceedings*
Verlag, *publishing house* (1.6.1)
Verlag von, *published by* (1.8.3)
vermehrt, *enlarged*
veröffentlicht, *published*
Versammlung, *conference*
Versand, *dispatch*
vervielfältigt, *duplicated*
vierteljährlich, *quarterly* (1.8.5)
Vierteljahrsschrift, *a quarterly* (1.8.5)
vierzehntägig, *fortnightly*
Vorbemerkung, *preface*
Vorbereitung, *preparation*
Vorrede, *preface*
Vorwort, *preface*

Woche, *week*
Wörterbuch, *dictionary*

Zeitschrift, *periodical, review*
Zusammenfassung, *summary*
zusammengestellt, *compiled*

GRAMMATICAL INDEX: WORDS

aller-, 5.3.2
als, 11.3
am, 5.3.2, 10.2.2
ans, 10.2.2
auch, 11.3

beim, 10.2.2
bewußt, 8.19.4
bin, bist, 8.10.3, 8.19.2

da, 11.2, 11.3
da(r)-, 7.1.2
damit, 8.7.4
darf, 8.17.2
das, 3.1.1, 7.1.2, 7.2.2
daß, 8.7.4
dein(er), 7.3.1
dem, den, der, 3.1.1,
7.1.2, 7.2.2
deren, derer, 7.1.2, 7.2.2
des, 3.1.1

dessen, 7.1.2, 7.2.2
dich, 7.3.1, 8.14.1
die, 3.1.1, 7.1.2, 7.2.2
dies, 7.1.3
dir, 7.3.1
drei, -en/-er, 6.1.2
durfte(-), dürf-, 8.17.2

ein(-), 3.2.1
er, es, 7.3.1, 7.3.3
euch, 7.3.1, 8.14.1
eu(r)er, 7.3.1

gegangen, -gangen, 8.12.2
getan, 8.12.2
gewesen, 8.19.2
geworden, 8.19.3
gewußt, 8.19.4
ging, 8.3.2

habe(n), habt, hast, hat,

8.10.3, 8.19.1
hatt-, hätt-, 8.19.1
hoh-, 5.1.3

ihm, ihn, ihnen, ihr(er),
7.3.1
im, 10.2.2
ist, 8.10.3, 8.19.2

kam, 8.3.2
kann, konnte(-), könn-,
8.17.3

mag, 8.17.4
mein(er), mich, mir, 7.3.1
mochte(-), 8.17.4
möchte(-), 8.7.3, 8.17.4
mög-, 8.17.4
muß-, müss-, müß-, 8.17.5

nächst, 5.3.2

sei(-), 8.19.2
seid, sind, 8.10.3, 8.19.2
sein(er), 7.3.1
sich, 7.3.1, 7.3.2, 8.14.1
sie, 7.3.1, 7.3.3
so, 7.2.4, 11.1
soll-, 8.17.6, 8.17.7

uns, 7.3.1, 8.14.1
uns(r)er, 7.3.1

vom, 10.2

war(-), wäre(-), 8.19.2
weil, 11.3
weiß, 8.19.4
wem, wen, 7.2.2
wenn, 11.3
werde(n), werdet, 8.10.1,
    8.15.1, 8.19.3
wessen, 7.2.2
will, 8.17.7
wird, wirst, 8.10.1, 8.15.1,
    8.19.3
wiss-, 8.19.4

woll-, 8.17.7
wo(r)-, 7.2.3
worden, wurde(-), 8.15.1,
    8.19.3
würde(-), 8.10.2, 8.15.1,
    8.19.3
wußt-, wüßt-, 8.19.4

zu, 8.1.1, 8.11.2, 8.12.1,
    10.5
zum, zur, 10.2.2
zwei, -en/-er, 6.1.2

GRAMMATICAL INDEX: ENDINGS

- (no ending), 4.3.2,
    4.3.3, 8.3.2

-a, 4.3.7

-end, 8.12.1

-e, 4.3.1, 4.3.3, 5.2.1,
    5.2.2, 5.4.1, 5.4.2,
    7.1.1, 8.2.1, 8.7.1, 8.7.2
-̈e, 4.3.3, 8.7.2
-te, 8.3.1, 8.7.2

-i, 4.3.7

-am, 4.3.7
-em, 5.2.1, 5.4.1, 5.4.2,
    7.1.1

-um, 4.3.7

-n, 4.3.1, 4.3.5
-en, 4.3.1, 4.3.4, 4.3.5,
    4.3.7, 5.2.1, 5.2.2, 5.4.1,
    5.4.2, 6.1.2, 7.1.1,
    8.2.1, 8.3.2, 8.7.1,
    8.7.2, 8.11.1, 8.12.2
-en (with prefix ge-),
    8.12.2
-ten, 8.3.1, 8.4.2

-o, 4.3.7

-er, 5.2.1, 5.3.1, 5.4.1,
    5.4.2, 7.1.1
-̈er, 4.3.3, 5.3.1

-s, 4.3.2, 4.3.7, 4.6.1
-es, 4.3.2, 5.2.1, 5.4.1,
    5.4.2, 7.1.1
-ens, 4.3.4, 4.3.5

-t, 8.2.1, 8.12.2
-t (with prefix ge-), 8.12.2
-et, 8.2.1, 8.3.2, 8.7.1,
    8.7.2
-tet, 8.3.1, 8.7.2
-st, 5.3.2, 8.2.1
-est, 5.3.2, 8.2.1, 8.3.2,
    8.7.1, 8.7.2
-test, 8.3.1, 8.7.2

-̈ indicates that the pre-
    ceding vowel is modi-
    fied, (2.1.2, 2.6.1).

DANISH

SPECIMENS

Denne bogs titel er forsåvidt utilstrækkelig, som bogen i virkeligheden rummer en undersøgelse af H. C. Andersens forbindelse med England og Skotland; dette kan imitlertid ikke udtrykkes på dansk i en kort, koncis titel. (*H. C. Andersen og England*, 1954)

The title of this book is to this extent inadequate, that the book in fact contains an investigation of H. C. Andersen's connexion with England and Scotland; that cannot, however, be expressed in Danish in a short, concise title.

Det er jo Poul Martin Møller vi har tænkt paa med Titlen til denne Samling—paa et Digt saa kendt og elsket, at det af sig selv har banet sig Vej ind i en af Teksterne. (*Glæde over Danmark*, 1958)

It is of course Poul Martin Møller we have thought of in the title of this collection—of a poem so known and loved that it has of itself made itself a way into one of the texts.

The later text is more conservative (2.1.1, 2.2.1) than the earlier one.

0 GENERAL CHARACTERISTICS

0.1 DEGREE OF INFLEXION
Danish is on balance almost as analytical as English, in some respects more so. It has only one form for each tense of the verb and has generalised the possessive -s to all genders and numbers. On the other hand the definite article and the passive voice are to some extent expressed by suffixes.

0.2 ORDER OF WORDS
Genitives as well as adjectives precede the nouns they qualify but prepositional phrases follow them. The normal sentence order, SVOC, is not changed, as it is in German, in dependent sentences, but if the complement is first, the order of subject and verb is reversed. In fact, in word order and general behavior Danish is very like English, even to the omission of the relative and the placing of a preposition at the end of the sentence. (See Specimen 2.) The position of the adverb may be momentarily puzzling especially in compound verbs (8.23), and the article sometimes has long insertions between it and the noun, e.g. **de i snævrere forstand driftsøkonomiske emner,** *the subjects which pertain to business economics in the narrower sense.*

0.3 RELATION TO OTHER LANGUAGES
Germanic in its general structure, though with Romance borrowings in vocabulary, Danish, like Norwegian and Swedish, has lost the th-sound which persists in English and Icelandic but does not turn every initial **th** into **d** as the German does. Thus: **tak,**

c

thanks; but **det**, *that* (De **Dank, das**). On the other hand it retains the original **k** in words like **skib**, *ship*; **skam**, *shame*. As **tak** shows, it shares the common Scandinavian assimilation of **n** to following **k**. (See General note on the Germanic languages.) It is alone, however, in voicing a large number of consonants after vowels, e.g. **bog**, *book*; **ud**, *out*; **dyb**, *deep*; and in inserting an unetymological silent **d** after l and n, e.g. **fuld**, *full*; **ind**, *in*.

1 BIBLIOLINGUISTICS

1.1 NAMES

The spelling of older names may give rise to some awkwardness. Reference books usually preserve the old spelling but may file according to modern conventions. Names in **Th-** may be filed as **T**, **œ** treated as **ø** and more recently **aa** as **å**. It is peculiarly difficult for those unfamiliar with the language to look for **oe** and **aa** at the end of the alphabet. Rules for names with prefixes are given in Chaplin.

1.2 NAMES OF AUTHORS, EDITORS, ETC.

1.2.1 The names of authors may stand at the head of the title-page or follow the title and be preceded by **af**. Where the work is a dictionary or catalogue or some other composition not felt to involve pure authorship, **ved** may take the place of **af**. The form of the words is not affected. As occasion requires, such words as **fremstillet**, *recounted*; **afgivet**, *submitted*; **udført**, *carried out*, may be added before **af**.

1.2.2 In collected works, memoirs, letters and new editions of standard works the name may have the genitive **-s**, e.g. **H. C. Andersens|Eventyr og Historier**; **Oehlenschlägers Erindringer**; **Salmonsens Konversations Leksikon**; but **H. C. Andersen| Eventyr|Første Samling** in the original edition. Sometimes care is needed as in **Henrik Steffens|Et Livsbillede|af Richard Peterson**, a biography of Steffens.

1.2.3 The names of editors usually follows the title. The usual word for *edit* is the vague **udgive**, which also means *publish* in a broad sense; but **redigeret** and the cognate **redaktion** are also common, **under H. Weitermeyers redaktion**, with the genitive **-s** or **under Redaktion af P. Tuken**. **Bearbejdet** suggests the working over of an existing text; collections may be described as **samlede og udgivne** and selections as **uddraget**, *extracted*; **udvalgt**, *selected*. (But note that the *noun* **udvalg** also means a committee.) With society publications one often meets simply **udgivet af** [society] **ved** [editor]. Here the relations of the two parties to the text are obviously different; but **af** and **ved** as such do not imply a different relation. In editions of existing texts the usual **udgivet** may be qualified by references to **indledning, noter, oplysninger, kommentarer** (*introduction, notes, explanations, commentaries*). It is a question whether **udgivet** necessarily excludes original authorship. Probably **udgivet af Victor Eremita** in Kierkegaard's *Enter-eller* should be taken as a deliberate mystification.

1.2.4 For collaborators, apart from the simple collocation of names, with or without **og**, one finds such expressions as **under medvirkning/medarbejderskab af, i samråd med, i forbindelse med**. Where the part played by the various authors is unequal such expressions as **med bidrag af**, *with a contribution by*, may be substituted.

1.2.5 The standard expressions for translation are **oversættelse, oversat af**, but one also meets **fordansket**, and a free version may be described as **gendigtet**, *recreated*, or **udlagt**, *interpreted*.

1.2.6 The names of bodies responsible for the preparation of a book are given in much the same way as those of individual authors, usually in the **nominative**, occasionally with the possessive -s. Sometimes such names may be those of the publishing or sponsoring institutions, but the latter are more likely to be given in a note and distinguished by such words as **tilskud**, *contribution*; **(under)støtte(lse)**, *support*; **understøttet**, *supported*; **subventioneret**, *subsidised*. Very often the body ultimately responsible, e.g. that to which a report is made, appears at the head, while the body that has prepared the work follows the title.

1.2.7 In Danish it makes no difference to the form of a corporate name whether it is in a connected context or isolated in a heading. In English we have *Ministry of Labour* as a heading, but *prepared by the Ministry of Labour*; in Danish we have **Arbejdsministeriet**, with the suffixed article (3.2.1) in both cases. Other names may have no article in either context. With the prefixed article the principle is the same: either the article on both occasions, e.g. **Det kongelige nordiske Oldskriftselskab** and **udgivne af Det kongelige . . .**, or on neither, e.g. **(af) Jysk Selskab for Historie**.

The catalogue heading should follow the practice of the body in question, retaining the article if need be. The prefixed article, which would be ignored in filing, may be awkward to retain in its proper position but it can be transferred to the end, e.g. **Kongelige Nordiske Oldskriftselskab, Det**. In view of the rules governing strong and weak adjectives (5.2.2) its omission results in a grammatical oddity. Nevertheless, if one decides for reasons of convenience to omit it, one should not follow the German model and substitute the strong form. As we have seen, if the body had wished to use the strong form (as in **Jysk Selskab**), it could have done so, but it would have used it in all contexts.

1.2.8 Where a main and a subordinate body are mentioned together there are three possibilities:

(a) **Folketingets Bibliotek**. The main body, **Folketinget** has the article and the genitive **-s**, the subordinate body has no article. If one arranges this in a catalogue under **Folketinget** and not as an independent heading, it would seem reasonable to put either **Folketinget. Folketingets Bibliotek**, treating the latter as an unalterable name, as is done in *Impressa publica Regni Danici*, or **Folketinget. Biblioteket**, treating the phrase as simply descriptive, breaking it up as one would *House of Commons. Library*, and giving **Bibliotek** the customary article.

(b) **Husholdningsudvalget under Landbrugsministeriets produktivitetsudvalg**. Here the superior body is already complex as in (a); further subdivision is expressed by putting the subordinate body first and following it with the appropriate preposition. The catalogue entry here could be **Landbrugsministeriet. Produktivitetsudvalget. Husholdningsudvalget**. (Here again *Impressa publica* does not break up **Landbrugsministeriets produktivitetsudvalg**.)

(c) The bodies may be simply set out in hierarchical order as in the catalogue entry just given.

It should perhaps be mentioned that the phrases of type (a) do not necessarily imply a subordinate body. The genitive may be descriptive, as in **Arbeiderbevægelsens Bibliotek**, *Library of the Labour Movement*.

1.3 TITLES

1.3.1 Most titles are fairly transparent, consisting mainly of nouns, adjectives and prepositions, though belles lettres, propaganda and intimate literature may produce titles which include verbs. The genitive before the noun may pull one up for a moment, as in **Af mit livs og min tids historie**, *From the history of my life and times*; **45 timers ugens indførelse**, *The introduction of the 45 hour week*.

1.3.2   In the filing of the title entries under the Anglo-American rules the article **den, det, de** is ignored, but not the demonstrative with the same form. Thus **Det STORE cirkus**, *The big circus*; **Den STORE fjende**, *The great enemy*; but **DET Danmark vi bygger**, *The Denmark we are building*; **DE kampe glemmer jeg aldrig**, *Those struggles I shall never forget*; and also **DEN ene — og de seks**, *The one — and the six*. Note that the English translation is not an adequate guide: den, etc., is ignored in the combination article, adjective, noun, but not otherwise.

The suffixed article **-en, -et, -ne** cannot be ignored: e.g. **Familie og ægteskab, Familiekundskab, Familien Ataka** in that order.

The indefinite article **en** or **et** is ignored, but the numeral (sometimes distinguished as **én, ét**) is not.

Under British Museum rules genitive **-s** and suffixed article would be removed to produce the anonymous heading.

1.4   VOLUMES AND PARTS

1.4.1   The usual word for volume is **bind**, smaller divisions being **halvbind, del, afdeling, hæfte (hefte)**. **Del** and **afdeling** are ambiguous, for they can indicate a part or division either of the whole work or of the volume. **Del** may even be synonymous with **bind** or **halvbind**, as in **Danmarks gamle folkeviser, tiende del**; but in the preface **Bd X**. **Hæfte** most often means *fascicule*. In old books **tomus** is occasionally found for **bind**.

1.4.2   The numeration is frequently given in the form **Første binds første afdeling, andet binds tredie hefte**, with **bind** in the genitive.

The numeration is sometimes explicitly closed, e.g. **4de og sidste** (*last*) **bind**, or there may be a statement of intention such as **Den foreliggende udgave . . . vil udgøre 4 bind, af hvilke det 4de indeholder kommentaren**, *The present edition will comprise 4 volumes of which the 4th contains the commentary.*

1.5   EDITIONS

1.5.1   The relevant words are **udgave**, *edition*, and **oplag** (less commonly **optryk**) *impression*, e.g. **Trettende udgave, V oplag** *5th impression of the 13th edition*, **3. udgave, 5. optryk**. But the distinction between **udgave** and **oplag** is often ignored. (For another meaning of **optryk** see below.)

1.5.2   Revision is indicated by such additions as **ny** (*new*), **ændrede, omarbejdede, gennemsete, reviderede** (all *revised*), **forøgede** (*enlarged*) **rettede** (*corrected*). Reprints are denoted by **optryk** (but see above), offprints by **særtryk**.

1.6   IMPRINTS

1.6.1   Most publishers imprints include the word **forlag**, preceded by a personal name in the possessive, e.g. **G.E.C. Gads Forlag**, or an adjective derived from a name, e.g. **Det Schønbergske Forlag**. Here, as in **Universitetsforlaget** and in descriptive or arbitrary names such as **Nordisk Forlag**, the word **forlag** simply means *press*. But in **trykt på forfatterens forlag**, *printed at the authors expense*, it has the original meaning, which is common in earlier imprints. In these one also meets the verb **forlagt af**, *undertaken by*, and such vague expressions as **fås hos**, *obtainable from*, or **sælges på**, *sold by*. When the publishing firm is an agent, the fact is usually expressed by **i kommission hos**. **Trykt, trykkeri** indicate the printer.

1.7   SERIES

1.7.1   The titles of series may be singular, e.g. **Danmarks Nationallitteratur** (*Danish National Literature*), **Dansk Bogsamling** (*Danish Library*) or plural, as **Danske**

middelalderlige **Regnskaber** (*Danish mediaeval accounts*) or the numerous **Skrifter udgivne af** . . . (*Publications of* . . .). Implied series, e.g. **Rapport nr. 1**, are less common. It is worth noting that they are left in the singular in the headings in *Impressa publica Regni Danici*, not turned into the plural, as is usual in English catalogues.

Titles of series may form a single grammatical whole with the name of the issuing body, e.g. **Arbejds- og Socialministeriernes Økonomisk-Statistiske Undersøgelser**, *Economico-Statistical Investigations of the Ministries of Labour and Social Affairs* (catalogue heading: Denmark. Arbejdsministeriet *and* Socialministeriet. Økonomisk-Statistiske Undersøgelser. (Cf. 3.1.1, 4.2.1, 4.3.1.)

1.7.2 Numeration is by **bind, hæfte** or **nummer**, and the series are often divided into sub-series, either consecutive, as 1, 2 [etc.] **række**, or concurrent, e.g. **A, B**, etc.

1.7.3 The names of long continued series may be affected by the change from **aa** to **å** (2.1.1).

1.8 PERIODICALS

1.8.1 Titles do not differ grammatically from those of books. Some types of title, e.g. **Acta**, are common to series and periodicals. **Årbog** and **årbøger** (both singular and plural are found in titles) usually denote periodicals, but **Gyldendals Julebog**, containing each year a single work or collection of essays and stories by one author, is more a series. (On **aarbog/årbog** and the like see 2.1.1.)

1.8.3 **Udgivet** usually indicates the issuing body, *edited* being here **redigeret**.

1.8.4 The numeration may again be by **bind**, but **årgang** (*annual volume*) is perhaps commoner, and very occasionally **serie** is found. For individual numbers **hæfte** is used, e.g. **pr. årgang a 7 hæfter**, *per volume of 7 parts*.

1.8.6 The statements of price and directions for obtaining distinguish between subscription (**i abonnement**) and the sale of separate volumes or parts (**løssalg** or **enkeltsalg**), and in the case of societies between members (**medlemmer**) and others.

2 ALPHABET, PHONETICS, SPELLING

2.1 ALPHABET

2.1.1 The alphabet reads: **a–z æ ø å**. V and w are interfiled in most reference books and in Dahlerups dictionary, but are separated in Vinterberg and Bodelsen. In 1948 it was officially recommended that **aa**, indexed at the beginning of the alphabet, should be replaced by **å**. For a time both forms were allowed (cf. the specimens at the beginning), and Vinterberg and Bodelsens dictionary, published in 1954, uses **aa**. *Danske Bogfortegnelse* adopted å in its title, årskatalog, but filed å with aa. In 1956 it followed the more definite recommendations of 1955 and 1956 and transferred **aa** with **å** to the end. Some writers still use **aa**, and names may or may not be changed. Those which keep their old spelling **aa** are now indexed as if they were spelt with **å**.

Danish was formerly printed in gothic type. (See German.)

2.1.2 An acute accent is used in some French words, e.g. **armé** (but not before an ending, e.g. armeen); to indicate stressed **-ér**, or for distinction or emphasis, e.g. **én, ét** (*one*), **dér, fór, lét**.

2.2 CAPITALISATION

2.2.1 Formerly all nouns had initial capitals. This is still found today, and one needs to guard against mistaking common nouns such as **forfatter**, *author*; **udgiver**, *editor*; forening, *society*, for names, when they occupy similar positions.

The following are the current rules. Names of persons (when used in their proper sense), geographical features, political and administrative divisions, societies and institutions, political parties, books and works of art, synonyms for God, such adjectives in -ske as **den Bohrske familie**, *the Bohr family*, have initial capitals. Such names continue to be written with a capital when joined to a common noun, e.g. **Versaillestraktaten.**

2.2.2 Where a name contains two elements, both are spelt with capitals, but if the expression is descriptive, as in **Århus stift, Handelsministeriets produktivitetsudvalg** the common noun may be written small. If there are more than two, it is possible either to capitalise all the important words or only the first and last. This is also done when quoting the titles of books, but not when making entries in a catalogue.

2.2.3 The following begin with a small letter: days of the week, festivals, months, seasons, points of the compass; political and religious designations such as **social-demokrater, protestanter**; names that have become or form part of common nouns, e.g. **sankthansurt** (contrast *St John's wort*), **celsius, dieselmotor**, derivatives such as **grundtvigianer, dansk, englænder, den lutherske kirke**. The titles of official bodies may be considered to be names and spelt with capitals or as descriptions and spelt with small letters.

2.2.4 Titles and prefixes are written with a small initial, as in **kongen**, *the King*; but **Deres Majestæt, Deres kongelige Højhed, Sankt Peter, Jomfru Marie.**

2.2.5 Note especially that when the name of an institution customarily begins with the article, the article begins with a capital even in the middle of a sentence.

2.3 DIVISION OF WORDS

2.3.1 The following rules (p. xiii) apply; 1, 2, 3, 4, 5a, 6c, 7a, 8.

2.3.2 The following relaxations and exceptions are allowed:

(a) **sk, sp, st** may be taken over, and after a long vowel or in a word accented on the last syllable, any 'possible' combination, e.g. **pro-blem**;

(b) Etymological division of derivatives is not insisted on, nor the preservation of suffixes that are not obvious.

Possible initial combinations include some that may be strange, viz, **bj, dj, fj, hv, kj, kv, pj, sj, skj, spj, stj, tj, tv, vr.**

2.4 PUNCTUATION

2.4.1 An apostrophe is used before suffixes and endings in some special cases, e.g. **å'et**, *the letter å*; **wc'et** (without full-stops or capitals), *the lavatory*; **buffet'er** (silent t), *buffets*.

2.4.2 Danish, unlike English, puts a comma before a relative clause when the relative is omitted: **De linier, dit øie her først falder paa, ere skrevne sidst**, *The lines your eye first falls on here are written last.*

2.4.3 There is a hyphen at the beginning or end of a word in such phrases as **rationaliserings- og organisationsteori og -praksis**, *the theory and practice of rationalisation and organisation.* In this rather extreme example both **teori** and **praksis** are combined with both **rationalisering** and **organisation.** (Cf. also 1.7.1.)

2.6 VARIATION OF VOWEL

2.6.1 Monosyllables ending in a consonant may have a short or long vowel. If the vowel is short, the consonant is doubled before a termination beginning with a vowel, e.g. **søn, sønnen.**

2.6.2 Unaccented -e- in a final syllable may disappear when an ending is added, e.g. **frøken, frøknen.**

2.7 SPELLING

Danish spelling has changed little in the last two hundred years, though in the early 18th century, it was still somewhat fluid. The following are the principle earlier changes: **c >k; ee > e; ey > ei; fv > v; oe > ø; ph > f; sch > s; th > t; v > f** (occasionally); **x > ks.**

The 1948 orthographical recommendations (for which see *Retskrivningsordbog*, 1957) restored some French spellings, such as **Accoucheur** for **Akkuchør**, while Danicising other words, such as **distrait** to **distræt**, **cortege** to **kortege**. At the same time **æ** replaced **e** in a number of words, and to a much lesser extent vice versa, and **j** replaced **i** between vowels. (In words like **tredje** and **afbejde** the change had taken place long since.)

3 ARTICLES

Danish has definite and indefinite articles, but their use is only roughly the same as in English. Along with the strong form of the adjective (5.2.1) they reveal the gender of Danish nouns, viz. common or neuter.

3.1 DEFINITE

3.1.1

C	N	P
-(e)n	-(e)t	-(e)ne

attached to the S or P of the noun, e.g. **bog|en, kirke|n, hus|et, hæfte|t, bøger|ne, hæfter|ne, hus|ene.** But note **studium, studiet; danskere, danskerne.**

3.1.2

C	N	P
den	det	de

Used before adjectives, e.g. **det gamle hus,** *the old house.* The same forms are demonstratives. See 7.2 and 1.3.2.

3.2 INDEFINITE

C **en**	*N* **et**

4 NOUNS

4.2 PLURAL

4.2.1 Most words add **-e, -er** or nothing. Nouns ending in **-um** substitute **-er**, e.g. **centrum, centrer;** or **-e** or **-a,** e.g. **spektrum, spektre** or **spektra.**

4.2.2 In some common words the vowel is changed as well, e.g. **fader, fædre; moder, mødre; bog, bøger; mand, mænd; barn, børn.**

4.1.3 Good dictionaries give the plural form.

4.3 CASES

4.3.1 An **-s,** without apostrophe, is added to singular and plural, with or without article, and to the last of a group of nouns to indicate the genitive, e.g. **fra alle landets egne,** *from all parts of the land;* **ideernes krise,** *the crisis of ideas;* **Foreningen af Statsautoriserede Revisorers Bibliotek,** *Library of the Association of State-authorised Auditors.*

It will be apparent that the genitive corresponds as often to *of* (or even some other preposition) as to *'s*. Note also such words as **femårs**, *five-year*. (Cf. 1.3.1.)

4.3.2 Traces of other cases are found in stereotyped expressions, e.g. **på tid|e**, *about the time*.

5 ADJECTIVES

5.1 AGREEMENT
So far as there are separate forms adjectives agree with the nouns they qualify.

5.2 ENDINGS
5.2.1

	C	N	P
Strong	-	-t	-e
Weak	-e	-e	-e

with changes as in 2.6.

Adjectives ending in **-sk** or **-t** do not add **-t**.
Adjectives ending in **-e**, **-s** or a stressed vowel may be invariable.
Note: **viis** > **vise**; **vis** > **visse**.

5.2.2 The weak form is used after the definite article, demonstratives, possessives and genitives, and in address, e.g. **Det danske Forlag, denne nye udgave, mit eventyrlige liv, Københavns største plads**; otherwise the strong form, e.g. **dansk litteratur, Socialt Tidsskrift, et dansk selskab, et nyt selskab, tidsskriftet er nyt, gamle danske minder samlede og udgivne af . . ., små bøger.**

5.3 COMPARISON
Comparative **-(e)re**, superlative **-(e)st**. Irregular comparisons, e.g. **god, bedre, bedst**, are given in the dictionary.

6 NUMERALS

6.1 CARDINAL
6.1.1

1 en, et	11 elleve	21 enogtyve
2 to	12 tolv	22 toogtyve
3 tre	13 tretten	30 tredive
4 fire	14 fjorten	40 fyrre(tyve)
5 fem	15 femten	50 halvtreds(indstyve)
6 seks	16 seksten	60 tres(indstyve)
7 syv	17 sytten	70 halvfjerds(indstyve)
8 otte	18 atten	80 firs(indstyve)
9 ni	19 nitten	90 halvfems(indstyve)
10 ti	20 tyve	100 hundrede

101 **(et) hundrede (og) et**
102 **(et) hundrede (og) to**
200 **to hundrede**
1000 **tusind(e)**
1204 **et tusind to hundrede (og) fire**

6.2 ORDINAL

1	første	11	ellevte	21	enogtyvende
2	and|en, -et	12	tolvte	22	toogtyvende
3	tredje	13	trettende	30	tredivte
4	fjerde	14	fjortende	40	fyrretyvende
5	femte	15	femtende	50	halvtresindstyvende
6	sjette	16	sekstende	60,	etc. tresindstyvende, etc.
7	syvende	17	syttende	100	hundrede
8	ottende	18	attende	102	(et) hundredeanden
9	niende	19	nittende	1000	tusinde
10	tiende	20	tyvende		

6.3 FIGURES

Simple arabic figures represent cardinals. Ordinals are represented by arabic figures followed either by a full stop or by the ordinal ending, e.g. lste, 2den, 3dje, 4de, 5te. Occasionally roman figures may be used for ordinals.

6.4 DATES

6.4.1 The months are:

januar, februar, marts, april, maj, juni,
juli, august, september, oktober, november, december

6.4.2 (*On*) *the 18th of October 1961* is expressed thus:

den 18de oktober nitten hundrede enogtres(indstyve)

As cardinals are invariable, expressions like 1848–1948 cause no difficulty.

7 PRONOUNS

7.1 DEMONSTRATIVE, ETC.

7.1.1 The various forms of possessives, demonstratives, interrogatives, relatives and the like are given in good dictionaries. Some forms and usages may cause a little trouble.

7.1.2 **Den, det, de,** besides the obvious meaning *that, those,* may mean *he, she, it, they.* (Example at the end of 10.)

7.1.3 Used adjectivally as antecedents of relatives, they are usually translated *the,* but they are still demonstratives. (See 1.3.2.)

7.3 PERSONAL

7.3.1 De, Dem with initial capitals are polite forms for *you.* The corresponding possessive is **Deres.**

7.3.2 Some uses of the reflexive **sig** are idiomatic, e.g. **Femte og sjette udgave lader sig bruge samtidig,** *The fifth and sixth editions may be used simultaneously* (literally *let themselves use*).

8 VERBS

8.1 STRUCTURE

8.1.1 Verbs are entered in the dictionary under the infinitive (8.11).

8.1.2 The following is the commonest pattern of endings, **V** denoting a vowel other than **e**:

Active			*Passive*	
Infinitive	-e	-V	-es	-Vs
Present	-er	-Vr	-es	-Vs
Past (1)	-de, -te, -ede	-Vede	-des, -tes, -edes	-Vedes
(2)	See 8.3.2		Add -(e)s	
Present participle	-ende	-Vende	——	——
Past participle	——	——	(1) -(e)t	
			(2) See 8.12	
			See also 8.15	

For further details and for compound tenses see below.

8.2   PRESENT

8.2.1 The forms given above now apply to both singular and plural. At one time the plural form was the same as the infinitive, except for **ere**, *are*. For irregular presents see 8.19.

8.3   PAST

8.3.1 The weak past is far more common—examples:

    læse > læste, høre > hørte, bygge-de, bo-ede

Occasionally there is also a change of vowel, e.g. **følge > fulgte**.

8.3.2 The strong past, which is a relic, is got by removing the -e of the infinitive and changing the vowel, e.g. **give > gav** (*give, gave*). Possible changes are:

	Past	*Infinitive*
	-a-	-i-, -y-, -æ-
	-e-	-i-
	-o-	-a-
	-ø-	-y-
also	bad	bede
	lå	ligge
	så	se

Some dictionaries list such verbs separately; Vinterberg and Bodelsen give the past tense and participle in the entry itself.

8.10   COMPOUND TENSES

8.10.1 The future is expressed by **skal** and **vil**, and also **får** and **kommer at,** all with the infinitive.

8.10.2 The perfect (pluperfect, future perfect) are expressed by the present (past, future) of **have** or **være** (8.19) with the past participle (8.12.2), e.g. **vi har udgivet; bogen er udkommet.**

8.11   INFINITIVE

This corresponds also to the English verbal noun ending in -*ing* and is commonly preceded by **at,** e.g. **ved at benytte,** *in using.*

8.12 PARTICIPLES

8.12.1 The present participle is used as an adjective. (Cf. 8.23.)

8.12.2 The past participle, when used as a verb, ends in **-et**. Some verbs with strong past tenses change the vowel, viz.

Past participle	Infinitive
-e-	-i-
-u-	-i-, -y-, -æ-
-a-	-æ-
-ø-	-y-

8.12.3 When used adjectivally, the participles of some strong verbs may end in **-en**, **-ne**; but participles that follow the noun now often have the **-t** form, e.g. **Aarbøger for nordisk Oldkyndighed, udgivne af . . .**; and **Skrifter udgivet af . . . .**

8.15 PASSIVE

8.15.1 The **-s** form (8.1.2) is common in general statements and to express possibility, e.g. **fås**, *is obtainable*; **sælges**, *is on sale*.

8.15.2 **Blive** with the past participle emphasises the action, e.g. **bogen bliver udgivet**, *the book is being (will be) published*.

8.15.3 **Være** with the past participle emphasises result or state, e.g. **bogen er udsolgt**, *the book is sold out*.

8.19 IRREGULAR VERBS

Some common verbs are irregular in the present or have anomalous past tenses, viz.

Infinitive	Present	Past	Past participle
være, *be*	**er**	**var**	**været**
have, *have*	**har**	**havde**	**haft**
bringe, *bring*	**bringer**	**bragte**	**bragt**
burde, *ought*	**bør**	**burde**	**burdet**
flyve, *fly*	**flyver**	**fløj**	**fløjet**
få, *get*	**får**	**fik**	**fået**
gå, *go*	**går**	**gik**	**gået**
kunne, *can*	**kan**	**kunne***	**kunnet**
måtte, *may, must*	**må**	**måtte**	**måttet**
skulle, *shall, ought*	**skal**	**skulle***	**skullet**
vide, *know*	**ved**	**vidste**	**vidst**
ville, *will*	**vil**	**ville***	**villet**

* earlier **kunde, skulde, vilde.**

8.23 COMPOUND VERBS

As in English (*go out, look over, overlook*), there exist in Danish verbs compounded with attached or unattached adverbs. Often there are pairs, with the same meaning, e.g. **udbringe** and **bringe ud**, *to deliver*, or a different one, e.g. **udgive**, *to publish*; **give ud**, *to spend*. The members of these pairs are entered independently in the dictionary and maintain their differences in nearly all their various parts, e.g. **kaste bort, kastede bort, har kastet bort**. But when the present and past participles are used as adjectives, the adverb is always attached, e.g. **sammenhørende emner**, *subjects which belong together* (høre sammen); **udgået træ**, *dead tree* (**gå ud**). As far as its form goes, **udgået** could equally well come from **udgå**, which exists but has a different meaning. As this is often the case, caution is needed in translating.

9 ADVERBS

The strong neuter form of most adjectives may be used adverbially.

10 PREPOSITIONS

Despite their similarity to English ones, it is not always safe to guess at the meaning of Danish prepositions, since their use differs considerably. Thus **ved** (etymologically *with*) may mean *about, at, by, in, on, to*, while **af** has many other meanings besides *of* and *off*. It is refreshing therefore to meet such phrases as **som det koster meget arbejde at få noget ud af**, *which it costs one a good deal of labour to get anything out of*.

GLOSSARY

abonnement, *subscription*
adresse, *address*
afdeling, *part* (1.4.1), *volume*
afhandling, *essay*
aftryk, *edition*
anmærkning, *note*

bearbejdet *revised*
bemærkning *note*
bestille, *to order*
bestilling, *order*
bibliotek, *library*
bibliotekar, *librarian*
bidrag, *contribution*
bilag, *supplement*
billigbog, *cheap paperback*
bind, *volume* (1.4.1)
bog, *book*
boghandel, *bookshop*
boghandler, *bookseller*
brev, *letter*
brochure, *pamphlet*
bytte, *exchange*

del, *part* (1.4.1)
digtning, *poetry*
død, *died*

eksemplar, *copy*
ekspedition, *dispatch*
enkelt, *single*
enkelthefte, *issue*

fjortendags-, *fortnightly*
forening, *society, association* (2.2.1)
forestående, *forthcoming*
forfatterret, *copyright*
forhandlinger, *proceedings*
forlag, *press; publishing house* (1.5.1)
forlagt, *published*
formeret, *enlarged*
forord, *preface*
forsøg, *essay, research*
fortale, *preface*
fortsat, *continued*
fortælling, *short story*
forøget, *enlarged* (1.5.2)
fri, *complimentary, free*
født, *born*
følge, *series*

gammelt nummer, *back number*
gennemset, *revised* (1.5.2)
genoptryk, *offprint, reprint*
granskning, *research*

halvbind, *part* (1.4.1)
halvmånedlig, *fortnightly*
halvårlig, *half-yearly*
hefte, hæfte, *part* (1.4.1)
håndskrift, *manuscript*

indbundet, *bound*
indholdsfortegnelse, *index*
indledning, *introduction* (1.1.4)

kartonneret, *in boards*
kvartalsskrift, *a quarterly*
kvartårlig, *quarterly*

levering, *issue*

medlem, *member*
månedlig, *monthly*
månedsskrift, *a monthly*
møde, *conference*

novelle, *short story*
ny, *new* (1.5.2)
nytryk, *reprint*

omarbejdet, *revised* (1.5.2)
omredigeret, *revised*
ophavsret, *copyright*
oplag, *edition*; *impression* (1.5.1)
optryk, *impression* (1.5.1); *reprint* (1.5.2)
ordbog, *dictionary*
oversigt, *summary*
oversættelse, *translation*

planche, *plate*
prøveeksemplar, *sample*

rabat, *discount*
redaktion, *editing* (1.1.4); *editorial office*
redaktør, *editor*
redigeret, *edited* (1.1.4)
register, *index*
regning, *bill*
rettede, *corrected* (1.5.2)
rettelse, *correction*
revideret, *revised* (1.5.2)
roman, *novel*
række, *series*

samarbejde, *collaboration*
samlede, *compiled, collected*

samling, *collection*
serie, *series*; *volume* (1.8.1)
side, *page*
skuespil, *play*
småfortælling, *short story*
småtryk, *pamphlet*
sælges, *is on sale* (8.15.1)
særtryk, *offprint* (1.5.2)

tabel, *table*
tale, *speech*
tavle, *plate, table*
tidsskrift, *periodical, review*
til gennemsyn, *on approval*
til salg, *on sale*
tilføjelse, *addition*
tillæg, *appendix, supplement*
trykkeri, *printer's*

udarbejdet, *compiled*
uddragne, *selected*
udgave, *edition* (1.5.1)
udgiver, *editor* (1.1.4); *publisher*
udgivet, *edited*
udkomme, *come out*
udsolgt, *out of stock*
udvalg(et), *committee* (1.1.4)
udvalgt, *selected* (1.1.4)
udveksling, *exchange*
udvidet, *enlarged*
ugeblad, *week*
under trykking, *being printed*
utrykt, *unpublished*

vedlagt, *added*

ændrede, *revised* (1.5.2)

år, *year*
årbog, *yearbook*
årgang, *volume* (1.8.1)
årlig, *annual*

GRAMMATICAL INDEX: WORDS

andet, 6.2
at, 8.11

blive, 8.15.2
bragt(e), 8.19

burde(t), 8.19
bøger, 4.2.2
bør, 8.19
børn, 4.2.2

de, 3.1, 7.1.2
De, Dem, 7.3.1
den, 3.1
Deres, 7.3.1
det, 3.1

en, et, 3.2
er, 8.19

haft, har, havde, 8.19
have, 8.10.2, 8.19

skulde, skulle(t), 8.19
studiet, 3.1

fik, 8.19
fløj, fløjet, 8.19
fædre, 4.2.2
fået, 8.19
får, 8.10.1, 8.19

kan, kunde, kunne(t), 8.19
kommer at, 8.10.1

mænd, 4.2.2
mødre, 4.2.2
må, måtte(t), 8.19

var, 8.19
ved, 8.19, 10
vidst(e), 8.19
vil, 8.10.1, 8.19
vilde, ville(t), 8.19
vise, 4.3.1
visse, 4.3.1
være, 8.10.2, 8.15.3, 8.19
været, 8.19

gik, 8.19
gået, 8.19

sig, 7.3.2
skal, 8.10.1, 8.19

GRAMMATICAL INDEX: ENDINGS

- (no ending), 4.2.1,
  5.2.1, 8.3.2

-V(owel) (not otherwise
  listed, 8.1.2

-a, 4.2.1

-e, 4.2.1, 5.2.1, 8.1.2, 9
-de, 8.1.2

-ede, 8.1.2
-ende, 8.1.2
-ne, 3.1, 8.12.3
-ene, 3.1
-re, 5.3
-te, 8.1.2

-n, 3.1.1
-en, 3.1.1, 8.12.3

-r, 8.1.2

-er, 4.2.1, 8.1.2

-s, 4.3.1, 8.1.2, 8.15.1
-es, 8.1.2
-(e)des, 8.1.2
-tes, 8.1.2

-t, 3.1, 5.2.1, 8.1.2
-et, 3.2, 8.1.2
-st, 5.3

NORWEGIAN

SPECIMENS

Bokmål

Dette lille skrift saa først dagens lys i 'Aftenpostens' spalter i løbet af juli maaned dette aar. Det gir sig ikke ud for at være 'videnskabens sidste ord' i vor maalstrid, ligesaalidt som retsmaalets historie kan tjene som almindelig maalestok for vor sprogudvikling overhode. (1900)

Disse studier indeholder en del enkeltbidrag til forklaring og udnyttelse af gamle nordiske stednavne. Først kommer 4 kapitler fra omraader, hvor navneforskningen mere direkte synes at kunne give bidrag til den egentlige historie. (1912)

Det er en slik samling jeg her våger å legge frem. Den gjør ikke fordring på å være fullstendig og utdragene her nødvendigvis måttet bli kortfattede. Jeg har forsøkt å finne de mest karakteristiske 'Norwegica' fra de forskjellige århundrede og utdragene er gjort med særlig henblikk på kulturhistorien. (1932)

Dette er en sterkt omarbeidet utgave av 'Hvordan sproget blir til' som første gang utkom i 1934. Foruten å føre alle opplysninger à jour etter de siste ti års begivenheter har jeg gjort en del tilføyelser. (1948)

Den første del av verket, skrevet av fil. dr. Gunnar Christie Wasberg, følger utviklingen frem til 1920, fra de første funn av jernalderredskaper til industriens stilling under den første verdenskrig og den allerførste etterkrigstid. (1969)

The first part of the work, written by Dr Gunnar Christie Wasberg, traces the development up to 1920, from the first finding of Iron Age tools until the shutting down of the industry during the First World War and the period immediately after the war.

Nynorsk

I denne andra utgåva av Norsk grammatikk for skuleungdom er den nye rettskrivingi frå 1917 gjenomførd; dei valfrie formene er umrødde i §33. Av andre brigde sem eg hev gjort, kann eg nemna at ljodlære er vorti noko meir utfyllt og at ordlære er noko umlage ... Elles er boki i det store og heile som fyrr. (1931)

Desse stykki som her er samla, er eit utval av utgreidingar og livsskildingar som eg hev skrive framigjenom åri, ofte på grunnlag av talar. Det er mest utgreidingar um spursmål i målreising og kulturarbeid på historisk bakgrunn og skildringar av menn som hev vore med i norsk reisingsarbeid. (1953)

Det var i 1936 Det Norske Samlaget sende ut fyrste bandet i serien Norsk Folkedikting, Eventyr I. Planen var å laga eit allsidig og representativt utval av det beste i folkdiktinga vår etter denne ordninga: 2. band eventyr, 1 band segner og 1 band rim, gåter og ordtøke.

Professor Knut Liestøl stod sjølv for utgjevinga av dessa 4 banda. Seinare har serien vorti utvida med ei samling stev og med folkevisene i 2 band.

Denne andre utgåva av de fyrste eventyrbandet, som har vori utselt ei tid, er i det meste lik fyrste utgåva. (1960)

It was in 1936 that Det Norske Samlaget issued the first volume in the series Norsk Folkedikting, Eventyr I. The plan was to make an all-round and representative selection of the best in our folk poetry after this arrangement: a second volume of fairy tales, 1 volume of traditions and 1 volume of rhymes, riddles and sayings. Professor Knut Liestøl undertook the editing of these 4 volumes. Later the series was enlarged with a collection of ballads and with folk-songs in 2 volumes.

This second edition of the first volume of fairy tales, which has been out of print for some time, is for the most part like the first edition.

0 GENERAL CHARACTERISTICS

0.1/0.2 In its most general features, what is said of Danish is true of Norwegian.

0.3 THE LINGUISTIC PROBLEM

0.3.1 From the union of the crowns of Norway and Denmark in 1450 the literary language of Norway was Danish, always more or less Norwegianised and in its development by writers like Ibsen, Bjørnson and Knudsen growing steadily more so. The local dialects also persisted in speech and by 1855 'the speech of the Norwegian people' (**det norske Folkesprog**) had been recognised for educational and literary purposes alongside Dano-Norwegian.

0.3.2 When the question of spelling became pressing, the educational authorities were faced with four problems: the unphonetic nature of the traditional orthography, the discrepancies between the Danish written language and Norwegian pronunciation and morphology, divergences within Norwegian, and the coexistence of two officially recognised forms of language. In the spelling reform of 1907 the second problem was partially settled.

(a) **b, d, g** after a long vowel were replaced in a number of words by **p, t, k**; but related words often retained the voiced consonants, in some words the spelling was left optional, and some words that had **p, t, k** in Old Norse retained **b, d, g** in accordance with urban pronunciation.

(b) In names and (principally to avoid ambiguity) in a few other words, a single consonant after a short vowel was replaced by a double one, e.g. **tal, tall; vis, viss**; likewise **visst** for **vidst**; and in neuters of adjectives ending in **-t**, e.g. **fett** from **fet**.

(c) A number of short forms were enjoined or permitted, e.g. **fjær** not **fjæder, hoved** or **hode, fader** or **far**; and among verbs **bli(ve), ha(ve), ta(ge), la(te), la(gde), sa(gde)**.

(d) Accidence was brought into line with Norwegian practice in the following points: P in **-er** or **-**, not in **-e**; **nogen** not **nogle**; past tense in **-et** and **-dde**, e.g. **kastet, naadde**, not in **-ede**; past participle in **-t** and **-dd** as well as **-et**.

(e) **å** was permitted instead of **aa**.

0.3.3 The reform of 1907 applied only to the official language, variously called **skriftsprog, riksmål** and finally **bokmål**, as opposed to **landsmål** or **nynorsk;*** those of

---

* The changes of name were made official in 1929. I have adopted the current forms, abbreviated as BM and NN, irrespective of date. It should be noted that the term **riksmål** persists, as the name of a conservative form of **bokmål**.

1917 and 1938 and the textbook norm of 1959, which was a continuation of the latter, applied to both forms of the language and had as part of their aim a rapprochement between them. All four problems were tackled, but the complete elimination of Danish forms or unphonetic spellings was not attempted.

The reform of 1917 carried through the substitution of unvoiced consonants, reintroduced the historical distinction between **ld** and **ll**, **nd** and **nn**, identical in pronunciation, systematically doubled final consonants after short vowels and allowed peculiarly Norwegian grammatical forms. Few wide-spread general changes have been made since, but changes of detail have increased the difference from Danish, and numerous by-forms (**sideformer**) both in BM and NN have made rapprochement possible while preserving a marked difference between the extremes. With some words there have been gradual reversals of the type $A > A[B] > A$ or $B > B$, where brackets indicate a by-form, permitted but not recommended for textbook use. Details of changes, so far as they affect spelling, are given in 2.7; changes in grammatical forms are noted under the part of speech concerned. (In 1966 another committee, Vogtkomitéen, reported but did not lay down further reforms.)

0.3.4 The attention paid since 1917 to nynorsk is one indication of its increasing importance. Another is its use in government publications. The differences between nynorsk and bokmål are partly in vocabulary, including differences in word-formation such as BM **størrelse** NN **storleik**, and the NN avoidance of 'fast' compound verbs (8.23), partly in phonetics and morphology, e.g. BM **bare** NN **berre**; BM **kommer** NN **kjem**, *comes*. Phonetic differences are listed in 2.7.5, and morphological ones under the part of speech concerned. (For a nynorsk dictionary see 0.3.5.)*

0.3.5 The grammatical notes that follow, being general, apply for the most part to all stages of the language since 1907; but where there are important changes, they have been noted, as well as nynorsk forms which differ. Changes chiefly affect spelling and make the use of the appropriate dictionary desirable. 'Dano-Norwegian' dictionaries cover the period before 1907; the great Brynildsen, even in the third edition of 1927, gives the 1907 spelling, and occasionally even that of the previous period; Scavenius 1933, as reprinted by Blackwell in 1941, gives the 1917 spelling, while the revision by Christophersen and Scavenius (Blackwell 1954) gives that of 1938, but omits many of the permitted variants. The American school dictionary of Jorgenson (1943; rev. ed. 1955) includes grammatical information and gives more prominence to permitted forms. All these are of bokmål only. Haugen (1965) has an excellent grammatical introduction and gives 'all the spellings of any word that has been in use since 1917, within the limits of space available, for both languages and the manifold varieties of each down through the Textbook Norm of 1959'. Failing this one can get help for nynorsk from the dictionary by Ragnvald Iversen and Ove Bakken: *Bokmål—nynorsk, nynorsk—bokmål* (Oslo, Damm, 1958) or the earlier *Nynorsk ordbok* of Matias Skard, which often, though not always, gives the bokmål equivalent.

It must always be remembered, however, that official spellings are obligatory only in official contexts. **Språk,** for instance, may have come out in 1938, but sprog is still used by some; and officially Norwegian still has two forms of the language, extremely hard to reconcile, plus numerous variants permitted some in one context and some in another.

---

* Those who are interested in the details of the language question will find it fully treated in Einar Haugen: *Language conflict and language planning* (Harvard U.P.).

1 BIBLIOLINGUISTICS

1.2 NAMES OF AUTHORS, EDITORS, ETC.

1.2.1   The names of authors, editors and the like cause little grammatical difficulty, though changes in spelling may give rise to some awkwardness. (See 2.1.) Before 1907 the treatment of names in Norwegian is the same as in Danish.

1.2.2   The names of authors quite often stand at the head of the title-page, those of editors less commonly; or they may follow the title and be preceded by a preposition. Where there is also a past participle which defines the relation of the writer to the book, e.g. **udvalget besørget av**, *selection made by*; **utgitt** (NN **utgjeve**) **ved, under redaksjon av**, *edited by*; **samlet av**, *collected by*; **oversatt av, oversættelse ved**, *translated by, translation by*, it does not matter whether the preposition is **ved** or **av**. But when the preposition stands alone, we find **av** with authors and **ved** with editors, compilers and the like, e.g. **Norsk sogukunst ved Rikard Berge . . . Skildringar og uppteikningar av Rikard Berge** [and others]; **en antologi ved . . .; et forsøg ved** (a bibliography); and, at the head of the title-page, **H. Eitrem ved Edvard Stang og Johs. Krogsrud**, where Stang and Krogsrud are in part collaborators (but **ved** does not mean *with*) but more importantly posthumous editors. Neither preposition has any effect on the name. As **av** basically denotes origin, one must not be surprised to find it in a quite different sense in such a phrase as **utdrag av utenlandske reisebeskrivelse**, *selection of accounts by foreign travellers*.

1.2.3   In the case of correspondence and the like the name may precede the title in the genitive, e.g. **Bjørnstjerne Bjørnsons brevveksling med svenske; Doktor Holmsens dagbok**. This used also to be so with collected works, e.g. **Henrik Wergelands Samlede skrifter** (1852); but the 1937 edition has **Henrik Wergeland|Samlede skrifter** as in 1.2.2. New editions of classics may still show it, e.g. **Asbjørnsen og Moes Folkeeventyr**.

1.2.4   Collaboration, where it is not simply indicated by a collocation of names or a plural word such as **redaktører**, is usually indicated by such words as **medarbeidare, under medvirkning** (NN **medverking**) **av**. Where joint editorship is involved there may be a **redaksjonskomité** usually with a **høvedredaktør** (*editor-in-chief*).

1.2.5   The names of corporate authors are given in the same way as those on individuals, but names at the top of the title-page are frequently those of an issuing body, not of one responsible for the preparation of the text. Similarly **utgitt av** in this case will simply mean *published by*, though in the alternative **utgitt for** [name of society] **ved** [name of editor] one would translate it *edited*.

Sponsoring bodies may appear without further note on the title-page but are more likely to appear overleaf or in the preface, distinguished by such expressions as **tilskott** (**tilskudd**) or **økonomisk bidrag**.

1.2.6   What is said under Danish (1.2.8) about the definite article in corporate names applies *mutatis mutandis* to Norwegian, e.g. **Norsk Forening for Sosialt Arbeide**, but **Den Norske Historiske Forening** and also **Det Norske Samlaget** with two articles. Not but that a body is at liberty to change its style; but whatever style it adopts appears in all contexts (cf. 1.7). In view of such expressions as **hele dagen, kjære venn**! the omission of the prefixed article in headings, though not in accordance with Norwegian practice (the *Årskatalog* transfers it to the end of the heading), would appear to be grammatically permissible.

In so far as official changes of spelling are reflected in corporate names, great care may have to be exercised in the case of bodies with a long history, e.g. **Videnskabs-selskabet i Christiania** afterwards **Videnskapsselskapet i Kristiania** (afterwards **Videnskapsakademi i Oslo**).

1.2.7 Subordinate bodies are either simply put after the main body, perhaps on a separate line, e.g. **Sosialdepartementet|Den alminnelige avdeling**, or the main body has the genitive **-s** and the two are run together, e.g. **Norges Eksportråds informasjonstjeneste**. If this is split into **Norges Eksportråd. Informasjonstjeneste** for a heading, there is the difficulty that it is unidiomatic for the second half not to have the suffixed article **-n**.

1.3 TITLES

1.3.1 The grammar of plain titles is fairly stereotyped, involving mainly nouns, adjectives (including past participles), prepositions and occasionally possessives, e.g. **Omstridde spørsmål i norsk språkutvikling**, *Disputed questions in the development of Norwegian*; **Fra vårt styringsverk**, *From our administration*; apart from the genitive before the noun, as in **En norsk diplomats liv**, *The life of a Norwegian diplomat*, they have much the same order as in English. Belles-lettres, propaganda and popular literature give rise to greater variety, e.g. **Hva skal vi gjøre med mor?**, *What shall we do with mother?*; **Veien går videre**, *The road goes on*.

1.3.2 In filing titles one needs to distinguish the different uses of **den, det, de**. In **Det store spranget**, *The great leap*, **det** is an article, to be ignored; but **Det var deg jeg elsket**, *It was you I loved*; **De som styrer Norge**, *Those who govern Norway*; **Det mennesket glemmer jeg ikke**, *That person I shall not forget*; and even **Dei tre på Lang-øy**, *The three on Lang-øy*, all begin with demonstratives, to be retained. Den, etc., is reckoned as an article only before adjectives.

The suffixed article (3.1.1) cannot be ignored in filing: on a word by word basis **Faren** follows **Far og sønn**, though by British Museum rules, both would have to be filed under the heading FAR if they were anonymous, and so would **En fars valg**. (Incidentally **faren** could come from **fare**, *danger*, as well as from **far**, *father*.)

The indefinite article (3.2) is ignored in filing but the numeral *one* (6.1.1), some forms of which are the same, is not. **En mot mange**, *One against many*, is filed under **En**.

Owing to changes in spelling care may have to be exercised in choosing a British-Museum-type anonymous heading, and Anglo-American title entries may need cross-referencing.

1.4 VOLUMES AND PARTS

1.4.1 The usual words are **bind** (NN **band**) and **hefte**, though **halfbind** and **del** are also found. **Del**, a division of a work, may be more than one volume, one volume, or part of a volume. (Wergeland's collected works are numbered I.1–3, II.1–6, etc., the arabic numerals being **bind**, while the roman ones are unspecified.)

1.4.2 The numeral usually precedes, e.g. **tredje** (3dje, III.) **bind**, **annet/andre hefte**, and even long numerals like **enogtyvende** are frequently spelt out. Forms like **bind III** are read **tre**.

1.4.4 The total number of volumes in a work is sometimes given on the opposite page to the title, e.g. **Skrifter i 12 bind**, or at the end of the volume.

1.5 EDITIONS

1.5.1 The words in use are **utgave**, earlier **udgave**, NN **utgåve**, and **opplag**. Though **utgave** is the only possibility in expressions like **hundreårsutgave**, *centenary edition*, while in **2det opplag af omarbeidet udgave** it is obvious that **opplag** means *impression*, there are cases where the two words mean much the same.

1.5.2 The word for *edition* will usually be preceded by an ordinal number or by some adjective indicating revision such as **ny**, *new*; **revidert**, **omarbeidet**, *revised*; **forøket (-de, NN auka)** *enlarged*, and so on.

1.5.3 Reprints are denoted by **opptrykk**, offprints by **særtrykk**.

1.6 IMPRINTS

1.6.1 Forms of imprint are various. **Forlag**, *press*, occurs frequently, usually preceded by a name in the genitive, e.g. **Ernst G. Mortensen|s Forlag** or an adjective, e.g. **Norsk Forlag** but sometimes by a plain name **Johan Grundt Tanum-Forlag**. The last appears also as **(Forlagt av) Johan Grundt Tanum**.

1.6.2 Where societies are involved, the name of the society may appear at the top of the page, the imprint being that of a printer, e.g. **A.s John Griegs Boktrykkeri** or a publishing firm acting as agent, e.g. **i kommissjon hos J. M. Stenersens Forlag**.

1.7 SERIES

1.7.1 The titles of series may be singular, e.g. **Sak og Samfunn, Norges Offisielle Statistikk** or plural, e.g. **Forelesninger, Smaaskrifter fra Det Litteraturhistoriske Seminar**. Implied series occur of the type: **Norges almenvitenskapelige forskningsråd. Gruppe: Språk og historie A 191–12**. Here the main series has no title, only the sub-series. Sometimes the main series and the sub-series are run together in one expression, e.g. **Skrifter fra Norges Handelhøyskole i rekken Språklige avhandlinger**.

1.7.2 The numeration is often by figures only as in the example above, but **Nr.** or **No.** is also found. Concurrent sub-series are indicated by **serie**, **rekke** or **gruppe**, consecutive ones as a rule only by **rekke**. (Note, however, that **rekke** as such does not necessarily imply a series in the bibliographical sense, e.g. **Norges gamle love|anden række|1388–1604**, *The ancient laws of Norway, second set* . . . .)

1.7.3 Changes of spelling are likely to affect very long series, e.g. 1911: **Norges Officielle Statistik, række V, utgit av Det statistiske Centralbyraa** (earlier **-bureau**); 1919: **Norges Offisielle Statistikk, rekke VI, utgitt av Det statistiske Centralbyrå**; 1939: do., **rekke IX, utgitt av Det statistiske Sentralbyrå**; 1941: do., **rekke X, utgitt av Statistisk Sentralbyrå**; and in Nynorsk, **Noregs Offisielle Statistikk**.

1.8 PERIODICALS

1.8.1 Titles do not differ grammatically from those of books, e.g. **Historisk tidsskrift**, though they may be vaguer, e.g. **Syn og segn** (*Vision and tradition*).

1.8.3 **Utgitt, utgjeve** usually indicate the issuing body, the editor being **redaktør**. Occasionally it is stated by whom the periodical was founded, **grunnlagt**.

1.8.4 Individual parts are **hefte(r)**, several such making up a **bind (NN band)** or **årgang**.

1.8.5 Periodicity is mostly indicated as so many parts a year (**for året, om året, pr. år**) or by an adverb such as **månedsvis**, *monthly*.

1.8.6/1.8.7 The statements of price and directions for obtaining distinguish where necessary between **redaksjon**, *editorial office*, and **ekspedisjon**, *dispatch*, and between subscription—**abonnement(spris), årspeng|er, -ar, årstinging**—and separate numbers— **løssalg, laussal**, and may list special rates outside Skandinavia—**utanom Skandinavia**. In the case of irregular periodicals one may be invited to place a standing order—**tegne seg som fast kjøper**. Where a periodical is obtained through membership of a society the annual subscription may be described as **medlemskontingent**, and provision made for life membership—**en gang for alle**.

2 ALPHABET, PHONETICS, SPELLING

2.1 ALPHABET

2.1.1 The present alphabet runs as follows: a–z æ ø å.

Until about 1910 å was written aa and indexed at the beginning of the alphabet. For some time after that å and aa co-existed. Now names in aa which keep their old spelling are usually indexed with å at the end, though the opposite is sometimes found. Ü in names may be interfiled with u, may follow it or be interfiled with y; v and w are kept separate in the national bibliography but may be found interfiled in some indexes and reference books.

Norwegian was formerly printed in gothic type (see German). The type as such has no effect on spelling.

2.1.2 An acute accent may occur in words of foreign origin with an unusual stress, e.g. komité(en), or other ambiguity, e.g. européisk.

The numeral en is sometimes written én to distinguish it from the indefinite article, and fór is the past tense of fare.

Emphatic forms are distinguished by the grave accent, e.g. òg, *also*; og, *and*.

2.2 CAPITALISATION

2.2.1 At one time all nouns in Norwegian were spelt with an initial capital letter, but this has been long discontinued.

In principle only proper names are now spelt with a capital, this including personal, geographical, administrative and corporate names and the names of books and works of art. But not all parts of a complex name will necessarily have a capital. Thus we find **Olav den hellige, Grue herred**, *Grue Rural District*; **Kirke- og undervisningsdepartementet**, *Church and Education Department* (this is standard for government departments); **Londons brann**, *the Fire of London*. The names of firms and societies are treated as arbitrary names and capitalised according to the practice of the body concerned. Among countries both **De forente stater** and **De Forente Stater** are found.

2.2.2 Small letters are used for days of the week, points of the compass, political and religious descriptions, names that have become or form part of common nouns, derivatives, nouns and adjectives of nationality, titles and prefixes. But adjectives in -ske derived from personal names have capitals, e.g. **den Ritter-Kellnerske metode**. For the king both **Kongen** and **kongen** are found. The names of historical events which can be considered as descriptive phrases are written with small letters, e.g. **første verdenskrig**, *the First World War*.

2.2.3 Note that where the name of a body begins with the prefixed article, this has a capital even in the middle of a sentence, e.g. **Bergens Privatbank og Den norske Creditbank**.

2.3 DIVISION OF WORDS

2.3.1 Rules 1, 2, 3, 4, 5a, 6a (p. xiii) apply with modification as indicated in 2.3.2.

2.3.2 Suffixes need be kept intact only if desired, e.g. **bøk-er** or **bø-ker**; but the more obvious ones such as -aktig and -skap should not be broken up. Combinations of letters that stand for a single sound, such as **gj, kj, sj, skj**, are not divided, nor **ng** in native words.

2.4 PUNCTUATION AND ABBREVIATIONS

2.4.1 When two compound words have the second element in common, only the first half of the first compound is written, ending with a hyphen, e.g. **Kirke- og**

undervisningsdepartementet, *Church and Education Department*, in which **departementet** goes with both. In the rarer case where the first element is common, the hyphen comes at the beginning of the second word, e.g. **tømmerkjørere og -fløtere.**

2.4.2 Apostrophes are found in words like **Hans's**, as in English, or like **Cadillac'en**, and to denote omission.

2.4.3 Abbreviations have a stop if the last letter is not included, e.g. **t. eks.**, *til eksempel* (*e.g.*), similarly **o.fl.**, **m.m.** (both meaning *etc.*), **dvs.**, **det vil si** (*i.e.*), with no intermediate stops; but **jfr** with no stops for **jevnfør**, *cf.*

2.5 VARIATION OF CONSONANT

2.5.1 Though most words with a short vowel in the last syllable now end in two consonants and are not affected by the addition of endings, a single **m** may be doubled, or vice versa, e.g. **dom, dommer; gammel, gamle.** Before 1917 such doubling was commoner: the positive of **tryggere** was **tryg** (now **trygg**).

2.5.2 There is variation between **t** and **d** in past participles. (See 8.12.2.)

2.5.3 For historic changes in consonants see 2.7.3.

2.6 VARIATION OF VOWEL

2.6.1 Unaccented **-e-** (and its alternative **-a-**) may be omitted when an ending is added, e.g. **utkommen, -mne.**

2.6.2 Changes of vowel take place in the plural (4.2.2) and there are a number of verbs in which a change of vowels takes place between different tenses (8.2, 8.3, 8.12).

2.6.3 For historical changes in vowels see 2.7.2, and for the differences between bokmål and nynorsk see 2.7.5.

2.7 SPELLING

2.7.1 The history of the reforms of 1907, 1917 and 1938/1959 has been given in 0.3.2 and 0.3.3. Possible variations are given below under the earliest in the alphabet of the vowels or consonants concerned.

2.7.2 *Vowels*

a/e: In a few words **a** has displaced **e** or **en** or is allowed as well. (Many more in NN.) Notably **frem** > **fram** 1938.

a/o, å: **å** > **a** progressively, e.g. 1907 **hård**, 1917 **hård** [hard], 1938 **hard.**

au/ø: The characteristic N **au** has been allowed alongside **ø** and is preferred in some words, e.g. 1907 **løv**, 1917 **lauv** [løv], 1938 **lauv**, 1959 **lauv/løv**; 1907, 1917, 1938 **øst**, 1959 **øst/aust.**

aug/øy (earlier **øi**): The N **-aug** has gained on the D **-øy**, e.g. 1907 **fløi**, 1917 **fløi** [flaug], 1938 **flaug** or **fløy.**

e/ei: **e** > **ei**, e.g. 1907 **sten**, 1917 **sten** [stein], 1938 **stein.** Some more words of this type were changed in 1959, but usually with by-forms in **-e-**.

e/i: N **e** alongside or ousting D **i**, e.g. 1907 **kilde**, 1917 **kilde** [kjelde], 1938 **kilde/kjelde**; and vice versa 1907 **læbe**, 1917 **lebe** [lepe], 1938 **lepe** [leppe, lippe], 1959 **leppe** [lippe]; 1907, 1917 **levne**, 1938 **livne/levne**, 1959 **livne** [levne].

e/je: 1907 **stæle**, 1917 **stjele**, 1938 **stele/stjele.**

e/æ: The complicated rules taken over from D were simplified in 1917, with few changes since. Mostly **æ** > **e**.

e(æ)/ø(jø): **e** > **ø**, e.g. 1907 **sne**, 1917 **sne** [snø], 1938 **snø**; 1907 **selv**, 1917 **selv** [sjøl], 1938 **selv/sjøl(v)**, 1959 **sjøl(v)** preferred except for stylistic reasons; 1907 **fjær**, 1917 **fjær** [fjør], 1938 **fjær/fjør.**

ed/ei(d): 1907–1938 led, 1959 lei(d)/led.

ei/je: 1907 hjem, 1917 hjem [heim], 1938 hjem/heim.

ju/y: See u/y.

o/u: D o survives to some extent alongside N u, and vice versa, though not usually recommended, e.g. 1907 bo, 1917 bo [bu], 1938 bu; 1907 skudd, 1917 skudd [skott], 1938 skudd/skott, 1959 do. with -skott preferred in compounds.

Before m(m), ng, nk, kk, kC short close o is usually spelt u, but here too there have been changes, e.g. 1907 grum, 1917 grum [grom], 1938 grom; 1907–1938 kronglet, 1959 krunglet [kronglet].

o/ø: 1907–1917 fore, 1938 fore/føre; 1907–1917 sønn, 1938 sønn/son.

u/y, ju/y: 1907 skyld, 1917 skyld [skuld], 1938 skyld/skuld; 1907 syv, 1917 syv [sju], 1938 sju [syv], 1959 sju.

u/å: 1907 nu, 1917 nu [nå], 1959 nå.

y/ø: 1907 fyrti (or D fyrretyve); 1917 førr [fyrti, firti], 1938 førti.

ø/øy (øi): 1907 ø, 1917 ø [øi], 1938 øy; 1907 røk [røik], 1959 røyk [røk].

2.7.3 *Consonants*

b/p, d/t, g/k: The changes initiated in 1907 (b > p, etc.) were continued in later reforms, but the voiced consonants still persist in some words, e.g. 1907 aapen, but aabenbar, 1917 åpen, åpenbar; 1907, 1917 sprog, 1938 språk; 1907–38 -tagelse, 1959 -takelse [-tagelse]. NB 1907, 1917 modig/motig, 1938 motig, 1959 modig (motig was a hypercorrection).

single and double consonant: In accordance with N pronunciation double consonants were introduced after a short vowel, mostly in 1917, e.g. 1907 tryk, 1917 trykk; 1907 tryg, 1917 trygg; (but pre-1907 tag, with a long vowel, 1907–59 tak); 1907–17 op; 1938 opp; 1907 placere, 1917 plasere [-c-], 1959 plassere.

d: d is often silent after l, n, r or a vowel. Hence in traditional spelling it was often introduced without historical justification. It was generally eliminated in 1917.

> ld/ll: 1907 fuld, 1917 full; but 1907–59 holde with silent d.
>
> nd/nn: 1907 finde, 1917 finne (ON finna); but 1907–59 binde.
>
> rd/r: Words traditionally spelt with rd retain it, and it is now permissible in some words formerly spelt with r.
>
> after a vowel: Verb forms with d exist alongside forms without d, e.g. 1907 ride, red, 1917 ri(de), red [rei], 1959 ri(de), red/ri(de).
>
> In certain other combinations d was eliminated, e.g. 1907 bedst, bundt, 1917 best, bunt.

g: Alternates with zero and v.

> In selge, salg; velge, valg and the like g is D. The N forms selle, sal; val also occur. Conversely 1907 due [duge], 1917 duge [due], 1938 duge. Variation between g and diphthong occurs in veg, høg: 1907 høi, 1917 høi [høg], 1959 høg [høy] but only høg- in some compounds. Note also D meget, N mye.
>
> v/g, e.g. 1907 farve, flyve, savn; 1917 farve [farge], flyve [flyge], savn [sakn]; 1938 farge, flyve/flyge, savn/sakn; 1959 farge, fly(ge) [flyve], savn/sakn.

hv/v/kv: Silent h has usually been preserved, especially in relatives and interrogatives, e.g. hvem (*who*), hvorledes. In 1938 hvorledes had as alternatives hoss(en), åssen and koss, but only **åssen** survives in the 1959 textbook norm. **Erverv** lost its unetymological **h** in 1938.

mn/vn: In a number of words -mn- is permitted alongside the old -vn-, mostly since 1938, e.g. **havn**, 1938 **havn/hamn**; but **nevnd** was eliminated in favour of **nemnd**.

nk/kk: The elimination of the n sound is sometimes peculiar to N and Icelandic; forms in -nk- persist for varying periods, e.g. 1907 **tanke**, 1917 **takke**; 1907, 1917 **tankefull**; 1907–59 **senke** (NN **søkkja**).

v/-: **gav** is now preferred to **ga**, but a number of words are found with or without **v**, e.g. 1917 **stue**, 1959 **stu/stove**.

2.7.4 There have been various miscellaneous changes, some of which preceded the spelling reforms. The most important are: **c** > **k** or **s**, **ee** > **e**, **oe** > **ø**, **ph** > **f**, **-sion**, **-tion** > **sjon**, **th** > **t**, **x** > **ks**, e.g. **sirkel, fonetikk, nasjonal, teater, eksklusiv.**

2.7.5 The following are some of the commonly occurring differences, obligatory or permissible, between bokmål and nynorsk. Forms in brackets are permissive.

BM	NN	Examples
a	å, o	allmenn [almen]; allmenn [ålmen]
e	a	frequently in the infinitive ending
e	ei	fett; feitt
e	i	levnet; livnad
e	æ	seter; seter [sæter]
i	e	fikk [fekk]; fekk [fikk]
om(m)	um	som; som [sum]
y	u	syd-; sud-
y	ju, jo	skyte; skyta [skjota]
æ	e	særskilt; særskild [serskild]
ø	au	drøm/draum; draum [drøm]
(j)ø	y	søster; syster [søster]
å	o	åpen; open
double consonant	single	sommer; sommar [sumar]
-ge	-gja, -gje	egge; eggja
-ke	-kja, -kje	rekke; rekkje

There are slight differences in suffixes:

-ig	-ug
-lig	-leg
-løs	-laus
-som	-sam

3 ARTICLES AND GENDER

Norwegian has definite and indefinite articles, but they only roughly correspond in use with English. They are the only complete indication of gender.

Up to 1917 BM recognised two genders: common (M and F) and N. Since then a separate feminine gender has been recognised and to some extent prescribed, but usage is still fluid (cf. 0.3). NN has always had three genders. Gender may vary between BM and NN.

3.1 DEFINITE

3.1.1 *Suffixed*

| | S | | | P | |
	M	F	N	MF	N
Either	-(e)n		-(e)t	-(e)ne	
or	-(e)n	-a	-(e)t	-(e)ne	-a

The article **-a** is much commoner in NN, which has also FS and NP **-i**, and leaves plurals in **-o** unchanged.

This article is suffixed to S and P forms of nouns: **publikasjon|en, utgave|n, bok|en** or **bok|a** (NN also **boki**), **rekkja** (from **rekkje**), **år|et, hefte|t**; **publikasjona|ne, bøke|ne, år|ene** or **år|a (åri)**. The **-r** of the plural (**bøker**) is usually dropped before **-ne**, as is the **-e(r)** of words like **arbeidere(r)**, viz **arbeiderne**.

3.1.2 *Prefixed*

MFS	NS	P
den	det	de(i)
dei is NN

Used before adjectives, e.g. **Det Norske Samlaget**; **dei tidligare publikasjonar**. Note the optional suffixed article.

3.2 INDEFINITE

	M	F	N
BM	en	(ei)	et
NN	ein	ei	eit

For the feminine cf. 3.1. The use of **ei** is less common than that of **-a** (3.2.1), so that **boka** and **en bok** may occur in the same text.

4   NOUNS

4.2 PLURAL

4.2.1 *BM*   Before 1907: **-e, -(e)r** or nothing
1907 onwards: mostly **-(e)r** or nothing

Latin-derived words in **-um** may have plural in **-a**, e.g. **sentra, halvfabrikata**.

NN   M: **-ar** (optionally **-er** in some words)
F: **-er** (optionally **-ar** in some words)
F in **-ing**: **-ar**
Words ending in **-e**: **-r** (or change to **-or**)
Words ending in other vowels: **-r**
Words ending in **-a** may change to **-o**
Neuters usually have no ending

4.2.2   Both in BM and NN the stem vowel is changed in some common words, e.g. **bok, bøker**; **barn, born**. Note also **mann, menn**; **far, fedre**; **mor, mødre**.

4.2.3   Jorgenson's dictionary gives 1938 plurals, Haugen's those of 1959.

4.3 CASES

4.3.1 An -s, without an apostrophe, is added to singular and plural, with or without article, and to the last of a group of nouns to form the genitive. It corresponds to English *of* as well as *'s*, and is occasionally used after the preposition **til**, e.g. **Norge|s Offisielle Statistikk**. *Official Statistics of Norway*, **Lag|et|s faste publikasjon**, *The company's regular publication*, **Arbeider|ne|s faglige Landesorganisasjon**, *Norwegian Trade Union Federation* (lit. *Professional National Organisation of Workers*); **for hustru og barn|s skyld**, *for the sake of wife and child*; **til sal(g)s**, *on sale*. Note also such expressions as **10-års**, *ten-year*.

4.3.2 Traces of other cases are found in stereotyped expressions such as **i live**. NN sometimes has a definite dative plural in **-om**.

5 ADJECTIVES

5.1 AGREEMENT

5.1.1 So far as there are distinctive forms adjectives agree with the nouns they qualify.

5.2 ENDINGS

5.2.1

	C	N	P	
Strong form	-	-t(t)	-e	With changes
Weak form	-e	-e	-e	as in 2.5, 2.6

Some adjectives, especially national adjectives in **-sk**, do not add **-t**, and some are invariable, especially past participles in **-e** or **-a**.

In NN adjectives in **-en** had F **-i**, N **-e**; e.g. **liti**, but the only surviving F forms are **lita** (NN and BM) and **eiga** (BM **eia**). N **-e** is found in BM in some words.

5.2.2 The weak form is used after the definite article, demonstratives, possessives and genitives, with names, and in some stereotyped expressions, e.g. **den første utgaven, denne nye serien, Norges Offisielle Statistikk, Lille Eyolf**; otherwise the strong form, e.g. **Norsk Forening, Norsk** (5.2.1) **tidsskrift, et nytt tidsskrift, tidsskriftet er nytt, Norske studier, utdragene har måttet bli kortfattede**.

5.3 COMPARISON

5.3.1 *Comparative*: BM **-ere**; NN **-are**
       Superlative: BM **-(e)st**; NN **-(a)st**

5.3.2 Some common adjectives change the vowel in the comparative and superlative thus **a > e, o > ø, u > y, å > æ**, e.g. **lang, lengre, lengst**. These and irregular comparisons such as **god, bedre** (NN **betre**), **best** have independent entries in good dictionaries.

6 NUMERALS

6.1 CARDINAL

6.1.1

1 **e(i)n, e(i)tt**	5 **fem**	9 **ni**
2 **to**	6 **seks**	10 **ti**
3 **tre**	7 **sju (syv)**	11 **elleve**
4 **fire**	8 **åtte**	12 **tolv**

13 tretten	20 tjue (tyve)	80 åtti
14 fjorten	21 tjueen (enogtjue)	90 nitti
15 femten	30 tretti (tredve)	100 (ett) hundre
16 seksten	40 førti (førr, firti)	101 hundre og en
17 sytten	50 femti	128 hundre og tjueåtte
18 atten	60 seksti	200 to hundre
19 nitten	70 sytti	1000 (ett) tusen

6.1.2 ein, eitt are NN; the forms in brackets are not now recommended, but compounds of the type **enogtjue**, officially changed in 1951, are still commonly used. In tjueen, the **-en** is officially stated to be invariable, e.g. **tjueen år.**

6.2 ORDINAL
6.2.1

1 første, fyrste	11 ellevte	21 tjueførste (e(i)n-
2 annen	12 tolvte	ogtjuende)
3 tredje	13 trettende	30 trettiende (tredevte)
4 fjerde	14 fjortende	40 førtiende
5 femte	15 femtende	50, etc. femtiende, etc.
6 sjette	16 sekstende	100 hundrede
7 sjuende (syvende)	17 syttende	101 hundrede og første
8 åttende	18 attende	1000 tusende
9 niende	19 nittende	
10 tiende	20 tjuende (tyvende)	

6.2.2 fyrste is NN alternative.

annen, earlier **anden**, has N **annet** or **anna** and may have F **anna**. There is also an alternative, weak, form **andre**, e.g. **annet** or **andre hefte**, *part 2*. For tjueførste and bracketed forms see 6.1.2.

-ande is found for **-ende** in NN.

6.3 FIGURES
Simple arabic figures usually represent cardinals. Ordinals are represented by arabic figures followed by a full stop, e.g. **det 70. år**, or by the ordinal ending, e.g. **1ste, 2nen, 3dje, 4de**, etc. Roman figures are used much as in English, e.g. **Haakon I (Haakon den første), I. del (første del), Del II (del to)**.

6.4 DATES
6.4.1 The months are:

**januar, februar, mars, april, mai, juni,
juli, august, september, oktober, november, desember**

6.4.2 (*On*) *the 22nd of October 1961* is expressed thus:

den 22. (22dre, 22de) oktober nitten hundre og sekstie(i)n

As numerals are invariable, expressions like **1848–1948** or **1870–80-åra**, *the 1870's and 80's*, need cause no difficulty. Note also **1800-tallet**. ('„1800-tallet" er bedre enn „det 19. hundreår" eller „de 19. århundrede".')

7 PRONOUNS

7.1 DEMONSTRATIVE, INDEFINITE, ETC.

7.1.1 The various forms of these pronouns are given in good dictionaries. More recently allowed forms and those current in NN (listed in 7.1.2) as well as some usages, may cause difficulty if one has to rely on one of the earlier dictionaries.

7.1.2

annan M, **anna** F or N, **onnor** F: BM **annen, anne**
deira, *their, of those, of them*
dessa P of **denne**
han also *him*
honom, *him*
inga, ingi F of **ingen**
nogen antiquated form of **noen**
no(k)a, nokor F of **noen**
noko N of **noen**; **nokre** P of **noen**
sume, sumt, *some*

7.2 RELATIVE AND INTERROGATIVE

7.2.1 The relative as object is often omitted, e.g. **regler rettskrivningskomitéen sendte ut,** *the rules the orthographical committee issued.*

7.2.2 Prepositions with interrogatives and relatives are put at the end of the sentence, e.g. **spørsmål som jeg ikke har kunnet få plass til,** *questions that I have not been able to make room for.*

7.2.3 Note **kva, kven,** *what, who(m)* in NN.

7.3 PERSONAL

7.3.1 Possessives may follow the noun, e.g. **boka mi, forretninga hans.**

7.3.2 **De(i), Dem** with initial capital are polite forms for *you* (NN oblique cases **Dykk, Dykkar**).

7.3.3 Some uses of **seg** (*himself, itself,* etc.) are idiomatic, e.g. **det viste seg at,** *it turned out that.*

8 VERBS

8.1 STRUCTURE

8.1.1 Like English verbs, to which they bear a family resemblance, Norwegian verbs have very few different forms. They are entered in the dictionary under the infinitive (8.11).

8.1.2 The commonest pattern of endings in bokmål is as follows, V standing for unspecified vowel:

	Active		*Passive*	
Infinitive	**-e/-a**	**-V**	**-(e)s/-as**	**-Vs**
Present	**-er/-ar**	**-Vr**	**-(e)s/-as**	**-Vs**
Past (*1*)	**-et/-a, -te, -de**	**-Vdde**	**-es, -tes, -des**	**-Vddes**
(*2*)	See 8.3.2		add **-(e)s**	
Present participle	**-ende/-ande**	**-Vende**		
Past participle			**-et/-a, -t, -d**	**-Vdd, -Vtt**

For details, compound tenses and nynorsk forms see below.

8.2 PRESENT

8.2.1 The **-r** forms are found both in BM and NN, but many verbs in NN may also have the bare stem, e.g. **finne/finn**; **selja/sel**, sometimes with changes of vowel: **a/e, o/ø, a/æ**.

For irregular presents see 8.19.

8.3 PAST

8.3.1 The weak past, much the commonest, is got by removing the **-e/-(j)a** of the infinitive and adding **-et/-a, -te, -de, -dde**, e.g. **kaste: kastet/kasta**; **tenke/-kja: tenkte**; **leve: levde**; **bo: bodde**.

Occasionally there is a change of vowel (**e/a; e/o; ø/u**), e.g. **fortelle/-lja: fortalte/-de**. Jorgenson's and Haugen's dictionaries give such changes.

8.3.2 As in English, some verbs (known as strong verbs) make their past by changing their vowel, at the same time removing the **-e/-(j)a** of the infinitive, e.g. **finne/fann**.

Possible changes are:

	Past	*Infinitive*
BM	**-a-**	**-e-, -i-, -æ-**
	-au-	**-y-**
	-e(i)-	**-i-**
	-o-	**-a-, -o-**
	-ø-	**-y-**
NN	**-a-**	**-e-, -i-**
	-au-	**-y-**
	-e-	**-a-**
	-ei-	**-i-**
	-o-	**-a-, -o-, -ø-**

Jorgenson gives past tenses and past participles under the infinitive, with 1938 alternatives; Haugen makes a separate entry as well.

8.10 COMPOUND TENSES

8.10.1 The future is expressed by **skal** and **vil** and also by **komme/koma til å**, all with the infinitive.

8.10.2 The perfect (pluperfect, future perfect) are expressed by the present (past, future) of **ha** or **være** with the past participle (8.19, 8.12), e.g. **har gitt**, *has given*; **er blitt**, *has become*.

8.11 INFINITIVE

8.11.1 The infinitive, under which verbs are listed, ends in a vowel, usually **-e** or (especially in NN) **-a**. Often NN **-ja** corresponds to BM **-e**.

8.11.2 The infinitive is used both with and without **å** (*to*) but keeps **å** after prepositions, e.g. **til å gå**. It corresponds to our verbal noun in *-ing* as well as to the infinitive.

8.12 PARTICIPLES

8.12.1 The *present participle* (8.1.2) is used as an adjective, e.g. **tilhørende**, *corresponding*.

8.12.2 *Past participle, weak*: **-et/-a, -t, -d, -dd/-tt**.

-tt is rare except in NN; **-dd** may be the result of **-d-** in the stem, e.g. **rådd** from **råde**, but **nådd** from **nå**.

With the adjectival ending -e, -et changes to -ede.

8.12.3 *Strong*: -et, -t (NN -e, -i). In BM the vowel is usually the same as in the infinitive. The following are possible changes of vowel:

	Past participle	*Infinitive*
BM	-e-	-i-
	-u-	-i-, -y-
	-ø-	-y-
	-å-	-æ-
NN	-e-	-a-
	-o-	-e-, -o-, -y-, -ø-
	-u-	-e-, -i-

8.12.4 When used as adjectives the past participles of some strong verbs may end in **-en, -ne**; but where they follow the noun they usually have the **-t** form, e.g. **Tidligere utkomne nummer,** *Previously published numbers*; but **Skrifter utgitt av . . . ,** *Works published by . . . .*

8.15 PASSIVE

8.15.1 The -s form (8.1.2; NN also -st) is often subject to simplification, e.g.

Active	*Passive*
finne, finner	**fin(ne)s**
fant, fann	**fan(te)s**
funnet	**funnes**
solgte	**solgtes**

Verbs with past tense in **-et** may have alternatives, e.g. corresponding to **lykket**: **lykkes, lyktes, lykkedes** (D). The form in commonest use is the present, which often has a general or potential meaning, e.g. **få(e)s,** *obtainable*; **sendes i tillegg,** *is sent as a supplement*. With some verbs the **-s** form has a special meaning.

8.15.2 **Bli** (8.19) with the past participle emphasises the action, e.g. **boka er blitt sterkt forsinket,** *the book has been seriously delayed.*

8.15.3 **Være** (8.19) with the past participle emphasises result or state, e.g. **I første hefte er det gjeve oppgåver . . .** (NN), *In the first part are given data . . . .*

8.17 AUXILIARIES
Included in 8.19.

8.19 IRREGULAR VERBS
Some common verbs are irregular in the present or have anomalous past tenses, viz. (R = regular):

Infinitive	*Present*	*Past*	*Past participle*
være, *be*	**er**	**var**	**vært (vori NN)**
ha, *have*	**har (hev NN)**	**hadde**	**hatt**
bli, *become*	R	**ble(i)**	**blitt**
bringe, *bring*	R	**brakte**	**brakt**

burde, *ought*	bør	burde	burdet
fly(ge), *fly*	R	flaug/fløy	flydd/fløyet
få, *get*	R	fikk (fekk NN)	fått
gi (gjeve NN), *give*	gir (gjev)	ga(v)	git (gjeve)
gå, *go*	R	gikk (gjekk NN)	gått
kunne, *can*	kan	kunne	kunnet
måtte, *may, must*	må	måtte	måttet
se (sjå NN), *see*	R	så (såg NN)	sett/sedd
skulle, *shall, ought*	skal	skulle	skullet
stå, *stand*	R	sto(d)	stått
ta(ke), *take*	R (tek NN)	tok	tatt (teke)
ville, *will*	vil	ville	villet
vite, *know*	vet	visste	visst

8.23 COMPOUND VERBS

Verbs compounded with adverbs or nouns are classed in N as fast, e.g. **tilgi**, or loose, e.g. **legge til**. Fast verbs do not differ from simple verbs; loose ones become fast in the present participle and often in the past participle (cf. En *incoming*), though these forms are usually avoided and a relative clause used instead. Sometimes there may be a fast verb with the same meaning, e.g. **gi ut** and **utgi**; but often there is no such verb or it may have a different meaning. Unless therefore the meaning is clear it is as well to look up the corresponding loose form also. Conversely some verbs which are now loose were formerly fast, and if looked for in old dictionaries will have to be sought under the fast form. Many verbs are loose in NN which are fast in BM.

9 ADVERBS

The strong neuter form of most adjectives may be used adverbially: example under 8.15.2. With some adjectives and nouns **-vis** (-*wise*) may be added.

10 PREPOSITIONS

The caution given under Danish applies also to Norwegian. (Cf. also 7.2.2.)

GLOSSARY

abonnement(spris), *subscription* (1.8.6)
anmerkning, *note*
arbeit, *work*
auka, *enlarged* (1.5.2)
avhandling, *essay*
avtrykk, *impression*

band, *binding;* (NN) *volume* (1.4.1)
bearbeidet, *revised*
bemerkning, *note*

bestille, *order* (vb.)
bestilling, *order* (sb.)
bibliotek, *library*
bibliotekar, *librarian*
bidrag, *contribution*
bilag, *supplement*
bild, *plate*
billigbok, *cheap paperback*
bind, *volume* (1.4.1)
bokhandel, *bookshop; publishing house*

bokhandler, *bookseller*
boktrykker, *printer*
brev, *letter*
brevveksling, *correspondence*
brosjyre, *pamphlet*
bytte, *exchange*

del, *part; volume* (1.4.1)
dupliseret, *duplicated*
død, *died*

eksemplar, *copy*
enkelthefte, *single issue*
expedisjon, *dispatch*

fjortendaglig, *fortnightly*
flyveskrift, *pamphlet*
forbedret, *improved*
forfatterrett, *copyright*
forhandlingar/-er, *proceedings*
forkortet, *abridged*
forlag, *press* (1.6.1); *publishing house*
forlagt, *published*
forord, *preface*
forsatt, *continued*
forskning, *research*
forstørret, *enlarged*
forsøk, *essay*
fortelling, *story*
forøkelse, *addition*
forøket, *enlarged* (1.5.2)
fri(-), *complimentary, free*
født, *born*

gammelt nummer, *back number*
gave-, *complimentary*
gjennomsett, *revised*
til gjennomsyn, *on approval*
gruppe, *series*

halvbind, *half-volume* (1.4.1)
halvårlig, *half-yearly*
handskrift, *manuscript*
hefte, *issue, number, part* (1.8.4); *volume* (1.4.1)
høvedredaktør, *chief editor* (1.5.1)

innbundet, *bound*

a jour, *up to date*

kartonnert, *in boards*
kommende, *forthcoming*
korrigert, *corrected*
kvartalsskrift, *quarterly*

laussal, *separate sale* (1.8.6)
levering, *issue, number*
løssalg, *separate sale* (1.8.6)

meddelelser, *proceedings*
medlem, *member*
månedlig, *monthly*
månedsvis, *monthly* (1.8.5)
møte, *conference*

novelle, *short story*
nummer, *number*
ny, *new* (1.5.2)

omarbeidet, *revised* (1.5.2)
omredigert, *revised*
opphavsrett, *copyright*
opplag, *edition, impression* (1.5.1)
opptrykk, *reprint* (1.5.3)
ordbok, *dictionary*
oversettelse, *translation*

plansje, *plate*
prøveeksemplar, *sample copy*

rabatt, *discount*
redaksjon, *editing, editorial office* (1.2.2, 1.8.3)
redaksjonskomité, *editorial board* (1.2.4)
redaktør, *editor* (1.2.4, 1.8.3)
redigert, *edited*
register, *index*
regning, *bill*
rekke, *(sub)series* (1.7.2)
rettelse, *correction*
rettet, *corrected*
revidert, *revised* (1.5.2)
roman, *novel*
række, see rekke

til sal(g)s, *on sale* (4.3.1)
samfunn, *society*
samling, *collection*

sammendrag, *summary*
selskap, *society*
ser-, see sær-
side, *page*
sjefredaktør, *chief editor*
skuespill, *play*
småskrift, småtrykk, *pamphlet*
særprent, særtrykk, *offprint* (1.5.3)

tabell, *table*
tale, *speech*
tidsskrift, *periodical, review*
tillegg, tillægg, *appendix; supplement*
trykk, *impression*
trykkeri, *printer's*
under trykking, *being printed*

ud-, see ut-
uke, *week*

utarbeidet, *revised, compiled*
utenlandsk, *foreign*
utgave, *edition* (1.5.1)
utgitt ved, utgjeve ved, *edited by* (1.2.2, 1.2.5)
utgiver, *editor*
utgåve, *edition* (1.5.1)
utkomme, *come out*
utselt, utsolgt (fra forlaget), *out of print*
utvalg, *committee*
utvalgt, *selected*
utveksling, *exchange*
utvidet, *enlarged*

år, *year*
årbok, *yearbook*
årgang, *volume of a periodical* (1.8.4)
årspenger/-ar, *subscription* (1.8.6)
årsskrift, *yearbook*
årstinging, *subscription* (1.8.6)

GRAMMATICAL INDEX: WORDS

andre, 6.2.2
anna, annet, 6.2.2, 7.1.2
annen, 6.2.1, 7.1.2

blei, bli(tt), 8.15.2, 8.19
brakt(e), 8.19
burde(t), bør, 8.19

de(i), 3.1.2
De(i), 7.3.2
deira, 7.1.2
Dem, 7.3.2
den, 3.1.2
dessa, 7.1.2
det, 3.1.2
Dykk(ar), 7.3.2

ein, ei(t), en, 3.2
er, 8.19
et, 3.2

fekk, fikk, 8.19
flaug, flydd, fløy(et), 8.19

fått, 8.19

ga(v), 8.19
gikk, 8.19
gir, gitt, gjev(e), 8.19
gått, 8.19

ha, 8.10.2, 8.19
hadde, 8.19
han, 7.1.2
har, hatt, hev, 8.19
honom, 7.1.2

inga, ingi, 7.1.2

kan, kunne(t), 8.19
koma/komme til å, 8.10.1
kva, kven, 7.2.3

må, måtte(t), 8.19

nogen, no(k)a, noko(r), nokre, 7.1.2

onnor, 7.1.2

sedd, sett, 8.19
seg, 7.3.3
skal, 8.10.1, 8.19
skulle(t), 8.19
sto(d), stått, 8.19
sume, sumt, 7.1.2
så(g), 8.19

tatt, tek(e), tok, 8.19

var, 8.19
vet, 8.19
vil, 8.10.1, 8.19
ville(t), 8.19
visst(e), 8.19
vori, 8.19
være, 8.10.2, 8.15.2, 8.19
vært, 8.19

å, 8.11.2

D

GRAMMATICAL INDEX: ENDINGS

SWEDISH

SPECIMEN

Den upplaga av Strindbergs samlade brev, vars första del härmed föreligger, är beräknad att omfatta 12 volymer och att utkomma med 1 volym om året. Den syftar icke till absolut fullständighet, utan sådana brev uteslutas, som kunna anses sakna varje person-historiskt intresse eller litterärt värde. Upplagan inrymmer såväl förut tryckta som otryckta brev, i vissa fall även brevkoncept.

I slutvolymen inrymmas eventuellt även sådana brev, som återfunnits under utgivnings-arbetets gång men icke kunnat medtagas i de tidigare delarna av verket.

This edition of Strindberg's collected letters, the first volume of which is presented here, is reckoned to comprise 12 volumes and to come out at the rate of one volume a year. It does not aim at absolute completeness, but such letters are excluded as may be thought to lack biographical interest or literary value. The edition includes both already published and unpublished letters, in certain cases also drafts.

In the final volume there may be accommodated also such letters as were discovered in the course of publication but could not be included in the earlier parts of the work.

0 GENERAL CHARACTERISTICS

Swedish agrees with Danish (q.v.) and Norwegian in its most general features, but has a greater variety of forms.

1 BIBLIOLINGUISTICS

1.1 NAMES

1.1.1 The make-up of modern Swedish names is the usual one of Christian name and surname, in that order, sometimes with a preposition such as **av** or the German **von** between. Among the surnames are many that originate in patronymics, but are obviously so no longer, as in **Märta Eriksson**. In medieval names these may still be genuine patronymics, as the feminine counterparts in **-dotter** invariably are, e.g. **Ingeborg Gerhardsdotter**, filed under **Ingeborg**. Hence notes like '**Personer med faders namn hava förts på förnamnet om de levat före 1650**' (*Persons with patronymics have been put under the Christian name if they lived before 1650*). A similar distinction has to be made between a modern name like **Agnes av Krusenstjerna** (filed under **Krusenstjern(-a)**) and a medieval name of the same form where the **av** indicates territorial origin.

1.1.2 Swedish includes a number of names of German origin and a number which preserve otherwise antiquated spellings. In general, reference books follow the spelling given but may make a reference from other spellings, e.g. **Ohlson**: se även **Ohlsson**. They also distinguish between, say, German **Goedecke** (filed between **God-** and **Gof-**)

and Swedish **Gödecke** (filed after **Gy-**), and most of them distinguish German **ü**, spelt out as **ue**, from **ü** in identical Swedish names, which is equated with **y**. But they all equate **V** and **W**, e.g. **Vasa, Wassen, Vastovius**. (On **aa** and **å** see 2.1.1.)

1.2 NAMES OF AUTHORS, EDITORS, ETC.

1.2.1 In most cases statements of authorship have no effect on the form of the name. This is obviously so when the name is simply put at the head of the title-page, as is often the case with authors.

1.2.2 Alternatively an author's name may follow the title, preceded by **av** (*by*). When appropriate a word such as **författad**, *composed*; **sammanställd**, *compiled*; **skildrad**, *described*, may be inserted.

With a word like **utarbetad**, *prepared*, we come to the borderline between authorship and editing, more explicitly indicated by **utgiven** or **redigerad**. The latter is somewhat commoner in the case of collective enterprises. The verb **utgiva** is also used of the publishing of works by a society, so that one may meet, e.g. **Uppländska domböcker utgivna av Kungl. Humanistiska Vetenskapssamfundet I. Vendels Sockens Dombok; utgiven genom Nils Edling**. Here **utgivna av** means *published by* and **utgiven genom** *edited by*. Such changes of preposition are common, but by itself **utgiven av** for *edited by* is quite normal. Information not on the title-page may have a finite verb, e.g. **har redigerats av**, *has been edited by*.

1.2.3 As an alternative to participles there may be nouns, e.g. **under redaktion av**, *under the editorship of*; (i) **urval av**, (*in a*) *selection by*; and of translations **översättning av**, *translation by*; **i svensk tolkning av**, *in a Swedish version* (i.e. a free translation) *by*; **översättare**, *translator*.

1.2.4 In the case of collected works, correspondence, memoirs, encyclopedias and the like, the name may have the genitive **-s**, e.g. **August Strindbergs brev**, *A.S.'s letters*. In view of 1.2.1 one should be sure that the author's name does not itself end in **-s**.

1.2.5 Apart from simple collocation, with or without **och**, collaboration may be indicated by such phrases as **under medverkan av**, *with the cooperation of*; or the word **medförfattare**, *co-author*, may be used.

1.2.6 The names of corporate authors appear in much the same fashion as those of individuals, but in the nature of things societies and institutions will usually be publishers and sponsors. For instance **Promemorior överlämnade till Beredningen för internationella bistandsfrågor**, *Memoranda delivered to the Committee for International Aid Questions*, cannot have been produced by the committee, and we discover from the preface that they are the work of 'en särskild arbetsgrupp med O. Palme som ordförande' (*a special working party under O.P.*).

Subordinate departments may precede the main body, joined by **inom** (*at*), or follow it, in which case the name of the main body will normally have the genitive **-s**, e.g. **Göteborg|s Drätselkammare|s Gatunamnsberedning**. The peculiar difficulties arising from the article in corporate names in Danish and Norwegian do not affect Swedish since such names always have the article suffixed but not prefixed, e.g. **Statsvetenskapliga Föreningen** as well as **Institutionen för Nordiska Språk**. The names are usually unaltered as headings, the article being retained.

Changes of spelling do not particularly affect the names of Swedish bodies.

1.3 TITLES

1.3.1 The grammar of modern titles, which consist mainly of nouns, adjectives and prepositions, causes little difficulty. Older titles with relative clauses **and numerous**

participles take more working out. Apart from the genitive the order is much as in English. More varied titles are found in belles lettres and popular literature, e.g. **Giv oss jorden!** (*Give us the earth!*); **Saker och ting du kan göra själv** (*Things you can do and make yourself*).

1.3.2 As in Danish and Norwegian, the articles are ambiguous: **Den lustgård som jag minns** (in English *The garden I remember*) is filed under **Den**; **Det gamla Floda** (*Old Floda*) under **Gamla**. For details see Norwegian.

1.4 VOLUMES AND PARTS

1.4.1 The usual words for *volume* are **del** and **band**, **del** emphasing the division of the whole work, **band** the physical unit. (Another synonym is **volym**, little used in actual numeration. See Specimen.) Since **del** literally means *part* it can denote also an internal division of the work, or a broad division of the whole enterprise (1.4.2). Occasionally **avdelning** is substituted. A separate part is indicated by **häfte**.

1.4.2 Numeration is by preceding numeral, e.g. **Tredje delen, första bandet,** *Division 3, vol. 1*; or a following cardinal, **Band I.** (Note the presence or absence of the article.) Where there are only two volumes or parts, **förra** and **senare** are used for *first* and *second*.

1.5 EDITIONS

1.5.1 The usual word is **upplaga(n)**, preceded by an ordinal number, e.g. **tredje upplagan** (*third edition*), revision of various sorts, or its absence, being denoted by **ny** (*new*), **bearbetad, omarbetad, reviderad** (*revised*), **utökad, utvidgad, kompletterad** (*enlarged*), **oförandrad** (*unaltered*), **oförkortad** (*unabridged*); **delvis** (*partially*) or **helt** (*entirely*).

1.5.2 More complicated relationships may be stated elsewhere than on the title-page, e.g. **original-upplagan från 1945 i reviderat skick,** *original edition of 1945 in revised form*; **Folkskolans läsebok utgör elfte upplagan av Läsebok för folkskolan,** *F.l. forms the 11th edition of L.f.f.*

1.5.3 Reprints are indicated by **omtryck**, off-prints by **särtryck**.

1.6 IMPRINTS

1.6.1 The full names of Swedish presses, which by law must appear somewhere in the book, tend to produce forms such as **Bokförlaget P. A. Norstedt och Söner AB, AB** being short for **Aktiebolag** (*joint-stock company*), **Tidskriftsförlaget Allhem A.-B.**, but especially over a period of time numerous variations occur, e.g. **P. A. Norstedt & Söners (S:rs) Förlag**, or just **Norstedts**; **Albert Bonniers Förlag** and plain **Bonniers**; **C. W. K. Gleerup, Gleerupska Universitets-Bokhandeln, CWK Gleerups Förlag** and plain **Gleerups**. Most of the presses involve personal names but there are some like **(Bokförlaget) Natur och Kultur**, or **Studentlitteratur**.

1.6.2 Some of the big publishers are also printers, but except in older books **tryckt** and **boktryckeri**, should be taken purely as printers' imprints. Usually they will be found with some other indication of the publisher, e.g. **utgifna af Sveriges Kristliga Studentrörelseförlag** in the title and **tryckt hos Almqvist & Wicksells Boktryckeri A:B** in the imprint.

1.6.3 No inference can be drawn from the use, rare nowadays, of the preposition **hos** (*by*) by itself, for it occurs in contexts like **tryckt hos** on the one hand and **hos bokhandleren W. Isberg** on the other.

1.6.4 Occasionally one may find a series note in place of the imprint, e.g. **Skånes Konstförenings publikation n:r 14**, where **Skånes Konstförening** has the genitive **-s**.

1.7 SERIES

1.7.1   Titles of series are commonly in the plural, as in the universal **Skrifter utgivna av . . .**, *Publications of . . .*, best abbreviated to plain **Skrifter**; but they may be singular, e.g. **Lychnos-Bibliotek**, or with the name of the issuing body first in the genitive, **Jernkontorets Berghistoriska Skriftserie**. If this is catalogued as **Jernkontoret. Berghistoriska Skriftserie**, the series title will not be in the usual form (cf. **Nordisk Statistisk Skriftserie**). As this is inadmissable, it is better to retain **Jernkontorets** than to alter -iska to -isk.

1.7.2   The numeration of series may be by **nummer**, abbreviated **n:r, nr, no., no:,** by **band**, or by **häfte**, but the number is often without prefix of any sort.

Double series are found, each with its own numeration, e.g. **Skrifter utgivna av Svenska Litteratursällskapet i Finland 347 | Studier i nordisk filologi | Fyrtiotredje bandet.**

Occasionally title and numeration are run together, e.g. **Försäkringsjuridiska föreningens publikation nr. 15**, *Publication no. 15 of F. föreningen.* (The plural is **publikationer.**)

1.8 PERIODICALS

1.8.1/1.8.2   The titles of periodicals have the same grammatical structure as the titles of books, e.g. **Svenska landsmål och svenskt folkliv | Tidskrift utgiven av Landsmåls- och Folkminnesarkivet i Uppsala genom Dag Strömbäck**, where **utgiven av** indicates the publishing body and **(utgiven) genom** the editor. Transactions and proceedings may involve names in the genitive, e.g. **Skytteanska Samfundet|s Handlingar.**

1.8.3   The editor usually appears as **redaktör**, occasionally **utgivare**, the editorial department, **redaktion**, being distinguished from dispatch, **expedition**. (The **ansvarig utgivare** is a titular figure, legally responsible for the periodical.)

1.8.4   An individual part is usually **häfte**, an annual volume being **årgång**, sometimes with the number following, sometimes preceded by an ordinal number.

1.8.5   Periodicity is variously indicated, e.g. **en gång i kvartalet**, *once a quarter*; **kvartalsvis**, *quarterly*; **med fyra häften årligen**, *four numbers a year*; **monatligen**, *monthly*.

1.8.6   The price may be given as **boklådspris**, *over-the-counter price;* **prenumerationspris**, *subscription-price*, and provision may be made for the sale of *separate numbers*, **lösnummer** or **lösa häften**. (Mention of the **annonspris**, *charge for advertisements*, in the same context may cause confusion.)

2   ALPHABET, PHONETICS, SPELLING

2.1 ALPHABET

2.1.1   The order is **a–z å ä ö**.

Note the difference from the order in Danish and Norwegian. **W** in names is interfiled with **v**, and **ü** is filed as **y**. **Q** may be followed by **v** in names. At one time Swedish was printed in Gothic type.

2.1.2   Some borrowed words end in **-é(n)**, e.g. **armé, komité**, and many names end in **-én**. The diaeresis, not to be confused with the umlaut on **ä** and **ö** (and in names on **ü**), is found in names like **Michaël.**

2.2 CAPITALISATION

2.2.1   In principle capitals are used for names, the difficulties arising over the definition of names, and the treatment of names consisting of more than one word. As regards the first, **Gud** (*God*), **Konungen** (*the King*) are treated as names; the words for the days of the week and the months are not. Nor are adjectives like **svensk, luthersk** or nouns like **stokholmare**, though **Bergska**, derived from a personal name, is. Words like **dieselmotor** and **vichyvatten** (*mineral water*) where the proper name is lost in the common noun have small letters but most authorities prefer to write words like **Lapplandsresa** (*Lapland journey*) with a capital.

2.2.2 The treatment of institutional names depends on how they are regarded. Learned institutions and public buildings have capitals, but a word like **socialstyrelsen** may well be regarded as simply descriptive as, e.g. **armén, drätselkammaren** (*finance committee*), **finansdepartementet** always are. **Kungl. Finansdepartementet** (the full official name) has capitals.

2.2.3 There is economy in names consisting of more than one word: **den helige Ande** (*the Holy Ghost*), **Johannes döparen** (*John the Baptist*), **Svenska museet** (*the Swedish Museum*). When, however, the first word is one such as **Sveriges, Stockholms, Norra, Stora**, or when, as in **Föreningen Rädda barnen**, the first word is not grammatically connected with what follows, the second too has a capital. Firms and periodicals have registered names of which the capitalisation is part, but only the first word of book titles has a capital.

2.3 DIVISION OF WORDS

2.3.1 Rules 1, 2, 3, 4, 5, 6a (p. xiii) apply except as under.

2.3.2 The following special rules are to be observed:

(a) In words (usually of foreign origin) such as **problem, cypress**, which are accented on the last syllable, both consonants belong to this syllable, provided that they can begin a word.

(b) Combinations of letters that stand for a single sound are not divided, e.g. **ma-skin** (*machine*), **du-scha, cre-scendo**; but **mis-sion** is correct. Similarly **dräng-ar** has to be divided after the g, though **tan-gent**, in which the g is separately sounded, is not. The complex sound x goes with the earlier syllable.

(c) When a word ending in a double consonant is compounded with one beginning with the same letter, the three are reduced to two. On division the omitted consonant is restored, e.g. **tillåta** > **till-låta**, **rättrogen** > **rätt-trogen**. Similarly **-mm-** is expanded into **mm-m**.

2.3.3 '**Man skriver ogärna ä-ta.**' In other words it is wiser to apply rule 8.

2.4 PUNCTUATION AND ABBREVIATIONS

2.4.1 The use of the interior colon in abbreviations, e.g. **n:r** for **nummer**, **förf:s** for **författares**, is less frequent than formerly, and the use of the first and last letters without any stop, e.g. **nr, dr**, or the first few consonants (usually ending in a consonant) followed by a full stop, is growing, e.g. **bl.a.** (*inter alia*), **dvs.** or **d.v.s.** (*i.e.*), **m.fl., m.m., osv.** or **o.s.v.** (*etc.*), **t.e(x).** (*e.g.*).

2.4.2 When two compound words have the second element in common, or a complex expression is formed in which two elements combine in the same way with a third, the first element stands by itself and ends with a hyphen, e.g. **gross- och detaljhandeln**, *wholesale and retail trade*; **låne- och uthyrningslagen**, *Lend-lease Act*. Similarly the less common **kraftproduction och -förbrukning**, *power production and consumption*.

2.4.3 When a complex name is joined to a common noun, only the second element is joined by a hyphen, e.g. **Nathan Söderblom-samfundet**. (Some writers join the last two words or sometimes all three together without a hyphen.)

2.5 VARIATION OF CONSONANT

2.5.1 A vowel may be short before final -m, which is then doubled before an ending beginning with a vowel, e.g. **kam, kammen,** (*the*) *comb*, as opposed to **ram, ramen,** (*the*) *frame*.

2.5.2 In some verbs there are alternations of plain and palatalised consonants, e.g. **stal/stjäla**. But in the apparently similar **gör/gjorde** there is no change, for **g** is palatalised before **ö** in any case.

2.6 VARIATION OF VOWEL

Unstressed -e- in a final syllable is often dropped before an ending, e.g. **tecken, tecknet.** For changes in strong verbs see 8.3, 8.12, 8.19.

2.7 SPELLING

Before 1906 a number of superfluous consonants are found, since removed, and some conventional spellings, e.g. **hvad, öfver, haf, godt, händt** (now **vad, över, hav, gott, hänt**). In the 18th century **w** is still found for **v, g** for **k, qu** for **kv, th** for **d** in words such as **det**, and **ä** and **ö** are written **ȧ** and **ȯ**. In combination these deviations from present practice may be puzzling, e.g. **hwålfning = välvning**.

3 ARTICLES

3.1 DEFINITE

3.1.1 The definite article is most often appended to the noun and is dealt with there (4).

3.1.2 Before adjectives there is a separate article: S **den, det**; P **de**, but the noun has the appended article also, e.g. **den första upplagan**. Note that the same form may count as a demonstrative (1.3.2).

3.2 INDEFINITE

Common gender: **en**   N: **ett**

4 NOUNS

4.1 GENDER AND FORM

Nouns may be of common (M & F) or neuter gender, but the form is no indication of gender, which is revealed by the article: C -(e)n, N -(e)t, e.g. **man, mannen; kvinna|n, bok|en, artikel|n, arbete|t, hus|et.** Note **ministerium, ministeriet**.

4.2 PLURAL

4.2.1 The plural, without and with the article, may end in:

-ar, -arna: nouns of common gender in unstressed -e, -el, -en, -er (except those of foreign origin), in -dom and -ing.

-er, -erna: nouns in -ad, -else, -skap; nearly all those of foreign, especially Latin origin; neuter nouns in -eri and -um.

-or, -orna: most nouns of common gender in -a.

-n, -na: neuter nouns ending in a vowel, except -eri.

-, -en: neuter nouns ending in a consonant, also **män(nen)** plural of **man(nen)**.

-, -na: nouns ending in -are, -ande, -iker, e.g. S läkare|n, P läkare, läkarna;
S främmande|n, P främmande|na.

Note the ambiguity of the ending -en.

4.2.2 If it is necessary to form the plural, it is as well to check it in a good dictionary, since the above are for the most part only rough rules. Borrowed foreign words may take -s, pending naturalisation.

4.3 CASES

4.3.1 The genitive ending -s may be added to any noun, singular or plural, with or without appended article, or to an adjective if it follows the noun it qualifies. But note, in contrast to Danish and Norwegian, **k(on)ungen|s av Danmark bröstkarameller,** *the King of Denmark's cough sweets.*

4.3.2 In use the Swedish genitive corresponds to both *'s* and *of* in English, e.g. **Stockholm|s stad|s historia,** *the history of the city of Stockholm* (but **Uppsala stads historia**); **kvinnor|na|s andel,** *women's share*; and occurs in set phrases after **i** and **till.**

4.3.3 Obsolete case-endings -e, -er, -om are found in some stereotyped expressions.

5 ADJECTIVES

5.1 AGREEMENT

So far as there are distinct forms, adjectives agree with the nouns they qualify.

5.2 ENDINGS

5.2.1

	MF	N	P
Strong form	-	-t(t)	-a
Weak form	-e, -a	-a	-a

In older texts -e is found for -a.

5.2.2 The addition of the neuter -t is not always straightforward, e.g. **liten, litet; sann, sant; god, gott; blind, blint; trodd, trott; fast, fast.** Adjectives in -a and -e do not change.

5.2.3 The weak form is used when the noun is preceded by the definite article or a demonstrative, in which case the noun has the suffixed article also, e.g. **det(ta) politisk|a livet,** when it is preceded by a possessive, a genitive or **någon,** *some,* e.g. **Jernkontorets Berghistorisk|a Skriftserie,** very commonly in names, when the noun has the suffixed article only, e.g. **Svensk|a Dagbladet, Stads historisk|a Institutet,** with personal names and in stereotyped expressions such as **näst|a vecka,** *next week.* (Here there is no strong form in existence.) Otherwise the strong form is used, e.g. **Nordisk Statistisk Skriftserie, tidskriften är ny, Svensk|a Landsmål (pl.) och Svensk|t Folkliv, Skrifter utgivn|a av . . . .**

5.2.4 The strong neuter form is used adverbially, e.g. **sterkt,** *strongly.*

5.3 COMPARISON

Comparative: **-(a)re**   Superlative: **-(a)st**

Some common adjectives change the vowel in the comparative and the superlative thus: o/ö, u/y, å/ä, e.g. **lång, längre, längst.** These and irregular comparisons such as **god, bättre, bäst,** have independent entries in good dictionaries.

6 NUMERALS

6.1 CARDINAL

6.1.1

1 en, ett	11 elva	21 tjugoen, -ett
2 två	12 tolv	22 tjugotvå
3 tre	13 tretton	30 trettio
4 fyra	14 fjorton	40 fyrtio
5 fem	15 femton	50 femtio
6 sex	16 sexton	60 sextio
7 sju	17 sjutton	70 sjuttio
8 åtta	18 aderton	80 åttio
9 nio	19 nitton	90 nittio
10 tio	20 tjugo (tjugu)	100 hundra

101 hundraen, -ett	1000 tusen
128 hundratjugoåtta	1500 ett tusen fem hundra
200 två hundra	2000 två tusen

6.1.2 Apart from **en**, N **ett**, cardinal numbers are invariable.

6.2 ORDINAL

6.2.1

1 första	6 sjätte	11 elfte	21 tjugoförsta
2 andra	7 sjunde	12 tolvte	30 trettionde
3 tredje	8 åttonde	13 trettonde	90 nittionde
4 fjärde	9 nionde	19 nittonde	100 hundrade
5 femte	10 tionde	20 tjugonde	1000 tusende

6.2.2 Ordinals are weak adjectives.

6.2.3 **Andra** (*second*) is to be distinguished from **annan** (*other*).

6.3 FIGURES

6.3.1 Cardinals are represented by simple arabic numerals, ordinals also may be so represented, e.g. **den 11 maj**, or by the addition of a colon and the appropriate ending, e.g. **11:e divisionen**. Roman figures more often stand for ordinals, e.g. **efter Karl IX:s död**. **Sidan 10** (*p. 10*) is read as a cardinal (cf. 1.3).

6.4 DATES

6.4.1 The months are:

**januari, februari, mars, april, maj, juni,
juli, augusti, september, oktober, november, december**

6.4.2 *11 May 1966* is den 11 (**elfte**) **maj nittonhundrasextiosex**.

6.4.3 Note **1800-talet, adertonhundratalet,** *1800–1899*; **nittonde århundradèt,** *1801–1900*; **40-talet (fyrtiotalet),** *the 40's*, and even **90-talesteticismen.**

7 PRONOUNS

7.2 RELATIVE, INTERROGATIVE

7.2.1 The relative as object is often omitted, **e.g. Människor jag mött,** *People I have met.*

7.2.2 With relatives and interrogatives the preposition is often put at the end of the sentence, e.g. **Allt (som) vi arbetat för,** *Everything we have worked for.*

7.3 PERSONAL

7.3.1 The plural form of the second person is the prescribed polite form, as in **Tycker ni om Brahms** (*Aimez-vous Brahms*), but it is not popular.

7.3.2 The use of **sig** (*himself, herself, itself*) is often idiomatic, e.g. **det måste löna sig att arbeta,** *it must pay to work.*

8 VERBS

8.1 STRUCTURE

8.1.1 The verb in Swedish has very few different forms—only slightly more than in English or the other Scandinavian languages. In many respects it resembles the English verb.

8.1.2 Verbs are listed under the infinitive, which ends in a vowel, usually an -a. It is used with or without **att,** *to,* but keeps **att** even after a preposition, e.g. **Bryt strömmen genom att trycka på knappen,** *Cut the current by pressing the button.*

8.2 PRESENT

8.2.1 All forms now end in **-r,** and correspond to the infinitive as in the examples below:

P	kallar	säger	tror	hör
I	kalla	säga	tro	höra

8.2.2 The plural used to be the same as the infinitive, but such forms are now stylistic archaisms. For irregular presents see 8.19.

8.3 PAST

8.3.1 *Weak*: remove the -a or -ja, if any, of the infinitive and add -ade, -de, -dde, -te, e.g. **kalla** > **kallade; höra** > **hörde; skilja** > **skilde; tro** > **trodde; köpa** > **köpte.** There may be a change of vowel before -de and -te, especially with infinitive in -ja, e.g. **böra** > **borde; spörja** > **sporde.** The plural is the same as the singular.

8.3.2 *Strong*: the singular has no ending, but usually a different vowel from the infinitive, viz.

Past		*Infinitive*
S	P	
-a-	-u-	-i-, -ä-, -jä-
-e-	-e-	-i-
-o-	-o-	-a-
-å-	-å-	-ä-
-ä-	-ä-	-å-
-ö-	-ö-	-a-, -u-, -ju-, -y-, -å-

e.g. **springa sprang**

The distinctive plural, which had the ending -o, e.g. **sprungo,** is even less used than that of the present.

8.3.3 Some important verbs diverge from the patterns given above. As some of them have other irregularities also, they are given together at 8.19.

8.7 SUBJUNCTIVE

8.7.1 The present ends in -e, corresponding to the infinitive, e.g. höre, Inf. höra.

8.7.2 The past also ends in -e and has the same stem as the plural of the past indicative, e.g. om jag vore, *if I were.*

8.7.3 The subjunctive was used in wishes and unfulfilled conditions, but is now avoided by using an auxiliary verb.

8.10 COMPOUND TENSES

8.10.1 The future is expressed by komm-er/-a att or skall/skola with the infinitive. Skall often has a suggestion of intention, threat or promise.

8.10.2 The perfect and related tenses are formed as in English. The neuter of the past participle is used, the strong participle having a special form in -it, e.g. jag har kommit. (Swedish grammars call this the supine.)

8.12 PARTICIPLES

8.12.1 *Present*: -ande/-ende

8.12.2 *Past, weak*: -ad, -d, -dd, -t. The neuter substitutes -t(t) for -d(d).

8.12.3 *Past, strong*: -en, N -et. Participles with the vowel -u- may correspond to infinitives in -i-, -y-, -ä-, or -jä- as well as -u-. For other irregularities see 8.19.

8.12.4 The past participle is an adjective and behaves as such when used to form the passive (8.15).

8.15 PASSIVE

8.15.1 Most commonly in writing -s is added to the active; to form the present the -s is added to the infinitive. In the present this form usually refers to habitual action, but not in the past, e.g. distribueras av, (*is*) *distributed by*; har beretts, *has been prepared.* In some verbs it has a special meaning, e.g. behövs, *it is necessary*; jag minns, *I remember*; in others it may be reciprocal.

8.15.2 bli(va) and vara (8.19) with the past participle differ roughly in emphasising respectively action and state, e.g. hade blivit utsatta, *had been turned out*; tredje upplagan är starkt omarbetad, *the 3rd edition is much revised.*

8.19 IRREGULAR VERBS

Some common verbs are irregular in the present or have anomalous past tenses, viz.

Infinitive	Present	Past	Past participle
vara, *be*	är, äro	var, voro	varit
ha(va), *have*	har	hade	haft, havd
be(dja), *ask*	be(de)r	bad, bådo	bett, -bedd
bli(va), *become*	blir	blev	bliv-en/-it
bringa, *bring*	bringar	bragte	bragt
dö, *die*	dör	dog -o	dött
få, *get*	får	fick, fingo	-fådd, -fången, fått
ge, giva, *give*	g(iv)er	gav, gåvo	given, gett

gå, *go*	går	gick, gingo	gången, gått
kunna, *can*	kan	kunde	kunnat
ligga, *lie*	ligger	låg -o	legat (-legad)
lägga, *lay*	lägger	lade	lagd, lagt
se, *see*	ser	såg -o	sedd, sett
slå, *strike*	slår	slog -o	slagen
stå, *stand*	står	stod -o	-stådd, -stånden, stått
säga, *say*	säger	sade	sagd, sagt
varda, *become*	varder	vart, vordo	vorden
veta, *know*	vet	visste	vetat
vilja, (*be*) *will*(*ing*)	vill	ville	velat

8.23 COMPOUND VERBS

8.23.1 Adopting Norwegian terminology, verbs compounded with adverbs or nouns may be classed as 'fast', e.g. **förbjuda**, *forbid*, or 'loose', e.g. **gå av**, *break*, *get off*. Fast verbs are no different from any others, but loose verbs become fast in the present and past participles, e.g. **avgående**, **avgången**, which could equally well come from **avgå**, *leave*. Sometimes the corresponding fast and loose verbs differ little, if at all, in meaning; sometimes the difference is substantial. Where both verbs exist, both possibilities should be entertained in translating; but fast participles from loose verbs tend to be avoided by using a relative clause.

8.23.2 The detached part of a loose verb is not placed right at the end as in German but even precedes a pronoun-object, and may therefore be mistaken for a preposition, e.g.

De körde genast ut honom, *They turned him out immediately.* German: Sie jagten ihn sofort hinaus.

9 ADVERBS

See 5.2.4. It is also possible that new adverbs formed of a noun plus **-vis** (*-wise*) may appear, which are not in the dictionary.

10 PREPOSITIONS

The caution given under Danish applies to Swedish. (Cf. also 7.2.2.)

GLOSSARY

anteckning, *note*
avdelning, *section, department*
avdrag, *discount, rebate*

band, *volume* (1.4.1)
bearbetad, *revised* (1.5.1)

beredning, *committee* (1.2.6)
beställning, *order*
bibliotek, *library*
bibliotekarie, *librarian*
bidrag, *contribution*
bifogad, *added*

bilaga, *appendix, supplement*
billigbok, *cheap paperback*
bokförlag, *publishing house*
bokhandlare, *bookseller*
boktryckeri, *press*
brev, *letter*
broschyr, *pamphlet*
byte, *exchange*

del, *volume, part* (1.4.1)
dikt, *poem*
död, *dead*

eftertryck, *reprint*
exemplar, *copy*
expedition, *dispatch*

forskning, *research*
fortsättning följer, *to be continued*
född, *born*
följd, *series*
författarrätt, *copyright*
förhandlingar, *proceedings*
förlag, *publishing house*
förlagd, *published*
förord, *preface*

genomsedd, *revised*

halvårs-, *half-yearly*
handskrift, *manuscript*
häftad, *sewn, stitched*
häfte, *part, number* (1.4.1)

inbunden, *bound*
inledning, *introduction*

korrigering, *correction*
kostnadsfri, *free*
kvartalsvis, *quarterly* (1.8.5)

lösnummer, *single number*

meddelande, *communication(s)*
medlem, *member*
månadsskrift, *monthly publication*
månatlig, *monthly*
möte, *meeting, congress*

nota, *bill*
novell, *short story*
ny, *new*
ny tryckning, *reprint* (1.5.3)

omarbetad, *revised* (1.5.1)
omtryck, *reprint* (1.5.3)
ordbok, *dictionary*
otryckt, *unpublished*

pjäs, *play*
plansch(blad), planschsida, *plate*
pocketbok, *paperback*
prenumeration, *subscription* (1.8.6)
pris, *price*
prov, *sample*
til påseende, *on approval*

rabatt, *discount*
redaktion, *editing* (1.2.3, 1.8.3),
    editorial office
redaktör, *editor*
redigerad, *edited* (1.2.2)
register, *index*
revy, *review*
räkning, *bill*
rättad, *corrected*

til salu, *on sale*
samfund, *society*
samling, *collection*
samma, *same*
sammandrag, sammanfattning, *summary*
sammanställd, *compiled*
sida, *page*
skådespel, *play*
små|skrift, -tryck, *pamphlet*
sällskap, *society*
särtryck, *offprint* (1.5.3)

tabell(blad), *table*
tal, *speech*
tidskrift, *periodical*
tillägg, *supplement, appendix*
tillökad, *enlarged*
tillökning, *addition*
tryckning, *impression*

undersökning, *investigation*

upplaga, *edition, impression* (1.5.1)
uppsats, *essay*
utanskrift, *address*
utarbetad, *prepared* (1.2.2)
utbyte, *exchange*
utgivare, *editor* (1.8.3)
utgiven, *edited, published* (1.2.2, 1.8.1)
utgången, *out of print*
utkomma, *appear, come out*
utkommen, *published (already)*
utskott, *committee*
utsåld, *sold out*
utvald, *selected*

utvidgad, *enlarged* (1.5.1)

vecka, *week*
verk, *work*

är, *year*
årgång, *volume* (1.8.4)
års-, *annual*
årsbok, *yearbook*

äldre nummer, *back number*

översättning, *translation*

GRAMMATICAL INDEX: WORDS

att, 8.1.2

bad, be(de)r, 9.19
(-)bett (with prefix), 8.19
blev, blir, bliv-en/-it, 8.15.2, 8.19
bragt(e), 8.19
bådo, 8.19

de(n), det, 3.1.2
dog(o), 8.19
dött, 8.19

en, ett, 3.2, 6.1.2

fick, fingo, 8.19
fådd, fången, fått, 8.19

gav, ger, 8.19
gett, 8.19

gick, gingo, 8.19
given, giver, 8.19
gången, 8.19
gått, 8.19
gåvo, 8.19

hade, haft, har, havd, 8.19

kan, 8.19
komm-er/-a att, 8.10.1
kunde, kunnat, 8.19

lag-d/-t, 8.19
-legad, legat, 8.19
ligger, 8.19
lägger, 8.19
låg(o), 8.19

männen, 4.2.1

sade, sag-d/-t, se-dd/-tt, 8.19
sig, 7.3.2
skall, skola, 8.1
slagen, slog(o), 8.19
säger, 8.19
såg(o), 8.19

var(it), 8.15.2, 8.19
varder, vart, 8.19
velat, 8.19
vet(at), 8.19
vill(e), 8.19
viste, 8.19
vord-en/-o, 8.19
voro, 8.15.2, 8.19,

är(o), 8.15.2, 8.19

GRAMMATICAL INDEX: ENDINGS

- (no ending), 4.2.1, 5.2.1, 8.3.2

-a, 5.2.1
-na, 4.2.1
-rna, 4.2.1

-(d)d, 8.12.2
-ad, 8.12.2

-e, 4.3.3, 5.2.1, 8.7.1, 8.7.2

-(d)de, 8.3.1
-nde, 8.12.1
-re, 5.3
-te, 8.3.1

-om, 4.3.3

-n, 4.1, 4.2.1
-en, 4.1, 4.2.1, 8.12.3

-o, 8.3.2

-r, 4.2.1, 8.2.1
-er, 4.2.1, 4.3.3

-s, 4.2.2, 4.3.1, 8.15.1
-vis, 9

-t, 4.1, 5.2.1, 5.2, 8.12.2
-et, 4.1, 8.12.3
-it, 8.10.2
-st, 5.3
-tt, 5.2, 8.12.2

ICELANDIC

SPECIMEN

Hér á landi er ekki til neitt tímarit, sem hefur það hlutverk að birta aðgengilegar upplýsingar og greinar um efnahag þjóðarinnar og fjármál. Er þó mikil nauðsyn, að allur almenningur geri sér ljóst eðli þeirra vandamála, sem við er að etja. Einnig hefur vantað hér vettvang fyrir ritgerðir og umræður um hagfræðileg efni, en því fer fjarri, að einkenni hins íslenzka hagkerfis hafi verið könnuð til nokkurrar hlítar.

In this country there exists no periodical, which has the task of publishing available information and articles on national economic conditions and finance. It is however very necessary that the general public should make clear to itself the nature of the problems that have to be dealt with. There has also been lacking a forum for essays and discussions on economic subjects, though it is far from being the case that the characteristics of the Icelandic economy have been investigated in any sufficiency.

Marks of Icelandic are the letters ð and þ, accented vowels, the endings **-ar, -ir, -ur**, and the various forms of the suffixed article **-inn** (cf. **þjóð|ar|inn|ar** above).

0 GENERAL CHARACTERISTICS

0.1 DEGREE OF INFLEXION
Though modern Icelandic differs from the Icelandic of the sagas, of which it is a development, it has a more primitive structure than the other Scandinavian languages, retaining four cases in noun, article, adjective and pronoun, and different forms for different persons of the verb. To this extent it is a synthetic language; nevertheless it uses prepositions freely and subject pronouns with verbs.

0.2 ORDER OF WORDS
Adjectives usually precede their nouns, while genitives follow, but neither rule is absolute; possessives vary. The basic sentence order SVOC is varied (a) when something other than the subject comes first, or a subordinate clause precedes the main clause; (b) in impersonal constructions, when the logical subject comes first; (c) after the relative and certain conjunctions, e.g.

(a) $\overset{1}{\text{Í}}$ $\overset{2}{\text{bókaverzlunum}}$ $\overset{3}{\text{kostar}}$ $\overset{4}{\text{hvert}}$ $\overset{5}{\text{hefti}}$ $\overset{6}{\text{10}}$ kr., $\overset{1}{\text{In}}$ $\overset{2}{\text{bookshops}}$ $\overset{4}{\text{each}}$ $\overset{5}{\text{part}}$ $\overset{3}{\text{costs}}$ $\overset{6}{\text{10 kr.}}$

(b) **Okkur vantar þessa bók**, i.e. *We lack this book*

(c) $\overset{1}{\text{Ef}}$ $\overset{2}{\text{dæma}}$ $\overset{3}{\text{má}}$ $\overset{4}{\text{eftir}}$ $\overset{5}{\text{reynslu}}$ $\overset{6}{\text{annarra}}$ $\overset{7}{\text{þjóða}}$, $\overset{8}{\text{mundi}}$ $\overset{9}{\text{það}}$ $\overset{10}{\text{taka}}$ $\overset{11}{\text{alllangan}}$ $\overset{12}{\text{tíma.}}$ $\overset{1}{\text{If}}$ $\overset{2}{\text{one}}$
$\overset{3}{\text{may}}$ $\overset{2}{\text{judge}}$ $\overset{4}{\text{from}}$(the) $\overset{5}{\text{experience}}$ $\overset{6}{\text{of-other}}$ $\overset{7}{\text{peoples}}$, $\overset{9}{\text{it}}$ $\overset{8}{\text{would}}$ $\overset{10}{\text{take}}$ $\overset{11}{\text{quite-a-long}}$
$\overset{12}{\text{time}}$

$\overset{1}{\text{Þau,}}$ $\overset{2}{\text{sem}}$ $\overset{3}{\text{boðin}}$ $\overset{4}{\text{hafa}}$ $\overset{5}{\text{verið}}$ $\overset{6}{\text{út,}}$ $\overset{1}{\text{Those}}$ $\overset{2}{\text{which}}$ $\overset{4}{\text{have}}$ $\overset{5}{\text{been}}$ $\overset{3}{\text{offered}}$

0.4 RELATION TO OTHER LANGUAGES

In vocabulary it is notably Germanic, preferring native compounds even where the other Scandinavian languages admit Latin and Greek derivatives, e.g. **ritstjóri**, *editor* (Da. and No **redaktør**); **hagfræðilegur**, *economic* (**økonomisk**). Many words and expressions recall archaic English, e.g. **dæma**, *to deem*; **mér þótti**, *me thought*. (See further General note on the Germanic languages.)

1 BIBLIOLINGUISTICS

1.1 NAMES

1.1.1 The number of Icelandic Christian names is large, and since the majority of them are compounded of interchangeable elements, e.g. **Hall|grímur**, **Þór|grímur**, **Hall|dór**, it is always theoretically possible that new ones will appear. But in fact many of the possibilities are very rare, while the simple imported name **Jón** is immensely popular.

1.1.2 Among the native names masculine ones mostly end in **-ur** (4.3.2) or **-i** (4.3.11), but other consonant endings are also found; feminine names commonly end in **-a** (4.3.12) or a consonant (4.3.2), though **-ur** is also possible. Imported names frequently end in a consonant without the termination **-ur**.

1.1.3 A list of final elements and terminations, and some imported names follow:

Masculine	*Feminine*
-an	-arna
-ar	-björg*
-arinn	-björt
-bergur	-borg*
-bjartur	-dís
-björn	-ey*
-dór, -ór, -þór	-finna
-finnur	-fríður
-freður	-gerður
-fús	-gríma
-geir	-gunnur
-gils	-heiður
-grímur	-hildur
-heðinn	-laug*
-kell	-leif*
-kon	-ný*
-laugur	-ríður
-leifur	-steina
-mann	-unn*
-steinn	-veig
-týr	-vör*
-vin	-þrúður
-þegn	
-þér	* See 4.3.2

M Andrés, Anton, Eggert, Jakob, **Jóhann(es)**, Jón, Jónas, Klemenz, **Kristinn**, **Kristján**, Lárus, Magnús, **Markús**, Páll, Pétur, Valdimar

F Mostly in -a, e.g. Anna, **Jóna, María**, Marta, Una; but note **Elísabet, Kristín**, Margrét

1.1.4   The parallel M and F elements **-laugur/-laug, -finnur/-finna** are distinguishable in all or most of the cases, viz.

	N	*A*	*G*	*D*
M	-laugur	-laug	-laugs	-laugi
F	-laug	-laugu	-laugar	-laugu

In the case of **Finnur** there is a third possibility: **Finni**, viz.

	N	*A*	*G*	*D*
M	Finnur	Finn	Finns	Finni
M	Finni	Finna	Finna	Finna
F	-finna	-finnu	-finnu	-finnu

The same is true of such similar names as **Grímur** and **Grímar**, viz.

N	*A*	*G*	*D*
Grímur	Grím	Gríms	Grími
Grímar	Grímar	Grímars	Grímri

1.1.5   The vast majority of Icelandic 'surnames' are in fact not family names but simply patronymics, e.g.

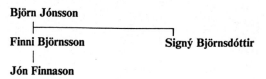

For this reason many Icelandic indexes and works of reference enter all personal names under the Christian name, while some enter under Christian name only if there is no true surname. It is inadvisable to follow these practices in multilingual catalogues, or to attempt to guess whether a name in -son is as usual a patronymic or, as it sometimes is, a genuine surname, or possibly in the case of a woman the husband's patronymic. It is best to follow the practice of the national bibliography and treat them all as surnames, unless the patronymic is followed by a true surname, as in **Einar Gisli Hjörleifsson KVARAN**.

Where, however, a name is compounded with the preposition **frá** or **úr**, indicative of origin, it is entered under the part before the preposition, e.g. **GUÐRÚN** frá Lundi, **Bjarni JÓNSSON frá Unnarholti**.

1.1.6   As patronymics are formed by adding **-son** to the genitive of a Christian name, alternative forms are sometimes possible, e.g. in 1887 **Valdimar Ásmundarson** but in the 1899 edition of the same book **Valdimar Ásmundsson** (cf. 4.3.1).

1.1.7   Both Christian names and patronymics are declined as occasion arises after the pattern of common nouns (4), and some of the changes are quite marked (cf. 1.2). True surnames, e.g. Kvaran, **Briem, Nordal, Bergmann**, are rarely declined, though they may take the genitive **-s**; but note that some, such as **Aðils, Arnalds, Reynis**, already end in **-s**.

Herra, *Mr*; **frú,** *Mrs*; **ungfrú,** *Miss*; **Síra** or **Séra,** *Rev.*; **prófessor**; **d(okto)r**, precede the Christian name, but there are some terms like **biskup** that come between the Christian name and the patronymic.

1.2 NAMES OF AUTHORS, EDITORS, ETC.

1.2.1   The names of authors usually stand at the head of the title-page in the nominative. The nominative is also used in the order: title, active verb, name, e.g. **samið hefur Arni G. Eylands**, but this type is much commoner in the case of editors and translators, with such verbs as **valdi**, *chose*, **safnað hefur, tók saman**, etc., *collected*; **búið hefur** or **bjó** (P **bjuggu**) **til prentunar**, *prepared for printing*; **sá um útgáfuna**, *saw to the publishing*; **þýddi, íslenzkaði** (P **-u**), *translated* (*into Icelandic*). Note that there is agreement between the verb and subject; a plural verb such as **bjuggu** implies at least two names.

1.2.2   Less common, except in the case of dictionaries, is the use of prepositions such as **eftir** and **af** (*by*), the latter being used with or without a preceding participle (1.2.5). **Af** takes the dative; **eftir**, which takes the accusative, e.g. **Króka-Refs rímur eftir Síra Hallgrím Pétursson**, is more dangerous, for the accusative form is more familiar than the nominative **Hallgrímur**. In a suitable context, as in the example in 1.2.3, **eftir** may indicate an editor.

1.2.3   Collected works, letters, classics and some other types of work may have the name in the genitive, e.g. **Bréf Jóns Sigurðssonar**, *Letters of Jón Sigurðsson*; **Passiúsálmar Hallgríms Péturssonar með orðalykli, eftir Björn Magnusson**, *Hallgrímur Pétursson's Passion Psalms, with glossary, edited by Björn Magnússon*; **Ritdeila Sigurðar Nordals og Einars H. Kvarans**, *Controversy between Sigurður Nordal and Einar H. Kvaran.*

1.2.4   Collaborators are usually indicated simply by the use of the two names. In this connection it should be noted that surnames have plural forms which are used in instances such as **Magnús og Kjartan Helgasynir**, i.e. *Magnús Helgason and Kjartan Helgason.*

1.2.5   The names of institutions, societies, government departments and suchlike may likewise appear in the nominative, independently or with an active verb; in the genitive, dependent on some other noun; or in the accusative or dative, after prepositions: but the relation of the body to the work is often left vague, e.g. **Skrár Þjóðskjalasafns**, *Catalogues of the National Archives*. Here a note in one of the volumes runs: **skrá . . . rituð af dr. Birni K. Þórólfssyni skjalaverði**, *catalogue . . . written by Dr. Björn K. Þórólfsson, Archivist.*

1.2.6   Some corporate names have the article (3.1.2) appended, e.g. **Ættfræðifélag|ið**, *The Genealogical Society*; **Póststjórn|in**, *the G.P.O.*; others have none, e.g. **Stjórnarráð**, *Cabinet*; **Landsbanki Íslands**, *National Bank of Iceland*. This last is a common type, for a noun qualified by a genitive has no article. If the expression is abbreviated, e.g. **Landsbankinn**, the article is used. Others again seem to vary, e.g. **Landsskjalasafnið**, *the National Archives*, but also **í Þjóðskjalasafn|inu, sem þá hét** (*which was then called*) **Landsskjalasafn**. In such cases it does not seem to matter whether one uses the article or not; but generally speaking the form used in the catalogue should follow the practice in each particular case.

1.2.7   Where the name of the body begins with an adjective, it is normal to have the prepositive article, e.g. **Hið íslenzka þjóðvinafélag**, lit. *The Icelandic Friends-of-the-Nation-Society*, **af Hinu Íslenzka Bókmenntafélagi**, *by the Icelandic Literary Society*. Note that this is always spelt with a capital letter, even though the rest of the names need not be. In Icelandic catalogues the article is usually transferred to the end, e.g. **Almenni Kirkjusjóður, Hinn**. If the article is omitted, the rest of the name should be left unaltered, with a weak adjective, and not supplied with a strong one after the analogy of German (cf. 5.2). These names too may have abbreviated forms with an appended article, e.g. **Þjóðvinafélagið, af Bókmenntafélaginu**.

1.2.8 Subordinate departments and offices usually precede the main body, which is in the genitive, e.g. **Bókadeild Menningarsjóðs,** *Book Department of the Literary Fund;* **Skrifstofa Alþingis,** *Office of the Althing.* In accordance with the grammatical rule stated above neither **Bókadeild** nor **Skrifstofa** has the appended article. If in the catalogue one separates the expressions into **Menningarsjóður. Bókadeild,** and **Alþingi. Skrifstofa,** should one on the doubtful analogy of **Landsbankinn** above write **Bókadeildin** and **Skrifstofan?** Icelandic catalogues seem often to solve the problem by leaving the compound expression as it is, but such entries as **Almennar Tryggingar H.F. Lífdeild** (*General Insurance Co. Life Department*) indicate that it is correct to continue to omit the article.

1.2.9 **Félag,** the final element in the names of many societies, used to be written **fjelag;** other changes of spelling are of only minor importance.

1.3 TITLES

1.3.1 Once the difficulties of unfamiliar inflexions are overcome, Icelandic titles are straightforward, the order of the words being usually much the same as in English, e.g. **Alþýðlegur fróðleikur í bundnu máli og óbundnu,** *Popular knowledge in verse* (lit. *bound speech*) *and prose.*

1.3.2 Title entries are unlikely to cause difficulty except under British Museum rules, when the nominative may have to be got from some oblique case. This is somewhat perilous and a dictionary should be handy. **Hinn** is ignored in the filing; but note that **einn** is a numeral, **Einn dagur í lífi Sigga litla,** *One day in the life of little Siggi,* follows **Einarsson, A.K.**

1.3.3 In the context of a sentence the principal word in a title and adjectives in agreement may be put into an oblique case, e.g. **Fyrsti kafli Stundar og staða,** *the first chapter of 'Stund og staðir',* but if the title is in italics this may be considered enough to insulate it, e.g. **í Hrímvíta móðir** (í takes the dative, but the title remains in the nominative).

1.4 VOLUMES AND PARTS

1.4.1 The usual word for volume, **bindi,** is neuter, and unchanged in the plural: **I. (fyrsta) bindi,** *first volume;* **tvö bindi,** two volumes. The numeral usually precedes in the ordinal form. If there are only two volumes, **fyrra** and **síðara** are used instead of **fyrsta** and **annað.**

1.4.2 Both **hefti** and **hluti** could be translated *part.* **Hefti** is used for subdivisions of **bindi, hluti** for small books. Neither is common.

1.5 EDITIONS

1.5.1 Edition is **útgáfa,** e.g. **önnur útgáfa,** *second edition;* but this is not the only meaning of the word (cf. 1.2.1, 1.6.1).

1.5.2 Revision is indicated in various ways, e.g. **ný,** *new,* **endursamin,** *revised,* **endurbætt,** *improved,* **aukin,** *enlarged.* **Útgáfa** is also used in such terms as **heildarútgáfa** (*complete edition*). One also meets expressions such as **1. og 2. þúsund** (*1st and 2nd thousand*), **þriðja prentun** (*third printing*) and in older books such variations as **Prentaðar í þriðja sinn** (*Printed the third time*).

1.5.3 *Offprint* is **sérprent(un).**

1.6 IMPRINTS

1.6.1 The publisher's imprint frequently consists simply of the words **Bókaforlag** or **Bókaútgáfa(n),** *press,* with or without the appended article, followed by a personal or corporate name in the genitive, e.g. **Bókaútgáfa Guðjóns O. Guðjónssonar, Bókaútgáfa Menningarsjóðs**, or by an arbitrary name in apposition, e.g. **Bókaútgáfan Þjóðsaga**. The first two could well be abbreviated to **Guðjónsson** and **Menningarsjóður**, in line with the shorter types of imprint that are now more common, the last perhaps to **Þjóðsaga**, though Icelandic catalogues do not do so; but more elaborate examples such as **Íslendingasagnaútgáfan Haukadalsútgáfan** should be left as they are. The article **-n** should not be removed. As alternatives to **bókaútgáfa** we find **bókadeild**, *book department*, and **bókaverzlun**, *bookshop*. Note also **höfundurinn**, *the author*; **á kostnað höfundar**, *at the author's expense*.

1.6.2 The form of the name is unaffected by such additions as **útgefandi, kostnaðarmaður**, P **-menn**, *publisher(s)*, or **gáf út**, *published*; but **prentað (birt) á kostnað**, *printed (published) at the expense*, is followed by the genitive, as is the old-fashioned **á forlag**; **gefið út af**, *published by*, requires the dative.

1.6.3 The printer is implied by **prentsmiðja**, *printing press* (but printers often publish) and more directly indicated by **prentað (-uð) hjá**, followed by the dative.

1.7 SERIES

1.7.1 The titles of series are usually descriptive of the contents and in the plural; they often incorporate the name of the publisher, e.g. **Íslenzk sendibréf**, *Icelandic missives*; **Handbækur Menningarsjóðs**, *Handbooks of the Educational Fund*. Arbitrary titles in the singular are also found, e.g. **Lýðmenntun**, *Popular culture*, for a series of textbooks for Everyman.

1.7.2 More often than not the items are simply numbered, e.g. **Rit Rímnafélagsins VII**, *Writings of the Ballad Society VII*, but they may be specified as **hefti**, e.g. **Studia islandica 13. hefti**, or **bók**, e.g. **Annar Bókaflokkur Máls og Menningar. 4. bók**, *Second series of books of Mál og Menning, 4th book*.

1.8 PERIODICALS

1.8.1 The titles of periodicals have much the same form as those of series, but are more often singular, e.g. **Fjármálatíðindi**, *Financial news*; **Tímarit lögfræðinga**, *Lawyers' Journal*. In the context of a sentence the title is affected in the same way as that of a book, e.g. **áskrifendur að Nýju Helgafelli**, *subscribers to Nytt Helgafell*.

1.8.2 The title or sub-title may incorporate the name of the publishing body, e.g. **Tímarit Hins íslenzka náttúrufélags**, or this may follow **útgefandi** (*publisher*) or **gefið út af** (cf. 1.6.2).

1.8.3 The editor is usually indicated simply by **ritstjóri**, P **ritstjórar**, but there may be a committee, **ritnefnd**.

1.8.4 Numeration is commonly by **ár(gangur)**, *year*, and **hefti**, or **tölublað**, *part*, e.g. **fjórða ár, 1. hefti**, *vol. 4, pt. 1*, or occasionally **13. árs 1. hefti**, *no. 1 of vol. 13*. Words and figures are used indifferently. **Hefti** may also be used of a single annual number. Another term that occurs quite often is **arkir**, *gatherings*, referring to the compass of the resulting volume.

1.8.5 Periodicity may be indicated by a noun such as **mánaðarrit**, *monthly publication*, but is more likely to be an explicit statement of the form **þau komi út fjórum sinnum á ári**, *they come out four times a year*; **ritið kemur út einu sinni á ári**, *the publication comes out once a year*.

1.8.6 *Subscription* is **áskrift, áskriftarverð, áskriftagjald**, *subscriber* **áskrifendi**. (**Verð** alone simply means *price*.) It is contrasted with **lausasala**, *separate sale*, e.g. **verð hvers heftis verður 75 kr. til áskrifenda, en hærra í lausasölu**, *the price of each part* *will be 75 kr. to subscribers and higher for separate parts.* When not quoted per part, it is usually for a whole year (**árgangs**). Sometimes the price of odd numbers is given as **í bókaverzlunum**, *in book shops*.

With society publications one may meet statements such as **Félagar (meðlimir) fá bókina fyrir árgjaldið,** *Members get the books in return for annual subscription.*

1.8.7 Addresses (the general word is **heimilisfang**) may specify different departments, such as **ritstjórn,** *editorial office*; **skrifstofa,** *office*; **afgreiðsla,** *dispatch*; or may give directions such as **Öll bréf varðandi efni ritsins sendist til,** *All letters which concern editorial matters are sent to.*

2 ALPHABET, PHONETICS, SPELLING

2.1 ALPHABET

2.1.1 The alphabet officially runs as follows:

a á b d ð e é f g h i í j k l m n o ó p r s t u
ú v x y ý z þ æ (œ) ö (ø)

In some lists every letter has a distinct alphabetical place, but often the accents are ignored and **d** and **ð**, which represent different sounds but occur in different contexts, are treated as one letter. The bracketed letters, which are obsolete, are filed with the one which precedes each.

2.1.2 **Þ** represents the sound of *th* in *thin* (Is **þunnur**) and if not transliterated is filed as if it were; but it should be remembered that **th** is a possible Icelandic combination, so that the transliteration, if not distinguished in some way, is formally ambiguous. On the other hand **ð** may be represented by *d* if the special character is not available, and there is very little likelihood of ambiguity if *d* is used both for **d** and **ð**. In other than purely Scandinavian contexts **æ** is filed as **ae** and **ö** as **o**.

2.1.3 The acute accent on a vowel alters its quality as well as its length. Some alternation of accented and unaccented vowels occurs in the declension and conjugation and in the formation of compounds, e.g. **ég gaf, við gáfum; Þór, Þórunn, Þorsteinn.** In older books **é** was written **je** and may occasionally be found occupying that alphabetical position in lists today.

2.2 CAPITALISATION

2.2.1 The principle laid down is that names have an initial capital. The concept of a name is interpreted strictly: days of the week, months, seasons and festivals are not treated as names, nor are words beginning with **austur-** (*east*) and other points of the compass, unless like **Austur-Þýzkaland,** *Eastern Germany*, they are names of definite geographical entities. Adjectives like **íslenzkur** are written small.

2.2.2 Epithets attached to personal names do not have a capital, e.g. **Haraldur hárfagri,** *Harald the Fair*.

2.2.3 In corporate names such as **Hið íslenzka bókmenntafélag** it is recommended that only the article should have an initial capital, and this is what one usually finds, but not invariably. Bibliographical citations follow the internationally standard pattern, but in casual mentions of periodical titles consisting of two nouns, such as **Mál og Menning,** one is quite likely to find two capitals.

2.3 DIVISION OF WORDS

Compounds are divided according to sense, e.g. **tíma-rit**; otherwise division is after the consonant(s), e.g. **verzl-un, nokkr-ar, verkj-um.** The rules do not seem to apply to foreign names even in Icelandic forms, e.g. **Brazi-lía, Ung-verjaland**. A single letter should not be taken over.

2.4 PUNCTUATION AND ABBREVIATIONS

2.4.1 Where two successive compound words have the same final element the first omits it and ends in a hyphen, e.g. **úr Framsóknar- og Alþýðuflokknum**, *from the Progressive and Popular parties*. In general hyphens are not common, most compounds being written as one word, but they are always used in expressions like **á Weimar-tímunum**, *in the Weimar period*.

2.4.2 Abbreviations require a full stop, whether they include the last letter or not, e.g. **m.fl.** (**með fleiru**), *etc.*; **þ.e.** (**það er**), *i.e.*; **o.þ.h.** (**og þess háttar**), *and the like*; **bls.** (**blaðsíða**), *page*; **sbr.** (**samanber**), *cf.* The only exceptions are of the type **v/s** for **vélskip**, *motor-vessel*; **Rvík** for **Reykjavík**, and international symbols like **m** for **metri**. (See also 6.3 and 6.4.)

2.5 VARIATION OF CONSONANT

Initial **v-** disappears before **o** and **u**, e.g. **verða**, past **urðum**, p.p. **orðinn**; where a stem ends in a vowel a **-j-** may be inserted before another vowel, e.g. **nýr, nýir**, but **nýja, nýjum; Signý, Signýjar**. Conversely a **-j-** which belongs to the stem may be lost before certain endings, e.g. **verkur, verkjar, verkir, verkjum**.

2.6 VARIATION OF VOWEL

2.6.1 The vowels **-a-, -i-** and **-u-** in final syllables may disappear before an ending, e.g. **drottinn, drottnar; hamar, hamri**.

2.6.2 At an earlier stage in the history of the language the presence in an ending of an **i** or **j** on the one hand or a **u** on the other caused a change in the preceding vowels; the **i, j** or **u** may now have disappeared or been changed or a **u** may have appeared since which has no such effect, making the shifts appear arbitrary (cf. En *mouse, mice*). The shifts are as follows:

i-shift		*u-shift*	
a to e	o to e, y	a to ö	
á æ	ó æ	a	u
au ey	(j)u y	(v)i	y
e i	(j)ú ý		
jó ý			

Examples: **dagur, degi**, *day*; **háttur, hættir**, *manner(s)*; **eyrir, aurar**, *cent(s)*; **koma, kemur**, *come(s)*; **sonur, syni**, *son*; **bók, bækur**, *book(s)*; **kallaði, kölluðum**, *called*; **mörk, merkur, marka**, *field(s)*; **köttur, kattar, kettir**, *cat(s)*. These last types, with both shifts in one word, are common.

2.6.3 An allied change is the 'breaking' of an **e** before **r** or **l**, under the influence of a following **a**, e.g. **geld, gjalda**. This too may alternate with shifts in the forms of a single word, e.g. **Björn, Bjarnar, Birni**. (The basic **-e-** appears in none of these forms.)

2.7 SPELLING

2.7.1 Spelling is stable and regular, though not completely phonetic. As **z** and **s** represent the same sound, **z** merely indicating the loss of a dental, e.g. **betur, bezt, s** was for a time used instead, but **z** is now once more the standard spelling, except in **íslensk**.

Similarly **pt** is pronounced **ft**, and as a result words such as **eftir, oft** (cf. En *after, oft*) were at one time spelt **eptir, opt** as well as those like **keypti** (*bought*) from **kaupa**, where the stem actually has a **p**.

2.7.2 In compound words all the letters are retained, even if this results in combinations such as **-fll-, -lll-, -ttt-**, e.g. **alllangur**, *rather long*.

3 ARTICLES

3.1 DEFINITE

3.1.1 This corresponds in use only roughly to the English *the*. The forms are:

		S			P	
	M	*F*	*N*	*M*	*F*	*N*
N	hinn	hin	hið	hinir	hinar	hin
A	hinn	hina	hið	hina	hinar	hin
G	hins	hinnar	hins		hinna	
D	hinum	hinni	hinu		hinum	

3.1.2 The article is most often shortened by omitting **h-** or **hi-** and appended to the noun, e.g. **bók|in**, *the book*; **bókar|innar**, *of the book*; **banki|nn**, *the bank*; **banka|ns**, *of the bank*; **bækur|nar**, *the books*; **bankar|nir**, *the banks*; **ár|ið**, *the year*; **árs|ins**, *of the year*; **á áru|num**, *in the years* (cf. 4.2.4). Where there is an adjective the article usually precedes, in full, e.g. **hin fyrsta bók**, *the first book*; but here too it may be appended to the noun, especially if the adjective is a numeral or superlative, e.g. **þriðja (ákjósanleg-asta) leiðin**, *the third* (*the most desirable*) *way*.

3.2 INDEFINITE

None; **einn** means *one*.

4 NOUNS

4.1 GENDER AND FORM

Declensions fall into two main classes: strong, in which the GS (and very often the NS) ends in a consonant; weak, ending in a vowel. Within these classes the endings are different for the three genders. Dictionaries give the GS and NP. Inanimate nouns may be of any gender.

4.2 PLURAL See under 4.3.

4.3 ENDINGS

4.3.1 *Strong nouns*

The endings of the singular are:

	M	*F*		*N*
N	-(u)r, -, -CC	-,	-ur, -	-
A	-	-, -u	-i	-
G	-s, -ar	-(a)r, -ur	-ar	-s
D	-i, -	-, -u	-i	-i, -

4.3.2 The nominative forms are distributed thus:

> **-ur**: Most M nouns, some F especially names. Note that **-ur** is not necessarily an ending.

-r: M nouns with vowel stems, e.g. **vísir**.

-: M nouns in -r, -s; in -l or -n preceded by another consonant; some in simple -n; nouns of foreign origin; most F nouns (AD -, -u); F nouns in -dís and -unn (AD -i); all N nouns. Examples: M **Þór, Pétur** (stem **Pét(u)r-**), **Magnús, afl, Björn, vin(ur), Björnsson** (but **sonur**), **Kristján, biskup, ágúst**; F **bók, Ingibjörg, á, Signý** (stem **Signýj-**), **Þórunn, Ásdís**; N **safn, klaustur** (stem **klaust(u)r-**), **bindi, tré**.

Doubled consonants are found in M nouns with stems in -l, and most M nouns with stems in -n, e.g. **miðill** (stem **mið(i)l-**), **steinn**.

4.3.3 The other endings call for a few comments.

-i is ambiguous. It may be a case ending, e.g. **Sigurði, Þórunni**, or the final vowel of the stem as in **vísi**, A of **vísir, bindi** (NAD identical). (See also 4.3.4.)

-r is found where the stem ends in a stressed vowel.

-ar, the normal G ending of the F, is not uncommon in the M, especially as an alternative. It is not related to any particular nominative ending.

-ur is comparatively rare as G.

-s is common to M and N.

-u is found in names (marked* in the list in 1.1.3). But cf. 4.3.12, 4.3.13.

4.3.4 The forms of the plural are:

N   **-ar, -ir, -or, -ur, -r, -**
A   **-a(r), -i(r), -or, -ur, -r, -**
G   **-a**
D   **-um** (with article **-unum**)

4.3.5 The nominative forms are distributed thus:

-ar: most M, some F
-ir: most F, some M
-or: a few F
-ur: some F and a few irregular nouns
-r: F with stems ending in a vowel
-: all N; a few irregular M

4.3.6 The accusative forms are less complicated:

-a, -i: M   **-ar**, etc.: F   **-**: N and a few irregular M

4.3.7 The G and D may displace or coalesce with existing vowels, e.g. **á** (F): G **áa**, D **ám**; **bindi** (N): **binda, bindum**.

4.3.8 Fugitive vowels (2.6.1) disappear before -ar, -i and plural endings. Fugitive -j- appears before S **-ar** in a few words, and before **-a** and **-um**.

4.3.9 Vowel shifts (2.6.2) are found in both S and P:

i-shift: in DS of some words; before GS -ur; often before -ir; sometimes before P **-ur**.

u-shift: in NAS of some M words; in NADS of some F; in NAP of some neuters; before **-um**.

The unshifted vowel is restored before -ar, but breaking occurs. Examples are given in 2.6.2 and 2.6.3.

4.3.10 *Irregular strong nouns*

M   faðir: AGD föður; P feður, feðra, feðrum
     bróðir: bróður; bræður, etc.
     maður: mann, manns, manni; menn, manna, mönnum
F   móðir: móður; mæður, etc.
     dóttir: dóttur; dætur, etc.
N   fé: G fjár

4.3.11 *Weak masculine nouns* have the following endings:

	S	P
N	-i	-(j)ar/-ur
A		-(j)a/-ur
G	-(j)a	-(j)a
D		-(j)um

4.3.12 *Weak feminine nouns* have the following endings:

	S	P		S	P
N	-a	-ur			-ar/-ir
A		-ur	-i		-ar/-ir
G	-u	-(n)a			-a
D		-um			-um

kona has GP **kvenna**

4.3.13 *Weak neuter nouns* have the following endings:

	S	P
NA		-u
G	-a	-na
D		-um

4.3.14 The u-shift (2.6.2) occurs before **-u** and **-um**, e.g. **tafla, töflu(m)**; **saga, sögu(m)**.

4.6 USE OF CASES

Besides the typical uses of the cases one should note the accusative by itself denoting direction and destination, and the dative denoting manner, instrument, time, where English uses prepositions *with, at*.

5 ADJECTIVES

5.1 GENERAL

Adjectives have the same number, gender and case as the nouns they qualify. They have two sets of forms, strong and weak.

5.2 ENDINGS

5.2.1 *Strong forms*

There are 4 main types, which are all basically the same.

	S			*P*		
	M	*F*	*N*	*M*	*F*	*N*
N	-ur/-	-	-t*	-ir	-ar	-
A	-an	-a	-t*	-a	-ar	-
G	-s	-rar	-s		-ra	
D	-um	-ri	-u		-um	

The commonest type. If the stem already ends in **-ur**, the NM has no ending, e.g. **fagur** (F **fögur** N **fagurt**). *Note **nýr, nýtt, nýjan**, etc.; **sannur, satt; glaður, glatt; prentaður, prentað; sagður, sagt; þýddur, þýtt**.

5.2.2

	S			*P*		
	M	*F*	*N*	*M*	*F*	*N*
N	-inn	-in	-ið	-nir	-nar	-in
A	-inn	-na	-ið	-na	-nar	-in
G	-ins	-innar	-ins		-inna	
D	-num	-inni	-nu		-num	

Mostly participles (8.12.2).

5.2.3 As 5.2.2 but with **-da, -ða** or **-ta**, etc., instead of **-na** and other endings beginning with **-n**. Participles: e.g. **talinn, talda**, etc., *counted*; **barinn, barða**, *beaten*; **rakinn, rakta**, etc., *traced*. (Cf. 8.12.2, 8.12.3.)

5.2.4 N **-ill, -il, -ið** A **-inn, -la, -ið**, then as 5.2.2 with **-l-** for **-n-**.

Lítill (*little*), **mikill** (*big*) and **gamall** (*old*). Gamall has N **gamalt** ASM **gamlan**.

5.2.5 The u-shift (2.6.2) is found in FS and NP, where there is no ending, e.g. **sannur, sönn** (*true*), and before endings in **-u** and **-um**, e.g. **talinn, töldu**.

5.2.6 *Weak forms*

	S			*P*
	M	*F*	*N*	
N	-i	-a	-a	-u
AGD	-a	-u	-a	-u

5.2.7 Some adjectives that have only weak forms, especially comparatives (5.3.1) and present participles (8.12.1), have **-i** everywhere except in the neuter singular.

5.2.8 *Use of forms*

Strong forms are used when there is no article or pronoun, e.g. **bókin var uppseld**, *the book was sold out*; **í flestum löndum**, *in most lands*. Weak forms are used with the article, e.g. **hin mikla þensla**, *the great extension*; **þriðja leiðin**, *the third way*; with demonstratives and the like, e.g. **þessi fyrsti árgangur**, *this first volume*; and in some stereotyped phrases without the article, e.g. **í fyrsta lagi**, *in the first place*.

5.3 COMPARISON

5.3.1

	Comparative -(a)ri	*Superlative* -(a)stur	
e.g. **alvarlegur**	**alvarlegri**	**alvarlegastur**	*serious*
stór	**stærri**	**stærstur**	*large*
nýr	**nýrri**	**nýjastur**	*new*

Note the possible vowel mutation.

Irregular forms such as **góður, betri, beztur** are entered separately in some dictionaries.

5.3.2   The comparative endings are **-i, -a** (5.2.7); the superlative is declined regularly with strong feminine **-ust**.

5.4 POSSESSIVES

The only ones that decline are **minn**, *my*; **þinn**, *your*; **sinn**, *his, her, their*; **vor**, *our*. **Minn**, etc., are declined like **hinn** (3.1.1) except that the neuter is **mitt**, etc., not **mið**. **Vor, vor, vort** has ASM **vorn**, but is otherwise like a strong adjective (5.2.1).

6 NUMERALS

6.1 CARDINAL

   6.1.1

1 einn	11 ellefu	21 tuttugu og einn
2 tveir	12 tólf	22 tuttugu og tveir
3 þrír	13 þrettán	30 þrjátíu
4 fjórir	14 fjórtán	40 fjörutíu
5 fimm	15 fimmtán	50 fimmtíu
6 sex	16 sextán	60 sextíu
7 sjö	17 sautján, seytján	70 sjotíu
8 átta	18 átján	80 áttatíu
9 níu	19 nítján	90 níutíu
10 tíu	20 tuttugu	100 (eitt) hundrað

101 (eitt) hundrað og einn
122 e.h. tuttugu og tveir
200 tvö hundruð
300 þrju hundruð
1000 (eitt) þúsund
2462 tvö þúsund (tvær þúsundir)
       fjögur hundruð sextíu og tveir

   6.1.2   **einn–fjórir** are declined as follows:

      einn, ein, eitt like **hinn**: also weak **eini, eina**

tveir	tvær	tvö	þrír	þrjár	þrjú	fjórir	fjórar	fjögur
tvo	tvær	tvö	þrjá	þrjár	þrjú	fjóra	fjórar	fjögur
tveggja			þriggja			fjög(ur)ra		
tveim(ur)			þrem(ur)			fjórum		

Hundrað, hundruð and **þúsund(ir)** are declined when used as nouns. The remaining cardinals are invariable.

   6.1.3   Masculine forms are used in counting.

6.2 ORDINAL

   6.2.1

1 fyrsti	5 fimmti	9 níundi
2 annar	6 sjötti	10 tíundi
3 þriðji	7 sjöundi	11 ellefti
4 fjórði	8 áttundi	12 tólfti

13 etc., þrettándi, etc.	50 fimmtugasti	100 hundraðasti
20 tuttugasti	60 sextugasti	101 hundraðasti og fyrsti
21 tuttugasti og fyrsti	70 sjötugasti	1000 þúsundasti
30 þrítugasti	80 átttugasti	2000 tvö þúsundasti
40 fertugasti	90 nítugasti	

6.2.2 Fyrsti has strong and weak forms (5.2.1; 5.2.6), **annar** is declined as follows:

	S			P		
	M	*F*	*N*	*M*	*F*	*N*
N	annar	önnur	annað	aðrir	aðrar	önnur
A	annan	aðra	annað	aðra	aðrar	önnur
G	annars	annarrar	annars		annarra	
D	öðrum	annarri	öðru		öðrum	

The rest have only weak forms (5.2.6).

6.3 FIGURES

Plain figures, whether arabic or roman, stand for cardinal numbers, figures followed by a full stop for ordinals, e.g. **42 bl(að)s(íður)** (=42pp.), **töflur nr. I-IV; III. tafla, 42.bl(að)-s(íða)** (=p.42). Decimals are written with a comma, read **komma**.

6.4 DATES

6.4.1 The months are:

> janúar, febrúar, marz, apríl, maí, júní,
> júlí, ágúst, september, október, nóvember, desember

They are indeclinable.

6.4.2 *16 December 1953* = **hinn 16. desember (árið) 1953**, read **hinn sextándi desember árið nitján hundruð fimmtíu og þrjú**; *on 16 December* is also **(hinn) 16. desember** but is read **(hinn) sextánda desember**.

1939-1945 is read for catalogue purposes with simple juxtaposition.

17. öld (G 17. aldar): *17th century.*

7 PRONOUNS

7.1 DEMONSTRATIVE AND INDEFINITE

7.1.1 **þessi**, *this*

	S			P		
	M	*F*	*N*	*M*	*F*	*N*
N	þessi	þessi	þetta	þessir	þessar	þessi
A	þenna(n)	þessa	þetta	þessa	þessar	þessi
G	þessa	þessarar	þessa		þessara	
D	þessum	þessari	þessu		þessum	

7.1.2 **sá**, *that* (*it*)

	S			P		
	M	*F*	*N*	*M*	*F*	*N*
N	sá	sú	það	þeir	þær	þau
A	þann	þá	það	þá	þær	þau
G	þess	þeirrar	þess		þeirra	
D	þeim	þeirri	því		þeim	

7.1.3 hinn, *that, the other*
like **hinn,** *the* (3.1.1) but with the neuter **hitt.**

7.1.4 *Indefinite*
The following peculiarities are noteworthy:

> **engi(nn), engi(n), ekkert (ekki),** *no(ne)* has stem **eng- (öngv-),**
>   ASM **engan,** GSM & N **ein(s)kis.**
> **báðir, báðar, bæði,** *both,* a plural adjective (5.2.1), has G **beggja.**
> **einhver,** *someone:* N **eitthvert.**

7.2 RELATIVE
Sem and **er** are both indeclinable. A preposition is put after **sem,** and may be postponed to the end of the sentence, e.g. **vandamál sem við er að etja,** *problems that have to be contended with;* **það sem ég spurði þig um,** *what I asked you about.*

7.3 PERSONAL

		N	*A*	*G*	*D*
	1	ég	mig	mín	mér
	2	þú	þig	þín	þér
S	3*m*	hann	hann	hans	honum
	3*f*	hún	hana	hennar	henni
	3*n*	See 7.1.2			
S and *P*	3*r*	-	sig	sín	sér
	1	við (vér)	okkur (oss)	okkar (vor)	okkur (oss)
P	2	þið (þér)	ykkur (yður)	ykkar (yðar)	ykkur (yður)
	3	See 7.1.2			

hann and **hún** can both mean *it.*

8 VERBS

8.1 STRUCTURE
8.1.1 Icelandic verbs resemble English ones but have many more different forms, and the subjunctive is still distinct.
8.1.2 They are entered in the dictionary under the infinitive, which ends in **-a,** rarely **-u.** In a few verbs the **-a** is lost after the **-á-** of the stem. In use the infinitive is usually preceded by **að,** *to.* It corresponds to the English verbal noun in *-ing* as well as to the infinitive.

8.2 PRESENT
8.2.1 The indicative endings are:

> **-a, -ar, -ar**
> **-i, -ir, -ir** ⎬ ; **-um, -ið, -a**
> **-, -ur, -ur**

-um causes u-mutation (2.6.2).
8.2.2 Changes of stem may occur in the singular.

Present indicative	*Infinitive*	
-æ	-á	e.g. fæ, fá
-e-	-o-	kem, koma
-e-	-(j)a-	held, halda
-ý-	-jó-, -jú-, -ú-	býð, bjóða

8.3 PAST

8.3.1 *Weak*

-(a)ði, -(a)ðir, -(a)ði; -(u)ðum, -(u)ðuð, -(u)ðu
-di, etc.
-ti, etc.

e.g. prenta, prentaði; sá, sáði; spyrja, spurði; leifa, leifði; þýða, þýddi; þekja, þakti; reisa, reisti with u-mutation in the plural. Note the loss of -j- and change of vowel.

8.3.2 *Strong*

-, -(st), -; -um, -uð, -u

with change of stem vowel both from the infinitive and usually between singular and plural, viz.

Past	*Infinitive*	*Example*
a/á	e, i	gaf, gáfu, gefa
a/u	e, i	fann, fundu, finna
au/u	jó, jú, ú	kaus, kusu, kjósa
é	a, á	féll(u), falla
ei/i	í	skein, skinu, skína
ó	a	tók(u), taka
dó	deyja	
át	éta	
fékk, fengum	fá	
kom	koma	
óx, uxum	vaxa	
sá	sjá	
svaf, sváfum	sofa	

Note the assimilation of consonants in the singular of some verbs, e.g. fékk, fann; also batt, bundum.

8.7 SUBJUNCTIVE

8.7.1 *Present:* -i, -ir, -i; -um, -ið, -i, with the same stem as the infinitive.

8.7.2 *Past, weak:* same as indicative (8.3.1).

Past, strong: -i, -ir, -i; -um, -uð, -u. The stem is that of the strong past, but with i-shift, e.g. gaf/gæfi, fundu 'fyndu.

8.7.3 The subjunctive is used in direct and indirect wishes, commands, hopes, etc. and in indirect statements.

8.10 COMPOUND TENSES

8.10.1 The future and conditional are expressed by the present and past of munu with the infinitive. Skulu (*shall*) is also used, conveying a more definite idea of intention or obligation than in English.

8.10.2 The perfect, pluperfect, etc., are expressed by the present or other appropriate tense of **hafa**, followed by the 'supine,' which is usually the same as the neuter of the past participle, e.g. **ég hefi sent**, *I have sent*.

In some verbs of motion and change these tenses can be formed with **vera**, *to be*. The past participle agrees, e.g. **ég er kominn**, *I have come*. (But **hefur hann komið ?**, *has he been here ?*)

8.12 PARTICIPLES

8.12.1 *Present:* -andi (5.3.2)

8.12.2 *Weak past*

M	F	N	
-aður	-uð	-að⎫	
-ður	-ð	-t ⎬ cf. 5.2.1	
-dur	-d	-t	
-tur	-t	-t ⎭	
-inn	-in	-ið	cf. 5.2.2 and 5.2.3

with stem as in 8.3.1.

8.12.3 *Strong past*

-inn,   -in,   -ið (5.2.2)

with change of the stem vowel as follows:

Participle	Infinitive
-o-	-e-, -jó-, -jú-, -ú-
-u-	-e-, -i-

e.g. **brostinn** from **bresta**; **boðinn** from **bjóða**; **bundinn** from **binda**.

8.15 PASSIVE/REFLEXIVE

8.15.1 -st may be added to the active, -(u)r being omitted, and -ðs-, -ds- and -ts-becoming -z-, e.g. **það seljast**, *it is sold (habitually)*; **það hefur selzt**, *it has been sold*. This form is known as the middle, and has also intransitive, reflexive and reciprocal meanings.

8.15.2 The name 'passive' is given to the combination of **vera** (8.19.2), or in some tenses **verða** (8.19.5) with the past participle, e.g. **bókin var upp seld**, *the book was sold out*. This form commonly indicates a state. The present of **verða** may by itself indicate the future, e.g. **það verður selt**, *it will be sold*.

8.17 AUXILIARIES
See 8.19.1–7.

8.19 IRREGULAR VERBS
Most of these have the same endings in 1 and 3 PS and are regular in the plural.

8.19.1 **hafa**, *to have*
     Present indicative: **hef(i), hefur, hefur; höfum, hafið, hafa**
     Past subjunctive: **hefði**, etc.

8.19.2 **vera**, *to be*
     Pres. ind.: **er . . . erum**, etc.
     Pres. subj.: **sé**, etc.

Past ind.: var . . . vorum, etc.
Past subj.: væri, etc.

8.19.3 munu, *shall, will*
Pres. ind.: mun, etc.

8.19.4 skulu, *shall*
Pres. ind.: skal, etc.

8.19.5 verða, *to become* (cf. 8.19.2)
Past ind.: varð . . . urðum, etc.
Past subj.: yrði, etc.
Past part.: orðinn

8.19.6 eiga, *to own, have, ought*
Pres. ind.: á, etc.
Past ind.: átti, etc.
Past subj.: ætti, etc.

8.19.7 mega, *may*
Pres. ind.: má, etc.
Past ind.: mátti, etc.
Past subj.: mætti, etc.

8.19.8 muna, *to remember*
Pres. ind.: man, etc.

8.19.9 unna, *to love*
Pres. ind.: ann, etc.

8.19.10 vilja, *to want, be willing*
Pres. ind.: vil, etc.

8.19.11 vita, *to know*
Pres. ind.: veit, etc.
Past ind.: vissi, etc.

8.19.12 þurfa, *to need*
Pres. ind.: þarf, etc.

8.19.13 þykja, *to seem*
Past ind.: þótti, etc.

8.23 COMPOUND VERBS

There are two sorts: with prefixes, e.g. afnema; with a separate adverb or preposition, e.g. gefa út, *to publish.* Such verbs keep the same character in most other tenses, e.g. afnam, afnumið; gaf út, gefið út; but the present participle, like derived words, is always of the first form, e.g. útgefandi.

9 ADVERBS

Those derived from adjectives end in -a, e.g. árlega, *annually,* from árlegur, with comparative and superlative in -(a)r and -(a)st respectively, or are the same as the neuter. Some other adverbs have comparative in -ur, e.g. fram, fremur.

10 PREPOSITIONS

10.2 SYNTAX

Prepositions govern specific cases, and some take two cases with different meanings, notably eftir, *after,* which with the dative refers to place, but with the accusative to

E

time, as well as meaning *by* (authorship). The commonest prepositions with their cases are:

> Accusative: **um**
> Dative: **að, af, frá, hjá, mót, undan**
> Accusative (direction) and Dative (location): **á, eftir, fyrir, í, með, undir**
> **við, yfir**
> Genitive: **án, auk, til**

10.5 MEANING

Many of these resemble English ones but their meaning may be different; viz. **að**, *to* not *at*; **af** has other senses besides *of*(*f*); **eftir** see 10.2; **til** means *to*, *for* as well as *till*; **við** does not mean *with*. It is rarely possible to assign a single translation to a preposition. Double prepositions like **á undan**, *in front of*, may be unfamiliar.

GLOSSARY

afgreiðsla, *dispatch* (1.8.7)
afsláttur, *discount*
andlitsmynd, *portrait*
aukin, *enlarged* (1.5.2)

áður útkomið, *already published*
ár, *year* (1.8.4, 3.1.2)
árgangur, *volume of a periodical* (1.8.4)
árlegur, *annual*
ársbók, *yearbook*
ársrit, *yearbook*
áskrift (-arverð/-argjald), *subscription* (1.8.6)

band, *binding*
í bandi, *bound*
bindi, *volume*
bjó (bjuggu) til prentunar, *prepared for printing*
blaðsíða, *page* (2.5.2)
bók, *book* (3.1.2)
bókaflokkur, *series*
bókaforlag, *press, publishing house* (1.6.1)
bókasafn, *book collection, library*
bókaútgáfa, *press, publishing house* (1.6.1)
bókaverzlun, *bookshop* (1.6.2)
bókavörður, *librarian*
bóksali, *bookseller*
bréf, *letter*
búið til prentunar, *prepared for printing*

bæklingur, *pamphlet*
bætt, *corrected*

dáinn, *dead*

efnisyfirlit, *contents*
einn, einstakur, *single*
eintak, *copy*
eldri númer, *back number*
endurbætt, *improved* (1.5.2)
endurprentun, *reprint*
endursamin, *revised* (1.5.2)
endurskoðuð, *revised*
erlendis, *abroad*

(-)félag, *society* (1.2.7, 1.2.9)
félagi, *member*
flugrit, *pamphlet*
formáli, formálsorð, forspjall, *preface*
fylgirit, *supplement*
fæddur, *born*
færa til nútímans, *bring up to date*

gaf út, *published* (1.6.2)
gefið út, *edited; published* (1.2.2, 1.6.2)
grein, *article*
greinargerð, *preamble*

halfsmánaðar-, *fortnightly*
hefti, *issue, part* (1.8.4)
heimilisfang, *address* (1.8.7)
heldur áfran, *to be continued*

hluti, *part* (1.8.4)
hætta, *stop, cease*
höfundur, *author*

inngangsorð, *preface*
inngangur, innleiðsla, *introduction*

koma út, *come out*
kveðskapur, kvæði, *poetry*

leiðrétting, *correction*
leikrit, *play*
ljóðmæli, *poetry*

mánaðarlegur, mánaðarrit, *monthly*
meðlimur, *member*
mynd, *illustration, plate*

nefnd, *committee*
númer, *number*
ný, *new* (1.5.2)

orðabók, *dictionary*

óbirt, *unpublished*
ókeypis, *free*

pappírskylja, *paperback*
partur, *part*
prentað hjá, *printed at*
prentari, *printer*
á prenti, *in print*
prentsmiðja, *printer's*; *press* (1.6.3)
í prentun, *being printed*

rannsókn, *research*
ráðstefna, *conference*
registur, *index*
reikningur, *bill*
ritgerð, *essay*
ritgjörð, *contribution*
ritstjóri, *editor* (1.8.3)

ritstjórn, *editing*; *editorial board* (1.8.7)
ræða, *speech*

safn, *collection*
safn greina, *collected articles*
saga, sagnfræði, *history*
samur, *same*
sérprent(un), *offprint* (1.5.3)
skáldsaga, *novel*
skáldskapur, *poetry*
skifti, *exchange*
skýringarrit, *commentary*
skýrslur, *proceedings*
smásaga, *short story*

tafla (töflur), *table(s)*
tekið saman af, *compiled*
til sölu, *on sale*
tímarit, *periodical, review*
tölublað, *number* (1.8.4)

undirbúningur, *preparation*
upp seld, *sold out*

úrdráttur, *summary*
útgáfa, *edition* (1.5.1)
útgáfuréttur, *copyright*
útgefandi, *editor*
í útlöndum, *abroad*
útskýring, *commentary, explanation*
útvalin, *selected*

valin, *selected*
verð, *price* (1.8.6)
verk, *work*
viðbót, *addition*
viðbætir, *appendix, supplement*
vika, *week*

yfirlit, *summary*

þýðing, *translation*

öll réttindi áskilin, *all rights reserved*

GRAMMATICAL INDEX: WORDS

aðr-, 6.2.2
af, 1.2.2, 10.2
ann(-), 8.19.9
anna-, 6.2.2

á, etc., 8.19.6, 10.2
át, 8.3.2
átt-, 8.19.6

báð-, 7.1.4
beggja, 7.1.4
bræð-, 4.3.10
bæði, 7.1.4

GRAMMATICAL INDEX: ENDINGS

-(a)ð (+adj. term.—5.2.1),
  8.12.2
-ið, 3.1.2, 5.2.2, 5.2.3,
  5.2.4, 8.2.1, 8.2.3,
  8.12.2, 8.12.3
-uð, 8.7.2, 8.12.2
-duð, 8.3.1, 8.7.2
-(u)ðuð, 8.3.1, 8.7.2
-tuð, 8.3.1, 8.7.2

-i, 1.1.2, 4.2.1, 4.2.2,
  4.2.3, 4.2.6, 4.2.8,
  4.3.11, 4.3.12, 5.2.6,
  5.3.2, 8.2.1, 8.7.1,
  8.7.2
-di, 8.3.1, 8.7.2
-andi, 8.12.1
-(a)ði, 8.3.1, 8.7.2
-illi, 5.2.4
-inni, 3.1.2, 5.2.2, 5.2.3
-ri, 5.2.1
-(a)ri, 5.3.1
-ti, 8.3.1, 8.7.2

-il, 5.2.4
-ill, 5.2.4

-um, 4.3.4, 4.3.8, 4.3.9,
  4.3.11, 4.3.12, 4.3.13,
  4.3.14, 5.2.1, 8.2.1,
  8.3.2, 8.7.1, 8.7.2

-(un)um, 4.3.4, 4.3.8,
  4.3.9, 4.3.11, 4.3.12,
  4.3.13, 4.3.14
-j(un)um, 4.3.11
-dum, 5.2.3, 8.3.1, 8.7.2
-(u)ðum, 5.2.3, 8.3.1,
  8.7.2
-lum, 5.2.4, 5.2.5
-num, 5.2.2, 5.2.5
-tum, 5.2.3, 8.3.1, 8.7.2

-an, 5.2.1
-in, 3.1.2, 5.2.2, 5.2.3,
  8.7.2, 8.7.3
-inn, 3.1.2, 5.2.2, 5.2.3,
  8.7.2, 8.7.3
-son, 1.1.5, 1.1.6

-r, 4.3.1, 4.3.2, 4.3.3,
  4.3.4, 9
-ar, 4.3.1, 4.3.3, 4.3.5,
  4.3.6, 4.3.8, 4.3.9,
  4.3.11, 4.3.12, 5.2.1,
  8.2.1, 9
-dar, 5.2.3
-ðar, 5.2.3
-jar, 4.3.11
-lar, 5.2.4
-illar, 5.2.4
-nar, 3.1.2, 5.2.2
-innar, 3.1.2, 5.2.2, 5.2.3
-rar, 5.2.1
-tar, 5.2.3

-ir, 4.3.4, 4.3.5, 4.3.6,
  4.3.9, 4.3.12, 5.2.1,
  8.2.1, 8.7.1, 8.7.2
-dir, 8.3.1, 8.7.2
-(a)ðir, 8.3.1, 8.7.2
-lir, 5.2.4
-nir, 3.1.2, 5.2.2
-tir, 8.3.1, 8.7.2
-or, 4.3.4, 4.3.5, 4.3.6
-ur, 1.1.2, 4.3.1, 4.3.2,
  4.3.3, 4.3.4, 4.3.5, 4.3.9,
  4.3.11, 4.3.12, 5.2.1,
  8.2.1, 9
-(a)stur, 5.3.1

-s, 4.3.1, 4.3.3, 5.2.1
-ils, 5.2.4
-ins, 3.1.2, 5.2.2, 5.2.3

-t, 5.2.1, 8.7.2
-t + adj. term. (5.2.1),
  8.7.2
-st, 8.3.2, 8.15.1, 9
-ast, 9
-ust, 5.5.2

-u, 4.3.1, 4.3.2, 4.3.3,
  4.3.12, 4.3.13, 4.3.14,
  5.2.1, 5.2.5, 5.2.6,
  5.3.2, 8.3.2, 8.7.2
-du, 8.3.1, 8.7.2
-(u)ðu, 8.3.1, 8.7.2
-tu, 8.3.1, 8.7.2

LATIN and THE ROMANCE LANGUAGES

General note
Latin
Portuguese
Spanish
Catalan
French
Italian
Rumanian

GENERAL NOTE: ROMANCE LANGUAGES

The Romance languages dealt with here—from west to east, Portuguese, Spanish, Catalan, French, Italian, Rumanian—owe their similarities to their common derivation from the spoken Latin of the Roman Empire, and their differences partly to differences in the original languages of the peoples that adopted it, partly to their isolation from each other during the early stages of their development, partly to differences in the material they borrowed, in the west from Germanic conquerors (not all the same) and to a less extent from the Moors, in Rumania from the Slavs.

Even before it gave place to Romance, Latin had begun to diverge, so that a common word like *to speak* goes back to *fabulare* in Portuguese and Spanish, to *parabolare* in Catalan, French and Italian, while the Rumanian *vorbi* may not be of Latin origin at all, a not uncommon situation. Thereafter the different nations developed their inheritance differently. The resulting similarities and differences, or some of them, can be judged from the following table:

Latin	Portuguese	Spanish	Catalan	French	Italian	Rumanian	English
bibere	beber	beber	beure	boire	bere	bea	*drink*
clamare	chamar	llamar	clamar	-clamer	chiamare	chema	*call*
dicere	dizer	dizer	dir	dire	dire	zice	*say*
factum	feito	hecho	fet	fait	fatto	făcut	*done*
flores	flores	flores	flors	fleurs	fiori	flori	*flowers*
gaudium	gozo	gozo	goig	joie	gioia	(bucurie)	*joy*
oculum	olho	ojo	ull	oeil	occhio	ochi	*eye*
patrem	padre	padre	pare	père	padre	(tată)	*father*
pluvia	chuva	lluvia	pluja	pluie	pioggia	ploaie	*rain*
rationem	razão	razón	raó	raison	ragione	rațiune	*reason*
actionem	accão	acción	acció	action	azione	acțiune	*action*
noctem	noite	noche	nit	nuit	notte	noapte	*night*
venit	vem	vien	ve	vient	viene	vine	*comes*

To the extent that there are regular correspondences, a knowledge of one Romance language helps with the others.

Approaching the Romance vocabulary from English, we find that the more everyday words tend to be different, while the less common ones, which English has often borrowed from French or Latin, are similar. Typical examples in the above list are *reason* and *action*, less typical *flowers* and *joy*.

In their structure the western Romance languages are very similar, having lost all trace of case and using much the same set of prepositions to remedy the deficiency, and having at their disposal the same basic verb forms. Here again some differences have developed: French cannot do without subject pronouns; Catalan has a peculiar periphrastic past, distinct from the perfect; Portuguese and Spanish have retained Latin tenses which the other languages have lost. Rumanian, by contrast, is often the odd one out, having for instance retained a genitive-dative case, developed a suffixed article, found a different way of expressing the future, and created a set of prepositions sufficiently different to be traps for the unwary.

LATIN

SPECIMEN

Praefationis loco de ratione et norma elenchi bibliographici concinnandi pauca tantum mihi dicere liceat. Comprehenduntur in his bibliographiae fundamentis non solum opera ad medium saeculum praeteritum usque typis excusa, quae a scriptoribus natione Slovenis Latine conscripta intra fines Sloveniae, quae nunc est, vel extra eos emissa sunt, sed etiam illa, quae a cuiuscumque nationis scriptoribus e finibus Sloveniae oriundis variis locis typis edita sunt. (1971)

By way of preface let me say just a few words about the system and standard by which the bibliography was compiled. There are included in this basic bibliography not only works printed up to the middle of last century which were written in Latin by writers of Slovene nationality and published inside or outside the boundaries of present-day Slovenia, but also those that were printed and published in various places by writers of any nationality who were of Slovene origin.

Though straightforward technical Latin, the passage illustrates some of its differences of idiom. For **norma elenchi concinnandi** see 8.11.3, for **conscripta . . . emissa sunt** see 8.15.2. Note also **bibliographiae fundamentis**, '*foundations of bibliography*' and conversely **medium saeculum**, '*mid-century*'; **natione Slovenis**, '*Slovene by nation*'.

0 GENERAL CHARACTERISTICS

0.1 DEGREE OF INFLEXION

Latin is a highly synthetic language, person, tense, mood and voice in the verb and simpler relationships of nouns all being expressed by endings, e.g. **edentur**, *they will be published*, only the perfect tenses of the passive being compound.

0.2 ORDER OF WORDS

In view of this the order of words is fluid. The governing principle is rhetorical, that the important words should come where the emphasis will naturally fall on them. So the verb usually comes at the end of the clause and the subject at the beginning, reversal giving heightened emphasis to the subject. Qualifying phrases are quite likely to procede what they qualify, e.g. **foris pax et domi concordia**, *peace abroad and harmony at home*, but there is no mechanical rule. The relative order of clauses too is often different from that usual in modern languages, and as Latin tends to build up hierarchies of subordination, with comparatively few main verbs, the resulting complications may require patience to unravel.

0.3 HISTORY

The Latin texts now extant may be classical (in the widest sense: the Latin of the Romans), medieval or modern. Medieval Latin departs in varying degrees from the classical norm, particularly in vocabulary and idiom; modern Latin, that is, Latin from the Renaissance onwards, is once more based on the classical, especially nowadays, when it is largely written by professed Latinists. But as Latin was for some centuries the normal language of all forms of scholarship and was used by a very large number of writers, it is not to be expected that it is all of classical purity. Nevertheless the basic grammar is the same, and although the parts of the book that we are especially concerned with are all modern, it is the ordinary classical grammar that is given here.

1 BIBLIOLINGUISTICS

1.1 NAMES

1.1.1 Roman names under the republic usually consist of three elements, e.g. **Marcus Tullius Cicero**. The first is personal, the second that of the clan, the third, not always found, that of the particular family. In formal contexts the father's name or initial is inserted after the middle name, e.g. **M. Tullius M. f(ilius) Cicero**. Some families, e.g. the Scipios, found it necessary to add one or more names distinguishing branches of the family, and individuals may have additional honorific names, e.g. **P. Cornelius Scipio Africanus**. A similar effect is produced by adoption, e.g. **P. Cornelius Scipio Aemilianus**, before adoption **L. Aemilius Paulus**. Under the Empire the pattern is much less clear. Women's names were usually simpler, e.g. **Cornelia**, though other elements might be present, and names like **Agrippina**, daughter of **M. Vipsanius Agrippa**, are found later. A wife took her husband's name in the genitive, e.g. **Caecilia Q. Cretici f. Metella Crassi**, *Caecilia Metella, daughter of Q. (Caecilius Metellus) Creticus, wife of Crassus*, but only in formal contexts.

1.1.2 The earlier personal names, which are few, have standard abbreviations, e.g. **P.** for **Publius**, **L.** for **Lucius**, which are given in Lewis and Short's Latin dictionary. The abbreviations for **Gaius** and **Gnaeus** are **C.** and **Cn.** (C is the old form of G), which has had the unfortunate result of producing the false forms **Caius** and **Cnaeus**.

1.1.3 Romans are usually referred to by one or other of their family names, or both, e.g. **Pompei Crassique potentia** (**Cn. Pompeius Magnus, M. Licinius Crassus**); in English *Cicero* (earlier *Tully*), *Scipio Africanus*, *Aemilius Paulus*, *Horace* (**Q. Horatius Flaccus**), *Quintilian* (**M. Fabius Quintilianus**).

1.1.4 The names of medieval writers usually consist of a Christian name and an epithet and are often interchangeable with vernacular forms, e.g. **Paulus Diaconus** or *Paul the Deacon*, **Joannes Sarisberiensis** or *John of Salisbury*.

1.1.5 Later names are Latinisations of vernacular names, usually by the simple addition of Latin endings but some by a more thoroughgoing transformation, e.g. **Georgius Buchananus, Georgius Agricola** (*Bauer*). One singularity is the addition of **-us** to unstressed **-er** (4.3.4), e.g. **Simlerus**. The vernacular forms are often not known with certainty, hence the practice of leaving in their Latin forms names of authors who write only in Latin.

1.2 NAMES OF AUTHORS, EDITORS, ETC.

1.2.1 The names of ancient authors are usually put before the title in the genitive, e.g. **M. Tulli Ciceronis orationes, Cornelii Taciti Annales**. In names of the republican period the ending **-i** is ambiguous (4.3.4), unless it is clear that the editor adopts the later practice of using **-ii** as the genitive of **-ius**.

1.2.2 The names of more recent authors may be given in the same way but are more likely to follow the title and be in the accusative preceded by **per** or in the ablative preceded by **a(b)**, e.g. **ab Alano Copo editi**, *edited by Alanus Copus (Alan Cope)*; **per Jacobum Noüet explicata**. Not infrequently, phrases like **Jo. Antonio Vulpio auctore** are found, again involving the ablative (4.6.6).

1.2.3 The same types occur, with a passive participle, in the case of editors and translators, but it is perhaps more common to find a word like **cura** (*by the labour of*) with the name in the genitive, or a finite verb with the name in the nominative, e.g. **recognovit brevique adnotatione critica instruxit Cyrillus Bailey**, *Cyril Bailey reviewed (the text) and furnished it with a short critical apparatus*. With a simple word like **scripsit**, *he wrote*, this form serves for authors, but not commonly. **Editionem curavit**, *edited* or *saw through the press*.

1.3 TITLES

1.3.1 The titles of classical works are simple, often consisting of a single word, singular or plural, e.g. **Aeneis, Historiae**, or a short phrase like **De re rustica** (*On country life*), to which there may be added at will a general noun, as in **De bello gallico (commentarii)**. Later titles have much the same characteristics as vernacular titles of the period and can be very elaborate, e.g. **Alphonsi de Vargas Toletani relatio ad reges et principes christianos de strategematis et sophismatis politicis Societatis Iesu ad monarchiam orbis terrarum sibi conficiendam** (*The report of Alphonsus de Vargas of Toledo to Christian kings and princes on the strategems and political sophisms of the Jesuits for world domination*).

1.3.2 Title entries under Anglo-American rules present no difficulties except the filing problems arising out of the letters I and J, U and V (2.1.1), which recur in the filing of entries under authors. Printers and editors provide one with every variation from the I, i; V, u of the Roman alphabet to the full complement of upper and lower case for i, j, u and v. If you file what you find blindly, you may create separate entries under IUS, IVS and JUS; but choosing a standard form brings you up against the fact that the present convention of equating i and j but distinguishing u and v has no justification. British Museum rules entail the restoration of the nominative and in some cases translation: both require care.

1.3.3 Titles like **Aeneis** are declined if the context requires, e.g. **in Aeneide, in primo libro Aeneidos** (4.3.7), and in later titles words like **tractatus, liber, quaestiones** are affected in the same way together with any adjectives that agree with them. A title like **De ecclesiastica et politica potestate** cannot be altered, so we find a reply entitled **Libelli de ecclesiastica . . . potestate elenchus**. (Sometimes all attempt at reproducing the title exactly is abandoned.) For the possible effect of numeration on titles see 1.4.3.

1.4 VOLUMES AND PARTS

1.4.1 The native word **volumen** (*a roll*) is less common than **tomus** (*a slice*) for *volume*. **Liber** (*book*), which in classical times indicates a comparatively small division of a work, no more at times than a chapter in a modern book, is occasionally used in more recent times for a volume. *Part* is almost always **pars**.

1.4.2 The numeral, invariably ordinal, usually follows. If there are only two parts or volumes the first is **prior**, the second **posterior** or **alter(a)**. Otherwise the numerals given in 6.1.2 are used. Quite often, where a volume is divided into parts, the whole numeration is given in one grammatically connected phrase, e.g. **Tomi primi pars altera**, *second part of the first volume*.

1.4.3 A similar connexion is often found between the numeration and the title, either in the form **P. Vergili Maronis Georgicon libri IV**, *The four books of Virgil's Georgics*, or with the number of a particular volume, e.g. **Observationum medicarum decas prima, Operum miscellaneorum tomus primus.**

1.5 EDITIONS

The word **editio** is followed (usually) by an ordinal numeral and where necessary some word indicating revision such as **emendatior, correctior,** *more correct,* or **auctior, complectior,** *enlarged.* Note also the implication of **denuo,** *afresh.* See also 1.6.3.

1.6 IMPRINTS

1.6.1   The name of the printer or publisher, frequently the same in the Renaissance period, appears in a variety of ways involving different cases. Thus **typis** (*with the types*), **litteris** or **formis** may precede the printer's name, **sumptibus** or **impensis** (*at the expense*) the publisher's, the name being in the genitive. Or the prepositions **apud** (*at*), **per** (*by*) may be used, both taking the accusative. **Prostant venales apud** (*on sale at*) obviously indicates the bookseller/publisher; so less obviously does **apud**: but **per** (and even **impressum per**) is ambiguous. In other books one finds a verb like **imprimebat** or **excudebat** (*was the printer*) with the name in the nominative, sometimes coupled with the publisher in the dative, e.g. **Conradus Badius excudebat Roberto Stephano.** Finally there are expressions like **ex officina Roberti Stephani,** *from the workshop of Robert Estienne,* with a genitive, **ex officina Hackiana,** with an adjective, or more specifically **e typographia.**

1.6.2   The place is given in the locative (4.6.3), e.g. **Romae, Londini.** With plural names one gets forms like **Parisiis** (often fancifully spelt **Parrhisiis**). Practically all of them are of the first or second declension. Most names are easy enough to recognise, but imprints like **Trajecti ad Rhenum** (*at Utrecht*), **Rotomagi** (*at Rouen*) require a dictionary of Latin names, while **Lugdunum** is the Latin for both *Lyons* and *Leiden* (in full **Lugdunum Batavorum**).

1.6.3   An institutional publisher, possibly not responsible for the business details, may be indicated by such a phrase as **Editio Academiae scientiarum,** *published by the Academy of Sciences.*

1.7 SERIES

1.7.1   The titles of series are straightforward, describing the series as in **Bibliotheca Teubneriana, Scriptorum Classicorum Bibliotheca Oxoniensis,** or the contents, e.g. **Collectanea spiritualia, Miscellanea historiae pontificiae.**

1.7.2   Numeration is by **tomus, volumen** or **fasciculus** or by a combination of the last with one of the others, the number being dealt with as in books. Sub-series are not uncommon, e.g. **Analecta Gregoriana vol. 188, Series Facultatis theologiae, Sectio B, n(umerus)58.**

1.8 PERIODICALS

1.8.1   Latin periodicals are fewer nowadays than formerly, when numbers of learned societies published their proceedings in Latin, but classical studies, theology and related disciplines, international law, medicine and botany still produce them. (Not that a Latin title indicates a Latin periodical.) Their titles are sober and linguistically straightforward, e.g. **Gregorianum; Verbum Domini,** *The Word of the Lord;* **Ius romanum medii aevi,** *Medieval Roman Law;* **Periodica de re morali,** etc. (as it were *Journal of ethical studies*).

1.8.2 The body responsible (Latin periodicals tend to be institutional) may be part of the title, e.g. **Analecta romana Instituti danici**. The name is in the genitive, as it is in the more common type **editum cura professorum Pontificii Athenaei Antionani de Urbe**, *published by the care of the professors of Pontificium Athenaeum Antonianum de Urbe*, i.e. the Pontificio Ateneo Antoniano in Rome. For **cura** may be substituted **studio, opere** or **opera** meaning much the same or **consilio** (*by counsel*) or **iussu** (*by order*) or they may be variously combined with each other or with **impensis** (*at the expense*). Somewhat less common are the use of a finite verb, e.g. **edidit** (*published*), with the name in the nominative, or an ablative absolute (4.6.6), e.g. **auspice Collegio Antiqui Iuris Studiis Provehendis,** *under the auspices of the Collegium*, etc.

1.8.3 Editorship is about equally often expressed by a noun, abstract or concrete, e.g. **moderator, redactor, director, consilium moderatorum**, or a verb in the present, e.g. **redigit, redigunt**, or the past, e.g. **redegit, digessit, edenda curavit**. In all these instances the name or names are in the nominative, but the verb has different forms in the singular and plural. A phrase like **Consilium Commentariis edendis** (*Council for publishing the Commentarii*) is in itself more complicated but makes no difference; but assistant editors preceded by **adiuvantibus** will be in the ablative—if, that is, their names are in Latin at all. Other names mentioned may be those of **distributores**, alternatively called **depositarii**.

1.8.4 Numeration is by **volumen, tomus** or **annus**, divided by **fasciculus** or **numerus**. **Pars** is uncommon. Details are as for books (1.4).

1.8.5 Periodicity may be expressed by an adjective, e.g. **periodicum semestre**, *half-yearly*; **periodica publicatio trimestris**, *quarterly*; **commentarii bimestrales**, *bi-monthly*, or by an adverbial phrase, e.g. **prodit (prodeunt) bis (quater) in anno, tertio quoque mense**, *come(s) out twice (four times) a year, every three months*; **singulis annis editur volumen**, *a volume is published every year*.

1.8.6 Subscription is annual (**subnotatio annua, annuae subscriptionis pretium, pretium subscriptionis in annum**). One journal refers vaguely to **pecuniae solvendae** (*money to be paid*), but one must always remember when dealing with Latin that the classics do not furnish ready-made technical terms for modern situations. Distinctions may involve such expressions as **per tabellarios**, *by post*; **pro Italia**, *for Italy*; **extra Italiam**, *outside*; and the usual warnings take such forms as: **Subscriptio censetur continuata quoad contrarium non significatur**, *Subscription is considered to be renewed so long as the contrary is not indicated*; **Pretium pro anno sequenti solvendum statim post ultimum fasciculum receptum**, *Next year's subscription is to be paid immediately after receipt of the last number*. Provision is usually made for single copies, e.g. **separatim veneunt**, *they are sold separately*, and for back numbers (**numerus praeteritus, volumen praeteritum**) as opposed to current numbers (**vertentis anni**).

1.8.7 Addresses distinguish, even if they usually combine, **redactio (directio)** and **administratio**, but simple specification is less common than detailed instructions of the following types: **Qui cum Consilio Commentariorum quavis de ratione communicare velint, ita litteras inscribant**, *Those who wish to communicate with the board of Commentarii on any matter, are to address letters thus*; **Inscriptio litterarum tam pro administratione quam pro redactione**, *Address both for business and editorial matters*. Common are **mittenda sunt** and **mittantur** (*are to be sent*) with subjects such as **manuscripta, periodica quae mutuo dantur, quaecumque spectant ad subnotationem, petitiones, omnia** (*MSS, periodicals on exchange, whatever concerns subscription, orders, everything*). And please, **nominis ac domicilii inscriptio clare signetur**, *write your name and address clearly*.

2 ALPHABET, PHONETICS, SPELLING

2.1 ALPHABET

2.1.1 The alphabet frequently used for Latin is the one we are familar with, less **W** and with **K** scarcely used; but to the Romans **I** and **J**, **U** and **V** were simply variant forms and were not differentiated as vowel and semi-vowel respectively. Nor were they during the Renaissance, when for the most part **j** was used, if at all, initially or in the combination **ij**, while only **V** was used in the upper case and **v** and **u** were initial and non-initial respectively. Later **j** and **v** stood for the semi-vowels, but **j** has now been dropped by all scholars, and **v** by a few. So from the Renaissance onwards one would find successively:

> **EIVS, eius, VIVVS, viuus, VNIVS, vnius**
>
> **EJUS, ejus, VIVUS, vivus, UNIUS, unius**
>
> **EIUS, eius, VIVUS, vivus** (occasionally **VIVVS, UIUUS, uiuus**), **UNIUS, unius**

In transcribing upper into lower case the practice of the book should be followed.

A capital **I** among lower-case letters or a taller **I** among capitals was re-introduced in the 17th century in those words in which earlier Latin used **-i** and later Latin **-ii**. So for instance **HelmestadI** for **Helmestadii** as an imprint.

2.1.2 Accents are not an essential part of the alphabet and are not used in modern scholarly texts, but are found earlier. The acute accent was used before enclitics like **-ne** and **-que**; the grave on **à** and **è** and the **-è** of adverbs; the circumflex as a means of distinction on words like **hîc**, *here* (**hic**, *he*); **quî**, *how* (**qui**, *who*), on the **-â** of the ablative singular, and on supposed contractions like **dî** (4.3.4).

2.1.3 The ligatures **Æ æ, Œ œ** are likewise obsolete, as well as the use of the diaeresis on words like **aëris** (*of the air*).

2.1.4 Early printed books contain a mass of variously barred letters by way of abbreviation, but only the bar over vowels, e.g. **ā** = **am** or **an**, and **q̣** or **q₃** for **que** remain common.

2.2 CAPITALISATION

2.2.1 Latin has been used for so long in so many different countries that no fixed rules can be laid down. Modern scholars for the most part write both proper nouns and proper adjectives with capitals, but in transcribing titles it is better to follow the usage of the book in question. Institutions are usually spelt with capitals throughout, e.g. **Academia Scientiarum Imperialis**.

2.3 DIVISION OF WORDS

2.3.1 Subject to the following notes, rules 1, 2, 4, 5b, 6c, 7a, 8 apply (p. xiii).

2.3.2 Rule 2 is not followed pedantically: **trans-igit** but **tran-scriptam** (to preserve the integrity of **scriptam**), and in the same Oxford text **super-atum** but **praete-rita**.

2.3.3 Suffixes like **-per**, **-quam**, **-que**, **-cumque**, which are simply tacked on to a word, are kept intact, e.g. **paulis-per** contrary to 5b, but not the great mass of endings and formatives, e.g. **ege-stas** not **eges-tas**.

2.3.4 Rule 4 admits of no exceptions.

2.3.5 Possible combinations include some like **ct, mn, pt** (**do-ctus, conde-mnare, pro-pter**) which do not in fact begin any native word.

2.4 PUNCTUATION

2.4.1 Full stops were not specially characteristic of abbreviations; in inscriptions they often stood between every word. But in modern texts they are usual.

2.4.2 The apostrophe has been used to indicate the omission of a letter, but it is not usual in the best texts nowadays, e.g. **satin** rather than **sati'n'** for **satisne**.

2.5 VARIATION OF CONSONANT

2.5.1 S is involved in a number of changes: Cs is often simplified to (s)s, sC to C, so that the consonant or s is present in some forms but not in others, e.g. **cedo/cessi** (<**cedsi**); **pono** (<**posno**)/**posui**; s between vowels may change to r, e.g. **corpus/corporis**; **dt** and **tt** produce (s)s, e.g. **fundo/fusum**.

2.5.2 A number of consonants are completely or partially assimilated before the following consonant, or can be, e.g. **ad + fui > affui** or **adfui**; **in + p** or **b > im-**, and conversely **tum/tunc**, etc.

2.5.3 A p is inserted between m and s, m and t, e.g. **hiem(p)s/hiemis**; **demo/demptum**.

2.5.4 The presence or absence of **-n-** and **-sc-** is significant in the conjugation of verbs.

2.6 VARIATION OF VOWEL

2.6.1 Many changes of vowel are modes of inflexion, e.g. **agit/egit**, but some are incidental to it or to composition, e.g. a/e, a/i and a/u: **damno/condemno**, **ago/adigo**, **calco/inculco**; e/i: **nomen/nominis**, **rego/corrigo**; o/i: **homo/hominis**; u/o: **corpus/corporis**; ae/i: **aequus/iniquus**; au/ō, au/ū: **plaudo/explodo**, **claudo/concludo**.

2.6.2 Unstressed e may vanish in declension: **liber/libri** (*book*); also, less frequently, i, e.g. **valde** for **valide**, **fert** for **ferit**.

2.6.3 In a number of forms o early gave place to u, but was retained much longer after u, e.g. **voltis** for **vultis**, **quom** for **cum**.

2.7 SPELLING

2.7.1 The changes in the pronunciation of Latin which are evidenced by the development of the Romance languages led to a good deal of confusion in the spelling of it during the Middle Ages; and though the manuscripts of classical authors might be expected to preserve more carefully the classical spelling, there was a good deal of variation, and what are now held incorrect spellings were for a long time accepted as standard. So one finds **coelum** for **caelum** and **caeteri** for **ceteri**, **coda** for **cauda**, **adolescens** for **adulescens**, **myrrha** for **murra**. Single and double consonants are confused, e.g **littus** for **litus** and **litera** for **littera**; **-ti-** and **-ci-** interchange, e.g. **conditio** for **condicio** and **nuncio** for **nuntio**; so do **ct** and **t** (or **th**), e.g. **aut(h)or** for **auctor**, **auctumnus** for **autumnus**. H is inserted where it should not be and omitted where it should be present, e.g. **umus** for **humus**, **humerus** for **umerus**, **lachryma** for **lacrima**.

2.7.2 Some such differences are still in dispute, and there is considerable variation in the matter of assimilation (2.5.2).

3 ARTICLES

There are no articles.

4 NOUNS

4.1 GENDER AND FORM

4.1.1 Latin nouns are arranged in different declensions by the characteristic vowel, or lack of one, at the end of the stem: 1 **-a-**; 2 (**-o**); 3 **-i-/-**; 4 **-u-**; 5 **-e-**. There is some correspondence between gender and form, viz. 1 mostly F; 2 mostly M or N; 4 mostly M; 5 nearly all F.

4.1.2 Some nouns are compound, consisting of a noun and an adjective run together such as **respublica**, or a noun and a qualifying genitive such as **paterfamilias**. Both parts of **respublica** are declined but only **pater** in **paterfamilias**.

4.3 DECLENSIONS

4.3.1 The general pattern of the singular is as follows, but the notes in 4.3.3–4.3.6 should be consulted.

	1	2	3	4	5
N	-a	-us/-, -um	see 4.3.5	-us, -u	-es
A	-am	-um	-em/-im or as N	-um, -u	-em
G	-ae	-i	-is	-us	-e(i)
D	-ae	-o	-i	-ui	-e(i)
Ab	-a	-o	-e	-u	-e

4.3.2 The plural forms are:

	1	2	3	4	5
N	-ae	-i, -a	-es, -a, -ia	-us, -ua	-es
A	-as	-os, -a	-es/-is, -a, -ia	-us, -ua	-es
G	-orum	-orum	-um, -ium	-uum	-erum
D Ab	-is	-is	-ibus	-ubus/-ibus	-ebus

The -a endings are neuter.

4.3.3 In the first declension the DAbP of some nouns, e.g. **dea**, ends in **-abus**, and some may have GP **-um**.

4.3.4 In the second declension most M nouns in **-r** have NS **-er** not **-erus** and may drop the **-e-** in the other cases, e.g. **numerus** but **puer**, G **-eri**; **liber** (*book*), G **libri**. So also **vir**. The usual neuter ending is **-um** but **vulgus** and **virus** (A **-us**, no P) are neuter too. The GS of nouns in **-ius** and **-ium** may be **-i** as well as **-ii**. The GP of some nouns may be plain **-um**. **Deus** has P **di**, etc. Some nouns hesitate between M and N, e.g. **locus** P **loci** or **loca**.

4.3.5 The NS of third-declension nouns (except for neuter nouns, which end in **-e** or the stem consonant) is mostly **-es**, **-is** or **-s**, e.g. **urbs, nubes, orbis**, GS **-bis**; but some stems are peculiar.

Variation between **-e-** and **-i-** is common, e.g. **index** GS **indicis; hospes, hospitis;** but not invariable, e.g. **radix, radicis; rex, regis.**

> Stems in **-d-**: N **-s** for **-ds**.
> Stems in **-l-**: N **-l** (M or N), **-le** (N), **-les, -lis**; also N **-l** GS **-llis**.
> Stems in **-n-**: N **-en** GS **-inis; -o, -inis/-onis**; also N **-nis**.
> Stems in **-r-**: N **-ar/-are/-as** GS **-aris; -er/-es/-is/-us** GS **-eris**, also **-er, -ris;**
>   **-or/-os/-us, -oris**; also N **-ris**.
> Stems in **-t-**: N **-s** for **-ts**.

Somewhat isolated are **caro** GS **carnis; senex, senis; iter, itineris; vis** A **vim** Ab **vi** P **vires** etc.; **lac, lactis; nix, nivis.**

4.3.6 In the fourth declension **-u** (P **-ua**) is the neuter ending.

4.3.7 Nouns taken over from Greek have some peculiar forms and stems. Ignoring proper names the following should be noted:

1	N -e	A -en	G -es	Ab -e				
	-es	-en	(-ae	-a)				
2	N -os	A -on	D -o	P -oe	GP -on			
3	A -a; nominative and stem: -as, -ad-/-ant-; -o(n), -on-/-ont-; -us, -od-; -ma, -mat-							

4.6 USE OF CASES

4.6.1 Crude as it may seem, many of the uses of the cases can be reasonably well indicated by the traditional English prepositions: G *of*, D *to* or *for*, Ab *at, in, by, with, from*.

4.6.2 The accusative is the case of limitation. Apart from expressing the direct object, it is used for extent of time, space or action (adverbial), and for the goal.

4.6.3 The locative has no distinctive forms, being identical in the singular with the genitive of the first and second declensions, and the ablative (or dative) of the third. In the plural it coincides with the ablative. Its typical preposition is *at*, being used of place, time and value.

4.6.4 Apart from the uses typically translated *of*—possession, partitive, quality, etc.—the genitive is used (even where not identical with the locative) for value.

4.6.5 Besides uses which may be translated *to* or *for*, the dative may denote the agent (cf. 8.11.3), and is used for a certain class of predicates, e.g. **auxilio est**, *it is a help*. The translation *by way of* is then sometimes appropriate.

4.6.6 The ablative is a mixture of older cases and its uses are accordingly diverse: place where, time at or within which; place whence, separation, *than* after comparatives; instrument, means, cause, circumstances, description, manner, price, amount of difference. See also 4.6.3. An extension of the ablative of circumstances is the 'ablative absolute' in which a noun in the ablative with a participle in agreement is equivalent to a subordinate clause. e.g. **vivente marito**, *while her husband was alive*. Cf. 1.2.2.

5 ADJECTIVES

5.1 GENERAL

5.1.1 Adjectives are variable nouns. When used to qualify substantives they agree, and when used alone the endings which are tied to gender are significant, e.g. **bonus**, *good man*; **bona**, *good woman*; **bonum**, *good thing*. Unfortunately most cases of the M and N are the same so that, for example, **libera nos a malo** is ambiguous.

5.1.2 The adjective may precede or follow a noun which it qualifies and may be separated from it by a number of words, e.g.

1 2 3 4 5 6 7
Nova nuper exorta est de clausulis Tullianis doctrina

1 7 3 2 3 4 6 5
A new theory has lately appeared about Ciceronian cadences

5.2 ENDINGS

5.2.1 Some adjectives have the forms of the first and second declensions (4.3.1–4.3.2), viz.

M	N	F
-us	**-um**	**-a**
-er	**-(e)rum**	**-(e)ra**
-erus	**-erum**	**-era**

5.2.2 The remainder take all their forms from the third declension. Only those in -er have three distinct forms, viz. M -er N -re F -ris. Others have MF -is (including -ris) N -e; MF -or N -us. The rest have only one form, but the neuter as usual has the same form for N and A, and plural -(i)a. Except in N and A none of the forms distinguish gender.

5.3 COMPARISON

5.3.1 So far as they exist the comparative and superlative forms are usually -ior and -issimus added to the stem. (In the third declension the stem is shown by the oblique cases.)

emendat -us	-ior	-issimus
grav -is	-ior	-issimus
audax GS -cis	-cior	-cissimus

Adjectives in -er(us) have superlative -errimus, and some in -ilis have -illimus.

5.3.2 Some comparatives and superlatives have no positive or are irregular. The dictionaries, however, have separate entries or references.

6 NUMERALS

6.1 CARDINAL

6.1.1

1 unus	11 undecim	21 {viginti unus / unus et viginti}	100 centum
2 duo	12 duodecim	28 duodetriginta	200 ducenti
3 tres	13 tredecim	30 triginta	300 trecenti
4 quattuor	14 quattuordecim	40 quadraginta	400 quadringenti
5 quinque	15 quindecim	50 quinquaginta	500 quingenti
6 sex	16 sedecim	60 sexaginta	600 sescenti
7 septem	17 septemdecim	70 septuaginta	700 septingenti
8 octo	18 duodeviginti	80 octoginta	800 octingenti
9 novem	19 undeviginti	90 nonaginta	900 nongenti
10 decem	20 viginti	99 undecentum	1000 mille

1,000,000 **deciens centum mil(l)ia**

6.1.2 All the numerals are adjectives, except (to some extent) **mille**. **Unus, duo, tres, ducenti**, etc. are declined: **unus** like a pronoun adjective (7.1.2), **tres, tria** like a third declension adjective, the hundreds like a first/second declension adjective (5.2.1). The forms of **duo** are:

	MN	*F*
N	duo	duae
A	duo	duas
G	du(or)um	du(ar)um
DAb	duobus	duabus

6.1.3 **Mille** is an indeclinable adjective; the plural **mil(l)ia** (4.2.2) is a noun: **mille passus**, *a thousand paces, a mile*; duo millia **passuum**.

6.2 ORDINAL, ETC.

6.2.1

1 primus	11 undecimus	21 unus (primus) et
2 secundus, alter	12 duodecimus	vice(n)simus
3 tertius	13 tertius decimus	30 trice(n)simus
4 quartus	14 quartus decimus	40, etc. quadrage(n)simus,
5 quintus	15 quintus decimus	etc.
6 sextus	16 sextus decimus	100 cente(n)simus
7 septimus	17 septimus decimus	200, etc. ducente(n)simus,
8 octavus	18 duodevice(n)simus	etc.
9 nonus	19 undevice(n)simus	1000 mille(n)simus
10 decimus	20 vice(n)simus	2000 bis mille(n)simus

6.2.2 There are also forms in -(e)ni, meaning *so many each*, and adverbs in -e(n)s meaning *so many times*. The last are important owing to the habit of shortening 1,000,000 and the like to **deciens**, etc.

6.3 FIGURES

6.3.1 The basic elements of Roman figures, which denote cardinals and ordinals alike, are familiar enough, but present-day usage is not quite that of the Romans.
I = 1, V = 5; X = 10; L (from ↓) = 50; C = 100; CIƆ or ∞ = 1000; CCIƆƆ = 10,000, and so on. Taking the right hand half of the last two we have IƆ (D) = 500; IƆƆ = 5000. There is also a symbol Q for 500,000. Despite the coincidence of the word **mille** M for 1000 is a late development.

6.3.2 Intermediate numbers are produced by repetition and collocation of the basic elements, e.g. VIIII or IX for 9. The subtraction method is not so common in Roman times but it includes XXC for 80 (as well as LXXX). The date 1919 in a modern book would usually be MCMXIX.

6.3.3 The practice of distinguishing numerals by a line over the top begins in the Augustan period. Earlier they were distinguished, if at all, by a line through them, as in the abbreviation **HS** (2½) for **sestertius**, and a line over the top indicated multiplication by 1000.

6.4 DATES

6.4.1 The months are:

**Ianuarius, Februarius, Martius, Aprilis, Maius, Iunius,
Iulius (Quinctilis), Augustus (Sextilis), September, October, November,
December**

They are all adjectives (6.4.3), but with **mensis**, *month*, expressed or understood they function as nouns.

6.4.2 In modern dating the day and the year are in the ablative, and the month in the genitive, e.g. *on 31 May 1972*, **die trice(n)simo primo Maii anno mille(n)simo non-gente(n)simo septuage(n)simo secundo.**

6.4.3 The Roman system was based on three fixed points in each month, Kalendae, the 1st; Nonae, the 5th, or in the case of March, May, July, October the 7th; Idus, the 13th or 15th. Other days were expressed by reckoning back from the next fixed point, e.g. *2 March* is **ante diem sextum Nonas Martias (a.d. VI Non. Mart.)**—an idiomatic way of saying *the sixth day* (by inclusive reckoning!) *before the Nones of*

March; *31 March* is **pridie Kalendas Apriles**. If the year is given by reference to the foundation of Rome—A(nno) U(rbis) C(onditae), 753 B.C.—the year B.C. can be got by subtracting from 753 for dates before **a.d. XI Kal. Mai.** and from 754 for the rest of the year.

7 PRONOUNS

7.1/7.2 DEMONSTRATIVE, ETC.

7.1.1 The non-personal pronouns share certain peculiarities, others are peculiar to certain pronouns or groups of pronouns. Otherwise they follow the pattern of first/second declension adjectives.

All have GS **-ius** and D **-i** for all genders.

7.1.2 (N)ullus, solus, totus, unus; alter, neuter, uter; ipse (ipsa, ipsum) have no other peculiarities.

7.1.3 Alius (GS alius), ille, iste have neuter in -d, viz. aliud, illud, istud.

7.1.4 Hic incorporates the affix -c(e), optional with other pronouns, to produce:

	S			P		
	M	*N*	*F*	*M*	*N*	*F*
N	hic	hoc	haec	hi	haec	hae
A	hunc	hoc	hanc	hos(ce)	haec	has(ce)
G		huius(ce)			horum	harum
D		huic			his(ce)	
Ab	hoc		hac		his(ce)	

7.1.5 Is (*this, that, he, she, it*) mostly has the stem e-:

	S			P		
	M	*N*	*F*	*M*	*N*	*F*
N	is	id	ea	ei/ii	ea	eae
A	eum	id	eam	eos	ea	eas
G		eius			eorum	earum
D		ei			eis/iis	
Ab	eo		ea		eis/iis	

In **idem** (=is + dem) note **eundem, eorundem**, etc. NPM (e)idem, DAbP (e)isdem.

7.1.6 Qui(s) (*who, which, what, any*) relative, interrogative, indefinite, has the following forms:

	S			P		
	M	*N*	*F*	*M*	*N*	*F*
N	qui(s)	quod/quid	qua(e)/quis	qui	qua(e)	quae
A	quem	quod/quid	quam	quos	qua(e)	quas
G		cuius			quorum	quarum
D		cui			qui(bu)s	
Ab	quo/qui		qua/qui		qui(bu)s	

Some of the alternatives have special uses. The indefinite sense is found after ne, nisi, num and si.

Likewise **aliqui(s)**, etc., *someone, something, some*.

7.1.7 There are a number of appendages which combine with the basic pronouns to make further ones, viz. -cunque, -dam, -libet, -nam, -quam, -que, -vis, e.g. quidam, quisquam, uterque. Only the first part is declined.

7.1.8 Compound pronouns are found such as alteruter, quisquis, unusquisque. Both parts are declined, e.g. alterius utrius, quemquem, unicuique.

7.2 RELATIVE AND INTERROGATIVE
See 7.1/7.2.

7.3 PERSONAL
7.3.1

	S		S & P	P	
	1	2	3r	1	2
N	ego	tu	—	nos	vos
A	me	te	se(se)	nos	vos
G	mei	tui	sui	nostri/-rum	vestri/-rum
D	mi(hi)	tibi	sibi	nobis	vobis
Ab	me	te	se	nobis	vobis

7.3.2 The genitive is not used as a possessive, there being adjectives meus, noster, etc., except in the case of eius (illius, istius) (7.1.5, 7.1.3) which contrasts with the adjective suus in meaning. Suus is used for *his, her, their* when the subject and the possessor are the same, eius when they are different.

8 VERBS

8.1 STRUCTURE

8.1.1 Latin verbs, which are cited nowadays by the 1PS of the present, are traditionally grouped into four conjugations. This grouping is used here for the present tense, but as each tense is dealt with separately, it is ignored where not helpful.

8.1.2 The endings express simultaneously person, number, tense and mood, and there are highly characteristic recurrent elements which are given in full for the present tense only. In relation to a given conjugation they show little ambiguity, but in themselves they may be equivocal. Thus -et may be present indicative, future indicative or present subjunctive according to the conjugation. It is also possible for forms which differ in pronunciation to be written the same, e.g. fugit (fŭgit, *he flees*; fūgit, *he fled*).

8.2 PRESENT

8.2.1 *Endings*

I   -o, -as, -at; -amus, -atis, -ant
II -eo, -es, -et; -emus, -etis, -ent
III -(i)o, -is, -it; -imus, -itis, -(i)nut
IV -io, -is, -it; -imus, -itis, -iunt

8.2.2 The sense corresponds both to the simple and continuous present of English, and may also refer on-occasion to the future and the past.

8.3 IMPERFECT

8.3.1 The endings are the same for each conjugation, only the connecting vowel being different:

$$
\left.\begin{array}{l}\text{-a} \\ \text{-e} \\ \text{-ie}\end{array}\right| \text{bam, -bas, -bat; -bamus, -batis, -bant}
$$

Present:
-o
-eo, -o
-io

8.3.2 The imperfect expresses continuous or habitual action, or action begun in past time. In letters it may refer to the time of writing, past by the time the letter is received, e.g. **scribebam haec,** *I am writing this.*

8.4 PERFECT, PLUPERFECT, FUTURE PERFECT

8.4.1 The endings of the perfect are the same for all verbs:

-i, -isti, -it; -imus, -istis, -erunt

but there are varieties of perfect stem.

8.4.2 These stems with the 1P ending are:

-avi: present -o, -avo.

-evi: pr. -eo, -esco, -o; also **sprevi/sperno.**

-i(v)i: pr. -io, -o, -eo; **trivi/tero.**

-si (-xi): pr. -o, -eo, -io. Note **scripsi/scribo** but **sumpsi/sumo**; -d- and some-times -r- vanish before -s-; -c-, -g-, -qu- may vanish or more commonly combine to form -x-; -x- also comes from -ct- and -h-. Note **vixi** from **vivo,** and **iussi** from **iubeo.**

-ui: pr. -eo, -o, -io.

-i with a long vowel in the stem. The present in -o inserts -n-, e.g. **fudi/fundo;** or simply has a short vowel with ending -o, -eo, -io. The long vowel corre-sponding to -a- may be -e-, e.g. **cepi/capio.**

-i with reduplication, sometimes with change of vowel as in 2.6.1, e.g. **cecini/cano.** The present may have an inserted -n-, e.g. **tetigi/tango.**

8.4.3 The 'perfect' usually has the force of a simple past tense.

8.4.4 The pluperfect and future perfect have the perfect stem with the following endings:

Pluperfect: -eram, -eras . . . -erant
Future perfect: -ero, -eris . . . -erunt

See also 8.5.2.

8.5 FUTURE

8.5.1

Endings	Present
-a |	-o
| bo, -bis . . . -bunt	
-e |	-eo
-am, -es . . . -ent	-o
-iam, -ies . . . -ient	-io

8.5.2 The tense is used precisely, so that the English translation may be the present, e.g. **cum (si) lucem videbis** (or **videris,** 8.4.4), *when (if) you see the light.*

8.7 SUBJUNCTIVE

8.7.1 *Present*

```
I    -em, -es . . . -ent
II   -eam, -as . . . -ant
III  -(i)am, etc.
IV   -iam, etc.
```

See 8.2.1 for the corresponding indicative.

8.7.2 *Imperfect*

```
    I    -a|
II, III   -e|rem, -res . . . -rent        Pr. ind. 8.2.1
   IV    -i|
```

8.7.3 *Perfect*, from the perfect stem:

-er|im, -is . . . -int

8.7.4 *Pluperfect*, from the perfect stem:

-issem, -isses . . . -issent

8.7.5 The subjunctive expresses not a simple fact but a wish, a supposition, a consequence or the like.

Without a conjunction: a wish, command or supposition: **valeat**, *good luck to him*; **dicat aliquis**, *suppose someone says* (*someone may say*).

With **si, nisi**: **si veniat**, *if he should come*; **si veniret**, *if he were* (*now*) *coming*; **si venisset**, *if he had come*. Similarly, expressing what would happen under such conditions: **venisset**, *he would have come*.

With **ut, qui** expressing purpose or result: **ut veniat**, *that he may come* (**ut venit**, *as he comes*).

With **cum** (*when, since, although*) and many other conjunctions, expressing circumstances: **cum verum sit**, *since it is true*.

With **quod**, expressing a reported reason: **laudat quod fuerit abstinens**, *he praises him for having been abstinent* (**quod fuit**, *because in fact he was*).

With interrogatives, in indirect questions: **Plauti comoedias quantum fecerit antiquitas, ignorare arbitror neminem**, *I think no-one is unaware how much store antiquity set by Plautus's comedies*.

With relatives, expressing a type: **editionem quae memoratu digna sit**, *an edition worth mentioning*.

A good many conjunctions are habitually followed by the subjunctive, but the meaning is adequately conveyed by the conjunction itself.

8.11/8.12 VERBAL NOUNS AND ADJECTIVES

8.11.1 Latin verbs in the active have present and future participles, a gerund (to which there corresponds a passive adjective in **-us**, the gerundive), present and perfect infinitives and a supine (to which there corresponds the perfect passive participle). The forms of the four conjugations (see 8.2.1) are:

	Pr. part.	*Gerund*	*Infinitives*		*Supine*	*Fut. part.*
I	**-ans**	-andum	**-are**	-isse	-atum	**-aturus**
II	**-ens**	-endum	**-ere**	-isse	-itum	*et sim.*
III	**-(i)ens**	-(i)endum	**-ere**	-isse	see 8.11.5	
IV	**-iens**	-iendum	**-ire**	-isse	-itum	

The supines given are the typical ones; for exceptional ones see 8.11.5. On the perfect infinitive see 8.4.2, 8.11.4.

8.11.2 The present participle is an adjective (4.3.5: stems in -t-) and can be used simply as such or as a noun, e.g. **sapiens**, *wise, a sage*. But more often it has its proper verbal force, e.g. **exeunti obviam venit**, *he met him as he was coming out*; **contra dicente nullo**, *no-one objecting*; **legentibus**, *to those who read*.

8.11.3 The gerund answers roughly to our verbal noun in *-ing*, but it rarely has an object, for the gerundive, agreeing with what would have been the object, is nearly always used instead. Both are found in the following example: **et diligendi aliquos et referendae gratiae principia**, *the instinct to love people and show gratitude* (lit. *of loving*). In other cases: **ad imprimendum**, *for printing*; **de contemnenda morte**, *about despising death*. (See also Specimen.)

The gerundive, as an adjective meaning *fit to be done*, is also used to express obligation. The logical object is the subject of the verb *to be* with the gerundive in agreement, and the agent in the dative. If there is no object the neuter is used, e.g. **nunc est bibendum nunc pede libero pulsanda tellus**, *now is (the time) to drink and beat the ground with unrestrained foot*; **gratiae agendae sunt mihi**, *I have to thank*.

8.11.4 The infinitives are mostly used as subject or object, e.g. **licet dicere**, *it is permissible to say*; **divinare possumus**, *we can guess*. Equally common is the infinitive with an accusative as its subject, dependent on a verb of saying, thinking or the like, **bona sese dicit emisse**, *he says he has bought the property*. The perfect infinitive is formed from the perfect stem: **emi**, *I bought*; **emisse**, *to have bought*.

8.11.5 The supine is a noun in the accusative (**-um**) or ablative (**-u**). The accusative expresses purpose, the ablative is used in phrases such as **mirabile dictu**, *strange to say*. (Sometimes the noun has all its cases and is entered separately in the dictionary.) The correspondence of the supine stem to the present, like that of the perfect (8.4.2) is not altogether simple. Basically the stem is **-tu-** with or without a vowel, but in a number of verbs it is changed to **-su-**. Hence:

> **-(s)sum** usually corresponds to **-(n)do**, less commonly to **-deo, -dio, -go, -teo, -tio, -to**. Note **cursum/curro**; **falsum/fallo**; **haesum/haereo**; **iussum/iubeo**.
> **-xum** (i.e. **-csum**) corresponds to **-cto**.
> **-itum** to **-o** as well as **-eo** and **-io**.

Note also for themselves or as patterns: **cautum/caveo**; **cretum/cerno**; **cultum/colo**; **fletum/fleo**; **gestum/gero**; **iutum/iuvo**; **notum/nosco**; **situm/sino**; **solutum/solvo**; **vectum/veho**; **victum/vinco** or **vivo**.

8.12 PARTICIPLES
See 8.11/8.12.

8.15 PASSIVE
8.15.1 In all except the perfect and related tenses the passive has its own endings which correspond to the active as follows:

Passive:	-i	-mini	-ari	-eri	-iri	-ar	-er	-or	-mur	-tur
Active:	-ere	-tis	-are	-ere	-ire	-am	-em	-o	-mus	-t
Passive:	-aris	-eris								
Active:	-as	-es, -is								

8.15.2 The passive has one participle, the perfect, which can be used simply as an adjective, e.g. **libri impressi**, *printed books*, or with verbal force, as in **libros impressos edidit**, *when the books had been printed, he published them* (or *he printed and published the books*), or (4.6.6) **libris impressis codices reddidi**, *when the books had been printed I returned the manuscripts*. The participle has the supine stem (8.11.5) and the endings of a first/second declension adjective (5.2.1).

8.15.3 The participle with the present of **esse**, *to be*, makes the perfect passive, **liber impressus est**, *the book was (has been) printed*. With the imperfect and future it makes the pluperfect and the future perfect.

8.15.4 Some verbs, known as deponents, are passive in form and active in meaning, e.g. **sequor**, pf. **secutus sum**, *I follow*. Others are deponent in the perfect, e.g. **audeo**, pf. **ausus sum**, *I dare*. **Fio**, pf. **factus sum**, inf. **fieri** means either *I become* or *I am made*.

8.17 AUXILIARIES
See 8.19.1.

8.19 IRREGULAR VERBS
    8.19.1   **sum**, *I am* (see also 8.15.3)
        Present: **sum, es, est; sumus, estis, sunt**
        Imperfect: **eram**
        Future: **ero**
        Perfect: **fui**
        Present subjunctive: **sim, sis . . . sint**
        Imperfect subjunctive: **essem**
        Present participle: -**sens**, e.g. **absens**
        Infinitives: **esse, fuisse;** *future:* **fore**
        Future participle: **futurus**
    8.19.2   **possum**, *I am able*, is a compound of **sum**. Typical forms are **potest, poteram, potui, possim, possem, potens**.
    8.19.3   **volo**, *I wish, will*
        Present: **volo, vis, vult; volumus, vultis, volunt**
        Imperfect: **volebam**
        Future: **volem**
        Perfect: **volui**
        Infinitive: **velle**
    8.19.4   **malo**, *I prefer:* **mavult, malle**
    8.19.5   **nolo**, *I will not*
n- for **v**-, except **nonvis, nonvult(is), nolle**.
    8.19.6   **eo**, *I go*
        Future: **ibo**
        Present participle: **iens** (stem **eunt**-)
        Gerund: **eundum**
Otherwise as if **io**.
    8.19.7   **fero**, *I bear*
        Present: **fero, fers, fert; ferimus, fertis, ferunt**
        Perfect: **tuli**
        Infinitive: **ferre**
        Supine: **latum**
But **sustuli, sublatum** from **tollo**.

9 ADVERBS

9.1 FORMATION

There are a great many adverbial terminations, but the ones most commonly used to form adverbs are -e, e.g. **iustus**, *just*, **iuste**, *justly*, and -ter, e.g. **amans**, **amanter**; **acer**, **acriter**; **humanus**, **humaniter**. A dictionary such as Lewis and Short makes reference from all adverbs to their corresponding adjectives.

9.2 COMPARISON

The comparative is the same as the neuter of the adjective and the superlative has -e for -us.

10 PREPOSITIONS

10.1 POSITION

Most prepositions precede the noun or pronoun that they govern, but **mecum**, **tecum**, **secum**, **nobiscum**, **vobiscum**, **quocum**, **quacum** and sometimes **quibuscum** are found, and **erga** and **versus** follow but are not attached.

10.2 SYNTAX

Prepositions are used to make precise the meaning of a case. There are usually, therefore, cases proper to them, but **in**, **sub**, **subter** and **super** may have either the accusative or the ablative. **In** with the accusative is translated *into*, with the ablative *in*; the translation of the others is not affected by the case, though there is a comparable difference in meaning.

11 CONJUNCTIONS

11.1 COORDINATING

11.1.1 There are distinctions in usage between **et**, **-que** and **atque** (**ac**) but they all translate as *and*, or when repeated as *both . . . and*; but **et** can mean *also* or *even*. They may be omitted entirely. An elegant variation on **et . . . et** is **cum . . . tum**, not to be confused with **tum . . . tum**, which means *now . . . now*.

11.1.2 There is a difference of meaning between the words for *or* in that **aut** makes a real or important distinction, **vel**, **-ve** or **sive** one that is formal or unimportant.

11.2 SUBORDINATING

11.2.1 Some require the subjunctive (8.7.5), some the indicative. This can be important in the case of **ut** (indicative *as*, *how*; subjunctive *so that*, *in order that*) and **cum**: (see 8.7.5).

GLOSSARY

accessit, *has been added*
acta, *proceedings, transactions*
adiuvare, *assist* (1.8.2)
anecdota, *unpublished materials*
annales, *annals, yearbook*
annus, *year*
auctus, -tior, *enlarged* (1.5.1)
auspice, see 1.8.2

bibliopola, *bookseller*
bibliotheca, *library* (1.7.1)
bibliothecarius, *librarian*

collectanea, *collection* (1.7.1)
complectior, *enlarged* (1.5.1)
concinnare, *compile, arrange*
consilio, see 1.8.2

consilium, *board* (1.8.3)
cura, see 1.2.3, 1.8.2

decessio, *reduction*
depositarii, *distributors* (1.8.3)
digerere, *edit*
directio, *editorial office* (1.8.7)
director, *editor* (1.8.3)

edere, *publish, edit*
edenda curare, *edit* (1.8.3)
editio, *edition* (1.5.1); *publication* (1.6.3)
eiusdem auctoris, *by the same author*
elenchus, *critique, critical apparatus*
emendatus, -tior, *corrected* (1.5.1)
emittere, *publish*
excudere, *print*
exemplar, *copy*
explicare, *explain* (1.2.2)

fasciculus, *issue, part* (1.7.1; 1.8.4)
figura, *illustration*
foris, *abroad*
formis, *see* 1.6.1

illustrare, *make clear, edit*
imago, *portrait, illustration*
impensis, *at the expense* (1.6.1; 1.8.2)
imprimere, *print* (1.6.1)
indagatio, *investigation, research*
inscriptio, *address* (1.8.7)

libellus, *pamphlet*
liber, *book*
libraria, *bookshop*
librarius, *bookseller*
litterae, *letter(s)*; see also 1.6.1
in lucem dare, *publish*

menstruus, *monthly*
mittere, *send*
moderator, *editor* (1.8.3)
mortuus, *dead, died*
mutuo dare, *exchange*
mutuum dare, *lend*

natus, *born*
novus, *new*

officina, (printing) *workshop* (1.6.1)
opera, opere, see 1.8.2
opus, *work*
oratio, *speech*

petitio, *order* (1.8.7)
praeteritus, *back* (number) (1.8.6)
sub prelo, *in the press*
pretium, *price* (1.8.6)
prodere, *publish*
prodire, *come out* (1.8.5)
prooemium, *preface, introduction*
prostare, *be on sale*

ratio, *account*
recensere, *edit*
recognoscere, *edit* (a text)
redactio, *editorial office* (1.8.7)
redactor, *editor* (1.8.3)
reddere, *translate*
redigere, *edit*
relatio, *report, account*

scriptor, *writer*
semestralis, *half-yearly* (1.8.5)
series, *sub-series* (1.7.2)
socius, *member, fellow*
studio, see 1.8.2
subnotatio, *subscription*
sumptibus, *at the expense* (1.6.1)

tabellarii, *postal service*
trimestris, *quarterly* (1.8.5)
typographia, -eum, *press* (1.6.1)

unicus, *single*

venalis, *on sale*
venire, *be sold*
vertentis anni, *current* (1.8.6)

GRAMMATICAL INDEX: WORDS

aut, 11.1.2

carn-, 4.3.5
cautum, 8.11.5

cretum, 8.11.5
cui(us), 7.1.6
cultum, 8.11.5
cursum, 8.11.5

duabus, duae, etc., 6.1.2

ea, earundem, eius, eo,
etc., 7.1.5

GRAMMATICAL INDEX: ENDINGS

PORTUGUESE

SPECIMEN

Ao apresentarmos esta 3.ª edição da Antologia da Novíssima Poesia Portuguesa, e em virtude das modificações que nela introduzimos, tornam-se indispensáveis umas breves notas iniciais tendentes a explicar a mecânica interna do nosso trabalho, para que o leitor possa mais ràpidamente orientar-se e mais ùtilmente fazer uso do vasto e complexo material coligido.

Na nova Introdução encontram-se as razões e os modos pelos quais esta 3.ª edição apresenta profundas modificações em relação à 1.ª e à 2.ª edições. Esta Introdução substitui também as antigas Introduções.

In presenting this 3rd edition of the Anthology of Recent Portuguese Poetry, and in virtue of the modifications which we have introduced into it, some brief introductory remarks become indispensable, designed to explain the inner mechanics of our work, so that the reader can find his bearings more quickly and make more profitable use of the vast and complex material that has been assembled.

In the new Introduction will be found the reasons why this 3rd edition presents profound modifications in comparison with the 1st and 2nd, and the way in which these modifications have been carried out. This Introduction also replaces the old ones.

0 GENERAL CHARACTERISTICS

0.1 DEGREE OF INFLEXION
Portuguese is a moderately synthetic language, with a wealth of verb forms, but expressing the relations of nouns by means of prepositions.

0.2 ORDER OF WORDS
Qualifying phrases follow the noun, but the position of adjectives depends on style and function. In a plain style, where adjectives convey additional information, they tend to follow the noun. The standard order SVO can be varied by putting the verb first, and in sentences which have no object this order is not uncommon. (See Specimen: **tornam-se indispensáveis**, etc.)

0.4 RELATION TO OTHER LANGUAGES
On the relation of Portuguese to Latin and the other Romance languages see General note on the Romance languages. The Greco-Latin element in Portuguese vocabulary is very strong.

1 BIBLIOLINGUISTICS

1.1 NAMES
1.1.1 Modern Portuguese names in their full form consist of one or more Christian names (or a compound like **Maria da Graça**) and a compound surname composed of

the mother's surname followed by the father's, the last being the entry word. In theory; and no doubt in practice too with most ordinary people. But their composition is often far more complicated, as one can see from the two brothers **Alexandre José da Silva de Almeida Garrett** and **João Baptista da Silva Leitão de Almeida Garrett**, where the father's surname is **da Silva**, the mother's **Almeida**, and **Garrett** is that of the paternal grandmother. Nevertheless **Almeida Garrett** or **Garrett** is the name by which they are known. Such permutations are always possible where there are illustrious connexions; in fact the Brazilian sociologist Antônio Candido said that the name expressed less the tie of filial relationship than participation in a vast kinship system. (Quoted in Wagley: *An Introduction to Brazil*, p. 189.) Nor, quite apart from compounds of the form **Pires de Castro**, does every collocation of two surnames arise in the same way. For instance, the 14th-century **Alvaro Gonçalves Pereira**, as his name implied, was the son of **Gonçalo Pereira** and **Gonçalves Pereira** is still current as a compound surname. His mother's surname **Pires** was ignored. Again, the last element may be one of the words **Filho, Junior, Net(t)o, Sobrinho**, in which case the preceding word will be the father's, grandfather's or uncle's surname as the case may be. It would be easier if the mother-and-father compounds were always joined by e (*and*), but the presence or absence of e is quite arbitrary, and the same name may be cited in both forms. In any case the mother's surname may be omitted.

Formerly the order of the two surnames was the opposite of what it is now, and in the Middle Ages surnames are sometimes unstable or absent. Thus the son of **Alvaro Gonçalves Pereira** bore the surname, or rather the patronymic, **Alvares**, and many names of the form **João de Barroca** will be found indexed under the Christian name.

For cataloguing rules applicable to these complications one must consult such works as the A.L.A. Rules or A. H. Chaplin's *Names of person: national usage*, etc. (1967).

1.1.2 Christian names are naturally of different genders, but while in **Pedro** and **Maria**, for example, the gender is apparent from the form, in **Inês** (F) and **Andrés** (M) it is not. **Maria** may be part of a man's name.

1.1.3 Both Christian names and surnames can take the plural -s if their form admits of it, e.g. **as três Marias, os Monteiros**; but not in such cases as **João e Pedro Monteiro**. As surnames in de frequently originate in the name of some family property the plural form is here inappropriate and one finds for instance **os de Castro**.

1.2 NAMES OF AUTHORS, EDITORS, ETC.

1.2.1 The names of authors, editors and the like may precede the title or follow it. In the latter case they will usually have a preposition in front of them, but this has no effect on the form of the name. A complication does however occur when such words as **Dr., professor** and so on, which take the article, come between the preposition and the name. The prepositions **a, de** and **por** coalesce with the article (10.2.1), and the phrase, if cited, must be cited as a whole, unless one is prepared to make such changes as **do** to **d[e]** and **pelo** to **p[or]**.

1.2.2 The names of corporate authors present little grammatical difficulty, though their exact relation to the work may not always be easy to specify. The name of a subordinate body may be linked to that of the principal one, but this is not difficult to sort out.

1.3 TITLES

1.3.1 Fiction apart, the titles of books usually consist of nouns and adjectives, linked if necessary by prepositions, e.g. **Licões práticas de português**, *Practical lessons*

F

in Portuguese; **As ondas de frio da Bacia Amazônica,** *Cold waves in the Amazon Basin.* Belles-lettres and the literature of persuasion produce more varied types of construction, e.g. **A terra vai ficando ao longe,** *The land goes on into the distance*; **Como receber alguns benefícios do Ipase,** *How to obtain civil service benefits*; **Os povos exigem: independência nacional,** *The peoples demand: national independence.*

Older titles can be very complicated: **Carta que um amigo de Lisboa escreveu a outro da provincia da Beira, em a qual lhe da circumstanciada noticia do modo comque se fez a transladação do Sanctissimo Sacramento da freguezia de Nossa Senhora da Encarnação para a sua nova igreja,** *Letter which a friend in Lisbon wrote to another in the province of Beira, in which he gives him a circumstantial account of the way in which the most Blessed Sacrament was transferred from the parish of Our Lady of the Incarnation to its new church.*

1.3.2 Title entries should cause no difficulties, unless, under British Museum rules, there are combinations involving proper adjectives (of which Portuguese has many). These will have to be freely translated, e.g. **Cartas Transtaganas** would presumably require the heading **Tagus.**

When filing titles, it is necessary to remember that the indefinite article, which is ignored, has the same form as the numeral *one*, which is not. Similarly the definite article may function as a demonstrative pronoun in the contexts **o de** and **o que.** Thus **O que deve saber um mestre mação,** *What a master mason should know* is filed under **O.**

1.3.3 Titles in the context of a sentence are now usually kept distinct, e.g. one writes **n'os Lusíadas** or **em Os Lusíadas** (less commonly **n-os Lusíadas**) rather than **nos.** A different sort of complication arises from titles like **Do Banco de Lisboa,** *On the Bank of Lisbon.* They are difficult to cite without inserting some word like **tratado** which can then be mistaken for part of the title.

1.4   VOLUMES AND PARTS

1.4.1 The usual words are **volume** or **tomo** and **parte.** There is no difference in meaning between **volume** and **tomo.**

1.4.2 Numeration is by ordinal number which may be in words or figures, e.g. **tomo 1, parte 1; V tomo, primeira parte.**

1.4.3 In older books the numeration may be one with the title, e.g. **Terceira parte da Monarchia Lusitania,** *Third part of A Monarchia,* etc. (cf. 1.3.3).

1.5   EDITIONS

1.5.1/1.5.2 The usual word is **edição** (but cf. 1.6.1) preceded by a number in ordinal form, e.g. **10.ª edição** or by **nova** or some other qualifying word. Revision is indicated by a variety of adjectives, from the plain **revista** to more specific phrases such as **refundida e aumentada** (or **ampliada**), *thoroughly revised and enlarged*; **melhorada,** *improved*; **acrescentada,** *expanded*; **actualizada,** *brought up to date*; **corrigida,** *corrected.* A text may be **segundo** (or **conforme**) **as primeiras edições,** *in accordance with the earliest editions.*

1.5.3 *Offprint* is **separata.**

1.6   IMPRINTS

1.6.1 Most modern imprints will be that of the publisher. Often enough this will be obvious from the name, e.g. **Livraria Académica, Empresa Nacional de Publicidade, Edições Atica,** or the presence of **edição de** meaning *published by*, or **editor(a),** as opposed to words like **tipografia, imprensa** (but see below). In some books publication and distribution are explicitly distinguished.

1.6.2 In earlier books one should note the implications of different words and phrases: **por** (in full **impresso por**) and **oficina** indicate the printer, **a custa de** the publisher, **vendese, acharse ha** the bookseller; **em casa de** is equivocal. But one frequently finds **na oficina de** . . . **e a sua custa** and similar combinations. The printer-publisher continues into the 19th century, and **imprensa** (*press*) occurs in the imprints of academic publishers still.

1.6.3 One may find the terms for *widow* (**viuva**) *heirs* (**heredeiros**), *successors* (**successores**) and *brothers* (**irmãos**) prominent in older imprints.

1.7 SERIES

1.7.1 The titles of series, which are to be found in various places—at the head of the title-page, or on the half title-page, or even on the cover only—are mostly simple, e.g. **Colecção de Clássicos Sá da Costa** (cole(c)ção, the generic word, is common); **Biblioteca de escritores portugueses**; or in the plural, **Textos de cultura portuguesa, Publicações do Centro de Estudos Filológicos** (cf. 1.8.2).

1.7.2 Series are frequently not numbered, or bear a simple number; but **volume** and **número** are found, and **série** for sub-series.

1.8 PERIODICALS

1.8.1 The titles of periodicals do not differ in language from those of books and series: a title like **Cadernos** might be a periodical or a series, though words like **Boletim, Revista, Anais** point clearly enough to a periodical. Fanciful titles such as *O ramalhete, The nosegay*, are somewhat more likely with periodicals than with books. For the effect of prepositions on titles beginning with the article cf. 1.3.3, but note that **no Mundo**, in '*O Mundo*' is possible, but not obligatory.

1.8.2 Institutional periodicals, in which the name of the institution forms part of the title or sub-title, are common, e.g. **Revista do Conselho Nacional de Economia**. The name begins at **Conselho** and extracting it presents no difficulty.

1.8.3 Ways of indicating the persons responsible for editing (**dire(c)ção** or **reda(c)-ção**) vary. Frequently there is a **Conselho de Dire(c)ção** with a **Dire(c)tor Responsável** (or simply **Dire(c)tor** or **Responsável**) at the head, assisted by a **Reda(c)tor-Chefe** and various **Colaboradores** or **Dire(c)tores Associados**. Alternatively the principal executive may be called **Coordenador**.

The publisher, immediate or remote, may be indicated by derivatives of the roots **ed-** and **public-**, e.g. **edição, editado, publicado**, but is sometimes simply named at the foot of the title-page, imprint-wise. Occasionally some other agency, appropriately entitled **distribuidora**, is responsible for the commercial side.

1.8.4 Numeration is principally by **volume** or **ano**, i.e. *annual volume*, but sometimes both occur, e.g. **ano XXIX, vol. 98**, where **ano** simply means *year of publication*. A part is usually **número**, but **tomo** is also found in conjunction with **volume**.

1.8.5 Periodicity may be indicated by the appropriate adjective, usually in the sub-title or the description, e.g. **publicação trimestral**, *quarterly publication*, or by the corresponding adverb, e.g. **publica-se (editada) semestralmente**, *published half-yearly*, or by a phrase such as **sai quatro vêzes por ano**, *comes out four times a year*.

1.8.6 Subscription is usually annual (**assinatura anual**) with provision for single numbers and back numbers (**número avulso, atrasado**) or the price of a single number may be stated as **preço dêste número**, *price of this number*. Different rates are quoted for foreign countries (**para o exterior, para o estrangeiro**) or when the rates for Portugal and Brazil are the same, other countries (**outros países**).

1.8.7   Addresses may distinguish between **Diretores** (*editors*) and **Editora** (*Publishing Agency*) or specify **Reda(c)ção e Administração**, or all branches may have the same address: **Tôda correspondência deve ser dirigida a . . .**, *All correspondence is to be addressed to . . . .*

2   ALPHABET, PHONETICS, SPELLING

2.1.   ALPHABET

2.1.1   The alphabet is the same as in English, except that **k, w** and **y** occur only in words derived from foreign names and in certain abbreviations, e.g. **byroniano, darwinismo, kg. (quilograma), W (oeste)**. Although **i** and **j, u** and **v** have quite distinct sounds, they are not always distinguished in early printing, the use of **V** for both **U** and **V** and of initial **v** and medial **u** for both **u** and **v** persisting until the middle of the 17th century.

2.1.2   An acute or circumflex accent according to the quality of the vowel is used

(a) to distinguish words with the same spelling but different meanings, e.g. **do**, *of the*; **dô**, *pain*; **da**, *of the*; **dá**, *gives*; **este**, *east*; **êste**, *this*. (In this use the acute accent is found only on monosyllables.)

(b) to indicate an abnormal stress. The stress normally falls on the last syllable but one if the word ends in **-a, -am, -as, -au(s), -e, -em, -ens, -es, -o(s)**, otherwise on the last syllable; **-ia(s), -io(s)** follow the rule. Hence **ignorância, público, também, avô** (*grandfather*), **avó** (*grandmother*), **conténs** (verb; plural nouns have no accent even if the last syllable is stressed); **fácil, bênção**; and see 2.1.6. Even the Portuguese sometimes use the wrong accent.

2.1.3   The grave accent is used on unstressed syllables

(a) to indicate a contraction, e.g. **às** for a **as**; **àquele** for a **aquele**; **còrar** (*to colour*);

(b) since 1927, in a derived word, when the original word has an acute accent, e.g. **rápido, ràpidamente** (but **cortês, cortêsmente**);

(c) to indicate that the vowel is open, e.g. **prègar**, *to preach*. As it happens there is also a verb **pregar** without an accent meaning *to nail*.

2.1.4   A cedilla is attached to **c** to give it the sound of **s**; **ç** does not have a separate place in the alphabet.

2.1.5   The til indicates a nasal vowel or diphthong. It is written over the first vowel of a diphthong, e.g. **edição**.

2.1.6   The diaeresis is written over **u** when it is pronounced separately in the combinations **gue, gui, que, qui**, and does not bear the stress, e.g. **argüir** (but **arguo, argúis**). See also 2.5.

2.2   CAPITALISATION

2.2.1   Some writers are more prone to use capitals than others, and they are not so frequently used today as formerly. In principle, proper names are spelt with capitals, but the corresponding adjectives are not, e.g. **Portugal, português; Lisboa, lisboeta; os brasileiros** and so on. The days of the week and the months are not now spelt with capitals.

2.2.2   Personal, geographical and astronomical names, and the names of historical events and religious feasts, of institutions and government departments are spelt with capitals throughout except for articles, prepositions and the generic part of geographical names, e.g. Lancelote do Lago, cabo de Boa Esperança, Natal (*Christmas*), Academia das Ciências.

2.2.3 Book titles are still usually spelt with capitals throughout except for articles and prepositions (including prepositional phrases), but a number of writers have adopted the practice normal in bibliographies of using capitals only where they would be required in any case. Inconsistencies will in fact be found, e.g. **Pequeno Vocabulário Ortográfico, O português em Florença** in the same book. Periodical titles are regularly capitalised throughout, e.g. **Gazeta de Noticias.**

2.2.4 Titles of office and nobility begin with a small letter except in ceremonial contexts, e.g. **o profesor Dr. Magnus Bergström, o duque de Caxias**; but **Senhor Profesor,** and at the beginning of a letter, **Caro Doutor.** Abbreviations such as **Dr., B.^{el} (bacharel), L.^{do} (licenciado)** always have a capital.

2.3 DIVISION OF WORDS

Rules 4, 5a, 6a, 7a, 8 (p. xiii) apply, with the proviso that **l** and **r** are not usually separated from a preceding **b, c, d, f, g, p, t** or **v.** Rule 2 no longer applies, e.g. **cir-cuns-tân-cia,** though it is still customary to separate **ab-** and **sub-** from a following **l** or **r** if the word is an obvious compound, e.g. **ab-legação** as against **a-blução.** The digraphs **ch, lh** and **nh** are not divided.

2.4 PUNCTUATION

2.4.1 The full stop is customary after abbreviations, whether or not they include the end of the word, e.g. **pg. (pago), Rev^o (Reverendo), Sr. (Senhor).**

2.4.2 Many of the uses of the hyphen are as in English, but the following should be noted:

(a) Compounds like **agua-de-colonia, segunda-feira,** where the whole has a different meaning from the parts; and the title **el-rei,** (*the*) *king*;

(b) Names involving the article, such as **Entre-os-Rios,** or **grão,** such as **Grã-Bretanha.**

(c) The phrases **hei-de, ha-de, hão-de** (*I, he, they must*) as opposed to all other forms of this construction.

(d) The suffixing of the object pronoun to the verb, e.g. **vi-o,** *I saw him.*

It may also be used in the same way as the apostrophe (b).

2.4.3 The apostrophe is rare. It is used

(a) In a few compound nouns and names, e.g. **mãe-d'água,** *reservoir*; **Nun'Alvares; Sant'Iago.** But **mão-de-obra** is now spelt without an apostrophe, and in most such expressions the **de** is either given in full or coalesces with the following word.

(b) When **de, em** or **por** is followed by an article beginning with a capital letter, e.g. **d'Os Lusíadas,** *of the Lusiads*, **n'A Noite,** *in A Noite.* (But see also 1.8.1.)

(c) After a capital **A** or **E,** instead of an acute accent, e.g. **A'sia.** The practice may still conceivably be found among old-fashioned printers, but cannot be confused with the normal uses.

2.4.4 Inverted question marks and exclamation marks, after the Spanish fashion (Spanish 2.4), may be encountered, but are not normal.

2.5 VARIATION OF CONSONANT

This is largely a matter of spelling. As in English, **c** and **g** have different values before **a, o, u** and **e, i.** Before the latter group they have the same value as **s** and **j** respectively. To preserve the same consonant sounds the consonants are changed thus:

ca	que	qui	co	cu
ga	gue	gui	go	gu

ça	ce	ci	ço	çu
ja	ge	gi	jo	ju

Hence **rico**, rich; **riquíssimo**, *very rich*; **distinguir**, *to distinguish*; **distingo**, *I distinguish*; **dirigir**, *to direct*; **dirijo**, *I direct*; **começar**, *to begin*; **comecei**, *I began*. (This does not mean that j is not often found before e and i.)

For other changes found in adjectives see 5.3.

2.6 VARIATION OF VOWEL

2.6.1 Some changes take place in the stem vowel of verbs as the stress changes, e.g.

Unstressed	*Stressed*	
-e-	-ei-	verbs in -ear
-i-	-ei-	some verbs in -iar
-e-	-i-	some verbs in -ir
-u-	-o-	before endings containing e, some verbs in -ir

e.g. **passear**, *to walk*; **passeia**, *he walks*; **(negociar) negoceiam**, *they negociate*; **(progredir) progridem**, *they progress*; **(consumir) consome**, *consumes*.

2.6.2 Similar changes take place both in stressed and unstressed syllables before **a** and **o**, viz.

Normal	*Before a and o*
-e-	-i-
-o-	-u-

e.g. **(sentir) sintamos**, *we may feel*; **(dormir) durmo**, *I sleep*.

2.7 SPELLING

2.7.1 Apart from minor changes, the present spelling in Portugal itself goes back to 1916. The changes made at that time, if given in full detail make a formidable list, but the general look of the average page is not so very different. Learned words in the old spelling are nearer to English. (Some Renaissance writers used spellings like **nocte, epses, non, cognescido**, instead of **noite, esses, não, conhecido**; but the surviving complications were much less marked than this.) The principal modern changes are:

(a) Elimination of purely etymological letters, e.g. **escrito** not **escripto**, **salmo** not **psalmo**, **beleza** not **belleza**; and further **pronto** not **prompto**, **aceitar** not **acceptar**. (But c and p are retained in Portugal in many words in which they are not themselves pronounced, e.g. **excepção, acção**, because they affect the quality of the preceding vowel, cf. 2.7.3.)

(b) A more phonetic spelling of words of Greek origin, e.g. **filosofia, teatro, reumatismo, química**.

(c) The replacement of **k, w** and **y** by **c** or **qu**, **v** and **i**.

(d) The omission of silent **h** in the middle of a word, e.g. **sahir** > **sair** (preserved in the Brazilian proper name **Bahia**), **desumano**, and of unetymological **h** at the beginning. (The results are not quite consistent: **ombro** lost its **h**, but **húmido** did not, though the **h**'s in **humerus** and **humidus** are equally traditional and equally incorrect.)

(e) The respelling of the diphthongs **ae, ao, eo, oe, oa** as **ai, au, eu, oi, ua**.

2.7.2 The most notable subsequent change has been the change of sc to c at the beginning of words like **ciência, cena** and so on. But Portuguese orthography still often admits alternative spellings.

2.7.3 The present Brazilian spelling, governed by the Vocabulary of 1943, does not make the exceptions referred to in 2.7.1 (a). The examples given there are spelt **exceção, ação,** the **e** and **a** being pronounced in Brazil like any other unaccented **e** and **a**. There are also variants such as **quatorze** as well as **catorze**. An official attempt in 1945 to reintroduce Portuguese spelling was abortive and was eventually disavowed, but in spite of this statements will still be found in grammars and encyclopaedias which suggest that the spelling of the two countries is identical.

Slight as the differences are, it is as well to be aware of them when selecting and using dictionaries. To take three examples, *A new dictionary of the Portuguese and English languages* by H. Michaelis, 'brought up to date 1945' and 'including official reformed spelling rules as authorised by the Brazilian government' follows the 1931 Brazilian rules, which do not differ from those of Portugal. Taylor's *Portuguese–English dictionary*, published by Harrap in 1959, says nothing more on the title-page, but reveals in the introduction that it follows current Brazilian spelling. It nowhere states the differences explicitly but makes some references from Portuguese forms. *The new Appleton dictionary of the English and Portuguese languages*, 1964, makes no comment and no references and follows Brazilian norms.

3 ARTICLES

3.1 DEFINITE

3.1.1 The forms are the following:

SM	SF	PM	PF
o	a	os	as

All formerly began with **l**, which comes out in the contractions **pelo, pela,** etc. (10.2.1).

3.1.2 The article is frequently used in Portuguese where it is not used in English and occasionally vice versa, e.g. **a humanidade,** *humanity*; **o viajar,** *travelling*; **o Brazil** (but **Portugal**); **o Porto** (i.e. *the Port*); **o Camões; o senhor Fulano de Tal,** *Mr X*; **Alexandre Magno,** *Alexander the Great*.

3.1.3 The same forms are used as pronouns (7.1.1).

3.2 INDEFINITE

3.2.1 The forms are:

SM	SF	PM	PF
um	uma	uns	umas

3.2.2 The plural forms mean *some* or *a pair of*, and in such expressions as **Ela tem uns olhos azuis tão bonitos!** (*She has such lovely blue eyes!*) there is no English equivalent. Conversely we find **correr risco** (*to run a risk*) and many other expressions in which the article is absent in Portuguese.

4 NOUNS

4.1 GENDER AND FORM

Nouns are either masculine or feminine. With a few exceptions those in **-o, -eu, -u** are masculine and those in **-a** feminine, words like **clima** being masculine. With other endings there is less certainty: those in -ã are mostly feminine, those in -ão are likely to be masculine if concrete, e.g. **sermão**, and feminine if abstract, e.g. **edição**, along with other abstracts in **-ade**.

4.2 PLURAL

4.2.1   The plural of simple nouns is formed as follows:

S	P
most vowels	add -s
-ão (M)	-ães, -ãos, -ões
-ão (F)	-ões
-l	-is

(Note **carril/carris**; **têxtil/têxteis** and the like)

-m	-ns
-n, -r, -s, -z	add -es
-x	-ces

Words like **post scriptum** are unchanged.

4.2.2   In compound nouns either the first element only may be affected or the second or both; but it is not wise to follow the light of nature, as the examples show: **caminho(s) de ferro** (noun and qualifying phrase); **lugar-tenente(s)** (noun governed by participle); **grão-mestre(s)** (adjective and noun); **passa-tempo(s)** (verb and noun); **re-dactor(es)-chefe(s)** (equal nouns); **obra(s)-prima(s)** (noun and adjective); **banho(s)-maria(s)** (!). In some cases time has brought a more common-sense view, e.g. **os padre-nossos** not as formerly **os padres-nossos** (*paternosters*).

5   ADJECTIVES

5.1 GENERAL

Adjectives agree in number and gender with the nouns they qualify. As already stated (0.2), they may either precede or follow the noun, but **belo, bom, caro, certo, grande, longo, mau, novo, pobre**, among others, have different shades of meaning in the different positions, e.g. **um certo amigo**, *a certain friend*; **um amigo certo**, *a reliable friend*.

5.2 ENDINGS

5.2.1   The feminine is formed thus:

M	F
-o	-a
-eu	-eia
-u	-ua
-ão	-ã
-dor	-dora
adjectives of nationality	add -a

The remainder do not change; but **bom** makes **boa**.

5.2.2   The plural is formed in the same way as that of nouns, except that adjectives in -z are unchanged.

5.3 COMPARISON

The comparative is regularly expressed by **mais**, the superlative by putting the article before the comparative. Irregular comparatives like **melhor** (*better*) are given in the dictionary. The absolute superlative can be expressed by **mui(to)** (*very*) or some synonym, or by using forms in **-íssimo** and **-imo**. Most adjectives add **-íssimo** to the positive stem, but there are some regular changes of stem exemplified by **são/saníssimo, terrível/terribilíssimo, feliz/felicíssimo, comum/comuníssimo**, and there are some sixty adjectives which have forms, often in **-imo**, going back to the Latin as well as or instead of the regular ones, e.g. **antigo/antiquíssimo, cruel/crudelíssimo, fácil/facílimo, livre/libérrimo, sabio/sapientíssimo, bom/óptimo**.

5.4 POSSESSIVES

Possessive adjectives may take the place of a phrase in English, e.g. **notícias suas,** *news of you.*

6 NUMERALS

6.1 CARDINAL

6.1.1

1 um, uma	11 onze	21 vinte e um	101 cento e um
2 dois, duas	12 doze	22 vinte e dois	200 duzentos, -as
3 três	13 treze	30 trinta	300 trezentos
4 quatro	14 catorze (see 2.7.3)	40 quarenta	400 quatrocentos
5 cinco	15 quinze	50 cincoenta	500 quinhentos
6 seis	16 dezasseis	60 sessenta	600 seiscentos
7 sete	17 dezassete	70 setenta	900 novecentos
8 oito	18 dezoito	80 oitenta	1000 mil
9 nove	19 dezanove	90 noventa	2000 dois mil
10 dez	20 vinte	100 cento, cem	

6.1.2 Only **um** and forms in **-entos** have feminine forms.

6.2 ORDINAL

6.2.1

1 primeiro	12 duodécimo	80 octagésimo
2 segundo	décimo segundo	90 nonagésimo
3 terceiro	13 décimo terceiro	100 centésimo
4 quarto	19 décimo nono	200 ducentésimo
5 quinto	20 vigésimo	300 tricentésimo
6 sexto	21 vigésimo primeiro	400 quadringentésimo
7 sétimo	30 trigésimo	500 quingentésimo
8 oitavo	40 quadragésimo	600 sexcentésimo
9 nono	50 quinquagésimo	700 septingentésimo
10 décimo	60 sexagésimo	800 octingentésimo
11 undécimo	70 septuagésimo	900 non(in)gentésimo
décimo primeiro		1000 milésimo

6.2.2 All ordinals have feminine forms in **-a**.

6.2.3 Cardinals are substituted in the enumeration of sovereigns and centuries beyond 10.

6.3 FIGURES

Cardinals are represented by simple arabic figures, ordinals by arabic figures with a superscript o or a, e.g. **10.ª edição**. Roman figures may represent either (cf. 6.2.3).

6.4 DATES

6.4.1 The months are:

janeiro, fevereiro, março, abril, maio, junho,
julho, agôsto, setembro, outubro, novembro, dezembro

6.4.2 Dates, with the exception of the first of the month, are expressed by cardinals, e.g.

(On) 23.5.1969	**(Em) vinte e três de maio de mil novecentos e sessenta e nove**
1 May	**O primeiro de maio**
In the nineties	**nos anos noventa**

Centuries are read as cardinals when the numeral follows (up to the 10th they are in any case spelt out), e.g. **século XX (vinte)**.

7 PRONOUNS

7.1 DEMONSTRATIVE

7.1.1 There is nothing much to notice about these, many of which can be indifferently pronoun or adjective.

The forms in **-o**: **isto, isso, aquilo**, do not refer to a specific thing, but to a whole situation, e.g. **Que é isto?**, *What is that?*

7.1.2 **Êste**, *this*, and **êsse**, *that*, are often used in correspondence with reference to the writer and the recipient respectively, so that they are almost equivalent to *my (our)* and *your*.

7.1.3 The forms of the definite article (3.1.1) have the force of a pronoun when followed by **de** and **que** (cf. 1.3.3).

7.2 RELATIVE AND INTERROGATIVE

7.2.1 These mostly have the same form. As an interrogative **quem** refers to persons and **que** to things, but as relatives **que** may mean *who* or *which*, while **quem** means *the one who*.

7.2.2 **Cujo**, *whose* (?), *of what* (?), *of which* (?), is an adjective agreeing with the following noun, e.g. **o livro, cuja segunda edição . . .**, *the book whose second edition . . . .*

Onde and **donde** are adverbs but can be used in the senses *in which* and *from which*.

7.3 PERSONAL

7.3.1

			Subject	*Object*	*Disjunctive*
		1	eu	me	mim
		2	tu / see 7.3.2	te / as 3*m*, 3*f*	ti
	S				
		3*m*	êle	o (lo, no); lhe	êle
		3*f*	ela	a (la, na); lhe	ela
S & P		3*r*	—	se	si
		1	nós	nos	nós
		2	vós / see 7.3.2	vos / as 3*m*, 3*f*	vós
	P				
		3*m*	êles	os (los, nos); lhes	êles
		3*f*	elas	as (las, nas); lhes	elas

7.3.2 The pronouns of the second person are commonly replaced by polite peri-phrases such as **Vossa(s) Excelência(s)**, **Vossa(s) Senhoria(s)**, **Vossa(s) Mercê(s)** (shortened **Você(s)**, etc.), **o senhor**, **a senhora**. All these as common nouns take the third person and the corresponding object pronouns and possessives are naturally of the third person also: **avisá-los-ei**, for instance, is as likely to mean *I will inform you* as *I will inform them.*

lo and **no**, etc. are substituted for **o**, etc. as follows:

> **lo**: after **-r**, **-s**, **-z**, which are omitted, e.g. **publicá-los**, *to publish them*, not **publicar-os**
>
> **no**: after **-ão** and **-m**, e.g. **não no sei**, *I do not know* (*it*)

lhe and **lhes** denote the indirect object, the rest either; but **detalhar-lhe a organização** means *to describe its organisation in detail*. On **se** see 8.14.

7.3.3 **Me**, **te**, **lhe(s)** combine with **o(s)**, **a(s)** to form **mo(s)**, **ma(s)**, **to(s)**, **ta(s)**, **lho(s)**, **lha(s)**, e.g. **vender-lhos**, *to sell them to him* (*to her*, *them*, *you*).

7.3.4 Object pronouns sometimes precede the verb, and are sometimes suffixed by means of a hyphen; with the future and the conditional (8.5) they may be sandwiched. (See 7.3.2 for examples.) When one verb depends on another the pronoun may be dis-placed, e.g. **pode-se fazer**, *it can be done*.

8 VERBS

8.1 STRUCTURE

8.1.1 There are different forms for the different persons, making the use of subject pronouns unnecessary except for emphasis, and for the different moods and tenses. Some simple tenses correspond to compound ones in English.

8.1.2 Most verbs have the same stem throughout, but in some the present stem is modified, and in some of the commonest the past stem differs from that of the present and the infinitive. These are listed in 8.19.

8.2 PRESENT
8.2.1 *Endings*

I	-o, -as, -a; -amos, -ais, -am	inf. -ar
II	-o, -es, -e; -emos, -eis, -em	inf. -er
III	-o, -es, -e; -io, -is, -i; -imos, -is, -em	inf. -ir

8.2.2 Consonant variation (2.5) affects the first person singular of classes II and III, and a number of verbs have softened stems, e.g. **ouço (ouvrir)**, **pairo (parir)**, **peço (pedir)**, **valho (valer)**.

8.2.3 Vowel variation (2.6) occurs in verbs of all classes.

8.2.4 The present has sometimes to be translated by an English perfect.

8.3 IMPERFECT
8.3.1 *Endings*

I	-ava, -avas, -ava; -ávamos, -áveis, -avam	inf. -ar
II	-ia, -ias, -ia; -íamos, -íeis, -iam	inf. -er, -ir

8.3.2 The imperfect has sometimes to be translated by an English pluperfect.

8.4 PRETERITE AND PLUPERFECT

8.4.1 The preterite has these endings:

I	-ei, -aste, -ou; -ámos, -astes, -aram	inf. -ar
II	-i, -este, -eu; -e, -este, -e; -emos, -estes, -eram	inf. -er
III	-i, -iste, -iu; -imos, -istes, -iram	inf. -ir
	See also 8.19	

8.4.2 The pluperfect has these endings:

I	-ar⎫
II	-er⎬ a, -as, -a; -amos, -eis, -am
III	-ir⎭

It has the same stem as the preterite.

8.4.3 The preterite answers usually to the English simple past, occasionally to the perfect or pluperfect. The pluperfect is sometimes used in place of the conditional.

8.5/8.6 FUTURE AND CONDITIONAL

8.5.1 *Future*

I	-ar⎫
II	-er⎬ ei, -ás, -á; -emos, -eis, -ão
III	-ir⎭

8.5.2 *Conditional*

I	-ar⎫
II	-er⎬ ia, -ias, -ia; -íamos, -íeis, -iam
III	-ir⎭

8.5.3 These tenses are formed from the infinitive and the present and past of **haver**. Pronoun objects (7.3) may be inserted between the infinitive and the ending, e.g. **publicar-se-á** (formerly written **publicar-se-há**), *it will be published*.

8.5.4 Both the future and the conditional may be used to express what is possible or conjectural, e.g. **teria oito anos**, *he must have been eight years old*.

8.7 SUBJUNCTIVE

8.7.1 *Present*

I	-o, -es, -e; -emos, -eis, -em	inf. -ar
II	-a, -as, -a; -amos, -ais, -am	inf. -er, -ir

Changes of vowel, consonant or stem as in the indicative (8.1.2–3).

8.7.2 *Imperfect*

I	-ass⎫	inf. -ar
II	-ess⎬ e, -es, -e; -emos, -eis, -em	inf. -er
III	-iss⎭	inf. -ir

8.7.3 *Future*

I	-ar⎤		inf. -ar
II	-er⎥	-, -es, -; -mos, -des, -em	inf. -er
III	-ir⎦		inf. -ir

8.7.4 The imperfect and future subjunctive are both based on the past stem, in irregular as well as regular verbs, e.g. **fizeste, fizesse, fizer** from **fazer**.

8.7.5 The subjunctive is used to express wishes and commands and is also obligatory in certain dependent clauses. In others it may alternate with the indicative, expressing uncertainty, supposition or generality as against the factual statement of the indicative, e.g. **não imaginem**, *do not imagine*; **o que me der** (8.7.3), *whatever you give me*; **não quere dizer que se não viaje**, *it does not mean that nobody travels*. It is also used in unfulfilled conditions, e.g. **o pai as repartisse como quisesse**, *his father would divide them as he pleased*. The English equivalent varies.

8.7.6 The future subjunctive may cause difficulty in that in most verbs its forms are identical with the infinitive, plain or personal (8.11); but it is only found in subordinate clauses, whereas the infinitive normally follows another verb or a preposition, e.g. **a obra impressionará quem a contemplar**, *the work will impress whoever beholds it* (future subjunctive, **a** object pronoun), but **continuava a contemplar a obra**, *he continued to behold the work* (infinitive, **a** preposition).

8.10 COMPOUND TENSES

8.10.1 *Perfect indicative and subjunctive*

Formed with the present indicative and subjunctive of **ter** (8.17.4), rarely **haver** (8.17.5), with the past participle (8.12.2), e.g. **tinha baixado os olhos**, *I had lowered my eyes*, **acabado que tinha**, *after he had finished*. The participle is invariable; but if **deixar** (*to leave*), **levar** (*to get*), **trazer** (*to bring*) are substituted for **ter**, the participle agrees with the object.

8.10.2 *Pluperfect, future perfect, conditional perfect*

Formed with the imperfect, future and conditional instead of the present.

8.11 INFINITIVE

8.11.1

> *Impersonal:* I -ar   II -er   III -ir
> *Personal:* as above with the addition of the following endings: -, -es, -; -mos, -des, -em

In all regular verbs the forms are the same as those of the future subjunctive (8.7.3) but the use is quite different.

8.11.2 Both types of infinitive are freely used as nouns, as subject or object and after prepositions and other verbs, e.g. **o escrever cansa**, *writing is wearisome*; **o prepararmos um volume**, *the fact that we are preparing a volume*; **se foi embora sempre a chorar**, *he went away, still crying*; **água a ferver**, *boiling water*; **ao formarmos a frase relacionamos** ..., *in forming the phrase, we relate* ..., **pode deixar de vir precedida de** ..., *it may cease to be preceded by* ...; **Não nos deixeis cair em tentação**, *Suffer us not to fall into temptation*; **creio ser verdade**, *I believe it is true*.

8.11.3 The special function of the personal infinitive is to make its subject clear. As the examples show, it is not necessary that the subject should be different from that of the main verb, nor does a difference of subject make its use obligatory.

8.12 PARTICIPLES

8.12.1 *Present participle active*

I -ante inf. -ar   II -ente inf. -er   III -inte (rare) inf. -ir

Used as an adjective or more often as a noun. Most examples are entered separately in the dictionary, e.g. **seguinte**, *following*, but some must be deduced, e.g. **partícula apassivante**, *passive-forming particle*, from **apassivar**, *to make passive*.

8.12.2 *Past participle*

I -ado inf. -ar   II -ido inf. -ir, -er

A few verbs, otherwise regular, have irregular past participles, e.g. **aberto** from **abrir**, and others have two participles, one regular, used to form the perfect tense, the other, much closer to the Latin original, used as an adjective, e.g. **concluido** and **concluso** from **concluir**. All these irregular forms are given separately in the larger dictionaries such as Taylor.

Apart from its use to form compound tenses (8.10) and the passive (8.15), and as an adjective, the past participle is used more freely than in English in such constructions as **passados momentos**, *after some moments had passed*; **(depois de) concluidos os estudos**, *after his studies had been completed*.

8.13 PRESENT GERUND

I -ando inf. -ar   II -endo inf. -er   III -indo inf. -ir

Invariable, used adverbially like the English participle, e.g. **passava um bando de andorinhas, chilreando**, *there passed a flight of swallows, twittering*, and with **estar** and other verbs to express continuous action, e.g. **estava (ia, vinha) pensando**, *I was thinking*; **continuava sorrindo**, *he went on smiling*.

8.14 REFLEXIVE

8.14.1   These are made by adding the personal pronoun of the same person to the verb, as in the examples below.

8.14.2   The uses of the reflexive are varied, viz.

simple reflexive: **nos ocupamos com**, *we busy ourselves with*
reciprocal: **êles se feriram**, *they struck each other*
intransitive: **mover-se**, *to move (oneself)*
passive: **os vocábulos se dividem em . . .**, *words are divided into . . .*
passive or impersonal: **diz-se**, *is said* or *one says*
impersonal (not passive): **abre-se o mapa . . . e parte-se**, *one opens out the map . . . and off one goes*; **uma mulher a quem se ama**, *a woman whom one loves*; **se era amado**, *one was loved*

Note that in the impersonal use the verb may be intransitive or already passive or have an object.

8.15 PASSIVE

When the reflexive (8.14) is not substituted, which it often is, the passive is expressed by means of a number of verbs followed by a past participle agreeing with the subject. The verbs are principally **ser** (*to be*), expressing action, and **estar** (*to be*), expressing state, but one or other of the verbs **achar-se** (*to find oneself*), **andar** (*to go*), **ficar** (*to become*), **ir** (*to go*), **jazer** (*to lie*), **ver-se** (*to be seen*), **vir** (*to come*) may be substituted as appropriate, e.g. as grandes novidades serão guardadas para a estação, *the great novelties will be kept for the season*; a casa está construída, *the house is finished*; ficou aterrado, *he was terrified.*

8.17 AUXILIARIES

8.17.1 *Forms of* ser
Present indicative: sou, és, é; somos, sois, são
Imperfect: era, etc.
Past: fui, foste, foi; fomos, fostes, foram
Present subjunctive: seja, etc.
Future subjunctive: for, etc.

8.17.2 *Forms of* estar
Present indicative: estou, estás, etc.
Past: estive, estiveste, esteve; estivemos, etc. (cf. 8.7.4)
Present subjunctive: esteja, etc.

8.17.3 Both verbs mean *to be*, but roughly speaking ser denotes permanent, essential qualities, estar temporary qualities and states. Note also estava a dormir or dormindo, *he was sleeping*; está para, *it is about to*, and cf. 8.15.

8.17.4 *Forms of* ter
Present indicative: tenho, tens, tem; temos, tendes, teem/têm
Imperfect: tinha, etc.
Past: tive, tiveste, teve; tivemos, etc. (cf. 8.7.4)
Present subjunctive: tenha, etc.

8.17.5 *Forms of* haver
Present indicative: hei, hás, há; havemos, haveis, hão
Past: houve, etc. (cf. 8.7.4)
Present subjunctive: haja, etc.

8.17.6 The normal word for *have* in all its uses is ter. Though haver can be used to form compound tenses, it rarely is nowadays, being common only in the phrase haver de and in certain impersonal uses, e.g. hei-de escrever, *I must/intend to write*; não ha tempo, *there is no time*; há quem, *some people*; há-os metafísicos, *there are some which are metaphysical*; há pouco, *a little while ago.*

8.19 FURTHER IRREGULARITIES

8.19.1 caber, *to be contained, to hold*
Present indicative: caibo, cabes, etc.
Past*: coube, etc.
Present subjunctive: caiba, etc.

8.19.2 dar, *to give*
Present indicative: dou, dás, etc.
Past*: dei, deste, deu; demos, etc.
Present subjunctive: dê, dês, dê; dêmos, etc.
Future subjunctive: der, etc.

8.19.3 dizer, *to say*
Present indicative: digo, dizes, diz; dizemos, etc.
Past*: disse, etc.
Future†: direi, etc.

* cf. 8.7.4
† cf. 8.5

8.19.4 fazer, *to do, make*
  Present indicative: **faço, fazes, faz; fazemos,** etc.
  Past*: **fiz, fizeste, fêz; fizemos,** etc.
  Future†: **farei,** etc.
  Present subjunctive: **faça,** etc.
  Past participle: **feito**

8.19.5 ir, *to go*
  Present indicative: **vou, vais, vai; vamos, ides, vão**
  Past*: **fui,** etc. (see 8.17.1)
  Present subjunctive: **vá, vás, vá; vamos, vades, vão**

8.19.6 poder, *to be able*
  Present indicative: **posso, podes,** etc.
  Past*: **pude, pudeste, pôde; pudemos,** etc.
  Present subjunctive: **possa,** etc.

8.19.7 pôr, *to put*
  Present indicative: **ponho, pões, põe; pomos, pondes, põe(m)**
  Imperfect: **punha,** etc.
  Past*: **pus, puseste, pôs; pusemos,** etc.
  o may be substituted for **u** in all except 1PS, and **z** for **s** throughout
  Present subjunctive: **ponha,** etc.

8.19.8 prazer, *to please*
  Present indicative: **praz**
  Past: **prouve**
  used only in 3PS

8.19.9 querer, *to wish*
  Past*: **quis, quiseste, quis; quisemos,** etc.
  Present subjunctive: **queira,** etc.

8.19.10 saber, *to know*
  Present indicative: **sei, sabes,** etc.
  Past*: **soube,** etc.
  Present subjunctive: **saiba,** etc.

8.19.11 trazer, *to bring*
  Present indicative: **trago, trazes,** etc.
  Past*: **troux,** etc.
  Future†: **trarei,** etc.
  Present subjunctive: **traga,** etc.

8.19.12 ver, *to see*
  Present indicative: **vejo, vês, vê; vemos, vedes, vêem**
  Past*: **vi, viste, viu; vimos,** etc.
  Present subjunctive: **veja,** etc.

8.19.13 vir, *to come*
  Present indicative: **venho, vens, vem; vimos, vindes, veem/vêm**
  Imperfect: **vinha,** etc.
  Past: **vim, vieste, veio; viemos,** etc.
  Present subjunctive: **venha,** etc.

* cf. 8.7.4
† cf. 8.5

9 ADVERBS

9.1 FORMATION

A large number of adverbs are formed regularly by the addition of **-mente** to the feminine form of the adjective. If two or more adverbs follow each other only the last has the termination, e.g. **política e econòmicamente**.

9.2 COMPARISON

The same as for adjectives.

10 PREPOSITIONS

10.2 FORMS

Some prepositions contract with the article and certain pronouns.

    10.2.1 With the definite article:

	o	a	os	as
a	ao	à	aos	às
de	do	da	dos	das
em	no	na	nos	nas
por	pelo	pela	pelos	pelas

    10.2.2 With the indefinite article and pronouns:

a + aquele > àquele	em + um > num
de + um > dum	em + êle > nêle
de + êle > dêle	em + isto > nisto
de + isto > disto	em + aquilo > naquilo
	and so on

10.4 COMPOUND PREPOSITIONS

There are a number of compound prepositions, e.g. **além de**, *beyond*; **de sôbre**, *from on*.

10.5 USES

    10.5.1 The uses of prepositions are too varied to admit of summary treatment, and stock equivalents are deceptive. The following points may be noted.

    10.5.2 A is sometimes used before the direct object, especially (though not necessarily) if it is personal, e.g. **a quem se ama**, *whom one loves*; **vence o inverno ao verão**, *winter overcomes summer*. For **a** with the infinitive see 8.11.2.

    10.5.3 De and do que are used after the comparative meaning *than*.

    10.5.4 A, de, para, and por often do not require translating before the infinitive.

11 CONJUNCTIONS

For the most part conjunctions are grammatically straightforward, even if the multiplicity of them and the fact that many of them are phrases, not single words, may make them hard to find and remember. It is worth bearing in mind that prepositions come before the conjunction **que** in sentences of the following type: **admiro de que êle ignore**, *I am surprised at his not knowing/that he does not know*.

GLOSSARY

à venda, *for sale*
abatimento, *discount*
acrescentado, *expanded* (1.5.2)
actas, *proceedings*
actualizado, *brought up to date* (1.5.2)
adicionamento, *addition*
ampliado, *enlarged* (1.5.2)
anais, *yearbook* (*annals*)
anexo, *supplement*
ano, *year; volume* (1.8.4)
anuário, *yearbook*
apenso, *added*
assinatura, *subscription* (1.8.7)
associado, *member*
aumentado, *enlarged* (1.5.2)
avulso, *single* (1.8.7)

biblioteca, *library*
bibliotecário, *librarian*
brochura, *pamphlet, paperback*

câmbio, *exchange*
carta, *letter*
colaboradores, *editorial board* (1.8.3)
cole(c)ção, *series* (1.7.1)
coletânea, *collection*
coligido, *collected*
comissão, comitê, *committee*
conferência, *conference*
conselho de dire(c)ção, *editorial board* (1.8.3)
conta, *bill*
conto, *short story*
coordenador, *editor* (1.8.3)
correção, *correction*
corrigido, *corrected* (1.5.2)

desconto, *discount*
dire(c)ção, *editing* (1.8.3)
dire(c)tor responsável, *editor* (1.8.3)
dire(c)tores associados, *editorial board* (1.8.3)
direitos autorais, *copyright*

edição, *edition, publication* (1.5.1, 1.6.1)
editado, *edited, published* (1.8.6)
editor, *publishing house* (1.6.1)

editôra, *publishing house* (1.6.1)
emenda, *correction*
encadernação, *binding*
endereço, *address*
ensaio, *essay*
escolhido, *selected*
esgotado, *out of print*
estrangeiro, *abroad* (1.8.7)
exemplar, *copy*
expedição, *dispatch*

fascículo, *pamphlet, part*
fatura, *bill*
folheto, *pamphlet*
franco, *free*

imprensa, *press* (1.6.1)
impresso, *pamphlet, printed* (1.6.1)

livraria, *bookshop*
livreiro, *bookseller*
livro, *book*
livro brochura, *paperback*

melhorado, *improved* (1.5.2)
mensal, *monthly*
mesmo, *same*
morreu, *died*

nasceu, *was born*
no prelo, *in press*
nota, *note*
nota preambular, *preface*
notas iniciais, *preface*
novela, *short story*
novo, *new*
número atrasado, *back number* (1.8.7)

obra, *work*
oficina, (printer's) *shop*

página, *page*
peça, *play*
pesquisa, *research*
preâmbulo, *introduction*
preço, *price* (1.8.7)
prefação, prefacio, *preface, introduction*

prestes a aparecer, *forthcoming*
prólogo, *preface*
publicado, *published* (1.8.6)
publica-se, *is published* (1.8.7)

quadro, *table*
quinzenal(mente), *fortnightly*

reda(c)ção, *editing* (1.8.3)
reda(c)tor (-chefe), *editor* (1.8.3)
refundido, *revised* (1.5.2)
regist(r)o, *index*
resumo, *summary*
retrato, *portrait*
revisado, *revised*
revista, *review*

revisto, *revised* (1.5.2)
romance, *novel*

sai, *comes out* (1.8.5)
semana, *week*
semestral(mente), *half-yearly* (1.8.5)
separata, *offprint* (1.5.3), *reprint*
série, (*sub-*)*series* (1.7.2)
sob condição (de devolver), *on approval*
sociedade, *society*
socio, *member*

tabela, *index, table*
tábua, *table*
tipografia, *press* (1.6.1)
tradução, *translation*
trimestral(mente), *quarterly* (1.8.5)

GRAMMATICAL INDEX: WORDS

houve (-mos, -ram, -ste(s)),
 8.17.5

ides, 8.19.5
ir, 8.13, 8.15

jazer, 8.15

(-)la(s), 7.3.1, 7.3.2,
 7.3.4, 8.5.3
levar, 8.10.1
(-)lha(s), 7.3.3, 8.5.3
(-)lhe(s), 7.3.1, 7.3.2,
 7.3.4, 8.5.3
(-)lho(s), 7.3.3, 8.5.3
(-)lo(s), 7.3.1, 7.3.2,
 7.3.4, 8.5.3

(-)ma(s), 7.3.3, 8.5.3
mais, 5.3
(-)me, 7.3.1, 7.3.4, 8.5.3
(-)mo(s), 7.3.3, 8.5.3
mui(to), 5.3

(-)na(s), 7.3.1, 7.3.2,
 7.3.4, 8.5.3, 10.2.1
naquilo, 10.2.2
nêle, 10.2.2
nisto, 10.2.2
(-)no(s), 7.3.1, 7.3.2, 7.3.4,
 8.5.3, 10.2.1
num, 10.2.2

(-)o(s), 3.1.1, 7.3.1, 7.3.4,
 8.5.3
onde, 7.2.2
ouço, 8.1.2

pairo, 8.1.2
peço, 8.1.2
pela(s), 10.2.1
pelo(s), 10.2.1
pôde, 8.19.6
põe (-m, -s), 8.19.7
pomos, 8.19.7
pondes, 8.19.7
ponha (-is, -m(os), -s),
 8.19.7
ponho, 8.19.7
por, 1.2.1, 1.6.2, 2.4.3,
 10.5.4

pôs, 8.19.7
pose-/poze-mos, -ram,
 -ste(s), 8.19.7
possa (-is, -m(os), -s),
 8.19.6
posso, 8.19.6
praz, 8.19.8
prouve, 8.19.8
pude (-mos, -ram, -ste(s)),
 8.19.6
punha (-m(os), -s), 8.19.7
punheis, 8.19.7
pus, 8.19.7
puse-/puze-mos, -ram,
 -ste(s), 8.19.7

que, 1.3.2, 7.1.3, 11
queira (-is, -m(os), -s),
 8.19.9
quis (-emos, -eram,
 -este(s)), 8.19.9

riquíssimo, 2.5

saiba (-is, -m(os), -s),
 8.19.10
são, 8.17.1
(-)se, 8.14, 8.5.3
sei, 8.19.10
seja (-is, -m(os), -s), 8.17.1
ser, 8.15, 8.17.3
so-is, -mos, -u, 8.17.1
soube (-mos, -ram, -ste(s)),
 8.19.10

(-)ta(s), 7.3.3, 8.5.3
(-)te, 7.3.1, 7.3.4, 8.5.3
teem, 8.17.4
têm, 8.17.4
tem(os), 8.17.4
tendes, 8.17.4
tenha (-is, -m(os), -s),
 8.17.4
tenho, 8.17.4
tens, 8.17.4
ter, 8.10.1, 8.17.6
teve, 8.17.4
têxteis, 4.2.1
tinha (-m(os), -s), 8.17.4
tinheis, 8.17.4

tive (-mos, -ram, -ste(s)),
 8.17.4
(-)to(s), 7.3.3, 8.5.3
traga (-is, -m(os), -s),
 8.19.11
trago, 8.19.11
trar-á(s), -ão, -ei, -emos,
 -eis, 8.19.11
trazer, 8.10.1
trouxe (-mos, -ram,
 -ste(s)), 8.19.11

um, 3.2.1
uma, 3.2.1
umas, 3.2.1
uns, 3.2.1

vá, 8.19.5
va-des, -i(s), -mos,
 8.19.5
valho, 8.1.2
vão, 8.19.5
vás, 8.19.5
ve-des, -jo, -mos, 8.19.12
veem, 8.19.12, 8.19.13
vêem, 8.19.12
veio, 8.19.13
veja (-is, -m(os), -s),
 8.19.12
vem, 8.19.13
vêm, 8.19.13
venha (-is, -m(os), -s),
 8.19.13
venho, 8.19.13
vens, 8.19.13
ver-se, 8.15
vês, 8.19.12
vi (-mos, -ram, ste-(s), u),
 8.19.12
vie-mos, -ram, -ste(s),
 8.19.13
vim, 8.19.13
vimos, 8.19.13
vindes, 8.19.13
vinha (-m(os), -s),
 8.19.13
vinheis, 8.19.13
vir, 8.13, 8.15
(-)vos, 7.3.1, 7.3.4, 8.5.3
vou, 8.19.5

GRAMMATICAL INDEX: ENDINGS

SPANISH

SPECIMEN

Esta nueva serie de "La Historia de España en sus Documentos" aproxima la obra a nuestra personalidad de hoy. Quien cuente con más de cincuenta años recordará fácilmente los episodios aquí contenidos; los otros los considerarán igualmente familiares por haberlos oído comentar en la primera de las escuelas a que un niño se asoma: el propio hogar. Los nombres son conocidos, las fechas fáciles de recordar. Siendo ya total, íntegramente, historia de España, sucedió sólo ayer.

This new series of 'The history of Spain in its documents' brings the work close to us as men of today. Anyone who is more than fifty will easily recall the episodes contained herein; the others will find them equally familiar from having heard them discussed at the first school which a child attends: his own home. The names are known, the events easy to recall. It is totally and inalienably Spanish history, but it happened only yesterday.

0 GENERAL CHARACTERISTICS

0.1 DEGREE OF INFLEXION

Spanish is a moderately synthetic language, distinguishing the various persons and tenses by different forms, thus dispensing for the most part with subject pronouns. The relations of the noun, however, are indicated by prepositions.

0.2 ORDER OF WORDS

The position of adjectives depends largely on style and function, and they are as likely to precede the noun as to follow it, but qualifying phrases follow. The order SVO is normal but is often varied by putting the verb first, and adverbial phrases are variously placed, e.g. **De los artículos firmados responden sus respectivos autores,** *Their respective authors are responsible for signed articles.*

0.4 RELATION TO OTHER LANGUAGES

On the relation of Spanish to Latin and the other Romance languages see General note on the Romance languages.

1 BIBLIOLINGUISTICS

1.1 NAMES

1.1.1 Modern Spanish names in their full form consist of a Christian name and a compound surname, the first element of which is the father's surname and the second the mother's or some such word as **Hijo** (*son*). The two surnames may or may not be joined by y (*and*), and the second can be omitted or abbreviated: e.g. **R. Menéndez Pidal, Juan de Ávila y Zúñiga, Juan Valera (y Alcalá Galiano), Guillermo Guerra J.,**

Carlos Malpica S(ilva) S(antisteban). Either element may involve a preposition and there are other forms of compound surname, notably those of married women and also double compounds. The implications for cataloguing cannot be dealt with here but must be studied in such publications as the Anglo-American code, or in A. H. Chaplin's *Names of persons: national usages*, etc. (1967).

1.1.2 The forms of some medieval names are ambiguous: in **Gonzalo de Berceo** for instance **Berceo** is a place name, indicating his provenance, and the rules prescribe entry under **Gonzalo**; but it looks no different from a surname, and some reference books enter under **Berceo**.

1.1.3 Modern surnames are ambiguous in a different way. Since compound surnames are not obligatory and two Christian names are not uncommon, three names without **y** may be two plus one as well as one plus two. Unless one has some experience of Spanish names, **Juan Gonzalo Vidal** (2/1) is not readily distinguishable from **Juan González Vidal** (1/2), so it is as well to check. The Christian names which can also be surnames, e.g. **Alonso**, are very few.

1.1.4 Christian names are naturally of different genders, but the gender is not always obvious from their form. Not only are many neutral in form (4.1), e.g. **Andrés** (M), **Inés** (F), but the numerous synonyms of **María** are nearly all common nouns, which may be obviously masculine like **Amparo** and **Rosario** or plural like **Dolores** and **Mercedes**. Conversely **María** and its synonyms, some of which do happen to be feminine abstract nouns, can be borne by men, e.g. **José Asunción Silva**.

1.1.5 Most Spanish surnames can have plural forms (4.2), e.g. **la casa de los Mendozas**, *the Mendozas' house*, but there is a tendency nowadays to rely entirely on the plural article, e.g. **los Quintero**.

1.1.6 The Christian names of foreign authors are usually hispanised, e.g. **Emilio Zola**, **Ricardo Pattee** (a Canadian).

1.2 NAMES OF AUTHORS, EDITORS, ETC.

1.2.1 Whether names occur in isolation at the head of the title page or follow the title, in which case they may be preceded by a preposition, they are grammatically unaffected. The only complication arises from nouns denoting status, which require the article. As the prepositions **de** (*of*) and **a** (*to*) combine with the article **el**, shortening of titles has to be done with caution: one cannot simply omit the descriptive noun without violating the grammar, e.g. **edición del padre Angel Custodio Vega**.

1.2.2 The names of corporate authors present little grammatical problem, though their relation to the work may not be so easy to decide. The name of the subordinate body may be linked with that of the principle body, e.g. **Gabinete de Documentación y Publicaciones de la Secretaría General Técnica del Ministerio de Justicia**, but it is a simple matter to separate them: **Ministerio de Justicia. Secretaría General Técnica. Gabinete de Documentación y Publicaciones**. But not every **de** indicates subordination: **de Justicia** defines **Ministerio**.

1.3 TITLES

1.3.1 The great majority of titles consist of nouns, adjectives and prepositions, e.g. **Apuntaciones críticas sobre el lenguaje bogotano**, *Critical notes on the language of Bogotá*; **Orígenes del español**, *Origins of Spanish*. There is little to cause difficulty, even the contraction of preposition and article (**del** for **de el**) being pretty transparent.

Imaginative and persuasive literature has a more varied grammar, e.g. **La dictadura me honró encarcelandome**, *Dictatorship honoured me by putting me in prison*; **El mundo** es ansí, *The world is like that*; and older titles may be more complicated, containing subordinate clauses. The following is an extreme example, **Real cedula de S.M. y Señores de su Real, y Supremo Consejo, por la qual se manda cumplir, y observar la ley, y auto acordado, que comprehende otra Real Cedula que va inserta, y traten de lo que se ha de observar por los prelados en quanto a dar licencia para la impresia de papeles,** etc. In such cases care must be taken when transcribing the title not to mutilate the sense.

1.3.2   Title entries pose no problems, except in so far as under British Museum rules combinations involving proper adjectives need to be translated, or proper names extracted therefrom.

Certain ambiguities can arise in connexion with filing. The indefinite article (3.2), which is ignored, is similar to or identical with the numeral *one* (6.1.1), while the forms of the definite article (3.1) can also be demonstrative or personal pronouns (7.1.1, 7.3.1). In that case they would be followed by a verb or the words **que** or **de**. Such titles are naturally not common, but when they do occur as in **Los que triunfan** and **La de Bringas,** they are filed under L.

1.3.4   References to titles should be treated with some caution. Although titles beginning **Discurso sobre . . . , Memorial sobre . . . , Tratado de . . . ,** etc. are very much commoner than those which begin simply **Sobre . . . ,** the latter would almost certainly attract some prop like **discurso** when cited. One must therefore check that it is actually part of the title.

1.4   VOLUMES AND PARTS

1.4.1   The usual words are **volumen** or **tomo** and **parte. Volumen** and **tomo** are synonyms, so that **tomo primero** may be described in the preface as **este volumen.**

1.4.2   Numeration is by a following ordinal, in words, as above, or figures, e.g. I,1,1°. It is also possible to use **libro** (*book*) but this a logical rather than a physical division. **Parte** can stand by itself.

1.4.3   In older books the numeration may precede the title, e.g. **Segunda parte de la Vniversal redencion**; or come between the title of the particular volume and that of the whole work, e.g. **Rimas Sacras: tomo tercero de las obras poeticas de,** etc.

1.5   EDITIONS

1.5.1   The usual word is **edición,** but in the example in 1.2.1 **edición de** means *edited by,* in other contexts *published by* (see also 1.6). **Impresión** is also found, coupled with adjectives as below.

1.5.2   Numeration is by a preceding ordinal, supplemented as necessary by words like **(muy, esmeradamente) aumentada, adicionada, corregida, revisada,** (*much, carefully*) *enlarged, added to, corrected, revised.*

1.5.3   An *offprint* is **separata,** *to reprint* is **reimprimir.**

1.6   IMPRINTS

1.6.1   Modern imprints are mostly the names of firms, and may be personal, e.g. **Jiménez-Frand, editor; Aguilar, S.A. de Ediciones**; or arbitrary, e.g. **Editorial Planeta; Atenea, S.E.** (Such abbreviations for *publishing house* are common.) As these examples show the publisher's imprint is usually clearly marked by **editor** and the like; **librería** (*bookshop*) and its cognates amount to the same thing. **Imprenta** nowadays would simply indicate the printer, e.g. **Imprenta de la librería y casa editorial Hernando** in a work published as a supplement (anejo) to the **Revista de filología española.** Outside

Spain institutional imprints such as **Fondo de Cultura Económica, Ediciones de la Universidad Nacional Autónoma**, are somewhat more common.

1.6.2 In older imprints the distinction between the printer and publisher is often a matter of inference. **Imprenta, impres(s)o por**, and presumably plain **por** indicate the printer, but if nothing more is said, he is presumably also the publisher. Sometimes he says so, as in **sacalos a luz Manual Roman en su propia imprenta**, *M.R. published them in his own printing shop*; **oficina de . . . donde se hallará** (*where they are obtainable*). At other times this last expression, like **a costa de, a cargo de, véndese en casa de**, distinguishes the publisher.

1.6.3 Widows, e.g. **por la viuda de Alonso Martin de Balboa**, heirs (**herederos**) and successors (**sucesores**) are not uncommon.

1.6.4 Occasionally a book may be expressly printed **en comandita**, that is, the printer is acting as an agent.

1.7 SERIES

1.7.1 The titles of academic series usually appear at the head of the title-page or on the preceding leaf, but those of popular series may be tucked away at the back of the book or appear on the cover only. They may be singular or plural, e.g. **Biblioteca Selecta de Clásicos Españoles, Colección "Sepan cuantos"** (**colección** is the generic word for *series*), **Clásicos Castellanos, Cuadernos de la Facultad de Filosofía y Letras, Universidad Veracruzana**. This last requires the extraction of the body responsible, beginning with the university, but the task is not difficult.

1.7.2 Quite often series are not numbered or simply bear a figure. If any word is used it is **número** or **volumen**. There may be sub-series, e.g. **nueva serie, serie II**.

1.8 PERIODICALS

1.8.1 The titles of periodicals do not differ linguistically from those of books, though most learned periodicals in Spain have distinctive titles like **Revista Internacional de Sociología, Anuario de Derecho Penal y Ciencias Penales**. Such a title as **De Economía** (*On Economics*) might however belong to anything. (Incidentally, it is frequently misfiled under **Economía**, disregarding the preposition as if it were an article.) Other types of periodical may have fanciful titles, e.g. **El Lagarto** (*The Lizard*) or the untranslatable **La sopa boba; alimento ministerial**, which implies that politicians live at other people's expense. But the grammatical form is still stereotyped. Titles such as **El Lagarto** do not usually coalesce with the preposition **de** (10.2) to form **del** but remain separate and retain the capital **El**.

1.8.2 Institutional periodicals are common. The name of the institution may simply appear at the head or foot of the title-page or it may be part of the title, e.g. **Boletín del Centro de Estudios Sociales**, or sub-title, as in **Estudios Empresariales: revista de la Escuela Superior de Técnica Empresarial**, or again it may follow a verb such as **edita** (*publishes*) or more likely a passive participle, **editada/publicada por . . .** (*published by . . .*). The less common **para** (*for*) occurs when one body acts as agent for another. The name of the institution is not affected by any of these contexts.

1.8.3 Persons concerned with editing appear under a variety of terms, not very precisely distinguished. There is usually a **director**, who seems often to correspond to the editor, but who may be accompanied by a **redactor** or **redactor-jefe** or **jefe de redacción**; or there may be several **directores** or **redactores**, who would not then be very different from the **consejo de dirección** (*board of management*) and the **consejo** (**comité**) **de redacción** (*editorial board*) respectively. Alternatively **one may have a junta editora**

or **junta rectora** or a **consejo asesor**, a sort of advisory board. Managerial, if not honorific, functions, rather than editorial would seem to be indicated by **administrador** and **presidente**.

Colaboracion usually means *contribution*, but at times **colaboradores** are clearly identical with the **consejo de redacción**.

1.8.4 Numeration is by **volumen** or **tomo** (occasionally **año**, which also, however, indicates the calendar year) and **número, fascículo** or **cuaderno**, e.g. **volumen XIX, cuaderno III; tomo XVII, fascículo II; año XXI, núm. 104**; or by **número** alone. The numeral is a cardinal one. There may be more than one series of numeration, e.g. **2° época, N° 13**.

1.8.5 Periodicity may occasionally be implicit in the title, e.g. **Trimestre económico**, *Economic quarterly*, or the periodical may be described in the sub-title as e.g. **revista trimestral** or **semanario**. But more often one has to look in the general information given in some such place as inside the front cover for phrases like **publicada trimestralmente**, *published quarterly*; **aparece (se publica) tres veces al año (al final del cuatrimestre)**, *appears (is published) three times a year (at the end of every four months)*; **cada volumen anual se compone de tres fascículos cuatrimestrales**, *each annual volume is composed of three four-monthly parts*.

1.8.6 Subscription (**suscripción, precio de suscripción**) is usually annual (**anual; anualidad**, *annual subscription*) with different rates for the country of origin and the rest of the world (**los demás países, otros países, extranjero**). Quotations are usually also given for a single number (**número/fascículo/ejemplar suelto**) occasionally for a double number (**número doble**), and back numbers (**números atrasados**), and offprints (**separatas**).

2 ALPHABET, PHONETICS, SPELLING

2.1 ALPHABET

2.1.1 The alphabet is as follows:

a b c ch d e f g h i j k l ll m n ñ o p q r s t
u v w x y z

Each of these has a distinct place in the alphabet, so that **ocho** comes after **ocurrir**, **año** after **antiguo**. This does not apply to **rr**, though it sometimes appears separately in presentations of the alphabet (cf. 2.3). W occurs only in names and foreign words. Into the 17th century **u** and **v** are treated as one letter, which can be vowel or consonant. The capital is **V**, the lower case is either **u** everywhere or **u** medially and **v** initially. Earlier still **i** and **j** are not distinguished.

2.1.2 An acute accent is used (a) to distinguish words with the same spelling but different meanings, e.g. **mí**, *me*; **mi**, *my*; **éste**, *this one*; **este**, *this*; (b) to indicate an abnormal stress. The stress normally falls on the last syllable but one if the word ends in a vowel, **n** or **s**, and on the last syllable if the word ends with any other consonant: for this purpose it is assumed that any combination of **a, e** or **o** with **i, u** or **y** which can be a diphthong or triphthong is one. Hence **económico, edición, después**; **Cristóbal, lápiz; teoría, raíz, caída, habíais**. If a suffix is added, the accent remains, e.g. **rápidamente**, although there is also a normal stress on **-men-**; **abrióla** (*opened it*), although that is the normal stress.

The accent is often omitted on capitals. Common endings such as **-ión**, and familiar proper names like **López** may be found, irregularly, without the accent. In the past grave and circumflex accents were used instead, and the alphabet included ç, with the same value as z.

2.1.3 A diaeresis is found on **u** in the combinations -**güe**- and -**güi**- when the **u** is separately pronounced.

2.2 CAPITALISATION

2.2.1 There is no absolute uniformity, so that divergences will be found from the current norms set out below. In principle names are spelt with capitals but the corresponding adjectives are not, e.g. **Andalucía, andaluz, Buenos Aires; bonaerenses; Fernando VII, fernandino**; and some nouns which might be regarded as names, such as the months and the days of the week, are not treated as such, e.g. **sábado**, *Saturday*.

2.2.2 Personal, geographical·and astronomical names, and the names of historical events and religious feasts, institutions and government departments, are spelt with capitals throughout, except for prepositions and articles and the generic part of geographical names, e.g. **Pedro el Cruel, cabo Verde, Guerra Civil de los Siete Años, Sábado de Gloria** (*Holy Saturday*), **Escuela de Bellas Artes**. But one finds variations like **Puerta del Sol** against **la puerta del Ayuntamiento**.

2.2.3 Book titles are usually found in bibliographies and catalogues with the first word only spelt with a capital, e.g. **Los amores tardíos**, though it used to be common for a short title of this sort to be capitalised throughout. Periodicals are still written so, e.g. **El Pobrecito Hablador**.

2.2.4 Titles of office and nobility preceding names are written small, e.g. **don Marcos Giménez de la Espada, el general Ocampo**; but note **San, Sor, Fray**, and the abbreviations **Sr.** for **señor**, **Vd.** for **Usted**.

2.3 DIVISION OF WORDS

2.3.1 Rules 4, 5a, 6a, 7a, 8 (p. xiii) apply, with the proviso that apart from **nr** pairs of consonants the second of which is **l** or **r** are not divided. This includes **rr**, e.g. **co-pla, en-tre, ce-rrar, hon-rar**. Nor of course can **ch** and **ll** be divided, since they count as single letters.

2.3.2 Prefixes may be kept intact but need not be: **des-engáñese** and **de-sautorizado** occur in the same book, published by a university press.

2.4 PUNCTUATION AND ABBREVIATIONS

2.4.1 Note that the question mark and the exclamation mark are inverted at the beginning of the question or exclamation, e.g. **Señora, ¿sabe Vd. lo que se dice?**, *Madam, do you know what you are saying?*

2.4.2 The abbreviation **Vd.** above for **Usted** illustrates the usual practice in the use of stops, but one will also find examples like **Sres** for **Señores** and **ptas** for **pesetas**, as well as the universal acronyms of type **PNV** for **Partido Nacional Vasco**.

2.5 VARIATION OF CONSONANT

2.5.1 This is largely a matter of spelling. As in English, **c** and **g** have different values before **a, o, u** on the one hand and **e, i** on the other; before the latter they have the same values as **z** and **j** respectively. To preserve the same consonant sound the consonants are changed as follows:

Hard	ca	que	qui	co	cu
	ga	gue	gui	go	gu
Soft	za	ce	ci	zo	zu
	ja	ge/je	gi/ji	jo	ju

e.g. **rico**, *rich*; **riquísimo**, *very rich*; **seguir**, *to follow*; **sigo**, *I follow*; **coger**, *to get*; **cojo**, *I get*; **capaz**, *capable*; P **capaces**. (But **j** is not changed to g, e.g. **caja**, *box*; **cajita**, *little box*.)

2.5.2 Another frequent change is the insertion of **y** between two vowels or the change of **i** to **y**, e.g. **contribuyen** from **contribuir**, **leyó** from **leer**.

2.6 VARIATION OF VOWEL

2.6.1 Some changes take place in the stem vowel of verbs as stress changes, viz.

Unstressed	Stressed	
-e-	-ie-	all conjugations
-e-	-i-	verbs in -ir only
-o-	-ue-	all conjugations

e.g. **probar**, *to test, prove*; **prueba**, *he proves*; **sentir**, *to feel*; **sienten**, *they feel*; **servir**, *to serve*; **sirve**, *serves*. Initially ie- is spelt **hie-** or **ye-**, ue- as **hue-**.

2.6.2 Other changes take place in unstressed syllables if -a, -ie or -ió occurs in the following syllable, viz.

Normal	Before -a, etc.
-e-	-i-
-o-	-u-

e.g. **sirvió**, *he served*; **durmió**, *he slept* (**dormir**).

2.7 SPELLING

2.7.1 Modern spelling was all but established by the 17th century. Some changes that were taking place then and have remained are: c, ç (as in **cabeça**) > z; ch (as in **Christo**) > c; g (as in **magestad**) > j; i (as in **rei**) > y; ph > f; ss > s; x (as in **dixo**) > j; y (as in **cuydado**) > i; ye- (as in **yerro**) > hie (but **yerba** may still be so spelt); z (as in **haze**) from Lat. **facit**) > c.

2.7.2 The spelling of Spanish words can prove a trap; e.g. **inocente**, **comercio**, **inmenso**, **pasar**.

3 ARTICLES

3.1 DEFINITE

3.1.1 The forms are as follows:

	M	F	N
S	el	la, el	lo
P	los	las	

F **el** is used before stressed a- and ha-, e.g. **el alma**; N **lo** is used with adjectives, including the past participle, to express abstractions, e.g. **de lo contrario**, *on the contrary*.

3.1.2 The article is often used in Spanish where it is not used in English, e.g. **la virtud**, *virtue*; **el señor X, el Perú**.

3.2 INDEFINITE

3.2.1 The forms are as follows:

	M	F
S	un	un(a)
P	unos	unas

The plural forms mean *some*.

3.2.2 The indefinite article is often omitted in Spanish.

4 NOUNS

4.1 GENDER AND FORM

4.1.1 Nouns may be masculine or feminine, those in -o being masculine, those in -a being feminine. All others may be either, e.g. **la actividad** and many similar abstract nouns, **el huésped**; **la especie, el detalle**; **la acción** and such like, **el bastón**; **la flor, el calor**; **la luz, el juez**.

4.2 PLURAL

S	P
unstressed vowel	add -s
stressed vowel	add -es, -s
consonant	add -es
-z	-ces
-sis	-sis

5 ADJECTIVES

5.1 GENERAL

Adjectives agree in number and gender with the nouns they qualify. As already stated (0.2) they may either precede or follow the noun, but **buen(o), cierto, gran, nuevo** and **pobre** have different shades of meaning in the different positions, e.g. **un buen hombre**, *a good sort*; **un hombre bueno**, *a good man*.

5.2 ENDINGS

5.2.1 *The feminine* is formed thus:

M -o	F -a
M -or, -ón, -án	F -ora, -ona, -ana

All others, including comparatives in -or, are unchanged.

5.2.2 *The plural* is formed like that of nouns.

5.3 COMPARISON

The comparative is usually expressed by **más**, the superlative by putting the article before the comparative. Irregular comparatives like **mejor** (*better*) are given in the dictionary. The absolute superlative can be expressed either by **muy** (*very*) or the ending -isimo, e.g. nuevo > **novísimo**.

6 NUMERALS

6.1 CARDINAL

6.1.1

1 un(o), una	11 once	21 veintiun(o)	101 ciento un(o)
2 dos	12 doce	30 treinta	200 doscientos, -as
3 tres	13 trece	31 treinta y un(o)	300 trescientos
4 cuatro	14 catorce	40 cuarenta	400 cuatrocientos
5 cinco	15 quince	50 cincuenta	500 quinientos
6 seis	16 dieciséis	60 sesenta	600 seiscientos
7 siete	17 diecisiete	70 setenta	700 setecientos
8 ocho	18 dieciocho	80 ochenta	800 ochocientos
9 nueve	19 diecinueve	90 noventa	900 novecientos
10 diez	20 veinte	100 cien(to)	1000 mil
			2000 dos mil

dieci- and veinti- may be written diez y, veinte y. The long forms uno and ciento are used when the numeral is not followed by a noun.

6.1.2 Only uno and forms in -ientos have feminine forms.

6.2 ORDINAL

6.2.1

1 primer(o)	4 cuarto	7 séptimo	10 décimo
2 segundo	5 quinto	8 octavo	11 undécimo
3 tercer(o)	6 sexto	9 noveno	12 duodécimo

Beyond 12 cardinals are substituted, and for 11 and 12 also in the names of kings and the like.

6.2.2 All ordinals have feminine forms in -a.

6.3 FIGURES

Cardinals are represented by simple arabic figures, ordinals by arabic figures with a superscript o or a. Roman figures can be cardinal or ordinal, e.g. **Alfonso II (segundo), Alfonso XIII (trece).**

6.4 DATES

6.4.1 The months are:

enero, febrero, marzo, abril, mayo, junio,
julio, agosto, se(p)tiembre, octubre, noviembre, diciembre

6.4.2 Dates, with the exception of the first of the month, are expressed by cardinals, e.g.

(on) 25.3.1969	el veinticinco de marzo de mil novecientos sesenta y nueve
in 1848	en mil ochocientos cuarenta y ocho
1 May	el primero de mayo

7 PRONOUNS

7.1/7.2 DEMONSTRATIVE, INTERROGATIVE, ETC.

7.1.1 These pronouns and their corresponding adjectives, which are given in the dictionary, have few grammatical peculiarities. The following points may be noted.

Adjective and pronoun are often distinguished by the accent, e.g. **este, éste**; but **el, la, lo** mean both *the* and *that* in such phrases as **lo que**, *(that) which*, **el de él**, *his (that of him)*.

> **cuyo** (*whose*) is an adjective
> **quien** (*who*) has a plural **quienes**
> **el cual** (*who, which*): both parts vary

7.1.2 In formal correspondence **este** (*this*) and **ese** (*that*) often refer to the sender and the recipient respectively.

7.3 PERSONAL

7.3.1

			Subject	Object
		1	yo	me
		2	tú	te
			Usted	la, le, se
S	3m		él	lo, le, se
	f		ella	la, le, se
	n		ello	lo, le, se
S & P	3r		—	se
		1	nosotros, -as	nos
		2	vosotros, -as	os
P			Ustedes	los, las, les, se
	3m		ellos	los, les, se
	f		ellas	las, les, se

7.3.2 After prepositions the subject forms are found, except in 1 and 2S and the reflexive, where **mí, ti** and **sí** are used. **Usted(es)**, abbreviated **Vd(s)** are the usual forms; as contractions of **vuestra(s) merced(es)** they take the 3rd person, and the possessive **su(yo)** is as likely to mean *your(s)* as *his*. Except when it is reflexive, **se** is indirect object, being used in place of **le** and **les** before **lo, la, los, las**. Of the 3rd person pronouns **él, ella, la, ellos, los, ellas, las** refer equally to persons and things, **ello** has no specific reference, while **lo, le, se** either refer to persons or things which are masculine, or have no specific reference, being often translated *so* or not at all.

For reflexive uses see 8.14.

7.3.3 The object pronouns usually precede all parts of the verb except the infinitive, imperative and gerund, e.g. **Vais a saberlo**, *You will know it*; **Prepárate**, *Prepare yourself*; **poniéndose colorado**, *blushing*. But the pronoun can be attached to a finite tense, especially if this comes at the beginning, e.g. **Despues de esto, sentáronse todos; háblose de la otoñada**, *After that they all sat down; there was talk of the autumn.*

8 VERBS

8.1 STRUCTURE

8.1.1 There are different forms for the different persons and for the different moods and tenses, subject pronouns being unnecessary except for emphasis. There is rather a plethora of subjunctive forms. Some simple tenses correspond to compound ones in English.

8.1.2 Most verbs have the same stem throughout, but in some of the commonest the past stem differs from the present and the infinitive, under which the verb is entered in the dictionary, and the past participle may be irregular.

8.2 PRESENT
8.2.1 *Endings*

I	-o, -as, -a; -amos, -áis, -an	inf. -ar
II	-o, -es, -e; -emos, -éis, -en	inf. -er
III	-o, -es, -e; -imos, -ís, -en	inf. -ir

8.2.2 Consonant variation (2.5) affects the 1st person singular of classes II and III, and many verbs in **-cer** and **-cir** have 1PS **-zco**. Other verbs insert or substitute **-g-**, e.g. **caigo, pongo, valgo** from **caer, poner, valer**; **yazco, yazo**, or **yazgo** from **yacer**.

8.2.3 Verbs of all classes are affected by vowel variation as set out in 2.6.

8.2.4 The present has sometimes to be translated as an English perfect.

8.3 IMPERFECT
8.3.1 *Endings*

I	-aba, -abas, -aba; -ábamos, abais, -aban	inf. -ar
II	-ía, -ías, etc.	inf. -er, -ir

8.3.2 The imperfect has sometimes to be translated as an English pluperfect.

8.4 PAST
8.4.1 *Endings*

I	-é, -aste, -ó; -amos, asteis, -aron	inf. -ar
II	-í, -iste, -ió; -imos, -isteis, -ieron	inf. -er, -ir
III	-e, -iste, -o; -imos, -isteis, -(i)eron	see 8.4.2

8.4.2 The endings of class III are accompanied by a change of stem, viz.

change of vowel: **pude** < **poder**; **vine** < **venir**
change of consonant: **-duje** < **-ducir**; **traje** < **traer**
insertion of **-s-** with change of vowel: **puse** < **poner**; **quise** < **querer**

Other examples occur in irregular verbs (8.19).

8.5 FUTURE
8.5.1 *Endings*

-ar		-ar
-er	é, -ás, -á; -emos, -éis, -án	inf. -er
-ir		-ir

8.5.2 In some verbs the future is contracted e.g. **podré, pondré, querré, tendré, valdré, vendré** from **poder, poner, querer, tener, valer, venir**.

8.6 CONDITIONAL
8.6.1 *Endings*

-ar		-ar
-er	ía, -ías, -ía; -íamos, -íais, -ian	inf. -er
-ir		-ir

Contractions are the same as for the future (8.5.2).

8.6.2 The conditional is sometimes used to express doubt or conjecture, e.g. **en la duda de si habría salido . . .** , *in doubt whether it had gone . . .* ; **Serían las diez de la noche,** *it must have been 10 p.m.*

8.7 SUBJUNCTIVE
8.7.1 *Present*

> I   -e, -es, -e; -emos, -éis, -en   inf. -ar
> II -a, -as, -a; -amos, -áis, -an   inf. -er, -ir

Changes of vowel and stem as for the indicative (8.1.2-3).

8.7.2 *Imperfect* (see also 8.7.5)

> I   -as|e, -es, -e; -emos, -eis, -en   inf. -ar
> II -(i)es| inf. -er, -ir

8.7.3 *Future* (see also 8.7.5)

> I   -ar|e, -es, -e; -emos, -eis, -en   inf. -ar
> II -(i)er| inf. -er, -ir

8.7.4 *Conditional* (see also 8.7.5)

> I   -ar|a, -as, -a; -amos, -ais, -an   inf. -ar
> II -(i)er| inf. -er, -ir

8.7.5 The stem of the imperfect, future and conditional subjunctive, despite their names, is that of the past, regular or irregular as the case may be, e.g. **produjese, pudiere, pusieran.** As to their meaning, there is no distinction between the present and the future, or between the imperfect and the conditional.

8.7.6 The subjunctive does not express a fact. It may express a wish, command or concession, e.g. **vamos,** *let us go*; **sea lo que fuere,** *be that as it may.* In subordinate clauses, where it is frequently required by Spanish grammar, it may, like **fuere** in the last example, require *may* in English, but quite often does not, as in **antes que llegase,** *before he arrived,* or the equivalent may be an infinitive, e.g. **para que la educación los fecunde,** *for education to make them fruitful.* The imperfect and conditional are also much used in conditional sentences, either of them in the if-clause, and the conditional subjunctive (or the plain conditional) in the main clause, e.g. **Así la pintaría yo, si tuviese el pincel de Ticiano,** *So I would paint it, had I Titian's brush*; **Si yo fuera tu padre . . . ,** *If I were your father. . . .* Quite frequently there is no if-clause, and one meets expressions like **dijerase,** *one would have said*; **no debiera,** *ought not,* and so on.

8.10 COMPOUND TENSES
8.10.1 *Perfect indicative and subjunctive*
Formed with the present indicative and subjunctive of **haber** (8.17.4), occasionally **tener** (8.17.5) or **llevar** with the past participle (8.12.2). In sentences with **haber,** like **no ha probado las uvas, no las ha probado,** the participle is invariable, but with **tener** and **llevar** it agrees with the object, e.g. **tengo sufridas muchas penas.**

8.10.2 *Pluperfect, future perfect, conditional perfect (indicative and subjunctive)*
Formed with the imperfect (or past), future, etc. instead of the present.

G

8.11 INFINITIVE

      I -ar   II -er   III -ir

The infinitive is freely used with prepositions, e.g. **la necesidad de añadir,** *the necessity of adding*; **sin pretender,** *without claiming*, and with the article: **al salir,** *as he (etc.) was going out.* After a verb it may correspond to an English clause with the same subject, e.g. **creía ver,** *I thought I saw.*

8.12 PARTICIPLES

    8.12.1 *Present participle*

      I   -ante   inf. -ar
      II -iente   inf. -er, -ir

Used as noun or adjective, and in consequence frequently entered separately in the dictionary, e.g. **con vista penetrante,** *with penetrating gaze*; **siguiente,** *following*; **la corriente,** *the current*; **los agonizantes,** *the dying.* Not particularly common, apart from certain words.

    8.12.2 *Past participle*

      I   -ado   inf. -ar
      II   -ido   inf. -er, -ir
      III -so, -to   a few verbs in **-er** and **-ir**, otherwise regular, viz.
                     abierto/abrir; cubierto/cubrir; escrito/escribir; impreso/imprimir; puesto/ poner; roto/romper; vuelto/volver
                     and the irregular verbs listed in 8.19
      IV various other endings for which see 8.19

Apart from its use in forming compound tenses (8.10) and the passive (8.15) the participle is used, as in English, as an adjective and with the article as a noun, and also in the formation of or instead of temporal clauses, e.g. **(después de) escritas las cartas,** *having written the letters.*

8.13 PRESENT GERUND

      I   -ando   inf. -ar
      II -iendo   inf. -er, -ir

Invariable. Used adverbially like the English participle, and with the verbs **estar, ir,** and **venir** to express continuous action, e.g. **en llegando al siglo XVI,** *on reaching the 16th century*; **se está vistiendo,** *he is dressing*; **parece que va diciendo,** *he seems to be saying.*

8.14 REFLEXIVE

    8.14.1 These are made by adding the personal pronoun of the same person to the verb, e.g. **se lava,** *he washes himself*; **nos observábamos,** *we watched one another*; **hacerse daño,** *to do oneself a mischief.*

    8.14.2 The uses of the reflexive are varied and subtle, including not only the true reflexive and the reciprocal, as illustrated above, but also intransitive and passive uses, such as **se alegró,** *he was glad*; **se venden,** *they are sold*, and others which are difficult to classify, such as **morirse**, *to be dying*; **me caí**, *I fell off.* The passive use can often be regarded as impersonal and the same construction is found with intransitive verbs (even **ser**). In the example in 7.2.2 the -se of **hablóse** must be object, but more often the **se** is so placed that it could be taken as subject, and so one arrives at such sentences as: **Se terminó de imprimir este libro,** *The printing of this book was completed*; **Se llama así a la anotación en que se describe el contenido de los libros compuestos,** *This is what we call the note in which are described the contents of composite books.*

8.15 PASSIVE

8.15.1 The passive is not much used (**se usa poco**!). In the third person the reflexive (8.14.2) often does duty for it, or active phrases can be substituted, e.g. **A Macbeth le entró la melancolía,** *Macbeth was attacked by melancholy.*

8.15.2 There are, however, occasions when passive forms are appropriate, e.g. **Este volumen no está concebido con un criterio geográfico,** *This volume is not conceived on the basis of a geographical criterion*; **Su obra ha sido editada en Argentina,** *His work was published in Argentina*; **El volumen queda reducido a . . . ,** *The volume is thus reduced to . . . .* The pattern is the same in each case, an auxiliary and a past participle agreeing with the subject, the different auxiliaries conveying different nuances: **estar** (*to be*) and **hallarse** (*to find oneself*) express states; **ser** (*to be*), **quedar** (*to remain*), **ir** (*to go*) and **venir** (*to come*) express actions.

8.17 AUXILIARIES

8.17.1 *Forms of* **ser**
Present indicative: **soy, eres, es; somos, sois, son**
Imperfect: **era**
Past: **fui . . . fue; . . . fueron**
Present subjunctive: **sea**
(and see 8.7.5).

8.17.2 *Forms of* **estar**
Present: **estoy, estás,** etc.
Past: **estuve** (8.4.1 type III; see also 8.7.5)

8.17.3 Both verbs mean *to be*, but roughly speaking **ser** refers to permanent, essential qualities, **estar** (originally *to stand*) to temporary qualities and states, including those which, though lasting, are thought of as being the result of change. Note also **estoy leyendo,** *I am reading*, and see 8.15.2.

8.17.4 *Forms of* **haber**
Present indicative: **he, has, ha; hemos, habéis, han**
Past: **hube** (8.4.1 type III; see also 8.7.5)
Future: **habré**
Present subjunctive: **haya**

8.17.5 *Forms of* **tener**
Past: **tuve** (8.4.1 type III; see also 8.7.5)
Other irregularities are covered by 2.5 and 8.2.2.

8.17.6 Apart from certain idioms such as **hay,** *there is* (*are*); **había,** *there was;* and similarly with other tenses; **hay niebla,** *it is foggy*; **haber de,** *to have to*; **muchos días ha,** *many days ago*, **haber** is only used to form compound tenses (8.10).

Tener ('*to hold*') denotes possession, and has idioms resembling those of haber, e.g. tengo calor, *I am hot*; tener que, *to have to*. It may be used as an auxiliary (8.10.1), but its basic meaning comes through: an expression like **en tenerse ganada la voluntad de regidores** (*in having gained the good will of councillors*) suggests that the good will has been kept.

8.19 FURTHER IRREGULARITIES

8.19.1   andar, *to go* (see also 8.19.6)
   Past*: **anduve** (8.4.1 type III)

8.19.2   caber, *to be contained*
   Present indicative: **quepo, cabes,** etc.
   Past*: **cupe** (8.4.1 type III)
   Present subjunctive: **quepa**

8.19.3   dar, *to give*
   Present indicative: **doy, das,** etc.
   Past*: **di**

8.19.4   decir, *to say*
   Present indicative: **digo, dices,** etc.
   Past*: **dije** (8.4.1 type III)
   Future: **diré**
   Present subjunctive: **diga**
   Past participle: **dicho**

8.19.5   hacer, *to do, make*
   Present indicative: **hago, haces,** etc.
   Past*: **hice . . . hizo,** etc. (8.4.1 type III)
   Future: **haré**
   Present subjunctive: **haga**
   Past participle: **hecho**

8.19.6   ir, *to go*
   Present indicative: **voy, vas,** etc.
   Imperfect: **iba**
   Past*: **fui** (cf. 8.17.1)
   Present subjunctive: **vaya**

8.19.7   placer, *to please* (impersonal)
   Past*: **plugo**
   Present subjunctive: **plega/plegue/plazca**

8.19.8   saber, *to know*
   Present indicative: **sé, sabes,** etc.
   Past*: **supe** (8.4.1 type III)
   Present subjunctive: **sepa**

8.19.9   ver, *to see*
   Present indicative: **veo, ves,** etc.
   Imperfect: **veía**
   Present subjunctive: **vea**

9   ADVERBS

A large number of adverbs are formed by the addition of -mente to the feminine of the adjective, e.g. **nuevo, nuevamente.** When two such adverbs follow one another, only the second has the ending, e.g. **deliberada y voluntariamente.**

* see also 8.7.5

10 PREPOSITIONS

10.2 FORMS

The prepositions **a** and **de** combine with the article **el** to form **al** and **del**.

10.5 USES

10.5.1 It is impossible to set out briefly all the often subtle uses of prepositions and their idiomatic combination with verbs, such as **dar con**, *to find*, but the following should be noted:

A is used before the *direct* object if this is a noun denoting a definite person or animal, or a personified thing, e.g. **Algunas madres buscaban a sus hijas**, *Some mothers were looking for their daughters*; **El gatito busca a su madre**, *The kitten seeks its mother*; **Interrogué al mar**, *I questioned the sea*. Sometimes it distinguishes even a non-personal object, e.g. **uno al que llama "la cruz de amor"**, *one which he calls the 'cross of love'*.

10.5.2 A, **de**, and **para** before infinitives do not usually require translating.

11 CONJUNCTIONS

11.1 Y and **o** become **e** and **u** before **(h)i** and **(h)o** respectively, e.g. **carácter e instintos**.
11.2 Provided that one remembers that some of them require the subjunctive, conjunctions cause no grammatical difficulty.

GLOSSARY

acta(s), *proceedings*
actualizado, *brought up to date*
adición, *addition*
adicionado, *added to* (1.5.2)
advertencia, (*prefatory*) *note*
agotado, *out of print*
anejo, *appendix, supplement* (1.6.1)
anualidad, *annual subscription* (1.8.6)
anuario, *yearbook*
año, *year* (1.8.4)
aparecer, *come out* (1.8.5)
atrasado (número, etc.), *back* (*number*) (1.8.6)
atrasarse, *to be late*
aumentado, *enlarged* (1.5.2)

biblioteca, *library*
bibliotecario, *librarian*
bimensual, *fortnightly*

cambio, canje, *exchange*
carta, *letter*
casa editora, *publishing house*
colaboración, *contribution* (1.8.3)
colaboradores, *editorial board* (1.8.3)

colección, *collection, series* (1.7.1)
comisión, *committee*
conferencia, *conference; lecture*
corregido, *corrected* (1.5.2)
cuaderno, *issue, number, part* (1.8.4)
cuadro, *table*
cuento, *short story, tale*

derecho de autor, *copyright*
descuento, *discount*
dirección, *address; management*
director, *editor* (1.8.3)

edición, *edition; publication* (1.5.1)
editado por, *published by* (1.8.2)
editor, *publisher*
ejemplar, *copy*
encuadernación, *binding*
ensayo, *essay*
entrega, *issue, part*
enviar, *send*
espécimen, *sample*
estampa, *press*
expedir, *dispatch*

factura, *bill, invoice*
fascículo, *issue, number* (1.8.4)
folleto, *pamphlet*

imprenta, *press* (1.6.1)
impresión, *impression, edition* (1.5.1)
inédito, *unpublished*

jefe de redacción, *chief editor* (1.8.3)
junta editora/rectora, *editorial board*
   (1.8.3)

lámina, *plate*
librería, *bookshop* (1.6.1); (editorial)
   publishing house
librero, *bookseller*
libro, *book*

mejorado, *improved*
mensual, *monthly*
mismo, *same*
muerto, *dead*
muestra, *sample, complimentary copy*

nacido, *born*
nota, *bill; note*
novela, *novel*
novela corta, *short story*
nuevo, *new*

obra, *work*
obra de teatro, *play*
opúsculo, *pamphlet, bulletin*

palabras preliminares, *foreword*
para examinar, *on approval*

pedido, *order*
plancha, *plate*
precio, *price*
(precio de) suscripción, *subscription* (1.8.6)
prefacio, *preface, introduction*
prensa, *press*
proemio, *preface, introduction*
prólogo, *preface*
proximas publicaciones, *forthcoming*
   publications
a prueba, *on approval*

rebaja, *discount, reduction*
recopilación, *collection*
redacción, *editing, editorial office*
redactor (jefe), (*chief*) *editor* (1.8.3)
refundido, *revised*
reimpresión, *reprint*
repertorio, *index*
retrato, *portrait*
revista, *review, periodical*
rústica, *paperback, paper covers*

semana, *week*
semestral, *half-yearly*
señas, *address*
separata, *offprint* (1.5.3)
solo, *single*

tirada aparte, *offprint*
trabajos, *writings, transactions*
trimestral(mente), *quarterly* (1.8.5)

único, *single*

a la venta, en venta, *on sale*

GRAMMATICAL INDEX: WORDS

GRAMMATICAL INDEX: ENDINGS

CATALAN

SPECIMEN

Si no temés de repetir-me, diria que intento d'escriure una "aproximació" a la vida catalana del Vuitcents. Però, en tot cas, una aproximació meditada i més que mai exigent i rigorosa, pel mètode emprat i per la prudència en els inevitables judicis de valor. La senyoreta Montserrat Llorens, llicenciada en Història i apassionada pels temes del segle XIX, sobre els quals porta ja escrit un notable article, ha accedit a la meva invitació perquè redactés la segona part d'aquest llibre, o sigui les biografies dels polítics i dels industrials.

If I were not afraid of repeating myself, I would say that I intend to write an approximation to the Catalan life of the eighteen hundreds. But in any case, a studied approximation and (one that is) more than ever searching and rigorous, in the method employed and in its caution in the inevitable value judgements. Senyoreta Montserrat Llorens, a graduate in history and an enthusiast for nineteenth century themes, about which she has already written a notable article, has acceded to my invitation to compile the second part of this book, namely the biographies of the politicians and industrialists.

Characteristic of Catalan as compared with Spanish are forms like **escriure, -ació, llibre**, etc., **segona, polítics, industrials**, and endings in **-e** and **-es**.

0 GENERAL CHARACTERISTICS

0.1 DEGREE OF INFLEXION
Having a more differentiated set of verbs than French, so that subject pronouns are not necessary except for emphasis, Catalan is to that extent more synthetic, but otherwise it shares the analytic characteristics, using prepositions to define relationships between nouns.

0.2 ORDER OF WORDS
Qualifiers both precede and follow. Dependent phrases with **de** invariably follow, while the position of adjectives is variable, their position depending to some extent on their stylistic function.

0.4 RELATION TO OTHER LANGUAGES
On the relation of Catalan to Latin and the other Romance languages see General note on the Romance languages.

1 BIBLIOLINGUISTICS

1.1 NAMES
1.1.1 The structure of Catalan names is identical with that of Spanish ones. In some instances there is nothing to show whether the name is Catalan or Spanish, in

others authors with names like **Bosch**, pronounced [Bosk], which is Catalan, may write exclusively in Spanish. One should not in those cases Catalanise their Christian names or replace Spanish **y** by Catalan **i**.

1.1.2 Surnames come in early in Catalonia, but one finds names such as **Arnau de Vilanova, Francesc d'Olesa** indexed under the Christian name.

1.2 NAMES OF AUTHORS, EDITORS, ETC.

1.2.1 *Mutatis mutandis* what is said of Spanish applies to Catalan. The prepositions **de** and **per** before authors' names do not affect them but coalesce with the article (10.2). If therefore one has **pel P. Miquel Batllori**, one must keep the **P.**

1.2.2 Names at the head of the title should be treated with due caution and read in conjunction with what follows. **Joan Maragall | Conferències en commemoració del centenari de la seva naixença** is hardly likely to be by Maragall himself.

1.3 TITLES

1.3.1 The great majority of titles, even of collections of verse, are grammatically straightforward concatenations of nouns, adjectives and prepositions, as instanced by the one quoted above. But popular literature has more variety, e.g. **On va l'home?** *Where is man going?*

1.3.3 Titles in context do not present much difficulty. In a phrase like **la publicació de El català bàsic**, the article and preposition do not usually coalesce.

1.4 VOLUMES AND PARTS

The usual word is **volum**, but often enough there is a number and nothing more. The number may precede, **tercer volum**, or follow, **vol. 3**, but in either case it is an ordinal. **Part** is found in internal divisions.

1.5 EDITIONS

1.5.1 The word is **edició**, which occurs in other contexts (cf. 1.6) meaning publication. **Tiratge** occurs also but only in contexts such as **Un altre tiratge d'aquesta edició ha estat fet ... dins la Biblioteca Selecta,** *Another printing of this edition has been made ... forming part of the Biblioteca Selecta.*

1.5.2 Numeration is by a preceding ordinal number, e.g. **segona edició**, accompanied if necessary by epithets such as **corregida**, *corrected*; **ampliada**, *enlarged*; **revisada**, *revised*, or comments such as **amb esmenes i addicions**, *with corrections and additions.*

1.5.3 A reprint is **reimpresió**, an offprint **separata** or **tiratge separat.**

1.6 IMPRINTS

1.6.1 Modern imprints nearly all include the words **editorial** (*publishing house*) or **edicions** (*publications*), e.g. **Editorial Teide, S.A.; Editorial Alpha; Edicions 62; Edicions Ariel.** Most of them are arbitrary firm names. Less common nowadays is **Llibreria**, e.g. **Llibreria Catalònia**, which somewhat earlier is found with personal names, e.g. **Llibreria Cientifich-Literaria Joseph Agustí; Llibreteria de E. Fernando Roca.**

1.6.2 Printers may also be publishers, but an imprint like **Imprenta Ariel** nowadays would imply that the firm was concerned as printer. Similarly **imprès per** (*printed by*).

1.6.3 Older imprints are sometimes less clear cut. There may be indications of both parties, as in **Vense en Valencia en casa de Borbo librer ab despeses del qual fonch estampat, en casa de Ioan de Mey** (*Sold at Valencia at the house of Borbo bookseller at* *whose expense it was printed, at the house of Joan de Mey*). Three relationships—printer, entrepreneur, bookseller—among two persons, which is common enough. A(b) **despeses, a costa** indicate the entrepreneur, **vense** the bookseller, **imprenta (emprempta), estampa** and their various derivatives the printer; but it is clear that **en casa de** is equivocal. It is probable that **per** refers to the printer, but as with the other indications, it does not exclude publishing, clearly not in such an instance as **per Pau Rivera, estamper y llibreter.**

1.6.4 Up to the 19th century at least the imprint may be that of a widow (**viuda**) or heirs (**hereus**). One even finds **Hereus de la Viuda Pla.**

1.7 SERIES

1.7.1 The titles of series, which frequently include the generic name **col·lecció**, are mostly simple, in the singular describing the series, e.g. **Col·lecció "Que cal saber"** (*What you should know series*); **Biblioteca selecta**; or in the plural describing the contents, e.g. **Biogràfies catalanes; Publicacions de l'Oficina Romànica.** In this last type the name of the body concerned (**Oficina Romànica**) forms part of the title as stated, but in suitable contexts this could be reduced to **Publicacions.**

1.7.2 Numeration, if the unit is specified, is by **volum**, or **número**, followed by an ordinal. Quite often the series is subdivided, e.g. **secció Novel·la, sèrie Assaigs** (*Essays*), **segona sèrie, Col·lecció A (volums en dotzau)** i.e. 12mo.

1.8 PERIODICALS

1.8.1 The titles of periodicals are linguistically straightforward, even if sometimes semantically obscure, and are very like those of series, e.g. **La nova revista, Ilustració catalana, Serra d'or** (i.e. Montserrat), **Poemes, Estudis franciscans.**

1.8.2 The title may include the name of the body concerned, or this may appear in a formal imprint such as **Publicacions de l'Abadia de Montserrat** (publishers of **Serra d'or**).

1.8.3 *Editor* is literally **redactor** (**redactor en cap**, *editor-in-chief*) but he may be described as **director literari**. **Direcció** is sometimes equated with and sometimes distinguished from editorship (**direcció i redacció**). The editor may also double as **administrador** (*manager*). Occasionally there is a board of editors (**cos de redacció**). **Editat** means *published*; **edita**, *publishes*.

1.8.4 Terms used in numeration include **any, volum, fascicle, número** and **quadern**. Any (*year*) and **volum** are often interchangeable but are not synonymous, as the following statement shows: **any XXX, volum 48, fasc. 1 (núm. 268)**. There is no essential difference between the terms for parts. The number of the volume or part is read as an ordinal and may be spelt out, e.g. **volum vuitè** (*eighth volume*).

1.8.5 Periodicity is frequently indicated by an adjective, e.g. **revista (publicació) setmanal, quinzenal, mensual, trimestral**, *weekly, fortnightly, monthly, quarterly review* (*publication*). Alternatively there may be a statement of the form **es publica el dia 20 de cada mes**, *is published on the 20th of each month*; often vague in the case of society publications which **els Srs Socis** receive by way of membership (1.8.6), e.g. **formarà un volum anual que apareixerà en dos o més fascicles**, *will form an annual volume which will come out in two or more parts.*

1.8.6 Subscription terms are stated as **preu(s) (de) subscripció** and are quoted by **l'any, semestre** and **trimestre**. Most periodicals quote for a single number (**número solt**), some do not commit themselves beyond the price of the volume in hand (**preu d'aquest volum**), some offer back numbers (**atrassats**).

1.8.7 Catalan periodicals are not prodigal of addresses. Some indicate **centres de subscripció** (often local agents), some give specific directions of the form **cal adresar-se a**, *one should apply to*. The editorial office is **redacció**.

2 ALPHABET, PHONETICS, SPELLING

2.1 ALPHABET

2.1.1 The alphabet is strictly **a–l**, **ll**, **m–z**: **l·l** (2.1.5) occupies the normal position between **lj** and **lm**, and so quite often does **ll**, interfiled with **l·l**.

2.1.2 Accents, acute on close vowels, viz. **é, í, ó, ú**, grave on open vowels, viz. **à, è, ò**, serve (a) to distinguish homonyms, e.g. **mes**, *but*, *month*; **més**, *more*; (b) to indicate an unusual stress. The stress falls by rule on the last syllable but one of words which end in a vowel, vowel + **s**, **-en** or **-in**; on the last syllable of all other words. So **acció** has an accent to indicate stress on the last syllable; its plural **accions** has none. (The Spanish convention which assumes that the ending -ia for instance is a diphthong unless it is accented -ía does not obtain. It is words like **història** which have the accent in Catalan.)

2.1.3 A cedilla is attached to **c** when it has the sound of **s**: the resulting **ç** is interfiled with **c**. (See also 2.5.1, 2.7.2.)

2.1.4 A diaeresis is placed on a letter when it is necessary to show that it is pronounced separately, e.g. **plaïa**. It is common after **g**: **hagué** (*he had*) and **llengües** (*tongues*) differ in the same way as English *plague* and *linguist*; but **llengua** does not need the diaeresis.

2.1.5 A dot is used in **l·l**, pronounced as two l's, to distinguish it from **ll**, which is a palatalised l.

2.2 CAPITALISATION

2.2.1 In principle proper names are spelt with initial capitals, even though in form they may be common nouns, while the corresponding adjectives are written small even when they are used as nouns. As to what are names, Catalan usage is not necessarily the same as English: in particular, months, days, and titles of rank and office are not so regarded. So one has **Vuitcents** (*the 1800's*), **Renaixença**, **Ponent** (*West*), **Catalunya**, **Carles**, but els **catalans**, **carlins** (*Carlists*), **agost**, el general **Prim**, el marqués de **Mataflorida**. But note **Dr.** and (sometimes) **En**, the Catalan equivalent of **don**.

2.2.2 Complex personal, geographical and astronomical names, and the names of historical events and religious feasts, institutions and government departments are written with capitals throughout except for prepositions and articles, and particularly with geographical names, the generic noun, e.g. **Pere el Ceremoniós**, **Vall d'Aran**, la **Setmana Tràgica** (but also **Revolució francesa**), **Junta de Comerç**; la plana de **Vic**, la guerra de **Set Anys**.

2.2.3 In bibliographies and catalogues book titles are usually written with the first word only in capitals, e.g. **L'aptitud econòmica de Catalunya**, but in citations such variants as **La Nacionalitat catalana** and **Moralitats i Pretextos** are found. Periodicals, such as **El Poble Català**, are still usually given capitals throughout.

2.3 DIVISION OF WORDS

2.3.1 Rules 4, 5a, 6a and 8 (p. xiii) apply, subject to the provisos below.

2.3.2 Prefixes which end in a consonant are not divided but may be added **to**, e.g. **des-afiant** (and **pen-insular**) but **cons-trucció** (2.3.3) and the like not **con-**. In compounds we find **autòc-ton** despite the familiarity of **auto-**.

2.3.3   Rules 5a and 6a are modified where **b, c, d, g, p** or **t** are followed by **l** or **r**, e.g. **po-ble**; but unlike Spanish, Catalan divides **rr**.

2.3.4   The combinations **ll** and **ny** are not divided.

2.3.5   The only divisions of vowels that I have come across are of the type **re-acció**. (Some, such as the separation of **ig** and **ix** from a preceding vowel, would be monstrous: **goig** for instance is pronounced [gotʃ], **baix** [baʃ].)

2.3.6   Note that the division **d'a-gost** does not break rule 8, since **d'agost** (with no space after the apostrophe) counts as one word.

2.4   PUNCTUATION

2.4.1   As in Spanish the exclamation mark and the question mark may be inverted at the beginning of the phrase (not necessarily the beginning of the sentence), e.g. **Però ¿qui érem nosaltres per atansar-nos a promoure'l? ¿quins títols teníem per posar-ho tot en revolt?**, *But who were we . . ., what right had we . . .?* But it is not usual.

2.4.2   The hyphen has two principal uses: in compounds, and to attach object pronouns to the verb. Examples of the latter will be found in 2.4.1. If, as in **promoure'l**, the vowel of the pronoun is elided, the apostrophe takes the place of the hyphen. Its use in compounds is not completely covered by rules. Thus compounds which are condensed phrases may be written as separate words, with hyphens or in one word; e.g. **cop d'ull, cul-de-sac, potser** (Spanish **quizá**). It depends to some extent on familiarity and the extent to which the literal meaning is transcended.

2.4.3   Words formed with prefixes are not generally treated as compounds but are written as one, e.g. **semicircular**. The exceptions are **arxi-, ex-, pre-, pseudo-, quasi-, sots-, vice-**.

2.4.4   Nouns formed of a verb and a noun, e.g. **guardacostes**, adjectives formed of a noun and an adjective, e.g. **barbablanc**, verbs formed of a noun and a verb, e.g. **ullprendre** are written as one word unless this is phonetically misleading, e.g. **guarda-roba, barba-serrat, para-xocs** because **r, s** and **x** have a different pronunciation at the beginning and in the middle of a word; **front-ample** because **nt** differs at the end of a word. Likewise **pèl-llarg** to avoid ambiguity.

2.4.5   Nouns formed of a noun and an adjective agreeing with it, such as **pell-roja**, take a hyphen.

2.4.6   Most words formed of the combination of two elements of the same sort, including adjectives of the type **històrico-arqueològic**, have hyphens, e.g. **nord-est**, but there are exceptions both ways, e.g. **paper moneda, vaivé** (*coming and going*).

2.4.7   An expression consisting of an adjective followed by a noun, of the type represented by **lliure canvi**, *free trade*, is usually written as two words, but there are some long-established exceptions like **plataforma**. But where the new expression has a different function a hyphen is used, e.g. **un poca-vergonya**, *a man without shame*; **un escrit poca-solta**, *a bromide*.

2.4.8   Further derivatives are written as one word, e.g. **lliurecanvista**, *free-trader*.

2.5   CHANGE OF CONSONANT

2.5.1   This arises largely from the fact that **c** and **g** have different values before **a, o, u** on the one hand and **e** and **i** on the other. To preserve the same sound the consonant has to be changed thus:

ca	**que**	**qui**	co	cu
ga	**gue**	**gui**	go	gu

and on the other hand:

ça	ce	ci	ço	çu
ja	ge (je)	gi (ji)	jo	ju

Changes accordingly occur in the course of declension and conjugation, e.g. roca, P roques; començo *I begin*, comencen *they begin*; pujar *to go up*, pugí *I went up* (-je- and -ji- only in learned words like objecte). Similarly verbs whose infinitives end in -guar and -quar have -gü- and -qü- before e and i.

2.5.2   In many words n is omitted when final but appears medially, e.g. català but catalana, catalans. Words like convenir were once cov-, but have been brought back to the Latin original.

2.5.3   The combination nd is simplified to n in many words but retained in related or more literary ones, e.g. prenen, prendre; món (*world*), mundial; fonamental, profund.

2.5.4   A good many changes of consonant occur in the conjugation of irregular verbs: see 8.19.

2.6   CHANGE OF VOWEL

2.6.1   Very few changes take place in the stem vowel in Catalan, though one must remember that the same letter may have different pronunciations depending on the placing of the stress. In some irregular verbs, however, the changes go farther and one meets with the alternations a/e, e/i (or both), o/u. See in 8.19 the verbs eixir, fer, néixer, poder, riure, sortir, voler for examples.

2.7   SPELLING

2.7.1   The present standard spelling dates from the Normes ortogràfiques of 1913. Although early manuscripts show remarkably few fundamental differences from modern spelling, there were more at a later date owing to Spanish influence or misplaced erudition.

2.7.2   The following letters are those principally affected by the standardisation. (The changes do not affect every occurrence of the letters.)

Old	*New*
b	v
ç	s
ch	c
h	omitted between vowels
je, ji	ge, gi
ph	f
s(s)	ç
x	ix pronounced [ʃ]
y	i

The word ab became amb, pronounced [am], and mitg and similar words became mig.

2.7.3   In medieval texts l is used for ll, e for i (*and*) and -tio for -ció.

3   ARTICLES

3.1   DEFINITE

3.1.1   The forms are:

	M	*F*
S	el, l'	la, l'
P	els	les

El is shortened to l' before any vowel, la is not shortened before unstressed i, u, hi, hu, e.g. la influència. The old forms lo and los still survive in some parts, but the use of lo for the neuter, e.g. lo contrari for el contrari, is frowned on as a Castilianism.

3.1.2 The article is used with abstract nouns and names, e.g. el catalanisme, *Catalanism*; l'Alfons Maseras, la Matilde; but en Lluís, en Rovira. This en has the same origin as don, but as el is considered vulgar and the forms na and n' are little used, we are left with en, la, l', all regarded as articles. The article is not indispensable with names: in the text in which en Rovira and l'Alfons Maseras occur we find el va llegir Antoni Rovira i Virgili, and so frequently.

3.2 INDEFINITE

3.2.1 The forms are:

	M	F
S	un	una
P	uns	unes

Una is not elided before a vowel: una obra. The plural forms mean *some*.

3.2.2 The indefinite article is often omitted, e.g. era anarquista i revolucionari, *he was an anarchist, etc.*

4 NOUNS

4.1 FORM AND GENDER

4.1.1 Nouns may be masculine or feminine, but though certain formative suffixes regularly have a particular gender, e.g. -ment M, -ció, -tat of abstract nouns F, endings in general are not a very certain guide. Most words ending in a consonant are M, most words ending in -a are F, but there are exceptions. Even the gender of the Latin originals cannot be relied on, for abstract nouns in -or have mostly changed to F.

4.2 PLURAL

4.2.1 A very large number of nouns simply add -s, e.g. títols, col·legis, pares, índexs.

4.2.2 The numerous feminines in -a have plural -es; but note that -es may well result from -e+s.

4.2.3 Masculines in -ç, -sc, -st, -xt, -x, -tx (except índex and words similarly stressed) and most of those ending in -Cs, add -os.

4.2.4 Masculines in -'Vs add -os or -sos. Similarly monosyllables, e.g. compàs, compassos; cas, casos.

4.2.5 Nouns in -ig usually add -s, which looks right, but as -ig is pronounced [itʃ] or after a vowel [tʃ], the plurals -itjos and -jos, as pronounced, are also found, e.g. desig, desitjos; raig, rajos.

4.2.6 Nouns in -à, -é, -í, -ó, -ú and monosyllables which have lost -n recover it in the plural, e.g. mà, mans; fí, fins; acció, accions (a very common type). A knowledge of Latin or other Romance languages is useful, for though -ans, for instance, always comes from -à, a word like clixé (Fr cliché) has P clixés. (Note, however, that only words with the stress on the last syllable have P -ns: home makes homes despite Latin homines.)

4.2.7 Nouns ending in -Vs not stressed on the last syllable are unchanged in the plural, e.g. els òmnibus. So is temps.

5 ADJECTIVES

5.1 AGREEMENT AND POSITION

5.1.1 Adjectives agree in number and gender with the nouns they qualify.

5.1.2 In general adjectives may either precede or follow the noun (0.2), but there are some, like **gran, bo, petit** that are nearly always found in front, and others such as **pobre, trist**, which have their literal meaning when they follow but a transferred one, like En *poor, sorry*, when they precede, e.g. **trista situació**, *sorry state of affairs*.

5.2 ENDINGS

5.2.1 The majority of adjectives make the feminine by adding, or substituting -a, e.g. **famós, famosa**; **pobre, pobra**; **flonjo, flonja**. Other changes may take place, as detailed in the following paragraphs.

5.2.2 Final **p, t, c, s** may change to **-ba, -da, -ga, -ssa**: e.g. **grec, grega**; but **sec, seca**. The converse is not necessarily true, e.g. **fred, freda**. Note also **oblic, obliqua**.

5.2.3 Adjectives which end in a stressed vowel, with the exception of **nu, cru** and **escrú** (F **nua**, etc.), add **-na** (cf. 4.2.6), e.g. **català, catalana**.

5.2.4 Adjectives in **-ig** preceded by a consonant have F **-itja**, e.g. **mig, mitja**; if a vowel precedes the F is simply **-(t)ja**, e.g. **roig, roja**; **lleig, lletja**.

5.2.5 The F of **-au, -iu, -ou** is **-ava, -iva, -ova**; of **-eu, -ea**, or, for possessives, **-eva**.

5.2.6 The following have no special F form: those ending in **-ç**, most of those in **-al, -el, -il** (exc. **mal, parallel, tranquil**); most of those in **-ar** (exc. **car, clar, rar**); comparatives in **-or**; most of those in **-ant, -ent**; a number in **-e**, especially **-ble**.

5.2.7 The formation of the plural is the same as for nouns. Note, however, that adjectives in **-ç** have P **-ços, -ces**. Changes of consonant (2.5.1) may occur before **-es**.

5.2.8 The possessives **mon, ton, son** have the forms **ma, mos, mes**, etc.; **llur(s)**, *their*, has no separate F form. The remaining possessives, including the commoner **(el) meu**, etc., are regular.

5.3 COMPARISON

5.3.1 The comparative is expressed by **més**, *more*.

5.3.2 The superlative is expressed by **el més**, *the most*, but there are also forms in **-íssim**, which seem to be made at will, with the meaning *very*, e.g. **brillantíssima carrera**; and even **el crit barceloníssim**, *the typically Barcelonian cry*.

5.5 USAGE

5.5.1 As in English but much more freely, adjectives, usually with the article, are used as nouns or with nouns understood, e.g. **el nombre d'aprovats**, *the number of successful pupils*; **en llenguatge parlat es diu Sarral; en l'escrit, oficial i administratiu és Sarreal**.

5.5.2 An adjective that qualifies two nouns is plural, e.g. **l'observació i la formulació gramaticals**.

6 NUMERALS

6.1 CARDINAL

6.1.1

1 **un, una**	4 **quatre**	7 **set**	10 **deu**
2 **dos, dues**	5 **cinc**	8 **vuit**	11 **onze**
3 **tres**	6 **sis**	9 **nou**	12 **dotze**

13 tretze	30 trenta	101 cent un
14 catorze	31, etc. trenta-un, etc.	200 dos-cents,
15 quinze	40 quaranta	dues-centes
16 setze	50 cinquanta	1000 mil
17 disset	60 seixanta	
18 divuit	70 setanta	
19 dinou	80 vuitanta	
20 vint	90 noranta	
21, etc. **vint-i-un**, etc.	100 cent	

6.1.2   Only 1, 2, 21, 22 and the like, and the hundreds have feminine forms. The plural **un(e)s** is usually a pronoun but there are expressions like **unes tisores**, *a pair of scissors*. See also 7.3.3. **Un** may be reduced to **u** when not followed by a noun.

6.2   ORDINAL
6.2.1

1 **primer**	11 **onzè**
2 **segon**	21 **vint-i-unè**
3 **terç(er)**	22 **vint-i-dosè**
4 **quart**	23 **vint-i-tresè**
5 **cinquè**	24 **vint-i-quatrè**
6 **sisè**	30 **trentè**
7 **setè**	etc.
8 **vuitè**	
9 **novè**	
10 **desè**	

Cinquè has an alternative **quint**.

6.2.2   All the ordinals are variable adjectives, those in -**è** have the forms -**è**, -**ena**, -**ens**, -**enes**, e.g. **la dinovena centúria**.

6.2.3   Those above 20 are uncommon, it being always possible to substitute a cardinal number, which is invariable and follows the noun, e.g. **la pàgina vint-i-u**. **Vuitè, dotzè, setzè** have also the specialised meanings *octavo, duodecimo, sexto-decimo* as alternatives to **en octau**, etc.

6.3   FIGURES
6.3.1   Cardinals are indicated by plain arabic figures, ordinals by the forms **1.°**, etc. Roman numerals may indicate either, e.g. **Pere III (tercer), Alfons XIII (tretze)**.

6.4   DATES
6.4.1   The months are:

> **gener, febrer, març, abril, maig, juny,**
> **juliol, agost, septembre, octubre, novembre, desembre**

6.4.2   Except for *first*, dates are expressed by cardinals.

> *28.viii.1955*, **el vint-i-vuit d'agost de mil nou-cents cinquanta-cinc**
> *1 May*, **el primer (dia) de maig**; but **l'u** is not unknown
> **el segle XVIII** is read **el segle divuit**
> *the 1800's*, **el Vuitcents**

7 PRONOUNS

7.1 DEMONSTRATIVE AND INDEFINITE

7.1.1 As in Spanish, the demonstratives are three-fold: **aquest**, *this*; **aqueix**, *this, that*; **aquell**, *that*; but **aqueix** is not popular, despite its usefulness in letters to denote things in the neighbourhood of the recipient (almost, *your*), contrasting with **aquest** ('*our*').

7.1.2 The adjective and pronoun are identical and have the usual four forms (5.2). There are also neuter pronouns, **açò, això, allò,** of which **açò** is uncommon.

7.1.3 Before **de** and **qui/que** the article is used as a pronoun, e.g. **la millor denominació ens ha semblat la d'Obres essencials**; and see 7.2.2.

7.1.4 The indefinite pronoun and the corresponding adjective tend to differ, e.g. **algun, alguna,** etc. *some*; **algú,** *somebody*.

7.1.5 **Qualsevol** and **qualsevulla,** *any*(*body*), have invariable suffixes, so that the plural is **qualssevol,** etc.

7.1.6 **Un** may be a pronoun equivalent to **hom,** e.g. **quan un no té res a dir,** *when one has nothing to say*.

7.1.7 **Mateix** is said to mean *same* before a noun and *self* after it, but **el mateix Tort i Martorell** can hardly mean anything but *T. i. M. himself*.

7.2 INTERROGATIVE AND RELATIVE

7.2.1 The interrogatives are **qui?** *who?*, **què?** *what?*, **quin(a)?** *what?, which?* (adj.), whether they are subject, object or follow prepositions.

7.2.2 The relatives are like the interrogatives but confusingly different. As subject **que** is generally used both for persons and things, though **qui,** the old personal form, is still found; as object only **que**; after prepositions **qui** for persons, **què** for things. Where the relative has no noun as antecedent we have **qui** or more often **el qui** of persons (**campi qui pugui,** *sauve qui peut*; **tots els qui no parlen el català,** *all those who do not speak Catalan*), **el que** of things. You will however find **el que** of persons in contexts such as the following: **El passat de Catalunya no existeix per al català que només sap el que li han ensenyat a l'escola oficial primària. No existeix gaire, tampoc, per al que ha pogut freqüentar l'Institut,** *Catalonia's past does not exist for the Catalan who only knows what they have taught him at the official primary school. It hardly exists, either, for the one who has been able to attend the grammar school.* The first **el que** is the neuter *what*, but **al que** stands for **al català que.** (Small wonder that even educated Catalans sometimes write **els que ho fan** for *those who do so*.)

7.2.3 An alternative relative is **el (la,** etc.) **qual(s).**

7.2.4 The relative adverb **on** (*where*) can mean *in which*.

7.3 PERSONAL

7.3.1 The personal pronouns have two basic sets of forms: those used as subject and, for the most part, after prepositions; and those used as objects, e.g. **jo crec,** *I believe*; **entre tu i jo,** *between you and me*; **a mi,** *to me*; **em sembla,** *it seems to me*; **m'emportà,** *carried me away*; **comptar-me,** *to count myself*; **veure'm,** *to see me*. (Paradoxically **m'** is the reduced form of **em,** and **'m** of **me.**) Only the full forms are given in the table.

		Subject/Disjunctive	Object
	1	jo (D jo, mi)	em, -me
	2	tu	et, -te
S	3m	ell	D el, -lo; I (-)li
	3f	ella	D (-)la; I (-)li
	3n	—	(-)ho
S & P	3r	D si	es, -se
	1	nosaltres	ens, -nos
P	2	vós; vosaltres	(-)us, -vos
	3m	ells	els, -los
	3f	elles	D (-)les; I els, -los

Except to some extent in the 3rd person no distinction is made between direct and indirect objects. For reflexive uses see 8.14.

7.3.2 Vós and vosaltres both take a plural verb, but vós is singular in sense. More common than vós is vostè, pl. vostès, which takes the 3rd person. Hence the 3rd-person pronouns may mean *you*, as in jo li asseguro, *I assure you*.

7.3.3 The adverbs en, -ne and hi function as personal pronouns. En (*thence*) corresponds to a noun with de, e.g. en resultaren, *resulted from it*. With expressions of quantity, where it means *of it*, *of them*, it will often be omitted in translation, and in phrases like no en tinc the translation would be *I haven't any*. Note also a cantar-ne les excel·lències, *to sing its excellences*.

Hi (*there*) corresponds to a noun with any other preposition, e.g. menja-hi pa, *eat some bread with it*; insistir-hi, *to insist on it*; comptant-hi, *including*. With haver it gives forms such as hi ha, *there is*. It is also used idiomatically instead of li when another 3rd-person pronoun is present, e.g. l'hi estic llegint a la cara, *I read it in his face* (lit. *to him in the face*).

7.3.4 When the object or adverbial complement stands before the verb the corresponding pronoun is used as well, e.g. de la pobresa antiga en parlava l'àvia paterna, *of the poverty of past times my paternal grandmother used to speak*, in which en simply takes up de la pobresa.

7.3.5 When pronouns are found with a pair of infinitives, one needs to be careful to note which they are to be construed with: el fet de poder-se'n passar means *the fact of being able to do without them*.

8 VERBS

8.1 STRUCTURE

8.1.1 Differences of person, tense and mood are almost always unequivocally indicated by differences of ending, so that subject pronouns are only needed for contrast or emphasis.

8.1.2 The majority of verbs have a regular relationship between the infinitive, under which they are listed, and the other parts; and though they differ from each other in the vowel of the stem show a marked similarity of pattern. Some, while otherwise regular, change in spelling (2.5; 2.1.4). About fifty verbs, including some very common ones, are irregular (8.19).

8.2 PRESENT

8.2.1 *Endings*

    I   -o, -es, -a; -em, -eu, -en   inf. -ar
    II -o, -s, -; -em, -eu, -en   inf. -er, -re
    III -(eix)o, -(eixe)s, -eix/-; -im, -iu, -(eix)en   inf. -ir

8.2.2 The usual English equivalent is the simple present, occasionally the continuous present (but cf. 8.12.2), and as in English, the time referred to may sometimes be past or future.

8.3 IMPERFECT

8.3.1 *Endings*

    I   -ava, -aves, -ava; -àvem, -àveu, -aven   inf. -ar
  II, III -ia, -ies, -ia; -íem, etc.   inf. -er, -re, -ir

8.3.2 The imperfect typically expresses duration or habit in the past and is usually translated by the English continuous past. With some verbs, however, the simple past is more appropriate, e.g. **això no semblava preocupar gaire el director**, *this hardly seemed to bother the director.*

8.4 PAST

8.4.1 *Endings*

    I   -í, -ares, -à; -àrem, -àreu, -aren   inf. -ar
    II -í, -eres, -é; -érem, -éreu, -eren   inf. -er, -re
    III -í, -ires, -í; -írem, -íreu, -iren   inf. -ir

Note the accentuation.

8.4.2 The English equivalent is the simple past.

8.5 FUTURE

8.5.1 *Endings*

    I   -aré, -aràs, -arà; -arem, -areu, -aran   inf. -ar
   IIa   -eré, etc.   inf. -er
    b   -ré, etc.   inf. -re
   III   -iré, etc.   inf. -ir

Contrast the accentuation of the plural with that of the preterite (8.4.1).

8.5.2 The future sometimes expresses doubt.

8.6 CONDITIONAL

8.6.1 *Endings*

    I   -aria ⎫
    II -(e)ria ⎬ etc. as 8.3.1.
   III -iria ⎭

8.6.2 Apart from uses corresponding to the English conditional, the Catalan conditional expresses inference or probability.

8.7 SUBJUNCTIVE

8.7.1 *Present endings*

    I & II   -i, -is, -i; -em, -eu, -in   inf. -ar, -er, -re

    III   -(eix)i, -(eix)is, -(eix)i; -im, -iu, -(eix)in   inf. -ir

8.7.2 *Imperfect endings*

    I & II   -és, -essis, -és; -éssim, -éssiu, -essin

    III   -ís, -issis, -ís; -íssim, -íssiu, -issin

8.7.3 The subjunctive is very common, both in clauses expressing desire or purpose and in those which have vague, emotional, general or negative antecedents, e.g. **perquè tingueu,** *so that you may have*; **no penso pas que això avui hagi millorat del tot,** *not that I think that that has improved at all today*; **el lector benevolent que m'hagi acompanyat fins ací,** *the kind reader who has followed me thus far.* Despite the definite article no particular reader is meant: if one had been, the verb would have been **ha,** the factual indicative. As the examples show, the subjunctive rarely requires special translation. In conditional sentences the imperfect indicative and the imperfect subjunctive can both be used in unreal conditions, but **si era** usually means *if it was, if it were* being **si fos.**

8.10 COMPOUND TENSES

8.10.1 The compound preterite has the following forms:

    vaig, vas, va; vam, vau, van + infinitive

(For **vaig** see 8.19.6.) Similarly, with **vagi,** etc., the past subjunctive; and with **vaig haver** + the past participle, the pluperfect (8.10.2). These periphrastic forms do not differ in meaning from the simple ones: in potted biographies you will meet **va néixer** and **nasqué** indifferently for *was born.* This use of **anar,** *to go,* to form a past tense takes a little getting used to, for **anar a,** also with the infinitive, means *to be going to,* while **anar** with the gerund denotes continuous action (8.12.2).

8.10.2 The present, imperfect or preterite, future, etc. of **haver** (8.17.4), with the past participle, form the perfect, pluperfect and future perfect, etc. The difference in usage between the two pluperfects need not detain us.

8.10.3 The past participle agrees in gender and number with a preceding pronoun object, e.g. **havia acabat la feina,** *he had finished his task*; **l'havia acabada,** *he had finished it.* But *the task which he had finished* is once again **la feina que havia acabat.** (In older Catalan, in Llull for example, it always agrees, e.g. **hac dites aquestes paraules.**)

8.10.4 If tenir is used instead of **haver** the participle agrees in all circumstances, e.g. **creia que té la prosperitat assegurada,** but the meaning is *he has prosperity safe* rather than *he has secured prosperity.*

8.11 INFINITIVE

8.11.1 The possible endings are **-ar, -er, -ir** and with a number of irregular verbs **-re.**

8.11.2 The infinitive is a verbal noun and may be the subject or object of another verb, e.g. **la vivacitat que dòna fer-los parlar textualment,** *the vivacity which making them speak in their own words confers* (**fer** subject, **parlar** object).

8.11.3   More commonly the infinitive follows a preposition, e.g. **invitava a ésser llegit**, *asked to be read*; **sense parlar**, *without speaking*; **en morir el rei**, *on the death of the king*.

8.12/8.13   PARTICIPLES (GERUND)

8.12.1   The present participle and gerund have the same form except for verbs in -ir, viz.

> -ant; -ent; P -ent, G -int

These two parts, so far as they are distinguished, cover most of the uses of the English participle. In Catalan the name participle is confined to the adjectival uses, e.g. **l'absorbent aprenentatge**, *the absorbing apprenticeship*; **una còrpora imponent**, *an imposing corporation* (possessed by **un italà ventripotent**—not all such words are Catalan participles). The participle has plural forms like any other adjective and at the same time retains something of its verbal character, e.g. **una seixantena d'alumnes pertanyents a l'estament obrer**, *some sixty pupils belonging to the working class*. The term gerund is applied to the adverbial uses, e.g. **m'he deturat una mica descrivint-vos aquesta escola**, *I have lingered a little in describing to you this school*.

8.12.2   The gerund is used with parts of **estar** and **anar** to express duration, e.g. **estic llegint**, *I am reading*; **van anar desapareixent**, *they gradually disappeared*. (Both uses of **anar** simultaneously.)

8.12.3   The past participle has the forms -at, -ut, -it (inf. -ar, -er, -ir), the F forms being -ada, -uda, -ida, and the P regular. Besides entering into compound tenses (8.10) and the passive (8.15) it is used as an adjective, e.g. **llenguatge parlat**, *spoken language*, and as the equivalent of a clause, with or without a conjunction, e.g. **després d'iniciat el segle actual**, *after the present century had begun*; **destruïda la ciutat**, *as the city was in ruins*.

8.14   REFLEXIVE

8.14.1   The coupling of the pronoun object of the same person with the verb produces reflexive forms, e.g. **em poso a escriure**, *I set myself to write*; **proveir-se d'aquest aliment**, *to provide oneself with this food*; **s'ho emporta tot**, *carries it all away with it*.

8.14.2   The perfect of reflexive verbs is formed with **haver**, though the archaic use of **ésser** survives in a few set phrases.

8.14.3   The meaning of reflexive forms is varied. Besides the properly reflexive meaning illustrated above, they may be reciprocal, e.g. **es saludaven**, *they would greet each other*; intransitive, **s'accentua i aguditza**, *becomes more marked and acute*; **es feia**, *happened*; passive, e.g. **la vila es diu Sarral**, *the town is called Sarral*; or impersonal, **no es menjava tant de pa**, *they did not eat so much bread*. Sometimes the force of the reflexive is not clear, e.g. **la vinya es moria**, *the vine was dying*.

8.15   PASSIVE

8.15.1   The passive form is got by coupling the appropriate part of **ésser,** sometimes **anar** or **quedar** (rarely estar) with the past participle, which agrees with the subject, e.g. **el pa era repartit als concurrents,** *the bread was distributed to the participants*; **coses que van juntes amb la meva jovenesa,** *things which are connected with my youth*; **quedaren castigats,** *they were punished*.

8.15.2 The substitution of the reflexive (8.14) is much more restricted than in Spanish. Occasionally the English passive is the appropriate translation of a phrase with the impersonal **hom**, e.g. **hom els veia sovint,** *they might often be seen.*

8.16 IMPERSONAL

8.16.1 There are some verbs which are found only in the third person, one of the commonest being **cal,** *it is necessary,* e.g. **trobaven que calia respondre amb les mateixes armes,** *they found that they had to reply with the same weapons;* **ni ens cal saber-ho,** *nor do we need to know it.* Commonest with the infinitive or by itself, it can also be followed by **que** and the subjunctive, as in **calia que les personalitats que havien establert el programa li administressin el temps,** *the personalities who had set up the programme had to manage his time for him.*

8.16.2 Other verbs not essentially impersonal have impersonal uses, e.g. **s'ha de jutjar,** *one has to judge;* **hi ha,** *there is;* but impersonal turns of phrase are not particularly common in Catalan (cf. 8.15.2).

8.17 AUXILIARIES

8.17.1 *Forms of* **ésser** (ser), *to be*
    Present indicative: **sóc/só, ets, és; som, sou, són**
    Imperfect: **era,** etc.
    Preterite: **fui, fores, fou; fórem, fóreu, foren** (or **vaig ésser,** etc.)
    Future: **seré,** etc.
    Conditional: **seria,** etc.; **fóra,** etc.
    Present subjunctive: **sigui,** etc.
    Imperfect subjunctive: **fos, fossis,** etc.
    Present participle: **essent**
    Past participle: **estat** (8.17.2)

8.17.2 *Forms of* **estar,** *to be*
    Present indicative: **estic, estàs, està; estem, esteu, estan**
    Preterite: **estigui, estigueres,** etc.
    Present subjunctive: **estigui,** etc.
    Imperfect subjunctive: **estigués,** etc.
All other parts are regular.

8.17.3 The basic distinction between **ésser** and **estar** is that **ésser** expresses qualities, states and situations that are lasting or does so without reference to time, **estar** expresses ones that are temporary or accidental, much as in Spanish, though there are many instances where Spanish uses **estar** and Catalan **ésser. Estar** in Catalan can also mean *to stop, to stand* and *to live somewhere.* The auxiliary of the passive is **ésser** (8.15).

8.17.4 *Forms of the auxiliary* **haver** (8.10.2)
    Present indicative: **he/haig, has, ha; h(av)em, h(av)eu, han**
    Preterite: **haguí, hagueres,** etc.
    Future: **hauré,** etc.
    Conditional: **hauria,** etc.
    Present subjunctive: **hagi . . .; hàgim, hàgiu, hagin**
    Imperfect subjunctive: **hagués,** etc.
    Past participle: **hagut**
Other forms regular.

8.17.5 *Forms of* haver/heure, *to get*
  Present indicative: hec, heus, heu; havem, haveu, heuen
  Present subjunctive: hegui; haguem, heguin
All other forms like the auxiliary.

8.17.6 *Forms of* tenir, *to have, hold*
  Present indicative: tinc, tens, té; tenim, etc.
  Preterite: tinguí, tingueres, etc.
  Future: tindré
  Conditional: tindria, etc.
  Present subjunctive: tingui, etc.
  Past subjunctive: tingués, etc.
  Past participle: tingut
Other forms regular.

8.17.7 The auxiliary is used to form the perfect group of tenses and the periphrasis **haver de**; **haig** occurs only in **haig de**. The sense of **haver de** is commonly *to have to*, but not always, e.g. **que no sabem si hem de retrobar mai més,** *which we do not know if we shall ever find again.* **Haver/heure** does not mean *to have*, which is **tenir**. In some uses **tenir** too comes close to being an auxiliary (8.10.4) and **tenir de** can be used as well as **haver de**.

8.19 IRREGULAR

8.19.1 The irregular verbs are a much smaller class than the regular ones but include many that are common. The majority of them derive from Latin verbs of the third conjugation but there has been considerable analogical development, so that a large number of them can be subsumed under two patterns. What follows applies to the commoner verbs, viz. **anar,** *to go*; **aprendre,** *to learn*, and other verbs in **-ndre**; **cabre,** *to contain*; **caldre,** *to be necessary*; **caure,** *to fall*; **conèixer,** *to know*; **córrer,** *to run*; **creure,** *to believe*; **deure,** *to owe, to be obliged, to be probable*; **dir,** *to say*; **dur,** *to take, carry*; **eixir,** *to go out*; **escriure,** *to write*; **fer,** *to do, make*; **moure,** *to move*; **néixer,** *to be born*; **plaure,** *to please*; **poder,** *to be able*; **rebre,** *to receive*; **riure,** *to laugh*; **saber,** *to know, to be able*; **soler,** *to be accustomed*; **sortir,** *to go out*; **tenir,** *to have*; **treure,** *to draw out*; **venir,** *to come*; **veure,** *to see*; **viure,** *to live*; **voler,** *to wish, want.*

8.19.2 *The present tense* has two common patterns:

> I   -c, -s, -; -em, -eu, -en   inf. **-dre**
>   All verbs in **-ndre** and **caldre**
> IIa -c, -us, -u; -vem, -veu, -ven
> b   do.   -(i)em, -(i)eu, -(i)en   inf. **-ure**
>   All other verbs not dealt with below (8.19.6 foll.)

There are small divergences, e.g. **dic . . . diem** from **dir**; **duc . . . duem** from **dur**; **caic** from **caure**; **traiem** from **treure**; **visc** from **viure**.

8.19.3 *The imperfect* usually follows the plural of the present, e.g. **creure, creiem, creia**: but **deia** is from **dir**; **feia** from **fer**; **queia** from **caure**; **reia** from **riure**.

8.19.4 *The preterite* commonly ends in **-guí**, e.g. **aprenguí, caiguí** (**caure**), **traguí** (**treure**); **coneguí** (**conèixer**) but **visquí** from **viure**. See also 8.19.6 and following.

8.19.5 *The present subjunctive* also ends in **-gui**, but without the accent. See also 8.19.6 and following.

8.19.6 anar

Present indicative: vaig, vas, va; anem, aneu, van
Future: aniré, etc.
Present subjunctive: vagi . . . ; anem . . . vagin

For **anar** as auxiliary see 8.7.1.

8.19.7 cabre

Present indicative: cabo, caps, cap; cabem, etc.
Present subjunctive: càpiga, càpigues, etc.

8.19.8 conèixer

Present: conec, coneixes, etc.

8.19.9 eixir

Stem: eix- or ix-

8.19.10 fer

Present indicative: faig, fas, fa; fem, feu, fan
Preterite: fiu, feres, féu; férem, etc.
Future: faré, etc.
Present subjunctive: faci, etc.

A common idiomatic use of **fer** is found in **fa** (or **feia**) **anys**, *years ago*.

8.19.11 néixer

Stem: neix- or naix-

8.19.12 poder

Present indicative: puc, pots, pot; podem, etc.
Present subjunctive: pugui, etc.

8.19.13 saber

Present indicative: sé, saps, sap; sabem, etc.
Present subjunctive: sàpiga, etc.

8.19.14 sortir

Stem: sort- or surt-

8.19.15 tenir (and similarly **venir**)

See 8.17.6

8.19.16 veure

Present indicative: veig . . . ; veiem, etc.
Preterite: viu, v(ei)eres, veié/véu; v(ei)érem, etc.
Present subjunctive: vegi, etc.

8.19.17 voler

Present indicative: vull, vols, etc.
Present subjunctive: vulgui, etc.

8.19.18 The past participles of these and some other verbs are irregular, viz.

P	I	P	I	P	I
-(i)gut	-ure	dut	dur	pogut	poder
-mès	-metre	establert	establir	sofert	sofrir
atès	atènyer	estret	estrènyer	tingut	tenir
(c)obert	(c)obrir	fet	fer	tret	treure
(c)omplert	(c)omplir	imprès	imprimir	vingut	venir
conegut	conèixer	mort	morir	vist	veure
corregut	correr	nascut	néixer	viscut	viure
dit	dir	ofert	oferir	volgut	voler

8.22 NEGATIVE

8.22.1   The adverb no is sufficient to make a verb negative, e.g. **no sap,** *he does not know*; but it may be combined with one or more of the words **cap,** *any*; **enlloc,** *anywhere*; **gens,** *at all, any*; **mai,** *ever*; **ningú,** *anybody*; **res,** *anything*; **tampoc,** *either*; e.g. **Ningú no havia vist mai res de semblant,** *No-one had ever seen anything like it.*

8.22.2   The special words, like the corresponding English ones, are restricted to negative, interrogative and some subordinate sentences. Unlike the English ones they can in certain contexts function as negatives by themselves, e.g. **són els del tot o res que s'han quedat amb no res,** *they are the all-or-nothing men who have finished up with nothing.*

8.22.3   No . . . pas is not equivalent to the French ne . . . pas, but introduces a correction, a denial of what might have been expected, e.g. **L'exacerbació anticlerical sembla atenuar-se. No és pas que hi hagi convertits,** *Anticlerical bitterness seems to be lessening. Not that there have been converts.* **No pas** on the other hand is the normal negative for a single word or phrase, e.g. **feina no pas sempre fàcil,** *a task which was not always easy.*

8.22.4   Both no and no pas are found in sentences which are not strictly speaking negative, after expressions of doubt or fear and in the second member of a comparison, e.g. **tinc por que no sigui mort,** *I am afraid he is dead*; **això era més litúrgia externa . . . que no pas intimitat i caritat,** *that was outward ceremony . . . rather than inwardness and charity.*

9 ADVERBS

9.1 FORMATION

9.1.1   A good many primitive adverbs have no distinctive form. Those formed from adjectives are obtained by adding **-ment** to the feminine.

9.1.2   Note that in a phrase like **joiosament i solemne** both are adverbs; but contemporary writers would be more likely to repeat the **-ment,** e.g. **purament i simplement.**

9.2 COMPARISON

9.2.1   Apart from a few special forms like **millor,** *better*; **pitjor,** *worse,* the comparative is got by putting **més,** *more,* in front. Absolute superlatives in **-issimament** are also found.

10 PREPOSITIONS

10.2 FORMS OF SIMPLE PREPOSITIONS

The prepositions **a, de** and **per** combine with the article to form **al, als, del, pel,** etc. Before a vowel or **h** de becomes **d'.**

10.4 COMPOUND PREPOSITIONS

Besides the simple prepositions there are a number of prepositional phrases ending in **a** or **de,** e.g. **cap a,** *towards*; **prop de,** *near*; but **per a,** *for* (as opposed to **per,** *by, through*) is considered to be a simple preposition.

10.5 USES

10.5.1   The uses are not likely to surprise anyone familiar with other Romance languages, except for the wholly strange **amb,** *with, by means of.* (Its old form **ab** is more recognisably related to the French **avec**.) There are a few constructions where **a** is used with the direct object, but only a few. On the other hand **a** is regularly used with **com** in phrases like **com a adversaris**, *as opponents*.

10.5.2 A, de and per a are usually untranslated before infinitives.

11 CONJUNCTIONS

11.1 Provided one is not put off by the conjunctions, mostly compounded with **que**, which require the subjunctive, the translation of conjunctions should not cause much difficulty. Note, however, that **perquè** is ambiguous: both senses occur together in **perquè no hi manqués res, i perquè a Catalunya sempre hi ha lloc per a coses pinto-resques . . .**, *so that nothing might be wanting, and because Catalonia always has room for things that are picturesque . . . .* **Per què**, however, means *why*, while **per bo que fos** means *good though it is*.

11.2 When **o**, *or*, is used to introduce an equivalent or amplification, it is often re-inforced by **sia** or **sigui**, e.g. **la segona part, o sigui les biografies**, *the second part or biographies*. But this can introduce an afterthought, e.g. **o sigui que no es menjava tant de pa**, *or else it was just that they did not eat so much bread*.

GLOSSARY

actualitzat, *brought up to date*
advertiment, *prefatory note*
ampliada, *enlarged* (1.5.2)
anuari, *yearbook*
any, *year* (1.8.4)
aparèixer, *appear*
aplec, *collection*
assaig, *essay*
atrassat, *back* (*number*) (1.8.6)

biblioteca, *library* (1.7.1)
bibliotecari, *librarian*
butlletí, *bulletin*

carta, *letter*
col·lecció, *series* (1.7.1)
comanda, *order*
corregida, *corrected* (1.5.2)

diari, *journal*
drets reservats, *all rights reserved*

edició, *edition* (1.5.1), *publication* (1.6.1)
editat, *published*
editorial, *publishing house*
enllestit, *ready*
enviar, *send*
esmena, *correction* (1.5.2)

estranger, *abroad, foreigner*
exemplar, *copy*
expedir, *dispatch*

factura, *invoice*
fascicle, *issue* (1.8.4)
de franc, *free*

impremta, *press* (1.6.2)
inèdit, *unpublished*

llibre, *book*
llibret, *pamphlet*
llibreter, *bookseller*
llibr(et)eria, *bookshop*

mateix, *same*
mensual, *monthly* (1.8.5)
mes, *month* (1.8.5)
morí (**va morir**), *died*
mostra, *sample*

narració, *short story*
nasqué (**va néixer**), *born*
nou, *new*
novel(·l)a, *novel, short story*

obra, *work*

pamflet, *libel*

en premsa, *in the press*

preu, *price* (1.8.6)

pròleg, *preface, introduction*

és proprietat, *copyright*

quadern, *issue* (1.8.4)

quadre, *table*

quinzenal, *fortnightly* (1.8.5)

redacció, *editing* (1.8.3), *editorial office* (1.8.7)

redactat, *edited*

redactor, *editor* (1.8.3)

reimpressió, *reprint* (1.5.3)

retrat, *portrait*

revista, *review*

sèrie, (*sub*)*series* (1.7.2)

setmanal, *weekly* (1.8.5)

soci, *member* (1.8.5)

solt, *single* (1.8.6)

(relligat en) tela, *hard back*

tiratge separat, *offprint* (1.5.3)

traducció, *translation*

trametre, *dispatch*

triat, *selected*

trimestral, *quarterly* (1.8.5)

vegeu, vegi's, *see*

venda, *sale*

GRAMMATICAL INDEX: WORDS

a, 10.5.1

al, 10.2

algú, algun(a), 7.1.4

als, 10.2

amb, 10.5.1

aqueix, aquest, 7.1.1

atès, 8.19.18

caic, 8.19.3

cal(ia), 8.16.1

cap, càpiga, etc., 8.19.7

cobert, 8.19.18

complert, 8.19.18

conec, 8.19.8

conegut, 8.19.18

corregut, 8.19.18

deia, 8.19.3

del(s), 10.2

dit, dut, 8.19.18

el qual, 7.2.3

el(s), 3.1.1, 7.1.3, 7.3.1

em, 7.3.1

en, 3.1.2, 7.3.3

ens, 7.3.1

era, etc., 8.17.1

es, 7.3.1

està(s), etc., 8.17.2

estat, 8.17.1

estic, estig-, 8.17.2

estret, 8.19.18

et, 7.3.1

fa, faci, faig, etc., 8.19.10

feia, 8.19.3

fet, 8.19.18

feu, fiu, 8.19.10

for-, fos(sis), etc., fou, fui, 8.17.1

ha, hag-, haig, han, hau-, 8.17.4

hav-, 8.15, 8.17.4

he, 8.17.4

hec, heg-, heu(en), heus, 8.17.5

hi, 7.3.3

ho, 7.3.1

imprès, 8.19.18

ix-, 8.19.9

l', 3.1.1, 7.3.1

'l, 7.3.1

la, les, 3.1.1, 7.1.3, 7.3.1

'ls, 7.3.1

m', 'm, 7.3.1

ma, mes, 5.2.8

mateix, 7.1.7

més, 5.3

mi, 7.3.1

mort, 8.19.18

mos, 5.2.8

n', 'n, 7.3.3

n', na, 3.1.2

naix-, 8.19.11

nascut, 8.19.18

'ns, 7.3.1

o sia, o sigui, 11.2

obert, 8.19.18

on, 7.2.4

pas, 8.22.3–4

pel(s), 10.2

per a, 10.4

perquè, 11.1

pod-, 8.19.12

pogut, 8.19.18

pot(s), 8.19.12

puc, pug-, 8.19.2

qualsevol, qualsevulla, 7.1.5

que, 7.2.1–2

queia, 8.19.3

qui, 7.2.1–2

GRAMMATICAL INDEX: ENDINGS

FRENCH

Beuueurs tresill stres, et vous verollez trespretieux (car a vous non a aultres sont dediez
Buveurs très illustres   vérolés très précieux   à   à autres   dédiés

mes escriptz), Alcibiades louant son precepteur Socrates . . . le dict estre semblable
    écrits   pré—   dit être

es Silenes . . .
(aux) Silènes

Tel disoyt estre Socrates; par ce que, le voyans au dehors et lestimans par lexteriore
    disait-il être   voyants   l'estimants l'extérieure

apparence nen eussiez donné vng coupeau doignon, tant laid il estoyt de cors, et ridicule
    (vous) n'en (auriez)   un   d'o—   était   corps

en son maintien; le nez poinctu, le reguard dung taureau, le visaige dung fol . . . tousiours
                          pointu   regard d'un   visage d'un fou   toujours

riant, tousiours beuuant dautant a vng chascun, tousiours dissimulant son divin scavoir.
       buvant d'autant à un chacun   savoir

(Rabelais)

es is for en les, but French no longer uses en in this way.
voyans: modern French would have voyant, the participle no longer agreeing.
eussiez: the form has not changed, but the subjunctive is not now used in this way.

De quoy estant tres-asseuré, ie supplieray treshumblement vostre Maiesté de recevoir
    quoi étant très-assuré   -ai très   votre

d'aussi bonne main ce mien labeur, comme d'vn cœur treshumble et tresaffectionné ie luy
                                                  très   très   lui

presente. Priant Dieu, Madame, qu'il doint à vostre Maiesté autant d'heur et de felicité,
présente   donne votre   fé—

que vostre bon frere vous souhaite de mal et d'encombre. (1573)
    votre   frère

209

Que pendant que le mesme Prince apportoit toutes les précautions que la guerre conseille,
          même   -ait

particulierement pour passer le grand Escaut, au delà duquel les Espagnols estoient
     -ère-   étaient

postez pour l'empescher; ce Mareschal ayant rencontré quelques basteaux le passa avec
postés   -êch-   -êch-   bat-

cinq cens chevaux et donna la chasse aux Ennemis, qui creurent que toute l'Armee estoit
     cents   crurent   -ée était

passee. (1651)
  -ée

Ces ouvrages forment une espèce de cours sur la grave matière que les malheurs pressans,
l'entêtement du ministre, et la prochaine session des chambres, peuvent rendre propre à
jeter quelque jour dans le dédale de notre crédit public. Si je n'avais pas cru à leur utilité,
je ne les aurais pas publiés. (1826)

Only **pressans** for **pressants** remains of the old forms. The Academy insisted on **avois,
aurois** until 1835, but most writers had by now changed to **-a-**.

L'élaboration de l'ouvrage remonte aux années 1932–1939. J'en savais alors la témérité.
Entreprendre seul une histoire de toute notre littérature passant les cadres de la pédagogie
élémentaire: je suis sans doute le dernier qui ait risqué l'aventure . . . . Mais il me tentait
de construire une histoire littéraire fondée non plus sur la division par genres, selon moi
dépassée, mais essentiellement sur les mouvements d'idées, qui seuls permettent d'atteindre
aux pensées profondes, et dont l'évolution à travers les générations successives . . . suit le
cours même de la vie. (1965)

*The preparation of the work goes back to the years 1932–1939. I realised even then my
recklessness. To undertake on my own a history of our whole literature which went beyond
the bounds of elementary instruction: I was doubtless the last to have taken the risk . . . . But
I found it tempting to construct a literary history which was based not on the division into
genres—to my mind we had got past that—but essentially on the movements of ideas,
which alone permit one to penetrate to men's deeper thoughts, and whose evolution
through successive generations . . . follows the very course of life.*

0 GENERAL CHARACTERISTICS

0.1 DEGREE OF INFLEXION
French is a predominantly analytical language. Many forms of the verb have become
identical in pronunciation, so that subject pronouns are now obligatory, as in English,
and though French has a simple past tense, the spoken language and styles based on it
prefer to use the compound past both for the perfect and the simple past.

0.2 ORDER OF WORDS
Adjectives and qualifying phrases mostly follow the noun they qualify. The standard
phrase order is SVO and reversals such as those quoted in 8.16.2 are stereotyped and
not very common.

0.4 RELATION TO OTHER LANGUAGES

On the relation of French to Latin and the other Romance languages see General note on the Romance languages.

1 BIBLIOLINGUISTICS

1.1 NAMES

1.1.1 Modern French personal names consist of Christian name and surname, but during the Middle Ages both phrases denoting territorial origin and descriptive terms may be regarded rather as epithets. So one has **Adam de la Hal(l)e**, alias **Adam le Bossu** indexed under **Adam**, and the 14th-century **Jean le Bel**, son of **Gilles le Beal**, indexed sometimes under **Jean** and sometimes under **Lebel**.

1.1.2 The ramifications of French families produce a large number of surnames of the general form **X de (la) Y**, with holders frequently known simply as **Y**, if indeed they are not known instead by their title. So we have **Fénelon (François de Salignac de la Motte-Fénelon)** and **Montesquieu (Charles Louis de Secondat, Baron de la Brede et de Montesquieu)**. Holders of ecclesiastical dignities may be known as, e.g. **l'abbé de Boisrobert (François de Metel, sieur de Boisrobert)**, **le cardinal de Retz (Jean François Paul de Gondi)**, **M. de Genève** (St. Francis de Sales, Bishop of Geneva). (Incidentally it should be noted that **M., Mme, Mlle** are by no means confined to commoners.)

1.1.3 Despite the rule that names in **Du** and **Des** are so indexed while those in **De La** fall under **La**, **Du Bellay** will sometimes be found under **Bellay** while names like **De La Haye** may be spelt as one word.

In a sentence it is possible to have, e.g. **l'œuvre de Du Bellay**, but **Jean de La Fontaine** and **Alfred de Musset** are reduced to **La Fontaine** and **Musset** in all contexts, so the question of **de de** does not arise.

1.1.4 A plural **-s** is occasionally added to surnames, e.g. **les Bourbons**, but more often the name is unchanged.

1.1.5 Classical names and well-known foreign names are often given French forms, sometimes throughout, sometimes only in the Christian name, e.g. **Aristote, l'Arétin** (Aretino), **François Bacon, Cicéron, Gaufrei de Monmouth, Pic de la Mirandole, Zwingle**.

1.2 NAMES OF AUTHORS, EDITORS, ETC.

1.2.1 The names of authors, if not simply placed at the head of the title-page, follow the title and are usually preceded by **par**. The names of editors, translators and so on usually follow, some participle indicative of the special activity being inserted, e.g. **revu(e)(s), mis(e)(s) en français, avec introduction et notes de** (or **par**). The name is not affected by the grammatical relationship.

1.2.2 In editions of complete works, selections and correspondence, as well as in new editions of classics and in citations, the preposition **de** is common, e.g. **Œuvres de François Rabelais; Lettres choisies de Madame de Sévigné; Fables de J. de La Fontaine**. If the name is preceded by a title which includes the definite article, phrases like **du R. P. (révérend père) M.-J. Lagrange** may occur, which cannot be shortened without upsetting the grammar (10.2).

1.2.3 The names of corporate bodies as authors should not cause difficulty. They may be preceded by **par** or **de**, e.g. **publié sous les auspices de la Commission des Archives diplomatiques au Ministère des Affaires Étrangères**. The subordinate body has to be extracted, viz. **Ministère des Affaires Étrangères. Commission des Archives Diplomatiques.**

H

1.3 TITLES

1.3.1 Most titles consist simply of nouns, adjectives and prepositions, e.g. **Histoire de la littérature française,** *History of French Literature*; **Lettres sur divers sujets de métaphysique et de religion,** *Letters on various matters of metaphysics and religion.* Imaginative and persuasive literature introduce more elements, e.g. **Où en est le marché commun?,** *How does the Common Market stand?*; **On ne badine pas avec l'amour,** *Love is not to be trifled with.* Older titles may contain subordinate clauses, e.g. **Avertissement très utile du grand profit qui reviendrait à la Chrétienté s'il se faisait inventaire de tous les corps saints et reliques qui sont tant en Italie qu'en France,** *A very useful notification of the great profit which would accrue to Christianity if an inventory were made of all the bodies of saints and relics which are to be found as well in Italy as in France*—a title which it is difficult to shorten without mutilation.

1.3.2 Title entries pose no problems except in so far as under British Museum rules combinations involving proper adjectives need to be translated, so that **Noëls bourguignons** appears under BURGUNDIAN CAROLS—if that is how one translates **noëls.** There are many local adjectives in French and not all of them have English equivalents.

In the filing of titles most bibliographies make a distinction between the indefinite article and the numeral *one*, filing **Un curé de montagne** under **Curé,** but **Une vie, trois guerres** under **Une;** but **La librairie française** files all under **Un(e).** (The definite article is consistently ignored.)

1.3.3 Titles beginning with a preposition were often shortened when cited by the omission of the preposition. So one finds **Commentaire sur l'Esprit des lois** and the like more often than the more formal **Observations sur un livre intitulé: De l'esprit des lois.** A less common type of departure is found in such a phrase as **contenus au livre de la République de Bodin.** The title of Bodin's work is neither **La république** nor **De la république** nor **Livre de la république** but **Les six livres de la république.**

When a title begins with **le** or **les** this may combine with a preceding **à** or **de** (10.1), e.g. **l'auteur du Monde primitif,** *the author of 'Le monde primitif'.*

1.4 VOLUMES AND PARTS

1.4.1 The usual words are **volume** or **tome** on the one hand and **partie** on the other. **Livre,** *book*, not much used nowadays, is at all times more a division of the subject matter and has no necessary relation to physical divisions. Works which are continued may indicate subsequent parts in terms derived from the title, e.g. **Second recueil,** etc; **Troisième lettre,** etc; **Suite de l'Histoire,** etc.

1.4.2 Numeration in words by an ordinal number, e.g. **Troisième volume,** is common, but not to the exclusion of the type: **tome 3,** now read **tome trois,** earlier **tome troisième.**

1.4.3 Except in the cases already mentioned the numeration is usually distinct from the title, but phrases like **La seconde partie du Censeur du temps et du monde** are occasionally found.

1.5 EDITIONS

1.5.1 The usual word is **édition,** but the word may simply mean publication (1.6.1). The number precedes in ordinal form, e.g. **troisième édition,** or sometimes simply **nouvelle édition,** to which may be added words indicating revision such as **(entièrement) revue, corrigée, mise à jour, refondue,** etc.

1.5.2 It should be noted that new numbered editions are commoner in French than in English books. Not merely does one find **Troisième édition conforme à la**

deuxième, indicating a straight reprint, but high numbers are rapidly reached, probably impressions rather than new editions. **Impression** itself is also found.

1.5.3 **Réimpression** means *reprint*; **tirage à part** *offprint*.

1.6 IMPRINTS

1.6.1 Modern imprints are usually those of publishers. This may be made explicit by the use of **édition(s)**, *publication(s)*, **société d'édition** (*publishing company*), by **librairie**, literally *book-shop*, or by **éditeur(s)**, *publisher(s)* or **libraire(s)-éditeur(s)** after the name.

Printers are indicated by **imprimeur** or the abstract **imprimerie**, less commonly by words from the stem **typograph-**. Up to the 18th century at least the functions could be combined, e.g. **De l'imprimerie de Pierre le Petit, Imprimeur et Libraire ordinaire du Roy**, but in the 19th one finds **de l'imprimerie** of the printer contrasted with **chez** (1.6.2) of the publisher.

1.6.2 Not too much can be made of the use of different prepositions. **Pour**, *for*, indicates a publisher, **chez** probably does, **par** is more likely to indicate the printer; but **par Jean Pillehotte, Libraire de la S. Vuion** (1591) and **chez Jean B. Besougne le Fils, Imprimeur ordinaire du Roy** (1725) show the contrary. **Aux dépens de**, *at the expense of*, is sometimes found in earlier books for the publisher. Today prepositions, as in **Aux Éditions du Seuil**, are very rare.

1.6.3 Publishers' styles have developed from the simplicity of **Jean Martin** to a variety ranging from the laconic **Plon** to such names as **Société d'Édition d'Enseignement Supérieur** (naturally enough abbreviated to **S.E.D.E.S.**) or **Librairie de Droit et de Jurisprudence Durand-Auzias** or the names of periodicals like **Mercure de France**. Sometimes **éditions** (1.6.1) is optional—one finds both **Bernard Grasset, éditeur** and **Éditions Bernard Grasset**—sometimes an essential part of the title (cf. 1.6.2). The same is true of **librairie**. A few firms have names like **J'ai lu** (*I have read*) and **Le Livre de Poche** (*The Pocket Book*). Names like **Garnier Frères** (*Garnier Bros*), **Boivin et Cie** are now among the least common.

1.6.4 Heirs (**héritiers**) or a widow, e.g. **Chez la veuve Mathurin Dupuis**, are found in earlier books. In this instance one must either reduce the imprint to **Dupuis** or give it in full since **Mathurin** is the husband's name.

1.7 SERIES

1.7.1 Series are very common in French publishing. Sometimes the name appears at the head of the title-page, sometimes only on the cover or half-title. Apart from **collection, bibliothèque**, e.g. **Bibliothèque d'histoire**, *Historical library*, is fairly common in the names of series, sometimes **cahiers**, as in the famous **Cahiers de la quinzaine**, sometimes **études**. (But both **cahiers** and **études** may equally well occur in the titles of periodicals, e.g. **Cahiers de la république**.) Less commonly the title of the series suggests the subject matter rather than describes the series as such, or is purely evocative, e.g. **Être et penser** (*Being and thinking*); **Nous deux** (*Us two*). Sometimes the title of the series incorporates the name of the publishing institution, e.g. **Publications de l'Observatoire de Haute Provence**, which might be reversed in the catalogue. Whether one should perform such reversals on a joint series like **Bibliothèque des Écoles françaises d'Athènes et de Rome** is another matter.

1.7.2 By far the commonest form of numeration is by **numéro**, though **fascicule** and **cahier** are also found. Learned series may be divided by **tome**, sometimes subdivided into **fascicules**, or by **volumes** and **numéros**. Sub-series are indicated by **nouvelle série, 15me série** and so on, or by **série A**, etc.

   1.7.3   Sometimes the series is implied by such statements as **Document technique n° 67** or **Cahier 55 de la Fondation Nationale des Sciences Politiques**, which would usually appear in catalogues in the plural, viz. FONDATION NATIONALE DES SCIENCES POLITIQUES. Cahiers.

1.8 PERIODICALS

   1.8.1   The titles of periodicals differ little linguistically from those of books and series (1.7.1), e.g. **Politique étrangère, Revue d'histoire économique et sociale**, but may be more fanciful, e.g. **Le lys rouge** (*The red lily*), and may not mean what they appear to. **L'abeille de France** is indeed about bees, but **L'abeille de Neufchateau** contains legal notices.

   1.8.2   The title, or more often the sub-title, may include the name of an institution, e.g. **Bulletin d'information de l'Association auxiliaire de l'action sociale et familiale**, which some libraries may prefer to enter under the Association.

   1.8.3   The persons concerned with the editing, grouped as **rédaction**, are indicated individually by various terms, the meanings of which in isolation are not obvious. There may be a **directeur (de la publication)** or **directeur général**, either alone or with a **rédacteur en chef** and various **collaborateurs**; or there may be several **directeurs** and a **secrétaire de la rédaction**. Sometimes a periodical may have a **rédacteur en chef** and a **rédacteur**. Which of these is 'the editor' cannot be decided from language alone. Behind these may be found a large **comité de direction** and a small **comité de rédaction**. In such a case the **comité de direction** is a sort of advisory board, much the same as the **conseil d'administration** or the **comité de patronage (scientifique)** or **comité de parrainage** (*sponsoring committee*), but where it is contrasted with these it is likely to be of the same sort as what is elsewhere called the **comité de rédaction**.

   The publisher is usually given simply as **éditeur**, or a phrase such as **publié(e) par** may follow the title.

   1.8.4   Numeration is most commonly of the form **47ᵉ année, n° 12**, or with continuous numeration of the parts **N° 442 - LXXXᵉ année**. **Volume** and **tome** are found instead of **année**, and **cahier** instead of **numéro**. Individual parts are sometimes described as **fascicules**, but more often in connexion with subscriptions than in the numeration. Occasionally words are used instead of figures.

   1.8.5   Periodicity may be apparent from the title, or more often from the sub-title, e.g. **revue (publication) mensuelle (bimestrielle, trimestrielle)**; **revue paraissant tous les deux mois** (*appearing every other month*). Alternatively there may be a separate statement such as: **La revue parait quatre fois par an**, *The review appears four times a year*, or the periodicity may be implied by the subscription rates (1.8.6).

   1.8.6   Details of subscriptions are given under such rubrics as **Tarif(s) (des abonnements), Commandes et abonnements**. Here will be found the **prix de l'abonnement d'un an (annuel) (X numéros)** or for six months **(six mois)**, or occasionally there will be a quotation for a **vol. relié** (*bound volume*). Usually there will also be rates for single numbers (**vente au numéro, prix du numéro**, or simply **le numéro** or **numéro simple**).

   All this applies to the current year (**l'année courante**). Back numbers usually come under the heading **année(s) écoulée(s)**, or may be implied in **années disponibles**, *volumes available*; or there may be a quotation for individual back numbers, **e.g. chaque fascicule ancien se vend** . . . .

1.8.7 Addresses usually distinguish **rédaction**, the editorial, and **administration**, the business side, but the two may be linked or there may be an instruction to direct all correspondence to one address: **adresser toute correspondance à** . . . .

2 ALPHABET, PHONETICS, SPELLING

2.1 ALPHABET

2.1.1 The alphabet is the same as in English. The use of some letters was different in the earlier period from what it is today, viz.

i represents present-day **i** and **j** in all positions. Lower-case **j** comes in gradually in the second-half of the 17th century, J somewhat later on the whole, so that for example **SVIET** and **sujet** may be found in the same book.

u and **v** also are treated as one letter. In the upper case only V is found, while in the lower case **v** is usually found at the beginning of a word while **u** occurs elsewhere, e.g. **LIVRE, liure; IVRE, iure** (modern **jure** or **ivre!**); **vne vie.** Sometimes **u** is found in all positions. As with **i** and **j** the change to the modern practice is gradual and inconsistencies will be found. It is usual in transcribing titles to follow the convention of the book, substituting **u** for V when not initial, though this raises problems in filing title entries. (See the first two specimens.)

2.1.2 There are three accents, all of which are essential to the correct spelling of the words on which they occur. The acute accent is found on e, indicating a close vowel, as in **côté**, a different word from **côte**.

The grave accent on e, in the combinations **-èCe-** and **-ès**, indicates an open vowel, but on the other letters it simply serves to distinguish homonyms, such as **où** *where*, **ou** *or*; **à** *to*, **a** *has*.

The circumflex accent is a grammarian's delight. It indicates the loss of a letter in **bête**, *beast*; **côte**, *coast*; **flûte** (earlier **fleute**) and so on, but not in **extrême** or **dôme**. It almost always indicates that **a** and **o** are close; but **rose**, for instance, does without it; and **chrême** and **crème** are both derived from **chrisma**. So when in doubt, consult the dictionary.

Very occasionally one may find on or after E an apostrophe instead of an acute or circumflex accent. Accents in capitals are sometimes omitted, the grave accent on A more often than not.

2.1.3 Other orthographical signs are the cedilla, used to indicate that **c** has the sound it has in *city*, and the diaeresis. With changes of ending one form of a word may have **c** and another **ç**, e.g. **placer, plaça**. The diaeresis indicates that two vowels are not to be taken together in the usual way, e.g. **archaïque** [arkaik]. In the case of **aiguë**, where the **ë** is silent, the diaeresis indicates that the **u** is pronounced, whereas in **blague** it is not. But when medial **u** stands for both **-u-** and **-v-** (2.1.1) a spelling like **auoüe** denotes **avoue** as against **avove**.

2.1.4 The apostrophe, regularly used to indicate the omission of a letter at the end of a word, is found in the middle in words like **presqu'île, grand'mère**. There is no space after it. (See also 2.1.2)

2.2 CAPITALISATION

2.2.1 In principle proper names are spelt with capitals, but adjectives derived from them, e.g. **français, rabelaisien**, are not; nor are some types of names, those of months and days of the week, counted as proper names in French as they are in English. Historical periods and events vary: **la Réforme**, but **le Moyen Age** or **moyen âge**.

2.2.2 Most parts of personal, geographical and astronomical names have capitals. Prepositions nearly always begin with a small letter, e.g. **Joachim du Bellay, cap de Bonne Espérance**; but **la poésie de Du Bellay**. The article usually has a capital in personal names, e.g. **Jean de La Fontaine** but when the surname is compound we tend to find forms like **Restif de la Bretonne**. In astronomical names adjectives do not begin with a capital letter unless they begin the name, e.g. **Grande Ourse** but **Couronne australe**. The common part of a geographical name, e.g. **cap**, has a small letter.

2.2.3 In the names of institutions, societies and the like, including government departments, the practice of the Ministère de l'éducation nationale is to use a capital for the first word only, excluding the article; but this austere norm is not always observed, and either all words except prepositions and articles are capitalised, e.g. **Association de la Jeunesse Ouvrière Chrétienne**, or all nouns, e.g. **Union mondiale des Organisations féminines catholiques**. **Président de la République**, however, is not an exception: **République** (= **France**) would have a capital in any case.

Book titles are treated in the same way, with the same inconsistencies.

2.2.4 Titles of nobility and office are commonly spelt with a small letter, though contrary instances are found in the case of titles of office, e.g. **le duc de Liancourt; M. du Gué, président des trésoriers de France; le cardinal de Lyon; le Président Cassin; Jérôme Carcopino, Directeur de l'École française de Rome**.

2.3 DIVISION OF WORDS

2.3.1 For the most part rules 1, 4, 5a, 6a, 7b and 8 (p. xiii) apply, with the proviso that **l** and **r** are not separated from a preceding **b, c, d, f, g, p, t** or **v**: **no-ble** not **nob-le**. With clusters of three or more consonants there is some freedom: divisions like **in-struire** are found as well as the commoner **ins-truire**.

2.3.2 Combinations which represent a single sound, viz. **ch, ph, th**, are not divided. The same applies to **gn**, as in **témoi-gnage**; but **ll** is divided whether in **vil-lage** (vilaʒ) or **sil-lon** (sijɔ̃). Divisions involving **x** between two vowels are simply avoided.

2.4 PUNCTUATION AND ABBREVIATIONS

2.4.1 Apart altogether from the modern tendency to omit stops in abbreviations consisting of a series of initials, French usually omits them if the last letters are included, e.g. **Mgr** for **Monseigneur**.

2.4.2 Hyphens are often (but not always) used between initials standing for Christian names.

2.5 VARIATION OF CONSONANT

2.5.1 The consonants **c** and **g** each have different values before different vowels, as they do in English. To keep the sound the same **qu** and **gu**, **ç** and **ge** have to be substituted as follows:

> *Hard:* **ca, que, qui, co, cu; ga, gue, gui, go, gu**
> *Soft:* **ça, ce, ci, ço, çu; gea, ge, gi, geo, geu**

In practice, however, matters are not so simple. **Attaquer** has **-qu-** throughout not **attaca**, and **vaincre** makes **vainquons** as well as **vainquez**. (In this connexion note that **convaincant**, *convincing*, is an adjective; the participle is **convainquant**.)

2.5.2 Some changes of consonant in verbs are common enough to warrant a general note. A number of consonants vanish, especially before **s**, e.g. **craindre/crains; bouillir/bous; dormir/dort; mentir/mens; suivre/suit**.

In some verbs normal consonants alternate with palatalised ones, e.g. **craindre/craignez; vouloir/veuille.**

2.5.3 Final -l and -il become -u- in the plural of nouns, and similar changes are found in verbs. For i/y see 2.6.2, and for the alternation of single and double consonants 2.6.1.

2.6 VARIATION OF VOWEL

2.6.1 The not very marked stress in French falls on the final syllable; there is often a change of vowel according as it is stressed or unstressed. This occurs both in the conjugation of verbs, viz.

e è	lever	lève	[ləve, lɛv]
eC eCC	jeter	jette	[ʒəte, ʒɛt]

(Different ways of indicating the same change)

e ie	tenir	tient
e oi	recevoir	reçoit
é è	céder	cède
ou eu	vouloir	veut

and between allied words, viz.

a ai/e/è	marine	mer
o eu	cordial	coeur

They were commoner in old French, e.g. **je treuve,** now **je trouve.**

2.6.2 Between two vowels **i** changes to **y,** e.g. **voit** but **voyons.** Note however that a word like **crier,** with ending -ions, makes **criions.**

2.7 SPELLING

2.7.1 The main lines of French spellings are established by the time the printed book appears, but there have been a number of changes of detail, especially in the earlier period. Most striking among these early points of spelling is the presence of 'etymological' letters which are not pronounced and are now omitted, e.g. **droi(c)t, a(d)vis, sou(b)s, escholier (écolier), c(h)olere;** similarly **void** for **voit.** Except for -s- these letters nearly all fade out by the 18th century, earlier in some writers than in others. (See specimens.)

2.7.2 In the 16th century -ez is found not only in **vous aimez,** *you love,* but in the past participle, viz. S -é, -ee P -ez, ees (now regularised into -é, -ée, -és, -ées), and in the plural of abstract nouns in -té.

2.7.3 Nouns and adjectives ending in -nt made their plural in -ns. The present-day -nts appears sporadically in the 17th century but -ns persists in some printers until the early 19th century.

2.7.4 In the imperfect and conditional of verbs and in adjectives which now end in -ais one formerly had -oi-, pronounced [wɛ], or in the earlier period -oy-, e.g. **étoit, françois.** Similarly **reine,** formerly **royne.** The old spelling is found alongside the modern even in the late 18th century, and was not officially abandoned until 1835. In view of the pronunciation one occasionally finds spellings like **mirouer** for **miroir.**

2.7.5 The modern system of accents on **e** took some time to establish. The persistence of **s** in words like **estat (état), neufiesme (neuvième), mesme (même)** makes them unnecessary for a long time even by modern rules, and one finds **complette, fidelle** for the modern **complète, fidèle**. But even a word like **première** is regularly found without an accent in the 16th and 17th centuries, while in the 18th -ere, -ére and -ère are all found. Spellings like **regne, regle** are found in the 19th century, and in place names the acute accent instead of the grave, e.g. **Liége**, persisted in some quarters until well into the present century.

As -eCe stood for the modern -èCe, an accent was necessary when the e's had some other value, as in **arriéré**, though even here **arriéré** was considered enough. Similarly **augmenté** requires an accent, since **augmente** is also possible, but **augmentee** does not. No accent is found at first on **mémoire**, but it begins to appear sporadically in the 17th century and with increasing regularity in the 18th. (To some extent these differences are a matter of pronunciation: in the 17th century **désir** was pronounced [dzir].)

3 ARTICLES

3.1 DEFINITE
    3.1.1 The forms are as follows:

        MS **le**   FS **la**   P **les**

Both **le** and **la** are reduced to **l'** before vowels and usually before **h**.
    3.1.2 The article is more common in French, being used for instance before abstract nouns and many geographical names.

3.2 INDEFINITE
    3.2.1 This article has the forms M **un** F **une**; no plural.
    3.2.2 The article is identical with the numeral *one* (6.1.1).

3.3 PARTITIVE
    3.3.1 The combination of the preposition **de** with the definite article, producing **du, de la, de l'** and **des**, has the meaning *some* or *some of the*.
    3.3.2 Parallel to these forms are **de** alone, after negatives and before adjectives, and combinations of **de** with demonstratives and possessives, e.g. **des différences de ce genre**, *differences of this kind*; **il n'y a pas de différence**, *there is no difference*; **de semblables différences**, *similar differences*; **de ses éditions**, *editions of him*.

4 NOUNS

4.1 GENDER AND FORM
Nouns are either masculine or feminine. Except for certain suffixes there is little obvious correlation between form and gender. At times one needs to be specially careful, since there may be two identical words, one masculine, the other feminine, with different meanings, e.g. **pendule**: M *pendulum*, F *clock*; **tour**: M *turn*, F *tower*.

4.2 PLURAL
    4.2.1 Nearly all nouns make their plural by adding **-s**, unless they already end in **-s** or **-x**, in which case they are unchanged.
    4.2.2 A number of nouns in **-l** and **-u** make their plural in **-x**, viz. most of those in **-al** and some in **-ail**: P **-aux**; **aieul** P **aieux**; **œil** P **yeux**; **ail** P **aulx**; those in **-eau** and most of those in **-ou**.
    4.2.3 The plural of compound words is complicated, though basically logical, viz. Adjective + noun; noun + noun: **grand(s)-livre(s)**, **libraire(s)-éditeur(s)**, but **timbre(s)-poste**.

Verb + noun: **couvre-lit(s)**, *coverlet(s)*, but **un/des couvre-feu**, *curfew(s)*. The word garde causes peculiar trouble: e.g. **le(s) garde-fou(s)**, *the hand-rail(s)* but **le(s) garde(s)-côte(s)**, *the coast-guard(s)*.

If the first element is an adverb or preposition, the noun takes a plural ending, e.g. **des en-têtes**, *headings*. Otherwise compounds are invariable.

4.2.4 Of words ending in **-um** some make their plural in **-a**, some in **-ums** and others in either. The number of plurals in **-a** tends to diminish.

5 ADJECTIVES

5.1 GENERAL

5.1.1 Adjectives agree in number and gender with the nouns they qualify and may therefore have different forms for masculine and feminine, singular and plural.

5.1.2 A few simple adjectives such as **grand, petit, bon, beau** and all ordinal numbers precede the noun.

5.1.3 Other adjectives may precede or follow, but their usual position is after the noun. Sometimes, as with **certain, grand, propre, seul, simple**, the difference of position implies a distinct difference of meaning. More often the difference is one of nuance.

5.2 ENDINGS

5.2.1 *The feminine* is usually formed by the addition of **-e**, which may entail some further changes, such as doubling or change of consonant, e.g.

M	F
formel	formelle
public	publique (2.5.1)
faux	fausse
heureux	heureuse
bref	brève
blanc	blanche
-eur	-euse, -eresse
-teur	-trice

Exceptionally:

frais	fraîche
malin	maligne
favori	favorite

If the masculine already ends in **-e**, there is no change.

5.2.2 The adjectives **beau, nouveau; vieux; fou** and **mou** have three forms, viz.

M	F
beau/bel	**belle**
vieux/vieil	**vieille**
fou/fol	**folle**

The forms in **-l** are used before vowels.

5.2.3 There are some invariable adjectives.

5.2.4 *The plural* of adjectives is made in the same way as that of nouns, the masculine and the feminine independently.

5.2.5 Adjectives which are invariable as regards gender are equally so as regards the plural.

5.3 COMPARISON

5.3.1 The comparative of nearly all adjectives is got by putting **plus** before the positive, **le plus**, etc. being used for the superlative.

5.3.2 A few common adjectives have special comparative forms, such as **bon**, **meilleur**. Such forms are entered separately in most dictionaries.

5.4 POSSESSIVES

Mon, *my*, F **ma** P **mes**; similarly **ton**, *your*; **son**, *his, her*; **notre, nos** *our*; **votre, vos** *your*; **leur, leurs**, *their*.

6 NUMERALS

6.1 CARDINAL
6.1.1

1 **un(e)**	11 **onze**	21 **vingt et un**	100 **cent**
2 **deux**	12 **douze**	22 **vingt-deux**	101 **cent un**
3 **trois**	13 **treize**	30 **trente**	200 **deux cents**
4 **quatre**	14 **quatorze**	40 **quarante**	210 **deux cent dix**
5 **cinq**	15 **quinze**	50 **cinquante**	1000 **mil(le)**
6 **six**	16 **seize**	60 **soixante**	
7 **sept**	17 **dix-sept**	70 **soixante-dix**	
8 **huit**	18 **dix-huit**	80 **quatre-vingts**	
9 **neuf**	19 **dix-neuf**	81 **quatre-vingt-un**	
10 **dix**	20 **vingt**	90 **quatre-vingt-dix**	

6.1.2 Only **un** has a special feminine form. The numerals from **deux** on, including compounds of **un**, are followed by the plural.

6.2 ORDINAL
6.2.1

1 **premier**   2 **deuxième, second**   3 **troisième**

and so on, adding **-ième** to the cardinal, after cutting off final **-e** and the **-s** of **quatre-vingts**, **deux cents**, etc. **Vingt et un** and similar compounds make **vingt et unième**, etc.

6.2.2 Ordinals are adjectives and therefore agree with the noun, e.g. **en premières noces**.

6.2.3 It is permissible to reduce the first of two successive ordinals to the cardinal.

6.3 FIGURES

6.3.1 Plain figures, arabic or roman, are used for cardinals, ordinals having the last letter, or more, added, e.g. **1ᵉʳ, 7ᵉ, XXᵉᵐᵉ**. In the names of monarchs **I** stands for **premier**.

6.3.2 **1°, 2°**, etc. stand for **primo, secundo** (see Latin for the whole series).

6.4 DATES

6.4.1 The months are:

janvier, février, mars, avril, mai, juin,
juillet, août, septembre, octobre, novembre, décembre

6.4.2 With the exception of the first of the month, dates are expressed entirely by cardinals.

> *(On) 25.1.1971,* le vingt-cinq janvier dix-neuf cent soixante et onze (or **mil neuf cent,** etc.)
>
> *the 70's,* les années soixante-dix

7 PRONOUNS

7.1 DEMONSTRATIVE, INDEFINITE, ETC.

7.1.1 The adjectival form of the demonstrative is **ce, cet, cette;** P **ces.** It means *this* or *that,* and if greater precision is needed, **-ci** or **-là** is added to the noun.

7.1.2 The pronoun is **celui, celle** P **ceux, celles** referring to persons or things; **ce,** referring to abstractions, situations, etc. Apart from **ce** they are always followed by **de** or **que** or have **-ci** or **-là** appended, e.g. **la cuisine ne vaut pas celle de l'Union Interalliée,** *the cuisine is not as good as that of the U.I.;* **celles que vous avez lues,** *those that you have read* (**les nouvelles**). Ce is used in the same way, but it can also be subject in phrases like **ce n'est pas le même,** *it is not the same.* Ce combines with **-ci** and **-là** to make **ceci, cela** (**ça**).

7.1.3 The interrogative coupled with **que** and the subjunctive has the sense *whoever,* etc. Distinguish, however, **quoi que,** *whatever,* from **quoique,** *although,* and **quel que,** *whatever* from **quelque,** *however* or *some.*

7.1.4 Quelque with **un(e)** makes **quelqu'un(e),** *somebody, anybody,* the plural of which is **quelques-un(e)s.**

7.1.5 Même varies in meaning according to its position: **la même chose,** *the same thing;* **la chose même,** *the very thing.* It is appended to the disjunctive forms of the personal pronouns, e.g. **moi-même,** *(I) myself.* (cf. 7.3.2).

7.2 RELATIVE AND INTERROGATIVE

7.2.1 The relatives are **qui** subject and after prepositions, **que** object, referring to both persons and things; **lequel, laquelle, lesquel(le)s,** especially after prepositions; **dont,** *of which, of whom, whose.* **Lequel,** etc. combine with **à** and **de** to form **auquel,** etc. (see 10.2). There is also a relative **quoi** as in **ce à quoi je pense,** *what I am thinking of.*

7.2.2 The interrogative **qui** refers to persons, *what?* being **que,** or after prepositions **quoi.**

7.3 PERSONAL

7.3.1

		Subject	Object	Disjunctive
	1	je	me	moi
	2	tu	te	toi
S	3m	il	le; lui; y; en	lui
	3f	elle	la; lui; y; en	elle
S & P	3r	—	se	soi
	1	nous	nous	nous
	2	vous	vous	vous
P	3m	ils }	les; leur; y; en	{eux
	3f	elles }		{elles

7.3.2   **Lui** and **leur** denote the indirect object. The disjunctive forms are used by themselves, after prepositions, as complements of the verb *to be*, and after the imperative.

7.3.3   **Y** (also *there*) is equivalent to **à lui**, etc. and is nearly always used of things; **en** (also *from there*) is equivalent to **de lui**, etc. and quite often refers to persons. Note particulary **il n'en a pas**, *he hasn't one (any)*; **les retouches n'en changent pas l'esprit**, *the revisions do not change its spirit*. Both are found in a number of idiomatic expressions, whose meaning cannot be guessed.

7.3.4   The object pronouns are placed before the verb but follow the positive imperative: **il le lui donne**, *he gives it to him (her)*; **donnez-le-lui**, *give it to him*. Note also **me voici**, *here I am*; **le voilà**, *there he is*.

8   VERBS

8.1   STRUCTURE

8.1.1   Although differences of person and tense are largely indicated by differences of ending, many of these endings are now pronounced if not spelt the same, so that subject pronouns are essential.

8.1.2   Regular verbs have a straightforward relationship between the infinitive, under which verbs are listed, and the remaining parts. A number of verbs have minor irregularities, mentioned here in the form of general notes, and some (including some very common verbs) show marked changes in the course of conjugation. These are listed in the better dictionaries, so they will not be given in full here unless they are very irregular.

8.2   PRESENT

8.2.1   *Endings*

I	-e, -es, -e; -ons, -ez, -ent	inf. -er, rarely -ir
II	-s, -s, -t/-; -(C)ons, -(C)ez, -(C)ent	inf. -(C)re, -(C)ir, rarely -Coir
III	-is, -is, -it; -issons, -issez, -issent	inf. -ir
IV	-ois, -ois, -oit; -evons, -evez, -oivent	inf. -evoir

8.2.2   The consonant in type II may be one of several: some commoner ones are found in the following examples, **crains, craignons, craindre**; **conduis(ons), conduire**; **connais(sons), connaître**; **pars, partir**; **suit, suivre**; **écrivons, écrire**; **voyons, voir**. See also 2.5.2.

8.2.3   Vowel changes of the types mentioned in 2.6.1 are found in the more irregular verbs, e.g. **sait, savoir**; **meurt, mourir**; **meu(ven)t, mouvoir**. So also **pouvoir** which has both **je peux** and **je puis**.

8.2.4   **Dire** and **faire** have **vous dites, faites**. Note also **ils font**.

8.2.5   The French present translates both the simple and the continuous present: **je vais**, *I am going*, and in expressions like **paraît depuis six ans**, the perfect, viz. *has been coming out for six years*.

8.3   IMPERFECT

8.3.1   *Endings*

-ais, -ais, -ait; -ions, -iez, -aient

The stem is the same as the plural of the present.

8.3.2   The imperfect, which typically expresses continuous or habitual action in the past, is frequently used in description. It is not necessarily translated by the English continuous past.

8.4 PAST HISTORIC

8.4.1 *Endings*

I	-ai, -as, -a; -âmes, -âtes, -èrent	inf. -er
II	-is, -is, -it; -îmes, -îtes, -irent	inf. -ir, -re
III	-us, -us, -ut; -ûmes, -ûtes, -urent	inf. -evoir

8.4.2 Types II and III are found also in irregular verbs. The stem is sometimes the same as the plural of the present, but the relation is often more complicated, so that recourse must be had to a list of verbs. Note particularly **vis, vit** which may be either present, from **vivre**, or past, from **voir**; similarly **dis**, present or past of **dire**.

8.4.3 The past historic is essentially a narrative tense. cf. 8.10.1.

8.5 FUTURE

8.5.1 *Endings*

I	-er	inf. -er
II	-ir	ai, -as, -a; -ons, -ez, -ont	inf. -ir
III	-r	inf. -re
IV	-vr	inf. -voir

8.5.2 All types are found with irregular verbs, but the future is more regular than the other tenses, being derived directly from the infinitive: **-drai** is found not only from verbs in **-dre**, but in **tiendrai, viendrai** (tenir, venir) and **vaudrai** (valoir); **-rrai** is found from **acquérir, courir, mourir, envoyer** (enverrai), **pouvoir** (pourrai).

8.6 CONDITIONAL

The conditional substitutes **-ais**, etc. (as 8.3.1) for the **-ai**, etc. of the future.

8.7 SUBJUNCTIVE

8.7.1 *Present endings*

-e, -es, -e; -ions, -iez, -ent

The stem is usually the same as that of the 3PP of the indicative (8.2.1): so **reçoivent, reçoive**, etc., **recevoir**.

8.7.2 There are a few changes of vowel (2.6.1), e.g. **recevions; meure** but **mourions** from **mourir; viennent, venions** from **venir; vaille, valions** from **valoir; veuille, voulions** from **vouloir; prenne, prenions** from **prendre**. The forms in **-ions** and **-iez** are ambiguous (8.3.1) except in the more irregular verbs, viz. **pouvoir** (puisse), **savoir** (sache), **faire** (fasse).

8.7.3 *Imperfect endings*

-sse, -sses, -t; -ssions, -ssiez, -ssent

The 3 PS has a circumflex accent.

8.7.4 This tense corresponds regularly to the past definite in form thus: **aimas, aimasse**, and so on (8.4.1).

8.7.5 The subjunctive often has no special significance and will be translated by an indicative or by an infinitive: the French construction simply happens to require it. Sometimes, however, either the indicative or the subjunctive is possible and the indicative will express an actual fact and the subjunctive an idea, a generality or a purpose.

Thus: **je cherche un livre qui me plaise**, *I am looking for a book such as will please me*, while **qui me plaît** means *which actually pleases me*. After conjunctions like **de sorte que** (*so that*), **jusqu'à ce que** (*until*) indicative and subjunctive express respectively fact and purpose. In independent clauses the subjunctive expresses a wish: **puisse l'ouvrage répondre aux curiosités nouvelles**, *may the work satisfy new interests*.

8.10   COMPOUND TENSES

8.10.1   *Perfect indicative and subjunctive*
Formed from the present, indicative or subjunctive, of **avoir** or **être** (8.19) according to the verb in question, and the past participle. Despite its form this tense must be translated quite often by the simple past (cf. 0.1).

8.10.2   *Pluperfect, future perfect, conditional perfect*
Formed like the perfect (8.10.1) but with imperfect (indicative or subjunctive) or past definite, future and conditional instead of the present.
8.10.3   In the same way one can form the perfect infinitive and perfect active participle.

8.11   INFINITIVE

8.11.1   The possible endings are **-er, -ir, -oir, -re.**
8.11.2   The French infinitive is equivalent to the English verbal noun as well as the infinitive, e.g. **il s'agissait d'apporter l'essentiel**, *it was a matter of furnishing the essentials*. Sometimes where English has two clauses with the same subject French will have a phrase with the infinitive, e.g. **avant de partir**, *before he left*.
8.11.3   The infinitive is used as an impersonal imperative: cf. 1.8.8.

8.12   PARTICIPLES

8.12.1   *The present participle* ends in **-ant** and has the same stem as the plural of the present (8.2.1), except in the case of **savoir**, where the participle is **sachant** and **savant** is an adjective meaning *learned*. (On the other hand **pouvant** is the participle of **pouvoir** and **puissant**, *powerful*, the adjective. There are a number of these pairs.)
8.12.2   Like the English participle it may be an adjective, e.g. **suivant**, *following*, or the equivalent of a clause, e.g. **la plupart des questions s'étant récemment renouvelées**, *most of the questions having been recently revived*; **en assemblant une vaste matière**, *in* (or *while*) *bringing together a mass of material*.
8.12.3   *The past participle passive* has the following regular forms:

-é (inf. **-er**); **-i** (**-ir**); **-u** (**-evoir, -re**)

and a number of irregular ones. Most of these end, confusingly enough, in **-u**, and where the word is short, as are **bu, cru, mû, plu, pu, su, vu**, the infinitive may be a long way off in the dictionary. Similar difficulties are found with **mis** (**mettre**) and **pris** (**prendre**), and with **mort** (**mourir**) among those in **-t**.
8.12.4   Apart from its use as an adjective, the past participle enters into the formation of the compound tenses (8.10) and the passive (8.15). If the direct object is a pronoun and therefore comes first, the participle agrees with it. In the case of **que**, which is itself invariable, it is not always easy to remember this, if in correcting proof, say, one finds **Voyages qu'il a fait** instead of **faits**.

8.14   REFLEXIVE

8.14.1   These are got by using the object pronoun of the same person, e.g. **se laver**, *to wash* (*oneself*), **je me lave**; **se donner de la peine**, *to take pains*. Note that the **se** here is indirect, *to give to oneself*, while in **se donner pour exhaustifs**, *to claim to be exhaustive*, it is direct.

8.14.2 The auxiliary of the compound tenses is always **être**, e.g. **les changements se sont accusés surtout pour le XVIIe siècle**.

8.14.3 This last example illustrates the variety of uses of the reflexive. It can be reciprocal (**ils s'aiment**, *they love one another*) as well as plain reflexive; but here it is neither of these but a sort of passive; *the changes have become more marked*, etc. Similarly with **une révision s'imposait**, *a revision was called for*; **se vend** (1.8.6) *is sold*. But **se tromper**, for instance, *to make a mistake*, is distinct from **être trompé**, *to be deceived* (8.15.1).

8.15 PASSIVE

8.15.1 The passive form is got by coupling the parts of **être** with the past participle, agreeing with the subject: **une réédition a été envisagée**, *re-publication was contemplated*.

8.15.2 Apart from the reflexive (8.14.2) the passive may be replaced by the active with **on** or some other impersonal verb (8.16).

8.16 IMPERSONAL

8.16.1 Some verbs exist only in the third person, e.g. **il faut**, *it is necessary*, others are used both personally and impersonally. They are frequently turned some other way in English, e.g. **il me faut**, *I must*; **il me tentait** (see last specimen) *I was tempted, I found it tempting*.

8.16.2 The impersonal forms with subject **on** can sometimes be translated by *one*, as in **à quelles erreurs on s'expose**, *to what errors one is exposed*; but **on le confond avec**, *it is confused with*; **qu'on le sache bien**, *you may be sure*; **peut-être nous saura-t-on gré**, *perhaps people will thank us*.

8.17 AUXILIARIES
See 8.19.1, 8.19.2.

8.19 IRREGULARITIES (other than those already mentioned)

8.19.1 avoir, *to have*
  Present: **ai, as, a; avons, avez, ont**
  Imperfect: **avais**, etc.
  Past definite: **eus**, etc.
  Future: **aurai**, etc.
  Present subjunctive: **aie, aies, ait; ayons**, etc.
  Present participle: **ayant**
  Past participle: **eu**

8.19.2 être, *to be*
  Present: **suis, es, est; sommes, êtes, sont**
  Imperfect: **étais**, etc.
  Past definite: **fus**, etc.
  Future: **serai**, etc.
  Present subjunctive: **sois ... soyons**, etc.
  Present participle: **étant**
  Past participle: **été**

8.19.3 aller, *to go*
  Present: **vais, vas, va; allons, allez, vont**
  Future: **irai**, etc.
  Present subjunctive: **aille ... allions**, etc.

8.21 INTERROGATIVE

8.21.1   The interrogative can be expressed by reversing the order of subject pronoun and verb, which are joined by a hyphen. The final -e of the first person takes an acute accent, and if the third person ends in a vowel a -t- is inserted between it and the pronoun, e.g. **quels messages la littérature apportera-t-elle?**, *What messages will literature bring?*

8.21.2   In colloquial styles these reversals are largely avoided and **est-ce-que** is placed before the affirmative instead.

8.21.3   Not every such reversal implies a question, any more than it does in English: cf. **nous saura-t-on gré** in 8.16.2.

8.22 NEGATIVE

8.22.1   The negative **ne** is complemented normally by **pas** or by one or more specialised words such as **rien** (*nothing*), **jamais** (*never*) and so on, the verb being sandwiched between them, except in the infinitive. Note particularly **ne . . . que**, *only*. The adjuncts themselves were not originally negative, so that when used by themselves they may in different contexts be either positive or negative, e.g. **je doute que personne le sache**, *I doubt whether anyone knows it*; **Qu'est-ce que vous voulez? Rien**, *What do you want? Nothing.*

8.22.2   Ne by itself is sometimes negative, as in **il n'est de page où nous n'ayons utilisé des travaux antérieurs**, *there is no page where we have not used earlier works*; but after comparatives and expressions of doubt and the like, e.g. **il est plus difficile qu'on ne pense**, *it is more difficult than you think*, it adds nothing to the sense.

9   ADVERBS

9.1 FORMATION

The regular adverbial termination is **-ment**, added to the feminine form of the adjective. Adverbs in **-amment** and **-emment** correspond to adjectives in **-ant** and **-ent**. The primary adverbs, however, such as **bien**, *well*, have no special form, and some, e.g. **fort**, are indistinguishable from adjectives.

9.2 COMPARISON

The same as that of adjectives (5.3).

10   PREPOSITIONS

10.2   À and de combine with **le** and **les** to make **au, aux, du, des**. Similarly with **lequel**.

10.4   There are a number of compound prepositions such as **autour de**, *round*.

10.5   The simpler the preposition the more difficult it seems to be to translate: beware therefore of **à** (which often means *from* not *to*), **de** and **par**.

11   CONJUNCTIONS

The translation of conjunctions does not cause much difficulty. Those which take the subjunctive, and end in **que**, are not repeated but are replaced the second time by **que** alone. More surprisingly, this **que** can replace **si** and takes the subjunctive even though **si** has the indicative.

GLOSSARY

abonnement, *subscription*
achevé d'imprimer, *printing completed*
ancien (fascicule, etc.), *back (number)*
année, *year*
année écoulée, *back number*
annexe, *supplement*
annuaire, *yearbook*
avant-propos, *preface*
avertissement, (*prefatory*) *note*

bibliothécaire, *librarian*
bibliothèque, *library*
broché, *paper-covered*
brochure, *pamphlet*

cahier, *issue, number, part; pamphlet*
choisi, *selected*
commande, *order*
y compris, *including*
à condition, *on approval*
conférence, *lecture; conference*

déjà paru, *already published*
discours, *speech*
disponible, *available*

échantillon, *sample, specimen*
éditeur, *publisher*
édition, *edition; publication*
envoyer, *send*
épuisé, *out of print*
à l'essai, *on approval*
été, *summer*
étranger, *foreign, abroad*
exemplaire, *copy*
expédier, *dispatch*
extrait, *extract(ed)*

facture, *bill*

gratuit, *free*
hebdomadaire, *weekly*
hiver, *winter*
hommage de, *with the compliments of*

imprimeur, *printer*
inédit, *unpublished*

libraire, *bookseller*
librairie, *bookshop*
livraison, *issue*
livre, *book*

maison d'édition, *publishing house*
même, *same*
mensuel, *monthly*
mis à jour, *brought up to date*
mis en ordre, *arranged*
mort, mourut, *dead, died*

naquit, né, (*was*) *born*
nouveau, -velle, *new*
nouvelle, *long short story*

œuvres, *works*
opuscule, *pamphlet*
ouvrage, *work*

paraître, *to come out*
à paraître, *forthcoming*
pièce, *play*
planche, *plate*
sous presse, *being printed*
printemps, *spring*
procès-verbal, (*minutes of*) *proceedings*
propriété littéraire, *copyright*

quinzaine, quinze jours, *fortnight*

recueil, *collection*
recherche, *research*
rédacteur, *editor*
rédaction, *editing, editorial office*
rédigé, *edited, compiled*
réimpression, *reprint*
reliure, *binding*
remise, *discount, reduction*
reprendre, *resume*
revu(e), *revised*
revue, *review*
roman, *novel*

semaine, *week*
sémestriel, *half-yearly*
simple, *single*

suite, *continuation*
à suivre, *to be continued*

table, *index, table*
tableau, *table*
tirage à part, *offprint*

à titre gracieux, *complimentary*
traduction, *translation*
travaux, *transactions*
trimestriel, *quarterly*

en vente, *on sale*

GRAMMATICAL INDEX: WORDS

a, ai, aie(s), 8.19.1
aille, etc., 8.19.3
ait, as, 8.19.1
au, 10.2
aur-, 8.19.1
aux, 10.2
av-, ay-, 8.19.1

bel(le), 5.2.2

celle(s), 7.1.2
ces, cet(te), 7.1.1
ceux, 7.1.2

de(s), du, 3.3.1, 10.2
dites, 8.2.4

en, 7.3.3
es(t), ét-, êtes, 8.19.2
eu, 8.19.1

faites, 8.2.4
fol(le), 5.2.2
furent, fus, fut, etc., 8.19.2

irai, 8.19.3
l', la, le(s), 3.1.1, 7.3.1

leur, 5.4.1, 7.3.1

ma, 5.4.1
même, 7.3.3
mes, 5.4.1
mol(le), 5.2.2

nos, 5.4.1
nouvel(le), 5.2.2

que, 7.2.1, 7.2.2, 7.1.3,
   11.1

sa, 5.4.1
ser-, 8.19.2
ses, 5.4.1
sois, soit, sommes, sont,
   soy-, 8.19.2
suis, 8.2.2, 8.19.2
suit, 8.2.2

un(e), 3.2.1, 6.1.1

va(is), 8.19.3
vieil(le), 5.2.2
vont, 8.19.3
vos, 5.4.1

y, 7.3.3
yeux, 4.2.2

GRAMMATICAL INDEX: ENDINGS

(no ending), 4.2.1

-a, 4.2.4, 8.4.1
-là, 7.1.1
-ra, 8.5.1

-e, 5.2.1, 8.2.1, 8.7.1
-é, 8.12.3
-sse, 8.7.3

-i, 8.12.3
-ai, 8.4.1
-rai, 8.5.1
-ci, 7.1.1

-s, 4.2.1, 5.2.4, 8.2.1
-as, 8.4.1
-ras, 8.5.1
-es, 5.2.4, 8.2.1, 8.7.1
-mes, 8.4.1
-sses, 8.7.3
-tes, 8.4.1

-is, 8.2.1, 8.4.1
-ais, 8.3.1
-rais, 8.6
-ois, 8.2.1
-ons, 8.2.1
-ions, 8.3.1, 8.7.1
-rions, 8.6
-ssions, 8.7.3
-rons, 8.5.1
-issons, 8.2.1
-evons, 8.2.1
-us, 8.4.1

-t, 8.2.1, 8.7.3, 8.12.3
-it, 8.2.1, 8.4.1
-ait, 8.3.1
-rait, 8.6
-oit, 8.2.1
-ant, 8.12.1
-ent, 8.2.1, 8.7.1

-aient, 8.3.1
-raient, 8.6
-ment, 9.1
-rent, 8.4.1
-ssent, 8.7.3
-issent, 8.2.1
-oivent, 8.2.1
-ront, 8.5.1
-ut, 8.4.1

-u, 8.12.3

-(u)x, 4.2.2, 5.2.1

-ez, 8.2.1
-iez, 8.3.1, 8.7.1
-riez, 8.5.3
-ssiez, 8.7.3
-rez, 8.5.1
-issez, 8.2.1
-evez, 8.2.1

ITALIAN

SPECIMEN

Esaurita la prima edizione del mio commento alla Commedia di Dante, ho creduto bene, siccome già feci per le Opere minori, di riprodurlo in una forma più conveniente e più ampia, la quale facesse anche questo volume, per ogni riguardo, degno compagno degli altri tre. Ond'è che tutto ebbi l'animo a migliorarlo (per quanto mi fosse dato) così nell'ordine come nella sostanza, sia ritoccando e ripulendo in molte parti il lavoro, sia accrescendolo, e anche notevolmente, là dove pareami non essere abbastanza.

Now that the first edition of my commentary on Dante's Commedia is out of print, I have thought it well, as I did for the Minor works, to reproduce it in a more convenient and ample form, which would make this volume also in every respect a worthy companion to the other three. Accordingly I gave my entire mind to improving it (so far as I might) both in arrangement and in substance, either by rehandling or refashioning the work in many places, or by enlarging it, even considerably, where it seemed to me to be inadequate.

0 GENERAL CHARACTERISTICS

0.1 DEGREE OF INFLEXION
Italian is a moderately synthetic language with a wealth of verb forms but no cases. It is thus able to dispense with subject pronouns, but indicates the relations of names by means of prepositions.

0.2 ORDER OF WORDS
Most adjectives and all qualifying phrases follow the noun they qualify. The order SVO is normal but may be varied by putting verb or object first, and adverbial phrases are variously placed.

0.4 RELATION TO OTHER LANGUAGES
On the relation of Italian to Latin and the other Romance languages see General note on the Romance languages.

1 BIBLIOLINGUISTICS

1.1 NAMES
1.1.1 Modern Italian personal names consist of Christian name and surname, with or without a preposition, but in the Middle Ages and Renaissance names are found which consist of a Christian name followed by a phrase indicating origin, e.g. **Jacopone da Todi,** or authors who have surnames are better known, like Dante and **Michelangelo,** by their Christian names. There is no formal way of distinguishing a name like **Jacopone da Todi** from one like Lorenzo **da Ponte,** and some would index both under the last

element. Italian catalogues and reference books, it should be noted, index modern names under the preposition, **Da Ponte, De Rossi, Degli Occhi** and so forth, but older ones under the last element, e.g. **Pazzi, Jacopo de'**. There are also compound names such as **Alberto Paveri Fontana Di Fontana Pradosa**.

One might add that some of the most famous Italian artists are commonly known by nicknames, e.g. **Botticelli** (real name **Alessandro Filipepi**). These may take the article, but should not be combined with Christian names, though it is often done.

1.1.2 Christian names, not being declined, give little trouble except through their variants, such as **Gian, Gianni, Giovanni; Pier, Piero, Pietro**. With earlier names it is not always easy to decide which form to adopt. Nor is the habit of combining names any easier to cope with. In a modern name **Giambattista** may be taken at its face value, but in the eighteenth century one might find it in one book alongside **Giovanni Battista** in another. Similarly **Giampaolo, Giampietro** and so on.

1.1.3 Surnames nowadays are grammatically indifferent, whatever their form, be it a singular noun like **Croce**, a plural noun like **Leopardi**, a Latin ablative plural like **(de) Sanctis**, or an adjective like **Gentile**; and if it is necessary to use them in the plural, they are unchanged, e.g. **i Croce**, *the Croces*. But at an earlier period names might be given a plural form if more than one member of the family is referred to, sometimes by simple substitution of the appropriate plural ending (4.2) sometimes by means of a derivative, e.g. **i Gioliti**, viz. G. P. Giolito and others of the family, **la famiglia de' Colonnesi**, *The Colonna family*. (But **dalli Giolito** is found in 1592.) Some names are used only in the plural, e.g. **Lorenzo de' Medici**, and sometimes, as in **Francesco Ferruccio** or **Ferrucci**, the name itself fluctuates between singular and plural.

1.2   NAMES OF AUTHORS, EDITORS, ETC.

1.2.1 The names of individual authors may occur in isolation at the head of the title-page or after the title, but in the latter position they are more likely to be preceded by a preposition. Words in isolation after the title should be treated with caution, lest **CENNI MEDICI** (*Medical notes*) should appear in the catalogue as the latest scion of that noble family.

Editors' and translators' names will normally be preceded by prepositions, e.g. **annotato e illustrato da Pietro Fraticelli; con traduzione italiana . . . e note e illustrazioni di Pietro Fraticelli**. This has no effect on names but if the name is preceded by a description, such as **dottor(e)**, which requires the definite article, the preposition may combine with the article (10.2), e.g. **dal dottor X. Y.** One cannot then omit **dottor** without violating the grammar.

1.2.2 The names of corporate authors present little grammatical problem, though the factual problem of the exact relationship of the body to the work may be less tractable. The name of a subordinate body may be linked grammatically with that of the principal body, e.g. **a cura del Servizio Studi economici della Banca d'Italia**, but no great ingenuity is required to disentangle this into **Banca D'Italia. Servizio Studi Economici.**

1.3   TITLES

1.3.1 The great majority of titles consist of nouns, adjectives and prepositions, e.g. **Storia della letteratura italiana**, *History of Italian literature*; **Indagine sugli istituti di ricovero, i refettori, gli iscritti negli elenchi comunali dei poveri al 31 maggio 1948,** *Investigation into public assistance institutions, canteens and persons entered in the local registers of poor persons on 31 May 1948*. Here the chief difficulty lies in the contractions of preposition and article, **della, sugli, negli, dei, al** (10.2), and the much freer use of article plus adjective as a noun: **gli iscritti**, literally *the inscribed.*

Imaginative and persuasive literature shows more variety, e.g. **Cristo si è fermato a Eboli**, *Christ stopped at Eboli*; **Che cosa ha veramente detto Gramsci?**, *What did Gramsci really say?* and older titles may be more complicated, containing subordinate clauses, e.g. **Ricordi ne quali si ragiona di tutte le materie che si ricercano a vn vero gentilhuomo**, *Memorials in which are discussed all the matters that are required of a true gentleman.* In such cases one needs to be careful, when transcribing the title, that one does not mutilate the sense.

1.3.2 Title entries pose no problems except in so far as under British Museum rules combinations involving proper adjectives need to be translated, e.g. **Canzoni italiane** would be entered under ITALIAN SONGS.

In filing titles one should remember that the indefinite article and the numeral and pronoun *one* have forms in common (3.2). Thus **Uno . . . due . . . tre . . .**; **Uno mandato da un tale** are filed under **Uno**. **Lo, la** and **le** can be pronouns as well as articles, but it is not very likely.

1.3.3 Peculiar problems arise with titles beginning with prepositions, a type formerly common and not unknown today, e.g. **Dei delitti e delle pene**, *On crimes and punishments.* The difficulty arises not when dealing with the book itself or the filing of the catalogue card (under **Dei**), but in the citation of the book by other authors. As the title begins with a preposition it is not easy to incorporate into a sentence and phrases like **nel suo trattato Dei delitti e delle pene**, *in his treatise On crimes and punishments* are apt to occur. But printers were not over-punctilious in their use of capitals, and the phrase might well appear as **nel suo Trattato dei delitti e delle pene**, producing the plausible non-title: **Trattato dei delitti**, etc. Or the title may be shortened as in **Discorsi sopra la Ragion di stato del signor Giovanni Botero**. Botero's work was entitled **Della ragione di stato**.

1.3.4 This use of **di** should not be confused with that found in **De' ragguagli di Parnaso . . . centuria prima** (see 1.4.3), where the title is **Ragguagli di Parnaso**.

1.4 VOLUMES AND PARTS

1.4.1 The usual words are **volume** or **tomo** on the one hand, and **parte** on the other.

1.4.2 Numeration is by an ordinal number, usually following, in words or figures, e.g. **volume terzo (III, 3°)**; **parte prima**. (But **voll. 4** in bibliographies will mean *4 vols.*) **Libro**, *book*, is also found but is more likely to indicate an internal division of a work, as in Guicciardini's one-volume **Historia d'Italia . . . divisa in venti libri**.

1.4.3 Title and numeration are sometimes run together in one grammatical whole, as in **De' ragguagli di Parnaso . . . centuria prima**, *of the dispatches from Parnassus . . . first hundred.* Here one is forced by the grammar to include the numeration in the title.

1.5 EDITIONS

The usual word is **edizione** (but see 1.6.1), the number preceding in ordinal form, e.g. **seconda edizione** or sometimes simply **nuova edizione**, to which may be added words indicating revision, as **riveduta**, *revised*; **con correzioni e aggiunte**, *with corrections and additions*; **notevolmente ampliata (accresciuta)**, *substantially enlarged*, to quote a few. Or a new edition may be implied by phrases like **di nuovo ristampato con correzioni**, *reprinted with corrections.* But **nuovamente stampato** could be used of a first edition. The word **impressione** also occurs meaning *printing*, and **ristampa**, *reprint.* For **edizioni** in the sense simply of *publications* see 1.6.1.

1.6 IMPRINTS

1.6.1   Most modern imprints will be that of the publisher and this may be made explicit by phrases like **edizioni, casa editrice, editore, libreria**, or as was very common in former times the word **(ap)presso** before the name of the publisher. Conversely **stampato, stamperia, tipografo** and the like indicate the printers, and so usually does the preposition **per**, but one must remember that printer and publisher might be one and the same, and this practice persists longer in Italy than in England.

1.6.2   Most publishers' imprints take the form of personal names, e.g. **Vincenzo Valgrisi, Fratelli Treves** (*Treves Brothers*), but arbitrary names like **'Il Solco'** (*The Furrow*), **Casa Editrice Vita e Pensiero** (*Life and Thought Press*) are found. Institutional imprints such as **per conto della Confederazione della municipalizzazione** are not common. Latterly acronyms such as **CEDAM** for **Casa Editrice Dott(or) A. Milani** have come into being. In earlier imprints a widow (**vedova**) or successors (**eredi, successori**) may have to be watched for.

1.7 SERIES

1.7.1   Indications of series appear in various places, but usually at the top of the title-page, on the page facing it or in the reverse of it. In form the title is usually descriptive of the series as a whole or of its members, e.g. **Collana di studi economici e finanziari**, *Collection of economic and financial studies*; **Quaderni della Sezione lombarda dell'Istituto nazionale di Studi sul Rinascimento**, *Note-books of the Lombard Section of the National Institute of Renaissance Studies*. In the latter example, as often happens with institutional series, title and institution are merged, and the entry in the catalogue will appear refashioned as **Istituto Nazionale di Studi sul Rinascimento. Sezione Lombarda. Quaderni**.

1.7.2   In the example in 1.7.1 **quaderni** is part of the title. It might also occur in the singular as a unit of numeration, though **numero** is commoner. Other series are numbered by **volume** or by **fascicolo**, and one may find many-volumed works of the 'Handbuch' type divided successively by **sezione** and **volume**, with **tomo** kept in reserve in case any of the individual items (**volumi**) are in more than one volume. Sub-series are called **serie**.

1.7.3   Occasionally the series itself has no title, but one is implied by the description of the individual items, e.g. as **Pubblicazione No. 2** implying a series of **Pubblicazioni** (4.2.1). Obviously, not every occurrence of a word as colourless as **pubblicazione** should be allowed to generate a series.

1.8 PERIODICALS

1.8.1   Linguistically, the titles of periodicals are no different from those of books and series; in fact it is impossible always to distinguish periodicals and series by the title alone. **Rivista di economia agraria** is obviously a periodical, **Quaderni di sociologia** could as easily be a series. More fanciful titles, such as **Avanti!, Belfagor, Dedalo**, are somewhat more likely with periodicals than with books. Titles beginning with the article are often kept intact when they follow a preposition, e.g. **in** or **ne Il Telegrafo, ne La Stampa** (not **nel, nella**, 10.2).

1.8.2   Institutional periodicals are common in which the name of the institution forms part of the title or sub-title. Extracting the name of the institution presents no difficulty, viz. **Rassegna economica della Associazione fra le società italiane per azioni**, where the name begins at **Associazione**.

1.8.3   Persons concerned with editing may be grouped under **Direzione e redazione**, but though these terms are distinguished, the distinction is not always applied in the same way: one periodical may have a score of **redattori** and two or three **direttori**, one of whom appears to be 'the editor', another may have only one **redattore** or a **redattore capo**, equally obviously the editor. Most often the **direttori** are what would normally be called the editorial board or committee (**comitato direttivo**).

The publisher, immediate or remote, is indicated by some form of the roots **ed-** and **pubblic-**, e.g. **edita sotto gli auspici dell' Università di . . .; pubblicata da . . .; Licinio Capelli editore.**

1.8.4 Numeration is by **anno**, very rarely **volume**, and **numero** or **fascicolo**. Annual volumes are usually described elsewhere as **annate**. Occasionally numeration may go into a new series (**nuova serie**).

1.8.5 Periodicity may be implicit in the title, e.g. **Rivista trimestrale di diritto pubblico**, but more often such adjectives (**settimanale, mensile, bimestrale, quadrimestrale**) appear in the sub-title or description. Alternatively such phrases as **esce (uscirà, si pubblica) in quattro numeri (fascicoli) all'anno (ogni semestre)**, *comes out* (*will come out, is published*) *in four numbers a year* (*every six months*), may be used.

1.8.6 Subscription (**abbonamento**) may be **annuale (annuo), semestrale** or **trimestrale**, and runs usually from January but occasionally **da qualsiasi mese** (*from any month*). Single numbers (**numeri/fascicoli separati**) are quoted, sometimes with the addition of **ogni** or **ognuno** (*each*), and special prices for abroad (**per l'estero**). Back numbers, whether single (**numeri arretrati**) or whole volumes (**annate arretrate**), are distinguished from those **in corso**, but sometimes they are simply stated to be **senza aumento** (*without price increase*) or to bear a fixed relation to the price on the cover (**prezzo di copertina**). Stringent rules are usually given for cancellation (**disdetta**).

1.8.7 Addresses usually distinguish **direzione e redazione**, the literary side, from **edizione e amministrazione**, the business side, but the information may be given in other ways, such as **I manoscritti vanno inviati a . . .** (*Manuscripts are to be sent to . . .*), **I pagamenti vanno effettuati presso . . .** (*Payments are made at . . .*).

2 ALPHABET, PHONETICS, SPELLING

2.1 ALPHABET

2.1.1 The alphabet is the same as in English, but the letters **j, k, w, x, y** occur nowadays only in names and words of foreign origin. Earlier uses of some letters call for comment:

I: formerly used in the plural of nouns and adjectives in **-io** instead of the present-day **-i** or **-ii**, e.g. **studI** (**studi**), **templI** (**tempii**).

j: used at first as a variant of **i** in the combination **-ij**, e.g. **varij**, but in the 18th and 19th century in the same way as **I** (cf. 2.1.2).

i and j are sometimes interfiled.

u, v, V: treated at first as one letter, which may be either a vowel or a consonant. In the upper case only V is found, e.g. **GLI VLTIMI QVATTRO LIBRI** (**gli ultimi quattro libri**). In lower case v is usually found at the beginning of a word and u elsewhere, e.g. **rompeuano tutte le vie, eccetto vna** (**rompevano, una**); but with some printers **u** is found in all positions. It is usual in transcribing titles to follow this convention, substituting **u** for **V** when not initial: but this raises problems in filing title entries.

2.1.2 Accents are obligatory (a) to indicate a stress falling on the last syllable, (b) on monosyllables to avoid ambiguity. The usual practice is to put either an acute **or** a grave accent on **e**, according to the quality of the vowel, and a grave accent on all other vowels, e.g. **città**, **ciò**, **più**; **dì** (*day*), **di** (*of*), **né** (*nor*), **ne** (*of it*), **è** (*is*), **e** (*and*). (Cio would be read like **pio** with the stress on the **i**.) Some printers still use an acute accent on **i** and **u**, while there is a growing tendency on the other hand to use the grave accent everywhere.

Accents are optional on syllables other than the last either to distinguish words spelt alike but stressed differently, such as **àncora** (*anchor*) and **ancora** (*still*), **balìa** (*power*) and **bàlia** (*nurse*), or simply to indicate a doubtful or unusual stress. No-one, I imagine, would accent **ancòra**, but either or neither of the other pair might carry the accent. Whether a stress needs marking is very much a matter of opinion, and examples include **l'isole Egée** and **Tróade** in Foscolo, words like **natìo** (*native*) and poetic stresses like **edúchi** (*may educate*). The practice was common at one time of accenting the -ia of the imperfect and the conditional (**dormía**, **potrìa**). Italian, unlike Spanish, has never formulated a rule about such endings, and nowadays the accent is pretty well confined to names, the stressing of which is notoriously uncertain, e.g. **Barbèra**.

It was also used, optionally, to distinguish words that differ neither in spelling nor stress, e.g. **sòle** (= **suole**, *is accustomed*), **sole** (*sun*); **párti** (*seems to you*), **parti** (*you go away*).

The circumflex accent might be used in the same way, e.g. **vôlto** (*turned*), **volto** (*face*); **vôti** (*empty*), **voti** (*vows*); but more often it indicated a real or supposed contraction, e.g. **fûr** (**furono**), **côri** (= **cuori**), as opposed to **cori**, *choirs*. Nowadays it is used, and even then not often, in the ending -**î**, in the same way as -**j** was earlier (2.1.1), e.g. **varî** (**varii**).

2.1.3 A practice which can be disconcerting to the foreign librarian is the substitution of a following apostrophe for the grave accent on a final capital letter, e.g. **E'**, **CITTA'**. It is often found in newspapers, periodicals and cheap books where the saving of space is important, but is not unknown on title-pages. The grave accent would be restored when transcribing into lower-case. Final apostrophes, indicating the truncation of a word, as opposed to those in the middle of a word (2.1.4, 2.3), are rare in present-day Italian, though **Ca'** for **Casa** is found in imprints. Unfortunately, the shortening of such common words as **ai**, **dei** and the like (10.2) to **a'**, **de'**, etc. had not disappeared by the time this new typographic trick was introduced. Both uses are found together in this title-page of 1749: **DELLA PUBBLICA FELICITA', OGGETTO DE' BUONI PRINCIPI.**

2.1.4 A number of Italian words—articles, adjectives, pronouns, adverbs, prepositions, conjunctions, but also occasionally verbs—may lose an unstressed final vowel before the initial vowel of the next word, and take an apostrophe. The vowel may be -**a**, e.g. **quest'opera**; -**e**, e.g. **anch'essa**, **ch'egli**, **dev'essere**; -**i**, e.g. **d'ogni**, **c'è**; -**o**, e.g. **tutt'uno**. The article is now governed by fixed rules (3.1.1), and the abbreviation of the preposition **da** is forbidden, lest it be confused with **di**; but otherwise it is a matter of taste and custom.

The practice was much commoner in earlier texts, where forms such as **c'hanno** for **che hanno** are found and initial vowels are elided, as in **terranno'l mondo**. (See also 2.3.)

2.1.5 The diaeresis was formerly not uncommon to indicate that two contiguous vowels did not form a diphthong, e.g. **fïata**, **fëudale**, **ardüo**.

2.2 CAPITALISATION

2.2.1 Practice in the use of capitals is not altogether uniform, and one may expect to find divergences from the norms set out below. In principle names are spelt with capitals, but the corresponding adjectives are not, e.g. **Roma**, **romano**; **Dante**, **dantesco**;

and some nouns which might be regarded as names are not usually treated as such, in particular the names of days and months.

2.2.2 Personal, geographical and astronomical names are spelt with capitals throughout, except for articles and prepositions and the generic part of geographical names, e.g. **la penisola di Muggia**. But this should not be interpreted too widely: **Campi Flegrei** has a capital C.

Names of government departments are spelt with capitals throughout except for prepositions, e.g. **Ministero degli Affari Esteri**, *Ministry of Foreign Affairs*.

2.2.3 In the names of institutions, societies and the like standard practice is to spell only the first word, excluding the article, with a capital, e.g. **il Centro nazionale di documentazione scientifica**, but short names will often be found capitalised throughout, e.g. **Unione Velocipedistica Italiana**, and longer ones may have capitals for the nouns.

In book titles standard practice is to spell the first word only with a capital, even if it is an article, e.g. **Nuovo mondo**; **Gli archivi e le moderne ricerche**, but sometimes the first word after the article, or the remaining nouns, or all the words of a short title are so spelt, e.g. **La Grammatica italiana**; **I Promessi Sposi**; **Dialogo di Torquato Tasso e del suo Genio familiare**. In any case prepositions always begin with a small letter.

2.2.4 Titles of office and nobility prefixed to names are put in lower-case, e.g. **il presidente Gronchi, il conte Sforza**; but note **Fra Angelico, Don Arcangiolo Venerati, San Francesco d' Assisi**.

2.3 DIVISION OF WORDS

Rules 4, 5b, 6c, 7a and 8 (p. xiii) apply.

On rule 8 note that neither **del-l'uscio** nor **dell'u-scio** breaks the rule: a combination involving the apostrophe is regarded as a single word, and it is therefore **dell'-uscio**, breaking at the apostrophe, which is the improper division.

2.5 VARIATION OF CONSONANT; PALATALISATION

2.5.1 The consonants **c** and **g** each have different values before different vowels, as they do in English. To keep the sound the same **h** or **i** is added as follows:

> *Hard:* **ca, che, chi, co, cu**
> *Soft:* **cia, ce, ci, cio, ciu**

and the same with **g**. The alternations **c/ch, g/gh, c/ci, g/gi** may therefore be found in the same word as the ending changes, e.g. **fuoco P fuochi**; but not always, e.g. **amico P amici**, with a different pronunciation.

2.5.2 The change of pronunciation of **c** and **g** before **e** and **i** is an instance of palatalisation (see General note on the Slavonic languages). More striking examples of this phenomenon, and alternatively of gutturalisation, occur in some parts of verbs, the changes being as follows:

d	**l**	**n**
ggi and **gg**	**gli** and **lg**	**gn** and **ng**

By an analogous change **r** vanishes before consonantal **i**, e.g. **muoio** from **morire**.

Simple alternation of **gn** and **ng**, e.g. **piagnere** for **piangere** is of more general occurrence.

2.5.3 There is a strong tendency to reduce combinations of dissimilar consonants, resulting in the production of the characteristic **-ss-** and **-tt-**, and the disappearance before **-s-** not merely of **d** and **f** but also of the **g, n,** and **v** found in other parts of verbs. For examples see 8.4.2; 8.12.3.

2.5.4   Consonants are also doubled after a number of prefixes, e.g. **soprannaturale**, when suffixed pronouns or articles immediately follow a stressed vowel (cf. 7.3.3, 10.2), and in the middle of many words, e.g. **femmina**. Conversely **comunale** has now only one **m**.

2.6 VARIATION OF VOWEL

2.6.1   Change of vowel is one of the devices of Italian morphology inherited from Latin, but apart from this there are certain alternations dependent on the position of the accent, viz. e/ie, o/uo, e.g. **tiene** from **tenere**, **si duole** from **dolersi**; and with a more complex history, the alternations e/i and o/u, e.g. **detto** from **dire**, **prodotto** from **produrre**.

⸱**2.6.2**   Final -**e** may be dropped after **r, l, n**; and before a suffix infinitives, including those in -**rre**, are regularly shortened to -**r**. Less frequently -**o** is dropped after **n**.

2.7 SPELLING

Italian spelling has been stable for a very long time, and variations are minor, e.g. **j** for **i** between vowels. Generally speaking, earlier spelling is more Latinised. Thus in the sixteenth century one finds spellings like **intentione** for **intenzione**, while in some authors one finds -**tia** where one now has -**zia**, and in others, though not consistently, even where the modern spelling is -**za**, e.g. **notitia, gratia**; and **eccellentia, ub(b)idientia, sententia** alongside **licenza, prudenza, sapienza**. In the same vein silent **h** is retained in words like **(h)onore**, but not every difference is a simple difference of spelling: forms once current have become obsolete and permissible variations of dialect have yielded place to standardisation.

Occasionally even more extreme Latinisms are found, e.g. **maximamente** (-ss-), **facto** (-tt-), **excesso** (-cc-).

It should also be noted that older texts sometimes omit the customary apostrophes, producing **mabbiate** for **m'abbiate**, **daltro** for **d'altro** and so on; and conversely may separate words now joined, as **de i** for **dei**, **de la** for **della**.

3 ARTICLES

3.1 DEFINITE

3.1.1   The definite article has the following forms:

	M	*F*
S	**lo** before **s** + consonant, **z, gn, ps** **l'** before vowels **il** elsewhere	**l'** before vowels **la** before consonants
P	**gli** corresponds to **lo, l'** **gl'** before **i**- **i** corresponds to **il** (**li** obsolete)	**le**

In the past **le** became **l'** before **e**, **lo** was more freely used and **gl'** is found before vowels. Conversely **gli** is sometimes found before **i**-.

3.1.2   The definite article is used not only as in English, but also with abstract nouns and many geographical names and **surnames**.

3.2 INDEFINITE

	M	F
S	un, uno	una, un'

Uno and **una** may also be numerals (6.1.1) and **uno** a pronoun.

3.3 PARTITIVE

The combination of the preposition **di** with the definite article, producing **del**, **dell'**, **dello**, **della**, **dei**, **degli**, **delle**, gives the meaning *some*.

4 NOUNS

4.1 GENDER AND FORM

Nouns may be either masculine or feminine, there being some correlation between ending and gender. The commonest endings are -o (usually M), -a (usually F), -e (either), followed by -à (F), -ù (F).

4.2 PLURAL

4.2.1 *Masculine*

Nouns in unstressed -o and -e and a number in -a, like **poeta**, **economista** make their plural in -i. Some nouns in -io make -i, others -ii, or î (2.1.2).

There are a few common nouns ending in various other ways which do not change in the plural, e.g. **il re**, **il cinema**, **l'autobus**.

Spelling variation (2.5.1) is found with nouns in **-co** and **-go**.

Note **uomo** P **uomini**; **Dio** P **dei**.

4.2.2 *Feminine*

The most frequent types are:

S	P
-a	-e
-e	-i
-à	-à
-ù	-ù
-ie	-ie/-i

There are also a few invariable nouns in -i and -o, some of which like **la crisi**, **la radio**, **l'auto** are common.

Spelling variation is sometimes found with nouns in **-cia** and **-gia**, e.g. **fascia**, P **fasce**.

4.2.3 *Mixtures*

Some masculine nouns have feminine plurals in -a, e.g. **il dito**, **le dita**, *finger(s)*; **il miglio**, **le miglia**, *mile(s)*; **mille**, **mila**, **il migliaio**, **le migliaia**, *thousand(s)* (numeral and noun respectively).

5 ADJECTIVES

5.1 GENERAL

5.1.1 Adjectives agree in number and gender with the nouns they qualify. All but the commonest follow the noun.

5.2 ENDINGS

5.2.1 Forms for the feminine and the plural are as follows:

	S			P	
	M	F		M	F
	-o	-a		-i	-e
	-io	-ia		-i	-ie
		-e			-i

5.2.2 Bel(lo) has MP forms **bei** or **begli**

5.3 COMPARISON

The comparative is expressed by **più**, *more*, the superlative by **più** with the article. There are also irregular comparatives, entered separately in the dictionary, and absolute superlatives in -issimo and -errimo, e.g. **ricchissimo**, *very rich*, which are not.

5.4 POSSESSIVES

Mio, tuo, suo have MP **miei, tuoi, suoi.**

6 NUMERALS

6.1 CARDINAL

6.1.1

1 uno, una	11 undici	21 ventun(o)	200 duecento
2 due	12 dodici	22 ventidue	300 trecento
3 tre	13 tredici	30 trenta	900 novecento
4 quattro	14 quattordici	40 quaranta	1000 mille
5 cinque	15 quindici	50 cinquanta	2000 duemila
6 sei	16 sedici	60 sessanta	
7 sette	17 diciassette	70 settanta	
8 otto	18 diciotto	80 ottanta	
9 nove	19 diciannove	90 novanta	
10 dieci	20 venti	100 cento	

6.1.2 Only **uno** has a special feminine form. Compounds of **uno** may be followed by singular or plural; all other numerals by the plural.

6.2 ORDINAL

6.2.1

1 primo	11 undecimo
2 secondo	decimoprimo
3 terzo	undicesimo
4 quarto	12 duodecimo
5 quinto	decimosecondo
6 sesto	dodicesimo
7 settimo	13 decimoterzo
8 ottavo	tredicesimo
9 nono	19 decimonono
10 decimo	diciannovesimo

The remaining ordinals are formed by adding **-esimo** to the stem of the cardinal.

6.2.2 Ordinals are adjectives and have corresponding feminine forms in **-a**.

6.3 FIGURES

Cardinals are represented by plain arabic figures, ordinals by roman numerals, or by arabic with a superscript o or a, e.g. **1°, 1ª**.

6.4 DATES

6.4.1 The months are:

> gennaio, febbraio, marzo, aprile, maggio, giugno,
> luglio, agosto, settembre, ottobre, novembre, dicembre

6.4.2 Dates are expressed by cardinals with one exception:

> (*On*) *21.1.1969*, **il (giorno) ventuno gennaio millenovecentosessantanove**
> *In 1848*, **nel milleottocentoquarantotto**
> *1 May* (*January*, etc.), **il primo (di) maggio (gennaio, etc.)**
> *in the 90's*, **negli anni novanta**

Centuries may be expressed as in English by ordinals, or by the cardinal for the appropriate hundred. Thus *the 16th century*, **il secolo decimosesto** or **il Cinquecento**.

7 PRONOUNS

7.1/7.2 DEMONSTRATIVE, INTERROGATIVE, RELATIVE, ETC.

   7.1.1 Demonstrative, interrogative and similar pronouns, and the corresponding adjectives, which are all given in the dictionary, present few forms that call for comment.

> **quello** (adj.) has P **quei, quegli**.
> **quegli, questi** are ambiguous: they may be MP from the adjectives **quello, questo**, or singular pronouns.
> **il quale**: both parts vary; **la quale, i quali, le quali**.

   7.1.2 The demonstratives **questo, codesto, quello** correspond respectively to the first, second and third persons, and **questo** and **codesto** are accordingly found in commercial correspondence meaning *our* and *your* respectively.

7.3 PERSONAL

   7.3.1

			Subject	*Object* (*unemphatic*)	*Disjunctive emphatic*
		1	io	mi, me	me
		2	tu	ti, te	te
S		Lei	Le	Lei
		3*m*	egli	lo; gli(e), ci, ce	lui
		3*f*	ella	la; le	lei
		3*n*	esso, essa	lo, la; vi, ve, ci, ce	lui
S & *P*		3*r*	—	si, se	sé
		1	noi	ci, ce	noi
		2	voi	vi, ve	voi
P		Loro	Loro	Loro
		3*m*	(eglino), loro	li; loro	loro
	f		(elleno), loro	le; loro	loro
	n		essi, esse	li, le; ci, ce	essi, esse

As unemphatic object pronouns **me, te, glie, ce, se, ve** are contextual variants of the forms in **-i**, e.g. **ci parlano**, *they are talking to us*, **ce ne parlano**, *they are talking to us about it*. 3M **gli, ci, loro**, 3F **le, loro**, 3N **vi** express the indirect object, where with nouns the preposition **a** would be used. Other forms are indifferently direct or indirect. See also 8.14.1.

7.3.2 **Ci** and in part **vi** are adverbs by origin and are still used as such. So is **ne**, which is used of persons and things instead of **di** and a 3rd person pronoun, e.g. **se ne prende cura**, *he takes care of them*.

7.3.3 Nowadays the unemphatic object pronouns are placed before the tenses of the verb as in the examples above, but suffixed to the infinitive, participle, gerund and imperative, e.g. **parlarne**, *to talk about it*; **mandatogli**, *sent to him*; **dammi**, *give me*. In the past they might also be suffixed to finite tenses, e.g. **mostrommi**, *he showed me* (=**mi mostrò**); **hollo havuto**, *I have had it* (**l'ho avuto**). Note the truncated infinitive (2.6.2) and the doubled consonants (2.5.4).

8 VERBS

8.1 STRUCTURE

8.1.1 There are different forms for most of the different persons, so that subject pronouns are not obligatory, and for the different tenses and moods. Some simple tenses in Italian correspond to compound ones in English. Verbs are entered under the infinitive.

8.1.2 Regular verbs have one stem throughout, that of the infinitive, under which verbs are entered in the dictionary. In the irregular verbs, which include some of the commonest, parts of the past tense have a different stem.

8.2 PRESENT

8.2.1 *Endings*

I	-o, -i, -a; -iamo, -ate, -ano	inf. -are
II	-o, -i, -e; -iamo, -ete, -ono	inf. -ere
III	-(isc)o, -(isc)i, -(isc)e; -iamo, -ite, -(isc)ono	inf. -ire

8.2.2 Consonant variation (2.5.1) occurs with verbs in **-care, -gare** on the one hand and **-ciare, -giare** on the other and palatalisation or gutturalisation (2.5.2) in various verbs of types II and III. Of these **pongo** (stem **pon-**) has inf. **porre**. Note also **piaccio, taccio** (2.5.4) from **piacere, tacere**.

8.2.3 Vowel variations o/u, uo/o occasionally occur, e.g. **odo** from **udire**.

8.3 IMPERFECT

I	-a	
II	-e	vo, -vi, -va; -vamo, -vate, -vano
III	-i	

Infinitive as in 8.2.1.

The ending -va was formerly used for the first person also.
The -v- is often omitted in poetry, and sometimes in prose.

8.4 PRETERITE

8.4.1 *Endings*

    I   -ai, -asti, -ò; -ammo, -aste, -arono
    IIa -ei/-etti, -esti, -é/-ette; -emmo, -este, -erono/ettero
    b   †-i, -esti, †-e; -emmo, -este, †-ero
    IIIa -ii, -isti, -ì; -immo, -iste, -irono
    b   †-i, -isti, †-e; -immo, -iste, †-ero
    Infinitive as in 8.2.1.

8.4.2 Stem changes, indicated by †, occur in types IIb, IIIb, The commonest change is the addition of -s-, which usually affects the preceding consonant. The following represent the more usual types: **rimasi, rimanesti, rimase; rimanemmo, rimaneste, rimasero; risi, ridere; difesi, difendere; colsi, cogliere; dolsi, dolere; porsi, porgere; ressi, reggere; discussi, discutere; riflessi, riflettere; scrissi, scrivere;** but there are other types in **-si,** and a number of common verbs like **venire, venni** which vary their stems in other ways. In some the vowel is changed. A great many dictionaries list all verbs with irregularities of this sort.

8.5 FUTURE

8.5.1 *Endings*

    I, II -er|
    III   -ir|ò, -ai, -à; -emo, -ete, -anno
    Infinitive as in 8.2.1.

8.5.2 The tense is obviously based on the infinitive, but in some common words telescoping takes place, e.g. **cadrò, cadere; vorrò, volere; verrò, venire.**

8.6 CONDITIONAL

    I, II -er|
               |ei, -esti, -ebbe (-ia); -emmo, -este, -ebbero
    III   -ir|
    Infinitive as in 8.2.1.

The stem is the same as that of the future (8.5.2).

8.7 SUBJUNCTIVE

8.7.1 *Present*

    I   -i, -i, -i; -iamo, -iate, -ino
    II   -a, -a, -a; -iamo, -iate, -ano
    III -(isc)a, -(isc)a, -(isc)a; -iamo, -iate, -(isc)ano
    Infinitive as in 8.2.1.

8.7.2 *Past*

    I   -assi, -assi, -asse; -assimo, -aste, -assero
    II   -essi, etc.
    III -issi, etc.
    Infinitive as in 8.2.1. The stem does not change.

8.7.3 The subjunctive will nearly always be translated by an English indicative.

8.10 COMPOUND TENSES

8.10.1 *Perfect indicative and subjunctive*

Formed from the present (indicative or subjunctive) of **avere** (8.19.1) or **essere** (8.19.2), according to the verb in question, and the past participle (8.12.2).

8.10.2 *Pluperfect, future perfect, conditional perfect*

Formed like the perfect (8.10.1) but with the past (indicative or subjunctive), future and conditional instead of the present.

8.10.3 The use of **essere** is more widespread than that of **être** in French and extends to the modal if the main verb takes **essere**, e.g. **ho dovuto scrivere** but **sono dovuto andare**.

8.11 INFINITIVE

> I -are   II -ere   III -ire

The **-e** is always dropped before a suffix, and may be dropped for reasons of euphony elsewhere.

The infinitive can be used as a noun with the article, e.g. **l'aprirsi della nuova epoca**, *the opening of the new epoch*.

8.12 PARTICIPLES

8.12.1 *Present participle active*

> I -ante   II -ente   III -ente/-iente
> Infinitive as in 8.2.1.

Always an adjective or noun, e.g. **sequente**, *following;* **comandante**, *commander*.

8.12.2 *Past participle passive*

> I   -ato, -ata, -ati, -ate (5.1)
> IIa   -uto, etc.
>   b   (see 8.12.3)
> IIIa -ito, etc.
>   b   (see 8.12.3)
>   Infinitive as in 8.2.1.

8.12.3 A good many common verbs in **-ere** and **-ire** have irregular past participles in **-to** or **-so**, usually going back to Latin. Thus the verbs given in 8.4.2 have or may have participles **rimasto, riso, difeso, colto, (doluto), porso, retto, discusso, riflesso, scritto, venuto**. Once again it is best to consult a good dictionary.

8.12.4 The past participle is used more freely in Italian, e.g. **Esaurita la prima edizione**, *when the first edition had gone out of print*, and **gli iscritti** in 1.3.1.

8.13 GERUND

> I -ando,   II, III -endo
> Infinitive as in 8.2.1.

Used adverbially like the English participle, and also with the **verb venire** to express continuous action, e.g. **si veniva esaurendo**, *it was becoming exhausted*; and with **andare** action in the immediate future.

8.14 REFLEXIVE

8.14.1 These are formed by adding the personal pronoun of the same person to the verb, e.g. **lavarsi**, *to wash* (oneself); **mi lavo**; **procurarsi un impiego**, *to get oneself a job*.

8.14.2 The uses of the reflexive form are diverse. The English equivalent may be not only reflexive, but reciprocal, e.g. **si accordarono**, *they agreed with each other*; intransitive **si mosse**, *he moved*; passive, **si vendono**, *they are sold*; or impersonal, **si va**, *one goes*. The last two types are almost indistinguishable; the point to note is that intransitive verbs can be reflexive.

8.15 PASSIVE

8.15.1 The passive is not very common in Italian, frequent use being made of the reflexive in its place. When it is used it is formed by the combination of the verbs **essere** (8.19.2) or **venire** with the past participle passive, e.g. **è pubblicato**, **vien pubblicato**, *it is published*; **era usato**, *was used* (habitually); **furono staccati**, *they were detached* (once for all); **è stato pubblicato**, *has been published*. No absolute distinction can be drawn between these and the corresponding tenses of the reflexive, e.g. **si pubblica**, but the latter are peculiarly appropriate to express continuous or habitual action, while the forms with **essere** and the participle must be used where a state is described.

8.15.2 Another verb which can be used with the participle, but less commonly than **essere** and **venire**, is **andare** (8.19.3). For examples see 1.8.7.

8.17 AUXILIARIES

See 8.19.1–8.19.3.

8.19 IRREGULARITIES

8.19.1 avere, *to have*
> *Present:* **ho, hai, ha; abbiamo, avete, hanno**
> *Past:* **ebbi, avesti**, etc.
> *Present subjunctive:* **abbia**, etc.

8.19.2 essere, *to be*
> *Present:* **son(o), sei, è; siamo, siete, son(o)**
> *Imperfect:* **ero, eri, era; eravamo, eravate, erano**
> *Past:* **fui, fosti, fu; fummo, foste, furono**
> *Future:* **sarò**, etc.
> *Past participle:* **stato**

8.19.3 andare (ire), *to go*
> *Present:* **vado/vo, vai, va; andiamo, andate, vanno**
> *Imperfect:* **andavo**, etc. (archaic: **ivo**, etc.)
> *Future:* **andrò**, etc.

8.19.4 dare, *to give*
> *Present:* **do, dai, dà; diamo, date, danno**
> *Past:* **diedi, desti, diede/dette/d(i)è; demmo, desti, diedero/dettero/dierono**
> *Present subjunctive:* **dia**, etc.

8.19.5 dire, *to say*
Forms most of its parts from the stem **dic-**.
> *Past:* **dissi, dicesti**, etc.

8.19.6 dovere, *ought*
> *Present stems:* **dev-, debb-, deggi-, de-** (also 1P **dobbiamo**)

I

8.19.7 fare, *to do, make*
Stems: *fac-, facci-*
Present: *fò/faccio, fai, fa; facciamo, fate, fanno*
Past: *feci, facesti,* etc.
Past participle: *fatto*

8.19.8 potere, *to be able*
Present: *posso, puoi, può; possiamo, potete, possono*

8.19.9 sapere, *to know*
Present: *so, sai, sa; sappiamo, sapete, sanno*
Present subjunctive: *sappia,* etc.

8.19.10 stare, *to stand*
Present: *3P stanno*
Past: *stetti, stesti,* etc.
Present subjunctive: *stia,* etc.

8.19.11 uscire, *to go out*
Alternate stem: *esc-*

8.19.12 volere, *to wish*
Present: *voglio/vo', vuoi, vuole; vogliamo, volete, vogliono*
Future: *vorrò,* etc.
Present subjunctive: *voglia,* etc.

9 ADVERBS

9.1 FORMATION
The only adverbial formative is **-mente**, e.g. **nuovamente, facilmente**; but some adjectives, such as **forte** are used unchanged, and combinations of preposition and adjective, e.g. **di certo**, *certainly*, are not uncommon.

9.2 COMPARISON
The comparative is formed in the same way as that of adjectives (5.3).

10 PREPOSITIONS

10.2 FORMS
Many prepositions combine (or may do) with the article

> **a:** al, allo, all', alla, ai, (alli), agli, alle
> **con:** col, etc.
> **da:** dal, etc.
> **di:** del, etc.
> **in:** nel, etc.
> **per:** pel, etc.
> **su:** sul, etc.

Forms such as **ai, dei** may all be shortened to **a', de'** though the practice is not so widespread as it was.

> **di** may become **d'** before vowels; **da** does not.

10.4 COMPOUND PREPOSITIONS
There are a number of compound prepositions such as **contro di**, *against*; **dentro a**, *inside*.

10.5 MEANINGS

The meanings of the simple prepositions are anything but simple. A typical Italian grammar will give as many as 15 different senses for **di**, not all of them to be translated *of*.

11 CONJUNCTIONS

Italian has a wide variety of conjunctions, but they cause no grammatical difficulty provided one remembers that some of them require the subjunctive.

GLOSSARY

abbonamento, *subscription* (1.8.7)
aggiornato, *up to date*
aggiunta, *addition* (1.5)
allestimento, *preparation*
ampliato, *enlarged* (1.5)
annata, anno, *year, volume* (1.8.4)
annuario, *yearbook*
appresso, (published by) (1.5.1)
arretrato, *back number* (1.8.7)
atti, *proceedings*
aumentato, *enlarged*

biblioteca, *library*
bibliotecario, *librarian*

cambio, *exchange*
casa editrice, *publishing house* (1.6.1)
cenno, *note*
collana, collezione, *collection* (1.7.1)
in corso, *current* (1.8.7)
in corso di stampa, *being printed*
a cura di, *edited by* (1.2.2)

disponibile, *available*
domanda, *order*

edito, *published* (1.8.6)
edizione, *edition* (1.5), *publication* (1.6.1)
edizione, non di nostra, *not published by us*
esaurito, *out of print*
esemplare, *copy*
estratto, *offprint*

fascicolo, *number, issue* (1.7.3, 1.8.4)
fattura, *invoice*

giunto, *added*

illustrato, *illustrated, with notes*
indirizzo, *address*
inedito, *unpublished*
inviare, *send* (1.8.8)

libraio, *bookseller*
libreria, *bookshop* (1.5)
libro, *book*

mensile, *monthly* (1.8.5)
migliorato, *improved*
morto, *dead*

nato, *born*
novella, *short story*
nuovo, *new* (1.5)

in omaggio, *complimentary*
opera, *work*

prezzo, *price*
pronto per la stampa, *ready for printing*
proprietà letteraria, *copyright*

quaderno, *part, number, pamphlet* (1.7.1, 1.7.3, 1.8.1)
quindicinale, *fortnightly*

raccolta, *collection*
recato in ordine, *arranged*
redattore, *editor* (1.8.3)
redazione, *editing, editorial office* (1.8.3)
ricerca, *research*
rimettere, *send*

ristampa, *reprint(ing)* (1.5)
ritratto, *portrait*
riveduto, *revised* (1.5)
rivista, *review*
romanzo, *novel*

saggio, *essay*
saggio, numero di, *trial number*
scelto, *selected*
seguito, *continuation*
semestrale, *half-yearly* (1.8.5)
separata, *offprint*
separato, *single* (1.8.7)
settimana(le), *week(ly)*
spedire, *dispatch*

stampa, *press*
stesso, *same*
storia, *history*

tavola, *plate, table*
tipografo, *printer*
traduzione, *translation*
tratto, *taken*
trimestrale, *quarterly*

unico, *single*
uscire, *come out,* (1.8.5)

in vendita, *on salǝ*

GRAMMATICAL INDEX: WORDS

a, 10.2
abbia, etc., 8.19.1
ai, agli, al, alla, etc., 10.2
andare, 8.15.2
andate, andiamo, andrò,
    8.19.3

bei, begli, 5.1.3

ce, 7.3.1
ci, 7.3.1, 7.3.2
codesto, 7.1.2
col, etc., 10.2
contro di, 10.4

d', 10.2
da(i), 8.19.4, 10.2
dal, dalla, etc., 10.2
danno, de, 8.19.4
degli, 3.2
dei, 3.2, 4.2.1, 10.2
del, della, etc., 3.2, 10.2
demmo, 8.19.4
dentro a, 10.4
desti, dettero, detti,
    8.19.4
di, 10.5
di certo, 9.1
dia, etc., 8.19.4
dicesti, 8.19.5

diedero, diedi, dierono,
    8.19.4
dissi, 8.19.5
do, 8.19.4
dobbiamo, 8.19.6

e, 2.1.2
è, 2.1.2, 8.19.2
ebbi, 8.19.1
era, etc., 8.19.2
esc-, 8.19.11
essere, 8.10.3, 8.15.1

fa, facciamo, etc., 8.19.7
feci, fò, 8.19.7
forte, 9.1
foste, fu, etc., 8.19.2

gl', 3.1.1
gli, 3.1.1, 7.3.1
glie, 7.3.1

ha, ho, etc., 8.19.1

i, il, 3.1.1
iva, etc., 8.19.3

l', 3.1.1
la, le, 3.1.1, 7.3.1
lei, 7.3.1
li, 3.1.1

lo, 3.1.1, 7.3.1
lui, 7.3.1

me, mi, 7.3.1
miei, mio, 5.4.

ne, 7.3.2
né (nè), 2.1.2
nei, nel, etc., 10.2
noi, 7.3.1

pei, pel, etc., 10.2
piaccio, 8.1.2
pongo, 8.1.2
posso, potete, può, etc.,
    8.19.8

quale, quali, 7.1.1
quegli, quei, 7.1.1
quello, 7.1.1, 7.1.2
questi, 7.1.1
questo, 7.1.1, 7.1.2

sa, sapete, sarò, etc.,
    8.19.9
se, 7.3.1
sei, 8.19.2
si, 7.3.1
siamo, siete, 8.19.2
so, 8.19.9
son(o), 8.19.2

stanno, 8.19.10

stato, 8.19.2

stesti, stetti, stia, 8.19.10

suo(i), 5.4

sul, 10.2

taccio, 8.1.2

te, ti, 7.3.1

tuo(i), 5.4

un', una, uno, 3.3, 6.1.1

uomini, 4.2.1

vanno, 8.19.3

ve, 7.3.1

venire, 8.15.1

vi, 7.3.1, 7.3.2

vo, 8.19.3, 8.19.12

voglia, etc., 8.19.12

voi, 7.3.1

volete, vorrò, vuoi, vuole,
  8.19.12

GRAMMATICAL INDEX: ENDINGS

-a, 4.2.1, 4.2.2, 5.2.1, 6.2.2,
  8.2.1, 8.7.1

-ᵃ, 6.3

-ea, 8.3

-ia, 5.2.1, 8.3, 8.6

-ta, 8.12.2

-va, 8.3

-e, 4.2.1, 4.2.2, 5.2.1, 8.2.1,
  8.4.1

-ebbe, 8.6

-ie, 4.2.1, 5.2.1

-re, 8.11

-se, 8.4.2

-sse, 8.7.2

-te, 8.12.2

-ate, 8.2.1, 8.7.1, 8.12.2

-vate, 8.3

-ete, 8.2.1

-rete, 8.5.1

-ite, 8.2.1

-ante, -(i)ente, 8.12.1

-mente, 9.1

-ste, 8.4.1, 8.7.2

-ette, 8.4.1

-i, 4.2.1, 5.2.1, 8.2.1, 8.4.1,
  8.7.1

-ai, 8.4.1

-rai, 8.5.1

-ei, 8.4.1

-rei, 8.6

-ii, 4,2.1, 8.4.1

-si, 8.4.2, 8.14.1

-ssi, 8.7.2

-ti, 8.12.2

-sti, 8.4.1

-etti, 8.4.1

-vi, 8.3

-o, 4.2.1, 5.2.1, 8.2.1

-ò, 8.4.1

-°, 6.3

-ando, -endo, 8.13

-iamo, 8.2.1, 8.7.1

-(v)amo, 8.3

-remo, 8.5.1

-errimo, 5.3

-ssimo, 8.7.2

-issimo, 5.3

-mmo, 8.4.1

-remmo, 8.6

-ano, 8.2.1, 8.3, 8.7.1

-eano, -iano, 8.3

-vano, 8.3

-ranno, 8.5.1

-ono, 8.2.1

-rono, 8.4.1

-rò, 8.5.1

-ero, 8.4.1

-ebbero, 8.6

-sero, 8.4.2

-ssero, 8.7.2

-ettero, 8.4.1

-so, 8.12.3

-to, 8.12.2, 8.12.3

-vo, 8.3

-ù, 4.2.2

RUMANIAN

SPECIMEN

Abonamentele la „Revista română de drept" se contractează numai prin administraţia revistei în următoarele condiţii:
  (a) pentru instituţii, intreprinderi, organizaţii cooperatiste şi obşteşti: 200 lei pe an, plata făcîndu-se pe întreg anul;
  (b) pentru jurişti: 120 lei pe an, 60 lei pe 6 luni şi 30 lei pe 3 luni.
Administraţia nu-şi asumă răspunderea în cazul pierderii revistelor, trimise instituţiilor sau intreprinderilor abonate, care nu au indicat adresa exactă cu stradă şi număr sau a căror titulatură ne-a fost comunicată cu iniţiale.

Subscriptions to 'Revista română de drept' are now being placed with the management of the review on the following conditions:
  (a) *for institutions, enterprises, co-operative organisations and societies: 200 lei per annum, payment being made for a whole year;*
  (b) *for jurists: 120 lei per annum, 60 lei for 6 months and 30 lei for 3 months.*
The management takes no responsibility in case of loss of the reviews, sent to subscribing institutions or enterprises which have not indicated their exact address with street and number or whose representation (i.e. the name of whose representative) *has not been communicated* (*complete*) *with initials.*

0 GENERAL CHARACTERISTICS

0.1 DEGREE OF INFLEXION
In as much as it still has a genitive case, it is somewhat more synthetic than any of the other members of the family, but cannot be called a markedly synthetic language.

0.2 ORDER OF WORDS
Qualifiers, including most adjectives, follow the noun they qualify. The usual order of words in the sentence is subject, verb, object, but the verb may come first.

0.4 RELATION TO OTHER LANGUAGES

Although Rumanian is a member of the Romance family, its divergent phonetic and morphological development, and the influence of Slavonic languages on its vocabulary lead to marked differences from the Western Romance languages.

1 BIBLIOLINGUISTICS

1.1 NAMES
1.1.1 Modern Rumanian personal names consist of Christian names and surnames, dealt with separately below, but names of medieval type in which the second element

is a descriptive adjective or noun in apposition persist into the 19th century, e.g. **Dionisie Eclesiarhul,** indexed under D.

1.1.2 Christian names are masculine or feminine nouns as the case may be. Masculine names are not declined (cf. 4.3.2) but most feminine ones are (4.3.5), e.g. **scrieri ale Rosei Luxemburg,** *writings of Rosa Luxemburg.* Note that they incorporate the definite article (3.1), whereas masculine names do not.

1.1.3 Native surnames mostly end in a vowel; among those that end in a consonant are a number borrowed from other languages. They may all be regarded as masculine nouns. They have no case-endings, but the native ones can have plural forms, which incorporate the definite article (3.1), e.g. **Ionescu; Ioneştii,** *the Ionescus.* The singular cannot always be unequivocally derived from such plurals, but the problem very rarely arises. Double-barrelled surnames occur, but present no problem.

1.1.4 Foreign names need no special treatment, though Christian names may be found in a Rumanian form. For the Rumanian transcription of Russian names see Russian 2.1.2.

1.2 NAMES OF AUTHORS, EDITORS, ETC.

Names are given in a variety of ways but are rarely affected grammatically.

1.2.1 The name commonly appears at the head of the title page, in the nominative.

1.2.2 It may follow the title, sometimes without connexion but more often preceded by the equivalent of the preposition *by,* e.g. **Istoria bisericii româneşti de N. Iorga.** In either case the name is unaffected. The genitive is not usual: **Opera lui Mihai Eminescu** is a book about Eminescu, **Omagiu lui George Oprescu** is a Festschrift, **lui** here indicating the dative. In any case masculine names are not affected.

1.2.3 The agent may be specified by a noun. The name then follows in the nominative, e.g. **Redactor Liviu Marcu; Colectivul de redacţie: V. Popovici** [followed by other names].

1.2.4 The activity may be specified by a noun. The name follows, with or without **de,** e.g. **Sub redacţia: H. D. Sterian, M. Resiga; prefaţa şi note de Ileana Berlogea.** The names are not affected.

1.2.5 The activity may be specified by a passive verb, e.g. **Lucrarea a fost elaborată de . . .,** *The work was prepared by . . .;* **Capitolele sint scrise de . . .,** *The chapters were written by . . . .* The name is unaffected.

1.2.6 Corporate authorship involves the same types of construction, but the names are more often affected, e.g. **Academia Republicii Populare Romine|Institut(ul) de Cercetări Economice** at the head in the nominative in the order: main body, subordinate body; **elaborată sub ingrijirea Institutului de Cercetări Economice al Academiei RPR,** *under the care of* the same bodies, both in the genitive, in the opposite order. The omission of the article **-ul** is very unusual, and the article should be preserved in headings.

1.3 TITLES

1.3.1 Most titles are straightforward combinations of nouns, adjectives and prepositions. e.g. **Aspecte ale dezvoltării capitalismului premonopolist in Rominia,** *Aspects of the development of pre-monopoly capitalism in Rumania.* More variety is found in belles lettres and the literature of persuasion, e.g. **Acolo şezum şi plânsem,** *There we sat down and wept;* **Din lumea celor care nu cuvintă,** *From the world of those who do not speak;* **Cum putem economisi concentratele?,** *How can we save concentrates?*

1.3.2 Title entries according to Anglo-American rules pose no grammatical problems. Since genitives are usually dependent on other nouns and follow them, the 'first noun' of the British Museum rules will usually be in the nominative/accusative, but feminine proper names may be in the genitive. In any case, the suffixed article will have to be removed, e.g. **Cheia înțelesului** (heading **Cheie**). Needless to say, the definite article cannot be ignored in filing, but neither is the indefinite article (or numeral): not only is **Un pas înainte** . . . (*One step forward* . . .) indexed under **Un** but **O istorie a literaturii române** (*A history of Rumanian literature*) appears under **O**. Similarly **Cele 23 întrebări ale lui Den** (*The 23 questions of Den*) and **Al treilea ochi al lui Shiva** (*Shiva's third eye*), both under the first word, though it counts (3.3, 3.4) as an article.

1.3.3 In the context of a sentence the chief noun in a title may appear in the genitive instead of the nominative, e.g. **paternitatea „Istoriei Țării Românești** . . .", *the authorship of 'Istoria etc.'*; but this can be avoided by interposing the appropriate descriptive noun before the title, e.g. **în centrul romanelor „Roxana" și „Doctorul Taifun"**, *at the heart of the novels 'Roxana' and 'Doctorul Taifun'*.

1.4 VOLUMES AND PARTS

1.4.1 The usual words are **volum(ul)** and **parte(a)** respectively, though **tom(ul)** is also found.

1.4.2 Numeration is by a following ordinal number, usually in figures, e.g. **volumul I-iu**; **partea 1**. **Carte(a)**, *book*, is also found, denoting a more or less independent member of a work in several parts: it may or not be physically separate. Occasionally numeration occurs without any descriptive word, e.g. **Carul de foc | III. Desculț**, *The chariot of fire: vol. 3 (of) The tramp* (more explicitly at the end: **urmează volumul al patrulea**, *vol. 4 follows*). Sometimes **parte** denotes a major division, e.g. **Opere complete. Partea antêia. Teatru. volumul II**.

1.5 EDITIONS

The usual word is **ediție** or **edițiune**, the number of the edition following in ordinal form, e.g. **edițiunea întâia**, or an adjective denoting some form of revision, e.g. **îmbunătățită**, *improved*; **completată**, **adăugită**, *enlarged*; **revăzută** or **revizuită**, *revised*. (Alternatively: **nevarietur**, *unaltered*.) For another meaning of **edițiune** see 1.6.1.

1.6 IMPRINTS

1.6.1 These show little grammatical variety, neither the name of the publisher nor place being usually affected. The publisher's name is usually in the nominative. Sometimes **edițiunea** may be prefixed, meaning *publication* and followed by the genitive; but the following expression will only be affected if it is a noun with the article, e.g. **edițiunea Academiei Române** (N: **Academia Română**); so also **editura autorului**, i.e. *published by the author*. In the 19th century, where printer and publisher are less distinct, expressions like **În tipografia lui Anton Pann**, *At the press of A. P.*, are found; but masculine names are invariable (1.1.2).

1.6.2 The place is almost always in the nominative. If a preposition precedes, e.g. **în Buda**, it makes no difference to the form.

1.6.3 Present-day publishing is institutional, and the publishing houses have names descriptive of their function, e.g. **Editura (de stat) pentru literatură (și artă)**, (*State*) *Publishing House for Literature (and Art)*. The names and number of these vary from time to time. They include the press of the Academy, **Editura Academiei R.P.R.** (now **R.S.R.**), the only one that might admit of abbreviation—to **Academia R.P.R.**

Earlier imprints are either personal names or arbitrary names or a combination of both, e.g. **Adevărul** (*Truth*); **Cugetarea** (*Thought*)—**Georgescu Delafras**; **Editura librăriei şcolelor Fraţii Şaraga**, *Publishing House of the Schools Bookshop Şaraga Bros.*

1.7 SERIES

1.7.1 The titles of series appear most often at the head of the title-page, sometimes on the previous leaf or the cover, or even above the imprint. Most series titles are descriptive of the series as a whole or the individual items, e.g. **Biblioteca pentru toţi**, *Library for All*; **Biblioteca şcolarului**, *Scholar's library*; **Scriitori români**, *Rumanian writers*; or more elaborately, **În ajutorul celor care studiază economia politică**, *To assist those who are studying economics*, or arbitrarily: **Colecţia Ceres**. Sometimes a series must be inferred, e.g. **Aşezămantul cultural Ion C. Brătianu. LV**, where one must understand [*Publications*].

Academic series may include the name of an institution in the genitive, e.g. **Memoriile Secţiunii Istorice**, *Memoirs of the Historical Section* (**Secţiunea Istorică**).

1.7.2 Numeration is often absent, and in any case is usually a simple numeral, on the cover or on the spine.

1.8 PERIODICALS

1.8.1 There is no linguistic difference between the titles of periodicals and those of books and series, e.g. **Revista de etnografie şi folclor**, *The review of ethnography and folklore*; **Legalitate populară**, *People's law*, but, as might be expected, titles are often more allusive, e.g. **Sburătorul**, *The flier*; **Linia dreaptă**, *The straight line*.

As with books (1.3.3) the title may be grammatically affected by its connexion with the rest of a sentence, e.g. **Suplement al ,,Gazetei matematice"**, *Supplement to 'Gazeta matematică'*; or isolated, as in **conducerea revistei ,,Luceafărul"**, *the running of the review 'Luceafărul'*.

1.8.2 If the name of the body responsible forms part of the title or sub-title it will usually appear in the genitive, e.g. **Analele Institutului de istorie a partidului**, etc., *Annals of the Institute of Party History*; **Muncitorul: organ al partidei muncitorilor**, *The worker: organ of the Workers' Party*. But a good many genitives will simply be descriptive, as in **Gazeta învăţămintului**, *Education Gazette*. Also in the genitive is the name of an institution preceded by a noun denoting activity, e.g. **apare sub îndrumarea (ingrijirea, egida)**, *appears under the direction (care, aegis)*.

1.8.3 Editorial activity is usually indicated by the stem **redac-**, e.g. **redactor (şef or responsabil)**, (*chief or responsible*) *editor*. Where editing is collective the differences between the various terms are difficult to sort out. If one has a large **colegiu redacţional** or **ştiinţific** and a small **colectiv redacţional** or **de redacţie**, it is obvious that the **colegiu** is an advisory body, but sometimes **colegiul de redacţie** or **de conducere** or **colectivul de coordonare** is the only term given and the body includes the responsible editor.

Sometimes the editor is indicated by **alcătuit din**, *arranged by*; **condus(ă) de**, *conducted by*; **de sub conducerea**, *under the management (of)*.

1.8.4 Numeration is most often by **an** and **numar**, e.g. **anul 16 (1971) nr 1**, with **volum** and **tom(ul)** as synonyms for **anul**. Nr is sometimes reinforced by **caietul**.

Parte should be treated with caution. In a publication such as the official gazette it can indicate a section devoted to a particular type of material.

1.8.5 Periodicity may be implicit in the title or sub-title, e.g. **revistă lunară**, *monthy review*; **publicaţie trimestrială**, *quarterly publication*. It is more likely however to be stated in a phrase beginning **apare**, *appears*, e.g. **apare de 4(6) ori pe an**, *4(6) times a* *year*; o dată la două luni, *once in two months*; **lunar, bilunar, trimestrial, anual,** *monthly, bi-monthly, quarterly, annually*. Sometimes it can only be deduced from words such as **12 numere, 12 apariţii,** *12 numbers, issues* in the terms of subscription.

1.8.6 Details of subscription are often missing, even though one may be implored to subscribe **din timp şi pe termene cît mai lungi,** *in time and for the longest possible period*. If so, one simply finds **preţul,** *the price* (of a single number), on the back.

If subscription terms are given (**plată** or **abonament**), the formula is usually **costul (preţul) unui abonament (individual) (anual) este de . . .,** *the cost (price) of an (individual) (annual) subscription is . . .*. **Anual** may be replaced by **pe 6 (şase) luni, pe tre luni.** Subscriptions are often greater for institutions and enterprises, (**instituţii, întrepinderi**). Separate numbers (**numere izolate**) are sometimes quoted for, e.g. **costul unui numar,** and occasionally sets of back numbers are offered, e.g. **un set din XI–XXVI se poate obţine după achitarea sumei de 236 lei,** *a set of vols XI–XXVI can be obtained on payment of the sum of 236 lei*.

1.8.7 Addresses may specify **redacţia** or **administraţia**, but they are often the same. Alternatively directions are given for specified approaches, e.g. **orice comandă din străinătate se face prin,** *all orders from abroad to be made to*; **manuscrisele . . . şi revistele pentru schimb precum şi orice corespondenţă se vor trimite pe adresa,** *Mss and journals for exchange as well as all correspondence are to be sent to the address . . . .* Instead of **se vor trimite** (future) one may have **se trimit** or **se primesc** (present).

2 ALPHABET, PHONETICS, SPELLING

2.1 ALPHABET

2.1.1 The Latin alphabet used in Rumania runs thus:

a ă â b c d e f g h i î j k l m n o p q r s ş
t ţ u ǘ w x y z

of which **k, q, w** and **y** are found only in foreign words. Subscript commas are more usual in **ş** and **ţ**. Except in **România** and related words, **â** has been replaced, as at times in the past, by **î**, which has the same pronunciation. Each letter should have a separate place in the alphabet, but the different **a**'s and **i**'s are often equated.

2.1.2 Until about the last quarter of the 19th century the alphabet was wholly or partly Cyrillic. What should be an authoritative statement on the Cyrillic alphabet in its latest stages, with its obsolescent variants, is given below. As will be seen, the alphabet given does not include the letter, ↑ (**i**), which the writer himself uses as well as ж (**â**).

'The Slavonic letters which have remained in use among the Rumanians are the following:

а є б г д є ж з і к л м н о п
р с т ф х ȣ ц ч ш ψ ж з у

Note

The letters:

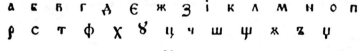

have been removed by the honourable Society of letters of Bucharest from the number of the Slavonic alphabet, since they were not only superfluous, but the cause also of difficulty and loss of time to innocent children '

In fact the older versions of the Cyrillic alphabet amounted to 43 letters—a good reason for leaving them to the experts. One of the letters which the writer fails to notice is и, which he uses himself instead of ʌ at the beginning of a word.

2.1.3 The semi-cyrillic alphabet follows the Cyrillic order, substituting some Latin letters. A textbook of 1856 gives the following table:

A	а	a	П	п	p
Б	б	b	Р	p	r
B	в	v	C	c	s
Г	г	g(h)	T	т	t
D	d	d	Ꙋ	ꙋ	u
E	e	e	Ф	ф	f
Ж	ж	j	X	x	h
Z	z	z	Ц	ц	ţ
I	i	i	Ч	ч	c (ce ci)
К	к	c(h)	Ш	ш	ş
Л	л	l		ъ	ă
M	m	m	Ѧ	ѧ	î
N	n	n	Џ	џ.	g (ge gi)
O	o	o			

This tir-ѧ: alone is given in the table, but ж is freely used in the text. The disconcerting effect of the mixture is well illustrated by the following sentence from a pamphlet of 1867.

Nꙋ есте Ромънꙋ каре астъзi съ nꙋ сiмцъ печессiтатеа de а iнтродꙋче лiтерiле латiпе ѫп алфабетꙋ пострꙋ

In the present-day alphabet: **Nu este Românŭ care astăzi să nu simţă necessitatea de a introduce literile latine în alfabetu postru** (sic). In view of the misprint (**n** for **n**) one can only echo the sentiment: *There is not a Rumanian who today does not feel the necessity of introducing the Latin letters into our alphabet.*

2.1.4 The alphabet used today for Moldavian in the Soviet Union is much the same as the old Cyrillic one, viz.

С	а	б	в	г	д	е	ж	з	и	й	к	л	м	н	о	п	р	с	т
L	a	b	v	g(h)	d	(i)e	j	z	i	i	c(h)	l	m	n	o	p	r	s	t

С	у	ф	х	ц	ч		ш	ы	ь	э	ю	я
L	u	f	h	ţ	c (ce, ci)		ş	i	i	ă	iu	ia

2.1.5 Both alphabets call for a certain amount of comment. The Cyrillic alphabet is phonetic, whereas the Latin alphabet as used in Rumania is not. Hence the alternative equivalents. It should also be noted that the British Standard transliteration given under Moldavian, though based on Rumanian spelling, usually gives one equivalent only, and may therefore result in spellings different from the Rumanian. Notes on difficult letters follow.

г: g before a, î, o, u; gh before e, i.

е: usually corresponds to e, but in Moldavian equals ie at the beginning of some words and after vowels. (Some Ro words in ie- begin with ие- in Mo.)

ж: corresponds to Ro j and in Moldavian also to g before e and i. Though this makes it ambiguous, it can safely be said that at the end of a word, or before o, у, а or a consonant, it will represent j; before ю, я it will represent g; while in же and жи it could represent either, e.g. прилеж, prilej; мижлок, mijloc; жустэ, justă; грижа, grija; лежя, legea; пажинь, pagini; ынгрижире, îngrijire; леже, lege; ангажезе, angajeze.

й: occurs after and occasionally before a vowel, e.g. луй, lui; й-ау, i-au.

к: c before a, î, o, u; ch before e.

кз, кс: x.

ч: the statement in the standard transliteration 'c (before e or i)' is inadequate. Before a, o and у it corresponds in itself to Ro ce and ci, e.g. ачастэ, această; чобан, cioban; чуф, ciuf. How the BSI recommends it should then be transliterated I do not know. (Ro Cyrillic used ачеастъ.)

ь: occurs at the end of a word, or in the middle of a compound, after a consonant, e.g. орь, ori; орькаре, oricare; and in words like обьект, obiect.

я: The standard transliteration ia is the least likely Rumanian equivalent. In about 80% of cases this will be ea, as in the common endings -ря, -яскэ, -язэ (-rea, -ească, -ează). Of the remainder a as in жустиция (justiţia) is at least as likely as ia, as in яр, кяр (iar, chiar).

2.1.6 The accents and diacritical marks on the letters ă, â, î, ş, ţ, are an essential part of them, but despite this the omission of the circumflex accent in upper-case was not uncommon. In the past ĭ and ŭ were also used, and also é and ó (see 2.7).

2.2 CAPITALISATION

2.2.1 There are slightly different conventions in Rumanian and Moldavian, though in principle all names are spelt with initial capitals in both. If, however, a name consists of several elements, it is not invariably the case that all of them are capitalised, and some words that might be thought to be names are not treated as such. Among these are the months and the days of the week, nouns of nationality, such as **român**, and the word **dumnezeu**, *God*.

2.2.2 The following are spelt with capitals throughout: personal names, including such names as **Petru cel Mare** (*Peter the Great*); geographical, topographical and astronomical names, e.g. **Capul Bunei Speranţe, Piaţa Concordiei** (пяца in Moldavian), **Calea Laptului** (*Milky Way*), but note that **fluviul**, *river*, is not usually considered to be part of the name, except in such expressions as **Fluviul Galben**, *Yellow River*; names of orders; in Rumanian, names of historical events, e.g. **Marea Revoluţie Socialistă din Octombrie**, but not of periods such as **evul mediu**; names of central or supreme political organs and organisations, national, foreign and international, e.g. **Partidul Muncitoresc Român, Camera Comunelor, Organizaţia Naţiunilor Unite**. (In Moldavian only the central organs and organisations of the Soviet Union are so treated.)

2.2.3 In the following only the first word has an initial capital: anniversaries, unless the word is a figure, e.g. **Anul nou, 1 Mai**, though Moldavian has **Зия Конституцией**; institutions and organisations other than those mentioned in 2.2.2, e.g.

Frontul unic muncitoresc, Institutul de lingvistică, Comunitatea economică europeană; books and periodicals. In Moldavian the names of historical events have only the first word capitalised.

2.3 DIVISION OF WORDS

2.3.1 Rules 1, 2, 4, 5a, 6b, 7a, 8a (p. xiii) apply, with the following modifications: both consonants are taken over if the second is **l** or **r**; if **i** or **u** stands between two vowels, it is taken over. Examples: **nord-estul; trans-unite; a-pa-rat; per-sis-ten-te**, but **re-flecta, demo-cratica; cen-tru, punc-tuaţie; une-ori, ule-iuri**. There is no objection to **x** at the beginning of a line.

2.3.2 Moldavian practice is fundamentally the same but **бл** is found divided, e.g. **пуб-личитэций**, and **ст** can begin a syllable after a vowel, e.g. **ача-ста**. On the other hand there is no objection to such divisions as **обш-теск** instead of **об-штеск**, **ност-ру** instead of **нос-тру**.

2.5 PALATALISATION (See General note on the Slavonic languages)

2.5.1 Palatalisation occurs in nouns and verbs as a result of a following **i** or occasionally **e**, but the palatalisation of **c** and **g** is not reflected in the spelling. Instead **c** and **g** have different pronunciations before **a, o, u** on the one hand and **e, i** on the other. The remaining changes are as follows:

d	l n r	s	sc	st	şc	t	x	z
z	vanish	ş	şt	şt	şt	ţ	cş	j

Examples: **a auzi**, *to hear*; **aude**, *he hears*; **românesc, româneşti**, *Rumanian*; **frate** P **fraţi**, *brother(s)*. (The dictionary form is given first.)

2.5.2 It may be a help to remember that similar changes take place between Latin and Rumanian, e.g. **dicet** > **zice**, *he says*; **filius** > **fiu**, *son*.

2.5.3 Endings preceded by a palatalised consonant are indicated by an asterisk.

2.6 VARIATION OF VOWEL

2.6.1 This usually occurs under the influence of the vowel in the following syllable and is a notable feature of Rumanian. The commonest effects are those produced in nouns and adjectives by a following **e** or **i**, viz.

Vowel	*Effect*
a	e (or ă before i)
ă	e
ea	e
î	i
oa	o (only occasionally before e)

or **a, ă**, viz.

e	ea
o	oa

The changes do not occur in all circumstances, but when they do not the reader has no problem. Examples: **fată**, *girl*, P **fete**; **făt**, *boy*, P **feţi**; **mare**, *sea*, G **mări**; **sfînt**, *saint*, P **sfinţi**; **veac**, P **veci**; **oaie**, *sheep*, P **oi**; **acest**, *this*, F **această**.

2.6.2   Similar changes, though not always for the same reasons, take place in verbs, e.g. **a face**, *to do*, **mult de făcut**, *much to do*; **a vedea**, *to see*, **văd**, *I see*, **vadă**, *he may see*; **a putea**, *to be able*, **poate**, *he can*, **pot**, *they can*; **vin**, *I come*, **a veni**, *to come*.

2.7 SPELLING
   2.7.1   The change from the Cyrillic to the Latin alphabet produced controversies, since the Latin alphabet lent itself more readily to etymological spellings. Spelling has gradually become more phonetic and more regular, discarding final **-u** and either changing **-i** to **i** or omitting it; expanding **ó** and **é** to **oa** and **ea**, and introducing other simplifications. Examples of 19th-century spelling with modern equivalents are: **astădi**, **astăzi**; **nevoe**, **nevoie**; **douĕ**, **două**; **ţéră**, **ţară**; **vedé**, **vedea**; **věḑênd**, **văzînd**; **sciintifica**, **ştiintifica**.
   2.7.2   The spelling reform of 1953 abolished the letter **â** (only temporarily in **român** and related words). It had the same pronunciation as **î** and had alternated with it in many words. Also abolished were silent **-u** after **i**, e.g. **ochi** for **ochiu**; **zb-**, **zd-** and the like were substituted for **sb-**, **sd-** and **dez-** for **des-** before a vowel or voiced consonant, e.g. **dezinfectare**, **dezvoltare**; and single for double letters except for **înn-** at the beginning of words. On the other hand the ending **-şi** was restored for **-ş** in a number of demonstratives and adverbs, e.g. **acelaşi**, *the same*. (The Moldavian spelling of such words varies between **-ш** and **-шь**.) Most of these changes had had some currency even before the reform.

3   ARTICLES

Rumanian has four articles: the definite, the indefinite, the possessive and the adjectival, the forms and uses of which are given below.

3.1 DEFINITE
   3.1.1   This corresponds roughly to the English definite article, but is used with abstract nouns and names of countries and in headings. It may also be used in addition to or instead of a possessive. On the other hand it is usually omitted after prepositions, e.g. **linguistica**, *linguistics*; **Institutul de linguistică**, *Institute of Linguistics*.

   3.1.2   *Forms*

	S		P	
	M	*F*	*M*	*F*
NA	-(u)l, -le	-a	-i	-le
GD	-(u)lui	-i	-lor	-lor

These are added to the appropriate form of the noun (see 4), e.g. **tată|l, foc|ul, nume|le, nume|lui, carte|a, cărţi|i,** but **familiei** not **familiii.** Short **-ă** disappears and so does the **-e** of **-ie,** e.g. **limbă, limba; istorie, istoria.**
   3.1.3   If an adjective precedes the noun, the article is attached to it instead. The article **-lui** is not added to masculine names but precedes them as a separate word, e.g. **Iliada lui Homer.** It is also used before indeclinable feminine names.

3.2 INDEFINITE
   3.2.1   The indefinite article, which is identical in form with the numeral *one*, is used much as in English.

3.2.2 *Forms*

	S		P	
	M	F	M	F
NA	un	o	unii	unele
GD	unui	unei	unor	unor

3.4 POSSESSIVE

3.4.1 This stands between the noun, with which it agrees, and a following genitive (except in simple constructions) or an ordinal numeral, or less frequently a possessive adjective, e.g. **Congresul al doilea al ligii,** *the second congress of the league*; but in **nordul Angliei,** *in the north of England.* See also 3.4.

3.4.2 *Forms*

S		P	
M	F	M	F
al	a	ai	ale

3.5 ADJECTIVAL

3.5.1 This is a special use of the demonstrative **cel,** but is traditionally treated as an article. Its commonest use is with superlatives, e.g. **cea mai mare parte,** *the greatest part*; **asigurarea profiturilor celor mai ridicate,** *the securing of the highest profits.* It is also used with numerals, both cardinal, e.g. **cele şase şcoli,** *the six schools,* and ordinal, e.g. **in timpul celui de-al doilea război mondial,** *at the time of the Second World War*; and with adjectives when there is no noun, e.g. **clerul musulman cît şi cel hindus,** *Moslem as well as Hindu clergy.*

3.5.2 *Forms*

	S		P	
	M	F	M	F
NA	cel	cea	cei	cele
GD	celui	celei	celor	celor

4 NOUNS

4.1 GENDER AND FORM

So far as forms are concerned there are two genders, masculine and feminine. Nouns which are masculine in the singular and feminine in the plural, e.g. **adjectivul, adjectivele,** *the adjective(s),* are classed as neuter.

4.3 ENDINGS

4.3.1 *Masculine*

These end in the singular in a consonant, -u, -i, -e; rarely -ă. Some of the last behave in the singular as if they were feminine, e.g. papă, *pope*; **papii,** *of the Pope.*

4.3.2 There is one form for the singular and one for the plural, the case being indicated by the article. The plural is got by adding -i or changing the existing vowel to -i.

4.3.3 Palatalisation and change of vowel take place in the plural. For tables of changes and examples see 2.5 and 2.6.

4.3.4 The plural of **om,** *man* is **oameni.**

4.3.5 *Feminine*

These end in the nominative singular in -ă, -e, -a, -ea, plus the word zi, and have the following case endings:

		-ă	-e	-a	-ea	zi
S	NA	-ă	-e	-a	-ea	zi
	GD	-e/-i	-i	-ale	-ele	zile
P		-e/-i/-uri	-i	-ale	-ele	zile

4.3.6 Palatalisation takes place before -i and change of vowel before -e, -i and -uri. For tables of changes and examples see 2.5 and 2.6.

4.3.7 Soră, *sister*, has P surori.

4.3.8 *Neuter (mixed)*

The plural is got by adding -e or -(u)ri or by changing the -u of the singular to -e or -i.

Palatalisation and vowel changes take place in the plural. For examples see 2.5 and 2.6.

4.3.9 *Place names*

Place names like Bucureşti, Iaşi are plural, but they may be found with singular articles, e.g. Flăcara Iaşului (title of a periodical).

Compound place names may give trouble. The second element may be an adjective, e.g. Tîrgu Frumos, in which case both elements will be declined, or a noun, in the genitive, as Sighetul Marmaţiei, or in apposition, e.g. Turnu Severin. In both these cases only the first element is declined, e.g. Turnului Severin. (In the nominative Turnul-Severinului is also found.)

5 ADJECTIVES

5.1 GENERAL

Adjectives vary according to number, gender and case and agree with the nouns they qualify.

5.2 ENDINGS

5.2.1 The feminine is formed as follows:

M	consonant	-u	-iu	-i	-tor	-e
F	add -ă	-ă	-ie	-e/-ie	-toare	-e

-e- and -o- usually change to -ea- and -oa-; nou makes nouă; greu, grea; rău, rea; roş(u), roş(i)e.

5.2.2 The declension of adjectives is the same as that of nouns (4.2; 4.3); but some have FP -i where -e might be expected, e.g. largi from larg, and some of those in -ace are unchanged in the plural.

5.3 COMPARISON

> Comparative: mai and positive
> Superlative: cel mai and positive (cf. 3.5)

5.4 POSSESSIVES

(al) meu, tău, său, nostru, vostru, F (a) mea, sa, ta, noastră, voastră are regular. They take second place in the phrase and require the article, e.g. şcoala sa, *his school*; clasica sa lucrare, *his classic work*.

6 NUMERALS

6.1 CARDINAL

6.1.1

1 un(u)	11 unsprezece	21 douăzeci şi un(u)
2 doi	12 doisprezece	22 douăzeci şi doi
3 trei	13 treisprezece	30–90 treizeci, etc., as 13–19
4 patru	14 paisprezece	100 o sută
5 cinci	15 cincisprezece	101 o sută un(u)
6 şase	16 şaisprezece	200 două sute
7 şapte	17 şaptesprezece	300 etc. trei sute, etc.
8 opt	18 optsprezece	1000 o mie
9 nouă	19 nouăsprezece	2000 două mii
10 zece	20 douăzeci	

6.1.2 *Declension*

un, o before a noun, as 3.2.1; unu(l), una, unuia, uneia when standing alone.
doi has F două but no separate GD.
3–99 are indeclinable, except in so far as they incorporate unu and doi.
o sută, o mie, etc. are feminine nouns, declined as such.

6.1.3 *Construction*

The numerals from douăzeci onwards are followed by de.

6.2 ORDINAL

6.2.1

1 prim|ul, -a	9 nou(ăle)a	
intîi|ul, -a	10 zec(el)ea	
2 doilea, doua	11–19 unsprezec(el)ea, etc.	
3 treilea, treia	20–90 douăzec(el)ea, etc.	
4 patr(ule)a	21 douăzeci si un(ule)a	
5 cinc(il)ea	100 o sut(ăle)a	
6 şas(el)ea	200 două sut(ele)a	
7 şapt(el)ea	1000 o mi(ile)a	
8 opt(ule)a		

6.2.2 intîi, indeclinable, is also found. The ordinals from doilea onwards, though they have separate M and F forms, behave also like nouns in that they are preceded by the possessive article al, a or the phrase cel de-al (cea de-a, etc.) (cf. 3.4, 3.5 and examples). The expression cel dintîi, *the first*, is also found.

6.3 FIGURES

6.3.1 Cardinals are expressed by simple arabic figures, ordinals either by arabic figures with the termination -(le)a or by roman figures with similar suffixes, e.g. pe linea a 3-a, *in line 3*; din secolul al XVIII-lea, *in the 18th century*.

6.3.2 Moldavian may use simple arabic numerals, and more frequently roman numerals, without al, but the al is inserted when the text is read, e.g. Конгресул VIII (ал оптулеа); Капитолул ал патрулеа; but in the table of contents Капитолул 4.

6.4 DATES

6.4.1   The months are:

ianuarie, februarie, martie, aprilie, mai, iunie,
iulie, august, septembrie, octombrie, noembrie, decembrie

6.4.2   Both day and year are expressed by cardinals, viz. (*On*) *28 March 1962*: (**la**) **28 martie 1962**, i.e. (**la**) **douăzeci și opt martie o mie nouă sute șaizeci și doi**. As no declension is involved, more complicated dates do not call for special comment.

7   PRONOUNS

7.1/7.2   DEMONSTRATIVE, INTERROGATIVE, RELATIVE, ETC.

7.1.1   The endings of these pronoun/adjectives are much the same as the definite article, viz.

	S		P	
	M	*F*	*M*	*F*
NA	-/-l	-a	-i	-(l)e
GD	-(l)ui	-(l)ei	-(l)or	-(l)or

7.1.2   Palatalisation (2.5) and vowel changes (2.6) occur, e.g. **acest**, F **această**, P **acești**.

7.1.3   The following have forms that call for notice:

cel(ă)lalt, cest(ă)lalt, *the other*, are compounds, both halves of which decline, the first half as a pronoun and the second as an adjective, e.g. GD celuilalt, celeilalte.
ce, *what ?, what*, is indeclinable.
cine, *who ?* has GD cui. So also fiecine, *anyone*.
care, *who, which*, has cărui, etc. So also fiecare, *anyone*.
vreun F vreo, *some*, is a compound of un.

7.1.4   Several pronoun/adjectives add -a to all forms, especially when used as pronouns, acea becoming aceea, e.g. in cazul acesta, *in that case*; unul dintre acestea, *one of these*. Other additions are -ași meaning *the same*, and -va, as in cineva, *somebody*.

7.1.5   The feminine is used when no noun is referred to, as in **Asemenea linii au fost observate și în spectrul stelelor, ceea ce dovedește . . .**, *similar lines have been observed in the spectrum of the stars, which proves . . . .*

7.3 PERSONAL

7.3.1   *Declension*

		1	2	3m	3f	3r
S	N	eu	tu	el	ea	-
	A	mine; m(ă)	tine; te	el; l, îl	ea; o	sine; s(e)
	G	-	-	lui	ei	-
	D	mie; mi, îmi	ție; ți, îți	lui; i, ii	ei; i, îi	sie; și, iși
P	N	noi	voi	ei	ele	
	A	noi; ne	voi; v(ă)	ei; i, ii	ele; le	as *S*
	G	-	-	lor	lor	
	D	nouă; ne, ni	vouă; v(ă), vi	lor; le, li	lor; le, li	

7.3.2 The commoner, unemphatic forms (following the semi-colon), are prefixed to the auxiliary and suffixed to the gerund, and in the case of **o** to the past participle, e.g. **l-a denumit**, *called him*; **limba poporului, care a creat-o şi o vorbeşte**, *the language of the people, which has created and speaks it.*

7.3.3 The dative may be appended to a noun, as a possessive, or precede the verb, like the French **en**, e.g. **el ii suferă efectele**, *he suffers the effects of it.*

7.3.4 Sometimes **o** is used as a neuter, without reference to any definite thing.

7.3.5 The element **în|su, -să, -şi, -se**, *self*, enters into several pronouns, e.g. **dînsul, -sa, -şii, -sele**, *he, she, they.*

7.3.6 There are polite forms for *you* and *he*, viz.

		2	3	3*m*	3*f*
S	NA	dumnea|ta	-sa	dumnea|lui	dumnea|ei
	GD	dumi|tale	-sale		
P		dumnea|voastră		-lor	

abbreviated **d-ta**, etc. (also **dv.** for **dumneavoastră**). **Dumneavoastră** may refer to a single person.

8 VERBS

8.1 STRUCTURE

8.1.1 The Rumanian verb has different forms for most of the different persons, making subject pronouns often unnecessary, and for the different tenses and moods. Some simple tenses in Rumanian correspond to compound ones in English, and vice versa.

8.1.2 Verbs have two stems. The present stem is the same as that of the infinitive, under which verbs are entered. The relation of the past stem to the present varies according to the conjugation.

8.2 PRESENT

8.2.1 *Endings*

I	-(ez), -(ez)i, -(eaz)ă/-e; -ăm/-em, -aţi, -(eaz)ă	inf. **-a**
II	-, -*i, -e; -em, -eţi, -	inf. **-e(a)**
III	-(esc), -(eşt)i, -(eşt)e; -im, -iţi, -(esc)	inf. **-i/-*i**
IV	-(ăsc), -(ăşt)i, -ă(şte); -im, -iţi, -ă(sc)	inf. **-i**

8.2.2 Verbs with infinitive in **-Cla** and **-Cra** have 1PS in **-Clu, -Cru**. So also **scriu** for **scrie, viu** from **veni** and cf. 8.19.

8.2.3 Palatalisation (2.5), indicated above by *, and change of vowel (2.6) occur.

8.3 IMPERFECT

I	-am, -ai, -a; -am, -aţi, -au	inf. **-a** or **-î**
II	-eam, -eai, etc.	inf. **-e(a)**
III	-iam, -iai, etc.	inf. **-i**

8.4 PAST

8.4.1 *Endings*

I	-ai, -aşi, -ă; -arăm, -arăţi, -ară	inf. **-a**
II	-*ui, -*uşi, -*u; -*urăm, -*urăţi, -*ură	inf. **-(e)a**
III	-sei, -seşi, -se; -serăm, -serăţi, -seră	inf. **-e**
IV	-ii, -işi, -i; -irăm, -irăţi, -iră	inf. **-i**
V	-îi, -îşi, -î; -îrăm, -îrăţi, -îră	inf. **-î**

8.4.2 Palatalisation (2.5) and change of vowel (2.6) may occur. In type III the -s- of the ending may affect the previous consonant, viz. **c**+**s**, **g**+**s** > **s** or **ps**; **d**+**s**, **n**+**s**, **t**+**s** > **s**, e.g. **frig**+**se** > **fripse**; **plâng**+**se** > **plânse**. In **rămase** from **a rămîne** (earlier **rămâne**) denasalisation also occurs.

8.4.3 There are old forms without -**ră**-, e.g. **şezum**, *we sat*.

8.7 PRESENT SUBJUNCTIVE

8.7.1 This tense, what there is of it, may express a wish, e.g. **să trecem**, *let us go on*, but more often either corresponds to an English infinitive, e.g. **ele pot să existe**, *they can exist*, or is a simple grammatical necessity, translated in English by the indicative. It is always preceded by **să**. See also 8.10.1.

8.7.2 It differs from the indicative (8.1) only in the 3PS, which substitutes -**e** for -**ă** and -**ă** for -**e**, changing the stem vowel in accordance with 2.6, e.g. S -**eze**, I -**ează**; S **meargă**, I **merge**; S **vadă**, I **vede**.

8.7.3 The subjunctive of **a ţine** and **a veni** may be **ţie, vie**.

8.10 COMPOUND TENSES
8.10.1 *Future*

> **voi, vei, va; vom, veţi, vor** + infinitive

Colloquial **o să** + subjunctive.

8.10.2 *Perfect*

> **am, ai, a; am, aţi, au** + past participle (8.7.2)

8.10.3 *Future perfect*

> **voi** (etc.) **fi** + past participle (cf. 8.10.1, 8.12.1, 8.15.2)

The sense conveyed is often one of inference: '*must have*'.

8.10.4 *Perfect subjunctive*

> **să fi** (all persons) and past participle (cf. 8.7.1, 8.12.1)

8.10.5 *Conditional*
aş, ai, ar; am, aţi, ar + infinitive, e.g. **aş crede**; or the other way round, with long infinitive, e.g. **credere-aş**. Besides its expected meaning, e.g. **ar fi interesant**, *it would be interesting*, it is used for hearsay statements: **am văzut scris că broşura ar fi având un scop politic**, *I saw it stated that the pamphlet had a political purpose*.

8.10.6 *Conditional perfect*

> **aş** (etc.) **fi** and past participle

8.11 INFINITIVE AND SUPINE

8.11.1 Short forms, -**a**, -**ea**, -**e**, -**i**, -**î**, are the forms under which verbs are entered in dictionaries, and correspond both to the English infinitive and the verbal noun. The infinitive is nearly always preceded by **a**, even with a preposition, e.g. **fără a gîndi**, *without thinking*; **pentru a-şi putea îndeplini funcţia**, *in order to be able to fulfil its function*.

8.11.2 Long forms, **-are, -ere, -ire, -îre,** are used as nouns, as abstract nouns corresponding to the range of meanings of the verb, or in specialised senses. They usually have independent entries in the dictionary. (See also 8.10.5.)

8.11.3 For the supine see 8.12.3.

8.12 PARTICIPLE

8.12.1 Only the perfect passive exists, with endings

PP	-at	-*ut, -s, -t		-it	-ît
I	-a	-e(a)		-i	-î

Follows the past (8.3) in form, e.g. **crezut** (**crezu, a crede**).

8.12.2 It is an adjective, invariable when used to form the perfect tense (8.10.2, etc.) but agreeing when forming the passive (8.15.1).

8.12.3 The same form functions as a verbal noun, called the *supine*, corresponding to the English infinitive and verbal noun, e.g. **interesant de ştiut,** *interesting to know*; **fumatul oprit,** *smoking prohibited.*

8.13 GERUND

8.13.1 *Endings*

    I   **-ind(u):** inf. **-a, -i; -îndu/-*îndu:** inf. **-e(a)**

Formerly spelt **-ând** from verbs in **-a** and **-e(a).**

    II   **-ind(u):** inf. **-i**

8.13.2 It is invariable, and is used much like the English present participle (see Specimen).

8.14 REFLEXIVE

8.14.1 These are formed by adding the personal pronoun, A or D, of the same person to the verb, e.g. **mă spăl,** *I wash* (*myself*); **şi-a adus aminte,** *He called to mind.*

8.14.2 Rumanian grammarians recognise several different types of reflexive verb, but for present purposes it is enough to remember that the English equivalent may be reflexive, reciprocal (**ei se înţeleg reciproc,** *they understand each other*), intransitive (**ma trezesc,** *I wake up*) or passive (**se ştie,** *it is known*). Sometimes, as in **mă tem,** *I am afraid*; **se pare,** *it seems*, no trace of any reflexive sense remains, and the basic verb in the last example is intransitive.

8.15 PASSIVE

8.15.1 This tends to be avoided, the active or reflexive being used instead. When it is used it is formed by the appropriate tense of **a fi,** *to be* (8.19.2) and the past participle, which agrees with the subject.

8.15.2 Some forms with **fi** are ambiguous (cf. 8.10).

8.17 AUXILIARIES
See 8.19.1, 8.19.2.

8.19 IRREGULARITIES

8.19.1 **a avea,** *to have*

    Present: am, ai, are; avem, aveţi, au
    Present subjunctive: 3PS and P să aibă

8.19.2   a fi, *to be*
  Present: sînt/-s, eşti, e(ste)/-i, sîntem, sînteţi, sînt/-s
    -u- may be substituted for -î-
  Present subjunctive: să fiu, fii, fie; fim, fiţi, fie
  Imperfect: eram
  Past: fu(se)i
  Gerund: fiind
  Past participle: fost

8.19.3   a da, *to give*
  Present: dau, dai, dă; dăm, daţi, dau
  Present subjunctive: 3PS and P să dea or deie
  Imperfect: d(ăde)am
  Past: dădui or detei

8.19.4   a lua, *to take*
  Present: iau, iei, ia; luăm, luaţi, iau

8.19.5   a sta, *to stand*
  Present: stau, stai, stă; stăm, staţi, stau
  Present subjunctive: 3PS and P să stea or steie
  Imperfect: st(ăte)am or steteam
  Past: stătui or stetei

8.19.6   a vrea, *to want*
  Present: vreau, vrei, vrea; vrem, vreţi, vreau

9   ADVERBS

The masculine form of the adjective is commonly used as an adverb, e.g. **precis**, *precisely*. Specifically adverbial forms can be obtained by adding **-eşte** or changing **-esc** to **-eşte**. These are also a few instances of adverbs in **-mente**, e.g. **fatalmente**, **realmente**.

10   PREPOSITIONS

10.1   FORMS AND CONSTRUCTION

10.2.1 Most prepositions do not affect the following noun, but there are some, especially those formed from nouns, which are followed by the genitive or a possessive, e.g. **asupra tuturor chestiunilor**, *on all the questions*; **în faţa casei**, *in front of the house*; **contra noastră**, *against us* (cf. *in his stead*).

10.2.2 **din**, **în** and **prin** have longer forms **dintr(u)**, **intr(u)**, **printr(u)** before a vowel. They should not be confused with **dintre**, **intre**, and **printre**, meaning *among*.

10.5   USES

10.5.1 Resemblances to other Romance languages may be deceptive. Thus **a** is rarely a preposition nowadays: in the following example it is successively the ' possessive article' (3.4), part of the verb **a avea** (8.19.2), and the sign of the infinitive (8.8.1), „Gramatica Romînă" a lui H. Titkin a avut la bază metoda justă de a exemplifica regulile gramaticale. And when it is a preposition, it may have to be translated *of* or *like*. As for **al**, it is always an article.

10.5.2 **Cu** is obviously *with* — sometimes; not so obviously *by* or *in*, e.g. **cu numele**, *in name*; and **cu totul**, *quite*, and **cu greu**, *hardly*, are anything but obvious.

10.5.3 Though **de** is usually clear enough, **de cap** means *per head*, **de-o săptămînă**, *for a week*, and **cel de-al doilea** simply *the second*; **de la** may be used adverbially meaning *from*, e.g. **pornind de la convingerea că** . . ., *setting out from the conviction that* . . ., or adjectivally meaning *at* or *of*, e.g. **un om de la ţară**, *a countryman*; similarly **de pe, din** (i.e. **de** + **în**), **de lîngă**, e.g. **Din publicaţiunile Ministerului Cultelor din Bucureşti**, *From the publications of the Ministry of Religious Observances in Bucharest*. (See also 11.)

10.5.4 It is easy to forget that **la** is a preposition, usually to be translated *at*, *in*, *on*, *to*, but also *per*; while **pe**, though it may mean *by* or *through*, more commonly means *on*, and frequently simply marks the direct object, e.g. **pe ei nu-i interesează**, *it does not interest them*, **limbă pe care o cunoaşte**, *a language which he understands*, or it may make the sense of another preposition more general.

11 CONJUNCTIONS

The conjunctions are among the least guessable of Rumanian words, but do not cause any special grammatical difficulty. One should distinguish **ca să**, *so that*, from **că**, *that*, *because*. Note also that **de** may be a conjunction, with the basic meaning *and*, but often amounting to *so that*, *if* and even *who*.

GLOSSARY

abonament, *subscription*
acte, *proceedings*
adăugit, *enlarged* (1.5)
adunat, *collected*
alcătuit, *compiled*
alegere, *selection*
ales, *selected*
an, *year* (1.8.4)
anuar, *yearbook*
apare, *comes out*
apariţie, *issue* (1.8.5)
apărut, *published*

bibliotecar, *librarian*
bibliotecă, *library*
bilunar, *semi-monthly*
broşat, *paper-covered*

caiet, *number*, *part*
carte, *book*, *letter*
cercetare, *research*
colecţie, *series* (1.7.1)
colegiu de conducere, *managing* (editorial) board
comandă, *order*
completare, *addition*
culegere, *collection*

cuvînt înainte, *preface*
cuvîntare, *speech*

drept de autor, *copyright*

editat, *published*
ediţie, *edition* (1.5)
ediţiune, *edition* (1.5), *publication* (1.6.1)
epuizat, *out of print*
exemplar, *copy*
expedia, *dispatch*
extras, *offprint*

factură, *invoice*

imprimare, *impression*
imprimerie, *press*
inedit, *unpublished*
introducere, *introduction*
izolat, *single* (1.8.6)

îmbunătăţit, *improved* (1.5)
îndrepta, *to correct*
întocmi, *compile*

librar, *bookseller*
librărie, *bookshop*

lucrare, *work*
lucrări, *proceedings*
lunar, *monthly*

mort, *dead*

născut, *born*
nevarietur, *unaltered* (1.5)
nou, *new*
număr, *number*
nuvelă, *short story*

piesă, *play*
planşă, *plate*
povestire, *story*
presă, *press*
prescurtat, *abridged*
preţ, *price*
probă, exemplar de, *specimen copy*

rabat, *discount*
redactor, *editor* (1.2.3, 1.8.3)
redacţie, *editing* (1.8.7)
referat, *abstract*

retipărire, *reprint*
revăzut, *revised* (1.5)
revistă, *review* (1.8.1)
revizuit, *revised* (1.5)
roman, *novel*

săptămînă, *week*
schimb, *exchange*
străinătate, *abroad* (1.8.7)

tabel, tablă, *table*
teatru, *plays*
tipărire, *impression*
tipografie, *press* (1.6.1)
traducător, *translator*
traducere, *translation*
tragere separată, *offprint*
trimestrial, *quarterly* (1.8.5)
trimite, *dispatch*

urmează să apară, *forthcoming*

va urma, *to be continued*
de vînzare, *on sale*

GRAMMATICAL INDEX: WORDS

a, 3.4.2, 8.10.2, 8.11.1,
  10.5.1
ai, 3.4.2, 8.10.2, 8.10.5,
  8.19.1
ai fi, 8.10.6
al(e), 3.4.2
am, 8.10.2, 8.10.5, 8.19.1
am fi, 8.10.6
ar (fi), 8.10.5, 8.10.6
are, 8.19.1
aş (fi), 8.10.5, 8.10.6
aţi, 8.10.2, 8.10.5
aţi fi, 8.10.6
au, 8.10.2, 8.19.1
avem, 8.19.1
aveţi, 8.19.1

căr-, 7.1.3
cea, 3.5.2
cei, 3.5.2
cel dintîi, 6.2.2

cel mai, 5.3
cel(-), 3.5.2
cellalt, etc., 7.1.3
cestlalt, etc., 7.1.3
cu, 10.5.2
cui, 7.1.3

da(i), dam, daţi, dau,
  8.19.3
dă, dăd-, dăm, 8.19.3
de, 10.5.3, 11
det-, 8.19.3
din, 10.5.3
din(tru), 10.2.2
d-lor, 7.3.6
d-sa(le), 7.3.6
d-ta(le), 7.3.6
două, 6.1.2
d-voastră, 7.3.6
dumisale, dumitale, 7.3.6
dumnea-, 7.3.6

e, 8.19.2
ei, 7.3.1
ele, 7.3.1
era-, 8.19.2
este, eşti, 8.19.2

fiecăr-, fiecui, 7.1.3
fiind, 8.19.2
fost, 8.19.2
fu(se)-, 8.19.2

grea, 5.2.1

i, 7.3.1
ia(u), 8.19.4
iei, 8.19.4

ii, il, îmi, 7.3.1
în(tru), 10.2.2
îşi, îţi, 7.3.1

GRAMMATICAL INDEX: ENDINGS

* indicates forms which are joined to the preceding word with a hyphen.

CELTIC, GREEK and ALBANIAN LANGUAGES

Irish

Welsh

Ancient Greek

Modern Greek

Albanian

IRISH

SPECIMEN

Ós ag caint ar 'Writing in Irish To-day' atá mé, ní mór tagairt a dhéanamh do *Ag troid*
ar son na saoirse le Dónall Ó Braoin. Aistriúchán é ar *My fight for Irish freedom* le
Dan Breen. Tá dhá rud gur féidir a rá ina thaobh; tá sé leagtha amach go snasta, idir
chló, cheangal agus dhearadh. Tríd is tríd tá sé ar aon dul le leabhar ar bith a thiocfadh
chuigainn ón Mór-Roinn. Rud eile, tá an t-aistriúchán le Séamus Daltún mar shampla
foirfe den ardchaighdéan atá sroiste againn in Éirinn san ealaíon seo.

Besides talking about '*Writing in Irish To-day*', I must make mention of Ag troid ar
son na saoirse (*Fighting on behalf of freedom*) by Dónall Ó Braoin. It is a translation
of My fight for Irish freedom *by Dan Breen*. There are two things which it is possible
to say about it; outwardly it is elegantly laid out, as regards printing, binding and design.
Through and through it is on one footing with any book that might come to us from the
Continent. Secondly, the translation by Séamus Daltún is by way of being a prime
example of the high standard we have reached in Ireland in this art.

References to sections

2, 3: 8.20.2	34: 8.12.2
6, 7: *which I am*, unrepresented in English	36, 37: 9.1
8, 9: *is not great*, idiom for *must*	57: 10.3.1
17, 18: 7.3.3	58, 70: 10.3.5
26: 7.2.2	72–74: 8.20.3
30, 31: 10.4.2	77: 10.3.5

0 GENERAL CHARACTERISTICS

0.1 DEGREE OF INFLEXION

Irish is basically synthetic, but becoming less so. The verb has different endings for the
persons and tenses, making the use of pronouns unnecessary, but the third person
singular can be used, with the appropriate pronouns, for all persons, and use is made
of the verbal noun with the verb *to be* as well as numerous phrases with verbs like

271

cur, *to put*. The noun has four cases, but the dative is only used with prepositions and is losing some of its distinctive forms.

0.2 ORDER OF WORDS

The normal sentence order is VSO, and even if it is varied for emphasis this is done by making a new sentence beginning with is, *it is*. It is not uncommon, however, for adverbial expressions to be put before the verb. Adjectives and genitives both follow the noun, but the sequences will usually be article—noun—adjective and noun—article—genitive, respectively. (Not that this criterion should be too slavishly relied on.)

0.4 RELATION TO OTHER LANGUAGES

Historically, Irish is an Indo-European language, as the numerals, among other things, show. But its relationship to English is distant, and in practice nearly all the vocabulary is strange.

0.5 PROBLEMS OF TRANSLATION

Irish does not lend itself overwell, any more than English, to grammatical analysis on traditional lines, and the ordinary man will have to take a good many phrases as he finds them, looking beyond the individual words. To complicate matters words have a wide spread of meaning, related or simply homonymous. Thus **nach** means *not ?*, *is not ?*, *that . . . not*, *that . . . is not*, *which . . . not*, *which is not*; **go** may be a preposition, a relative, a conjunction, an adverb-former or a sign of predication; **a** may be a possessive, a relative, or a particle that stands before a vocative, verbal noun or numeral; **is** is most likely to be the copula (*is, am, are*) but can mean *and*. So one must not jump to conclusions.

There is need therefore of a comprehensive and up-to-date dictionary. Unfortunately, that by An Seabhac, valuable as it is, is understandably small: it is, as it proclaims itself to be, a *Learner's Irish-English pronouncing dictionary*. To save space it groups allied words together, and so sometimes loses them. Recourse may be had to section 13 on derivation, but alterations of stem can complicate matters: thus **laethúil**, *daily*, is entered under **lá**, *day*. Section 13 shows that -**úil** is an adjectival ending and the index under **laethe** leads to 4.3.8 where the forms of **lá** are given. But it is a long haul.

1 BIBLIOLINGUISTICS

1.1 NAMES

1.1.1 Present-day Irish names consist of the usual Christian name and surname, though there are a fair number of Bardic names in use, which may take any form, and are not confined to belles-lettres. There is for instance the dictionary already mentioned, compiled by **An Seabhac** (*The Hawk*). Some guidance is given here on the problems that arise in connexion with names, but anyone who is likely to have much to do with them will need to refer constantly to the handbooks of Woulfe* and MacLysaght†.

1.1.2 Christian names may be distinctively Irish, such as **Conn**, Irish forms of common European ones or Irish names that have been equated with English ones,

---

* Woulfe (Patrick) *Sloinnte Gaedhael is Gall* [Revised edition] M. H. Gill and Son, 1923.
  † MacLysaght (Edward) *A guide to Irish surnames* [Reprinted with corrections] Irish University Press, 1973.

such as **Seán** and **Liam** (*William*). As the Irish and English forms are often interchanged according to the language, some of the ambiguous or less obvious equivalents are given here. Conventional equivalents are given in brackets.

Amhlaoibh	*Auliffe, Olave, (Humphrey)*
Aodh	*(Hugh)*
Aonghus	*Angus, Aeneas, Neece*
Brian	*Brian, (Bernard)*
Calbach, Cathal, Cathaoir	*(Charles)*
Conchobhar	*Conor, (Cornelius)*
Diarmaid	*Dermot, (Jeremiah)*
Dónall, Domhnall	*Donall, (Daniel)*
Éamonn	*Edmond, (Edward)*
Eibh(i)lín	*Eileen, Evelyn, Ellen, Helen*
Eoin	*John*
Feidhlim(idh)	*Phelim(y), (Felix, Philip)*
Fitheal	*(Florence)*
Gobhnait	*(Abigail, Deborah)*
Labhrás	*Laurence*
Mael(sh)eachlainn	*Melaghlin, Lanty, (Malachi, Miles)*
Mathghamhain	*Mahon, (Matthew)*
Parthalán	*Bartholomew, Barclay*
Proin(n)sias	*Francis*
Raghnall	*Reginald, (Randal)*
Ruai(dh)rí, Ruaraí	*Rory, Roderick, (Roger)*
Síle	*Sheila, Cecily, (Julia, Judith, Sally)*
Sinéad	*Jane(t)*
Siobhán	*Joan, Hannah*
Somhairle	*Sorley, (Samuel)*
Tadhg	*Teague, (Thady, Timothy)*
Uaithne	*(Antony)*

They are nouns and are declined like nouns, and the initial consonant is softened (2.5.4) in the genitive.

1.1.3 As far as their form goes surnames belong to six types: names in **Mac** and **Ó**, names in **de**, adjectival names, names in **an**, names in **a**, and other names without prefix.

1.1.4 Names formed (in the case of men) by prefixing **Mac** (*son*) **Ó** or **Ua** (*grandson, descendant*) to a personal or occupational name or description, e.g. **Mac Cormaic, Ó Briain, Mac an Bhaird** (*Ward, son of the poet*), **Mac-an-tSaoi** (*MacEntee, son of the scholar*) are usually patronymics, but names like **Mac an Ghabann** or **Mac Gabhann** may be anglicised as *Smith* as well as *MacGowan*. Hence **Mac Siubhlaigh** as the equivalent of *Walker*. Linguistic usage being different in different parts of the country, the part following **Mac** or **Ó** is sometimes softened and sometimes not, producing names which differ only minutely in Irish spelling but whose English equivalents are far apart, e.g. **Mac Diarmada,** *MacDermott* and **Mac Dhiarmada,** *Kermode*; **Ó Flaith-(bh)eartaigh,** *O'Flaherty* and **Ó Fhlaith(bh)eartaigh,** *O'Lafferty*.

Both **Mac** and **Ó** are nouns and are declined accordingly, with G **Mhic** and **Uí(Í)**, but the following portion is already in the genitive and incapable of any further variation except softening, if not already soft, after **Mhic** or loss of its initial **h-** after **Uí**.

The standard feminine equivalents are **Bean Mhic (Uí)** for married and **Iníon Mhic (Uí)** for unmarried women, but the latter pair are usually reduced to **Nic** and **Ní.** The following portion is softened. **Bean** and **Iníon** are both declinable, but **Nic** and **Ní,** incorporating masculine genitives, are not. Women's names are now filed separately, not as in the British Museum catalogue, subsumed under the masculine form, e.g. **Uí Néill (Máire, *Bean*).** (In Munster Irish **Mhac,** without **Iníon,** is used instead of **Mhic,** though the most illustrious example, **Máire Mhac an tSaoi,** is not a Munster name.) Matters are a little complicated by the use of **Mac,** followed by the genitive of the whole name, for *Mr,* e.g. **Mac Mhic Shuibhne,** *Mr MacSweeny.*

1.1.5 The English forms do not always retain the **Ó**—**Ó Ceallaigh** may be either *O'Kelly* or *Kelly*—and **Mac** is replaced in some names, e.g. **Mac Gearailt,** by *Fitz.* Apart from this, names include far more silent consonants than is usual in present-day spelling (2.7.2), and though one might convert some names into their Anglicised forms safely enough by reading them aloud, it would be a bold Englishman who would attempt the reverse. Even the passage from Irish to English is made perilous by the use of conventional equivalents and translations of the real or supposed meaning of the Irish original. Thus one finds *Armstrong* for **Mac T(h)réinfhir** (*Traynor* or *Mac Crainor*) and for **Ó Labhradha** (*Lavery* or *Lowry*), and *Fox* for four different names, only one of which, **Ó Sionnaigh** (*Shinagh* or *Shinnock*), has anything to do with foxes.

1.1.6 Some conventional equivalents are included in the following list, which is intended to give some idea of what one is up against rather than to attempt the impossible task of listing all the names that are likely to give trouble.

Mac Aodha	*MacCoy, MacHugh, MacKay, MacKee, Cox*
Ó hAodha	*Hayes, Hughes, O'Hea*
Mac Aonghusa	*Guinness*
Ó hAonghusa	*Hennessy*
Ó Coileáin, Ó Cuilleáin	*Collins*
Mac Connmara	*MacNamara*
Mac Fhiodhbhuidhe	*MacEvoy, MacVeagh*
Mac Fhionnghail	*Ginnell*
Mac Giolla Bhride	*MacBride, Kilbride*
Mac Giolla Domhnaigh	*MacEldowney*
Mac Giolla Phádraig	*Fitzpatrick*
Ó Loinsigh	*Lynch*
Ó Muircheartaigh	*Moriarty, Murtagh*
Mac Oisdealbhaigh	*Costello*
Mac Sheonín	*Jennings*

Some simpler forms are used nowadays, such as **Mac Coisdealla** for *Costello.*

1.1.7 Theoretically names in **Mac** and **Ó** have alternatives without the prefix but with the adjectival ending **-ach** (1.1.9) e.g. **Pádraig Carthach, Máire Chartach,** *Patrick* (*Mary*) *MacCarthy;* **Mac an Chartaigh,** *Mr MacCarthy.* But their use is very variable.

1.1.8 Anglo-Norman names in most cases prefix **de** (representing not only *de* but *le, the* and *atte*), are invariable and are the same for men and women. Like patronymics they may take the article instead and add the adjectival ending **-ach,** and it is this form (in the genitive) which follows **Mac =** *Mr* or **Iníon,** *Miss:* e.g. **Seán (Síle) de Búrca,** *John* (*Sheila*) *Burke;* **Mac an Bhúrcaigh,** *Mr Burke;* **Iníon an Bhúrcaigh,** *Miss Burke.* The English forms are not always easy to guess, e.g.

de Barra	*Barry*
de Faoite	*White* (see also 1.1.9)
de Léadús	*Ledwich*
de Leis	*Lacey*
de Londra	*Landers*
de Paor	*Power*
de Roiste	*Roche*

1.1.9 Adjectival names behave like other adjectives, that is, they are declined and the initial consonant of the feminine is softened (2.5.4). Hence **Seán Caomhánach**, *John Kavanagh*; **Mac an Chaomhánaigh**, *Mr Kavanagh*; **Máire Chaomhánach**, *Mary Kavanagh*. The English equivalents may be transcriptions, easy in the case of **Glas**, not so easy in **Craobhach** (*Creagh*) or **Seoigheach** (*Joyce*); or translations, one way or the other, as **Uaithne** (*Green*), or **Breathnach** for *Walsh*. **Breathnach** in its turn is sometimes re-transcribed, e.g. as *Brannock*, and similarly **Bán** may be transcribed as *Bane* or *Bawn* or translated as *White*. Names in -ach may also be substituted for names of other types (1.1.7, 1.1.8).

1.1.10 Names in **an**, the definite article (3.1), are rare. They comprise names derived from places, e.g. **an Mhachaire**, *Maghery*, (*of the field*) or from activities, e.g. **an tSiubhail**, *Walker* (*of walking*). In both cases the noun is in the genitive—hence the softening and the initial **t-** (3.1.1)—and cannot change any further.

1.1.11 Names in **a**, which are also rare, are invariable. The English forms are usually transcriptions, without the **a**, rarely translations.

1.1.12 Names without prefix which are not Irish adjectives, such as **Puirséil** (*Purcell*), **Beinéid** (*Bennett*), **Táilliúir** (*Taylor*), **Gabha** (*Gow* or *Smith*) (cf. 1.1.4), are invariable but some of them have alternative forms in -ach (1.1.9), which are particularly useful for forming a plural, e.g. **na Puirséalaigh**, *the Purcells*. The Irish spelling of what are often familiar English names can be disconcerting, e.g. **Aghas** for *Ashe*, **Bároid** or **Bairéad** for *Barrett*, **Comartún** for *Comerford*.

1.1.13 Older Irish names are not necessarily of the form Christian name and surname, and in any case will be filed under the forename, e.g. **Fionn mac Cumhaill** under **Fionn**.

1.2 NAMES OF AUTHORS, EDITORS, ETC.

1.2.1 The names of authors, editors and the like are given in various ways, but few of them have any effect on the form of the name.

1.2.2 The name may stand by itself, in its basic form, before or after the title.

1.2.3 The name may be preceded or followed by a finite verb in the past tense indicating the relationship of the person to the book, e.g. **Pádraig Ó Móráin do chum**, (*it was*) *P. O'M. who made* (*them*); **an t'Athair Raghnall Mac Siubhlaigh a d'aistrigh ón téacs Laidine**, *the Rev. Reginald Walker who translated from the Latin text*; **Aodh Mac Dhubháin a chóirigh**, *A. Mac D. who edited*. Unless the name has to be anglicised, it needs no alteration.

1.2.4 The name may be preceded by an abstract or semi-abstract noun of agency, in which case it will be in the genitive, e.g. **ó láimh Thomais Bairéad**, *from the hand of Thomas Barrett*; **arna gcur in eagar fá stiúradh Ghearóid Í Mhurchadha**, *put in order under the direction of Gearód Ó Murchadha (Gerald Murphy)*. The Christian name will have the genitive appropriate to its form (4.3), mostly a slender consonant (2.5.4) instead of the broad one of the nominative, and the initial consonant will be softened. For the effect on surnames see 1.1.

K

1.2.5 It is possible, though not common, for the name to follow directly in the genitive if the title denotes simply works or correspondence or the like: **Dánta Phiarais Feiritéir**, *Poems of Fiaras Feiritéir* (*Pierce Feriter*), **Scríbhinní Phádraig mhic Phiarais**, *Writings of Pádraig Mac Piarais*. For the effect on the name see previous paragraph.

1.2.6 The name may be preceded by the preposition **le** (*by*). This has no effect on the name, but **le** itself takes the form **leis** when it precedes the article, so that one cannot abbreviate **leis an Dr Cormac Ó Cuílleanáin** by leaving out **an Dr**.

1.3 TITLES

1.3.1 Titles of all types fall largely into the patterns formed of noun, adjective and preposition, e.g. **Ainmneacha Gaeilge na mbailte poist i gCúige Mumhan**, *Irish names of post towns in Munster*; **Eachtra dheireanach Réamoinn Óig**, *The last adventure of Réamonn Óg*; **Le grá ó Úna**, *With love from Una*. Belles-lettres and the literature of persuasion are more likely to produce more varied titles such as **So, súd agus súd eile**, *This, that and the other*, and titles are still found of a type which elsewhere would be medieval, e.g. **Sa leabhar seo tá an dá ráiteas phápúla** *Vigilanti cura*, *In this book are the two papal statements* Vigilanti cura; **Aistriú é seo ar Ireland's loyalty to the Mass**, *This is a translation of Ireland's*, etc.

1.3.3 If a title is in a context which normally affects a noun or adjective, the appropriate nouns and adjectives in the title will be suitably modified, e.g. **Nua-aistriú ar Fhaoistin Phádraig**, *New translation of the Confession* (**Faoistin**) *of Patrick* (**ar** softens); **i bhFinnegan's Wake**. But some writers simply leave the titles unmodified, e.g. **de Cúirt an Mheadhon Oidhche** (not **Chúirt**).

1.4 VOLUMES AND PARTS

1.4.1 Only **cuid**, literally *part*, is at all common, and often the numeration is not accompanied by any designation. In citations of long sets **imleabhar** (cf. 1.7.2, 1.8.3) is found, e.g. **The letters of the Rev. John Wesley, A.M., iml. VI.**

1.4.2 The numeration is by cardinal number, following the noun, e.g. **cuid a haon**, *part 1*.

1.5 EDITIONS

1.5.1 The fundamental words are **cló** (*printing*), **eagrán** (*edition*; but see 1.8.4) and **foilsiú**, *to publish*. Hence **an chéad chló**, *first impression*; **eagrán nua**, *new edition*; **foilsíodh** (older **foillsigheadh**) **don chéad uair**, *published for the first time*. (Not that **cló** excludes the possibility of changes.)

1.5.2 Revision may produce yet other expressions, such as **atheagrú** (*re-edition*), **nua-chóiriú** (*new arrangement*), **nua-réitithe** (*re-arranged*), but their meaning can be got from the dictionary, with patience. (The words above must be sought, in An Seabhac's dictionary, under **ath-, eagar, nua-, cóir** and **réiteach**.)

1.6 IMPRINTS

1.6.1 Many imprints will be names of a familiar type, sometimes in less familiar guises, e.g. **Brún agus Ó Nualláin** (*Brown and Nolan*), **Cló Ollscoil Chorcaí** (*Cork University Press*), and a good many will be names of an institutional type, e.g. **An Clóchomhar Tta** (*The Printing Corporation Ltd*), **Comhlucht Oideachais na hÉireann** (*Educational Company of Ireland*). These now include acronyms such as **FAS** for **Foillseacháin Adhbhar Spioradálta** (*Publications of religious subjects*).

1.6.2 The basic terms are **clóbhualadh**, *to print*, and **foilsiú**, *to publish*, as in Cahill & Co. Ltd a chlóbhuail agus Oifig an tSoláthair d'fhoilsigh (*C. & Co. Ltd printed and the Stationery Office published*). Various combinations of these and other terms are possible, especially when books are published through agents, e.g. **Arna fhoilsiú le hagaidh na mBráithre Críostaí ag M.H. Mac an Ghoill agus a Mhac**, *Published for the Christian Brothers by M.H. Gill and Son*; **arna gcur ar f(agh)áil ag**, *made available at.*

1.6.3 Where the publisher and place are baldly stated or the publisher is the subject of a verb, as above, the names will have their basic form, but in other expressions changes may be expected. Thus **Bráithre**, being in the genitive plural, is eclipsed (2.5.4) by the definite article **na**, but otherwise the genitive is the same as its nominative; **oifig** on the other hand makes G **oifige**. In **Arna fhoillsiú faoi Chomhartha na dTri gCoinneal i mBaile Átha Cliath** (*Published at the Sign of the Three Candles in Dublin*), **faoi** softens the initial letter of **Comhartha**, but in an imprint of this sort the preposition would be retained; while the **B** of **Baile Átha Cliath** is eclipsed by **i**, but eclipsis is fortunately a transparent phenomenon.

1.6.4 Place-names will naturally be left in their Irish forms, but one needs to be able to link them with their English equivalents. The differences are not usually so great as between **Áth Cliath** or **Baile Átha Cliath** (or even **Bleá Cliath**) and *Dublin* (though **Dubh Linn** is also good Irish) or **Port Láirge** and *Waterford*; but such names as **Luimneach** and **Tiobraid Árann** (*Limerick, Tipperary*) are tricky enough.

1.7 SERIES

1.7.1 Series are not common in Irish publishing. The titles may be singular, such as **Saíocht ár sean**, *Our ancient learning*; or plural, e.g. **Teaxaí Gaelge as Lss**, *Gaelic texts from MSS.*

1.7.2 More often than not the parts are simply numbered, without designations, but if a word is used it is likely to be **imleabhar**, e.g. **Leabhair Thaighde. An 17ú hImleabhar** (*Research Books, vol. 17*).

1.8 PERIODICALS

1.8.1 Grammatically the titles of periodicals are much the same as any others, in fact their frequent brevity tends to simplicity. But there is more room for fantasy and besides titles like **Dinnsheanchas** (*Local history*) one may find **Agus** (*And*) or **Feasta** (*Henceforward*).

In the context of a sentence a title may suffer grammatical change (1.3.2) but the titles of periodicals seem to be even more immune than those of books.

1.8.2 A body concerned with publication (and a good many Irish journals are society publications) may appear in the sub-title, e.g. **timire an Chroí Naofa**, *The Messenger of the Sacred Heart*, but it is just as likely to appear simply as an imprint, e.g. **arna fhoilsiú ag Conradh na Gaeilge**, *published by C. na G.*; or in another context, e.g. **foilseofar iris an Chumainn, Dinnsheanchas . . ., D.**, *the journal of the Society, will be published . . ..*

1.8.3 The name of the editor(s) is usually given under the **eagarthóir(í)**, though matters may be in the hands of a committee (**coiste**). Also mentioned may be **éarlamh** (*patron*), **rúnaí** (*secretary*) and **cisteoir** (*treasurer*). Sometimes editorship is not stated but implied (example in 1.8.7).

1.8.4 By far the commonest way of numbering periodicals is in terms of **imleabhar** (*volume*) and **uimhir** (*number*) or one of these, though it is possible for units given as **imleabhair** in the numeration to be described as **uimhreacha** elsewhere. Occasionally one finds **eagrán 1** (cf. 1.5.1) or the like on the cover, but its commonest occurrence is in citations, e.g. **Beidh cuid a trí i gcló in eagrán Eanáir de 'Comhar'**, *Part 3 will be in print in the January number of 'Comhar'* (actually numbered **iml. 32, uimh. 1**).

1.8.5 Periodicity is usually stated in some such phrase as **foilseofar dhá uair sa bhliain**, *will be published twice a year*; **foilsítear sa Mhárta, sa Mheitheamh**, etc., *published in March, in June*, etc.; or even **cuirfimid uimhir a trí amach go luath**, *we shall issue no. 3 soon*.

1.8.6 *Subscription* is properly **síntiús** (**bliantúil**, *annual*; **bliana**, *of the year*), but **táille bliana** (*annual payment*, used also of membership subscription) is also found, and by implication, **riar bliana: £1**, *a year's order: £1*. Various words for *price* can also be used, e.g. **fiacha, luach** and **praghas** with the alternatives of **cóip amháin** (*single copy*) and **go ceann bliana**, *till the end of the year*. **Rátaí speisialta** may be quoted for multiple copies or for classes of readers, e.g. **mic léinn** (*students*), but beware of **rátaí fógraíochta** (*advertising rates*).

1.8.7 Addresses may specify manuscripts, e.g. **Láimhscríbhinní go dtí an tEagaithóir** (*MSS to the Editor*) or distinguish editorial from business matters, e.g. **Seoltar litreacha faoi chúrsaí eagarthóireachta go dtí ... Faoi chúrsaí gnó scríobhtar go dtí ...**, *Letters on editorial matters are to be addressed to ... On business matters one should write to ....*

2   ALPHABET, PHONETICS, SPELLING

2.1   ALPHABET

2.1.1   The alphabet is as follows:

ᴀ b c ᴅ e ꜰ ᵹ h ı ʟ m n o p ʀ ɼ ꜱ ꞇ u
a b c d e f g h i l m n o p r s t u v

The forms of the letters are based on those found in Irish manuscripts, but the ordinary roman forms can be used equally well, as they have been for centuries and are here. The forms ʀ and ɼ (the latter originally initial or medial only) are old-fashioned. Capital letters differ only in size. The letters which are omitted may occur in indexes of names; they occupy their usual positions.

2.1.2   Vowels may bear an acute accent, and some consonants a superscript dot. The acute accent is a sign of length and may distinguish words, e.g. **ait**, *funny*; **áit**, *a place*; it must not therefore be omitted. The dot (replaced by an **h** after the letter in roman) has basically the effect of turning a stop into a spirant. (The details are a matter of pronunciation and are given in 2.5.2.) Thus a dotted letter is a different letter from its undotted counterpart, and in the middle or end of a word may produce a quite different word, e.g. **loc**, *a pen*; **loċ** (**loch**), *a lake*. At the beginning it may convey a grammatical distinction (2.5.4). Neither sign affects alphabetical order, though the addition of **h** may.

2.2   CAPITALISATION

Basically as in English, with prepositions, article and conjunctions in compound names written with a small letter. It should be noted however that when a proper name is eclipsed (2.5.4), the eclipsing consonant is written small: examples in 1.6.2. So is a prefixed **h**.

2.3   DIVISION OF WORDS

This is more a matter of tendencies than of fixed rules. A break is commonly made between stem and ending or between root and suffix, even if the ending begins with a vowel, e.g. **gléas-aimid** (*we dress*), but examples are also found in which part of the stem is taken over, such as **antra-thach** (*untimely*) a derivation of **antrath**. And if a stem is telescoped, so that the taking over of the termination would leave a nasty clutter of consonants at the end of the line, part of the stem will certainly be taken over, e.g. **ceang-lóidh** (*will fasten*): cf. **ceangal**, *a fastening*. Where there is no obvious ending the tendency is to divide between consonants. Prefixes should be kept intact and compounds divided according to sense.

In dividing words written in the roman alphabet care should be taken never to separate **h** from the preceding consonant: **bh** for example is in effect a different letter from **b**.

2.4 PUNCTUATION

2.4.1 The hyphen is not used in compounds to the same extent as it is in English, but only for the sake of clarity and nicety. Thus it separates:

(a) The prefixes **n-** and **t-** from a lower-case vowel (but **Tír na nÓg** is unambiguous and needs no hyphen).

(b) Prefixes and suffixes from words that begin or end with same letter, and prefixes that end in a vowel from words that begin with one, e.g. **ceann-na**, **mí-ordú**.

(c) The prefixes **do-, fo-, so-** from words beginning with **bha, bhla, bhra, dha, gha, ghla, ghra, mha**, all of which normally have a tendency to form diphthongs. Thus **domhan** is pronounced much like *down*, but in **do-mharfa** the prefix is distinct and the **mh** is pronounced as a consonant (w).

(d) The prefixes **an-** (*very*) and **dea-** (*well*) from the rest of the word. (There is another prefix **an-** (*not*) which is not so separated.)

Usage is not completely governed by explicit rules. In similar cases to the above if a word would be unrecognisable or ambiguous without it, the hyphen would be used.

2.4.2 The apostrophe replaces the vowel in the words **ba** (*was*), **de** (*from*), **do** (*to*; *your*; sign of past tense), **mo** (*my*), when they come before a vowel or **fh** (which is silent).

2.4.3 Abbreviations require a full stop at the end, unless they include the last letter of the full word, in which case the stop is optional. Thus **teor.**, **tta** and **tta.** are all possible abbreviations of **teoranta** (*limited*).

2.5 PHONETICS OF CONSONANTS

2.5.1 In order to make the pronunciation of names and the effects of mutation (2.5.4) a little more intelligible, some broad notion of the values of the letters is given; but it is far from complete, and there are times when the relation between spelling and pronunciation seems as ambiguous as in English.

2.5.2 The following peculiarities in the pronunciation of the consonants should be noted:

> **bh** = [v] or [w]
> **c** = [k]; **sc** = [sg]
> **ch** as in German. One value is familiar in the word **loch**, the other is similar but further forward.
> **dh** like **ch** but voiced; often silent. Before or after e and i has the sound of y, I.P.A. [j]; when final = [g].
> **fh** silent

gh as **dh**
lt = [lh]
mh = [v] or [w]; or nasalises the preceding vowel
nn sometimes = [ng]
sp = [sb]; **ph** = [f]
s before or after **e** and **i** = sh, I.P.A. [ʃ]
sh = [h]
st = [sd]
th = [h]

2.5.3   Consonants are divided into 'broad' and 'slender,' broad consonants being mostly what we should consider normal, and slender ones more or less palatalised. The distinction is marked in spelling: **caol** has broad **c** and **l**, **céile** narrow ones. (Broad **c**, pronounced at the back of the mouth, is one of the few broad consonants we should not feel to be normal.) In the four words **mín, mbíonn, maoin, mbuíon** (the **b**'s are silent) what is basically the same vowel [i·] occurs in four different contexts— between slender **m** and slender **n**, slender **m** and broad **n**, broad **m** and slender **n**, broad **m** and broad **n**. The **u** and **o** are primarily indicators, but as the broad **m** pulls the **i** back and the broad **n** causes a slight vowel-glide, the spelling is appropriate enough. In a name like **Súilleabháin** the sounded vowels are **ú**, **a** and **á**, the **i**, **e** and **i** being buffers between the broad vowels and the slender **l** and **n**. The following table gives the conventions, so far as they can be relied on. The varied spellings of the simple vowels in the left-hand column are arranged according to the nature, broad or slender, of the consonants that surround them.

	b-b	*b-s*	*s-b*	*s-s*
a	a	ai	ea	eai
á	á	ái	eá	eái
e			ea	ei
é	ao	ae	éa	éi
i	uio	ai, oi, ui	io	i
í	aío, uío	aí, aoi, uí	ío	í
o	o	oi	eo	
ó	ó	ói	eó	eói
u	u	ui	iu	iui
ú	ú	úi	iú	iúi

2.5.4   The mutations are sets of systematic changes in initial consonants which were originally phonological but now show no signs of their origin, and have in any case been extended by analogy. By now they are part of the morphology and syntax. Thus the definite article has now only two forms **an** and **na** but the consonants that follow are affected differently according to case and gender, e.g. **an fear**, *the man*; **an fhir**, *of the man*; **ar an bhfear**, *on the man*; **bean**, *a woman*; **an bhean**, *the woman*. (The old forms of the article in these instances ended in **-s**, a vowel, **-n**, a vowel, respectively, producing the various phonetic changes.)

There are two types of mutation—softening (also misleadingly called aspiration) represented by a dot over the letter or an **h** after it, which basically turns stops into spirants (see 2.5.2 for details), and eclipsis, which voices unvoiced stops and nasalises voiced ones. The new sound, which is written in front of the old one, as in **bhfear** above, eclipses it and reduces it to silence.

There are occasions when the presence of mutation or its character is in itself grammatically significant: for instance **arna cur** means literally *after her putting*, **arna chur** *after his putting*, **arna gcur** *after their putting*. (Any of these could appear on a title-page as the equivalent of the past participle *put*.) More often than not, however, mutation is redundant: it may be obligatory but it adds nothing to the meaning: **fear**, *man*; **aon fhear**, *one man*; **blianta beaga**, *a few years*; **cait bheaga**, *little cats*. Unless therefore one is writing or speaking Irish, one is mainly concerned to recognise mutation when it occurs, and here one is helped by the fact that very few words in their radical form start with dotted consonants, and none with such combinations as **bp**, **gc**, **mb**, **nd**, which are characteristic of eclipsis. No attempt will therefore be made to specify all the occasions when mutation, occurs; but where it is part of a declension, or a word invariably causes mutation, this will be indicated, using the symbol * for softening and § for eclipsis and the prefixing of **n-** (2.5.5).

2.5.5 Words beginning with a vowel may have the consonants **h-**, **n-**, and **t-** prefixed: **t-** is only found following the article **an** (3.1.2), **h-** and **n-** are more universal, **n-** occurring as a rule in those cases where a consonant would be eclipsed. The principal occasions will be mentioned in the appropriate places, but as with mutation, it is more important in reading Irish to know that these phenomena occur than when, for **n-** is clearly marked with a hyphen, and there are very few words in the dictionary beginning with **h**.

2.5.6 Assimilation takes place occasionally when consonants of different classes come together. The instance most frequently encountered is **bean**, *woman*; **mná**, *women*.

2.6 PHONETICS OF VOWELS

2.6.1 Simple vowels approximate to their standard continental values, but the following peculiarities are found:

> **a** ≃ [ɔ]   cf. **cailín**, *colleen*
> **o** ≃ [ʌ]   cf. **boc**, *buck*
> **á** ≃ [ɔ·]   cf. **seál**, *shawl*

Combinations of vowels more often represent spelling conventions (2.5.3) but **ao** is pronounced [ɛ·] and **aoi** [i·]; **ua** is sometimes pronounced [o·] and sometimes as written; **ai** and **oi** are sometimes pronounced [ɛ].

2.6.2 Most cases of variation in the vowel from one case or person of a word to another are in fact the mark or accompaniment of changes of consonant from broad to slender or vice versa, e.g. **leabhar**, *book*; GS **leabhair** with a slender **r** (4.3.2); **muir**, *sea*; GS **mara**.

The less obvious changes are:

B	↔	S
a		ui
ea		i
éa		éi
ía		éi
io		i
o		ui

and in similar circumstances:

ea   io

In irregular nouns and verbs and in the conjugation of prepositions more striking changes take place, which will be noted in the appropriate section.

2.6.3   A vowel of the stem may be omitted when an ending is added, e.g. **doras**, *door*, NP **doirse** (note how the **r**, which was broad, now becomes slender too); **labhairt**, *speaking*, **labhraim**, *I speak*.

2.7 SPELLING

2.7.1   The spelling prevalent in Ireland until the 1950's is said to have been a fair representation of 12th-century pronunciation and in some respects already out of date in the thirteenth. Some religious propagandists of the 17th century tried to write as they spoke, anticipating modern standard spelling, but their example was not generally followed. Dialect cleavage hampered the development of a new standard spelling, and the learned societies and dictionary makers fastened the antiquated spelling on the language. Despite difficulties, however, a standard spelling was brought out in draft in 1945, and finally introduced in 1958.

2.7.2   The changes which had made the old spelling unrepresentative were not so uniform as to make it possible to give a simple list of equivalents, but some sorts of change are commoner than others, viz. disappearance of spirants between vowels, with lengthening or modification of the vowel:

-idhe, ighe > -í
-idheacht, igheacht > -íocht
-ochad > -ód
-(e)amhail > (i)úil
-mh(e)adh > (i)ú
-(i)ughadh > (i)ú

and so on; simplification of groups of consonants:

-bhth- > -f-
-ngc- > -nc-

thinning of vowel sounds:

-eas > -íos

It will be obvious that though one might conceivably try to read a text in old spelling with a modern dictionary (finding **seiseadh** under **séú**?), the reverse process would be hopeless.

3 ARTICLES

Irish has only the definite article. When there is no article the indefinite article must often be supplied in English (but see 3.1.2).

3.1 DEFINITE

3.1.1   The article itself has only two forms, but the initial letter of the noun or adjective is subject to variations which reflect old differences in the forms of the article.

	S		P
	M	F	
NA	an, an t-	an*	na, na h-
G	an*	na, na h-	na §, na n-
D	an §	an §	na

The letters **t-**, **n-** and **h-** are inserted before vowels (2.5.5); * indicates softening (2.5.4), which for historical reasons does not affect **d** or **t**, changes **s** not to **sh** but to **ts** (pronounced [t]), and leaves most combinations of **s** and another consonant unaffected; § indicates eclipsis (2.5.4).

3.1.2 The article is used with demonstratives, e.g. **an leabhar seo**, *this book*, but otherwise there are few instances where it is used in Irish but not in English. On the other hand in phrases such as **udair an leabhair seo**, *the authors of this book*, the first noun very rarely has the article.

4 NOUNS

4.1 GENDER AND FORM

Nouns may be masculine or feminine. Some feminine nouns are declined differently from masculine ones, but though a few endings are distinctively masculine there is for the most part no difference in the nominative between masculine and feminine nouns. Omitting the vocative there are three cases, of which the dative plural is obsolescent and the dative singular only rarely distinct from the nominative.

4.3 DECLENSIONS

4.3.1 There are five classes of nouns arranged according to the genitive singular. They include verbal nouns (8.11). Cases are often marked not by endings but by change of consonant from broad to slender (2.5.3).

4.3.2 GS slender, NS broad, masculine:

	S	P
NA	B	S, -e
G	S	B
D	B	-aibh or as N

e.g. **leabhar**, *book* (see 3.1.2). Nouns in **-each** have GS **-igh**.

4.3.3 GS **-e** NS usually broad, feminine:

	S	P
NA	B, S	-a, -(e)acha, -(e)anna, -e, -í, -ta, -te, -tha
G	-e	B, or as N
D	S	-aibh or as N

Nouns in **-each** have GS **-í**; so has **deoch**.

P **-acha**, **-anna**, **-ta** are added to broad consonants, **-e**, **-eacha**, **-eanna**, **-í**, **-te**, **-tha** to slender ones, **-a** (the commonest ending) to either.

A broad ending will broaden a slender consonant, e.g. **tír, tíortha** (2.5.3, 2.6.2) and vice versa, **pian, péine**. Note that **-(e)acha** may be **-(e)ach + a** or zero +**e(acha)**, e.g. **obair**, *work*: P **oibreacha**; **cláirseach**, harp: P **cláirseacha**.

4.3.4   GS -a, NS broad or slender, masculine or feminine:

	S	P
NA	B, S	-a, -(a)í, -acha, -anna, -ta, -te
G	-a	B, or as N
D	B, S	-(a)ibh or as N

P -í and -te are added to slender consonants only; the rest to either, with broadening effect (2.5.3, 2.6.2), e.g. **cuid**, *part* GS **coda** P **coda(nna)**. The change N -io- G and P -ea- occurs in a good many words.

4.3.5   GS (and D) unchanged, N mostly in a vowel:

P -(a)í, -te, -the, -acha, -anna, -anta throughout
D (optional) -íbh

Example: **garda** P **gardaí; cluiche, cluichí; cailín -í; baile, bailte; ainmhí, ainmhithe; bus-anna; oíche-anta**. Note: **duine** P **daoine**.

4.3.6   GS -(e)(a)ch, -(a)d, -(a)n(n), N mostly in a vowel:

	S			P
NA	(V)	S	-a, -e	As DS; -de, -ne, -(a)cha
G	n-(n)	-(e)ach	-ad, -ead	As GS; -(a)cha
D	-in(n)	-(s)	-id	-(a)ibh

Examples: **teanga, teanga(n), teanga(in), teangacha; cathair, cathrach, cathracha** (cf. 2.6.3); **fiche, fichead, fichid**.

4.3.7   The class to which a noun belongs is not always fixed: thus **ainm** may belong to 4.3.3 or 4.3.5, **teanga** to 4.3.5 or 4.3.6.

4.3.8   A small group of nouns make GS by broadening the final consonant, e.g. **athair**, *father* GS **athar**. Others are more irregular, viz.

bean	G mná	D mnaoi	NP mná GP ban
Dia	G Dé		NP déithe
lá	G lae	D ló	P laethe(annta)
teach	G tí	D tigh	P tithe

4.3.9   The change of consonants and the addition of endings are accompanied by changes of vowels, details of which are given in 2.6.

5 ADJECTIVES

5.1 POSITION
Adjectives nearly always follow the noun. If they precede it, as a few may, they form a compound and cause softening (2.5.4), e.g. **nuachúrsa** (nua + cúrsa) *new course*; or **cúrsa nua**. These compounds are not given separately in the dictionary.

5.2 ENDINGS
Adjectives have different declensions according as they end in a broad consonant, a slender consonant, a vowel.

5.2.1   *Broad consonant*

	S		P
	M	F	
NA	B	*B	-a
G	*S	-e	B, or as N
D	B	*S	-a

Adjectives in (e)ach have GS -(a)igh, -(a)í. The ending -e makes the consonant slender, e.g. **leathan, leithne.**

5.2.2   *Slender consonant*

	S		P
	M	F	
NA	S	*S	-a, -e
G	*S	-e, -a	S, or as N
D	S	*S	-a, -e

The ending **-a** (which has a broadening effect) is used for adjectives in **-úil**; **cóir**, *right*; **deacair**, *difficult*; **socair**, *quiet* (GS **-cra**).

5.2.3   *Vowel*
A few have plural endings, e.g. **breá**, *fine*, P **breátha**; **te**, *hot*, **teo**. Otherwise they do not vary.
   5.2.4   The softening indicated by * is part of the declension, but there are circumstances when other forms, not so marked, are softened (cf. 2.5.4).

5.3   COMPARISON
The regular comparative and superlative have the same form, which is usually identical with the GSF, e.g. **óg**, *young*: **óige**, *younger*; but **breá**: **breátha**; **minic**: **minice**, **-cí** or **mionca**. The comparative is often preceded by **níos** (**ní ba*** in past time) the superlative invariably by **is** (**ba***), e.g. **an bealach is éifeachtaí**, *the most effective way*.

5.4   POSSESSIVES
   5.4.1   *Forms*

	S				P		
1	2	3m	3f	1	2	3	
mo*, m'*	do*, t'*	a*	a	ár§	bhur§	a§	

For * and § see 2.5.4, 2.5.5; a (3f) aspirates a following vowel.
   5.4.2   Suffixes 3SM, 3P -s(e)an; 1P, -na -ne; all other persons -sa, -se may be added to the noun for emphasis, e.g. **mo leabharsa**, *my book*.

5.5   IDIOMATIC USE
   5.5.1   The GSF, which is rare in its literal sense, produces an abstract noun, e.g. **minice**, **-cí**, *frequency*, which may or may not have a separate entry in the dictionary. Preceded by the possessive a it is equivalent to a phrase with *so* or *how*, e.g. **a mhinice a úsáidtear focail**, *how frequently words are used*.
   5.5.2   When used with **tá** adjectives are preceded by **go**.

6 NUMERALS

6.1 CARDINAL

6.1.1 *Forms*

1 aon*	11 aon déag		(aon) is fiche
2 d(h)á*, dó	12 dó dhéag	21	aon fichead
3 trí*	13 trí déag		aon ar fichid
4 cheithre*, ceathair	14 ceathair déag		fiche a haon
5 cúig*	15 cúig déag	30	tríocha
6 sé*	16 sé déag	33	trí is tríocha
7 seacht§	17 seacht déag	40	daichead, dathad, ceathracha
8 ocht§	18 ocht déag	50	caoga
9 naoi§	19 naoi déag	60	seasca
10 deich§	20 fiche	70	seachtó

80 ochtó	200 dhá chéad
90 nócha	900 naoi gcéad
100 céad	1000 míle
101 céad (is) a haon	

If it is necessary to spell out figures the forms given should be used, but the system of counting by scores which prevails in **daichead** is found with higher numerals, e.g. 70 **deich is trí fichid.**

6.1.2 In counting **a** is prefixed, aspirating **aon**, and the forms **dó** and **ceathair** are used, e.g. **cuid a dó**, *part two*; **fiche a haon**, *21*. Otherwise there are a number of alternatives, with a strong tendency to sandwich the noun, e.g. **aon fhear déag**, *11 men*; **aon mhíle dhéag**, *11,000*; **leabhar is fiche, aon leabhar fichead/ar fichid**, *21 books*.

6.1.3 **Fiche, céad** and **míle** are nouns, but it makes no difference nowadays to the construction, all numerals being usually followed by the NS. **Dhá** is followed by forms historically dual but identical with DS, which is usually, but not always, the same as the NS, e.g. **dhá leabhar**, *two books* (but **dhá láimh**, not **lámh**, *two hands*). The numbers 3–10 may be followed by the plural (cf. **trí fichid** for 60), 3–6 without the indicated softening, and may be preceded by the plural article. With other numerals the article is in the singular.

6.1.4 Sometimes **amháin** (*only, single*) is used where English would have *one*.

6.2 ORDINAL

6.2.1 *Forms*

1 céad*	11 aonú . . . déag
2 dara	12 dara . . . déag
3 tríú	13 tríú . . . déag
4 ceathrú	19 nao(i)ú . . . déag
5 cúigiú	20 fichiú
6 séú	21 aonú . . . is fiche (fichead), etc.
7 seachtú	
8 ochtú	
9 nao(i)ú	
10 deichú	

Higher ordinals do exist, ending in **-ú** or **-dú**, but they are hardly ever used, counting cardinals (6.1.2) being used instead.

6.2.2 Nouns and adjectives are usually invariable nowadays after all ordinals except **céad**.

6.3 FIGURES

Plain arabic figures stand for cardinals, except in dates, ordinals being followed by **-ú**, e.g. **an 21ú lá**, *the 21st day*, which is read as **an t-aonú lá is fiche (fichead)**. Roman numerals will usually be read as counting cardinals.

6.4 DATES

6.4.1 The months are:

> **Eanáir, Feabhra, Márta, Aibreán, Bealtaine, Meitheamh,**
> **Iúil, Lúnasa, Meán Fómhair, Deireadh Fómhair, Samhain, Nollaig**

Sometimes they will be found with **mí na** (*month of the*) prefixed, e.g. **mí na Samhna, mí na Nollag**. February can be **mí na Féile Bríde**, 1 February being St Bride's day.

6.4.2 24/10/1969 is read **an ceathrú lá** (*day*) **is fiche (fichead) de Dheireadh Fómhair, míle naoi gcéad seasca a naoi.**

In phrases like **1798–1898** the two numbers should be simply expanded, but the only effect of a preposition would be to cause softening or eclipsis (2.5.4) of the first word.

1 May, 1 August, and *1 November* may be expressed as above but as they are all festivals they may appear simply as **Lá Bealtaine** (*May Day*), **Lá Lúnasa** and **Lá Samhna**. **Lá Nollag** however is *Christmas Day*.

Do not confuse **Márta**, *March*, and **Máirt**, *Tuesday*.

7 PRONOUNS

7.1 DEMONSTRATIVE AND INDEFINITE

7.1.1 There are strictly no pronouns of this sort, but only nouns like **cách**, *everybody*, or adjectives, which are invariable. Thus *this book* is **an leabhar seo**; complete with definite article. To function as pronouns these adjectives need a noun, e.g. **duine**, *person*, or a personal pronoun as a prop, e.g. **é sin, í sin**, *that*; (**ansin**, *there*; cf. **ann**, *in it*, 10.2.1); **ina theannta sin**, *along with that* (literally *in its support that*).

7.2 RELATIVE

7.2.1 Relative clauses are somewhat bewildering, for though the relative has few forms, these have a variety of other meanings and enter into peculiar combinations. The relative is more of a particle than a pronoun, and there are relative forms of the present and future tense, which are in fact older than the relative. There is no distinction between *who* and *which*.

7.2.2 Words which introduce relative clauses include:

> **a*** subject or object: **a thóg na pictiúir**, *who took the pictures*; **a rinne siad**, *which they made*. (More examples in 1.2.3.)
>
> **a §** other cases. The meaning is shown by other words in the sentence, e.g. **a bhfuil guta ar a lorg**. The first **a** (*which*) and the second (*its*) are taken together and the whole means literally *of whose tracks is a vowel*, i.e. *which is followed by a vowel*. Similarly in **daltaí a bhfuil roinnt eolais acu**, **a** and **acu** make *to whom* (*pupils who have some knowledge*). Alternatively, it can combine with prepositions, as below.

ab: *which was*

ar* (1): is used with the past of most verbs instead of **a** §

ar (2) (**arb** before a vowel): equivalent to **a** § + **is** or **tá** (*is*), e.g. **ar múinteoir a mhac**, *whose son is a teacher*

ar* (3) (**arbh** before a vowel): the same in past time

dá: **de** + **a**, **do** + **a**, *to/from which*

dar(b): **de** (**do**) + **ar** (2): *to* (*from*) *which is*

dar*(bh): **de** (**do**) + **ar*** (3): *to* (*from*) *which was*

dár*: **de** (**do**) + **ar** (1)

do*: the same as **a***

faoina(r)(b)(h): **faoi** + **a** (**ar, arb, arbh**)

go §: the same as **a** §

gur(b)(h): **ar(b)(h)**, e.g. **gur mian leo**, *who wish* (*whom is desire to them*)

ina(r)(b)(h): **i** + **a** (**ar, arb, arbh**)

lena(r)(b)(h): **le** + **a** (**ar, arb, arbh**)

na, nach §: negative of **a*** and **a** §

nár*: negative of **ar***

óna(r)(b)(h): **ó** + **a** (**ar, arb, arbh**)

It must be emphasised that many of these forms have other meanings as well, some, like go, *that*, connected with their meaning here, others, like ar, *on*, mere homonyms.

7.3 PERSONAL

7.3.1

	S					P		
	1	2	3	3*f*		1	2	3
N	mé	tú	sé	sí		sinn	sibh	siad
A	mé	t(h)ú	é	í		sinn	sibh	iad

The 'accusative' forms **é, í, iad** are used with parts of the verb *to be* and after certain prepositions, as well as for the direct object.

7.3.2 Emphatic forms are got by adding the suffixes **-sa**, etc. (cf. 5.4.2) viz. **mise, tusa, (s)eisean, (s)ise; sinne, sibhse, (s)iadsan**.

7.3.3 The presence of **é**, for instance, may imply predication, e.g. **aistriúchán é**, *it* (*is*) *a translation*.

8 VERBS

8.1 STRUCTURE

8.1.1 The verb has a wealth of forms, for the simple forms are supplemented with periphrastic ones using the verb *to be* (8.20). A few verbs have what are known as dependent forms, but as the distinction between dependent and absolute concerns the writing of Irish, both forms are given here without distinction.

8.1.2 Apart from the verb *to be* and certain irregular ones, verbs are either normal, syncopated or contracted. Syncopated verbs have stems in **-il, -in, -ir, -is** which are shortened before endings, e.g. **labhair** 1PS **labhraim; inis, insím**. Contracted verbs have stems in **-igh**, which coalesces with the following vowel.

8.1.3 Normal stems may end either in a broad or a slender consonant (2.5.3), the endings varying accordingly, e.g. **creidim, creideann; díolaim, díolann**. Sometimes the quality of the consonant is not what you might expect.

8.1.4   The 3PS may be used, with the appropriate pronoun, for any person except 1PP, regularly so with the past, future and subjunctive.

8.1.5   Verbs are entered in dictionaries and vocabularies under the verbal noun or the stem (past tense 3PS, unsoftened in regular verbs).

8.2   PRESENT

> -(a)im, -(a)ir, -(e)ann; -(a)imid, -(e)ann, -(a)id
> -(a)ím, -(a)ír, -(a)íonn; -(a)ímid, -(a)íonn, -(a)íd

The forms in **-í-** are used with all contracted and some syncopated verbs.

8.3   PAST HABITUAL
8.3.1   *Endings*

> -(a)inn, -th(e)á, -(e)adh; -(a)imis, -(e)adh, -(a)idís
> -(a)ínn, -(í)th(e)á, -(a)íodh; -(a)ímis, -(a)íodh, -(a)ídís

On forms in **-í-** see 8.2.

8.3.2   See 8.4.2.

8.4   PAST
8.4.1   *Endings*

> -(e)as, -(a)is, -; -(e)amar, -(e)abhair, -(e)adar
> -(a)íos, -(a)ís, -igh; -(a)íomar, etc.

The forms in **-í-** are used with contracted and syncopated verbs, the latter having the full stem in the 3PS.

8.4.2   The past and conditional tenses have a softened initial consonant. This is the effect of the particle **do** which formerly preceded these tenses but is now usual only before vowels and the silent letter **fh**, e.g. **d'aistrigh**, *translated*; **d'fhoilsigh**, *published*.

8.5   FUTURE
8.5.1   *Endings*

> -f(e)ad, -f(a)ir, -f(a)idh; -f(a)imid, -f(a)idh, -f(a)id
> -(e)ód, -(e)óir, -(e)óidh; -(e)óimid, etc.

8.5.2   The forms in **-ó-** are used in syncopated verbs and in most contracted ones.

8.6   CONDITIONAL
8.6.1   *Endings*

> -f(a)inn, -f(e)á, -f(e)adh; -f(a)imis, -f(e)adh, -f(a)idís
> -(e)óinn, -(e)ófá, -(e)ódh, etc.

On forms in **-ó-** see 8.5.2.

8.6.2   See 8.4.2.

8.7   SUBJUNCTIVE
8.7.1   *Present*

> -(e)ad, -(a)ir, -a/-e; -(a)imid, not used
> -fod, -ir, -i; -imid

8.7.2 *Past*

$\left.\begin{array}{l}\text{-(a)inn}\\ \text{-(a)ínn}\end{array}\right\}$ as 8.3.1 but not softened (8.4.2)

8.7.3 Contracted and syncopated verbs mostly have forms in -í-, but those with a vowel before the -igh- of the stem have forms such as léad, lé, (léigh); clód, cló (clóigh).

8.7.4 Apart from its use in wishes the subjunctive occurs after a few conjunctions and in conditional clauses; but its use is declining.

8.11 VERBAL NOUN

8.11.1 The verbal noun is used freely, mostly in senses where the infinitive or gerund is used in English. (See also 11.4.) The fact that it is a noun is often shown by the construction and by its use in the genitive and the plural, e.g. **cleachtaí**, *exercises*; but the logic of some of its commonest uses is ambiguous.

8.11.2 It is frequently used after prepositions, e.g. **taithí ar labhairt**, *practice in speaking*; **ag gabháil buíochais**, *thanking (on getting of thanks)*; **le m'fheicéail**, *to see me (to my seeing)*; **níl an t-eolas ar fáil**, *the knowledge is not to be got*. When the verbal noun has an object it may follow in the genitive, as above, or it may be sandwiched between the preposition and the verbal noun, e.g. **chun an Ghaeilge a labhairt**, *to speak Irish*. In this case it is in the nominative/accusative and the verbal noun is preceded by **a*** or **d'**. A number of uses with prepositions amount to periphrastic tenses (8.20.2).

8.11.3 Not infrequently it is the subject or object of some other verb or phrase, e.g. **Tá áthas orm tú a fheiceáil**, *I am glad (Is gladness to me) to see you*.

8.11.4 In the genitive it may qualify another noun, e.g. **cumas labhartha**, *ability to speak*, **lucht foghlamtha**, *learners*.

8.11.5 The verbal noun is sometimes the same as the stem, but usually one of the following endings is added: -(e)adh, -ail, -(e)amh, -í, -(a)int, -t, -(i)ú, -(i)úint. The genitive may be the same as that of any ordinary noun (4.3.2, 4.3.3, 4.3.4), e.g. **lucht óil**, *drinkers* (**ól**, *to drink*), or, more often, as the past participle (8.12.2), especially if it has an objective genitive depending on it, e.g. **lucht múchta tinte**, *fire brigade* (**múchadh**, *to quench*).

8.12 PARTICIPLES

8.12.1 Irish manages without a present participle.

8.12.2 The past participle, known as the 'verbal adjective', ends in -t(h)a or t(h)e according to the quality of the preceding sound, e.g. **díolta**, *sold*; **forbartha**, *developed*; **briste**, *broken*; **aontaithe**, *united*. Note also **scríofa** (*written*) for **scríobhtha**.

8.12.3 The term 'participle' is reserved in Irish for certain derivatives of the verbal adjective, viz. **sobhriste**, *breakable*, *fragile*; **dobhriste**, *hard to break*, *unbreakable*; **inchreite**, *credible*.

8.16 IMPERSONAL

8.16.1 These are sometimes referred to as 'passive', but the Irish name means *free* (of number and person) and is officially rendered *autonomous*. They simply state an action and are formed from both transitive and intransitive verbs. No doubt the passive is the usual translation, e.g. **Leathnaítear iad (is é sin fágtar ar lár an i) nuair a chuirtear foirceann leo**, *They are broadened (that is i is left out) when an ending is added to them*. But the first subject in the English is object in Irish, as the form **iad** shows (7.3.1).

8.16.2

	Normal	Contracted and syncopated
Present	-t(e)ar	-(a)ítear
Past habitual	-t(a)í	-(a)ítí
Past	-(e)adh	-íodh, -(a)dh
Future	-f(e)ar	-(e)ófar
Conditional	-f(a)í	-(e)ófaí
Present subjunctive	-t(e)ar	-(a)ítear

8.16.3 The softening of past tenses (8.4.2) is regularly found only in the past habitual, but the particle **do** is sometimes found, with or without softening, with the simple past, e.g. **Do ceapadh an foclóir so do mhicléinn,** *This dictionary was planned for students.*

8.17 THE VERB *to be*

8.17.1 beith

Present: **táim, táis/taoi, tá; táimid, tá, táid**
    fuil|im, -is, -; -imid, -, -id

There are relative forms, **atáim,** etc. **Fuilim,** etc., which are always preceded by some particle, combine with **ní** to make **nílim,** etc.

Present habitual: **bím,** etc. (8.2)
Past habitual: **bhínn** (8.3.1)
Past: **bhíos,** etc.; **rabhas,** etc. (3PS **raibh**) (8.4.1)
Future: **bead, beir, beidh; beimid, beidh, beid**
Conditional: **bheinn, bheifeá, bheadh; bheimis, bheadh, bheidís**
Present subjunctive: **rabhad,** etc. (8.7.1)
Past subjunctive: **beinn** (as Conditional)
Imperative: 3PS **bíodh** (used for *although*)

8.17.2 *Impersonal forms*

Present: **táthar, fuiltear**
Present habitual: **bítear**
Past habitual: **bhítí**
Past: **bhíothas, rabhthas**
Future: **beifear**
Conditional: **bheifí**
Present subjunctive: **rabhthas**
Past subjunctive: **beifí**

8.17.3 The parts of **beith** describe; when identity is asserted other words are used, viz.

Present: **is**
Past: **ba**
Future: **bhus**
Subjunctive, Conditional: **ab, ba**

These serve for all persons.

The copula is omitted with **an** (8.21), **ar, gur(bh), nach, nár(bh)** (7.2.2), **ní** and **níor(bh)** (8.21), e.g. **ní ceart,** *it is not right.* Some forms coalesce with pronouns and conjunctions to make the following:

cérbh	who was . . .?
gur	that he (etc.) is (am, are)
gura	may he (etc.) be
gurb	used for gur and gura before vowels
nára, nárb	may he (etc.) not be

and see 7.2.2.

8.17.4   Both **beith** and is enter into the formation of idioms with nouns or adjectives and prepositions. The commonest is **tá ag** as the equivalent *to have*, e.g. **Tá leabhar agam**, *I have a book*. With the addition of the preposition **ar** it means *to owe*, e.g. **Tá punt agam ort**, *You owe me a pound*, and with abstract nouns forms various expressions denoting states of mind, e.g. **Tá aithne agam air**, *I know him*.

The uses of **is (ba)** are not very different, e.g. **Is liom an leabhar**, *The book belongs to me*; **Is dóigh liom**, *I think (it likely)*; **Is fearr liom é**, *I prefer it*. Compare also **bíodh gurb eol dóibh**, *although they know (be it that is knowledge to them)* with **daltaí a bhfuil roinnt eolais acu**, *pupils who have some knowledge*.

Is is also used to emphasise a word, e.g.

Tháinig sé inné	He came yesterday
Is é a tháinig inné	HE came yesterday
Is inné a tháinig sé	He came YESTERDAY

8.19   IRREGULARITIES

A number of common verbs are more or less irregular. Some form different tenses from different roots, others appear to, while others are related in origin and are thus confusingly similar. Only the irregular tenses are given and of these only so much as is needed to establish the irregularity. The past habitual and the subjunctive follow the present.

8.19.1   **breith,** *to bear*
Stem: **beir- (béar-)**, except
Past: **rugas**, etc.

8.19.2   **cloisteáil, clos, cloisint,** *to hear*
Past: **chualas, chualais, chuala**, etc.
Past impersonal: **chualathas**

8.19.3   **déanamh,** *to do, make*
Past: **rinneas, rinnis, rinne**, etc.
       dearnas, dearnais, dearna, etc.

8.19.4   **dul,** *to go*
Principal stem: **té-**
Past: **chuas, chuais, chuaigh**, etc.
       deachas, deachais, deachaigh, etc.
Past impersonal: **chuathas**
Future: **raghad (rachad)**, etc.

8.19.5   **fáil,** *to get*
Present: **gheibhim/faighim**, etc.
Past: **fuaireas**, etc.
Past impersonal: **fuarthas**
Future: **gheobhad/faighead**, etc.
Future impersonal: **gheofar/faighfear**
Past participle: **fachta**

8.19.6   feiscint, feiceáil, *to see*
    Principal stem: feic-
    Present: feicim/chím, etc.
    Past: chonaiceas, etc.
        facas, facais, faca, etc.
    Past impersonal: chonacthas, facthas
    Future: chífead/feicfead, etc.
8.19.7   ithe, *to eat*
    Future: íosfad, etc.
8.19.8   rá, *to say*
    Present: deirim/abraim, etc.
    Past: dúras, dúrais, dúirt, etc.
    Future: déarfad/abród, etc.
8.19.9   tabhairt, *to give*
    Present: bheirim/tugaim, etc.
    Past: thugas, etc.
    Future: bhéarfad/tabharfad, etc.
    Past participle: tugtha
8.19.10 teachı, tíocht, *to come*
    Present: tagaim, etc.
    Past: thángas, thángais, tháinig, etc.
    Past impersonal: thángthas
    Future: tiocfad, etc.

8.20   PERIPHRASTIC

8.20.1   There is a great variety of periphrastic forms, usually with parts of **beith**, *to be* (8.17). Not all correspond to recognised English tenses, but they are given together here for convenience.

8.20.2   Forms with the verbal noun include the following:

beith + **ag** + v.n.	*to be doing* (continuous action)
+ **ar** + v.n.	(continuous state)
+ **ar tí** ⎫ + v.n.	*to be about to do* (intention)
+ **chun** ⎭	
+ **do** + possessive + v.n.	(continuous passive)
+ **i** + possessive + v.n.	(continuous state)
+ **i ndiaidh** + v.n.	(perfect; immediate past)
tá + **le** + v.n.	*is to be done*
do. + **ag** + person	*to have something to do*
beith + **tar éis** + v.n.	(immediate past)

Constructions are as indicated in 8.11.2, but it should be noted that after **chun** and **tar éis** the verbal noun is in the genitive, except when it is preceded by the object noun.

Examples: **táthar ag tathaint**, *people are urging*; **gach ceart ar cosaint**, *all rights protected*; **tá an leabhar dá dhíol**, *the book is being sold*; **tá siad i ndiaidh teagasc éifeachtúil a fháil**, *they have had effective teaching*; **tá sé le tuiscint**, *it is to be understood*; tá leabhar le díol agam, *I have a book to sell*.

8.20.3   With the past participle **tá** makes the perfect tense, with a suggestion of lasting effect, **atá sroiste againn**, *which we have reached* (Specimen: 72–74).

8.21/8.22 NEGATIVE AND INTERROGATIVE

In themselves the negative **ní** §, the interrogative **an** §, the interrogative-negative **nach** § and the dependent **nach** §/**ná** cause no trouble so far as reading Irish goes; but it should be noted that they all have special forms for use with the past tense of most verbs, viz. **níor(bh)**, **ar(bh)**, **nár(bh)**. These soften the initial consonant. See also 8.17.3.

9 ADVERBS

9.1 FORMATION

Adverbs are regularly formed from adjectives by placing **go** in front, e.g. **maith**, *good*; **go maith**, *well*. (But see 5.4.2.)

9.2 COMPARISON

In the comparative and superlative the adverb is identical with the adjective.

10 PREPOSITIONS

10.2 SIMPLE PREPOSITIONS, FORMS AND SYNTAX

10.2.1 Most simple prepositions, viz. **ag, ar, as, chuig/chun, de, do, faoi/fé, i(n), idir, le, o, roimh, thar, trí(d), um**, have special personal forms which are used instead of the basic form followed by a personal pronoun (10.3.1). All the above soften the following consonant, except **ag, as, chun, le, thar**, which have no effect, and **i**, which eclipses.

10.2.2 Of the remaining prepositions, which are followed by personal pronouns, **gan** softens, **go, timpeall** and **trasna** have no effect.

10.2.3 All prepositions take the dative, except **chun, timpeall** and **trasna**, which take the genitive.

10.3 DERIVATIVES OF SIMPLE PREPOSITIONS

10.3.1 The personal forms are different for each person and number, and though there is a marked similarity between corresponding forms of different prepositions, it is not simply a matter of adding endings, viz.

	S				*P*		
	1	2	3m	3f	1	2	3
ag	agam	agat	aige	aici	agaínn	agaibh	acu
ar	orm	ort	air	uirthi	orainn	oraibh	orthu
as	asam	asat	as	aisti	asainn	asaibh	astu
⌈**chuig**	chugam	chugat⌉	chuige	chuici	chugainn	chugaibh	chucu
⌊**chun**	chúm	chút⌋		chúithi	chúinn	chúibh	chúthu
de	díom	díot	de	di	dínn	díbh	díobh
do	dom	duit	dó	di	dúinn	daoibh	dóibh
faoi/fá/fé	fúm	fút	faoi/fé	fúithi	fúinn	fúibh	fúthu
i	ionam	ionat	ann	inti	ionainn	ionaibh	iontu
idir	—	—	—	—	eadrainn	eadraibh	eatarthu
le	liom	leat	leis	léi(thi)	linn	libh	leo(thu)
ó	uaim	uait	uaidh	uaithi	uainn	uaibh	uathu
roimh	romham	romhat	roimhe	roimpi	romhainn	romhaibh	rompu
thar	tharam	tharat	thairis	thairsti	tharainn	tharaibh	tharstu
trí	tríom	tríot	tríd	tríthi	trínn	tribh	tríothu
um	umam	umat	uime	uimpi	umainn	umaibh	umpu

10.3.2 The emphatic endings -sa, etc. (5.5.2) can be added to prepositional pronouns, e.g. fúmsa, *under ME.*

10.3.3 For the combination of prepositional pronouns and demonstratives see 7.1.1; for their use with relatives see 7.2.2.

10.3.4 Some prepositions combine with possessives (5.5.1), viz.

	mo	do	a	ár	a
ag			á, ghá		á
ar			arna		arna
de			dá		dá
do			dá		dá
faoi			faoina		faoina
i	im	id	ina	inár	ina
le	lem	led	lena	lenár	lena
ó	óm	ód/ót	óna	ónár	óna
trí			trína		trína

Some of these are common in idioms with the verbal noun (8.10.2) and tá ina is almost equivalent to is (8.17.3), but suggests a temporary rather than a permanent state.

10.3.5 Some prepositions combine with the article, viz.

	an	na
de	den	—
do	don	—
fé	fén	—
í	(in)san	(in)sna
le	leis an	leisna
ó	ón	—

10.4 COMPOUND PREPOSITIONS

10.4.1 Compound prepositions are usually formed of a simple preposition followed by a noun, current or obsolete, like *instead*, but go dtí, *until, to,* is a verb phrase and is followed by the nominative.

10.4.2 Those formed with nouns, e.g. i dtaobh, *about*; os cionn, *above*, are too numerous to list. The nouns which they govern are naturally in the genitive, but when they are construed with personal pronouns these appear as possessives (cf. *in his stead*) and changes take place in the second element of the preposition, thus: i dtaobh, *about*; im thaobh, *about me*; os cionn, *above*; os a chionn, *above him*; os a gcionn, *above them.* The reason for the changes is that i eclipses but m' softens; os has no effect, but a (*his*) and a (*their*) soften and eclipse respectively. In most cases one will have to find the preposition in the dictionary under the basic form of the noun, e.g. taobh, ceann.

11 CONJUNCTIONS

11.1 As in English some of the numerous conjunctions show clear traces of their connexion with adverbs and prepositions or derivation from nouns, e.g. chun go, *in order that* (chun, *towards*; go, *that*); toisc nach, *because . . . not* (toisc, *purpose*); nuair a, *when* (uair, *hour*; a, *which*).

11.2 One needs to be on the watch for negative conjunctions such as nach, ná, *that not*, and for forms specially used with past tenses. These end in -r(bh), which can usually be simply cut off to obtain the basic form, e.g. **murar(bh)**, **sular(bh)**. But the past form of **go** is **gur(bh)** and of **ní**, **níor(bh)**. For combinations with the copula see 8.17.3.

11.3 Some conjunctions require the subjunctive, but this is not usually critical for meaning.

11.4 There is a tendency to avoid subordinating conjunctions by substituting **agus** (*and*) or by using a verbal noun, e.g. **Bheinn buíoch díot ach sin a dhéanamh**, *I should be grateful if you would do so* (**ach** = *but*).

13 WORD-FORMATION

13.1 There are a number of regular formative elements in Irish and in view of what is said in 0.5 about dictionaries it is useful to be acquainted with them. As some of the examples given below show, stem changes as in 2.6 may take place with suffixes.

13.2 PREFIXES

Adjectives, nouns and numerals can all be prefixed to nouns, with obvious results, e.g. **nuachúrsa**, *new course*; **bun-chúrsa**, *elementary course*; **dó-lámhach**, *two-handed*. In addition there are a number of prefixes which have no separate existence, of which the most important are:

> **aimh-, ain-, amh-, an-**(1), negative
> **an-**(2), see 2.4.1 (4)
> **ais-**, back, again
> **ath-**, again, another, *ex-*, very
> **comh-**, equal, together: **comhchosach**, *isosceles* (**cos**, *leg*); **comhfhocal**, *compound* (word)
> **dea-**, good, well
> **dí-**, negative
> **do-**, difficult, impossible: **do-bhriste**, *unbreakable*
> **dó-**, very
> **eadar-, idir-**, *inter-*
> **fo-**, *under-*, *sub-*, occasional
> **for-**, *super-*, more: **formhór**, *majority*
> **il-, iol-**, many
> **im-, iom-**, round, *circum-*
> **leas-**, *vice-*
> **leath-, leith-**, *half-*, *semi-*
> **mí-**, negative
> **réamh-**, *pre-*, *fore-*
> **ró-**, too
> **sár-**, very, *super-*

13.3 SUFFIXES

The most important and prolific suffixes are the following. The basic word is given where necessary in brackets.

> **-ach, -t(e)ach, -theach**, adjectives: **acrach**, *convenient* (**acaire**, *handy tool*); **deon(t)ach**, *willing* (**deoin**, *will*); **éiritheach**, *successful* (**éirí**, *to rise up*)
> **-(e)acht**, abstract nouns: **milseacht**, *sweetness* (**milis**)

-(a)í, agent; also adjectives: **oibrí**, *worker* (**obair**)

-aire, agent: **diaire**, *theologian* (**Dia**)

-amh, agent: **breitheamh**, *judge* (**breith**, *judgement*)

-án, classed as a diminutive but in practice makes nouns of many sorts, e.g.
   eitleán, *aeroplane* (**eitilt**, *to fly*)

-(e)as, abstract noun: **iontas**, *wonder* (**ionadh**)

-dóir, agent, *-er*, *-or*: **clódóir**, *printer*

-eolas, *-ology*

í, -(i)ú (stem -igh-), verbs derived from nouns

-ín, diminutive: **boithrín**, *lane* (**bothar**, *road*)

-(a)íocht, abstract nouns

-lann, place: **leabharlann**, *library*

-mhar, adjectives from nouns

-(i)óir, see **-dóir**

-ra, collective nouns: **glasra**, *greenery*

-t(e)ach, see -ach

-t(h)a, adjectives: **ceachtartha**, *mutual* (**ceachtar**, *each*)

-theach, see -ach

-ú, see -í

-úil, adjectives: **laethúil**, *daily* (**lá**)

GLOSSARY

achomair, achoimre, *summary*

aguisín, *addendum, appendix*

aiste, *essay*

aistriú(chán), *translation*

aitheasc, *address, talk*

aithne, *order*

amháin, *single* (1.8.6, 6.1.4)

athchló, *reprint*

atheagrú, *revise, revision*

bailiúchán, *collection*

ball, *member*

bhfuair bás, *died*

bliain, *year* (1.8.6)

bliantúil, *annual* (1.8.6)

breis, *addition*

brollach, *introduction*

cailleadh, *died*

ceangal, *binding*

céanna, *same*

clár, *table*

cló, *printing, impression, edition* (1.5.1);
   press (1.6.1)

clóbhualadh, *to print* (1.6.2)

clólann, *press*

clúdach crua, *hardback*

clúdach páipéir, *paperback*

cnuasach, *to collect*

cóip, *copy* (1.8.6)

cóipceart, *copyright*

cóiriú, *to edit* (1.2.3)

coiste, *committee* (1.8.3)

comh-chomhairle, *conference*

cuid, *part, volume* (1.4.1)

cumadh, *to form* (write)

cumann, *society*

cur in eagar, in oiriúint, *to edit* (1.2.3)

dánta, *poems*

d'éag, *died*

le dea-mhéin, *with compliments*

díoltóir leabhar, *bookseller*

díonbrollach, *preface*

díreach foilsithe, *just published*

eagarthóir, *editor* (1.8.3)

eagrán, *edition* (1.5.1); *issue* (1.8.4)

earrach, *spring*

ar fáil, *available*

faisnéis, *bulletin, information*

feabhsaithe, *improved*
fiacha, *price* (1.8.6)
filíocht, *poetry*
foclóir, *dictionary*
foilseachán, *publishing house*
foilsiú, *to publish* (1.5.1, 1.6.2)
fomhar, *autumn*
forlíonadh, *supplement*

gach ceart ar cosaint, *all rights reserved*
gan foilsiú, *unpublished*
gearrscéal, *short story*
geimhreadh, *winter*

imleabhar, *volume* (1.4.1, 1.7.2, 1.8.4)
innéacs, *index*
iris, *journal*

lacáiste, *discount*
láimhscríbhinn, *manuscript* (1.7.1, 1.8.7)
leabhar, *book*
leabharlann, *library*
leabharlannaí, *librarian*
leagan, *version*
leanfar de, ar lean(úint), *to be continued*
leasaithe, *corrected*
leathanach, *page*
leathbhliain, *half year*
litir (P litreacha), *letter*
luach, *price* (1.8.6)

méadaithe, *enlarged*
mí, *month*
míosúil, *monthly*

núa, *new*
núa-réitithe, *revised, revision* (1.5.2)

ordaithe, *order*
óráid, *speech*

paimfléad, *pamphlet*
praghas, *price* (1.8.6)

ráitheachán, *quarterly*
réamhrá, *preface*
ríar, *order* (1.8.6)
(a) rugadh, *was born*

samhradh, *summer*
saor, *free*
saothar, *work*
Sasana, *England*
scríbhinn, *writing*
seach-chló, *offprint*
seachtain, *week*
seoladh, *address*
síntiús, *subscription* (1.8.6)
sleachta, *selections*
sraith, *series*
stair, *history*

taighde, *research*
tráchtaireacht, *commentary*

údar, *author*
uimhir, *number* (1.8.4)
úrscéal, *novel*

GRAMMATICAL INDEX: WORDS

* soft, and § eclipsis, see 2.5.4

GRAMMATICAL INDEX: ENDINGS

B, and S, see 2.5.3

* soft, and § eclipsis, see 2.5.4

WELSH

SPECIMEN

Ychydig cyn i'r rhyfel *ddechrau gwelsom *fod angen am *eiriadur newydd a *fyddai'n gweddu i *blant ysgol ac i'r lliaws sydd o *bryd i *bryd am *ddysgu'r iaith *Gymraeg. Bu'r Athro T. Gwynn Jones yn *garedig iawn tuag atom ar hyd y blynyddoedd, a gofynnwyd iddo fel arfer am ei *farn. Yna, gyda'r parodrwydd hwnnw a oedd yn un o'i nodweddion amlycaf, ymgymerodd yr Athro â †pharatoi'r Geiriadur hwn.

Pan *ddechreuodd iechyd yr Athro *wanhau, rhoddodd Mr. Arthur ap Gwynn *lawer o help i'w *dad, ac ymhen ychydig amser cymerodd holl *faich y Geiriadur ar ei ysgwyddau ei hun.

(For * and † see 2.5.2.)

Shortly before the war began we saw that there was need for a new dictionary which would be suitable for school children and for the many people who from time to time propose to learn the Welsh language. Professor T. Gwynn Jones has been very kind to us throughout the years and he was asked as usual for his opinion. Thereupon, with that willingness which was one of his most conspicuous characteristics, the Professor undertook to prepare this Dictionary.

When the health of the Professor began to weaken, Mr. Arthur ap Gwynn gave a good deal of help to his father, and within a little while he took the whole burden of the Dictionary on his own shoulders.

0 GENERAL CHARACTERISTICS

0.1 DEGREE OF INFLEXION
Welsh is a moderately synthetic language, more so in its traditional written form than in conversation and styles based on conversation. A full conjugation of the verb is available, in which subject pronouns are unnecessary, but periphrastic tenses (8.20) are freely used in conversational style. The noun has no cases, but on the other hand there are many compounds of prepositions and pronouns.

0.2 ORDER OF WORDS
Genitives and most adjectives follow the noun. The usual sentence order is VSO, but adverbial phrases may be placed at the beginning; the putting of the subject or object first emphasises it, and the syntax is slightly modified (7.2.2).

0.4 RELATION TO OTHER LANGUAGES
A look at the numerals demonstrates the place of Welsh in the Indo-European family of languages, but when the words derived from Latin are discounted, the relationship is not a great deal of practical help.

0.5 GRAMMATICAL STRUCTURE

0.5.1 Although Welsh has a large number of endings, especially those of the verb, which unmistakably indicate their grammatical significance, e.g. -asom 1PP Past tense, the structure in many respects approaches the fluidity of English. Thus, though *front* may not always be the appropriate translation of **blaen**, **blaen**, like *front*, can be either noun or adjective (**erthygl flaen**, *leading article*) and goes to form prepositional phrases, e.g. **o flaen**, *in front of*. The verbal noun (8.11) may be used as an ordinary noun or even as an adjective, e.g. **ateb** (*to answer, answering, an answer*); **byw** (*to live, alive*). Nouns have no cases, and the same form can function as subject, object, genitive or adverb without the aid of prepositions.

0.5.2 A noun functioning as object or adverb usually suffers a change of its initial consonant known as mutation, and there are numerous other circumstances in which this takes place. This is dealt with in 2.5.2; I am concerned here to note the marked effect that it has on the form of a word when combined say with other features such as vowel change (2.6). Thus a sentence may contain the phrase **a barodd**: **a** turns out to have a number of meanings, and though **-odd** looks like a verb ending (8.4.1), the dictionary produces no verb with a stem **bar-**. However, the relative **a** (7.2.1) causes the soft mutation which produces **b-** from **p-**. Alas, there appears to be no verb **par-** either, for in fact the verb-noun ends in **-i**, and that causes the stem vowel to change to **-e-**: the stem is **par-**, but the verb-noun under which the word appears in most dictionaries is **peri** (8.1.3), and the phrase means *which caused*. On the other hand **parhau**, *to continue* makes **pery**, *continues* (2.6, 2.7); **ellir** has to be looked up under **gallu**. It is important therefore to read section 2, dealing with general features, and having found an ending to read all that is said about the tense or class of word concerned.

1 BIBLIOLINGUISTICS

1.1 NAMES

1.1.1 Welsh names are for the most part thoroughly Anglicised, e.g. **Ambrose Jones, Hugh Bevan.** The pure Welsh equivalents are **Emrys ap Iwan** (among other possibilities) and **Huw ap Efan.** (**Ap** may be spelt **ab** before vowels.) Ambrose Jones writes under the Welsh form, and the son of T. Gwynn Jones uses the name **Arthur ap Gwynn,** but there is no very marked tendency to substitute such forms, even among Welsh nationalists, though Welsh spellings and forms of Christian names are perhaps commoner again, as well as peculiarly Welsh names. Surnames in **ap** are filed under **Ap,** but cf. 1.1.3. The great majority of surnames are patronymics of one sort or the other, but there are names like **Llwyd** (Lloyd) which are descriptive adjectives (*Grey*). At one time such names were commonly mutated (2.5.2), hence *Vaughan* representing **Fychan** from **bychan**, *small*.

1.1.2 More common at all times than the straightforward conversion of surnames has been the adoption of bardic names. Such names may be simple, like **Elfed** (H. Elvet Lewis), territorial like **Iolo Morgannwg** (i.e. of Glamorgan, Edward Williams), adjectival like **Taliesin Hiraethog** (John Davies) or occasionally patronymic like **Robert ap Gwilym Ddu** (Robert Williams). Whatever their form they tend to be filed under the Christian name (cf. 1.1.3).

1.1.3 Welsh names up to the sixteenth century, those of literary figures at any rate, include a number which are filed under the Christian name, e.g. **Llywarch Hen, Dafydd ap Gwilym, Iolo Goch, Guto'r Glyn, Siôn Cent,** where **hen** and **goch** (from **coch**) are adjectives, **ap Gwilym** a patronymic, **'r glyn** a dependent genitive (*of the glen*) and **Cent** is a surname.

1.2   NAMES OF AUTHORS, EDITORS, ETC.

1.2.1   None of the varied ways of expressing authorship and the like has any effect on the form of the name. The commonest way is to use **gan** (*by*), preceded if necessary by some form of the passive (or rather, impersonal) verb or less commonly a noun of action, e.g. **gan D. Simon Evans**; **golygwyd** (*edited*) **gan Henry Lewis**; **wedi ei drosi i'r Gymraeg gan E. T. Davies**, *translated* (8.11.2) *into Welsh by E.T.D.*; **cyfieithiad gan John Edwards**, *translation by J.E.*; **wedi ei chymreigio gan . . .**, *Welshed by . . .*. (**Trosi** is now specialised in the sense *to translate*; it does not need **yn Gymraeg**, *Welsh-wise* or **i'r Gymraeg**, *into Welsh* or some similar phrase to complete the sense, but **troi**, *to turn*, obsolete in this sense, does.) On the absence of the regular mutation after **gan** see 2.5.2.

1.2.2   For simple authorship it is enough to put the name after the title, e.g. **Hanes Cymru | T. P. Lewis**. As far as form goes the name could be in the genitive, like **Cymru** (*The history of Wales of T. P. Lewis*). It hardly seems necessary to suppose so in cases like the above, but it obviously is in **Gwaith y Parch. Walter Davies**, *The work of the Rev. W. D*.

1.2.3   It is not usual for the names of authors to precede the title and a name at the head of the page is more likely to have some other significance, as in **William Carey er clod**, *In honour of W. C.*

1.2.4   With corporate authors the statements are liable to be more complicated and there is more likelihood of common nouns being affected by mutation (2.5.2), e.g. **Lluniwyd y rhestrau gan panel o athrawon o Gyfadran Addysg Golegol Aberystwyth a chan gydbwyllgor yn cynrychioli'r Gyfadran honno a Chyfadran Addysg Golegol Bangor**, *The lists were compiled by a panel of teachers from the College Faculty of Education, Aberystwyth and by a joint committee representing this Faculty and the College Faculty of Education, Bangor*. The key word **Cyfadran** appears under two different mutations and would have to be restored if used as a heading. **Gydbwyllgor** and **golegol** too are mutated, but in the latter case the relationship which causes the mutation (feminine adjective following its noun) would not be affected by the removal of the entire corporate name from the context. (The unmutated **panel** was still felt to be a borrowed word.)

1.3   TITLES

1.3.1   Most titles consist of nouns, adjectives and prepositions in various combinations, e.g. **Emynau a'u hawduron**, *Hymns and their authors*; **Hanes Cymru**, *History of Wales*; **Gramadeg Cymraeg Canol**, *Middle Welsh grammar*; **Ar wib yn Sweden**, *Out and about in Sweden*. Belles-lettres and the literature of persuasion, as well as sub-titles, call for more varied grammatical forms, e.g. **FY NGHYMRU I**, *My Wales*; **Ditectif Inspector Hopkin yn datrys achos y gadair wag**, *D.I. Hopkin solves the case of the empty chair*—short title **Y gadair wag**; **Y llyfr ordinhadau, sef Ffurfiau gwasanaeth wedi eu hawdurdodi i'w defnyddio yn yr Eglwys Fethodistaidd**, *The book of ordinances*; *or, Forms of service authorised to be used in the Methodist Church*. The title **Fy Nghymru i** above is printed in capitals to draw attention to a possible confusion with the roman numeral.

1.3.2   Title entries according to Anglo-American rules should cause little difficulty provided one does not get confused between **y**, **yr** (*the*) and **yn** (*in*), though it is possible, even if statistically improbable, for a title to begin with **Yr wyf** (*I am*), which would be filed under **YR**.

British Museum rules cause more complications: **Y genhinen**, if anonymous, would have to be filed under **cenhinen** (4.3), **Fy Nghymru i** under **WALES**, **Dramâu Cymraeg** under **WELSH PLAYS**.

1.3.3 The first word of a quoted title may undergo mutation (2.5.2) in the appropriate context, e.g. **Detholion o 'Gannwyll y Cymry'**, *Selections from* Cannwyll y Cymry, but the insertion of a word like **nofel** or **llyfr** will stop the mutation by separating the title from the mutating word.

1.4 VOLUMES AND PARTS

1.4.1 The usual words are **cyfrol** and **rhan** respectively, but **llyfr** (*book*), which can be used of an internal formal division of a work, is not infrequently found in much the same sense as **cyfrol**. **Rhan**, like *part*, is used in the sense of *instalment*, e.g. **cyhoeddir yn rhannau**, *published in parts*.

1.4.2 Numeration usually precedes, in ordinal form, e.g. **Yr ail ran**, *part 2*; but **cyntaf** (*first*) follows. If other numbers follow, e.g. **cyfrol II**, they are read as cardinals.

1.5 EDITIONS

The usual word is **argraffiad** (literally *printing*) coupled with a numeral, e.g. **argraffiad cyntaf**, *first edition*, or the word **newydd** with or without some expression denoting revision, such as **wedi ei ddiwygio gydag ychwanegiadau**, *revised with additions*. Sometimes expressions denoting special kinds of edition are found, e.g. **argraffiad beirniadol ac eglurhaol**, *critical and explanatory edition*.

1.6 IMPRINTS

1.6.1 The names of publishers are of the same types as in England, e.g. **J. D. Lewis a'i Feibion**, *J. D. Lewis and Sons*; **Gwasg y Brython**, *Briton Press*; **Gwasg Prifysgol Cymru**, *University of Wales Press*; **Llyfrau'r Dryw**, *Wren Books*, and a good many society imprints such as **Cymdeithas Lyfrau Ceredigion Gyf.**, *Cardiganshire Book Society Ltd.*; **Mudiad Efengylaidd Cymru**, *Evangelical Movement of Wales*.

1.6.2 Commissioned publishing and printing occurs, as instanced by **Cyhoeddwyd ar ran Cyngor yr Eisteddfod Genedlaethol gan Hugh Evans a'i Feibion**, *published on behalf of the Council of the National Eisteddfod by H. E. and Sons*; **Argraffwyd dros y Gymdeithas gan . . .**, *Printed for the Society by . . .*; and also sponsorship, as in **Cyhoeddir trwy gydweithrediad Bwrdd Gwybodau Celtaidd**, *Published through the cooperation of the Board of Celtic Studies*; **Cyhoeddir dan gynllun Pwyllgorau Addysg Caernarfon, Ceredigion . . . .** , *Published in the programme of the Education Committees of Caernarvonshire, Cardiganshire . . . .* Most publishers are still printer-publishers.

1.6.3 The place of publication may be stated baldly or preceded by the preposition **yn**. If the former, one has only to remember that the larger towns have their own forms in Welsh, and that a good many English towns have Welsh forms too. So one finds **Gwrecsam, Dinbych, Caerdydd, Caerfyrddin** (*Carmarthen*), **Abertawe** (*Swansea*), **Glyn Ebwy** (*Ebbw Vale*); **Lerpwl, Llundain, Rhydychen** (*Oxford*). If **yn** is used, it nasalises the initial consonant of the name, viz. **yng Ngwrecsam, yn Ninbych, yng Nghaerdydd, ym Mangor** (*at Bangor*).

1.7 SERIES

1.7.1 The titles of series mostly appear at the head of title-page and begin with the word **cyfres** (*series*). The specific name is usually descriptive as in **Cyfres barddoniaeth y siroedd**, *County poetry series*; **Cyfres clasuron y plant**, *Series of children's classics*, but may be more allusive, e.g. **Cyfres Pobun**, *Everyman Series*. More rarely **cyfres** is omitted, e.g. **Atgofion Ceredigion**, *Cardiganshire Recollections*; **Help llaw**, *Helping hand*.

1.7.2 Numeration is usually by **rhif**, followed by a number, but **cyfrol** and **llyfr**

are also found. Occasionally the numeration is given in the form of a continuous statement, e.g. **Dyma'r drydedd gyfrol yng nghyfres Atgofion Ceredigion,** *Here is the third volume in the series Atgofion Ceredigion.*

1.7.3 Information about other volumes in the series is frequently given under such rubrics as **Yn yr un gyfres,** *In the same series;* **Wedi'u cyhoeddi,** *Published;* **I ddilyn yn fuan,** *To follow shortly;* **I'w cyhoeddi'n fuan,** *To be published shortly.*

1.8 PERIODICALS

1.8.1 The titles of periodicals are not linguistically different from those of books, but naturally they include many such as **Bore da** (*Good morning*) or **Y ddraig goch** (*The red dragon*) which are more allusive than descriptive. In context mutation of the first word may occur (cf. 1.3.3), but isolation of the title is more likely.

1.8.2 Institutional periodicals are common, with the name of the institution forming part of the title, as in **Cylchgrawn Llyfrgell Genedlaethol Cymru,** *Magazine of the National Library of Wales,* or more often of the sub-title, e.g. **Yr Haul: cylchgrawn chwarterol yr Eglwys yng Nghymru,** *The Sun: quarterly magazine of the Church in Wales.* Sometimes the information may appear as a note, e.g. **Cyhoeddiad y Cylch Catholig Cymreig yw Efrydiau Catholig,** *Efrydiau Catholig is a publication of the Welsh Catholic Circle.* Or, **Argraffwyd gan . . . ar ran . . . ,** *Printed by . . . for . . . .*

1.8.3 Editorship is usually expressed by some form of the root **golyg-,** e.g. **golygydd (ymgynghorol),** (*consultative*) *editor;* **dan olygiad (olygyddiaeth),** *under the ,editorship of.* Occasionally one may find a **bwrdd golygyddol,** *editorial board.*

1.8.4 Numeration is by **cyfrol** (*volume*) and **rhif** (*number*). **Cyfres** (usually *series*) is sometimes found for **cyfrol,** even alongside its normal use: e.g. **Cyfres XX, rhif 10. Cyfres newydd** (*Vol. 20, no. 10. New series*). **Rhifyn,** the usual word for *issue,* sometimes replaces **rhif,** or the two may be used in conjunction, e.g. **Rhifyn Gorffennaf, 1971. Cyfrol CXXVI, rhif 540** (*July number 1971. Vol. 126, no. 540*).

1.8.5 Periodicity may be expressed by an adjective as in **Yr Haul** above, or by an adverb: **yn chwarterol,** *quarterly;* **pob chwarter,** *every quarter;* by implication, **naw ceiniog y mis,** *ninepence a month.*

1.8.6 Subscription rates or terms (**telerau**) are rarely given very explicitly, as in **Trwy'r post gan y Cyhoeddwyr am y tanysgrifiad blynyddol o 12/- (cludiad yn rhad),** *By post from the publishers on a yearly subscription of 12/- (post free),* or more simply **Drwy y Post 11s. 6d. y flwyddyn,** *By post 11s. 6d. a year.*

1.8.7 Addresses (**cyfeiriadau**) are given pretty uniformly. The following example is one of the more elaborate: **Anfoner—erthyglau a gohebiaeth i'r golygydd . . . Llyfrau i'w hadolygu i'r is-olygydd . . . Cyfraniadau i Adran Ysgolion i . . . Archebion a hysbys-ebion i . . . :** *To be sent—articles and correspondence to the editor . . . Books for review to the assistant editor . . . Contributions to the Schools Department to . . . Orders and advertisements to . . . .* Sometimes the list includes **taliadau,** *payments.* Instead of **anfoner** (or **danfoner**), which is the impersonal subjunctive (8.16.2), the phrase **i'w hanfon** (7.3.2, 8.11.2) may be used, or **gellir anfon,** *can be sent.*

2 ALPHABET, PHONETICS, SPELLING

2.1 ALPHABET

2.1.1 The present-day alphabet is as follows:

a b c ch d dd e f ff g ng h i l ll m n o p ph r rh s
t th u w y

Each of these symbols has its distinctive place in the alphabet. When they are initial the dictionary gives ample warning, but it is not so easy to remember that **cyngor** comes before **cyhyd**, and even more difficult then to remember that words like **dangos** come among the **dan**'s.

For the better understanding of mutation the values of some of the letters should be noted:

> **c** as in **can**, no matter what vowel follows
> **ch** is the corresponding fricative, as in *loch*
> **dd** like th in *the*
> **f** as in *of*
> **ff** as in *off*
> **ll** unvoiced l ('Press the tongue against the roof of the mouth and hiss like a goose!')
> **ph** as in *philosophy*
> **th** as in *thin*
> **mh, nh, ngh** and **rh** are the unvoiced varieties of **m, n ng** and **r** (as the English *wh* is of *w*)

This alphabet dates in essentials from 1621. Before that date various other attempts had been made, and scholarly editions of old texts may reproduce the early spellings. The main points to notice are the use of **d, đ, dh** and **z** for **dd**, **k** for **c**, **l** and **lh** for **ll**, **u** and **v** for **f**, **u** for **w**; and **ġ** for the mutation (that is to say the absence) of **g** (2.5.2).

2.1.2 The circumflex accent may be put on a stressed long vowel:

(a) It may indicate that the vowel is long, e.g. **gŵr, ânt**. In a word like **gwên**, *a smile*, it serves incidentally to distinguish it from **gwen**, *white*, with a short e.

(b) It may simply distinguish one word from another: **tŷ**, *house* (mutated form **dŷ**); **dy**, *your*; **nâd**, *cry*; **nad**, *that not*.

(c) It distinguishes the different ways of stressing the diphthong **-wy-** (provided it has a long w), when there is more than one word with the same spelling, e.g. **gŵydd**, *presence*; *wild*; *goose*; **gwŷdd**, *trees*.

(d) It indicates an unusual stress, e.g. **dramâu**, *dramas*; **iachâd**, *a cure*. The normal stress is on the penultimate. But **-had** is invariably stressed and needs no accent, e.g. **parhad**, *continuation*. (N.B.: **ch** is a different letter from **h**.)

2.1.3 The acute accent is put on a short vowel to indicate an unusual stress, e.g. **nesáu**, *to approach*; but **parhau**, *to continue*, with the same stress, requires no accent (cf. 2.1.2d).

2.1.4 The grave accent indicates that a vowel is short, e.g. **clòs**, *close*. (Monosyllables ending in -s are regularly long.) Like the acute accent it is of rare occurrence.

2.1.5 The diaeresis indicates that a succession of vowels does not form a diphthong, e.g. **storïau**, *stories*; **töwr**, *tiler*.

2.2 CAPITALISATION
The use of capitals is the same as in English.

2.3 DIVISION OF WORDS
2.3.1 Compounds are divided according to sense.

2.3.2 Prefixes are kept intact, e.g. **an-ialwch**. If there is a nasal mutation (2.5.2), the division is after the **m** or **n** and between **ng** and **h**, e.g. **cyn-gor**, **am-hosibl**, **cyng-horion**.

L

2.3.3 Terminations and formative elements are taken over, e.g. **cystr-awen** (*but* **cys-trawen** is also possible), **esiampl-au, wrth-ych**.

2.3.4 Apart from this there is a tendency to divide before a vowel and between two consonants. The latter causes deviations from the previous rules even in good printers, e.g. **syl-wodd** (root **sylw-**), **dych-rynasant** (prefix **dy-**). **Ch, dd, ff, ll, ph, th** must not be separated. If **d-d** is found split between two lines, retain the hyphen in transcribing (2.4.1).

2.4 PUNCTUATION

2.4.1 The hyphen is used to indicate an equal-stressed compound, e.g. **ail-wneud,** *re-make*; in words which are condensed expressions, e.g. **di-alw-amdano,** *uncalled for* (13.2); and in words like **priod-ddull** (*idiom*), **prudd-der** (*sadness*), **cyd-destun** (*context*), which would otherwise be ambiguous or misleading.

2.4.2 The apostrophe denoting missing letters is *de rigueur* in **mae'n** (for **mae yn**), **a'i** (for **a ei**) and the like, but **roedd** and the like are as common as **'roedd** (8.17). See also 8.22.2.

2.5 VARIATION OF CONSONANT, MUTATION

2.5.1 Apart from those dealt with in 2.7 few consonant changes occur in the course of inflexion. Consonants are unvoiced in the comparison of adjectives (5.3.2) and the subjunctive of verbs (8.7), and there is variation between **-C** and **-Ci-**, e.g. **meddwl, meddyliaf**. Similarly **lluniwr, llunwyr**. But in syntactical contexts and in compounds there are a number of important changes known as mutations, e.g. (1) **Pwllheli, ym Mhwllheli** (*in Pwllheli*); **posibl, amhosibl** (*impossible*); (2) **tŷ,** *house*; **hen dŷ,** *old house*; **llythyrdy,** *post office*; (3) **cân,** *song*; **ei chân,** *her song*; **dychan,** *satire*. Most compounds are of type 2.

2.5.2 The mutations, a set of regular changes of initial consonant, though phonological in origin, are now determined not by the adjacent sounds but by the syntactical relations of the mutated word. The possible mutations are as follows:

| | | *Mutations* | |
Original consonant	Soft	Nasal	Spirant
p	b	mh	ph
t	d	nh	th
c	g	ngh	ch
b	f	m	
d	dd	n	
g	-	ng	
ll	l		
m	f		
rh	r		

Where no mutation is indicated, the consonant is unaffected; but under soft mutation **g** vanishes.

In some instances the spirant mutation appears not to conform with this table, for historical reasons. For instance one finds such a phrase as this: **gan panel o athrawon** . . . **a chan** . . . , *by a panel of teachers* . . . *and by* . . . . The mutation **chan** goes back to **can**, of which **gan** is itself a permanent mutation. Similarly **yma a thraw,** *here and there*: the dictionary form is **draw**.

It is helpful to remember that **dd, mh, nh, ngh, ng** and **ph** are not found at the beginning of unmutated words, **ch** only before **w**, and **f, l, r** and **th** very rarely. On the other hand **f** may come from **b** or **m**, **l** from **gl** or **ll**, **r** from **gr** or **rh**, and any vowel may result from a word beginning with **g**.

The circumstances in which mutation occurs are stated wherever possible under the category of word involved, viz.

> Nouns (4.7)
>
> Feminine adjectives (5.2.2)
>
> Adjectives and nouns after **yn** (5.1.2, 9.1, 10.2.2)
>
> After certain cardinal numerals (6.1.3)
>
> After ordinals (6.2.2)
>
> After the relative **a** (7.2)
>
> After possessives (7.3)
>
> After the negatives **na, ni** (7.2.3, 8.22.1)
>
> After certain adverbs (9.2)
>
> After certain prepositions (10.2.1)
>
> After certain conjunctions (11.2)

If a word always causes mutation this may be indicated by * soft, † spirant, § nasal; but something must be said about those instances which cannot easily be dealt with under parts of speech. The principal instances of such 'syntactical' mutation are:

(a) Adjectival genitives are softened like ordinary adjectives, e.g. **neuadd bentref,** *village hall* (**pentref**), **neuadd** being feminine. Occasionally even after masculine nouns.

(b) Nouns in apposition to proper names, e.g. **Dafydd frenin,** *King David* (**brenin**), and in reverse order, with feminine nouns, e.g. **y Forwyn Fair,** *the Virgin Mary*.

(c) Nouns and noun phrases used adverbially. Traditionally softening occurs only in the middle of a sentence, as in **Teimlasom gywilydd droeon . . .,** *We have felt shame at times* (**troeon**), but apart from some set phrases most writers now find it natural to soften such expressions even when they occur at the beginning.

(d) The verb is softened after a personal pronoun or pre-verbal particle, e.g. **chi gofiwch** or **fe gofiwch chi,** *you remember* (**cofiwch**).

(e) The object of a finite verb is softened: **dymunaf ddiolch,** *I wish to thank.* But **yr wyf yn dymuno diolch** (8.20.2), where **diolch** is a genitive dependent on the verb-noun **dymuno** and not a direct object.

(f) The predicate is softened after **oes** and **bu**; and so is **bod** whenever it is predicate.

(g) The subject is softened after an adverb, prepositional phrase or personal form of the verb, and so is an objective genitive: **mae gennyf ddiddordeb,** *I am interested* (10.5); **am ganiatáu imi ddefnyddio,** *for allowing me to use*; and cf. 10.5 for another example. Similarly after **dyma** and other words meaning *here is* and the like.

(h) Softening occurs after a parenthesis, e.g. **fe geir, fodd bynnag, ddigonedd o enghreifftiau;** but **digonedd** if **fodd bynnag** is omitted.

(i) There are some standing mutations. In some cases the radical forms have become obsolete, though they leave traces (cf. what is said earlier about **gan** and **chan**); in others both forms are found, without difference of meaning; in others the mutated form is a special use. Dictionaries vary in their treatment of them. *Geiriadur Prifysgol Cymru* enters under the mutated form only if the radical form is obsolete, though it distinguishes **beth**, *what*, from **peth**, *thing*. The similar **fodd**, *how*, must, however, be sought under **modd**, *manner*, and **fawr**, *not much, no great*, under **mawr**. In this it is followed by smaller dictionaries, even if they enter simple variants like **trwy/drwy** in both places.

The mutation of personal names is subject to severe limitations. Sir John Morris Jones says flatly that they are not mutated, and we find '**gan Gwilym Rhysiart**' in a book of 1773 and '**gan Megan Morgan**' and numerous other examples in books of today. Nevertheless, in a major work on the subject, *Y treigladau a'u cystrawen*, Professor T. J. Morgan contends that from a purely grammatical point of view proper names are no different from common nouns. Reverting to the older tradition he writes **gan Oronwy Owen, gan Ddafydd William**. Only un-Welsh forms are exempt, e.g. **gan Lloyd-Jones, yn Daniel Owen**. In Thomas Parry we find **gan Dafydd Jones o Drefriw** and **gan Ddafydd ap Gwilym** within a few lines; and on another page **a chan Ddafydd Jones**. It would be unwise therefore to exclude altogether the possibility of mutation, even on a title-page. For the permanent mutation of some surnames see 1.1.1.

Borrowed words and foreign place-names resist mutation so long as their alien origin is remembered: **un moment** and **y talent** (feminine) in the Bible (but **am foment** in a recent text); **gan panel** (**banel** nowadays) in the example in 1.2.4. Some Welshmen say **i Dwickenham**, but they may regard it as part of Wales.

2.5.3 Words beginning with a vowel prefix an **h** when preceded by certain words. This sometimes corresponds to a mutation, e.g. **ein Harglwydd**, *our Lord* (no mutation); **ei henw**, *her name* (spirant); **ei enw**, *his name* (soft mutation, but no **h**). For another change involving **h** see 2.7.

2.6 VARIATION OF VOWEL

2.6.1 Changes in the quality of a vowel take place:

(a) as a result of adding an ending;

(b) in the last syllable, under the influence of a following -**i**- or similar vowel, now lost;

(c) in the last syllable but one, under the influence of such a vowel in the last syllable;

(d) in the last syllable, under the influence of a now lost -**a**.

2.6.2 The possible changes are:

Root vowel	(a)	(b)	(c)	(d)
a		ai, ei, y	e, ei	
ae		ai		
ai	ei		ei, eu, ey	
au	eu			
aw	o	au, y	ew	
e		y	ei	
o		y		
oe		wy		
uw	u			
w	y	y		o
y				e

Examples: **iaith**, P **ieithoedd** (a); **bardd**, P **beirdd** (b); **arall**, P **eraill** (b) and (c); **gwyn**, F **gwen** (d). The changed vowel may be in the dictionary form, e.g. **prawf** 3PS of **profi**.

2.6.3 *Concordance*

Resulting vowel	Possible origin
ai	a
au	aw
e	a, y
ei	a, ai, e
eu	ai, au
ew	aw
ey	ai
o	aw, w
u	uw
wy	oe
y	a, aw, e, o, w

2.7 SPELLING

Since the beginning of printing spelling has been pretty stable, except for some uncertainty about doubled letters and a recent tendency to spell out words like **ochr, dwfn** as **ochor, dwfwn**. In some words **h** has been dropped after **ng, m, n** and **r**, unless the syllable beginning with **h** is stressed, e.g. **cyngor (cynghor)** P **cynghorion; cynnwrf, cynhyrfau; cynhyrfiad, cynyrfiadau**. A similar alternation occurs between vowels in words like **dihareb** P **diarhebion**. In some cases the **h** is not original but inserted by analogy.

Editions of old manuscripts may preserve spellings which rest on a different alphabet: see 2.1.1.

3 ARTICLES

3.1 DEFINITE

3.1.1 Welsh has only the definite article. When there is no article, the indefinite article must often be supplied in English. (But see 3.1.2.)

The article has three forms:

> **y** before a consonant
> **yr** before a vowel or **h**
> **'r** after a vowel

These forms apply to both genders, singular and plural.

3.1.2 The article is used sometimes in Welsh where it is not in English, e.g. **yn yr Eglwys,** *in church*. The reverse is commoner: in phrases like **achos y gadair wag** (*the case of the empty chair*) the first noun never has the article in Welsh.

4 NOUNS

4.1 FORM AND GENDER

Nouns may be masculine or feminine. There is some correspondence between form and gender in simple nouns, but the rules are not easy to remember, and there are many exceptions. Suffixes are much more clearly associated with gender, e.g. **-aeth** and **-fa** with F, **-ad** and **-dod** with M.

4.2 PLURAL

Nouns have number but no cases. Relations between nouns are indicated by preposi-tions, except the genitive (*of*) which is indicated by simple juxtaposition (cf. 3.1.2).

The plural, irrespective of gender, is formed in three ways:

(a) By adding an ending, with or without change of vowel (2.6). The principal endings are **-(i)aid, -(i)au, -edd, -i, -od, -oedd, -(i)on, -ydd**, e.g. **llyfr-au**, *books*; **ysgol-ion**, *school(s)*; **nant, nentydd**, *valley(s)*.

(b) By changing the vowel (2.6), e.g. **bardd, beirdd**, *poet(s)*; **gŵr, gwŷr**, *man, men*; (similarly compounds in **-wr**).

(c) By removing an ending, sometimes with reverse change of vowel, e.g. **plentyn, plant**, *child(ren)*.

Finding the singular in the dictionary is not difficult, provided one remembers the possibility of change of vowel, or even two, e.g. **bachgen**, P **bechgyn**. It is rarely necessary to form a plural, which is just as well, for no simple rules can be given. It is better to use a dictionary which gives plurals.

4.7 MUTATION

Feminine singular nouns undergo soft mutation after the article, e.g. **y wraig**, *the woman* (**gwraig**); **y ferch**, *the girl* (**merch**); but plural **y gwragedd**, without mutation. All nouns are softened by a preceding adjective.

5 ADJECTIVES

5.1 GENERAL

5.1.1 Most adjectives follow the noun.

5.1.2 An adjective used as a predicate is preceded by **yn*** (2.5.2), e.g. **nid yw'n debyg**, *it is not likely* (**tebyg**). The same applies to nouns. Expressions like **yn dyrrau**, *in(to) heaps*, if not adverbial (9.1), are to be regarded as predicates. On **yn Gymraeg** see 10.2.1.

5.2 ENDINGS

5.2.1 A few adjectives have different forms for the feminine singular. Rather more have plural forms, common in gender; but the masculine singular is sometimes used instead.

5.2.2 Where there is a distinct feminine, it is formed by internal change of vowel (cf. 2.6).

M	F
-w-	-o-
-y-	-e-

The initial consonant is softened (2.5.2) after the article or a noun.

5.2.3 The plural, when there is one, is formed by adding **-on** or **-ion**, or by change of vowel (2.6). The addition of **-ion** is accompanied by change of vowel, e.g. **tlws, tlysion**.

5.3 COMPARISON

5.3.1 The regular comparative ending is **-ach**, the superlative **-af**, added to the masculine form. There is also an 'equative' form **-ed** used to express *as . . . as, how . . .* and similar phrases. Comparatives cause no mutation.

5.3.2 Adjectives ending in **-b**, **-d**, **-g** change these to **-p-**, **-t-**, **-c-**, in the other degrees, e.g. **drud, druted, drutach, drutaf,** *dear*, etc. Some vowels change (2.6) e.g. **amlwg, amlycaf.**

5.3.3 As often happens, some of the commonest adjectives have irregular comparison, e.g. **da, gwell, gorau,** *good, better, best*; **hen, hŷn,** *old(er)*. Such forms will be found entered separately in the dictionary.

5.4 POSSESSIVES
See 7.3.1.

6 NUMERALS

6.1 CARDINAL

6.1.1 *Traditional forms*

1 **un**	11 **un ar ddeg**	21 **un ar hugain**
2 **dau, dwy**	12 **deuddeg**	39 **pedwar ar bymtheg ar**
3 **tri, tair**	13 **tri ar ddeg**	**hugain**
4 **pedwar, pedair**	14 **pedwar ar ddeg**	40 **deugain**
5 **pum(p)**	15 **pymtheg**	50 **deg a deugain, hanner**
6 **chwe(ch)**	16 **un ar bymtheg**	**cant**
7 **saith**	17 **dau ar bymtheg**	60 **tri(u)gain**
8 **wyth**	18 **tri ar bymtheg,**	80 **pedwar ugain**
9 **naw**	**deunaw**	100 **cant**
10 **de(n)g**	19 **pedwar ar bymtheg**	101 **cant ac un**
	20 **ugain**	120 **cant ac ugain,**
		chweugain

140 **cant a deugain, saith ugain**
160 **cant a thrigain, wyth ugain**
180 **cant a phedwar ugain, naw ugain**
200 **deucan(t)**
300 **trichan(t)**
400 etc. **pedwar** (etc.) **can(t)**
1000 **mil**

6.1.2 A simplified method of expressing numbers is often used nowadays, especially in numeration, viz.

11–19 **un deg un–un deg naw**
30 **tri deg**
40 etc. **pedwar** (etc.) **deg**

6.1.3 The noun following a cardinal number may follow immediately (in fact in the middle of a compound numeral) in the singular, or may be joined to it by the preposition **o***, in which case the plural is used, e.g. **pedwar llyfr ar ddeg** or **pedwar ar ddeg o lyfrau,** *fourteen books.*

Some numerals cause mutation (2.5.2), unless otherwise stated, universally, viz.

un, soft: F nouns, except ll. rh; nasal: **blynedd** and **blwydd** (*years*) only.
dau, dwy, soft. They themselves are mutated by y.
tri, spirant.
pum, nasal: **blynedd, blwydd, diwrnod.**

chwe, spirant.

saith, wyth, soft: words beginning with **p, t, c**; nasal: **blynedd, blwydd, diwrnod.**

naw, nasal: **blynedd, blwydd, diwrnod.**

deng, soft: words beginning with **g**; nasal: **blynedd, blwydd** and words begining with **d**. (Note the form **deng,** which occurs also before original **m** and **n**.)

ugain and its derivatives, nasal: **blynedd, blwydd, diwrnod.**

can, nasal: **blynedd, blwydd.**

6.2 ORDINAL

6.2.1

1 cyntaf	6 chweched	11 unfed ar ddeg
2 ail	7 seithfed	12 deuddegfed
3 tryd|ydd -edd	8 wythfed	20 ugeinfed and similarly its
4 pedwerydd, pedwaredd	9 nawfed	derivatives
5 pumed	10 degfed	100 canfed
		1000 milfed

Compound ordinals follow the pattern of **unfed ar ddeg** in that only one element has the ordinal form, e.g. *93rd,* **trydydd(-edd) ar ddeg a phedwar ugain.**

Nowadays ordinals above 40 are little used, the new style cardinals being used, after the noun, instead.

6.2.2 Ordinals are adjectives, but do not all have the same mutating effect, viz.

cyntaf follows the noun
ail precedes the noun, soft mutation

All others precede the noun but mutate only feminines.

6.3 FIGURES

Plain figures are used for cardinals in the usual way. Ordinals may be represented by figures with ordinal terminations attached, e.g. **5ed, 11fed, 3ydd.** Roman figures are usually ordinal: **Edwart IV (Edwart y Pedwerydd).**

6.4 DATES

6.4.1 The months are:

**Ionawr, Chwefror, Mawrth, Ebrill, Mai, Mehefin,
Gorffennaf, Awst, Medi, Hydref, Tachwedd, Rhagfyr**

Note that **Mawrth** also means *Tuesday* and **Hydref,** *Autumn.*

6.4.2 Days are reckoned in ordinals, years in cardinals, viz.

17 March 1953 **Yr ail ar bymtheg o Fawrth (2.5.2) mil naw cant a thri ar ddeg a deugain (or mil naw cant pum deg tri,** or **a thri)**

Numerals are subject to mutation, e.g. after prepositions, but apart from this, expressions of time which involve only years should not cause difficulty.

7 PRONOUNS

7.1 DEMONSTRATIVE AND INDEFINITE

7.1.1 These and their corresponding adjectives are adequately given in the dictionary. So far as the plural forms are not given, they are the same as those of nouns and adjectives, e.g. **y llall, y lleill,** *the other(s).*

Dim, *anything*, which is frequent in negative sentences (8.22.2) especially in conversation, and thus acquires the meaning *nothing*, *not*, combines with **o** (*of*) and its personal forms to make **mo**, **mohonof**, etc. (8.22.3). For details of forms see 10.2.1. After the verb, a common position, it has the mutated form **ddim**.

7.2 RELATIVE

7.2.1 These are few in number and simple in form, but the constructions are more complicated.

> **a***, *who(m)*, *which*, is used universally.
>
> **y(r)**, with the same meaning, is used where the relative is not subject or object.

e.g. **G. J. Williams, a ddarllenodd y gwaith**, *G. J. Williams, who read the work*; **y peth a welaist**, *the thing that you have seen*; **y gwledydd yr** (or **a**) **es iddynt**, *the countries I went to*; **y dyn y gwelais (a welais) ei dŷ**, *the man whose house I saw*. In the last two sentences **a** and **y(r)** amount simply to particles indicating a relative sentence; the particular sense is conveyed by the following pronoun or possessive, viz. **iddynt**, *to them*; **ei dŷ**, *his house*. (Those who are interested will find parallels in Balkan languages, in Maltese and in Chaucer.)

7.2.2 A relative sentence is obligatory when the subject, object or adverbial complement is emphasised, e.g. **Fi a'i gwelodd hi gyntaf**, *I (am the one) who saw it first;* **y pethau hyn a garaf**, *these (are the) things I love*; **Ar gyfer plant ysgol y bwriadwyd y Geiriadur hwn**, *It was for the use of school children that this Dictionary was intended.* Not that the sentences need necessarily be translated so in every case.

7.2.3 The corresponding negative forms are **na(d)** and **ni(d)**. The form **na(d)**, formerly restricted to certain constructions, is now used in any type of sentence and is commoner than **ni(d)**. Both **na** and **ni** produce the spirant mutation of **p, t, c**, and the soft mutation of **b, d, g, ll, rh, m** (2.5.2).

7.3 PERSONAL

7.3.1 Personal pronouns have a large number of forms some of which they share with possessives:

			S			*P*	
	1	2	3*m* 3*f*	1	2	3
Simple	mi/i	ti	ef hi	ni	ch(w)i	hwy(nt)
Post-vocalic	'm	'th	'i/'w/-s	'n	'ch	'u/'w/-s
Possessive	fy§	dy*	ei* eit†	ein	eich	eu

7.3.2 The simple forms are used as subject, as object, to reinforce a possessive or post-vocalic form and after a few prepositions, e.g. **Chwi gofiwch**, *You remember*; **Yr wyf fi**, *I am*; **Mab i bwy wyt ti?**, *Whose son are you?*; **Credwch chwi fi**, *Believe you me*; **Fy Nghymru i**, *My Wales*; **â mi**, *with me*. Note that **hi** frequently means *it*. As object, as reinforcements and in certain circumstances as subject, **mi** and **ti** undergo soft mutation (2.5.2).

7.3.3 The post-vocalic forms serve both as object and as possessives: **fe'i gwelais**, *I saw him*; **Hughes a'i Fab**, *Hughes and Son*; but **'w** is always possessive, being used after **i**: **i'w fab**, *to his son*. It mutates or not according as **ei** and **eu** do; **'i** as object does not cause mutation. The termination **-s** is added to **na, ni, oni** and **pe** to express the object, e.g. **Nis gwelais hwy,** *I did not see them.* An **h-** is prefixed to the initial vowel of any word which follows **'m, 'i** (obj.), **'i** (*her*), **'w** (*her*), **'n, 'u, 'w** (*their*).

7.3.4   **Ei** (*her*), **ein,** and **eu** aspirate a following vowel, e.g. **ein Harglwydd,** *our Lord.* Owing to the frequent occurrence of the verb-noun or infinitive the possessives have often the force of an object or subject, e.g. **Yr ydym ni wedi ei argraffu,** *We have printed it* (*we are after its printing*); **am fy mod . . . ,** *since I am . . .* (*by my being*). See further in section 8 and other examples in 1.2.1, 1.3.1, 1.5, 1.7.3, and for possessives with compound prepositions 10.4.

7.3.5   The possessives are not used as pronouns. For these the noun **eiddo** (*property*) is used with personal suffixes: **eidd|of, -ot, -o, -i; -om, -och, -ynt,** *mine,* etc.

7.4   MUTATIONS

The effect of personal pronouns is given in 7.3. Of other pronouns, **ambell, aml, y fath, holl, naill, rhyw** and its derivatives and **ychydig** cause soft mutation (2.5.2).

8   VERBS

8.1   STRUCTURE

8.1.1   The verb has two complete sets of forms, the simple tenses, commoner in writing than in speech, and a parallel set of periphrastic tenses (8.20) got by using the tenses of the verb **bod,** *to be,* with the verb-noun. Pronouns are not needed, but they are often used, expecially with the verb *to be,* e.g. **Cefais (Fe gefais i) lawer iawn o help gan,** *I got a great deal of help from.*

8.1.2   The endings of nearly all verbs are the same, the exceptions being the contracted verbs and a certain number of irregular ones.

8.2   PRESENT/FUTURE
8.2.1   *Endings*

-af, -i, see 8.2.2; -wn, -wch, -ant

8.2.2   An **-a-** in the stem changes to **-e-** in the 2nd person. The 3rd person of some verbs ends in **-a,** but in most cases it has no ending but a different vowel from the 1st person, viz. **a > ai, ei; ae > y; ei > ai; o > aw, wy, y; y > w;** e.g. **collaf, cyll; profaf, prawf; atebaf, etyb; arhosaf, erys** (2.6, 2.7).

8.2.3   In a number of verbs with **-a-** in the stem, the verb-noun has **-e-,** e.g. **paraf, peri; safaf, sefyll;** and in some with **-y-** the verb noun has **-w-** e.g. **cyffyrddaf, cyffwrdd.**

8.2.4   The meaning of the simple tense is usually future, the present meaning being conveyed by periphrastic forms.

8.3   IMPERFECT
8.3.1   *Endings*

-wn, -it -ai; -em, -ech, -ent

8.3.2   An **-a-** in the stem is changed to **-e-** before **-it.**
8.3.3   See 8.2.3.
8.3.4   The meaning is usually past habitual or conditional.

8.4   PAST (PERFECT AND PLUPERFECT)
8.4.1   *Perfect*

-ais, aist, -odd; -asom, -asoch, -asant

8.4.2 -a- changes to -e- before -ais, -aist. A few verbs omit the -a- of the ending in the plural. 3rd person -as, -es, -is, are occasionally found.

8.4.3 See 8.2.3.

8.4.4 The meaning can be either simple past or perfect, with a tendency to substitute periphrastic forms for the perfect.

8.4.5 *Pluperfect*

-aswn, etc. as imperfect

The -a- is omitted in a few verbs.

8.4.6 See 8.2.3.

8.4.7 The meaning is more often than not simple conditional.

8.5 FUTURE
See 8.2.

8.7 SUBJUNCTIVE

8.7.1 *Present*

-wyf, ych, -o; -om, -och, -ont

8.7.2 *Imperfect*

-wn, -it, -ai; -em, -ech, -ynt/ent

8.7.3 A -b-, -d-, -g- at the end of the stem is changed in many verbs to -p-, -t-, -c-. This is the effect of the -h- with which the endings once began. But in most verbs the imperfect is indistinguishable from the imperfect indicative.

8.7.4 The subjunctive is used in wishes: **Duw a'ch bendithio**, *God bless you*, to express purpose, and in indefinite and conditional sentences.

8.7.5 See 8.2.3.

8.11 VERB-NOUN

8.11.1 The uses of the verb-noun are so many and varied that it seems better to use the Welsh term and not 'infinitive'. There will of course be many instances where an infinitive or gerund will be the natural translation, but it is not always so, particularly when it is preceded by a possessive. It is also important that it is always a noun, construed as such.

8.11.2 Most commonly it follows prepositions in a variety of uses, e.g. **i roi enghraifft**, *to give an example*; **er eu bod**, *although they are (in spite of their being)*; **am/trwy fy mod**, *because I am*; **cof yn aros**, *a lingering memory*; **dan fynd, wrth fynd**, *while going*; **wedi mynd**, *having gone*; **ar fynd**, *about to go*; **heb wybod**, *without knowing*; **gan wneuthur ohonot** (10.4), *since you have done it*; **wedi canu'r gloch**, *when the bell rang (after the ringing of the bell)*; **wedi ei drosi (throsi) i'r Gymraeg**, *translated into Welsh (after its turning)*; **i'w hanfon**, *to be sent*. See also 8.20.

8.11.3 It can also be the subject or object of a verb or in apposition to or qualification of a noun, e.g. **Un o effeithiau yw fod geiriau fel 'braf' yn cadw'r gysefin**, *One of the effects is that words like 'braf' keep the radical*; **arwydd fy mod wedi clywed**, *a sign that I had heard*; **papur sgrifennu**, *writing paper*; **dywedasant eu bod yn gweithio**, *they said they were working*; **credir i Ddafydd gael ei eni rhwng 1320 a 1330**, *it is believed that Dafydd was born between 1320 and 1330*. See also 8.17.3.

8.11.4   The verb-noun not infrequently replaces a finite form, sometimes in isolation, e.g. **gobeithio**, *I hope so*; more often the later members of a series, e.g. **cododd ef
a mynd allan**, *he got up and went out*.

8.11.5   The endings are various, e.g. **dysg|u, cofi|o, clyw|ed, tro|i**, to cite the com-
monest. Often, however, there is no ending, or the verb-noun is shorter than the stem,
e.g. **meddwl**, present **meddyli|af**. The stem-vowel may be changed (8.2.3) or the stem
telescoped, as in **cymryd**, *to accept*, stem **cymer-**, or expanded, as in **taro**, *to strike*; past
trawais. The rules are complicated and of no practical use in the present context.

8.12   VERBAL ADJECTIVES

There are not reckoned to be any participles, recourse being had to periphrases with
the verb-noun (8.11.2); but the derivative in **-edig** (13.3) is in effect a verbal adjective,
usually passive, sometimes active. The derivative in **-adwy** (ibid.) could be counted as
a gerundive. See also 10.5.

8.16   IMPERSONAL

8.16.1   These are often called passive, and more often than not are so translated in
English. The past in particular is common on title-pages where English would have a
passive participle, e.g. **golygwyd**, *edited*, and the agent is expressed by **gan**, *by*. But
there is only one form to each tense; what would in English be the subject is the object
in Welsh, e.g. **fe'm dysgir**, *I am taught* (cf. **fe'm dysg**, *he teaches me*); and they can be
formed from intransitive verbs, e.g. **ar yr hwn yr eisteddid y dydd**, *on which one sat by day*.
The present subjunctive is often used as a general imperative, e.g. **gweler**, *see*.

8.16.2
> *Present:* **-ir**
> *Imperfect:* **-id**
> *Past:* **-wyd**
> *Pluperfect:* **-asid/-esid**
> *Present subjunctive:* **-er**

8.16.3   **-a-** changes to **-e-** before **-ir, -id**. Conversely the verb-noun may have **-e-**
instead of **-a-**.

8.17   AUXILIARIES

8.17.1   A number of verbs are used idiomatically, apart from their ordinary meanings, in the formation of various tenses.

8.17.2   **bod**, *to be* (see also 8.20)
> *Present:* **(yd)wyf, (yd)wyt, (yd)yw/mae/oes/sy(dd); ydym/ŷm, ydych/ŷch,
> ydynt/ŷnt/maent/sy(dd)**

Apart from local differences of usage, the alternative forms are used in different
contexts, but this only affects the comprehension of Welsh in the case of **sy(dd)**. This
is a relative form meaning *who/which is/are*, and is used also when the subject is
emphasised, whatever the person **(y) fi sydd wedi ennill**, *I've won* (*It is I who have won*).
Despite the existence of a future tense the present can have a future meaning.

> *Present habitual/Future:* **byddaf**, etc. (8.2.1)
> *Imperfect:* **oeddwn, oeddit, (yd)oedd**, etc.
> *Past habitual:* **byddwn**, etc. (8.3.1)
> *Past (Perfect):* **bûm, buost, bu; buom, buoch, buont**
> *Pluperfect:* **buaswn**, etc.
> *Present subjunctive:* **b(ydd)wyf**, etc.

Imperfect subjunctive: **byddwn**, etc. or **bawn, bait, bai; baem, baech, baent**

Bawn etc. combine with **pe(d)**, *if,* to make **petawn**, etc. So also **petaswn** for **pe buaswn**.

Impersonal forms are mostly regular, on the roots **bydd-, oedd-** and **bu-** respectively. There are also:

Present: (yd)ys

Present habitual: **byddys**

Many parts of **bod** are preceded by the untranslated particle **y(r)**.

8.17.3 cael, *to get* (8.19.4)

The present tense, with the verb-noun; makes a coloured future, e.g. **A gawn ni fynd i mewn?**, *Shall we go in?*, or indicates permission: **A gawn ni ddod i mewn?**, *May we come in?* Note that the verb-noun has the soft mutation.

Any tense, followed by a possessive and the verb-noun, expresses the passive, e.g. **cafodd ef ei sgrifennu,** *it was written.*

8.17.4 darfod, *to happen* (8.18.1)

The past **darfu,** *it happened,* is used with **i** and the appropriate pronoun, followed by the verb-noun, as the equivalent of a past tense, e.g. **darfu i mi ysgrifennu,** *I wrote (It happened to me to write).*

In indirect speech one may have **darfod,** but the usual equivalent is the idiom illustrated in the last example in 8.11.3. and in 10.5, without **darfod.**

8.17.5 gwneuthur, gwneud, *to do* (8.19.2)

Used much as in English, and also to express intention, e.g. **A wnewch chwi roi help llaw i mi?**, *Will you give me a helping hand?*

8.17.6 peidio (â), *to refrain (from)*

Used in the imperative and verb-noun as the equivalent of a negative, e.g. **tadl gref dros beidio â'u treiglo,** *a strong argument for not mutating them.* See further 8.22.4.

8.18 COMPOUNDS OF **bod** AND CONTRACTED VERBS

8.18.1 Canfod, cydnabod, darganfod, cyfarfod, darfod (see also 8.17.4), gorfod, hanfod follow the conjunction of **bod**, e.g. **canfod:** present **canfyddaf, cenfydd** (8.17.2).

8.18.2 Adnabod and gwybod form certain tenses from other stems, and share other peculiarities, viz.

adnabod

Present: **adwaen, adwaenost, edwyn; adwaen-om, -och, -ant**

Imperfect: **adwaenwn,** etc.

Present subjunctive: **adnapwyf,** etc.

Imperfect subjunctive: **adnapwn,** etc.

Impersonal present: **adwaenir**

Impersonal subjunctive: **adnaper**

gwybod

Present: **gwn, gwyddost, gŵyr, gwydd-om,** etc.

Imperfect: **gwyddwn**

Impersonal present: gwyddys/gwŷs

Other tenses like **adnabod.**

8.18.3 In verbs whose stem ends in **-o** or **-ha-** an ending may coalesce, e.g. **trof** for **troaf** from **troi, troesom** for **troasom;** similarly **parhaf, parhewch** (8.2.2). The 3PS of the present may be peculiar; try, **para/pery,** likewise **rhy(dd)/dyry** from **rho(dd)i;** and **troed** and **rhoed** are alternative forms for the past impersonal.

8.18.4   C(aff)ael (see also 8.17.3) has come contracted forms. The tenses are:

Present: caf, cei, caiff; cawn, cewch, cânt

Imperfect: cawn, cait, câi, caem, etc.

Past: cefais/ces, cefaist/cest, cafodd/cadd; cawsom, etc.

Pluperfect: cawswn, etc.

Subjunctive: caffwyf, etc.; caffwn, etc.

Impersonal: ce(ff)ir

            ceid

            cafwyd/caed

            cawsid

            caffer

            ce(ff)id

8.19   OTHER IRREGULARITIES

8.19.1   dyfod, dod, *to come*

Present: deuaf, etc.; or dof, doi, daw; down, dowch, dônt

Imperfect: deuwn, etc.; or down, doit, dôi, doem, etc.

Past: deuthum, daethost, daeth; daethom, etc.

Pluperfect: daethwn, etc.

Present subjunctive: delwyf, etc.

Impersonal: deuir

           deuid/doid

           daethpwyd/deuwyd

           daethid/delsid

           deler; delid

8.19.2   gwneud, gwneuthur, *to do* (see also 8.17.5); myn(e)d, *to go*

Present: gwn|af, -ei, -a; -awn, -ewch, -ânt, *I do*

        af, etc., *I go*

Imperfect: (gwn)awn, -ait, -âi; -aem, etc.

Past: (gwn)euthum, like deuthum (8.19.1.)

    also 1PS (gwn)es, 2PS (gwn)est

Pluperfect: (gwn)aethwn, etc.

Present subjunctive: (gwn)elwyf, etc.

Imperfect subjunctive: (gwn)elwn, etc.

Impersonal: (gwn)eir

           (gwn)eid

           (gwn)aethpwyd/(gwn)aed

           (gwn)aethid/(gwn)elsid

           (gwn)eler; (gwn)elid

8.20   PERIPHRASTIC

8.20.1   There are periphrastic forms for every tense. They are formed by using the appropriate tenses of **bod** (8.17.2) as an auxiliary, and as **bod** has more forms than other verbs, the periphrastic tenses are sometimes more precise than the simple ones, which they have to a great extent supplanted in conversation.

8.20.2   *Present*

Present of bod + yn + verb-noun

Expresses both the continuous present (its natural meaning) and the simple present, as in **Ydyw ef yn aros ym Mhentref-du?** (*Does it stop at Pentref-du?*). Like the simple form it can have a future meaning, but see also 8.20.3.

8.20.3 *Present habitual/Future*

Present habitual/Future of **bod** + **yn** + verb-noun

8.20.4 *Imperfect*

Imperfect of **bod** + **yn** + verb-noun

Tends to be used for the past continuous, leaving the simple form for the conditional and habitual. (Cf. also 8.20.5.)

8.20.5 *Imperfect habitual*

Imperfect Habitual of **bod** + **yn** + verb-noun

8.20.6 *Perfect*

Present of **bod** + **wedi** + verb-noun

Usually has a perfect meaning: cf. 8.4.4.

8.20.7 *Perfect habitual or continuous*

Perfect of **bod** + **yn** + verb-noun

8.20.8 *Pluperfect*

Imperfect of **bod** + **wedi** + verb-noun

The usual way of expressing the pluperfect, the simple form having a conditional sense, except in subordinate clauses.

8.21 INTERROGATIVE

The interrogative **a***, is liable to confusion with the relative (7.2.1) and other partial homonyms such as **a**, *and*. (See also 8.22.2.)

8.22 NEGATIVE

8.22.1 The negatives **ni(d)**, **na(d)**, **na(c)** are a little confusing: nowadays **ni(d)** is chiefly used in statements; **na(d)** in relative and other subordinate clauses, so that it is equivalent to *who . . . not*, *that . . . not* as well as plain *not*; **na(c)** in answers and prohibitions, and for *nor*.

More important, they cause mutations, the spirant mutation of p, t, c, and the soft mutation of b, d, g, ll, rh, m. Nid also means *it is not*, in which sense it occurs before consonants.

8.22.2 The negative **ni(d)** is reduced in conversational style to d- or omitted altogether, **ddim** (*anything*) being inserted by way of compensation. Similarly **a** (8.21) is often omitted. In both cases the mutation remains: hence, **Ddeui di gyda mi? Wn i ddim**, *Are you coming with me? I don't know.* The omitted ni or a may be represented by an apostrophe.

8.22.3 Mo(ho)no, etc. (7.1.1), literally *nothing of him*, etc., are frequently simply an emphatic negative, e.g. **nid beirniad cymdeithasol mono**, (whatever else he is) *he is not a social critic.*

8.22.4 Negation is often expressed by **heb** (*without*) or **peidio** (*to refrain*, 8.17.6), e.g. **beth sydd yn newyddion a pheth sydd heb fod**, *what is news and what is not*; **yn amlach na pheidio**, *more often than not.*

8.24 SYNTAX
The 3PS is often used instead of the plural.

9 ADVERBS

9.1 FORMATION
These may be formed from most adjectives, positive, comparative and superlative, by prefixing **yn** (5.1.2) which softens (2.5.2) initial consonants other than **ll**, **rh**, e.g. **yn dda**, *well*; **yn well**, *better.*

9.3 MUTATIONS
The adverbs **cyn**, **go**, **mor**, **pur**, **rhy** soften (2.5.2) initial consonants, except **ll**, **rh**. **Tra** turns **c**, **p**, **t** into spirants.

10 PREPOSITIONS

10.2 SIMPLE PREPOSITIONS: FORMS AND SYNTAX
10.2.1 Most of the common prepositions, viz.: **am**, **ar**, **at**, **er**, **i**, **gan**, **heb**, **o**, **rhag**, **rhwng**, **tan** (**dan**), **tros**, **trwy**, **wrth**, **yn**, have special personal forms which are used instead of the basic form followed by a personal pronoun (10.3). All the above, except **er**, **rhag**, **rhwng** and **yn**, soften the following consonant: **er**, **rhag**, **rhwng** have no effect, **yn** nasalises (2.5.2). In most contexts *in Welsh* is not **yng Nghymraeg** but **yn Gymraeg**. This may be for **yn y Gymraeg**, but cf. 5.2 and 9.1.

10.2.2 The remaining simple prepositions except for **â** (*with*, etc.), have no effect on the following noun and are not used with personal pronouns at all. **A** causes spirant mutation: for its use with pronouns see 7.3.

10.3 PERSONAL FORMS
10.3.1 The possible endings are:

S		P	
1	-af/-of/-yf	1	-om/-ym
2	-at/-ot/-yt	2	-och/-ych
3	M -(dd)o, F (dd)i	3	-(dd)ynt

10.3.2 Combined with the prepositions, in the order of 10.2.1, they make e.g. **amdanaf**, **arnaf**, **ataf**, **erof**, **iddo** (3 only; otherwise **i mi**, etc.), **gennyf** (but **ganddo**), **hebof**, **ohonof**, **rhagof**, **rhyngof**, **o danaf**, **trosof** (3P **trosto**, etc.), **trwof**, **wrthyf**, **ynof**. (On **mohonof**, etc. see 8.22.3.)

10.4 COMPOUND PREPOSITIONS
These end either in a preposition, in which case they behave like the preposition they end with, e.g. **oddi wrth**, *from*, making **oddi wrthyf**, *from me*, or in a noun. Those

that end with a noun may govern personal pronouns, but these become possessives as in E *in his stead*, e.g. **ar fy ôl**, *after me*; **o'm hôl** (7.3.2), *behind me*. (Note that in **i mewn** there is no softening of the **m**.)

10.5 IDIOMS

There are numerous idioms with prepositions. There are, for instance, the common types like **y mae gennyf i**, *I have* (*there is by me*), **y mae arnaf i eisiau**, *I want*, **y mae'n dda gennyf**, *I like*, and there are the trickier ones by which the prepositions **i** and **o** have come in one type of sentence to indicate the logical subject of a dependent verb-noun and usually the past tense, **cyn i'r rhyfel ddechrau** (note the mutation), *before the war began*, or **cyn dechrau o'r rhyfel** (cf. 8.11.2). Note also **nodedig o hynaws**, *remarkably genial*.

Yn makes phrases or compounds that serve as adjectival past participles. Though normally written as one word, they tend to be entered in the dictionary under the second element, e.g. **ynghadw**, *preserved*, under **cadw**, *to keep*; **ynghlo**, *locked up*, under **clo**, *a lock*.

11 CONJUNCTIONS

11.1 SYNTAX

11.1.1 Conjunctions are a varied class. Apart from coordinating conjunctions like **a(c)**, *and*; **ond**, *but*, and so on, there are some which are regularly followed by a verb in the indicative, perhaps also in the subjunctive with a different shade of meaning, e.g. **pan**, *when*, *whenever*, while others, like **gan**, are sometimes prepositions and sometimes conjunctions. For instance **oherwydd** (*because, on account of*) is regularly followed by the indicative when the reason follows the main statement (*for* in literary English), e.g. **Yr oedd y plant yn effro gyda'r wawr, oherwydd disgwylid . . .**, *The children were awake at dawn, for it was expected . . . .* Apart from this it is construed in affirmative sentences with the verb-noun, e.g. **oherwydd fy mod**, *because I am*, where **oherwydd** is just as much a preposition as it is in **oherwydd y dull y trinir geiriau**, *on account of the manner in which words are treated*. But in negative clauses like **oherwydd na siaredais**, *because I did not speak*, a finite verb is always used. This pattern is common in Welsh.

a(c) must be translated *with* in **a'i geg ar agor**, *with his mouth open*, and omitted in phrases like **ond—a dweud y gwir—**, *but—to tell the truth—*.

11.1.2 Other prepositions are converted into conjunctions by the addition of **y(r)**, e.g. **er y**, *although*; **wedi y**, *after*. As with the relative, the negative of **y** is **na**. By itself **y(r)** can mean *that* and **na(d)** *that not*. There is another **na** (**nag** before vowels) which means *than*.

11.2 MUTATIONS

Some conjunctions cause mutation, viz.

Soft	*Spirant*
neu	a
oni (before **b, d, g, ll, rh**)	na
pan	o (*if*)
tra (forms of **bod** only)	**oni** (before **p, t, c**)

12 PARTICLES

There are a number of words, viz. **a, fe, mi, y(r)**, which besides their other meanings are used before verbs or to begin sentences (which is often the same thing) but when so used have no meaning of their own, e.g. **Ni a welsom, Fe** (or **Mi**) **welsom ni**, *we saw*. **Fe** and **mi** here are not pronouns but are used before all persons of the verb. **Y(r)** is chiefly used before parts of **bod**, *to be*.

13 WORD-FORMATION

13.1 GENERAL

Derivatives are freely formed in Welsh. Even the best dictionaries do not list all the words that may be encountered, though *Y Geiriadur Mawr* has lists of prefixes and suffixes. The most important of these, with the complications that they may cause, are dealt with below.

13.2 PREFIXES

A number of these are still apt to form compounds, viz.

> **ail-**: (1) again, e.g. **ailwerthu**, *to re-sell*; (2) secondary, e.g. **ail-law**, *second-hand*. Softens.
>
> **ang(h)-, am(h)-, an-**: negative. The variants are due to the effect of **an-** on initial consonants: it softens **b, g** and **m**, and nasalises **c, d, p** and **t**. (See 2.5.2 and 2.7.) The results are complicated: **anh-** results from **an + h-**, **anhr-** from **an + tr-**, while **an + t-** gives **annh-**; **an-** followed by a vowel may presuppose an original beginning with **g-** or **h-** as well as with the vowel in question.
>
> **cam-**: wrong, e.g. **camargraff**, *misprint*.
>
> **cy-, cyd-, cyf-, cyng-, cym-, cyn-**: together (*co-, com-, con-, fellow-*) e.g. **cydweithred**, *cooperation* (**gweithred**); **cyfateb**, *to correspond* (**ateb**); **cynnwrf**, *commotion* (**twrf**).
>
> **cyn-**: *former, ex-*, e.g. **cyn-filwr**, *ex-soldier* (**milwr**). Softens.
>
> **di-**: negative. A very prolific formative, mainly producing adjectives from nouns. The resulting meaning is often wide, e.g. **diateb** may mean *unanswering, unanswered, unanswerable* or *not bound to answer*. The original may be a phrase, e.g. **di-droi'n-ôl**, *resolute* (**troi'n ôl**, *to turn back*). Note the softening.
>
> **gor-**: extreme degree, excess, e.g. **gor-ddweud**, *overstate(ment)* (**dweud**, *to say*).
>
> **ym-** imparts a reflexive or reciprocal meaning to the verb or makes it intransitive, e.g. **ymgynnal**, *to hold out, to last* (**cynnal**, *to uphold*). The meaning of some of the older compounds is not obvious, e.g. **ymosod**, *to attack* (**gosod**, *to place*), so try the dictionary first. The prefix softens.

13.3 SUFFIXES

These are freely used to form one part of speech from another. The meanings given in the following list are not the only ones, but they are the most usual.

> **-fa**: place, e.g. **(y)storfa**, *store*.
>
> **-deb**: abstract nouns from adjectives, e.g. **cyfrifoldeb**, *responsibility*. Frequent after **-ol** and **-lon**. Similarly **-ineb**, e.g. **doethineb**, *wisdom*.

-wch: the same, e.g. **tegwch**, *beauty*. Frequent after -gar.

-(i)ad, P -(i)adau: nouns of action or result, from verbs, e.g. **mudiad**, *movement* (-iad, P -iaid denotes an agent).

-dod, -tod: like -deb, e.g. **Cymreictod**, *Welshness*.

-edd: abstract nouns from adjectives or nouns, e.g. **magnetedd**, *magnetism*.

-aidd: adjectives, e.g. **algebraidd**, *algebraic*; **plentynnaidd**, *childish*.

-ydd: agent or instrument, e.g. **golygydd**, *editor*; **golchydd**, *detergent*.

-rwydd: like -deb, e.g. **odrwydd**, *oddity*. Frequent after -ig.

-eg: nouns denoting languages, arts and sciences, e.g. **Saesneg**, *English*; **arianneg**, *finance*.

-edig: verbal adjectives corresponding to passive or active participles, e.g. **helaethedig**, *enlarged*; **siomedig**, *disappointing*.

-(i)og: adjectives, mostly from nouns, e.g. **geiriog**, *wordy*.

-ni: like -deb, e.g. **oerni**, *cold*.

-(i)ol: adjectives from nouns and verbs, e.g. **geiriol**, *verbal*.

-lon: adjectives from nouns (*-ful*), e.g. **ffyddlon**, *faithful*.

-(i)o: verbs, e.g. **sganio**, *to scan*.

-gar: adjectives, much like -lon, e.g. **diolchgar**, *grateful*.

-der, -ter: like -deb, e.g. **mwynder**, *gentleness*; **dwyster**, *importance*.

-wr: agent, occasionally instrument, e.g. **addysgwr**, *educationalist*.

-us: adjectives from nouns, e.g. **niferus**, *numerous*.

-iant: nouns denoting activity, e.g. **moliant**, *praise*.

-(i)aeth: nouns denoting action, quality, office, e.g. **amcaniaeth**, *conjecture*; **amrywiaeth**, *diversity*; **arolygiaeth**, *editorship*.

-yddiaeth (see preceding) frequently answers to *-ology*.

-adwy: possibility, e.g. **gwerthadwy**, *saleable*.

GLOSSARY

aelod, *member*

anghyhoeddedig, *unpublished*

ailargraffiad, *reprint*

allan o brint, *out of print*

anfon, *send*

araith, *speech*

archeb, *order* (1.8.7)

argraffiad, *edition, printing* (1.5)

argraffwyd, *printed*

atodiad, *appendix, supplement*

awdur, *author*

barddoniaeth, *poetry*

i'w barhau, *to be continued*

blwyddiadur, blwyddlyfr, *yearbook*

blwyddyn, *year*

blynyddol, *annual*

casgliad, *collection*

clawr caled, *hard back*

clawr papur, *paper back*

crynodeb, *summary*

cydweithrediad, *cooperation* (1.6.2)

cyfeiriad, *address* (1.8.7)

cyfieithiad, *translation* (1.2.1)

cyfnewid, *exchange*

cyfnodolyn, *periodical*

cyfraniad, *contribution* (1.8.7)

cyfres, *series* (1.7.1, 1.8.4)

cyfrol, *volume* (1.4.1, 1.7.2, 1.8.4)

cyngor, *council*

cyhoeddir, *is published*

cyhoeddwyd, wedi'u cyhoeddi, *published*

cylchgrawn, *magazine*

cymdeithas, *society*

cymreigio, *translate into Welsh*

cynhadledd, *conference*

cywiro, *to correct*

chwarterol, *quarterly* (1.8.2)

chwedl, *story*

detholedig, *select(ed)*
diwygiedig, *revised*

eglurhaol, *explanatory*
enghraifft, *example, sample*

ganwyd, *was born*
geiriadur, *dictionary*
gohebiaeth, *correspondence*
golygiad, *editing* (1.8.3)
golygwyd, *edited* (1.2.1)
golygydd, *editor* (1.8.3)
golygyddiaeth, *editorship* (1.8.3)
gwaith, *work*
gwasg, *press* (1.6.1)
gyda chyfarchion, *with compliments,*
   complimentary

hanes, *history*
helaethedig, *enlarged*

lluniwyd, *compiled*
llyfr, *book* (1.7.2)
llyfrgell, *library*
llyfrgellydd, *librarian*
llyfrwerthwr, *bookseller*
llythyr, *letter*

mis, *month*
mynegai, *index*

newydd, *new* (1.5)
nifer, *number* (1.8.6)
nodiadau, *notes*

ôl rifyn, *back number*

paratoi, *prepare*
i'w parhau, *to be continued*
plât, *plate*
pris, *price*
pwyllgor, *committee*
pythefnos, *fortnight*

yn rhad, *free*
rhagair, *preface*
rhagymadrodd, *introduction*
rhan, *part* (1.4.1)
rhif, *number* (1.7.2, 1.8.4)
rhifyn, *issue* (1.8.4)

Saesneg, *English*
sampl, *sample*
stori fer, *short story*
sylwadau, *notes*

tabl, *table*
taflen, *pamphlet*
tanysgrifiad, *subscription* (1.8.6)
troi, *to turn*
trosi, *to translate*
tudalen, *page*

yr un, *the same*

wedi ei (g)eni, *born*
ar werth, *on sale*
wythnos, *week*

ychwanegiad, *addition* (1.5)
ymchwil, *research*

GRAMMATICAL INDEX: WORDS

*, †, § see 2.5.2. Mutation is not indicated in this index except to distinguish homonyms.

GRAMMATICAL INDEX: ENDINGS

ANCIENT GREEK

SPECIMEN

Κατέβην χθὲς εἰς Πειραιᾶ μετὰ Γλαύκωνος τοῦ Ἀρίστωνος προσευξόμενός τε τῇ
θεῷ καὶ ἅμα τὴν ἑορτὴν βουλόμενος θεάσασθαι τίνα τρόπον ποιήσουσιν ἅτε νῦν
πρῶτον ἄγοντες. καλὴ μὲν οὖν μοι καὶ ἡ τῶν ἐπιχωρίων πομπὴ ἔδοξεν εἶναι, οὐ
μέντοι ἧττον ἐφαίνετο πρέπειν ἣν οἱ Θρᾷκες ἔπεμπον. προσευξάμενοι δὲ καὶ
θεωρήσαντες ἀπῇμεν πρὸς τὸ ἄστυ. κατιδὼν οὖν πόρρωθεν ἡμᾶς οἴκαδε ὡρμημένους
Πολέμαρχος ὁ Κεφάλου ἐκέλευσε δραμόντα τὸν παῖδα περιμεῖναί ἑ κελεῦσαι.

I went down to Peiraeus yesterday with Glaucon the son of Ariston both to pray to the
goddess and also because I wanted to see how they would conduct the festival, this being
the first time they had done it. The local procession certainly seemed to me to be good,
but the one which the Thracians put on appeared to be no less distinguished. We had
made our prayers and seen the sights and were on our way back to town when Polemarchus
the son of Cephalus caught sight of us from afar homeward bound and told his servant
to run and tell us to wait for him.

0 GENERAL CHARACTERISTICS

0.1 DEGREE OF INFLEXION
The main lines of the structure of Greek are very similar to those of Latin, in that
practically all the differences of voice, mood, tense, number and person in the verb
are indicated by endings, as are the principal relations of nouns.

0.2 ORDER OF WORDS
The order of words is fairly fluid: Plato is said to have written the opening words of
the Republic (see specimen) in several different ways before choosing the one in the
text. The position of adjectives in prose is fixed, however, and the same rule applies
to qualifying phrases (5.1.2).

0.3 HISTORY
Except during the early period ancient Greek was dominated by the Attic dialect and
its simpler successor the κοινή or common dialect. The natural changes to which
any language is subject were strenuously and to a great extent successfully opposed

by the grammarians, and even the Fathers of the Church retreated from the language of the New Testament to the archaic splendours of classical Greek. Influences from Latin and other languages there certainly were on Byzantine Greek, but the basic structure of the language remained largely unchanged, and it continued to be written in this form, alongside various types of modern Greek, until the nineteenth century.

0.4 RELATION TO OTHER LANGUAGES
Greek is distantly related to English. In addition many Greek words are familiar from learned borrowings; but the sort of relations which link the word κάνναβις with *hemp* are of little immediate help to its understanding.

0.5 MISCELLANEOUS
The late manifestations of ancient Greek are not likely to be the concern of any but experts, and the sections that follow will be confined to the elucidation of the title-pages of classical and medieval texts. Expressions relating to editions, imprints, series and periodicals do not arise.

1 BIBLIOLINGUISTICS

1.1 NAMES
1.1.1 Ancient Greek names usually consist of a single element, a personal name, the father's name and a local epithet being added in those contexts where specific identification is required. Later writers not infrequently have epithets (*Dionysius of Halicarnassus*) and a number of them have Roman names (*Ammianus Marcellinus*). Late Byzantine writers often have names of a modern type, though they are likely to be known by the personal name not the surname. All names are traditionally Latinised, e.g. Aeschylus (Αἰσχύλος). This is a little disconcerting with later writers, as when Ἰωάννης Σκυλίτζης becomes **Joannes Scylitza** (under Scylitza in the B.M. catalogue) but a later Ζάννης Σκυλίτζης is **Zannēs Skulitzēs**.

1.1.2 I do not think it is the practice to Latinise the names of eighteenth and nineteenth-century writers who still write in ancient Greek.

1.2 NAMES OF AUTHORS, EDITORS, ETC.
1.2.1 The names of classical and Byzantine authors are put in the genitive before the title, e.g. Αἰσχύλου τραγῳδίαι, *The tragedies of Aeschylus*; Γεωργίου τοῦ Κεδρηνοῦ σύνοψις ἱστοριῶν, *Synopsis of histories by Georgius Cedrenus*.

1.3 TITLES
1.3.1 The titles of older works are simple and descriptive. Mostly they consist of nouns in various cases, as in 1.2.1. A number begin with περὶ (*about*), e.g. Περὶ τῆς τῶν Χριστιανῶν πίστεως, *On the faith of the Christians*. As, however, Greek has a definite article and uses it freely with adjectives, participles and prepositional phrases to make substitutes for nouns, one must be prepared for occasional titles like that cited in 1.4.3.

1.3.3 When a title is quoted it is subject to the grammar of the phrase in which it occurs. Those elements which are in the nominative may be altered into some other case, e.g. ἐν Χαρίτων πρώτῃ, *in the first of the* (*poems entitled*) Χάριτες. Titles which are already in oblique cases (cf. 1.3.1) cannot be treated so, and some descriptive word has to be added, e.g. ἐν τῇ περὶ τῆς τῶν Χριστιανῶν πίστεως πραγματείᾳ, *in the treatise on the faith of the Christians*, which could as far as the form goes just as well be part of the title.

For the possible effect of numeration on the title see 1.4.3.

1.4 VOLUMES AND PARTS

1.4.1 Ancient works are divided into books. These are much smaller than our volumes, but scholarly editions of single books are sometimes published. More often than not the numeration of these is given in Latin or some modern language, but one does sometimes meet the Greek, especially in citations in other Greek authors and where the total number of books is stated. The word translated *book* is properly βίβλος or βιβλίον, but λόγος (in the sense *discourse*) is also used (cf. 1.4.3).

1.4.3 The numeration is usually combined with the title, so that the key words of this are in the genitive, e.g. Τῶν καθ᾽ Ὑσμίνην καὶ Ὑσμινίαν λόγοι ια᾽, *The 11 books of the story of (the things concerning) Hysmine and Hysminias.* For the numeral signs see Modern Greek 6.3.

2 ALPHABET, PHONETICS, SPELLING

2.1 ALPHABET

2.1.1 The alphabet in its final form, with the British Standard equivalents, is as follows:

A	B	Γ	Δ	E	Z	H	Θ	I	K	Λ	M	N	Ξ	O	Π	P	Σ	T	Y
α	β	γ	δ	ε	ζ	η	θ	ι	κ	λ	μ	ν	ξ	ο	π	ρ	σ	τ	υ
a	b	g	d	e	z	ē	th	i	k	l	m	n	x	o	p	r	s	t	u

Φ	X	Ψ	Ω
φ	χ	ψ	ω
f	h	ps	ō

Note the order and value of the signs Γ, Z, H, P, Y and X.

2.1.2 The British (and International) Standard transliteration, which applies to Modern Greek as well, is not universally accepted, the transliteration inherited from Latin being used instead. In this no visible distinction is made between ε and η, ο and ω; γ is transliterated *n* before γ, κ and χ; κ is often transliterated *c*; υ by itself is *y*, φ is *ph* and χ is *ch*. (See also 2.1.3.) Names (cf. 1.1.1) are more thoroughly Latinised, except those like Athens and Corinth which have peculiarly English equivalents. There are some exceptions, notably Κνωσ(σ)ός, now usually Knossos not Cnossus or Gnosus.

2.1.3 The aspirate H became a vowel sign in Greek, but its two halves developed into what are known as the rough and smooth breathings, the rough breathing (᾽) being an aspirate and the smooth breathing (᾽) an obligatory embellishment on any initial vowel which does not carry a rough breathing. The breathings stand above small letters: ά, ἁ; to the left of capitals: ῾A, ᾽A and on the second member of a diphthong: Aἱ, αἱ. The rough breathing is taken over unchanged or replaced by an apostrophe in the B.S. transliteration, but is read as *h* in the traditional transliteration. The smooth breathing is ignored. Initial ρ was always aspirated and written ῾P, ῥ and -ρρ- even without the breathings was always read as *-rrh-*. A smooth breathing is found over some contractions, e.g. προὔφερε for προέφερε.

2.1.4 In Greek manuscripts there are a great many ligatures or combinations of two or three letters. They were taken over into printing. The early ones are matters for experts, and those that survived into the 18th and 19th century are dealt with under Modern Greek. One such convention, however, is universal: both long and short vowels form diphthongs with ι, but when the vowel is long the iota is written under it, viz. ᾳ, ῃ, ῳ. The iota follows capitals, but ᾠδή in capitals becomes ᾿ΩιΔΗ with the breathing before the Ω and the ι written small. It is transliterated *j* in B.S. and ignored in the traditional transliteration.

2.1.5 The diaeresis is placed on ι and υ when they do not form a diphthong with the preceding vowel, e.g. Ταΰγετος, *Taygetus*. At the beginning of a word the diaeresis is not needed, as the position of the breathing is sufficient distinction, e.g. αἰδώς with a diphthong, ἀίδιος, with separate sounds.

2.1.6 Accents were invented by Alexandrian grammarians to guide intonation, and now serve no practical purpose, so far as classical Greek is concerned, except occasionally to distinguish different words with the same spelling, e.g. ἀλλά, *but*; ἄλλα, *other things*. In Byzantine and later Greek they are stress accents. There are three accents: acute, which may fall on any of the last three syllables; circumflex, which may fall on the last two, and only on long syllables; and grave, which is substituted for acute on the last syllable, except before a pause. If the last syllable is long, the acute accent may not go farther back than the last but one, and a circumflex accent is found only on the last: φιλόσοφος but φιλοσόφου; δῶρον, δώρου.

2.2 CAPITALISATION

2.2.1 Capital letters are used only for proper nouns, not for proper adjectives; nor are the names of common institutions and magistracies, such as βουλή and ἄρχων given capitals.

2.3 DIVISION OF WORDS

2.3.1 Rules 4, 5b, 6c, 7a (p. xiii) apply.

2.3.2 Prefixes which end in a consonant, e.g. προσ-, are kept distinct, but not those which have lost a vowel, e.g. παρ- from παρα-.

2.3.3 Any combination of β, γ, δ, θ, κ, π, τ, φ, χ with λ, μ, ν, ρ, can begin a syllable, as well as βδ, γδ, κτ, πτ, φθ, χθ and combinations of any of these with a preceding σ or a following ρ. (Not that all these combinations are actually found.)

2.4 PUNCTUATION

Peculiarities of Greek punctuation are the colon (·) and the question mark (;).

2.5 VARIATION OF CONSONANT

2.5.1 The letters θ, φ, χ are aspirated and take the place of τ, π, κ when another aspirate or an aspirated vowel follows, e.g. ἐπί but ἐφ᾿ ᾧ. But two aspirates are not found separately in the same syllable, and this results in curious alternations. Thus the root θριχ- is impossible and becomes τριχ-, but θριχ + σ (the nominative) makes θρίξ and the θ- remains.

2.5.2 Voiced and unvoiced consonants do not come together, and various simplifications take place before -μ-, e.g. πράσσω (-ττω) (stem πραγ-) has passive participles (8.12.6–7) πραχθείς and πεπραγμένος; verbs in -ίζω have -ισθείς and -ισμένος; κρύ/πτω and similar verbs -φθείς and -μμένος. Combinations of consonant + σ are simplified.

2.5.3 The alternatives exemplified by πράσσω/πράττω, ἄρσην/ἄρρην are respectively common Greek and Attic.

2.6 VARIATION OF VOWEL
There is frequent alternation between α and η, the latter not being found after a vowel or ρ. (See 4.3.1.) Similar alternations of long and short vowels—ε/ει, ε/η, ο/ου, ο/ω, as well as the disappearance of vowels, are found, e.g. ἑνός/εἷς; πατέρα, πατρός/πατήρ; ποδός/πούς; μείζονος/μείζων.

3 ARTICLES

3.1 DEFINITE

3.1.1 The forms are as follows:

		S			P	
	M	N	F	M	N	F
N	ὁ	τό	ἡ	οἱ	τά	αἱ
A	τόν	τό	τήν	τούς	τά	τάς
G		τοῦ	τῆς		τῶν	
D		τῷ	τῇ	τοῖς		ταῖς

3.1.2 The article, especially the M and NP, is used with adjectives, participles, adverbs and adverbial phrases, the whole having the force of a noun, e.g. οἱ πλούσιοι, *the rich*; οἱ τεθνηκότες, *the dead*; τά πάλαι, *antiquity* (πάλαι, *long ago*); τὰ καθ' Ὑσμίνην (1.4.3).

3.1.3 The article is used with abstract nouns and some proper names, where it is not used in English, e.g. ἡ σοφία, *wisdom*; ἡ Χίος, *Chios*.

4 NOUNS

4.1 GENDER AND FORM

4.1.1 The general pattern of Greek nouns is much the same as that of Latin, though with fewer declensions and even more variety in the third declension. The characteristic vowels of the stem are: 1 α/η, 2 ο/ω; 3 other vowels or no vowel.

4.1.2 Some forms are characteristic of particular genders, viz. 1 -α, -η F; -ας, -ης M; 2 -ος M (a few F), -ον N; 3 -μα, -ος N, the rest M or F.

4.1.3 The dual number, used for pairs of things, is ignored here.

4.3 DECLENSIONS

4.3.1 The forms of the first and second declensions and the basic forms of the third declension are as follows. Variations in the third declension are given in 4.3.3.

	1			2	3
			S		
N	-α, -ας, -ης, -α/-η			-ος, -ον	See 4.3.3, 4.3.4
A	-αν	-ην	-αν/-ην	-ον	-α/-
G	-ας	-ου	-ης	-ου	-ος
D	-ᾳ		-η	-ῳ	-ι
			P		
N	-αι			-οι, -α	-ες, -α
A	-ας			-ους, -α	-ας, -α
G	-ων			-ων	-ων
D	-αις			-οις	-σι

4.3.2 The plural ending -α is peculiar to neuter nouns.

4.3.3 The endings given for the third declension apply to most consonant stems and a few vowel stems. With the remaining stems contraction or vowel lengthening takes place, e.g.

	N	-ης	-ις	-ος	-υς	-ευς
S	A	-η	-ιν	-ος	-υν	-εα
	G	-ους	-εως	-ους	-εος	-εως
	D	-ει	-ει	-ει	-ει	-ει
	N	-εις	-εις	-η	-εις	-εις
P	A	-εις	-εις	-η	-εις	-εις (later -εας)
	G	-ων	-εων	-εων	-εων	-εων
	D	-εσι	-εσι	-εσι	-εσι	-ευσι

Of these -ις is a common ending of abstract nouns, and -υς of adjectives. (Most nouns in -υς have stem in -υ- and endings as in 4.3.1.)

4.3.4 The nominative most commonly ends in -ς, stems in -δ-, -θ-, -τ- and sometimes -ντ- losing the consonant, e.g. Ἑλλάς G Ἑλλάδος, -κως G -κοτος, -εις/-ης G -εντος. The vowel of the nominative is lengthened. Stems in -β-, -π-, -φ- make -ψ, those in -γ-, -κ-, -χ- make -ξ.

Stems involving ν and ρ usually have no ending in the nominative, and the stem vowel, if short, is lengthened, e.g. -ων G -ονος, -ωνος, -οντος; -ηρ G -ηρος, -ερος.

Neuters in -ματ- have N -μα.

4.3.5 The relation between the stem and nominative is peculiar in some nouns, e.g. ἀνήρ: stem ἀνδρ-, DP ἄνδρασι; similarly μήτηρ: st. μητρ-; πατήρ: st. πατ(ε)ρ-; γυνή: st. γυναικ-; ὕδωρ: st. ὑδατ-.

A few nouns are quite irregular, notably ναῦς (*ship*): A ναῦν, G νεώς, D νηί, P νῆες, ναῦς, νεῶν, ναυσί. (There is another word νεώς, itself an example of a peculiar declension which has -ω- throughout, which means *temple*.)

4.6 USE OF CASES

The names of the cases in Greek are misleading, for the genitive would be more accurately termed the genitive-ablative and the dative the dative-instrumental. With this proviso the use of the cases is understandable enough, at any rate in the composition of titles.

5 ADJECTIVES

5.1 GENERAL

5.1.1 Adjectives are variable nouns. When used to qualify substantives they agree, and when they stand alone the endings which are tied to gender are significant, e.g. ὁ δίκαιος, *the just man*; τό δίκαιον, *justice* (that which is just); Ἐκκλησιάζουσαι, *Women in Parliament*. It is uncertain, however, whether some forms are M or N.

5.1.2 Attributive adjectives are either sandwiched between the article and the noun or if placed after the noun have the article repeated, e.g. ἡ μαθηματικὴ θεωρία or ἡ θεωρία ἡ μαθηματική. The same is true of dependent genitives, e.g. τὰ τῶν φιλοσόφων δόγματα or τὰ δόγματα τὰ τῶν φιλοσόφων.

5.2 ENDINGS

5.2.1 The majority of adjectives have the forms of the first and second declensions, viz. M -ος, N -ον, F -η/-α. (The forms in -η are used after consonants, those in -α, which is found in all cases, after vowels and ρ.) For the cases see 4.3.1. Compound adjectives and negative adjectives with the prefix ἀ(ν)- have MF -ος, N -ον.

5.2.2 A number of adjectives, including some common ones, have MN forms of the third declension (4.3.1–4) and F forms of the first, with a slightly different stem, e.g. -υς, -υ, -εια; -εις, -ες, -εσσα; and see 8.12.

5.2.3 A few adjectives have MF -ης, N -ες, GMFN -ους, PMF -εις, N -η (see 4.3.3). Comparatives have MF -ων, N -ον (5.3.2).

5.2.4 Some very common adjectives have peculiar forms, e.g.

μέλας: N μέλαν, st. μελαν-, F μέλαινα, *black*

μέγας: N μέγα, F and all other forms as if from μεγάλος, *great*

πολύς: N πολύ, AM πολύν, F and all other forms as if from πολλός, *much, many*

5.3 COMPARISON

5.3.1 The regular endings are: comparative -τερος, superlative -τατος, which with the stem vowel or consonant produce -ότερος, -έστερος, -ύτερος, etc.

5.3.2 Some very common adjectives have C -(ι)ων, S -ιστος, e.g. μέγας, μείζων, μέγιστος; καλός, καλλίων, κάλλιστος. Πλείων from πολύς varies between πλε- and πλει-. There are entries in dictionaries under the irregular forms. The stem of the comparative is -ον- but contraction may occur, e.g. μείζους for μείζονος and μείζονας.

6 NUMERALS

As the necessity of deducing the words from the figures does not arise in the case of ancient Greek, the numerals are not listed. The figures, used in the numeration of books and the dates of modern publications, are given under Modern Greek.

7 PRONOUNS

7.1/7.2 DEMONSTRATIVE, ETC.
Some of these pronouns are very complex, but the likelihood of their occurrence in the titles of books is remote.

7.3 PERSONAL

	S		*P*	
	1	2	1	2
N	ἐγώ	σύ	ἡμεῖς	ὑμεῖς
A	ἐμέ, με	σέ	ἡμᾶς	ὑμᾶς
G	ἐμοῦ, μου	σοῦ	ἡμῶν	ὑμῶν
D	ἐμοί, μοι	σοί	ἡμῖν	ὑμῖν

8 VERBS

8.1 STRUCTURE
8.1.1 The Greek verb is very rich, having three voices—active, middle and passive—three moods and three numbers and a large number of participles. Only a selection of the participles and the infinitive and their relation to the 1PS of the present indicative,

under which verbs are entered in the dictionary, are dealt with here. For the declension of participles see 5.2.1–2.

8.11 INFINITIVES

8.11.1 Of the large number of infinitives only the present and aorist are considered here, in their capacity as nouns.

8.11.2 *Present active:* -ειν, 1PS -ω; -εῖν, 1PS -ῶ (for -έω); -ᾶν, 1PS -ῶ (for -άω); -οῦν, 1PS -ῶ (for -όω). Ζῆν, *to live*, is peculiar.

8.11.3 *Aorist active:* weak, -(σ)αι; strong, -εῖν. See 8.12.2.

8.11.4 *Present middle and passive:* -εσθαι, 1PS -ω (-ομαι); -ᾶσθαι, 1PS -ῶ (-ῶμαι); -εῖσθαι, 1PS -ῶ (-οῦμαι); -οῦσθαι, 1PS -ῶ (-οῦμαι).

8.11.5 *Aorist middle:* weak, -(σ)ασθαι; strong, -εσθαι. See 8.12.2.

8.11.6 *Aorist passive:* -(θ)ῆναι. See 8.12.6.

8.11.7 There are some other infinitives in -ναι, e.g. ἱστάναι, στῆναι; τιθέναι, θεῖναι; διδόναι, δοῦναι, from ἵστημι, τίθημι, δίδωμι; εἰδέναι (grammatically perfect) from οἶδα, *I know*; εἶναι, *to be*.

8.11.8 The infinitive is freely used with the article in all cases as a noun, e.g.

τίς οἶδεν εἰ τὸ ζῆν μέν ἐστι κατθανεῖν —
τὸ πνεῖν δὲ δείπνειν τὸ δὲ καθεύδειν κῳδῖον;

(Aristophanes)

'*Who knows if life be death*'—*and breathing dining, and going to sleep a pillow?*

8.12 PARTICIPLES

8.12.1 *Present active*

-ων, N -ον, st. -οντ-, F -ουσα
-ῶν, N -ῶν, st. -ωντ-, F -ῶσα
-ῶν, N -οῦν, st. -ουντ-, F -οῦσα

The 1PS is -ω/-ῶ.

Peculiar participles are ἱστάς, N -άν, st. -άντ-, F -ᾶσα, from ἵστημι; τιθείς, N -έν, st. -έντ-, F -εῖσα from τίθημι; διδούς, N -όν, st. -όντ-, F -οῦσα from δίδωμι.

8.12.2 *Aorist (past) active*

Weak   -ας, N -αν, st. -αντ-, F -ασα
Strong   -ων (as 8.12.1), with different stem

The weak participle usually has a stem formed by adding -σ- to that of the present, e.g. παύσας: παύω; δηλώσας: δηλῶ. Modifications are common, e.g. -σας: -ζω, -νω; -ψας: -βω, -π(τ)ω, -φω; -ξας: -γω, -κω, -σσω, -χω. Participles in -νας are found from presents in -νω, usually with a different vowel, e.g. μείνας: μένω; ξηράνας: ξηραίνω.

The strong participle invariably has a simple stem, that of the present being enlarged, usually by the insertion of ν or ι, e.g. τυχών: τυγχάνω; λιπών: λείπω.

Peculiar are εἰπών: λέγω; ἰδών: ὁρῶ; πεσών: πίπτω; παθών: πάσχω; ἀποθανών: ἀποθνήσκω; στάς (intransitive), στήσας (transitive): ἵστημι; θείς (like τιθείς, 8.12.1): τίθημι; δούς (like διδούς, 8.12.1): δίδωμι.

8.12.3 *Perfect active*

-(κ)ώς, N -(κ)ός, st. -(κ)ότ-, F -(κ)υῖα

The first syllable is repeated with vowel -ε-, e.g. πεπτωκώς: πίπτω; τεθνηκώς: θνήσκω; γεγονώς: γίγνομαι; ἐστηκώς: ἵστημι; εἰδώς: οἶδα (no present).

8.12.4   *Present middle and passive*

-όμενος (-ούμενος, -ώμενος): 1PS -ω (-ῶ)

Some verbs are found only in the middle or passive: 1PS -ομαι (-οῦμαι, -ῶμαι).

8.12.5   *Aorist middle:* -(σ)αμενος, -ομενος. Cf. 8.12.2.

8.12.6   *Aorist passive:* -(θ)είς like τιθείς, 8.12.1. The forms without -θ- are strong forms (cf. 8.12.2), e.g. ταφείς: θάπτω (2.5.1). For modifications caused by -θ- see 2.5.2.

8.12.7   *Perfect middle and passive:* -μένος with reduplication (8.12.3). The ending is added direct to the stem, which may be modified (2.5.2), e.g. πεπεισμένος: πείθω; γεγραμμένος: γράπτω.

8.12.8   Participles are widely used as in the specimen, as equivalents of temporal and other adverbial clauses, but their chief importance here is in their combination with the article to form noun-equivalents, e.g. οἱ πάσχοντες (παθόντες), *the victims* (those who are suffering, suffered); τὰ γεγονότα, *past events, history* (the things which have come to pass).

9   ADVERBS

9.1   FORMATION

Adverbs have many endings, but the commonest way of making an adverb from an adjective is to turn the adjectival ending into -ως. In some instances the neuter plural is used adverbially.

9.2   COMPARISON

The comparative and superlative endings are -τερον (-ῑον) and -τατα (-ιστα) See 5.3.

10   PREPOSITIONS

The function of prepositions is to make precise the meaning of a case. Some prepositions have proper cases but most of them can be used with two or three cases, with different meanings. Care must therefore be used when looking them up in the dictionary.

GRAMMATICAL INDEX: WORDS

παθών, 8.12.2

πατ(ε)ρ-, 4.3.5

πεσών, 8.12.2

πολ-, πολλ-, 5.2.4

σέ, σοί, σοῦ, 7.3

στάς, 8.12.2

στῆναι, 8.11.7

τά, ταῖς, τάς, 3.1.1

τῇ, τήν, τῆς, 3.1.1

τιθείς, 8.12.1

τιθέναι, 8.11.7

τό, τοῖς, τόν, τοῦ, τούς, 3.1.1

τῷ, τῶν, 3.1.1

ὕδατ-, 4.3.3

ὑμεῖς, etc., 7.3

GRAMMATICAL INDEX: ENDINGS

-α, 4.3.1, 5.2.1, 8.12.7

-ᾳ, 4.3.1, 5.2.1, 5.2.2

-εα, 4.3.3

-εῖα, 5.2.2

-υῖα, 8.12.3

-ασα, 8.12.2

-(θ)εῖσα, 8.12.6

-ουσα, 8.12.1, 8.12.2

-εσσα, 5.2.2

-τατα, 9.2

-(σ)αντα, 8.12.2

-έντα, 5.2.2, 8.12.6

-οντα, -οῦντα, -ῶντα, 8.12.1

-ότα, 8.12.3

-ιστα, 9.2

-η, 4.3.1, 4.3.3, 5.2.1, 5.2.3

-ῃ, 4.3.1, 5.2.1, 5.2.3

-ι, 4.3.1, 5.2.2

-αι, 4.3.1, 5.2.1, 5.2.2, 5.2.3, 8.3.3

-(σ)ασθαι, 8.11.5

-εσθαι, 8.11.4, 8.11.5

-(θ)ῆναι, 8.11.6

-σαι, 8.11.3

-ει, 4.3.3, 5.2.2, 5.2.3

-οι, 4.3.1, 5.2.1, 8.2.7

-σι, 4.3.1, 8.12.1, 8.12.2, 8.12.3

-(σ)ασι, 8.12.2

-εσι, 4.3.3

-εῖσι, 8.12.6

-όσι, 8.12.3

-εσσι, 5.2.2

-ουσι, -ῶσι, 8.12.1

-(σ)αντι, 8.12.2

-εντι, 5.2.2, 8.12.6

-οντι, -οῦντι, -ῶντι, 8.12.1

-ότι, 8.12.3

-αν, 4.3.1, 5.2.1, 5.2.2

-ᾶν, 8.11.2

-ην, 4.3.1, 5.2.1, 8.12.7

-ιν, 4.3.3

-ειν, 8.11.2, 8.11.3

-ον, 4.3.1, 5.2.1, 5.2.2, 5.2.3, 9.2

-ῖον, 9.2

-τερον, 9.2

-ύν, 4.3.3

-οῦν, 8.11.2

-ων, 4.3.1, 5.2.1, 5.2.2, 5.2.3, 5.3.2

-(σ)άντων, 8.12.2

-έντων, 5.2.2

-όντων, -ούντων, -ώντων, 8.12.1

-ότων, 8.12.3

-ας, 4.3.1, 5.2.1, 5.2.2

-έας, 4.3.3

-(σ)αντας, 8.12.2

-εντας, 5.2.2, 8.12.6

-οντας, -οῦντας, -ῶντας, 8.12.1

-ότας, 8.12.3

-ες, 4.3.1, 5.2.2, 5.2.3

-(σ)αντες, 8.12.2

-εντες, 5.2.2, 8.12.6

-οντες, -οῦντες, -ῶντες, 8.12.1

-ότες, 8.12.3

-αις, 4.3.1, 5.2.1, 5.2.2, 5.2.3

-εις, 4.3.3, 5.2.2, 5.2.3

-(θ)εις, 8.12.6

-οις, 4.3.1, 5.2.1

-ος, 4.3.1, 4.2.3

-μένος, 8.12.7

-άμενος, 8.12.5

-όμενος, 8.12.4, 8.12.5

-ούμενος, -ώμενος, 8.12.4

-τερος, 5.3.1

-τατος, 5.3.1

-(σ)αντος, 8.12.2

-εντος, 5.2.2, 8.12.6

-οντος, -οῦντος, -ῶντος, 8.12.1

-ότος, 8.12.3

-ιστος, 5.3.2

-ους, 4.3.1, 4.3.3, 5.2.1, 5.2.3, 5.3.2

-ως, 8.12.3, 9.1

-εως, 4.3.3, 5.2.2

-ύ, 5.2.2

-ου, 4.3.1, 5.2.1, 8.12.7

-ῳ, 4.3.1, 5.2.1, 8.12.7

MODERN GREEK

Βρισκόμαστε στὰ 1970, δηλαδὴ πενῆντα χρόνια ὕστερα ἀπὸ τὴν ἵδρυση τοῦ " 'Αρχείου τῶν Οἰκονομικῶν 'Επιστημῶν " ἀπὸ τὸν καθηγητὴ κ. Δ. Ε. Καλιτσου- νάκη. Σ' αὐτὰ τὰ πενῆντα χρόνια ποὺ πέρασαν πολλοί, ἴσως οἱ περισσότεροι, ἀπὸ τοὺς προκομένους διανοούμενους καὶ κοινωνικοὺς ἐπιστήμονες τοῦ ἔθνους εἰδο- ποίησαν τοὺς 'Ελληνικοὺς ἐπιστημονικοὺς κύκλους γιὰ τὴν ὕπαρξή τους σὰν τέτοιοι ἀπὸ τὸ " Αρχεῖο ". "Αλλοι μὲ τὰ πρῶτα δοκίμια ποὺ μόλις ξεπερνοῦσαν τὸ στάδιο τῆς δουλικῆς μίμησης, ἄλλοι μὲ πιὸ πρωτότυπες ἐργασίες καὶ ἄλλοι στὸ στάδιο τῆς ὡριμότητάς τους μὲ ἐργασίες ποὺ ἀποτελοῦσαν σημαντικὴ συνεισφορὰ στὴ σχετικὰ πτωχὴ ἐπιστημονικὴ βιβλιογραφία τοῦ τόπου. (1971) (D)

We find ourselves in 1970, fifty years that is since the foundation of the 'Arheio tōn Oikonomikōn kai Koinōnikōn Epistēmōn' by Professor D. E. Kalitsounakēs. In those fifty years many, perhaps most, of the distinguished intellectuals and social scientists of the nation have made Greek learned circles aware of their existence as such through the 'Arheio'. Some with their first essays, which scarcely passed the stage of slavish imitation, others with more original works and others at the stage of their maturity with works that constituted a significant contribution to the relatively scanty scientific literature of this country.

Εἶμαι πολὺ εὐτυχής, εὑρισκόμενος εἰς τὴν εὐχάριστον θέσιν νὰ προλογίσω τὸ ἀνὰ χεῖρας δημοσίευμα, διότι ἀποτελεῖ ἐπιβράβευσιν σπανιωτάτου ἐπιτεύγματος εἰς τὰ ἐπιστημονικὰ χρονικὰ τῆς Χώρας μας. Εἶναι, πράγματι, ἐξαιρετικὸν τὸ γεγονός, ὅτι συμπληρώνει ὁλόκληρον πεντηκονταετίαν ἀδιακόπου ἐκδόσεως ἕν ἐπιστημονι- κὸν περιοδικόν, εἰς μίαν πολυτάραχον περίοδον, χωρὶς μεγάλα οἰκονομικὰ μέσα. Ἔτι πλέον ἀξιοσημείωτον εἶναι τὸ γεγονός, ὅτι ὁ ἱδρυτὴς τοῦ περιοδικοῦ αὐτοῦ, ὁ Καθηγητὴς Δημήτριος Καλιτσουνάκης εἶναι ἐν ζωῇ καὶ ἐν δράσει κατὰ τὸ τέλος τοῦ μακροῦ αὐτοῦ χρονικοῦ διαστήματος. (1971) (K)

I am very happy to find myself in the agreeable position of prefacing the present publi- cation, since it constitutes a recognition of a very rare achievement in the scientific annals of our country. It is in fact an exceptional event, that a scientific periodical is completing a whole fifty years of unbroken publication, in a tumultuous period, without great economic means. Even more noteworthy is the fact that the founder of this periodical, Professor Dēmētrios Kalitsounakēs is alive and active at the end of this long period of time.

For the two styles see 0.3.

0 GENERAL CHARACTERISTICS

0.1 DEGREE OF INFLEXION
Modern Greek is a natural development from the ancient language, resulting from

M

phonetic change and semantic development, coupled with borrowing from other languages, particularly Turkish, Italian and French. There are many words of foreign origin in the dictionary, but in an average piece of modern prose only about 5% of the vocabulary is foreign. Words like νερό, *water*, or ψάρι, *fish*, are as Greek as the ancient ὕδωρ and ἰχθύς. Like most modern languages it is a good deal more analytic than its ancestor, the verb having periphrastic forms for the future and the perfect, though it still has a complete set of passive forms.

0.2 ORDER OF WORDS
Sentences are mostly in the order SVO, but as subject and object are usually different in form there is nothing to prevent the subject following the verb. In translating one would retain the order and change the construction, e.g. δὲ λείπει ἡ μπύρα, *there is no shortage of beer.*

A peculiar feature of modern Greek, not so marked now as formerly, and characteristic of dēmotikē rather than kathareuousa (0.3) is the use of clauses joined by καί, *and*, instead of by some form of subordination (cf. 11.1.2).

0.3 HISTORY
A very trying feature of modern Greek is the continued existence of two forms of the language, not altogether appropriately called dēmotikē (popular) and kathareuousa (purizing). (Up to the nineteenth century one might have three, for ancient Greek was still being written by some.) Greek pride in the language has always engendered a marked conservatism, and a comparison of the Greek of the New Testament with that of more self-conscious writers of the same period provides evidence of a growing gap between literary and everyday Greek. By the twelfth century some modern Greek is found side by side with ancient in literature, and in the 17th century there was a flourishing modern literature in Crete.

The Turkish domination, however, destroyed the unity and continuity of linguistic and literary development, and when the kingdom of Greece was established there were still many who despised the language of the people as incoherent, degenerate and ungrammatical. It was obviously useless to try to impose ancient Greek on all, but many hoped that by successive approximations the regression might be achieved in a few generations. It never was, but an intermediate form resulted, basically modern but brought back in this or that particular to the old norms. This is kathareuousa. Being artificial it is inherently unstable, for its exponents do not agree among themselves how far the archaising should go. It is now completely rejected as a vehicle of creative literature, but all laws and government documents, reports of learned societies, many text books and some newspapers are written in it. (Some ancient forms survive as fossils in demotic also, e.g. ἐν τάξει, *O.K.*)

No attempt is made here to set out a grammar of kathareuousa. The core of the grammar is demotic, with a note of kathareuousa variants or a reference to ancient Greek where appropriate. The abbreviations D and K will be used to distinguish forms and examples.

1 BIBLIOLINGUISTICS

1.1 NAMES
1.1.1 Modern Greek names usually consist of a single Christian name, an initial representing the father's Christian name, which if given in full is in the genitive, and

a surname. Except in legal contexts the father's name is always abbreviated. Medieval names in which there is an epithet instead of a surname are naturally few, but the pseudonym Ρήγας Βελεστινλής (or Φεραῖος, Βελεστῖνο and Φεραί being the modern and ancient names) may be considered to be of this form. As Κωνσταντῖνος Ρήγας Βελεστινλής it could also be taken as a compound name.

1.1.2 Christian names are for the most part either the names of saints or ancient Greek names, e.g. Πέτρος, Σωκράτης, Μαρία, Ἕλλη. As might be expected, a number, e.g. Σπυρίδων, Χαραλάμπης, belong to an unfamiliar tradition. For the most part they fit demotic and kathareuousa equally well, but Σπυρίδων is pure K, and some names have variant forms, e.g. Ὀδυσσεύς (K) and Ὀδυσσέας (D), while others have one form which is neutral and one which fits only demotic, e.g. Ἀντώνιος and Ἀντώνης. Most feminine names fit D and K equally well, but those in -ω, originally diminutives, e.g. Φρόσω (Φροσύνη, Εὐφροσύνη) are purely D. There are many such short forms, e.g. Γιάννης (Ἰωάννης), Κώστας or Κωστής (Κωνσταντῖνος), Νῖκος (Νικόλαος). Sometimes they alternate with the full forms, but more often they are, if not the only form of the writer's name, at any rate the one he is known by. They are not likely to cause much trouble unless affected by dialect, as in the Cypriot Ττοουλῆς for Χριστόδουλος. Dialect in any case is an occasional complication on its own, e.g. Cretan Βιτζέντζος as against Βικέντιος.

1.1.3 Surnames show the usual variety, some of them being of Turkish and some of Italian origin. The majority, however, are patronymics with suffixes -όπουλος, -ίδης, -άδης, -άκης (-άκις), all declinable, or less commonly the indeclinable Turkish suffix -ογλου (declinable form -ογλους). More simply, a patronymic surname may consist of a Christian name in the genitive case, and as there are some surnames which are identical with Christian names, it may be impossible without other evidence to establish the name (1.2.1).

1.1.4 Until fairly recently many such names in Cyprus were genuine patronymics so that Ἀντώνιος (Παπᾶ, Χατζῆ) Νικολάου would mean *Antonios son of* (the priest, the pilgrim) *Nikolaos*. They have to be treated as surnames, but when in the thirties there was a widespread adoption of surnames, their bearers tended to adopt independent ones and not to convert the patronymic into a surname: Χαραλάμπης Μιχαήλ became Χαραλάμπης Μ. Ἄζινος and Κυριακὸς Παπανικολάου became Κυριακὸς Ν. Παπαδόπουλος.

1.1.5 Compound surnames such as Ρίζος Ραγκαβῆς are not common but when they do occur both parts are declined. For Ρήγας Βελεστινλής see 1.1.1.

1.1.6 Women take their father's or husband's surname in the genitive, which can be trying when the name is in the genitive in any case and the Christian name is represented by an initial.

1.1.7 The Romanisation of Greek names and the reconstruction of the original forms present many problems. The British Standard transliteration (see 2.1.1) is less familiar to English-speaking librarians than those of the British Museum and the Library of Congress, and it will be a long time before gh, logical as it is, will immediately suggest γχ (LC and BM nch). H by itself is often used by Greeks to represent χ: indeed it would strike most people as just as absurd to spell a name beginning Hatzi- with Ch- as to spell one beginning with Christo- with H-. But one must stomach one or the other. Individual Greeks are not bound to be consistent with each other, and usually represent their names more or less phonetically. So β will usually be v; γ may be g or gh or y, but gh will sometimes represent γχ (a hard g); η and ι will both be i; φ will be f. So when a name may end either in -ης or -ις it is usually impossible to tell from the transcription how the original is spelt. Sometimes the final -ς is dropped: **Κ. Π. Καβάφης** is always **C. P. Cavafy**, with a final -y as in **Philip Pandely** (Παντελῆ), **Argenti** (patronymic in full as if it were a second Christian name, and 'Αργέντης given its original Italian form) and **Elly Lambridi** (῎Ελλη Λαμπρίδη). It is obvious that unless the names are well known one will need either expert advice or very good reference books. (For further phonetic details see 2.1.2.)

1.2 NAMES OF AUTHORS, EDITORS, ETC.

1.2.1 The names of authors are most often placed at the head of the title-page in the genitive. This will be so even if the name is separated from the title by a rule. There are two complications. First, the name may be one of those (1.1.3, 1.1.6) that are already of the genitive form. Secondly, it is not unknown for the name at the head of the title-page to be in the nominative.

1.2.2 Alternatively, especially in the case of editors and translators, the title may be followed by the appropriate participle (8.12.3, 8.12.4), a preposition and the name in an oblique case. With titles in K the preposition will usually be ὑπό or παρά and the case the genitive, e.g. συντεθὲν παρ' 'Αγαπίου μοναχοῦ, *composed by the monk Agapios*; ἐκδιδομένη ὑπὸ Κ. Δυοβουνιώτου, *edited by K. Duobouniōtēs*. With titles in D the preposition will be ἀπό and the case accusative, e.g. ἐκδομένη ἀπὸ τὸν Ι. Βασιλικό, *edited by I. Basilikos*.

1.2.3 The aorist participle in -θείς is an archaic survival, and the perfect participle is sometimes reduplicated in K, but never in D. Heart-searchings can be avoided by using abstract nouns instead of verbs, with the name, alas, sometimes in the genitive and sometimes in the nominative, e.g. εἰσαγωγή, κείμενα, μεταφράσεις, γλωσσάριον Νικολάου Β. Τωμαδάκη, *introduction, texts, translations, glossary by Nikolaos B. Tōmadakēs*; σύγγραμμα Κωνσταντίνου Ν. Σάθα, *composition of K. N. Sathas*; ἐπιμελείᾳ Ν. Δαμαλᾶ, *by the care of N. Damalas* (typical K); ἐπιμέλεια Γιῶργος 'Ιωάννου (the surname is already in the genitive); ἐπιμέλεια Κωνστ. Τσάτσου—the surname is in fact Tsatsos, but how are you to know? ('Επιμελείᾳ, the dative, is always followed by the genitive, but the construction with the nominative varies.)

A following genitive is also found in cases like 'Εκλογὴ ἀπὸ τὸ ποιητικὸ ἔργο τοῦ Κωστῆ Παλαμᾶ, *Selection from the poetical work of Kōstēs Palamās*; 'Ανέκδοτοι ἐπιστολαὶ Μελετίου τοῦ Πηγᾶ, *Unpublished letters of Meletios Pēgas*.

1.2.4 Rarely in older books an active verb is used, e.g. ἅσπερ μετήνεγκεν εἰς τὴν κοινὴν γλῶτταν 'Ιωάννης ὁ Ναθαναήλ, *which Iōannēs Nathanaēl translated into the common tongue*. (Here the title-page and preface are practically in ancient Greek.)

1.3 TITLES

1.3.1 Titles of technical works consist for the most part of nouns and adjectives, including participles, in the nominative and genitive, e.g. 'Ιστορία τῆς νεοελληνικῆς λογοτεχνίας, *History of modern Greek literature*; or there may be prepositions, e.g. 'Η ποίηση στὴ ζωή μας, *Poetry in our life*. Belles-lettres and propaganda literature introduce more varied types, e.g. Γιὰ νὰ περνᾶ ἡ ὥρα, *To help time pass* (D); Πῶς ἐκπαιδεύονται τὰ ἀπαχθέντα ἑλληνόπουλα, *How the abducted Greek children are educated* (K); Καθὼς χάραζε ἡ λευτεριά, *As freedom was dawning* (D).

1.3.2 Title entries and filing do not present any special problems, apart from the more general one of transliteration. The articles, however, are not unambiguous. The definite article shares most of its forms with the pronoun of the third person, but an article is always followed by an adjective or a noun, the pronoun never. The indefinite article is identical with the numeral *one*, and only the context will indicate which is meant, e.g. Μιὰ παράτολμη ἑρμηνεία τοῦ " Πόρφυρα", *A rash interpretation of 'Porphuras'*; Μία τῶν παρὰ τοῖς Βυζαντινοῖς ποινῶν, *One of the punishments (practised) at Byzantium.* (Μιὰ D; μία K.) As title-pages printed in capitals rarely have breathings and accents, ΕΙΣ and ΕΝ (K forms) may be εἰς, ἐν or the prepositions εἰς, ἐν.

1.3.3 A title which is quoted will be subject to the grammar of the sentence in which it is quoted, so that nouns and adjectives in the nominative may have their case changed, e.g. στὴν πρώτη ἔκδοση τῆς Ἱστορίας τῆς νεοελληνικῆς λογοτεχνίας, *in the first edition of* Ἱστορία, etc. (cf. also 8.12.1). Greek is usually quite content to do this (cf. 1.3.2), but it is possible to insulate the title, as in Ἀνασκευὴ τῶν ἐν τῷ βιβλίῳ " Οἱ ξένοι ἐν Κερκύρᾳ " ἀνακριβειῶν, *Refutation of the inaccuracies in the book* Οἱ ξένοι . . . .

1.4 VOLUMES AND PARTS

1.4.1 The usual words are τόμος and μέρος respectively, but βιβλίον (*book*) and τεῦχος (*fascicule*), the latter commoner with periodicals, are also found, usually as primary divisions. (Not always: μέρος Α', τεῦχος Α', *vol. 1, pt. 1.*)

1.4.2 Numeration is by an ordinal number, πρῶτος τόμος, τόμος πρῶτος, τόμος Α' (see 6.3.2).

1.5 EDITIONS

1.5.1 The Greek equivalent is ἔκδοση (ἔκδοσις), a word with all the usual ambiguities, implying in other contexts editing and publication. Ἐκτύπωσις, *impression*, is not common.

1.5.2 The numbering of editions is by ordinal numbers in words or figures, e.g. πρώτη ἔκδοση, ἔκδοση 7η (or more often Ζ'), accompanied where necessary by participles indicating forms of revision, e.g. βελτιωμένη, *improved*; ἀναθεωρημένη, *revised*; συμπληρωμένη, *supplemented*; διορθωμένη, *corrected.*

1.5.3 The proper word for *offprint* is ἀνάτυπο(ν), but ξανατύπωμα, strictly *reprint* (ξανατυπώνω means *to reprint*), is also found. Ἀνατύπωσις is a reprint.

1.6 IMPRINTS

1.6.1 Modern imprints tend to incorporate ἐκδότης (*publisher*) or some related word, e.g. Ἐκδόσεις " Κέδρος " (as we should say *Kedros Books*), Ἐκδόσεις Πέτρου Τζουνάκου (Petros Tzounakos, the personal name being in the genitive), Ἐκδοτικὸς οἶκος Ἀθηνᾶ, ἐκδοτικὴ Ἑρμῆς Ε.Π.Ε. (*Ltd*), both meaning *publishing house* and both capable of being followed by a personal name in the genitive or the nominative. Ἔκδοση in this context means *published by* and is followed by the genitive. Alternatively there may be a straight name, institutional, personal, or arbitrary such as Ἀετός Α.Ε. (*Eagle Co.*), or a bookshop, e.g. βιβλιοπωλεῖον Ἰωαν. Ν. Σιδέρη. Here again the personal name is in the genitive.

1.6.2 Printers' imprints are distinguished by τύπος, τύποις, ἐκτύπωση (*type, with the types, printing*) followed by a genitive or an adjective in agreement; τυπογραφεῖο(ν) (*printing shop*), which exhibits the same grammatical variety as ἐκδοτική; or τυπώθηκε (*was printed*) usually followed by σέ (*at*). Τυπογραφεῖο(ν) even today does not exclude a publisher.

1.6.3 The place nowadays is for the most part in the nominative. Some places have D and K forms, e.g. Ἀθήνα, Ἀθῆναι, or at any rate popular and learned forms: Κορφοί, Κέρκυρα; Πόλη, Κωνσταντινούπολις. Note also **Λευκωσία**, *Nicosia*.

In K books imprints like ἐν ᾿Αθήναις, ἐν Κωνσταντινουπόλει and other phrases involving ἐν with the dative (see Ancient Greek) occur, and in earlier books ancient Greek locatives such as ᾿Αθήνησι, ᾿Ενετίησι (*in Venice*).

1.7 SERIES

1.7.1 The names of series, found usually either at the head of the title-page, facing it or on the half-title leaf, are mostly descriptive, e.g. Τὰ καλύτερα βιβλία τσέπης, *The best books for the pocket*; Νέα ἑλληνικὴ βιβλιοθήκη, *Modern Greek library*; Βιβλιοθήκη Κολλεγίου ᾿Αθηνῶν. ᾿Εγχειρίδια βιβλιοθηκονομίας, *Athens College Library. Library science handbooks.*

1.7.2 The separate parts, if specified and not simply numbered, are usually designated ἀριθμός, *number*; or τόμος in the case of more substantial volumes. The number which follows would be read as an ordinal. A sub-series is described as σειρά.

1.8 PERIODICALS

1.8.1 The titles of periodicals are grammatically no different from those of books, e.g. ᾿Αρχεῖον οἰκονομικῶν καὶ κοινωνικῶν σπουδῶν, *Archives of economic and social studies*; Κομμουνιστικὴ ἐπιθεώρηση, *Communist review*, though they may be much more laconic, such as Γράμματα, *Literature*; or Βυζαντινά, *Things Byzantine*; or even Βεντέτα, *Vedette*, a popular show-business magazine. In the context of a sentence the titles of periodicals behave like those of books (1.3.3), e.g. ἵδρυση του ᾿Αρχείου κλπ., *foundation of ᾿Αρχεῖον*, etc.; τοῦ περιοδικοῦ " Γράμματα ", *of the periodical Γράμματα.*

1.8.2 The name of the body responsible may be in the title, e.g. Πρακτικὰ τοῦ ῾Ελληνικοῦ ῾Υδροβιολογικοῦ ᾿Ινστιτούτου, *Proceedings of the Greek Hydrobiological Institute*; or in the sub-title, e.g. ἐπιστημονικὸν ὄργανον Κέντρου Βυζαντινῶν ᾿Ερευνῶν Φιλοσοφικῆς Σχολῆς ᾿Αριστοτελείου Πανεπιστημίου, *scientific organ of the Centre for Byzantine Research of the Philosophical School of Aristotle University*, a trying sequence of genitives producing a catalogue heading 'Aristoteleion Panepistēmion. Filosofikē Shole. Kentron Buzantinōn Ereunōn'. Less trouble is caused when the name is at the head of the page or follows some such word as ἐκδότης, *publisher*.

1.8.3 The persons responsible for running the periodical are variously described, and the functions variously combined. Remotest (unless he also performs some other function) is the ἰδιοκτήτης, *proprietor* (corresponding abstract noun ἰδιοκτησία). The functions of the διευθυντής (*director, manager*) are less easy to determine. Sometimes the διευθυντής, who may also be ἐκδότης (*publisher* or *editor*), is the only name mentioned and must be counted as editor; at other times he is distinguished from διεύθυνσις συντάξεως, those managing the putting together of the periodical, in other words, the editors. On the other hand the contrast may be between διεύθυνσις and ἔκδοσις-διαχείρισις, and the διαχειριστής is quite clearly the business manager. But ἔκδοσις itself is ambiguous: ἐπιτροπὴ ἐκδόσεως is the same as ἐπιτροπὴ συντάξεως, *editorial committee*; ἐκδίδεται (ἐκδιδόμενον), (*is*) *edited*, the same as διευθύνεται, *is managed*. Both in fact are general and embrace not only the actual editor but the advisory board—συντακτικὴ ἐπιτροπή, διοικητικὸν συμβούλιον—whose part is τακτικὴ συνεργασία, *regular collaboration*. (But alas, συνεργασία can also mean *contribution*.)

Alternative expressions for editorship, like σύνταξη unambiguous, are ἐπιμελεία (ἐπιμελητής) with or without ὕλης (*of the material*).

1.8.4 Numeration is commonly by τόμος sub-divided by τεῦχος, or by either. Τόμος is frequently supplemented (occasionally replaced) by ἔτος or by χρόνος, *year*, and τεῦχος by φυλλάδιο, *fascicule*. The numeral, in ordinal form, usually follows, but not necessarily. Academic periodicals not infrequently run into more than one series or cycle (περίοδος).

1.8.5 Periodicity is occasionally implicit in the title itself, e.g. Μηνιαῖον δελτίον στατιστικῆς, *Monthly bulletin of statistics*. Similar adjectives, ἑβδομαδιαῖος, τριμηνιαῖος (*weekly, quarterly*), may occur in the sub-title or in such phrases as θὰ ἐκδίδηται εἰς μηνιαῖα τεύχη (*will be published in monthly parts*). Such phrases, however, are more likely to contain prepositional constructions such as ἀνὰ τρίμηνον, καθ᾽ ἑξάμηνον (*every quarter, every six months*). Alternatively the number of parts or the date of appearance may be given: βγαίνει σὲ 4 ἀριθμοὺς τὸ χρόνο, *comes out in four numbers a year*; ἐκδίδεται την 1ην καὶ 15ην κάθε μηνός, *published on the 1st and 15th of each month*.

1.8.6 Subscription is συνδρομή (D also συντρομή), often in the plural -μές (K -μαί), in full ὅροι συνδρομῶν, *terms of subscription*. It may be annual (ἐτήσια, γιὰ ἕνα χρόνο) or half-yearly (ἐξαμηνιαία, ἐξάμηνη, γιὰ ἕξι μῆνες) or by volume (ὁ τόμος), and will often be different for individuals (φυσικὰ πρόσωπα) and societies (ἑταιρίαι), and certainly between inland (ἐσωτερικοῦ) and foreign (ἐξωτερικοῦ, γιὰ τὸ ἐξωτερικό). The price of single parts is stated simply as τιμὴ (ἑκάστου) τεύχους and back numbers may be offered as τόμοι προηγουμένων ἐτῶν. (Διαφήμησις is an *advertisement*.)

1.8.7 Addresses (διευθύνσεις!) may or may not separate the various activities: on the one hand there may be a simple statement such as τὰ γραφεῖα εἶναι σὲ . . ., *the offices are at . . .*; or γραφεῖα συντάξεως, *editorial offices*, may be specified. Most commonly there is a direction in the form νὰ στέλλονται, θὰ ἀποστέλλωνται, θ᾽ ἀπευθύνεται, *are to be sent, is to be addressed*, specifying ὅ τι ἀφορᾶ τὴν σύνταξιν ὕλης (*what concerns the editing of material*), τὰ χειρόγραφα (*manuscripts*) or συνεργασία καὶ ἐπιστολές (*contributions and letters*) on the one hand, and πᾶσα χρηματικὴ ἀποστολή or ἐμβάσματα (meaning *remittances*), παραγγελία or ἐπιταγαί (*orders*) on the other. Sometimes there is κεντρικὴ πώλησις, a *central selling office*.

2 ALPHABET, PHONETICS, SPELLING

2.1 ALPHABET

2.1.1 The alphabet and the British Standard transliteration are the same as for ancient Greek, viz.

Α	Β	Γ	Δ	Ε	Ζ	Η	Θ	Ι	Κ	Λ	Μ	Ν	Ξ	Ο	Π	Ρ	Σ	Τ	Υ	Φ	Χ	Ψ	Ω
α	β	γ	δ	ε	ζ	η	θ	ι	κ	λ	μ	ν	ξ	ο	π	ρ	σ	τ	υ	φ	χ	ψ	ω
a	b	g	d	e	z	ē	th	i	k	l	m	n	x	o	p	r	s	t	u	f	h	ps	ō

ς is used at the end of a word.

For the numerical value of the letters see 6.3.2.

2.1.2 In the BS transliteration the equivalents have to be pronounced like the corresponding Greek letters in a given context; other transliterations are to some extent affected by the varying values of the Greek letters, about which something must therefore be said.

αι is identical in pronunciation with ε [ε].

β is pronounced much like *v* and is often so transliterated. German uses *w*. British Museum and Library of Congress retain the transliteration *b*.

γ has four pronunciations: (1) Before αι, ε, η, ι, οι and υ it is approximately like En *y* and is often so represented. The combinations για and γιο are often represented by *ya* and *yo*. (2) Before γ, κ, ξ and χ it has the sound [ŋ] and is usually transliterated *n*. (3) After γ it has the sound of *g* in *get*, no matter what follows. (4) Elsewhere it is a voiced velar fricative, a *g* which is continuous rather than stopped. Standard transliterations use *g*, but unofficially *gh* is sometimes used to suggest the sound of the fricative.

γκ at the beginning of a word is a single sound, the same as γ (3). In the middle of a word it has the sound of [ng], except in a few foreign words, e.g. Καραγκιόζης = Turkish **Karagöz**. BM uses *g* initially, *nk* medially; L of C *nk* always. Unofficially *ghi-* (Italian fashion) is found for γκι-.

δ has the sound of *th* in *the*. The difference is not usually marked in transliter- ation but *dh* is sometimes found.

η and ι have precisely the same sound [i], to English ears *ee*. Hence the story of the magistrate who asked a defendant's occupation, and being told κριτικός, replied: 'I asked what you did, not where you came from.' BM uses the transliteration *e* for η as for ε; L of C uses *ē*; but elsewhere the use of *i* for η is very common. Somewhat surprisingly *-dès* is sometimes found in French for -δης. The combinations ει, οι and υι also have the sound [i], and this may affect their representation, e.g. *Evvia* for Εὔβοια.

κ see γκ.

μπ and ντ have the sounds [b] and [d] at the beginning of a word, [mb] and [nd] (sometimes simply [b] and [d]) in the middle. BM uses the trans- literations *b* and *d* initially, *mp* and *nt* or *b* and *d* medially according to pronunciation. L of C uses *mp*, *nt* in all positions.

ο and ω are identical in sound. BM does not distinguish in transliteration. (But οι [i] and ωι [ɔi] do differ in pronunciation.) L of C uses *ō* for ω.

π, τ see μπ and ντ.

υ has the sound [i] except in the combinations αυ [af or av], ευ [εf or εv] and ου [u]. L of C uses *y* for υ on its own. Informally one may find *i*, and phonetic representations of the combinations. These can be ambiguous.

φ: BM and L of C *ph*. Greeks more often use *f*.

χ: BM and L of C *ch*. It has in fact the two sounds of the German *ch*, but Greeks equate it with *h* and often use *h* in transliterating.

2.1.3 A breathing is alas still necessary on an initial vowel, but neither the smooth breathing, e.g. Ἀ, ἀ, Αἰ, nor the rough, Ἁ, ἁ, Αἱ makes any difference. They are frequently omitted on capitals, and if the system of transliteration distinguishes them (BM and L of C: smooth ignored, rough *h*; BS: smooth ignored, rough taken over as it stands, except in typing where an apostrophe may be substituted), the word, if not known, will have to be checked. The expert (*crede mihi*) is as likely to transliterate ΙΔΡΥΜΑ as IDRUMA instead of HIDRUMA or 'IDRUMA as anyone else, since he habitually ignores the breathing in pronunciation. The use of the rough breathing on initial ρ and of both in words like ἄρρωστος (cf. Ancient Greek) is found only in the extremest form of kathareuousa. The smooth breathing is still found (but is not obligatory) when words are run together, e.g. νἄχω for νὰ ἔχω.

2.1.4 The placing of a small iota under long vowels (ᾳ, ῃ, ῳ) survives in K, but is now obsolete in D. Originally diphthongs (κωμῳδία became comoedia in Latin) they long ago ceased to be distinguished in pronunciation from the simple vowels.

Many ligatures are found in earlier printed books, and even those found in the 18th century are too numerous to be dealt with here. Some idea of their general character can be found from this extract, though it is not in modern Greek.

Οὐδεὶς μᾶλλον Παύλ8 τ̄ Χειστὸν (26) ἠγάπησεν, 8δεῖς μέ-ζονα ἐκείν8 απ8δ̄λω ἐπιδείξᾱτο, 8δεῖς πλείον⊙ ἠξιώθη χάρῑ⊙· ἀλλ' ὅμως μ̄ ̄τσαῦτα δέδοικεν ἔτι καὶ ̄τέμει, ̄περὶ ταύτης δ̄ ἀρ-χῆς καὶ τ̄ω ἀρχομένων ῡπ' αὐτ8.

Οὐδεὶς μᾶλλον Παύλου τὸν Χριστὸν ἠγάπησεν, οὐδεὶς μείζονα ἐκείνου σπουδὴν ἐπεδείξατο, οὐδεὶς πλείονος ἠξιώθη χάριτος· ἀλλ' ὅμως μετὰ τοσαῦτα δέδοικεν ἔτι καὶ τρέμει, περὶ ταύτης τῆς ἀρχῆς καὶ τῶν ἀρχομένων ὑπ' αὐτοῦ.

One still finds ς for στ and 8 for ου in the 19th century. (On ς cf. 6.3.2.)

2.1.5 When the digraphs ending in ι or υ do not have the special values given in 2.1.2 but the values of the separate letters, a diaeresis is placed over the second letter, as in φαΐ [fai], *food*. A word like τσάι, *tea*, however, can dispense with it, since if it were pronounced [tse] it would be accented τσαί (2.1.6); but it often has it, as do words like ρωμαίικος and πρωινός whose pronunciation is never in doubt. At the beginning of a word the position of the breathing suffices to distinguish, say, ἄυλη or ἄϋλη [aili], *immaterial*, from αὐλή [avli], *courtyard*.

2.1.6 The three accents—acute as in λόγος, grave as in ἀπὸ, circumflex as in μπορῶ—no longer have distinct values but all indicate stress. Where the words are inherited from ancient Greek the old rules (Ancient Greek 2.1.6) prevail: ἡ ὥρα but τὰ δῶρα, because the α's were once respectively long and short. But not entirely in D: the feminine of τέταρτος (*fourth*) is τέταρτη. (The old feminine Τετάρτη means *Wednesday*.) Where there is no tradition there is sometimes uncertainty: πενήντα or πενῆντα, παπάς or παπᾶς. The modern feeling is for the acute. Some would abolish all accents, or retain them solely for the sake of distinction, e.g. between ἀλλά, *but* and ἄλλα, *other things*.

2.1.7 Short final vowels are often, but not always, cut off and represented by an apostrophe, e.g. μ' ἕνα (μὲ ἕνα), γι' αὐτό (γιὰ αὐτό), ἀπ' τό (ἀπὸ τό).

2.2 CAPITALISATION

2.2.1 Capital letters are used for proper nouns but not for national or local adjectives. The names of the months and the days of the week count as proper nouns, and these may also include personifications like Πατρίδα, Φύση, Δημιουργία, but not consistently.

2.2.2 All elements in personal names are capitalised, but words like κύριος (*Mr.*), καθηγητής (*Professor*) placed before them do not have capitals. Practice with ἅγιος is subject to subtle variations. When equivalent to *Saint* it has a capital, but one also finds ὁ ἅγιος Ἱερομάρτυς Εἰρηναῖος, *the holy martyr Irenaeus*.

2.2.3 In institutional names all elements except articles and prepositions have capitals, but shortened forms, e.g. ἡ ἐκκλησία, *the Church*, may have a small initial, unlike ἡ Ὀρθόδοξος Ἀνατολικὴ Ἐκκλησία in full.

2.2.4 In geographical names consistently and in names of historical events to a great extent the generic element has a small initial, e.g. τὸν ποταμὸ Στρυμόνα, τῶν Ἰονίων νήσων, ὁ Ρωσοτουρκικὸς πόλεμος, ἡ ἅλωση τῆς Κωνσταντινουπόλεως, τὸν

Ἐνωτικὸν ἀγῶνα. But in the same bibliography ἡ Ἅλωσις τῆς Καλαμάτας. When used alone ἡ Ἅλωση (i.e. the Fall of Constantinople) like ἡ Τουρκοκρατία, ἡ Ἕνωση, ὁ Διαφωτισμός (*the Enlightenment*) would always have a capital.

2.2.5 Entries in bibliographies do not use capitals except where the word would have one in any case, but casual citations often use capitals for all important words.

2.3 DIVISION OF WORDS
The rules for division are the same as in ancient Greek.

2.4 PUNCTUATION; ABBREVIATIONS
2.4.1 The only important points to note are the colon (·) and the question mark (;).

2.4.2 Abbreviations are customarily followed by a full stop, e.g. ἴ.β.: ἴδιο βιβλίο, *op. cit.*; λ.χ.: λόγου χάρη (χάριν), *e.g.* Occasionally words are contracted, e.g. πρβ.: παράβαλε, *cf.*, or several are run together with only one stop, as in κτλ. or κλπ.: καὶ (τὰ) λοιπά, *etc.*

2.5 VARIATION OF CONSONANT
2.5.1 Some changes are an essential feature of conjugation or declension and are dealt with in the appropriate place. Besides these a number of types of assimilation have been inherited from ancient Greek and extended by analogy, viz.

β, π + θ > φθ/φτ, e.g. λείπω, λείφτηκε. Similarly, γ, κ + θ > χθ/χτ; ζ + θ > σθ/στ or χθ/χτ; θ + θ > σθ/στ.

β, π, φ(τ) + μ > (μ)μ, e.g. γράφω, γραμμένος; αυ, ευ (pronounced αβ, εβ) also give (μ)μ, e.g. παντρεύω, παντρεμένος. Similarly, ζ + μ > σμ or γμ.

β, π, φ(τ) (and usually αυ and ευ) + σ > ψ, e.g. γράφω, ἔγραψα; παύω, ἔπαψα, ἔπαυσα.

γ, χ(ν), χτ + σ > ξ; ζ + σ > ξ or σ; ν + σ > σ.

2.5.2 The variations φθ/φτ, χθ/χτ and σθ/στ above are dissimilations subsequent to the original assimilation, and are usually present in pronunciation if not in spelling. A similar dissimilation turns σχ into σκ, as in ἄσκημος for ἄσχημος, and a reverse one turns κτ, πτ into χτ and φτ, e.g. ἔχτος, *sixth* as well as ἔκτος. If one is working with a dictionary which is conservative in its spelling one may need to look up φτ and χτ in both places.

2.6 VARIATION OF VOWEL
Most changes of vowel (e.g. μένω, *I remain*, θὰ μείνω, *I shall remain*) are an essential feature of declension or conjugation. In others, like στέλνω (στέλλω), *I send*, σταλμένος, *sent*, the change is only part of the inflexion. Notes of such changes are given under nouns and verbs.

2.7 SPELLING
2.7.1 A number of letters or combinations of letters have come to stand for the same sound (2.1.2). This has sometimes resulted in the almost exclusive use of one or the other of the equivalents, e.g.

Ελαβαμε ιδισι οπου ισαστε αγαναχτισμενι. (Ἐλάβαμε εἴδηση ὁποὺ εἴσαστε ἀγαναχτισμένοι.)—Lord Nelson, 1798

Κε αφτο το σκελεθρο το αφησηκο δεν ηνε ντροπη μας να κατατηραγναι το γενος μας κοντα διο χιλιαδες χρονια; (Καὶ αὐτὸ τὸ σκέλεθρο τὸ ἀφύσικο δὲν εἶναι ντροπή μας νὰ κατατυραγνάει τὸ γένος μας κοντὰ δυὸ χιλιάδες χρόνια;)—Bēlaras, 1821

2.7.2 Such phonetic radicalism, however, is not general, and traditional spelling, if any, dominates. But where phonetic change makes the old spelling impossible, there is uncertainty. Thus παλαιός has come to be pronounced [paljos]: keeping close to the old spelling it was written παλῃός, then παληός and finally παλιός. Similarly γέλοιον has become γέλιο. The alternation [-εnɔ/-ina] in verbs may appear as -ένω/ -εινα, -αίνω/-υνα or -αίνω/-ηνα. Similarly where there is no tradition, e.g. κοιτάζω, κυττάζω.

2.7.3 Some combinations of letters have changed their sound (2.5.2). In such cases some writers retain the traditional spelling while others spell phonetically, and some spell differently according to the type of word, e.g. all from the same essay: περιοριστεῖ, εὐαισθησία, πέφτω, ἀναπτύχθηκε, γράφτηκε. In most cases -νδ- has become -ντ-, reflecting the usual pronunciation.

3 ARTICLES

3.1 DEFINITE

3.1.1 *Forms*

		S			P	
	M	N	F	M	N	F
N	ὁ	τό	ἡ	οἱ	τά	οἱ (ἡ)
A	τό(ν)	τό	τή(ν)	τούς	τά	τίς (τές, ταἱς)
G		τοῦ	τῆς		τῶν	

The alternative plural forms are obsolete. For K forms see Ancient Greek.

3.1.2 The article is used with abstract nouns (ἡ παιδεία, *education*), proper names (ἡ Ἑλλάδα, *Greece*; and cf. 1.2.3), general plurals (οἱ ἄνθρωποι, *men*) and clauses (τὸ νὰ ποῦμε, *our saying*; τὸ πότε θὰ λειτουργήσῃ, *the question when will it function*).

3.2 INDEFINITE

3.2.1 *Forms*

	M	N	F
N	ἕνας	ἕνα	μιά
A	ἕνα		μιά(ν)
G	ἑνός(ἐνούς)		μιᾶς

K has N εἷς, ἕν, μία; AN ἕν; D ἑνί, μιᾷ

3.2.2 The article is omitted in expressions of the type μοῦ **φάνηκε μεγάλο ἄδικο**, *it seemed to me a great injustice*.

4 NOUNS

4.1 FORMS AND GENDER

4.1.1 Although some of the old anomalies, such as ἡ ὁδός, have come back into use, modern Greek on the whole has developed a remarkable correspondence between form and gender by which M nouns end in -ς in the nominative, F and N in a vowel.

4.1.2 Apart from nouns in -ος, the nature of the stem vowel makes no difference to the pattern of declension (cf. 4.3.2, 4.3.3).

4.1.3 K retains some or all of the ancient Greek forms.

4.2 PLURAL

4.2.1 Apart from those given in 4.3.1, 4.3.4, and 4.3.5, there are two types of plural, NA -ες, G -ων from nouns ending in -α, -η, -ας, -ης; -δες, -δων from all types of noun, but limited in scope:

> -ες: πατέρας, πατέρες; γραμμή, γραμμές
>
> -δες: κυρά-δες; ἀδερφή, ἀδερφάδες; βασιλιάς, βασιλιάδες; ἀφέντης, ἀφεντάδες; μενεξές, μενεξέδες; μάγκας, μάγκηδες; κόντες, κόντηδες; χατζής, χατζῆδες; παππούς, παπποῦδες

4.2.2 The ending -ες used to be written -αις.

4.3 ENDINGS

4.3.1 *Masculine nouns (and adjectives)*

	S	P
N	-ος	-οι
A	-ο(ν)	-ους
G	-ου	-ων

4.3.2 All other M nouns, in -ας, -ες, -ης, -ους, make A and G by dropping the -ς, e.g. πατέρας, AG πατέρα.

For their plural see 4.2.

4.3.3 *Feminine nouns (and adjectives)* end in a vowel (-α, -ε, -η, -ο, -ου, -ω) in N and A and add -ς in G, ἡ/τὴν Ἑλλάδα, τῆς Ἑλλάδας.

4.3.4 Most nouns in -ση (-ξη, -ψη), formerly also -σι (K -σις), usually have plural NA -σεις, G -σεων rather than the regular plural, for which, as for other F plurals, see 4.2.

4.3.5 *Neuter nouns (and adjectives)*

S	NA	-μα	-ι	-ο	-ιμο	-ος
	G	-ματος (-μάτου)	-ιοῦ	-ου	-ιματος (-ιμ(άτ)ου)	-ους (ου)
P	NA	-ματα	-ια	-α	-ιματα	-η(-ια)
	G	-μάτων	-ιῶν	-ων	-ιμάτων	-ῶν

The forms in brackets (extreme demotic) are obsolete, as is GP without the final -ν.

4.3.6 The first and last types, important survivals from the ancient language, do not square with the usual patterns. Hence the once popular alternatives. Another survival is φῶς, *light*, G φωτός, P φῶτα.

4.6 USE OF CASES

4.6.1 The nominative is sometimes found after γιά and ἀπό (10.2.1).

4.6.2 The accusative, besides being the case of the direct object and the complement of prepositions, is typically the adverbial case, e.g. τὸ ἴδιο, *likewise*; ἔμεινε τρεῖς μῆνες, *he stayed three months*. Note also phrases like γεμάτο φῶς, *full of light*.

4.6.3 The genitive, besides its expected uses, descriptive or possessive—χαρτὶ ἐφημερίδας, *newsprint*; τὸ βιβλίο τοῦ πατέρα μου, *my father's book*—can be used for the indirect object, e.g. ἔδωσα τοῦ πατέρα μου ἕνα βιβλίο, *I gave my father a book*. Note the order. The genitive is obligatory for pronouns, but nouns more often take the preposition σέ (*to*), viz. στὸν πατέρα μου.

5 ADJECTIVES

5.1 GENERAL

5.1.1 Adjectives vary for gender and number. When they qualify nouns they agree in both, but they can be used alone, in which case the gender is significant, e.g. οἱ διανοούμενοι, *intellectuals*; ἡ φαρμακωμένη, *the poisoned woman*; τὸ ἰδανικό, *the ideal*.

5.1.2 When used with an article the adjective precedes the noun. When there is no article it may follow, especially if it is the beginning of a long phrase, e.g. προλήψεις ζυμωμένες μὲ χιλιόχρονη ἐκπαιδευτικὴ παράδοση, *prejudices formed by a thousand-year educational tradition*.

5.2 ENDINGS

5.2.1 Most adjectives have three forms for the different genders, viz.

M	N	F
-ος	-ο	-η/-α
-ής	-ί	-ιά
-ης	-ικο	-(ισσ)α
-ύς	-ύ	-(ε)ιά

Each of these follows the declension of nouns of the same forms, -υς, -υ being treated like -ης, -ι, from which they are phonetically indistinguishable. There are M plurals in -δες but not F ones.

5.2.2 The third-declension adjectives in ancient Greek which had the same form for M and F have mostly been transformed into one of the above types, but the more learned of them tend to crop up in technical writing, e.g. ὁμοιογενής, *homogeneous*. Possible forms are:

	S		P	
	MF	N	MF	N
N	-ής	-ές	-εῖς	-ῆ
A	-ῆ	-ές	-εῖς	-ῆ
G	-οῦς		-ῶν	

5.2.3 πολύς (*much, many*) has most of its forms as if from πολλός.

5.3 COMPARISON

5.3.1 There is a comparative ending -τερος, though πιό, *more*, can also be used. Adjectives in -ος make -ότερος or -ώτερος, occasionally, like those in -υς, -ύτερος, also spelt -ήτερος, -(ε)ίτερος.

5.3.2 The superlative adds the article to the comparative.

6 NUMERALS

6.1 CARDINAL

6.1.1

1 ἕνας (K εἷς)	9 ἐννιά	30 τριάντα
2 δυό	10 δέκα	40 σαράντα
3 τρεῖς	11 ἔνδεκα (ἐντ-)	50 πενῆντα
4 τέσσερεις	12 δώδεκα	60 ἐξῆντα
5 πέντε	13 δεκατρεῖς	70 ἐβδομῆντα
6 ἔξι	19 δεκαεννιά	80 ὀγδόντα
7 ἐφτά	20 εἴκοσι	90 ἐνενῆντα
8 ὀχτώ	21 εἴκοσι ἕνας	100 ἐκατό

200 διακόσ(ι)οι	700 ἐφτακόσ(ι)οι
300 τρ(ι)ακόσ(ι)οι	800 ὀχτακόσ(ι)οι
400 τετρακόσ(ι)οι	900 ἐννιακόσ(ι)οι
500 πεντακόσ(ι)οι	1000 χίλιοι
600 ἐξακόσ(ι)οι	

6.1.2 ἕνας, τρεῖς, τέσσερεις and their compounds, διακόσοι, etc. and χίλιοι are declinable adjectives: ἕνας like the indefinite article; τρεῖς: N τρία, G τριῶν. Τέσσεροι, τέσσερις have been used for τέσσερεις, which has N τέσσερα.

6.2 ORDINAL

6.2.1

1 πρῶτος	8 ὄγδοος
2 δεύτερος	9 ἔνατος
3 τρίτος	10 δέκατος
4 τέταρτος	11 ἐνδέκατος
5 πέμπτος	12 δωδέκατος
6 ἔκτος (ἐχ-)	13 δέκατος τρίτος
7 ἔβδομος	20 εἰκοστός

Higher ordinals are little used.

6.2.2 The ordinals are all adjectives, with F -η.

Note the following distinctions in D: δεύτερη, *second*; Δευτέρα, *Monday*; τέταρτη, *fourth*; Τετάρτη, *Wednesday* (ambiguous in K).

6.3 FIGURES

6.3.1 Arabic numerals can be used both for cardinals and, with a full stop or the adjectival endings, as ordinals, e.g. **7** or **7η**: ἐβδόμη.

6.3.2 In the numeration of preliminary pages, volumes, parts, years and centuries, the letters of the alphabet are often used as figures, e.g. ͵αωλα΄, *1831*; ὁ ΙΖ΄ αἰώνας, *the 17th century*. The values are as follows:

1	2	3	4	5	6	7	8	9	10	20	30	40	50	60	70	80
α΄	β΄	γ΄	δ΄	ε΄	ϛ΄	ζ΄	η΄	θ΄	ι΄	κ΄	λ΄	μ΄	ν΄	ξ΄	ο΄	π΄

90	100	200	300	400	500	600	700	800	900	1000
ϟ΄	ρ΄	σ΄	τ΄	υ΄	φ΄	χ΄	ψ΄	ω΄	ϡ΄	͵α

6.4 DATES

6.4.1 The months are:

'Ιανουάριος, Φεβρουάριος, Μάρτιος, 'Απρίλιος, Μάιος, 'Ιούνιος,
'Ιούλιος, Αὔγουστος, Σεπτέμβριος, 'Οκτώβριος, Νοέμβριος, Δεκέμβριος

Though K forms, these are widely used. In pure demotic -ης replaces -ιος and the first two months are Γενάρης and Φλεβάρης.

6.4.2 The first day of the month is expressed as an ordinal number, 2–31 in cardinals. The month is in the genitive, the year in cardinals, e.g.

on 12 July 1972, στὶς δώδεκα (τοῦ) 'Ιουλίου χίλια ἐννιακόσα δυό
in May '41, τὸ Μάη τοῦ σαράντα ἕνα

K uses ordinals, and so does D for dates which signify events, such as ἡ τέταρτη Αὐγούστου, ἡ εἰκοστὴ πρώτη 'Απριλίου.

7 PRONOUNS

7.1 DEMONSTRATIVE, ETC.

The non-personal pronouns, when used adjectivally, behave like any other adjective, except for the position of some of them, e.g. αὐτὴ (τούτη) ἡ ἔκδοση, *this edition.* As pronouns they have optional long forms in the genitive, e.g. αὐτ(ουν)οῦ, αὐτ(ην)ῆς, αὐτ(ων)ῶν; (ἐ)τουτου(νοῦ), etc.; ποιανοῦ, ποιανῆς, etc. from ποιός.

7.2 RELATIVE

The commonest relative is πού, which is indeclinable and is supplemented by the demonstrative thus: πού . . . του (της, etc.) *whose;* πού τοῦ, etc., *to whom;* πού γι' αὐτούς, *about whom;* πού ἀπο κεῖ, *whence.*

7.3 PERSONAL

7.3.1

	S		P	
	1	2	1	2
N	ἐγώ	ἐσύ	ἐμεῖς	ἐσεῖς
A	ἐμένα, μέ	ἐσένα, σέ	(ἐ)μᾶς	(ἐ)σᾶς
G	ἐμένα, μοῦ	ἐσένα, σοῦ	(ἐ)μᾶς	(ἐ)σᾶς

The third person pronoun is the demonstrative αὐτός, with short forms identical with the article (3.1.1) except that τούς serves as the genitive plural.

7.3.2 When the short (unemphatic) forms follow a noun or preposition they have no accent, being treated as if they were part of the preceding word: κοντά μου.

8 VERBS

8.1 STRUCTURE

8.1.1 The Greek verb has endings characteristic of person and number which make subject pronouns unnecessary. The same endings serve more than one tense, the tenses being distinguished by differences of stem.

8.1.2 There is basically only one system of endings, but some verbs have stems ending in a vowel which has combined with the endings, resulting in different vowels. The endings are:

I(a) -ω, -εις, -ει; -ο(υ)με, -ετε, -ουν(ε)
(b) -ῶ, -ᾶς, -ᾶ; -ᾶμε, -ᾶτε, -ᾶν(ε)
(c) -ῶ, -εῖς, -εῖ; -οῦμε, -εῖτε, -οῦν(ε)

K has, additionally or instead, -ομεν, -ῶμεν, -οῦμεν; -οῦτε; -ουσι(ν), -ῶσι(ν).

II(a) -α, -ας, -ε; -αμε, -ατε, -αν(ε)
(b) -οῦσα, -οῦσας, etc.
(c) -ον, -ες, -ε; -ομεν, -οτε, -ον (K)

8.1.3 Verbs are entered in the dictionary under the 1PS of the present (present passive if there is no active).

8.2 PRESENT

8.2.1 *Endings* I(a)–(c) according to the verb.

8.2.2 Variants with η or ῃ for ει and ε are found after νά and θά.

8.2.3 Telescoped forms are found with some vowel stems, e.g. λένε from λέω, ἀκοῦμε from ἀκούω.

8.2.4 When used with νά and θά (8.7.2, 8.10.1), the present forms express continuous action or emphasise its concreteness, the aorist subjunctive single acts or abstract notions, e.g. Θὰ βλέπουμε καὶ θακοῦμε. "Αχ τί θὰ δοῦμε καὶ τί θακούσουμε;, *We shall have sights and sounds. Ah, what shall we see and what shall we hear?*

8.3 IMPERFECT

8.3.1 *Endings* II(a) with present stem: καταλαβαίνω, *I understand*; καταλάβαινα, *I understood*. Verbs with monosyllabic stems usually prefix ἔ-, e.g. λέγω, ἔλεγα, λέγαμε.

Endings II(b) from presents in -ῶ, e.g. μποροῦσα, *I could* (μπορῶ).

8.3.2 K has II(c) endings and all simple verbs prefix ἐ- throughout. (Verbs with prefixes insert -ε-, e.g. καταλαμβάνω, κατελάμβανον.) Some verbs in K, and a few in D, lengthen the initial vowel of the stem, e.g. ἔχω, εἶχα; ὑπάρχω, ὑπῆρχα (K -χον).

8.3.3 The imperfect by itself expresses continuous or habitual action in past time. For its use with θὰ see 8.10.2.

8.4 AORIST

8.4.1 The aorist has a different stem from the present. Many stems end in σ or its combinations ξ and ψ, corresponding thus to the present:

Aorist	Present
-σ-	-δω, -ζω, θω, -νω, -τω, -ω
-ασ-	also -(ν)ῶ (Ib)
-εσ-	also -ῶ (Ic)
-ησ-, -υσ-	also -αίνω, -ένω, -ῶ (Ib; Ic)
-ωσ-	also -ώνω
-ξ-	-(γ)γω, -ζω, -κω, -χ(ν)ω
-αξ-	also -ῶ (Ib)
-ηξ-	also -(ν)ῶ (Ib)
-ψ-	-βω, -πω, -φ(τ)ω
-αψ-, -εψ-	also -αύω, -εύω

Peculiar stems are:

-δωσ-	δίδω, δίνω
καθισ-	κάθομαι (8.15.5)

8.4.2 Stems which do not take σ have a different vowel from the present, or omit -(αι)ν-, or both, viz.

Aorist	Present
-	-αίνω
-λ-	-λλω/-λνω
-αν-	-αίνω
-ειν-, -ην-, -υν-	-αίνω, -ένω
but κριν-	κρίνω
-ειρ-, -ηρ-, -υρ-	-αίρνω, -έρνω

In K the stems are sometimes the same. Alternations of the type τυχ-/τυχαίνω, λαβ-/λαβαίνω have τυγχάνω, λαμβάνω in K.
Peculiar are:

βαλ-: βάζω/βάνω/βάλλω (similarly βγαλ-, μπαλ-)
γιν-: γίνομαι (8.15.5)
καμ-: κάνω
φαγ-: τρώγω
φυγ-: φεύγω
εἶδα, δῶ: βλέπω
εἶπα, πῶ: λέγω
ἤπια, πιῶ: πίνω
ἤξερα, ξέρω: ξέρω, ξεύρω
ἦρθα, ἔρθω/(ἐ)ρθῶ: ἔρχομαι (8.15.5)

8.4.3 The aorist stem takes both type I and type II endings. (K has II(c) endings for some aorists without σ). With II(a) endings and occasional ἔ- (cf. 8.3.1) it is the usual past tense, e.g. ὅπως εἴδαμε, *as we saw*; καταλάβατε; *have you understood?* (*do you understand?*); ἀφοῦ μᾶς πάτησαν, *after they had trampled on us*. With type I endings (type I(c) in forms like δῶ) it forms the aorist subjunctive, found in subordinate clauses, and especially after νά and θά (8.7.2, 8.10.1). For the force of the tense see 8.2.3.

8.7 THE SUBJUNCTIVE; νά

8.7.1 The old subjunctive endings became phonetically identical with those of the indicative in the present tense, and though for a time the difference of spelling lingered, most writers have now dropped it. In the aorist, however, the indicative endings are type II and the subjunctive endings type I, so the η spelling characteristic of the old subjunctive is found more often. I have therefore kept the term 'subjunctive,' though tempted to follow Sofroniou in using 'indefinite' (a Latinisation of 'aorist') for the aorist subjunctive, and 'past' for the aorist indicative.

8.7.2 The aorist subjunctive is found only in subordinate clauses and is commoner than the vivid present (8.2.3). Typical uses are ἄς ὑποθέσουμε, *let us suppose*; προτοῦ (or πρίν) ἀρχίσει, *before it begins*; ὥσπου νά συναντήσουν, *until they meet*; ἄν ἐξαιρεθοῦν, *if they are excepted*. (Those who know ancient Greek must not be horrified to learn that ἄν, ὅταν and the like are also used with the past indicative, e.g. ἄν μπορούσα, *if I could*.)

8.7.3 Some subordinating conjunctions incorporate νά, derived from the old conjunction ἵνα, *in order that*. It now goes closely with the verb, being separated only by object pronouns and the negative μή(ν), and the subject must either precede νά, e.g. πρέπει μερικοί ἐκδρομεῖς νὰ ἐκφράσουμε τὴν εὐγνωμοσύνη μας, *many of us excursionists have to express our gratitude*, or follow the verb, as in κανένας τρόπος γιὰ ν' ἀποδείξει κανείς, *no way for anyone to show*. So νά itself is hardly felt as a conjunction, and though it can be translated *that*, most of its uses correspond to the English infinitive as above, or after prepositions to the gerund, e.g. χωρὶς νὰ ἔχω ἀσχοληθεῖ εἰδικά, *without having made a special study*. (Modern Greek has no infinitive.)

8.10 COMPOUND TENSES

8.10.1 The future is formed by means of the particle θά (earlier θενά) with the present or more often the aorist subjunctive, e.g. θὰ δοῦμε, *we shall see* (see also 8.2.3).

8.10.2 The conditional is θά with the imperfect. (Θά with the aorist indicative means *must have*—probability.) Note the common contraction θἄτανε for θὰ ἤτανε, θἄχα for θὰ εἶχα, and so on.

8.10.3 The perfect (pluperfect, etc.) is formed from the present (imperfect, etc.) of ἔχω, *I have*, with the 3PS of the aorist subjunctive, e.g. ἔχω γράψει, *I have written*; δὲν εἶχε γραφεῖ, *it had not been written*. The perfect sense is stronger than in English: ἔχω ξεχάσει, *I have forgotten* (and am no longer aware), the English perfect being often represented by the aorist. The pluperfect, however, is used when it is necessary to indicate the priority of an event.

8.10.4 Forms like ἔχω γραμμένο are best taken literally, as in 8.12.3, rather than as normal compound tenses.

8.12 PARTICIPLES

8.12.1 *Present active:* -οντας, -ῶντας (from -ῶ). Indeclinable, and only used adverbially or as the equivalent of a relative clause, e.g. κρίνοντας τὸν " Ἐρωτόκριτο " συναντοῦμε δυὸ λογιῶ δυσκολίες, *in judging the Erotokritos we meet two sorts of difficulties*; ἕνας λεβέντης κοιτάζοντας ἀγριωπά, *a cavalier with a grim look on his face*. Declinable in K as in ancient Greek.

8.12.2 *Present passive:* -άμενος, -ούμενος. Only from a few verbs. Now used almost exclusively adjectivally, e.g. τρεχάμενο νερό, *running water*. K has it from all verbs: ending -όμενος.

8.12.3 *Perfect passive:* -μένος. Mostly used adjectivally, e.g. τὰ ξαφνιασμένα πρόσωπα, *the surprised faces*; τὰ εἴχανε γραμμένα, *they had them in written form*; οἱ τραγικοί, ἐπηρεασμένοι ἀπὸ τὴν ἰωνικὴ ποίηση, *the tragedians, influenced by Ionian poetry*.

The precise forms are parallel to those of the aorist, and thus to the present forms given in 8.15.3:

Participle	Aorist
-μένος	-θ-
-σμένος	-στ-
-(μ)μένος	-φτ-
-γμένος	-χτ-

Forms in -εμένος may thus correspond to a present in -ῶ, -εύω, -έβω, -έπω, -έφ(τ)ω, but there is sometimes a change of vowel, e.g. -στραμμένος from -στρέφω.

K may have an extra syllable at the beginning, e.g. κεκομμένος, γεγραμμένος (D κομμένος, γραμμένος).

8.12.4 K also uses the aorist active and passive participles in -ας (-ων) and -(θ)είς for which see Ancient Greek 8.12.6 (and 8.15.3 below).

8.15 PASSIVE

8.15.1 The endings of the *present* are:

- (a) -ο(υ)μαι, -εσαι, -εται; -ο(υ)μαστε, -εστε, -ο(υ)νται
- (b) -ιέμαι, -ιέσαι, etc.
- (c) -ᾶμαι, -ᾶσαι, -ᾶται; -ούμαστε, -ᾶστε, -οῦνται
- (d) -εῖμαι, -εῖσαι, -εῖται; -ούμαστε, -εῖστε, -οῦνται

K has -ομεθα, -εσθε. Forms such as -ουμαι (type a) are extreme demotic.

Type (b) corresponds to (b) and (c) of the active; (d) to (c). Type (c) has no active form.

8.15.2 The endings of the *imperfect* are:

- (a) -όμουν(α), -όσουν(α), -όταν(ε)/-ονταν; -όμασταν, -όσασταν, -όντουσαν/ -ο(υ)νταν(ε)
- (b) -ιόμουν(α), etc.

K has -ομην, -εσο, -ετο; -ομεθα, -εσθε, -οντο, together with the prefix ἐ-.

8.15.3 The *aorist* has the endings -(θ)ηκα (type II); and -(θ)ῶ (type I(c)) after νὰ and θά and subordinating conjunctions. Aorist passive stems correspond to the present active as follows:

Aorist		Present
-θ-		-ω, -νω
-α(ν)θ-	also	-αίνω
-εθ-		-ῶ (Ic)
-ηθ-		-ῶ (Ib, Ic) or -ᾶμαι (8.15.1)
-υθ-	also	-αίνω, -ένω
-ωθ-	also	-όνω
-αλθ-, -ελθ-		-έλλω/-έλνω
-αρθ-, -ερθ-		-αίρνω, -έρνω
-υρθ-		-έρνω
-στ-		-ω, -ζω, -θω, -νω
-αστ-, -εστ-	also	-ῶ
-φτ-		-βω, -πω, -φ(τ)ω
-χτ-		-(γ)γω, -ζω, -κω, -χ(ν)ω
-αχτ-, -ηχτ-	also	-ῶ (Ib)

(For -στ-, etc. instead of -σθ- see 2.5.2.)

-αν-	-αίνω
-π-	-φτω
-απ-	-έπω, -έφτω
-αρ-	-αίρω
-αφ-	-έφω

Peculiar stems are:

ἀφεθ-	ἀφίνω
βαλθ-	βάζω, etc. (8.4.2)
βρεθ-	βρίσκω
δοθ-	δίδω, δίνω
εἰπωθ-	λέγω
σταθ-	στέκω
φαγωθ-	τρώγω

8.15.4 The endings -ηκα, etc. are sometimes active, as in -βῆκα from -βαίνω and similarly βγῆκα, μπῆκα; βρῆκα (as well as ηὗρα) from βρίσκω; ἔθηκα (as well as ἔθεσα) from θέτω.

8.15.5 The passive forms not only have a passive sense, but may also be reflexive, intransitive or reciprocal. Some verbs have no active voice, e.g. θυμᾶμαι, *I remember*; some like γίνομαι, ἔρχομαι have some forms of one voice and some of the other.

8.17 THE VERB *to be*

8.17.1

Present: εἶμαι, εἶσαι, εἶναι; εἴμαστε, εἶστε, εἶναι

Imperfect: ἤμουν(α), ἤσουν(α), ἤταν(ε); ἤμασταν, ἤσασταν, ἤταν(ε)
or εἴμουν, etc.

Future and Conditional as in 8.10.1, 8.10.2.

8.17.2 K has εἴμεθα in the present; imperfect ἤμην, ἦσο, ἦτο.

9 ADVERBS

9.1 FORMATION

9.1.1 Adverbs derived from adjectives usually end in -α, the ending of the neuter plural, but there are a number with the old ending -ως, such as ἀλλιῶς, *otherwise*; ἑπομένως, *consequently*, including some, like δυστυχῶς, *unfortunately*; συνήθως, *usually*, whose adjectives do not fit the demotic scheme. In a few cases the neuter singular in -o is used.

9.1.2 The adverbial ending in K is almost invariably -ως.

9.2 COMPARISON

9.2.1 The scheme is much the same as for adjectives, e.g. καλύτερα, *better*, or sometimes the neuter singular, e.g. λιγότερο, *less*, the superlative being τὸ πιὸ καλύτερα or simply τὸ καλύτερο.

9.2.2 K has C -τερον, S -τατα, and one finds, e.g. ἀπλούστατα, *quite simply*, occasionally in demotic.

9.2.3 *Than* is ἀπό or παρά.

10 PREPOSITIONS

10.2 SIMPLE

10.2.1 Simple prepositions in D are few in number and all take the accusative. The preposition σέ, εἰς (*in, at, into, to*) combines with the article to make στόν, στή, etc. Those who know ancient Greek should beware of changes of usage: ἀπό, for instance, can now mean *through, by* (1.2.2 and ἀπὸ τὸ τηλέφωνο, *by telephone*), *of*, as well as *from*. (᾽Από meaning *from being* and γιά meaning *as* are followed by the nominative.)

10.2.2 K tries to preserve the ancient Greek scheme in which some prepositions have different meanings with different cases, e.g. μετά + G *with* (D μέ), μετά + A *after* (D ὕστερα ἀπό), and elides ἀπό, ἐπί, κατά, ὑπό to ἀφ᾽, ἐφ᾽, καθ᾽, ὑφ᾽ before a rough breathing. (D ἀπ᾽: 2.1.7.)

10.4 COMPOUND

The remaining prepositions consist of an adverb followed by ἀπό or σέ, e.g. κάτω ἀπό, *below*; μπροστά σέ (or ἀπό), *before*. With unemphatic pronouns the adverb is used alone and the pronoun is in the genitive, e.g. μπροστά μου, *in front of me*. ᾽Αντί(ς), *instead*, is followed by γιά.

11 CONJUNCTIONS

11.1 COORDINATING

11.1.1 The forms are much the same as in ancient Greek, and differences of usage can be disconcerting. Thus οὔτε now usually means *not even* or *not . . . either*, as in οὔτε ἀπό τὸν ἐπίλογο—ἀλλά οὔτε καὶ ἀπὸ ἄλλα στοιχεῖα, *not even from the epilogue— or for that matter from other elements either*; nor is μήτε any longer confined to the subjunctive and the imperative, but is used like οὔτε: δὲ βλέπει τίποτε ἀπὸ ὅλα αὐτὰ τὰ πράγματα, μήτε κἄν τὸ πρόσωπο ποὺ ὀνομάζεται " Σύ ", *he sees none of all these things, not even the person who is called 'Thou'*. *Neither . . . nor* may be either οὐδέ . . . οὐδέ or οὔτε . . . οὔτε. K on the other hand uses οὐδέ for *nor* or *not even*, οὔτε . . . οὔτε for *neither . . . nor*.

11.1.2 A peculiar feature of modern Greek is the use of καί, *and*, where one might expect subordination, e.g. ἄν τύχει καὶ ξυπνήσει, *if he happens to wake*; κάνει καὶ λέγονται, *results in their being called*.

11.1.3 The word ἄν is ambiguous. Usually it is a conjunction, *if* (ἄν καὶ, *although*), but καὶ ἄν after relatives has the meaning *-ever*, e.g. ὅπως κι᾽ ἄν εἶναι, *however that may be*.

GLOSSARY

ἀλληλογραφία, *correspondence*
ἀμοιβή, *exchange*
ἀναθεωρημένος, *revised* (1.5.2)
ἀνάτυπο(ν), *offprint*
ἀνατύπωσις, *reprinting, reprint* (1.5.3)
ἀνέκδοτος, *unpublished*
ἀντίτυπο(ν), *copy*
ἅπαντα, *complete works*
ἀπευθύνω, *I send, dispatch*
ἄρθρο(ν), *article*
ἀριθμός, *number* (1.7.2)

βγαίνει, *comes out*
βελτιωμένος, *improved* (1.5.2)
βιβλιοθηκάριος, *librarian*

βιβλιοθήκη, *library*
βιβλίο(ν), *book*
βιβλιοπωλεῖο(ν), *bookshop*
βιβλιοπώλης, *bookseller*

γεννήθηκε, *was born*
γραφεῖο(ν) συντάξεως, *editorial office*

δεῖγμα, *sample, specimen*
δεκαπενθήμερος, *fortnightly*
δελτίο(ν), *bulletin* (1.8.5)
δεμένος, *bound*
δημοσιευμένος, *published*
διάσκεψις, *conference*

διεύθυνση, *address* (1.8.7); *management, editorship; directorate*
διευθυντής, *editor, manager* (1.8.3)
διήγημα, *story*
διορθωμένος, *corrected* (1.5.2)
δοκίμιο, *essay*
δωρεάν, *free*

ἑβδομαδιαῖος, *weekly* (1.8.5)
εἰκόνα, *illustration*
εἰσαγωγή, *introduction*
ἐκδιδόμενος, *being published*
ἐκδομένος, *published*
ἔκδοση, *edition* (1.5.1), *publication* (1.6.1, 1.8.3)
ἐκδότης, *editor, publisher* (1.8.3)
ἐκδοτική, ἐκδοτικὸς οἶκος, *publishing house* (1.6.1)
ἐκλογή, *selection*
ἐκτύπωσις, *impression*
ἐξαμηνιαῖος, καθ' ἐξάμηνο, *half-yearly* (1.8.5, 1.8.6)
ἐξαντλημένος, *out of print*
ἐξήγηση, *interpretation, commentary*
ἐξηντλήθη, *is out of print*
ἐξωτερικός, *foreign, abroad*
ἐπετηρ|ίς, -ίδα, *yearbook*
ἐπιθεώρηση, *review* (1.8.1)
ἐπιμέλεια, *care (editorship, etc.)* (1.2.3, 1.8.3)
ἐπίμετρο(ν), *appendix*
ἐπιστολή, *letter*
ἐπιταγή, *order* (1.8.7)
ἐπιτροπή, *committee, board*
ἐργασία, ἔργο(ν), *work*
ἔρευνα, *research*
ἑταιρία, *society*
ἐτήσιος, *annual*
ἑτοιμασία, *preparation*
ἕτοιμος, *ready*
ἔτος, *year* (1.8.4)
εὑρετήριο(ν), *index*

ἰδιοκτήτης, *proprietor*
ἴδιος, *same*
ἱστορία, *history*

λεξικό(ν), *dictionary*
λογαριασμός, *bill*

μέλος, *member*
μέρος, *part*
μεταφράζω, *I translate* (1.2.2)
μετάφραση, *translation* (1.2.3)
μηνιαῖος, *monthly*
μυθιστόρημα, *novel*

νέος, *new*

ξανατύπωμα, *reprint, offprint* (1.5.3)

παραγγελία, *order* (1.8.7)
παράρτημα, *appendix, supplement*
πεθαμένος, *dead*
πεπραγμένα, *proceedings*
περίληψις, *summary*
περίοδος, *series, period* (1.8.4)
πίνακας, *index; list; plate; table*
πρακτικά, *proceedings*
πρόλογος, *preface*
προσθήκη, *addition*
πωλοῦνται, *are on sale*

ρομάντσο, *novel*

σειρά, *(sub)series* (1.7.2)
σελίδα, *page*
σημείωση, *note*
στέλνω, *I send*
σύγγραμμα, *composition, work* (1.2.2)
συγγραφέας, *author*
συγγραφικὸ(ν) δικαίωμα, *copyright*
συλλογή, *collection*
σύλλογος, *association, club*
συμπλήρωμα, *supplement*
συμπληρωμένος, *enlarged* (1.5.2)
συνδιάσκεψις, *conference*
συνδρομή, *subscription* (1.8.6)
συνέδριο(ν), *congress*
συνεργασία, *collaboration, contribution*
συνέχεια, *continuation*
συνεχίζεται, *is (to be) continued*
συνθέτω, *compile*
σύνταξις, *editing* (1.8.3)
συντρομή, *subscription* (1.8.6)
σχόλιο(ν), *commentary*

τεῦχος, *part*
τιμή, *price*

τόμος, *volume*

τόμοι προηγουμένων ἐτῶν, *back numbers*

τριμηνιαῖος (1.8.5)

τυπογραφεῖο(ν), *printing shop* (1.6.2)

τυπογράφος, *printer* (1.6.2)

γιὰ τύπωμα, *to be printed*

φυλλάδιο, *issue* (1.8.4)

χειρόγραφο, *manuscript*

χρόνος, *year* (1.8.4)

GRAMMATICAL INDEX: WORDS

GRAMMATICAL INDEX: ENDINGS

-ουνα, 8.15.2
-τερα, 9.2.1
-σα, 8.4.3
-ισσα, 5.2.1
-οῦσα, 8.1.2, 8.3.1
-(ί)ματα, 4.3.5
-τατα, 9.2.1
-ψα, 8.4.3

-ε, 4.3.2, 8.1.2, 8.3.1,
   8.4.3
-εσθε, 8.15.1, 8.15.2
-κε, 8.15.3
-με, 8.1.2, 8.2.1
-αμε, 8.1.2, 8.3.1, 8.4.3
-καμε, 8.15.3
-οῦμε, 8.1.2, 8.3.1
-θοῦμε, 8.15.3
-νε, 8.1.2, 8.2.1, 8.4.3
-ανε, 8.1.2, 8.3.1, 8.4.3
-κανε, 8.15.3
-οῦσανε, 8.1.2, 8.3.1
-(ν)τανε, 8.15.2
-θοῦνε, 8.15.3
-σε, 8.4.3
-οῦσε, 8.1.2, 8.3.1
-ατε, 8.1.2, 8.3.1, 8.4.3
-κατε, 8.15.3
-ε(ι)τε, 8.1.2, 8.2.1, 8.4.3,
   8.15.3
-θεῖτε, 8.15.3
-(μα)στε, 8.15.1
-οῦτε, 8.1.2, 8.3.1
-ψε, 8.4.3

-η, 4.3.2, 4.3.3, 4.3.5,
   5.2.1, 8.2.2
-ῆ, 5.2.2
-η, 8.2.2

-ί, 5.2.1
-μαι, -σαι, -ται, 8.15.1

-ει, 8.1.2, 8.2.1, 8.4.3
-εῖ, 8.1.2, 8.2.1, 8.4.3,
   8.15.3
-θεῖ, 8.15.3
-οι, 4.3.1
-σι, 8.1.2

-αν, 8.1.2, 8.3.1, 8.4.3
-ᾶν, 8.1.2, 8.2.1
-καν, 8.15.3
-ξαν, -σαν, 8.4.3
-οῦσαν, 8.1.2, 8.3.1
-ντουσαν, 8.15.2
-ταν, 8.15.2
-ψαν, 8.4.3
-αμεν, 8.3.1, 8.4.3
-ομεν, 8.1.2, 8.4.3
-ομην, 8.15.2
-σιν, 8.1.2
-ον, 4.3.1, 8.1.2, 8.4.3
-τερον, 9.2.1
-ουν, 8.1.2, 8.2.1, 8.4.3
-οῦν, 8.1.2, 8.2.1, 8.4.3,
   8.15.3
-θοῦν, 8.15.3
-μουν, 8.15.2
-σουν, 8.15.2
-ων, 4.2.1, 4.3.1, 4.3.5,
   8.12.4
-ῶν, 4.3.5, 5.2.2
-δων, 4.2.1
-σεων, 4.3.4
-ιῶν, 4.3.5
-(ί)ματων, 4.3.5

-ο, 4.3.1, 4.3.3, 4.3.5,
   5.2.1, 9.1.1
-ικό, 5.2.1
-τερο, 9.2.1
-εσο, 8.15.2
-οντο, 8.15.2
-ετο, 8.15.2

-ς, 4.1.1, 4.3.1, 4.3.2,
   4.3.3
-ας, 8.1.2, 8.3.1, 8.4.3,
   8.12.4
-ᾶς, 8.1.2, 8.2.1, 8.4.3
-κας, 8.15.3
-ξας, -σας, 8.4.3
-οῦσας, 8.1.2, 8.3.1
-ντας, 8.12.1
-ψας, 8.4.3
-ες, 4.2.1, 4.3.2, 8.1.2,
   8.4.3
-ές, 5.2.2
-δες, 4.2.1, 5.2.1
-ής, 5.2.1, 5.2.2
-αις, 4.2.2
-εις, 8.1.2, 8.2.1, 8.4.3,
   8.12.4
-εῖς, 5.2.2, 8.1.2, 8.2.1,
   8.4.3, 8.15.3
-θείς, 8.12.4
-θεῖς, 8.15.3
-σεις, 4.3.4
-μενος, 8.12.2
-μένος, 8.12.3
-τερος, 5.3.1
-(ί)ματος, 4.3.5
-ους, 4.3.1, 4.3.5
-οῦς, 5.2.2
-ως, 9.1.1

-ύ, 5.2.1
-ου, 4.3.1, 4.3.2, 4.3.5
-ιοῦ, 4.3.5
-ιμου, 4.3.5
-(ί)ματου, 4.3.5

-ω, 8.1.2, 8.2.1, 8.4.3
-ῶ, 8.1.2, 8.2.1, 8.4.3,
   8.15.3
-θῶ, 8.15.3
-(ί)ματω, 4.3.5

ALBANIAN

Tosk

Në këtë vëllim janë dhënë burimet për historinë e lashtë të Shqipërisë, për ilirët dhe Ilirinë. Kronologjikisht ato përfshijnë një periudhë të gjatë që fillon me Homerin dhe mbaron me shek. VII të e. sonë. Meqenëse ndonjë burim antik me rëndësi nuk na është ruajtur veçse në dorë të dytë e të tretë, nëpërmjet autorësh më të vonë, u pa e nevojëshme që përsa i përket zgjedhjes së autorëve të mos i përmbaheshim rigorozisht këtij rregulli dhe përmblodhëm në listën e burimeve tona edhe veprën e Zonarës.

In this volume are given the sources for the early history of Albania, for the Illyrians and Illyria. Chronologically they cover a long period which begins with Homer and ends with the 7th century A.D. Seeing that no ancient source of importance is preserved except at second or third hand, through the medium of later authors, it seemed necessary that so far as concerns the selection of authors we should not abide rigorously by this rule, and we have included in the list of our sources the work also of Zonaras.

Geg

Ndër ato 25 vepra të Kristoforidhit, përkthime e origjinale, rândësinë mâ të madhe e ka Fjalori i tij, pse âsht i pari fjalor i shqipes i punuem me kriter e me kujdes, dhe i krahasuem me dy fjalorët e mâparshëm del shumë mâ i naltë e mâ i plotë. Punimin e këtij fjalori Kristoforidhi e ka nisë bashkë me hartimin e vepravet të tjera të tij, por mbledhjen e materialit për tê do ta ketë fillue mâ parë.

Among those 25 works of Kristoforidhi, translations and originals, his Dictionary has the greatest importance, since it is the first dictionary of Albanian made with a criterion and with care, and in comparison with two previous dictionaries it comes out far superior and much fuller. K. began the work of this dictionary along with the composition of his other works, but the assembly of the material for it he will have begun earlier.

The accentuation of the text has been made consistent (2.1.3).

For the dialects see 0.5. Their essential sameness is apparent from the specimens. Forms typical of one or other of them, with the equivalents in the other, are listed below. (The forms in brackets do not occur in the specimens.)

Tosk	*Geg*
vëllim	**(vĭlim)**
dhënë	**(dhânë)**
Shqipëri	**(Shqipní)**
një	**(nji)**
ndonjë	**(nonji)**

Tosk	*Geg*
rëndësi	rândësi
është	âsht
ruajtur	(ruejtë)
më	mâ
(-uar)	-uem, -ue
(të)	tê

0 GENERAL CHARACTERISTICS

0.1 DEGREE OF INFLEXION
Despite its suffixed article, and the possession of three noun inflexions and of verb endings sufficiently characteristic to enable subject pronouns to be dispensed with, Albanian does not present quite so synthetic a picture as might be expected, on a naïve statistical count, being about on a level with English. This is due to the balancing effect of the attributive particle (3.4).

0.2 ORDER OF WORDS
Adjectives and other qualifying phrases generally follow the noun they qualify. The order of words in a sentence is free: the object is easily distinguishable from the subject, and though in simple narrative it is more likely to follow the verb, the order OVS and OSV are by no means excluded, e.g. **rândësinë e ka Fjalori** and **punimin Kristoforidhi e ka nisë** in the second specimen.

0.4 RELATION TO OTHER LANGUAGES
Albanian is an Indo-European language, but as it belongs to a family of its own, its connexion with other European languages is not very apparent, except in some of the numerals. To link **thom** (*I say*) with old Persian or **pjek** (*I roast*) with *cook* may be interesting but is not of much immediate help. Many of the more obvious similarities are in fact due to borrowings from Latin and Slavonic languages, or the adoption of what one might call international words.

0.5 DIALECTS
There is no one standard Albanian, since it is divided into two dialect groups, Geg in the north and Tosk in the south, and each of these has its varieties. Standard grammars of the written forms of both have been composed, for the official language of the state was at first Geg but since World War II has been Tosk. They are bound to be somewhat arbitrary but are followed here. Now that the official language is Tosk, it is possible to find a book with the title-page in Tosk and the text in Geg. Of recent years the dialects have tended to become mixed and compromise spellings are found.

Except in their extreme forms the two dialects are mutually intelligible, though there are differences of vocabulary, in the forms of words and in syntax. Some of the phonetic differences are fairly regular, viz.

G	â	-b	-d	ê	-g	i	î	ie	j	m	n	nj	sh-	û	ue	uer
T	ë	-p	-t	ë	-k	ie	ë/i	je	nj	mb/r	nd/r	ngj	ç-	u	ua	or

In addition T ë is often simply absent in G. More than one change may occur in the same word, e.g. G bâna T bëra; G shtypshkroja T shtypëshkronja. Particular changes in particular parts of speech are dealt with in the appropriate section. See also the specimens.

1 BIBLIOLINGUISTICS

1.1 NAMES

1.1.1 Modern Albanian names consist of one or more given names followed by a surname, few of them having any obvious meaning. There are no important names in which the second element is an epithet instead of a surname, but **i riu**, *the younger*, may be met with at the end. A few names may be either given names or surnames. If unfamiliar with the language it is as well to keep in mind the further possibility that the first component may be a title, as in **At Gjergj Fishta**, *Father G. F.*

1.1.2 Male given names usually have the form of indefinite nouns (4.1.1). As far as their grammatical form goes they may be masculine or feminine: thus -o is a feminine ending but **Nelo** is a man's name. Women's names mostly end in -(j)a, which is the feminine definite ending, that is, it incorporates the definite article (3.1.2). When they are declined (on which see 1.1.4), they all have definite endings, e.g. **Thimiut**, *of Thimi*.

1.1.3 Surnames may be masculine or feminine in form, irrespective of the sex of the bearer, e.g. **Aleksandër Xhuvani, Gjergj Fishta; Mamica Kastrioti, Andromija Gusho.** Here **-i** is a masculine definite ending, **-o** feminine indefinite. The endings of the oblique cases are always definite, and for this reason names belonging to the -o declension can cause trouble: the nominative usually has the indefinite -o, but forms like **Thimi Mitkua**, with a definite ending, also occur, as well as **Mitko**.

1.1.4 In a sequence of names and titles only one is declined. If there is a title it will usually be the title, as in **prej peshkopit Theofan**, *by Bishop Theofan*. But this is not true of **At**, *Father*, nor is it possible when the title is abbreviated. In the absence of a declinable title it is normally the surname which is declined, e.g. **prej Prof. Aleksandër Xhuvanit.** The opposite, however, as in **Mamicës Kastrioti**, is sometimes found. As a rule given names are only declined when they stand alone. A name in apposition to a common noun may remain in the nominative case, e.g. **nën redaktimin e juristëve të Kryeministrisë: Kristo Çevi, Vangjel Meksi, Dhimo Dhima.** In the absence of **juristëve**, etc., the names would have to be in the genitive case (4.1.2).

1.2 NAMES OF AUTHORS, EDITORS, ETC.

1.2.1 The commonest way of indicating authorship is by means of the prepositions **prej** and **nga**; **prej** is followed by the genitive case, **nga** by the nominative. The preposition may be preceded by **hartuar** (G -uem), *composed*, but more often stands alone unless some special relationship is intended, e.g. **përk(ë)thyer**, *translated*; **përpunuar**, *edited*; **përshtatë** or **adaptuar**, *adapted*. (See also 1.1.4.)

1.2.2 Also common is the placing of the name, in the nominative, before the title. This naturally can only be used for simple authorship.

1.2.3 Collections of letters, collected works, and new editions of well-known works may have the author's name in the genitive case, e.g. **Fjalori i Marko Boçarit**, *The dictionary of Marko Boçari*; **Bleta Shqypëtare e Thimi Mitkos**, *Thimi Mitko's 'Albanian bee'*.

1.2.4 Occasionally a noun denoting the agent may be used, e.g. **Auktori: Mehdi Frashëri**, or a collective noun such as **redaksia** followed by a list of names. In both instances the names are in the nominative.

1.2.5 Where we have not a collective noun but one denoting an activity, such as **redaktim** in the last example of 1.1.4, or more vaguely **nën kujdesin e**, *by the care of*, the name is in the genitive case.

1.2.6 A further possibility is the use of a finite verb; the name is once more in the nominative, e.g. **e përktheu shqyp dhe e radhiti Dr. Gjergj Pekmezi**, *translated it into Albanian and arranged it Dr. G. P.*

1.2.7 Where a name is left in the nominative for the reason given in 1.1.4, one should be careful how one shortens the title.

1.3 TITLES

1.3.1 For the most part titles are composed of nouns and adjectives together with prepositions and connecting particles and conjunctions, e.g. **Fillime të pedagogjis për shkollat normale e për mësuesit e fillores**, *Elements of pedagogy for teacher-training schools and elementary school teachers.* Imaginative literature for the most part produces much the same types, though more varied titles, e.g. **Kur hapet perdja**, *When the curtain is drawn back.*

1.3.2 Title entries of the Anglo-American type should cause no difficulty, and the translations required by British Museum rules, e.g. **Historija e Shqipërisë** (heading ALBANIA) are uncomplicated. As for filing, the definite article is a suffix, but note that **I huaj** (3.4.1) **në vendin e tij**, *Stranger in his own land*, is filed under **I**, the attributive particle not being ignored in filing. Nor is **një** (3.2.2).

1.3.3 When a title forms part of a sentence the principal noun in it may be declined like any other noun, e.g. **shtypi « Bletën Shqyptare »**, *he printed 'Bleta Shqyptare'*. Likewise if the title is in apposition to a descriptive word, e.g. **kemi dhe një poemë tjetër Hadikanë**, *we have also another poem* Hadikaja.

1.4 VOLUMES AND PARTS

1.4.1 The usual words are **vëllim (vllim)** or **tom** and **pjesë**, which literally means *piece* (and can mean *play*). Though **pjesë** should no doubt be translated *part*, it is often used where one might expect **vëllim**. One also finds **librë (libër)**, *book*, as in **Libri I i këtij romani u botua . . . 1952**, *Book I of this novel was published . . . 1952*; but this is a formal rather than a material division.

1.4.2 Numeration may be in figures or words, after the noun, which may be definite or indefinite, e.g. **libri I (d.), vëllim i parë (i.), pjesa e dytë (d.)**. The numeral is ordinal.

1.4.4 The total number of volumes is sometimes stated, in the form **në tre vëllime**, *in three volumes.*

1.5 EDITIONS

1.5.1 The word **botim** has the general meaning *publication*. In the appropriate context it will mean *edition*, but it is also found in imprints (1.6). **Edicje** also occurs.

1.5.2 Numeration is by ordinal number, which follows the noun, e.g. **botim i dytë, botimi i tretë**. The definite and indefinite forms of the noun (*second edition, the third edition*) are used indifferently. Qualifying adjectives such as **përpunuar** or **ripunuar**, *revised*; **korrektuar, koregjuar** or **ndrequr**, *corrected*; **plotësuar**, *enlarged*, are also used, but the fact of revision may also be implied by phrases in the general description, as in **hartuar së pari me alfabet greqisht dhe botuar në Athinë me 1904—transkriptuar tani me alfabet shqip dhe përpunuar prej . . .** , *first composed in the Greek alphabet and published at Athens in 1904—now transcribed into the Albanian alphabet and revised by . . . .*

1.6. IMPRINTS

1.6.1 Modern imprints are those of state institutions of one sort or another, e.g. **Botim i Ministrisë s'Aresimit dhe Kulturës** (*Publication of the Ministry of Education* *and Culture*). Earlier imprints mostly give the name of a printing press, e.g. **Shtypë-shkronja e Diellit** (*The Sun Press*), **Shtypshkroja «Nikaj»**, which may have variants in neighbouring languages, e.g. **Shtyp. e Zojës s'Paperlyeme** and **Tipografia Immacolata**. The name of the proprietor may follow in the genitive, e.g. **në shtypëshkronjët shqipe «Mbrothësia» të Kristo P. Luarasit** or in apposition, e.g. **shtypur në shtyp. Mbrothësia Kristo P. Luarasi**. This last type should not be confused with cases where the name is honorific, e.g. **Sh. B. (Shtëpia botonjëse) «Naim Frashëri»**, *Naim Frashëri Publishing House*.

1.6.2   The name of the publisher or press is usually in the nominative, but after **botim** (*publication*) it will be in the genitive case, and after **n(d)ë** (*at*) it will be in the accusative. Examples of both are given in 1.6.1.

1.6.3   The place is almost invariably in the nominative. Sometimes it follows **n(d)ë** and is in the accusative, but this makes no difference unless, as rarely happens, the place-name is in the definite form.

1.7   SERIES

1.7.1   The titles of series usually appear at the head of the page, or on the half-title-page. They may be descriptive of the series as a whole, e.g. **Biblioteka e mërgimit**, *Library of the Emigration*, or of the items, e.g. **Burime dhe materiale për historinë e Shqipërisë**, *Sources and materials for the history of Albania*.

1.7.2   The numeration is by **vëllim** or **numër**. For grammar see 1.4.2.

1.8   PERIODICALS

1.8.1/1.8.2   The titles of periodicals are linguistically simple, e.g. **Ylli**, *The Star*; **Jeta e re**, *The new life*; **Studime historike**, *Historical studies*; or incorporate the name of the publishing body, e.g. **Buletin i Universitetit Shtetëror të Tiranës**, *Bulletin of the National University of Tirana*. The same sort or information may be given in the sub-title using **botim** (*publication*) or **organ**, or occasionally an active verb may be used, e.g. **e boton Komiteti Kombëtar Demokrat**, or a passive, e.g. **botuar nga**, *published by*; **botohet nga**, *is published by*. **Universitetit** above is in the genitive case, definite form, and the nominative, usually definite, will have to be extracted (3.1.2). The other modes do not affect the name.

A title itself may be affected by being part of a larger grammatical whole, e.g. **botim i «Zërit të Popullit»**, *published by 'Zëri i Popullit'*.

1.8.3   Editorial indications almost always involve the stem **redak-**, e.g. **kolegjumi i redaksisë**, **këshilli redaktues**, and permutations of these; or just plain **redaksia**. The **këshilli** is an advisory body. In charge is usually a **kryeredaktor**, *chief editor*, assisted by a **sekretar shkencor**, *scientific secretary*. Alternatively there may be a **drejtonjës**, *director*, or a verb, e.g. **e drejton**, *he (she) directs it*, may be used instead.

1.8.4   Numeration is commonly by **viti**, *year*, with the alternative of **vëllim**, *volume*, subdivided by **n(umu)r**. It is expressed simply in the form **viti XVII, nr. 2**. Change of numeration consequent on change of title may be expressed thus: **Duke filluar nga numri i ardhshëm ... merr emrin ... dhe fillon me Nr. 1**, *beginning with the next number ... takes the name ... and begins at No. 1*.

1.8.5   Periodicity may be expressed by an adjective forming part of the title or the sub-title, e.g. **organ dymujor**, *bimonthly organ*, **revistë e përmuajshme**, *monthly review*, but more common are phrases beginning with **del**, such as **del një herë në (çdo) tre muaj**, *comes out once in (every) three months*; **në 12 numura**, *in 12 numbers*; or less commonly **mbyllja bëhet në çdo tremujor**, *completion takes place every quarter*.

1.8.6 Subscriptions (**pajtimet** or singular **pajtimi**, alternatively **abonimi**) are quoted **për një vit**, *for one year* or **për gjashtë muaj**, *for six months* and are different **brënda shtetit** and **jashtë shtetit**, *at home* and *abroad*. More often than not, however, no subscription rates are quoted: there is simply a note **çmimi**, *price*, on the back.

1.8.7 Addresses may specify the editorial office, **adresa e redaksisë**, and may or may not couple it with the business side, **dhe administratës**, *and of the administration*. Alternatively the information may be put the other way round, e.g. **redaksia dhe informacioni pranë**, *editorial office and information at*; **abonimi bëhet pranë**, *subscription takes place at*.

2 ALPHABET, PHONETICS, SPELLING

2.1 ALPHABET

2.1.1 The present alphabet was adopted at the Congress of Monastir in 1908. It was preceded by systems of spelling based upon neighbouring languages, e.g. Greek and Serbocroatian, but there were also in existence some peculiarly Albanian forms which are given here in brackets after the modern form.

a   b   c   ç   d   dh (Б, ä)   e (ε)   ë (Ԑ, e)   f   g   gj (Г, ҕ)   h   i   j

k   l   ll (Λ, λ)   m   n   nj (И, ҥ)   o   p (Π, ҏ)   q   r   rr (Р, p)   s

sh (Ҁ, ҕ)   t   th (θ, ð)   u   v   x   xh (x)   y   z   zh (ҙ)

Each letter or digraph has a distinct alphabetical position, so that **baltë** will precede **ballë**.

It should be noted that ε is sometimes found after 1908 to denote ë (e.g. in 1921 in Boston), a reversal of its value in the old alphabet, and also é for e and e for ë, e.g. **vjéter (vjetër)**. Even more disconcerting, Ë is not always distinguished even now from E, e.g. **NJE VEPER E RE** for **NJË VEPËR E RE**.

2.1.2 Modified Greek alphabets were also formerly used. The commonest follows with the modern equivalents. Digraphs occupy the position given.

A	α	a		Λ	λ	ll	
B	β	v			λj	l	
B	b	b		M	μ	m	
Γ	γ	g		N	ν	n	
Δ	δ	dh		O	o	o	
D	d	d		8	ου	u	
	dσ	x		Π	π	p	
	dö	xh		P	ρ	r	
E	ε	e	(ε̰ = ë)	Σ	σ	s	
Z	ζ	z		Ӟ	ö	sh	
Ž	ξ̈	zh		T	τ	t	
Θ	θ	th			τσ	c	
I	ι	i			τö	ç	
J	j	j		Y	υ	y	
K	κ	k		Φ	φ	f	
	κj	q		X	χ	h	

ι and **j** are sometimes confused and ε̰ is sometimes distinguished from ε and sometimes not.

2.1.3 Accents are used in Geg, but not consistently: grave for distinction, acute for length and stress and circumflex to indicate nasality.

2.1.4 Apostrophes indicate omissions, which may occur even before a consonant, e.g. **s'ka**, *has not*. They are often omitted, or the elision does not take place.

2.2 CAPITALISATION

2.2.1 Capitals are used for proper nouns and adjectives (but **shqip**, *Albanian*, is nowadays spelt small). These are stated in the official grammars to include personal names, whether of human beings or of animals, geographical names, e.g. **Mali i Thatë** (*Dry Mountain*), names of peoples and of books and periodicals. In practice the treatment of books and periodicals varies, e.g. **Bagëti e Bujqësija** (*Sheep and Agriculture*) alongside **Letërsija jonë** (*Our literature*). Certainly in bibliographies books are not capitalised throughout. No ruling is given about the names of days, months and seasons, but modern practice is that days of the week, feast days, months and seasons are not capitalised. One may also add to the list names of institutions and departments and historic events.

2.2.2 When a common noun is not an integral part of the name, e.g. **në malin Dajt**, *to Mount Dajti*; **shkolla «Qemal Stefa»**, *Qemal Stefa School*, it is not capitalised.

2.2.3 The chief organs of state such as **Presidiumi i Kuvëndit Popullor**, and such institutions as **Banka e Shtetit**, as well as learned institutions, are capitalised throughout, but one also finds ministries with only the first word spelt with an initial capital.

2.3 DIVISION OF WORDS

2.3.1 For the purposes of the rules each alphabetical symbol counts as one letter even if it is a digraph: one must not divide, for instance, **dh**, **gj** or **rr**.

2.3.2 Rules 1, 2, 4, 5a or b, 6d, 7a and 8 (p. xiii) apply. There is a preference for rule 5a unless the second letter is **j**, **l** or **r**. Division after consonants is not unknown.

2.4 PUNCTUATION; ABBREVIATIONS

2.4.1 If a hyphenated word is divided between two lines, a hyphen is put at the beginning of the second line also.

2.4.2 Abbreviations are indicated, as in English, by stops after the initial letter (or digraph), e.g. **d.m.th.** for **do me thënë** (G **thânë**), *i.e.*; **p.sh.** for **për shembull**, *e.g.*; **etj.** for **e të tjera**, *etc.*

2.4.3 The abbreviated names of institutions are treated, according to their sound, as independent nouns ending in a stressed vowel and as such are feminine, e.g. **S.M.T.--ja**, even though this is short for the masculine **Stacioni i makinave dhe traktorëve**. Similarly **S.M.T.-së** for **Stacionit**, etc., **N.B.SH.-të** for **Ndërmarrjet bujqësore shtetërore**.

2.5 VARIATION OF CONSONANT; PALATALISATION

2.5.1 In Tosk voiced consonants become unvoiced when final, e.g. **bregu**, *the hill*; **breg**, pronounced and formerly spelt **brek**, *hill*. The reverse is not true: **mik-u**, *(the) friend*.

2.5.2 A number of consonants have been palatalised (see General note on the Slavonic languages) by a following **e** or **i**. Thus **q**, the palatalised form of **k**, is found in words like **qershi** (*cherry*), **qëndrë** (*centre*), **qind** (*hundred*). (This does not mean that as words now are **q** must always be followed by **e** or **i** and **k** never. Both are followed by all vowels.) Linguistic history apart, palatalisation occurs in the declension of nouns and conjugation of verbs, e.g. **mik**, *friend*; **miq**, *friends*; **pjek**, *I cook*; **poqa**, *I cooked*.

Apart from **k/q**, the only palatalisations important in this way are **g/gj** and **ll/j**; but **t/ç** and **r/j** are sometimes found.

2.5.3   A number of verbs show an alternation between **t** and **s**.

2.6   VARIATION OF VOWEL

2.6.1   Changes in nouns are few, the only important ones being **u/o, ue/o** and between singular and plural in some nouns, **a/e**.

2.6.2   There are a number of changes in verbs. In various circumstances **-ua-** (G **-ue-**) alternates with **-o-**. When the 1PS of the present (the basic form) ends in a consonant, the corresponding 2PP and the imperfect, both of which involve adding an ending beginning with a further consonant, show the following changes: **a > e, a > i, e > i, ë > i, ie (je) > i, o > i** and more rarely **i > e**.

Between the 1PS and the 3PS **a > e** and **o > e** are found.

Between the present and the past: **a > o, e, je > o, e > i**.

2.6.3   With the addition of a syllable **-ë-** may vanish, as in the common adjectival ending **-shëm, -shme**, etc.

2.7   SPELLING

2.7.1   As the alphabet has only recently been standardised (2.1.1), there has been very little change in spelling. What looks like variation in spelling may be due to dialect differences or varying choice of alternative forms, e.g. **xbukuroj/zbukuroj** (**x** is pronounced dz).

2.7.2   Words are spelt sometimes with and sometimes without **ë**, the tendency being to use it less than in the past, e.g. **prej I. Vretosë** (1886), **të Jan Vretos** (1959), but in many instances that too is dialect difference. There are also variations between **ë** and **e** and between **r** and **rr**.

2.7.3   There is a tendency to use **k** for **q**, **l** for **ll** and **r** for **rr** in learned borrowings, e.g. **arkeologyí** instead of **arqeollogyí**.

2.7.4   More disconcerting in some ways is uncertainty about breaks between words, e.g. **megjithatë**, *nevertheless* (**me gjith' atë**, *for all that*); **parasysh**, *in view* (*before eyes*).

3   ARTICLES

The number of articles in Albanian depends on one's view of what is an article. Three are treated here: definite, indefinite and attributive.

3.1   DEFINITE

3.1.1   This corresponds roughly to the English definite article, but it is used with proper names and abstract nouns, and in expressions like **në pasqyrën 23**, *in table 23*. On the other hand in **sipas regjistrimeve të popullsisë të viteve 1950 dhe 1955**, *according to the population censuses of the years 1950 and 1955*, the expected **-t** of the definite article is absent both from **regjistrimeve** and **viteve**.

3.1.2   It is suffixed to the basic form of the noun, singular or plural, as follows, making what is usually known as the definite form.

		S		*P*
	M	*F*	*N*	
N	**-i/-u**	**-(j)a**	**-t**	**-t(ë)/-ët/-it**
A	**-in/-un**	**-(ë)n(ë)**	**-t**	
M	**-it/-ut**	**-(ë)s(ë)**	**-it**	**-vet**

For the cases see 4.1.

Some forms could be analysed into case ending (cf. 4.3.2) plus article proper, but this is not always possible.

3.1.3   Final -ë is dropped before forms beginning with a vowel. As masculine nouns may end in a consonant or -ë, there is some ambiguity: **burri** comes from **burrë, derri** from **derr**. Feminine nouns are less ambiguous: possible endings are -ël, -ëll, -ëm, -ën, -ër, -ërr, -ëz, -ul, -ull, etc., forms which have lost their final -ë. In either dialect a form like **udha** can only come from **udhë**. Vowels other than i take the article -ja, so that -ija would now come from -ijë, i producing -ia. Formerly, however, i also might produce -ija. Final -e is dropped before -ja, e.g. **regullore, regullorja** (but -ja may also correspond to -je).

3.1.4   Vowel alternation of o and u occurs, e.g. -o/-oja or -ua, -ua/-oi, -uar/-ori, -uall/-olli; and in Geg -uer/-ori.

3.1.5   Some masculine nouns ending in a long vowel insert -r- (G -n-) before -i, e.g. **sy-ri**, (*the*) *eye* (G **sy-ni**).

3.2   INDEFINITE

3.2.1   The use is much the same as that of the English indefinite article.

3.2.2   There is only one form in each dialect:

T **një**   *G* **nji**

(For **njëri** and the like see 7.1.3.)

3.4   ATTRIBUTIVE PARTICLE

3.4.1   This has many other names, such as Connective (p)article, Proclitic of concord. None of them is altogether satisfactory. It stands before most adjectives, even when they are used as nouns, usually before the genitive when used as such and before some nouns denoting kinship, e.g. **botim i dytë**, *second edition*; **burimet e të dhënave**, *the sources of data* (**e** before genitive, **të** for the adjective used as a noun); **fjalori âsht shumë mâ i plotë** (G), *the dictionary is much fuller*; **mbas vdekjes së të shoqit**, *after the death of her husband*; but **mjete prodhimi**, *means of production*. Where it connects a noun with an adjective or genitive, or stands before the predicate, its gender and case are those of the noun: **botim i, burimet e, fjalori . . . i, vdekjes së**; but the **të** before **dhënave** and **shoqit** is determined by those words alone.

3.4.2   It has the following forms:

	S			P
	M	*F*	*N*	
N	i	e	e/të	e/të
A	e/të	e/të	e/të	e/të
M	të	së/të	të	të

For the cases see 4.1.

3.4.3   The alternatives **e/të** and **së/të** are not completely interchangeable, but the variation does not affect translation from Albanian. In **për klasën e V-të dhe të VI-të**, *for the 5th and 6th class*, both **e** and **të** fulfil the same function.

3.4.4   In view of its similarity to the definite article it is as well to remember that the attributive particle is neutral in this respect: it follows an indefinite noun equally, e.g. **simbas nji dëshmie të Jan Vretos** (G), *according to a testimony of J. Vreto*.

N

4 NOUNS

4.1 GENDER AND FORM

4.1.1 On the evidence of the definite article there are three genders but the only mark of a neuter noun is the article -t: in other respects it behaves either as masculine or feminine. Gender to a great extent follows form, though the ending -ë is common to both, and many M nouns are F in the plural.

4.1.2 The official Albanian grammars still recognise five cases, but there are only three inflexions, for which I use the terms nominative, accusative and genitive.

4.1.3 Some words which are nouns in function are adjectives in form, e.g. **e metë**, *a fault* (5.1.1).

4.2 PLURAL

4.2.1 The plural is most often formed by adding an ending, but a number of feminine nouns are unchanged, and some common nouns change the internal vowel (2.6.1) or palatalise the final consonant (2.5.2). As usual some of the commonest nouns are irregular.

4.2.2 The principal endings are:

Ending	Use	Caution
-a	Replaces -ë in F nouns and **burrë**, *man*. Added to consonant in some M and F (cf. 2.6.3; 3.1.3)	A few nouns end in -a in the singular and are unchanged. See also -ra
-ra G -na	Added to F nouns ending in a vowel	There is a rare plural ending -ëra, but -ëra is more likely to be -ë + ra
-e	Added to M nouns ending in a consonant, especially -im and -nd. Accompanied by palatalisation of -k (-g) and -ll. Occasionally replaces -ë	May represent an unchanged F in -e
-ë	Added to M nouns ending in a consonant. Sometimes accompanied by palatalisation, and in Geg by change of vowel	May represent an unchanged F -ë. Endings -lë, -rë occur infrequently in M nouns in -i
-nj G -j	Added to M nouns ending in a vowel, principally -i	Merges with palatalisation in Geg. There is also a rare ending -ërinj

The endings -ër (G -ën), -lerë are rare.

4.2.3 The analysis of some plural forms follows:

> **informatash,** *of facts:* informatë + a + sh
> **vepravet,** *of the works:* vepër/veprë + a + vet
> **gjuhëra,** *languages:* gjuhë + ra
> **shpenzimet,** *the expenses:* shpenzim + e + t

origjinale, *originals:* no change
(e) **Shqiptarëvet,** *of the Albanians:* **Shqiptar** + **ë** + **vet**
tri herë, *three times:* no change
(e) **Bektashinjvet,** *of the Bektashi:* **Bektashi** + **nj** + **vet**
historitë, *the histories:* no change + **të**
nxânësit (G), *the pupils:* no change + **it**

4.2.4 The following irregular plurals may be noted: **derë, dyer,** *door(s);* **djalë, djem,**
boy(s); **dorë, duar** (G **duer),** *hand(s);* **grua, gra,** *woman (-men);* **kal(ë), kuaj,** *horse(s);*
njeri, njerës (G **njerz),** *person(s);* **thes, thasë,** *bag(s).*

4.3 ENDINGS
4.3.1 *Masculine nouns*
These end, when in their basic, or, as it is usually called, 'indefinite' form, in a
consonant. The few that end in a vowel behave quite differently from the corresponding
feminines.

4.3.2 *Case endings*

	S	P
NA	-	see 4.2
G	-i/-u	-ve/-sh added to P stem

The ending **-u** follows gutturals and most vowels. Some vowels, however, take **-ri**
(Geg **-ni**).
4.3.3 For the formation of the plural see 4.2.

4.3.4 *Feminine*
The commonest feminine endings are **-ë, -e** and **-i.** Nouns in **-o** (which are not common) are grammatically feminine but are often masculine names, or nouns whose
natural gender is masculine; nouns in **-a** are few in number but include **grua,** *woman.*
For consonant endings see 3.1.3.

4.3.5 *Case endings*

	S	P
NA	-	see 4.2
G	-e/-je	-ve/-sh added to P stem

The ending **-je** follows vowels other than **-e,** but of recent years **-e** has become common
after **-i,** e.g. **simbas nji dëshmie** (from **dëshmi).**

4.6 USE OF CASES
4.6.1 The accusative case is often adverbial (cf. 6.4.2), the genitive case follows
many prepositions, indicates the indirect object or person interested (dative) or, in the
broadest sense, the possessor. (See 3.4.1.)
4.6.2 The ending **-sh,** sometimes called the ablative, is used as a partitive or
adjectival genitive after an indefinite expression, e.g. **një grup emrash,** *a group of*
nouns (but **shumica e emrave,** *the majority of nouns);* **fletë drandofillesh** (G), *rose-*
leaves.

5 ADJECTIVES

5.1 GENERAL

5.1.1 Adjectives usually follow the noun, simple adjectives, as well as derived adjectives in -shëm and -ët/-të, being preceded by the attributive particle. They agree in number and gender but have no case endings or article unless they precede, in which case the noun has none, e.g. **i pari fjalor**, *the first dictionary*, or stand alone, e.g. **numëri i të lindurve**, *number of born*; **ka të meta**, *has faults*.

5.1.2 In so far as they agree with nouns they are M or F, but they are used with the N article to make abstract expressions. Nevertheless the F is used in such phrases as **pa qenë e nevojshme që**, *without its being necessary that*. It should be noted that MP nouns in -e take F adjectives.

5.2 ENDINGS

5.2.1 Adjectives end in either a consonant or -ë. Those which end in a consonant have the following forms:

	S		P	
M	F	M	F
-	-e	-ë/-	-e

except those in -ët, -uar (G -uem), -ur (G -un) which behave like adjectives in -ë. Those which end in -ë change only FP -a. See also 5.2.3.

5.2.2 A few common adjectives show irregularities, viz.

	S		P	
	M	F	M	F
	keq	keqe	këqi(n)(j)	këqi(n)(j)a
	lig (lik)	ligë	ligj	liga
	madh	madhe	mëdhaj	mëdha(ja)
	ri	re	ri(n)j	reja
	zi	zezë	zes (G zez)	zeza

5.2.3 Adjectives used as nouns take the definite article when appropriate.

5.3 COMPARISON

5.3.1 Both comparative and superlative are expressed by **më** (G **mâ**), the superlative naturally taking the article, e.g. **autorët më të vjetër**, *older authors*; **rândësinë mâ të madhe**, *the greatest importance*. The superlative may either precede or follow the noun.

5.4 POSSESSIVES

5.4.1 These agree with the noun like other adjectives and follow the noun, in most cases with the attributive particle. The noun has the definite article. They differ from other adjectives in having some special forms when the noun is not in the nominative, and these are given in brackets. The attributive particle often coalesces with the adjective, so the whole expression is given.

5.4.2 The forms are as follows:

Noun

		S		P	
		M	*F*	*M*	*F*
	1	(i) im (t'im)	(e) ime (t'ime, s'ime)	e mij	e mija
	2	(i) yt (tënd)	(e) jote (tënde, s'ate)	e tu	e tua
S	3*m*	i tij	e tij	e tij	e tija
	3*f*	i saj	e saj	e saj	e saja
	1	(i) ynë (t'onë)	e jonë (t'onë, s'onë)	t'anë (t'onë)	t'ona
P	2	(i) juaj (t'uaj)	e juaj (t'uaj, s'uaj)	t'uaj	t'uaja
	3	i tyre	e tyre	e tyre	e tyre

(Pronoun)

The apostrophes may be omitted. For the third person cf. 7.3.2.

5.4.3 Some Geg forms exemplify the regular phonetic differences, viz. t'ând-, (j)uej, tyne (0.5).

5.4.4 The addition of the definite article converts the adjectives into the pronouns *mine*, etc.

6 NUMERALS

6.1 CARDINAL

6.1.1

1 një (G nji)	11 njëmbëdhjetë (G nji-)	200 dy qind
2 dy (or dý G)	19 nëntëmbëdhjetë	1000 një mijë
3 tre (G trí)	20 njëzet (G nji-)	2000 dy mijë
4 katër	21 njëzet e një	
5 pesë	30 tridhjet (tridhetë)	
6 gjashtë	40 dyzet (or katërdhetë G)	
7 shtatë	50 pesëdhjet	
8 tetë	90 nënddhjet (nândëdhetë)	
9 nënd (G nândë)	100 një qind	
10 dhjetë (dhetë)	101 një qind e një (njiqindenji)	

6.1.2 Though they are adjectives, cardinals are not declined when they precede the noun; nor do they take the article except when standing alone, e.g. **me dy fjalorët e maparshëm** (G), *with the two earlier dictionaries*. The noun is plural and has the appropriate endings.

6.2 ORDINAL

6.2.1

1 parë	7 shtatë
2 dytë	8 tetë
3 tretë	9 nëntë (G nândët)
4 katërt	10 dh(j)etë
5 pestë	20 njëzettë (G njizetët)
6 gjashtë	21 njëzet (nji-) e njëjtë

Variants **katërtë, gjashtët**, etc. are found but are not current.

6.2.2   Ordinals take the article or not like other adjectives (5.1.1). Only the last element of a compound numeral has the ordinal form.

6.3   FIGURES

Cardinals are represented by simple arabic figures. Ordinals have the ending attached, e.g. **I-rë**, **2-të**, and roman figures are common.

6.4   DATES
6.4.1   The months are:

>   **janar, fruer (shkurt), mars, prill, maj, qershor,**
>   **korrik, gusht, shtator, tetor, nëntor, dhjetor**

Older names for *September–December* are:

>   **Vjesht e Parë, Vjesht e Dytë, Vjesht e Tretë, Shëndre**

Geg forms are:

>   **Kall(ë)n(d)uer, Fruer, Mars, Prill, Maj, Qershuer,**
>   **Korrik, Gusht, Shtatuer, Tetuer, Nânduer, Dhetuer**

The forms in **-uer** change to **-or-** before the article. The names of the months may be used with or without the article. The initial letters may be lower-case in Geg also.

6.4.2   Dates are usually expressed thus:

>   *(On) 10 February 1958*: **(më) dh(j)etë shkurt (fruer) një mijë (njimijë) nëntëqind**
>   **(nândëqind) e pesëdh(j)etë e tetë**
>   *The census of 2 October 1960*: **Regjistrimi i popullsisë së 2 tetorit 1960**

Since cardinals do not take case endings expressions involving years only present no problems.

7   PRONOUNS

7.1   DEMONSTRATIVE, INDEFINITE, ETC.
7.1.1   Except in a few forms there is no distinction between pronouns and adjectives.
7.1.2   The demonstratives **ky**, *this*, and **ay/ai**, *that*, have parallel forms. **Ay** serves also as personal pronoun of the third person (7.3.2). The long forms are used only as pronouns. The alternatives **kësi**, etc., are used as in 4.6.2 and after prepositions.

	S		*P*	
	M	*F*	*M*	*F*
N	ky	kjo	këta	këto
A	këtë	këtë (G këtê, kët)	këta	këto
G	këtij/kësi	kësaj/këso	këtyre(ve)/	këtyre(ve)/
			kësi(sh)	këso(sh)

Ay substitutes **a-** for **k-** or **kë-**.
7.1.3   The indefinite pronouns **n(d)okush**, **dikush**, *someone*, **kushdo**, *whoever* are compounds of **kush** (7.2.1).
    njëri (G **njëni, njâni**), *the one, someone* behaves like a noun and also means *person*.
    tjetër P **të tjerë, të tjera**, *other* is used with and without the article, e.g. **e vepravet të tjera**, *of the other works*; **të gjith tjerat**, *all the others*; **së palës tjetër**, *of the other party*; **tjetra derë**, *the other door*.
    atillë, *such*, is frequently abbreviated to **tillë**.

7.2 INTERROGATIVE AND RELATIVE

7.2.1 The interrogative **kush** (*who?*) has A **kë** (G **kê**) G **kuj(t)**; **cili, cila, cilët, cilat** (*which?*) has adjectival forms with the definite article (GPM **cilvet** in Geg); **çë, ça** (*what?*) is often reduced to **ç'**.

7.2.2 The relatives **që** (G **qi**), **kush** have no other forms, but **që** is supplemented by the parts of **ay**, as in **që për atë folëm**, *of whom we spoke*; **i cili, e cila**, etc., is like **cili**.

7.3 PERSONAL

7.3.1 The forms of the first and second person are:

	S		*P*	
	1	2	1	2
N	unë	ti	na/ne	ju
A	mua (G mue)/më	ty/të	na (G also né)	ju(ve)
G	mua/më/meje	ty/të/teje	neve/na/nesh	ju(ve)/jush

7.3.2 The pronoun of the third person **ay** is a demonstrative (7.1.2). As a personal pronoun it may drop the **a-** and has special unemphatic forms **e** (AS), **i** (GS, AGP) and **u** (GP). They combine with others as follows:

$$\text{më} + \text{e} > \text{m'a} \qquad \text{ju} + \text{e} > \text{jua}$$
$$\text{të} + \text{e} > \text{t'a (ta)} \qquad \text{ju} + \text{i} > \text{jua}$$
$$\text{i} + \text{e} > \text{ja (ia)} \qquad \text{u} + \text{e} > \text{ua}$$

The form **ta** holds also for the **të** of the subjunctive (8.7.2) and in this context **ti** and **tu** are also found.

7.3.3 The forms **e, i** and **u** are frequently used in addition to a definite noun object or even to the full pronoun, e.g. **e pati menden me e botue**, *he had the mind to publish it* (G); **Të gjithë shtetasve u garantohet liria e fjalës**, *To all citizens is guaranteed freedom of speech.*

8 VERBS

8.1 GENERAL

The Albanian verb has different forms for most of the different persons, making subject pronouns unnecessary, and for the different tenses and moods. In some verbs there are variations between the stems of the different tenses. Verbs are entered under the 1PS of the present.

8.2 PRESENT

8.2.1 Verbs with a vowel stem have the endings:

    I   **-j, -n, -n; -jmë, -ni, -jnë**
    II **-, -, -; -më, -ni, -në**

Verbs with a consonant stem have the endings:

    -, -, -; -im, -ni, -in (G also **-i, -ë, -ë**)

The majority of verbs end in **-oj**, but a good many old and common ones have consonant stems. (The Tosk variant **-onj** is old-fashioned.)

8.2.2 Verbs in **-ij** are peculiar: **vij** (*I come*) has 2 and 3PS **vjen** but others have the pattern **-ij, -ën, -ën; -im, -ini, -in**. The ending **-ini** may come from **-ej, -e, -ë** and **-ie** as well as **-ij**.

8.2.3 Consonant stems exhibit various peculiarities:

(a) There is a common alternation: -s, -t, -t; -sim, -tni/-sni, -sin.

(b) The consonant in the singular may have become unvoiced (2.5.1), but in 1 and 3PP the voiced form is found, e.g. **zbras, zbrazin.**

(c) The consonant before **-ni** may be palatalised (2.5.2).

(d) Vowel changes occur, for which see 2.6.2. These changes may occur simultaneously.

8.2.4 The continuous present is expressed by **po,** e.g. **po shkon,** *he is going.*

8.3 IMPERFECT

8.3.1 The standard endings today for most verbs are:

-ja, -je, -nte; -nim, -nit, -nin

but **-nja, -nje, -te, -jim,** etc., are also found in various combinations with the above.

G **-(j)shem, -(j)she, -(n)te; -(j)shim, -(j)shit, -(j)shin**

8.3.2 The correspondence with the present follows the following pattern: **-oja/-oj** and similarly with other vowels + **j; -ija/-ë, -i, -ie** as well as **-ij; veja** corresponds to **vij.** With consonant stems there is the same change of vowel as in the 2PP of the present, and the consonant may be voiced or palatalised or both, e.g. **shoh/shihja** (G **shifshem**); **djek/digjia.**

8.3.3 The imperfect may sometimes have to be translated by a simple past. The continuous sense is emphasised by the use of **po,** e.g. **po punonja,** *I was working.*

8.4 PAST

8.4.1 The following are the possible endings:

$$\left.\begin{array}{l} \text{-a, -e, -i} \\ \text{-va, -ve, -u} \\ \text{-ra, -re, -ri} \\ \text{(G -na, -ne, -ni)} \end{array}\right\} \left\{\begin{array}{l} \text{-më, -të, -në} \\ \text{-ëm, -ët, -ën} \end{array}\right.$$

Consonant stems usually have the endings:

-a, -e, -i; -ëm, -ët, -ën

Verbs in **-oj** have the endings:

-ova, -ove, -oi; -uam, -uat, -uan (G -uem, etc.)

Similarly **-yem,** etc., from verbs in **-ej** and **-yej.**

8.4.2 The relation of the past to the present depends on the nature of the stem. Verbs with a vowel stem have a consonant before the ending, or have endings beginning with a consonant, viz.

Past	**-ajta, -ava**	**-eta**	**-eva**	**-ijta**	**-ita**	**-iva**	**-ova**
Present	**-aj**	**-ej, -ë**	**-ej**	**-i**	**-e, -ij**	**-i, -ij**	**-oj, -uaj**

Past	**-ujta**	**-ura (G -una)**	**-yra (G -yva)**	G **-ina**
Present	**-uj (G -uej)**	**-ë, -ie (-je)**	**-ie (-je), -yj**	G **-i**

With a consonant stem the ending may be simply added, e.g. **shtypa/shtyp.** But quite often there is a change of vowel (2.6.2) or of consonant (2.5.1, 2.5.2) or both, e.g.

Past	mbolla	hoqa	zbraza	shkava	hodha	poqa	dogja	prita	ngrita
Present	mbjell	heq	zbras	shkas	hedh	pjek	djeg	pres	ngreh

Past	vdiqa	fola
Present	vdes	flas

Similar changes take place in Geg.

8.7 SUBJUNCTIVE

8.7.1 The subjunctive hardly differs from the indicative. The 3PS of the present has an additional -ë (-jë, -rë after a simple vowel), e.g.

Subjunctive	shtypë	botojë	pijë	verë	rrahë
Indicative	shtyp	botoj	pi	vë	rreh

8.7.2 The subjunctive is required after some conjunctions and enters into the formation of the future. It is preceded by **të**. (For the form **ta** see 7.3.2.) Clauses with the subjunctive are found in Tosk where Geg and English use the infinitive.

8.10 COMPOUND TENSES

8.10.1 *Future:* **do të** + subjunctive (8.7.1); G also **kam** (8.19.1) **me** + verbal noun (8.11); T also **kam për të** + verbal noun (a weak future)
8.10.2 *Conditional:* **do të** + imperfect (8.3); or **kishem** (8.19.1) **me** + verbal noun
8.10.3 *Perfect:* **kam** + verbal noun
Other tenses and moods of **kam** produce the pluperfect, perfect subjunctive and so on.

8.11 VERBAL NOUN OR ADJECTIVE

8.11.1 This part of the verb functions both as a verbal noun and as a verbal adjective (past participle passive). As a verbal noun it is usually preceded by some preposition e.g. **pa qënë**, *without being*; **me folur**, *by speaking* (T); or by a particle such as **për të**, *in order to*; **duke** (or **dyke**, G **tue**) the latter making the equivalent of a present participle, e.g. **tue fillue nga viti 1504**, *beginning with the year 1504*. In Geg **me** + verbal noun functions as an infinitive. As a participle it is commonly used as an adjective, with the appropriate attributive particle.
8.11.2 The usual endings are:

T -në, -rë, -tur, -uar or -ur
G -në, -m(ë)/-, -tun/-të, -ue(m), -un/-, -ë (See also 8.11.3)

In vowel stems they correspond to the present tense thus:

V.n.	-arë/-ajtur	-erë/-ejtur	-etur	-ënë		-irë	-itur	-uar
P	-aj	-ej	-ë	-ë/-ie (-je)	-i/-ij	-e/-i/-ij	-oj

V.n.	-ujtur	-urë	-yer	-yjtur	-yrë
P	-uj	-ie (-je)	-ej	-yj	-ie (-je)

In consonant stems the verbal noun is usually got simply by adding -ur, but there may be changes of consonant or vowel similar to those which take place in the past tense, e.g. **bërtitur/bërtas**; djegur/djeg; **folur/flas**; **ngritur/ngre(h)**; zbritur zbres; **vdekur/vdes**; or the verbal noun may end in -ë, e.g. **marrë/marr**; nxjerë/nxjer; shkarë/shkas. See also 8.19 for irregular verbs. The correspondences in Geg are similar.

8.11.3   There is only one form in Tosk for all uses, e.g. **i mbaruar,** *finished*; **i ndarë,** *divided*; **i ngritur,** *raised*; **ka ngritur,** *has raised*; **për të marrë në dorezim,** *in order to take delivery*; **duke paguar shpenzimet,** *paying the expenses.* In Geg, however, only the adjectival participle has the full form; in the other uses the shorter alternative is used, e.g. **i botuem,** *published*; **i rritun,** *full grown*; **i falun,** *excused*; **me e botue,** *to publish it*; **kishte vojtë,** *had gone*; **me falë,** *to excuse.*

8.12   PARTICIPLES
See 8.11.

8.14   REFLEXIVE AND PASSIVE
8.14.1   These forms, also called 'middle', function as reflexive; where appropriate, as passive; and supply corresponding intransitives. They are characterised by an inserted **-e-** or **-he-,** e.g. **garantohet,** *is guaranteed*; **bëhem,** *I become, am made* (**bëj,** *I do*); **mbrohet,** *he defends himself,* or by the particle **u.**

8.14.2   *Present*

> **-(h)em, -(h)e(sh), -(h)et; -(h)emi, (h)(en)i, -(h)en**

The forms beginning with **h-** are added to vowel stems, e.g. **-ohem/-oj** and so with other vowels; **-ihem/-i** or **-ij.** With consonant stems there may be change of vowel, e.g. **ngrihem/ngre(h).**

8.14.3   *Imperfect*

> **-(h)esh|(ja), -(j)e, -; -(j)im, -(j)it, -(j)in**

G also **-(h)eshem, -(h)eshe, -(hej)**; or **u** before the active.
The stem is the same as that of the present.

8.14.4   *Past*
The active form (8.4.1) is preceded by **u** except that the 3PS has no ending and **-ua** (G **-ue**) is substituted for **-oi.**

8.14.5   *Future (Conditional)*

> **do të** + present (imperfect)

8.14.6   *Perfect, etc.* (cf. 8.10.3)

> Parts of **jam** (8.19.2) + verbal noun

Note that the verbal noun does not have the characteristically adjectival attributive particle, e.g. **është caktuar,** *has been specified* (**është e caktuar,** *it is definite*).
Alternatively **u** may be prefixed to the active.
8.14.7   The verbal noun is got by prefixing **u** to the active, e.g. **pa u dërguar përgjigja** *without the answer being sent.*

8.15   PASSIVE
See 8.14.

8.17 AUXILIARIES

See 8.19.1, 8.19.2.

8.19 IRREGULARITIES

    8.19.1   kam, *I have* (see also 8.10)

        Present: kam, ke, ka; kemi, keni/kini, kanë

        Imperfect: kish(j)a, kish(j)e, kishte; kishim, etc. (G kishem)

        Past: pata (G also paçë)

        Present subjunctive: ke|m, -sh, -të; -mi, -ni, -në

        Verbal noun: patur/pasur (G pasun, pasë)

    8.19.2   jam, *I am* (see also 8.14.6)

        Present: jam, je, është (G âsht); jemi, jeni/jini, janë

        Imperfect: ish(j)a (G ishem) as 8.19.1

        Past: qeshë, qe, qe; qemë, etc.

        Present subjunctive: je|m as 8.19.1

        Optative: 3PS qoftë

        Verbal noun: qënë (G qênë)

(Qoftë is one of the few optatives in current use, e.g. sido qoftë, *be that as it may*, and see 11.2.)

    8.19.3 bie, *I bring* (G also bij)

        Past: prura (G prûna)

        Verbal noun: prurë (G prû)

    8.19.4 bie, *I fall*

        Past: rashë, re, ra; rame, etc.

        Verbal noun: rënë (G ra-m)

    8.19.5 dal, *I go out, come out*

        Present: 3PS del

        Past: dol(l)a, dol(l)e, dol(l)i (G duel); duallmë (G duelëm), etc.

    8.19.6 dua (G due), *I want*

        Present: dua, do(n), do(n); duam, doni, duan (G -e- for -a-)

        Imperfect: donja (G dojshem)

        Past: desh(t)a

        Verbal noun: dashur (G dash(t)un/dash(t)ë)

    8.19.7 ha, *I eat*

        Past: hëngra (G hângra)

        Verbal noun: ngrënë (G hângrun/hângër)

    8.19.8 jap, *I give* (G also ap, nap)

        Past: dhashë, dhe, dha; dhamë, etc.

        Verbal noun: dhënë (G dhânë)

    8.19.9 jes, *I stay* = mbes, to which all other parts correspond regularly.

    8.19.10 lë (G lâ), *I leave, let*

        Past: lashë, etc., as 8.19.8

    8.19.11 rri (G also rrij), *I sit, stand, stay*

        Past: ndejta/ndënja (G ndêj(t)a)

        Verbal noun: ndejtur/ndënjur (G ndêj(t)un/ndêjtë)

    8.19.12 shoh (G shof), *I see*

        Past: pashë, etc., as 8.19.8

        Verbal noun: parë (G pa-m)

        Passive: shihem, etc.

8.19.13   thom/them, *I say*

   Present: thom/them, thua (G thue), thotë; thomi/themi, thoni, thonë

   Imperfect: thoshja (G thojshem), etc.

   Past: thashë, etc., as 8.19.8

   Verbal noun: thënë (G thânë)

8.19.14   vete, *I go*

   Present: vete, vete, vete; vemi, veni, venë

   Imperfect: veja (G vejshem)

   Past: vajta (G vojta)

   Present subjunctive: 3PS vejë

   Verbal noun: va(j)tur (G vojtë)

8.19.15   vij, *I come*

   Present: see 8.2.2

   Past: erdha

   Verbal noun: ardhur (G ardhun/ardhë)

9   ADVERBS

9.1   FORMATION

9.1.1   Apart from those which are based on pronominal stems or have no obvious connexions, all of which must be sought in the dictionary, and those which are oblique cases of nouns, e.g. ditën, *by day*; motit, *once upon a time*, adverbs can be derived from adjectives and also from nouns and verbs.

9.1.2   An adverb may be the same as the corresponding adjective, without any attributive particle, e.g. keq, *badly* (burrë i keq, *a bad man*).

9.1.3   An adverb may consist of the corresponding adjective preceded by me të, e.g. me të madhe, *greatly*.

9.1.4   Some adverbs are formed from adjectives and nouns by adding -isht, e.g. frëngisht, *in French*; lirisht, *freely*. Variants are -ërisht, -ësisht, -tërisht; e.g. tërësisht, *entirely*; pjesërisht, *partially*.

9.1.5   A number of adverbs are formed from adjectives, nouns and verb stems by the addition of -as and -azi, e.g. rishtas (G), *recently*; lehtazi, *easily*.

10   PREPOSITIONS

10.2   SYNTAX

Most prepositions are followed by the genitive or the accusative case, but a few take the nominative. These are tek, te (G also ke, tu, tuk), *at, to, in*; nga (G kah), *from, by*. (They are said to be equivalent originally to phrases such as *where X is* rather than to normal prepositions—hence the nominative—and are also used as adverbs, e.g. Nga vjen, *Where is he coming from?*)

10.3   MEANINGS

As in other languages the standard translations are only an approximate guide. Thus nga (10.2) is often equivalent to *than* and sometimes to *of*; me is given as *with*, but me vendim të gjykatës means *by decision of the court*.

11   CONJUNCTIONS

11.1   Conjunctions may be simple or compound. The only difficulties arise from the fact that small dictionaries such as that of Drizari may not specify all the possible meanings, or have no convenient place for citing compound conjunctions, which in any case are sometimes written as one word, sometimes as two or more. Thus **se** is given as *for, because*; but it also means *than* and quite frequently *that*; **po** means not only *but* but also *if* (when it is not the sign of a continuous tense: 8.2.4, 8.3.3); so does **në**, more familiar as a preposition.

11.2 Among compound conjunctions may be noted:

> **edhe pse,** *although*
> **me qënë se,** *seeing that*
> **mjaft që,** *if (so be that)*
> **nëse,** *whether*
> **nga që,** *because* (not to be confused with **që nga,** *as from*)
> **para se,** *before*
> **po që se,** *if*
> **se mos,** *lest, that*
> **sidhe,** *as well as*

There are many others, a common type being an adverb followed by **që** or **se**.

13 WORD-FORMATION

13.1 A knowledge of the meaning of the commoner suffixes and prefixes is useful in supplementing a small dictionary.

13.2 SUFFIXES

These are numerous, and most of those listed below are still productive. The list that follows is in order of final letters.

> **-je (-ie) (F), -esë (F), -im (M):** all form nouns expressing the action or result of a verb, e.g. **ndërmarrje,** *undertaking, enterprise* (**marr,** *I take*); **kërkesë,** *request* (**kërkoj,** *I seek*); **vendim,** *decision* (**vendoj,** *I decide*). The endings **-esë** and **-im** are sometimes contrasted as action and result, e.g. **me shkresë,** *in writing,* **shkrim,** *a written text*; but **një ndërtesë** means *a building.*
>
> **-ore, -tore (F):** form abstract nouns allied in meaning to the corresponding adjective (or noun) in **-or** or **-tor,** e.g. **rregullore,** *set of rules*; **fitore,** *victory* (**fitoj,** *I win*).
>
> **-esë:** see **-je** above.
>
> **-të:** see **-ët** below.
>
> **-i (F):** forms abstract nouns from adjectives, nouns and adverbs, e.g. **veprimtari,** *activity* (**veprim-tar** < **veproj,** *I act*). Sometimes there are pairs of nouns in **-imi** and **-im,** e.g. **trashëgimi,** *inheritance,* **trashëgim,** *estate,* and as the latter with the article also ends in **-imi,** this can be disconcerting.
>
> **-ri (F):** forms abstract nouns from adjectives, e.g. **qëndruarshmëri,** *stability* (< **qëndruar-shëm** < **qëndroj,** *I stand*).
>
> **-si (F):** forms nouns denoting qualities from adjectives and adverbs, e.g. **zotësi,** *capacity* from **i zoti,** *capable.*
>
> **-o(n)j:** forms verbs from nouns and adjectives, e.g. **lajmëro(n)j,** *I notify* (**lajm,** *news*). Usually **-oj** nowadays.

-shëm: forms adjectives from nouns, verbal nouns, verb stems, adverbs and phrases, e.g. ndërgjegjëshëm, *conscientious* (ndërgjegje, *conscience*); pa-çmueshëm, *invaluable* (çmoj, *I value*); ngjashëm, *similar* (ngjan, *is like*); brendëshëm, *internal* (brenda, *inside*); aty-për-atyshëm, *summary* (aty për aty, *there and then*).

-an: forms adjectives denoting origin, e.g. shkodran, *of Scutari*; amerikan. In rrethana, *circumstances*, we have the FP used as a noun (rreth, *circle*).

-ar: is like -an but is also useful for naturalising words like revolucionar.

-tar: also forms adjectives or nouns of wider application, e.g. përfundimtar, *concluding, final* (përfundim < përfundoj, *I conclude*); pjes(ë)-tar, *member* (pjesë, *part*).

-or: forms adjectives, e.g. popullor, *popular*. A number end in -ror or -sor, e.g. shtetëror (G shtetnor) *national*; bujqësor, *agricultural* (cf. -ri and -si above). Where appropriate they can be nouns, e.g. malësor, *mountaineer*.

-tor (-tuer): forms nouns denoting agents, e.g. punëtor, *worker*. (The -t- may of course be part of the stem as in vjetor, *annual*, for which see -or.)

-as: is like -an and -ar, e.g. shtetas, *citizen*.

-(nj)(ë)s: the nearest thing Albanian possesses to an active present participle. It may be either a noun (E -er) or an adjective (E -*ing*, -*ant*, -*ent*, -*ive*) but does not form adverbial phrases like an English participle. Verbs in -oj may have derivatives in -onjës (characteristically Tosk) or -ues (characteristically Geg, but found frequently in the Tosk statutes). Other verbs have forms in -ës, which generally speaking are got by adding -s to verbal nouns (8.11) in -ë and changing those in -ur to -ës—in Geg more simply by adding -s or -ës to the short form of the verbal noun (8.11.3)—e.g. përkatës, *relevant* (përket, *pertains*; përkatur); huadhënës, *lender* (jap, *I give*; dhënë). There are also some words such as nëpunës, *employee*, which seem to be formed from phrases.

-ët, -të: form adjectives from verb stems and adverbs, e.g. fshehtë, *secret* (fsheh, *I hide*); hapët, *open* (hap, *I open*); përbashkët, *common* (bashkë, *together*).

13.3 PREFIXES

The meaning of these is less easy to fix: për- for instance is found in many words that have little in common, and in a word such as përcaktoj, *I define*, it adds little or nothing to the simple caktoj. But its existence is worth remembering. More obvious are:

bashkë-: *co-*, e.g. bashkëpunim, *collaboration*
ç-, s-, sh-: *dis-*, e.g. çdukem, *I disappear*; shpërndarje, *dissolution*
mos-: *non-*, e.g. mospranim, *non-acceptance*
pa-: *un-*, etc., e.g. paligjëshëm, *illegal*
para-: *pre-*, e.g. parafabrikoj, *I prefabricate*
ri-: *re-*, e.g. rishtyp, *I reprint*

The English equivalents are typical, not exclusive. Thus mosmarrëveshje would be *disagreement*.

GLOSSARY (Tosk forms; Geg see 0.5)

abonim, *subscription* (1.8.5)

bashkëpunim, *collaboration*
biblioteka, *library*
bibliotekar, *librarian*
botim, *edition* (1.5.1), *publication* (1.6.1, 1.8.1)
botohet, *is (being) published*
boton, *publishes* (1.8.1)
botuar, *published* (1.8.1)
broshurë, *pamphlet*

copë, *piece, copy*

çkëmbim, *exchange*
çmim, *price* (1.8.5)

darovisht, *complimentary, free*
del, *comes out*
dorëshkrim, *manuscript*
të drejtat, *rights*
dymujor, *bi-monthly*

faqe, *page*
fjalë, fjalim, *speech*
fjalor, *dictionary*

gati për t'u shtypur, *ready for printing*
gati të dali, *forthcoming*

hartuar, *composed, compiled* (1.2.1)
hesap, *bill*
hyrje/hymje, *introduction*

jashtë shtetit, *abroad*
jashtë teksti, *on a separate leaf* (plate)
javë, *week*

kartuç, *board*
kërkim, *research*
këshillë, *committee*
koleksionë, *collection, series*
konspekt, *summary*
kopje, *copy*
koregjuar, korektuar, *corrected* (1.5.2)
kumtesë, *contribution*

letër, *letter*
libër, *book* (1.4.1)

i lidhur, *bound*
ligjëratë, *speech*
lindi, i lindur, *(was) born*

marrë, *taken*
i mbaruar, *finished, out of print*
mbledhje, *meeting*
muaj, *month*

ndrequr, *corrected* (1.5.2)
numër, *number* (1.7.2, 1.8.3)

pabotuar, *unpublished*
pajtim, *subscription* (1.8.5)
i pandrruar, *unaltered*
paraqitur, *submitted*
parathënie, *preface*
pasqyrë, *table*
përgatitur, *prepared*
e përkohëshme, *periodical*
përkthim, *translation*
përmbledhje, *assembly, collection, summary*
e përmuajshme, *monthly* (1.8.4)
përpiluar, *compiled*
përpunuar, *edited* (1.2.1), *revised* (1.5.2)
përshtatur, *adapted* (1.2.1)
përrallë, *folk-tale*
pjesë, *part* (1.4.1), *play*
pjesëtar, *member*
plotësuar, *enlarged* (1.5.2)
po ai, po ay, *same*
poligrafuar, *duplicated*
porosi, *order*
pregatitur, *prepared*
pronë letrare, *copyright*

radhiti, *edited* (1.2.6)
redaksia, *editing, editorial office* (1.8.2, 1.8.7)
redaktim, *editing* (1.2.5)
redaktor, *editor* (1.8.2)
referat, *report*
revista, *review*
i ri, *new* (5.2.2)
ribotim, *republication*
ripunuar, *revised* (1.5.2)

rishtypje, *reprinting*
roman, *novel*

shtypje, *impression*
të shtypur, *printed, published*

shënim, *note*
në shitje, shitet, *on sale*
shkëmbim, *exchange*
shkrim, *writing*
shkrimtar, *writer*
shoqëri, shoqni, *society*
shqipëruar, *translated into Albanian*
shtëpi botonjëse, *publishing house* (1.6.1)
shtesë, *addition, appendix*
shtojcë, *appendix, supplement*
i shtuar, *added*
nën(ë) shtyp, *being printed*
shtypëshkronjë, *printer's*

tregim, *short story*
tremujor, *quarterly* (1.8.4)

vdiq, *died*
vepër, *work*
i vetëm, *single*
v(ë)llim, *volume* (1.4.1, 1.7.2)
vijon, *to be continued*
vit, *year*
vjersha, *verses, poetry*
vjetor, *annual, yearbook*

zgjedhur, *selected*

GRAMMATICAL INDEX: WORDS

ai, ajo, 7.1.2, 7.3.2
ardh-, 8.19.15
as-, at-, ay, 7.1.2, 7.3.2
âsht, 8.19.2

bashkë-, 13.3

cil-, cilvet, 7.1.3

ç-, 13.3
ç', 7.1.3

dashur, dash(t)ë, dash(t)un, 8.19.6
del, 8.19.5
desh(t)-, 8.19.6
djem, 4.2.4
do, 8.19.6
do të, 8.10.1, 8.10.2, 8.14.5
doja, dojsh-, 8.19.6
dol(l)-, 8.19.5
don(i), donja, donte, 8.19.6
dua, 8.19.6
duall-, 8.19.5
duam, duan, 8.19.6
duar, 4.2.4
due, 8.19.6
duel-, 8.19.5

duem, duen, 8.19.6
duer, 4.2.4
duke, 8.11.1
dyer, 4.2.4
dyke, 8.11.1

dha(më), dhanë, dhashë, dhatë, dhânë, dhe, dhënë, 8.19.8

e, 3.4.2, 7.3.2, 7.3.3
edhe pse, 11.2

është, 8.19.2

gra, 4.2.4

gjatë, 10.5

hângr-, hëngr-, 8.19.7

i, 3.4.2, 7.3.2, 7.3.3
ia, 7.3.2
im(e), 5.4.2
ish-, -ishj-, 8.19.2

ja, 7.3.2
jam, 8.14.6, 8.19.2
janë, je, jem-, jen-, 8.19.2

jes, 8.19.9
jeshë, jetë, 8.19.2
jonë, jote, 5.4.2
jua, 7.3.2
juaj, 5.4.2
juej, 5.4.3
jush, ju(ve), 7.3.1

kam, 8.10.3, 8.19.1
kam për të, 8.10.1
ka(në), 8.19.1
ke, 7.1.3, 8.19.1
kem-, ken-, 8.19.1
keq, 5.2.2
kesh, 8.19.1
ketë, 8.19.1
kë, 7.1.3
këqi(a), etc., 5.2.2
kës-, kët-, 7.1.2
kini, kish-, 8.19.1
kishem me, 8.10.2
kjo, 7.1.2
kuaj, 4.2.4
kuj(t)(-), 7.1.3
ky, 7.1.2

la(më), lanë, lash(ë), latë, le, 8.19.10
lig-, ligj, 5.2.2

m'a, 7.3.2
madhe, 5.2.2
mâ, 5.3.1
mbes, 8.19.9
me, 8.10.1, 8.11.1, 10.5
me qënë se, 11.2
meje, 7.3.1
më, 5.3.1, 7.3.1
mëdha, mëdhaj(a), 5.2.2
mij(a), 5.4.2
mjaft që, 11.2
mos-, 13.3
mua, mue, 7.3.1

na, 7.3.1
ndejt-, ndêj(t)-, ndënj-,
    8.19.11
nej, 5.4.3
nesh, neve, 7.3.1
në, 11.1
nëse, 11.2
nga, 10.2, 10.5
nga që, 11.2
ngrënë, 8.19.7

njerës, njerz, 4.2.4, 7.1.5
një, nji, 3.2.2

pa, 8.19.12
pa-, 13.3
pam(ë), panë, 8.19.12
para se, 11.2
para-, 13.3
parë, 8.19.12
pasë, 8.19.1
pasun, pasur, 8.19.1
pashë, 8.19.12
pata, 8.19.1
patë, 8.19.12
patur, 8.19.1
pe, 8.19.12

për, 13.3
po, 8.2.4, 8.3.3, 11.1
po që se, 11.2
prur-, prû, 8.19.3

qe(më), qenë, qeshë, qetë,
    qênë, 8.19.2
që, 7.1.4, 11.2
që nga, 11.2
qënë, 8.19.2
qoftë, 8.19.2

ra(m), ramë, ranë, rashë,
    ratë, 8.19.4
re(ja), 5.2.2
rënë, 8.19.4
ri-, 13.3
ri(n)j, 5.2.2

s', 2.1.4; 5.4.2
s-, 13.3
saj(a), 5.4.2
s'ate, 5.4.2
se, 11.1, 11.2
se mos, 11.2
së, 3.4.2
sidhe, 11.2
s'ime, 5.4.2
s'onë, 5.4.2
s'uaj, 5.4.2

sh-, 13.3
shih-, 8.19.12

ta, t'a, 7.3.2
t'anë, 5.4.2
t'ând-, 5.4.3
te, tê, 7.3.2
teje, 7.3.1
të, 3.4.2, 7.3.1, 7.3.2,
    8.7.2
tënd(e), 5.4.2

ti, 7.3.1, 7.3.2
tij(a), 5.4.2, 7.3.2
tillë, 7.1.5
t'im(e), 5.4.2
tjera, tjerë, 7.1.5
to, 7.3.2
t'ona, t'onë, 5.4.2
tu, 5.4.2, 7.3.2
tua, tuaj(a), 5.4.2
tue, 8.11.1
ty, 7.3.1
tyne, 5.4.3
tyre, 5.4.2

tha(më), thanë, 8.19.13
thasë, 4.2.4
thashë, thatë, thânë,
    8.19.13
the, them(i), thënë,
    8.19.13
thoj(sh)-, thom(i), thonë,
    thosh-, thotë, 8.19.13
thua, thue, 8.19.13

u, 7.3.2, 7.3.3, 8.14.1,
    8.14.6, 8.14.7
ua, 7.3.2

vajt-, vatur, ve, vej-,
    8.19.14
veja, 8.3.2, 8.19.14
vejsh-, vem-, ven-, vete,
    8.19.14
vjen, 8.2.2
vojt-, 8.19.14

ynë, 5.4.2
yt, 5.4.2

zes, zez(a), zezë, 5.2.2

GRAMMATICAL INDEX: ENDINGS

- (no ending), 5.2.1, 8.2.1
    8.11.2, 8.14.3, 8.14.4
-a, 3.1.2, 4.2.2, 5.2.1,
    8.4.1
-ja, 3.1.2, 8.3.1

-nja, 8.3.1
-(h)eshja, 8.14.3
-na, 4.2.2, 8.4.1
-ra, 4.2.2, 8.4.1
-ëra, 4.2.2

-ua, 8.14.4
-va, 8.4.1

-e, 4.2.2, 4.3.5, 5.2.1,
    8.4.1, 8.14.2

-he, 8.14.2
-ie, 13.2
-je, 4.3.5, 8.3.1, 13.2
-nje, 8.3.1
-(h)eshje, 8.14.3
-ne, 8.4.1
-re, 8.4.1
-(t)ore, 13.2
-(j)she, 8.3.1
-(h)eshe, 8.14.3
(-n)te, 8.3.1
-ue, 8.11.2, 8.14.4
-ve, 4.3.2, 4.3.5, 8.4.1

-ë, 4.2.2, 5.2.1, 8.2.1,
    8.7.1, 8.11.2
-jë, 8.7.1
-më, 8.2.1, 8.4.1, 8.11.2
-jmë, 8.2.1
-në, 3.1.2, 8.2.1, 8.4.1,
    8.11.2
-jnë, 8.2.1
-rë, 4.2.2, 8.7.1, 8.11.2
-lerë, 4.2.2
-së, 3.1.2
-esë, 13.2
-të, 3.1.2, 8.4.1, 8.11.2,
    13.2

-i, 3.1.2, 4.3.2, 8.2.1,
    8.4.1, 8.7.1, 8.14.2,
    13.2
-hi, 8.14.2
-(h)emi, 8.14.2
-ni, 3.1.2, 4.3.2, 8.2.1,
    8.4.1
-(h)eni, 8.14.2

-ini, 8.2.2
-sni/-tni, 8.2.3
-oi, 8.4.1
-ri, 3.1.2, 4.3.2, 8.4.1,
    13.2
-si, 13.2
-azi, 9.1.5

-j, 4.2.2, 8.2.1
-hej, 8.14.3
-oj, 8.2.1, 13.2

-m, 8.11.2
-uam, 8.4.1
-(h)em, 8.14.2
-(j)shem, 8.3.1
-(h)eshem, 8.14.3
-uem, 8.11.2
-ëm, 8.4.1
-shëm, 13.2
-im, 8.2.1, 8.2.2, 13.2
-jim, 8.3.1
-(h)eshjim, 8.14.3
-nim, 8.3.1
-sim, 8.2.3
-(j)shim, 8.3.1
-(h)eshim, 8.14.3

-n, 8.2.1
-an, 13.2
-uan, 8.4.1
-(h)en, 8.14.2
-ën, 4.2.2, 8.2.2, 8.4.1
-in, 3.1.2, 8.2.1, 8.2.2
-jin, 8.3.1
-(h)eshjin, 8.14.3
-nin, 8.3.1

-sin, 8.2.3
-(j)shin, 8.3.1
-(h)eshin, 8.14.3
-un, 3.1.2, 8.11.2
-tun, 8.11.2

-nj, 4.2.2
-onj, 8.2.1, 13.2

-(t)ar, 13.2
-uar, 8.11.2
-ër, 4.2.2
-(t)or, 13.2
-ur, 8.11.2
-tur, 8.11.2

-s, 3.1.2, 8.2.3, 13.2
-as, 9.1.5, 13.2
-(nj)ës, 13.2

-sh, 4.3.2, 4.3.5
-(h)esh, 8.14.2, 8.14.3

-t, 3.1.2, 8.2.3
-uat, 8.4.1
-(h)et, 8.14.2
-vet, 3.1.2
-ët, 8.4.1, 13.2
-jit, 8.3.1
-(h)eshjit, 8.14.3
-nit, 8.3.1
-(j)shit, 8.3.1
-(h)eshit, 8.14.3
-sht, 9.1.4

-u, 3.1.2, 4.3.2, 8.4.1

SLAVONIC LANGUAGES

General note
Russian
Byelorussian
Ukrainian
Polish
Czech
Slovak
Slovene
Serbocroatian
Macedonian
Bulgarian

GENERAL NOTE: SLAVONIC LANGUAGES

COMMON FACTORS

The Slavonic languages—Russian, Byelorussian, Ukrainian, Polish, Czech, Slovak, Slovene, Serbocroatian, Macedonian, Bulgarian—are a sufficiently close family to have a number of common characteristics, as well as phonetic correspondences between the languages which to some extent enable a knowledge of one to throw light on another. They fall into groups, as indicated by the order above: Russian to Ukrainian; Polish to Slovak; Slovene to Bulgarian.

The sort of phonetic correspondences that are found are shown in the following table, the languages which use the Cyrillic alphabet being transliterated according to the standard published by the International Organization for Standardization. As usual consonants are more reliable than vowels.

Ru	Br	Uk	Pl	Cz	Sk	Sn	Sh	Ma	Bu
mat'	maci	maty	(matka)	(matka)	(matka)	mati	mati	(majka)	(maĭka)
vera	vera	vira	wiara	víra	viera	vera	v(j)era	vera	vjara
son	son	son	sen	sen	sen	sen	san	son	săn
den'	dzen'	den'	dzień	deň	deň	dan	dan	den	den
pjat'	pjac'	p'jat'	pieć	pět	päť	pet	pet	pet	pet
četyre	čatyry	čotyry	cztery	čtyri	štiri	četiri	četiri	četiri	četiri
tretii	treci	tretii	trzeci	třetí	treti	tretji	treći	treti	treti
gorod	gorod	(misto)	gród	(mesto)	(mesto)	(mesto)	grad	grad	grad

One must not, however, place too blind a reliance on this sort of correspondence. Not only have differences grown up in the declensions and conjugations, but it is apparent from the table itself that there are differences of vocabulary between the groups. To take another example, the word for *preface* is Ru **predislovie**; Br **pradmova** Uk **peredmova** Pl **przedmowa** Cz **předmluva**; Sn, Sh, Ma and Bu **predgovor**.

HARD AND SOFT CONSONANTS

In most languages, even when the spelling is said to be phonetic, a given consonant is not a unique sound but a wider or narrower range of sounds. Thus [k] in *key*, *cart* and *cool* is not one identical sound nor is [t] in *tea*, *try* and *too*, since the position of the tongue is accommodated to the succeeding sound. Though the differences in English are not so marked as in the Slavonic languages, the consonants in *key* and *tea*, with the tongue forward, may be classed as soft, those in *cart*, *cool*, *too*, with the tongue more or less retracted, as hard. (The [t] in *try* is palatalised.)

In standard English the differences are contextual, automatic, and usually unperceived; but in dialects one may hear *cart* pronounced with the [k] of *key*, giving the pronunciation 'kyart,' with a perceptibly soft [k]. In Slavonic languages this combination of a forward consonant with a back vowel is common, and it is therefore necessary to distinguish two series of consonants, hard and soft. Furthermore, it is possible for a word to end with a soft consonant. Thus we have, for example, [p] in Ru **pyl', pal, put'** (пыль, пал, путь), Pl **pytanie, padł, punkt**; [p̓] in Ru **pit', pjat', p'jut** (пить, пять, пьют), Pl **pić, piasek, pióro.**

In the representation of soft consonants we either have a sign following the consonant, viz. **ь** in Russian and **i** in Pl **piasek** and **pióro**, or a diacritical mark, e.g. **ć**, or we must infer the softness of the consonant from the following vowel, viz. Ru **е, и, ю, я**, Pl **i** in **pić**. Similarly, Sk **ä** invariably, **e** and **i** usually indicate a preceding soft consonant, but there are also special soft consonants, **ď, ľ, ť**; Sh **lj, nj** and their Cyrillic equivalents are soft consonants, and a following **j** softens other consonants, there being only a single series of vowels. The completeness of the two series varies from language to language, and in every language there are some consonants which are only hard or soft: thus sz is hard in Polish, but š is soft in Czech. The classification of consonants is set out under each language.

The classification of consonants is sometimes important for the spelling of the basic form of words, but (pronunciation apart) its chief importance lies in the existence of parallel hard and soft declensions, and to lesser extent conjugations, and in its effect on individual endings in each class.

PALATALISATION AND DISPALATALISATION

The accommodation of certain consonants to [e], [i] and [j], whereby the tongue approaches nearer to the hard palate than would otherwise be the case, may proceed farther than is necessary and produce the effect known as palatalisation; indeed soft consonants, whatever their origin, tend to become palatalised, some in one way and some in another. The best known example is the Latin [k̓] in, say, **civilis**, which produced [tʃ] in Italian, [ts] in German, [s] in French and English, [θ] in Spanish. The Latin **caput**, whose [k] was later softened in some parts of the empire, produced En *chief*, Fr *chef*. Similarly, the discrepancy between spelling and pronunciation in such words as *nation* springs from the palatalisation of the [t].

Whereas in most languages palatalisation is a matter of linguistic history, in the Slavonic languages the consonants [t], [d], [r], [s], [z], [k], [g], [x] and their combinations may be palatalised in the course of inflexion, e.g. Pl **mogę, możesz,** *I can, you can*; Ru **hotit', hoču,** *to want, I want*; Cz **Amerika, v Americe,** *(in) America,* and so on. The extent, occasions and nature of the palatalisation vary somewhat from language to language, and the details are given under the language concerned.

It follows from their generation that Slavonic palatals were originally soft consonants, but in itself [tʃ] for instance is just another consonant and need not be any softer than [t]. They tended therefore, to a greater or less extent in the several languages to be 'dispalatalised' and to become hard. This is particularly so in Polish, where it has a disturbing effect on the declensional pattern. The i of a termination softens a preceding consonant and in some cases palatalises it. If the resulting palatal is one that has become hard, it cannot be followed by **i**, which is a sign of softness; so y must be substituted. Thus in the plural of **robotnik** we have ***robotniki*** > ***robotnici*** > **robotnicy** as against **chłop, chlopi,** where there is no palatalisation. (See Polish 4.3.2 for details.)

ASPECTS OF THE VERB

The distinction of aspects—between momentary and continued or repeated action, between one that is beginning and one that is ending—is present to some extent in most languages, but it is not necessarily indicated as it is in the Slavonic languages by differences in the basic form of the verb, so that there is both a perfective and an imperfective infinitive.

The ways of indicating the differences (apart from the use of completely different verbs) are common to the various languages, but the use made of them is not always the same. They fall into two categories: modification of the stem and the use of prefixes. Two of the most universal modifications are the use of **-n-** to indicate the perfective aspect, e.g. Ru **dvinut'/dvigat'**, *to move*, and of **-v-** to indicate the imperfective, e.g. Ru **dat'/davat'**, *to give*.

Most prefixes not only make the verb perfective but also narrow its meaning, and a verb like **dat'**, which is itself perfective, can take a prefix. There is little difference, other than aspect, between the imperfective **delat'** and the perfective **sdelat'**, but **dat'** means *to give* and **sdat'** *to give up* (among other things). So we find as well **sdavat'**, where the **-va-** makes the imperfective. Again **platit'**, *to pay*, has a corresponding perfective **vyplatit'**, where **vy-** (*out*) has little to do but indicate aspect: this time we find a second imperfective **vyplačivat'**, *to keep paying off*. The infix **-va-** tends in all the Slavonic languages to indicate repeated action.

In the nature of things some tenses fit one aspect better than another. The present is naturally imperfective, so the corresponding perfective tense is either used as a future, as in Russian, or is confined to subordinate clauses. But whereas Russian uses the imperfective past much as we use the imperfect, and the perfective past like our simple past or perfect, the southern languages have imperfect and aorist tenses too, which they use in conjunction with the aspects to make subtle distinctions.

If the forms of the different aspects are adequately entered in available dictionaries, little will be said about the relations between them, but where this is not so, the principal ways of indicating aspect are set out under the language concerned.

RUSSIAN

SPECIMENS

Настоящее собрание сочинений А. И. Герцена является первым научным изданием литературного и эпистолярного наследия выдающегося деятеля русского освободительного движения, революционного демократа, гениального мыслителя и писателя, сыгравшего, по словам В. И. Ленина, «великую роль в подготовке русской революции».

The present collection of the works of A. I. Gertsen (Herzen) constitutes the first scholarly edition of the literary and epistolary remains of a prominent agent of the Russian liberation movement, a revolutionary democrat, a thinker and writer of genius, who played, in the words of V. I. Lenin, 'a great role in the preparation of the Russian revolution'.

Не считаемъ нужнымъ разъяснять пользы или значенія *Энциклопедическаго Словаря*. Различные методы составленія изданій этого рода, равно какъ и существовавшее въ различныя времена отношеніе между ними, возникавшую между ними необходимую связь и зависимость читатели найдутъ въ нашемъ словарѣ, подъ словами: *Азбуковникъ, Букварь, Энциклопедія, Энциклопедическій Словарь.*

The specimen exhibits the following divergences from present-day spelling:

> ъ: final, now omitted. (Medial ъ was for a time replaced by '.)
> i: и
> -аго: -ого
> -ыя: -ые
> ѣ: е

0 GENERAL CHARACTERISTICS

0.1 DEGREE OF INFLEXION
The language is synthetic, with a rich system of inflexions.

0.2 ORDER OF WORDS
Adjectives precede the nouns they qualify, genitives follow. The order SVOC is usual but the order of verb and subject is not infrequently reversed, especially on title-pages, where the order may well be CVS or OVS (cf. 1.2.4).

0.4 RELATION TO OTHER LANGUAGES
The Russian vocabulary contains a number of 'international' words derived from Greek and Latin, whose meaning is soon grasped, such as экономическій, республика,

культурный; but the basic vocabulary is peculiarly Slavonic and its affinities with other Indo-European languages do not reveal themselves to casual inspection.

1 BIBLIOLINGUISTICS

1.1 NAMES

1.1.1 Russian names are either nouns or adjectives and are so declined. Personal names consist of a Christian name (имя), a patronymic (отчество) and a surname (фамилия).

1.1.2 Christian names are nouns, e.g. Павел (4.3.1), Василий (4.3.1), Никита (4.3.4), Илья (4.3.4); Ольга (4.3.4), Мария (4.3.4). Note that not all names ending in -а or -я are borne by women; apart from Никита and Илья given above there are a large number of male diminutives such as Ваня (Иван), Алеша (Алексей). Furthermore the new names invented after the revolution, continuing in Russia proper until the thirties but in remoter parts of the Union long after that, are often anomalous: Коммуна for instance has been used by men and women and so have Идеал and Юность (4.3.4). Долорес is found as a man's name and Маркс as a given name instead of a surname. In Estonia traditional Russian names may be substitutes for the native ones, e.g. Кирилл for Kaarel.

1.1.3 Patronymics are regularly formed from the father's name and end in -ович, -евич, -ыч or -ич for men, -овна, -евна or -(ин)ична for women. The precise form depends on the ending of the Christian name, thus:

Борис	Борисович	(hard consonant)
Павел	Павлович	
Игорь	Игоревич	(soft consonant)
Николай	Николаевич	(final -й)
Василий	Васильевич	(-ий)
Илья	Ильич (F Ильинична)	
Никита	Никитыч (F Никитычна)	(most names in -а and -я)
Гаврила	Гаврилович	(colloquial forms in -а)
Яков	Яковлевич	(exceptional)

Both the -ич and the -на forms are nouns (4.3).

In Soviet Asia non-Russian forms of patronymic are found, e.g. Адиль Мейраб-оглы Эльдаров, especially of recent years.

1.1.4 Surnames may be nouns or adjectives.

(a) Those that end in a consonant, apart from those in -ин, -ын, -ев, -ов, are nouns (4.3), e.g. Засулич, Радек. They have no feminine forms, and when borne by women are indeclinable, e.g. Веры Засулич, *of Vera Zasulich*. They are not common. The letter -й counts as a consonant, as in Бурий (4.3.1), but most of those in -ий, -ой, -ый belong to type (d) below.

(b) Surnames in -ка, е.g. Глинка, and -ко, e.g. Шевченко, are masculine nouns; those in -ка are declined like other nouns in -а (4.3.4), those in -ко are not declined. Names of foreign origin which end in a vowel are treated like foreign names (1.1.7).

(c) Pure Russian surnames in -ев, -ов, -ин (-ын after -ц) are possessive adjectives in origin and form the feminine by adding -а, e.g. Павлов(а), Голицын(а). Their declension is given in 5.2.4. They are very common. It will be noted that most of the feminine and plural forms are identical with those of the adjectival names given under (d), so that care is needed. To these names are assimilated Russian names of foreign origin such as **Фон-Визин**, but not foreign names like **Грин** (Green) or **Бюлов** (Bülow), for which see 1.1.7. As the GM and NF both end in -a, the construction (1.2) needs to be noted in order to distinguish them (cf. **Попова** in 1.2.4, **Струмилина** in 1.2.6).

(d) Those that end in **-ий, -ой, -ый** are usually adjectives. The corresponding feminine form is nearly always **-ая**, e.g. **Крупский/Крупская, Толстой/Толстая, Подольный/ Подольная**. If there is any surname which is an adjective in **-ий** (not **-кий**), its feminine will be **-яя**. The hard endings of the masculine are ambiguous. Apart from the fact that **к** and **г** are followed by **и**, not **ы**, so that **Троцкого** comes from **Троцкий, -ого** is equally the genitive of names in **-ой**; and so with the other cases. Names in **-ой** are not numerous but include some that are well known. Both the **-ов** and **-ий** types of names have plural forms which can be used where two or more members of the same family are mentioned, e.g. **Братья Карамазовы**, *The Brothers Karamazov*. They will more usually be husband and wife as in **Е. и М. Никольские**, explained as **Евгения Ана- тольевна Никольская и Михаил Осипович Никольский**, members of other family combinations being mentioned separately, e.g. **Д. И. Улянов и М. И. Улянова**. But grammatically the plural is neutral as between masculine and feminine and can indicate any combination.

1.1.5   Both halves of a compound name are appropriately declined.

1.1.6   Grammar apart, it is as well to remember that the serfs in 19th-century Russia had no surnames and may therefore be known by different names at different stages. Thus the revolutionary Petr Anisimovich Moiseenko, b. 1852, called himself first Petr Anisimov (the usual procedure) before adopting Moseenok (also found in the forms Moseenka and Moseenko) in 1883. Likewise the names of non-Russian inhabitants of the Soviet Union show at different times varying degrees of Russification and in some cases a similar lack of surnames.

1.1.7   Foreign names follow where possible the Russian grammatical pattern. This is easy where surnames end phonetically in a consonant, e.g. **Шекспир**, *Shakespeare*, G **Шекспира**. (Like similar Russian names they are indeclinable when borne by women.) Surnames that end in -a, e.g. **Варга** (*Varga*), are usually declined (1.1.4b) but some- times not. Those that end in the other vowels are indeclinable. Christian names may be declined if they are sufficiently like Russian ones in form, e.g. **два разы в год перечитывала Памелу**, *twice a year she would re-read Pamela*; but most of them are not. The chief difficulty with foreign names is to restore their original forms; having been rendered more or less phonetically into Russian, they cannot be blindly restored unless the spelling of the original language is phonetically unequivocal or the original name has only one possible form (cf. 2.1.5). Slavonic and Baltic names, on the other hand, including Ukrainian and Byelorussian ones, are usually (but not necessarily) Russified, e.g. **Дмоховский** or **Дмоховски** for Polish **Dmochowski**, and can be much more surely restored provided one knows the forms of the names in the language concerned (cf. 2.1.5 and the sections on those languages). But unless a library holds materials in the original languages also there is much to be said for leaving Soviet names in their Rus- sian forms.

1.2 NAMES OF AUTHORS, EDITORS, ETC.

1.2.1   The ways of indicating authorship, editorship and the like require the name to be in various cases.

1.2.2   The name stands at the head of the title-page and needs no alteration for the catalogue. This is the usual way of indicating simple authorship.

1.2.3   The name follows the title in the genitive or the nominative. The genitive, without break between title and name, is still fairly common for complete or selected works, e.g. **Воспоминания Бориса Николаевича Чичерина**, *Memoirs of Boris Nicolaevich Chicherin*. It was formerly much commoner and found in all types of works, e.g. **Лекціи и изслѣдованія по древней исторіи русскаго права. Третье изданіе дополнено. В. Сергѣевича**, *Lectures and studies in the early history of Russian law. By V. Sergeevich.* In a modern instance such as **Выплаты и возмещения хозорганам средств и бюджета. А. Дьяченко, Б. Мохов, Т. Фрейман**, the names are in the nominative.

1.2.4   The work done may be indicated by an active verb, following the title and preceding the name. The normal tense is the past, which has the form of a participle and agrees in gender as well as in number with the subject, i.e. the author or authors. Care is therefore needed in abbreviating titles, but the name needs no alteration, e.g. **сборник составил Г. Марягин**, *G. Maryagin compiled the collection*; **избрала Т. Попова**, *T. Popova selected*; **в редактировании принимали участие** . . . (followed by a list of names), *took part in the editing*; **перевел с литовского В. Чепайтис**, *V. Čepaitis translated from the Lithuanian*. This is one of the commoner ways of indicating editors and compilers; but verbs like **написал**, *wrote*, denoting simple authorship, are little used nowadays, and translators are more often indicated as in 1.2.6.

1.2.5   The agent may be denoted by a noun, e.g. **составитель**, *compiler*; **редактор(ы)**, *editor(s)*; **авторский коллектив**, *team of authors*; **редакционная коллегия**, *editorial college*. Here too the names follow in the nominative and need no alteration. The expressions **группа авторов, коллектив авторов**, however, may be followed by names in the genitive in apposition to **авторов** (cf. 1.1.4c). More elaborate expressions are found in prefaces such as **авторами отдельных глав являются** . . ., *authors of individual chapters are* . . .. Names follow in the nominative.

1.2.6   The work done is indicated by a noun, e.g. **сочинение**, *composition*; **перевод**, *translation*; **редакция**, *editing*; **под общей редакцией**, *under the general editorship*; similarly **руководство**, *leadership*. The names follow in the genitive, e.g. **предисловие С. Г. Струмилина**, *preface by S. G. Strumilin*.

1.2.7   The work done is indicated by a passive participle agreeing with some preceding noun. The name of the author, editor or the like is in the instrumental case, e.g. **издан Н. С. Таганцевым**, *edited by N. S. Tagantsev*; **главы I, II и V написаны С. И. Винокуром и А. В. Могилевичем, III и IV С. В. Свойкиным, глава XII З. Д. Косаревой**, *Chapters 1, 2 and 5 written by S. V. Vinokur and A. V. Mogilevich, 3 and 4 by S. V. Svoikin, chapter 12 by Z. D. Kosareva.* The last phrase by itself would require **написана** agreeing with **глава**.

1.2.8   Corporate authors may be indicated in most of the ways already mentioned, but the nominative at the head of the page (1.2.2) is much the most frequent. The instrumental (1.2.7) is often used to denote the section actually responsible for the preparation of a volume, e.g. **Сборник подготовлен Управлением по проводению Всесоюзного переписи населения** of a work which appears under the name of the **Центральное статистическое управление**. The genitive (1.2.3) is found in the case of transactions or series, e.g. **Материалы Всесоюзного Совещания заведуючих кафедрами овщественных наук**; **Труды Башкирского филиала Академии наук СССР**. Where the body is named at the head of the page, there may well be no precise indication of its relation to the work.

When corporate names need altering for the heading, only the key noun and its qualifying adjectives have to be put in the nominative, e.g. in the examples above **Всесоюзное совещание** and **Башкирский филиал**. Long runs of genitives can be trying, e.g. **Доклады Всесоюзной ордена Ленина Академии сельскохозяйственных наук им. В. И. Ленина**: only **Всесоюзная Академия** will appear in the nominative, all the other genitives being in one way or other descriptive.

Subordinate bodies are usually placed before the parent body, which is either in the genitive or preceded by a preposition such as **при**, *at*; or occasionally the parent body may be sandwiched. For the catalogue the order will have to be reversed or sorted out and nominatives restored where appropriate. Sometimes, however, both bodies will appear in the nominative with the subordinate body second; but caution is needed here since coordinate bodies may be shown in the same way. The first type is exemplified by **Башкирский филиал** etc. above, which becomes **Akademiya Nauk. Bashkirskiĭ Filial**. A sandwich occurs in **Комиссия при Президиума ЦИК Союза ССР по изданию документов эпохи империализма** (USSR. Tsentral'nyĭ Ispol'nitel'nyĭ Komitet. Prezidium. Komissiya po Izdaniyu Dokumentov Épokhi Imperializma). Groups of institutions such as **Кафедры марксистско-ленинской философии Высшей партийной школы ... и местных высших партийных школ** (*Chairs of Marxist-Leninist Philosophy at the Higher Party School ... and the local higher party schools*) defy sorting out.

1.3 TITLES

1.3.1 The great majority, fiction apart, consist of nouns and adjectives in various cases with or without prepositions, e.g. **Роль общественности в борьбе с преступниками,** *The role of public opinion in the struggle against criminals*; **Незабываемые годы,** *Unforgettable years*. The literature of persuasion includes more varied types, e.g. **Никто не забыт, ничто не забыто,** *Nobody forgotten, nothing forgotten*; **А что ответишь ты?,** *And what is your answer?*, and is fond of the infinitive, e.g. **Улучшить снабжение рабочих,** *Improving the supply of workers* (but with an implied exhortation).

1.3.2 Title entries on the Anglo-American pattern pose no problems, but unless the titles are transliterated, present difficulties of filing. It seems that at least the catchword must be transliterated but this can produce difficulties of its own by creating the appearance of a heading. The British Museum rules, which require in every case a heading, avoid this difficulty, but necessitate the picking out of the nouns, the restoration of nominative forms and sometimes translation.

The filing of titles in Cyrillic where there are also titles in the Latin alphabet under the same heading involves either concealed transliteration or separation of alphabets or the production of a 'super-alphabet' such as the following:

а	б	в	г	д	е		ж	з	и	й	к	л	м	н	о	п		р
a	ʌ b	c		d	e	f	g	h		i	j		k	l	m	n	o	p	q	r

с	т	у		ф	х	ц	ч	ш	щ	ь	ы	ъ	э	ю	я
s	t	u	v	w	x	y	z

in which equated letters are interfiled. Each system has its disadvantages.

1.3.3 When a title forms part of a sentence the case of the principal noun or nouns and any adjectives that agree with it may be affected, e.g. **одна из глав «Евгения Онегина»,** *one of the chapters of 'Evgeniĭ Onegin'*; **о «Капитанской дочке»,** *about 'Kapitanskaya dochka'*. If, however, there is a noun to which the title is in apposition the noun takes the appropriate case and the title is unaffected, e.g. **из главного про-**

изведения Данте «Божественная комедия», *from Dante's main work 'The divine comedy'.*

1.4 VOLUMES AND PARTS

1.4.1 These are usually indicated by том and **часть** respectively. **Книга,** *book,* which often indicates an internal division of a large work without necessarily corresponding to a physical volume, is sometimes equivalent to том and sometimes used where two physical units have the same volume number, e.g. **том 28, книга 1, книга 2.** **Выпуск** usually denotes, in this context, a part of a work issued in instalments (cf. also 1.8.4), but sometimes simply replaces том or часть.

1.4.2 Numeration is given in ordinal numbers, which may be in words or figures, e.g. **том 3, часть первая.**

1.4.4 Many-volumed works often have a second title-page on which the total number of volumes is stated, e.g. **Д. И. Писарев | Сочинения в четырех томах,** or the information may be given in various ways in the preface, e.g. **Все издание рассчитано на 26 томов,** *The whole edition is estimated at 26 volumes.*

1.5 EDITIONS

1.5.1 The usual word is **издание,** a verbal noun which also has the more general meaning *publication* (1.6.6). The number may be expressed either by a word or figure, preceding or following, e.g. **третье издание, издание 2-е.** Occasionally the information is given incidentally in the preface, e.g. **Второе издание учебного пособия подготовлено . . .,** *the second edition of the educational handbook (was) prepared . . ..*

1.5.2 Revision is indicated by a variety of terms, usually participles (8.12.5). They may precede the word **издание,** in which case they have the long form (5.2.1), e.g. **второе дополненное издание,** *second, enlarged, edition,* or follow it, with the short form (5.2.4), e.g. **второе издание, дополнено.** Other words commonly used are: **исправленное,** *corrected;* **переработанное,** *reworked* (a greater degree of revision); and **пересмотренное,** *revised.* The degree of revision may be indicated by an adverb such as **значительно,** *considerably.*

1.6 IMPRINTS

1.6.1 The imprints of modern books rarely cause any grammatical difficulty, both press and place being in the nominative. Soviet presses are institutional and until recently the state publishing houses have had long descriptive names, e.g. **Государственное издательство политической литературы,** abbreviated to **Госполитиздат** **Гос-ое изд-во детской литературы** abbreviated to **Детгиз.** The abbreviations, if used in place of the full name, may be found on the cover; if not, they must be sought in a standard list such as *Словарь сокращений русского языка* produced under the editorship of B. F. Kovutskiĭ (ГИИНС 1963); they cannot be predicted.

1.6.2 Standard abbreviations (2.4) of individual words can of course be safely used, as in the second example; but it is risky to combine syllabic abbreviations with unabbreviated adjectives. Thus **государственное издательство** (neuter) becomes **госиздат** (masculine); **Латвийское госиздат** with a neuter adjective, though it could be justified *ad sensum,* is against normal usage, while the grammatically correct **Латвийский госиздат** cannot be regarded as a legitimate abbreviation of **Латвийское гос-ое изд-ство** in view of the changed adjective. (There are in fact complete abbreviations: **Латгосиздат** and **ЛГИ.**)

1.6.3 In a recent reorganisation the naming of the state publishing houses was changed; short names consisting of a single abstract noun, e.g. **Мысль**, have been substituted. A few such names existed before the change.

1.6.4   Academy and university imprints also usually incorporate the word **издатель-ство**, e.g. **Издательство Академии наук**, *Press of the Academy of Sciences*. It is perhaps legitimate to abbreviate this to **Академия наук** or **АН**.

1.6.5   Pre-revolutionary imprints (which may well be foreign) include personal names, e.g. **Издание М. и С. Сабашниковых**, *published by M. and S. Sabashnikov*; **Берлинъ, Издание Гуго Штейница**, *Hugo Steinitz Verlag*; but it is quite common to find simply a printer's imprint, e.g. **Университетская типография** and a note of the distributor, e.g. **Складъ изданія у С. П. Льдова**, *stock at S. P. L'dov's*. Such notes may also accompany a publisher's imprint. Sometimes a printer's imprint may occur in the usual place, while **издание** and a name appears as part of a title.

1.6.6   Grammatical complications may be introduced by the use of the preposition **в** before the place of publication, which is in the locative case, e.g. **в Петрограде**, *at Petrograd*, and by the use of **издание**, *publication*, before the name of the publisher, which is in the genitive as above.

1.7   SERIES

1.7.1   The titles of series are given either at the head of the title-page or on an extra title-page facing that of the individual volume. Most of them are simple descriptions, either collectively of the series, e.g. **Рабочая библиотека**, *Workers' library*, **Библиотека Жизни**, *Zhizn' library*; or of items, e.g. **Труды Ленинградского отде-ления института истории**, *Works of the Leningrad section of the Institute of History*. It is very rarely such a plural title has to be inferred from a single item: in particular the occurrence of **издание** (1.6.6) must not be taken as evidence of a series of **Издания**.

In the catalogue some rearranging and grammatical disentangling may be necessary, e.g. **Институт Истории. Ленинградское Отделение. Труды.**

1.7.2   Series may be divided into sub-series, sometimes indicated by **серия**, e.g. **Серия историческая**, but often simply by a further title, e.g. **Труды, вып. 171: Исторические науки, книга 36**, *Works, No. 171: Historical sciences, book 36*. Numeration is usually by **выпуск**, but **том** and **книга** are also found.

1.8   PERIODICALS

1.8.1   Linguistically the titles of periodicals are of a piece with those of books and series, e.g. **Вопросы экономики**, *Questions of economics*; **Международная жизнь**, *International affairs*; but more fanciful titles, e.g. **Искра**, *The spark*, are encountered more often. **Сборник** (*collection*) is so common in the names of irregular serials as almost to be a technical term. As with titles of books (1.3.3) the title may be grammatically connected with or insulated from the rest of the sentence.

1.8.2   The name of the body responsible may be put at the head of the title-page in the nominative like that of the author of a book (1.2.2), or it may be in the genitive as part of the title, e.g. **Вестник Академии наук**, or of the sub-title, e.g. ... **орган Ин-ститута государства и права Академии наук СССР**, ... *organ of the Institute*, etc. Occasionally the information is given only in the preface in such a form as **По реше-нию ЦК КПСС возобновляется ежегодное издание «Справочника партийного работника»**, *By decision of the Central Committee of the CPSU annual publication of the Party Worker's Handbook has been resumed*.

1.8.3   Editorship is indicated by some form of the root **редак-**, e.g. **редактор(ы)**

or more commonly nowadays **редакционная коллегия**, followed by the names of the editors in the nominative.

1.8.4 Numeration is usually by **год**, *year*, and **номер**, *number*, abbreviated **№**, or **выпуск**. (I have once seen **тетрадь** in an émigré publication: = *cahier*?) The years may be numbered serially from the beginning, e.g. **41-й год издания, год издания тридцать третий**, *41st (33rd) year of publication*, in which case it is equivalent to *volume*, or only the calendar year may be given, e.g. **№ 18, Декабрь 1964 г.**

1.8.5 Periodicity is indicated by such phrases as **выходит раз (два раза) в месяц**, *comes out once (twice) a month*; **6 номеров в год**, *6 numbers a year*; **ежемесячно**, *monthly*; **ежемесячный журнал**, *monthly magazine*.

1.8.6 Subscription (**подписка**) is usually quoted for the year, e.g. **подписная цена на год 3р. 60к.**, occasionally for less, e.g. **на шесть месяцев**, *for six months*. The price of a single number (**одного** or **отдельного номера**) may also be given.

1.8.7 Addresses given distinguish between the editorial side (**адрес редакции**) and the business side (**адрес издательства**).

2 ALPHABET, PHONETICS, SPELLING

2.1 ALPHABET

2.1.1 *Alphabet and transliteration*

		B.S.		*B.M.*	*L.C.*
А	а	a			
Б	б	b			
В	в	v			
Г	г	g			
Д	д	d			
Е	е	e			
Ж	ж	zh	ž		
З	з	z			
[I	i]	ī	ī		ï
И	и	i		ий = y	
Й	й	ĭ	j		
К	к	k			
Л	л	l			
М	м	m			
Н	н	n			
О	о	o			
П	п	p			
Р	р	r			
С	с	s			
Т	т	t			
У	у	u			
Ф	ф	f			
Х	х	kh	h		
Ц	ц	ts	c		
Ч	ч	ch	č		

(Continued overleaf)

		B.S.		B.M.	L.C.
Ш	ш	sh	š		
Щ	щ	shch	šč		
—	ъ	” (and see below)			
—	ы	ȳ	y	ui	
				ый = uy	
—	ь	’			
[Ѣ	ѣ]	ê	ě	ye	ie
Э	э	é	ė	e	ė
Ю	ю	yu	ju		iu
Я	я	ya	ja		ia
[Ѳ	ѳ]	ḟ		th	
[Ѵ	ѵ]	ў	ẏ		ẏ

e is sometimes pronounced yo or o; it may then be written ё, but outside school texts and dictionaries this is only done if the word is ambiguous or obscure, e.g. все, *every-one*, but всё, *everything*; Олёкма (proper name). Й, usually the second component of a diphthong, is occasionally found at the beginning of a borrowed word, e.g. йод. The letters in brackets are now obsolete in Soviet Russia: i is replaced by и, ѣ by e, ѳ by ф and ѵ by и. The ъ at the end of a word, which was neither pronounced nor transliterated, is now omitted, and may be replaced in the middle of a word by a single or double apostrophe. The variants in the second column are the international trans-literations recommended (like those in the first column) by the British Standards Institution in B.S.2979:1958 and taken from the International Organization for Standardization's recommendation ISO/R9. Those in the remaining columns derive from the practice of the British Museum and the Library of Congress. In other trans-literations *y* is found for й.

2.1.2   Other countries have certain national variants, viz.

	German	French	Italian	Polish	Hungarian	Norwegian	Rumanian
в	w			w			
ж	sh	j		ż	zs	sj(zj)	j
з	s					s	
с					sz		
у		ou					
х	ch					ch	
ц							ţ
ч	tsch	tch	c(i)	cz	cs	tsj	c(i)
ш	sch	ch	sc(i)	sz	s	sj	ş
щ	schtsch	chtch		szcz	scs	sjtsj	şc(i)
ь	j					j	
ы	ü						î

2.1.3   In addition e is often transliterated ie, je or ye, ё as io, jo or yo, or occasionally o; books and newspapers modify the strict transliteration, sometimes in order to indicate the pronunciation more clearly, sometimes because they are following a traditional transcription, sometimes for simplicity's sake, e.g. *Kruschoff* not *Khrushchev* (1 and 3), *Tchaikovsky* not *Chaikovskiĭ* (2). The last example illustrates the influence of foreign systems of transliteration, which by introducing ambiguities may well make it impossible to reconstruct the original.

2.1.4 The apostrophe representing the soft sign ь is sometimes confused in transliterated titles with the English apostrophe, e.g. Kak rabotat's for Kak rabotat' s.

2.1.5 Transliteration of the Latin alphabet as such is very little used. If it is necessary to represent a foreign word in Cyrillic it is transcribed, having regard to the form and more particularly the sound of the original word and the conventions of Russian spelling. Thus the Russian equivalent of a letter will be different for different languages, or, especially in the case of English and French, in different contexts, though the representation may not be exactly phonetic, e.g. En *gorge* is гордж, Fr *gorge* is горж. More strikingly Ir *Seabhac* is Шавак though Шаук would be nearer the sound, and in De *Goethe* (Гёте) the representation of the first vowel sound is conventional. The desire not to be too outlandlish (but cf. 2.5.2) results sometimes in avoidable ambiguities, and even the distinctions that are acceptable are not always exploited.

2.1.6 In most languages the number of possible equivalents for which a given Russian letter can stand is very limited, so that it is possible to make a table. In that on pages 404-9, from which English and French are omitted, the foreign equivalents of Russian letters and combinations of letters are given language by language, but not vice versa: where no equivalent of a combination is given the letters have the same equivalents as they have separately. The restriction of an equivalent to a particular position in a word is not stated unless there is another equivalent which is unrestricted, e.g. Russian o is Tr *o* anywhere, but *ö* only initially. A consonant followed by a soft sign is to be understood to indicate also that consonant followed by any soft vowel; the soft sign is retained as well in Pt, Es, Ca, It, Ir, Ee, Su, Hu and Ba, but not in Al, Pl, Cz, Sk, Sn, Sh, Le, e.g. Hu *Nyaregy* is Ru Ньяредь and Al *Quka* is Кюка. Note that я and ю must be interpreted as (ь)a and (ь)y respectively. In Tr the soft sign is retained for î, but not for û.

The following conventions apply:

> [ ]: obsolete
> ( ): contextual letters, e.g. Is a(rn) denotes **a** before **rn**
> /: regular alternation, e.g. It gi/g denotes **gia, ge, gi, gio, giu**; g gh: **ga, ghe, ghi, go, gu**

o

CYRILLIC EQUIVALENTS OF RO[

Ru	Nl	Af	De	Da	No	Sv	Is	La	Pt	Es	Ca	It	Ro	Ir
а	a, aa, ae	a, aa, ae	a, aa, ah	a	a	a	a	a	a	a	a	a	a	a
ай			ej, eg				æ [œ]		айн <āe					
ан									ã, ão					
ау	ou						á, a(rn), a(ng)							
б	b	b	b	b	b	b	b	b	b	b	b	b	b	b
в	v, w	w	w	v	v	v	f	v	v	v	v	v	v	b, b, r
г		gh	g	g	g	g	g	g, h	g/gu	g/gu	g/gu	g/gh	g/gh	g, c
гь														
д	d	d	d	d	d	d	d, ð	d	d	d	d	d	d	c
дь														
дж											gi/g	ge/g		
джь														
дз											z, zz			
дл(ь)							ll, rl							
дн							nn, rn							
е	æ, e, ee	e, ee	ä, äh, e, ee, eh	e, æ	e, ge-, e, ä æ	e	e	e	e, ye	e, ye	e, ye	e, ie	e, ie	e, e, g
ей	ij, y	y	ei, eu, äu				e(ng)							
ем, ен											-ен <cm			
ё	eu	eu	ö	ø	ø	ö	ö	oe						
ёй	ui, uy						au, ö(ng)							
ём, ён														
ёу				au										
Ru	**Nl**	**Af**	**De**	**Da**	**No**	**Sv**	**Is**	**La**	**Pt**	**Es**	**Ca**	**It**	**Ro**	**Ir**

TTERS ACCORDING TO LANGUAGE

:	Al	Pl	Cz	Sk	Sn	Sh	Le	Li	Ee	Su	Hu	Tr	Ba		Ru
	a	a	a	a	a	a	a	a, ą	a, aa	a, aa	a	a	a		а
ai, ei, ey															ай
															ан
															ау
	b	b	b	b	b	b	b	b	b	b	b	b	b		б
	v	w	v	v	v	v	v	v	v	v	v	v	v		в
	g	g	h	h	g	g	g	g	g	g	g	g, ğ	g		г
	gj														гь
	d	d	d	d	d	d	d	d	d	d	d	d	d		д
			ď	ď							gy				дь
	xh											c			дж
						đ [dj, gj]									джь
	x														дз
															дл(ь)
															дн
	e	e, ie	e	ä, e	e	e	e	e, ę, ie, jie	e, ee, ä-, ää-	e, ee, ä-, ää-	e	e, ye	e		е
															ей
		ę													ем, ен
		io							io		ö, ő, jö-, jö-				ё
															ёй
		ią													ём, ён
															ёу

:	Al	Pl	Cz	Sk	Sn	Sh	Le	Li	Ee	Su	Hu	Tr	Ba		Ru

Ru	Nl	Af	De	Da	No	Sv	Is	La	Pt	Es	Ca	It	Ro	Ir
ж									g(e, i), j		g(e, i), j		j	
з	z	z	s					z	-s-, z		-s-, z	s	z	
зь														
и	i, ie	i, ie	i, ie, ih, ü-, y	i, y-	i, y-	i, y-	i, y	i, y	e, i, y	i, y	i, y	i	i	i, ia io, uio
й	i, [y]	i	i, [y]	j	g-, gj-, -j	g-, -j	g		y	y	y		i	dh·
к	k	k	k, ck	k	k	k, ck	c	c	c/qu	c/qu	c/qu	c/ch	c/ch	c
кв	qu	qu	qu	qu, kv	qu, kv	qu, qv, kv		qu				qu		
къ														
кс	x	x	chs, x	x	x	x	x	x	x	x		x	x	
л	l	l	l	l	l	l	l	l	l	l	l, lt	l	l	l
лл(ь)			ld	ld							l·l			
ль		l	l	l, ld	l, ld	l	l	l	l, lh	l, ll	l, ll	l, gli		
м	m	m	m	m	m	m	m	m	m	m	m	m	m	m, mb
н	n	n	n	n, nd	n, nd	n	n	n	n	n	n, nt	n	n	n,
нь									nh	ñ		gn		
о	o, oo	o, oo	o, oh, oo	o, å [aa]	o, å [aa]	o, å	o	o	o, ou	o	o	o	o	o,
п	p	p	p	p	p	p	p	p	p	p	p	p	p	p
р	r	r	r	r	r	r	r	r	r	r	r	r	r	r
рж, рш														
с	s, c(e, i)	s, c(e, i)	s, ß	s, z, c(e, i), t(ion)	s, z, c(e, i)	s, z	s, z, ts	s	s, ç, c(e, i)	s, z, c(e, i)	s, ss, c(e, i)	s	s	s
сь														
т	t	t	t	t	t	t	t, þ	t	t	t	t	t	t	t
ть														
у	oe, u	oe, u	u	u	o, u	o, u	u-, u(ng)	u	u, o	u	u	u	u	u
уо														
Ru	Nl	Af	De	Da	No	Sv	Is	La	Pt	Es	Ca	It	Ro	Ir

Al	Pl	Cz	Sk	Sn	Sh	Le	Li	Ee	Su	Hu	Tr	Ba	Ru
zh	ż, rz	ž	ž	ž	ž	ž	ž	ž		zs	j		ж
	z	z	z	z	z	z				z	z		з
	ź												зь
i, y-	i	i, y	i, y	i	i	i, j, ji	i, į, j, ji	i, ii	i, ii	i, ü-, ü-	i	i, y	и
j	j	j	j	j	j	j	j	j	j	j, ly, lly	y	i, y	й
k	k	k	k	k	k	k	k	k	k	k	k	k	к
													кв
q													къ
		x						x		x			кс
ll	ł	l	l	l	l	l	l	l	l	l	l	l	л
													лл(ь)
l	l	l	l, ľ	lj	lj	ļ	l		l	l	l	l, ll	ль
m	m	m	m	m	m	m	m	m	m	m	m	m	м
n	n	n	n	n	n	n	n	n	n	n	n	n	н
	ń, ni	ň	ň	nj	nj	ņ				ny		ñ	нь
o	o	o	o	o	o	o	o	o, oo	o, oo	o	o, ö-	o	о
p	p	p	p	p	p	p	p	p	p	p	p	p	п
r	r	r	r	r	r	r	r	r	r	r	r	r	р
		ř											рж, рш
s	s, ś	s	s	s	s	s	s	s	s	sz	s	s, z	с
	ś												сь
ı, t	t	t	t	t	t	t	t	t	t	t	t	t	т
		ť	ť									tt	ть
u	u, ó	u, ů	u	u	u	u, ų	u, uu	u, uu	u		u, ü-	u	у
		ô											уо

Al	Pl	Cz	Sk	Sn	Sh	Le	Li	Ee	Su	Hu	Tr	Ba	Ru

Ru	Nl	Af	De	Da	No	Sv	Is	La	Pt	Es	Ca	It	Ro	Ir
ф	f	f, v	f, v	f	f	f	f	f, ph	f	f	f	f	f	f,]
х	h, ch, g	h, ch, g	h, ch	h	h, k(e, i, y)	h	h			g(e, i), j					h, sh
хь					kj, tj									
х(с, т)							g(s, t)							
ц			c, t(i), tz, z									z		ţ
ч		tj	tsch		k(e, i, y, ä, ö), kj, tj					ch	ch, tx, -ig	ci/c	ce/c	
ш	sj		sch	sj	sj, skj sk(e, i, y, ö, ø, æ)	skj			ch, s, x, z		x	sci/sc	ş	s(e se
щ														
ы													î	
ь				i		j	j	i	i, y	i, y	i			
э	e, ee	e, ee	e, eh, ä, äh, ö-	e, æ, ø-	e, æ, ö-	e, ä ö-	e, ö-	e	e	e	e	e	ă, e-	ae ao e-,
эй	ui, ij								ö(ng)-, au-					
ю	u	u	ü	y	y	y	y	u	yu	yu	yu	iu	iu	
я	ja	ja	ja	ja	ja	ja	ja	ja	ya, -(i)a	ya, -(i)a	ya, -(i)a	ia, -(i)a	ia	
Ru	Nl	Af	De	Da	No	Sv	Is	La	Pt	Es	Ca	It	Ro	Ir

Al	Pl	Cz	Sk	Sn	Sh	Le	Li	Ee	Su	Hu	Tr	Ba	Ru
f	f	f	f	f	f	f	f	f	f	f	f	f	ф
h	h, ch	ch	ch	h	h	h	h, ch	h	h	h			х
													хь
													х(с, т)
c	c, ць <ć	c	c	c	c	c	c			c			ц
ç	cz	č	č	č	č, ć	č	č			cs	ç	tx [tch]	ч
sh	sz	š	š	š	š	š	š	š		s		x [ch]	ш
	szcz												щ
	y						i	õ				i	ы
			ье <ie			ьи <ji				j			ь
e	e	e	e	e	e	e	e	e, ee, ä-, ää-, ö-, öö-	e, ee, ä-, ää-, ö, öö-	e, ö-, ö-	e	e	э
													эй
ju	iu, ju	ju	ju	ju	ju	ju	iu, ju	ü, üü, ju	y, yy, ju	ü, ű, ju	(k, g, l)u, yu	yu	ю
ja	ia, ja	ja	ja	ja	ja	ja	ia, ja	-ä, -ää, ja	-ä, -ää, ja	ja	ya	ya	я
Al	**Pl**	**Cz**	**Sk**	**Sn**	**Sh**	**Le**	**Li**	**Ee**	**Su**	**Hu**	**Tr**	**Ba**	**Ru**

2.2 CAPITALISATION

2.2.1 Capitals are used less freely in Russian than in English, and the practice with institutional names is somewhat complicated. Both columns of the following table should be consulted.

Capitals	*Lower case*
The following expressions begin with an initial capital throughout unless otherwise stated:	The following elements begin with a small letter:
Personal names of every sort, e.g. **Александр Сергеевич Пушкин, Иван Грозный** (*Ivan the Terrible*), **Фон-Визин, Мак-Дональд, Ким Ир Сэн.**	Separate articles and particles forming part of names, e.g. **фон дер Гольц**; the last element in Chinese names, e.g. **Мао Цзэ-дун**; names transferred to things, e.g. **форд, ампер.**
The particular part of astronomical, geographical and official or popular topographical names, even if composed of common nouns, e.g. **Сатурн, Новая Земля, Советский Союз.** Geographical names used figuratively, e.g. **Рубикон.**	Generic words forming part of geographical and topographical names, e.g. **Балтийское море**, *Baltic Sea*; **улица . . .**, *. . . Street*. Geographical names used as common nouns, e.g. **бостон** (the dance).
Orders, all words except **орден** and **степень** (*class*), e.g. **орден Отечественной Войны 1 степени.**	
The highest state, party and trade union organisations of the USSR and a few international bodies, e.g. **Верховный Суд СССР** (*Supreme Court of the USSR*), **Коммунистическая партия Советского Союза** (*the CPSU*), **Организация Объединенных Наций** (*the UN*).	Foreign names of political parties, e.g. **лейбористская партия**, *the Labour Party*. Names beginning with the word **партия**, e.g. **партия социалистов-революционеров**, *Social Revolutionary Party*. The word **партия** itself, wherever it occurs.
All other organisations, Soviet, foreign or international, including ministers and political parties (first word only), e.g. **Российская социал-демократическая рабочая партия**, *Russian Social-Democratic Workers' Party*; **Институт истории Академии наук СССР** (*The Historical Institute of the Academy of Sciences of the USSR*).	

Capitals	*Lower case*
Historical events, eras and documents (the first word, or the first and second if the first is **Великий**), e.g. **Столетняя война** (*Hundred Years' War*), **Великая Отечественная война** (*The Great Patriotic War, i.e. The Second World War*).	Phrases describing historical events or eras, if not considered to be names, e.g. **средние веки** (*Middle Ages*), **вторая мировая война** (*the second world war*).
Revolutionary holidays and anniversaries (first only unless a numeral), e.g. **Первое мая, 1 Мая**.	Religious holidays, days of the week, months.
Names of works of art and titles of books and periodicals (the first word), e.g. **Капитанская дочка** (*The captain's daughter*).	
Adjectives in **-ев, -ов** and **-ин** denoting possession.	Adjectives in **-ев, -ов** and **-ин** that no longer denote possession, e.g. **сизофов труд** (*Sisyphean toil*).
Adjectives in **-евский, -овский, -инский**, derived from names, when used commemoratively, e.g. **Пушкинский дом**, *Pushkin House*.	Adjectives in **-евский, -овский, -инский** not used commemoratively, e.g. **в пушкинское время**, *in Pushkin's time*.
	Adjectives derived from geographical names, as such, and nouns of nationality, e.g. **русский язык**, *Russian language*; **русские**, *Russians*.

2.3 DIVISION OF WORDS

2.3.1 Rules 1, 4, 5a or b, 6d, 7a, 8 (p. xiii) apply.

2.3.2 Prefixes need only be kept intact if a consonant follows, and it is incorrect to divide between a prefix and **ы**. The letters **й, ъ** and **ь** must not be separated from the preceding letter. On rule 5 it should be noted that although double letters may begin a few words, one may divide before them only after a prefix, e.g. **по-ссорить** but **кас-са**.

2.4 PUNCTUATION AND ABBREVIATIONS

2.4.1 Abbreviations are much commoner in Russian than in English and certain points should be noted.

Initial letters or the first few letters up to a consonant, with full stops, are used as in other languages, e.g. **ж.д.** for **железная дорога, обл.** for **область**; but note that **ж.-д.**

stands for **железнодорожный** (one word) and similarly **с.-х.** for **сельскохозяйствен-ный**. However, a hyphenated original too will have a hyphenated abbreviation. Doubled letters indicate the plural, e.g. **гг.** for **годы**.

2.4.2 Most words can be abbreviated by replacing the middle portion by a hyphen, e.g. **изд-во** for **издательство**.

2.4.3 Parts of several words can be run together to form a compound abbreviation, e.g. **колхоз** for **коллективное хозяйство**, *collective farm*. Although the original expression is neuter, the abbreviation, which ends in a consonant, is treated as a masculine noun (4.2) and so declined. Conversely **облоно** (**областной отдел народного образования**, *District Board of Education*) is neuter, and being stressed on the last syllable, is indeclinable. If the last part of a compound is unabbreviated there is of course no problem. (Cf. also 1.6.2.)

2.4.4 Initial letters, usually written in capitals without stops, sometimes combined with initial syllables, are an equally common form of abbreviation. In some the individual letters are read out, e.g. **РСФСР** [эр-эс-эф-эс-эр], **АзССР**, in others the resulting word is read, e.g. **ТАСС** (*TASS*). Both sorts of abbreviations may follow the gender of the principal noun, viz. **республика, агентство**; or endings may be added as if they were ordinary masculine nouns, viz. **РСФСРа, ТАССа**; and when the latter type results in a common noun such as **вуз** (**высшее учебное заведение**, *higher educational establishment*), ending in a consonant, it is never treated as anything but a masculine noun.

2.4.5 It should be noted that the hyphen is used in Russian in many cases where it would not be used in other languages. The majority of compounds are written as one word, even compound adjectives derived from two separate words, and independent words are not normally hyphened together; but there are a number of exceptions. Full rules are given in *Правила русской орфографии и пунктуации*; ред. Д. А. Чешко. Москва, Учпедгиз, 1956 (trans. *Russian orthography*. Pergamon Press, 1963), but some brief notes may nevertheless be helpful.

The hyphen is used:

(a) in many non-Russian names, e.g. **Мак-Дональд, Сен-Симон, Нью-Йорк, Алма-Ата, -оглы, -паса**; but **де Валера**, and also **Лафонтен**;

(b) in place-names involving prepositions, e.g. **Ростов-на-Дону**;

(c) in the less common place-names in **Ново-**, and in most names of compound territorial units, e.g. **Австро-Венгрия, Эльзас-Лотарингия**; but **Чехословакия**;

(d) after non-Russian prefixes such as **экс-, унтер-**, and the like;

(e) in a number of adjectives and some nouns in which the first element is on the same level as in the second, e.g. **англо-русский**, *Anglo-Russian, English-Russian*, or expresses some modification of quality or degree, e.g. **ярко-красный**, *bright-red*;

(f) for the sake of clarity, e.g. **пол-листа**, *folio* (*half-sheet*); **пол-оборота**, *half-turn*; but **полгода**, *half-year*;

(g) the prepositional prefix **по-** is hyphenated in adverbs of the type **по-русски**, *in Russian*; but in other adverbs it and other prepositions are written as one word without a hyphen.

It also occurs at the end of the earlier members of a succession of compounds with the same termination, e.g. **паро-, электро-, и тепловозы**, *steam, electric and diesel engines*.

2.4.7 The apostrophe is now used in various foreign names whose original form has one, e.g. **Н'Дама, О'Кейси, Д'Аннунцио, Д'Антркасто**. At one time it was not: **Данте** could stand both for **Dante** and **D'Anthès**. It is no longer used in forms such as **СССР'а** (2.4.4), nor as a substitute for **ъ** (2.1.1).

2.5 HARD AND SOFT CONSONANTS; PALATALISATION

2.5.1 The quality of a consonant in Russian is shown by the succeeding vowel, the series being:

Hard а э ы о   у
Soft я е и е[ё] ю

or by the absence or presence of the soft sign **ь**. The corresponding vowels are found in parallel hard and soft declensions and conjugations, with the exception of э, which occurs in few pure Russian words, and never in endings. (Some endings are soft even in hard declensions.)

2.5.2 The consonants г, ж, к, х, ц, ч, ш, щ, present peculiarities:

Г, к, х are followed by the one set: **а, е, и, о, у**
ж, ч, ш, щ by **а, е, и, о/е, у**, of which **о** occurs only when it bears the accent
ц by **а, е, и/ы, о, у**

ы being found chiefly in endings, including -ын. In consequence nouns, adjectives and verbs whose stems end in one of these consonants present a mixed appearance: instead of the alternations а/ы, я/и one finds а/и; instead of -/ом, ь/ем one may have -/ем, and so on. These limitations do not apply to foreign names, e.g. **Цюрих**, *Zürich*, or foreign-derived words such as **кюре**, *curé*.

2.5.3 A prefix ending in a hard consonant hardens the following vowel, unless, paradoxically, a hard sign is inserted to separate them, e.g. **с-играть** becomes **сыграть**, *to play*, but **съезд** (earlier **съѣздъ**), *congress*. Similarly in foreign words such as **объект**, *object*, to preserve the pronunciation.

2.5.4 No palatalisation (see General note on the Slavonic languages) now takes place before noun endings, e.g. **река, на реке**; but changes may take place in verbs as the result of endings beginning with a soft vowel or [j], viz.

	г	д	з	к	с	ск	ст	т	х
into	ж	ж	ж	ч	ш	щ	щ	ч/щ	ш

For the peculiarities of the resulting consonants see 2.5.2. Akin to palatalisation is the change of б, в, м, п, ф to бл- etc. before certain soft endings, e.g. **люблю** from **любить**, *to love*.

2.5.5 Assimilation in spelling occurs when a prefix ending in з is followed by an unvoiced consonant, but other prefixes are left unassimilated, e.g. **из-ход** becomes **исход**, but **подпись** not **потпись**. (Pronunciation is assimilated in all cases.)

2.6 VARIATION OF VOWEL

2.6.1 An е or о in the last syllable of the NS may be absent when endings are added, e.g. **Павел**, G **Павла**; **Лев**, patronymic **Львович** (note the **ь**, preserving the softness of the л). Conversely an е or о may be present when there is a zero-ending, e.g. **книжка**, GP **книжек**; **сестра, сестер; окно, окон; копейка, копеек**. (Note in the last example the double change: й becomes unnecessary when the two е's come together; cf. 2.1.)

2.7 SPELLING

2.7.1 Mention has already been made (2.1) of the disappearance of certain letters. Apart from this the only important changes in recent times has been from з to с before unvoiced consonants, e.g. **искусство**, previously **изк-** and the re-spelling of certain endings.

2.7.2 The soft sign **ь** is found before vowels, e.g. **третье**, but only rarely in contexts which superficially resemble those where **ъ** occurs (2.5.3), e.g. **вьюнок)(въезд**.

2.7.3 Changes of case endings, e.g. **-aгo** to **-oгo**, are all dealt with under the appropriate part of speech, even if the change is orthographical.

3 ARTICLES

There are no articles.

4 NOUNS

4.1 FORM AND GENDER
4.1.1 There are three genders, the gender for the most part corresponding to the form of the noun. Inanimate nouns may be of any gender. Omitting the vocative there are six cases, the endings varying according to the form of the noun.

4.3 DECLENSIONS
4.3.1 *Masculine and neuter nouns*
These are the same in many of their endings. Masculine nouns end in the NS in a hard or soft consonant; neuters mostly in **-o** or **-e**. (For masculines in **-a**, **-я** see 4.3.4.)

Hard type

	S		P	
	M	N	M	N
N	-	-o	-ы	-a
A	As N or G	-o	As N or G	-a
G	-a		-ов	-
D	-y		-ам	
I	-ом		-ами	
L	-e		-ах	

Soft type

	S		P	
	M	N	M	N
N	-й/-ь	-e	-и	-я
A	As N or G	-e	As N or G	-я
G	-я		-ев/-ей	-ей/-й
D	-ю		-ям	
I	-ем		-ями	
L	-e	-е/-и	-ях	

4.3.2 For the explanation of mixed types see 2.5.2. Variation of vowel (2.6.1) occurs.

4.3.3 NPM **-a** and **-я** are found, e.g.

дом, дома; край, края; учитель, учителя;
брат, братья (GP братьев); друг, друзья (GP друзей);
муж, мужья, мужей; сын, сыны/сыновья, сыновей

Some masculine nouns have no ending in GP, e.g. человек.

Nouns in -анин have NP -ане, GP -ан.

The ending -у is sometimes partitive and sometimes locative.

Neuter nouns in -мя have S stem -мень- (GS -мени), P -мен- (but семя: GP семян); око, ухо have P stem оч-, уш-, NP очи, уши.

4.3.4 *Feminine nouns*

These end in -а, -я or a soft consonant. Masculine nouns in -а and -я are declined like feminine ones.

	Hard type S	Hard type P	Soft type S	Soft type P
N	-а	-ы	-я	-и
A	-у	As N or G	-ю	As N or G
G	-ы	-	-и	-ь/-й/-ей
D	-е	-ам	-е/-и	-ям
I	-ой/-ою	-ами	-ей/-ею	-ями
L	-е	-ах	-е/-и	-ях

Consonant type

	S	P
N	-ь	-и
A	-ь	As N or G
G	-и	-ей
D	-и	-ям
I	-ью	-ями/-ьми
L	-и	-ях

4.3.5 For the explanation of mixed types see 2.5.2; for the appearance of vowels in GP see 2.6.

4.3.6 Мать and дочь behave as if they were матерь and дочерь.

4.6 USE OF CASES

Much might be said about the use of the cases, but it is more relevant to composition than to the construing of title-pages and prefaces. The object of the verb is not always in the accusative; negative verbs more often take the genitive. The instrumental is commonly used as a predicate after быть and other verbs, e.g. Пушкин был противником «поэтической прозы», *Pushkin was an opponent of 'poetic prose'*; авторами являются, *are authors* (1.2.4). It is used with nouns of action where the corresponding verb takes the instrumental, e.g. управление делами, *administration of affairs* (*administrative dept.*). For the use of different cases after prepositions see section 10.

5 ADJECTIVES

5.1 GENERAL

5.1.1 Adjectives vary for gender, number and case, and agree with the nouns they qualify. They precede the noun.

5.1.2 Most adjectives have both long forms and, so far as they exist, short forms. Some have only long ones, and some have short forms in some cases and long ones in others.

5.2 ENDINGS

5.2.1 *Long forms, hard type*

	M	N	F	P
	S			**P**
N	-ый/-ой	-ое	-ая	-ые [-ыя]
A	As N or G	-ое	-ую	As N or G
G	-ого [-аго]		-ой	-ых
D	-ому		-ой	-ым
I	-ым		-ой/-ою	-ыми
L	-ом		-ой	-ых

Bracketed forms are obsolete.

5.2.2 *Long forms, soft type*

	M	N	F	P
	S			**P**
N	-ий	-ее	-яя	-ие [-ія]
A	As N or G	-ее	-юю	As N or G
G	-его [-яго]		-ей	-их
D	-ему		-ей	-им
I	-им		-ей/-ею	-ими
L	-ем		-ей	-их

Bracketed forms are obsolete.

5.2.3 Adjectives such as **другой, русский, хороший, большой** and participles in -ший and -щий are mixed. For details see 2.5.2.

5.2.4 *Short forms*

Only the following distinctive short forms are found:

	M	N	F	P
	S			**P**
N	-	-о	-а	-ы
A	As N or G	-о	-у	As N or G
G	-а			
D	-у			

The NSM may have an inserted e or o (2.6).

5.2.5 Apart from some stereotyped adverbial phrases, the short forms of most adjectives are used only as predicates in the nominative, e.g. **хорошая книга**, *a good book*, but **книга хороша**, *the book is good* (cf. 1.5). Possessive adjectives in -ов and -ин use all the forms. They are not very common except as proper names (1.1.3c).

5.2.6 Ordinary adjectives are given in the dictionary under the long form. This is got from the short form of the NSM by adding the ending -ый or -ий and omitting e or o between the last two consonants if it is merely euphonic (2.6), e.g. **нужен, нужный**, *necessary*. Conversely **дополненный**, *enlarged*, short form дополнен, a participle (8.12.5).

5.3 COMPARISON

5.3.1 There is a comparative ending -ee, which is invariable and only predicative.

5.3.2 The superlative is expressed by inserting самый (a declinable adjective) before the positive, e.g. самые дорогие книги, *the most expensive books.*

5.3.3 A number of common words make the comparative in -*e (-ше, -же), and the superlative in -(ей)ший or -*айший, e.g. дорогой, дороже, дражайший, *dear, dearer, dearest*; старый, старше, стар(ей)ший, *old, older, oldest.*

5.4 POSSESSIVES

5.4.1 The possessives мой, твой, свой, чей, наш, ваш have mostly long forms of the soft or mixed type. The following are short:

		S		P
	M	*N*	*F*	
N	мой	мое	моя	мои
A	мой	мое	мою	

So also **твой**, etc.

N	наш	наше	наша	наши
A	наш	наше	нашу	

So also **ваш**, etc. (**Ваш**, with an initial capital, refers to one person.)

6 NUMERALS

6.1 CARDINAL
6.1.1

1 один	11 одиннадцать	21 двадцать	101 сто один
2 два	12 двенадцать	один	200 двести
3 три	13 тринадцать	30 тридцать	300 триста
4 четыре	14 четырнадцать	40 сорок(а)	400 четыреста
5 пять	15 пятнадцать	50 пятьдесят	500 пятьсот, etc.
6 шесть	16 шестнадцать	60 шестьдесят	900 девятьсот
7 семь	17 семнадцать	70 семьдесят	1000 тысяча
8 восемь	18 восемнадцать	80 восемьдесят	
9 девять	19 девятнадцать	90 девяносто	
10 десять	20 двадцать	100 сто	

6.1.2 **Один–четыре** are adjectives. Один, одно, одна has partly short and partly long forms with *I* -им.

Два, три, четыре:

	MN	*F*	*All genders*	
N	два	две	три	четыре
A	As N or G		As N or G	
G	двух		трех	четырех
D	двум		трем	четырем
I	двумя		тремя	четырьмя
L	двух		трех	четырех

пять onwards are nouns in form, declined as follows:

> 5–20, 30: as 4.3.4 (consonant)
> 40: NA сорок[а], other cases сорока
> 50–80: both halves as 4.3.4, e.g. пятидесяти
> 90: NA in -о, other cases in -а
> 100: oblique cases ста
> 200–300: both halves are declined. Apart from двести, which is a survival, сто is a normal neuter noun (GP сот) (4.3.1).
> 1000: as 4.3.4 (mixed)

6.1.3 The following noun or adjective is in the same case as the numeral except when this is in the nominative or accusative. When that is so the case is as follows:

	Noun	Adjective
With один	NS	NS
два, три, четыре	GS	GP/NP
all other simple numerals	GP	GP

Except with один, the verb may be either in the neuter singular or in the plural, e.g. вышло [вышли] из печати три новых тома, *three new volumes have issued from the press*; вышел один том, *one volume came out*; вышла книга в трех томах, *the book came out in three volumes*. Compounds numerals behave like their last element.

6.2 ORDINAL
6.2.1

1 первый	11–19 одиннадцатый, etc.	200 двухсотый
2 второй	20 двадцатый	300 трехсотый
3 третий	30 тридцатый	400 четырехсотый
4 четвертый	40 сороковый	500 пятисотый, etc.
5 пятый	50 пятидесятый	1000 тысячный
6 шестой	60 шестидесятый	
7 седьмой	70 семидесятый	
8 восьмой	80 восьмидесятый	
9 девятый	90 девяностый	
10 десятый	100 сотый	

6.2.2 третий, третье, третья has stem треть-.

6.2.3 In compound ordinals only the last element has the form of an ordinal. For examples see 6.4.2.

6.3 FIGURES

6.3.1 Plain arabic numerals normally stand for cardinals, ordinals being expressed by either roman figures or by the addition of the appropriate ending to the arabic, e.g. X съезд, *10th congress*; 3-е издание, *3rd edition*.

6.4 DATES

6.4.1 The months are:

> январь, феьраль, март, апрель, май, июнь,
> июль, август, сентябрь, октябрь, ноябрь, декабрь

For declension see 4.1.

6.4.2

1 May is translated **Первое мая**

On 28.ii.1962: **28-ого февраля тысяча девятсот шестьдесят второго года** (6.2.3)

1848 is read: **тысяча восемьсот сорок восьмой год**

В 1848 г.: **в . . . восьмом году**

1848–1948: **от** (*from*) and **до** (*to*) can be read before the numerals, which will then be in the genitive; but in spelling out titles it is better to read both numbers in the nominative, without additions.

80-ые гг.: **восьмидесятые годы**, *the 80's*

Революция 1905–1907 гг. [годов]: the numerals are in the genitive (**пятого, седьмого**) and the hyphen is ignored.

Note however that after cardinals requiring the genitive plural **лет** is used instead of **годов**, e.g. **сорок лет**, *forty years*.

7 PRONOUNS

7.1/7.2 DEMONSTRATIVE, INTERROGATIVE, RELATIVE, INDEFINITE

7.1.1 These have much the same case endings as adjectives (the long forms of which incorporate a pronoun). Note:

этот, это, эта, *this*: ISM and N **этим**, AF **эту**, P **эти**

тот, то, та, *that*: **тем, ту**; P **те, тех, тем, теми, тех**

кто, *who?*: **кого, кому, кем, ком** (so also **никто, некто**, which may be split)

что, *what?*: **чего, чему, чем, чём** (so also **ничто, нечто**); **низачто**, *for no reason*, with the preposition sandwiched

весь, всё, вся, *all*: **всем, всю**, P **все**, etc. like **те**

7.1.2 The suffixes **-же, -либо, -нибудь, -то** are suffixed to some pronouns, altering their meaning. The suffixes are invariable, e.g. **тогоже, кому-нибудь** from **тот же, кто-нибудь**.

7.2 RELATIVE AND INTERROGATIVE
See 7.1.

7.3 PERSONAL
7.3.1

	S		S & P	P	
	1	2	R	1	2
N	я	ты	—	мы	вы
AG	меня	тебя	себя	нас	вас
D	мне	тебе	себе	нам	вам
I	мной	тобой	собой	нами	вами
L	мне	тебе	себе	нас	вас

The instrumental may end in **-ою**. **Себя**, *self*, refers to all persons and both numbers. **Вы**, with an initial capital, is the polite substitute for **ты**.

7.3.2 Он, оно, она, *he, she, it*, P они [F онъ] has oblique cases from another root:

	S		P
	MN	F	
AG	(н)его	(н)ее [ея]	(н)их
D	(н)ему	(н)ей	(н)им
I	(н)им	(н)ей	(н)ими
L	нем	ней	них

онъ and ея are obsolete. The genitives его, etc. serve as possessives, *his*, etc.

8 VERBS

8.1 STRUCTURE

Subject pronouns are usual. In the present and future, which have distinctive endings, they may be dispensed with, e.g. пишу, *I write*: but in the past писал would usually mean *he was writing*; unless the context made it clear, *I was writing* would have to be я писал(а). Verbs are entered in most dictionaries under the imperfective infinitive (see General note on the Slavonic languages) with a reference from the perfective.

8.2 PRESENT AND FUTURE

(The tenses have the same endings; the present is formed from the imperfective, the future from the perfective stem.)

8.2.1 *Endings*

> I -ю/-у, -(*)ешь, -(*)ет; -(*)ем, -(*)ете, -ют/-ут
> II -(л)ю/-(*)у, -ишь, -ит; -им, -ите, -ят/-(*)ат

In the parts marked (*) the preceding consonant may be palatalised. (2.5.4), eg. могу, может; хожу, ходит.
Similarly люблю, любит.

8.2.2 *Relation to infinitive*

P	-аю	-яю	-ею	-ую	-юю	-[л]ю (II)
I	-ать	-ять	-еть	-овать	-евать	-ить, -еть

P	-ну	-жу, -чу, -шу, -щу	-у (I)	
I	-нуть*	See 8.2.3	See 8.2.4	

* See also 8.2.4.

8.2.3 Verbs with presents in -жу, -чу, -шу, -щу mostly have the infinitives with corresponding unpalatalised consonants (2.5.4). This is always so with verbs in set I above, e.g. пишу, писать, *write*. The present is palatalised throughout. In verbs in set II only the first person singular is palatalised as a rule, and the infinitive ends in -еть or -ить, e.g. вижу, видеть, *see*; хожу, ходить, *go*; but they may be palatalised throughout and have an infinitive in -ать, e.g. держу, держать, *hold*.

8.2.4 *Some peculiar stems*

P	беру	бью	веду	везу	возьму	встаю
I	брать	бить	вести	везти	взять	вставать

P	даю	еду	живу	крою	иду (-йду)	лягу
I	давать	ехать	жить	крыть	идти (-йти)	лечь

P	могу, может	начну	несу	пью	расту	сплю
I	мочь	начать	нести	пить	расти	спать

P	стану	сяду	умру	шлю	-аду	-йму
I	стать	сесть	умереть	слать	-асть	-нять

8.2.5 Irregularities

Дам, дашь, даст; дадим, дадите, дадут from дать

Ем, ешь, ест; едим, едите, едят from есть

Хочу, хочешь, хочет; хотим, хотите, хотят from хотеть

8.3 PAST

This tense is in form a participle, and has two numbers of three genders, but no distinction of persons.

8.3.1 Usual endings

	S		P
M	N	F	
-л/-	-ло	-ла	-ли

8.3.2 Relation to infinitive

(a) Substitute -ть for -л, etc. (See also table below.)

(b) If there is no ending in the masculine (in which case the other endings are added directly to the root consonants) the infinitive is got by adding -еть or -нуть, or from the table below:

P	вез	вел	ел	клал	лег	мог	нес
I	везти	вести	есть	класть	лечь	мочь	нести

P	пал	рос	сел	-чел, -чло	шел, шло		
I	пасть	расти	сесть	-честь	идти (-йти)		

8.5 FUTURE

See 8.2; 8.10.

8.10 COMPOUND TENSES

8.10.1 Future imperfective

Буду (8.17.2) with the imperfective infinitive.

8.11 INFINITIVE

The infinitive ends in -ть, -ти, -чь. Instructions for deriving it are given under the other parts of the verb.

8.12 PARTICIPLES

8.12.1 Both active and passive participles are formed from both the perfective and imperfective stems. They are either purely adjectival or equivalent to a relative clause. Those which are active in form may be given a passive meaning by the addition of the reflexive suffix. (See 8.14.1, and for an example, 8.12.3.) For declension see 5.2.

8.12.2 *Present active participle*

-щий, follows the 3PP of the present (8.2), e.g. настоят, настоящий, *present*; следуют, следующий, *following*; настоящие в этой книге статьи, *the articles which are to
be found in this book*.

8.12.3 *Past active participle*

-(в)ший, formed from the past (8.3), e.g. читал, читавший; шел, шедший; лег,
легший; обзоров печатавшихся в газете, *of surveys printed in the newspaper*.

8.12.4 *Present passive participle*

-м(ый), there being both long and short forms (5.2). The short form is identical with
the 1PP of the present (8.2), e.g. издаваемый, *(which is being) published*; видимый,
being seen, visible; пишемый, *being written*; слова употребляемые в разговорной речи,
words which are used in colloquial speech.

8.12.5 *Past passive participle*

-н(ый), -т(ый), there being both short and long forms (5.2). The short forms are
given here.

P -ан	*I*	-ать, е.g. сдан, *given up*: сдать
-ен		-еть, -ти, -чь, е.g. виден, *seen*: видить; переведен, *translated*: перевести (cf. 8.1.4)
-(*)ен		-ить, е.g. дополнен, *enlarged*: дополнить; изображен, *shown*: изобразить; исправлен, *corrected*: исправить (cf. 2.5.4)
-т		-ть, е.g. открыт, *open*: открыть

8.13 GERUNDS

8.13.1 The gerunds, which are adverbial, are active, but may take the reflexive/
passive suffix (8.14).

8.13.2 *Present gerund*

-я/*а, follows the 3PP of the present (8.2), e.g. следуют, следуя; смотрют, смотря;
пишут, пиша. It frequently replaces an adverbial clause, e.g. минуя церковные каноны,
as the church canons became things of the past.

8.13.3 *Past gerund*

-(в)ши, formed like the participle and used like the present gerund.

8.14 REFLEXIVE AND PASSIVE

8.14.1 Reflexive forms are obtained by adding -ся/-сь to the active. They can also
have a reciprocal or a passive sense (cf. 8.12.3 and 8.14.2 for examples), and sometimes
there is no corresponding active or the two forms differ in meaning in some other way,
e.g. защититься, *defend oneself*; бороться, *to wrestle*; продаться, *to be sold*; бояться,
to be afraid; браться за, *to take up* (брать, *to take*).

8.14.2 The passive, if not avoided, is expressed by reflexive forms (8.14.1) or by
passive participles (8.12): *the book is sold* may be книгу продают (*they sell the book*)
or книга продана (*has been sold*) or книга продаеться (*sells itself*) according to context.

8.17 THE VERB **быть**, *to be*

> *Present:* only **есть**, *there is*, survives; negative **нет**. *Am, is* and *are* are understood.
>
> *Future:* **буду** (8.2.1, type I)
>
> *Past:* **был**
>
> *Present gerund:* **будучи**

The participles **будущий** and **бывший** are used as adjectives, meaning *future* and *former*.

8.23 PREFIXES

The Russian verb has a rich assortment of prefixes. Sometimes they merely indicate the perfective aspect (for which see General note on the Slavonic languages), but usually they alter the sense. As short words may not be easily recognised when they have a prefix, these are listed here:

в, во, вз, воз, вы, до, за, из, изо, ис, на, над, о, об, обо, от, ото, пере,

по, под, пре, пред, при, про, раз, рас, с, со, у

The bracketed forms are variants depending on what follows. Prefixes that end in a consonant are followed by **ъ** before most soft vowels, e.g. **съезжаться**, *to assemble*.

9 ADVERBS

Adverbs can be formed from adjectives by substituting **-о**, comp. **-ее**, for the adjectival ending. Nouns in the instrumental case, used adverbially, and compound adverbs beginning with **по-** are usually to be found in the dictionary, either as independent entries or under the noun or adjective concerned.

10 PREPOSITIONS

Prepositions govern particular cases. Some may be used with more than one case, and where this affects the translation, care is needed: **по** with the dative may be translated by almost any preposition indicating locality, and has an idiomatic distributive use, viz. **по рублю**, *one rouble each*; with the accusative it means *up to*, and with the locative it means *after*. Good dictionaries distinguish.

GLOSSARY

бесплатно, *free*
библиотека, *library* (1.7.1)
брошюра, *pamphlet*
бумажная обложка, *paper cover*

введение, *introduction*
вестник, *bulletin*
вклад, *contribution*
возобновлять, *renew*
воспоминания, *memoirs*

все права охранены, *all rights reserved*
вступительная статья, *introductory essay*
выйдет, *is forthcoming*
выйти, выходить (1.8.5), *to come out*
выпуск, *issue* (1.4.1, 1.7.2, 1.8.4)

год, *year* (1.8.4)
годовой, *annual*
готов, *ready*

двухнедельный, *fortnightly*
доклад, *report*
дополненный, *enlarged* (1.5.2)
дополнительный, *additional*

ежегодник, *yearbook*
ежегодный, *annual*
ежеквартальный, *quarterly*
ежемесячный, *monthly* (1.8.5)
еженедельный, *weekly*

за границей, *abroad*
заказ, *order*
заменять, *replace*
записки, *studies*

избранный, *selected*
известия, *news*
издание, *edition* (1.5.1), *publication* (1.6.5, 1.6.6)
издательство, *publishing house* (1.6, 1.8.7)
изменение, *correction*
исправленный, *corrected* (1.5.2)
исследования, *investigations, research*

книга, *book* (1.4.1, 1.7.2)

лет, *years*
летопись, *chronicle*

месяц, *month* (1.8.5)
множительный аппарат, *duplicator*

неизданный, *unpublished*
новый, *new*
номер, *number* (1.8.4)

обмен, exchange
общество, *society*
один, *one, single* (1.8.6)
отдельный, *separate* (1.8.6)
отдельный оттиск, *offprint*
очерк, *essay*

перевел, перевод, *translated* (1.2.4), *translation* (1.2.6)

перепечатание, *reprinting*
переписка, *correspondence*
переплет, *binding, hard cover**
переработанный, *revised* (1.5.2)
пересмотренный, *revised* (1.5.2)
перестать, *stop*
печать, *press*
письмо, *letter*
повесть, *story*
подготовляеться, *is being prepared*
подписка, *subscription* (1.8.6)
полугодовой, *half-yearly*
полный, *complete*
послать, *to send*
посылка, *dispatch*
предисловие, *preface* (1.2.6)
приложение, *appendix, supplement*
примечание, *annotation*
пробный экземпляр, *specimen copy*
продажа, *sale*
продолжение (следует), *continuation (follows)*
просмотр, *approval*
пьеса, *play*

размножать, *to duplicate*
разошлось, *out of print* (type distributed)
распродано, *sold out*
рассказ, *story*
расширенный, *enlarged*
редактирование, *editing* (1.2.4)
редакция, *editing, editorial office* (1.2.6, 1.8.7)
реферат, *abstract*
речь, *speech*
р(одился), *born*
роман, *novel*
ротапринт, *offset press*

самиздат, *circulated clandestinely*
сборник (статей), *collection (of articles)* (1.2.8, 1.8.1)
скидка, *discount*
словарь, *dictionary*
смотри, *see*
собрание, *collection*
сообщение, *communication*

* Books not distinguished as hardbacks should be assumed to be paperbacks, not vice versa.

составил, *compiled, composed* (1.2.4)

сочинение, *composition* (1.2.6), pl. *works*

старый номер, *back number*

статья, *essay, article*

стихотворение, *verse*

страница, *page*

счет, *bill*

том, *volume* (1.4.1, 1.7.2)

труды, *transactions*

указатель, *index*

умер, *died*

цена, *price*

тамиздат, *published in the West*

типография, *printing, press*

того же автора, *by the same author*

часть, *part* (1.4.1)

член, *member*

экземпляр, *copy*

GRAMMATICAL INDEX: WORDS

бер-, 8.2.4

буд-, 8.10, 8.17

бь-, 8.2.4

бывший, был, etc., 8.17

вам(и), вас, 7.3.1

ваш-, 5.4.1

вед-, 8.2.4

вез, везла, etc., 8.3.2

вез-, 8.2.4

вел, etc., 8.3.2

возьм-, 8.2.4

времен-, 4.3.3

вс-, 7.1.1

встаю, etc., 8.2.4

дад-, дам, etc., 8.2.5

даю, etc., 8.2.4

дву-, 6.1.2

дочер-, 4.3.6

его, 7.3.2

ед-, 8.2.4, 8.2.5

ее, ей, 7.3.2

ел, etc., 8.3.2

ем, 8.2.5

ему, 7.3.2

ест, 8.2.5

есть, 8.17

ид-, 8.2.4

им, 7.3.2

имен-, 4.3.3

ими, их, 7.3.2

жив-, 8.2.4

кем, 7.1.1

клал, etc., 8.3.2

кого, ком(у), 7.1.1

кро-, 8.2.4

лег, etc., 8.3.2

ляг-, etc., 8.2.4

матер-, 4.3.6

меня, мн-, 7.3.1

мо-, 5.4.1

мог, могла, etc., 8.3.2

нам(и), нас, 7.3.1

начн-, 8.2.4

наш-, 5.4.1

него, нее, ней, 7.3.2

нек-, 7.1.1

нем(у), 7.3.2

нес, несла, etc., 8.3.2

нес-, 8.2.4

нет, 8.17

неч-, 7.1.1

нея, 7.3.2

ник-, 7.1.1

ним(и), них, 7.3.2

нич-, 7.1.1

он-, 7.3.2

оч-, 4.3.3

пал, etc., 8.3.2

пь-, 8.2.4

раст-, 8.2.4

самый, 5.3.2

сво-, 5.4.1

себ-, 7.3.1

сел, etc., 8.3.2

соб-, 7.3.1

сплю, etc., 8.2.4

стан-, 8.2.4

та, 7.1.1

тво-, 5.4.1

те, 7.1.1

теб-, 7.3.1

тем(и), тех, то, 7.1.1

тоб-, 7.3.1

тре-, 6.1.2

ту, 7.1.1

умр-, 8.2.4

уш-, 4.3.3

хоч-, 8.2.4

чего, 7.1.1

чел, 8.3.2

чем(у), 7.1.1

четыр-, 6.1.2

чла, etc., 8.3.2

шел, шла, etc., 8.3.2

шлю, etc., 8.2.4

эт-, 7.1.1

GRAMMATICAL INDEX: ENDINGS

-а, 4.3.1, 4.3.3, 4.3.4,
　5.2.4, 8.13
-ла, 8.3.1

-ев, 4.3.1
-ов, 4.3.1

-е, 4.3.1, 4.3.4, 5.3.3
-ее, 5.2.2, 5.3.1
-же, 7.1.2
-ане, 4.3.3
-ое, 5.2.1
-ете, -ите, 8.2.1
-ые, 5.2.1

-и, 4.3.1, 4.3.4
-ли, 8.3.1
-ами, 4.3.1, 4.3.4
-ими, 5.2.2
-ьми, 4.3.4
-ыми, 5.2.1
-ти, 8.11
-(в)ши, 8.13

-й, 4.3.1, 4.3.4
-ей, 4.3.1, 4.3.4, 5.2.2
-ий, 5.2.2, 5.2.3
-(в)ший, 8.12
-(ей)ший, -айший, 5.3.3
-щий, 8.12
-ой, 4.3.4, 5.2.1, 5.2.3
-ый, 5.2.1
-мый, -ный, -тый, 8.12

-л, 8.3.1

-м, 8.12
-ам, 4.3.1, 4.3.4
-ем, 4.3.1, 5.2.2, 8.2.1
-им, 5.2.2, 8.2.1
-ом, 4.3.1, 5.2.1
-ым, 5.2.1
-ям, 4.3.1, 4.3.4

-н, 8.12
-ан, 4.3.3

-о, 4.3.1, 5.2.4
-аго, -ого, 5.2.1, 5.2.3
-его, 5.2.2, 5.2.3
-ло, 8.3.1
-то, 7.1.2

-т, 8.12
-ат, -ет, -ит, -ут, -ют,
　-ят, 8.2.1

-у, 4.3.1, 4.3.4, 5.2.4,
　8.2.1
-аду, 8.2.4
-жу, 8.2.3
-ему, 5.2.2
-йму, 8.2.4
-ому, 5.2.1
-ну, 8.2.2

-шу, 8.2.3
-щу, 8.2.3

-ах, 4.3.1, 4.3.4
-их, 5.2.2
-ых, 5.2.1
-ях, 4.3.1, 4.3.4

-ь, 4.3.1, 4.3.4
-нибудь, 7.1.2
-сь, 8.14.1
-ть, -чь, 8.11
-ешь, -ишь, 8.2.1

-ы, 4.3.1, 4.3.4, 5.2.4

-ю, 4.3.1, 4.3.4, 8.2.1
-аю, 8.2.2
-ею, 4.3.4, 5.2.2, 8.2.2
-лю, 8.2.2
-ою, 4.3.4, 5.2.1
-ую, 5.2.1, 8.2.2
-ью, 4.3.4
-юю, 5.2.2, 8.2.2
-яю, 8.2.2

-я, 4.3.1, 4.3.4, 8.13
-ая, 5.2.1
-ся, 8.14.1
-ыя, 5.2.1
-яя, 5.2.2

BYELORUSSIAN

SPECIMEN

Гэты слоўнік мае на мэце даць па магчымасці поўнае ўяўленне аб уласных асабовых імёнах, якімі ў сучасны момант шырока карыстаецца беларускі народ. Разам з тым слоўнік прызначаецца ў якасці даведніка па такіх пытаннях, як адрозніваць гутарковую форму ад афіцыяльнай формы імя, поўную ад скарочанай, як правільна ўжываць тое ці іншае імя ў жывой мове і ў разнастайнай пісьмовай дакументацыі: пасведчаннях ад нараджэнні, пашпартах, ваенных і партыйных дакументах, паштовых адрасах і іншых паперах афіцыяльнага характару.

This dictionary has as aim to give so far as possible a complete notion of personal proper names which at the present moment the Byelorussian nation uses widely. Together with this the dictionary is designed in the character of a guide to such questions as distinguishing the conversational form from the official form of a name, the full from the shortened, as correctly using this or other name in the living language or in written documentation of various sorts: certificates of birth, passports, military and party documents, postal addresses and other papers of an official character.

This over-literal translation does not aim to be elegant.

0 GENERAL CHARACTERISTICS

0.4 RELATION TO OTHER LANGUAGES

0.4.1 Byelorussian is closely akin to Russian and Ukrainian, but differs in its phonology, and shares much of its vocabulary with Polish.

0.4.2 Some frequent phonetic correspondences with Russian are:

Byelorussian	Russian
а	о
ра, жа, ча, ша	ре, же, че, ше
я	е
я	a after vowels
ё	o after vowels and л
ы	и
э	е
лы, ры	ле, ре
у (ў)	в, л
дж	ж

(Continued overleaf)

427

Byelorussian	*Russian*
дз	д before е, и, ю, я, ь
ц	т before е, и, ю, я, ь
x (в)	ф
-анне, -енне	-ание, -ение
-ыцце, -iцце	-итие
-цца	-ться

The sounds дз and ц above, as against the Russian д and т, e.g. дзве (Ru две), цябе (Ru тебе), *to you*, result from palatalisation. This is also found in the declension of the noun, where it has been eliminated in Russian, e.g. на фронце, *on the front*; Ru фронте. Examples of divergent vocabulary are: Br пытанне, Ru вопрос; Br мова, Ru язык (cf. Ukrainian); Br лiтара, Ru Uk буква; and see also 6.4.1.

1 BIBLIOLINGUISTICS

1.1 NAMES

1.1.1 Byelorussian names are similar to Russian names, but patronymics, though used, are uncharacteristic.

Christian names (iмёны) are nouns, e.g. Павел, Васiль, Якаў, Цiмафей, *Timothy* (all 4.3.2), Пятро (standard form Пётр, both 4.3.2), Данiла, Iлья; Анна, Агапiя (all 4.3.6).

There are a number of masculine names ending in -a, some corresponding to Russian or Ukrainian names in -a, others to names in -o, others peculiar to Byelorussian. There are also a few in accented -o.

Russian and Byelorussian names are for the most part linguistic variants and are usually changed to suit the language, e.g. Васiль, Васiлiй, Ru Василий; Цiмафей, Тимофей; Яўгенiй, Евгений; Улалзiмiр, Владимир and vice versa. Equivalents can be found in M. R. Sudnik: *Слоўнiк асабовых уласных iмён.* Мiнск, *Акадэмiя Навук БССР*, 1965.

1.1.2 Patronymics (iмёны па бацьку) are regularly formed from the father's Christian name. They nearly all end in -вiч for men, -вна for women. The preceding vowel depends on the form of the name from which the patronymic is derived, e.g.

Вiктар: Вiктаравiч (hard consonant)
Багуслаў: Багуславaвiч (do.; 2.5.5)
Пётр: Пятровiч (do.; stress on ending)
Леў: Львовiч (do. do.; 2.5.5, 2.6.2)
Васiль: Васiлевiч (soft consonant)
Ерафей: Ерафеевiч (final -й)
Васiлiй: Васiльевiч (final -iй)
Кузьма: Кузьмiч
Iлья: Iльiч (most names in -a and -я)
Мiкiта: Мiкiтавiч (sic)
Якаў: Якаўлевiч (sic)
Збiгнеў: Збiгневiч (sic)

The feminine forms are -аӯна, -еӯна, etc.; but note Кузьмінічна and the like. Current forms are listed in Sudnik.

1.1.3 Surnames (прозвішчы) may be of native or foreign origin. The foreign names belong to classes (a), (b) and (e). Among native names are here included Russian names, which nearly always have different forms in Byelorussian books, so as to conform to Byelorussian phonetics and morphology, and vice versa. The changes may be extensive or may represent little more than a different spelling convention, e.g. Ru Пе'тровский Br Пя'троӯскі; Ru Вышинский Br Вышынскі; Ru Соловьев Br Салаӯёӯ; Br 'Каменшчыкаӯ Ru 'Каменщиков; Br Салад'коӯ Ru Солод'ков; Br Яр'моленка, 'Краӯчанка Ru Ер'моленко, 'Кравченко; Br Дзя'менцьеӯ Ru Де'ментьев; Br 'Дземчанкава Ru 'Демченкова.

The information given in 0.4.1 and 0.4.2 will enable one to recognise known names in Russian or Byelorussian disguise, but it is unwise to attempt to convert unfamiliar names without a good knowledge of the languages.

Surnames may be nouns or adjectives.

(a) Those that end in a consonant or semi-vowel are, except for the very common endings -аӯ, -ін and the like, for which see (c) below, nouns, e.g. Юзепчук, Вейс, Багамолец. They have no feminine forms, and when borne by women are indeclinable, e.g. работа Я. Н. Казановіч, *work of Ya. N. Kazanovich*. (See also (e) below.)

(b) Surnames in -о and a good many of those in -а and -я are masculine nouns, e.g. Юхо, Шаціла, Броӯка, Друя, Бядуля. Those in -а are declined like feminine nouns (4.3.6). As women's names they are not declined. (For other names in -а and -я see (c) and (d), and for names in -о see (e).)

(c) Surnames in -аӯ, -еӯ, -ёӯ, -оӯ, -эӯ, -яӯ, -ін, -ын are possessive adjectives in origin. The corresponding feminines end in -ава, -ева, (etc.) -іна, -ына. Information on their declension is given in 5.4. The cautions and qualifications given in the corresponding Russian section apply here also.

(d) Names in -кі and -ы are adjectives (5.2), with feminine forms in -ая, e.g. Георгіеӯскі, -кая. (On the anomalous correspondence -кі, -кая see 2.5.2, 5.2.1.) The adjectival nominative -кі (usually -скі or -цкі) should not be confused with the genitive of nouns in -енка and -анка.

Names of type (c) and (d) have plural forms which can be used where two or more members of the same family, of the same or opposite sexes, are mentioned. For further details see Russian 1.1.3.

(e) Names, usually foreign, which do not fit the pattern of declension, are invariable, e.g. Мелкіх (GP of an adjective), Лано (stressed on the last syllable), Дантэ.

1.1.4 Both halves of a compound name are appropriately declined, e.g. выяӯлены В. Д. Міхайлавай-Лукашовай, *established by V. D. Mikhailava-Lukashova*.

1.2 NAMES OF AUTHORS, EDITORS, ETC.

1.2.1 The ways of indicating authorship, editorship and the like are grammatically the same as in Russian, where full details are given. Some Byelorussian examples follow:

Active verb with name in the nominative: **Апрацаваӯ Васіль Друя,** *Vasil' Druya worked it up*; **склалі М. Г. Крэканэ і А. А. Сакольчык,** *M. G. Krekane and A. A. Sakol'chyk compiled*; **асобныя раздзелі і часткі кнігі напісалі наступныя аӯтары** (followed by a list), *the following authors wrote particular sections and parts.*

1.2.2 *Agent as noun,* name in the nominative: **Укладальнык М. Р. Суднік,** *compiler M. R. Sudnik*; similarly **складальнікі,** *compilers*; **адказны (галоӯны) рэдактар,**

responsible (*chief*) *editor*; **рэдакцыйная калегія** (*editorial committee*): **Міхаль Клім-ковіч** (and others); similarly **аўтарскі калектыў** (*author-collective*).

1.2.3   *Activity as noun*, name in the genitive: **пад рэдакцыяй І. С. Краўчанкі**, *under the editorship of I. S. Krawchanka* (*Kravchenko*); **зверка тэкстаў, заўвагі і тлума-чэнні да іх А. Д. Атаевай**, *selection of texts, notes and translations to them by A. D. Ataeva*.

1.2.4   *Passive participle* with instrumental case: **Асобныя параграфы напісаны . . . З. У. Доктаравым . . . кандыдатам юрыдычных навук І. А. Юхо**, *particular sections written by Z. U. Doktaraw . . . I. A. Yukho, Cand. Iur.*

1.2.5   On corporate authors see Russian 1.2.7. For example **Інстытут літаратуры і мастацтва Акадэміі навук БССР** will have the catalogue entry *Akademiya Navuk B[elaruskaĭ] S.S.R. Instytut Literatury i Mastatstva*; **Інстытут гісторыі партыі пры ЦК КП Беларусі**: *Kamunistychnaya Partyya Belarusi. Tséntral'ny Kamitét. Instytut Historyi Partyi.*

1.3   TITLES

1.3.1   What is said about Russian titles applies equally to Byelorussian, whether straightforward ones such as **Нарысы па гісторыі беларускай літаратуры**, *Sketches on the history of Byelorussian literature*, or more coloured ones like **Калі ўзыходзіла сонца**, *When the sun rose*; **Ты і яна**, *You and she*. Titles quoted may be integrated in the grammar of the sentence in which they are quoted, e.g. **да «Беларускага слоўніка»** (title *Беларускі слоўнік*) or isolated by being put in apposition, e.g. **у кнізе «Правілы беларускай арфаграфіі і пунктуацыі».**

1.3.2   Russian and Byelorussian titles can be interfiled since if Br **і** and Ru **и** are equated the Russian alphabet contains all the Byelorussian letters except **ў**. But where-as Russian treats **е** and **ё** as one letter, in the Byelorussian alphabet **ё** follows **е**.

1.4   VOLUMES AND PARTS

1.4.1   The usual words are **том** and **частка**. **Раздзел** denotes a division of a work, without necessary connexion with binding units.

1.4.2   Numeration is given in ordinal numbers in words or figures, e.g. **том першы, частка II.**

1.4.4   The total number of volumes may be given, e.g. **Звор твораў у чатырох тамах**, *Collected works in four volumes.*

1.5   EDITIONS

1.5.1   The word is **выданне**, a verbal noun which also has the more general meaning *publication* (1.6). The number is usually given in words, e.g. **выданне другое**, *second edition*, accompanied if necessary by some such word as **перароблеnae**, *revised*; **дапоўненae**, *enlarged*.

1.5.2   Necessary information may be given more discursively in the preface, e.g. **Першае выданне выходзіла ў якасці пробнага падручніка ў 1955 годзе**, *The first edition came out in the form of a trial textbook in 1955.*

1.6   IMPRINTS

1.6.1   Soviet imprints are institutional, with either long descriptive names or short symbolic ones, such as **Выдавецтва Навука і Тэхніка, Беларусь**, the latter being the commoner today. The commonest imprint over the years has been **Дзяржаўнае**

выдавецтва БССР (abbreviated Дзяржвыд) with its subordinate рэдакцыі — Рэдакцыя сацыяльна-эканамічнай літаратуры, Рэд. палітычнай літ. Though there have
also been separate presses covering the same areas of interest, e.g. Дзяржаўне выдавецтва палітычнай літаратуры or Дзяржпалітвыдавецтва (and compare the
Russian Соцэкгиз and Госполитиздат: Russian 1.6), these рэдакцыі are usually
ignored when giving the imprint. The abbreviations may be used if known, but they
are unpredictable and should not be invented.

1.6.2 Learned institutions still have long descriptive names, e.g. **Выдавецтва
Беларускага Дзяржаўнага Універсітэта** (abbreviated **Выд. Белдзяржуніверсітэта**)
Выд. Акадэміі Навук БССР.

The last could no doubt be abbreviated to Акадэмія Навук without ambiguity, but
with university presses it would be more prudent to retain the word выдавецтва.

1.6.3 Outside the Soviet Union presses may be commercial, involving personal
names, or institutional, e.g. выданьне Беларускае рэлігійнае місіі. Note that выданьне
(Soviet spelling выданне) is a verbal noun equivalent in meaning to *published by* but
followed by the genitive. If it is omitted, the imprint becomes Беларуская рэлігійная
місія.

1.6.4 The place is regularly in the nominative. If it should be preceded by у it will
be in the locative.

1.7 SERIES

1.7.1 The names of series are usually descriptive of the series as a whole, e.g.
Беларуская народная творчасць, *Byelorussian national creation* (i.e. literary works),
or of the individual items, e.g. Матарыялы і каталёгі, *Materials and catalogues.*

1.7.2 Numeration is usually by №, i.e. нумар.

1.8 PERIODICALS

1.8.1 Byelorussian periodicals, the few that I have seen, are not very forthcoming
as far as formal details are concerned. Titles, whether of Soviet or expatriate periodicals,
are usually simple, e.g. Беларусь, *Byelorussia*; Маладосць, *Youth*; Божым шляхам,
On God's highway. The last involves an oblique case.

1.8.2 The name of the body concerned is frequently part of the title or sub-title
and is in the genitive, e.g. **Працы Інстытута мовазнаўства АН БССР,** *Transactions
of the Institute of Linguistics of the Academy of Sciences of the BSSR*; орган Саюза
пісьменнікаў БССР, *organ of the Writers' Union of the BSSR.* Nominatives Інстытут
and Саюз will need to be extracted for catalogue purposes. It may however appear
in the nominative preceded by выдае or выдаюць, *publish(es).* In the Soviet Union
the publisher may be different from the body whose organ the periodical is, being one
of the state or party publishing houses.

1.8.3 Editorship is stated with little variety, usually рэдакцыйная калегія (abbreviated рэдкалегія) and a list of names, one of whom may be singled out as галоўны
or адказны рэдактар (*chief* or *responsible editor*). Small expatriate periodicals may
be run by a **vydaviec-redaktar.** In one case no name was given (apart from that of the
technical editor, who is part of the production side) except that of a мастацкі рэдактар,
artistic editor, whom also one would normally be inclined to ignore.

1.8.4 Numeration is primarily by год (выдання), *year (of publication),* coupled
with № (i.e. нумар) or выпуск. Very often an alternative, continuous numeration is
given. Occasionally numeration is simply by кніга, literally *book.*

1.8.5 Periodicity, if given, may be by adjective as part of the title, e.g. штомесячны (квартальны) часопіс, *monthly (quarterly) periodical*, or by the corresponding noun, e.g. **dvumiesačnik**, *bi-monthly*. More often than not it is not stated, or only in the terms of subscription (1.8.6).

1.8.6 Usually there is simply a price (**цана**) on the individual numbers. Subscription (**падпіска** or **падпісная цана**) is quoted for a period, e.g. **на год (12 кніжак)**, **на поўгода**, **на 3 месяца**, *for a year (12 issues), for a half-year, for 3 months*. In such cases the price of a separate issue may be given: **кошт асобнага нумару**, or **tsana adnaho exemplara**.

1.8.7 The only address I have seen is that of the editorial office: **адрас рэдакцыі**.

2 ALPHABET, PHONETICS, SPELLING

2.1 ALPHABET
2.1.1 The standard alphabet is:

А	Б	В	Г	[Ґ]	Д	Е	Ё	Ж	З	І	Й	К	Л	М	Н	О
а	б	в	г	[ґ]	д	е	ё	ж	з	і	й	к	л	м	н	о

П	Р	С	Т	У	Ў	Ф	Х	Ц	Ч	Ш	Ы	Ь	Э	Ю	Я
п	р	с	т	у	ў	ф	х	ц	ч	ш	ы	ь	э	ю	я

The transliteration is the same as that of Russian except for Г І Ў, for which the equivalents are as follows:

	BS	BM and LC	ISO
г	h	h	g
ґ	g	g	ġ
і	i	i	ī
ў	w	ŭ	ŭ

ISO/R9 permits variants h, i (and ch for x). Ґ is now obsolete in the Soviet Union. Properly speaking ё is a separate letter, but it is occasionally equated with е. It is transliterated ë. ў, which like й is the second member of a diphthong, can be a contextual variant of у, e.g. **барацьба ў Мінску**.

The apostrophe ' is used, as it once was in Russian, to separate a hard prefix from a succeeding soft vowel, e.g. **з'явілася**; but it is also found, as in **сям'я**, where Russian has always had ь, viz. **семья**.

One occasionally finds Byelorussian written in the Latin alphabet. The only correspondences that need to be noted specially are:

Cyrillic	в	г	е	ё	ж	ў	х	ц	ч	ш	ю	я
Latin	v	h	ie	io/jo	ž	ŭ	ch	c	č	š	iu/ju	ia/ja

The soft sign ь is replaced by an acute accent on the preceding consonant, e.g. **шэсць = šeść**, and hard ł is distinguished from soft l.

2.1.2 What is said under Russian (2.1.2 and 2.1.3) of national and loose transcriptions applies to Byelorussian. In particular, Byelorussians writing in foreign languages may be found with their names spelt Polish fashion.

2.2 CAPITALISATION
As in Russian.

2.3 DIVISION OF WORDS

Rules 1, 4, 5a or b, 6d, 7a, 8 (p. xiii) apply. Obvious divisions between words and prefixes or suffixes are respected, but no great pains are taken, e.g. пад-ворныя [двор], проз-вішчы [званця], and the proviso of Rule 7a takes precedence, e.g. прый-шлося.

2.4 PUNCTUATION AND ABBREVIATIONS

The principles are the same as in Russian.

2.5 HARD AND SOFT CONSONANTS; PALATALISATION; VARIATION OF CONSONANT

(See General Note on the Slavonic languages.)

2.5.1 The quality of a Byelorussian consonant is indicated by the following vowel or by the presence or absence of the soft sign ь. The vowel series are:

Hard а э ы о у
Soft я е і ё ю

Both э and ы are commoner than they are in Russian. The corresponding vowels are found in parallel hard and soft declensions and to a less extent conjugations, but the correspondences are not absolutely regular (cf. 4.3.2). A few endings are always soft, even in hard declensions.

2.5.2 The consonants г, ж, к, р, х, ч, ш present peculiarities:

г, к, х are followed only by endings beginning with а, е, і, о, у, so that declensions appear to be mixed, though in the body of a word г and к may be followed by other vowels;

ж, р, ч, ш are invariably hard.

2.5.3 A prefix ending in a hard consonant hardens the following vowel, unless separated from it by an apostrophe, e.g. с + іграць > сыграць, *to play*, but з'езд, *congress*. Similarly in foreign words such as аб'ект, *object*.

2.5.4 Palatalisation takes place both in nouns and verbs before certain endings. (For palatalisation as a factor differentiating Byelorussian from Russian see 0.4.2.)

The changes due to palatalisation are:

	г	д	з	к	с	ск	т	х
into	з	дз		ц			ць	с
or	ж	дж	ж	ч	ш	шч	ч	ш

The second set of changes is found only in verbs. For the peculiarities of some of the resulting consonants see 2.5.2. Akin to palatalisation is the change of б, в, м, п, ф to бл, ўл, мл, etc. before certain soft endings, e.g. любіць, люблю.

2.5.5 в and л are replaced by ў at the end of a syllable, e.g. слова/слоў; быў/было.

When a prefix ending in -з is followed by an unvoiced consonant, the з is changed to с, e.g. бясспрэчка [без-]. Other prefixes are left unassimilated, e.g. ад|сылка.

2.6 VARIATION OF VOWEL

2.6.1 The difference in quality between accented and unaccented vowels, found also in Russian, is reflected in Byelorussian spelling. If the accent shifts in declension or conjugation the spelling will alternate, viz. о/а, е/я, э/а, e.g. 'свой/сва'ім; '.іепш/.ля'пей, and the systems of endings are different according as they are accented or not, e.g. '-ага/-'ога/-а'го. Further details of this will be found in the appropriate places.

2.6.2 An а, е or о in the last syllable of the NS may disappear when endings are added, e.g. майстар, G майстра; Леў, Львовіч, with soft л preserved; M ішоў, F ішла. Conversely an a, e, or o may be inserted when there is a zero ending, e.g. кніжка, кніжак; сястра, сястёр; акно, акон; (NP вокны [2.6.1]).

2.7 SPELLING

2.7.1 The Latin script before 1918 followed Polish conventions, e.g. cz for č. In the same year ъ, ѣ and и were dropped, and шч was substituted for щ.

2.7.2 In 1933 some minor spelling changes were made in the USSR: a consonant preceding a soft consonant is assumed to be soft, hence снег not сьнег, выданне not выданьне; e is not changed to я or a except immediately before the stress, hence выданне not выдання, or after ж, ш, and ч; words of foreign origin keep their o, hence соціаліст not сац-, and э is used only after д and т.

3 ARTICLES

There are no articles.

4 NOUNS

4.1 FORM AND GENDER

There are three genders. Correspondence between form and gender of the noun is blurred, as compared with Russian, by Byelorussian's more phonetic spelling, e.g. кніга is feminine, слова (Ru слово) neuter. Inanimate nouns may be of any gender. Omitting the vocative, there are six cases, the endings varying according to the form of the noun, and the place of the stress.

4.3 FORMS

4.3.1 *Masculine and neuter*

These are the same in many of their endings. Masculine nouns end in the NS in a hard or soft consonant, neuters mostly in -o or -ё (-a or -e when the ending is unstressed). For masculine nouns in -a see 4.3.6.

4.3.2 *Hard type*

	S			*P*		
	M	*M & N*	*N*	*M*	*M & N*	*N*
N	-/-o		-o/-a		-ы	
A	N or G		-o/-a	N or G		-ы
G	-y	-a		-оў/-аў		-/-аў/-ей
D		-y		-ом	-ам	
I		-ом/-ам			-амі	
L		-*е/-ы/-у			-ах	

Soft type

	S			*P*		
	M	*M & N*	*N*	*M*	*M & N*	*N*
N	-ь, -й		-е/-ё		-i	
A	N or G		-е/-ё	N or G		-i
G	-ю	-я			-ёў/-яў	
D		-ю			-ём/-ям	
I		-ем/-ём			-ямі	
L		-i			-ях	

4.3.3 For the explanation of mixed types see 2.5.2. Variation of vowel (2.6) occurs.

4.3.4 Some names have by-forms in the nominative only, e.g. Пятро = Пётр.

4.3.5 Some masculine nouns have no ending in GP, e.g. чалавек, раз; дзень makes дзён; nouns in -анін (-янін) have NP -ане, GP -ан.

імя has a long consonant stem in some cases, viz.

NA	G	D	I	L	P stem
(ім) -я	-ені/-я	-ені/-ю	-(ен)ем	-(ен)і	-ён-

вока and вуха have palatalised plural stems, viz. воч|ы, вуш|ы, G -эй, I -мі.

4.3.6 *Feminine*

These end in -a or -я or consonant (originally soft). Masculine nouns in -a follow the same declension but have IS -ам.

	-a *type*		-я *type*	
	S	P	S	P
N	-a	-ы	-я	-i
A	-у	N or G	-ю	N or G
G	-ы	-/-аў	-i	-ь/-й/-яў
D	-*е/-э/-ы	-ам	-i	-ям
I	-ой/-ай†	-амі	-ей/-яй†	-ямі
L	-*е/-э/-ы	-ах	-i	-ях

† -ю is sometimes found for -й, viz. -ёю, -аю, etc., especially in earlier texts.

4.3.7 *Consonant type (soft)*   *Consonant type (hardened)*

	S	P	S	P
N	-ь	-i	-	-ы/-i
A	-ь	-i	-	-ы/-i
G	-i	-ей	-ы/-i	-аў/-эй/-ей
D	-i	-ям	-ы/-i	-ам
I	-ю	-ьмі/-ямі	-у/-ю	-амі
L	-i	-ях	-ы	-ах

Before -ю consonants may be doubled.

Люд makes plural людзі (soft).

4.3.8 Palatalisation (2.5.4) occurs in DS and LS of -a types. For the explanation of mixed types see 2.5.2.

4.6 USE OF CASES
See Russian 4.6.

5 ADJECTIVES

5.1 GENERAL

5.1.1 Adjectives vary for gender, number and case, and agree with the nouns they qualify. They precede the noun.

5.1.2 Most adjectives have both long forms, and, so far as these exist, short forms. Some have only long forms, and some have short forms in some cases and long ones in others.

P

5.1.3 The chief uses of the short forms are as predicates, in the nominative, and in possessive adjectives. Possessive adjectives like **бацькаў** have short forms only for the nominative, but surnames of the same type (1.1.3 (c)) use all the forms that exist and make up with long forms in the other cases.

5.1.4 Adjectives are given in the dictionary under the long form. This can be got from the short form of the NSM by adding the ending given in 5.2.1 and omitting any inserted vowel (2.6), e.g. **чоран, чорны; повен, поўны** (2.5.5). Conversely **пашы-раны**, *wide-spread*, short form **пашыран**, a participle (8.12.3).

5.2 FORMS

5.2.1 Long forms

Hard type

	M	N	S F	P
N	-ы	-ое/-ае	-ая	-ыя
A	as N or G		-ую	N or G
G	-ога/-ага		-ой/-ай (-ое/-ае)	-ых
D	-ому/-аму		-ой/-ай	-ым
I	-ым		-ой/-ай (-ою/-аю)	-ымі
L	-ым		-ой/-ай	-ых

Soft type

	M	N	S F	P
N	-i	-яе	-яя	-ія
A	as N or G		-юю	N or G
G	-яга		-яй (-яе)	-ix
D	-яму		-яй	-ім
I	-ім		-яй (-яю)	-імі
L	-ім		-яй	-ix

Bracketed forms are now less usual.

Adjectives like **другі, беларускі** are of the hard type, but have **i** for **ы** throughout (2.5.2).

5.2.2 Short forms

Only the following distinctive short forms are found:

Hard type						*Soft type*			
	M	S N	F	P		M	S N	F	P
N	-	-о/-а	-а	-ы		-ь	-я	-я	-i
A	as N or G		-y						
G	-а								
D	-y								

5.3 COMPARISON

5.3.1 There is a comparative ending **-ейшы**, less commonly **-эйшы**, added to the stem left after removing the **-ы, -кі, -окі** of the positive.

5.3.2 The superlative is formed by prefixing **най-** to the comparative or adding **самы** (a declinable adjective) before the positive, e.g. **самае багатае** (N), *richest*.

5.3.3 Irregular comparatives such as **лепшы**, *better*, are entered separately in the dictionary.

5.4 POSSESSIVES

The possessives **мой, твой, свой, наш, ваш** have short forms in the nominative and accusative and long forms elsewhere. The forms of **мой**, etc. are:

	S			*P*
	M	*N*	*F*	
N	мой	маё	мая	мае
A	as N or G		маю	as N or G
G	майго		маей	маіх
D	майму		маёй	маім
I	маім		маёй	маймі
L	маім		маёй	маіх

6 NUMERALS

6.1 CARDINAL

6.1.1

1 адзін	11 адзінаццаць	21 дваццаць адзін	101 сто адзін
2 два	12 дванаццаць	30 трыццаць	200 дзвесце
3 тры	13 трынаццаць	40 сорак	300 трыста
4 чатыры	14 чатырнаццаць	50 пяцьдзесят	400 чатырыста
5 пяць	15 пяцьнаццаць	60 шэсцьдзесят	500 пяцьсот
6 шэсць	16 шаснаццаць	70 семдзесят	900 дзевяцьсот
7 сем	17 семнаццаць	80 восемдзесят	1000 тысяча
8 восем	18 восемнаццаць	90 дзевяноста	
9 дзевяць	19 дзевяцьнаццаць	100 сто	
10 дзесяць	20 дваццаць		

6.1.2 адзін–чатыры are adjectives.

адзін, адно, адна (stem **адн-**) has most of its forms as 5.2.1, GM **-аго** GF **-ой/-ае** ILF **-эй**.

два, тры, чатыры:

	MN	*F*	*All genders*	
NA	два	дзве	тры	чатыры
G	двох/двух	дзвёх/дзвюх	трох	чатырох
D	двом/двум	дзвём/дзвюм	тром	чатыром
I	двума	дзвяма/дзвюма	трыма	чатырма
L	двох	дзвёх/дзвюх	трох	чатырох

пяць onwards, though nouns in origin, are not significantly different. The endings for 5–99 are:

	-і	-і	-ю	-і
or	-ёх	-ём	-ьма| -ёх	(less common now)

шэсць, сем, восем have stems шасц-, сям-, васьм- (2.6.1, 2.6.2).

сорак has GD and L -a, and 50–90 are declined in both parts, e.g. пяццюдзесяццю, if they are not left undeclined.

сто (4.3.2) and тысяча (4.3.6) are nouns (дзвесце is a survival). Both halves of 200–900 are declined.

6.1.3 *Construction*

With два, тры, чатыры the following noun or adjective is to all intents and purposes in the same case as the numeral, e.g. два рады, дзве спецыяльныя працы, з трох раздзелаў, у чатырох тамах. Strictly speaking, when the numeral is in the nominative or accusative, a feminine noun is in the genitive singular, but this is rarely any different from the NP. (Note, however, акно NP вокны but два акны.)

All other numerals in the nominative or accusative are followed by nouns or adjectives in the genitive plural, e.g. **40 асобных форм**. Otherwise numeral, noun and adjective agree. The verb is usually in the neuter singular, e.g. з'явілася дзве працы, *two works have appeared.*

6.1.4 Compound cardinal numerals are declined throughout, e.g. двухсот сарака пяці, *of 245.*

6.2 ORDINAL
6.2.1

1 першы	10 дзесяты	90 дзевяносты
2 другі	11–19 адзінаццаты, etc.	100 соты
3 трэці	20 дваццаты	200 двухсоты
4 чацвёрты	30 трыццаты	300 трохсоты
5 пяты	40 саракавы	400 чатырохсоты
6 шосты	50 пяцідзесяты	500, etc. пяцісоты, etc.
7 сёмы	60 шасцідзесяты	1000 тысячны
8 восьмы	70 сямідзесяты	
9 дзевяты	80 васьмідзесяты	

6.2.2 трэці, трэцяе, трэцяя. The rest are hard or mixed (5.2). In compound ordinals only the last element has the ordinal form and is variable.

6.3 FIGURES

Plain arabic numerals usually stand for cardinals, ordinals being expressed either by roman figures as in **III Дзяржаўнай думы**, *of the 3rd National Duma*, or by the addition of the appropriate ending to the arabic.

6.4 DATES
6.4.1 The months are:

студзень, люты, сакавік, красавік, май, чэрвень,
ліпень, жнівень (G жніўня), верасень, кастрычнік, лістапад, снежань

люты is declined like an adjective, the rest as in 4.3.

6.4.2

1 May is translated першы май or **першае мая**
Between 18 and 21 November: паміж **18-м** і **21-м** лістападам

On 5.ii.1967: пятага лютага тысячя дзевяцьсот шэсцьдзесят сёмага года
у **1848** г.: the ending is -ы год
у **90-х гг.**: у дзевяностых гадах, *in the 90's*

On expressions such as **1848–1948** and **рэвалюцыя 1905–07** see Russian 6.4.2. The same considerations apply. In contrast to Russian note **40 гадоў**, *40 years*.

7 PRONOUNS

7.1/7.2 DEMONSTRATIVE, INTERROGATIVE, RELATIVE, INDEFINITE

7.1.1 All these pronouns have much the same case endings as adjectives, the long forms of which incorporate a pronoun. Note:

> **той, тое, тая**, *that*: GSM **таго**; alternatives ASF **ту** GDIL **тэй** (**гэты**, *this*, as in 5.2.1)
> **хто**, *who?*: G **каго/кога** D **каму** IL **кім**. So also **нехта, ніхто**
> **што**, *what?, which*: G **чаго/чога** D **чаму** IL **чым**. So also **нешта, нішто**
> **сам, само, сама** has some short forms (5.2.2)
> **увесь, усё, уся**, *all*: stem **ус-** (soft), e.g. GSMN **усяго** GDILF **усёй** G also **усяе** I also **усёю** P **усе**, etc.

7.1.2 Some pronouns have invariable suffixes such as **-небудзь, -сь(ці), -сьць**, e.g. **хто-небудзь**, *whoever*, G **каго-небудзь**. Others, like **сякі-такі** consist of two elements both of which are declined, e.g. G **сякога-такога**.

7.2 RELATIVE AND INTERROGATIVE
See 7.1/7.2.

7.3 PERSONAL
7.3.1

	S		S & P	P	
	1	2	R	1	2
N	я	ты	-	мы	вы
AG	мяне	цябе	сябе	нас	вас
D	мне	табе	сабе	нам	вам
I	мною	табою	сабою	намі	вамі
L	мне	табе	сабе	нас	вас

сябе, *self*, refers to all persons.

7.3.2 **ён, яно, яна**, *he, it, she*, P **яны** has oblique cases from another root:

	S		P
	M	F	
AG	яго	яе	іх
D	яму		ім
I	ім	ей	імі
L	ім		іх

8 VERBS

8.1 STRUCTURE
The general characteristics of the verb are the same as in Russian, q.v.

8.2 PRESENT AND FUTURE

8.2.1 The present is formed from the imperfective stem, the perfective forms having usually a future meaning. The endings are the same, and in what follows the symbol P refers only to the forms.

8.2.2 *Endings*

Ia	-у, -эш, -э(ць); -ом, -аце, -уць
b	-*у, -*аш, -*а(ць); -*ам, -*аце, -*уць
c	-у, -еш, -е(ць); -ем, -яце, -уць
d	-у, -*еш, -*е(ць); -*ем, -*яце, -уць
II	-ю, -еш, -е(ць); -ем, -еце, -юць
IIIa	-ю/-у, -іш, -іць; -ім, -іце, -яць
b	-у, -ыш, -ыць; -ым, -ыце, -аць

8.2.3 *Relation to infinitive*

P	-*у (Ib)	-у (Ic)	-у	-ну	-ю (II)	-аю (II)
I	-аць	-аць	-уць	-нуць	-яць	-аць

P	-аю (IIIa)	-яю (II)	-ую	-юю	-ю (IIIa)	-у (IIIb)
I	-аяць	-яць	-аваць	-яваць	-іць, -ець	-ыць, -аць

8.2.4 *Some peculiar stems*

P	бяру	б'ю	вяду	вязу	даю	еду	жыву
I	браць	біць	весці	везці	даваць	ехаць	жыць

P	іду	йму		лягу	магу/можа	маю	начну
I	ісці	яць/няць		легчы	магчы	мець	начаць

P	нясу	паду	памру	расту	стану	сяду
I	нясці	пасці	памерці	расці	стаць	сесці

8.2.5 *Irregularities*

дам, дасі, дасць; дамо, дасцё, дадуць *I* даць
ем, ясі, есць; ямо, ясцё, едуць *I* есці
хачу, хочаш, хоча; хочам, хочаце, хочуць *I* хацець

8.2.6 The future imperfective is a compound tense. See 8.10.

8.3 PAST

8.3.1 This tense is a participle in form, having three genders and two numbers, but no distinction of persons.

Usual endings

	S		P
M	N	F	
-ў/-	-'ло/-ла	-ла	-лі

8.3.2 *Relation to infinitive*

Substitute -ць for -ў, etc. (See also table below.) If there is no ending in the masculine, the other endings are added direct to the root consonant.

8.3.3 *Irregularities*

P	вёў, вяла	вёз	ішоў, ішла	клаў	мог	нёс
I	весці	вязці	ісці	класці	магчы	нясці

P	памёр	сеў	упаў
I	памерці	сесці	упасці

8.5 FUTURE

See 8.2 and 8.10.

8.10 COMPOUND TENSES

Future imperfective: either буду (8.17) followed by the imperfective infinitive, or -іму, etc. suffixed to it, e.g. пісаціму, *I shall be writing.*

8.11 INFINITIVE

The infinitive ends in -ць or -ці, rarely -чы. Instructions for deriving it are given under the other parts.

8.12/8.13 PARTICIPLES AND GERUNDS

8.12.1 The participles are adjectives and variable, the gerunds adverbs and invariable.

8.12.2 *Present active participle and gerund:* -чы

8.12.3 *Past active participle and gerund:* -шы

8.12.4 *Present passive participle:* -емы, -імы

8.12.5 *Past passive participle:* -н(ы), -т(ы)

P	-ан	-ян	-ен, -*ен, -*ан	-ен	-нен	-т
I	-аць	-яць	-іць, -ець	-ець	-нуць	-ц

Note also -несен/-несці, ведзен/весці.

8.14/8.15 REFLEXIVE AND PASSIVE

8.14.1 Reflexive forms are got by adding -ся to the active. This -ся coalesces with the third person of the present, and with the infinitive, to give in both cases -цца, e.g. з'яўляецца, *reveals itself, is*; з'яўляюцца, *are* (active: з'яўляе(ць), з'яўляюць); паказацца, *to seem.* As in Russian they have reciprocal, passive, or intransitive senses.

8.14.2 The passive, if not avoided, is expressed by reflexive forms or passive participles (8.12), e.g. асіміляваліся, *they were assimilated*; некаторая колькасць была сабрана, *a certain quantity was collected.*

8.17 THE VERB **быць**, *to be*

> *Present:* **е(сць)** all persons
> *Future:* **буду, будзеш,** etc. (8.2.2 Ic)
> *Past:* **быў, была,** etc.
> *Gerunds:* **будучы, быўшы**

8.23 PREFIXES

Many verbs are compounded with prefixes, and may not always be easy to sort out. A list of these prefixes is therefore given here:

> **а, аб, аба, ад, ада, вы, да, за, на, над, па, пад, пера, перад, по, под, пра,**
>
> **пры, раз, рас, у, уз, узы**

The bracketed forms are variants depending on what follows. Prefixes that end in a consonant are followed by an apostrophe before most soft vowels, e.g. **з'езд**, *congress*. The prefixes used are often different from those in the corresponding Russian verbs.

9 ADVERBS

9.1 FORMATION

Most adjectives make adverbs in **-a**.

9.2 COMPARISON

Comparatives in **-ейшы** make adverbs in **-ейш**; similarly **лепш**, *better*; **горш**, *more bitterly* (but alternatively **ляпей, гарей**).

Adjectives in **-скі** make compound adverbs such as **па беларуску**. Adverbs formed from the oblique cases of nouns or pronouns, such as **зусім**, *altogether*, are mostly entered separately in the dictionary.

9.3 MEANINGS

Some common adverbs, none too easily recognisable on the basis of Russian are:

> **вельмі, вяльмі**, *very*; **дзе**, *where?*; **дужа**, *very*; **калі**, *when?*; **ніколі**, *never*; **сёлета**, *this year*; **сягоння, сяёння**, *today*; **тады**, *then*

10 PREPOSITIONS

Prepositions behave generally as in Russian (q.v.), though phonetic changes may make some of those shared with Russian a little strange at first sight, and some are peculiar to Byelorussian, e.g. **аб** (= Ru **о**), *about, against*; **ад** = Ru **от**; **апрача**, *except*; **да** = Ru **до**; **дзеля** = Ru **для**; **з** = Ru **из** or **с**; **з-за**, *because of*; **ля**, *by, near*; **між**, *among, between*; **пад** = Ru **под**; **п[е]рад** = Ru **перед**; **пра, праз**, *through, because of*; **у (ва, ува)** = Ru **в, у**; **уздоўж**, *along*.

11 CONJUNCTIONS

These have no grammatical difficulties. Some of the commonest ones differ widely from their Russian equivalents, viz. **але**, *but*; **бо**, *because*; **ды**, *but*; **дык**, *so, then*; **каб**, *that, so that, in order that*; **як**, *as*.

GLOSSARY

абмен, *exchange*
адбітак, *offprint*
апавяданне, аповесць, *short story*
апрацаваў, *edited* (1.2.1)
асобны, *single* (1.8.6)

бібліятэка, *library*
бібліятэкар, *librarian*
брашура, *pamphlet*
бясплатна, *free*

верш, *poem*
выбраны, *selected*
выдавецтва, *publishing house*
выданне, *edition* (1.5.1), *publication* (1.6.3)
выпуск, *issue, number* (1.8.4)
выходзіць, *come out, appear*
вышлы ў апошні час, *already published*

гісторыя, *history*
год, *year*

дадатак, *appendix, supplement*
дапоўнены, *enlarged*
даследаванні, *researches*
двухтыднёвы, *fortnightly*
у друку, *in the press*

замежны, *foreign*
замест уступу, *by way of introduction*
запіскі, *proceedings*
заўвага, *note* (1.2.3)
збор, *collection*
зверка, *selection* (1.2.3)
з'езд, *congress*

квартальны, *quarterly*
кніга, *book*

ліст, *letter*

нарадзіўся, *was born*
нарыс, *essay*
новы, *new*

нумар, *number*
нявыдадзены, *unpublished*

падпіска, *subscription*
памёр, *died*
папраўлены, *corrected*
партрэт, *portrait*
перадрук, *reprint(ing)*
пераклад, *translation*
перапіска, *correspondence*
пераплёт, *binding*
перароблены, *revised*
п'еса, *play*
пісьмо, *letter*
поўгадавы, *half-yearly*
поўгодзе, *half-year*
прадмова, *preface*
прамова, *speech*
працы, *transactions*
працяг будзе, *to be continued*
пробны, *sample*
у продажы, *on sale*
прыкладанне, *addition*

раздзел, *division*
раман, *novel*
распрадзены, *out of print*
рэдактар, *editor* (1.2.2, 1.8.3)
рэдакцыя, *editing, editorial office* (1.8.7)
рэдкалегія, *editorial board* (1.8.3)
рэферат, *abstract*

сабраны, *collected*
складальнік, *compiler* (1.2.2)
склаў, *compiled* (1.2.1)
слоўнік, *dictionary*
старонка, *page*
стары нумар, *back number*

табліца, *table*
таварыства, *society*
твор, *work*
тлумачэнне, *translation*

уводзіны, *introduction*
указальнік, *index*

цана, *price*

штогодні, *annual*
штогоднік, *yearbook*
штомесячны, *monthly*
часопіс, *periodical* (1.8.5)   штотыднёвы, *weekly*
частка, *part* (1.4.1)
член, *member*

экземпляр, *copy*

GRAMMATICAL INDEX: WORDS

GRAMMATICAL INDEX: ENDINGS

UKRAINIAN

SPECIMENS

Contemporary standard

У колективній праці «Розвиток народного господарства Української РСР» досліджуються питання розвитку соціалістичного народного господарства Української РСР як складової і невід'ємної частини СРСР.

Монографія складається з двох томів. У першому томі висвітлюється історія економічного розвитку УРСР в період будівництва і перемоги соціалізму. Порівняно з попередніми аналогічними виданнями в даній монографії більшою мірою використані геніальні ленінські праці, а також документи Комуністичної партії і Радянської держави.

In the collective work 'The development of the national economy of the Ukrainian SSR' are investigated questions of the development of the socialist national economy of the Ukrainian SSR as a constituent and integral part of the USSR.

The monograph consists of two volumes. In the first volume is expounded the history of the economic development of the UkSSR in the period of the building and victory of socialism. As compared with previous similar publications there are used to a greater extent in the present monograph Lenin's works of genius as well as documents of the Communist Party and the Soviet state.

Obsolete variants

Нам здаєтьсья, шчо крашче говорити про Ірландіју осібно от Англіји, бо в Ірландіји треба звернути увагу не тілько на звичайні державні j господарські справи, а шче j на національні (народні) j релігійні (церковні) одліки ціјеji землі.

(From Громада, 1881)

The alphabet used dispenses with є, ї, й, щ, ю, я: є is replaced by je or ьe, ï by ji, й by j, щ by шч, ю by jу or ьу, я by ja or ьа.

Наш край, Подкарпатска Русь составляет восточну часть Чешскословенской републики. Найвысшим урядом Подкарпатской Руси есть Цивильна (гражданска) управа в Ужгородѣ, при которой суть разны отдѣлы, а то: политичный, школьный, земледѣлскій . . . .

Ja uznal, čto v Vašem sadu jest' mnoho prekrasnych ovočevych derev i Vy usilujetesja jich s velikoju starannostju v svojem selji i okolicji poširiti.

Two passages from a reader sponsored by the Czech authorities for use in Subcarpathian Ruthenia, in the 1920's. Apart from a few endings like -a for -ая, formations like политичный, and words like the now obsolete суть, there is little that could not be Russian.

Украи́на, зложивъ П. Кулъшъ. Одъ початку Вкрайны до Батька Хмельницького. Кіевъ. Въ университетской типографіи. 1846.

In this type of spelling the letters generally have their Russian values (и for i, ы for и), but й corresponds to ї and the и in зложивъ and Хмельницького has its modern Ukrainian value. The letter ъ was already pronounced i. (The second line is in Russian.)

0 GENERAL CHARACTERISTICS

Ukrainian developed as a dialect in medieval Russian along with those that gave rise to Russian proper, but it must now be regarded as an independent language. In general characteristics it does not differ from Russian (q.v.), but it does in phonology, forms and vocabulary. The differences are naturally slighter than those between Russian and the other Slavonic languages, and a knowledge of some of the regular correspondences goes some way to make Ukrainian understandable to those already familiar with Russian, viz.

Ukrainian	Russian
i in closed syllables	o/e
ї, i	e (formerly ъ)
и	ы and и
o after ж, ч, ш, щ, й	e
-в at the end of a syllable	-л
-дж-	-ж-
-ж-	-жд-
-ждж-	-зж-
x in names	ф
-ння	-ние
-ття	-тие
-ський	-ский

Another notable difference is that palatalisation of consonants (see General note on the Slavonic languages), which has been eliminated in Russian in the declension of nouns, still occurs in Ukrainian, e.g. Ru Uk рука, *hand*; locative case Ru руке, Uk руці. In vocabulary Ukrainian sometimes agrees with Polish rather than Russian.

1 BIBLIOLINGUISTICS

1.1 NAMES

1.1.1 Ukrainian names are either nouns or adjectives and are so declined. Personal names consist in full of a Christian name (ім'я), a patronymic (по батькові) and a surname (прізвище). The patronymic is frequently omitted.

1.1.2 Christian names are nouns, e.g. Семен, Василь, Олексій, Петро (4.3.1), Ївга, Марія, Мар'я (4.3.6). Not all names ending in -a and -я are borne by women: men have names of biblical or Greek origin, e.g. Микита (*Nicetas*), Лука (*Luke*), Ілля (*Elias*) or short forms such as Олекса. It should also be remembered that Ukrainians may write in Russian or appear in Russian translation, or vice versa:

the Christian names will almost certainly be converted. A useful list of corresponding forms will be found in *Словник власних імен людей* compiled by S. P. Levchenko and others (Kiev, 1972). The first edition was compiled by N. P. Dzyatkivs'ka (1954).

1.1.3 Patronymics are formed from the father's name, nearly always by adding **-ович** for men, **-івна** for women. Exceptions are:

> Петро: Петрович (final -о)
> Сава: Савич
> Ілля:Ілліч (most names in -а and -я)
> Микита: Микитович
> Яків: Яковлевич or Якович

After a vowel the feminine form is **-ївна**. If it is necessary to form patronymics (and in many Soviet books they are given only in Russian form) the above rules should be applied, but in earlier and extra-Soviet literature other forms will be found, viz. **Володаревич, Тарасевич, Войткевич** (from **Войтко**), **Васильєвич, Сергієвич**. These forms, when found, should of course be respected and transliterated (2.1.1) accordingly.

1.1.4 Surnames may be of native or foreign origin (1.1.7). Among native names are here included Russian, which in Ukrainian books have their terminations modified when necessary to conform to Ukrainian morphology and are in any case spelt in accordance with Ukrainian values, e.g. **Виссарион Григорьевич Белинский** appears as **Вісаріон Григорович Бслінський** (the Ukrainian form of the name is **Білинський**), **Хрущев** as **Хрущов**, since е is never pronounced о in Ukrainian. The first example illustrates the complications that can arise: Uk і corresponds in value to Ru и, Uk и to Ru ы, but in **Григорович** and **-кий** we have the same letter in both languages, but different values, the phonetic habits of the two languages being different. When Ukrainian surnames occur in Russian books and works of reference they are more drastically altered: **Білодід** becomes **Белодед**, **Півторадні** becomes **Полторадня**. The characteristically Ukrainian **-ів** becomes **-ов** or **-ев**, but not vice versa: Ukrainian accommodates surnames in **-ов** and **-ев** and one finds them in native authors.

Though, therefore, one may recognise known Ukrainian names in Russian dress, it is unwise for the inexperienced to try to convert any that are unfamiliar.

1.1.5 Surnames may be nouns and adjectives:

(a) Those that end in a consonant (**й** is a consonant, but see (d) below), apart from those in **-ин**, **-ів** and the like, are nouns (4.3.1), e.g. **Мамай, Шойлевич, Білодід, Оренштайн**. They have no feminine forms and when borne by women are indeclinable, e.g. **Надії Стогній**, *of Nadiya Stohnii*. They include foreign surnames and a fair number of native ones.

(b) Surnames in **-о** (especially **-енко**) and many of those in **-а** and **-я**, e.g. **Кашуба, Гребінка**, are masculine nouns. Those in **-о** are declined like masculine nouns ending in a consonant (4.3.1). If found undeclined, as in 1.2.6, they are women's names, which are not declined. Those in **-а** and **-я** are declined like feminine nouns (4.3.6).

(c) Names in **-ев, -єв, -ів, -їв, -ов, -ин, -ін, -їн** are mostly possessive adjectives by origin and derived from Christian names or professions. The feminines end in **-ева, -єва, -йова, -ьова, -ова, -ина, -іна, -їна**. Declension is given in 5.2.2. The cautions and qualifications given in the corresponding Russian section apply here also. Note also that names like **Волошин** and **Сербин** are not possessives and have no feminine. Nor are all names in **-ина** feminine possessives. They may be nouns and male surnames of type (b).

(d) Names in -ий are normally adjectives (5.2.1). The corresponding feminine form is -a. Though this is a possible noun ending, e.g. Гребінка, noun; Ліпська, adjective, the confusion between them is not likely to cause trouble unless it leads one to confuse the sex of the writer. (Names in -ій are more often type (a) nouns, but may be soft-stem adjectives (5.2.1).)

1.1.6 Both halves of a compound are appropriately declined.

1.1.7 Foreign names and Ukrainian names of foreign origin are declined like native ones if they fit the pattern. A good many of them end in a consonant and accordingly belong to type (a). Most of those that end in a vowel, e.g. Ладані, are indeclinable. The treatment of Russian names has been dealt with above; other Slavonic names may have their endings modified, Polish ones rather more so than others, e.g. **Lipiński** becomes **Липинський** and not **Ліпіньський**. See further Russian 1.1.6.

1.1.8 Names of expatriate Ukrainians are frequently given in transcription as well as in Cyrillic. As they may also occur writing in other languages and the transcriptions are not quite the standard ones given in 2.1.1, the cribs are useful, e.g. **Olexa Woropay (Олекса Воропай), Osyp Diakiv-Hornovyj (Осип Дяків-Горновий), Vasyl' Borodacz (Бородач), Donzow (Донцов).**

1.2 NAMES OF AUTHORS, EDITORS, ETC.

The ways of indicating authorship, editorship and the like are grammatically the same as Russian, where full details are given. Some Ukrainian examples follow.

1.2.1 Not every name at the head of the page is that of the author, e.g. in **Андрієві Головку: збірник**, etc., we have a Festschrift to Andrii Holovko.

1.2.2 Name in the genitive: **Переписка Михайла Драгоманова з Михайлом Павликом**, *Correspondence of Mykhailo Drahomanov with Mykhailo Pavlyk*.

1.2.3 Active verb with name in nominative: **Написав Богдан Лепкий**, *Bohdan Lepkyi wrote it*; **Виготував до друку А. Шойлевич**, *A. Shoilevych prepared it for the press*; **у розробці матеріалів брали участь: С. І. Зв'ягіна, С. Я. Локшина . . .**, *In the working up of materials took part: S. I. Zv"yagina, S. Ya. Lokshyna . . . .* (Similarly **підготував**, *prepared*; **зладив**, *arranged*; **уклав**, *prepared*, **видав**, *edited*. But see 1.6.)

1.2.4 Agent as noun, name in nominative: **Відповідальний редактор О. І. Кисельов**, *Responsible editor O. I. Kysel'ov* (Ru Kiselev); **Автори розділів** [followed by list of names], *Authors of sections . . .*; **Редакційна колегія**, *Editorial board . . .*; **Авторський колектив**, *Author collective*.

1.2.5 Activity as noun, name in genitive: **За загальною редакцією О. І. Білецького**, *Under the general editorship of O. I. Bilets'kyi*; **Упорядкування, вступна стаття і примітки М. Сиротюка**, *Arrangement, introductory essay and annotation by M. Syrotyuk*; **переклади Миколи Зерова**, *translations by Mykola Zerov*.

1.2.6 Passive participle with instrumental case: **Складання хронології і підбір документальних матеріалів проведені науковим співробітником Інституту історії Н. С. Сидоренко**, *The compilation of the chronology and selection of documentary materials conducted by N. S. Sydorenko, a member of the research staff of the Institute of History*; **написана авторським колективом у складі** (*consisting of*): **Середенко М. М.** [and other names in the nominative].

1.2.7 On corporate authors see Russian 1.2.7. Both orders are found, e.g. **Академія наук УРСР. Інститут історії**, and **Рада по вивченню продуктивних сил Української РСР Академії наук УРСР**, an awkward expression in which the first and second genitives (*of the productive powers of the Ukrainian SSR*) are part of the name of the council.

1.3 TITLES

1.3.1 What is said about Russian titles applies equally to Ukrainian ones, both straightforward ones such as **Курс історії української літературної мови,** *Course in the history of the Ukrainian literary language,* and more coloured or complicated ones such as **Про тих, хто в полі,** *About those who are in the field*; **Коли розлучаються двоє,** *When two are parted*; **Гіартія веде,** *The party leads.*

1.3.2 Where titles in both Ukrainian and Russian occur under the same heading they can be filed into one alphabetic sequence, since the letters peculiar to either alphabet have their places defined by letters common to both. But one has to decide whether to follow the Ukrainian or the Russian alphabet for the position of **ь**.

1.3.3 Titles may be grammatically affected when included in another title or sentence, e.g. **Коментар до «Кобзаря» Шевченка,** *A commentary on Shevchenko's 'Kobzar'*, but if it is in apposition to a word indicating the type of composition, it will be unaffected (see specimen).

1.4 VOLUMES AND PARTS

1.4.1 These are usually indicated by **том** and **частина** or **часть** respectively, but **частина** is sometimes found meaning *volume*, and so is **книга,** *book*.

1.4.2 Numeration is given in ordinal numbers, in words or figures, e.g. **том третій, частина 1**. The total number of volumes is stated thus: **Твори в чотирьох томах,** *Works in four volumes.*

1.5 EDITIONS

1.5.1 The usual word is **видання**, a verbal noun which also has the more general meaning *publication*. The number of copies printed is denoted by **наклад**.

1.5.2 The number is expressed either by a word or figure: **видання 2-е**; **друге видання**. Occasionally more elaborate information is given in the preface, e.g. **Оця історична студія вперше була надрукована польською мовою під заголовком Dwie chwile z dziejów porewolucyjnej Ukrainy,** *This historical study was first printed in the Polish language under the title, etc.*

Revision is indicated by a variety of terms, usually participles such as **виправлене,** *amended* (or **справлене**); **доповнене,** *enlarged*; **перероблене,** *reworked*.

1.5.3 Both **передрук** and **перевидано** (the latter meaning strictly *re-published*) are found in the case of reprints. *Offprint* is **відбиток**.

1.6 IMPRINTS

1.6.1 Publishing in the Ukraine is institutional, but most of the state presses have now short symbolic names such as **Дніпро, Наукова думка, Видавництво «Прапор»,** instead of long descriptive ones like **Державне видавництво художньої літератури,** *State publishing house for literature.* Some such names, e.g. **Молодь, Радянська школа,** had been in use long before the general change. **Наукова думка** is the present name of what was formerly **Видавництво АН УРСР,** *Press of the Ukrainian Academy of Sciences.* This in most catalogues might reasonably have its **Видавництво** omitted; **Видавництво Львівського університету,** *Lvov University Press,* had better not.

1.6.2 The long names of state and regional presses had standard abbreviations such as **Держлітвидав.** These are not predictable and should not be invented, though abbreviations for individual words can safely be used. (See also the corresponding Russian section.)

1.6.3 The publisher is now given in the nominative and so frequently is the place, though **у Львові**, *at Lvov*, and the like are not uncommon.

1.6.4 Older imprints and those in the many Ukrainian books published outside the Soviet Union show other forms and constructions, sometimes involving the genitive of the name of the press after **накладом** (*at the expense*), **видання** (*publication*), or the instrumental case after a word such as **видано** (*published*), e.g. **Срібна Сурма** (Toronto), **накладом видавничої спілки Тризуб, Вінніпег**; **видано Українською Вільною Академією Наук у США.**

1.6.5 Words from the root **друк-** indicate the printers, e.g. **у друкарні Руської ради в Чернівцях**, *at the press of Rus'ka Rada at Chernivtsi.*

1.7 SERIES

1.7.1 The titles of series, found usually at the top of the title-page or on the page opposite, are usually severely descriptive of the series as a whole, e.g. **Українська духовна бібліотека**, *Ukrainian spiritual library*; or of the items, e.g. **Наукові записки,** *Scientific papers*. Many of them are academic series and not unnaturally include the name of the institution, **Праці Українського Наукового Інституту,** *Transactions of the Ukrainian Scientific Institute*, or **Збірник Філологічної Секції Наукового Товариства імени Шевченка,** *Magazine of the Philological Section of the Shevchenko Scientific Society*, necessitating the production of headings such as **Ukrains'kyi Naukovyi Instytut** and **Naukove Tovarystvo imeny Shevchenka. Filolohichna Sektsiya.** (Both titles would have led one to expect periodicals rather than series.)

1.7.2 Numeration is varied: **том** is frequently found, sub-divided by **випуск**, which in turn is sometimes found by itself. Alternatives are **№** and **книга**. When sub-series (**серія**) are involved the numeration can be complicated, as in **Статистика України. Серія Х. Статистичні праці. т. III, вип. 3. № 165**, where it is **№ 165** which is the numeration of the whole series. Sometimes the numeration is grammatically linked to the title, e.g. **Записок б. Українського Наукового Товариства в Києві том XXIII**, i.e. **Записки, том 23.** (The abbreviation **б.** is for **бувшого**, *former.*)

1.7.3 Not every apparent series should be taken at its face value: **Видання Української Господарської Академії** even at the top of the title-page means simply *published by the Ukrainian Academy of Economics*, **видання** being singular (cf. 1.6.4); but it could mean *publications of* . . . as a plural.

1.8 PERIODICALS

1.8.1 A fair number of periodicals are published outside the Ukraine, but there is little difference in practice apart from the spelling differences mentioned in 2.7.2. Titles are linguistically straightforward, e.g. **Іноземна філологія**, *Foreign philology*, **Український історичний журнал**, *Ukrainian journal of history*, though they may be less explicit than those of books, e.g. **Дніпро, Авангард.**

1.8.2 The body responsible for institutional periodicals is frequently put at the head of the cover or title-page in the nominative, but it may be part of the title or sub-title, e.g. **Вісник Академії наук Української РСР**, *Messenger of the Academy of Sciences of the URSR*; **видання Товариства культурних зв'язків . . .**, *publication of the Society for Cultural Relations . . . .* As the names are in the genitive one will need to extract the nominatives **Академія** and **Товариство** for catalogue purposes. Alternatively it may follow some such word as **видає** (*publishes*), e.g. **Збірник видає Львівський державний університет.** Here it is once more in the nominative.

1.8.3   Indications of editorship are stereotyped. Usually there is a **редакційна колегія** (*editorial board*), less frequently **редакція**, under a chief editor (**редактор**) who may be distinguished as **головний** or **начальний** (both meaning *chief*) or **відповідальний** (*responsible*). In the case of irregular serials individual numbers may have an ad hoc editor described as **відповідальний за випуск** (*responsible for issue*). In most cases the deputy (**заступник**) is also singled out. In all cases the names are simply listed in the nominative. Less frequently the name or names, again in the nominative, may follow a verb such as **редагує** (*edits*) or **редакцію веде** (*conducts the editing*).

1.8.4   Various styles of numeration are found, the commonest being the combination of **рік** (literally *year*) or **рік видання** (*year of issue*), sometimes **річник** (*annual volume*) with some word for *part*, be it **номер** (**№**), **число** (*number*) or **книга** (*book*). Sometimes no volume number is given but only the calendar year, and alternative numeration is not uncommon. Presumably the numbers, always given in figures, are read as ordinals.

As **рік** is not infrequently combined with the calendar year, one should not be misled by expressions such as **видається з 1924 року**, *published since 1924*; **рік заснування 1927**, *year of establishment 1927*; **журнал засновано в травні 1941 р.**, *journal founded in May 1941.*

1.8.5   Statements of periodicity may be part of the sub-title, the periodical being described as **місячник, тижневик, щомісячний журнал** (*monthly, weekly, monthly journal*), or frankly **неперіодичний бюлетень** (*irregular bulletin*). Equally common are expressions with adverbs or adverbial phrases, e.g. **виходить 1-го кожного місяця, два рази на місяць, 6 разів на рік, щомісяця** or **щомісячно, щотиждня**, *comes out on the first of each month, twice a month, six times a year, monthly, weekly.*

1.8.6   Terms of subscription are often absent, there being simply a price (**ціна**) on the cover. Where given, they are stated under the rubric **передплатна ціна** or **умови передплати** and the different periods may be distinguished by adjectives agreeing with **ціна** or **передплата**, e.g. **річна, піврічна, чвертьрічна** (*annual, half-yearly, quarterly*) or the corresponding adverbs **річно**, etc. or phrases such as **на рік, на півроку**. When terms are given, the price of a single number is stated explicitly under the heading **одне число, окреме число, ціна одного номера, ціна цього числа**. (The last means: *price of this number.*)

1.8.7   In most cases the only address given is **адреса редакції**, but **редакції і адміністрації** (or without **адреса**, in the nominative) and **редакційної колегії** are also found. More elaborate instructions usually involve hortatory infinitives such as **редакційне листування та матеріали надсилати на адресу редакції**, *send editorial correspondence and materials to the editorial office*; **з-за кордону передплати пересилати на . . .**, *remit subscriptions from abroad to . . .*; **звертатися до . . .**, *apply to . . ..* The periodical **Україна** is refreshingly direct: **пишіть нам**, *write to us*, **заходьте**, *drop in*, followed by the necessary instructions.

2   ALPHABET, PHONETICS, SPELLING

2.1   ALPHABET

2.1.1   The standard alphabet and the transliteration recommended in B.S. 2979: 1958 (with the divergences of ISO/R9, 2nd edition, 1968) are given below. ISO/R9 permits two sets of deviations, in both cases as wholes, viz.

(1) the B.S. characters, where they differ;

(2) the following: *h* for **г**; *y* for **и**; *i* for **і**; *ch* for **х**.

		B.S.	ISO			B.S.	ISO			B.S.	ISO
А	а	a		Ї	ї	yi	ï	Ф	ф	f	
Б	б	b		Й	й	ĭ	j	Х	х	kh	h
В	в	v		К	к	k		Ц	ц	ts	c
Г	г	h	g	Л	л	l		Ч	ч	ch	č
[Ґ	ґ]	g	g	М	м	m		Ш	ш	sh	š
Д	д	d		Н	н	n		Щ	щ	shch	šč
Е	е	e		О	о	o		Ю	ю	yu	ju
Є	є	ye	je	П	п	p		Я	я	ya	ja
Ж	ж	zh	ž	Р	р	r			ь	ʼ	
З	з	z		С	с	s			ʼ	”	
И	и	ӯ	i	Т	т	t					
І	і	i	ī	У	у	u					

The apostrophe occurs before soft vowels, more frequently than ъ or ' in Russian. It has no effect on alphabetical order.

The British Museum has *i* as the transliteration of и, і, ї and й; the Library of Congress has *ie, ï, iu, ia* instead of *ye, yi, yu, ya*; otherwise they agree with B.S. 2979.

2.1.2 As with Russian other countries have national variants: the table given under Russian applies. In this connexion the forms used by some expatriate Ukrainians should be noted. (See 1.1.8.)

2.1.3 Loose transcriptions, especially of endings like -ський (*-sky, -ski*), are found in newspapers and books. For their rationale and the difficulties that result see Russian 2.1.3.

2.1.4 The treatment of names written in the Latin alphabet is the same in principle in Ukrainian as in Russian.

2.2 CAPITALISATION
The principles of capitalisation are the same as in Russian (q.v.); but the Ukrainian rules state that proper names used typically begin with a small letter.

2.3 DIVISION OF WORDS
2.3.1 Rules 1, 2, 3, 4, 5a or b, 6d, 7, 8 (p. xiii) apply.

2.3.2 The following points should be noted. Rule 2 applies even to words like при-йшов. Rule 3: common suffixes like -ський and -ство are kept intact, but generally speaking suffixes are less easily recognised as such than prefixes. Rules 5 and 6: ьо, йо, дх, дз are not to be divided unless the first letter is part of the prefix, e.g. най-, під-; otherwise ь, like ', belongs to the previous syllable. Double letters are divided in the middle but divisions such as -ння, -ття are permitted.

2.4 PUNCTUATION AND ABBREVIATIONS
See Russian 2.4.

2.5 HARD AND SOFT CONSONANTS; PALATALISATION
(See General note on the Slavonic languages.)

2.5.1 The quality of a consonant in Ukrainian is shown by the succeeding vowel, the series being:

Hard	а	е	и	о	у
Soft	я	є	і, ї	[ьо]	ю

or by the absence or presence of the soft sign **ь**. The corresponding vowels are found in parallel hard and soft declensions and conjugations, but the parallelism is not exact. Some endings are always soft, and **e**, though it has become hard, is the usual soft equivalent of **o**; **є** is also found, after a vowel, and so is **ьо**. The letter **ї**, which is distinguished from **i** by a palatal on-glide (compare the B.S. transliteration) is now found in the Soviet Union only initially or after vowels. The appearance of **e** and **и** in the hard series, whereas in Russian they are soft, is not an arbitrary trick of spelling, for the pronunciation has altered. The Ukrainian **i** mostly derives from an earlier **e** or **o**.

2.5.2 The consonants **ж, ч, ц, ш, щ** present peculiarities: **ж, ч, ш, щ** as hard consonants are followed by **a, e, и, o, y**; but where hard and soft declensions present an alternation of **o** and **e**, **e** is used, and similarly **i** not **и**. Nouns ending with these consonants partly belong to the soft consonant declension (4.3.1). **Ц** is usually soft, but even so is followed by **e** not **є**.

2.5.3 Palatalisation alters consonants thus:

г	д	з	зд	зг	к	с	ск	ст	т	х
з					ц					с
ж	дж	ж	ждж	ждж	ч	ш	щ	щ	ч	ш

Those in the bottom row do not occur in nouns, except in the vocative.

2.5.4 Akin to palatalisation and occurring under similar conditions are the following phenomena:

(a) the change of **б, в, м, п, ф** to **бл**, etc.

(b) the doubling of **л, н, т** and other consonants before the endings **-я, -ю**.

2.5.5 Assimilation in spelling is not practised, e.g. **розкол** as against Ru **раскол**. It is true that **c-** remains in such words as **склад** just as in Russian, though by itself and before a voiced consonant it has become **з**.

2.6 VARIATION OF VOWEL

2.6.1 An **e, є** or **o** in the last syllable of the NS may disappear when endings are added, e.g. **рядок, рядка; німець, німця; італієць, італійця**. Conversely they may have to be inserted when there is a zero ending, e.g. **яйце** GP **яєць** (as it were **яйець**); **збірка, збірок; сестра, сестер**.

2.6.2 An **o** or **e** in an open syllable may be replaced by **i** (initially **ві**) and **є** by **ї** if the syllable becomes closed, and vice versa, e.g. **слово** GP **слів; Київ, Києва**. Both changes may occur simultaneously, e.g. **отець**, GS **вітця** (2.6.1). Note that **-й** before a consonant closes a syllable: corresponding to **доходити** we have **дійти**.

2.7 SPELLING

2.7.1 Standard spelling is of comparatively recent growth, and there were a number of rival systems, some of which are illustrated in the specimens. (Some are so aberrant that it is difficult to say what is spelling and what sheer Russification.)

2.7.2 Some changes have taken place in the last generation, not all of which have been adopted outside the Ukraine. They affect **г, i, ia, iy, ï, л** and some individual words, e.g. (modern spelling first):

вагон: вагон	баланс: балянс
філологія: фільольогія	аудитор: авдитор
-ості: -ости	кафедра: катедра
соціаліст: соціяліст	хімія: хемія
тріумф: тріюмф	

Except for **фільольогія** those in the second column are still accepted abroad. The letter ï was formerly found after **д, з, л, н, с, т, ц**, e.g. **сїм**, *seven*; **лїтература**, *literature*; **нїс**, *he bore* (but **ніс**, *nose*) to denote softening of the consonant, whereas **i** simply denoted a forward vowel. The distinction is no longer reflected in spelling (2.5.1).

2.7.3 An initial **i** after a final vowel becomes, rather disconcertingly, **й**, e.g. **Українські ймена**, *Ukrainian names*.

3 ARTICLES

There are no articles.

4 NOUNS

4.1 GENDER AND FORM

There are three genders, the gender for the most part corresponding to the form of the noun. Inanimate nouns may be of any gender. Omitting the vocative there are six cases, the endings varying according to the form of the noun.

4.3 ENDINGS

4.3.1 *Masculine and neuter nouns* are the same for many of their endings. Masculine nouns mostly end in the NS in a hard or soft consonant, including **-й**; but there are many names in **-o**; neuters end in **-o**, **-e** or **-я**. (For masculines in **-a** see 4.3.6.)

Hard type

	S M	S N	P M	P N
N	-/-о	-о	-и	-а
A	As N or G	-о	As N or G	-а
G	-а/-у	-а	-ів	-
D	-ові/-у		-ам	
I	-ом		-ами	
L	-ові/-у/-*i		-ах	

Soft type

	S M	S N	P M	P N
N	-ь/-й	-е/-я	-i/-ï	-я
A	As N or G	-е/-я	As N or G	-я
G	-я/-ю	-я	-ів/ïв	-ь/ïв
D	-еві/-сві/-ю		-ям	
I	-ем/-см/-ям		-ями	
L	-еві/-сві/-i/-ï/-ю		-ях	

4.3.2 Masculine nouns in **-ж, ч, ш, щ** have hard endings except for IS **-ем**, DLS **-еві** and NP **-i**. Nouns in **-p** may be hard, soft or mixed, with LS **-е**.

4.3.3 Palatalisation (2.5.3) occurs in the LS, and variation of vowel (2.6) as between forms with or without an ending.

4.3.4 Nouns in **-анин** have NP **-ани**, GP **-ан**; neuters in **-ння** have GP **-нь**; neuters in **-м'я** now have singular cases alternatively or exclusively from the soft stem **-мень-**, e.g. GS **ім'я** or **імені** (earlier **імени**) from **ім'я**, *name*, and plural cases from the hard stem **-мен-**. Neuters in **-ття** have GP **-ть**.

4.3.5 око, [в]ухо have peculiar plural forms which are dual in origin, viz.

$$\left.\begin{array}{l}\text{оч}\\\text{уш}\end{array}\right|\text{-і, -і, -ей, -ам, -ами/-има, -ах}$$

Instead of очі, вічі is sometimes found.

4.3.6 *Feminine nouns* end in -а, -я or a soft consonant, including ж, ч, ш, щ, for which see 4.3.7. Masculine nouns in -а, -я follow the same pattern.

Hard type			Soft type		
	S	P		S	P
N	-а	-и		-я	-і/-ї
A	-у	As N or G		-ю	As N or G
G	-и	-/-ів		-і/ї	-ь/-й/-ей
D	-і	-ам		-і/ї	-ям
I	-ою	-ами		-ею/-сю	-ями
L	-і	-ах		-і/	-ях

Consonant type

	S	P
N	-ь	-і
A	-ь	As N or G
G	-і	-ей
D	-і	-ям
I	-(')ю	-ями
L	-і	-ях

4.3.7 Stems ending in -ж, ч, ш, щ, have mixed endings (see 2.5): nouns in -жа, -ча, etc. have hard endings except IS -жею, NAP -жі, etc.; those of consonant type have no soft sign in the NS and have -ам, -ами, -ах in the plural, e.g. річ, *thing*, речі, річчю (!), речам, etc.

4.3.8 Palatalisation (2.5.3) occurs in D and LS, and variation of vowel as between open and close syllables (2.6): cf. річ above and conversely гора, GP гір; and between forms with or without endings: марка, GP марок (*stamp*).

4.3.9 Мати, *mother* has AS матір, stem матер- and soft endings as in 4.3.6, except GP -ів; дитина, *child* and людина, *person* have stems діт- and люд- in the plural and endings -и, -ей, -ям, -ями, -ях.

5 ADJECTIVES

5.1 GENERAL

5.1.1 Adjectives vary according to number, gender and case, and agree with the nouns they qualify. They precede the noun.

5.1.2 Most adjectives have only long forms, some have both long and a few short forms, and some have short forms for most cases in the singular and make up with long ones for the rest.

5.1.3 One of the most important occurrences of short forms is in the surnames derived from the possessive adjectives in -ів, -ів, -ев, -ов, -св, -ін, -ін, -ин, e.g. Петрів from Петро, *Peter*. (When used as adjectives, the possessives still have short forms.) The feminine counterparts, which end in -ева, etc., are declined throughout as other adjectives (5.2.1), while names of places, e.g. Київ, Лебедин, follow the noun declension throughout.

Otherwise the short forms are used, not very consistently, as predicates.

5.2 ENDINGS

5.2.1 *Long forms*

Hard type

	S			P
	M	N	F	
N	-ий	-е	-а	-і
A	As N or G		-у	As N or G
G	-ого		-ої	-их
D	-ому		-ій	-им
I	-им		-ою	-ими
L	-ому/-ім		-ій	-их

Soft type

	S			P
	M	N	F	
N	-ій	-є	-я	-і
A	As N or G		-ю	As N or G
G	-ього		-ьої	-іх
D	-ьому		-ій	-ім
I	-ім		-ьою	-іми
L	-ьому/-ім		-ій	-іх

This declension includes a few nouns such as **лютий**, *February*.

5.2.2 *Short forms* are found for the MS, excluding the instrumental, and for the NSN. The NSM has no ending, the remaining masculine endings are the same as those of nouns (4.3.1); the neuter ends in -o or -e. Where there is no short form, the long form is used instead.

5.3 COMPARISON

5.3.1 The comparative is formed by substituting -(і)ший for the -ий, -кий, -окий of the positive. By assimilation г + ш, ж + ш, з + ш = жч; к + ш = щ, e.g. **дорогий**, *dear*, **дорожчий**, *dearer*.

5.3.2 For the superlative **най-** is added, as a prefix, to the comparative.

5.3.3 Irregular comparatives (and superlatives) such as **кращий**, **найкращий**, *better*, *best* are given separately in the dictionary.

5.4 POSSESSIVES

Наш, ваш are declined as in 5.2.1. The remainder, **мій, твій, свій, чий**, have stems **мо-, тво-, сво-, чи-** and endings similar or identical with those of soft adjectives, viz.

мо-, тво-, сво-   **чи-**

	S			P	
	M	N	F	As 5.2.1 (soft)	As 5.2.1 (soft)
N	(мій, etc.)	-є	-я		except
A	As N or G		-ю		GM -його F -єї
D	-єму		-ій		DMN -єму/-йому
G	-го		-єї		IF -єю
I	-ім		-єю		
L	-єму/-ім		-ій		

6 NUMERALS

6.1 CARDINAL

6.1.1

1 один	11 одинадцять	21 двадцять один	300 триста
2 два	12 дванадцять	30 тридцять	400 чотириста
3 три	13 тринадцять	40 сорок	500 п'ятсот,
4 чотири	14 чотирнадцять	50 п'ятдесят	1000 тисяча
5 п'ять	15 п'ятнадцять	60 шістдесят	
6 шість	16 шістнадцять	70 сімдесят	
7 сім	17 сімнадцять	80 вісімдесят	
8 вісім	18 вісімнадцять	90 дев'яносто	
9 дев'ять	19 дев'ятнадцять	100 сто	
10 десять	20 двадцять	200 двісті	

6.1.2 один–чотири are adjectives.

один, одна, одно is declined as in 5.2.1, but has alternative forms GSF однієї, ISF однією.

два, три, чотири, п'ять:

G	двох	трьох	чотирьох	п'яти/п'ятьох
D	двом	трьом	чотирьом	п'яти/п'ятьом
I	двома	трома	чотирма	п'ять(о)ма
L	As G			

The rest of the numerals below 100, except 40 and 90, decline like п'ять.

сто   A сто   GDIL ста   (Similarly сорок and дев'яносто)
двісті   G двохсот   D двомстам   I двомастами   L двохстах
300–900 are similarly declined
1000 is a feminine noun (4.3.6)

6.1.3 With два, три, чотири the following noun is in the same case as the numeral. With all other simple numerals the noun is in the GP if the numeral is in the nominative, but if the numeral is in any other case the following noun agrees with it, e.g. два томи, в двох томах, десять томів, в десяти томах.

6.2 ORDINAL

6.2.1

1 перший	8 восьмий	50, etc. п'ятдесятий, etc.
2 другий	9 дев'ятий	100 сотий
3 третій	10 десятий	200 двохсотий
4 четвертий	11–19 одинадцятий, etc.	300 трьохсотий
5 п'ятий	20 двадцятий	900 девятисотий
6 шостий	30 тридцятий	1000 тисячний
7 сьомий	40 сороковий	

6.2.2 третій, третє, третя is a soft adjective, the rest are hard (5.2.1).

6.2.3 In compound ordinals only the last element has the form of an ordinal, e.g. сто перший, *101st*.

6.3 FIGURES

Plain arabic numerals stand for cardinals, ordinals being represented by roman figures, by plain arabic numerals, or by the addition of the appropriate ending to the arabic, e.g. **XXI з'їзд**, *21st congress*; **кінець 18–1-а половина 19 ст.**, *the end of the 18th–first half of the 19th century*.

6.4 DATES

6.4.1 The months are:

> **січень, лютий, березень, квітень, травень, червень,**
> **липень, серпень, вересень, жовтень, листопад, грудень**

For declension see 4.2.1, except for **лютий**, which has the form of a hard adjective (5.2.1).

6.4.2

> *1 May* is translated **Перше травня**
> *On 5.iv.1962*: **п'ятого квітня тисяча дев'ятсот шістдесят другого року**
> **1848 p.** is read **тисяча вісімсот сорок восьмий рік**
> **в 1848 p.: в ... восьмому році**
> **початки 20-х (двадцятих) років**: *the beginning of the 20's*

On expressions such as **1848–1948** and **революція 1905–1907 pp.** see Russian 6.4.2. The same considerations apply.

7 PRONOUNS

7.1 DEMONSTRATIVE, INDEFINITE

7.1.1 Demonstratives, interrogatives, relatives and indefinites have much the same case endings as adjectives, the long forms of which incorporate a pronoun. Note:

> **той, та, те**, *that*: alternative GSF **тієї**, ISF **тією**, otherwise like a hard adjective (5.2.1)
> **(о)цей, це, ця**, *this*: ISM **(о)цим**, GSF **(о)цієї**, ISF **(о)цією**, otherwise like an adjective (5.2.1), soft in the singular, hard in the plural
> **весь (увесь, ввесь)**, *all*: GSF **всієї**, ISF **всією**, LP **всіма**; otherwise like a soft adjective (5.2.1) with stem **вс-** or **ус-**

7.1.2 **Дехто, ніхто, дещо, ніщо** are compounds of **хто** and **що** (7.2), and so, with invariable suffixes, are words like **хтось**, *somebody*; **щобудь**, *anything*. **Кимсь**, from **хтось**, sometimes has the form **кимось**; similarly **чимсь**.

The compounds **ніхто, ніщо** may be split by a preposition, e.g. **ні з ким**, *with nobody*.

7.2 RELATIVE, INTERROGATIVE

> **хто**, *who?*: **кого**, etc.
> **що**, *what?*: **чого**, etc.
> **що** is also used as an indeclinable relative, and may then be combined with the 3rd person pronoun, e.g. **пропаганда, що її проводять**, *propaganda which they conduct*.

7.3 PERSONAL
7.3.1

	S 1	S 2	S & P R	P 1	P 2
N	я	ти	—	ми	ви
AG	мене	тебе	себе	нас	вас
D	мені	тобі	собі	нам	вам
I	мною	тобою	собою	нами	вами
L	мені	тобі	собі	нас	вас

себе, *self* refers to all persons and both numbers.

7.3.2 він, вона, воно, *he, she, it*, P вони, has oblique cases from another root:

	S MN	S F	P
AG	його, нього	її, неї	їх, них
D	йому	їй	їм
I	ним	нею	ними
L	ньому, нім	ній	них

8 VERBS

8.1 GENERAL
The general characteristics of the verb are the same as in Russian.

8.2 PRESENT AND FUTURE
8.2.1 The present is formed from the imperfective stems and the future from the perfective ones, the endings being the same. (The symbol P below refers simply to the forms.)

I	-у/-ю, -еш, -е; -емо, -ете, -уть/-ють
II	-ю, -сш, -с; -смо, -сте, -ють
IIIa	-[л]ю/-у, -иш, -ить; -имо, -ите, -[л]ять/-ать
IIIb	-ю, -іш, -іть; -імо, -іте, -ять

8.2.2 *Relation to infinitive*

P	-аю	-ію	-ую	-юю	-лю (I)	-[л]ю (III)
I	-ати	-іти, -іяти	-увати	-ювати	-лоти	-ити (8.2.3)

P	-рю	-ну	-джу, -жу, -чу, -шу, -щу	-у (I)
I	-рати	-нути	See 8.2.3	See 8.2.4

8.2.3 Verbs with presents in **-джу**, etc. mostly have infinitives with the corresponding unpalatalised consonants (2.5.3). This is always true of verbs of type I, e.g. пишу, пише, infinitive писати, *write*. The present is palatalised throughout. Type III verbs usually have palatalisation only in 1PS, e.g. ходжу, ходить, etc., I ходити, *go*; but люблю, любить has 3PP люблять, I любити, *love* (2.5.4). Some, however, like держу, are palatalised throughout, including the infinitive, which ends in **-ати**, viz. держати.

8.2.4 *Some peculiar stems*

P	беру	веду	везу	візьму	даю	живу	іду
I	брати	вести	везти	взяти	дати	жити	іти

P	іду	кладу	можу	несу	почну	стану	
I	їхати	класти	могти	нести	почати	стати	

P	сяду	умру	шлю	-німу, -йму	-паду	
I	сісти	умерти	слати	-няти	-пасти	

8.2.5 *Irregularities*

дам, даси, дасть; дамо, дасте, дадуть (future) from дати

їм, їси, їсть; їмо, їсте, їдять from їсти

хочу, хоч(еш), хоче; хочемо, хоч(е)те, хочуть from хотіти

8.2.6 The future imperfective is basically a compound tense. See 8.10.

8.3 PAST

8.3.1 This tense is a participle in form, having two numbers and three genders, but no distinction of persons, viz.

	S		P
M	N	F	
-в/-	-ло	-ла	-ли

Where there is no ending in the masculine, the alternation between e/o and i (2.6.2) may occur, e.g. ріс, росли.

8.3.2 *Relation to infinitive*

Substitute -ти for -в, etc. Where there is no ending add -ти or -нути (with vowel change, e.g. ніс, нести, as above) and see table below.

P	вів, вело	їв	ішов(-йшов)	клав	-пав
I	вести	їсти	іти(-йти)	класти	-пасти

8.5 FUTURE
See 8.2 and 8.10.

8.10 COMPOUND TENSES

8.10.1 *Future imperfective*

Formed either by буду (8.17) plus the imperfective infinitive or by -му, -меш, -ме; -мемо, -мете, -муть added to the infinitive.

8.11 INFINITIVE

The infinitive ends in -ти. Instructions for deriving it are given in other sections.

8.12/8.13 PARTICIPLES AND GERUNDS

8.12.1 *Present active participle:* -чий; *gerund* -чи

8.12.2 *Past active gerund:* -вши, got by adding -ши to the past (8.3.1)

8.12.3 *Past passive participle:* -ний, -тий

P	I
-аний	-ати
-ений	-ти, -(л)оти, -(р)оти, -(н)ути
-*ений	-ити
-тий	-ти

8.12.4 The participles are adjectives and similar in their behaviour to the corresponding Russian ones, except that a neuter passive participle can have an object (cf. 1.8.4). The gerunds are adverbial.

8.14/8.15   REFLEXIVE AND PASSIVE

8.14.1 Reflexive forms are got by adding -сь/-ся to the active, or -ться after -e and -є. Besides the basic reflexive meaning, e.g. показуватися, *to show oneself*, they may indicate reciprocity (сперечатися, *to argue*) or may be used for the passive (8.14.2); or the reflexive form may simply have a meaning of its own, as in намагатися, *to try*.

8.14.2 The passive, if not avoided, is expressed by reflexive forms or passive participles, e.g. друкується, *is (being) printed*; студія була надрукована, *the study was printed*; but видає Львівський університет, where we should say *published by the University of Lvov*.

8.17   THE VERB бути, *to be*

    Present: є for all persons and numbers
    Future: буду (8.1.1, type I)
    Past: S був, було, була; P були
    Gerund: present будучи; *past* бувши

8.23   PREFIXES

Many Ukrainian verbs begin with prefixes, some of which simply indicate the perfective aspect (see General note on the Slavonic languages). To assist in disentangling some of these verbs, especially short or irregular ones, a list of these prefixes is given here: в-, ви-, від-, ді-, до-, з-, за-, зо-, на-, над-, о-, об(i)-, пере-, перед-, під-, по-, пред-, при-, про-, роз-, с-, у-.

9   ADVERBS

9.1/9.2   FORMATION AND COMPARISON

Most adjectives make adverbs in -o or -e. Comparatives in -iший have the adverbs in -iше or -iш. Adjectives in -ський have compound adverbs in по- ——ськи or по- ——ському. Adverbs formed from the oblique cases of nouns or pronouns, with or without a prefixed preposition, e.g. зовсім, *altogether*, are mostly entered separately in the dictionary.

9.3   MEANINGS

Those who operate on the basis of a knowledge of Russian may find this list of common but not easily recognisable adverbs useful: вельми, *very*; де, *where*; коли, *when*; майже, *almost*; незабаром, *soon*; ніколи, *never*; скрізь, *everywhere*; сьогодні, *today*; тоді, *then*; щойно, *just*.

10   PREPOSITIONS

These behave generally as in Russian, and if account is taken of the phonetic changes mentioned in 0.1, many of them can be recognised from a knowledge of Russian.

The following may give trouble: **біля**, *beside*; **від** = Ru от; **з** = Ru из or с; **край**, *by*; **крізь**, *through*; **опріч**, *except*; **повз**, *past*; **у** = Ru у or в before a consonant; **уздовж**, *along.*

11 CONJUNCTIONS

These have no grammatical peculiarities. Some of them are not easily recognised even with a knowledge of Russian and the following short list may be useful: **але**, *but*; **ба**, *even*; **бо**, *because*; **буцім**, *as if*; **коли**, *if; when*; **мов**, *like*; **наче, неначе**, *like*; **ніби**, *as if*; **поки**, *until*; **проте**, *however*; **та**, *and, but*; **якщо**, *if.*

GLOSSARY

авторське право, *copyright*

безплатно, *free*
бібліотека, *library* (1.7.1)
бібліотекар, *librarian*
брошура, *pamphlet, paperback*

вибраний, *selected*
виготував, *prepared*
видав, *edited* (1.2.3), *published*
видавництво, *publishing house* (1.6.1)
видання, *edition* (1.5.1), *publication*
  (1.6.4, 1.7.3, 1.8.2)
виправлений, *corrected* (1.5.2)
випуск, *issue* (1.7.2)
виходити, *to come out*
відбиток, *offprint*
вірш, *verse*
вісник, *bulletin* (*messenger*) (1.8.2)
вісті, *news*
вклад, *contribution*
вступ, *introduction*
вступна стаття, *introductory essay* (1.2.5)

готовий, *ready*

далі буде, *to be continued*
дарунок автора, *with the author's
  compliments*
двотижневий, *fortnightly*
дивись, *see*
довідник, *reference book*
додатковий, *additional*
додаток, *supplement, appendix*
доповідь, *report*
доповнений, *enlarged* (1.5.2)

дослідження, *research*
друкарня, *printer's* (1.6.5)
друкується, *being printed*

журнал, *journal*

замовлення, *order*
записки, *papers, communications*
збірка, *collection*
збірник, *collective work, magazine*
  (1.2.1, 1.7.1, 1.8.2)
зібрання, *collection*
з'їзд, *congress*
зладив, *arranged* (1.2.3)
знижка, *discount*

квартальний, *quarterly*
книга, *book* (1.4.1, 1.8.4)
за кордоном, *abroad*
з-за кордону, *from abroad*

лист, *letter*

місячник, *monthly*
множний апарат, *duplicator*

надсилати, *to send* (1.8.7)
наклад, *expense* (1.6.4); *impression* (1.5.1)
написати, *to write* (1.2.3, 1.2.6)
нарис, *essay*
народився, *was born*
невиданий, *unpublished*
новий, *new*

обмін, *exchange*
один, окремий, *single* (1.8.6)

GRAMMATICAL INDEX: WORDS

GRAMMATICAL INDEX: ENDINGS

POLISH

SPECIMEN

Niniejsze wydanie *Dzieł wszystkich* Adama Mickiewicza ma być w zamiarze jego edytorów wydaniem krytycznym, czyli ma uczynić zadość dwom zasadniczym postulatom. Po pierwsze — na podstawie przekazów o możliwie najwyższym stopniu autentyczności ustalić poprawny tekst dzieł Mickiewicza; po drugie zestawić dokumentację, która by jak najwierniej i jak najpełniej odtwarzała sam proces twórczy powstawania utworów poety, a więc historię poszczególnych przekazów tekstu i pracę autora zarówno nad jego kształtowaniem do chwili ogłoszenia dzieła, jak i nad dalszym jego doskonaleniem w kolejnych wydaniach za życia autora.

The present edition of the Complete works *of Adam Mickiewicz is intended by its editors to be a critical edition, that is to satisfy two fundamental postulates. First—on the basis of documents of the highest possible degree of authenticity to establish the correct text of the works of Mickiewicz; secondly to put together documentation which would reproduce as accurately and as fully as possible the actual creative process of the formation of the compositions of the poet, and consequently the history of the individual documents of the text and the work of the author both in its formation from the moment of publication of the work and also in its protracted improvement in successive editions during the author's lifetime.*

0 GENERAL CHARACTERISTICS

0.1 DEGREE OF INFLEXION
The language is synthetic, with a rich system of declensions.

0.2 ORDER OF WORDS
Qualifiers sometimes precede and sometimes follow the words they qualify: adjectives may do either; genitives follow; in title-page Polish the object and other complements of the verb often precede it, e.g. **wstępem opatrzył**, *he furnished with an introduction*, and the subject follows it (cf. 1.2.2).

0.4 RELATION TO OTHER LANGUAGES
Polish has a fair number of learned words derived from **Greek** and **Latin**, e.g. **ekonomiczny**, **literacki**, **biblioteka**, **publikacja**; but for the most part the vocabulary is peculiarly Slavonic, the kinship with other Indo-European languages being rather of interest to the philologist than of help to the ordinary student.

Q

1 BIBLIOLINGUISTICS

1.1 NAMES

Polish names are either nouns or adjectives in form, or a mixture of both, and they are declined as such when occasion arises. Christian names are almost all nouns. Details of declension are given in 4.3, 5.2.

1.1.2 Male surnames may be:

(a) masculine adjectives, e.g. **Lipski**;

(b) masculine nouns, e.g. **Tyszkiewicz, Sinko**;

(c) mixed types, e.g. **Gosiów, Batory**.

Names like **Gosiów**, which in origin are possessive adjectives, are declined like nouns but have corresponding feminines which have adjectival endings; **Batory** has some noun endings and some adjectival ones.

1.1.3 Formerly all female surnames were adjectival, there being, as there still are, feminine forms of adjectival names, e.g. **Lipska, Gosiowa**, and adjectival suffixes that were added to masculine nouns, e.g. **Tyszkiewiczowa** (wife), **Tyszkiewiczówna** (daughter). The endings -owa, ówna are now obsolescent in Poland, the usual practice being to give the Christian name in full and decline it, but to make the surname invariable, e.g. **Irena** (etc.) **Majchrzak**. (But plain **Majchrzakowa** occurs elsewhere in the same book.)

1.1.4 Names of the **Gosiów/Gosiowa** type can give rise to ambiguity, for the genitive of **Gosiów** is also **Gosiowa**. As authors' and editors' name appear sometimes in the nominative (1.2.2) and sometimes in the genitive (1.2.5), it is necessary to make sure which construction is being used.

1.1.5 Surnames have plural forms, which are used when both writers are of the same family. Unfortunately these forms are ambiguous: **A. i F. Lipscy** may represent A. Lipski and F. Lipski, A. Lipski and F. Lipska, A. Lipska and F. Lipski, for where one noun is masculine the common adjective is masculine too. Similarly **Tyszkiewiczowie** may represent various combinations of Tyszkiewicz with Tyszkiewiczowa and Tyszkiewiczówna.

1.1.6 It is also worth noting that diacritical marks may be omitted in popular works in other languages published outside Poland. This applies particularly to names in -iński and -sław.

1.1.7 In compound names both parts are usually declined, e.g. **Vrtela-Wierczyńskiego** (4.3; 5.2), but sometimes only the last, e.g. **ministrowi Swiatopołk-Mirskiemu**.

1.2 NAMES OF AUTHORS, EDITORS, ETC.

1.2.1 The names of personal authors are usually put at the top of the title-page in the nominative and can then be adopted without alteration as the heading for cataloguing.

1.2.2 Less frequently in the case of authors but quite commonly with editors and translators the names follow the title or may appear on the back of the title-page preceded by an active verb, e.g. **napisał**, *wrote*; **wydał Dr Henryk Biegeleisen**, *Dr Henryk Biegeleisen edited*; **przejrzała i uzupełniła Helena Lipska**, *H. L. revised and supplemented*; **zebrali i opracowali Stanisław Kalabiński i Feliks Tych**, *S. K. and F. T. collected and edited*; **tłumaczyła A. Gosiowa**, *A. Gosiowa translated*. The form of the name is not affected by the construction but the verbs agree in gender and number (8.3.1): **zebrali** is plural and would look odd if followed by only one name.

1.2.3 Also in the nominative are names which follow a noun denoting an agent, a construction usually to be found in the case of collective works (1.2.7).

1.2.4 Collected works, correspondence and the like may have the author's name in the genitive immediately after the title, e.g. **Dzieła Wincentego Pola**, *Works of Wincenty Pol*; **Listy Jędrzeja Śniadeckiego do ks. Adama Czartoryskiego**, *Letters of Jędrzej Sniadecki to Count Adam Czartoryski.*

1.2.5 The genitive is also found after nouns denoting the activity of the editor or translator, e.g. **pod redakcją Celiny Bobińskiej**, *under the editorship of Celina Bobińska*; **z wstępem i komentarzem Tadeusza Sinki**, *with introduction and commentary of Tadeusz Sinko*; **przekład Henryka Bielskiego**, *translation of* (i.e. by) *Henryk Bielski.*

1.2.6 Less frequently a passive participle is used, followed by **przez** and the genitive, e.g. **tłumaczone przez A. Gosiowa**, *translated by A. Gosiów* (contrast 1.2.2).

1.2.7 A team of authors is often simply listed but if they are numerous the place of the names may be taken by **PRACA ZBIOROWA**. This is not, as might be thought, a feminine name but means *Collective work.* Collaboration among editors may be indicated by **Kollegium redakcyjne**, *editorial board*, followed by names in the nominative, or may be expressed in somewhat more complicated phrases: e.g. **w zespole pod kierownictwem Marii Stokowej opracowali Zofia Biłek, Maria Kukulska i Roman Loth**, *Z.B., M.K., and R.L. edited in a team under the direction of Maria Stokowa*; **w opracowaniu tego tomu uczęstniczyli** (names in nominative), *in the preparation of this volume there participated* . . . .

1.2.8 The presence of the name of an institution at the head of the title-page may indicate authorship or simply sponsorship. Names of branches and departments usually precede the name of the main body, which will either be in the genitive, e.g. **Wydział Historii Partii Polskiej Zjednoczonej Partii Robotniczej**, *Department of Party History of the Polish United Workers' Party*, or be joined by a preposition, e.g. **Rada Ekonomiczna przy Radzie Ministrów**, *Economic Council under the Council of Ministers*; but both may be in the nominative, with the name of the branch second, e.g. **Polska Zjednoczona Partia Robotnicza, Wydział Historii Partii**, as in English catalogues. The other example above would become **Rada Ministrów. Rada Ekonomiczna**. A number of institutions are named after persons, e.g. **Zakład Naukowy im(ienia) Ossolińskich**, *Ossoliński Scientific Institute*. In more elaborate names the **imienia**-element might well be omitted in the catalogue.

1.3 TITLES

1.3.1 The great majority, fiction apart, consist of nouns and adjectives in the nominative and other cases with or without prepositions, e.g. **Problemy handlu zagranicznego Polski**, *Problems of the foreign trade of Poland*; **Walki chłopów Królestwa Polskiego w rewolucji**, *Struggle of the peasants of the Polish Kingdom in the revolution.* More complicated ones involving verbs, adverbs and pronouns occur in persuasive and instructional material: **Ku czemu idzie „Mała Europa"**, *Where is 'Little Europe' going?*; **Co to są budżety rodzinne**, *What are family budgets?*; **Jak czytać liczby statystyczne**, *How to read statistical tables.* The infinitive is not uncommon in exhortations.

1.3.2 Title entries of the Anglo-American type present no problems. There are no articles to be ignored in filing. Those following British Museum rules will need to find the nominative of nouns (4.3) or their translation if accompanied by national adjectives. This is not very difficult, but it would be prudent to check with the dictionary.

1.3.3 When quoted in a sentence the main noun in a title often appears in an oblique case. e.g. **nowe wydanie „Gramatyki języka polskiego"**, *new edition of 'Gramatyka języka polskiego'*. It is also possible to isolate the title grammatically from the rest of the sentence as in **w wydaniu Z. B. Swietosławskiego** *Lud Polski w Emigracji*, *in the publication by Z. B. Swietoslawski 'Lud Polski w Emigracji'*. Here **wydaniu** has the necessary case-ending, so there is no need to alter **Lud Polski**. (On **wydanie** see 1.5, 1.6.)

1.4 VOLUMES AND PARTS

1.4.1/1.4.2 These are usually indicated by **tom** and **część** respectively, often with the numeration in words, e.g. **Tom pierwszy**, *Volume 1*; **Trzecia część**, *Part 3*.

1.4.3 The numeration is sometimes combined grammatically with the title, as in **Część III Dzienników** (=Dzienniki. Part 3).

1.4.4 A work in several volumes may have a second title-page on which the number of volumes of the completed work is indicated in some such phrase as **W czterech tomach**, *In four volumes*. Failing this, information may be found at the beginning or end of the preface, e.g. **Wydanie ukazuje się w pięciu tomach**, *The edition appears in 5 volumes*; **Tom niniejszy zamyka czterotomowe wydawnictwo**, *The following volume concludes the four-volume publication*, though in fact a supplement (**uzupełnienie**) appeared, numbered **tom V**.

1.5 EDITIONS

1.5.1 The standard word is **wydanie**, which normally means *edition*, but in other contexts may have the more general sense *publication*, especially when used as a verbal noun (see 1.6). **Druk**, which means *printing*, is not uncommon; **nakład**, which *inter alia* means *impression*, e.g. **nakład 10,000 egz.**, *10,000 copies printed*, occurs in the phrase **nakład ograniczony**, *limited edition*.

1.5.2 Revision is indicated by a variety of words, e.g. **dopełnione**, *supplemented*; **poprawione**, *corrected*; **przejrzane, przerobione**, *revised*; **rozszerzone**, *enlarged*; **uporządkowane, uzupełnione**, *supplemented*. Other words such as **kieszonkowe**, *pocket*; **masowe**, *for the masses*; **zbiorowe**, *collected*, indicate special sorts of editions.

1.5.3 Reprints are indicated by **przedruk**, e.g. **przedruk fotooffsetowy z wydania 1891 r.**, *photo-offset reprint from the edition of 1891*. Offprint is **nadbitka**.

1.6 IMPRINTS

1.6.1 As a rule the imprint of a modern book causes little difficulty, both the press and the place being given in the nominative. Most presses are institutional, e.g. **Państwowe Wydawnictwo Naukowe**, *State Scientific Press*; some are known by the names of periodicals; while others have arbitrary names such as **Książka i Wiedza**, *Book and Learning*. (For corporate names including **imienia** see 1.1).

1.6.2 The name of the press may appear in the genitive, preceded by **nakład(em)** or **wydanie**, here equivalent to *published by*. In reproducing the imprint one must either retain these words or turn the genitive into a nominative. The word **wydawnictwo** is ambiguous; it can mean either *publication* or *press*, e.g. **Nakładem Wydawnictwa „Prasa Krajowa"**, *published by 'Prasa Krajowa' Press*, but **wydawnictwo autora**, *published by the author* (not necessarily directly).

The original meaning of **nakład** is *expense*, and it properly indicates the person who takes the commercial risk, whereas **wydanie** indicates the person who initiates publication, e.g. **Własność i wydanie rodziny . . . Nakładem F. A. Richtera**, i.e. *Published by F. A. Richter for the family. . . Copyright by the family*. It occurs also in the phrases **nakład autora**, *published by the author* and **nakładem własnym**, *at his own expense*, i.e. privately printed. In derivatives the root simply means *to publish*, e.g. S(pół)ka **nakładowa**, *publishing company* (cf. also 1.5).

1.6.3 The use of **nakład(em)** is commoner in older imprints, in which personal names of publishers occur, e.g. **Gebethner i Wolff**, *G. and W.*; **nakładem Zygmunta Czaczki**, *published by Zygmunt Czaczko*. It should be noted that many masculine names in the genitive (e.g. after **nakład, wydanie** or **wydawnictwo**) have similar forms to feminine nominatives. Usually the context makes it clear, but after **wydawnictwo** one may have either a genitive, of a person or society, or a noun in apposition in the nominative (1.6.2).

1.6.4 Besides the publisher, proximate or remote, both the printer and the principal distributor may be named in the imprint. The printer is indicated by such words as **drukarnia (w drukarni, z drukarni), drukiem, czcionkami**, all followed by the genitive. Sometimes the printer is explicitly stated to be the publisher (**nakładem i drukiem**) and in the 19th century, if not later, may be so even when it is not so stated. The distributor is introduced by **skład główny (składy główne)**, *principal depot(s)*, either followed directly by a name, e.g. **Skład główny E. Wende i Ska**, or more often by the preposition **w**, e.g. **w księgarniach Gebethnera i Spółki**, *in the bookshops of Gebethner and Co.*; **w administracji „Prawdy"**, *at the office of 'Prawda'*.

1.6.5 Frequently in older books and occasionally today the place of publication is preceded by the preposition **w(e)**, e.g. **w Warszawie, we Lwowie** instead of the more usual **Warsawa, Lwów**.

1.7 SERIES

1.7.1 The names of series are given sometimes at the head of the title-page, sometimes on the half-title or occasionally on the back of the title-leaf, in much the same way as in English books, or even at the bottom of the page. They are usually severely descriptive, in the plural, e.g. **Wydawnictwa Instytutu Bałtyckiego**, *Publications of the Baltic Institute*; **Studya Ekonomiczno-Społeczne**, *Socio-Economic Studies*; or in the collective singular, e.g. **Biblioteczka Uniwersytetów Narodowych**, *Little Library of the Popular Universities*. More evocative titles, such as **Życie**, *Life*, **Polska w postęp**, *Poland on the move*, are rarer.

In the catalogue the first example could be shortened to **Wydawnictwa**, since the name of the institute will already have been given; but the occurrence of **wydawnictwo** (on which see 1.6) does not prove the existence of a series collectively entitled **Wydawnictwa**.

1.7.2 Series may be divided into sub-series, indicated by **seria**, e.g. **Seria: Sprawy Morskie** (*Maritime Questions*) or in one continuous expression, **Seria ekonomicznych nauk**, *Economic sciences series*.

Numeration is usually by **zeszyt**, but **tom** and **numer (nr.)** separately or in combination are not unknown.

1.8 PERIODICALS

1.8.1 The titles of periodicals (**czasopisma**) do not differ, linguistically, from those of books and series, e.g. **Państwo i Prawo**, *State and Law*; **Język polski**, *The Polish language*; **Kwartalnik Historyczny**, *Historical Quarterly*; **Wśród ludzi**, *Among the People*; though naturally periodicals more often have fanciful titles, such as **Sfinks**, than do books. Institutional periodicals will often have the name of the institution in the genitive.

When the title forms part of a phrase, one or more of the nouns may be put into an oblique case, e.g. **Treść numeru I „Państwa i Prawa"**, *Contents of no. I of 'Państwo i Prawo'*.

1.8.3 Editorship is almost invariably indicated by some form of the root **redak-**, e.g. **redaktor naczelny**, *editor-in-chief*; **pod redakcją**, *under the editorship* (cf. 1.1.2); **komitet redakcyjny, rada redakcyjna**, *editorial committee.*

1.8.4 Numeration of volumes is by **rok, rocznik** (*year, annual volume*) or **tom**, that of parts by **zeszyt** or **numer**, which are sometimes used indifferently in the same periodical. Occasionally the number in the whole run, e.g. **ogólnego zbioru tom XLV**, is given as well.

1.8.5 **Rocznik** is also one of a series of nouns indicating periodicity: **dziennik, tygodnik, miesięcznik, kwartalnik** (*daily, weekly, monthly, quarterly*), which sometimes form an essential part of the title, sometimes only of the description. (**Dziennik** also means *diary*.) The corresponding adjectives, ending in -ny, and adverbs in -nie also occur, as well as more complicated indications such as **Wychodzi w 5-arkuszowych zeszytach 5 razy rocznie**, *Comes out in parts of 5 gatherings 5 times a year*. (Such indications of bulk are not uncommon.)

1.8.6 Details of subscription (**prenumerata, cena prenumeraty**) are often given for various periods, using the adverbs of periodicity given above (+**półrocznie**, *half-yearly*); but single numbers (**numery, zeszyty, egzemplarze**) are usually obtainable (**do nabycia**), both back numbers (**zaległe, zdezaktualizowane**) and current (**bieżące**). Foreign subscriptions are naturally higher (**droższa, drożej**).

2 ALPHABET, PHONETICS, SPELLING

2.1 ALPHABET

2.1.1 The letters, each with its own alphabetical order, are:

a ą b c ć d e ę f g h i j k l ł m n ń o ó p q

r s ś t u v w x y z ź ż

Ą, Ň, Ž, ž are occasional variants of Ą, Ń, Ż, ż respectively.

2.1.2 In the past the order of ź and ż was sometimes reversed, or some or all of the distinctions between accented and unaccented letters might be ignored, as they are today in some indexes. According to the strict rule, however, each of the above letters is distinct: thus **spółka** will come after **spożycie** in the dictionary. When some forms of the same word have the accent and others not, it is very easy to forget this.

2.2 CAPITALISATION

2.2.1 The general rule is that all proper names have capital letters. These may be names of persons, natives of countries, feasts and festivals, titles of books and periodicals, geographical, astronomical and topographical names, and names of institutions.

2.2.2 Epithets attached to personal names have an initial capital, except for prepositions, e.g. **Aleksander Macedoński, Jędrzej z nad Rzeki. Bóg**, *God*, has a capital.

2.2.3 Names for the inhabitants of towns do not have a capital, so that **rzymianin**, *Roman*, may have one or not according to its meaning.

2.2.4 Possessive adjectives in -ów, -owy, -in, -yn, -owski have capitals.

2.2.5 All parts of periodical titles, if not grammatically subordinate, have capitals except conjunctions and prepositions (cf. 1.8.1); but only the first word of book-titles. **Nowy Testament** is an exception.

2.2.6 Names of countries, e.g. **Stany Zjednoczone Ameryki Północnej** (*U.S.A.*), have capitals throughout but names of common geographical features such as **góra** (*moun-*

tain), **jezioro** (*lake*) as parts of names have a capital only if they are determined by a noun in the genitive or by an adjective. **Ulica** (*street*) is always written small.

2.2.7 Names of historical events, e.g. **traktat versalski**, days of the week and months, ·and words like **prezydent, mahometanin, dekabrysta**, do not have capitals.

2.3 DIVISION OF WORDS

2.3.1 Rules 1, 2, 4, 5b, 6c (p. xiii) apply.

2.3.2 Many consonant combinations may begin a word in Polish that would be inadmissible in English; in fact unless the first consonant is **j, l, m, n** or **r**, or the letter is doubled, it is nearly always safe to take all the consonants over. Most English catalogues, however, admit divisions such as **jeź-dzić**, and they are not unknown in Polish books.

2.3.3 Note that **ch, cz** and **sz** represent single sounds and must not on any account be divided, e.g. **u-cho, u-szy**. So usually does **rz**, e.g. **któ-rzy**. Nor should **i** be separated from a following vowel: **bia-ły** not **bi-ały**.

2.5 HARD AND SOFT CONSONANTS; PALATALISATION

2.5.1 Consonant variation in different forms of the same word can be puzzling at first. A consonant may be hard, as in English, or soft, with a slight y-sound attaching to it or blending with it. Softness is usually indicated simply by a following **i** or an acute accent, but **d, ł** and **t** have as soft varieties **dzi (dź), l** and **ci (ć)**. If the following vowel is **i** the consonant is automatically soft, hard consonants being followed by **y**: **ba** (hard), **bia** (soft); **by** (hard), **bi** (soft).

2.5.2 Endings containing an **i** or **j** soften those consonants that admit of a soft variety and modify others; other changes in the noun or verb may have the opposite effect, according to the following table:

b	ch	d	f	g	k	ł	m	n	p	r	s	t
bi	sz*/si	dzi	fi	gi/dz*	ki/c*	l	mi	ni	pi	rz*	si ͵sz*	ci
bi	sz*	dzi/dz*	fi	ż*	cz*	l	mi	ni	pi	rz*	sz*	c*

w	z
wi	zi
wi	ż*

(At the end of a syllable **ci, ni, si, zi** are replaced by **ć, ń, ś, ż**.)

The changes between the first and second rows are found in nouns, e.g. **tło, L tle; tom, tomie; świat, świecie; numer, numerze; Polska, D Polsce; mucha, musze; Czech, P Czesi; twardy, twardzi**. Those between the first and third rows occur in verbs.

2.5.3 The consonants marked with an asterisk in 2.5.2 are palatalised; they were originally soft, but are now hard and are followed by **-y** instead of **-i**. For the effect of this see 4.3.2, 4.3.12, 5.2.1. (In this connexion note that **c** and **ci, dz** and **dzi** are distinct and unrelated consonants.) Conversely **k** and **g** are never followed by **-y**.

2.6 VARIATION OF VOWEL

2.6.1 Sometimes the vowel of the stem varies between one case of a noun and another, e.g. **miasto, mieście; ręka, rąk; czoło, czele; Lwów, Lwowie**.

2.6.2 In other instances a vowel may be inserted or left out, as in **okno, okien; dzień, dnia; orzeł, orły; osioł, osle**. Note the consequent changes of consonant (2.5.2).

2.7 SPELLING

There has been little change, except in words, nearly all of foreign origin, now ending in -ia and -ja, -ium, etc., and similarly in words such as **socjalizm**. During the 19th century practice varied:

> i after **b, f, g, k, l, m, n, p, w.**
>
> j or y after **c, d, r, s, t, z** (these letters are not normally followed by i) settling down to y in the later years of the century.

In the 1920's j was substituted both for i and y, except after g and k. Since 1936 i has been restored, and now only c, s, z are followed by j since i would radically affect the pronunciation.

The words are easy enough to find in the dictionary whatever the spelling; but a catalogue with entries in several languages, beginning with **Akademia, Akademie, Akademiia, Akademja** and **Akademya**, needs watching.

3 ARTICLES

There are no articles.

4 NOUNS

4.1 GENDER AND FORM

There are three genders, and a fair correspondence between the form of a noun and its gender. Inanimate nouns may be of any gender. Omitting the vocative there are six cases, the endings varying according to the form of the noun in question.

4.3 ENDINGS

4.3.1 *Masculine nouns*

These nearly all end in a consonant and have the following case-endings. (The few that end in -a or -o, follow, in the singular, the feminine declension, as in 4.3.9.)

	S				P		
N		-			-i, -y	-owie	-e
A		-a, -			-y	-ów	-e
G	-u		-a			-ów	-i, -y
D		-owi, -u				-om	
I	-iem		-em			-ami	-mi
L	-ie, *e		-u			-ach	

Where the endings are sorted into boxes, those on the left are found where the stem ends in a hard consonant, those on the right where it is soft or palatalised, while those in the middle are found with either (cf. 2.5).

4.3.2 NAP **-owie, -ów** are confined to animates; **-i** is personal, but it palatalises some consonants (2.5.3) and may therefore become **-y**; while **-y**, the inanimate ending, appears as **-i** after **k** and **g**. Hence magna|t, **-ci**, *magnate(s)*, but **robotni|k, -cy**, *worker(s)*; conversely **schema|t, -ty**, *scheme(s)*, but **roczni|k, -ki**, *annual(s)*.

4.3.3 Nouns in **-anin**, pl. **-anie**, and country names in **-y** (plural) have no ending in the GP, e.g. **mieszczanin, mieszczan**, *countryman*; **Niemcy, Niemiec,** *Germany* (2.6.2).

4.3.4 Changes of consonant (2.5) or vowel (2.6.1) may occur in LS and NP, loss of vowel (2.6.2) in all cases. Monosyllables in **-ą-** change to **-ę-** in oblique cases.

4.3.5 *Neuter nouns*

These end in -o, -(i)e, -(i)ę and have endings:

	S	P
NA	-o, -e	-a
G	-a	-; rarely -i, -y
D	-u	-om
I	-(i)em	-ami
L	-ie, -u	-ach

-o follows hard, -e soft or palatalised consonants.

Changes of consonant (2.5) and vowel (2.6) occur in oblique cases, e.g. **miasto, w mieście**; **sto, GP set**; **święto, świąt**; **słowo, słów.**

4.3.6 **Oko,** *eye,* and **ucho,** *ear,* make their plurals as follows:

ocz⎤
    ⎮y, -u, -om, -ami or -yma, -ach
usz⎦

4.3.7 Nouns in -ę have the same endings as in 4.3.5, but the stem changes. The most important is **imię**: singular stem **imieni-**, plural stem **imion-**.

4.3.8 *Feminine nouns*

These end in -a, -i or in soft or palatalised consonants. A few masculine nouns in -a and -o such as **specjalista, Kościuszko** also follow the pattern of 4.3.9. When, however, the case is specified in some other way a name in -o may be invariable, e.g. **pod redakcją Witolda Warkałło** and **pod redakcją W. Warkałły.**

4.3.9 Nouns in -a have the following endings:

	S	P
N	-a	⎱-y, -i, -e
A	-ę	⎰
G	-y, -i	-, -i
D	-ie, -e, -i, -y	-om
I	-ą	-ami
L	-ie, -e, -i, -y	-ach

NP -i after g, k; -e after i, j, and palatalised consonants (2.5.3); otherwise -y. Nouns such as **lekcja** make GP **lekcyj.**

Changes of consonant and vowel occur, of the same type as in 4.3.5.

4.3.10 **Ręka,** *hand,* has LS and P **ręku**; IP **rękoma.**

4.3.11 Nouns in -i behave as if NS were -ia, but **pani** (*Mrs*) has AS **panią.**

4.3.12 Nouns ending in a consonant have the following endings:

	S	P
NA	-	-e, -i, -y
G	-i, -y	-i, -y
D	-i, -y	-om
I	-ą	-ami
L	-i, -y	-ach

Soft consonants, other than **l**, are followed by **i** throughout; palatalised consonants are not, viz. **wieś, wsi, wsie, wsiach; rzecz, rzeczy, rzeczach.**

There is no rule for determining whether the NP is **-e** or **-i/y**, but abstract nouns in **-ość** have **-i**.

4.3.13 *Compound nouns*
There are a few nouns which consist of a noun and an adjective joined, e.g. **Białystok** (A + N), **rzeczpospolita**, *republic* (N + A). Each part has its own declension, viz. **w Białymstoku**, *at Białystok*; **rzeczypospolitej**, *of the republic*.

4.6 USE OF CASES
The names given to the cases are only rough guides to their use. In particular one should note the use of the genitive as the object of a negative verb, and of the instrumental as the predicate sometimes of the verb **być**, *to be*, more often of some similar verb, e.g. **Są one wynikiem dwukrotnych badań**, *they are the result of two-fold research.*

5 ADJECTIVES

5.1 GENERAL
5.1.1 These are variable. If there are several, some may precede the noun and some follow.

5.1.2 A few adjectives have a short and a long form, e.g. **rad** or **rady**, *glad*. The short forms have the same endings as nouns, but the oblique cases occur only in stereotyped phrases of an adverbial nature, such as **po polsku**, *in Polish.*

5.2 ENDINGS
5.2.1 *Long forms, hard type*

	S M	*S* N	*S* F	*P* M	*P* NF
N	-y	-e	-a	-i(-y), -e	-e
A	-ego, -y	-e	-ą	-ych, -e	-e
G	-ego		-ej	-ych	
D	-emu		-ej	-ym	
I	-ym		-ą	-ymi	
L	-ym		-ej	-ych	

Changes of consonant (2.5.2) may take place in NPM, e.g. **twardy, twardzi**; **dalszy, dalsi**; involving **-y** for **-i**, if there is palatalisation (2.5.3), e.g. **stary, starzy**.
On the NAPM ending **-e** see 5.2.2.

5.2.2 *Long forms, soft type*

	S M	*S* N	*S* F	*P* M	*P* NF
N	-i	-ie	-ia	-i(-y), -ie	-ie
A	-iego, -i	-ie	-ią	-ich, -ie	-ie
G	-iego		-iej	-ich	
D	-iemu		-iej	-im	
I	-im		-ią	-imi	
L	-im		-iej	-ich	

Adjectives in **-ki** and **-gi** have **-ka, -ką, -ga, -gą**, not **-kia**, etc. in FS: **-cy/-kie, -dzy/-gie** in NPM.

NAPM **-e** and **-ie** apply to inanimates, e.g. **instytuty naukowe**, *learned institutes*; but **pierwsi polscy biskupi**, *first Polish bishops*.

5.2.3 *Nouns with adjectival endings*

Some nouns which were originally adjectives, and others of similar form, including many proper names, are declined wholly or partly like adjectives, e.g. **Ossoliński** (P **Ossolińscy**), **Batory** (GS **Batorego**, P **Batorowie**), **Ossolińska, Pawłowa, Antoni**.

5.3 COMPARISON

5.3.1 The comparative is usually formed by substituting **-szy**, or sometimes **-(i)ejszy** for **-y** or **-i** (**-ki, -eki, -oki**), e.g. **twardy, twardszy; daleki, dalszy; łatwy, łatwiejszy**. Consonant and vowel alteration may take place, e.g. **długi, dłuższy; biały, bielszy**; and cf. 5.2.1.

5.3.2 The superlative is formed by adding **naj-** to the comparative.

5.4 POSSESSIVES

These have short forms in NS, viz. **mój, twój, swój** (*own*) **nasz, wasz**. **Mój, twój, swój** admit contracted forms such as **mego, mym**, as well as the normal **mojego, moim**, etc.

6 NUMERALS

6.1 CARDINAL
6.1.1

1 **jeden**	11 **jedenaście**	21 **dwadzieściajeden**	300 **trzysta**
2 **dwa**	12 **dwanaście**	30 **trzydzieści**	400 **czterysta**
3 **trzy**	13 **trzynaście**	40 **czterdzieści**	500 **pięćset**
4 **cztery**	14 **czternaście**	50 **pięćdziesiąt**	600 **sześćset**
5 **pięć**	15 **piętnaście**	60 **sześćdziesiąt**	700 **siedemset**
6 **sześć**	16 **szesnaście**	70 **siedemdziesiąt**	800 **osiemset**
7 **siedem**	17 **siedemnaście**	80 **osiemdziesiąt**	900 **dziewięćset**
8 **osiem**	18 **osiemnaście**	90 **dziewięćdziesiąt**	1000 **tysiąc**
9 **dziewięć**	19 **dziewiętnaście**	100 **sto**	
10 **dziesięć**	20 **dwadzieścia**	200 **dwieście**	

6.1.2 **jeden–cztery** are adjectives.
jeden, jedna, jedno is declined like a hard adjective (5.2.1) except in the nominative. **dwa, trzy, cztery** and **oba**, *both*, are declined as follows:

	dw-, ob-			**trz-, czter-**
	M	*N*	*F*	
N	-aj, -a	-a	-ie	-ej, -y
A	-óch, -u, -a	-a	-ie	-y
G	-óch, -u			-ech
D	-om, -u			-ema
I	-oma	-oma, -iema		-ema
L	-óch, -u			-ech

Instead of **dwaj panowie**, *two gentlemen*, and the like one may meet **dwóch (dwu) panów** (GP) as the subject of a sentence, with the verb in the singular.

6.1.3 **pięć** onwards are nouns in form. When subject or object they are construed as nouns, the objects numbered being in the GP and the verb in the singular, e.g. **pięć tomów ukazało się**, *five volumes have been published*. If the noun is personal the numeral is in the genitive too. When not subject or object they are treated as adjectives, e.g. **w pięciu tomach**, *in five volumes*.

6.1.4 The oblique cases are as follows:

5–10 **pięciu, sześciu,** etc.	50–90 **piećdziesięciu,** etc.
11 **jedenastu**	100 **stu**
12 **dwunastu**	200 **dwustu**
13–19 **trzynastu,** etc.	300 **trzystu**
20 **dwudziestu**	400 **czterystu**
30 **trzydziestu**	500–900 **pięciuset, sześciuset,** etc.
40 **czterdziestu**	1000 as 4.3.1

21, 31, etc. **dwudziestu** (etc.) **jeden** (sic)

151 **stu pięćdziesięciu jeden**

22–24, 32–34, etc. **dwudziestu dwóch (dwu, dwom,** etc.), **trzech** and so on. For details see 6.1.2.

6.1.5 Compound numerals ending in **jeden** are construed as if the **jeden** were not there, e.g. **dwadzięścia jeden tomów**, *21 volumes*. The others follow the construction of the final element, e.g. **dwadzieścia dwa tomy, dwadzieścia pięć tomów**, *22 (25) volumes*.

6.2 ORDINAL

1 **pierwszy**	8 **ósmy**	30, 40 **trzy(czter)dziesty**
2 **drugi, wtóry**	9 **dziewiąty**	50–90 **pięćdziesiąty,** etc.
3 **trzeci**	10 **dziesiąty**	100 **setny**
4 **czwarty**	11 **jedenasty**	200 **dwóchsetny**
5 **piąty**	12 **dwunasty**	300 **trzechsetny**
6 **szósty**	13–19 **trzynasty,** etc.	500–900 **pięćsetny,** etc.
7 **siódmy**	20 **dwudziesty**	1000 **tysięczny**

6.3 FIGURES

Plain figures normally stand for cardinals, ordinals being followed by part of the ending, e.g. **5-go** = **piątego, 13-stej** = **trzynastej**; but in older books at any rate one meets endings added to cardinals, e.g. **z 4-ma** (= **czterema**) **portretami**, *with four portraits*.

6.4 DATES

6.4.1 The months, genitives in brackets, are:

> **styczeń (-cznia), luty (-tego), marzec (-rca), kwiecień (-tnia), maj (-ja), czerwiec (-wca),**
>
> **lipiec (-pca), sierpień (-pnia), wrzesień (-śnia), pazdziernik (-ka), listopad (-da), grudzień (-dnia)**

(For the changes cf. 2.5 and 2.6.)

6.4.2 *On 16.v.1958* is translated (**Dnia**) **szesnastego maja tysiąc dziewięćset pięćdziesiątego ósmego roku.** Note the insertion of **dnia** (*day*) and **roku** (*year*), and the use of ordinals.

1 May is usually translated **Pierwszy Maj**.

Rok may also precede the numbers, e.g. **Rok 1848 (tysiąc osiemset czterdziesty ósmy) w Polsce.**

Double dates may cause difficulty in the reading, e.g. **Rewolucja 1905–1907 roku** (... **piątego** ... **siódmego**, with or without **do**). But **17.xi.1872–17.xi.1922** is best read with **siedemnasty** both times rather than (**od**) **siedemnastego** ... (**do**) **siedemnastego**; and **w latach 1897–1899** as **tysiąc osiemset dziewięćdziesiąt siedem tysiąc o.d. dziewięć**, with cardinal numbers.

7 PRONOUNS AND PRONOUN-ADJECTIVES

7.1/7.2 DEMONSTRATIVE, ETC.

7.1.1 Demonstratives, interrogatives and relatives have a similar declension to adjectives, but the nominative is somewhat unpredictable, viz.

> **ten, ta, to**: S **tego**, etc. (5.2.1) P **ci, te**, etc. (*this, that*)
> **kto**: AG **kogo**, D **komu**, IL **kim** (*who?*)
> **co**: stem **cz-** (*what?, who, which*)

7.1.2 **Tenże** (*the same*) follows **ten**, e.g. **tegoże**.

7.3 PERSONAL

7.3.1

	S 1	S 2	S & P R	P 1	P 2
N	ja	ty	—	my	wy
A	mnie, mię	ciebie, cię	siebie, się	nas	was
G	mnie, mię	ciebie, cię	siebie	nas	was
D	mnie, mię	tobie, cię	sobie	nam	wam
I	mną	tobą	sobą	nami	wami
L	mnie	tobie	sobie	nas	was

Się, which means *self*, applies to all persons, and can be attached to nouns derived from reflexive verbs, e.g. **spotkanie się**, *meeting*.

7.3.2 **on, ono, ona** (*he, it, she*) has oblique cases from another root, viz.

	MS	NS	FS	P
A	(je)go, niego	je, nie	ją, nią	MF (n)ich, MNF je, nie
G	(je)go, niego		jej, niej	(n)ich
D	(je)mu, niemu		jej, niej	(n)im
I	nim		nią	nimi
L	nim		niej	nich

8 VERBS

8.1 STRUCTURE

8.1.1 Differences of person are for the most part sufficiently expressed by endings, making pronouns unnecessary, e.g. **piszę**, *I write*.

8.1.2 Verbs are entered in the dictionary under the imperfective infinitive (see General note on the Slavonic languages). Where the perfective is formed by adding a prefix e.g. **pisać, napisać**, no special reference is to be expected, though there may be a general one under **na-**. Nor is there a reference from the frequentative **pisywać**. But where there is a more marked difference, special references are made.

8.2 PRESENT (impf.); FUTURE (pf.)

8.2.1 *Endings*

Ia	-ę, -esz, -e; -emy, -ecie, -ą
b	-ę, $\begin{cases} \text{-*esz, -*e; -*emy, -*ecie, -ą} \\ \text{-iesz, -ie; -iemy, -iecie, -ą} \end{cases}$
IIa	$\left.\begin{array}{l} \text{-ę,} \\ \text{-*ę,} \end{array}\right\}$-isz, -i; -imy, -icie, $\begin{cases} \text{-ą} \\ \text{-*ą} \end{cases}$
b	-ę, -ysz, -y; -ymy, -ycie, -ą
III	-em, -esz, -e; -emy, -ecie, -eją/-edzą
IV	-am, -asz, -a; -amy, -acie, -ają/-adzą

8.2.2 *Relation of present to infinitive* (see also 8.2.3)

P	-am	-ę (Ib)	-ę (II)	-*ę, -ie, (Ia)	-ję (Ia)
I	-ać, -ieć	see 8.2.3	-ić	-ać	-ć, -jać

P	-nę (Ib)	-uję (Ia)	-em
I	-(n)ąć	-ować, -ywać	-eć, -edzeć, -eść

8.2.3 *Some peculiar stems*

P	biorę	chcę	daję	idę	jadę	kładę	legnę
I	brać	chcieć	dawać	iść	jechać	kłaść	lec

P	mogę	niosę	rosnę (rośnie)	siądę/siędę	stoję
I	móc	nieść	róść	siadać/siąść	stać (impf.)

P	stanie się	tnę	wezmę	wiodę	wiozę
I	stać (pf.) się	ciąć	wziąć	wieść	wieźć

8.3 PAST TENSE

8.3.1 *Endings*

	S			P
M	N	F		
-ł	-ło	-ła		-li, -ły (old past participle)

followed by **-(e)m, -(e)ś, -; -śmy, -ście, -**, making **-łem/łam; -łeś/łaś**, etc.

Occasionally the endings **-em**, etc. are added to some other word in the sentence; or a particle may be inserted before them, e.g. **pisalibyśmy**.

8.3.2 *Relation to infinitive*

Usually P **-ł**, I **-ć**; fairly frequently **-iał, -ieć**. Note also:

jadł	kładł	mógł	niósł	szedł
jeść	kłaść	móc	nieść	iść

8.5 FUTURE

See 8.2, 8.10.1.

8.10 COMPOUND TENSES

8.10.1 *Future:* **będę**, etc. (8.1) with infinitive (8.11) or old past participle (8.3).

8.10.2 *Conditional:* formed from the past (8.3) by adding or inserting **by**.

8.11 INFINITIVE

Usually -ć but sometimes -c.

8.12 PARTICIPLES

8.12.1 *Present active*

-cy, added to the 3PP of the indicative. (With the reflexive pronoun it becomes passive, as in the example below.) An adjective, and very common as a substitute for a relative clause, e.g. **ukazujące się nowe wydanie,** *the present new edition;* **nie dające się realizować szybko,** *which cannot be realised quickly.*

8.12.2 *Past passive*

-ny/-ty, normally corresponding to infinitive -ć; fairly frequently -iany, -ieć; -*ony, -ić; and sometimes -(i)ęty, -ąć; -niony, -nąć.

Note also **kładziony, kłaść; niesiony, nieść; wyjedzony, wyjeść.**

8.14/8.15 REFLEXIVE AND PASSIVE

8.14.1 The reflexive pronoun **się** (all persons) with an active verb, produces a reflexive, reciprocal, intransitive or more often than not passive sense. **Nowe wydanie ukazuje się w pięciu tomach,** *The new edition is being published* (lit. presents itself) *in five volumes.*

8.14.2 The passive can also be expressed by means of the passive participle (8.12.2) with parts of the verb **być** or **zostać: zamówienia przyjmowane są,** *orders are accepted;* **drobna część została wydana w książkach, reszta ukryta jest w czasopismach,** *a small part was published in books, the rest is hidden in periodicals.*

8.14.3 As well as the passive participle agreeing with the subject, as in **pisownia i interpunkcja zostały zmodernizowane,** *orthography and punctuation have been corrected,* one finds the neuter participle governing an accusative, e.g. **pisownię i interpunkcję zmodernizowano,** with the same meaning. Similarly with **się: publikację przewiduje się . . . ,** *publication is expected . . . .*

8.17 THE VERB **być,** *to be*

   Present: **jestem, jesteś, jest; jesteśmy, jesteście, są**
   Future: **będę** (8.2.1)
   Past: **byłem** (8.3.1)

9 ADVERBS

9.1 FORMATION

They are regularly formed from adjectives, including participles, by substituting the endings -o or -ie (-*e), e.g. **zupełny, -nie,** *complete(ly);* **dobry, -brze,** *good, well;* **łatwy, -wo,** *wide(ly);* **długi, -go,** *long;* **krótki, -ko,** *short(ly).* (Cf. 5.1.2.)

9.2 COMPARISON

In the comparative the -o (-oko, -ieko) or -(i)e changes to -iej (-*ej), e.g. **zupełniej, łatwiej, dłużej, krócej** or **króciej.** Note the change of consonant (2.5). Irregular comparatives are entered separately in dictionaries.

The superlative is formed by prefixing **naj-** to the comparative.

10 PREPOSITIONS

These govern particular cases. Some may be used with more than one case and where this affects the translation, care is needed, e.g. **w pokoju,** *in the room;* **w pokój,** *into the room;* **który z panów,** *which of the men;* **z panami,** *with the men.*

GLOSSARY

abonament, *subscription*

badanie, *research*
bezpłatnie, *free*
biblioteka, *library*
bibliotekarz, *librarian*
bieżący, *current*
broszura, *pamphlet*

cena, *price* (1.8.4)
ciąg dalszy, *continuation*
czasopismo, *periodical* (1.8.1)
czcionka, *type* (1.6.4)
część, *part* (1.4.1)
członek, *member*

dodatek, *supplement*
druk, *printing, edition* (1.5.1)
w druku, *in the press*
drukarnia, *printer's* (1.6.4)
dwutygodniowy, *fortnightly*
dzieje, *history*
dzieło, *work* (1.2.4)

egzemplarz, *copy* (1.8.4)

faktura, *invoice*

gotowy, *ready*

książka, *book*
księgarnia, *bookshop*
kwartalnik, *quarterly*

lata, *years*
list, *letter* (1.2.4)

miesęcznik, *monthly*
mowa, *speech*

do nabycia, *obtainable* (1.8.4)
nadbitka, *offprint* (1.5.3)
nakład, *cost* (1.6.2), *impression* (1.5.1)
nowel(k)a, *short story*
nowy, *new*

objaśnienie, *explanation*
odbitka, *offprint* (1.5.3), *proof*
oddzielny, odrębny, *separate*

okazowy, *sample*
okładka, *cover*
opowiadania, opowieść, *story*
opracował, *compiled, edited* (1.2.8)
opracowanie, *editing* (1.2.5)
oprawa, *binding*

pisarz, *writer*
pisemko, *pamphlet*
plansza, *plate*
pojedynczy, *single*
poprawiony, *corrected* (1.5.2)
poprawka, *correction*
pos(y)lać, *send*
poszczególny, *individual*
poszerzony, *enlarged*
powiełacz, *duplicator*
powieść, *novel*
półroczne, *half-yearly*
praca zbiorowa, *collective work* (1.2.8)
prasa, *press*
prenumerata, *subscription* (1.8.4)
próbny, *specimen*
przedmowa, *preface*
przedpłata, *subscription*
przedruk, *reprint*
przejrzał, *he revised* (1.2.2)
przejrzany, *revised*
przekład, *translation*
przełożył, *translated*
przerobiony, *revised* (1.5.2)
przygotowany, *prepared* (1.2.7)

rabat, *discount*
rada, *committee*
redakcja, *editing* (1.2.5), *editorial office*
redaktor, *editor*
rocznik, *volume, yearbook* (1.8.3)
roczny, *annual*
rok, *year, volume* (1.8.3)
rozprawka, *essay*
rozprawy, *transactions*
rozsprzedany, *sold out*
rozszerzony, *enlarged* (1.5.2)

seria, *(sub)series* (1.7.2)
skład, *depot*

skorowidz, *index*
słownik, *dictionary*
słowo wstępne, *prefatory note*
spis, *list, table*
sprawozdanie, *proceedings*
do sprzedania, w sprzedaży, *on sale*
streszczenie, *summary*
stron(ic)a, *page*

tabela, *table*
tablica, *plate, table*
tenże, *the same* (7.1.2)
tłumaczył, -czenie, *translated, -tion*
towarzystwo, *society*
tygodnik, *weekly*

ukazało się, *was published*
urodzony, *born*
uzupełnienie, *supplement*
uzupełniony, *enlarged*

wiadomości, *news*
wiersz, *poem*
własność, *property* (*copyright*)

wstęp, *introduction* (1.2.4)
wszelkie (wszystkie) prawa zastrzeżone, *all rights reserved*
wybór, *selection* (1.2.5)
wybrany, *selected*
wychodzić, *to come out* (1.8.3)
wyczerpany, *out of print*
wydał, *edited* (1.2.2), *published*
wydanie, *edition* (1.5.1, 1.3.3), *publication* (1.6.2)
wydawnictwo, *publishing house* (1.6.1), *publication* (1.6.2, 1.7.1)
wymiana, *exchange*
wysprzedany, *sold out*
wys(y)łać, *dispatch*
wyszło, *came out*

zagranica, *foreign countries*
zamówienie, *order* (8.7.2)
zbiór, *collection*
zebrał, *collected* (1.2.2)
zespół, *team, set*
zeszyt, *issue, number, part* (1.7.2, 1.8.3)
zmarł, *died*
zobacz, *see*

GRAMMATICAL INDEX: WORDS

będę, etc., 8.10.1, 8.14.2, 8.17

biorę, etc., 8.2.3
by, 8.10.2
był(em), etc., 8.17

chcę, etc., 8.2.3
ci, 7.1.1
ciebie, cię, 7.3.1
czogo, czomu, 7.1.1
cztery, etc., 6.1.2
czym, 7.1.1

daję, etc., 8.2.3
dwa, dwóch, etc., 6.1.2

go, 7.3.2

ich, 7.3.2
idę, etc., 8.2.3

im, 7.3.2
imieni-, imion-, 4.3.7

jadę, 8.2.3
jadł, 8.3.2
ją, je(j), jego, jemu, 7.3.2
jest(em), etc., 8.17

kładę, etc., 8.2.3
kładł, 8.3.2
kim, kogo, komu, 7.1.1

legnę, etc., 8.2.3

mego, 5.4
mię, 7.3.1
mną, mnie, etc., 7.3.1
mogę, etc., 8.2.3
mógł, 8.3.2
moim, mojego, 5.4
mu, 7.3.2
mym, 5.4

naj-, 9.2
nam, nas, etc., 7.3.1
nią, nie(-), nich, nim(i), 7.3.2
niosł, 8.3.2
noszę, etc., 8.2.3

ocz-, 4.3.6

pani, etc., 4.3.11

rękoma, 4.3.10
rosnę, rośnie, etc., 8.2.3

siądę, etc., 8.2.3
siebie, 7.3.1
się, 7.3.1, 8.14
siędę, 8.2.3
sob-, 7.3.1
stanie się, 8.2.3
stoję, etc., 8.2.3
szedł, 8.3.2

ta, te, tego, temu, ten, to, etc., 7.1.1
tnę, etc., 8.2.3
tob-, 7.3.1
trzej, etc., 6.1.2

usz-, 4.3.6

wam, was, 7.3.1
wezmę, etc., 8.2.3

wiodę, etc., 8.2.3
wiozę, etc., 8.2.3

zostać, etc., 8.14.2

GRAMMATICAL INDEX: ENDINGS

-a, 4.3.1, 4.3.5, 4.3.9, 5.2.1, 8.2.1
-ga, -ia, -ka, 5.2.2
-ła, 8.3.1

-ą, 4.3.9, 4.3.12, 5.2.1, 8.2.1
-gą, -ią, 5.2.2
-ają, -eją, 8.2.1
-ką, 5.2.2
-adzą, -edzą, 8.2.1

-c, -ć, 8.11

-e, 4.3.1, 4.3.9, 4.3.12, 5.2.1, 8.2.1
-*e, 4.3.1, 8.2.1
-ie, 4.3.1, 4.3.5, 4.3.9, 5.2.2, 8.2.1
-acie, -(i)ecie, -icie, 8.2.1
-ście, 8.3.1
-ycie, 8.2.1
-anie, 4.3.3
-owie, 4.3.1
-że, 7.1.2

-ę, 4.3.9, 8.2.1

-ach, 4.3.5, 4.3.9, 4.3.12
-ich, 5.2.2
-ych, 5.2.1

-i, 4.3.1, 4.3.5, 4.3.9, 4.3.12, 5.2.1, 5.2.2, 8.2.1
-li, 8.3.1
-mi, 4.3.1
-ami, 4.3.1, 4.3.5, 4.3.9, 4.3.12
-imi, 5.2.2
-ymi, 5.2.1
-owi, 4.3.1

-ej, 5.2.1, 9.3
-iej, 5.2.2, 9.3
-yj, 4.3.9

-ł, 8.3.1

-(e)m, 8.3.1
-(i)em, 4.3.1, 4.3.5, 8.2.1
-im, 5.2.2
-om, 4.3.1, 4.3.5, 4.3.9, 4.3.12
-ym, 5.2.1

-o, 4.3.5, 9.1
-ego, 5.2.1
-iego, 5.2.2
-ło, 8.3.1

-(e)ś, 8.3.1

-u, 4.3.1, 4.3.5, 6.1.4
-iu, 6.1.4
-emu, 5.2.1
-iemu, 5.2.2

-ów, 4.3.1

-y, 4.3.1, 4.3.5, 4.3.9, 4.3.12, 5.2.1, 8.2.1
-cy, 8.12.1
-ły, 8.3.1
-amy, -(i)emy, -imy, 8.2.1
-śmy, 8.3.1
-ymy, 8.2.1
-ny, -ty, 8.12.2
-szy, 5.3.1
-(i)ejszy, 5.3.1

-asz, -(i)esz, -isz, -ysz, 8.2.1

CZECH

SPECIMEN

V tomto 2. vydání jsem leccos změnil a doplnil podle kritických připomínek svého žaka Dr. Fr. Kopečného ve Slově a slovesnosti XI, str. 170–182 a svého přítele prof. B. Havránka v Rudém právu ze 4.XII.1949. Srdečně jim za ně děkuji. Mnohé změny a doplňky vyplynuly z vlastního nového promýšlení celé obsáhlé látky v tomto díle zpracované. Nejednou mi k němu daly podnět dotazy čtenářů Jazykového zákampí neboť z nich jsem poznal, co je praktickému uživateli spisovného jazyka leckdy nezcela jasné. I těmto čtenářům srdečně děkuji za jejich podněty.

In this 2nd edition I have altered[1] and added various things in the light of critical comments of my pupil Dr Fr. Kopečný in Slovo a slovesnost *XI, pp. 170–182, and of my friend Prof. B. Havránek in* Rudé právo *of 4.XII.1949. I am heartily grateful to them for them. Many changes and additions resulted from my own new reflection on the whole extensive material dealt with in this part. Many times I was stimulated[2] thereto by the queries of readers of* Jazykové zákampí,[3] *for from them I learnt what (it is that) is sometimes not quite clear to the user of the literary language. To these readers also I am heartily grateful for their stimuli.*

1. **jsem změnil**: see 8.10.3.
2. Active in the original: *the queries gave me stimulus.*
3. This (*Language corner*) was a column conducted by the author.

0   GENERAL CHARACTERISTICS

0.1   DEGREE OF INFLEXION
Like most of the Slavonic languages Czech is predominantly synthetic, having numerous noun and verb endings, though phonetic changes have caused a number of these to coincide.

0.2   ORDER OF WORDS
Qualifiers sometimes precede and sometimes follow the words they qualify: adjectives may do either (5.1.1), genitives follow. Sentence order is fairly fluid: on title-pages in particular the predominant SVO(C) is frequently reversed, e.g. **K čtvrtému vydání upravila Ludmila Kudrnová,** *L. K. prepared for the fourth edition.*

0.4   RELATION TO OTHER LANGUAGES
There are a fair number of international words in Czech, such as **literatura, kulturní, universita** but the basic vocabulary is peculiarly Slavonic, revealing its family resemblances to other Indo-European languages to philological investigation rather than to cursory observation. For the relation of Czech to other Slavonic languages see General note on the Slavonic languages.

1 BIBLIOLINGUISTICS

1.1 NAMES

1.1.1 Modern Czech names are either nouns or adjectives and are declined as such. Christian names are almost all nouns in form (4.3; 5.2.2). Older names may be of the form **Sixt z Ottersdorfu**, *Sixt of Ottersdorf*. Only the first element then varies.

1.1.2 Male surnames may be:

(a) masculine adjectives (5.2), e.g. **Novotný**;

(b) masculine nouns (4.3.1), e.g. **Čapek**;

(c) nouns in **-a** or **-o**, mostly feminine or neuter in origin, e.g. **Svoboda** (*freedom*).

The last are declined like nouns in **-a** and **-o**, but with some characteristic masculine endings, e.g. **F. X. Svobodovi**, *to F. X. Svoboda* (but **svobodě**, *to freedom*) (see 4.3.1).

1.1.3 Women's surnames are always adjectival. If the corresponding man's surname is an adjective, the feminine of the adjective is used, e.g. **Novotná**. If the male surname is a noun the ending **-ová** is added, e.g. **Čapková, Svobodová**, and with foreign names, **Selma Lagerlöfová**. Declension as in 5.2.1.

1.1.4 When two persons of the same name are mentioned, plural forms are used. If one or both are male the forms are as follows:

(a) S **Novotný**   P **Novotní** (5.2)

(b) S **Čapek**   P **Čapkové, Čapků**, etc. (4.3)

(c) S **Svoboda**   P **Svobodové, Svobodů**, etc. (as if 4.3)

If both are female, adjectival forms may be used, e.g. **Novotní, Čapkové, Svobodové**; or the GP of the masculine name, e.g. **Čapků**. Other adjectival forms refer to families or married couples, e.g. **Čapkovi**, *the Čapeks*. It will be seen that many of the forms do not clearly indicate the sex of the writers.

1.1.5 Both parts of a compound name are usually declined, e.g. **romány K. M. Čapka-Choda**, *the novels of K. M. Čapek-Chod*; **skladby Boženy Vikové-Kunětické**, *the compositions of Božena Viková-Kunětická*.

1.1.6 Czech also uses with the greatest freedom possessive forms in **-ův** derived from masculine names and in **-in** from feminine ones (5.2.5). They are equivalent to and may be combined with genitives, e.g. **od dob Jungmannových a Palackého**, *from the times of Jungmann and Palacký*.

In narrative they are often used of authors, e.g. **Šolcova „Chaloupka"**, *Šolc's 'Chaloupka'*. Though this type of expression is common in the titles of series (1.7.1) and encyclopaedias, e.g. **Ottův slovník naučný**, *Otto's encyclopaedia*, authors' names are not so given on title-pages, so that in **Šaldův zápisník**, *Šalda's notebook*, **Šaldův** is best treated as part of the title. Possessive forms cannot be used with initials or Christian names.

1.1.7 Foreign names are adapted to Czech declensions. For details see 4.3.15 and 5.2.

1.2 NAMES OF AUTHORS, EDITORS, ETC.

1.2.1 The names of the authors are frequently put at the top of the title-page, e.g. **F. X. Šalda | Kritické projevy I**. In this position they are grammatically unaffected, but some forms are ambiguous and one needs to be sure that they are not genitive (1.2.4).

1.2.2 Somewhat less common in the case of authors but very common for editors and translators is the position after the title, preceded by the past tense active of the appropriate verb, e.g. **napsal**, *wrote*; **vydal**, *published*; **vydání (k vydání) připravil** (**upravil**), *prepared (for) publication*; **redigoval**, *edited*; **úvodem opatřil**, *furnished with an introduction*; **vybral**, *selected*; **přeložil**, *translated*.

The name follows in the nominative, and the only difficulty is with the verb. In the forms given above it is masculine singular: it may be feminine, e.g. **upravila**, or plural, **upravili, -ly**. If a plural verb is quoted in a catalogue entry, it is less awkward if at least two names are given; and if there is a mixed team, do not give two women's names with the masculine verb. Sometimes, especially if the work is in progress, a present tense is used, e.g. **reдiguje**, *is editing*; **řídí**, *directs*; **autorem je**, *is the author*.

1.2.3 The names will also be in the nominative if preceded by a simple statement such as **autor**, but this type is usually found with collective works, **autoři** (*authors*), **autorský kolektiv, redakční rada** (*editorial board*) being followed by a list of names.

1.2.4 Some publications, particularly collected works, correspondence, speeches and editions of classics give the author's name in the genitive, before or after the title, e.g. **Aloise Jiráska odkaz národu**, *Alois Jirásek's legacy to the nation* (elsewhere entitled **Spisy Aloise Jiráska**, *Writings of A. J.*); **Dílo Jiřího Wolkra**, *The work* (i.e. Complete works) *of Jiří Wolker*; **J. A. Komenského Labyrint světa a ráj srdce**, *Comenius' The labyrinth of the world and the paradise of the heart*. Except for this last type there is usually a descriptive phrase which goes naturally with the genitive rather than a title of the usual form.

Some endings, those in **-a** for instance, are grammatically ambiguous. **Jiráska** is genitive (**-ek**, G **-ka**, is a common ending, but so is **-ka**, G **-ky**) but **Šalda** in 1.2.1 was nominative. Fortunately **Soubor díla F. X. Šaldy** (*collection of works of F. X. Šalda*) occurs elsewhere in the same book, but it is as well to make sure of one's facts before choosing one's heading.

1.2.5 The genitive is also found after a noun denoting the activity of the person concerned, e.g. **Zpracoval kolektiv pod vedením Bedřicha Jecha**, i.e. *carried out by a collective under the leadership of Bedřich Jech*, but this type is by no means as common as it is in other Slavonic languages.

1.2.6 In earlier books the author's name is sometimes preceded by a preposition (see 10), e.g. **Růže stolistá. Báseň a pravda. Od F. L. Čelarowského**, *The rose with a hundred leaves. Fable and reality. By F. A. Čelarovský.*

1.2.7 Collaboration is usually indicated either by a plural verb (1.2.2) or by a descriptive noun (1.2.3) followed by a list of names. Where collaborators are distinguished as such from the main author the verb **spolupracovali** or the noun **spolupracovníci** (*collaborators*) is found. A chief editor may be distinguished as **vědecký redaktor**.

1.2.8 Societies and institutions as authors and editors are indicated in the same ways as individuals, but if their relation to the book is not specified it may be one of vague sponsorship. (They are often mentioned in the body of the title as 'publishing' works, for which see 1.6.) Names of branches and departments usually precede that of the main body, which is either in the genitive, e.g. **Ustav dějin Komunistickí strany Československa**, *Historical Institute of the Communist Party of Czechoslovakia*, or preceded by a preposition, e.g. **Komise pro vydávání pramenů českého hnutí náboženského ve století XIV. a XV. pri Českí akademie věd a umění**, *Commission for the publication of the sources of the Czech religious movement in the 14th and 15th cc. at the Czech Academy of Sciences and Arts*. In such cases the name of the main body, which appears first in the catalogue, will need turning into the nominative, viz. **Komunstická strana Československa**; **Česká akademie věd a umění**.

1.3 TITLES

1.3.1 The great majority, fiction apart, consist of nouns and adjectives in the nominative and other cases with or without prepositions, e.g. **Vliv vědeckotechnického rozvoje na strukturu zahraničního odchodu ve vyspělých kapitalistických státech**, *The influence of technological development on the structure of foreign trade in developed capitalist states*. Belles-lettres, popular works and propaganda produce more varied titles, e.g. **Sám a sám**, *All alone*; **Co víme a co nevíme o prvočíslech**, *What we know and what we do not know about prime numbers*; **Žena není nula**, *Woman is not a cypher*.

1.3.2 Titles entries, whether on the Anglo-American or the British Museum pattern, do not present any peculiar difficulties, though, as will be seen, some care is needed in deducing the nominative of the noun from the oblique cases. Where the title has to be translated there may be more difficulty: in **Anglické absurdní divadlo** the BM heading will be ENGLISH THEATRE; in **Z minulosti Děčínska** it will be DĚČÍN.

1.3.3 When quoted in a sentence the main noun in a title often appears in an oblique case, e.g. **autor ,, Malostranských povídek '' a ,, Arabesek ''**, *the author of 'Malostranské povídky' and 'Arabesky'*; and even **v ,, Bar Kochbovi ''**, *in 'Bar Kochba'*. It is also possible to isolate the title grammatically from the rest of the sentence by putting it in apposition, e.g. **starofrancouzské epiky ,, Karolinská epopeja ''**, *of the old French epic 'Karolinská epopeja'*.

1.4 VOLUMES AND PARTS

1.4.1 The words found are **svazek, díl, část** and **kniha**. **Díl** and **část** are translated literally *part*, the natural meaning of **svazek** is a physical volume and **kniha** means *book*; but they are often used interchangeably, e.g. on the title-page **Třetí díl** and in the introduction **V přítomném svazku vzpomínek** (*in the present volume of memoirs*) and again **první kniha mých vzpomínek**. Sometimes **díl** denotes a division of the whole enterprise, **svazek** a physical volume, but again one finds the several volumes of complete works described as **díl I**, etc., while the plays, which occupy two volumes, are described as **Divadlo část 1, část 2**. At another time **díl** and **část** seem to correspond to *volume* and *part*, e.g. **díl III, část 2**.

1.4.2 Whether the number precedes or follows, it is expressed as an ordinal.

1.4.3 In older books the numeration may affect the grammar of the title, e.g. **Veškerých spisů Jana Amosa Komenského svazek 1**, *Volume 1 of the complete works of J. A. Komenský* (**Veškeré spisy**).

1.4.4 The total number of volumes or plan of the edition may be indicated, **ve dvou částech**, *in two parts*; **celkem obsáhne 30 svazků**, *comprises in all 30 volumes*, or the termination may be stated, as in **Díl třetí a poslední**, *Third and last volume*; **Literární dílo Karoliny Světlé doplňují tyto dva svazky**, *These two volumes complete the literary work of Katolina Světlá*.

1.5 EDITIONS

1.5.1 The usual word is **vydání**, a verbal noun which also has the general meaning *publication* (cf. 1.2.2). The number is expressed either by a word or a figure, e.g. **I vydání, druhé vydání**. Occasionally the note of the edition is grammatically inseparable from other information, e.g. **k čtvrtímu vydání upravila**, *she prepared (it) for the fourth edition*.

1.5.2 Revision is indicated by a suitable adjective such as **přepracované, doplněné, přehlédnuté**. Conversely the edition may be described as **nezměněné**, *unaltered*, being a reprint.

1.5.3 An *offprint* is **zvláštní otisk**, **otisk** by itself being ambiguous.

1.6 IMPRINTS

1.6.1 Present-day publishing houses are mostly institutional, e.g. **Státní naklada-telství politické literatury**, *State Press for Political Literature*, or, with an arbitrary name, **Orbis**; **Československý spisovatel**. Earlier imprints include the names of indi-viduals and commercial companies, e.g. **Nakladatelství „Atlas" společnost s r.o.**, *Atlas Press Ltd.*

1.6.2 If standing alone any of these names will be in the nominative, and similarly if introduced by an active verb, e.g. **vydal Jan Laichter**. But **nákladem** (*at the expense*), **tiskem** (*with the type*), **v komisi** (*by the agency*), **péčí** (*by the care*), and the preposition **u** (*at X's*) all require a genitive. **Nakladatelství** occurs with a personal name either in the genitive, e.g. **Nakladatelství knih K. Viky**, *K. Vika's Book Publishing House* or nominative, e.g. **Nakladatelství Šolc a Šimáček**. More rarely the name may be preceded by a passive participle and will consequently be in the instrumental case, e.g. **vydáno A. Sauerem a J. Haškem**, *published by A. Sauer and J. Hašek*, or it may take the form of a possessive adjective (1.1; 5.2.5), e.g. **nakladatelský dům Vilímkův**, *publishing house of Vilímek*. Names of printing presses (which in earlier works may be publishers) are not infrequently preceded by **v** (*at*) and thus appear in the locative, e.g. **v arcibiskupské knihtiskárně**, *at the archiepiscopal press*.

1.6.3 The name of the place is either in the nominative, e.g. **Praha**, or preceded by **v** and in the locative, **v Praze**.

1.6.4 Some imprints may mention several bodies concerned in different ways with the publication of the book, e.g. **Péčí Ministerstva školství a národní osvěty vydalo Státní nakladatelství**, i.e. *Published for the Ministry of education by the State Press*; or, more complicated, **s podporou Ministerstva školství a národní osvěty nákladem Výboru I. sjezdu slovanských filologů tiskem Státní tiskárny v Praze v generální komisi Fy. [= Firmy] Orbis v Praze XII.**, *with the support of the Ministry of Education at the expense of* [i.e. *published by*] *Commission I of the Congress of Slavonic Philologists with the type of the State Printing Press at Prague by the general agency of Orbis, Prague XII.*

1.7 SERIES

1.7.1 The names of series and the general titles of works in progress usually but not invariably appear on the half-title, frequently on the verso facing the title. Series proper are more often than not in the collective singular, e.g. **Staročeská biblioteka**, *Old Czech library*; works in progress, such as **Divadelní hry Karla Čapka**, *Plays of Karel Čapek*, are more usually in the plural.

A not uncommon complication of Czech series is the incorporation of the publisher's name in the adjectival form, e.g. **Vikova malá knihovna**, *Vika's little library*; **Laichterův výbor nejlepších spisů poučných**, *Laichter's selection of the best instructional writings* (cf. 1.1.6. and 5.2.5).

1.7.2 Series may be divided into sub-series, indicated by **řada**. The unit is usually **číslo**, *number*, but may be **svazek**, *volume*, or **kniha**, *book*. Works in progress are numbered like books in several volumes (1.3). At times the numeration is grammatically connected with the title, e.g. **„Knih pro každého" svazek 5**, *vol. 5 of 'Knihy pro každého'*.

1.7.3 The word **edice**, *publication(s)*, occurs in the titles of series, e.g. **Edice Národní Knihovni v Praze**; but not every appearance of so vague a word should be taken to con-stitute a series, any more than **vydal Odeon jako svou 328. publikaci**, *published by O. as its 328th publication*.

1.8 PERIODICALS

1.8.1 The titles of periodicals (**časopisy**) do not differ linguistically from those of books, e.g. **Slovo a slovesnost**, *Word and literature*; **Právněhistorickí studie**, *Studies in legal history*—though they may be more cryptic, e.g. **Svedectví**, *Testimony*, at any rate without the sub-title, in this case **čtvrtletník pro politiku a kulturu**, *quarterly for politics and culture*. When the title is an element in a larger phrase, it may be grammatically affected (cf. 1.3.3), e.g. **v Času, Hlasu a v Národních listech**, *in Čas, Hlas and in Národní listy*.

1.8.2 Institutional periodicals often have the name of the institution in the genitive, e.g. **Sborník prací Filosofické fakulty University J. E. Purkyně v Brně**. Here the catalogue entry or reference would be: **Brno. Universita J. E. Purkyně. Filosofická Fakulta. Sborník prací**. (Cf. 1.1.5.) Alternatively, the name of the publisher may be in the nominative, preceded by **vydává**, *publishes*.

1.8.3 Editorship is almost invariably indicated by some form of the root **redak-**, e.g. **vedoucí redaktor**, *editor-in-chief*; **spoluredaktoři**, *joint editors*; **redakční rada**, *editorial committee*. The verb **řídí**, *directs*, may also be used.

1.8.4 Numeration of volumes is by **ročník**, *annual volume*, that of parts by **číslo**. The number of the volume may be given in words even when it is quite large, e.g. **ročník dvaačtyřicátý**, *forty-second volume*.

1.8.5 There are a number of other nouns of the same form as **ročník**, viz. **deník, týdeník, čtrnáctideník, měsíčník, čtvrtletník** (*daily, weekly, fortnightly, monthly, quarterly*). These may form part of the title of a periodical, or more frequently, of the description, but **ročník** is not so used. The corresponding adverbs, e.g. **denně, měsíčně**, occur in direct statements of periodicity; equally common are those in -krát, e.g. **vychází čtvrtletně, čtyřikrát do roka (ročně)**, *appears quarterly, four times a year* (*yearly*). Alternatively the number of parts may be given, e.g. **v pěti dvojčíslech do roka**, *in five double numbers a year*.

1.8.6 Details of subscription (**předplatné**) including postage (**i s poštovným**) are' given, using adjectives of periodicity, e.g. **roční předplatné**, *annual subscription* (or **na celý ročník**, *for the whole annual volume*); but single numbers are often quoted for, e.g. **cena jednoho čísla**, *the price of one number*; **jednotlivé číslo stojí**, *a single number costs*.

1.8.7 Addresses given distinguish between the editorial office (**redakce**) for editorial communication (**redakční sdělení**) and the business (**administrace**).

2 ALPHABET, PHONETICS, SPELLING

2.1 ALPHABET

2.1.1 The present alphabet is:

a á b c č d ď e é ě f g h ch i í j k l m n ň

o ó p q r ř s š t ť u ú ů v w x y ý z ž

Note the position of **ch** after **h**; **q, w** and **x** are used in foreign words only. The bracketed letters are interfiled.

2.1.2 The *háček* (e.g. **č, ď**) thus affects the alphabetical order of **č, ř, š** and **ž** only. (Some older dictionaries do not separate **r** and **ř**.) The attached hook which is used with lower-case **t** and **d** (the capitals are **Ť** and **Ď**) is easily overlooked. A following apostrophe can be substituted in typing if one has no special typewriter.

2.1.3 As Czech sometimes re-spells foreign names it is as well to know the pronunciation of the letters with *háček* and of c viz., in English values, **c** = ts, **č** = ch, **ď** is between dy and j, **ě** = ye in yet, **ň** = French gn, **ř** is a combination of a trilled r and the s in *pleasure*, **š** = sh, **ť** between ty and ch, **ž** = s in *pleasure*.

2.1.4 The acute accents denote length and must not be omitted. The letter **ů** has the same pronunciation as **ú** but a different origin; it is not used initially.

2.2 CAPITALISATION

2.2.1 Initial capitals are used for the names of persons, places and other geographical entities, states and institutions, orders and prizes, festivals and historic days. The following however, have small letters: months, days of the week, languages, points of the compass (but **Východ**, the *East*, as part of the world), such words as **černoch**, *negro*; **víla**, *fairy*; **stachanovec, husita**; but **Excelence, Mistr** and similar honorifics have capitals, though not **pan, paní, slečna**. Except for possessives in -**ův** (5.2.5), derived adjectives are written small, e.g. **český**.

2.2.2 The generic part of a geographical name is not spelt with a capital, e.g. **Severní ledový oceán**, *North Pacific Ocean*; **ulice Sedmého listopadu**, *7th of November Street*. Such names can be interpreted, to take the last example, as *the street which is called '7th of November'*. Hence **lázně Teplice**, *the spa Teplice*, but **Lázně Bělohrad**, *Bělohrad Spa*, where the whole expression is the name. Similarly with adjectives in connexion with personal names: **Petr Veliký**, *Peter the Great* (**Petr veliký**, *the great Peter*) but **Panna orleánská**, *the Maid of Orleans*, not as formerly **Orleánská**.

Where a complex of nouns and adjectives taken together form a proper name, only the first word is spelt with an initial capital unless any are themselves proper names, e.g. **Československá republika** or **Republika československá**; **Federativní lidová republika Jugoslávie**, *Federal People's Republic of Yugoslavia*. This is carried through consistently, without the exceptions found in some of the other Slavonic countries, e.g. **Velká říjnová socialistická revoluce**, *Great October Socialist Revolution*; **II. světový kongres obránců míru**, *2nd World Congress of Defenders of Peace* (not **Říjnová, Světový**).

2.3 DIVISION OF WORDS

Rules 1, 2, 3, 4 (p. xiii) apply. Rule 4 takes precedence over rule 3, and when the derivation is not obvious, over rule 2, e.g. **ro-zum**, *reason*, not **roz-um**, though there is a prefix **roz-**. The treatment of consonant clusters (rules 5 and 6) is free, subject to rule 3: **čes-ký** or **če-ský**; **sest-ra, ses-tra** or **se-stra**; but **starost-mi** (4.3.13) only. Foreign words are divided, as pronounced by Czechs, according to sound, e.g. **Rou-sseau, To-glia-tti** —a precarious and somewhat unnecessary exercise for English-speaking librarians.

2.5 HARD AND SOFT CONSONANTS; PALATALISATION

2.5.1 Consonants are classified as follows:

Hard	**d**	**g**	**h**	**ch**	**k**	**n**	**r**	**t**	
Soft	**c**	**č**	**ď**	**j**	**ň**	**ř**	**š**	**ť**	**ž**
Neutral	**b**	**f**	**l**	**m**	**p**	**s**	**v**	**z**	

The distinction is now of little importance for pronunciation, except in the case of **d/ď, n/ň, t/ť** (see 2.1); but it has an effect on the spelling, for hard letters are followed by **y** and soft by **i** (now identical in pronunciation). This in turn complicates the alternations given above; since **dy** is hard, **di** will automatically be soft and there is no need to write **ďi**, though that is how it is pronounced. Similarly **ni, ti** and **dě, ně, tě** not **ďe**, ňe, ťe. (Words of foreign origin may have **i** after a hard letter, e.g. **politický**, where **-ti-** is pronounced **-ty-**.)

Neutral letters may be followed by either **i** or **y**, **e** or **ě**.

There are parallel hard and soft declensions (4.3.1, 4.3.5, 4.3.9) according as the stem ends in a hard or soft consonant, with neutral consonants belonging sometimes to one and sometimes to the other.

2.5.2 Endings containing, now or originally, **i** or **j** soften the preceding consonant and may alter its character, thus:

	c	ck	g/h	ch	k	r	s	sk	z	
to	čť	z		š		c	ř		šť	in nouns
	č		ž		ť		š		ž	mostly in verbs

Thus **universita** has locative **universitě**, with softening indicated by the special vowel **ě**, but **Praha** makes **Praze**. The verb **krýt** has present **kryji**; **ukázat** makes **ukáži**. Endings which palatalise are indicated thus: **-*e**.

2.6 VARIATION OF VOWEL

Quite often the vowel of the stem changes its length or is altered to another one between one part of a noun or verb and another or between adjective and adverb, e.g. **dáma, dam**; **vůz, vozy**; **malý, málo**, and in verbs **mohu**, *I can*, **může**, *it can*; **být, byl**; or a vowel may be inserted or left out, e.g. **otec, otce**; **vajíčko, vajíček**. This applies also to derivatives, e.g. **Jirásek, Jiráskův**.

2.7 SPELLING

Czech spelling has been stable for two or three centuries. In the earliest books one meets **cz** for **č** and **rz** for **ř** (although **ž** is already used) and **yako** for **jako**, as well as the spelling found in the following title of a book by Komenský: **Theatrum universitatis rerum: to gest Diwadlo swěta a wssechněch wssudy přediwných wěcý geho, kteréž na nebi, na zemi, pod zemj, w wodách** [etc.]. Here **ge** = **je**, **w** = **v**, **ss** = **š**, **j** = **í**. Of these spellings **j** for **í** persists into the 19th century and **w** for **v** into the early 20th.

3 ARTICLES

There are no articles.

4 NOUNS

4.1 GENDER AND FORM

There are three genders, and where the endings are hard the form of the noun and its gender correspond closely. Soft endings are now all very much alike. Inanimate nouns may be of any gender. Omitting the vocative there are six cases, the endings varying according to the form of the noun in question.

4.3 ENDINGS

4.3.1 *Masculine nouns*

These nearly all end in a consonant, having no ending in the NS. There are some nouns in **-a**, including names, and some names in **-o**. Except for the masculine ending **-ovi** those in **-a** are declined in the singular like feminine nouns. Those in **-o** are now declined as below, hard type, with the ending **-ovi** characteristic of males, but formerly had AS -o and GS -y. A few Christian names in -e preceded by a hard consonant follow the same type if standing alone, but may be undeclined with surnames, e.g. **Arna** (or **Arne**) **Nováka**, *of Arne Novák*. Names that end in -ě or -*e follow the neuter declension (4.3.5), except again for D -*ovi.

In the plural all masculine nouns and names follow 4.3.1. For foreign names and names of foreign form see 4.3.15.

	Hard type			*Soft type*	
	S	P		S	P
N	See above	-i, -ové, -é; -y		-, -e	-i, -ové, -é; -e (-ě)
A	-a, -	-y		-e/-, -e	-e
G	-a, -u	-ů		-e (-ě)	-ů
D	-ovi, -u	-ům		-ovi, -i	-ům
I	-em	-y		-em (-ěm)	-i
L	-*e, -ě, -ovi, -u	-ech, -*ích		-i	-ích

4.3.2 The soft declension, consisting mostly of nouns ending in a soft consonant, includes also some that end in -l, -s, -z, and some in -ce, -le, -se, -ze. For the spelling of nouns ending in **ď, ň, ť** see 2.5.1.

4.3.3 Changes of consonant (2.5.2) occur before LS -ě (-*e), NP -i and LP -ích, e.g. **Čech, Češi; slucha, sluzích.** Variations of vowel (2.6) occur in some words, e.g. **dům, domu; vítr, větru; Karel, Karlovi.**

4.3.4 NP -y and -e (-ě) are confined to inanimates, e.g. **ročník, ročníky,** *volume(s)* (but **Slovák, Slováci**).

4.3.5 *Neuter nouns*
These end in -o (hard), in -e or -ě (soft) or -í (contracted).

	Hard type			*Soft type*	
	S	P		S	P
NA	-o	-a		-e (-ě)	-e (-ě)
G	-a	-		-e (-ě)	-í
D	-u	-ům		-í	-ím
I	-em	-y		-em (-ěm)	-í
L	-ě (-e), -u	-ech		-í	-ích

Euphonic -e- occurs in the GP, e.g. **vajíčko, vajíček.**

4.3.6 **Oko** and **ucho** are irregular in the plural, viz.

$$\left.\begin{matrix}\text{oč}\\\text{uš}\end{matrix}\right|\text{i, -í, -ím, -ima, -ích}$$

4.3.7 Stems in -et- and -ět- (soft) in the singular, -at- (hard) in the plural have NS in -e or -ě, e.g. **zvíře**, GS **zvířete**, Np **zvířata.** Similarly the masculine nouns **hrabě,** *count*; **kníže,** *prince.*

4.3.8 Nouns in -í have -í in all cases except IS -ím; DILP -ím, -ími, -ích.

4.3.9 *Feminine nouns*
These end in -a, -e (-ě), or a consonant, usually soft. The declension includes a few masculine nouns or names in -a (cf. 4.3.1).

	Hard type		Soft type	
	S	P	S	P
N	-a	-y	-e (-ě), -	-e (-ě)
A	-u	-y	-i, -	-e (-ě)
G	-y	-	-e (-ě)	-í
D	-ě (-*e)	-ám	-i	-ím
I	-ou	-ami	-í	-emi (-ěmi)
L	-ě (-*e)	-ách	-i	-ích

The choice between -e and -ě is determined by the preceding consonant (see 2.5.1, 2.5.2).

4.3.10 Some names have -a following a soft consonant, e.g. **Váša, Váňa, Fráňa** (masculine), **Baťa** (surname) with GS -i, DLS -ovi; **Mářa** (feminine) with GS -i, DLS -i or -e. **Maria** is declined like **Marie**.

4.3.11 **Noha**, *leg*; **ruka**, *hand*, and some others have G and LP -ou, IP -ama.

4.3.12 In the soft type the NS has no ending in words like **daň, píseň, mez, zář** (or **záře**) and there is a tendency for the number of such words to increase by migration from type 4.3.13. Place names in **-slav, -im** and soft consonants (2.5.1) may follow this declension or that of 4.3.13. The only difference is in the genitive.

4.3.13 The majority of feminine nouns that end in a consonant still have the following declension:

-, -, -i, -i, -í, -i; -i, -i, -í, -em, -mi, -ech

4.3.14 **Paní** has -í throughout except DILP: -ím, -ími, -ích.

4.3.15 *Foreign names*

These are adapted to Czech declensions.

Classical names have their classical stems with Czech endings, e.g. **Cicero**, G **Cicerona**, or are undeclined.

The following masculine names have the endings of 4.3.1, hard: those that end, phonetically speaking, in a hard consonant, e.g. **Wood**, G **Wooda**; **Lagarde**, G **Lagarda**; or, retaining the mute e, **Scribe, Scribea**; Romance names ending in a hard consonant followed by a sounded -e or -o, e.g. **Dante**, G **Danta** (or as **Heine** below).

Those that end in a soft consonant, followed or not by -e, are declined as in 4.3.1, soft, e.g. **u Dickense**.

Those that end in -a and such names as **Hugo** and **Otto** follow the mixed declension of Czech names in -a and -o (4.3.1, 4.3.9).

German names in -e usually have a mixed declension, e.g.

N	**Heine**
AG	**Heineho**
D	**Heinemu**
I	**Heinem**
L	**Heinem**

but may follow the patterns of 4.3.1, hard or soft as the case may be.

Feminine Christian names present no difficulty; a few names in -o follow 4.3.9.

Place names, which have no natural gender, are declined according to their form, e.g. **Oxford, Chicago**, 4.3.1; **Altona**, 4.3.9, **Bombaj**, 4.3.12.

4.6 USE OF CASES

Apart from obvious uses we find:

> *Genitive*: adjectivally; after certain verbs, adjectives, and prepositions; after negative verbs; in dates (6.4.2)
>
> *Dative*: after certain verbs, adjectives, prepositions and even nouns (where English has *of*)
>
> *Instrumental*: of place and time, and adverbially, e.g. **časem**, *from time to time*; **celkem**, *in all*; as predicate, e.g. **je významným příspěvkem**, *it is an important contribution*; and after certain verbs and prepositions

5 ADJECTIVES

5.1 GENERAL

5.1.1 Adjectives are variable and agree in gender with the nouns. They mostly precede the noun, but need not, e.g. **Československá akademie věd. Listy filologické**, *Czechoslovak Academy of sciences. Philological papers*. Two adjectives may sandwich a noun.

5.1.2 Some adjectives have both long forms and a few short ones (5.2); some have long forms for some cases and short ones for others; most have long forms only. Short forms are essentially the same as those of nouns.

5.1.3 Adjectives are formed from nouns principally by means of the endings **-ový, -ní, -ný**.

5.2 ENDINGS

5.2.1 *Long forms, hard type*

	S			P		
	M	N	F	M	N	F
N	-ý	-é	-á	-í, é	-á	-é
A	-ý/-ého	-é	-ou	-é	-á	-é
G		-ého	-é		-ých	
D		-ému	-é		-ým	
I		-ým	-ou		-ými	
L		-ém	-é		-ých	

5.2.2 *Long forms, soft type*

	S			P
	M	N	F	
N	-í	-í	-í	-í
A	-í/-ího	-í	-í	-í
G		-ího	-í	-ich
D		-ímu	-í	-ím
I		-ím	-í	-imi
L		-ím	-í	-ich

Includes such Christian names as **Jiří** (*George*). Foreign names in **-i** also follow this declension, but without the accents, e.g. **Petőfimu**, *to Petőfi*.

5.2.3 *Short forms*

	S			P		
	M	N	F	M	N	F
N	-	-o	-a	-i, -y	-a	-y
A	-a	-o	-u	-y	-a	-y
G	-a		-y	[-ých]		
D	-u		-é	[-ým]		
I	[-ým]		[-ou]	[-ými]		
L	-ě		-ě	[-ých]		

The forms in brackets are long forms.

5.2.4 Ordinary adjectives are given in the dictionary under long forms: the short form of the NSM is obtained by dropping the -ý, inserting -e- if necessary, e.g. svobodný: svoboden, -dno, -dna. Conversely the basic forms of past participles are short, e.g. napsán, *written*; but where appropriate they can be given long forms by adding -ý, etc., e.g. napsaný. Note the shortening of the -a-.

5.2.5 Short forms are found as predicates, in stereotyped adverbial phrases, and in possessive adjectives in -ův (F -ová) and -in, derived from proper names and nouns denoting relatives or generally persons, e.g. Čapkův, *Čapek's*; sestřin, *sister's*; básníkův, *poet's*.

5.3 COMPARISON

5.3.1 The comparative is usually formed by substituting -ši or -ejší (-ější) for -ý (-eký, -oký), e.g. mladý, mladší, daleký, další. Alteration of consonants (2.5.2) may occur, e.g. drahý, dražší; český, češtější.

5.3.2 The superlative is formed by adding nej- to the comparative.

5.4 PRONOMINAL POSSESSIVE ADJECTIVES

5.4.1 můj, tvůj and svůj are declined thus:

	S			P		
	M	N	F	M	N	F
N	můj	moje, mé	moje, má	{ moji, mí or moje, mé	moje, má	moje, mé
A	můj, mého	moje, mé	moji, mou	moje, mé	moje, má	moje, mé
G		mého	mé		mých	
D		mému	mé		mým	
I		mým	mou		mými	
L		mém	mé		mých	

Svůj refers to the subject and is translated *my, your, his*, etc., as the case may be.

5.4.2 náš, váš (stems naš-, vaš-) have the following endings:

	S			P		
	M	N	F	M	N	F
N	-	-e	-e	-í, -e	-e	-e
D	-, -eho	-e	-i		-e	
G	-eho		-i		-ich	
D	-emu		-i		-im	
I	-im		-i		-imi	
L	-em		-i		-ich	

6 NUMERALS

6.1 CARDINAL

6.1.1

1	jeden	11	jedenáct	21	jedenadvacet	101	sto jeden
2	dva	12	dvanáct		dvacet jeden	200	dvě stě
3	tři	13	třináct	30	třicet	300	tři sta
4	čtyři	14	čtrnáct	40	čtyřicet	400	čtyři sta
5	pět	15	patnáct	50	padesát	500	pět set
6	šest	16	šestnáct	60	šedesát	600	šest set
7	sedm	17	sedmnáct	70	sedmdesát	1000	tisíc
8	osm	18	osmnáct	80	osmdesát	2000	dva tisíce
9	devět	19	devatenáct	90	devadesát	5000	pět tisíc
10	deset	20	dvacet	100	sto		

6.1.2 jeden–čtyři are adjectives.

jeden, jedno, jedna (stem jedn-) is declined like ten (7.1.1), viz. GSM jednoho.
dva, tři, čtyři are declined as follows:

	M	N	F	All genders	
NA	dv|a	-ě	-ě	tř|i	čtyř|i
G		-ou		-í	—
D		-ěma		-em	
I		-ema		-emi	-mi
L		-ou		-ech	

6.1.3 pět onwards are nouns in form, all cases except N and A ending in -i; devět makes devíti, deset either deseti or desíti. If subject or object they are followed by the noun in the GP with verb in the singular; otherwise they are treated as adjectives: e.g. vyšlo pět svazků, *five volumes have appeared* but v pěti svazcích *in five volumes*.

6.1.4 Compound numerals such as dvacet jeden are declined throughout, and are construed like the numeral with which they end, e.g. v dvaceti jednom svazku, *in twenty-one volumes*.

6.2 ORDINAL

1	první	8	osmý	100	stý
2	druhý	9	devátý	200	dvoustý
3	třetí	10	desátý	300	třístý
4	čtvrtý	11–19	jedenáctý, etc.	400	čtyřstý
5	pátý	20–90	dvacátý, etc.	500–900	pětistý, etc. (cf. 6.1.3)
6	šestý	21	jedenadvacátý	1000	tisící
7	sedmý		dvacátý první	2000	dvoutisící
		2735	dvoutisící sedmistý třicátý pátý		

6.3 FIGURES

6.3.1 Plain figures normally stand for cardinals, ordinals being followed by a full stop, or written in roman figures.

6.4 DATES

6.4.1 The months, genitives in brackets, are:

leden (-dna), únor (-ra), březen (-zna), duben (-bna), květen (-tna), červen (-vna), červenec (-nce), srpen (-pna), září (-í), říjen (-jna), listopad (-du), prosinec (-nce)

6.4.2 *On 18.ii.1961* is translated: **Osmnáctého února roku devetenáctistého** (or **tisícího devítistého**) **šedesátého prvního** using the genitive of the ordinal and inserting **roku**, *of the year*.

The memorable 28 October appears as **památný 28. říjen**, with the month in the nominative.

In 1961 may be translated by the genitive or by **v** and the locative: **v roce devatenáctistém šedesátém prvním**. Alternatively cardinals may be used in the nominative, either for the whole date as in English, viz. **roku tisíc devět set šedesát jeden** or for the thousands and hundreds.

V létech (*in the years*) **1945–1960** is best read with cardinals in the nominative throughout. Note that different words are used for *year* in the singular and plural.

7 PRONOUNS AND PRONOUN-ADJECTIVES

7.1/7.2 DEMONSTRATIVE, ETC.

7.1.1 Demonstratives, interrogatives and relatives partly resemble adjectives in their declension and partly nouns, viz. (selected cases):

> **ten, to, ta**: MG **toho**, I **tím**, L **tom** (cf. 5.2), FA **tu** (4.3.9), G **té** (5.2), P **ti/ty, ta, ty** (5.2.3), G **těch** (*this, that*)
> **kdo**: **koho, kým** (*who?, who*)
> **nikdo**: **nikoho**, etc. (*nobody*)
> **co**: **čeho, čím** (*what?*)
> **nic**: **ničeho**, etc. (*nothing*)

7.1.2 **On, ono, ona** (*he, it, she*) has oblique cases from [**jen**], which is found only in the compound **jenž** (7.1.3), viz.

	S			*P*
	M	*N*	*F*	
A	jej, (je)ho, něj, něho	je, ně	ji, ni	je, ně
G	(je)ho, něho			jich, nich
D	(je)mu, němu		jí, ní	jim, nim
I	jím, ním			jimi, nimi
L	něm		ní	nich

7.1.3 A number of such pronouns have suffixes that are not declined, e.g. **ten|to**, P **ty|to**; **jenž, jež, jež**, *who* G etc. **jehož** etc. (see 7.1.2: **on**). In **týž**, *the same*, the first part is declined like a hard adjective: N and A also **tentýž**, i.e. **ten** (7.1.1) + **týž**, P **titíž, tytéž, tatáž, tytéž**.

7.3 PERSONAL

	S		*S & P*	*P*	
	1	2	*R*	1	2
N	já	ty		my	vy
AG	mě, mne	tě, tebe	se, sebe	nás	vás
D	mi, mně	ti, tobě	si, sobě	nám	vám
I	mnou	tebou	sebou	námi	vámi
L	mně	tobě	sobě	nás	vás

se, *self*, refers to all persons and numbers. For **se** indicating the passive see 8.14.2.

8 VERBS

8.1 STRUCTURE

8.1.1 Differences of person are for the most part sufficiently expressed by endings, making pronouns unnecessary, e.g. **píši**, *I write*.

8.1.2 Verbs are entered in most dictionaries under the imperfective infinitive (see General note on the Slavonic languages) with reference from the perfective, except where the entries would be adjacent. This economy can be disconcerting, as when **přinášet** is entered under **přinést**. The opposite arrangement is sometimes found.

8.2 PRESENT (impf.); FUTURE (pf.)

8.2.1 *Endings*

Ia	-u, -eš, -e; -eme, -ete, -ou
b	-i/-u, -eš, -e; -eme, -ete, -i/-u
II	-ím, íš, -í; -íme, -íte, -í/-ějí
III	-ám, -áš, -á; áme, áte, -ají

Ia follows hard consonants, Ib soft ones.

8.2.2 *Relation to infinitive*

P	-ám	-*i	-ji	-uji	-ím		-nu	-knu
I	-at	-at	-t	-ovat	-ít, -it, -et, ět		-nout, -t	-ci

8.2.3 *Some peculiar stems*

P	beru	čtu	chci	jdu	jedu	jím	kladu	mám	mohu
I	brát	číst	chtít	jít	jet	jíst	klást	mít	moci

P	nesu	píši	počnu	rostu	stojím	vedu	vezu	vím
I	nést	psát	počít	růst	stát	vést	vézt	vědět

8.3 PAST

Though its formation is the same essentially as in Russian and Polish, in Czech this tense is patently compound, and it is dealt with in 8.10.

8.10 COMPOUND TENSES

8.10.1 These involve either the infinitive (8.11) or the old past participle, which has the following forms:

	S			P	
M	*N*	*F*	*M*	*N*	*F*
-l	-lo	-la	-li, -ly	-la	-ly

8.10.2 The relation of the old participle to the infinitive is as follows:

P	-l after a vowel usually corresponds to
I	-t, e.g. **psal, psát; kryl, krýt**

Note also

-l	-il	-hl, -kl
-nout	-ít, -it, -et, -ět	-ci

R

and the following peculiar verbs:

P	četl	chtěl	jedl	kladl	měl	šel	vedl
I	číst	chtít	jíst	klást	mít	jít	vést

8.10.3 With the present tense of the verb **být**, *to be*, omitting the third person, we get the past tense. (See specimen for examples.) With **býval**, itself a past tense, we get the pluperfect. With

> **bych, bys, by; bychom, byste, by**

we get the conditional. Note also **kdybych**, etc., *if*.

8.10.4 The future imperfective is formed from **budu**, etc. (8.17) with the infinitive (8.11).

8.11 INFINITIVE
This now usually ends in **-t**, but the old ending **-ti** still persists in literary contexts. Some verbs have **-ci**.

8.12/8.13 PARTICIPLES AND GERUNDS
8.12.1 The participles are adjectives, e.g. **vedoucí redaktor**, '*leading*' editor (1.8.3); gerunds are used, like English participles, in adverbial phrases.

8.12.2 *Present active*

	Participle	Gerund
I	**-oucí**	**-a, -ouc, -ouc, P -ouce**
II	**-ící/-ějící**	**-e (-ě), -íc, etc.; -ěje, -ějíc, etc.**
III	**-ající**	**-aje, ajíc, etc.**

For the corresponding infinitives see 8.2.2. For the declension of the participle see 5.2.2.

8.12.3 *Past active*

	Participle	Gerund
I	**-(v)ší**	**-/v, -(v)ši, -(v)ši, P -(v)še**
II	**-evší/-ivší**	**-ev/-iv, etc.**
III	**-avší**	**-av, etc.**

Follows the past tense (8.10.2) in form, e.g. **psal, psavší; četl, četší; měl, měvší; but šel, šedší.**

8.12.4 *Past passive*
The participle ends in **-n** or **-t** (long form **-ný, -tý**, see 5.2.4), corresponding to an infinitive in **-t**. There may be a change of vowel length or quality, e.g. **psán** (*written*), inf. **psát**, but **kryt** (*covered*), **krýt**; **-nut**, inf. **-nout**. Participles in **-*en** correspond to infinitives in **-it, -ít, -nout**, e.g. **třen** (*rubbed*) **třít**; **prošen** (*entreated*) **prosit**; **tištěn** (as well as **tisknut**) (*printed*), **tisknout**; **obsažen** (*contained*) **obsáhnout**; but **sáhnut.**

Note also **nesen** (*carried*), **nest**; **řečen** (*said*), **říci**; **veden** (*led*), **vest**; **vezen** (*carried*) **vezt.**

8.13 GERUNDS
See 8.12.

8.14 REFLEXIVE

8.14.1 The addition of the universal reflexive pronoun **se** (7.3) makes a verb reflexive, e.g. **mýji se**, *I wash myself.*

8.14.2 The appropriate translation of a reflexive form may be an intransitive verb (*I wash*) or, as in 8.15.2, a passive.

8.15 PASSIVE

8.15.1 Using the passive participle (8.12.4) with parts of the verb **být: nejbližší svazky jsou (byly) rozvrženy takto,** *the next volumes are (have been) planned thus.*

8.15.2 Using the reflexive: **se prodává,** *is sold;* **se tisknou,** *are being printed, will be printed.*

8.17 THE VERB **být,** *to be*

    Present: **jsem, jsi, je(st); jsme, jste, jsou**
    Future: **budu** (8.2.1)
    Past: **byl jsem,** etc. (8.10.3)
    Pluperfect: **byl býval** (8.10.3)

není means *is not.*

8.22 NEGATIVE

The negative is formed by prefixing **ne-**: e.g. **dát,** *to give;* **nedat,** *not to give.*

9 ADVERBS

9.1 FORMATION

They are regularly formed from adjectives, including participles by substituting -**ě** (-**e*) or -**o**, e.g. **úplný, úplně,** *complete(ly);* **veliký, velice,** *extreme(ly);* **malý, málo,** *little.* National adjectives make adverbs in -**y**, e.g. **česky,** *in the Czech fashion.*

9.2 COMPARISON

The comparative ends in -**ěji** (-**eji*). Some common adverbs are irregular; but the comparatives are entered separately in dictionaries.

The superlative is formed by adding **nej-** to the comparative.

10 PREPOSITIONS

These govern particular cases. Some may be used with more than one case, and where this affects the translation, care is needed: **na universitě,** *at the university;* **na universitu,** *to the university.*

GLOSSARY

autorské právo. *copyright*

bádání, *research*
básně, *poems*
bezplatný, *free*
brožovaný, brožura, *paperback*
brožurka, *pamphlet*

cena, *price*

časopis, *periodical* (1.8.1)
část, *part* (1.4.1)
číslo, *number* (1.7.2, 1.8.4)
člen, *member*
čtrnáctideník, *fortnightly* (1.8.5)

čtvrtletník, *quarterly* (1.8.5)

dějiny, *history*
díl, *part* (1.4.1)
dílo, *work*
divadelní hra, *play* (1.7.1)
dodatek, *appendix*
dopis, *letter*
doplněk, *supplement*
doplněný, *enlarged* (1.5.2)
družstvo, *society*

edice, *publication* (1.7.3)
exemplář, *copy*

faktúra, *invoice*

hotov, *ready*

jednotlivý, *single*

kniha, *book* (1.4.1, 1.7.2)
knihkupec, *bookseller*
knihkupectví, *bookshop*
knihovna, *library* (1.7.1)
knihovník, *librarian*
knihtiskárna, *press* (1.6.2)

měsíční(k), *monthly* (1.8.5)

náklad, *impression*
nakladelství, *publishing house* (1.6.1)
nákladem, *at the expense* (1.6.2)
narozen, *born*
nevydaný, nevyšlo, *unpublished*
nezměněný, *unaltered*
novela, *long short story*
nový, *new*

objednávka, *order*
odeslat, *to dispatch*
oprava, *correction*
opravený, *corrected*
otisk, *impression*

podobizna, *portrait*
pokračování, *continuation*
pololetní, *half-yearly*
pos(í)lat, *to send*

povídka, *story*
poznámka, *note*
práce, *transactions*
prodej, *sale*
projev, *speech*
předmluva, *preface*
předplatné, *subscription*
přehlednutý, *revised* (1.5.2)
překlad, *translation*
přeložil, *he translated* (1.2.2)
přepracovaný, *revised* (1.5.2)
přetisk, *reprint*
příloha, *annexure, plate, supplement*
připravit, *to prepare* (1.2.2)
příspěvek, *contribution*
půl ročník, *semi-annual volume*

rabat, *discount*
rada, *committee, board* (1.8.3)
redakce, *editorial office* (1.8.7)
redaktor, *editor* (1.8.3)
redigoval, *he edited* (1.2.2)
referat, *report*
rejestřík, *index*
ročenka, *yearbook*
roční, *annual* (1.8.6)
ročník, *volume* (1.8.4)
rok, *year*
román, *novel*
rozebraný, *out of print*
rozmnožený, *duplicated*
rozšířený, *enlarged*

řada, *series* (1.7.2)
řeč, *speech*

sbírka, *series* (collection)
sborník prací, *transactions*
sebraný, *collected*
separátní výtisk, *offprint*
sestavil, *he compiled*
slovník, *dictionary*
soubor, *collection* (1.2.4)
souhrn, *summary*
spis, *writing* (1.2.4, 1.4.3)
společnost, *society*
spolupracovník, *joint author* (1.2.7)
sražka, *discount*

stránka, *page*
svazek, *volume* (1.4.1, 1.7.2)

tabulka, *table*
tentýž, *same*
tisk, *type, printing* (1.6.2)
v tisku, *being printed*
tiskárna, *press* (1.6.2)
týdeník, *weekly* (1.8.5)

ukazatel, *index*
ukázka, *sample, specimen*
na ukázku, *on approval*
umřel, *died*
upravit, *to arrange* (1.2.2)
úvod, *introduction*

vazba, *binding*
věstník, *bulletin*
veškerá práva vyhrazena, *all rights reserved*
viz, *see*
volný, *complimentary*
výbor, *selection*
vybral, *he selected* (1.2.2)
vycházet, *to come out*
vydal, *he published*
vydání, *edition* (1.5.1)
výměna, *exchange*
výtisk, *copy*

zahraniční, *foreign*
zakázka, *order*
zemřel, *died*
zvláštní otisk, *offprint*

GRAMMATICAL INDEX: WORDS

budu, etc., 8.10.4, 8.17
by, bych(om), 8.10.3
byl, 8.17
bys(te), 8.10.3
býval, 8.17

čeho, čím, 7.1.1
čtyři, etc., 6.1.2

dva, etc., 6.1.2

ho, 7.1.2

je, 7.1.2, 8.17
jeho, 7.1.2
jehož, 7.1.3
jej, jemu, 7.1.2
jest, 8.17
jich, jim, jím, jimi, 7.1.2
jsem, etc., 8.17

koho, kým, 7.1.1

má, mé, 5.4.1
mě, 7.3.1
mého, mém(u), 5.4.1
mi, 7.3.1
mne, etc., 7.3.1
moje, moji, 5.4.1
mu, 7.1.2
můj, mých, mým(i), 5.4.1

nám(i), nás, 7.3.1
ně(j), etc., 7.1.2
není, 8.17
ni, ní, 7.1.2
ničeho, etc., 7.1.1
nich, 7.1.2
nikoho, etc., 7.1.1
nim, ním, nimi, 7.1.2

sebe, sobě, etc., 7.3.1
své, etc., 5.4.1

ta, té, 7.1.1
táž, 7.1.3
tě, 7.3.1
tebe, tebou, 7.3.1
těch, 7.1.1
též, 7.1.3
ti, 7.1.1, 7.3.1
tím, 7.1.1
to, 7.1.1
tobě, 7.3.1
toho, tom, 7.1.1
třech, etc., 6.1.2
tu, 7.1.1
tvé, etc., 5.4.1
ty, 7.1.1, 7.3.1

vám(i), vás, 7.3.1

GRAMMATICAL INDEX: ENDINGS

-a, 4.3.1, 4.3.5, 4.3.9, 5.2.3, 8.12.2
-á, 5.2.1
-la, 8.10.1
-ima, 4.3.6

-íc, -ouc, 8.12.2

-e, 4.3.1, 4.3.5, 4.3.9, 5.4.2, 9.1

-é, 4.3.1, 5.2.1, 5.2.3, 8.12.2
-ě, 4.3.1, 4.3.5, 4.3.9, 5.2.3, 8.12.2, 9.1
-aje, -ěje, 8.12.2

-áme, -eme, -íme, 8.2.1
-áte, -ete, -íte, 8.2.1
-ové, 4.3.1

-ach, 4.3.9
-ech, 4.3.1, 4.3.5, 4.3.13
-ich, 5.4.2
-ích, 4.3.1, 4.3.5, 4.3.6,
 4.3.8, 4.3.9, 5.2.2
-ých, 5.2.1

-i, 4.3.1, 4.3.5, 4.3.6,
 4.3.9, 4.3.13, 5.2.3,
 5.4.2, 8.2.1
-í, 4.3.5, 4.3.6, 4.3.8,
 4.3.9, 4.3.13, 5.2.1,
 5.4.2, 8.2.1
-cí, 8.12.2
-ají, 8.2.1
-ějí, 8.2.1, 9.1
-li, 8.10.1
-ami, 4.3.13
-ami, -emi, 4.3.9
-imi, 5.4.2
-ími, 5.2.2

-ými, 5.2.1
-ši, 8.12.3
-ší, 5.3.1, 8.12.3
-ejší, 5.3.1
-vši, vší, 8.12.3
-ovi, 4.3.1, 4.3.9, 4.3.15

-l, 8.10.1

-ám, 4.3.9, 8.2.1
-em, 4.3.1, 4.3.5, 4.3.13,
 4.3.15, 5.4.2
-ém, 5.2.1
-ěm, 4.3.1, 4.3.5
-im, 5.4.2
-ím, 4.3.5, 4.3.8, 4.3.9,
 5.2.2, 5.4.2, 8.2.1
-ům, 4.3.1, 4.3.5
-ým, 5.2.1

-n, 8.5.4

-o, 4.3.5, 5.2.3, 9.1
-eho, 4.3.15, 5.4.2
-ého, 5.2.1

-ího, 5.2.2
-lo, 8.10.1
-to, 7.1.2

-áš, eš, -íš, 8.2.1

-t, 8.11, 8.12.4

-u, 4.3.1, 4.3.5, 4.3.9,
 5.2.3, 8.2.1
-ů, 4.3.1
-emu, 5.4.2
-ému, 5.2.1
-ou, 4.3.9, 5.2.1, 8.2.1

-v, 8.12.3

-y, 4.3.1, 4.3.5, 4.3.9,
 5.2.3
-ý, 5.2.1
-ly, 8.10.1
-ný, 8.12.4
-tý, 8.12.4

-ž, 7.1.2

SLOVAK

SPECIMEN

Táto práca mala byť pôvodne vlastne druhým, prepracovaným vydaním publikácie Príspevok k dejinám slovenského robotníckeho hnutia, ktorá vyšla v slovenčine roku 1951. V preklade českom (1952), maďarskom (1952) a ukrajinskom (1954) urobil autor iba nepatrné úpravy.

V čase, keď vyšla uvedená publikácia po prvý raz, nebolo v slovenskej historickej literatúre žiadnej samostatnej práce o dejinách slovenského robotníckeho hnutia pred vznikom ČSR.

This work was to be originally actually a second revised edition of the publication Contribution to the history of the Slovak labour movement, which came out in Slovak in the year 1951. In the Czech, Hungarian and Ukrainian translation the author made only slight corrections.

At the time, when the above publication came out for the first time, there was not in Slovak historical literature any independent work on the history of the Slovak labour movement before the beginning of the Czechoslovak Republic.

0 GENERAL CHARACTERISTICS

0.1 DEGREE OF INFLEXION
Slovak, like Czech, is predominantly synthetic.

0.2 ORDER OF WORDS
Reversal of standard order takes place (see specimen), especially on title-pages, as in

Pre tlač aktualizoval Teodor Fiš, *T.F. brought (it) up to date for printing.*

0.4 RELATION TO OTHER LANGUAGES
The relation of Slovak to other Slavonic languages is dealt with in the General note on the Slavonic languages. Slovak agrees generally with Czech in conventions of spelling and shows considerable similarity in forms and vocabulary; but there are quite a number of differences, and it should not be regarded as simply a dialect of Czech. Superficial distinguishing marks are the Slovak letters ä, ľ, ĺ, ó, ô, ŕ, the absence of ě, ř and ů, and the effects of the 'rhythmic law' (2.6.1). (Note the similarity and possibility of confusion between the Slovak word for *Slovakian*, **slovenský**, and the Slovene for *Slovenian*, **slovenski**.)

1 BIBLIOLINGUISTICS

1.1 NAMES
1.1.1 Slovak names are either nouns or adjectives, and are declined as such, and foreign names, so far as may be, are accommodated to the native declension. Christian names are almost all nouns in form (4.3).

1.1.2 Male surnames may be:
(a) masculine adjectives (5.2), e.g. Široký, Bánsky, Lepší, Rýdzi;
(b) masculine nouns (4.2.1), e.g. Holotík;
(c) nouns in -o or occasionally -a (4.3.6).

1.1.3 Women's surnames are always adjectival. If the corresponding man's surname is adjectival, the feminine of the adjective is used, e.g. Široká, Bánska, Lepšia, Rýdza. If the corresponding man's surname is a noun, the ending -ová is added to the stem, e.g. Holotíková, Grekovová, Hašková (Hašek), and with foreign names Dohnaniová. But Madame Curie is left without ending, as were many names in the past.

1.1.4 The plural ending is -ovci.

1.1.5 Surnames in -y which are not adjectives of the type Bánsky (1.1.2) are treated like foreign names (4.3.20), e.g. Fándly G Fándlyho, etc.

1.1.6 Usually both parts of a compound name are declined, e.g. s pomocou Hermíny Bunčákovej-Groeblovej, *with the assistance of Hermína Bunčáková-Groeblová.*

1.1.7 These are also possessive forms in -ov and -in, derived from masculine and feminine names respectively (5.4.1), which are freely used in narrative instead of or in combination with the genitive, e.g. Názory Tugana-Baranovského, Železnovove, Prokopovičove, Brentanove, *The views of Tugan-Baranovsky, Zheleznov, Prokopovich, Brentano.* They have a restricted use in indicating authors (1.2.4) and the publishers of series (1.6). They can be used, as here, with foreign names.

1.2 NAMES OF AUTHORS, EDITORS, ETC.

1.2.1 Authors' names are usually given at the top of the title-page, e.g. Alexander Markuš|Sedliacke povstanie v Zemplíne. They are in the nominative and need no alteration.

1.2.2 Also in the nominative are the names of authors, editors, translators, when they follow the title preceded by an active verb, e.g. napísal(i), *wrote*; vypracovala, *she elaborated.* Where the work is more of a compilation and some other verb is used, as in 1.2.6, or in case of editors, the position after the title is the regular one. Thus one finds such verbs as (z)redigoval, *edited*; k vydaní prihotovil, na vydanie pripravil, *prepared for publication*; posudzoval, *vetted*; zostavil (sostavil), *arranged*; preložil, *translated.* Note that the verb agrees in number and gender: one must be careful in shortening titles to preserve this agreement. (See 8.10.1.)

The forms given above are all past. The editor of a many-volumed work may be indicated by a present tense, e.g. rediguje, *is editing.*

1.2.3 In some sorts of publication such as collected works, letters, essays, speeches and editions of the classics the name may be in the genitive case, before or after the title, e.g. O Slovákoch. Článkov Jozefa Škultétyho sväzok I, *On the Slovaks. Vol. I of the essays of Jozef Škultéty.*

The ambiguity of the ending -a (Cz 1.2.4) applies to Slovak also.

1.2.4 When an existing work is referred to on the title-page of a new one its author's name may be in the form of a possessive adjective (1.1.7, 5.4.1) e.g. podľa Jursovho Slabikára, *based on Jurs's Primer*; Doplnky k Riznerovej Bibliografii, *Addenda to Rizner's Bibliography.*

1.2.5 Less common, but found in the case of translations, is the use of an abstract noun, e.g. preklad, *translation*, followed by the name in the genitive. (Cf. 1.2.3.)

1.2.6 For collaborators, apart from the simple use of a plural verb followed by a list of names, we commonly find autorský kolektiv, also with names in the nominative, sometimes with mention of the secretary, tajomnik; or the verb spolupracovali, *collab-*

orated. More elaborate phrases in **s** (**so**), *with*, are illustrated by **so slovenskými autormi spracoval R.W. Seton-Watson**, *R.W. Seton-Watson executed it along with Slovak authors*, **s pomocou Hermíny Bunčákovej-Groeblovej složil B. Vavrušek**, *B.V. compiled it with the help of Hermína Bunčáková-Groeblová.*

Editorial collaboration may be indicated by the same phrases as are used in periodicals (1.8) or these may be a phrase such as **za hlavnej redakcie Mikulaša Bakoša**, *under the general editorship of Mikulaš Bakoš* with the name in the genitive.

1.2.7 Societies and institutions as authors and editors are indicated in the same ways as individuals, but if their relation to the book is not specified it may be one of vague sponsorship. They are often mentioned in the body of the title (rather than in the imprint) as 'publishing' a work (cf. 1.5.1). Names of branches and departments may follow that of the main body, e.g. **Slovenská akadémia vied|Sekcia spoločenských vied**, *Slovak Academy of Sciences|Section of Social Sciences*; but they are more likely to precede it. The name of the main body will then be in the genitive, e.g. **Čitanková komisia Matice slovenskej**, *Commission for (the compilation of) a reader of Matica Slovenská*, or will be preceded by **pri** and be in the locative, e.g. **Edícia slovenskej historickej spoločnosti pri Slovenskej akadémii vied**. In such cases the name of the main body will have to be turned into the nominative in the catalogue, e.g. **Matica slovenská. Čitanková komisia**; **Slovenská akademia vied. Edícia slovenskej historickej spoločnosti.**

1.3 TITLES

1.3.1 The great majority, fiction apart, consist of nouns and adjectives in various cases with or without prepositions, e.g. **Pravidlá slovenského pravopisu**, *Rules of Slovak orthography*; **O niektorých otázkach roľníckej politiky na Slovensku**, *On some questions of agricultural policy in Slovakia*. The literature of persuasion produces more complicated titles, including verbs, adverbs and pronouns, e.g. **A svet sa hýbe**, *And the world moves*; **Život nie je majáles**, *Life is not all carnival.*

1.3.2 Title entries of the Anglo-American type present no problems. There are no articles to be ignored in filing. British Museum rules may entail the production of the nominative from oblique cases (4.3) or translation. Neither is very difficult, but it may be advisable to check with the dictionary.

1.3.3 When a title is quoted in a phrase the main noun may appear in an oblique case instead of in the nominative, e.g. **nové vydanie** (*new edition*) **Pravidiel slovenského pravopisu** (see 1.3.1); **Doplnky k Riznerovej Bibliografii**, *Additions to Rizner's 'Bibliografia'*; **v „Demokratoch"**, *in 'Demokrati'*. It is also possible to isolate the title grammatically from the rest of the sentence by putting it in apposition, e.g. **téma knihy Právne otázky odmeny za prácu**, *The theme of the book 'Právne otázky'*, etc. Here **knihy** has the necessary case-ending, so there is no need to alter **Právne otázky**.

1.4 VOLUMES AND PARTS

1.4.1 The words for *volume* and *part* are **zväzok** (older **sväzok**) and **časť** respectively, but the vaguer word **diel** will sometimes be found in place of **zväzok**. It does not necessarily denote a separate volume but only a division of a work.

1.4.2 The numeration may be in words or figures and may precede the word for volume or part, as an ordinal, or follow, as a cardinal: e.g. **Diel I, časť I**, but in the preface of the same work **prvého dielu (1. časti)**.

1.4.3 The numeration may be grammatically connected with the title of the work: e.g. **Člankov Jozefa Škultétyho sväzok 1**, *Of the articles of J. Škultéty volume 1.*

1.4.4 The actual or probable compass of many-volumed works is indicated by phrases such as **Dielo v piatich zväzkoch**, *Work(s) in five volumes*, usually on an additional title-page.

1.5 EDITIONS

1.5.1 The word for *edition* is **vydanie**, which as an abstract noun meaning *publication* can be used in other contexts, e.g. **vydanie Matice slovenskej** is equivalent to *published by Matica slovenská*. The word **náklad** may also be translated *edition*, but properly means *run* or *impression*. (See also 1.6.2.)

1.5.2 Numeration precedes, either in words or figures, e.g. **3. (tretie) vydanie.** Revision, or the lack of it, is indicated by various words, e.g. **opravené**, *corrected*; **prepracované**, *worked over*; **doplnené**, *filled out*; **rozšírené**, *enlarged*; **(z)revidované**, *revised*; or on the other hand **nezmenené**, *unchanged*.

1.5.3 *Offprint* is **separat**; *reprint* is **dotlač**.

1.6 IMPRINTS

1.6.1 Most present-day Slovak books are published by institutional publishing houses, e.g. **Vydavateľstvo Slovenskej akadémie vied** (*Press of the Slovak Academy of Sciences*), **Slovenská akadémia vied a umení** (*Slovak Academy of Sciences and Arts*), **Slovenské vydavateľstvo politickej literatúry** (*Slovak Publishing House for Political Literature*), **Slovenská rada družstiev v Oráči** (*Slovak Council of Cooperatives at Oráč*). This last is often cited just as **Oráč**. Occasionally the press is named after a periodical, e.g. **Nakladateľstvo Pravda**. Both the press and the place are usually in the nominative, but **v Prahe, v Bratislave**, *at Prague, at Bratislava* are not uncommon.

1.6.2 There is more variety in earlier books, both in the names of publishers and in the grammatical form of the imprint, e.g. **nákladom Kníhtlačiarskeho Učast(inár-skeho) Spolku**, *at the expense of the Book-Printing Company*; **v Komisii u firmy „Komenský"**, where **v komisii** indicates that the firm acts as agent, while the preposition **u**, like the French **chez**, indicates the publisher; **Vydavateľstvo Osveta**, *Osveta* (*Enlightenment*) *Press*; **v Prahe, v štatnom knihosklade**, *at Prague, at the State Bookstore*. **Nákladom, u** and **vydanie** (1.5) are followed by the genitive, **v** by the locative, **vydal** (-a, -o) by the nominative.

1.6.3 **Tlač, vytlačil**, indicate the printer, e.g. **tlačou Novej Kníhtlačiarne**, but words like **kníhtlačiarne**, though they denote a printing establishment, do not rule it out as publisher.

1.7 SERIES

1.7.1 The title of a series (**edícia**) may be descriptive of the collection, either in the collective singular, e.g. **Družstevná Knižnica**, *Cooperative library*, or in the plural e.g. **Spisy Slovenskej akadémie vied a umení**, *Writings of the Slovak Academy of Sciences and Arts*; or it may be a title equally appropriate to a book, e.g. **Slovaci v Maďarsku**, *Slovaks in Hungary*, or a fanciful one, such as **Žatva**, *Harvest*.

It usually appears on the half-title leaf but may also be found in the colophon, sometimes in a more complicated form, e.g. **vyšlo ako 2. sväzok Spisov Slovenskej akadémie vied a umení**, *appeared as 2nd volume of the Writings* (etc. as above).

1.7.2 Within a series there may be a sub-series (**séria**). Individual items are numbered by the **zväzok** (see example above), less commonly by **diel** or both.

1.7.3 Not every **edícia** is a bibliographical series. For instance the note: **Vydalo Slovenské vydavateľstvo politickej literatúry v edícii pôvodnej literatúry**, that is, *Published by S.V.P.L. in the series of original literature*, has much the same force as a subject heading in a publisher's list.

1.8 PERIODICALS

1.8.1 The titles of periodicals (**časopisy**) do not differ linguistically from those of books, e.g. **Čitateľ**, *The Reader*; **Slovenské divadlo**, *Slovak theatre*.

When the title is an element in a larger phrase nouns and adjectives which are normally in the nominative may have to obey the grammar of the larger phrase, e.g. **Tri ročniki „Hronky"**, *three volumes of Hronka*; but with **časopis** inserted, **v 9.č. časopisu „Živena"**, *in pt. 9 of the periodical Živena* (cf. 1.3.3).

1.8.2 Institutional periodicals often have the name of the institution in the genitive, e.g. **Ekonomický sborník Slovenskej akadémie vied a umení**, *Economic Magazine of the Slovak Academy of Sciences and Arts*. For the catalogue heading the nominative, **Slovenská akadémia**, etc. has to be produced. Alternatively the name of the publisher may already be in the nominative, preceded by **vydáva**, *publishes*.

1.8.3 Editorship is almost always indicated by some form of the root **redakt-**, whether there is a **hlavný redaktor** (*general editor*), **šefredaktor** (*chief editor*) or plain **redaktor** or **redaktorka** (*editress*), or **redakčná rada** or **redakčný sbor** (*editorial committee or body*) with its **tajomník** (*secretary*).

1.8.4 Numeration of volumes is by **ročník** (*annual volume*), that of parts by **číslo** or **zväzok** (**sv-**). The number of the volume usually follows **ročník** in Roman figures, but the order **5 XI. ročník** for **ročník XI, číslo 5** occurs.

1.8.5 There are a number of other nouns of the same form as **ročník**, viz. **týždenník, dvojtýždenník, mesačník, štvrťročník** (*weekly, fortnightly, monthly, quarterly*): these may form part of the title or description of a periodical, but **ročník** is not so used. The corresponding adverbs, ending in -ne, occur in direct statements of periodicity as well as those in -krát, e.g. **vychádza mesačne, štyrikrat do roka, štvrťročne raz, polročne** (*comes out monthly, four times a year, once quarterly, half-yearly*); **vychodí každoročne v týchto sväzkoch** (*will come out every year in the following numbers*); **vychádzajú mesačne, t.j. 12-krát ročne s dvojčíslom celoročného registra** (*come out monthly, i.e. 12 times a year with a double number containing the index for the whole year*).

1.8.6 Details of subscription (**predplatné**) with special rates for abroad (**pre cudzinu**) are quoted using adjectives of periodicity, e.g. **ročné predplatné**, *annual subscription* (or **na celý ročník**, *for the whole annual volume*); they may quote for single numbers separately, **pre jednotlivé sväzky osobitne**, or give ' *the price of this number* ' (**cena tohto čísla**).

1.8.7 Addresses given distinguish between the editorial office (**redakcia**) and the business side (**administrácia**).

2 ALPHABET, PHONETICS, SPELLING

2.1 ALPHABET

2.1.1 The alphabet in use today is as follows:

> **a ä b c č d e f g h ch i j k l m n o ô p [q] r**
> **s š t u v [w x] y z ž**

Each of the above letters has a separate alphabetical position.

2.1.2 Diacritical marks used are:

> acute accent, e.g. á = long **a**; **ĺ, ŕ** long syllabic **l** and **r**
> haček, viz. **ď, ľ, ň, ť**, indicating palatalisation

Unlike the háček on č, š, ž, these marks do not affect alphabetical order.

2.2/2.3 CAPITALISATION; DIVISION OF WORDS

Capitalisation and division of words are the same as in Czech.

2.5 HARD AND SOFT CONSONANTS; PALATALISATION

2.5.1 Consonants are classified as follows:

Hard	d	g	h	ch	k	l	n	t		
Neutral	b	f	m	p	r	s	v	z		
Soft	c	č	ď	dz	dž	j	ľ	ň	š	ť ž

The neutral consonants are often classed with the hard ones. The distinctions are of little moment, for i, the characteristically soft vowel, may follow hard consonants without necessarily affecting them, e.g. **slovenský**, MP **slovenskí**, with identical pronunciation.

Di, li, ni, ti, are usually equivalent to **ďi, ľi, ňi, ťi,** as always in Czech; **de,** etc. are sometimes equivalent to **ďe.**

One should also note that **i** is not used as a mere sign of a soft consonant as it is in Polish: **ia, ie, iu** in Slovak are always diphthongs. (Cf. 2.6.1.)

Most of the declensions are divided into two types according as the stem ends in a hard or soft consonant, but some of the differences are very slight (4.3.1).

2.5.2 The effects of palatalisation (see General note on the Slavonic languages) are as follows:

	d	h	ch	k	s	sl	t	z	
to			s	c					mostly in nouns
	dz	ž		č	š	šl	c	ž	mostly in verbs

e.g. **Slovák**, pl. **Slováci; písať,** pr. **pišem** (cf. **piť, pijem**). Palatalisation is less common in Slovak than in Czech: the locative ending **-e** (Cz **-ě**) has no effect, and the effect of the plural **-i** is limited, so far as concerns spelling, to **ch** and **k** (cf. 2.5.1) and does not occur in the declension of adjectives.

2.6 VARIATION OF VOWEL

2.6.1 By what is known as the 'rhythmic law' long vowels are not usually found in successive syllables. A long vowel in a prefix such as **vý-** will be shortened before an adjacent long vowel or diphthong; more important for practical purposes a long ending will be shortened by a preceding long vowel or diphthong. Thus endings such as **-ý, -á, ách** and so on occur equally often without the accent and **-ia** is shortened to **-a**, e.g. **horám** but **dievkam, uliciach** but **prácach, mestá** but **miesta** in nouns; **prvý, prvého,** but **piaty, piateho** in adjectives; **povedá** but **vydáva** in verbs. The resulting forms are characteristic of Slovak as opposed to Czech.

2.6.2 A more complicated variation of length and usually of quality occurs in stem vowels, viz. **a, ä** > **ia; i** > **í; o** > **ô.** The conditions are not easy to define succinctly except historically, but a common case is the occurrence of a short vowel when the ending contains a vowel, and of a long one when it does not, or there is no ending; e.g. **kniha,** *book*; knih, *of the books*; **môcť,** *to be able*; mohol, *could*; **legenda,** *legend,* legiend, *of the legends*; stôl, *table*; stola, *of the table*. (Historically the lengthening is here a compensation for the loss of an ultra-short vowel.) Conversely, päť, piati, *five*.

2.6.3 Vowels occur for the sake of euphony in the NS or GP though absent in other cases, e.g. jutár, vojen, učiteliek, robotníčok: GP of jutro, vojna, učiteľka, robotníčka; NS zväzok, stem zväzk-.

2.7 SPELLING

The principles of spelling have changed little in the last two hundred years. In the 19th century w is still found occasionally for v and j for i. The 1967 official orthography gives a large number of individual rulings but the only widespread change is the substitution of z- for s- in a number of words such as zväzok, the substitution of i for y in some words and the suppression of -ly in the past tense.

3 ARTICLES

There are no articles.

4 NOUNS

4.1 GENDER AND FORM

There are three genders, the gender for the most part corresponding to the form of the noun. Inanimate nouns may be of any gender. Omitting the vocative there are six cases, the endings varying according to the form of the noun in question.

4.3 ENDINGS

4.3.1 *Masculine nouns*

These nearly all end in a consonant (4.3.6).
The endings are:

	S	P
N	-	-i, -ia, -ovia, -y; -e
A	a, -	-ov, -y; -e
G	-a, -u	-ov/-
D	-ovi, -u	-om
I	-om	-(a)mi
L	-ovi, -e, -u; -i	-och

4.3.2 NAP -e is used only after soft consonants (2.5.1), LS -i both after soft consonants and also after -al, -ar, -el, -er.

4.3.3 NP -i, -ia, -ovia are used only with animate nouns (except deň, *day*) -i causing palatalisation of k and ch. Thus robotník has plural robotníci, but ročník (*yearbook*) makes ročníky.

4.3.4 Change or disappearance of vowel (2.6.2, 2.6.3) occurs.

4.3.5 The absence of ending in GP is confined to a few nouns, especially plural place-names, e.g. čas, čias; ráz, ráz; tisíc, tisíc; Sučany, Sučian.

4.3.6 The NS sometimes has an ending, e.g. **komunista** (AS **-u**), names in **-o** and classical and foreign names, for which see 4.3.20.

4.3.7 *Neuter nouns*

	Hard type		*Soft types*		
	S	P	S		P
NA	-o	-á	-e	-ie	-ia
G	-a	-	-a	-ia	-i, -
D	-u	-ám	-u	-iu	-iam
I	-om	-ámi, -y	-om	-ím	-(i)ami
L	-e, -u	-ách	-i	-í	-iach

4.3.8 The endings **-á, -ám, -ách** from nouns in **-o**; **-ia, -iam, -iach** from nouns in **-e** may be shortened to **-a, -am, -ach** by the rhythmic law (2.6.1), destroying the distinction between the types.

4.3.9 The stem vowel is lengthened (2.6.2) in the GP when there is no ending, but the converse is not true, for the vowel may be originally long, e.g. **mien** from **meno**, but **diel** from **dielo**. Insertion of vowel (2.6.3) also occurs.

4.3.10 **Dieťa**, *child*, GS **dieťaťa**, has irregular plural: **deti, detí, deťom, deťmi, deťoch**; **oko, ucho** have **oči, -í/-ú, -iam, -ami/-ima, -iach** and similarly **uši**, etc.

4.3.11 *Feminine nouns*

	Hard type		*Soft type*	
	S	P	S	P
N	-a	-y	-a, -	-e
A	-u	-y	-u, -	-e
G	-y	-	-e	-í, -
D	-e	-ám	-i	-iam
I	-ou	-ami	-ou	-ami
L	-e	-ách	-i	-iach

4.3.12 Nouns of the soft type have a soft consonant or **-i-** before the ending, e.g. **ulica, práca, baňa, demokracia**; or end in a soft consonant, e.g. **pieseň. Mať** (AS **mať**, **mater**, stem **mater-**) also belongs to this type. See further 4.3.17.

4.3.13 **-ám, ách, -iam, iach** are alike shortened by the rhythmic law (2.6.1) to **-am, -ach**.

4.3.14 For the GP cf. 4.3.9, e.g. **legenda, legiend; vojna, vojen**.

4.3.15 *Consonant type*
These usually end in a soft consonant.

S   -, -, -i, -i, -ou, -i
P   -i, -i, -i, -iam/-ám, -(a)mi, -iach/-ách

4.3.16 Vowels may be present in the nominative which are absent in other cases (2.6.3), e.g. **česť**, *honour* GS **cti**.

4.3.17 The distribution of nouns between 4.3.11 (soft) and 4.3.15, and hence the NP, is not altogether predictable. The following is a rough division:

4.3.11: -ň, -j; most of those in -ľ, ď, č, š, ž, dz, z, šť

4.3.15: -s, -p, -v; most of those in -c, -sť

4.3.18 ruka, *hand*; noha, *leg*, sometimes have old forms, viz. DLS ruce, noze; NP ruce, noze; GP rukú, nohú; IP rukama, nohama.

4.3.19 pani, *lady, Mrs*, has AS paniu, GDLS panej, IS paňou: P as if from pania.

4.3.20 *Foreign names*

The majority are fitted into the Slovak system, those that prove quite intractable being left undeclined. Details are given below.

Masculine in -as, -es, -os, -us, -o, -enko, -u, -ú, -ö, -ou, -au as 4.3.1 (hard), with a link consonant if necessary, e.g. Július GS Júliusa; Szabó-va, Montesquieu-a.

Masculine in a soft consonant, r or l as 4.3.1.

Masculine in -ta as 4.3.6.

Feminine in -Ca, -oa, -ea, -ua as 4.3.11 (hard); in -ia, -ya (soft).

Feminine names ending in a consonant as 4.3.15.

Neuter in -o, -on, um as 4.3.7, ignoring -on and -um, e.g. múzeum, GS múzea.

Russian names in -kij, -koj, Polish and Serbocroat names in -ki are treated as if they were native names in -ký, Russian names in -aja like the corresponding feminine (5.2.1).

French and English names sometimes follow the pronunciation, e.g. **Hume** G **Humea**; **Descartes, Descarta**; **Laplace, Laplacea**; but **Maurois, Mauroisa**.

Foreign names in -ä, -e, -é, -i, -y add in the singular: AG -ho; D -mu, IL -m, e.g. **Goetheho**, etc.

Czech names in -ě (non-existent in Slovak) follow the patterns: **Bičiště** GS **Bičišťa** P **Bičišťovi**; **Purkyně, Purkyňu, Purkyňovi**.

4.6 USE OF CASES

The standard names are only a rough guide. The genitive is used as the object of a negative verb, the instrumental as the complement of the verb *to be*.

5 ADJECTIVES

5.1 GENERAL

5.1.1 Adjectives vary according to gender, number and case, and agree with the nouns they qualify. Both long and short forms are found, but most adjectives have only long ones.

5.1.2 Common endings of adjectives derived from nouns are: -ný, -ský, -ový.

5.1.3 A good many proper names (1.1) and some common nouns e.g. predplatné, *subscription*, follow the adjectival declension.

5.2 ENDINGS

5.2.1 *Long forms*

The endings of the hard type (-ý, -é, -á) are the same as in Czech, except:

GDLSF	-ej
APM	-ých
NAPN	-é

The endings of the soft type are:

	S			P		
	M	*N*	*F*	*M*	*N*	*F*
N	-í	-ie	-ia	-í, -ie	-ie	-ie
A	-í, -ieho	-ie	-iu	-ích, -ie	-ie	-ie
G		-ieho	-ej		-ích	
D		-iemu	-ej		-im	
I		-ím	-ou		-ími	
L		-om	-ej		-ích	

5.2.2 Long vowels and the diphthongs **-ia, -ie**(-) are shortened by the rhythmic law (2.6.2), e.g. **vedúci, vedúca, vedúceho** but **vedúcou** unchanged.

5.2.3 *Short forms*

	M	*N*	*F*		
NAS	-	-o	-a	*NAP*	-i/-y

Except for possessives (5.4) and **jeden**, *one* (6.1.1) adjectives with short forms, e.g. **povinen, povinno**, etc., are used only as predicates.

5.3 COMPARISON

5.3.1 For the comparative substitute **-ší** or **ejší** for the **-ý, -ký, -cký, -oký** of the positive, e.g. **mladý, mladší; siroký, sirší; slavný, slavnejší**. Note **krátky, kratší; riedky, redší** (2.5.2).

5.3.2 For the superlative add **naj-** to the comparative.

5.4 POSSESSIVES

5.4.1 Possessive adjectives in **-ov** and **-in**, e.g. **Husov**, *of Hus*, **sestrin**, *sister's*, have short forms in NA, G **-ho**, e.g. **Husovho**, D **-mu** and the remaining cases as 5.2.1.

5.4.2 The ordinary possessives **moj, tvoj, svoj, naš, vaš**, have NAS **-, -e, -a** P **-i/-e**; other cases as 5.2.1 except for length, e.g. DP **mojim** (but IS **mojím**).

6 NUMERALS

6.1 CARDINAL

6.1.1

1 jeden	11 jedenásť	21 dvadsaťjeden	101 sto jeden
2 dva	12 dvanásť	jedenadvadsať	200 dvesto
3 tri	13 trinásť	30 tridsať	300, etc. tristo, etc.
4 štyri	14 štrnásť	40 štyridsať	1000 tisíc
5 päť	15 pätnásť	50 päťdesiat	2000 dva tisíce
6 šesť	16 šestnásť	60 šesťdesiat	5000 päť tisíc
7 sedem	17 sedemnásť	70 sedemdesiat	
8 osem	18 osemnásť	80 osemdesiat	
9 deväť	19 devätnásť	90 deväťdesiat	
10 desať	20 dvadsať	100 sto	

6.1.2 **jeden–štyri** are adjectives.
jeden, jedno, jedna as 5.2.1 except in the nominative.
dva has relics of the dual number, viz.

	M	NF
N	dva(ja)	dve
A	dvoch/dva	dve
G	dvoch	
D	dvom	
I	dvoma	
L	dvoch	

tri and štyri have:

N	traja/tri	štyri(a)
A	troch/tri	štyroch/štyri
G	troch	štyroch
D	trom	štyrom
I	troma	štyrmi
L	troch	štyroch

6.1.3 Päť onwards are nouns with the following endings:

N -/i   *A* -/ich   *G* -ich   *D* -im   *I* -imi   *L* -ich

The stem-vowel of **päť, deväť, desať, -sať** changes to **-ia-**; the **-e-** in **sedem, osem** is dropped.

6.1.4 In compound numerals of the type **dvadsaťdva, dvadsaťtri**, both parts are declined, but **dvadsaťjeden** is indeclinable.

6.1.5 *Construction*

1–4 agree like other adjectives
5 onwards are treated partly as nouns, partly as adjectives

Thus the most universal construction is: **päť vinníkov bolo dopravených**, *five culprits were transported*, with the verb in the neuter singular and the predicate in the genitive plural. This construction is obligatory with compound numerals ending in **-jeden** and with all feminine and neuter nouns.

In all other cases the numeral is treated as an adjective, though it may be undeclined, e.g. **v piatich zväzkoch**, *in five volumes* but also **pred dvadsať rokmi**, *20 years earlier*.

In relation to masculine animate beings we find this in the nominative and accusative also, viz.

N	**Piati (dvadsiati dvaja) mužovia**, *five (twenty two) men*
A	**piatich (dvadsiatich dvoch) mužov**

6.2 ORDINAL

6.2.1

1	prvý	11–19	jedenásty, etc.
2	druhý	20–90	dvadsiaty, etc.
3	tretí	100	stý
4	štvrtý	101	sto prvý
5	piaty	200	dvojstý
6	šiesty	300	trojstý
7	siedmy	400	štvorstý
8	ôsmy	500–900	päťstý, etc.
9	deviaty	1000	tisíci
10	desiaty	2000	dvojtisíci

See 2.6.1 for the short final vowels.

6.2.2 In compound numerals only tens and units have the form of ordinals. As in English, figures which follow the noun, e.g. **strana** (*page*) **238**, are read as cardinals.

6.3 FIGURES
As in Czech.

6.4 DATES
6.4.1 The months are:

> **január, február, marec, april, máj, jún,**
> **júl, august, september, október, november, december**

(All 4.3.1: soft, except **august**.)

6.4.2 *On 4.iv.1962* may be translated: **štvrtého apríla** (**po štvrtom apríle**) **tisíc deväť sto šesťdesiateho druhého roku**; but the year may follow **roku**, in which case it will be a cardinal and undeclined (**šesťdesiatdva**). This is the usual way with years alone, e.g. **r(oku) 1848** (. . . **osem**).

> *The 1st of May* is **prvý maj** in the nominative
> **1848–1948** would be read as cardinals
> Note also **v 40-tych** (**štyridsiatych**) **rokoch**, *in the '40's*

7 PRONOUNS

7.1/7.2 DEMONSTRATIVE, INTERROGATIVE, RELATIVE
7.1.1 These have much the same endings as adjectives, which indeed incorporate a pronoun, but the vowels are short.

> **ten, to, tá,** *this, that* (*one*): GSMN **toho**; D **tomu**, PN **tí/tie**, behaves otherwise as if it were **tý**
> So **tamten**
> **onen, ono, oná,** *that* (*one*) (not to be confused with **on**) behaves as if it were **oný** but has alternatives **onoho, onomu**
> **kto,** *who*: **koho, komu, kým, kom**
> **čo,** *what*: **čoho, čomu, čím, čom**
> Similarly **niekto, nik(to), nič**

7.1.2 Some of these pronouns have suffixes that are not declined, e.g. **tento** GSM **tohto**.

7.2 RELATIVE
See 7.1.

7.3 PERSONAL
7.3.1

	S		S & P	P	
	1	2	R	1	2
N	ja	ty	—	my	vy
AG	m(ň)a	teba, ťa	s(eb)a	nás	vás
D	mne, mi	tebe, ti	sebe, si	nám	vám
I	mnou	tebou	sebou	nami	vami
L	mne	tebe	sebe	nás	vás

sa, *self*, which enters into the formation of reflexive-passive verbs, refers to all persons and both numbers.

7.3.2 **on, ono, ona** (*he, it, she*) has oblique case from another root:

	S				P
	M		N	F	
N	on		ono	ona	oni, ony
A	jeho, (ne)ho, -ň(ho)			ju	(n)ich, ne
G	do.			jej, nej	(n)ich
D	jemu, (ne)mu, -ňmu			jej, nej	n(im)
I	ním			ňou	nimi
L	ňom			nej	nich

The suffixed forms are used with prepositions, e.g. **doň(ho)**, *to it*.

8 VERBS

8.1 GENERAL

8.1.1 Differences of person are for the most part sufficiently expressed by endings, making pronouns unnecessary, e.g. **môžem**, *I can*.

8.1.2 Verbs are entered in dictionaries under the imperfective infinitive (see General note on the Slavonic languages) with reference from the perfective.

8.2 PRESENT (impf.); FUTURE (pf.)

8.2.1 *Endings*

Ia	-em, -eš, -e; -eme, -ete, -(ej)ú
b	-iem, -ieš, -ie; -ieme, -iete, -(ej)ú
II	-ím, -íš, -í; -íme, -íte, -ia
III	-ám, -áš, -á; -áme, -áte, -ajú
	-iam, -iaš, -ia; -iame, -iate, -ajú

8.2.2 *Relation to infinitive*

P	-ám	-iam	-(*)em	-iem		-niem	-jem	-ujem
I	-ať	-ať	-ať	-ať, -ť (8.2.3)		-nuť	-ť	-ovať

P	-mem	-nem	-ím	
I	-ať (8.2.3)	-nuť, -ať (8.2.3)	-iť/ieť/ať (8.2.3)	

8.2.3 *Some peculiar stems*

-iem/-ať verbs have stem vowel in the present which is absent in the infinitive:
beriem/brať; ženiem/hnať (2.5.2)

-iem/-ť verbs lengthen the vowel (2.6.2) in the infinitive and change **d, t > s**;
č > c; ž > z, c, e.g. **mätiem/miasť; môžem/môcť**

-mem/-ať: note **snímem/sňať, vezmem/vziať**

-nem/-ať: note **rozožnem/rozžať**

-ím/-ať: mostly after **č, š, ž**, but note **spím/spať** and also **stojím/stať**

Note also:

P	chcem	idem	jem (3PP jedia)	viem (3PP vedia)
I	chcieť	ísť	jesť	vedieť
		pôjdem: future of ísť		

8.3 PAST

As in Czech the past is a compound tense (8.10.1).

8.10 COMPOUND TENSES

8.10.1 *Past tense*

Formed by combining the old participle:

	S		P
M	N	F	
-l	-lo	-la	-li

with the present tense of **byť**, *to be*, viz.

som, si, -; sme, ste, -

e.g. **pridal som**, *I* (*have*) *added, given*; **sme čím prv vydali druhé vydanie** *we have published the second edition all the sooner*. (Note the separation of the constituent elements.) Before 1953 the FP (and sometimes the M) was -**ly**.

8.10.2 *Relation to infinitive*

| P | -l, etc. after most vowels corresponds to |
| I | -ť; but note **vzal, vziať** |

| P | -el |
| I | -ieť |

| P | -ol |
| I | (a) -nuť; (b) -ť but with change of consonant, h to c, z; k to c; d, t to s, e.g. **viedol, viesť; mohol, môcť** (2.6.2) |

Note also **išiel, išlo**, etc. (in compounds -**šiel**, etc.) from **ísť** (-**jsť**).

8.10.3 *Future imperfective*

budem, etc. (8.2.1) with inf. (8.11).

8.10.4 *Conditional*

Formed from the past by adding **by**.

8.11 INFINITIVE

All infinitives end in -**ť**.

8.12 PARTICIPLES

8.12.1 *The present active* ends in -**ci**, which is added to the 3PP of the present, e.g. **vedúci**, *leading*. It is used as an adjective, sometimes with a special sense, so that it features, somewhat haphazardly, in dictionaries.

8.12.2 *The past participle passive* ends in -**ný** or -**tý** (5.2.1). This usually corresponds to an infinitive in -**ť**, but participles in -**ený** have I -**iť**, -**ieť**, or -**ť** with change of consonant, d, t, to s; č to c; ž to z, c: e.g. **vedený, viesť; premožený, premôcť**.

8.15 PASSIVE

8.15.1 The passive participle (8.12.2) is used, with or without parts of the verb **byť** (8.17) either as in English, e.g. **kniha je vydaná**, *the book is published*, or with the participle in the neuter and the noun in the accusative, e.g. **knihu bolo vydané**, *the book was published.*

8.15.2 Using the reflexive **sa**, which may be separated from its verb: **celý náklad sa minul**, *the whole impression was exhausted*; **na prvý pohľad sa môže zdať**, *at first sight it might be expected.*

8.15.3 Slovak often prefers to use the active: **rozširuje Poštová novinová služba**, i.e. *distributed by the P.O. Newspaper Service.*

8.17 THE VERB **byť**, *to be*

> *Present:* **som, si, je; sme, ste, sú**
>> Note: **niet,** (*there*) *is not*
> *Future:* **budem**
> *Past:* **bol som**

8.22 NEGATIVE

To form the negative **ne-** is prefixed to the verb.

9 ADVERBS

9.1 FORMATION

9.1.1 Adverbs formed regularly from adjectives end in **-o** or less frequently **-e**. Adjectives in **-cký**, **-ský** have adverbs in **-ky** and some phrases of the form **po ——sky**, e.g. **technicky**, *technically*; **po slovensky**, *in Slovak.*

9.1.2 A number of adverbs are derived from the combination of prepositions with nouns or adjectives, e.g. **zväčša**, *for the most part.*

9.2 COMPARISON

The comparative and superlative (5.3.2) end in **-(ej)šie**.

10 PREPOSITIONS

10.2 FORMS AND SYNTAX

10.2.1 Prepositions govern particular cases. Some, especially those relating to place, may be used with more than one case, and this may affect the translation, e.g. **na**: with A (*on*) *to*, with L *on, at*; **o**: with A *after, by* (of time), e.g. **o rok**, *in a year's time*; **o šesť rokov mladšia**, *six years younger*; with L *at, about*; **za**: with A *behind, for, instead of*; with G *during*; with I *behind.*

10.2.2 There are a number of peculiar prepositions compounded with **po-** expressing motion towards and with **spo-** (**zpo-**) expressing motion from, e.g. **ponad**, *to above*; **sponad**, *from above* (**nad**, *above*).

10.5 MEANINGS

Most Slovak prepositions can be recognised from other Slavonic languages, but the following may give trouble: **cez**, *through*; **kvôli**, *for the sake of*; **mimo**, *outside*; **okrem**, *except*; **skrz(e)**, *by means of*; **uprostred**, *in the middle of*; **vďaka**, *thanks to*; **voči**, *towards*; **vôkol**, *about.*

11 CONJUNCTIONS

Conjunctions call for no grammatical notice, except that their position in the sentence is often different from that in English. Many are similar to those in other Slavonic languages, especially Czech, but even so the following may give trouble: **aj**, *also, and*; **lež**, *but*; **čiže, alebo**, *or, as* (*well as*); **aby**, *in order that*; **keď**, *when.*

GLOSSARY

adresa, *address*

badanie, *research*
báseň, *poetry*
bezplatný, *free*
brožovaný, *paper-covered*
brožur(k)a, *pamphlet*

cena, *price*
cudzina, *foreign country* (1.8.6)

časopis, *periodical*
časť, *part* (1.4.1)
číslo, *number* (1.8.4)
článok, *article, essay*
člen, *member*

dejiny, *history*
diel, *volume* (1.4.1, 1.7.2)
dielo, *work*
divadelná hra, *play*
dodatok, *addendum, appendix*
doplnený, *enlarged*
doplnok, *addendum, appendix, supplement*
dotlač, *reprint, extra print* (1.5.3)
dvojtýždenník, *fortnightly*

edícia, *series* (1.7.1, 1.7.3)
esej, *essay*
exemplár, *copy*

faktúra, *invoice*

hotový, *ready*

jednotlivý, *single* (1.8.6)

každoročne, *annually*
kniha, *book*
kníhkupec, *bookseller*
knihovník, *librarian*
kníhtlačiareň, *printing shop* (1.6.3)
knižnica, *library*

list, *letter*

mesačník, *monthly* (1.8.5)
sa minul, *is out of print*

náklad, *impression, edition* (1.5.1), *expense* (1.6.2)
napísal, *he wrote* (1.2.2)
narodený, narodil sa, *(was) born*
nevydaný, *unpublished*
nezmenený, *unaltered* (1.5.2)
novela, *short story*
nový, *new*

objednávka, *order*
obraz, *illustration*
opravený, *corrected* (1.5.2)

pokračovanie (nabudúce), *(to be) continued*
polročne, *half-yearly* (1.8.5)
pos(ie)lať, *send, dispatch*
poviedka, *story*
poznámka, *note*
pozri, *see*
práce, *transactions*
predaj, *sale*
predplatné, *subscription* (1.8.6)
predslov, *preface*
prejav, *speech*
preklad, *translation* (1.2.5)
preložil, *he translated* (1.2.2)
prepracovaný, *revised* (1.5.2)
prihotoviť, *prepare*
prínos, *contribution*
pripraviť, *prepare*

rabat, *discount, reduction*
reč, *speech*
redakcia, *editing, editorial office* (1.8.7)
redaktor, *editor* (1.8.3)
redigovať, *edit* (1.2.2)
register, *index*
revidovaný, *revised* (1.5.2)
ročenka, *yearbook*
ročník, *(annual) volume* (1.8.4)
ročný, *annual*
rok, *year*
román, *novel*
rozmnožovač, *duplicator*
rozprava, *treatise, account*
rozprávka, *story*
rozšírený, *enlarged* (1.5.2)

separat, *offprint* (1.5.3)
séria, *(sub)series* (1.7.2)
schôdza, *meeting*
slovník, *dictionary*
složil, *he composed, compiled* (1.2.6)
sostavil, *compiled, arranged*
spis, *writing*
spoločnosť, *society*
spolupracovali, *they collaborated* (1.2.6)
spracoval, *he executed* (1.2.6)
správa, *report, account, communication*
staršie číslo, *back number*
stránka, *page*
sväzok, *volume* (1.4.1), *part* (1.8.4)

štvrťročník, *quarterly* (1.8.5)
štyrikrát, *four times* (1.8.5)

tabula, *plate*
tabuľka, *table*
ten istý, *the same*
tlač, *print(ing)*
týždenník, *weekly* (1.8.5)

účet, *bill*
ukázka, *sample, specimen*
úplný, *complete*
úvod, *introduction*

väzba, *binding*
viazaný, *bound*
voľný, *complimentary*
všetky práva vyhradené, *all rights reserved*
výbor, *selection*
vybraný, *selected*
vydanie, *edition* (1.5.1), *publication* (1.6.2)
vydať, *publish* (1.6.2, 1.8.1)
vydavateľstvo, *publishing house* (1.6.1)
vychodiť, vychádzať, *come out*
výmena, *exchange*
vyobrazenie, *illustration*
vypracoval, *he elaborated* (1.2.2)
vyšlo, *it came out*
vyťah, *abstract*
vytlačil, *he printed*
výtlačok, *copy*

zbierka, *collection*
zborník, *collective volume*
zhrnutie, *summary*
zľava, *discount*
zložil, *compiled* (1.2.2)
zobraný, *collected*
zomrel, *he died*
zostavil, *he compiled, arranged* (1.2.2)
zošit, *issue*
zoznam, *index*
zredigoval, *he edited* (1.2.2)
zrevidovaný, *revised* (1.5.2)
zväzok, *volume* (1.4.1), *part* (1.8.4)

GRAMMATICAL INDEX: WORDS

aby, 11
aj, 11
alebo, 11

beriem, etc., 8.2.3
bol, 8.17
budem, etc., 8.10.2, 8.17

cez, 10.5
cti, 4.3.16

čias, 4.3.5
čím, 7.1.1
čiže, 11
čoho, čom(u), 7.1.1

deť-, 4.3.10
dva(ja), dve, dvoch, etc.,
    6.1.2

ho, 7.3.2

ich, 7.3.2
idem, etc., 8.2.3
išiel, išlo, 8.10.2

je, 8.2.3, 8.17
jedia, 8.2.3
jeho, jej, 7.3.2
jem(e), 8.2.3
jemu, 7.3.2

ješ, jete, 8.2.3
ju, 7.3.2

keď, 11
koho, kom(u), 7.1.1
kvôli, 10.5
kým, 7.1.1

lež, 11

ma, 7.3.1
mätiem, etc., 8.2.3
mi, 7.3.1
mimo, 10.5
mňa, mne, etc., 7.3.1

GRAMMATICAL INDEX: ENDINGS

SLOVENE

SPECIMEN

Ko oddajam knjigo v tisk, čutim potrebo, da[1] vsaj na kratko pojasnim in opravičim njeno tako pozno objavo v slovenskem jeziku. Knjiga namreč ni v sedanji obliki povsem izvirna, temreč je po vsebini in sestavi nekakšna popravljena in dopolnjena izdaja moje knjigi Life and Death Struggle of a National Minority ki jo[2] prevedla ga[3] F. S. Copeland in jo[2] je[4] l. 1936 izdalo Društvo za Ligo narodov v Ljubljani. Dve leti pozneje je sledila francoska izdaja v prevodu J. Lacroixa. Takoj po vojni (1945) sta izšla[5] druga angleška izdaja in obširnejšie[6] izvleček v ruskem jeziku ter leto dni nato še druga dopolnjena francoska izdaja.

1. da...pojasnim, *that I explain* (11.2)
2. See 7.2.2
3. The abbreviation is usually **ga.**: ga means (*of*) *him, it*!
4. **je...izdalo** go together (8.12.5)
5. **sta izšla**, dual number
6. See 5.3.1

As I deliver the book to the press, I feel the necessity of at least briefly explaining and justifying its so late appearance in the Slovene language. The book, you see, is not in present form entirely original, but is in content and composition a sort of revised and enlarged edition of my book Life and Death Struggle of a National Minority, *which Mrs F. S. Copeland translated and which the League of Nations Society in Ljubljana published in the year 1936. Two years later followed the French edition in the translation of J. Lacroix. Just after the war (1945) came out the second English edition and a somewhat extended extract in the Russian language and a year later again the second enlarged French edition.*

0 GENERAL CHARACTERISTICS

0.1 DEGREE OF INFLEXION

In general lay-out Slovene resembles the majority of the Slavonic languages. It is nearest in its forms and syntax to Serbocroatian, but in various particulars, especially in the declension of the noun, it agrees rather with other Slavonic languages.

0.2 ORDER OF WORDS

Adjectives precede the noun they qualify, while dependent genitives almost always follow. Sentence order is free: the subject, the object, the verb or an adverbial phrase can all occupy the first place, though in the absence of any special emphasis the order SVO is more likely.

0.4 RELATION TO OTHER LANGUAGES.

As compared with other Slavonic languages Slovene shows a greater tendency to simplify awkward groups, e.g. **bn, dn, pn, tn** to simple **n, sk** to **šk** and even to simple **š**, as in **šola**, *school*, **šč** to **š**, **vl** to **l**. In morphology a notable feature is its retention of the dual number: for instance, where there are two authors, and also, quite logically, in expressions like **snov in njena razporeditev sta ostali isti**, *the subject matter and its arrangement have remained the same*.

1 BIBLIOLINGUISTICS

1.1 NAMES

1.1.1 What is said in the Serbocroatian chapter holds to a great extent for Slovenian names. The typical ending is **-ič** as opposed to Sh **-ić**. Names of Macedonian origin in **-ov, -ev, -ki** are much less likely to occur, while names of Italian and German origin, declined as foreign names, are much commoner.

1.1.2 Possessive adjectives in **-ov, -ev**, derived from names, occur in Slovene also. In view of what is said above they are not so ambiguous as in Serbocroatian, but changes like **Aškerc > Aškerčev** (2.5.3) need watching.

1.1.3 Names of the medieval type, e.g. **Ivan iz Ljubljani**, in which the second element is a descriptive epithet, are not of great importance, but the type does persist in pseudonyms, e.g. **Janež Svetokriški**, indexed under **Janež**.

1.2 NAMES OF AUTHORS, EDITORS, ETC.

1.2.1 Of the types set out in the Serbocroatian chapter the name at the head of the title-page and the use of an active verb are much the most common. Authors are most likely to be indicated by **napisal**, *he wrote*; **spisal**, *he composed* (F **-la** P-**li**); **sestavil**, *he compiled*; editors by a variety of verbs and phrases, e.g. **uredil**, *edited* (the commonest word); **uvod in opombe napisal**, *wrote the introduction and notes*; **zbral**, *collected*. The ending **-la** is not only feminine, e.g. **opremila Jakica Accetto**, *J. A. arranged*, but also dual, e.g. **sta utrdila Anton Breznik in France Ramovš**, *A. B. and F. R. consolidated*. Note that it is incorrect to use the plural when there are only two subjects, and that the dual usually has **sta** (*they two are*) while the feminine has the simple participle.

1.2.2 The possessive endings **-ev** and **-ov** are found in citations, e.g. **dramatizival je Jurčič-Kersnikove Rokovnjače ... in Jurčičevega Desetega brata**, *he dramatised Jurčič-Kersnik's Rokovnjače ... and Jurčič's Deseti brat*, and in Festschriften, e.g. **Aškerčev zbornik**, *Symposium for Aškerc*; but authorship of collected works and the like is more likely to be expressed by the genitive, e.g. **Poezije doktorja Francéta Prešérna** (2.1.3), *Poetry of Dr. Francè Prešeren*; **Simona Jenka zbrani spisi**, *Collected writings of Simon Jenko*.

1.2.3 Joint authorship, if not expressed simply by a plural or dual verb, or specifically **sodelovali**, *collaborated*, involves phrases like **s sodelovanjem Miroslava Ravbaja**, *with the collaboration of Miroslav Ravbaj*, **s prispevki Ivana Simoniča, Marjetke Kastelic, Bogomila Gerlanca**, *with contributions by Ivan Simonič, Marjetka Kastelic, Bogomil Gerlanc*. Note the indeclinable female surname **Kastelic**, masculine in form, and the ambiguous **Gerlanca**, the nominative of which could have been **Gerlanec**.

1.2.4 What is said about societies under Serbocroatian applies to Slovene, always remembering that two societies will require a dual verb. Both arrangements of subordinate bodies are found: **Univerza v Ljubljani, Pravno-ekonomska fakulteta** and **Fakultetna uprava Pravno-ekonomske fakultete** (*Faculty Board of the*. . .).

1.3 TITLES

1.3.1 The titles of learned works mostly consist of nouns and adjectives in various cases, e.g. **Kočevsko: zemljepisni, zgodovinski in umetnostno-kulturni oris Kočevskega okraja. Vodnik s adresarjem,** *Kočevsko: geographical, historical and artistico-cultural description of the Kočevje district. Guide-book with directory.* Artistic and popular productions may introduce more varied grammar, e.g. **Eno devo le bom ljubil,** *One maid alone shall I love;* **Narod si piše sodbo sam,** *The nation writes its own sentence.*

1.3.2/1.3.3 What is said of Serbocroatian title entries and titles in context applies here. Examples of titles affected by the context are given incidentally in 1.2.2. In the phrase **v Janežičevi zbirki Cvetje iz domačih in trujih logov,** *in Janežič's collection Cvetje,* etc., the title is insulated by the word **zbirki**.

1.4 VOLUMES AND PARTS

1.4.1 The usual words are found: **zvezek, zvezka,** *volume;* **knjiga,** *book;* **del,** *part;* but there is no clear distinction between them. For works issued in parts one may also come across **snopič,** *fascicule.*

1.4.2 Numeration is in words or figures, before or after the word for *volume,* e.g. **Prva knjiga,** *first book;* **I. zvezek, zvezek I.**

1.4.4 The total number of volumes is rarely stated, though one may find phrases like **štiri zvezke Župančičevih izbranih del,** *the four volumes of Župančič's selected works* in the text itself.

1.5 EDITIONS

1.5.1 The usual word is **izdaja,** but **natisk,** which in itself simply means *impression,* and is consequently imprecise, is also found.

1.5.2 Numeration is by a preceding ordinal, in words or figures, with a participle indicating revision if appropriate, e.g. **II. izdaja, drugi pregledani natisk** (*second revised impression*). Other words implying revision are **predelana,** *reworked* (**popolnoma,** *completely;* **delno,** *partially*); **popravljena,** *corrected;* **dopolnjena,** *supplemented;* **izpopolnjena,** *perfected;* the last two no doubt meaning much the same as **pomnožena,** *enlarged.*

1.5.3 An *offprint* is **osebni odbis,** *to reprint* **ponatisniti.**

1.6 IMPRINTS

1.6.1 Recent imprints are all institutional. Apart from the **Državna založba Slovenije,** *State Publishing House of Slovenia* and smaller official bodies like **Turistično olepševalno društvo,** *Society for Tourism and Amenities,* periodicals like **Uradni list LRS** (the Official Gazette) and **Slovenski poročevalec,** *the Slovenian Reporter,* we find a number of presses with more or less arbitrary names such as **Cankarjeva Založba,** *Cankar Press;* **Založba „Kenečka knjiga ",** *'Country Book' Press;* **Založba Obzorja,** *Horizon Press* (this time with the defining word in the genitive); **Akademska Založba,** *Academic Press.*

Older imprints produce simple personal names, e.g. **Ig. Pl. Kleimayr & Fed. Bamberg.**

1.6.2 The name of the publisher is nearly always in the nominative, and usually preceded by an active verb. Now and again it is preceded by the preposition **pri** and is in the locative, e.g. **pri Akademski Založbi.** The place may be in the nominative or in the locative preceded by **v,** e.g. **v Ljubljani,** *at Ljubljana.* Sometimes, as in **Slovenska kulturna akcija v Buenos Airesu** it is not clear whether the place name is part of the name of the society or not.

1.6.3 Four different activities are commonly referred to in imprints: publishing (i.e. distributing), indicated by **izdal;** financing, indicated by **založil** (naturally **izdala in**

založila is fairly common and **založil** alone is to be interpreted *published*); printing, indicated by **natisnil** or **tiskal**; and binding, indicated by **vezal**. (The participles are in fact nearly always feminine.)

1.6.4 Occasionally one finds a body like the *State Press* acting as an agent, e.g. **DZS založila za Universitetno študijsko komisijo**, where there is probably a case for treating DZS as the publisher and giving **Univerzitetna študijska komisija** an added entry.

1.7 SERIES

1.7.1 The names of series, usually to be found on the half-title leaf, may be arbitrary, e.g. **Knjižnica Kondor**, *Condor Library*; or descriptive of the contents severally or as a whole, e.g. **Zbrana dela slovenskih pesnikov in pisateljev**, *Collected works of Slovenian poets and writers*. Occasionally the title refers only to the individual member of the series, e.g. **Razprava Znanstvenega društva v Ljubljani 67**, *Dissertation 67 of the Ljubljana Scientific Society*. Libraries which prefer series titles to reflect the series as such will have to create the title **Razprave**.

1.7.2 Series published by societies may either have the form given above (catalogue entry: **Ljubljana. Znanstveno društvo. Razprave**) or a hierarchical one that can be taken over as it stands.

1.7.3 Numeration is often given by number alone. Where a noun is used it is, as usual, **zvezek**. Sub-series with independent numeration are found, e.g. in the case of the **Razprave** above, **Filološko-lingvistični odsek 17**. Sometimes there appear to be simultaneous series by two different bodies, but one would need to check the relationship between the two. Not all numeration is evidence of a series: **izdala kot svojo dvainpetdeseto publikacijo**, *published as its 52nd publication*, is best taken as an elaborate imprint, especially as a very similar statement occurs on an issue of a periodical with its own quite different numeration.

1.8 PERIODICALS

1.8.1 The titles of academic periodicals (**časopisi**) are mostly very straightforward, e.g. **Geografski vestnik**, *Geographical herald*; **Ekonomski zbornik**, *Economic magazine*, and so on. Political and cultural periodicals introduce more variety of wording but are often linguistically simple, e.g. **Sodobnost** (the abstract noun from *contemporary*, whatever that is); **Meddobje**, *Interval*.

1.8.2 The name of the body responsible may be simply put at the head of the title-page (cf. 1.2.1) or it may be incorporated in the title or sub-title, e.g. **Letopis Slovenske Akademije Znanosti in Umetnosti**; **Ekonomski zbornik Ekonomskega oddelka pravno-ekonomske fakultete Univerze v Ljubljani**, a chain of genitives leading to the heading: **Ljubljana. Univerza. Pravno-ekonomska fakulteta. Ekonomski oddelek**. Alternatively it may be preceded by a noun denoting the agent, e.g. **izdajatelj** (**in založnik**), or a verb such as **izdaja**, *publishes*, or **izdalo in založilo**, *published*. (For the distinction between **izda(ja)ti** and **založiti** see 1.6.3.) The **ustanovitelj** (*founder*) is sometimes given too.

1.8.3 Editorship is usually denoted by some form of the stem **ured-**. Often there is an **uredniški odbor**, *editorial committee*, perhaps with an **uredniški svet** or *editorial council* in the background. These are followed by a list of names, perhaps as subjects of a verb such as **sestavljajo**, *they compose*. In the simplest statement the names are preceded by the word **uredništvo**, an abstract noun for which in its collective sense we have no equivalent. One of the names is usually singled out as **glasni** (*chief*) or **odgovorni** (*responsible*) **urednik**. The notion of responsibility recurs in the form of a verb

in **za uredništvo in izdajatelja odgovarja dr Mitko Rupel.** Note that where there is a
verb two editors will produce a dual form, even if they do not act as a pair, viz. **uredila:
Ruda Furčec (začel), Tina Debeljak (končal),** where R.F. began and T.D. finished.

1.8.4 Numeration is by **letnik** (*annual volume*) alternatively **leto** (*year*), subdivided
by **številka** (*number*). Parts may also be described by the term **snopič** (*fascicule*) or
zvezek, another word with the primary sense of gathering. **Knjiga** also occurs, usually
of an individual volume.

1.8.5 Indications of periodicity are stereotyped, the term **letno,** *per annum,* occurring
in nearly all of them, e.g. **Revija izhaja letno v šestih številkah,** *the review comes out in
six numbers a year;* or **enkrat letno,** *once a year* (or if you prefer, **letno v eni knjigi,**
annually in one volume), or **dvakrat na leto ali enkrat v dvojni številki,** *twice a year or
once in the form of a double number;* or **četrtletno,** *quarterly.*

1.8.6 Subscription (**naročnina**) is not often given as such. It may be defined by an
adjective, e.g. **celoletna naročnina znaša,** *subscription for the whole year amounts to,*
and may be different **za člane** and **za nečlane,** for *members* and *non-members.* More
often one has **cena letniku** or **cena knjigi,** *price of a volume,* or **cena temu zvezku,** *price
for this part;* or there may be an explicit quotation for **posamezna številka,** *an individual
number.*

1.8.7 Addresses may distinguish the editorial and business sides, e.g. **rokopise
pošiljajte na naslov . . . , naročila in reklamacije na naslov . . . ,** *send MSS to address . . . ,
orders and complaints to address . . . .* The former may also be indicated by **sedež uredništva,** *seat of the editing,* the latter by **založba in uprava,** *publishing house and administration,* or by phrases such as **uprava revije je pri,** *the administration of the review is at;*
naroča se pri, *orders to* (impersonal passive); or more elaborately, **reklamacije in naročila
sprejema Založba Obzorja,** *Z. O. accepts complaints and orders* (*subscriptions*). But they
may be the same, e.g. **naslov uredništva in uprave,** and there may also be a separate
address for exchanges, **naslov za zamenjavo.**

2   ALPHABET, PHONETICS, SPELLING

2.1   ALPHABET

2.1.1 The present standard alphabet is as follows:

**a   b   c   č   d   e   f   g   h   i   j   k   l   m   n   o   p   r   s   š   t   u   v
z   ž**

Though **lj** and **nj** represent single sounds they do not have a special place in the alphabet.
Letters such as **q,** which are required for foreign names, occupy their usual place.

2.1.2 The present alphabet was settled in the middle of the nineteenth century.
Before that Cyrillic also was used (cf. Serbocroatian). In early books the conventions
$\int$ = s, $\int$h = š, s = z, sh = ž, z = c, zh = č are found.

2.1.3 Accents, indicating intonation, are used only in linguistic texts, and in
editions of Prešeren.

2.2   CAPITALISATION

2.2.1 In principle proper nouns are written with initial **capitals,** adjectives not.
Designations of days, months, seasons, events and occasions are not treated as proper
names, except to avoid ambiguity: the criteria are not always clear to an outsider, for
we have **vse Sveti,** *All Saints,* **trije kralji,** *Epiphany* (three kings). The same applies to
titles and to words like **kristjan.**

2.2.2　Adjectives in -ov, -ev, -in (possessive in meaning) derived from personal names are spelt with a capital, e.g. **Cankarjevi Zbrani spisi,** *Cankar's Collected works;* but **cankarski slog,** *Cankarian style,* by the general rule. Even adjectives in **-ski** may be spelt with a capital, if a small letter would be misleading, e.g. **Gorski,** *of Gora* (**gorski,** *mountainous*).

2.2.3　The extent to which all the parts of a complex proper name are capitalised varies:

(a) In geographical names all parts are capitalised except common nouns such as **gora,** *mountain*; **morje,** *sea*, which denote common geographical features. (**Bistrica,** *a mountain stream*; **Bela,** *white*; **Loka,** *meadow*; **Gradec,** *fortified place*; **Toplice,** *spa*, are all treated as proper names.)

(b) In personal names, both the name itself and essential epithets have a capital, e.g. **Aleksander Veliki,** *Alexander the Great*; but **Plinij starejši,** *Pliny the Elder*, with a merely distinguishing epithet.

(c) In the names of institutions and the like, of books and periodicals, only the first word has the capital, e.g. **Svet za prosveto in kulturo,** *Council for Education and Culture.* (There are a few traditional exceptions like **Slovenska Matica,** all consisting of two words.)

2.3　DIVISION OF WORDS

2.3.1　Rules 2, 4, 5b, 6c and 8 (p. xiii) apply.

2.3.2　Rule 1 has little application, but words like **triindvajset** are divided after **tri** or **in**.

2.3.3　Prefixes ending with a consonant are: **iz-, nad-, ob-, od-, pod-, pred-, raz-.**

2.3.4　Suffixes beginning with a consonant are kept intact, provided that **lj** and **nj** are not divided. Among common suffixes (apart from grammatical endings) are **-na, -ne,** etc. resulting from adjectives in **-en**; **-nik, -nost.**

2.3.5　No ruling is given on division of vowels, possibly because vowels rarely came together. The evidence is that division between vowels is avoided, except where prefixes are involved, e.g. **po-udarkom** or **pou-darkom.**

2.4　ABBREVIATIONS

2.4.1　All abbreviations have full stops, except those of weights and measures, e.g. **i.dr.** (**in drugo,** *etc.*); **dr.** (**doktor**); but **km** (it is to be hoped that **ga** for **gospa,** *Mrs*, in the specimen is a misprint). Note also **itd.** for **in tako dalje,** *and so on.*

2.4.2　Other abbreviations are **gl(ej),** *see*; **l(eto),** *year*; **n.pr.,** *e.g.*; **ok(oli),** *about*; **st(oletje),** *century*; **str(an),** *page*; **št(evilka),** *number*; **t.j.,** *i.e.*

2.5　HARD AND SOFT CONSONANTS; PALATALISATION; ASSIMILATION

2.5.1　There is no systematic alternation of hard and soft consonants (see General note on the Slavonic languages), since all consonants are now pronounced hard. Traces survive in the alternation of **-o-** and **-e-** in declensions, in the possessive endings **-ov** and **-ev,** e.g. **Aleksandrov, Gregorčičev,** in the behaviour of feminine nouns ending in a consonant (4.3.7), and in palatalisation (2.5.2, 2.5.3). Only the consonants **c, č, j, lj, nj, š, ž** are now counted soft.

2.5.2　**K** and **g** become **c** and **z** before **i**. In standard Slovene this is confined to the imperative and a few nouns.

2.5.3　Before some verb endings in **-e** (mostly from **-je**) and before the comparative ending **-[j]i,** consonants change as follows:

b	c	d	g	h	k	m	p	s	sk	st	t	z
blj	č	j	ž	š	č	mlj	plj	š	šč	šč	č	ž

2.5.4 Assimilations of the type common in Serbocroat are not found in Slovene. Thus the word for *subscription* is **podpis** not **potpis**; conversely **glasba** not **glazba**. But s and z are the same preposition and so are **k** and **h**.

2.5.5 On the other hand various simplifications are found which do not occur in other Slavonic languages, such as the disappearance in some instances of **b, d, p, t** before **n**, and **k** between s and n, e.g. **vrt|eti** but **vr|niti** (8.1.2), as well as others which are widespread, such as **dti, tti > sti, kti > či, dl > l**. Conversely **m, n** and **v** drop out before the **t** of the infinitive.

2.6 VARIATION OF VOWEL

2.6.1 There are no changes of stem vowels in the course of inflexion, but closely related verbs often show different vowels, e.g. **ponesti, ponositi, ponašati**.

2.6.2 To break up difficult complexes of consonants, a vowel (e, a, i) may be present in some forms, but not needed in others, e.g. **petak GS petka; dno GP dan**.

2.7 SPELLING

2.7.1 Spelling is not completely phonetic, e.g. **v** may be pronounced [v], [u], or [w] according to context and **l** may be [l] or [w]. But the conventions are well-established, and such changes as have occurred, e.g. **-ev** for **-iv** and more recently the fixing on **-alec** rather than **-avec** are due to a shifting of the balance between dialects.

2.7.2 When spelling some 'international' words one should remember that **x** is represented by **ks**; that s becomes z in words like **fizika, farizei**; that the German **st-** becomes **št-**, e.g. **študent**, and even (Austrian fashion) **inštitut**; and that words like **komisar** have one **m** and one **s**.

3 ARTICLES

There are no articles.

4 NOUNS

4.1 FORM AND GENDER

4.1.1 Nouns may be masculine, feminine or neuter. Inanimate nouns may be of any gender, and some neuter nouns denote persons. Correlation between form and gender, though obscured by sound changes, is still quite marked.

4.1.2 There are three numbers: singular, dual (4.3.11), plural.

4.1.3 There are six cases: nominative, accusative, genitive, dative, instrumental and locative.

4.3 ENDINGS

4.3.1 *Masculine nouns*

These mostly end in a consonant. The case endings are:

	S	P
N	-, -a, -e, -o	-(ov)i, -je
A	As N or G	-(ov)e
G	-a, -u	-ov, -ev
D	-u	-(ov)om, -em
I	-om, -em	-(ov)i
L	-u	-(ov)ih

4.3.2 Masculine nouns in -a include a few which denote occupation or office, e.g. **sluga**, *servant*, but far more are proper names. The endings are substituted for the N -a.

Those in -e, apart from **oče**, *father*, GS **očeta**, are all proper names. They all insert -t- before the ending (cf. 4.3.6).

Those in -o are nearly all names. The endings are substituted for the -o. Some of the forms that result are ambiguous, e.g. **Jožka** may be GS of **Jožko** or of **Jožek** (2.6.2). For foreign words and names see 4.3.13.

4.3.3 Fugitive -e- (2.6.2) is found in the NS of some nouns.

Some nouns of more than one syllable ending in -Vr have stems -Vrj-. Likewise foreign names in -er.

A few nouns, notably **mož**, *man*, have no ending in GP.

On -ov/-ev etc. see 2.5.1.

4.3.4 *Neuter nouns*

These end in -o after hard consonants, -e after soft ones (2.5.1). The endings are:

	S	P
NA	-o, -e	-a
G	-a	-
D	-u	-om, -em
I	-om, -em	-i
L	-u	-ih, -eh

4.3.5 A euphonic vowel (2.6.2) may be needed in GP. Nouns in -je (but not those in -lje, -nje) have GP -ij.

4.3.6 A few neuters have longer stems in the oblique cases: **ime-na**, **vreme-na**; **dete-ta** (P **dece** 4.3.7); **oko**, **očesa**; **uho**, **ušesa**, but the usual P of **oko** is **oči** (4.3.7).

4.3.7 *Feminine nouns*

These end in -a or a consonant, originally a soft one. The latter class includes numerous abstract nouns in -ost.

	Vowel type		Consonant type	
	S	P	S	P
N	-a	-e	-	-i
A	-o	-e	-	-i
G	-e	-	-i	-i
D	-i	-am	-i	-im, -em
I	-o	-ami	-(i)jo	-(i)mi
L	-i	-ah	-i	-ih, -eh

4.3.8 The vowel type includes, optionally for the most part, masculine nouns in -a (4.3.2). **Gospa**, *lady*, *Mrs*, has -e in D and LS and -e- throughout the plural.

4.3.9 Words like **misel**, **pesem** insert -e- in NS (2.6.2). **Cerkev** and other nouns in -kev and -tev are similar, but behave for the most part is if the NS were -va, so that -ev may also be GP.

4.3.10 The plural noun **ljudje**, *people*, has NA -je and all other cases as 4.3.7 (consonant type).

Mati, *mother*, **hči**, *daughter*, have AS **mater**, **hčer**, stem -er- (consonant type).

4.3.11 *The dual*

All nouns have dual forms for some cases: NA of masculine nouns -a, others -i; DI -(V)ma.

The dual forms must be used after **dva**, *two*; **oba**, *both*, but are not usual for objects that go in pairs!

4.3.12 *Irregular nouns*
Dan, *day*, has the following forms:

	N	A	G	D	I	L
S	dan,	dan,	dne(va),	dnevu,	dne(vo)m,	dne(vu)
D	dneva/dni			dne(vo)ma		
P	dnevi,	dni/dneve,	dni,	dne(vo)m,	dnemi/dnevi,	dne(vi)h

4.3.13 *Foreign nouns and names*
A large number of Central and East European names have Slovene forms, e.g. **Draždani**, **Lipsko**, **Dunaj** (Vienna), **Monakovo** (Munich), **Podenokli** (Bodenbach), **Solnograd** (Salzburg), **Tsarigrad** (Istanbul), and Slav names may be slightly modified to conform to Slovene spelling, e.g. **Praga** not **Praha**. Conversely the English forms of Slovene names, e.g. *Carinthia* (**Koroška**), *Carniola* (**Kranjska**) are not always such as to make the native form easily recognisable.

Greek and Latin names are largely respelt and accomodated to Slovene declension, but may preserve their classical stems, e.g. **Ajshilos** G **Ajshila**, *Aeschylus*; **Cicero** G **Cicerona**.

Names which end in a consonant, even one which is not sounded, are treated in writing like consonant stems (4.3.1) as are those which end in a consonant followed by a mute e. This -e is dropped before endings except after c and g: **Hegel** G **Hegla**; **Dumas**, **Dumasa**; **Shakespeare**, **Shakespeara**; **Wallace**, **Wallacea**; **Buenos Aires-a**.

Names which end in -e, stressed -a, stressed -o or other stressed vowels have also endings as in 4.3.1, inserting -j- before the ending, e.g. **Goethe-ja**, **Zola-ja**, **Defoe-ja**. Similarly common nouns such as **aranžma** and **nivo**.

Names which end in unstressed -a and -o are treated like the corresponding native nouns (4.3.7, 4.3.2), e.g. **Jena** G **Jene**; **Tasso** G **Tassa**; **v Jerez de la Fronteri**, **v Monte Carlu**.

4.6 USE OF CASES
4.6.1 The object is not necessarily in the accusative. Some verbs require a genitive or a dative. The accusative is also used to express length and duration.
4.6.2 The genitive, besides the uses which are extensions of the idea of possession, is used qualitatively and partitively, and expresses time at which. The object of a negative verb is in the genitive and there are other instances where the genitive of pronouns is used instead of the accusative.
4.6.3 The instrumental and locative are now used only after prepositions, except in so far as the instrumental is used by itself in such set phrases as **iti svojim potim**, *to go one's way*.

5 ADJECTIVES

5.1 GENERAL
5.1.1 Adjectives agree in number, gender and case with the nouns they qualify. They have definite and indefinite forms, but these differ in spelling only in the NSM. (The F and N forms differ, if at all, in intonation.)
5.1.2 The indefinite forms are used as predicate and when the phrase is indefinite, e.g. **ali je poudarek dolg ali kratek**, *the stress is either long or short*; **dolg poudarek**, *a*

S

long stress; **dolgi poudarek**, *the long stress*; **vsak omikan narod**, *every cilivised nation*; **naš knjižni jezik**, *our literary language*.

5.2 ENDINGS

5.2.1

	S				P		
	M	*N*	*F*		*M*	*N*	*F*
N	-, -i	-o, -e	-a		-i	-a	-e
A	As N or G	-o, -e	-o		-e	-a	-e
G		-ega	-e			-ih	
D		-emu	-i			-im	
I		-im	-o			-imi	
L		-em	-i			-ih	

5.2.2 The form without **-i** is indefinite (5.1.2). Adjectives in **-nji, -ski** and **-ški**, comparatives and a few others, notably **mali, obči, pravi**, have no short form.

5.2.3 An **-e-** may be present between the last two consonants of the short form but not of the long, e.g. **kratek, kratki**.

5.3 COMPARISON

5.3.1 The comparative ending is **-(ej)ši** or **-ji**, etc. as 5.2.1. It is added to the short form of the NSM. With some adjectives **bolj** (*more*) is used instead. It may have the meaning *rather*.

5.3.2 Before **-ši, d** becomes **j**, or if preceded by a consonant, is omitted altogether, e.g. **mlad, mlajši; trd, trši**.

5.3.3 The endings **-ji**, etc. result in palatalisation (2.5.3), e.g. **drag, dražji**.

5.3.4 The endings **-ak, -ek, -ok** are often removed before adding the comparative ending, e.g. **kratek: kračji** or **krajši**.

5.3.5 A few adjectives have irregular comparatives, viz. **dober** (*good*), **boljši; dolg** (*long*), **daljši; majhen** (*little*), **manjši; velik** (*big*), **večji**.

5.3.6 To obtain the superlative **naj-** is prefixed to the comparative.

5.4 POSSESSIVES

The possessives **moj** (*my*), etc. and the possessive adjectives in **-in** and **-ov/-ev** formed from names and from nouns denoting persons, e.g. **materin** (*mother's*), **bratov** (*brother's*) (cf. also 1.2.2), have only the short form (5.1, 5.2).

6 NUMERALS

6.1 CARDINAL

6.1.1

1 **ena**	11 **e(d)najst**	21 **enaindvajset**	101 **sto en**
2 **dva**	12 **dvanajst**	23 **triindvajset**	200 **dve sto**
3 **tri**	13 **trinajst**	30 **trideset**	300 **tri sto**
4 **štiri**	14 **štirinajst**	40 **štirideset**	500 **pet sto**
5 **pet**	15 **petnajst**	50 **petdeset**	1000 **tisoč**
6 **šest**	19 **devetnajst**	90 **devetdeset**	2000 **dva tisoč**
7 **sedem**	20 **dvajset**	100 **sto**	
8 **osem**			
9 **devet**			
10 **deset**			

6.1.2 The above are the counting forms. 1–4 are completely declinable: **en, eno, ena (eden, e(d)no, e(d)na** when used without a noun) as in 5.2.1; the others thus:

	M	FN	M	FN	M	FN
N	dva	dve	trije	tri	štrije	štiri
A	dva	dve	tri		štiri	
G	dveh		treh		štirih	
D	dvema		trem		štirim	
I	dvema		tremi		štirimi	
L	dveh		treh		štirih	

oba, *both* is declined like **dva**

pet–devetdeset have G -ih, D -im, I -imi, L -ih

sto (a neuter noun) is not declined

tisoč (a masculine noun) can be treated as such and declined as in 4.3.1, e.g. **v sto tisočih izvodov,** *in hundred(s of) thousands of copies,* but as a numeral it behaves like **pet,** except that it has no ending when used with a preposition, e.g. **naklada sto tisočih izvodov,** *an edition of 100,000 copies* (here **izvodov** depends on **naklada** and **tisočih** is G in agreement), but **v sto tisoč izvodih,** *in 100,000 copies.*

None of the numerals are declined in giving scores, temperatures and the like, or when cardinals are used as serial numbers, e.g. *on page 161,* **na strani sto enainšestdeset.**

6.1.3 **ena–štiri** are adjectives and agree with their nouns. With **dva** the dual (4.3.11) is usual. The rest, which are strictly speaking nouns, are followed when in the N or A by the GP and take a singular neuter verb, e.g. **izšlo je pet zvezkov,** *five volumes have appeared;* but in other cases are treated as adjectives, e.g. **v petih zvezkih,** *in five volumes.*

Compound numerals behave like the last element.

6.1.4 The forms given above are the standard forms: even **jetnik** (*convict*) **135974** is set out as **sto petintrideset tisoč devet sto štiriinsedemdeset** in the grammar by Bajec and others. But in some contexts it can be read **ena tri pet devet osem štiri,** and the otherwise antiquated **sedemdeset štiri** for **74** is permitted 'in announcements'.

6.2 ORDINAL

6.2.1

1 prvi	11–90 enajsti, etc. adding -i to
2 drugi	the cardinal
3 tretji	100 stoti
4 četrti	101 sto prvi
5 peti	200 dvestoti
6 šesti	201 dve sto prvi
7 sedmi	1000 tisoči
8 osmi	
9 deveti	
10 deseti	

6.2.2 The ordinal numbers are all adjectives in the definite form (**drug** is a pronoun: *another*). In such numbers as **tisoč sto prvi** only the last element is ordinal and declined.

6.3 FIGURES

6.3.1 Plain figures usually stand for cardinals, ordinals being followed by a full stop, except in the case of dates. Roman figures used for ordinals have the stop, e.g. **II. zvezek, 18. stoletje.**

6.4 DATES

6.4.1 The standard names of the months, which should be used if dates have to be spelt out, are:

> januar, februar, marcij, april, maj, junij,
> julij, avgust, september, oktober, november, december

All are masculine nouns with GS **-a** (4.3.1). In oblique cases **januar, februar, april** insert **-j-**, e.g. **aprilja**; **september**, etc. drop the last **-e-**.

6.4.2 There are also Slavonic names for the months, which are not all given in small dictionaries, viz.

> prosinec, svečan, sušec, mali traven, veliki traven, rožnik,
> mali srpan, veliki srpan, kimovec, vinotok, listopad, gruden

6.4.3

> *1 May* is **prvi maj**
> *On 1 May 1972,* **(dne) prvega maja (v prvi maj) tisoč devet sto dvainsedemdesetega leta**
> **1.v.1972** can be read with **petega** (*fifth*) for **maja**
> **Leto 1848** (without a stop) is read as a cardinal
> **1848–1948** as two cardinals, and even where **od** (*from*) and **do** (*to*) are understood, as in **1939–1945**, the numbers are unaffected.

7 PRONOUNS

7.1 DEMONSTRATIVE, INDEFINITE, ETC.

7.1.1 The endings of most of these pronouns are the same as those of adjectives (5.2.1), but there are some peculiarities:

> **ta,** *this* (N **to,** F **ta**) as if **ti**; IM **tem**; alternative D and LSF **tej**; dual NA **ta, te**; DI **tema**

Some of them have indefinite forms in NSM, some definite.

7.1.2 Demonstrative pronouns may have an indeclinable suffix **-le**, e.g. **tale** G **tegale**. Similarly **tistile, onile, takle**.

7.1.3 **Ves, vse, vsa,** *all*, otherwise like **ta**, has dual NA **vsa, vsi**, DI **vsema**.

7.1.4 **Vsakdo** and **nekaj** are compounds of **kdo** and **kaj** (7.2.1), G **vsakoga, nečesa**. Similarly **nikdo** and **nič**, which add **-r** to all oblique cases, e.g. **nikogar, ničesar**.

7.2 RELATIVE, INTERROGATIVE
7.2.1

> **Kdo,** *who?* makes **koga, komu, kom**
> **Kaj,** *what?* makes **česa, čemu, čim, čem**

7.2.2 The addition of **-r** converts the interrogatives into relatives, but the commonest words for *which* are **ki** and **kateri**. **Ki** is invariable and makes its oblique cases by appending the 3rd-person pronoun, making e.g. in the masculine **ki ga, ki mu, ki njim**

ki v njem, and similarly with other prepositions. Forms like **ki ga** are ambiguous, e.g. **ki ga je potrdil**, *who ratified it*; **ki so ga podpisali**, *which they signed.*

7.3 PERSONAL

7.3.1 The pronouns of the 1st and 2nd persons and the universal reflexive are as follows:

	S 1	*S* 2	*S & P* R	*P* 1	*P* 2
N	jaz	ti	-	mi, me	vi, ve
AG	me(ne)	te(be)	se(be)	nas	vas
D	m(en)i	t(eb)i	s(eb)i	nam	vam
I	menoj, mano	teboj, tabo	seboj, sabo	nami	vami
L	meni	tebi	sebi	nas	vas

Dual: 1 NA **naju,** DI **nama**; 2 **vaju, vama.**

7.3.2 The 3rd person pronoun **on** N **ono** F **ona** has oblique cases from another stem

	S M	*S* N	*S* F	*D*	*P* M	*P* N	*P* F
N	on	ono	ona	n(ji)ju	oni	ona	one
A	(nje)ga, -nj		(n)jo			nje/jih	
G	(nje)ga		(n)je			(n)jih	
D	(nje)mu		njej/ji	njima		(n)jim	
I	njim		njo			njimi	
L	njem		njej/nji			njih	

The short forms are the unemphatic and therefore commoner ones.

8 VERBS

8.1 STRUCTURE

8.1.1 As in other Slavonic languages, the verb in Slovene is characterised by two aspects, perfective and imperfective, dealt with more fully in the General note on the Slavonic languages. The two aspects have sets of tenses which are formally parallel, though there are some differences in their uses (cf. 8.2). In all the tenses the different persons are sufficiently distinguished without the use of subject pronouns, e.g. **jemljemo,** *we take*; **dobivajo,** *they receive.*

8.1.2 The entering of verbs in the smaller dictionaries is somewhat haphazard. Verbs whose perfective aspect differs from the imperfective by the addition of a prefix are usually entered in both places. Where the prefix also alters the meaning of the verb, this is recorded; but where the prefix does little beyond changing the aspect, as may be the case with **do-, iz-, na-, po-, s-, -u** and **z-** (not all with the same verb), the change of aspect is usually ignored: both **pisati** and **napisati** are simply *to write*. Where the perfective and imperfective differ internally, e.g. **pasti/padati,** the verb may be entered under the perfective (usually without reference from the imperfective), under both (with or without distinction of meaning) or occasionally under the imperfective with reference from the perfective. The following examples give some idea of the sort of changes that occur:

P	I
pasti (2.5.5)	padati
prinesti	prinasati
reči	rekati
pomoči	pomagati
umreti	umirati
našteti	naštevati
kupiti	kupovati
dati	dajati
načeti (pr. načnem, 2.5.5)	načenjati
odgovoriti	odgovarjati
pustiti	puščati (2.5.3)
krikniti	kričati

8.2 PRESENT

8.2.1 *Endings*

I	-am, -aš, -a; -ava, -ata; -amo, -ate, ajo
II	-em, -eš, -e; -eva, -eta; -emo, -ete, -ejo/-o
III	-im, -iš, -i; -iva, -ita; -imo, -ite, -ijo/-e

The dual sometimes has forms ending in -e if the subject is feminine or neuter.

8.2.2 *Relation to infinitive*

The commonest relations are given here. Exceptions and further explanations are given in 8.2.3–8.2.5.

P	-am	-em	-*em	-jem	-ujem		-nem
I	-ati	8.2.4	-ati	-ti/-jati	-evati/-ovati/-uti/-uvati		-niti

P	-im	-*im
I	-eti/-iti	-*ati

8.2.3 The presents in -*em (i.e. with the preceding consonant palatalised) have infinitives with normal consonants, according to the table in 2.5.3.

Presents in -ujem usually have infinitive -ovati, or -evati after a soft consonant.

Exceptions in -nem are **stanem/stati**; **denem/deti**; **-čnem/-četi**, and a number of others with the correspondence -nem/-eti.

8.2.4 *Some peculiar stems*

-bem: -bsti
-čem (3PP -ko): -či; but hočem: hoteti
-dem: -sti; but idem: iti (in compounds also -jdem)
-(a)mem: -eti
-rem: derem/dreti; mr(j)em/mreti; t(a)rem/treti; berem/brati;
 morem (3PP mogo)/moči
-s(t)em: -sti
-tem: -sti
-vem: -ti
-zem: -sti
-žem (3PP -go): -či

8.2.5 *Irregular*

> **dado** (3PP): **dati**
> **jem, jedo: jesti**
> **vem, veste: vedeti**
> **grem, gredo:** used as present of **iti**
> **imam: imeti**

8.2.6 The present of imperfective verbs may be a true (continuous) present or a historic present or may express a general (timeless) statement; the present of perfective verbs also may have the last two functions, but is more likely to refer to the future, especially in a subordinate clause.

8.3 PAST

The past is of a type common to all the Slavonic languages, but is an explicitly compound tense. See 8.10.2.

8.10 COMPOUND TENSES

8.10.1 *Future:* **bom,** etc. (8.17.2) + past active participle (8.12.3)

8.10.2 *Past:* **sem,** etc. (8.17.1) + p.a.p.
The participle may be derived from both perfective and imperfective verbs, the latter corresponding sometimes to the English imperfect, sometimes requiring to be translated by the simple past, e.g. **je skušal pisati kakor je govoril,** *he tried to write as he spoke* (both imperfective); **tako je ostalo,** *so the matter stood* (perfective). The past of of a perfective verb is sometimes used for the pluperfect (8.10.3). For the participle alone on title-pages see 1.2.1.

8.10.3 *Pluperfect:* **sem bil,** etc. (8.17.5) + p.a.p.

8.10.4 *Conditional present:* **bi** + p.a.p.; *past:* **bi bil** + p.a.p.

8.10.5 The components of a compound tense may be in either order and are frequently separated, as in **Težko narodu, ki** *je* **že v zibeli** *izgubil* **svobodo,** *It is hard for the nation that has lost its freedom even in the cradle.* The participle agrees in number and gender with the subject.

8.11 INFINITIVE AND SUPINE

8.11.1 The infinitive, which ends in **-ti** or **-či,** is used much like the infinitive in other languages, as a verbal noun and as the complement of various verbs, e.g. **molčati je zlato,** *silence is golden;* **so hoteli slovensko pisati,** *they wanted to write in Slovene.*

8.11.2 The supine, which lacks the final **-i** of the infinitive, is used instead of it after verbs of motion or phrases which imply motion.

8.12 PARTICIPLES AND GERUNDS

8.12.1 The participles are adjectives, e.g. **okupacija in sledeča ji aneksija,** *the occupation and the annexation which followed it;* but they are sometimes used, as the gerunds regularly are, in the same way as English participles, in adverbial phrases, e.g. **grede (gredoč),** *as I (he, etc.) was going.*

8.12.2 *Present active*

	Participle	Gerund
I	**-ajoč**	**-aje**
II	**-oč**	**-e**
III	**-eč**	**-e**

The forms correspond to the 3PP of the present, e.g. **gredo, gredoč, grede**. For the declension of the participle see 5.2.1.

8.12.3 *Past active*

Participle	Gerund
-l, -el (5.2.1, 4.3.11)	**-(v)ši**

With a few exceptions they correspond simply to the infinitive, e.g. **pisal, pisavši, pisati**; but there are some in **-el** and **-ši** which correspond as do the presents in **-em** listed in 8.2.4, e.g. **nesel, nesši, nesti** (Pr **nesem**). Those corresponding to infinitives in **-či** have **-kel, -kši** and **-gel, -gši**. To infinitives in **-reti** correspond participles in **-rl**, gerunds in **-rši**.

The irregular verbs in 8.2.5 are mostly regular in the past participle and gerund, but **iti** has **šel** and **šedši**. Note **vedel** F **vedla** I **vesti**; but **vedel, vedela, vedeti**.

The participle can be used as an adjective, e.g. **po kongresu začel izhajati časopis**, *a periodical which began to appear before the congress*, but its commonest occurrence is as a component of compound tenses (8.10).

8.12.4 *Past passive*

-t, -n, with endings as in 5.2.1

Those in **-t** and many of those in **-n** correspond to infinitives in **-ti**. Those in **-en** mostly come from the type of verb listed in 8.2.4, e.g. **nesen/nesti**; but **-nen** corresponds to **-niti** and **-jen** and **-*en** mostly to **-iti**, e.g. **mišljen/misliti**; **nošen/nositi** (cf. 2.5.3).

8.14/8.15 REFLEXIVE; PASSIVE

8.14.1 The passive can be expressed by the use of the passive participle with the appropriate part of **biti**, *to be*, e.g. **izrazi so razporejeni**, *the words are arranged*.

8.14.2 The reflexive forms, got by using the reflexive pronoun (7.2.1) in the appropriate case, may be truly reflexive, e.g. **ubil se je**, *he killed himself*; intransitive, e.g. **se vrnemo**, *we shall return*; or passive, e.g. **so se zgubile**, *they have been lost*. Non-reflexive uses are only possible where there is no ambiguity: *he was killed* has to be **ubit je bil**.

8.17 THE VERB **biti**, *to be*

8.17.1 *Present:* **sem, si, je; sva, sta; smo, ste, so**
    Negative: **nisem, nisi, ni**, etc.

8.17.2 *Future:* **bodem**, etc, as 8.2.1 (II)
    or **bom, boš, bo; bova, bo(s)ta; bomo, bo(s)te, bojo**

8.17.3 *Present participle:* **bodoč**

8.17.4 *Past gerund:* **bivši**

8.17.5 *Past:* **sem** [etc.] **bil** [etc.]

9 ADVERBS

9.1 FORMATION

These are regularly formed from adjectives by means of the endings **-o** and **-e** (2.5.1). Adjectives in **-ski** used to be unaltered but are now more often regular, There are, however, adverbs like **prav**, which have no ending (cf. English *right*).

9.2 COMPARISON

The comparative endings are **-e, -eje,** and **-še**: **-e** corresponds to **-ji** or **-ši** in the adjective (5.3), **-eje** to **-ejši,** **-še** to **-ši.** The superlative adds **naj-** to the comparative.

10 PREPOSITIONS

10.2 SYNTAX

Prepositions govern particular cases. Some may be used with more than one case, and where this affects the translation, care is needed. Thus, **s** or **z** with the genitive means *from*, with the instrumental *with*; **za** with the genitive *during*, with the instrumental and accusative *behind*. Here, as often, the instrumental denotes rest and the accusative motion. There is a similar distinction between the locative and the accusative.

10.3 PERSONAL FORMS

Prepositions are joined to personal pronouns (7.3), e.g. **name, nanj.** When the preposition ends in a consonant, forms like **podenj** are found.

10.5 MEANINGS

Most of the Slovene prepositions are part of the common Slavonic stock. Among those that are peculiar are **kljubu,** *despite*; **zoper,** *against*; **razen,** *except*; **zavoljo,** *because of.*

11 CONJUNCTIONS

11.1 These cause no grammatical difficulty though the distribution of meanings is a little unexpected. Thus there are three words which can mean *and*: **in, ter** and **pa.** Between **in** and **ter** there is no difference of meaning, but **pa** is more likely to mean *but* or *however* and to stand as second or third word.

11.2 Other conjunctions characteristic of Slovene are **če,** *if*; **da,** *(in order) that, because, if,* often used where English has the infinitive; **ko,** *when, as, if.*

GLOSSARY

bakrorez, *plate*
brezplačen, *free*
brošura, *pamphlet*

cena, *price* (1.8.6)

časopis, *periodical* (1.8.1)
četrtletno, *quarterly* (1.8.5)

del, *part* (1.4.1, 1.7.1)
delo, *work*
dopolnjen, *enlarged* (1.5.2)
društvo, *society* (1.6.1)

glasilo, *organ*
govor, *speech*

igra, *play*
v inozemstvu, *abroad*
isti, *same*
izbran, *selected* (1.4.4)
izdaja, *edition* (1.5.1), *publishes* (1.8.2)
izdajatelj, *publisher* (1.8.2, 1.8.3)
izdal, etc., *published* (1.6.3, 1.7.3, 1.8.2)
izhajati, iziti, *to come out* (1.8.5)
izpopolnjen, *perfected* (1.5.2)
izvleček, *abstract, extract, summary*
izvod, *copy*

kazalo, *index, table of contents*
knjiga, *book (volume)* (1.4.1, 1.8.4)
knjigarna, *bookshop*
knjižnica, *library* (1.7.1)
knjižničar, *librarian*

letak, *pamphlet*
leten, *annual* (1.8.5)
letnik, *volume* (1.8.4)
leto, *year, volume*
letopis, *chronicle* (1.8.2)

mehko vezana knjiga, *paperback*
mesečen, *monthly*
mesečnik, *monthly publication*

nadaljevanje, *continuation*
napisal, etc., *wrote* (1.2.1)
naročilo, *order* (1.8.7)
naročnina, *subscription* (1.8.6)
naslov, *address*
natisk, *impression* (1.5.1)
natisnil, *he printed* (1.6.3)
neizdan, *unpublished*
nov, *new*

obvestilo, *communication*
odbor, *committee* (1.8.3)
opomba, *note* (1.2.1)
opremil, *he arranged* (1.2.1)
osebni odtis, *offprint* (1.5.3)

pismo, *letter*
v platno, *in cloth*
poklon, *compliment, gift*
polleten, *half-yearly*
polmesečnik, *fortnightly*
pomnožen, *enlarged* (1.5.2)
ponatisniti, *to reprint* (1.5.3)
popravljen, *corrected* (1.5.2)
popust, *discount, reduction*
poročila, *proceedings, reports*
posamezen, *single* (1.8.6)
na/za poskušno, *on approval*
poslati, *to send*
posvetovanje, *conference*
pošiljati, *to send*
povest, *story*
predelan, *revised* (1.5.2)
predgovor, *preface*
pregledan, *revised* (1.5.2)
prevod, *translation*
prihodnjič, *continuation*
priloga, *appendix, supplement*
primerek na oglen, *specimen copy*
prispevek, *contribution*
na prodaj, *on sale*

račun, *bill*
raziskovanje, *research*
razlaga(nje), *commentary, explanation*
razprava, *dissertation* (1.7.1)
razpravica, *essay*
razprodan, *out of print*
referat, *communication*
revija, *review*
rojen, *born*
roman, *novel*

sestavil, *he compiled, composed*
slovar, *dictionary*
snopič, *fascicule, issue* (1.4.1, 1.8.4)
sodelova|li, -nje, *collaborated, -ation*
spis, *writing* (1.2.2)
spisal, *he wrote* (1.2.1)
stran, *page*

številka, *number* (1.8.4)

tabela, *table*
teden, *weekly*
se tiska, *is being printed*
tiskal, *he printed* (1.6.3)
tiskarna, *printing shop*

umrl, *he died*
uredil, *he edited* (1.2.1, 1.8.3)
urednik, *editor* (1.8.3)
uredništvo, *editing, editorial office*
    (1.8.3, 1.8.7)
uvod, *introduction* (1.2.1)
uvodna beseda, *preface*

vestnik, *herald* (1.8.1)
vezal, *he bound* (1.6.3)

založba, *publishing house* (1.6.1, 1.8.7)
založil, *he published* (1.6.3, 1.8.2)
založnik, *publisher* (1.8.2)
založniška pravica, *copyright*
zamenjava, *exchange* (1.8.7)
zbirka, *collection* (1.3.2)
zbornik, *symposium, magazine* (1.2.2,
    1.8.1)
zbran, *collected* (1.2.2, 1.7.1)
zgodovina, *history*
znižan, *reduced*

GRAMMATICAL INDEX: WORDS

GRAMMATICAL INDEX: ENDINGS

SERBOCROATIAN

Ekavština

Поред оне грађе која је поменута у предговору за прво издање, ваља поменути још и ову. После првог издања моје књиге, Живан Живановић објавио је прву свеску своје данас добро познате „Политичке историје Србије у другој половини деветнаестог века". Та свеска обухвата другу владу Милоша и Михаила у целини, и садржи, као и остале свеске, много важних података.

Besides that material which is mentioned in the preface to the first edition it is worth while mentioning this also. After the first edition of my book Živan Živanović published the first volume of his now well known 'Political history of Serbia in the second half of the nineteenth century'. That volume covers the second government of Miloš and Mihail in its entirety, and includes like the other volumes, many valuable data.

'Serbian' (0.5.1) in Cyrillic; but only века and целини, which would have -je for -e in *jekavština*, are peculiar.

Ekavština

Kad mi je „Kultura" predložila da izdam svoje članke, referate i govore iz posleratnog vremena, odabrao sam one radove koji pretstavljaju ili izvesnu pomoć čitaocu u razumevanje aktuelnih problema naše socijalističke izgradnje ili su sami po sebi dokumenta svoga vremena koji doprinosi objašnjenju pojedinih faza našeg unutarnjeg razvitka. U tekstovima nisam menjao ništa bitno.

'Serbian' (izvesnu, razumevanju, menjao not izvjesnu, razumijevanju, mijenjao) in *latinica* (0.5.4). Pretstavljaju would now be spelt predstavljaju.

Jekavština

I u ovoj drugoj knjizi morao sam da ponavljam izvjesne stvari kako bih čitaocima učinio neposrednijim i pristupačnijim politička zbivanja iz perioda diktature i petokolonaških režima, koji su doveli do kapitulacije.

'Croatian' (izvjesne).

0 GENERAL CHARACTERISTICS

0.1 DEGREE OF INFLEXION
The language is synthetic with a rich system of declensions and many forms.

0.2 ORDER OF WORDS

Adjectives precede the words they qualify; genitives follow. The order SVOC is usual but reversal of verb and subject is not uncommon, especially on title-pages where also the object or complement frequently precedes the verb. The present tense of the verb **biti**, *to be*, and various short pronouns tend to be placed early in the sentence after important words and not in what might be thought to be the logical position, e.g. **To me je osmelilo**, *this encouraged me* (*this me is having-encouraged*).

0.4 RELATION TO OTHER LANGUAGES

Serbocroatian has a number of words, mostly learned, derived from Greek and Latin, e.g. **stabilan**, *stable*; **gramatika**, *grammar*; **bibliografija**, *bibliography*; but most of the vocabulary is peculiarly Slavonic, and though it has affinities with that other Indo-European languages, these do not reveal themselves to casual inspection.

0.5 SERBIAN AND CROATIAN

0.5.1 The names of the language are somewhat confusing. In English 'Serbocroatian' is used for the whole language without distinction of dialect, 'Serbian' and 'Croatian' for the literary dialects. In fact 'Serbian' is not spoken throughout Serbia nor is 'Croatian' confined to Croatia. Linguistic works either prefer terms such as *eastern, western, southern* or use *ekavština* and *jekavština*, referring to the differing treatment of certain e's, e.g. **rečnik/rječnik**; **reč/riječ**; **deo/dio**. Except insofar as this difference occurs in inflexions, the dialects are nearly identical in structure, but besides the phonetics there are also some differences in vocabulary and idiom. A somewhat disconcerting instance is the use of **historija** in the West and **istorija** in the East.

0.5.2 The vernacular terms, apart from **srpski jezik** and **hrvatski jezik**, which are not much used nowadays, are:

(1) **srpskohrvatski jezik**   *Serbocroatian language*

(2) **srpski ili hrvatski jezik**   *Serbian or Croatian*

(3) **hrvatskosrpski jezik**   *Croatoserbian*

(4) **hrvatski ili srpski jezik**   *Croatian or Serbian*

These emphasise the unity of the language, but (1) and (2) take *ekavština* as standard, (3) and (4) *jekavština*.

0.5.3 Apart from Karadžić's historic *Српски рјечник*, and the 1971 dictionary by Morton Benson, which list all forms but give precedence to *jekavština* ('Croatian') and *ekavština* ('Serbian') respectively, dictionaries concentrate on one or other dialect as indicated by their titles. If the necessary adjustments are made, they are to a great extent interchangeable; but it is hardly worth the trouble.

0.5.4 Any form of the language can be equally well written in Cyrillic or Latin characters (2.1). Formerly *latinica* predominated in the Catholic west, so that Croatian could often be recognised from the characters alone; but the correspondence between dialect and alphabet was never exact and is even less so now that Serbian also is quite often written in Latin characters.

1 BIBLIOLINGUISTICS

1.1 NAMES

1.1.1 Serbocroatian surnames are nouns, the great majority masculine in form and ending in a consonant, for instance the ubiquitous names in -ić. (Names in -ič also occur, of Slovene origin.) A few end in -e or -o and are also masculine (for all of which see 4.3); a few end in -a and are feminine in form. Surnames of masculine form are not declined when borne by women, and the addition of **-ka** or **-eva** to form the surnames of married or unmarried women is antiquated. Typically Macedonian surnames in **-ov, -ev, -ki** (adjectives) are sometimes found: they have feminine forms in **-ova, -eva, -ka.**

1.1.2 Christian names are also nouns, masculine or feminine according to sex, and declined. Apart from consonant endings, a fair number of men's names end in **-e**, e.g. **Đorđe, Julije, Ante**, some in **-o**, e.g. **Matko, Ivo**, especially in Croatia; and some have forms in **-a**, e.g. **Aleksa**, especially in Serbia. (See 4.3.)

1.1.3 Plural forms may be used when referring to more than one man of the same name, e.g. **Braća Jovanovići,** *the brothers Jovanović.*

1.1.4 In compound names such as **Andrejević-Kun** both parts are declined, viz. **Andrejevića-Kuna.**

1.1.5 There are also possessive forms in **-ov** or **-ev** for men's names, and in **-in** for women's Christian names, for which see 5.2.1. The **-ov/-ev** ending is usually added to a surname but **Vuk Karadžić** produces **Vukov**. The forms are freely used where we should use *'s*, not only in narrative but on title-pages (1.2.5; but cf. 1.1.1).

1.1.6 Foreign names are adapted to Serbocroatian declensions and are usually respelt phonetically, e.g. **Šekspir, Šeli, Šo, Hemingvej; Labrijer, Igo; Gete, Šiler; Manconi; Jesenjin, Čajkovski.**

For grammatical details see 4.3.13.

1.2 NAMES OF AUTHORS, EDITORS, ETC.

1.2.1 The names of authors are quite likely to be put at the head of the title-page. If so they will normally be in the nominative. If, however, they appear to end in **-ev(a)** or **-ov(a)**, caution is needed: there are names, of Macedonian origin, with these endings, but they are not common, and the forms may be possessive adjectives (5.2.1).

1.2.2 More common in the case of editors, and not unknown in the case of authors, is the position after the title, preceded by a variety of active verbs, e.g. **napisao,** *he wrote* (F **napisala,** P **napisali**); **sastavio,** *compiled*; **pripremio, priredio,** *prepared*; **sredio, uredio,** *arranged*; **redakciju izvršili,** *they carried out the editing*; **sakupio, pribrao,** *collected*; **objasnio, objašnjenja napisao,** *explained*; **preveo,** *translated*, and so on. The names are once more in the nominative.

1.2.3 Also in the nominative are names following nouns denoting agent or activity, e.g. **urednici,** *editors*; **redakcioni (uređivački) odbor,** *editorial committee*; **uredništvo,** *editorial staff*; **izbor,** *selection*.

1.2.4 Less common is the use of **od,** *by,* followed by the name in the genitive, e.g. **od Stanislava Vulića,** *by Stanislav Vulić*. The obtaining of the nominative in such cases is not unattended by difficulties. The removal of the genitive **-a** usually suffices for masculine names, but **-e** or **-o** may have to be added (4.3.1) or a vowel inserted between the last two consonants (2.6.1). Thus so far as its form goes **Matka** could be the genitive of **Matko, Matak** or **Matek**. Surnames of feminine form present no difficulty: G **-e** gives N **-a**, but male Christian names with the same genitive ending may have nominatives in **-o** or **-e**.

1.2.5 In some sorts of publications, such as collected works, correspondence or new editions of established works the author's name may appear in the form of a possessive adjective (1.1.5; 5.2.1), e.g. **Vukova prepiska,** *Correspondence of Vuk* [*Karadžić*]; **Gavazzijev rječnik,** *Gavazzi's dictionary*. The same cautions apply as to the genitive, which is also found, e.g. **Sabrana dela Slobodana Jovanovića,** *Collected works of Slobodan Jovanović* (cf. 1.2.1, 1.2.4).

1.2.6 Joint works, apart from the collective nouns given in 1.2.3, may result in expressions such as **saradnici**, *contributors*, followed by a list in the nominative, or **uz saradnju**, *with the collaboration*, followed by the name in the genitive (1.2.4).

1.2.7 The names of societies and institutions are given in various ways, and their relation to the book is often left vague. Like personal authors, they may appear at the head of the title-page, or with an active verb, e.g. **uređuje Društvo istoričara NR Srbije**, *the Society of Historians of the People's Republic of Serbia edits*; **predložila za štampu Komisija za udžbenike i skripta pri Rektoratu Sveučilišta u Zagrebu**, *the Commission for Textbooks and Course-works of the Rectorate of the University of Zagreb proposed it for the press*. They may also be preceded by passive participles, e.g. **izdano s potporom Matice Hrvatske**, *published with the support of Matica Hrvatska*; **izrađeno u Sveučilišnoj knjižnici**, *produced at the University Library* (Sveučilišna knjižnica, 5.2.2, 4.3.9).

The second example illustrates ways of indicating subordinate bodies: the catalogue entry would be: **Zagreb** (4.3.1). **Sveučilište** (4.3.6). **Rektorat** (4.3.1). **Komisija za Udžbenike i Skripta.**

1.3 TITLES

1.3.1 The great majority, fiction apart, consist of nouns and adjectives in various cases, with or without prepositions, e.g. **Povijest Bosne u doba osmanlijske vlade**, *History of Bosnia in the period of Turkish rule*; **Naš narodni život**, *Our national life*. Some types of literature have more variety, introducing verbs and adverbs, e.g. **Srbija se budi**, *Serbia is awaking*; **Kako se kome čini**, *Each to his taste*.

1.3.2 Title entries of the Anglo-American type present no problems. There are no articles to be ignored in filing. British Museum rules may entail the production of the nominative from oblique cases (4.3) or translation. This is not particularly difficult, but those not experienced in the language should note that endings do duty for a number of cases and are therefore ambiguous.

1.3.3 When a title is quoted in a phrase the main noun may appear in an oblique case instead of in the nominative, e.g. **u Ljubavnom pismu**, *in The Love Letter* (**Ljubavno pismo**). The original form of the title is retained if a noun descriptive of the type of work is inserted, e.g. **u komedijama 'Čestitam' i 'Ljubavno pismo,'** *in the comedies*, etc.

1.4 VOLUMES AND PARTS

1.4.1 The commonest words are **tom** and **knjiga** respectively, but **tom** sometimes seems rather to denote a major division of the whole collection, while **knjiga**, which is in any case used by itself, comes nearer to meaning *volume*. One also finds S **deo** C **dio**, *part*, used as an internal division or for an independent volume, and also **svezak** and **sveska**, both in the sense *volume*.

1.4.2 Numeration is by ordinal numbers, which may precede or follow: **knjiga prva** or **prva knjiga**.

1.5 EDITIONS

1.5.1 The word for *edition*, **izdanje**, is a verbal noun meaning *publication*, whether as action or result, and is found with these meanings in imprints (1.6) and series (1.7). One must be guided by the position on the title-page.

1.5.2 Later editions are denoted by preceding ordinals, accompanied where necessary by words such as **prerađeno, pregledano**, *revised*; **popravljeno, ispravljeno**, *corrected*; **umnoženo, prošireno, dopunjeno**, *enlarged* (c(j)elokupno, *completely*); or conversely

neprom(ij)enjeno, *unaltered*. *Reprinted* is **preštampa(va)no**, and an offprint is **poseban otisak**.

1.6 IMPRINTS

1.6.1 In contemporary imprints both the place and the name of the publisher are likely to be in the nominative, but the place may be preceded by **u**, *at*, and be in the locative case, e.g. **u Zagrebu**, while the addition of **naklada** or **izdanje**, *publication*, will turn the publisher's name into the genitive, e.g. **Izdanje Izdavačkog preduzeća ,, Narodna knjiga "**, *published by Izdavačko preduzeće 'Narodna knjiga'*. The publisher, as here, is usually an institution. In this case it has a name, **,, Narodna knjiga "**, and the words **izdavačko preduzeće**, *publishing undertaking*, can be, and usually are, omitted; but in a simple descriptive phrase such as **Državno izdavačko preduzeće Hrvatske**, *State Publishing Enterprise of Croatia*, they obviously cannot be. Short names like **Nolit** are commoner now than heretofore.

1.6.2 In older imprints similar institutions, named or otherwise, are found, as well as personal names, firms and bookshops, e.g. **Izdavačko i knjižarsko preduzeće Geca Kon a.d. [akcionarsko društvo]**, i.e. *Geca Kon and Co., publishers and booksellers*, or with the name in the genitive **Knjižara braće Jovanovića**, *Bookshop of the brothers Jovanović*.

1.6.3 The root **izd-**, occurring frequently as above, rarely in the active verb forms **izdaje**, *publishes*; **izdao/izdalo** (8.10.1), *published*, specifies a publisher; **štampa** and its derivatives and the root **tisk-**, a printer, e.g. **Štampano u Državnoj Štampariji**, *printed at the national Press* (**Državna Štamparija**); **Tisak Dioničke tiskare**, *printing of the Joint-stock Press*.

1.7 SERIES

1.7.1 The title of a series may be descriptive of the collection, either in the collective singular, e.g. **Biblioteka kulturno nasljeđe**, *Cultural inheritance library*; or in the plural, e.g. **Udžbenici Zagrebačkog sveučilišta**, *Textbooks of Zagreb University*, or of its contents, e.g. **Savremeni hrvatski pisci**, *Contemporary Croatian Authors*; or it may be a title equally appropriate to a book, e.g. **Zemlje i narodi**, *Lands and peoples*. Learned series are frequently described as **Izdanja**, *Publications*, followed by the name of the society in the genitive, or the series may be implied by the singular **izdanje**, e.g. **18. izdanje Zadužbine dra Ljubomira Radivojevića**, *Publication 18 of the Dr Ljubomir Radivojević Foundation*. (But cf. 1.5.) Occasionally there is no series title, only numeration.

1.7.2 Simultaneous series and sub-series are found. For instance the last example bears also the following indications: **Srpska kraljevska akademija | Posebna izdanja | knjiga C | Filozofski i filološki spisi | knjiga 24**, *Royal Serbian Academy | Monographs | Book 100 | Philosophical and philological writings | Book 24*.

As these examples show, when **izdanje** itself does not suffice to carry the numeration, an individual item is frequently described as **knjiga**, *book*; but practice is pretty varied. Sometimes the **knjige** are gathered into a **kolo**, *cycle, set*; or the numeration may be by **kolo** and **broj**, *number*; or the **knjiga** may be the primary unit, with **svezak**, *volume* as a subdivision; or **svezak** may occur alone. The numbers, in words or figures, usually but not invariably follow.

1.8 PERIODICALS

1.8.1 The titles of periodicals (**časopisi**) do not differ from those of books, e.g. **Republika**, *The Republic*; **Naša knjiga**, *Our book*.

When the title is an element in a larger phrase, nouns and adjectives which are normally in the nominative obey the grammar of the larger phrase, e.g. **u izdanju „Ekonomskog pregleda "**, i.e. *published by Ekonomski pregled*; but the title can be grammatically isolated by the insertion of a suitable descriptive noun, as in **administracija časopisa „Finansije"**, *the management of the periodical Finansije*.

1.8.2 Institutional periodicals often have the name of the institution in the genitive, either in the title, e.g. **Anali Pravnog fakulteta u Beogradu** (*Annals of the Legal Faculty at Belgrade*) or in the sub-title. In some nouns the genitive plural is the same as the singular and care is needed, e.g. **Organ udruženja pravnika NR Srbije i NR Bosne i Hercegovine**, *Organ of the Associations of Lawyers*, etc. Alternatively the name of the publisher may be in the nominative preceded by **izdaje**, *publishes*, or **izdavač**, *publisher*.

1.8.3 Editorship is indicated by forms of the roots **ured-** and **redakt-**, e.g. **glavni, odgovorni, urednik**, *general, responsible, editor*; **redakcioni (uređivački) odbor**, *editorial committee*; **redakcijski savet**, *editorial council*; or, as verbs, **ovaj broj uredili su X, Y i Z**, *X, Y and Z edited this number*; **uređuju**, *are editing*.

1.8.4 Numeration of volumes can be complicated. The larger unit is commonly **godina** (or **godište**), *annual volume*, but may be **tom**, individual parts being denoted by **svezak, sveska** or **broj**. Though **broj** simply means *number*, whereas the usual dictionary equivalent of **svezak** and **sveska** is *volume*, there is in fact no difference between them here. Thus in god. XIX, br. 1 of *Socijalna politika* we read: **Za 12 mesečnih svezaka . . .**, *For 12 monthly parts . . . .* Basically **svezak** means a number of sheets fastened together, hence volume of a book or part of a periodical. In addition the word **knjiga**, *book*, is used.

1.8.5 Periodicity may be indicated by the appropriate adjectives, such as **(polu)godišnji, trom(j)esečni, (dvo)m(j)esečni**, (*half-*)*yearly, three-monthly*, (*two-*)*monthly*; adverbs, **polugodišnje, m(j)esečno**, etc.; or nouns, **godišnjak, m(j)esečnik**, etc., or by phrases such as **četiri puta godišnje**, *four times a year*; **svakog meseca izlazi po jedna knjiga**, *one part comes out every month*.

1.8.6 Details of subscription (**pretplata**) with special rates for abroad (**za inozemstvo, inostranstvo**) are quoted, using adverbs or adjectives of periodicity, e.g. **Pretplata: godišnja 120 dinara**; **godišnja pretplata**, or for a period, e.g. **za godinu**, or for a given number of parts, e.g. **za 12 svezaka**. They may quote a price for a single (this) number, **c(i)jena pojedin(ačn)om (ovom) broju**, or for a specimen (**primerak**) or double number (**dvobroj**). Society periodicals may quote special rates for members, **za članove**.

1.8.7 Addresses given may distinguish between the editorial office (**uredništvo, redakcija**) and the business side (**administracija**), exceptionally between **uredništvo** (*business office*) and **redakcija**. The publisher (see also 1.8.2) is very occasionally different again.

2 ALPHABET, PHONETICS, SPELLING

2.1 ALPHABET

2.1.1 All forms of Serbocroatian may be written either in the Cyrillic or the Latin alphabet, between which there is a fixed correspondence, viz.

Cyrillic	а	б	в	г	д	ђ	е	ж	з	и	ј	к	л	љ	м	н	њ	о	п
Latin	a	b	v	g	d	đ	e	ž	z	i	j	k	l	lj	m	n	nj	o	p

Cyrillic	р	с	т	ћ	у	ф	х	ц	ч	џ	ш
Latin	r	s	t	ć	u	f	h	c	č	dž	š

Latin	a	b	c	č	ć	d	dž	đ	e	f	g	h	i	j	k	l	lj	m	n
Cyrillic	а	б	ц	ч	ћ	д	џ	ђ	е	ф	г	х	и	ј	к	л	љ	м	н

Latin	nj	o	p	r	s	š	t	u	v	z	ž
Cyrillic	њ	о	п	р	с	ш	т	у	в	з	ж

Each character, including the digraphs, has a distinct place in the alphabet.

2.1.2 Obsolete variants are:

for **đ**:**dj** (same position), **gj** (after **ǵ**)
for **lj**:**ļ** (same position)
for **nj**:**ń** (same position)
for **dž**:**ǵ** (after **g**)

When **đ** is not available, e.g. on some typewriters, **dj** is still used.

2.1.3 Despite the existence of the standard equivalents, combinations of letters are often found in the transliteration of names, especially in newspapers, instead of accented letters, viz.

		En	*Fr*	*De*	
for	č, ć	ch	tch	tsch	Fr forms are found
	š	sh	ch	sch	in En also
	ž	zh	j	sh	

2.2 CAPITALISATION

2.2.1 All words capitalised:

Personal and geographical names (see also 2.2.4).
Possessives in **-ov**, **-ev**, **-ji**, **-in** derived from words spelt with capitals.

2.2.2 First word only capitalised:

Names of institutions, festivals, congresses, streets, firms, titles of books. (See also 2.2.5.)

2.2.3 Not capitalised:

Days of the week, months, geographical adjectives, words in **-ist**. (See also 2.2.4 and 2.2.5.)

2.2.4

Adjuncts of personal names, such as **sv(eti)**, **d(okto)r**, **g(ospodin)**, *Saint*, *Dr*, *Mr*; geographical features, e.g. **Dunavski basen**, *Danube Basin* are written small.

2.2.5 In **I Kongres jugoslovenskih geografa** (*1st Congress of Yugoslav Geographers*), the word following the numeral has a capital, but not in **Prvi kongres** .... A common noun has a capital when it is short for the full designation of persons, e.g. **Predsjednik**, *the President*.

2.3 DIVISION OF WORDS

2.3.1 Rules 1, 2, 3, 4, 5(a) or (b), 6(b) or (c), p. xiii, apply.

2.3.2 Practice is not rigid: divisions such as **še-snaesti**, **sugla-snik** are found, even though **šes-naesti** and **suglas-nik** are equally legitimate and accord better with the etymology. It is more important to remember not to divide **lj** and **nj** or, usually, **dž**.

2.3.3 Two vowels are usually divided, e.g. **ža-oka**, but **žao-ka** is admissible; **bi-o**, with a single vowel taken over is not. Note **pr-vi** with a vocalic **r**.

2.5 CONSONANTS AND CONSONANT CHANGES

2.5.1 As far as their pronunciation goes, nearly all consonants are hard, but for grammatical purposes the following consonants are 'soft':

ć č dž đ j lj nj š št ž žd (cf. 4.3.1)

2.5.2 The effects of palatalisation (see General note on the Slavonic languages) are as follows:

	b	c	ć	g	h	k	l	m	n	p	s	sk	st		t	v	z	zd
to				z	s	c												
or	blj	ć	č	ž	š	č/ć	lj	mlj	nj	plj	š	št	št/šć		ć	vlj	ž	žd/žd
	zg																	
to																		
or	žd																	

Where there are two possible changes, only the first is usual in nouns.

Examples: **Čeh**, pl. **Česi**; **mogu**, *I can*; **može**, *it can*

2.5.3 Assimilation occurs when a voiced and an unvoiced consonant come together, elimination when a consonant sound is repeated, or to avoid a difficult combination of consonants. This happens with prefixes, a fact worth remembering if you are used to other Slavonic languages, e.g. **s-bor** > **zbor**; **pod-pis** > **potpis**; **pod-tvrditi** > **potvrditi**; more disconcertingly it occurs in declension (cf. 4.3.3, 4.3.4).

2.6 VARIATION OF VOWEL

2.6.1 The vowel **a** occurs for historical reasons in the NS or GP though absent in other cases, e.g. **sestara** GP of **sestra**, *sister*; **ministar**, stem **ministr-**. In some verbs **e** similarly appears and disappears.

2.6.2 At the end of a word or syllable **l** becomes **o**, e.g. **napisala**, *she wrote*, but **napisao**, *he wrote*; **Beograd**, *Belgrade*; and with simplification, **stola** GS of **sto**, *table*.

2.6.3 In *jekavština* (0.5.1) variation between **-ije-** and **-je-** is found. (Both are **-e-** in *ekavština*.)

2.7 SPELLING

2.7.1 The present alphabets were introduced in 1818 (Cyrillic) and in the 1830's (*latinica*). Before 1818 the Cyrillic forms would be Church Slavonic, and if secular would embody conventions more like Russian, e.g. ѣ for present-day **ja**. Earlier *latinica* was chaotic, with c in different authors standing for both the present c and č, ch for ć and h and so on. In all 23 ways of representing ć are known.

2.7.2 Since the alphabets were established, changes have been minor, such as the disappearance of the hyphen in compounds like **dvadeset-drugi**, the change **št** to **šć** in some verbs, the obsolescence of variants like **august** for **avgust**.

3 ARTICLES

There are no articles.

4 NOUNS

4.1 GENDER AND FORM

There are three genders, the gender for the most part corresponding to the form of the noun. Inanimate nouns may be of any gender. Omitting the vocative there are six cases, the endings varying according to the form of the noun.

4.3 ENDINGS

4.3.1 *Masculine nouns*

Masculine nouns mostly have stems which end in a consonant or -l/-o (2.6.2), with no ending in the NS. Some names (mostly Christian names) have the ending -o or -e, e.g. **Marko, Tito, Blagoje, Đorđe, Nodilo**. For pet names in -o and -e and M nouns in -a, see 4.3.11. The endings are:

	S	P
N	- (-o, -e, -in)	-i/-ovi/-evi
A	-a/-	-e/-ove/-eve
G	-a	-a/-ova/-eva/-i/-ju
D	-u	
I	-om/-em	-ima/-ovima/-evima
L	-u	

The endings -em, -evi, etc., follow soft consonants.

4.3.2 The -v- plurals come principally from monosyllables, or disyllables with inserted -a- (2.6.1), e.g. **brojevi**, *numbers*, from **broj**; **poslovi**, *works* from **posao** (2.6.2).

4.3.3 Omission and insertion of -a- (2.6.1) and consequent assimilation or elimination (2.5.3) or alternation of l and o (2.6.2) produce effects such as **napredak**, *progress*, GS **napretka**; **otac**, *father* GS **oca** (< **otca**); **čitalac**, *reader* GS **čitaoca**.

4.3.4 Palatalisation (2.5.2) occurs before -i(ma), e.g. **rečnik**, *dictionary*, **rečnici(ma)**; **dodatak**, *supplement*, **dodacima** (2.5.3). Note also **otac**, *father*, NP **očevi**, **Turčin**, NP **Turci**, GP **Turaka**.

4.3.5 *Neuter nouns*

These end in -o or -e. Place names in -ovo, though neuter adjectives, follow the same declension.

The endings are:

	S	P
NA	-o/-e	-a
G	-a	-a
D	-u	
I	-om/-em	-ima
L	-u	

4.3.6 Inserted -a- (2.6.1) occurs in GP, e.g. **pismo, pisama**. This may cause consonant change (2.5.3).

4.3.7 **oko, uvo** (**uho**) have feminine plurals, **oči, uši** (4.3.8); **ime, vr(ij)eme** have stem **imen-, vr(ij)emen-**; **dete** stem **detet-**.

4.3.8 *Feminine nouns*

These end in -a, or more rarely, in a consonant. Of the latter the commonest are those in -ost.

In -a   In a consonant

	S	P	S	P
N	-a⎱		-⎱	
A	-u⎰	-e	-⎰	-i
G	-e	-a, -i, -*u	-i	-i(ju)
D	-i⎫		-i⎫	
I	-om⎬	-ama	-ju, -u⎬	-(i)ma
L	-i⎭		-i⎭	

4.3.9   Inserted -a- (2.6.1) occurs with GP -a, e.g. **tačka, tačaka,** *full stop,* occasionally with change of consonant (2.5.3) e.g. **sveska, svezaka** (though this could also come from **svezak).**

Note palatalisation (2.5.2) in **ruka, ruci.**

GP -u is found only with **ruka,** *hand;* **noga,** *leg;* **sluga,** *servant.*

4.3.10

     mati, *mother*   has AG, etc.   **mater, matere,** etc.
     kći, *daughter*   **kćer, kćeri,** etc.

4.3.11   The -a declension is followed by masculine names in -e and -o, originally pet names, such as **Arne, Ivo.**

4.3.12   *Foreign names*

These are usually respelt and declined on Serbocroatian models, e.g. **Šekspir,** G **Šekspira** (4.3.1), **Igo** G **Iga** (4.3.1). **Šo** and **Šeli** are treated as if they ended in a consonant G **Šoa, Šelija** (4.3.1), **Garsija Lorka, Glinka** and the like follow 4.3.8.

Russian names in -ski are declined as adjectives (5.2.2).

4.6   USE OF CASES

The names of the cases (see Introduction), are only a rough guide to their use. Note for instance that the genitive is used as the object of a negative verb.

5   ADJECTIVES

5.1   GENERAL

5.1.1   Adjectives vary according to gender, number and case and agree with the nouns they qualify. Surnames in -ki (F -ka), and place names such as **Hrvatska,** *Croatia,* and **Brčko** are adjectives.

5.1.2   Most adjectives have a short and a long form, e.g. **nov/novi; dobar/dobri.**

5.2   ENDINGS

5.2.1   *Short form*

The short form, which is used as a predicate, is also found when the noun is indeterminate, e.g. **nov svezak,** *a new volume;* **novi svezak,** *the new volume.* Possessive adjectives in -ov(-ev) and -in, e.g. **Vukov,** *Vuk's;* **materin,** *mother's;* **učiteljev,** *teacher's;* **njegov,** *his,* have short forms even when determinate, e.g. **Vukov rečnik,** *Vuk's dictionary.* Adjectives are entered in the dictionary under short forms.

Only the following short forms are different, as written, from the long ones:

	MS	NS
N	-	
A	-/-a	
G	-a	-a
DL	-u	-u

5.2.2 *Long forms*

	S			P		
	M	N	F	M	N	F
N	-i	-o/-e	-a	-i	-a	-e
A	N or G	-o/-e	-u	-e	-a	-e
G	-og/-eg(a)		-e	-i(je)h		
D	-om(e)/-em(u)		-oj			
I	-i(je)m		-om	-i(je)m/-ima		
L	-om(e)/-em(u)		-oj			

Changes of vowel (2.6) and of consonant (2.5.3) may occur with the addition of endings, e.g. **dobar, dobri**; **beo, beli**; **radostan, radosna**. Palatalisation may occur in the plural, e.g. **redak, reci**.

5.3 COMPARISON

5.3.1 *Comparative:* substitute **-(i)ji**, less commonly **-ši**, for the **-i(-ki, -oki, -eki)** of the long form of the positive. The addition of **-ji** causes palatalisation (2.5.2), e.g. **drag** > **draži**. Irregular comparatives, such as **dobar, bolji** (*good, better*) are given separately in the dictionary.

5.3.2 *Superlative:* add **naj-** to the comparative.

5.4 POSSESSIVES

5.4.1 For possessives in **-ov** and **-in**, see 5.2.1.

5.4.2 The pronominal possessives **moj, tvoj, svoj** (*own*)/**naš, vaš** have short forms in NS and other endings as 5.2.2, e.g. GSM **mojega**. Contracted forms are found, viz. in the masculine and neuter GS **moga**, DLS **momu/mome**.

6 NUMERALS

6.1 CARDINAL

6.1.1

1 jedan	11 jedanaest	21 dvadeset i jedan	200 dvesta, dve stotine
2 dva	12 dvanaest	25 dvadeset(i)pet	300 trista, tri stotine
3 tri	13 trinaest	30 trideset	400 četiri stotine
4 četiri	14 četrnaest	40 četrdeset	500 pet (etc.) stotina
5 pet	15 petnaest	50 pedeset	1000 hiljada (S), tisuća (C)
6 šest	16 šesnaest	60 šezdeset	2000 dve hiljade
7 sedam	17 sedamnaest	70 sedamdeset	5000 pet hiljada
8 osam	18 osamnaest	80 osamdeset	
9 devet	19 devetnaest	90 devedeset	
10 deset	20 dvadeset	100 sto(tina)	

6.1.2 **jedan–četiri** are adjectives.

jedan, jedna, jedno is declined as in 5.2.2 and 5.3.1.

dva, tri, četiri:

	MN	F	All genders	
NA	dva	dv(ij)e	tri	četiri
G	dvaju	dveju	triju	četiriju
DIL	dvama/dvema	dvema	trima	četirma

dva, tri, četiri are not usually declined after a preposition.

pet onwards are nouns. All except **sto(tina) hiljada** and **tisuća** are indeclinable, and even these are commonly found in the invariable forms **stotinu, hiljadu, tisuću.** No part of a compound numeral is declined except final **jedan.**

6.1.3 The noun following the numeral has the following endings:

		Numeral	
		dva, tri, četiri	**pet** onwards
Case	*NA*	MN -a F -e, -i	GP
	GDIL	normal endings as in 4.3	GP

For example: **za dv(ij)e godine,** *for two years*; **u pet svezaka,** *in five volumes*; **četrdeset i osam država,** *forty-eight states.*

6.1.4 Compound numerals behave like the numeral with which they end, except that **dva, tri, četiri** are then usually invariable.

6.2 ORDINAL
6.2.1

1 **prvi**		9 **deveti**	
2 **drugi**		10 **deseti**	
3 **treći**		11–19 **jedanaesti,** etc.	
4 **četvrti**		20–90 **dvadeseti,** etc.	
5 **peti**		21 **dvadeset prvi**	
6 **šesti**		100 **stoti**	
7 **sedmi**		200 **dvestoti**	
8 **osmi**		1000 **hiljaditi** or **tisuć(n)i**	

6.2.2 Only the last element of a compound ordinal has the ordinal form.

6.3 FIGURES
Plain arabic figures normally stand for cardinals, ordinals being followed by a full stop. Roman figures without stop also indicate ordinals.

6.4 DATES
6.4.1 The months are:

S **januar, februar, mart, april, maj, jun,
jul, avgust, septembar, oktobar, novembar, decembar**

C *alternatives* **siječanj, veljača, ožujak, travanj, svibanj, lipanj,
srpanj, kolovoz, rujan, listopad, stideni, prosinac**

All are masculine nouns (4.3.1, 4.3.3) except **veljača** feminine noun (4.3.8) and **studeni,** masculine adjective (5.2.2). Note the unusual meaning of **listopad.**

6.4.2

31 August is translated **trideset prvi avgust**

On 31.viii.1961: **trideset prvog avgusta hiljadu devet stotina šezdeset prve godine,** with day, month and year in the genitive and only the last element of compound ordinals having the ordinal form.

1848 (godina) is read: **hiljadu** (sic) **osam stotina četrdeset osma** (godina)

1939–1945 is read with cardinal numbers. Most speakers would insert **od** (*from*) and **do** (*to*), but if a title began with a similar date one could hardly file it under **od**.

Sedamdesete godine: *the 70's*

7 PRONOUNS

7.1 DEMONSTRATIVE, ETC.

7.1.1 Demonstratives and indefinites have much the same case endings as adjectives (which indeed incorporate a pronoun). Note:

> **ovaj**, *this*; **taj**, *this*, *that*; **onaj**, *that*: N -o, F -a, declined like an adjective in -i
>
> **Sav**, *all*: GP **sviju**

7.1.2 Some pronouns have an indefinite suffix **-god**, which is invariable, e.g. **kojigod, kojagod**, etc.

7.1.3 **Neko, niko** are compounds of **ko**; **nešto, ništa, išta** of **što** (7.2.1).

7.2 INTERROGATIVE AND RELATIVE

7.2.1 **(t)ko** and **što** likewise have more or less adjectival forms, viz.

> **(t)ko?**, *who?*, *who*: **(t)koga, (t)komu/kome, (t)kim(e), (t)kom(e)** (**tko** is Croatian)
>
> **što**, *what?*: **čega/šta, čemu, čim(e), čem(u)**

7.2.2 **što** has a special use as a universal relative, the oblique cases of which are formed with the aid of the third person pronoun, **on** (7.3.2) e.g. **članci što ih je izdala Srpska književna zadruga**, *articles which the Serbian Literary Society published.*

7.3 PERSONAL

7.3.1

	S 1	2	S & P R	P 1	2
N	ja	ti	—	mi	vi
AG	me(ne)	te(be)	se(be)	nas	vas
D	m(en)i	t(eb)i	s(eb)i		
I	mnom(e)	tobom	sobom	nam(a)	vam(a)
L	meni	tebi	sebi		

se, *self* refers to all persons and both numbers, and helps to form reflexive verbs.

7.3.2 **on, ono, ona**, *he, it, she* has oblique cases from another root:

	S MN	F	P
A	(nje)ga, nj	(n)ju, je	(nj)ih
G	(nje)ga	(n)je	
D	(nje)mu	(n)joj	(nj)im(a)
I	njim(e)	njom(e)	njima
L	njemu	njoj	

8 VERBS

8.1 GENERAL

8.1.1 As the different persons are expressed by endings, pronouns are usually dispensed with, e.g. **pišem,** *I write.*

8.1.2 In the smaller dictionaries verbs may be entered indifferently under either aspect (see General note on the Slavonic languages) or both, with or without a reference. The entry word is the infinitive.

8.2 PRESENT

8.2.1 *Endings*

I	-em, -eš, -e; -emo, -ete, -(ej)u
II	-im, -iš, -i; -imo, -ite, -e
III	-am, -aš, -a; -amo, -ate, -aju

8.2.2 *Relation to infinitive*

P	-am	-em (8.2.3)	-*em	-ijem	-nem (8.2.3)
I	-ati	-ći, -ti, -ati, -eti	-ati	-iti	-nuti, -ti

P	-ujem	-im (8.2.3)	
I	-ovati, -ivati	-ati, -(j)eti, -iti	

8.2.3 *Points to note*

-em/-ći, -ti: consonants are modified, as **-dem, -tem** > sti; **rečem** (3P **rek(n)u**) > **reći; mogu, možeš,** etc. > **moći**

-em/-ati: a vowel is inserted in the present, e.g. **zovem, zvati; berem, brati**

-nem/-ti: changes of consonant as for **-em/-ti,** e.g. **padnem, pasti.** Note also **stanem, stati; počnem, početi**

-im/-ati: the stem usually ends in a palatalised consonant (2.5.2) whereas the other **-im** verbs do not. Note also **stojim, stajati**

Irregular are **hoću, hoćeš,** etc./**hteti; idem/ići; odem/otići; dođem/doći; nađem/naći; šaljem/slati**

Note also **daje,** *gives,* from **dati**

8.3 PAST

Serbocroatian has imperfect and aorist tenses (cf. Bulgarian and Macedonian), but the tense most likely to be met on title-pages and in prefaces is the perfect, which is a compound tense (8.10).

8.5 FUTURE

The future is basically a compound tense (8.10.3).

8.10 COMPOUND TENSES

8.10.1 *Perfect*

Formed from the old participle:

S			P		
M	N	F	M	N	F
-o	-lo	-la	-li	-la	-le

together with **sam, si, je; smo, ste, su,** the present tense of the verb **biti,** *to be.*

The parts of **biti** are inserted early in the sentence and may accordingly be separated from the participle, e.g.

| 1 | 2 | 3 | 4 | 5 | 6 | 7 | 1 | 2 | 3 7 | 4 | 5 | 6 |

pesme koje su posle obih zbiraka izašle, *poems which came out after these two collections.*

On title-pages **je** and **su** are omitted (cf. 1.2.2).

8.10.2 *Relation to infinitive*

> P -o I -ti after most vowels: but **umro:umr(ij)eti**
> P -ao is ambiguous. The infinitive may be -ati or -ći/-ti, with change of consonant, e.g. **uzdao, izdalo,** etc., I **izdati,** but **mogao, moglo,** I **moći; rastao, raslo,** I **rasti**
> P -do, -to I -sti

Note also **išao** (in compounds -**šao**) from **ići(-ći).**

8.10.3 *Future*

> Formed from **ću, ćeš, će; ćemo, ćete, će** (present of **hteti,** *to wish*) followed, not necessarily immediately, by the infinitive.

The order may be reversed and the two parts run together, e.g. **ću napisati** or **napisaću,** *I shall write.*

8.10.4 *Conditional*

> **bih, bi, bi; bismo, biste, bi,** with the old past participle (8.10.1).

8.11 INFINITIVE
8.11.1 The infinitive mostly ends in -**ti**. A few common verbs have -**ći**.
8.11.2 The infinitive is used much as in English in Croatian, but Serbian tends to substitute a clause with **da**.

8.12 PARTICIPLES
8.12.1 There are no longer any active participles used as such, but a few words in -**ći** (cf. 8.13) are still declinable and function as adjectives, e.g. **idući,** *forthcoming.*

8.12.2 *Perfect passive participle*
This ends in -**n** or -**t** (5.2.2).

8.12.3 *Relation to infinitive*

P	-an, -at	-en		-en	-jen
I	-ati	-ti (cf. 8.2.3: -em/-ti)	-eti, -iti, -ći	-eti, -iti
P	-ijen, -it	-nut			
I	-iti	-nuti			

8.13 GERUNDS
There are two adverbial gerunds, functioning like the English participle.
> *Present:* -**ći** corresponding 3 PP, e.g. -**eći, -ajući**
> *Past:* -**vši** corresponding to the perfect

8.14/8.15 REFLEXIVE; PASSIVE

8.14.1 The passive participle may be used to express a state or past action, e.g. **ovaj udžbenik odobren je odlukom Saveta za prosvetu,** *this textbook is approved by resolution of the Council for Education;* **naslov pod kojim su bili naštampani,** *the title under which they were printed.*

8.14.2 Action, especially in the present, is more frequently expressed by a reflexive verb (7.3.1), e.g. **pretplata se šalje,** *the subscription is (to be) sent,* or the active is substituted, e.g. **uređuju Julije Benešić i Vladimir Gudel,** i.e. *edited by J.B. and V.G.*

8.17 THE VERB **biti,** *to be*
> *Present:* (je)sam, (je)si, je(st); (je)-smo, (je)ste, (je)su
> *Negative:* ni(je)sam . . . nije, etc.
> *Perfect:* bio sam, etc., as 8.10.1
> *Conditional:* bih, etc., as 8.10.4

8.22 NEGATIVE
The prefix **ne-,** common with adjectives where English has *un-, in-* is prefixed to verbs only if it makes a single concept, e.g. **nedostajati,** *to be lacking*; but *I do not know*: **ne znam.**

9 ADVERBS

9.1 FORMATION

9.1.1 Adverbs formed regularly from adjectives end in **-o/-e** (neuter) or less commonly **-om/-em** (instrumental case). Adjectives in **-ski** do not change.

9.1.2 Some adverbs are oblique cases of nouns, but they usually have a separate entry in the dictionary.

9.2 COMPARISON
Comparative and superlative are formed in the same way as from adjectives.

10 PREPOSITIONS

These govern particular cases, and with some prepositions the meaning varies with the case, e.g. **u** with locative = *at, in*; **u** with accusative = *to*; **u** with genitive = *of.*

GLOSSARY

autorsko pravo, *copyright*

bel(j)eška, *note*
besplatno, *free*
biblioteka, *library*
bibliotekar, *librarian*
broj, *number* (1.7.3, 1.8.4)

c(ij)ena, *price* (1.8.6)

časopis, *periodical* (1.8.1)
član, *member* (1.8.6)
članak, *article*

deo, dio, *part, volume* (1.4.1)
dodatak, *appendix, supplement*
dopuna, *appendix*
dopunjen, *enlarged* (1.5.2)
društvo, *society*
dvobroj, *double number* (1.8.6)

egzemplar, *copy*

godina, *year* (1.8.6), *volume* (1.8.4)
godišnjak, *yearbook*
godišnji, *annual* (1.8.5)
godište, *volume* (1.8.4)
govor, *speech*

inostranstvo, inozemstvo, *foreign
   countries*
ispitivanje, *research*
ispravljen, *corrected* (1.5.2)
isti, *same*
istraživanje, *research*
izabran, *selected*
izbor, *selection* (1.2.3)
izdanje, *edition* (1.5.1), *publication*
   (1.7.1, 1.8.2)
izdao, *he published*
izdavačko poduzeće, *publishing house*
   (1.6.1)
izlaziti, *to come out*
izm(j)ena, *exchange*
izrađen, *produced*
izv(j)eštaji, *communications, proceedings*
izvod, *abstract, extract*

knjiga, *book, part, volume* (1.4.1, 1.7.2,
   1.8.4)
knjižara, *bookshop* (1.6.2)
knjižica, *pamphlet*
knjižnica, *library*
kolo, *cycle, series* (1.7.3)

l(j)eto, *summer, year*
list, *leaf, page*; *newspaper*; *letter*

m(j)esečni, *monthly* (1.8.5)

naklada, *publication*
napisao, *wrote*
narudžb(in)a, *order*
naslov, *address*
nastavljati, *to continue*
neizdan, *unpublished*
neprom(ij)enjen, *unaltered* (1.5.2)
novela, *long short story*

objašnjenje, *explanation*
odabran, *selected*

odaslati, *to send, dispatch*
odbor, *committee* (1.2.3)

pesma, *poem*
pisac, *writer*
pismo, *letter* (4.3.6)
pjesma, *poem*
platnen, *of cloth*
pojedin(ačn)i, *single* (1.8.6)
poklon (od autora), *with* (*the author's*)
   compliments
polugodišnji, *half-yearly*
polum(j)esečni, *fortnightly*
popravljen, *corrected* (1.5.2)
popust, *discount*
posao (P poslovi), *work*
poseban otisak, *offprint* (1.5.3)
poslati, pošiljati, *to send*
povez, *binding*
pov(ij)est, *story*
predgovor, *preface*
pregled, *review*; *summary*
pregledan, *revised* (1.5.2)
prerađen, *revised* (1.5.2)
preštampa(va)n, *reprinted* (1.5.3)
pretplata, *subscription* (1.8.6)
preveo, *he translated*
pribrao, *he collected*
priča, *story*
pridodatak, *appendix*
prijegled, *review*; *summary*
prijevod, *translation*
prilog, *contribution*
primedba, *note*
prim(j)erak, *sample, specimen*
pripov(ij)est, pripovetka, *story*
pripremio, priredio, *he prepared*
   (1.2.2)
proširen, *enlarged* (1.5.2)

račun, *bill*
rasprava, *treatise*
rasprodan, *out of print*
razm(j)ena, *exchange*
reč, *speech*
rečnik, *dictionary*
redakcija, *editorial office* (1.8.7)
registar, *index*
riječ, *speech*

rječnik, *dictionary*
rođen, *born*

sabran, *collected*
sakupio, *he collected* (1.2.2)
saradnik, *contributor* (1.2.6)
sastavio, *he compiled* (1.2.2)
slati, *to send*
spis, *writing*
sredio, *he edited* (1.2.2)
stran(ic)a, *page*
sveska, *volume* (1.4.1), *part* (1.8.4)
sveučilište, *university*
svezak, see sveska

se šalje, *is sent*
štamparija, *printing shop* (1.6.3)

tabela, *table*
tablica, *plate*
tiskara, *printing shop* (1.6.3)
trom(j)esečni, *quarterly* (1.8.5)

umnožen, *enlarged* (1.5.2)
umro, *he died*
uredio, *he edited* (1.2.2)
urednik, *editor* (1.2.2, 1.8.3)
uredništvo, *editorial staff* (1.2.3),
   (*editorial*) *office* (1.8.7)
uvod, *introduction*
uvodna r(ij)eč, *preface*

zam(j)ena, *exchange*
zbirka, *collection*

GRAMMATICAL INDEX: WORDS

bi(h), 8.10.4, 8.17
bio, 8.17
bismo, biste, 8.10.4, 8.17

će, etc., 8.10.3

čega, čem(u), čim(e),
   7.2.1

daje, 8.2.3
detet-, 4.3.7
dođem, etc., 8.2.3
dva-, dve-, dvije-, 6.1.2

ga, 7.3.2

hoć-, 8.2.3

idem, etc., 8.2.3
ih, im(a), 7.3.2
imen-, 4.3.7
išao, išlo, 8.10.2

je, 7.3.2, 8.10.1, 8.17
jesam, jest, etc., 8.17
joj, ju, 7.3.2

kćer, 4.3.10
kim(e), koga, kom(e),
   komu, 7.2.1

mater-, 4.3.10
me-, mi, mnom, 7.3.1
mog-, 8.10.2
moga, mome, momu,
   5.4.2
mu, 7.3.2

nađem, etc., 8.2.3
naj-, 5.3.2
nam(a), nas, 7.3.1
ne-, 8.22
nek-, 7.1.3
nič-, 7.1.3
nije, etc., 8.17
nik-, 7.1.3
nj, nje-, nji-, njo-, 7.3.2

oca, 4.3.3
očevi, 4.3.4
oči, etc., 4.3.7
odem, etc., 8.2.3
on-, 7.1.1
ona, ono, 7.1.1, 7.3.2
ov-, 7.1.1

sam, 8.10.1, 8.17
se, seb-, 7.3.1
si, 7.3.1, 8.10.1, 8.17
smo, 8.10.1, 8.17
sobom, 7.3.1
ste, su, 8.10.1, 8.17
sviju, 7.1.1

šaljem, etc., 8.2.3
šta, 7.2.1
što, 7.2.1, 7.2.2

ta, 7.1.1
te, 7.1.1, 7.3.1
teb-, 7.3.1
ti, 7.1.1, 7.3.1
ti(je)h, ti(je)m, tima,
   7.1.1
tkim(e), tko-, 7.2.1
to, 7.1.1
tobom, 7.3.1
toga, toj, tomu, 7.1.1
tri-, 6.1.2
tu, 7.1.1

uši, 4.3.7

vam(a), vas, 7.3.1
vr(ij)emen-, 4.3.7

GRAMMATICAL INDEX: ENDINGS

MACEDONIAN

SPECIMEN

Книгата на Крсте П. Мисирков „За Македонските работи" издадена од самиот автор во крајот на 1903 год., печатена во Софија — печатница на „Либералниот клуб", требаше да минат 43 години за да ја види македонската општественост.

Вистина каков дар за младите македонски генерации и какво чесно воспоменание на македонскиот историк, публицист, филолог и политик и това точно на 20-то годишнината од неговата смрт и само неколку дни од 43-годишнината од Илинденската епопеја.

Krste P. Misirkov's book 'To the Macedonian workers', published by the author himself at the end of 1903, printed in Sofia — the press of the Liberal Club, has not been available to the Macedonian public for the last 43 years.

It is known what a gift (this is) for the young Macedonian generations, and what a fine commemoration of the Macedonian historian, publicist, philologist and politician, and that precisely on the 20th anniversary of his death and only a few days from the 43rd anniversary of the epic of Ilinden.

0 GENERAL CHARACTERISTICS

Macedonian is most closely allied to Bulgarian (q.v.), with which it shares the comparative absence of declension and the use of the appended article (in Macedonian -от, etc.), but it differs in its sound system and in vocabulary, and the apparent difference is accentuated by the use of the Serbocroatian form of the alphabet and the assimilation of consonants, plus the peculiar letters ќ, ѓ and ѕ. For instance:

Bu	*Ma*	*Sh*
опис	опис	опис
мъдър	мудар	мудар
нощ	ноќ	ноћ
ходи	оди	хода
дума	збор	реч
яйце	јајце	јаје

1 BIBLIOLINGUISTICS

1.1 NAMES

1.1.1 Macedonian surnames are almost all adjectives, some in -ев, -ов (5.4.2), F -ева, -ова, more in -ски, -ска (5.1.2). There are also some which are nouns, e.g. those in -иќ, corresponding to the Serbocroatian -ić. Christian names are nouns (4.3.1).

Until quite recent times both Christian names and surnames were fluid in form. Thus the 19th-century local worthy **Ѓурчин Кокалески** appears also as **Кокале**, and his father's Christian name is given variously as **Георгија** and **Ѓорѓи** and his grandson in 1943 as **Ефто Георгиев** or **Ѓорѓески** or **Кокалески**.

1.1.2 Confusion is possible between the accusative **-ва** of a masculine name in **-в** and the corresponding feminine **-ва**; but with the growing tendency not to decline masculine names either (e.g. **од Ефто Георгиев**) the likelihood is disappearing.

1.1.3 The plural is found in cases like **браќата Миладиновци**, *the brothers Miladinov*, but not with Christian names.

1.2 NAMES OF AUTHORS, EDITORS, ETC.

1.2.1 The names of persons connected with the production of a work may be stated in various ways. The name in isolation at the head of the title-page usually suffices for the authors of original works. It is in the nominative.

1.2.2 An active verb may be used to denote authorship, and is usual for editors, translators and so on. The verb may be in the past indefinite (8.10.2), aorist (8.3.3), or in the case of works in progress or series, in the present (8.2.1). It will agree with the names in number, and if in the past indefinite, in gender also.

> *Past:* редактирал Васил Иљоски; составиле Г. Милошев и К. Тошев
>
> *Aorist:* во прибирањето . . . на фактичниот материјал учествуваа М. Поп-Ангеловски и Т. Стефановски
>
> *Present:* уредува Редакционен одбор

The verb used depends on the relation of the agent to the work, e.g. **напишал**, *wrote*; **составил**, *composed, compiled*; **приредил**, **редактирал**, *edited*; **уредува**, *is editing*; **учествуваа**, *they took part.*

1.2.3 In the case of collected and selected works, correspondence and the like the name may follow the title, connected by **на**, *of*. The name is in the accusative, in so far as this makes any difference (4.3.1).

1.2.4 The work done is indicated by an abstract noun, usually followed by **на**, *of*, and the name in the accusative (4.3.1), e.g. **во редакција на Д-р Харалампие Поленаковиќ**, *under the editorship of Dr Haralampie Polenakoviḱ*; **заеднички труд на К. Џонов и А. Петровска**, *joint work of K. Džonov and A. Petrovska*; **превод и јазична редакција на**, etc., *translation and linguistic editorship by*, etc. The **на** may be omitted, making usually no difference, e.g. **подбор, редакција и коментар Љубен Лапе**, *selection, editing and commentary: Ljuben Lape.*

1.2.5 The specific relation may be indicated by a noun or phrase denoting the agent, followed by the name or names in the nominative, e.g. **уредник Ацо Шопов**, *editor Aco Šopov*; and similarly with words like **редактор(и)**, *editor(s)*; **составувач**, *compiler*; **редакциски одбор**, *editorial committee.*

1.2.6 Occasionally a passive verb is used with a preposition and the name in the accusative (4.3.1), **e.g. Овије белешки се земени од Ефто Георгиев**, *These notes are taken from Efto Georgiev.*

1.2.7 The names of corporate bodies usually appear at the head of the title-page, or as sponsors or editors rather than direct authors. The forms are not affected by any grammatical relationships but there may be appended articles to be coped with, e.g. **финансира Фондот за . . .**, *The Fund for . . . is financing.* Headings would omit the **-от**. An expression such as **Одделение за Општествени Науки на Македонската Академија на Науките и Уметностите** would need converting into the more usual

т

Makedonska Akademija na Naukite i Umetnostite. Oddelenie za Opštestveni Nauki. Similarly Уред за информации при Претседателството, etc. Conferences may produce expressions like Материјали од Научната средба одржана во Титов Велес на 8, 9 и 10 мај 1969 година по повод 40-годишнината од смртта на Васил Главинов, giving possible headings **Titov Veles** and **Naučna Sredba održana po povod 40-godišnata od Smrtta na Vasil Glavinov.**

1.3 TITLES

1.3.1　The titles of most books, other than novels and the like, consist of nouns and adjectives, with or without the article, and prepositions, e.g. **Развиток на земјоделството во Македонија,** *Development of agriculture in Macedonia*; **Македонски народни приказни,** *Macedonian folk tales.* More evocative titles may involve verbs, e.g. **Она што беше небо,** *That which was heaven.*

1.3.2　Title entries present few difficulties. What is said under Bulgarian applies to Macedonian.

1.3.3　As there is no separate accusative form, or where there is, its use is not obligatory, titles are not affected by forming part of a sentence.

1.4 VOLUMES AND PARTS

1.4.1　The use of terms is not very exact. **Том** is found subdivided by **книга,** which will naturally be taken as *volume* and *part,* but **книга** is found alone and so is **дел.**

1.4.2　Numeration is given in ordinal numbers or in figures, usually after **том** or **книга,** e.g. **том 1, книга прва.**

1.5 EDITIONS

1.5.1/1.5.2　The word for *edition* is **издание** (a word which also means *publication*), used with an ordinal numeral or an adjective denoting some form of revision. Occasionally the information may be given in the preface, e.g. **да се издаде ова ново издание,** *that this new edition should be published*; **во ова издание се извршени на извесни места скратувања,** *in this edition abridgements have been made in various places.*

1.5.3　*Offprint* is **посебен отпечаток**; *reprinted* **препечатен.**

1.6 IMPRINTS

1.6.1　Most presses nowadays are institutional, e.g. **Државно Книгоиздателство на Македонија,** *State Publishing House of Macedonia*; or with a commemorative name such as **Книгоиздателство „Кочо Рацин",** *Kočo Racin Press*, but shorter names are now common, e.g. **Култура,** and a personal name, e.g. **Христо Г. Данов** (1968), is sometimes found. Both place and publisher are usually in the nominative, the name of the publisher being sometimes preceded by **издава,** *publishes,* or **издавач,** *publisher.*

1.6.2　Printers are indicated by some form of the root **печат-,** e.g. **печатено во печатницата „Киро Димитровски-Дангаро",** *printed at the Kiro Dimitrovski-Dangaro Press.* Where the printer is prominent, information that such and such a body is responsible for publication (**издава,** etc.) may occur elsewhere on the title-page.

1.7 SERIES

1.7.1　The names of series occur in various places, at the top of the title-page or on a separate facing title-page being the commonest. They are usually descriptive of the series or its contents, e.g. **Библиотека Наши Современи Писатели,** *Our Contemporary Writers Library*; **Едиција Од нашето културно минато,** *From our cultural past* *series*; Домашни избори за македонската историја, *Home selections for Macedonian history*; Современа општествена мисла, *Contemporary social thought*; Посебни изданија, *Separate publications* (Monographs).

1.7.2 Numeration is by книга (*book*); том (*volume*) and книга; or коло (*series*) and книга.

1.8 PERIODICALS

1.8.1/1.8.2 The titles of periodicals are much the same grammatically as those of books, e.g. Македонски јазик, *Macedonian language*; Гласник на Институтот за национална Историја, *Messenger of the Institute for National History*. Sometimes, as in the preceding example or with such a title as Прилози, *Contributions*, the name of the institution publishing the periodical must be taken into account. Even if it is joined to the title of the periodical, it is not grammatically affected, except that the article (-от in the example above) will not appear in the catalogue heading. Alternatively it may follow издавач or издава (cf. 1.6.1).

1.8.3 Editorship is indicated by уредник, Р уредници, sometimes одговорен (главен) уредник, *responsible (chief) editor*, or more often collective, e.g. уредништво, редакција, redakcioni kolegium or редакционен (редакциски) одбор, *editorial committee*; or the information may be given by a verb, e.g. уредува, *is editing*; редактирале и уредиле, *they edited and arranged*, followed by the names, one of which may be distinguished as претседател, *chairman*. Соработници are *contributors*.

1.8.4 Numeration of annual volumes is by година (abbreviated год.) or том, individual parts being indicated by кн(ига) or број, e.g. Год. V, број 1.

1.8.5 Frequency, if not implicit in the title, may be indicated by such a phrase as излегува двапати годишно, *comes out twice yearly*.

1.8.6 Subscription is абонмент, usually appearing in some such phrase as годишниот абонмент изнесува, *annual subscription amounts to*, but subscription terms are often absent. A periodical may occasionally be stated to be само за размена, *only for exchange*.

1.8.7 In addresses editorial and managerial offices are often combined: уредништво и администрација, but there may be a specific direction about subscriptions, e.g. абонмент да се испраќа на адреса, *subscription to be paid at (the following) address* ....

2 ALPHABET, PHONETICS, SPELLING

2.1 ALPHABET

2.1.1 Macedonian uses the Serbocroatian form of the Cyrillic alphabet with ѓ and ќ after д and т instead of ђ and ħ and with the addition of s (= dz) after з.

2.1.2 Although Macedonian is almost invariably written in Cyrillic, *latinica* can be used as for Serbocroatian, and this is adopted as the British Standard transliteration. In this case ѓ becomes đ and ќ becomes ć. The international transliteration ISO/R9 prefers ǵ and ḱ, in accordance with its practice of transliterating a given Cyrillic letter by the same Latin one irrespective of language, and conversely. So does the British Museum. In non-standard transliterations one may find ki for ќ. (The British Standard practice does at any rate avoid the dilemma of names in -иќ, untypical names which may or may not be the names of Macedonians.)

2.2 CAPITALISATION

This is the same as in Serbocroatian.

2.3 DIVISION OF WORDS
This is the same as in Serbocroatian.

2.5 HARD AND SOFT CONSONANTS; PALATALISATION
(See General note on the Slavonic languages.)

2.5.1 There is no regular contrast of hard and soft consonants, but г, к, л, н have soft counterparts ѓ, ќ, љ, њ. Before е, и, ј one writes л not љ, and лј should be distinguished from љ.

2.5.2 The effects of palatalisation are as follows:

	в	г	д	з	к	л	н	с	ск	ст	т	х	ц
change to	с	з	ѓ		ц						ќ	с	
	ш	ж		ж	ч		њ	ш	шт	шт		ш	ч

The changes in the bottom row are confined to verbs. The peculiar (and occasional) palatalisation of в is due to its being sometimes a development of х.

2.5.3 Assimilation and simplification of consonant clusters occur as in Serbocroatian. For examples see 2.6: местен, тежок.

2.6 VARIATION OF VOWEL
As in Serbocroatian, **a**, **e** or **o** may be present in some forms of a word and absent from others, e.g. социјализам, социјализмот; местен, месна; тежок, тешка.

3 ARTICLES

3.1 DEFINITE

3.1.1 The definite article, which is suffixed to nouns, adjectives and numerals, has the following varieties:

	S			*P*
	M	*N*	*F*	
the	-от	-то	-та	-те
the . . . here, this	-ов	-во	-ва	-ве
the . . . there, that	-он	-но	-на	-не

3.1.2 Masculine nouns in **-a**, **-o** have articles **-та**, **-то**.

3.1.3 The definite article is used more freely than in English, e.g. **развиток на земјоделството**, *development of agriculture*.

3.2 INDEFINITE
This article is usually unexpressed, but the numeral **еден**, *one* (6.1.2), may be used in this sense.

4 NOUNS

4.3 ENDINGS

4.3.1 Nouns denoting male persons (especially names) are the only ones that show any difference of case, viz.

N	-/-o/-e	-и
A	-(т)а	-ија

Of Christian name and surname either or neither may be declined.

4.3.2 *Masculine nouns*

The majority of masculine nouns end in a consonant and form their plural by adding -ови, -ои, or -и. If the final consonant is ж, j, р, ч, or ш, they may have -е(в)и instead. Most monosyllables have plurals in -о(в)и; most others in -и.

> Nouns denoting inhabitants, ending in -(н)ин and most of those in -нец have plural in -(н)и.
> Surnames in -ов and -ев add -ци.
> Nouns in -ja preceded by a vowel have plural in -и.
> Consonant changes take place as in 2.5.2, e.g. S -ник, Р -ници, Влав, Р Власи.

Vowel changes as in 2.6, e.g. театар, театри.

4.3.3 *Neuter nouns*

> S -о; Р -а
> S -е; Р -иња: except nouns in -иште, verbal nouns in -ње and a few others, which have -а

4.3.4 *Feminine nouns*

Most of these end in -а; some, especially abstracts in -ост, end in a consonant. All have Р -и. The ending -ост, with article, makes -оста.

> Рака, нога have Р раце, нозе

5 ADJECTIVES

5.1 FORM AND GENDER
Adjectives agree in gender with the noun they qualify.

5.2 ENDINGS
5.2.1 They have three forms in the singular and one in the plural, viz.

M	N	F	P
-/-и	-о	-а	-и

The MS has -и when followed by the article, and in all circumstances in the case of adjectives in -ски and a few others, particularly in place-names.

5.2.2 A vowel may be absent from the stem where there is an ending (cf. 2.6).

5.2.3 Виши, нижи have N -е.

5.3 COMPARISON
Comparative по-; superlative нај-.

5.4 POSSESSIVES
5.4.1 Мој, твој, свој make мое, моја, мои, etc.

5.4.2 Masculine names and nouns of kinship make a possessive in -ов; their feminine counterparts, in -ин. Some names are of this form (cf. 1.1).

6 NUMERALS

6.1 CARDINAL

6.1.1

1 еден	11 единаесет	101 сто и еден
2 два	12 дванаесет	200 двесте
3 три	16 шеснаесет	300 триста
4 четири	20 два(д)есет	400 четиристотини
5 пет	30 три(д)есет	600 шестотини
6 шест	40 четиридесет	1000 илјада
7 седум	50 педесет	2000 две илјади
8 осум	60 ше(д)есет	
9 девет	70, etc. седумдесет, etc.	
10 десет	100 сто	

6.1.2 Еден and два vary according to gender, viz. еден, едно, една; два, две, две.

6.1.3 Два is followed by a special plural in **-а**, other numerals by this or the ordinary plural. Compounds ending in еден are followed by the singular.

6.2 OTHER

6.2.1 *Ordinals*

1 прв(и)	6 шести	11–99 единаесетти, etc.
2 втор(и)	7 седми	21 дваесет и прв
3 трет(и)	8 осми	100 стоти/стотен
4 четврт(и)	9 деветти	200, etc. двестотен
5 петти	10 десетти	1000 илјаден

6.2.2 The ordinals are adjectives.

6.2.3 Only the last element of a compound ordinal has the ordinal form.

6.2.4 There are also numeral adverbs ending in **-пати**, meaning *times*.

6.3 FIGURES

Both arabic and roman numerals are used in numeration (see 1.3, 1.7). Otherwise cardinals are usually expressed by plain arabic numerals, ordinals frequently by roman numerals, e.g. **IV клас**.

6.4 DATES

6.4.1 The months are:

јануари, февруари, март, април, мај, јуни,
јули, август, септември, октомври, ноември, декември

6.4.2

1 May is translated **Први мај**

На 24. vi. 1943 г. is read: **На дваесет и четврти јуни илјада осумстотини**
четириесет и трета година

50-(ти)те (i.e. **педесеттите**) **години**, *the 50's*

1935–1945 by itself should be read as cardinals

7 PRONOUNS

7.1 DEMONSTRATIVE, INDEFINITE, ETC.

7.1.1 M **овој**, N **ова**, F **оваа**, P **овије**, *this* and similarly **тој** and **оној**, *that*, have no cases.

7.1.2 сиот (сиов, сион), *all the*, has the forms:

N сето/се   F сета   P сите (сево, сено, etc.)

7.2 INTERROGATIVE/RELATIVE, ETC.

	M	*N*	*F*	*P*
N	кој	кое/што	која	кои
A	кого го	кое/што	која	кои
D	кому му	—	—	—

7.3 PERSONAL

7.3.1

	S		*S & P*	*P*	
	1	2	R	1	2
N	jac	ти	—	ние	вие
A	ме(не)	те(бе)	себе(си)/се	нас/не	вас/ве
D	мене/ми	тебе/ти	себе/си	нам/ни	вам/ви

The reflexive pronoun serves all persons.

7.3.2 The pronoun of the third person has some forms from a different stem.

	S			*P*
	M	*N*	*F*	
N	тој/он	то(в)а/оно	таа/она	тие/они
A	него/го		неа/ja	нив/ги
D	нему/му		нejзe/и	ним/им

7.3.3 Either or both of the double forms is used according to circumstances, and the short forms are often used pleonastically, e.g. **Обој број го редактирале . . .**, *This part they edited it* (i.e. *This part edited by . . .*).

7.3.4 The dative may have a possessive meaning.

7.3.5 Any of the genders may mean *it*.

8 VERBS

8.1 STRUCTURE

8.1.1 In its main characteristics the Macedonian verb is like the Bulgarian, but the distinction of aspects (see General note on the Slavonic languages) is very much alive, so that both perfective and imperfective aorists are in use where appropriate. The chief signs of the perfective aspect are the addition of a prefix to a simple verb, e.g. **пиша/напиша**, or a change in the system of endings such as:

I	-а	-а	-а	-aCa	-ува	-нува
P	-и	-*и	-не	-оСи	-а	-не

8.1.2 Dictionaries enter verbs (as is done above) under the 3 PS of the present. In the Macedonian-English dictionary of Crvenkovski and Grujić reference is made from derived imperfectives in **-ува** to the perfective aspect, but in other cases they are entered separately.

8.2 PRESENT

8.2.1 The endings of the present are:

I   -(ј)ам, -еш, -е; -еме, -ете, -(ј)ат
II -(ј)ам, -иш, -и; -име, -ите, -(ј)ат
III -ам, -аш, -а; -аме, -ате, -аат

8.2.2 The present is used much as in Bulgarian and Serbocroatian. Preceded by да it expresses an unrealised wish. See also 8.10.3.

8.3/8.4 IMPERFECT AND AORIST

8.3.1 *Imperfect endings*

$\begin{matrix} \text{-а} \\ \text{-е} \end{matrix}$ в, -ше, -ше; -вме, -вте, -ја

corresponding to the present in -а and -е/-и respectively. Imperfects of perfective verbs (8.3.2) have the vowel -е- only.

8.3.2 The imperfect, which expresses an action which is going on at the same time as something else, occurs as an independent tense in the imperfective aspect only; but imperfects of perfective verbs are found in subordinate clauses and with ќе; the aorist is usually of the perfective aspect, but can come from the imperfective where the action is presented as continuous but not contemporaneous. Its forms cannot then all be distinguished from those of the imperfect.

8.3.3 *Aorist endings*

I   -ов, -е, -е; -овме, -овте, -оа
II $\begin{matrix} \text{-а} \\ \text{-е} \\ \text{-и} \\ \text{-у} \end{matrix}$ в, -, -; -вме, -вте, -(ј)а

corresponding to presents in (I) -а, (II) -а, -е, -и, -yје respectively.

8.3.4 With да the imperfect expresses *if I had done*; with ќе, *was going to do, used to do* or *would have done*.

8.3.5 The aorist (perfective) can be used vividly in the sense *would have done*.

8.4 AORIST
See 8.3.

8.10 COMPOUND TENSES

8.10.1 *The perfect* is formed of имам, etc. in the case of transitive verbs, or сум, etc. (8.17) in the case of intransitive verbs, with the past participle passive.

8.10.2 *The past indefinite* is formed of сум, etc. with any of the forms of the past participle active (8.12.1). It may have the same meaning as the perfect, but is more likely to be a non-committal substitute for the aorist or imperfect. Sometimes it is hard to see why it is used, and one must always allow for the influence of Serbocroatian, in which the -л forms have no special significance.

8.10.3 *The future* is expressed by ќе or има да with the present (8.2.1).

8.10.4 *The conditional* is expressed by:

би with the past participle active
ќе with the imperfect (or imperfect indefinite)

8.12 PARTICIPLES

8.12.1 *The past participle active* is used in the formation of the past indefinite tense (8.10.2). Its endings are:

M	N	F	P
-л	-ло	-ла	-ле

It has imperfect and aorist forms.

8.12.2 *The imperfect participle* may be formed both from perfective and imperfective verbs, but those from perfective verbs have a limited use (cf. 8.3.2). The connecting vowel is the same as in the imperfect tense (8.3.1).

8.12.3 *The aorist participle* also can be formed from both aspects, but in imperfective verbs it is often indistinguishable from the imperfect participle. It usually has the vowel -o- where the aorist (8.3.3) is of type I, sometimes -e-; otherwise the same vowel as the aorist. Peculiar are вел, дал, зел, клал, corresponding to веде, etc. (See also 8.19.)

8.12.4 *The past participle passive* ends in -ан or -ен, or where the stem of the verb ends in -н-, in -ат or -ет. Stems ending in -к- change to -ч- before -ен.

When derived from intransitive verbs, it is active in meaning.

Like its English equivalent it can be used as an adjective, but it is commonest with parts of the verb *to be*, to express the passive.

8.13 GERUND

The present gerund, endings **-ејќи**, **-ајќи**, is used adverbially like the English present participle.

8.17 THE VERB сум, *I am*

Present: сум, си, е; сме, сте, се
Imperfect: бев
Future: ќе бидам, -еш, etc.
Gerund: бидеиќи
Past participle active: бил (бидел)

8.19 OTHER IRREGULAR VERBS

бере	aorist брав	past participle active брал
земе	зедов	зел
иде		ишол
најде		нашол
отиде		отишол
има negative нема		
-лезе	-легов	-легол

може past participle active neuter, etc. могло, etc.

| расте | | растол, расло, etc. |
| срете | | срел |

9 ADVERBS

9.1 FORMATION

9.1.1 Adverbs derived from adjectives end in -o (neuter). Adjectives in **-ки** are unchanged.

9.1.2 A number, derived from nouns, end in **-e** or less commonly **-a** or **-ум**.

9.1.3 Some are derived from verbs, also with the ending **-ум**.

9.2 COMPARISON

As for adjectives.

10 PREPOSITIONS

10.2 SYNTAX

Prepositions, which are construed with the accusat*i*ve of pronouns and the nominative of nouns, supply the absence of cases.

10.5 MEANINGS

A good many of the prepositions are identical in form and much the same in meaning as those in Russian, Serbocroatian or Bulgarian, but the following should be noted for one reason or another: **зад**, *behind*; **кај**, *at, to* (see 11, and cf. Albanian **kah**); **кон**, *towards, to*; **низ**, *through, down*; **од**, *from, of, than*; **поради**, *because of*; **спрема**, *according to*; **спроти**, *opposite*.

11 CONJUNCTIONS

These resemble to some extent those in Bulgarian and Serbocroatian, but the following should be noted: **ама**, *however*; **бидеики**, *seeing that*; **дека**, *that, because*; **додека**, *until*; **до каде, до кај**, *while*; **дури**, *until*; **едно**, *as soon as*; **каде што**, *where*; **кај**, *where* (see 10.5); **како**, *that*; **оти**, *that, because*; **па, потоа**, *then*; **чунки**, *because*.

GLOSSARY

абонмент, *subscription* (1.8.6)
авторско право, *copyright*
ажурен, *brought up to date*

белешка, *note*
бесплатен, *free*
библиотека, *library*
број, *number, part* (1.8.4)
брошура, *pamphlet*

говор, *speech*
година, *year, volume* (1.8.4)
годишен, *annual*
годишник, *yearbook*
готов, *ready*

двонеделен, *fortnightly*
дел, *volume, division* (1.4.1)
додаток, *addition, supplement*
дополнен, *enlarged*
дополнение, *addition*

едиција, *series* (1.7.1)

забелешка, *note*
записници, *proceedings*
збирка, *collection*
земен, *taken*

извештај, *report*
издавач, *publisher* (1.6.1)
издаден, *published*
издание, *edition, publication* (1.5)
излегува, *comes out* (1.8.5)
иследување, *research*
исправен, *corrected*
испраќа, *sends, dispatches*
исти, *same*
исчрпен, *out of print*

книга, *book, volume, part, number* (1.4.1, 1.7.2)
книгоиздателство, *publishing house* (1.6.1)

книжар, *bookseller*
книжарница, *bookshop*
книжница, *library*
книжничар, *librarian*
коло, (*sub*)*series* (1.7.2)

месечен, *monthly*

налог, наредба, *order*
неделен, *weekly*
неиздаден, *unpublished*
нов, *new*
новела, *long short story*

одбор, *committee*
одбран, *selected*
општество, *society*
отпечатен, *printed*
отпечаток, *offprint*

печатар, *printer*
печатница, *printing shop* (1.6.2)
пиеса, *play*
писмо, *letter*
повест, *history, story*
подбор, *selection* (1.2.4)
полугодишен, *half-yearly*
поправен, *corrected*
поправка, *correction*
попуст, *discount*
порачка, *order*
посебен отпечаток, *offprint* (1.5.3)
превод, *translation* (1.2.4)
преглед, *review*
предговор, *preface*
препечати, *reprints*
прилог, *appendix, contribution* (1.8.1),
    essay
примерок, *sample, specimen*
за продаја, *for sale*
продолжува, *to be continued*
продолжување, *continuation*

рабат, *discount*
размена, *exchange*
размножен, *duplicated*
расказ, *tale*
распродаден, *out of stock*
на распродаја, *on sale*
регистар, *index*
редактирал, *edited* (1.2.2)
редактор, *editor* (1.2.5)
редакција, *editorship* (1.2.3, 1.8.3)
резуме, *summary*
речник, *dictionary*
роден, *born*
роман, *novel*

сами, *same, self*
сметка, *bill*
соработник, *contributor*
составил, *compiled* (1.2.5)
составувач, *compiler* (1.2.5)
списание, *periodical*
средба, *conference*
стихови, *verses*
стран(иц)а, *page*
странство, *foreign countries*

табела, *plate*
тромесечен, *quarterly*
трудови, *transactions*

увод, *introduction*
умре, *died*
уредник, *editor* (1.8.3)
уредништво, *editorial board or office*
    (1.8.1, 1.8.7)
уредува, *edits* (1.2.2)

фактура, *invoice*

цена, *price*

член, *member*

GRAMMATICAL INDEX: WORDS

GRAMMATICAL INDEX: ENDINGS

BULGARIAN

SPECIMEN

Предложеният тук речник има пред вид преди всичко българина, който превежда
или съчинява на английски език. Затова тук не се цели толкова да се определи
точният смисъл на българската дума, колкото да се предложат съответствия, които
могат наистина да се употребят в даден контекст; по начало се отбягват обясни-
телни преводи дори и при понятия, които нямат и не могат да имат точни съответствия на английски.

*The dictionary offered here has in view above all the Bulgarian who is translating or
composing in (the) English language. Hence the aim is not so much to define the exact
meaning of the Bulgarian word as to offer equivalents which can really be used in a given
context; as a rule explanatory translations are avoided even for concepts which have
not and cannot have exact equivalents in English.*

0 GENERAL CHARACTERISTICS

0.1 DEGREE OF INFLEXION
Bulgarian, along with Macedonian, differs from the other Slavonic languages in
having greatly simplified the declension of the noun, adjective and pronoun. The
treatment of these parts of speech is very largely analytical. The Bulgarian verb on
the other hand is still synthetic and more complicated than in any other Slavonic
language.

0.2 ORDER OF WORDS
Adjectives normally precede the nouns they qualify, prepositional phrases follow. The
normal sentence order SVOC may be varied for emphasis, and verb and subject are
almost invariably reversed where author, editor, publisher and the like are designated,
producing the same order as in English but with an active verb, e.g. **написа Христо
Гандев, издаде Дирекцията на народната култура,** *Khristo Gandev wrote, the
Directorate of National Culture published.*

0.4 RELATION TO OTHER LANGUAGES
Bulgarian belongs with Serbocroatian, Slovene and Macedonian to the South Slavonic
group, but owing to the history of Russian a number of words, especially abstract
nouns, are the same in Bulgarian and Russian. Bulgarian is easily recognised by the
suffixed article **-ът, -то, -та,** etc., by the use of the preposition **на** instead of a genitive
and by the occurrence of **ъ** as a vowel. (Cf. Macedonian.)

1 BIBLIOLINGUISTICS

1.1 NAMES

1.1.1 Bulgarian names all behave like nouns (4.3.1, 4.3.4), though most surnames are in origin possessive adjectives and have corresponding feminine forms in -a.

1.1.2 Medieval names may consist of a Christian name with a distinguishing epithet, e.g. Паисий Хилендарски, filed under Paisiĭ.

1.1.3 Modern names include a few surnames that have been handed down by tradition, but the majority are patronymics. The traditional surnames may be derived from place-names and end in -ев(а) or -ов(а), e.g. Букорещлиев, Веселинов; or they may be adjectives in -ски (F -ска), e.g. Диловска; or they may have other origins and a variety of endings, e.g. Осинин, Руж, Бояджиев (Tr boyacı, *dyer*), Иван Атанасов Арабаджията (Tr arabacı, *coachman*).

1.1.4 Vastly more common are patronymic-surnames. Legally Bulgarians have three names, the second and third being derived from the Christian names of the father and grandfather respectively, and one or other patronymic is chosen as the customary surname. Thus Христо Ботев, the revolutionary poet, is in full Христо Ботев (or Ботйов) Петков, *Khristo the son of Botyo the son of Petko*, and may appear as Петков in documents: but Ботев is the customary form. His wife appears as Иван(к)а Ботева (or Ботйова), Иван(к)а Б(отьо) Петкова, Ивана Ботева Пет., or plain Ботьовица. On the other hand Кирил Цочев Братанов is known as Братанов. The forms themselves are now more stable, but it is impossible to predict whether the patronymic-surname will last two generations (or if the grandfather and grandson have the same Christian name, even longer) or change with each generation.

1.1.5 Since masculine names have an accusative in -a, while feminine names have only the one form -a in the singular, we can have on the one hand от Марина Дринова, *by Marin Drinov*, and on the other от Мариана Ев. Дадева, *by Mariana Ev. Dadeva*. The confusion is only likely where the name is ambiguous or there are initials, and grows altogether less likely as masculine names too cease to be declined. With the few names in -ски (F -ска) there is no confusion.

1.1.6 Names in -ев(а), -ов(а) have plural forms in -еви, -ови, e.g. Костови, *the Kostovs*; А. и П. Костови, *A. and P. Kostov, A. Kostov and P. Kostova, A. Kostova and P. Kostov*, or *A. and P. Kostova*.

1.2 NAMES OF AUTHORS, EDITORS, ETC.

1.2.1 The names of persons connected with the production of a work, author, editor, translator and so on, may be stated in various ways on the title-page or elsewhere in the book, as detailed in the following sections.

1.2.2 The name in isolation at the head of the title-page usually suffices for the authors of original works. The names are in the nominative.

1.2.3 An active verb may be used to denote authorship and is usual for editors, translators and the like. The order is: title, verb, name in the nominative. The verb may be in the perfect (8.10.2), aorist (8.3) or, in the case of works in progress or series, in the present (8.2). It will agree with the name in number, and if in the perfect, in gender also.

Perfect: съставил Иван П. Орманджиев
Aorist: написа Х. Гандев
Present: издава съпругата му Н. Л. Каравелова

The last example is taken from the complete works of L. Karavelov, published by his wife. The verb used depends on the relation of the agent to the work, e.g. написа(л), *wrote*; съставил, *composed, compiled*; редактирал, *edited*; подбрали и подготвили за печат, *selected and prepared for the press*.

1.2.4 The name may follow the title, connected by на, *of*. This occurs in collected and selected works, correspondence and the like. The name is in the accusative (4.3.1), e.g. съчинения на Любена Каравеловъ.

1.2.5 The work done may be indicated by an abstract noun. This may be followed by на (1.2.4), or it may be separated by a colon or typographically from the names, which will then be in the nominative, e.g. под редакцията на Димитър Осинин, *under the editorship of Dimitŭr Osinin*; подбор и редакция|Иван Руж, *selection and editorship|Ivan Ruzh*.

1.2.6 The specific relation may be indicated by a noun or phrase denoting the agent, followed by the name or names in the nominative, e.g. съставители: Елена Диловска, Виржиния Паскалева . . . , *compilers: Elena Dilovska, Virzhiniya Paskaleva . . .*; редакционна колегия, *editorial college*. The chief editor may be picked out as главен редактор, or as отговорен редактор, *responsible editor*. The latter is a legal concept, and where the book has a living author, it is impossible to tell what part the responsible editor has played, so bibliographically it is best to ignore him.

1.2.7 Least common is the use of a passive verb with от (or от by itself) and the name in the accusative (4.3.1), e.g. отделните глави са написани от следните автори, *the several chapters were written by the following authors*; общата редакция е извършена от Тодор Поляков и Давид Давидов. (In the first of the above instances the names are listed; thus isolated, none has the distinctive accusative form.)

1.2.8 The names of corporate bodies can be stated in any of the ways used for persons, but those given in 1.2.2 and 1.2.3 are much the most likely. Subordinate parts of the main body may either follow, grammatically detached, as in Българска Академия на Науките. Правен Институт, or come first, in which case they are usually linked by the preposition при, with the accusative, e.g. Институт по История на Българската Комунистическа Партия при Централния Комитет на БКП, *Institute for the History of the Bulgarian Communist Party at the Central Committee of the BCP*. (Note here that it is not на which links the two bodies: as the translation shows, it is part of the title of the institute.) The names have the article where appropriate in the context, but not in headings. Hence the catalogue entry would be: **Bŭlgarska Komunisticheska Partiya. Tsentralen Komitet. Institut po Istoriya na Bŭlgarskata Komunisticheska Partiya.** Note the dropping of -ta and the altering of **Tsentralniya** to **Tsentralen** (5.2).

1.3 TITLES

1.3.1 Imaginative literature apart, the titles of most books consist of nouns and adjectives, with or without the article, and prepositions. Less commonly relative clauses will be found, e.g. Погасителната давност при правоотношения в които участвуват и социалистически организации, *Prescription in legal relations in which socialist organisations also participate*. Propaganda and appeals to the emotions result in more complicated titles, e.g. Те загинаха, за да живеем ние, *They died that we might live*; Знаеш ли ти кои сме?, *Do you know who we are?*; И те са били деца, *They too were children*.

1.3.2 Title entries present few difficulties. The definite article, being a suffix (3.1), cannot be ignored in filing; but if a noun is isolated as a heading, as in the British Museum catalogue, the article would be removed.

1.3.3 Titles are rarely affected by their context. If they begin with a masculine name or noun or adjective with the article, they will be affected by prepositions, unless a word with some such meaning as *publication* is inserted to carry the preposition, e.g. в Иванка, *in 'Ivanko'*, but за драмата „ Иванко '', *for the drama 'Ivanko'*.

1.4 VOLUMES AND PARTS

1.4.1 The usual words are том and част respectively; or книга may be used for a part that is complete in itself. Sometimes дял is found.

1.4.2 The numeration may be in words or figures and may precede or follow, but it is always read as an ordinal, e.g. том 1 (първи), 1 (първа) част.

1.4.4 A work in several volumes may have a second title-page on which the number of volumes of the complete work is indicated in some such phrase as в осем тома, *in eight volumes*.

1.5 EDITIONS

1.5.1 The standard word for *edition* is издание, which in other contexts may have the more general meaning of *publication*, especially when used as a verbal noun (1.6.3).

1.5.2 Numeration is by ordinal number, revision being indicated most commonly by such adjectives as допълнено, *enlarged*; преработено, *revised*.

1.6 IMPRINTS

1.6.1 Present-day imprints are for the most part institutional. Grammatically they cause little trouble, since both place and publisher are usually in the nominative, but their forms are varied, e.g. Издателство на Бълг. Работническа Партия, *Publishing House of the Bulg. Workers' Party*; Издателство на ЦК ДСНМ „Народна Младеж", *Publishing House of the CC of the Dimitrov National Youth Union 'National Youth'*; (Държавно издателство) „Наука и Изкуство", (*State Publishing House*) '*Science and Art*'; Български Писател, *Bulgarian Writer* (a periodical). Where the press has a name, there seems no point in reproducing издателство and its adjuncts.

1.6.2 In earlier imprints personal names occur as well as commercial companies, e.g. Книгоиздателство Хр. Г. Дановъ, *Book Publishing House Khr. G. Danov*; Балканско издателство — О. О. Д-во, *Balkan Press Ltd*. Besides издателство is also found in earlier imprints книжарница, *bookshop*.

1.6.3 The printer is frequently indicated by печатница, often with a statement elsewhere on the title-page or in the colophon that some other body is responsible for publication. Such statements require a verb or verbal noun, e.g. издава, *publishes*; издаде, *published*; издание на, *publication of*, followed by the name of the publisher, which may be grammatically affected by на (4.3.1, 5.2.2, 10). The imprint too may be set out in the same way.

1.6.4 Earlier Bulgarian title-pages are not standardised, and one must be prepared to find the names of series and even всички права запазени, *all rights reserved*, occupying the place of the imprint.

1.7 SERIES

1.7.1 The names of series occupy various places on the front and back of the title-page (cf. 1.6.4), the position at the top of the page being the commonest. They may be descriptive of the series or its contents, e.g. Българска Библиотека, *Bulgarian*

Library; Български Писатели, *Bulgarian Writers*; or may be more of the nature of names, e.g. Библиотека Нива, '*Niva' Library*.

1.7.2 Numeration is indicated by № (номер), бр(ой), книжка (cf. 1.8.3). The volumes of a sub-series may at the same time be indicated by книга, e.g. Библиотека „Тракия" № 13: Приноси къмъ историята на възстаническото движение въ Тракия (1895–1903). Книга IV, *Thrace Library. No. 13: Contributions to the history of the insurrectionary movement in Thrace. Book 4.*

1.8 PERIODICALS

1.8.1 The titles of periodicals are much the same grammatically as those of books, e.g. Български книгопис: месечен библиографски бюлетин, *Bulgarian bibliography: a monthly bibliographical bulletin*; Пламък, *Flame*. As they rarely have the article, they are unaffected by being part of a phrase.

1.8.2 Titles may incorporate the name of an institution, e.g. Трудове на Висшия институт за народно стопанство, *Transactions of the Higher Institute for National Economy*; Септември: Орган на Съюза на българските писатели, *September: Organ of the Union of Bulgarian Writers*. The names of the institutions are affected grammatically: Висш and Съюз would be the forms in headings, not Висшия and Съюза (4.3.1, 5.2.2).

1.8.3 Editorship is denoted by редактор, frequently гл(авен) редактор, *chief editor*, or редакционна колегия, *editorial board*. The terms уредник and секретар-уредник also occur, meaning *manager* and *secretary-manager*.

1.8.4 Numeration of annual volumes, if present, is by година, which may also indicate the calendar year, e.g. год. LVII, година шеста (*vol. 6*), октомври 1961 година, *October 1961*. This numeration may be combined with the indication of the binding unit, denoted by том. Thus a година may be divided into four parts, each called книга, книжка or брой, two книги being bound together to form one том, e.g. кн. 1–2, год. VI, том 9; кн. 3–4, год. VI, том 10. The terms for *part* are interchangeable.

1.8.5 Periodicity may be indicated in the title itself, e.g. Славяни: месечно списание, etc., *The Slavs: monthly magazine*, etc., or by some such phrase as излиза годишно в 4 книжки, *issued in 4 parts a year*.

1.8.6 The subscription is usually quoted annually, viz. год(ишен) аб(онамент), but a price may also be given for a single number: отделен брой or отделна книжка. Special prices are quoted for foreign countries—за чужбина.

2 ALPHABET, PHONETICS, SPELLING

2.1 ALPHABET

2.1.1 The Cyrillic alphabet used in Bulgaria, with the standard British (BS 2979: 1958) and international (ISO/R9) transliterations, is as follows:

C	а	б	в	г	д	е	ж	з	и	й	к	л	м	н	о	п	р	с	т	у	ф
B	a	b	v	g	d	e	zh	z	i	ĭ	k	l	m	n	o	p	r	s	t	u	f
I							ž			j												

C	х	ц	ч	ш	щ	ъ	[ы]	ь	[ъ]	ю	я	[ж]
B	kh	ts	ch	sh	sht	ŭ		'	ê	yu	ya	ū
I	h	c	č	s	šč	"	"	'	ě	ju	ja	"

ISO/R9 permits the following variants: št for šč; ä for "; à for "

2.1.2 The letters in brackets have been discarded at various times, ы being replaced by и, ѣ by e or я, and ѫ by ъ. In fact ы has been obsolete so long that no transliteration is provided by either system. Either ī or î would serve if BS 2979 is followed, but the principles of ISO/R9 would require y. The only use of ь is now to indicate a soft consonant, e.g. Ботьо (approximately Botyo); as a vowel it has been replaced by ъ or я. At the end of a word ъ and ь served to distinguish hard and soft consonants, but all final consonants are now hard and both letters are omitted.

2.2 CAPITALISATION

2.2.1 In principle proper names are spelt with an initial capital, but months and days, nouns and adjectives of nationality, or of religion, e.g. католик, as well as titles such as доктор (д-р) and другар (др.) are not regarded as proper names.

2.2.2 In geographical and topographical names the use of capitals does not extend to common nouns like езеро (*lake*) or площад (*square*) when used in conjunction with names.

2.2.3 In societies, institutions and departments of state only the first word is given a capital, e.g. Министерство на народната просвета, Априлското въстание. Similarly with the titles of books and periodicals.

2.3 DIVISION OF WORDS

2.3.1 Rules 2, 4, 5a or b, 6d, 7a, 8 (p. xiii) apply.

2.3.2 On rule 4 note that й counts as a consonant: hence ра-йон, but by rule 5b най-лон.

On rule 6d the orthographical handbooks give only e.g. друже-ство and дружест-во. No doubt дружес-тво is inelegant, but not every 1 + 2 division is thereby excluded.

2.3.3 The combinations дж and дз are not divided unless the д forms part of a prefix such as над-.

2.5 HARD AND SOFT CONSONANTS; PALATALISATION

2.5.1 A good many originally soft consonants (see General note on the Slavonic languages) have become hard in Bulgarian, especially when final, but there are still traces of the original distinction, indicated by the vowels а, у (hard)/я, ю (soft) and less clearly by the alternations о/e, о/ьо.

2.5.2 The effects of palatalisation are as follows:

from	г	д	з	к	с	ст	т	х	ц	
to	з			ц			с			in nouns
	ж	жд	ж	ч	ш	щ	щ	ш	ч	in verbs

e.g. нога, Р нозе; могат, *they can*, може, *it can*; учебник, -ници, *textbook(s)*; писах, *I wrote*, пишат, *they write*.

2.5.3 Complex combinations of consonants are often simplified. This may be important for those who know Russian, e.g. Ru празник, Bu празник.

2.6 VARIATION OF VOWEL

2.6.1 The vowels e and ъ may be present in some forms of a word and absent in others, or the position of ъ may vary, e.g. социализъм, социализмът; седем, седми; Грък, Гърци.

2.6.2 Peculiar to Bulgarian is the alternation between e and я in the same or related words. (Formerly the now obsolete ѣ was used throughout with different pronunciations.) The letter **e** is found (a) in unaccented syllables, (b) when followed by ж, й, ч, ш, щ, (c) when followed by a syllable containing one of the vowels е, и, ьо, ю, я. Thus ¹сряда, *Wednesday*; сре¹да, *centre*; ¹някой, *someone*; ¹нещо, *something*; бял, P бели, *white*. But not every **e** alternates with **я** in this fashion nor vice versa: thus **пети**, *fifth*, has feminine **пета** not **пята**, and conversely **ясно** and **ясен**.

2.7 SPELLING

2.7.1   The simplification of the alphabet and its effect on spelling has been mentioned in 2.1; otherwise spelling has changed little in recent times, except for the suppression of mute consonants, e.g. **празник** for **праздник** (cf. 2.5.3), and replacement of -й- by -ь-.

2.7.2   In comparing Bulgarian spelling with that of other Slavonic languages one should note that the assimilation of consonants is not necessarily reflected in the spelling, e.g. Bu **изключение**, Ru **исключение**, *exception*; Bu **отговор**, Sh **odgovor**, *answer*.

3 ARTICLES

3.1 DEFINITE

3.1.1   The definite article is suffixed to the noun, adjective or numeral, e.g. **книгата**, **новата книга**, **моята нова книга** (*my new book*), **двете книги** (*the two books*). The resulting forms are given in 4, 5 and 6. It is more freely used than in English, e.g. **Академия на науките**, *Academy of Sciences*.

3.2 INDEFINITE

The indefinite article is usually unexpressed, but the numeral **един**, *one*, may be used in this sense.

4 NOUNS

4.1 GENDER AND FORM

There are three genders with a fair amount of correspondence between form and gender. Inanimate nouns may be of any gender. There are very few different endings, for most relations of the noun are now expressed by prepositions.

4.3 CASE ENDINGS

4.3.1   Nouns denoting male persons show traces of the old declensions, viz.

N	Петър	Петко	учител	Паиси(й)	Ботев
A	Петра	Петка	учителя	Паиси(я)	Ботев(а)
D	Петру	Петку	учителю	Паисию	—

Outside stereotyped phrases such as **слава Богу**, *Glory be to God*, the dative has been replaced by **на** with the accusative, and the accusative is now often identical with the nominative, e.g. **от Тодор Поляков**.

4.3.2   Other masculine nouns (mostly ending in a consonant) have these forms:

Singular, without article

NA	дом	път	край	дядо	слуга

Singular, with article

N	домът	пътят	краят	дядото	слугата
A	дома	пътя	края	дядото	слугата

Plural

N and A are the same. The chief endings are:

-ове|те from most monosyllables

-и|те (cf. 2.5.2, 2.6) polysyllables and a few monosyllables

-ища|та from a few monosyllables

For дядо and слуга see 4.3.3 and 4.3.4 respectively.

4.3.3   Neuter nouns are even simpler:

S	P
-о	-a, occasionally -еса
-це, -ще	-ца, -ща
-ие	-ия
-е	-ена, -ета
article -то	article -та

око, *eye*, and ухо, *ear*, make очите and ушите.

4.3.4   Feminine nouns mostly end in -а or -я.

S	P
-а, -я, -	-и
article -та	article -те

ръка, *hand*, and нога, *foot*, make ръце, нозе.

Among feminine nouns ending in a consonant are the abstract nouns in -ност (formerly -ность).

5   ADJECTIVES

5.1   GENERAL

These are variable and precede the noun. Only a trace remains of the distinction between long and short forms, in the masculine singular with and without article, and in the ordinal numerals (6.2).

5.2   ENDINGS

5.2.1   *Without article*

	S		P
M	N	F	
-/-и	-о	-а	-и
-/-и	-ьо/-е	-я	-и

The MS of most adjectives (except those in -ски) has no ending and frequently has an -е- inserted before the final consonant (2.6.1), e.g. пълен, пълно, etc., *complete*; техен, тяхно, *their*. Adjectives with soft forms (lower line) in N and F are comparatively few, e.g. син, синьо, синя, *blue*, but include possessives like мой, *my*, свой, *own*.

5.2.2   *With article*

	M	N, F *and* P
N	-ият	Add -то, -та, -те respectively
A	-ия	to forms given in 5.2.1

Added -e disappears in the masculine, e.g. **Правен институт**, *Law Institute*; **Правният (на Правния) институт**, *(of) the Law Institute*. The possessives **мой**, **твой**, **свой** have definite forms **моят**, etc. (cf. 3.1.1).

5.3 COMPARISON
The comparative and superlative are formed by prefixing **по-** and **най-** respectively to the positive.

6   NUMERALS

6.1 CARDINAL
6.1.1

1 един	11 единадесет, единайсет	101 сто и един
2 два(ма)	12 дванадесет, дванайсет	200 двесте, двеста
3 три(ма)	20–40 двадесет, двайсет,	300 триста
4 четири(ма)	etc.	400–900 четиристотин,
5 пет(има)	50 петдесет	etc.
6 шест(има)	60 шестдесет, шейсет	1000 хиляда
7 седем, седмина	70–90 седемдесет, etc.	2000 две хиляди
8 осем, осмина	100 сто	2124 две хиляди (и)
9 девет(мина)		сто и двайсет
10 десет(мина)		и четири

6.1.2   **Един** and **два** are variable, viz.

M	N	F
един	едно	една
два	две	две

6.1.3   Numerals ending in **един** are followed by the singular; the alternative forms for 2–10 (which refer to men) are followed by the plural; other numerals are followed by the plural if the noun is neuter or feminine, but masculine nouns have special plurals in -a, and some neuters in -e have plurals in -ета instead of the normal plural in -я.

6.1.4   The article may be added to numerals, the form -та to those ending in -a, and -те or -тях to the others.

6.1.5   **Един**, besides functioning as an indefinite article, is also a pronoun (7.1.2).

6.2 ORDINAL
6.2.1   *Long forms*

1 първи	10 десети
2 втори	11–19 единадесети, единайсети, etc.
3 трети	20–90 двадесети, двайсети, etc.
4 четвърти	21 двайсет и първи
5 пети	100 стотни
6 шести	200 двустотни
7 седми	300, etc. тристотни, etc.
8 осми	1000 хилядни
9 девети	2000 двехилядни

6.2.2 *Short forms*

Ordinals tend to have the article, but even when they do not, long forms are often used, e.g. **том първи** rather than **пръв**; indeed, many of the numbers have no short form. Where they do exist, they are got by dropping the final -**и** and inserting -**e**- if necessary, e.g. **стотен**.

6.3 FIGURES

Arabic numerals are used for cardinals. For ordinals arabic numerals are sometimes used, with or without full stops, but more often roman figures.

6.4 DATES

6.4.1 The months are as follows:

> **януари, февруари, март, април, май, юни**
> **юли, август, септември, октомври, ноември, декември**

6.4.2 (*On*) *26 September 1963* is written (**на**) **26 септември 1963 год.** and read: **двадесет и шести септември хиляда деветстотин шестдесет и трета година**, with ordinals, masculine for the day, feminine for the year. Prepositions do not affect the endings.

7 PRONOUNS

7.1 DEMONSTRATIVE, INDEFINITE

7.1.1 Demonstratives, when used as pronouns, have three cases in the masculine and neuter singular, but as adjectives are indeclinable. The forms are as follows:

този, тоя, *this*

	M	N	F	P
N	този, тоя	туй, това	тази, тая	тези, тия
A	тогози, тогова	—		—
D	томува			—

онзи, оня, *that*

	M	N	F	P
N	онзи, оня	онуй, онова	оназ, оная	онези, ония
A	оногози, оногова	—		—
D	ономува			—

7.1.2 **Някой,** *someone*; **едикой,** *a certain person*; **койгоде,** *anyone*; **никой,** *no-one*, are compounds of **кой** (7.2.1, 7.2.2).

7.2 INTERROGATIVE, RELATIVE

7.2.1 кой, *who?*

	M	N	F	P
N	кой	кое	коя	кои
A	кого	—	—	—
D	кому	—	—	—

7.2.2 In **който,** *who*, it is the first part only that varies; so also **чийто,** *whose*; **какъвто,** *such as, whatever*, where the first part behaves as an adjective.

7.3 PERSONAL

7.3.1 Those of the first and second persons, and the reflexive, all persons, are:

	S		S & P	P	
	1	2	R	1	2
N	аз	ти	—	ний, ние	вий, вие
A	ме, мен(е)	те, теб(е)	се(бе)	нас, ни	вас, ви
D	ми, мене	ти, тебе	си	нам, ни	вам, ви

7.3.2 Той, то, тя, *he, it, she*: P те, тие or тий, has some oblique cases from another root, viz.

	MN	F	P
A	(не)го	(не)я	тях, них, ги
D	(не)му	(не)и	тям, (н)им

The short forms of the dative are often equivalent to a possessive, e.g. книгата му, *his book*.

8 VERBS

8.1 STRUCTURE

8.1.1 As the different persons are expressed by endings, subject pronouns are usually dispensed with, e.g. пиша, *I write*. The infinitive is a rare survival, the English infinitive and the gerund being replaced by clauses, e.g. важно е да се знае, *it is important to know*; без да зная, *without (my) knowing*.

8.1.2 Verbs are entered in dictionaries under the first person singular of the present tense imperfective. The perfective aspect is noted in Stefanov's dictionary (1914) under the imperfective, and some references are made from perfectives in their proper alphabetical position. In Rusev (1947) and Minkov (1958) forms derived from the perfective may be given in examples, but there are no references. In Chakalov and others (1961) references are given from the perfective. As the perfective aspect is the source of past tenses (8.3/8.4) and of the passive participle (8.12), while the present perfective occurs frequently in subordinate clauses, it is necessary to have some idea of its relation to the imperfective. This is dealt with in broad terms in General note on the Slavonic languages and more particularly in the next paragraph.

8.1.3 One way of forming perfective verbs is to add a prefix such as до-, из-, на-, от-, по-, с-. Other possible relations are given in the table below. (The verbs are not necessarily common: the relationships are.)

I	P	I	P
запрашвам	запраша	умирам	умра
запърсквам	запърскам	предлагам	предложа
започвам	започна	запращам (2.5.2)	запраща
замазвам	замажа (2.5.2)	виждам (2.5.2)	видя
запоявам	запоя	направям	направя
намалявам	намалея	отговарям	отговоря
прочитам	прочета		

Note also давам/дам.

8.2 PRESENT AND FUTURE

8.2.1 *Endings*

> I   -а/-я, -*еш, -*е; -*еме, -*ете, -ат/-ят

Palatalisation (2.5.2), as indicated by asterisks, occurs after г and к.

> II   -я/-а, -иш, -и; -име, -ите, -ят/-ат

-а(т) follows ч, ш, щ.

> III   -ам, -аш, -а; -аме, -ате, -ат
> IV   -ям, -яш, -я; -яме, -яте, -ят

8.2.2 The ordinary present is derived from imperfective verbs; the corresponding perfective is uncommon except in subordinate clauses, e.g. **ставам**, *I stand, I am* (impf.), **за да стана**, *that I may be* (pf.). The present at times has the sense: *I have been doing*, or conversely may be substituted for the future (8.2.3).

8.2.3 The present preceded by **ще** (invariable) expresses the future.

8.3/8.4 IMPERFECT AND AORIST

8.3.1 *Imperfect endings*

> I   -ях, -еше, -еше; -яхме, -яхте, -яха
> II   -ех, -еше, -еше; -ехме, -ехте, -еха
> III   -ах, -аше, -ашо; -ахме, -ахте, -аха
> IV   -ях, -яше, -яше; -яхме, -яхте, -яха

8.3.2 *Relation to present*

I and II correspond to I and II; III to III; IV to IV.

8.3.3 *Aorist endings*

> I   -ох, -*е, -*е; -охме, -охте, -оха

Palatalisation of к and г (2.5.2).

> IIa   -ах, -а, -а; -ахме, -ахте, -аха
>   b   -ях, -я, -я; -яхме, -яхте, -яха
> III   -их, -и, -и; -ихме, -ихте, -иха
> IV   -х, -, -; -хме, -хте, -ха

8.3.4 *Corresponding present perfective*

> I   -а
> IIa   -а (sometimes with change of stem, e.g. **писах, пиша; звах, зова; брах, бера**), -ам
> IIb   -я, -ея, occasionally -а
> III   -я, -ия
> IV   -я

8.3.5 The imperfect is formed only from imperfective verbs, the aorist predominantly from perfective verbs. The imperfect implies both duration (or repetition) and that an action or state is going on at the same time as something else. The aorist of an imperfective verb implies the first but not the second. The perfective aorist is the ordinary narrative tense and should imply direct experience (8.10.6). It is used in newspapers, however, purely for the sake of vividness.

8.4 AORIST
See 8.3.

8.5 FUTURE
See 8.2.3.

8.10 COMPOUND TENSES

8.10.1 The active imperfect participle (8.12.3) with съм, etc. (8.17) forms the indirect imperfect or present tense (8.10.6).

8.10.2 The active aorist participle (8.12.4) with съм, etc. forms either the perfect tense, used much as in English, or the indirect past (8.10.6). The perfect may omit **e** or **ca**, the indirect past always does.

8.10.3 The same participle with бях, etc. (8.17) forms the pluperfect tense.

8.10.4 The same participle with съм бил, etc. (8.17) forms the indirect perfect or pluperfect (8.10.6).

8.10.5 The same participle with ще съм, etc. forms the future perfect.

8.10.6 The indirect tenses express what is not stated from direct experience or is alleged. Forms like съставил on title-pages should, however, be reckoned as perfects without **e**.

8.10.7 The future (ще with the present, 8.2.3) is historically a compound tense. The substitute има да (literally *I have to*) with the present (negative няма, etc.) obviously is. Other parts of ща (*I will*), e.g. щях, etc. (8.3.1) combine with the present and perfect to form conditional tenses.

8.12 PARTICIPLES

8.12.1 *Present active*

-ещ or -ящ. It has adjectival forms (5.2) and functions.

8.12.2 *Past active*

-л, -ло, -ла, -ли (5.2.1). It may be either imperfect (8.12.3) or aorist (8.12.4).

8.12.3 *Imperfect*

I -ял, II -ел, III -ал, IV -ял

corresponding to the types of present in 8.2.1. It is used solely to form the indirect imperfect (8.10.1).

8.12.4 *Aorist*

I -ъл/-л, II -ал/-ял, III -ил, IV -л

corresponding to the aorist forms in 8.3.3. Where the aorist stem ends in -т- or -д-, this vanishes before the -л, e.g. чел not четъл. It may be used as an adjective, e.g. пресъхнала река, *a dried-up river*; as a substitute for a temporal clause, e.g. дошъл, *having arrived*; but it is commonest in compound tenses (8.10.2–8.10.5).

8.12.5 *Past passive*

-н, -т. It is an adjective, and may be used to express the passive (8.14.2).

8.12.6 The form of this participle is related to that of the aorist, e.g. бран, брах (бера). Common relationships to the present perfective are:

-ан	-а, -ам
-ен	-а, -я
-*ен	-а
-нат	-на, -ная
-ит	-ия
-ут	-уя

8.14/8.15 REFLEXIVE AND PASSIVE

8.14.1 The addition of the reflexive pronoun (7.3.1) to an active verb makes it reflexive, intransitive (e.g. ядосвам се, *I am angry*) or passive (8.14.2).

8.14.2 The reflexive-passive is most commonly used of present action. A passive state or past action may be expressed by a passive participle. Both methods are illustrated in the following example: Понеже известни думи *се пишат* по един начин в Англия а по друг в Америка, *счетено е* за необходимо да *се дава* оригиналния правопис, *As certain words* are written *in one way in England and in another in America*, it was considered *essential* to give *the original orthography*. It is noteworthy that се дава, though reflexive, has an object. Reflexive verbs are often used impersonally, especially as infinitive equivalents, corresponding to an active infinitive in English.

8.17 THE VERB съм, *I am*

> *Present:* съм, си, е; сме, сте, са
> *Future:* ще бъда (8.2.1, type I)
> *Imperfect:* бях, беше, etc. (8.3.1: I)
> *Aorist:* бидох (8.3.3: I)
> *Perfect:* бил съм
> *Infinitive equivalent:* да бъда

8.19 IRREGULARITIES

The following should be noted:

> ям, *I eat*, as if яда, e.g. 3PS яде, aorist ядох
> дам, *I give*, as if дада
> -емам, *I take*, aor. -ех, participles -ел, -ет
> мога, *I can* (3PS може), aor. могох or могах
> ида means *come* or *go* according to aspect. Thus ида, *I come*; ще ида, *I shall go*; идох, шел съм, *I went*. (*I go* is ходя; *I shall come*, ще дойда.)

9 ADVERBS

9.1 FORMATION

9.1.1 Adverbs formed regularly from adjectives end in -o (neuter) or less commonly -ом (obsolete instrumental case). For the corresponding masculine adjective see 5.2.1. Adjectives in -ски are unchanged.

9.1.2 Some adverbs are old cases of nouns: accusative, e.g. вечер, *of an evening*; locative in -e or -y, instrumental in -ем, phrases with the genitive, e.g. отръки, *handy* (*from the hand*). Nearly all of these have separate entries in the dictionary.

9.2 COMPARISON

As for adjectives (5.3).

10 PREPOSITIONS

All prepositions take the accusative, so far as it is different from the nominative.

GLOSSARY

абонамент, *subscription* (1.8.4)

бележка, *note*
библиотека, *library* (1.7.1)
библиотекар, *librarian*
брой, *number* (1.7.2, 1.8.4)
брошура, *pamphlet*

всички права запазени, *all rights reserved* (1.6.4)
въведение, *introduction*

година, *year, annual volume* (1.8.4)
годишен, *annual* (1.8.5, 1.8.6)
годишник, *yearbook*
готвят се за печат, *are about to be printed*

двуседмичен, *fortnightly*
допълнен, *enlarged* (1.5.2)
дружество, *society*
дял, *part* (1.4.1)

екземпляр, *copy*

издаде, *published*
издание, *edition* (1.5.1), *publication* (1.6.3)
издателство, *publishing house* (1.6.1)
излиза, *comes out*
пзпращам, *I send, dispatch*
изследване, *research*
книга, *book* (1.4.1, 1.7.2, 1.8.4)
книгоиздателство, *publishing house* (1.6.2)
книжарница, *bookshop* (1.6.2)
книжка, *part* (1.8.4)

с меки корици, *paperback*
месечен, *monthly* (1.8.1)

намаление, *discount, reduction*
написа, *wrote*
научноизследователски, *of research*
неделя, *week, Sunday*
нов, *new*
новела, *long short story*
номер, *number* (1.7.2)

обмяна, *exchange*
обяснение, *explanation*
отделен, *separate, single* (1.8.6)
(отделен) отпечатък, *offprint*
очерк, *essay, sketch*

печат, *press*
печатница, *printing shop* (1.6.3)
пиеса, *play*
писател, *writer*
писмо, *letter*
повест, *long short story*
подбор, *selection* (1.2.4)
подбрал, *he has selected*
подвързан, *bound*
показалец, *index*
полугодишен, *half-yearly*
поправка, *correction*
пращам, *I send*
превод, *translation*
предговор, предисловие, *preface*
преработен, *revised* (1.5.2)
приложение, *supplement*
продава се, за продан, *on sale, for sale*

редактирал, *he has edited* (1.2.2)

редактор, *editor* (1.2.6, 1.8.3)
редакция, *editing, editorship* (1.2.5)
реч, *speech*
речник, *dictionary*
роден, *born*
роман, *novel*

следва, *to be continued*
слово, *speech, word*
списание, *periodical*
стихове, *verses*
страница, *page*
събрание, *meeting, assembly*
съставил, *he has compiled* (1.2.2)
съчинения, *works*
същ, *same*

тримесечен, *quarterly*
труд, *work*
трудове, *works; transactions* (1.8.2)

увод, *introduction*
указател, *index*
умира, *died*

фактура, *bill*

цена, *price*

част, *part* (1.4.1)
член, *member*
чужбина, *abroad* (1.8.6)

GRAMMATICAL INDEX: WORDS

беше, 8.10.3, 8.17
биде, бидох, etc., 8.17
бил, etc., 8.10.4, 8.17
бъда, etc., 8.17
бях, etc., 8.10.3, 8.17

вам, вас, ви, 7.3.1

ги, го, 7.3.2

дад-, 8.19
две, 6.1.2
до-, 8.1.3

е, 8.10.1, 8.10.2, 8.17
един, една, едно, 3.2,
6.1.2

и, 7.3.2
ида, etc., 8.19
из-, 8.1.3
им, 7.3.2
има да, 8.10.7

кого, кое, кои, кому,
коя, 7.2.1

ме, мен(е), ми, 7.3.1
може, 8.19
моя(т), 5.2.2
му, 7.3.2

на-, 8.1.3
най-, 5.3
нам, нас, 7.3.1
него, неи, нему, нея, 7.3.2
ни, 7.3.1
ним, них, 7.3.2
нозе, 4.3.4

он-, 7.1.1
от-, 8.1.3
очи(те), 4.3.3

по-, 5.3, 8.1.3

ръце, 4.3.4

с-, 8.1.3
са, 8.10.1, 8.10.2, 8.17
своя(т), 5.2.2
се, 7.3.1, 8.14

си, 7.3.1, 8.10.1, 8.10.2,
8.17
сме, сте, съм, 8.10.1,
8.10.2, 8.17

тази, тая, 7.1.1
твоя(т), 5.2.2
те, теб(е), 7.3.1
тези, 7.1.1
ти, 7.3.1
тия, 7.1.1
това, тогова, тогози,
томува, 7.1.1
туй, 7.1.1
тям, тях, 7.3.2

уши(те), 4.3.3

шел, шла, etc., 8.19

щеше, щях, etc., 8.10.7

я, 7.3.2
яд-, 8.19

GRAMMATICAL INDEX: ENDINGS

BALTIC
LANGUAGES
Latvian
Lithuanian

LATVIAN

SPECIMENS

Contemporary

Pēc dažiem gadiem latviešu valodā iespiestajai grāmatai būs 450 gadu jubileja: pirmā grāmata latviešu valodā izdota 1525. gadā. Tukši un mazsvarigi latviešu kultūrai bijuši grāmatniecibas pirmie gadu simti, jo nielielā skaitā izdotās grāmatas galvenokārt bija reliģiska satura. Uzplaukums latviešu grāmatniecibā sākās ar 19. gs. vidu lidz ar pāreju no feodālisma uz kapitālismu. Tieši pirms 100 gadiem—1867. gadā—pirmās grāmatas laida klajā latviešu tautibas pārstāvji (izdevēji K. Stālbergs un I. Alunāns). 19. gs. beigās un 20. gs. sākumā strauji pieauga grāmatas loma progresivo ideju izplatišanā.

In a few years it will be the 450th anniversary of the printed book in the Latvian language: the first book in the Latvian language was published in 1525. The first centuries of book production were empty and unimportant to Latvian culture, for the books, published in no great number, were generally of religious content. The growth in Latvian book-production began in the middle of the 19th century along with the transition from feudalism to capitalism. Just 100 years ago—in the year 1867—representatives of the Latvian nation (the publishers K.S. and I.A.) published their first books. At the end of the 19th century and the beginning of the 20th the role of the book in the diffusion of progressive ideas developed rapidly.

Nineteenth century

> Latwijai tàpat kà wiſai Kreewijai wiſa weh-
> riba bija jagreeſch uſ kara-lauku, tabehk warbuht
> paſchai baſchs lauzinſch palika neapkopts. Tomehr
> jaſaka, ka ta beeſgan zenſuſees, ſawas buhſchanas
> pahrlabot.

Modern transcription of preceding specimen

Latvijai tāpat kā visai Krievijai visa vēriba bija jāgriež uz kaṛa-lauku, tādēļ varbūt pašai dažs lauciņš palika neapkopts. Tomēr jāsaka, ka tā diezgan censusies, savas būšanas pārlabot.

0 GENERAL CHARACTERISTICS

0.1 DEGREE OF INFLEXION

Latvian is a predominantly synthetic language, expressing the commoner relations of nouns by means of case-endings, not prepositions, and having sufficiently distinct verb forms to dispense to a great extent with subject pronouns. On the other hand there are few simple tenses and recourse is had to auxiliaries.

u

0.2 ORDER OF WORDS

Qualifiers, including genitives, precede. In sentences the subject usually precedes the verb, and so may the object especially if there is no expressed subject. Adverbial expressions may be placed anywhere, and more than one may stand at the beginning of the sentence. With the verb *to be* and intransitive verbs, and more generally on title-pages, the subject may follow the verb. (Cf. the second sentence in the first specimen.)

0.4 RELATION TO OTHER LANGUAGES

Characteristics of Latvian which its shares with the Slavonic languages are the frequent omission of the verb *to be* and a preference for the active voice (cf. 8.15).

With Lithuanian it forms the Baltic group of Indo-European languages, but resemblances to the other members of the family, except Russian, are distant.

1 BIBLIOLINGUISTICS

1.1 NAMES

1.1.1 For grammatical purposes most Latvian names may be regarded indifferently as nouns or adjectives, since these do not differ in declension; but some are certainly nouns, and a few are recognisably adjectival.

The full legal style—Christian name, father's name in the genitive, d(ēls), *son*, or m(eita), *daughter*, surname—may be found in the colophon of Soviet books, e.g. **Irma Pētera m. Brakovska**, *Irma, daughter of Peter, Brakovska*; but the title-page has simply **I. Brakovska** and the patronymic is not used in catalogues.

1.1.2 Christian names conform for the most part to the appropriate declension, masculine names ending in **-s**, **-is** (4.3.1), feminine in **-a**, **-e** (4.3.5). There are a few borrowed masculine names in **-o** such as **Oto**, **Bruno**, which are indeclinable.

1.1.3 Most surnames have alternative masculine (4.3.1) and feminine (4.3.5) forms, e.g.

Vilks	Vilka
Petrovs	Petrova
Vējš	Vēja
Salmiņš	Salmiņa
Priednieks	Prieniece
Jansons	Jansone
Balodis	Balode
Bagrickis	Bagricka

A few like **Gudrais**, **Gudrā** are long adjectives (5.2.1) in form. There are also some, including borrowings from German, which end in **-a** or **-e**, whether borne by men or women, e.g. **Kārlis Skalbe**, **Lizete Skalbe**, **Jānis Roze**, **Prof. A. Švābe**, **Valters un Rapa a/s**. They are declined as feminine nouns (4.3.5), but if they are borne by men the DS has the masculine ending (4.3.6).

1.1.4 Surnames in **-u** are grammatically genitive plurals. As such they precede the Christian name, which is never omitted, and are invariable, e.g. **Ligotņu Jēkabs**. A good many of them are pseudonyms and may be derived from place names, but a number are variants of ordinary surnames, e.g. **Poruku Jānis**, who signed himself equally **Jānis Poruks**. There are also singular genitives, e.g. **Kaudzites Matiss**, which behave in the same way.

Surnames are capable of taking a plural form, e.g. **abi Ozoliņi**, *both Ozoliņšes*; **brāļu Kaudzišu**, *of the brothers Kaudzītes*.

1.1.5 There used to be some surnames of foreign origin which were not declined, e.g. **Alija Bauman, Lucija Zamaič, Anna Brigader**. The last two now usually appear as **Zamaiča** and **Brigadere**, declined regularly.

1.1.6 Foreign names are now usually made to conform to Latvian morphology, e.g. **prezidenta Džona Kenedija** (G) (N **Džons Kenedijs**), **sērs Alfreds Bosoms, Bts, Simona Siņorē, Vinnijs Pūks**, though they may be indeclinable, as **Benjamino Džilji**. Even Lithuanian names may be modified, e.g. **Guzevičus** for **Guzevičius**.

1.1.7 Latvian names in Russian are Russified as follows: final -s is dropped, **Harijs Šulcs** > **Харий Шулц**, but final -is is usually retained; feminine names in -ska become -ская, but other feminine names are converted into the corresponding masculine, if any, and are indeclinable, e.g. **A. Velniece** > **А. Велниек**, **Veltas Lines** (G) > **Велты Лине**.

1.2 NAMES OF AUTHORS, EDITORS, ETC.

1.2.1 The indication of authorship, editorship and the like results in various constructions, with the names in the nominative or the genitive. Often the name stands at the head of the title-page. It is usually in the nominative, unconnected grammatically with the title, e.g. **Kārlis Skalbe | Raksti**, *Kārlis Skalbe | Works*; **Bruno Kalniņš | Latvijas sociāldemokratijas piecdesmit gadi**, *Bruno Kalniņš | Fifty years of Latvian social democracy*. But such a name may not be that of the author, e.g. **Akademiķis Roberts Pelše | Bibliografia**.

1.2.2 In the first example the name could equally well have been in the genitive, e.g. **Rūdolfa Blaumaņa kopoti raksti**, *Complete works of Rūdolfs Blaumanis*. This construction is commonest with complete or selected works, correspondence and such like, but is also found with reprints, e.g. **Nicas un Bārtas mācitāja Jāņa Langija 1685. gada latviski-vāciskā vārdnica**, *The 1685 Latvian-German dictionary of Jānis Langijs, Pastor of Nīca and Barta*, and must be used elsewhere than on the title-page, e.g. **Kārļa Skalbes rakstus savākusi Lizete Skalbe**, *K.S.'s works were collected by L.S.*

As the genitive of a masculine name is often the same as the nominative of the corresponding feminine, care needs to be exercised in deciding on the heading for cataloguing.

1.2.3 The work done is often indicated by an active verb, following the title and preceding the name. This, being in the nominative, gives no trouble. The verb form used is the active past participle (8.12.3) which functions as a past tense (8.10). Being an adjective this participle agrees in number and gender with the names, e.g. **sastādijis A. Ģermanis**, *compiled by A. Ģermanis*; **savājusi Lizete Skalbe**, *collected L. Skalbe*; **sakārtojuši A. Gargulis un V. Austrums**, *arranged A. Gargulis and V. Austrums*; **savākušas M. Āboliņa un I. Alksne**, *collected M. Āboliņa and I. Alksne*. In view of this agreement care must be taken in abbreviating titles.

1.2.4 Alternatively, the agent is indicated by the appropriate noun, the name being in the nominative. This method is not common except to denote editors or joint authors, e.g. **redaktori K. Strazdiņš, J. Zutis**, *editors K.S., J.Z.*; **ši darba lidzstrādnieki ir**, *the contributors to this work are*, followed by a list of names.

1.2.5 A noun may be used to indicate the work done, the name being in the genitive, e.g. **K. Strazdiņa, J. Zuša redakcijā**, *under the editorship of K. Strazdiņš, J. Zutis*; **J. A. Jansona izlase un sakārtojums**, *selection and arrangement of J. A. Jansons*.

1.2.6 Very rarely the work done is expressed by a passive participle and the name is in the genitive case, e.g. **J. Endzelina un K. Mülenbacha sarakstita**, *written by J. Endzelins and K. Mülenbachs.*

1.2.7 Beware of the preposition **par**, which means *about*, e.g. **atmiņas** (*reminiscences*) **par Jāni Fabriciusu.**

1.2.8 Corporate authorship involves the same constructions as personal authorship. Thus we find **Latvijas PSR Zinātņu akademija | Vēstures un materialās kulturas instituts** at the head of the title-page where both the main body *Academy of Sciences of the Latvian SSR* and the subordinate *Institute of History and Material Culture* are in the nominative. In **Zemkopibas Ministrija | Lauksaimniecibas departamenta Gada grāmata** the superior ministry is again unconnected grammatically and therefore in the nominative, while the name of the department is linked in the genitive with the work published. On the other hand—and this is equally common—in **Latvijas PSR Ministru Padomes Preses Komiteja** the main body is in the genitive (so unfortunately are most of the nouns), viz. *Press Committee of the Council of Ministers* (catalogue heading: Latvia. Ministru Padome. Preses Komiteja).

There are no articles to worry about, but it should be noted that adjectives are in the definite form (5.2.1), e.g. **Komunistiskā Partija.**

The full official names of some institutions are inordinately long, e.g. **Ar Darba Sarkanā Karoga ordeni apbalvotā Pētera Stučkas Latvijas Valsts universitāte.** Fortunately the official bibliography shortens this to **Pētera Stučkas Latvijas universitāte.**

1.3 TITLES

1.3.1 Most titles consist of nouns and adjectives in various cases, occasionally with prepositions, e.g. **Latvijas sociāldemokratijas piecdesmit gadi**, *Fifty years of the social democracy of Latvia**; **Liduma dūmos**, *In the smoke of the clearance*; **Kvēlošā lokā**, *In a glowing arc.* The literature of persuasion includes more varied types, e.g. **Jo divu dzimteņu nav**, *But there are not two motherlands*; **Televizija? Tas ir ļoti vienkārši!,** *Television? That's very simple!*; **Neaiztiec mani—es neaiztikšu tevi**, *Don't touch me— I'll not touch you.*

1.3.2 Title entries on the Anglo-American pattern pose no grammatical problems, but Latvian word-order often brings genitives to the beginning, so that the 'first noun' of the British Museum rules will need to be turned into the nominative, and adjectival genitives may give rise to doubt. Should **Latviešu literatūra** appear under *Latvians* or *Latvian Literature?*

1.3.3 When a title forms part of a sentence the case of the principal noun or nouns and any adjectives that agree with it may be affected, e.g. **Par Ēriku Ādamsonu un «Sapņu pipi»**, *On Ēriks Ādamsons and 'Sapņu pipe'*, **«Zelta rozes» autoram 75 gadi**, *75 years to the author of 'Zelta roze'.* But if there is a noun to which the title is in apposition, this is in the appropriate case and the title is unaffected, e.g. **Par J. Germana trilogijas pirmo grāmatu «Tavs uzdevums»**, *On the first book of Y. German's trilogy, 'Tavs uzdevums'.* (For the name see 1.1.6.)

1.4 VOLUMES AND PARTS

1.4.1/1.4.2 The usual words are **sējums** and **daļa** respectively. The numeration is by a preceding ordinal number, in word or figure, e.g. **I** or **Pirmais sējums**, *Volume 1*; **otrā daļa**, *part 2*

---

* In idiomatic English the genitive would be represented by the adjective *Latvian*. The same is true of Latviešu, *of the Latvians.*

It should be noted that **dala** is not a precise technical term: like **nodaļa** it denotes any division of a work and itself may comprise several volumes, e.g. **Pirmajā daļā, kas iznāks trijos sejumos . . .**, *In the first part, which will come out in three volumes . . . .*

1.4.4 The total number of volumes is stated, if at all, as above; or using **daļa, Romāns 2 daļās**, *Novel in two parts*.

1.5 EDITIONS

The word for *edition* is **izdevums**, a word with the general meaning *publication*, another of whose uses is illustrated in 1.6.2. The edition is particularised by an ordinal numeral, or the appropriate indefinite or definite descriptive adjective, e.g. **(pār)labots**, *improved*; **papildināts**, *enlarged*; **pārstrādāts**, *revised*. The word **iespiedums** (*impression*) also occurs, as in **trešais, saisinātais, iespiedums**, *the third, abridged, impression*.

1.6 IMPRINTS

1.6.1 These show a certain amount of grammatical variety, so that those who are interested in the normal form of the press or place will need to distinguish the various types.

1.6.2 The publisher is often in the nominative, as in **Latvijas valsts izdevnieciba**, *Latvian State Press*; **Valters un Rapa**, *Valters and Rapa*; **Apgāds Tris Zvaugznes**, *Three Stars Press*; **Apgādnieciba «Spartaks»**, *Spartacus Press*; but with the addition of such words as **izdevums, apgādiens** (*publication*), **apgādibā** (*at the expense*) the name is put in the genitive, e.g. **Kultūras fonda izdevums**, *publication of Kultūras fonds*; **J. Rozes apgādibā**, *published by J. Roze*; and **apgāds** is often found with a personal name in the genitive, e.g. **Valtera un Rapas a/s apgāds**, *Press of Valters, Rapa and Co*. On the other hand **izdevis**, being an active verb, leaves the name in the nominative.

1.6.3 The place of publication is in the locative, e.g. **Rigā**, *at Riga*; **Stockholmā**, *at Stockholm*; **Kemptenē**, *at Kempten*. Some places outside Latvia have not very obvious Latvian forms, e.g. **Pleskava**, *Pskov*.

1.6.4 Soviet presses are institutional. Until recently they all had straightforward descriptive names, e.g. **Latvijas valsts izdevnieciba** (see above), **Latvijas PSR Zinātņu akadēmijas Izdevnieciba**, *Press of the Academy of Sciences of the Latvian SSR*. But since the reorganisation of 1965 the various state publishing agencies have had short symbolic names such as **Zvaigzne, Zinātne, Liesma** (*Star, Science, Flame*), the last two taking the place of the Academy press and the State press respectively. Earlier imprints and those in books published abroad, as we have seen, include personal names and commercial presses.

1.6.5 Not much can be done to shorten the long Latvian imprints, but the Academy of Sciences imprint above could no doubt be reduced to **Latvijas PSR Zinātņu akadēmija**.

1.7 SERIES

1.7.1 The titles of series may appear at the head of the title-page or on a separate page; but the latter position is also used for the general title of works in several parts. Most series titles are straightforward descriptions of the items, e.g. **Latvijas Universitātes Raksti**, *Works of the University of Latvia*, or of the series as a whole: **Sabiedriski Zinātniskā Biblioteka**, *Social Science Library*.

Where the name of the institution is part of the series it may be necessary to disentangle it when cataloguing, e.g. **(Pētera Stučkas) Latvijas universitāte. Raksti.**

1.7.2 Series may be divided into sub-series, indicated by **serija**, e.g. **Filoloģijas un**

filosofijas fakultātes serija; or simply by additional information, e.g. **Zinātniskie raksti. Valststiesibu zinātnes**, *Scientific works. Public law.*

In numeration the terms **sējums**, *volume*, and **izlaidums** or **laidiens**, ' *issue* ', are used, sometimes independently, as in **Zinātniskie raksti. Valststiesibu zinātnes. Piektais izlaidums. Sējums LXIV**, where **izlaidums** refers to the sub-series and **sējums** to the main series.

1.8 PERIODICALS

1.8.1   There is no linguistic difference between the titles of periodicals and those of books and series, e.g. **Ciņa**, *The struggle*; **Literatūra un Māksla**, *Literature and art*; but more fanciful titles such as **Sarkanā Zvaigzne**, *Red star*, are naturally encountered more often.

As is the case with books, the title may be grammatically connected with the rest of the sentence, e.g. **par «Zvaigznes» populāritāti**, *for the popularity of 'Zvaigzne'*, or isolated, e.g. **laikrakstam «Literatūra un Māksla»**, *to the newspaper 'L. un M'.*

1.8.2   The name of the body responsible may be prefixed to the title in the genitive, e.g. **LPSR Zinātņu Akadēmijas Vēstis**, *The Herald of the Academy of Sciences of the Latvian SSR*. But granted the commonness of the adjectival genitive in Latvian, titles in this form need watching: contrast **Padomju Latvijas Skola**, *The Soviet Latvian school*. Sometimes the body is stated separately, preceded by **izdevējs** or **izdevēja**, *publisher*.

1.8.3   Editorial activity is indicated by various forms. Most often there is a **redakcijas kolēģija**, *editorial committee*, with a **galvenais** or **atbildigais redaktors**, *chief* or *responsible editor*, or a **priekšsēdētājs** or *chairman*. Using a verb we have **rediģējuši**, the past active participle of **rediģēt**, followed by a list of names. In every case the names are in the nominative.

1.8.4   Numeration is commonly by **gads**, *year*, sometimes **pusgads**, *half-year*, divided usually by **numurs (№)**. Instead of **gads** we may have **sējums**, *volume*, and the numbers may be referred to as **burtnica**, *issue*. The numeral usually follows. Very occasionally the numeration and the periodicity may be stated together (1.8.5).

1.8.5   Periodicity may be implicit in a sub-title, e.g. **mēnešraksts**, *monthly periodical*, or it may be given in such phrases as **iznāk ik mēnesi, reizi mēnesi (kopš 1947. gada), 21. gadu divas reizes mēnesi**, *comes out every month, once a month (since 1947), in its 21st year twice a month.*

1.8.6   Subscription (**abonements** or **parakstišana**) is usually quoted **par gadu** or **par pusgadu**, *by the year* or *half-year*. Alternatively they may be (**atsevišķa numura**) **cena**, *the price (of a single issue)* or simply **atsevišķa burtnica**, *single issue*, or **maksā**, *costs*. A distinction is often made between the price **ar piesūtišanu uz ārzemēm** and **iekšzemē**, *for sending abroad* and *inland*, or there may be a simple reference to *other countries*, **citās valstis**.

1.8.7   Addresses sometimes distinguish **redakcija** and **pārstāvji**, *agents*; but usually there is only the one.

2   ALPHABET, PHONETICS, SPELLING

2.1 ALPHABET

2.1.1   The traditional alphabet is as follows:

a ā b c [ch] č d e ē f g ġ (G) h i i [ie] j k ķ l ļ

m n ņ o ō p r ŗ s š t u ū v z ž

Each of these letters formerly had a distinct alphabetical position, but in Latvia those which are bracketed together are interfiled, ie has its normal position after id, and ch and ŗ are obsolete.

2.1.2 The diacritical marks and long marks shown above are always used. The *haček* on capitals may be displaced, e.g. AUSTRINS^v.

2.1.3 For a long time Latvian used the Gothic alphabet, illustrated in the second specimen. The basic alphabet will be found under German 2.1.1, but some special letters or combinations of letters were needed. Soft consonants such as ļ were represented by letters with an oblique stroke through them, and the following letters and combinations of letters had the values indicated, viz.

ee	ſ	ſch	ſ	ȝ	ſch	tſch	w	ȝ
ie	z	ž	s	s	š	č	v	c

Grave and circumflex accents were both used to indicate long vowels, e.g. otrà, Peterburgâ. For spellings associated with this period see 2.7.

2.2 CAPITALISATION

2.2.1 In principle all names have initial capitals, but if a name consists of several elements, it is not invariably the case that all of them are capitalised; and some words that might be thought to be names are not treated as such. The chief of these are the months and the days of the week, and nouns of nationality and locality such as **latvietis**, *a Latvian*; **ridzinieks**, *a Rigan*.

2.2.2 The following are capitalised throughout: personal names, names of countries and regions, other geographical names which do not include generic terms, astronomical names, names of government organs, and honorifics, e.g. **Pēteris Lielais**, *Peter the Great*; **Amerikas Savienotās Valstis**, *U.S.A.*; **Tuvie Austrumi**, *Near East*; **Staraja Rusa**, but **Atlantijas okeans**; **Lielais Lācis**, *the Great Bear*; **Ministru Padome**, *Council of Ministers*; **Padomju Savienibas Varonis**, *Hero of the Soviet Union*.

2.2.3 In the names of orders all words are capitalised except **ordenis** itself, e.g. **Darba Sarkanā Karoga ordenis**, *Order of the Red Banner of Labour*.

2.2.4 In the names of periodicals all words except prepositions and conjunctions have capitals, e.g. **Literatūra un Māksla**, *Literature and Art*.

2.2.5 In all other cases only the first word has a capital, unless this is some form of lielais, e.g. **Grāmatu palāta**, *Palace of Books*; but **Lielā Oktobra sociālistiskā revolūcija**, *The Great Socialist October Revolution*. The same may happen when **Latvijas** or **Rigas** or some other town name is prefixed to a name which is complete in itself, e.g. **Rigas Medicinas instituts**, *Academy of Medicine, Riga*.

2.3 DIVISION OF WORDS

Rules 1–5, 7b and 8 (p. xiii) apply. For three consonants the rule is 6b, unless the first is a nasal or liquid and the second a stop: in this case either 6a or 6b is permissible. Four consonants are divided two and two.

Note that **ch** and **dž** count as single consonants. So does **dz**, unless, as in **vid-zeme**, *midland*, the **d** and **z** belong to different halves of the compound.

2.5 PALATALISATION

(See General note on the Slavonic languages.) Palatalisation occurs in nouns and verbs as the result of a following j. The effects of palatalisation are as follows:

	b	c	d	dz	g	k	l	m	n	p	s	sl	sn	st	t	v	z	zl	zn
become																			
	bj	č	ž	dž	dz	c	ļ	mj	ņ	pj	š	šļ	šņ	šķ	š	vj	ž	žļ	žņ

Formerly r was palatalised to ŗ, but this letter is now obsolete, and no change occurs. An ending which involves palatalisation is indicated by an asterisk, thus: -*a. The palatalisation of g and k occurs in derived words and in certain parts of verbs.

2.7 SPELLING

Differences of spelling connected with the use of the Gothic alphabet are dealt with in 2.1.3. Apart from this the chief difference in older spelling lies in the use of h to denote length, viz. ah, eh, ih, uh for ā, ē, i, ū. Alternatively length may be indicated by an accent, and in open syllables may not be marked at all (cf. the spelling of tāpat and tādēļ in the second specimen). Ee corresponds to the modern ie, e.g. dzeesmineeki, now dziesminieki. A number of borrowed words formerly spelled with ch are now spelled with h, e.g. (c)hameleons.

3 ARTICLES

There are no articles.

4 NOUNS

4.1 GENDER AND FORM

Nouns may be masculine or feminine, the gender corresponding for the most part to the form of the noun. There are three types of declension for each gender with different predominant vowels but a strong family resemblance. Omitting the vocative there are five cases, the endings of which vary according to the form of the noun.

4.3 ENDINGS
4.3.1 *Masculine*

		S		P
N	-s/-š	-(i)s (4.3.3)	-us	-i
A	-u	-i	-u	-us
G	-a	-*a/-a (4.3.4)	-us	-u
D	-am	-im	-um	-iem
L	-ā	-i	-ū	-os

The preceding consonant is palatalised (2.5) throughout the plural of nouns in -(i)s.

4.3.2 -š follows palatalised consonants other than č, š(ķ) and ž; -j- after a vowel is followed sometimes by -š and sometimes by -s. Where r represents the obsolete ŗ, it is followed by -š. Palatalised endings do not clearly determine the corresponding nominative: thus -ča may come from -čs or -cis, -ņa from -ņš or -nis, -ša from -šs, -sis or even -ts, -tis, e.g. **Andreja Upiša «Zaļa zeme»**, *Andrejs Upits's 'Zaļa zeme'*; **K. Strazdiņa, J. Zuša un A. Drizuļa redakcijā,** *edited by K. Strazdiņš, J. Zutis and A. Drizulis.* This may not matter with common names, but short names are unavoidably ambiguous, for both **Upitis** and **Upits**, **Osis** and **Ošs** are found, and **Bušs** alongside **Zutis**. In longer names such genitives mostly come from nominatives in -is, the only common endings of the other type being -ičs and iņš. As between -sis and -tis, both of which produce -š-, -aitis, -ietis and -itis are common, and on the other hand -esis.

4.3.3 A number of nouns with stems in -n-, as well as **mēness**, *moon*, follow the -is pattern but omit the -i- in the nominative. Most of them have -s in the genitive singular (cf. 4.3.5), e.g. **udens**, *water*, GS **udens** P **udeņi**, etc. (**Mēneša** is the genitive singular of **mēnesis**, *month*.)

4.3.4 The genitive singular of nouns in -is usually has a palatalised consonant (2.5). Important exceptions are surnames in -ckis, -skis and Christian names in -dis and -tis.

4.3.5 *Feminine*

	S	P	S	P	S	P
N	-a	-as	-e	-es	-s	-is
A	-u	-as	-i	-es	-i	-is
G	-as	-u	-es	-*u	-s	-*u
D	-ai	-ām	-ei	-ēm	-ij	-im
L	-ā	-ās	-ē	-ēs	-i	-is

4.3.6 Masculine nouns in -a and -e, which include names, differ only in DS -am, -em.

4.3.7 *Reflexive*

These serve for nouns and participles derived from reflexive verbs (8.14).

	M		F	
	S	P	S	P
N	-ies	-ies	-ās	-ās
A	-os	-os	-os	-ās
G	-ās	-os	-as	-os

4.6 USE OF CASES

4.6.1 *The Genitive* may be used as the direct object of some verbs, and of negative verbs generally, and to express the agent. It is freely used instead of an adjective, e.g. **Latvijas, latviešu**, *Latvian*; **Padomju**, *Soviet*.

4.6.2 *The Dative* denotes the person indirectly affected, requiring the translation *from* as well as *to* or *for*; the logical subject of impersonal expressions (cf. 8.9), and in the plural the instrument.

4.6.3 *The Locative* expresses both position and direction, and also point of time and manner.

5 ADJECTIVES

5.1 GENERAL

5.1.1 Adjectives vary for gender, number and case, and agree with the nouns they qualify. They precede the noun.

5.1.2 All adjectives have both short (indefinite) forms and long (definite) ones, e.g. **Tipiska aina**, *A typical sight*; **Mazā enciklopēdija**, *The little encyclopedia*. They are entered in the dictionary under the short forms, which end in the masculine in -s or -š and in the feminine in -a, and are declined like nouns (4.3.1, 4.3.5).

5.1.3 Short forms are used as predicates and when the noun is indefinite, i.e. usually, but not necessarily, in those cases where English has *a* or nothing. The long forms are common, for instance, in headings, where English has no article, e.g. **Centralā Komiteja**, *(The) Central Committee*; **Vispārigie jautājumi**, *General questions*.

5.2 LONG FORMS

5.2.1

	S		P	
	M	*F*	*M*	*F*
N	-ais	-ā	-ie	-ās
A	-o	-o	-os	-ās
G	-ā	-ās	-o	-o
D	-ajam	-ajai	-ajiem	-ajām
L	-ajā	-ajā	-ajos	-ajās

5.2.2 Adjectives with stems in **-ēj-** omit **-aj-** in the ending, e.g. **pēdējam** not **pēdējajam**.

5.3 COMPARISON

The comparative ends in **-āks** (**-ākais**, etc.); the superlative prefixes **vis-** to the comparative.

6 NUMERALS

6.1 CARDINAL

6.1.1

1 **viens**	11 **vienspadsmit**	21 **divdesmitviens**
2 **divi**	12 **divpadsmit**	22 **divdesmitdivi**
3 **tris**	13 **trispadsmit**	30 **trisdesmit**
4 **četri**	14 **četrpadsmit**	40 **četrdesmit**
5 **pieci**	15 **piecpadsmit**	50 **piecdesmit**
6 **seši**	16 **sešpadsmit**	60 **sešdesmit**
7 **septiņi**	17 **septiņpadsmit**	70 **septiņdesmit**
8 **astoņi**	18 **astoņpadsmit**	80 **astoņdesmit**
9 **deviņi**	19 **deviņpadsmit**	90 **deviņdesmit**
10 **desmit(s)**	20 **div(i)desmit**	100 **simt(s)**
		200 **divi simti, divsimt**
		205 **divsimt pieci**
		1000 **tūkstotis (-stoš)**
		2000 **divi tūkstoši, divtūkstoš**

6.1.2 **viens–deviņi** are adjectives, but being indefinite are declined in effect like masculine or feminine nouns, with the following exceptions or alternatives:

> **divi** may be used for all cases M and F
> **tris** stem **trij-**; contracted forms NALM & F **tris** D **trim**; or **tris** may be used for all cases
> **desmit(s)** and compounds leave off the -s and are undeclined before nouns
> **simt(s)** and **tūkstotis** may be either declined or undeclined

Only the last part of a compound numeral is declined.

6.1.3 Numerals are generally construed as adjectives, but the following should be noted:

> **viens** is followed by a singular noun even in compounds
> **2–9** when in the accusative or after prepositions are sometimes followed by the old dual forms in **-i**

desmit and its compounds may be treated as the nouns they once were and
followed by the GP

simt undeclined is an adjective; simts, a noun, is followed by the GP. Likewise
tūkstoš and tūkstotis

6.2 ORDINAL
6.2.1

1 pirmais	6 sestais	11–99 add -ais to the cardinal
2 otr(ai)s	7 septitais	100 simtais
3 trešais	8 astotais	200 div(i)simtais
4 ceturtais	9 devitais	1000 tūkstošais
5 piektais	10 desmitais	2000 divtūkstošais

6.2.2 All ordinals except **otrs** are definite adjectives (5.2.1).

6.2.3 In compound numerals only the last element has the form of an ordinal. For
examples see 6.4.

6.3 FIGURES
Plain arabic numerals are normally used for cardinals, ordinals being indicated by
arabic numerals with full stops or plain roman figures, e.g. **159 lpp.** (*159 pages*);
3.–4. lpp. (*p. 3–4*); **LKP VI kongress** (*6th Congress of the LCP*).

6.4 DATES
6.4.1 The months are:

janvāris, februāris, marts, aprilis, maijs, jūnijs,
jūlijs, augusts, septembris, oktobris, novembris, decembris

6.4.2

1 May is translated **Pirmais Maijs**
On 8.iii.1962: **tūkstoš deviņi simti sešdesmit otrā gada** (genitive) **astotajā
martā** (both locative); in figures **1962. g. 8. III.**
1848. g. is read: **tūkstoš astoņi simti četrdesmit astotais gads** (nominative)
1848. gadā: . . . **astotajā gadā**, *in 1848*
80-ie (astoņdesmitie) gadi: *the 80's*

7 PRONOUNS

7.1 DEMONSTRATIVE, ETC.
7.1.1 šis, *this*

	S M	S F	P M	P M & F	P F
N	šis	ši	šie		šis
A	šo	šo	šos		šis
G	šā/ši	šās/šis	šo		šo
F	šim	šai	šiem		šim
L	šajā/šai/šini		šajos	šais/šinis	šajās

7.1.2   tas, *that* (also *he, she, it*)

	S		P		
	M	*F*	*M*	*M & F*	*F*
N	tas	tā	tie		tās
A	to	to	tos		tās
G	tā	tās	to		to
D	tam	tai	tiem		tām
L	tajā/tai/tani		tajos	tais/tanis	tajās

7.1.3   pats F pati, *self*, behaves as if it were pašs, paša

7.2   INTERROGATIVE, RELATIVE, INDEFINITE

Kas, *who?, who*, though in sense both singular and plural, follows the masculine singular of **tas**, except in the locative, for which **kur**, *where*, is used. The indefinite pronouns compounded of **kas** follow **kas**.

7.3   PERSONAL

	S		P	
	1	2	1	2
N	es	tu	mēs	jūs
A	mani	tevi	mūs	jūs
G	manis	tevis	mūsu	jūsu
D	man(im)	tev(im)	mums	jums
L	mani	tevi	mūsos	jūsos

Sevi, *my-, your-, himself*, etc., is declined like **tevi**.

8   VERBS

8.1   STRUCTURE

8.1.1   For the most part the different persons are sufficiently distinct to dispense with pronouns, e.g. **būsim** or **mēs būsim**, *we shall be*.

8.1.2   Verbs with prefixes are of the perfective aspect (see General note on the Slavonic languages), but for present purposes all that need be noted is that the past of such verbs may have the sense of a perfect. Both forms are entered, under the infinitive, in the dictionary.

8.2   PRESENT
8.2.1   *Endings*

I	-u, (*)-/-i, -; -am, -at, -
II	-(*)u, (*)-, *-; -*am, -*at, *-
III	-u, -i, -a; -ām, -āt, -a
IV	-ju, -, -; -jam, -jat, -

The verbs in types I and II all have monosyllabic stems or are compounds of mono-syllables.

8.2.2 *Relation of present stem to infinitive*

I   (1) Add -t to obtain the infinitive

The following changes may also occur, singly or in combination:
(a) Change of vowel: **ej** to **ie**; **ē**, **ie** to **i**; **o** to **a**
(b) Shortening of vowel
(c) Change of consonant: **t**, **d** to **s**; **s** to **z**
(d) Removal of consonant, with lengthening of vowel
(e) Removal of **st** or **t**
Examples: **nes**, **nest**; **top**, **tapt**; **met**, **mest**; **skrej/skrien**, **skriet**; **mirst**, **mirt**; **lūst**, **lūzt**.

    (2) Add -(*)ēt, e.g. **māk**, **mācēt**
II   (1) Add -t, the palatalisation disappearing, e.g. **teic**, **teikt**; **laiž**, **laist** (< **laidt**)
    (2) Add -ēt. The palatalisation may disappear, e.g. **sēž**, **sēdēt**; **redz**, **redzēt**
III   Add -āt or -it. Most of the -āt verbs have stems ending in -in-

Before -it **k** and **g** change to **c** and **dz** respectively, e.g. **izsaka**, *expresses*, inf. **izsacit**.

IV   Add -t (the stem ends in a vowel)

8.2.3 The ending -(j)ot for all persons is used to express hearsay or reported speech, e.g. **viņš slimojot**, (*they say*) *he is ill.*

8.3 PAST
8.3.1 *Endings*

I   -u, -i, -a; -ām, -āt, -a
II   -ju, -ji, -ja; -jām, -jāt, -ja

8.3.2 To obtain infinitive add -t to the stem. The changes listed under 8.2.2; I.1.c,d and II.1 apply.
8.3.3 The tense expresses both continuous and momentary action.

8.5 FUTURE
8.5.1 *Endings*

-šu, -si, -s; -siem, -si(e)t, -s

8.5.2 To obtain infinitive add -t to the stem, except for some futures in -dišu, -sišu, -tišu, -zišu, which have infinitives in -st or -zt, e.g. **metišu**, **mest**; **gāzišu**, **gāzt**.
8.5.3 For the ending -šot see 8.2.3.

8.6 CONDITIONAL
This ends in -tu throughout and corresponds to an infinitive in -t.

8.9 OBLIGATION
The prefix **jā-** added to the 3PS expresses obligation. The logical subject is put in the dative and the logical object is usually in the nominative, e.g. **viņam jāraksta grāmata**, *he has to write a book.* To indicate the future and the past **būs** and **bija** are added.

8.10 COMPOUND TENSES

8.10.1 The present, imperfect and future of **būt**, *to be,* followed by the past active participle, produce the perfect, pluperfect and future perfect tenses. The present tense of **būt** is often omitted.

8.10.2 The meaning of the perfect tense is sometimes that of the simple past, with the implication of hearsay.

8.11 INFINITIVE

Ends in **-t**, more often than not preceded by a vowel. Instructions for finding the infinitive are given under the other parts of the verb. In sense it corresponds to the English infinitive and the verbal noun in *-ing.*

8.12 PARTICIPLES

8.12.1 The nomenclature of participles and related forms in Latvian is uncertain. Only those which are used as adjectives are here termed 'participles', but the name is sometimes applied also to what are here called 'gerunds' (8.13).

8.12.2 *Present active*

-oš(ai)s. Formed from the present stem, e.g. **tek,** *flows:* **tekošs ūdens,** *running water.*

8.12.3 *Past active*

-(*)is, F **-usi,** stem **-uš-.** Formed from the past, e.g. **sāku,** *he began:* **sācis, sākusi,** P **sākuši, sākušas,** *having begun.* It can be used as a noun, e.g. **kritušie,** *the fallen.* (See also 1.2.2, 8.10.)

8.12.4 *Present passive*

-ams/-āms, formed from the present stem, e.g. **lasāma grāmata,** *a reading book;* **grāmata ir lasāma,** *the book is readable.* It can be used to express obligation, e.g. **Mums rakstāms,** *We must write.*

8.12.5 *Past passive*

-ts, formed by adding **-s** to the infinitive. (See also 8.15.)

8.13 GERUNDS

8.13.1

-dams, -dama, -dami, -damas

This agrees with the subject and has no other cases. It is used liked the English participle as the equivalent of an adverbial clause and in such sentences as **Lai nāk kas nākdams,** *Come what may.*

8.13.2

-ot (indeclinable) formed from the present stem

This may be used like **-dams,** e.g. **atklājot latviešu lasitājiem citu tautu literārās bagātibas . . . iespiesti M. Gorkija u. c. darbi,** *works of M. Gorkiï and others were printed . . . revealing to Latvian readers the literary riches of other countries,* and also where English has a clause with no expressed subject or a different subject, e.g. **raksturojot grāmatas skaitļos, viens rāditājs . . .,** *if (we) characterise books in figures, one index ... ;* **sākoties** (8.14.2) **pirmajam pasaules karam, rūpniecibas evakuēja,** *when the first World War began, the businesses evacuated.* The logical subject **(karam)** is in the dative.

8.14 REFLEXIVE

8.14.1　Some verbs have a set of reflexive forms, e.g. **mazgāt**, *to wash* (something) **mazgāties**, *to wash* (oneself); **lūgt**, *to request*, **lūgties**, *to request for oneself*. Many, however have no active forms, being themselves active in meaning, e.g. **atcerēties**, *to remember*, and others correspond simply to English intransitive verbs. Nor is it always safe to guess the meaning from the active, e.g. **aprunāt**, *to slander*; **aprunāties**, *to converse*. (See also 8.15.)

8.14.2　The forms arise from suffixing the remains of a reflexive pronoun to the active. The stems therefore and their relation to the infinitive are the same.

> *Present:* **os, -ies,** $\begin{cases} \text{-ās; -āmies, -āties, -ās} \\ \text{-as; -amies, -aties, -as} \end{cases}$
> *Past:* **-os, -ies, -ās; -āmies, -āties, -ās**
> *Future:* **-šos, -sies, -sies; -simies, -si(e)ties, -sies**
> *Conditional:* **-tos**
> *Past Participle:* **-*ies, F -usies; P -ušies, -ušās** (cf. 4.3.7)
> *Gerunds:* **-damies, -oties**
> *Infinitive:* **-ties**

8.14.3　The 'hearsay' forms (8.2.3, 8.5.3) are **-oties** and **-šoties**.

8.15 PASSIVE

8.15.1　Though the participles (8.12.4, 8.12.5) are common enough, the tenses of the passive are little used, the active being usually substituted, whether the agent is expressed or not, e.g. **Stāstījuma teikumos . . . stāsta kādu spriedumu**, *In affirmative sentences . . . some thought is stated* (lit. *they state some thought*). Sometimes the reflexive is found where the passive might be expected, e.g. **izveidojās izdevniecības,** *presses were organised*.

8.15.2　The past participle passive alone can be used for the past tense, e.g. **Pirmā grāmata latviešu valodā izdota 1525. gadā**, *The first book in the Latvian language was published in 1525.*

8.15.3　With the appropriate tense of the verbs **tapt, tikt, palikt** or **kļut**, all meaning *to become*, the participle makes a continuous passive, but this is usually even less common.

8.15.4　State is expressed by the participle with **būt**, *to be*, e.g. **Valoda ir saistīta ar sabiedrību**, *Language is associated with society*.

8.17 THE VERB **būt**, *to be*

> *Present:* **esmu, esi, ir; esam, esat, ir**
> *Past:* **biju**
> *Future:* **būšu**
> *Participles:* **esošs, bijis**
> *Gerunds:* **budams, esam**
> '*Hearsay*' *forms:* **esot, būšot** (cf. 8.2.3, 8.5.3)

8.19 IRREGULARITIES

8.19.1　**dot,** *to give*
> *Present:* **dodu**
> *Past:* **devu**

8.19.2　**iet,** *to go*
> *Present:* **eju, ej, iet; ejam, ejat, iet**
> *Past:* **gāju**

8.22 NEGATIVE

Ne- is prefixed to the verb, and is used even if there is already a negative pronoun in the sentence, e.g. **Virs, kurš nevienam nepatika**, *The man whom nobody liked*. There is a special form **nav** for *is not*, *are not*.

9 ADVERBS

9.1 FORMATION

Adverbs are regularly formed from adjectives by substituting **-i**, **-am**, or **-u** for the adjectival ending, e.g. **viegls**, *easy*, **viegli**, *easily*; **lēns**, *slow*, **lēnām**, *slowly*; **tāls**, *distant*, **tālu**, *afar off*. Adverbs are sometimes found where adjectives might be expected: see 1.3.1 for an example.

9.2 COMPARISON

The comparative, where it exists, ends in **-āk** (cf. 5.3).

10 PREPOSITIONS

10.1 POSITION

A number of prepositions used to follow the noun, but the only one of these now in common use is **dēļ**, *on account of*.

10.2 SYNTAX

Prepositions govern various cases in the singular, but in the plural are all followed by the dative.

Pa and **uz** take two cases in the singular with differences of meaning, e.g. **uz vāka**, *on the cover*; **ceļš uz uzvaru**, *the way to victory*; but in the plural **uz laukiem** could be either *in the country* or *to the country*.

11 CONJUNCTIONS

The construction of conjunctions calls for no comment. It is worth noting that there are two words for *or*, viz. **jeb**, which connects alternative forms of expression, **vai**, which distinguishes real alternatives, e.g. **Kaukāza gūstekne jeb Šurika jaunie piedzivojumi**, *A Caucasian prisoner, or Šurik's new adventures*; **Kritizēt vai analizēt?**, *Criticise or analyse?*

13 WORD-FORMATION

As good dictionaries are few, it may be as well to note the meaning of some of the commoner suffixes:

> **-ājs**, **-ējs**, **-tājs**; F **-āja**, etc.: agent
> **-iba**: action of the verb, e.g. **izglitiba**, *education* (**izglitot**, *to educate*), abstract quality, e.g. **draudziba**, *friendship* (**draugs**, *friend*). Note the palatalisation (2.5). Also combined with **-niek-** to form **-nieciba**
> **-nieks**, F **-niece**: person connected with a place, agent, e.g. **ridzinieks**, *man of Riga*; **zemnieks**, *peasant* (**zeme**, *land*); **mākslinieks**, *artist* (**māksla**)
> **-šana**: action of the verb, e.g. **lietošana**, *employment* (**lietot**, *to use*)
> **-ums**: result of action, e.g. **sasniegums**, *achievement* (**sasniegt**); abstract quality, e.g. **skaistums**, *beauty* (**skaists**, *beautiful*)

GLOSSARY

abonements, abonēšana, *subscription* (1.8.6)

aktis, *proceedings*

apgādiens, *publication*

apgāds, *press* (1.6.2)

apmaiņa, *exchange*

apraksts, *essay*

ārzemes, *foreign countries*

atkārtots iespiedums, *reprint*

atsevišķs, *separate*

bezmaksas, *free*

bibliotēka, *library*

bibliotēkārs, *librarian*

biedriba, *society*

brošēts, *paperback*

brošūra, *pamphlet*

burtnica, *part, issue* (1.8.4)

cena, *price* (1.8.6)

daļa, *part* (1.4.1)

darbs, *work*

divnedēļu-, *fortnightly*

dzejolis, *poem*

dzimis, *was born*

eksemplārs, *copy*

faktūra, *invoice*

gadagrāmata, *yearbook*

gads, *year*

grāmata, *book*

ģimetne, *portrait*

iesiets, *bound*

iespiedējs, *printer*

iespiedums, *impression* (1.5)

iespiests, *in print*

ievads, *introduction*

ikgadējs, *annual*

izdevnieciba, *publishing house* (1.6.2)

izdevums, *edition* (1.5), *publication* (1.6.2)

izlaidums, *issue, part* (1.7.2)

izlase, *selection* (1.2.5)

izlasits, *selected*

iznāk, *comes out* (1.8.5)

izpārdots, *sold out, out of print*

kopsavilkums, *summary*

krājums, *collection*

labot(ai)s, *improved* (1.5)

laidiens, *issue, part* (1.7.2)

lappuse, *page*

loceklis, *member*

luga, *play*

maksa, *price*

maksā, *costs* (1.8.6)

ik mēnesi, *monthly*

par 3 mēnešiem, *quarterly*

mēnešraksts, *monthly publication*

miris, *died*

nedēļa, *week*

neizdots, *unpublished*

ar nodrošinātām autora tiesibām, *with the author's rights preserved*

novele, *short story*

numurs, *numbers* (1.8.4)

papildinājums, *addition*

papildināts, *enlarged* (1.5)

parakstišana, *subscription* (1.8.6)

paraugs, *sample, specimen*

pārdodamas, *on sale*

pārlabojums, *correction*

pārlabot(ai)s, *corrected, improved* (1.5)

pārstrādāts, *revised* (1.5)

pasūtit, *to order, subscribe*

pētnieciba, *research*

pielikums, *appendix, supplement*

piesūtit, -tišana, *to send, sending* (1.8.6)

piezime, *note*

priekšvārds, *preface*

pusgads, *half-year*

rāditājs, *index*

raksti, *works, proceedings*

redakcija, *editing* (1.2.5, 1.8.3), *editorial office* (1.8.7)

redaktors, *editor* (1.8.3)
rediģējuši, *they edited* (1.8.3)
rēķins, *bill*
romāns, *novel*
runa, *speech*

sagatavot, *to prepare*
saisināt(ai)s, *abridged*
sakārtotājs, *editor*
sastādijis, *compiled* (1.2.3)
satura rāditājs, *table of contents*
savilkums, *summary*
sējums, *volume* (1.4.1)
serija, (*sub*)*series*

skaties, *see*
spiestuve, *printing shop*

tabula, *table*
tēlojums, *description, essay*
tulkotājs, *translator*
turpinājums sekos, *to be continued*

vārdnica, *dictionary*
vecs numurs, *back number*
vēstule, *letter*
vēsture, *history*

ziņojumi, *reports, transactions*
žurnāls, *journal*

GRAMMATICAL INDEX: WORDS

bij-, 8.17
bija, 8.9, 8.17
būdams, 8.17
būs, 8.17
būšot, 8.17

dēļ, 10.1
dev-, 8.19.1
dod-, 8.19.1

ej(am), ejat, eju, 8.19.2
esam, esat, esi, esmu,
  esošs, esot, 8.17

gāj-, 8.19.2

iet, 8.19.2
ir, 8.17

jā-, 8.9
jeb, 11
jums, jūs(os), jūsu, 7.3

kā, kam, kas, 7.2
kļūt, 8.15.3
ko, 7.2
kur, 7.2

man(im), mani(s), mani,
  7.3
mums, mūs(os), mūsu, 7.3

nav, 8.22
ne-, 8.22

pa, 10.2
palikt, 8.15.3
par, 1.2.6
paš-, 7.1.3

sev(im), sevi(s), sevi, 7.3

ša(i)(s), šaj-, šās, 7.1.1
ši, ši, etc., 7.1.1
šo(s), 7.1.1

tā, tai(s), taj-, tam, tām
  tani(s), 7.1.2
tapt, 8.15.3
tās, 7.1.2
tev(im), tevi(s), tevi, 7.3
tie(m), 7.1.2
tikt, 8.15.3
to(s), 7.1.2
trim, 6.1.2
tris, 6.1.2

uz, 10.2

vai, 11
vis-, 5.3

GRAMMATICAL INDEX: ENDINGS

-, 8.2.1

-a, 4.3.1, 4.3.5, 8.2.1, 8.3.1
-ā, 4.3.1, 4.3.5, 5.2.1
-iba, 13
-ja, 8.3.1

-jā, 5.2.1, 5.2.2
-āja, 13
-ama, -āma, 8.12.4
-dama, 8.13.1
-šana, 13
-oša, 8.12.2

-uša, 8.12.3
-ta, 8.12.5

-e, -ē, 4.3.5
-niece, 13

LITHUANIAN

SPECIMENS

„Literatūros ir kalbos" antrašte Lietuvos TSR Mokslų akademijos Lietuvių kalbos ir literatūros institutas pradeda leisti savo Darbus. Šiame neperiodiniame serijiniame leidinyje bus spausdinami Instituto darbuotojų atlikti mokslo tiriamieji darbai iš lietuvių literatūros, kalbos ir tautosakos sričių, o taip pat darbai, nušviečią mūsų rašytojų, kalbininkų ir tautosakininkų ryšius su kitų tautų literatūromis bei mokslu.

Under the title 'Literatūra ir Kalba' (Literature and Language) the Institute of Lithuanian Language and Literature of the Academy of Sciences of the Lithuanian SSR is beginning to publish its transactions. In this non-periodical serial publication will be printed scientific research works produced by the staff of the institute from the field of Lithuanian literature, language and folklore, and also works elucidating the relations of our writers, linguists and folklorists with the literature and learning of other nations.

Two specimens of 19th-century spelling, with present-day equivalents:

Sułaukta amžiaus dienos ateja wałanda,
Riegiedamas pabajga, swietas nuosiganda.
Jau tranksmiausi perkunaj smarkej
    sugrumieja,
Duodami ženkłus bajsius, jog gałs
    prasidieja.
Oras wieł kitus grausmus nuog sawes
    padara
Ir isz wisur degamus dalijkus suwara.

Sulaukta amžiaus dienos atėjo valanda,
Regėdamas pabaigą, svietas nusigando.
Jau transkmiausi perkūnai smarkiai
    sugrūmėjo,
Duodami ženklus baisius, jog gals
    prasidėjo;
Oras vėl kitus griausmus nuog savęs
    padaro
Ir iš visur degamus dalykus suvaro.

Kas do nauda isz Pasakû Lietuv-Žemaj-tems tikt, kłausimas? Javgi, dar musû pri-gimta szalis, padiekavoti Dievuj, ne tejp atbuła arba iszlepusi, idant tiesybej rejktu slieptis.

Kas do nauda iš pasakų lietuv-žemai-čiams, tik klausimas? Jaugi dar mūsų pri-gimta šalis, padėkavoti Dievui, ne taip atbula arba išlepusi, idant teisybei reiktų slėptis.

0 GENERAL CHARACTERISTICS

0.1 DEGREE OF INFLEXION
Lithuanian is a predominantly synthetic language, having a variety of case-endings to express the commoner relations of nouns, and distinct forms for the different persons of the verb.

0.2 ORDER OF WORDS
Qualifiers, including genitives, precede the noun. In sentences the subject usually pre-cedes the verb, but when indicating the part played by particular persons in the pro-

duction of a book, especially on the title-page, the order object-verb-subject is very common (see 1.2.2 for examples).

0.4 RELATION TO OTHER LANGUAGES
Lithuanian is closely related to Latvian and fairly closely to the Slavonic languages in vocabulary and in some structural characteristics. Like them it frequently omits the verb *to be*.

1 BIBLIOLINGUISTICS

1.1 NAMES

1.1.1 For grammatical purposes most Lithuanian names must be regarded as nouns, even though some of them have corresponding feminine forms (1.1.3). Thus **Šarmas,** feminine **Šarmaitė,** has the dative **Šarmui** characteristic of a noun (4.3.1) not the -am ending of an adjective (5.2.1). In the full legal statement of a name the father's Christian name follows in the genitive, e.g. **Bronius Paulauskas s. Balio** or **Bronius Balio Paulauskas,** but is omitted in all ordinary contexts.

1.1.2 Christian names are nouns, masculine names ending in -as, -is, -us, -ys, feminine ones in -a, or -ė (4.3.1, 4.3.3).

1.1.3 Women's surnames have distinctive suffixes, -ienė for a married woman, -aitė for an unmarried woman. Many women use both their maiden and married names. They correspond thus:

-aitė	-a, -as
-ytė	-is, -ys
-aitytė	-aitis
-utė	-us
-ienė	-a, -as, -is, -ys, -ė
-(i)uvienė	-(i)us

Pseudonyms born by women are an exception, e.g. **Alė Rūta** (4.3.3).

1.1.4 There are also some men's surnames which end in -a or ė, e.g. **Petras Cvirka, Paulius Galaunė.** They are declined as feminine nouns, but have female counterparts, e.g. **Adelė Galaunienė.**

1.1.5 Surnames in -ų are genitive plurals. As such they precede the Christian name (which is always given in full) and are invariable. One such is **Rygiškių Jonas,** the pseudonym of J. Jablonskis, derived from his residence at Rygiškiai. There are also inclinable surnames in -os (genitive singular). In conjunction with names in -a they can be trying, e.g. **Vytauto Sirijos Giros,** genitive of **Vytautas Sirijos Gira.**

1.1.6 Both parts of a compound name are appropriately declined, e.g. **A. Gudaičio-Guzevičiaus „Broliai",** '*Broliai*' *by A. Gudaitis-Guzevičius.*

1.1.7 Foreign names are usually made to conform to Lithuanian morphology, e.g. **Čechovas, Gorkis, Tolstojus; Mickevičius** (Mickiewicz); **Getė** (Goethe); **Vitmenas** (Whitman); **Džonas Galsvortis, Tekerėjus; Mopasanas.** But if they end in a vowel other than -a or ė they are indeclinable; e.g. **Defo, Bernardas Šo, Sent-Egziuperi.** Women's names, other than Slavonic, have no ending and are indeclinable, e.g. **B. Poter, S. Unset, S. Lagerlef.**

1.1.8 Lithuanian names are rendered in Russian with very little change, but vowel length is perforce ignored, so that Cyrillic и represents both i and y. Cyrillic e also is ambiguous as between e and ie, and я represents not only ja but also e when it is so pronounced, as in **Гузявичюс, Guzevičius**. Feminine names retain their characteristic endings, but are not declined, e.g. **депутату Щумаускасу, депутату Барткене**, *to deputy Šumauskas . . . Bartkiene.*

1.2 NAMES OF AUTHORS, EDITORS, ETC.

1.2.1 Various constructions are used in indicating authorship, editorship and the like, but the name is most often in the nominative, less frequently the genitive. Often the name stands at the head of the title-page, in the nominative, unconnected grammatically with the title, e.g. **J. Jablonskis|Rinktiniai raštai** (*J. Jablonskis|Collected works*).

1.2.2 The work done is often indicated by an active verb following the title and preceding the name, which is in the nominative. The verb is almost invariably in the past tense (8.4), e.g. **redagavo K. Korsakas**, *K. K. edited*; **leidinj sudarė R. Carnytė ir J. Marcinkevičius**, *R. C. and J. M. compiled the publication*; **spaudai paruošė, spausdinimą prižiūrėjo**, *prepared for printing, supervised the printing*; **bendradarbiavo**, *collaborated*. Fortunately the singular and plural of the verb are the same. The activity, it will be noticed, is usually something other than simple authorship.

1.2.3 Alternatively, the agent is indicated by the appropriate noun and the name follows in the nominative, e.g. **sudarytojas**, *compiler*; **šio tomo autoriai**, *authors of this volume*; **(vyriausiasis) redaktorius**, (*chief*) *editor*; **redakcinė kolegija**, *editorial committee*.

1.2.4 A noun may be used to indicate the work done, and the name precedes in the genitive, e.g. **Prano Moncevičiaus pasakojimą užrašė A. Vaivutskas**, *A. V. took down the narrative of Pranas Moncevičius.* This type is not common.

1.2.5 Occasionally the author's name may be in the dative, as logical subject to a gerund (8.13.2), e.g. **Prof. Smirnickiui vadovaujant sudarytas**, *compiled under the leadership of Prof. Smirnitski.*

1.2.6 Corporate authors are usually isolated at the head of the title-page, in the nominative, but the other constructions are possible. One may also find the name in the genitive, e.g. **Lietuvos Komunistų partijos Centro komiteto kreipimas į visus Tarybų Lietuvos rinkėjus**, *Appeal of the Central Committee of the Lithuanian Communist Party to all electors of Soviet Lithuania.* Subordinate bodies may or may not be linked grammatically with the main body, e.g. **Lietuvos TSR Mokslų akademija|Istorijos ir teisės institutas** with the *Academy of Sciences of the Lithuanian SSR* and its offshoot the *Institute of History and Law* both in the nominative, or with the genitive **akademijos**, *Institute ... of the Academy*, etc. (It should be borne in mind however that most of the qualifying words, e.g. **mokslų, teisės, istorijos** will be nouns in the genitive as well.) Sometimes a preposition is used, e.g. **Lietuvos TSR Mokslų akademija. Filosofios, teisės ir sociologijos skyrius prie Istorijos instituto**—a sandwich: L—TSR M— a—ja. Istorijos institutas. F—, t— ir s— skyrius.

1.3 TITLES

1.3.1 Most titles consist of nouns and adjectives in various cases, e.g. **Lietuvos TSR istorijos šaltiniai**, *Sources of the history of the Lithuanian SSR*; **Sodžiaus menas**, *Village art*; **Ilgai brandintas grūdas**, *Long-ripened corn.* Belles-lettres and the literature of persuasion show more variety, e.g. **Pušis kuri juokėsi**, *The pine which laughed*; **Iš pelenų pakilęs kaimas**, *A village that rose from the ashes*; **Lietuva bus elektrifikuota**, *Lithuania shall be electrified.*

1.3.2 Title entries on the Anglo-American pattern pose no problems, but those who follow British Museum rules will not infrequently find the first noun in the genitive, and will need to provide a nominative as heading, or translate it. Where the genitive is adjectival it may be doubtful how it should be translated, e.g. **Lietuvių poezijos antologija**. Is the heading to be LITHUANIANS or LITHUANIAN POETRY?

1.3.3   When a title forms part of a sentence, the principal noun and any adjectives that agree with it may be affected by the grammar of the sentence, e.g. **Parengiant šį „Lietuvių kalbos gramatikos" leidimą**, *In preparing this edition of ' Lietuvių kalbos gramatika'*; if, however, there is a noun in apposition to the title, this is declined if necessary while the title is left unaltered, e.g. **romano „Žemė maitintoja"**, *of the novel 'Žemė maitintoja'*. (See however 1.4.3 and 1.8.1.)

1.4   VOLUMES AND PARTS

1.4.1/1.4.2   The appropriate words are **tomas** and **dalis** respectively. The numeration is by an ordinal, usually expressed in figures, e.g. **III tomas**, *vol. 3*; **I dalis**, *pt. 1*; **T. 1. Kn. 1**, *vol. 1, pt. 1*; **pirmoji knyga**, *first book*. **Dalis** should be treated with caution. Sometimes it is equivalent to **tomas**. The word **knyga**, *book*, is sometimes equivalent to **tomas**, but may equally well represent something more or less: e.g. **Raštai. T. 3. Broliai. Kn. 1, 2** (*Works. vol. 3. The Brothers. bks. 1, 2*).

1.4.3   Any of the words may be grammatically connected with the title, e.g. **Sodžiaus meno I-ai knygai**, *For Book I of ' Sodžiaus menas'*.

1.5   EDITIONS

1.5.1/1.5.2   The usual word is **leidimas**, e.g. **antras(is) (2-sis) leidimas**, *2nd edition*, or with appropriate adjectives indicating revision, such as **pataisytas**, *corrected*.

1.5.3   An *offprint* is **atspaudas**, *reprinting* **perspaudinimas**.

1.6   IMPRINTS

1.6.1   The constructions used are varied, and neither the place nor the publisher is necessarily in the nominative. The publisher's name appears in the nominative when it stands by itself, e.g. **Valstybinė politinės ir mokslinės literatūros leidykla**, *State Publishing House of Political and Scientific Literature*; equally when preceded by an active verb such as **išleido**, *published*, or **spaudė**, *printed*. But such expressions as **leidinys** (*publication*) require the name to be in the genitive, e.g. **Žemės ūkio rūmų leidinys**, *Publication of the Board of Agriculture* (**rūmai**).

1.6.2   The place of publication is usually in the nominative, e.g. **Kaunas, Vilnius**, but may be in the locative, e.g. **Chicagoje**, *at Chicago*; **Vilniuje**.

1.6.3   Soviet presses are institutional. Up to 1964 these had descriptive names like **Valstybinė grožinės literatūros leidykla**, *State Publishing House for [Artistic] Literature* (and cf. 1.6.1), though some might have the name of a periodical. Since 1964 short names such as **Vaga** (*Furrow*) and **Mintis** (*Thought*) have been substituted.

1.6.4   Earlier imprints nearly always give the name of the printer, e.g. **spaudinie** (i.e. **spaudinyje**)/**išspaustas pas C. Kray**, *printed by C. Kray*; **spaustuwieje Juzapa Zawadzia**, *at the press of Juzapas Zawadys*.

1.7   SERIES

1.7.1   The titles of series may appear at the top of the title-page, facing it, or even after the title of the individual volume. Most of them are straightforward descriptions of the items, e.g. **Lietuvių kalbos ir literatūros instituto darbai**, *Works of the Institute of Lithianian Language and Literature*; **Lituanistinė biblioteka**, *Library of Lithuanian studies*; or slightly more complicated, **Iš Lietuvių kultūros istorijos**, *From the history of Lithuanian culture*.

1.7.2   In numeration the terms **tomas**, *volume*, and **numeris (nr.)**, *number*, or **sąsiuvinis**, *fascicule*, are found. The numeration may be grammatically linked with the title, as in **Darbų t.11 (= Darbai. t.11)**.

Sub-series are usually indicated by **serija**, e.g. **Lietuvos TSR Mokslų akademijos darbai. Serija A**.

1.7.3   Occasionally the individual item is named and numbered, the series being implied, e.g. **Nidos knygų klubo leidinys nr. 3**, *Publication no. 3 of the Nida Book Club*. Here one will have to construct the name of the series as such, viz. **Nidos Knygų Klubas. Leidiniai**, but it will be clear from 1.6.1 that not every appearance of **leidinys** presupposes such a series.

1.8   PERIODICALS

1.8.1   The titles of periodicals are the same grammatically as those of books and series, e.g. **Tiesa**, *Truth*; **Liaudies ūkis**, *National economy*; **Literatūra ir menas**, *Literature and art*. As in the case of books, the title may be grammatically connected with the rest of the sentence, indeed it may appear in the genitive even when it qualifies a word like **leidinys** (*publication*) or **antraštė** (*title*), as in the specimen. (See also 1.8.4.)

1.8.2   The name of the body responsible may appear in the title in the genitive, e.g. **Lituanistikos instituto Metraštis**, *Yearbook of the Institute of Lithuanian Philology* (**Lituanistikos Institutas**), or there may be a similar statement elsewhere, e.g. **žurnalas yra Lietuvos TSR Mokslų akademijos Prezidiumo organas**, *the journal is the organ of the Presidium of the Academy of Sciences of the Lithuanian SSR*. As often the various sorts of genitives need distinguishing. If preceded by **leidžia** (*publishes*) or some other such verb or **leidėjai** (*publishers*) the name will naturally be in the nominative.

1.8.3   In indications of editorship the stem **redag-/redak-** is common, e.g. **redaguoja**, *edits*, followed by the name of the editor; (**atsakingasis, vyriausiasis**) **redaktorius** (*responsible, chief*) *editor*; or frequently **redakcinė kolegija** or **komisija**. The names in all these cases are in the nominative. Among the committee the chairman (**pirmininkas**) and members (**nariai**) are usually distinguished. On different lines we may have **sudaro**, *they put together*.

1.8.4   Numeration is by **metai** (*year*), alternatively **tomas** (*volume*), and **n(ume)r(is)** The numbers usually come first, read as ordinals, and may be combined with the title, e.g. **Darbų X tomas**, i.e. **Darbai, t.10**.

1.8.5   Periodicity is usually stated in the form **eina kartą per mėnesį**, *comes out once a month*; but special announcements may involve other tenses, e.g. **išeis aštuoni numeriai**, *eight numbers will come out*. (**Išeiti** is more explicit than **eiti** but in practice means the same.) **Eina** also appears in notices of foundation dates, e.g. **eina nuo 1947 metų**, *has been coming out since 1947*.

1.8.6   Subscription (**prenumerata**) may be for a whole year, a half year, quarter (**visiems metams, pusmečiui, ketvirčiui**). The same information using **kaina** appears as **metinių komplektų (pusmetinio) kaina**, *the price of annual sets (of a half-yearly set)*. The price of a single number (**atskiras numeris**) may be given in the same way by **šio numerio kaina** (*price of this number*) or with the dative, **vienam mėnesiui**, or using **kainuoja** (*costs*). **Skelbimai** are *advertisements*.

1.8.7   The editorial address (**redakcijos adresas**) is sometimes combined with that for administration, or one may be directed to send subscriptions to the editor (**prenumerata siunčiama redaktoriaus adresu**) but more often there will be some other direction such as **užsakymus siųsti šituo adresu**, *send orders to this address*.

2 ALPHABET, PHONETICS, SPELLING

2.1 ALPHABET

2.1.1 The alphabet is as follows:

a ą b c č d e ę ė f g h i į y j k l m n o p r

s š t u ų ū v z ž

As indicated by the brackets, diacritical marks on vowels are usually ignored for the purposes of order; otherwise each of the above letters has a distinct alphabetical position. Note the place of **y**.

2.1.2 The diacritical marks and long marks shown above must not be omitted.

2.1.3 The Gothic alphabet was formerly used, but though the spelling at the time was different (see the specimens), this alphabet as such did not involve any special letters, but was the same as that used for German.

2.2 CAPITALISATION

2.2.1 In principle all names have initial capitals, but if a name consists of several elements, it is not invariably the case that all of them are capitalised; and some words that might be thought to be names are not treated as such. The chief of these are the months and the days of the week, and nouns of nationality and locality such as **lietuvis**, *a Lithuanian*; **londonietis**, *Londoner*.

2.2.2 The following are capitalised throughout: personal names, geographical, topographical and astronomical names (except in so far as they include generic names), names of intergovernmental organisations, of the highest Soviet organs of state, and of Soviet festivals and honorifics, e.g. **Jonas Bežemis**, *John Lackland*; **Pietų Afrikos Sąjunga**, *Union of South Africa*; **Šiaurės Ledinuotas vandenynas**, *Arctic Ocean*; **Gorkio gatvė**, *Gorky Street*; **Grįžulo Ratai**, *Charles's Wain*; **Savienytųjų Nacijų Organizacijos generalinė asamblėja**, *General Assembly of the United Nations* (note that **generalinė asamblėja** is not treated as a name); **Aukščiausioji Taryba**, *Supreme Soviet*; **Gegužės Pirmoji**, *May Day* (contrast **balandžio pirmoji**, *April Fools' Day*); **Socialistinio Darbo Didvyris**, *Hero of Socialist Labour*.

2.2.3 In the names of other institutions and festivals, of orders (including Soviet orders), historical events and periodicals only the first word has a capital, unless this is some form of **didysis**, e.g. **Darbo žmonių deputatų taryba**, *Soviet of Workers' Deputies*; **Tarptitautinė moters diena**, *International Woman's Day*; but **Didžioji Spalio socialistinė revoliucija**, *The Great Socialist October Revolution*. The same may happen if the first word is **Lietuvos**, e.g. **Lietuvos Komunistų partija**.

2.3 DIVISION OF WORDS

Rules 1, 2, 4, 5a, 6a, 7a and 8 (p. xiii) apply, but four consonants may be divided two and two. These prefixes end with a consonant: **ant-, ap-, at-, im-, in-, iš-, per-, prieš-, tarp-, už-**; but it must not be assumed that every word that begins with one of these syllables has a prefix. The digraph **dž** must not be divided.

2.5 PALATALISATION

See General note on the Slavonic languages. Palatalisation occurs before **ia, ią, io, iu, ių**. It affects only **d** and **t**, which are changed to **dž** and **č** respectively in nouns, adjectives and verbs. Endings which cause palatalisation are indicated in the tables by a prefixed asterisk.

2.7 SPELLING

The present conventions are comparatively recent, and earlier spelling used some Polish devices such as sz for the present š, as well as ł for l, and l for li. The spelling adopted is connected with the standardisation of the language, and though the specimens give some idea of the differences, it is impossible to give rules for conversion. In some respects the older spelling was more phonetic but made morphology more complicated: cf. **perkunaj smarkej** in the second specimen.

3   ARTICLES

There are no articles.

4   NOUNS

4.1   GENDER AND FORM

Nouns may be masculine or feminine, the gender corresponding for the most part to the form of the noun. There are three types of declension for each gender, plus a few variations, but they all show a strong resemblance to each other. Omitting the vocative there are six cases, the endings of which vary according to the form of the noun. Diminutives are freely formed in **-elis** and **-elė**.

4.3   ENDINGS
4.3.1   *Masculine nouns*

	S			P	
N	-as	-ias, -is/-ys	-us	-(*i)ai	-ūs
A	-ą	-ią -į	-ų	-(*i)us	-us
G	-o	-*io	-aus	-(*i)ų	-ų
D	-ui	-*iui	-ui	-(*i)ams	-ums
I	-u	-*iu	-umi	-(*i)ais	-umis
L	-e/-uje	-yje	-uje	-(*i)uose	-uose

4.3.2   It is apparent from the table that the oblique cases do not all clearly indicate the nominative. In particular the dative -iui and the plurals in -iai, etc. (which cause palatalisation) may come from a nominative in -ias, -is, -ys, or ius.

For nouns with oblique cases in -enj etc. see 4.3.4.

Most of the endings hold for masculine adjectives (5.2.1).

4.3.3   *Feminine nouns*

	S			P		
N	-a	-ė	-is	-os	-ės	-ys
A	-ą	-ę	-į	-as	-es	-is
G	-os	-ės	-iės	-ų	-*ių	-*ių
D	-ai	-ei	-*iai	-oms	-ėms	-ims
I	-a	-e	-imi	-omis	-ėmis	-imis
L	-oje	-ėje	-yje	-ose	-ėse	-yse

The singular and plural columns correspond.

Pati, *wife* is adjectival (5.2.1) that is, it behaves as if it were **pačia** (see also 7.1.4).

For nouns with singular **-erį**, plural **-erys** and **-enys** see 4.3.4.

The endings hold for feminine adjectives.

4.3.4 *Nouns in* -uo *and* -e

Nouns in -uo are all masculine except **sesuo**, *sister*; nouns in -e are feminine.

Masculine nouns in -uo behave as if the nominative were -enis, with masculine endings (4.3.1) in the singular, but GS -ens, and feminine ones (4.3.3) in the plural; except **mėnuo**, *month*, which is declined as if it were **mėnesis**, with masculine endings throughout.

Sesuo and nouns in -e behave as if the nominative were -eris. The GS is -ers, as is that of **moteris**, *woman*.

4.6 USE OF CASES

4.6.1 *The Genitive* may be used as the object of negative verbs, and instead of adjectives, e.g. **sodžiaus menas**, *rural art*.

4.6.2 *The Dative* expresses the object or predicate with the infinitive, and the logical subject of impersonal expressions, e.g. **jums reikia**, *you ought*. (Cf. also 8.13.2.)

4.6.3 *The Instrumental* is used as a predicate, but not usually with **būti**, *to be*, e.g. **tapo prezidentu**, *he became president*.

5 ADJECTIVES

5.1 GENERAL

5.1.1 Adjectives vary for gender, number and case, and agree with the nouns they qualify. They precede the nouns. Feminine adjectives may express the neuter, e.g. **galima** (*it is*) *possible*.

5.1.2 All adjectives have both short (indefinite) forms, and long (definite) ones, e.g. **raudonas kryžius**, *a red cross*; **Raudonasis kryžius**, *Red Cross* (cf. 5.2.5). They are entered in the dictionary under the short form.

5.2 ENDINGS

5.2.1 *Short forms*

There are three types:

   M **-as**, F **-a**; **-is**, **-ė**; **-us**, **-i**

They are declined substantially like M or F nouns (4.3) **-i** being treated as if it were **-*ia**. There are the following differences in the masculine:

	S		P	
D	-am; -*iam; -*iam	N	-i from -as	
I	-*iu from -us	D	-iems; -*iams; -iems	
L	-ame; -*iame; -*iame			

Note that many of the M endings are ambiguous: e.g. -iam may come from -ias, -is or -us.

5.2.2 Endings in -i- followed by another vowel cause palatalisation (2.5), e.g. didis GS didžio, except -iems.

The endings -i and -iems swallow up a preceding -i-.

5.2.3 *Long forms*

These are made by the suffixation of the pronoun jis (7.1.2) with some phonetic modification, viz.

				S		
	M	*F*	*M*	*F*	*M*	*F*
N	-asis	-oji	-ysis	-*ioji	-usis	-ioji
A	-ąjį	-ąją	-įjį	-*iąją	-ųjį	etc.
G	-ojo	-osios	-*iojo	-*iosios	-*iojo	
D	-ajam	-ajai	-*iajam	-*iajai	etc., as columns 3 & 4	
I	-uoju	-ąja	-*iuoju	-*iąja		
L	-ajam(e)	-ojoj(e)	-*iajam(e)	-*iojoj(e)		

				P		
	M	*F*	*M*	*F*	*M*	*F*
N	-ieji	-osios	-ieji	-*iosios	-ieji	-*iosios
A	-uosius	-ąsias	-*iuosius	-*iąsias	etc., as columns 3 & 4	
G	-ųjų	-ųjų	etc., after the pattern			
D	-iesiems	-osioms	of columns 1 & 2			
I	-aisiais	-osiomis				
L	-osiuose	-osiose				

5.2.4 Many of the forms are equally consistent with short NM in -ias, -ys, or -us; -ieji and -iesiems with -as also.

5.2.5 *Use of forms*

Short forms are used as predicates, both short and long forms as attributes. In theory short forms are used where a definite object is not indicated, but which these cases are is not so easy to determine. The presence or absence of *the* in the corresponding English phrase is not critical, e.g. **Valstybinė pedagoginės literatūros leidykla**, *State Press for Pedagogical Literature* (short); **tikriniai daiktavardžiai**, *proper names* (short); **kietieji ir minkštieji priebalsiai**, *hard and soft consonants* (long); **didžioji raidė**, *capital letter* (long). The last example is disconcerting, but understandable, since every letter exists in one of two forms, the large one and the small one. Equally, the hard and soft consonants are completely enumerable. I cannot explain the first example.

When two adjectives jointly qualify the same noun, only one has the long form, e.g. **Būtasis dažninis laikas**, *past iterative tense*.

5.3 COMPARISON

The comparative ends in **-esnis**, the superlative in -iausias. Feminine and long forms are formed regularly.

6 NUMERALS

6.1 CARDINAL

6.1.1

1 vienas	11 vienuolika	21 dvidešimt vienas
2 du	12 dvylika	30 trisdešimt/
3 trys	13 trylika	trys dešimtys
4 keturi	14 keturiolika	40–90 keturiasdešimt/
5 penki	15 penkiolika	keturios dešimtys, etc.
6 šeši	16 šešiolika	100 šimtas
7 septyni	17 septyniolika	200 du šimtai
8 aštuoni	18 aštuoniolika	1000 tūkstantis
9 devyni	19 devyniolika	2000 du tūkstančiai
10 dešimt(is)	20 dvidešimt/	
	dvi dešimtys	

6.1.2 **vienas–devyni** are adjectives, declined, except for **du** and **trys**, in the usual way, e.g. **vienas, viena**; **keturi, keturios**, etc. (as if from adjectives in **-us**). **du** and **trys** have the following forms:

	M	F	M	F
N	du	dvi	trys	
A	du	dvi	tris	
G		dviejų	trijų	
D		dviem	trims	
I		dviem	trimis	
L	dviejuose	dviejose	trijuose	trijose

vienuolika and the like are declined like singular nouns.

dešimtis, šimtas, and **tūkstantis** are nouns, **dešimtis** being feminine, **šimtas** and **tūkstantis** masculine.

Every part of a compound cardinal numeral is declined.

6.1.3 The numerals **vienas–devyni** and compound numerals of which they form the last element are construed as adjectives, the noun having its appropriate case, e.g. **per dvi dienas**, *in two days*. The remainder, being nouns, are followed by the GP, e.g. **keturiasdešimt metų**, *40 years*.

6.2 ORDINAL

6.2.1 *Short forms*

1 pirmas	11 vienuoliktas	
2 antras	19 deviniolyktas	
3 trečias	20 dvidešimtas	
4 ketvirtas	21 dvidešimt pirmas	
5 penktas	30, etc. trisdešimtas, etc.	
6 šeštas	100 šimtas	
7 septintas	200 du šimtas	
8 aštuntas	1000 tūkstantas	
9 devintas		
10 dešimtas		

6.2.2 *Long forms* are formed in the usual way, e.g. **antrasis leidimas,** *(the) second edition.*

6.2.3 In compound numerals only the last element has the form of an ordinal.

6.3 FIGURES

Plain figures may represent either cardinals or ordinals, but to avoid confusion the endings are often added in case of ordinals, e.g. **40 metų,** 40 *years*; **2 dieną,** *on the 2nd day*; **XX suvažiavimo,** *of the 20th Congress* (roman figures are usually ordinal); **XII-jo suvažiavimo,** *of the 12th Congress*; **į 1980-tuosius,** *into the 1980's* (ordinal).

6.4 DATES

6.4.1 The months are:

> **sausis, vasaris, kovas, balandis, gegužė (-zis), birželis,**
> **liepa, rugpiūtis, rugsėjis, spalis, lapkritis, gruodis**

All except **gegužė** and **liepa** are masculine.

6.4.2

> *1 May* is translated **Gegužės Pirmoji**
> *On 2 October 1954*: **tūkstantis devyni šimtai penkiasdešimt ketvirtų metų** (genitive) **spalio mėnesio** (genitive) **antrą dieną** (accusative); in figures: **1954 m. spalio (men.) 2 (d.)**
> **1848 m.** is read **tūkstantis aštuoni šimtai keturiasdešimt aštuntieji metai**
> *in 1848, in 1940–41*: **1848 metais, 1940–41 metais; . . . aštuntais (keturiasdešimtais–keturiasdešimt pirmais).** (**Metai** and its oblique cases, being already plural, can mean either *year* or *years*.)
> Note the nominatives in **1941 m. birželis–1943 m. gruodis,** *June 1941–December 1943.*
> **1918–1919 m(etų) revolucija (. . . aštuonioliktų . . . devynioliktų).** See also 6.3.

7 PRONOUNS

7.1/7.2 DEMONSTRATIVE, INTERROGATIVE, RELATIVE, ETC.

7.1.1 Many of these are declined like adjectives, mostly that is like M and F nouns. The following have some special forms.

7.1.2 **Šis, ši,** *this*; **jis, ji,** *that, he, she, it*; **tas, ta,** *that.*

> *ISM*   **šiuo, juo, tuo**
> *NPM*   **šie, jie, tie**
> *APM*   **šiuos, juos, tuos**

Jis loses **i** before **a, o, u**; **ji** frequently means *it*, without particular reference. **Šitas,** *this*, is a compound of **tas.**

7.1.3 **Kas** (*who? what? who*) has SM forms only, with IS **kuo.** Despite this it is construed as feminine when it means *what*, e.g. **kas žinotina,** *what ought to be known.* **Niekas** (*nobody, nothing*) has IS **nieku,** GP **nieku. Koks, toks, visoks,** F **kokia,** etc. behave as if they were **kokis** (5.2.1), etc.

7.1.4 **Pats,** *self, same,* F **pati** has a mixture of forms in the masculine singular, viz.

> *N* pats   *D* **pačiam**
> *A* patį   *I* **pačiu**
> *G* paties   *L* **pačiame**

The plural is regular except for NM **patys**. With the feminine cf. 4.3.3 (**pati**).

7.2 RELATIVE AND INTERROGATIVE
See 7.1.3.

7.3 PERSONAL

		S		P	
	1	2	1	2
N	aš	tu	mes	jūs
A	mane	tave	mus	jus
G	manęs	tavęs	mūsų	jūsų
D	man	tau	mums	jums
I	manimi	tavimi	mumis	jumis
L	manyje	tavyje	mumyse	jumyse

Save, *my-, your-, himself, etc.* is declined like **tave**. For the third person see 7.1.2.

8 VERBS

8.1 STRUCTURE
    8.1.1 The verb having for the most part distinct forms for different persons can stand without subject pronouns, e.g. (**aš**) **prisiekiu**, *I swear.*
    8.1.2 Verbs with prefixes are all perfective. (See General note on the Slavonic languages). Both forms are usually entered, under the infinitive, in the dictionary, but the prefixes **pa-** and **su-** have frequently so little meaning that the verb has to be sought under the uncompounded, imperfective, form.

8.2 PRESENT
    8.2.1 *Endings*

        I   -(*i)u, -i, -(*i)a; -(*i)ame, -(*i)ate, -(*i)a
        II   -ju, -ji, -ja; -jame, -jate, -ja
        III -*iu, -i, -i; -ime, -ite, -i
        IV -au, -ai, -o; -ome, -ote, -o

    8.2.2 *Relation of present stem to infinitive*

        I   (1) Add **-ti** to obtain infinitive. The following changes may also occur in the infinitive singly or in combination:
           (a) Change of vowel: (i)e to i; uo to u; lengthening, shortening
           (b) Change of consonant: t(č), d(dž) to s
           (c) Removal of consonants d, m, st, t, v
           (d) Disappearance of **n** or replacement by 'nasal' vowel

    Examples: **béga**: **bégti**; **deda**: **déti**; **verda**: **virti** (a, c); **kyla**: **kilti** (a); **veda**: **vesti**; **leidžia**: **leisti** (b); **siunčia**: **siųsti** (b, d); **virsta**: **virsti**; **trūksta**: **trūkti** (c); **tinka**: **tikti** (d).
    Somewhat unusual is **reiškia**: **reikšti**.

        (2) Add **-éti**, or **-oti**, e.g. **dera**: **deréti**; **gieda**: **giedoti**

II   Add -ti, e.g. lyja: lyti
III   Add -ėti, e.g. tyli: tylėti
IV   Add -yti, or occasionally -oti, e.g. rašo: rašyti, bijo: bijoti

Note that set IV is shared with the past definite (8.4), but the relation to the infinitive is different.

8.3 IMPERFECT

8.3.1 *Endings*

-davau, -davai, -davo; -davome, -davote, -davo

8.3.2 *Relation to infinitive*
Add -ti to stem.

8.4 PAST DEFINITE

8.4.1 *Endings*

I   -au, -ai, -o; -ome, -ote, -o
II   -jau, etc.
III   -(*i)au, -ei, -ė, -ėme, -ėte, -ė

8.4.2 *Relation to infinitive*

I   Add -ti to stem

The following changes occur in the infinitive singly or in combination:
  (a) Change of vowel ⎫
  (b) Lengthening of vowel ⎬ usually combined with change (d)
  (c) Change of consonant: t, d to s
  (d) Omission of v (combined with changes a or b)
  (e) Replacement of n by 'nasal' vowel
Examples: keliavo: keliauti; redagavo: redaguoti (a, d); kliuvo: kliūti (b, d); virto: virsti (c); lindo: ljsti (c, e).

II   Add -ti to stem; lengthening of i to y

Examples: bijojau: bijoti; dalijo: dalyti:

III   Add -ti or -yti to stem

The following changes occur in the infinitive:
  (a) Shortening of vowel
  (b) Change of d, t (dž, č) to s
Examples: gynė: ginti; jautė: jausti; darė: daryti. Note davė: duoti; krovė and the like: krauti.

8.5 FUTURE

8.5.1 *Endings*

-siu, -si, -s; -sime, site, -s

By assimilation -ss- and -zs- change to -s-; -šs- and -žs- to -š-.

8.5.2 *Relation to infinitive*

Add -ti to stem, restoring any lost consonant

Examples: mokys: mokyti; mes: mesti; neš: nešti; veš: vežti.

In verbs with monosyllabic stems, the vowels i, u in the 3PS are lengthened to y, ū. Examples: lis: lyti; truks: trūkti.

8.7 SUBJUNCTIVE
8.7.1 *Endings*

-čiau, -tum, -tų; tume, -tute, -tų

8.7.2 To obtain infinitive add -ti to stem.

8.10 COMPOUND TENSES
Active participles may be used to form compound tenses with the appropriate part of **būti**, *to be*, though **yra**, *is/are*, is usually omitted. The present participle forms continuous tenses and the past participle the perfect, pluperfect and future perfect. The present participle usually has **be-** prefixed when so used, e.g. **Aš buvau beeinąs iš namų,** *I was leaving the house.*

8.11 INFINITIVE
This ends in -ti, frequently preceded by a vowel. Instructions for findings the infinitive are given under the other parts of the verb. In sense it corresponds both to the English infinitive and to the verbal noun in -*ing*.

8.12 PARTICIPLES
8.12.1 All participles follow the stem of the corresponding tense of the indicative, except the past participle passive and the passive participle of necessity, which follow the infinitive. The 3 PS or infinitive as the case may be is given in the final column.

8.12.2

	S		*P*		
	M	*F*	*M*	*F*	
Present active	-ąs/-antis	-anti	-ą	-ančios	-a, -o
	-įs/-intis	-inti	-į	-inčios	-i
Past active	-(dav)-ęs	-usi	-ę	-usios	-o, -ė
Future active	-siąs	-sianti	-sią	-siančios	-si
Present passive	-a				-a
	-i|mas	-ma	-mi	-mos	-i
	-o				-o
Past passive	-tas	-ta	-ti	-tos	-ti
Passive of necessity (8.12.2)	-tinas	-tina	-tini	-tinos	-ti

8.12.3 Participles are declined as in 5.2, the forms in -ąs, -įs, -ęs, being treated as if they were -antis, -intis, -usis, respectively, with definite forms (e.g. -antysis) based on these.

x

8.12.4 Participles are used as adjectives, in both definite and indefinite forms, often in contexts where a relative clause has to be used in English; with the force of an adverbial phrase or clause (cf. 8.13); instead of a clause after verbs saying and the like; to form compound tenses (8.10) and the passive (8.15).

Examples: **skaitoma knyga**, *a reading book*; **besimokantis jaunimas**, *young people who are studying on their own* (8.14.2, 8.23.1); **taip pasakęs senelis pranyko**, *so saying the old man vanished*; **ji sakosi daug žinanti**, *she is said to know a lot* (cf. also 1.3.1).

8.13 GERUNDS

8.13.1 *Present active:* **-dam/as, -a, -i, -os**, the 'semi-participle', corresponding to an infinitive in **-ti**, is used when both activities originate from the same subject, e.g. **Norėdama padėti ... biblioteka ... leidžia ...** , *Wishing to help ... the library ... is publishing. ...* It agrees with the subject.

8.13.2

> *Present active:* **-ant, -int** (invariable)
> *Past active:* **-(dav)us**
> *Future active:* **-siant**

These correspond in form to the active participles and are used when the subjects differ, or the adverbial expression has no definite subject, **Kalba auga ir vystosi, augant ir vystantis** (8.14) **gyvenimo poreikiams**, *Language grows and develops as the needs of life grow and develop*; **Sudarant žodyną naudotasi šiais šaltiniais**, *In the compilation of the dictionary the following sources were used.*

The logical subject of the adverbial expression is put in the dative (**poreikiams**).

8.14 REFLEXIVE

8.14.1 Some verbs have reflexive forms in addition to the active, others are much commoner in the reflexive or have no active forms. The latter may themselves be transitive, but are usually rendered by intransitive verbs, as may any reflexive verb, e.g. **prausti**, *to wash (something)*, **praustis** *to wash oneself*; **kalbėti**, *to talk*, **kalbėtis**, *to converse*; **juoktis**, *to laugh*; **pasiekti**, *to achieve*; **parodyti**, *to show*, **pasirodyti**, *to appear*.

8.14.2 The forms arise from the addition of **-si, -s** or occasionally **-is** at the end of the word, or **-si-** after the prefix if there is one. The first person in **-u** and the second person and some other endings in **-i** are slightly modified, e.g. **kalbuos(i), kalbies(i), nešdamies(i)** and in the subjunctive we have **-tumeis(i)** not **-tumsi**.

8.15 PASSIVE

8.15.1 Although an active construction may be preferred, or a verb which is passive in English may appear as a reflexive (8.14) in Lithuanian, e.g. **pasižymi pastovumu**, *it is distinguished by stability*, all the passive participles are used with the verb **būti**, *to be*, to express the passive, **yra**, *is, are*, being usually omitted, e.g. **Joje nurodyta pagrindinė literatūra**, *In it is indicated fundamental literature*; **Čia pateikiamas pirmasis tomas**, *Here is presented the first volume.* (Cf. also 1.3.1.)

8.15.2 With the participle of necessity the meaning *ought to be* is indicated, e.g. **Kas žinotina apie audinius**, *What ought to be known about textiles.*

8.17 AUXILIARIES
See 8.19.1

8.19 IRREGULARITIES

8.19.1 būti, *to be*

Present: **esu, esi, yra; esame, esate, yra**

Past: **buvau,** etc.

8.19.2 eiti, *to go*

Present: **einu,** etc.

Past: **ėjau,** etc.

8.22 NEGATIVE

All verbs may take the negative prefix **ne-**, e.g. **nesudaro,** *does not make*. Ne plus **yra** makes **nėra,** which frequently has the meaning *there is not,* followed by a genitive. The prefix may also be attached to the predicate. When emphatic it is written separately. Negatives are piled up without cancelling each other, e.g. **niekas niekada ten nebuvo,** *nobody has (n)ever (not) been there.*

8.23 PREFIXES

There are a good number of prefixes which alter the sense of the verb. The compound verbs are given in the dictionary and should give no trouble, except that verbs compounded with **pa-** and **su-,** are not entered separately but must be looked up under the simple verb when the prefix merely makes the verb perfective (8.1). The prefix **be-** is frequently attached to participles (cf. 8.12.4). It expresses duration, and **nebe-** (cf. 8.22) means *no longer.*

9 ADVERBS

9.1 FORMATION

9.1.1 The commonest ending for adverbs formed from adjectives, including participles, is -(***i)ai**, e.g. **dažnas,** *frequent,* **dažnai,** *often;* **nevykęs, nevykusiai,** *unfortunate(ly)* (**vykti,** *to succeed*).

9.1.2 Instead of adverbs prepositional phrases with adjectives or nouns may be found, e.g. **iš lėto,** *slowly;* **iš teisų,** *truly.*

9.2 COMPARISON

The comparative ends in -***iau**, e.g. **plačiau,** *more widely* (**platus,** *wide*), the superlative in -***iausiai**: **gerai,** *well,* **geriausiai,** *best,* except when the positive does not end in -**ai**, e.g. **arti, arčiausia,** *near(est).*

10 PREPOSITIONS

Different prepositions govern different cases, and **po** and **už** govern sometimes one case and sometimes another, with different meanings, viz.

> **po** with accusative, *in:* **po laukus,** *in the fields;* also **po du,** *two each*
> with genitive, *after:* **po pietų,** *after dinner*
> with dative, *to, until:* **po dešinei,** *to the right;* **po šiai dienai,** *until today*
> with instrumental, *under;* **po stalu,** *under the table*
> **už** with accusative, *for, than:* **už liaudies laimę,** *for the happiness of the people*
> with genitive: *beyond, by:* **už rankos,** *by the hand;* **už kalnelių,** *beyond the hills*

GLOSSARY

adresas, *address* (1.8.7)
apybraiža, *essay, sketch*
apsakymas, *tale*
atitrankimas, *discount*
atskiras, *single, separate*
atspaudas, *offprint* (1.5.3)
autoriaus teisė, *copyright*

biblioteka, *library*
bibliotekininkas, *librarian*
brošiūra, *pamphlet*
bukletas, *leaflet*

dalis, *part* (1.4.1)
darbai, *works, transactions*
draugija, *society*
dvisavaitinis, *fortnightly*

egzempliorius, *copy*
eileraščiai, *poetry*
eina, *comes out* (1.8.5)

faktūra, *invoice*

gimė, gimęs, *(was) born*

išaiškinimas, *commentary, explanation*
išleidėjas, *publisher*
išleidimas, *issue*
išleisti, *publish* (1.6.1)
išnaša, *note*
išsemtas, *out of print*
išsiųsti, *send, dispatch*
išspaustas rotoprintu, *lithographed*
išspaustas daugin(imo) prietaisu,
   duplicated
ištaisytas, *corrected*
įvadas, *introduction*
įžanga, *introduction*

kaina, *price* (1.8.6)
kainuoja, *costs* (1.8.6)
kalba, *speech, language*
ketvirtinis, *quarterly*
kietais viršeliais, *hardback*
knyga, *book* (1.4.1)
knygelė, *booklet*

laikraštis, *periodical*
laiškas, *letter*
lapas, *leaf,* (*plate*)
leidėjas, *publisher* (1.8.2)
leidimas, *edition* (1.5.1)
leidžia, *publishes* (1.8.2)

mainas, *exchange*
mėnesinis, per mėnesj, *monthly*
metai, *year* (1.8.4)
metinis, *annual*
metraštis, *yearbook* (1.8.2)
minkštais viršeliais, *paperback*
mirė, *died*

narys, *member* (1.8.3)
naujas, *new*
neišleistas, *unpublished*
nemokamai, *free*
novelė, *short story*
numeris, *number* (1.7.2, 1.8.4)

papildytas, *enlarged* (1.5.1)
parduodamas, *on sale*
parengimas, *preparation*
pataisytas, *corrected* (1.5.1)
pavyzdys, *sample, specimen*
perspaudinimas, *reprinting* (1.5.3)
pjesė, *play*
prakalba, pratarmė, *preface*
prenumerata, *subscription* (1.8.6)
priedas, *addition, appendix, supplement*
puslapis, *page*
pusmetis, *half-year* (1.8.6)

raštai, *works*
redagavo, *edited* (1.2.2)
redaguoja, *edits* (1.8.3)
redakcija, *editing, editorial office* (1.8.7)
redaktorius, *editor* (1,2,3, 1.8.3)
rinkinys, *collection*
rinktinis, *selected*
rodyklė, *index*
romanas, *novel*

santrauka, *summary*
sąsiuvinis, *part, fascicule* (1.7.2)

savaitė, *week*

serija, *(sub)series* (1.7.2)

siųsti, *send*

spaudė, *prints* (1.6.1)

spausdinamas, spaustuvėje, *in the press*

straipsnis, *article, essay*

subrošiūruotas, *sewn, stitched*

sudaryti, *compile* (1.2.2)

svetur, *abroad*

tas pats, *the same*

tęsinys, *continuation*

tomas, *volume* (1.4.1, 1.8.4)

tyrinėjimas, *research*

užsakymas, *order*

vertė, *he translated*

žodynas, *dictionary*

žurnalas, *journal, magazine*

GRAMMATICAL INDEX: WORDS

ant-, ap-, 2.3

apsi-, 8.14.2

aš, 7.3

at-, 2.3

atsi-, 8.14.2

be-, 8.10, 8.23

besi-, 8.14.2

būti, 8.10, 8.15.1, 8.19.1

buv-, 8.19.1

du, 6.1.2

duoti, 8.4.2

dvi, dviej-, dviem, 6.1.2

ein-, 8.19.2

ej-, 8.19.2

es-, 8.19.1

im-, in-, 2.3

yra, 8.19.1

iš-, 2.3

išsi-, 8.14.2

ji, jie, 7.1.2

jum-, 7.3

juo(s), 7.1.2

jus, jūs(-), 7.3

kas, 7.1.3

kok-, 7.1.3

krauti, 8.4.2

kuo, 7.1.3

man-, 7.3

mes, 7.3

mum-, mus, mūsų, 7.3

ne(-), 8.2.2

nebe-, 8.23

nebesi-, 8.14.2

nera, 8.22

nesi-, 8.14.2

niek-, 7.1.3

nusi-, 8.14.2

pa-, 8.23

pač-, 4.3.3, 7.1.4

parsi-, 8.14.2

pasi-, 8.14.2

pat-, 7.1.4

per-, 2.3

persi-, 8.14.2

po, 10

prasi-, 8.14.2

prieš-, 2.3

prisi-, 8.14.2

reikšti, 8.2.2

sau, 7.3

sav-, 7.3

su-, 8.23

sus-i, 8.14.2

šie, 7.1.2

ši(s), 7.1.2

šiuo(s), 7.1.2

ta, 7.1.2

tarp-, 2.3

tau, 7.3

tav-, 7.3

tie, 7.1.2

tok-, 7.1.3

trij-, trim-, tris-, trys,
  6.1.2

tu, 7.3

tuo(s), 7.1.2

už, 10

už-, 2.3

užsi-, 8.14.2

visok-, 7.1.3

GRAMMATICAL INDEX: ENDINGS

-(i)a, 4.3.3, 5.2.1, 8.2.1,
  8.12.2

-ą, 4.3.1, 4.3.3, 5.2.1,
  8.12.2

-iausia, 9.2

-sią, 8.12.2

-ja, 8.2.1

-ją, 5.2.4

-(i)ąja, 5.2.3

-ma, 8.12.2

-dama, 8.13.1

-tina, 8.12.2

-ta, 8.12.2

-e, 4.3.1, 4.3.3, 4.3.4,
  5.2.1

-ę, 4.3.3, 5.2.1, 8.12.2

FINNO-UGRIAN LANGUAGES
Estonian
Finnish
Hungarian

ESTONIAN

SPECIMEN

¹Hoopis ²raskema ³koormana ⁴lasub ⁵autoril ⁶tunne, ⁷et ⁸ta ⁹nii ¹⁰mõndagi ¹¹oleks ¹²pidanud ¹³esitama
¹⁴paremini ¹⁵ja ¹⁶et ¹⁷raamat ¹⁸vajaks ¹⁹tõlkevastete ²⁰alal ²¹veelgi ²²hoolikamat ²³ning ²⁴mitmekülgselt
²⁵täpsustatud ²⁶viimistlust. ²⁷Selle ²⁸ülesande ²⁹jõudumööda ³⁰täitmisel ³¹tulevikus ³²loodab ³³autor ³⁴ka
³⁵tarvitajaskonna ³⁶lahkele ³⁷abile.

There weighs as a much heavier burden on the author the feeling that he could have set out several things better and that in the field of translation equivalents the book would need still more careful and in many respects more meticulous polishing. In fulfilling this task to the best of his ability the author hopes also that he will have the kind help of the body of users.

References to sections

The nominative singular or infinitive is given, with a reference to the section where the ending or change of stem is dealt with.

2. **raske**: 5.3.1; 5.1.2	24. **mitmekülgne**: 9.1.1; 4.3.3(3e)
3. **koorem**: 4.4.3(3); 4.3.2(3f)	25. **täpsustama**: 8.16.2
4. **lasuma**: 8.2.1	26. **viimistlus**: 4.3.1(t)
5. **autor**: 4.4.3(9); 4.3.4(2e)	27. **see**: 7.1.1
10. **mõni**: 7.1.6.; 12.2	28. **ülesanne**: 4.3.3(3f)
11. **olla**, 12. **pidama**: 8.6; 8.10.1	30. **täitmine**: 4.4.3(9); 4.3.3(3e)
18. **vajama**: 8.6	31. **tulevik**: 4.4.3(10); 4.3.6(2f)
19. **tõlge** + **vaste**: 4.3.3(4)	32. **lootma**: 8.3.2(3)
20. **ala**: 4.4.3(9)	35. **-kond**: 4.1.3
22. **hoolikas**: 4.3.1(t); 5.3.1	36. **lahke**, 37. **abi**: 4.4.3(6); 5.1.2

0 GENERAL CHARACTERISTICS

0.1 DEGREE OF INFLEXION

Like Finnish, to which it is closely related, Estonian is a highly synthetic language, and omitting the reference to personal suffixes, of which there are none in Estonian, what is said of Finnish applies in a great measure to Estonian; but though the possibilities are much the same, Estonian borrows more freely from other languages and makes greater use of finite verbs, and thus has a somewhat less unfamiliar appearance.

0.2 ORDER OF WORDS

Qualifiers such as adjectives and genitives almost invariably precede the noun. Though the order of words in a sentence is freer, the 'natural' orders SVO and/or C far outnumber others in ordinary prose, and variants such as **sõnadel ei ole midagi ühist** (CVS) cease to be surprising if one follows the order but varies the syntax: *the words have nothing in common*. In statements of authorship and the like the name almost invariably follows the active verb as in English it does the passive.

0.4 RELATION TO OTHER LANGUAGES
Estonian is closely allied to Finnish and its wider connexions are dealt with under that language. Phonetic development has gone farther than in Finnish, making the language less uniform, e.g.

Finnish		*Estonian*	
N	*G*	*N*	*G*
kolme	kolmen	kolm	kolme
sata	sadan	sada	saja
näkö	näön	nägu	näo
silmä	silmän	silm	silma
ruotu	ruotun	rood	roodu
ruoto	ruodon	rood	roo
ruoko	ruovon	roog	roo

The Estonian series, which seems arbitrary on its own, becomes more intelligible in the light of the Finnish. Fortunately neither word **rood** is common.

0.5 STRUCTURAL PROBLEMS
Estonian grammatical forms do not always have unique endings. Thus **liimist** is analysed into **liimi**+**st**, -**st** being a relational suffix (4.4) and **liimi** the singular stem of **liim**; **loomist** may be **loomi**+**st**, **loomi** being the plural stem of **loom**, or **loomis**+**t**, being the partitive singular of **loomine** (4.3.1). **Realist** and **rist** are nominatives. In **abiks** and **oleks** the ending -**ks** is in one case a relational suffix and in the other indicates the conditional mood. Unless, therefore, one knows the language quite well, one has to be prepared for a certain amount of trial and error.

1   BIBLIOLINGUISTICS

1.1 NAMES
1.1.1   Modern Estonian names consist of Christian name and surname in that order. Earlier names, both native and foreign, may include ones in which a personal name is followed (or preceded) by an epithet, or an indication of origin, e.g. **Läti Henrik** (*Henricus de Lettis*), **Ludvig Püha**, **Thomas Aquinost**, *Thomas from Aquino*, i.e. *Aquinas*. Confusion between the two is not very likely but it is possible. The reverse order of names occurred in the earliest period, and a revival is found in the 19th-century pseudonym **Adra Mihkel** (real name **Mihkel Rein**), which is indexed under **Adra**.
1.1.2   Christian names belong largely to the common European stock, but there are some which are peculiarly Estonian, in form at any rate, e.g. **Ago, Ants, Mart, Rein**. When followed by a surname or any epithet they are invariable; it is the surname or epithet that varies, e.g. **Ludvig Pühalt, Saxo Grammaticuse**. Otherwise they take case-endings and suffixes like common nouns, e.g. **Läti Henriku kroonika**.
1.1.3   Surnames are nouns in form (even if some of them are adjectives in origin) and are declined accordingly (4.1.3), and the possible forms of Estonian names are so

varied that surnames of Scandinavian or German origin, such as Peterson or Kreutz-wald can be readily accommodated. Some have a definite pattern in a common noun, e.g. **Laas** like **laas** G **laane**, *forest*; others, especially those of foreign origin, take the reach-me-down -i in the oblique cases, e.g. **Kreutzwald|i**.

1.1.4 Some names are already genitive in form, and though they have good models in nouns ending in a vowel, they may be distinguished by the use of the apostrophe at the end of the genitive and before suffixes. Without the apostrophe one would assign these forms to the original. Thus **Silla'** comes from **Silla**, but **Silla** as a genitive comes from **Sild**. If the name is well known, the apostrophe is dispensed with, e.g. **A.H. Tammsaarest**.

1.1.5 In documents, where it is essential to establish the basic form of the name, the normal declension of the corresponding common noun may be ignored, and a name like **Loog** will have G and P **Loog'i**, though the common noun **loog** has **loo** and **loogu**. The same holds for less common names in any circumstances, if the noun is subject to change of grade (2.5.1). Note also the use of the apostrophe in **Jüris'e**; from **Jüris**; **Jürise** would come from **Jürine**, a common adjectival type.

1.1.6 Russian names follow the pattern of Estonian declensions, but the vowel of the genitive is invariably -i. Other foreign names, including Estonian names still felt to be foreign, almost all take -i if they end in a consonant sound and usually have an apostrophe, e.g. **Balzac'i, Buschmann'i, Marxi, Hone'i, Jacques'i** (but **Jamesi**), **Morris'e Berteliuse**. Those which end in a vowel sound, whatever their spelling, add an apostrophe in the genitive and append suffixes direct to the nominative, separated by an apostrophe, e.g. **Duclos** G **Duclos'** P **Duclos'd**.

1.1.7 Only the last part of a hyphenated name takes endings, e.g. **E. Peterson-Särgavale**, *to E. Peterson-Särgava*.

1.2 NAMES OF AUTHORS, EDITORS, ETC.

1.2.1 The names of authors are often placed at the head of the title-page in the nominative.

1.2.2 Equally common, if not more so, is the use of an active participle to denote the activity involved, followed by the name in the nominative, e.g. **toimetanud E. Sõgel** (*edited*); **koostanud G. Laugaste ja M. Teder** (*composed*); **Soome keeltest tõlkinud Helmi Eller** (*translated*). The participle is invariable.

1.2.3 Instead of a participle a noun may be used, such as **toimetaja** (*editor*), **toimetus-kolleegium** or **autorite kollektiv, redaktsiooni kolleegium** (*editorial board*). Once again the name is in the nominative. If there is more than one editor a word like **toimetaja** will have a final **-d**, which needs watching if one is abbreviating titles. Except on the title-page **toimetaja** should be regarded with caution: it may amount to little more than *imprimatur*.

1.2.4 Some constructions may involve names in the genitive, either dependent on a noun, as in **Dr. Jakob Hurda ja teiste kogudest**, *from the collections of Dr Jakob Hurt and others*, or before a postposition, e.g. **prantsuskeelne ülevaade on kokku seatud N. Buschmann'i poolt**, *the French synopsis has been composed by N. Buschmann*. It is more common when works are cited, e.g. **1940 aastal hakkas ilmuma H. Seppiku—V. Vihervälja «Eesti-inglise sõnaraamat»**, *in 1940 there began to appear H. Seppik and V. Vihervali's E.i.s.*

1.2.5 Other cases of nouns probably point to something other than a statement of authorship, e.g. **Valimik Kr. J. Petersonist tänapäevani**, *Anthology from K. J. Peterson to the present day*.

1.2.6 The indication of corporate authors is essentially the same as that of individuals, though some different suffixes may be involved, e.g. **kokku võetud Posti peavalitsuses**, *compiled at the G.P.O.* (**Posti peavalitsus**) (4.4.3).

The names of departments, branches, etc., usually follow that of the main body, which is in the genitive and needs to be turned into the nominative when separate, e.g. **Riigi Raudteevalitsuse statistika büroo** (*Bureau of Statistics of the State Railway Executive*)> ESTONIA. **Riigi Raudteevalitsus. Statistika Büroo**. Naturally, not every genitive denotes a superior body: **statistika** for instance is descriptive.

1.3 TITLES

1.3.1 Most Estonian titles consist of nouns and adjectives in various relations, e.g. **Eesti linnade sissetulekud ja väljeminekud 1922 a.**, *The revenue and expenditure of Estonian towns in 1922*; **Sõnalõpulise ülipika konsonandi märkimise kujunemisest eesti kirjakeeles**, *On the development of the marking of a word-final extra-long consonant in literary Estonian*. The characteristic feature is the use of suffixes rather than prepositions to specify the relations between nouns. Belles-lettres and intimate literature produce more varied forms of title, e.g. **Kas mäletad, mu arm?**, *Do you remember, my love?*; **Tulin kodumaalt**, *I come from the homeland*; **Inimesed olge valvsad!**, *Men, be vigilant!*

1.3.2 Title entries of the Anglo-American type should present no difficulty. There are no articles to be ignored. The application of British Museum rules runs up against the fact that the first noun will quite often be in the genitive and will need to be put into the nominative as a heading. When translating proper nouns and adjectives one should note that **eesti**, though originally the genitive of **Eesti**, *Estonia*, is now an indeclinable adjective. As title-pages will rarely show whether or not it is spelt with an initial capital, one must go by the context in translating.

1.3.3 When a title forms part of sentence the principal word and any adjectives that agree with it may be grammatically affected, e.g. **Minu «Tabamata imes»**, *in my 'Tabamata ime'*. When the title is short, this can be disconcerting, as when **Meri** (*The sea*) appears as **Meres** (in '*The sea*'; '*In the Sea*'?). This can be avoided by inserting some such word as **raamat** (*book*), **teos** (*work*), **draama, poeem**, which takes the ending. The title is then unaffected, e.g. **poeemis «Meri», draamas «Tabamata ime»**.

1.4 VOLUMES AND PARTS

1.4.1 The usual words are **köide** and **osa** respectively, not that the latter occurs very often; **anne** can mean either; **jagu** is sometimes found for *part*; **vihk** or **vihik** (see also 1.7) strictly means a fascicule of a work issued in parts but a 300-page book may be numbered **II köide, I. vihk**. In a good many instances a book has numeration only, without any word for volume or part. More specialised words like **kogu**, *collection* may be substituted in appropriate cases.

1.4.2 Numeration is given in ordinal numbers, the number preceding the word for volume or part.

1.4.3 Occasionally the numeration may be grammatically connected to part of the title, e.g. **Eesti kirjandusloo II**, i.e. **Eesti kirjanduslugu**, vol. 2.

1.4.4 Many-volumed works may have a second title-page on which the total number is stated, e.g. **Eesti kirjanduse ajalugu. Viies köites**, *History of Estonian literature. In five volumes*.

1.5 EDITIONS

1.5.1 The equivalent of edition is **väljaanne**, but **trükk** (*printing*) is found in much the same sense.

1.5.2 The number of the edition, in words or figures, precedes, and may be accompanied or replaced by a past participle indicating some form of revision, e.g. **ümbertöötatud, lühendatud en täiendatud väljaanne** (*re-worked, shortened and made more complete*); **viies, parandatud trükk** (*improved*).

1.5.3 The word **äratrükk** usually means *offprint*, *reprint* being **uustrükk**. Väljaanne literally means *giving out* and can mean publication (1.6.1).

1.6 IMPRINTS

1.6.1 The publisher usually appears in the nominative, but occasionally, in a colophon at any rate, the name may be followed by some such word as **toimetusel**, *by publication* (of) and will accordingly be in the genitive, e.g. **Keele ja Kirjanduse Instituudi toimetusel**, published by **Keele ja Kirjanduse Instituut**. (Toimetus is an ambiguous word: here it must mean *publishing*, but in a phase such as **Balti Humanistliku Ühingu väljaandel ning Arvo Hormi toimetusel** it is contrasted with **väljaanne** and the phrase means *published by Balti Humanistlik Ühing and edited by Arvo Horm.*)

1.6.2 The place of publication may either be in the nominative or have the suffix -s which denotes *at* or *in*. The addition of the suffix may affect the grade of the stem consonant (2.5.1) but the two most important places in Estonia, Tartu and Tallinn, are not affected (viz. **Tartus, Tallinnas**), and imprints like **New Yorgis** may be surprising at first sight but cause no real difficulty.

1.6.3 Soviet publishing houses are by nature institutional. Until recently the principal state press in Estonia was **Eesti Riiklik Kirjastus**. (Kirjastus is a common element in such names, e.g. **Eesti Kirjanike Liidu Kirjastus**, *Press of the Estonian Authors' League.*) Nowadays state publishing has been diversified and one finds short names like **Kirjastus «Valgus», Kirjastus «Kunst», Kirjastus «Eesti raamat»** (*Light; Art; Estonian book*).

Earlier publishers and publishers of Estonian books abroad may also have arbitrary names such as **Loodus** (*Nature*). **Eesti Raamat** had already been current as the name of a press in Sweden. Personal firms are rare, even in the earlier period. (An early printer-publisher's imprint is cited in 2.7.2).

1.7 SERIES

1.7.1 Many series are academic and their names, found at the head of the title-page or on the facing page, are soberly descriptive of the several items, e.g. **Keele ja Kirjanduse Instituudi Uurimused** (*Studies of the Institute of Language and Literature*). The name of the body responsible is here part of the title, and is in the genitive. In **Meie Kirjanikke** (*Our writers*) the title is more indirect. Less frequently the title describes, more or less straightforwardly, the series as a whole, e.g. **Elav teadus**, *Living knowledge*; **Kooli kirjavara**, *School treasury*.

1.7.2 Numeration is usually by **vih(i)k** or **anne**, but **köide** and **number** (no.) are found, and as with books the number may stand alone.

1.7.3 Not every form of words that stands opposite the title-page indicates a series: one would not create one from **Ajalooline romaan** (*Historical novel*) though one probably would for **«Uue Aja» hinnata kaasanne** (*Supplement included in the price of 'Uus Aeg'*) viz. **UUS AEG. Kaasandmed.**

1.8 PERIODICALS

1.8.1 The titles of periodicals do not differ linguistically from those of books, though they may well be less precise, e.g. **Eesti Keel**, *The Estonian Language*; **Tehnika ja tootmine**, *Technology and production*; **Tulimuld: eesti kirjanduse ja kultuuri ajakiri**, *Scorched earth: journal of Estonian literature and culture.* In the context of a sentence they behave like book titles, e.g. **Tulimulla esindajad**, or **ajakirja «Tulimuld» esindajad**, *agents for (the periodical) 'Tulimuld'*.

1.8.2 Institutional periodicals usually incorporate the name of the institution first in the genitive, e.g. **Eesti NSV Teaduste Akadeemia Toimetised**, *Transactions of the Academy of Sciences of the Estonian SSR*, leaving one with the problem of deciding whether to take it as it stands, initials and all, or sort it out into **ESTONIA. Teaduste Akadeemia. Toimetised.**

1.8.3 There may be a single editor (**toimetaja**) but quite often we find a (**toimetuse**) **kolleegium** under a chief editor (**peatoimetaja**) or president (**esimees**). Occasionally mention is also made of a **vastutav väljaandja**: although the dictionary translates **väljaandja** as *editor*, the fact that he is mentioned alongside **toimetaja**, together with the usual meaning of **välja andma**—*to publish*, suggest that this is the man responsible for publication rather than the literary editor.

1.8.4 Standard numeration is by **aastakäik**, *annual run*, which is usually synonymous with **köide**, *volume*, divided by **number**. But frequently the two figures are given baldly. Publications on the borderline between periodical and series, such as **Tartu Riiklik Ülikooli Toimetised**, *Transactions of the National University of Tartu*, may be numbered by **vihik**. Occasionally one finds a supplement: **lisa**.

1.8.5 Periodicity is usually stated in terms of the number of issues in a given period, e.g. **ilmub kord kuus**, *comes out once a month*; **kord kvartalis**, *once a quarter*; **neli korda aastas**, *four times a year*; **12 numbrit aastas**, *12 numbers a year*.

1.8.6 Subscription (**tellimishind**), if stated at all, is given by the year (**aasta**) or half-year (**poolaasta, 6 kuud**), but the single number (**üksiknumber, üksiknumbri hind**) is quite often the only quotation. Alternatively, after the number of annual parts has been given, the information may continue **tellides** (8.11.2) **maksavad**, *if one subscribes they cost . . .*; or one may be quoted **ette makstes**, *by payment in advance*. The taciturnity of a good many periodicals published in Estonia about subscriptions may be due to the existence of **Eesti NSV ajalehede ja ajakirjade preiskurant**, which gives the necessary information for newspapers and periodicals under the headings **tellimise kestus**, *period of subscription*; **tellimise hind rublades**, and **üksiknumbri hind kop(ikates)**.

1.8.7 The editorial address (**toimetuse aadress**) may or may not be the same as the business (**talituse**) address; the publishing of a good many current Estonian periodicals is a state affair, and the publisher will therefore be either the regular publishing house for the type of literature in question, e.g. **kirjastus «Kunst»** for art, or the one that specialises in periodicals, **Kirjastus «Perioodika»**.

2 ALPHABET, PHONETICS, SPELLING

2.1 ALPHABET

2.1.1 The current alphabet in its complete form is as follows:

a b [c č] d e f g h i j k l m n o p [q] r s š z ž
t u v [w] õ ä ö ü [x y]

The order of the modified vowels has been subject to variation and ü ä ö õ is still found in works published in Sweden. The letters in brackets occur only in foreign names, and f š z and ž are fairly recent additions; words like **finiš**, for instance, though naturalised, are obviously borrowings. Earlier borrowings like **potas**, or **tahvel** from German **Tafel**, were more thoroughly transformed and the Greek **y** is consistently represented by **ü**, e.g. **sünonüüm**. The combinations **aa**, **ee**, etc., denote long vowels, but are alphabetised as two letters.

2.1.2 Up to the earlier years of the present century Gothic letter forms were used, as in German, and there were difference of spelling, for which see 2.7.2.

2.2 CAPITALISATION

2.2.1 In principle, proper names are spelt with initial capitals, but some types of words which are proper names in English are not so treated in Estonian. In the case of names consisting of several words some are capitalised throughout while others have a capital for the first word only.

2.2.2 With the exceptions given below all words in the following have initial capitals: personal, geographical, topographical and astronomical names, names of government departments, international organisations and other institutions, Soviet festivals and honorifics. The generic part of certain types of names is spelt with a small letter, e.g. **Must meri**, *Black Sea*; **kolhoos «Rahva Võit»**, *Rahva Võit Collective Farm*; **Kolmekümne-aastane sõda**, *Thirty Years' War*, and so are all auxiliary words in corporate names, e.g. **NSV Liidu Ministrite Nõukogu juures asuv Geodeesia ja Kartograafia Peavalitsus** (**juures**, *at*; **asuv**, *situated*; **ja**, *and*). Likewise **nimeline**, *named after*. Shortened forms of names have capitals in the same way as the full forms, e.g. **Ajaloo Keskarhiiv**.

2.2.3 Only the first word has a capital in the titles of books, articles, laws, etc., and in the names of medals and orders.

2.2.4 The following do not have capitals: names of peoples, national and local adjectives, words derived from proper names, titles such as **professor**, months, days of the week and festivals, churches, faiths and religious books. A good many national adjectives are identical with the name of the country, so that what is apparently the same word is sometimes spelt with a capital and sometimes not.

2.3 DIVISION OF WORDS

2.3.1 Rules 1, 4, 5a, 6a and 8 (p. xiii) apply.

2.3.2 A long compound may be divided elsewhere than at the point of composition, but if so, it must be at a secondary stress, e.g. **mitme|sugu-seid** but not **mitme|su-guseid**. Most Estonian words are stressed on the odd syllables.

2.3.3 An international word which has a recognisable prefix or termination may be divided at the point of composition or may follow the general rule: **pro-gramm** or **prog-ramm**; **demo-kraatia** or **demok-raatia**.

2.3.4 Clusters of vowels which are not diphthongs may be divided, but if a syllable consists of a single vowel, it must go with the preceding syllable: **sai-al** is possible but not **sai-ata**. Doubled vowels are usually simply long vowels and are not divided, but there are words like **väljaanne** which are compounds.

2.4 PUNCTUATION AND ABBREVIATIONS

2.4.1 Abbreviations regularly have a full stop, whether, like **s.o.** for **see on** (*that is*) or **lk.** for **lehekülg** (*page*), they omit the last letter, or like **nr.** for **number** they include it. One does, however, find **jne(.)** as well as **j.n.e.** for *etc.*, and abbreviations which consist of a sequence of capital letters usually have neither stop nor spacing.

2.4.2 The acronyms mentioned above attach suffixes by means of a hyphen, e.g. **Eesti NSV-s.** A hyphen also appears at the end of a word when two connected words have the same final element, e.g. **üld- ja pärisnimi** for **üldnimi ja pärisnimi** (*common noun and proper noun*); and less commonly at the beginning, e.g. **modustamusviisi kui ka -kohta** (i.e. **modustamuskohta**).

2.5 VARIATION OF CONSONANT: GRADATION AND ALTERNATIVE STEMS

2.5.1 Like Finnish, Estonian has more than one grade or strength of consonant, but phonetic development has made the Estonian picture much less clear. Where Finnish has **ruoko/ruovon** (see Finnish 2.5.1) Estonian has **roog/roo**; where Finnish has **tupa/tuvan/tupaan** Estonian has **tuba/toa/tuppa**, with upgrading to compensate for the loss of the final syllable. Though experts differ, standard Estonian grammars recognise three grades. As however the contrast is usually between the strong stem and the weak one, the alternations are set out here on two levels. Repetition of the process will produce a still higher (or lower) grade.

S	pp tt kk	p t k	mb nd ld rd	b d g
W	p t k	b d g	mm nn/n ll/l rr/r	v/- j/- j/-
S	ff hk ht s sk ss šš			
W	f h h - s s/ss š			

Not every combination of letters is capable of change, and different changes may have similar results: thus **lj, ll, mm, ng, nn** and **rj** may result from **lg, ld, mb, nk, nd** and **rg** by down-grading or they may be original; **l** and **r** after a long vowel correspond to **ld** and **rd**, after a short vowel to **lg** and **rg**. (Weak **n** is not found after a short vowel.) Change of grade may be incidental to inflexion: **usun,** *I believe,* **uskuma,** *to believe;* **kaup** P **kaubad;** but owing to phonetic attrition it is often the only sign of it: thus **tuba** means *room;* **toa,** *of the room;* **tuppa,** *into the room;* conversely **aate** is the genitive of **aade.**

2.5.2 The regular alternation of stems which is a feature of Finnish is disguised in Estonian by phonetic change, but it does occur: **-e-** is found in some forms and not in others; in a word like **käsi,** *hand,* one finds variation between **kä-** and **kät-**, and verbs with stems in **-ks-** simplify this to **-s-** in some forms. Nouns which add syllables to cases other than the nominative are dealt with as they occur. A number of nouns show alternation between **s** and various grades of **t/d**, e.g. **vars, varre, varde.**

2.6 VARIATION OF VOWEL

2.6.1 When two vowels come together, e.g. by down-grading and the loss of **b, d** or **g** (cf. 2.5.1), **i, u** and **ü** are changed to **e, o** and **ö** respectively. So **rida/rea, ladu/lao, idu/eo, lugema/loen, tuua/tooma, lüüa/lööma.** This can result in ambiguity: **loo** is nearly always the genitive of **lugu,** but there is a word **loog** whose genitive is also **loo.** Similarly **peab** comes from **pidama, seab** from **segama.**

2.6.2 A long vowel followed by another vowel, and a diphthong followed by its second member, are simplified by reduction of the double vowel, e.g. **saag:** GS (saae >) **sae; tõug:** GS (tõuu >)tõu.

2.6.3 Both **oo** and **öö** before **i** are further changed to **õ** in some forms, e.g. **lööma lõin, jooma/jõin;** **i** before **i** become **e,** e.g. **numbri/numbreid.**

2.6.4 The vowel **e** between two other vowels changes to **j,** e.g. **aeg:** GS (aea >) **aja; ej** changes to **i,** e.g. **aed:** GS (aeja >)aia. Final **i** may appear as **j** before a vowel, e.g. **kiri** GS **kirja; soe** (by 2.6.2 and 2.6.1 for sooi) GS **sooja.**

2.6.5 The vowels **e**, **i** and **u** between two consonants may disappear when a syllable is added, e.g. **number/numbri**; **sünnis/sündsa**; **soodus/soodsa**. The vowel is usually **e**.

2.7 SPELLING

2.7.1 Spelling is not altogether phonetic. Thus **g** and **k** differ in length, not quality, and there are other differences of length both of vowel and consonant, between long and extra long, which are not marked. There is a difference of quality between the **l** in **palk**, *pay* (G **palga**) and that in **palk**, *beam* (G **palgi**), and similarly with **n**, **s** and **t**. Nevertheless compared with English the spelling of Estonian is phonetic. In its broad outline modern spelling dates from the latter half of the nineteenth century. Before that **h** had been used to lengthen vowels, instead of doubling, though it was also used after vowels as a consonant, and long vowels in an open syllable were not marked; instead the consonant after a short vowel was doubled. Until the eighteenth century **x** was used for **ks**, **-t** and **-nk** for **-d** and **-ng**; **õ** is not used. The use of **w** for **v** persists until the twentieth century and a number of borrowed words retain more of their original form, e.g. words in **-ismus**, now **-ism**, **kultur** for **kultuur**, **psychologia** for **psühholoogia**. (Not that all differences are merely differences of spelling; the standardisation of the literary language is comparatively recent.) Here is a seventeeth-century example:

Lõhikenne Palwe-Ramat Ehsti Mah-Rahwa tarbix kirjotut. Tal-Linnas trükkis sedda omma warra nink kullo lebbi Christoff Brendeken 1689. Ahstal.

In modern spelling:

Lühikene palve-raamat eesti maarahva tarbeks kirjutatud. Tallinnas trükkis seda oma vara ning kulu läbi Christoff Brendeken 1689. aastal.

The changes that need most to be noticed, which have taken place within the last fifty years are:

Modern standard	**e**	**o**	**ö**	before vowel	**v**	**õõ**	**ää**
Old or variant	**i**	**u**	**ü**		**w**	**õe**	**ea**

Neumann's 1924 dictionary uses the old spelling. On the change from **i**, **u** and **ü**, cf. 2.6.1.

3 ARTICLES

There are no articles in Estonian. One must add *the* or *a* or nothing in translation according to the context. The use of different cases (4.6) may provide some guide but not an automatic one.

4 NOUNS

4.1 GENDER AND FORM

4.1.1 There is no gender, and the number of cases depends on one's point of view: traditional Estonian grammar has names for 14 cases, but ten of them are simply invariable suffixes which can be added to any noun. On the basis of the other four the nouns are arranged in seven declensions; but the same endings keep recurring, so that it is the whole behaviour of the noun, not the presence of a particular ending which defines the declension.

The paradigms are not therefore of much help to the occasional enquirer, and after a general statement of the system of declensions in 4.1.2–4.1.3, it seems better to deal directly with the endings and state under each pattern of consonants and vowels what the possibilities are. This is done for the basic cases in 4.3, the relational suffixes being dealt with in 4.4. In deciding between the various possibilities one should check for relational suffixes, and also get what help one can from the context. Thus in **Tunnus võib näidata arvu, aega, kõneviisi, kesksõna** (*A characteristic may indicate number, tense, mood, a participle*), the four nouns at the end are all in the partitive singular (4.6.3); but in a combination of nouns such as **arva, aja, kõneviisi, kesksõna näitamine** or **juuni algul**, first words will be in the genitive (*the indication of number, tense, mood, a participle; at the beginning of June*). In **üksikuid sõnu** (*single words*) the recognisable partitive plural ending **-id** of the adjective shows the noun **sõnu** to be the same, just as the **-sse** in **viiendasse käändkonda** (*to the fifth declension*) clearly shows the illative, which **-konda** does not.

4.1.2 The four forms in each number which are here counted as cases are the nominative, genitive, partitive and illative. Originally each of these would have had a characteristic termination as is still the case in Finnish, but the phonetic development of Estonian has worn these away (0.3), so that in some instances one now has only secondary differences, in others none at all, while in others again new endings have been developed by analogy.

In some nouns the original vowel is preserved in the nominative, e.g. Su **jõki** Ee **jõgi**, in others, e.g. Su **tähti** Ee **täht**, where the preceding syllable is long, it is lost. (There are words like **aasta, teine, veski** on the one hand and **toimetus** on the other; but the patterns **-CVCV, -CVVC** and **CVCC** are far commoner.) A vowel which is lost in the nominative reappears in the oblique cases but there is no knowing what it will be, e.g. **-kond** GS-**konna**; **keel-e**; **kool-i**; **lind, linnu**.

4.1.3 The general pattern is as follows. (Nouns ending in a consonant and nouns ending in a vowel are treated separately in the singular for ease in stating the facts, but they follow the same basic pattern.)

Singular

N vowel

G may be the same, or may add **-da** or **-me**; the stem consonant may be downgraded* or, less frequently, upgraded*; **-i** frequently changes to **-e**; **-n-** may become **-s-**

P may be the same or may add **-d** or **-t** (occasionally **-dat**)

I may be the same or may double the stem consonant; or may add **-sse** or **-ha/-he/-hu**

N consonant

G adds a vowel or removes **-s**; the stem-consonant may remain the same but is frequently downgraded, less frequently upgraded; **-s-** may become **-n-**

P add a vowel, **-Vt** or **-t** (the last to stems in **-s** and **-r**)

I adds **-sse** to the GS; or adds a vowel, often with doubling of the stem consonant, or **-de**

---

* see 2.5.1

Plural

N adds **-d** to GS

G adds **-de** or **te**; for details see 4.3.3 (9)

P adds **-id** or **-sid** (4.3.1); adds **-i** to stems in **-s-**; or changes the vowel of the PS: **-a** to **-i** or **-u**; **-e** to **-i**; **-i** and **-u** to **-e**

I adds **-sse** to the GP. In many words **-sse** can be alternatively added to the PP, omitting **-d** and downgrading the consonant (not found with forms in **-sid**)

By way of illustration a few of the forty-three paradigms printed in Estonian grammars are given below. They cover most of the phenomena mentioned above.

S	N	aasta	ase	aade	järgmine	abi
	G	aasta	aseme	aate	järgmise	abi
	P	aastat	aset	aadet	järgmist	abi
	I	aastasse	asemesse	aatesse	järgmisesse	abisse/appi
P	N	aastad	asemed	aated	järgmised	abid
	G	aastate	asemete	aadete	järgmiste	abide
	P	aastaid	asemeid	aateid	järgmiseid	abisid/abe
	I	aastatesse/	asemetesse/	aadetesse/	järgmistesse	abidesse/
		aastaisse	asemeisse	aateisse		abesse

S	N	rikas	raamat	-kond	maa	jõgi
	G	rikka	raamatu	-konna	maa	jõe
	P	rikast	raamatut	-konda	maad	jõge
	I	rikkasse	raamatusse	-konnasse/konda	maha	jõkke
P	N	rikkad	raamatud	-konnad	maad	jõed
	G	rikaste	raamatute	-kondade	maade	jõgede
	P	rikkaid	raamatuid	-kondi	maid	jõgesid
	I	rikastesse/	raamatutesse/	-kondadesse/	maadesse/	jõgedesse
		rikkaisse	-tuisse	-konnisse	maisse	

4.3 CASE ENDINGS

For a systematic treatment of declensions, see 4.1.2–4.1.3.

Not all these endings are peculiar to nouns. The general index at the end should also be consulted.

The following abbreviations are used:

C	consonant	<	from
G	genitive	↑	of a higher grade*
I	illative	↓	of a lower grade*
N	nominative	↔	of the same grade* (2.5.1)
S	singular		(* The *apparent* grading: changes
P	partitive: plural		of grade which do not affect
V	short vowel		spelling are ignored)
VV	long vowel (e.g. **-aa-**) or diphthong		

A vertical line marks off the NS.

4.3.1   Possible consonant endings are:

b: after C or VV, NS: **halb, tiib** (not common)

d: (a) after C or VV

      NS: **põld, and, kord, keeld, mood, hoid**

      PS: **tuld** < **tuli**; **und** < **uni**; (but **lund** < **lumi**) **merd** < **meri**; **maa|d, partei|d**

    (b) after V or VV, NP: **-d** is added to the GS, e.g. **maa|d, sõna|d, rahvad** (N **-as**), **võimalused** (N **-us**), **inimesed** (N **-mene**), **nimed** (N **nimi**), **materjalid** (N **-al**), **reeglid** (N **-gel**), **lõpud** (N **lõpp**). For further details see the vowels (4.3.2)

    (c) **-(s)id**, PP: the endings are added to the GS of most nouns, to the PS of those which change their grade (2.5.1); changes as in 2.6.2 occur before **-id**, e.g. **maid, rahvaid, lauseid, nimesid, reegleid, jõgesid**

f, g, hh, k, l, m, n, p, r, s, š, ž are all possible endings for the NS, **-as** and **-us** being common; **f, hh, š,** and **ž** only in foreign borrowings

-l, -Vs and **-ks** may be relational suffixes (4.4.3 (9–11))

t: (a) after V, VV, h, r, s, t, NS

    (b) after V, r, s, PS: the **-t** is added sometimes to the NS and sometimes to the GS, e.g. **aasta|t, tegija|t, vahe|t, auto|t; rahvat** (N **-as**), **reeglit** (N **-gel**), **raamatut** (N **-mat**); **tütar|t, suur|t, teo|st, eest|ast** (N **-ane**), **loomist** (N **-ine**); also **-lt, -st**, relational suffixes (4.4.3 (12, 13))

v: NS: **arhiiv, võlv,** and many adjectives (participles) in **-av** and **-ev**

4.3.2   The vowel **a** may be the ending of a number of different cases, often with accompanying change of consonant, sometimes without. In what follows examples are given of the various possible cases for certain combinations of vowel and consonant. The nominative, if different, follows an oblique stroke, e.g. **tuha/tuhk** (i.e. GS **tuha** NS **tuhk**); precedes an upright stroke, e.g. **olev|a** (i.e. GS **oleva** NS **olev**); or has a hyphen, e.g. **jõuka-s** (i.e. GS **jõuka** NS **jõukas**).

(1) ending **-aa**: NS and GS, e.g. **maa**

(2) ending **-Va**:

    (a) NS and GS, e.g. **akadeemia** (foreign words)

    (b) GS (NS↑), e.g. **rea/rida, toa/tuba, sea/siga** (2.6.2); **roa/roog; laua/laud, aia/aed** (2.6.4); but **laia/lai**

(3) ending **-Ca**:

    (a) NS and GS, e.g. **tegija, andja, viija** and many such words; words in **-anna; summa, roosa, aasta**.

    (b) NS, GS and PS, e.g. **häda** (uncommon), **kaha, oja, küla, koma, vana, kära, pesa, lava**

    (c) NS, GS and IS, e.g. **Narva, Moskva**

    (d) NS and PS, e.g. **tuba, sõda, siga**

    (e) GS (NS↑), e.g. **kauba/kaup, nõrga nõrk, tuha/tuhk, sõja/sõda, poja/poeg** (2.6.4), **pika/pikk, õla/õlg, hinna/hind, piisa/piisk, ladva/latv, kurva/kurb**

    (f) GS (NS ↔), e.g. **sage|da, nädal|a, aus|a, olev|a, keev|a; jõuka-s, heeringa-s; padja/padi, poogna/poogen, sõbra/sõber, soodsa/soodus; üheksanda/-sas, viienda/viies**

(g) GS (NS↓), e.g. lamba/lammas, laeka/laegas, rikka/rikas, sündsa/sünnis, tõrksa/tõrges

(h) GS, PS and sometimes IS (NS ↔), e.g. king|a, sooja/soe, asja/asi, kael|a, silm|a, linn|a, mets|a, päev|a

(i) PS, and sometimes IS (NS ↔), e.g. kurb|a, leib|a, hind|a, raud|a, pikk|a, piisk|a, latv|a

(j) PS, and sometimes IS (NS↓), e.g. sõpra/sõber, patja/padi

(k) IS (-CCa, NS -Ca), e.g. majja/maja, külla/küla, ossa/osa, ritta/rida (NB)

(4) -ga, -ha, -na, -ta, may be relational suffixes (4.4.3)

4.3.3 Many different cases may end in -e, sometimes with change of consonant, sometimes without. Though -de and -te have a strong chance of being GP, the possibilities remain very varied. Possibilities for certain combinations of vowel and consonant are given below. (For the conventions see 4.3.2.)

(1) ending -ee: NS and GS, e.g. tee (*road* or *tea*), armee; and see (2)

(2) ending -Ve:

    (a) NS, e.g. kae, soe, oie, riie

    (b) GS (NS↑), e.g. poe/pood, õe/õde, sae/saag, jõe/jõgi, vee/vesi, käe/käsi, söe/süsi

(3) ending -Ce:

    (a) NS, e.g. läige, ehe, pale, -ne, mõte

    (b) NS and GS, e.g. kabe, reede, kõrge, lõhe, vale, komme, kaste

    (c) NS and PS, e.g. õde

    (d) GS (NS↑) köige/kõik, ühe/üks, lehe/leht, mehe/mees, viie/viis, jälje/jälg, rüpe/rüpp, varre/vars, vase/vask

    (e) GS (NS ↔) tuhande/tuhat, rehe/rehi, tule/tuli, keel|e, ese|me, rakme/rake, mitme/mitu, astme/aste, peen|e, lääne/lääs, tütre/tütar, -se/-ne, -us|e, teos|e

    (f) GS (NS↓), e.g. helbe/helve, ande/anne, palge/pale, läike/läige, randme/ranne, mõtte/mõte

    (g) GS and PS (NS ↔), e.g. lõhe/lõhi, nime/nimi, neem|e

    (h) PS (NS ↔), e.g. tõbe/tõbi, jõge/jõgi, sulg|e, retk|e, rüpp|e, leht|e, ühte/üks

    (i) PS and IS (NS ↔), e.g. kõik|e

    (j) IS (-CCe, NS usually -Ci), e.g. jõkke/jõgi, lumme/lumi, kätte/käsi; praegusse/-une; (-de NS -C), e.g. viide/viis, keeld|e, küünde/küüs, varde/vars

    (k) PP (NS -i, -u or -C with GS -i or -u), e.g. abe/-i, trage/-i, rahe/-u, rohte/rohu; jõud|e, saag|e, maastik|ke, tehnikum|e, seminar|e, poiss|e

(4) The GP ends in -de or -te. Removal of -de gives the PS in nouns which change their grade, the NS in nouns like tütar, the GS in all other instances, e.g.

    sõda|de, pikka|de, jõge|de (PS jõge NS jõgi); aken|de, katel|de; kõne|de, nimede (nimi), maa|de

The NS has the same consonant as the GP but may have a different vowel or none.

    Removal of -te leaves the GS or the corresponding consonant stem, or in the case of some nouns whose GS has a strong stem (2.5.1), the NS, e.g.

    aasta|te, numbrite (NS -ber), raamatute (-mat), liikmete (liige); -liste (-line), teos|te, küsimus|te; mõte|te, rikas|te

Here again the grade of the stem consonant is nearly always the same as in the N.S.

(5) **-he, -le** and **-sse** may be relational suffixes (4.4.3)

4.3.4 The ending **-i** is much less common but is likewise the ending of various cases. The possibilities for various combinations of consonant and vowel are:

(1) **-Vi**:

    (a) NS, e.g. **lai**
    (b) NS and GS, e.g. **partei, loterii, või**

(2) **-Ci**:

    (a) NS, e.g. **padi, jõgi, nimi**
    (b) NS and GS, e.g. **kummi, veski**
    (c) NS, GS and PS, e.g. **abi, südi, tragi**
    (d) GS (NS↑), e.g. **koti/kott, riigi/riik, vildi/vilt**
    (e) GS (NS ↔), e.g. **autor|i, meetri** (NS -ter), **peats|i**
    (f) GS and PS (NS ↔), e.g. **praktikum|i, seminar|i, kultuur|i, pärl|i, vorm|i**
    (g) PS (NS ↔), e.g. **kott|i**
    (h) PS and IS (NS ↔), e.g. **pood|i, riik|i**
    (i) IS (-CCi, NS -Ci), e.g. **appi/abi, kivvi/kivi**
    (j) PP (NS -a, -si, or -C with PS in -a or -e), e.g. **pesi/pesa, käsi, -us|i, mehi/mees, sepp|i, vars|i, poeg|i, viis|i, teisi/teine**

4.3.5 The vowel **-o** is rare as an ending. It occurs long as **-oo**, in various foreign words and as a result of changing **-u** (2.6.1):

(1) **-Vo**:

    (a) NS, e.g. **soo, depoo, kakao**
    (b) GS (NS in -bu, -du, -gu), e.g. **kao/kadu, leo/ligu, teo/tegu, loo/lugu**
    (c) GS (NS in -g), e.g. **roo/roog**

(2) **-Co**:

    (a) NS, GS and PS, e.g. **kino, takso**
    (b) IS (-CCo, NS -Co), e.g. **kinno**

4.3.6 The ending **-u**, like **-i** and **-a**, is moderately common and can represent any of five cases, usually with differences of consonant. The possibilities are:

(1) **-Vu**:

    (a) NS, e.g. **õu** (GS **õue**)
    (b) NS and GS, e.g. **kuu, puu**
    (c) NS, GS and PS, e.g. **au, nõu**
    (d) GS (NS ↔), e.g. **jõu/jõud**

(2) **-Cu**:

    (a) NS and GS, e.g. words in -tu and -matu (13.2), e.g. **õnnetu, parandamatu**
    (b) NS, GS and PS, e.g. **lõbu, kodu, rahu, himu, hapu, kasu**
    (c) NS, GS and IS, e.g. **kalju, Tartu**
    (d) NS and PS, e.g. **kubu, kadu, ligu**

(e) GS (NS↑), e.g. **vihu/vihk, ohu/oht, saju/sadu, luku/lukk, oru/org, põllu/põld, võrgu/võrk, sälju/sälg, niidu/niit**

(f) GS (NS ↔), e.g. **maastik|u, raamat|u**

(g) PS, and often IS (NS ↔), e.g. **põld|u, org|u, vihk|u, lukk|u, jõud|u**; but **maastik|ku**

(h) IS (-CCu, NS -Cu), e.g. **tujju, torru, ellu**

(i) PP (NS -a, or -C with PS -a), e.g. **vabu, ridu, vigu, kalu, kavu** (NS **vaba**, etc.); **hind|u, jalg|u, patju/padi, sõpru/sõber; leib|u, lõõg|u**

4.4 RELATIONAL SUFFIXES

4.4.1 Many of the relations expressed in English by prepositions and in some languages by case-endings are expressed in Estonian by invariable suffixes added to the singular and plural stems of all nouns alike. In practice this means that they are added to the GS and the GP. Alternatively some of them may be added to the stem of the PP of those nouns which have PP in -id or a vowel: if the PP ends in -si the suffixes are simply added, if it ends in -d the -d is removed and the suffixes added; otherwise it may be simply added, but in nouns that change their grade the stem consonant is down-graded (cf. -**konnisse** from -**kond** in the paradigms in 4.1.3).

4.4.2 The stem consonant is the same whatever the suffix, e.g. **lõpuks, lõpuna** (contrast Su **lopuksi, loppuna**).

4.4.3 The forms and basic meanings are as follows. (The suffixes are arranged in order of the last letter.)

(1) -**ga**, *with*
(2) -**ha**, illative case (4.6.4)
(3) -**na**, *as*
(4) -**ta**, *without*
(5) -**de**, -**he**, illative case (4.6.4)
(6) -**le**, *on, to*
(7) -**sse**, illative case (4.6.4)
(8) -**ni**, *up to*
(9) -**l**, *on, at*
(10) -**s**, *in*
(11) -**ks**, (predicate), *as, for*
(12) -**lt**, *off, from*
(13) -**st**, *out of, from, about; than*
(14) -**hu**, illative case (4.6.4)

4.4.4 As with prepositions in other languages the range of meaning of some of these suffixes is wide and calls for further comment.

(2) (5) (14) are used only with a few monosyllables, e.g. **maha, pähe, sohu, suhu** from **maa, pea** (N.B.), **soo, suu**.

(3) will nearly always be translated *as*, e.g. **iseseisva ainena õpitakse**, *is taught as an independent subject*; but *in the form of* or *for* may sometimes be better.

(6) is used with verbs, nouns, adjectives and adverbs. Its official name 'allative' implies motion towards, but it is used in a variety of analogous senses for which the term 'dative' would be as appropriate. The translation *to* is usually satisfactory, e.g. **kõige selgem vastus küsimusele**, *the clearest answer to the question*, but sometimes *for* or *on* or nothing, as with the verb **järgnema**, *to follow*, may be better. A good many postpositions (10.1.2) end in -**le**, and so do adverbs (9.1.1).

(9) indicates primarily rest upon or proximity (*on*, *at*, *by*) and analogous meanings, means (*by*, *with*), time at which, e.g. **sõna algul**, *at the beginning of a word*; **keele abil**, *with the help of language*; **praegusel ajal**, *at the present time*; **keelelise materjali alusel**, *on the basis of linguistic material*; with the verb **olla**, *to be*, it means *to have*, e.g. **on meil**, *we have*. There are also postpositions (10.1.2) and adverbs (9.1.1).

(10) indicates the place in which something is or with which it is intimately connected (*in*, *on*, *at*), but like *in* is extended to non-spatial relations; time within which; and is used with the infinitive to denote simultaneity or means (*while*, *on*, *by* doing); e.g. **sõna lõpus**, *at the end of a word*; **eesti keeles**, *in the Estonian language*; **neli korda aastas**, *four times a year*; **silmas pidades**, *keeping in view*.

(11) is the commonest ending of the predicate, e.g. **ta oli abiks**, *it was a help*; **Arve liigi tatakse kahte rühma: põhiarvudeks ja järgarvudeks**, *Numbers are classified into two groups: cardinals and ordinals*. Like its Finnish counterpart, it can indicate change of state, e.g. **sõnade lauseteks ühendamine**, *the combining of words to form sentences*; and it has other uses not easily classified, like **kolmeks aastaks valitud**, *elected for three years*; **valmivat 1. aprilliks**, *will be ready by the 1st of April*. There are also postpositions in **-ks** (10.1.2).

(12) literally indicates motion away from, e.g. **turult**, *from the market*, but the local sense is much less common than its adverbial uses, e.g. **nimeliselt**, *by name*; **nimelt**, *namely*, **pikemalt**, *longer*, and many others (cf. 9.1.1). There are also postpositions in **-lt** (10.1.2).

(13) literally indicates motion out of. By extension it covers origin, subject matter, material and the like, and is used with comparatives, e.g. **on nendest sõnadest tuletatud**, *is derived from these words*; **küsimus keele olemust**, *the question of the essence of language*; **terasest hapram**, *more brittle than steel*. There are also postpositions in **-st** (10.1.2).

4.6 USE OF CASES

4.6.1 The nominative is used as total subject (4.6.5) or as predicate and in the plural as total object (4.6.5). With the impersonal or passive (8.16.1) it is used as total object or subject according to one's viewpoint.

4.6.2 The genitive is used:

(1) to qualify what follows, being usually translated by a phrase with *of* or some other preposition, e.g. **eesti keele grammatika**, *grammar of the Estonian language*; **konstitutsiooni väljatöötamine**, *working out of the constitution*;

(2) in the singular as total object (4.6.5), e.g. **annab ülevaate**, *gives a survey*;

(3) with postpositions and prepositions (10.2.1), e.g. **N. Buschmann'i poolt**, *by N. Buschmann*.

4.6.3 The partitive is used:

(1) to indicate some or part of a large group or whole, e.g. **Erandjuhtumeid**, *Exceptions* (used as a heading); **mälestusi**, *reminiscences*. Hence the partitive (singular) is used after numerals other than 1 (6.1.3);

(2) as partial subject (4.6.5), with verbs which denote existence or change of state, the verb being singular;

(3) as partial object (4.6.5);

(4) with prepositions and postpositions, e.g. **enne sõda**, *before the war* (10.2.2).

4.6.4 The illative corresponds roughly to the English prepositions *into* and *to*, e.g. **tõlgitud eesti keelde**, *translated into Estonian*; **sisendab lugejasse**, *suggests to the reader*.

4.6.5 A subject, object or complement is partial:

(1) if it is part of a larger whole;

(2) if it only partially participates in the action of the verb:

    (a) because of the nature of the verb;

    (b) because of the circumstances;

    (c) because the action is incomplete;

    (d) because the action is negated.

Otherwise it is total.

Examples: **Lehti langeb puudelt**, *Leaves are falling from the trees* (1); **on tähtsamaid Emajõgi ja Narva**, *among the most important are E. and N.* (1); **järgmisi alasid ja andmete allikaid silmas pidades**, *keeping in view the following branches and sources of data* (2a); **püüdis parandada sisemisi olusid**, *tried to improve the internal conditions* (2c); **ei tehta vahet**, *it makes no distinction* (2d); contrariwise: **Eesti keel on saanud avarad võimalused arenemiseks**, *The Estonian language obtained ample opportunities for development.*

5 ADJECTIVES

5.1 GENERAL

5.1.1 There being no gender, adjectives have only one set of forms, which are the same as for nouns, though some types are particularly common as adjectives. Thus nearly half the adjectives in the dictionary end in **-ne** (GS **-se**), while the negative **-tu**, the participial **-v**, and the endings **-lik** and **-Vs** account for a good many of the rest. Most of these are derivative words, e.g. **sõnaline**, *verbal*; **kujutu**, *shapeless*; **kujatav**, *pictorial*; **riiklik**, *national*; **hapukas**, *sourish*, but the last type includes basic adjectives such as **rikas**, *rich*. Another fairly common ending for simple adjectives is **-e**, mostly with GS **-eda**. But simple adjectives like **hea**, *good*; **paha** or **kuri**, *bad*; **suur**, *large*; **külm**, *cold*; **must**, *black*, rarely belong to the types that are lexically most numerous. I repeat therefore: adjectives are formally indistinguishable from nouns.

5.1.2 For the most part adjectives agree with nouns, that is they have the same case or suffix, when they are attributive. They do not take the suffixes **-ga**, **-na**, **-ta** or **-ni**, the adjectives having the bare stem, that is in practice the GS or GP, e.g. **uued sõnad**, *new words*; **abi teistest eesti–võõrkeelsetest sõnaraamatutest**, *the help of other Estonian–foreign dictionaries* (NS: **uus, teine, -keelne**); but **iseseisva ainena** (not **iseseisvana**), *as an independent subject*. There are also some adjectives, notably **eesti**, *Estonian*, and participles in **-ud**, which are invariable.

When predicative the adjective agrees in number but has whatever ending is appropriate in the context, e.g. **Silpe on kahesuguseid**, *Syllables are of two sorts* (PP); **kus see on vajalik**, *when this is necessary* (NS); **terveks saama**, *to get well* (4.4.3(11)).

5.3 COMPARISON

5.3.1

    Comparative: **-m** (GS **-ma**) added to GS of positive, e.g. **rikas, rikkam**

    Superlative: **kõige** (*of all*) + comp.; or **-m** added to PP of positive, e.g.
       rikkaim

Many adjectives, however, with GS in **-a** or **-u** have comparatives in **-em** not **-am** or **-um**, e.g. **vana, vanem, vanim**; **pikk, pikem, pikim**.

5.3.2 Some common adjectives have irregular comparatives and superlatives, e.g. **hea** (*good*), **parem** (*better*). These are given in dictionaries, but lesser irregularities such as **lühike, lühem**; **õhuke, õhem** may not be.

6 NUMERALS

6.1 CARDINALS

6.1.1

1 üks (ühe)	8 kaheksa	21 kakskümmend üks
2 kaks (kahe)	9 üheksa	30 kolmkümmend
3 kolm (kolme)	10 kümme (kümne)	100 sada (saja)
4 neli (nelja)	11 üksteist	200 kakssada
5 viis (viie)	12 kaksteist	1000 tuhat (tuhanda)
6 kuus (kuue)	19 üheksateist	2000 kaks tuhat
7 seitse (seitsme)	20 kakskümmend	

6.1.2 All numerals are declined like nouns, the genitive where different being given in the table above. All parts of a compound numeral are declined but only the last takes suffixes, e.g. 357 appears as follows:

N   **kolmsada viiskümmend seitse**
G   **kolmesaja viiekümne seitsme**
P   **kolmesada viitkümmend seitset**

and with a suffix, **kolmesaja viiekümne seitsmes**. In **üksteist(kümmend)**, however, and in the other teens the **teist** is unalterable, since it means *of the second*. The units and the words for higher units such as *thousand* are now written separately, as in the table.

6.1.3 In the nominative numerals are followed by the partitive singular and usually take a singular verb. In other cases they agree with the noun, which is usually in the singular, e.g. **Meie keeles esineb 14 käänet**, *In our language there are 14 cases*; **kahes trükis**, *in two editions*.

6.2 ORDINAL

6.2.1

1 esimene	7 seitsmes
2 teine	8 kaheksas
3 kolmas	9 üheksas
4 neljas	10 kümnes
5 viies	11 üheteistkümnes
6 kuues	12, etc. kaheteistkümnes, etc.

The remaining ordinals are formed in the same way, by adding -s to the GS of the cardinal.

In compound ordinals only the last element has the -s (see 6.4 for example).

6.2.2 Ordinals are declined like nouns, **esimene** and **teine** have GS -se, the remainder **-nda**. They agree like other adjectives.

6.3 FIGURES

Simple arabic figures represent any form of the cardinal, arabic figures with a full stop or roman figures without a stop represent any form of the ordinal. In enumeration I. = **esimeseks**. Formerly the figures might be followed by the termination, e.g. **19st** = **üheksateistkümnendast**.

6.4 DATES

6.4.1 The months are:

jaanuar, veebruar, märts, aprill, mai, juuni,
juuli, august, september, oktoober, november, detsember

6.4.2 Dates are expressed as follows:

on 10 May 1953: **kümnendal mail tuhande üheksasaja viiekümne kolmandal
aastal** (in figures: **10 V (mail) 1953 a.**)

in 1953: **1953 a.**, read as above; or **aastal 1953** read **tuhat üheksasada viiskümmend kolm**

1940. aasta revolutsioon: tuhande üheksasaja neljakümnenda, etc.

in the thirties: **kolmekümnendatel aastatel**

7 PRONOUNS

7.1 DEMONSTRATIVE, INDEFINITE

7.1.1 These follow the same pattern as nouns but their stems need watching, viz.

	see, *this*			**too**, *that*	
	S	P		S	P
N	see	need		too	nood
G	selle	nende		tolle	nonde
P	seda	neid		toda	noid
Stems	se(lle)-	nende-/nei-		to(lle)-	nonde-/noi-

The forms of **need** are shared with the pronoun **nemad** (7.3.1).

7.1.2 **See** and **need** are extensively used both as adjective and pronoun in a variety
of ways, as the following extracts from the same text show: **selle küsimuse kohta,** *about
this question*; **see elab,** *it lives*; **üks neid jõude, mis** . . ., *one of those forces which* . . .;
selle progressini, mis . . ., *to the level of progress which* . . .; **vaadeldaksa seda,** *this is
observed*; **et neid alati õigesti tarvitada, selleks on vaja** . . ., *in order to use these correctly
on all occasions, it is necessary* . . . .

7.1.3 In **seesama** (*selfsame*) both parts vary, e.g. **sellessesamasse, neidsamu,** cf.
4.2.6 (2f).

7.1.4 Many of the combinations of **se(lle)-** with suffixes have specialised adverbial
uses and are given separately in the dictionary.

7.1.5 Indefinite pronouns are formed from the interrogatives by suffixation and
reduplication, e.g. **keegi,** *somebody, anyone*; **miski,** *something*; **kumbki, embkumb,**
either. The first part or both parts vary as the case may be, e.g. **kellegi, kellestki;
millegi; kummagi; emmakumma.** (On **-ki/-gi,** see 12.2.)

7.1.6 **Kõik** (GS **kõige**), *all, every, everybody, everything* has GP **kõikide/kõigi.**

Mõni, *some, several*, is declined like **jõgi** (4.1.3), but has PS **mõnd(a)**, IS **mõnda/
mõnesse.**

7.2 RELATIVE, INTERROGATIVE

The interrogative/relative pronouns **mis** (*what, which*) and **kes** (*who, which*) behave
like **see**, except that the only forms peculiar to the plural are the GP in **-de** and forms
derived from it. Thus **keda** is PS or PP, and there is a GP **kelle** as well as **kellede**, to

which suffixes may be added, e.g. **need rahvad, kellel . . .,** *those nations to which . . . .*
There is also a shortened singular form **kel** for **kellel. Kumb (G kumma),** *which (of the
two),* is regular.

7.3 PERSONAL
7.3.1 The forms are:

	S				P		
	1	2	3	1	2	3	
N	m(in)a	s(in)a	t(em)a	me(ie)	te(ie)	n(em)ad	
G	m(in)u	s(in)u	tema	meie	teie	nende	
P	mind	sind	teda	meid	teid	neid	
Stem	m(in)u-	s(in)u-	t(em)a-	mei-	tei-	nende-/nei-	

7.3.2 The third person pronoun is indifferent to gender, meaning equally in the
singular *he, she* or *it.* The plural stem is shared with **need** (7.1.1).

7.3.3 The genitives are used as possessives, e.g. **meie sõnavara,** *our vocabulary.*

7.3.4 The reflexive pronoun by itself refers to the third person but it may be combined with others. It has the following forms:

	S	P
G	enese/enda	eneste/endi
P	ennast/end	endid

Suffixes may be added to either form of the genitive. Combined with other pronouns
it may be intensive (*I myself*) rather than reflexive. If so there is also a nominative **ise.**

8   VERBS

8.1 STRUCTURE
8.1.1 The various parts of the verb are constructed by the addition of suffixes
indicating (1) person and number; (2) mood or tense.

This simple agglutinative structure is complicated by the alteration of (1) strong and
weak stems (2.5.1); (2) stems with and stems without a vowel (2.5.2); (3) change of
vowel (2.6.1).

More than one change may occur at a time, e.g. **vaadelda, vaatlema** (1 and 2); **peab,
pidada** (1 and 3). Verbs are usually given in the dictionary under the infinitive in **-ma,**
but some dictionaries cite the IPS of the present instead. Changes of stem between
these and other parts of the verb are set out in the following sections.

8.1.2 *Personal endings*

	S	P
1	-n	-me
2	-d	-te
3	(see tenses)	

8.2 PRESENT/FUTURE
8.2.1 The endings are added directly to the vowel stem, the stem consonant remaining unchanged throughout; 3P **-b; -vad.**

8.2.2 In a large number of verbs the present and the infinitive in **-ma** have the
same stem, e.g. **kirjutan, kirjutama.** In others changes occur, viz.

(1) change of grade, e.g. **õpin, õppima**

(2) ±V, e.g. **laulan, laulma; jooksen, jooksma**

(3) both (1) and (2), e.g. **saadan, saatma; annan, andma**

(4) change of grade and vowel, e.g. **loen, lugema** (2.6)

8.2.3 In verbs which denote the completion of an action this tense is naturally future; with other verbs it indicates present action if the object is partial (partitive case) but future action if it is total (see 4.6) or there is an adverb indicating futurity.

8.3 PAST

8.3.1 The tense suffix is **-i-** or **-si-**; 3P: **-i** or **-s**; **-(s)id**.

8.3.2 The stem is the same as that of the infinitive in **-ma** but the vowel may be eliminated or reduced when the suffix is **-i-**, e.g. **tulin, tulema; sain, saama; jõin, jooma**. The forms in **-si-** are ambiguous. The **-s-** is usually part of the ending but there are verbs like **pesema** and **seisma** in which it is part of the stem. In the plain **-si** ending, however, the **-s-** is nearly always part of the stem as in **pesi** from **pesema**; those verbs which add **-si-** have **-(i)s** in the 3 PS.

8.3.3 The tense usually corresponds to the English simple past, or to the imperfect; but sometimes the perfect is a more natural translation.

8.6 CONDITIONAL

8.6.1 The modal suffix is **-ksi-**; 3P **-ks(i)**; **-ksid**.

8.6.2 The stem is the same as the present: **kirjutaksin, õpiksin, laulaksin, saadaksin, loeksin**.

8.6.3 The tense indicates an event which is hypothetical, uncertain or dependent, e.g. **kui mul aega oleks**, *if I had time*; **vaevalt oleski** (12.2) **võimalik**, *it would scarcely be possible*; **silmas pidada, et käsikiri ei ületaks ettemääratud raame**, *to take care that the manuscript should not exceed the predetermined limits*.

8.10 COMPOUND TENSES

8.10.1 The present, past and conditional of **olla**, *to be*, with the past participle active, form the perfect, pluperfect and conditional perfect respectively, e.g. **Selle küsimuse kohta on marksismi klassikud korduvalt kirjutanud**, *On this question the classics of Marxism have repeatedly written*.

8.10.2 The present of **saama** (*to become*) with the first infinitive (8.11.1) expresses the future, e.g. **saame näha**, *we shall see* (cf. 8.2.3).

8.11 VERBAL NOUNS

8.11.1 The first infinitive, the one which corresponds most closely to the English infinitive, ends in **-da, -ta, -a**, and by assimilation **-la, -na, -ra**.

-da occurs after vowels and **-l-**. As regards correspondence with the infinitive in **-ma** and the present indicative, the following types are found:

saada	**saama**	**saan**
kirjutada	**kirjutama**	**kirjutan** (the commonest type)
lugeda	**lugema**	**loen** (2.6.1)
õppida	**õppima**	**õpin** (2.5.1) include some
laulda	**laulma**	**laulan** common words
kõnelda	**kõnelema**	**kõnelen**
võrrelda (2.5.1)	**võrdlema**	**võrdlen**

The last type includes the rather disconcerting **öelda/ütlema**.

In **anda, murda, jõuda** the **-d-** belongs to the stem:

| anda | andma | annan (2.5.1) |

-ta occurs after short vowels, **-s-** and **-t-**, e.g.

hinnata (2.5.1)	hindama	hindan
hakata (2.5.1)	hakkama	hakkan
joosta	jooksma	jooksen
seista	seisma	seisan
pesta	pesema	pesen
jätta	jätma	jätan

In **saata** and a number of similar verbs the second **-t-** is lost:

| saata | saatma | saadan (2.5.1) |

-a occurs after long vowels and diphthongs, e.g.

| tuua (2.6.1) | tooma | toon |

-la, -na, -va are found with a few verbs, the commonest being **tulla, minna, panna, surra**, with corresponding forms **tulema, tulen,** etc.

teha, näha correspond to **tegema, teen** and **nägema, näen.**

This infinitive occurs most frequently after verbs, e.g. **ei tohi katsuda,** *you are not allowed to touch*; **rauda on müüa,** *iron for sale*.

8.11.2 The second infinitive substitutes **-e** for **-a**, and always takes the suffix **-s**. It functions as a gerund, e.g. **silmas pidades,** *taking into consideration*.

8.11.3 The third infinitive is the infinitive in **-ma** under which verbs are now usually listed. (If a dictionary which lists verbs under the present is used, the correspondences can be found in 8.11.1). It is used after certain verbs and with the suffixes **-ta, -s, -st**. It corresponds roughly to the English infinitive and gerund, e.g. **lähen kirjutama,** *I am going to write*; **(ilma) kirjutamata,** *without writing*.

8.11.4 The fourth infinitive, in **-mine** (GS **-mise**) instead of **-ma**, is more of a noun than a verb and is often given separately in the dictionary. It takes all the usual suffixes, e.g. **sotsialistliku tootmise tekkimisega,** *with the coming into being of socialist production*.

8.11.5 The suffix **-ja** denotes the agent. The stem is the same as that of the third infinitive except that a number of words in **-ija** correspond to infinitives in **-ema**, e.g. **kirjastaja, tootja, lugeja, tegija (tegema).**

8.12 PARTICIPLES

8.12.1 Passive participles are dealt with in 8.16.2; the active participles are:
Present: **-v** (GS **-va**)
Past: **-nud** (invariable)

8.12.2 The corresponding **-ma** infinitive is usually got by substituting **-ma** for the participle ending, but note forms like **toitev, veenev** (Gs **toitva, veenva**) from **toitma** and **veenma** (2.6.5); **tulnud** from **tulema; hinnanud** (2.5.1) from **hindama, võrrelnud** from **võrdlema**; also **näinud; teinud** from **nägema, tegema.**

8.12.3 Participles are primarily adjectival, corresponding to English participles used in this way or to relative clauses, e.g. **1945 aastal ilmunud uus väljaanne,** *the new edition which came out in 1945*.

8.12.4 The past participle is a component of compound tenses (8.10.1) and is common by itself on title-pages as a verb (1.2.2: compare what is said below about hearsay). One also finds constructions like **torm raugenud,** *the storm having abated.* The partitive singular of the participles expresses hearsay or appearance, e.g. **näib veelgi suurenaks sirguvat,** *it seems to grow still bigger*; **see valmivat 1. aprilliks,** *it will be ready by 1st April.* It is formed equally with a plural subject.

8.16   IMPERSONAL OR PASSIVE

8.16.1   The impersonal forms of the verb express an action by an unnamed agent. Sometimes they may be translated by a passive, sometimes not, but it is important to note that they can be formed from transitive and intransitive verbs alike, and there is only one form per tense. They are nowadays usually regarded as impersonal rather than passive. The noun object (if the verb is thought of as impersonal) or subject (if it is thought of as passive) is in the partitive if partial (without the restrictions which apply to the active subject), in the nominative if total (4.6.5), and pronoun objects are always partitive.

Kirjutada nii, nagu hääldatakse, *to write as one pronounces*; **rahvusele omast keelt nimetatakse rahvus-keeleks,** *the language which is peculiar to a nation is called the national language*; **anti välja M. Varese «Eesti-inglise sõnaraamat»,** *there was published M. Vares's 'Eesti-inglise sõnaraamat'*; **tiitel, sisukord, tabeliosa ja lisad on trükitud Eesti Uhistrükikojas,** *the title-page, table of contents, plates and appendices were printed at the Estonian Cooperative Press*; **käsikirja revideerimisel on saadud kasutada ...,** *in the revision of the manuscript it has been possible to use ...* (**saama,** *to be able*).

8.16.2   The characteristic of the impersonal is **-t-/-d-,** giving the following forms:

> *Present/Future:* **-takse**
> *Past:* **-ti**
> *Ọonditional:* **-taks**
> *Participles:* **-tav, -tud**
> *Infinitive:* **-tama** (no suffixes)

Some verbs have **-d-** for **-t-,** and a few have no consonant.

8.16.3   The consonant is usually the same as in the first infinitive (8.11.1), e.g. **saadakse, hinnatakse, tuuakse,** but there are some discrepancies, e.g.

> **kirjutada: kirjutatakse**
> **lugeda: loetakse**
> **pidada: peetakse**
> **oppida: õpitakse**
> **anada: antakse**
> **saata: saadetakse**
> **tuua: tuuakse** but **toodud**
> **tulla: tullakse** but **tuldud**

8.16.4   The various forms of the impersonal are used in the same way as those of the active (8.3–8.12).

8.19   IRREGULARITIES

8.19.1   **olla,** *to be,* has present **olen, oled, on; oleme, olete, on**

8.19.2   **minna,** *to go,* has some tenses from another root:

> *Present:* **lähen**
> *Past:* **läksin**
> *Past participle:* **läinud**

8.22 NEGATIVE

8.22.1 Although the negative used with the verb has only one form **ei**, it is not used in the same way as *not* but is followed by the bare stem of the required tense, except for the past, where the participle is used, viz.

	Active	Impersonal
Present	-	-ta/-da
Conditional	-ks	-taks-/daks

e.g. **ei moodusta**, *does not form* (**moodustama**); **ei saaks**, *he would not be able* (**saama**); **ei olnud võimalik**, *it was not possible*; **ei taha**, *he does not want* (**tahtuma, tahan**); **ei anta seda**, *this is not given* (**andma**); **ei ole suutnud**, *has not managed*.

8.22.2 The stem is usually the same as in the positive, but where the present impersonal and the past participle disagree (8.16.3) the negative follows the participle, e.g. **tooda**.

8.22.3 The partitive of the present participle (8.12.2) is not affected by **ei**: **ei valmivat**, *it will not be ready*.

8.23 SEPARABLE VERBS

8.23.1 Estonian distinguishes between **liittegusõnad** and **ühendtegusõnad**. This is somewhat like the distinction in other languages between inseparable and separable verbs. The former are always written as one word, e.g. **ülehindama** (*to overestimate*), **ülehindav**; the latter are usually two words, but the present participles, and the past participles when used as adjectives, are written as one, e.g. **tähelepanev, tähelepandav, tähelepandud** from **tähele panema** (present **panen tähele**). Only **tähelepandav**, has a separate entry in Silvet's *Eesti–inglise sõnaraamat*: the rest must be deduced from the verb, which is entered under **tähele**.

9 ADVERBS

9.1 FORMATION

9.1.1 Various relational suffixes (4.4) can be used to form adverbs from adjectives and nouns; but the commonest suffixes for forming adjectives of manner from adjectives are -lt and -sti, added as usual to the GS, e.g. **vastav|alt**, *corresponding|ly*, **kiire|sti**, *quick|ly*.

9.1.2 Some adverbs are simply the PS of the adjective.

9.2 COMPARISON

9.2.1 Regular comparison follows the pattern of adjectives (5.2.1), adverbs in -lt making -(i)malt, those in -sti making -(i)mini.

9.2.2 Irregular comparatives are found, e.g. **paremini**, *better* (cf. 5.2.2).

10 PREPOSITIONS AND POSTPOSITIONS

10.1 POSITION

10.1.1 Estonian has comparatively few prepositions. Instead of simple prepositions like *on, in, to*, etc., it uses suffixes (4.4). Corresponding to compound prepositions like *behind, on top of*, it has some prepositions but more postpositions, which differ only in that they follow the noun.

10.1.2 English compound prepositions are mostly formed of simple preposition and noun, with or without a connecting *of*, and *in front of the house* corresponds formally to *on the roof of the house*. The latter in Estonian is **maja katusel**, with the genitive in its normal position in front of the noun it qualifies. Similarly *in front of the house* is **maja ees**: ees is formed from **esi**, *front part*, by means of the suffix -s and being preceded by the genitive becomes a postposition.

10.2 FORMS AND SYNTAX

10.2.1 Naturally enough, postpositions with the genitive are the commonest type. They often go in sets, with different suffixes, e.g. **ette, ees, eest**, indicating motion towards, rest at and motion from respectively. In this they are like adverbs, and quite often the same word may be either.

10.2.2 Prepositions with the partitive are the next commonest type, but there are some words which may precede or follow the genitive, with slight difference in meaning, e.g. **läbi metsa**, *through the word*; **hea juhuse läbi**, *by good luck*. Others may either precede or follow the partitive, and some are used as prepositions with the partitive and postpositions with the genitive, e.g. **pärast seda**, *after this*; but

$$\overset{1}{\text{viie}}\ \overset{2}{\text{minuti}}\ \overset{3}{\text{pärast}}\ \overset{4}{\text{kuus}}, \overset{3}{\textit{after}}\ \overset{1}{\textit{five}}\ \overset{2}{\textit{minutes}}\ \overset{4}{\textit{six}}, \textit{i.e. five minutes to six.}$$

10.2.3 A few words usually classed as prepositions and postpositions are used in conjunction with relational suffixes, e.g. **ühes minuga**, *together with me*. It is more natural to think of them in such cases as adverbs.

11 CONJUNCTIONS

11.1 Conjunctions call for little comment, except those meaning *and* and *or*. Of the two words for *and*, **ja** is said to join sentences and phrases and words with different meanings, whereas **ning** joins words with the same or closely connected meanings or denoting parts of the same action, e.g. **keel ja mõtlemine**, *language and thinking*; **küsivalt ning imestunult**, *questioningly and wonderingly*. But in practice ja will sometimes be found where the rule prescribes ning, as in **kolmas ja viimane album**, which means simply *a third and last album* and not *a third and then a final album*.

Ehk joins verbal alternatives, **või** real ones.

11.2 The conjunction **et**, which like *that* is very common and enters into many compounds, such as **sest et**, *because*, is followed by the infinitive in the meaning *in order to*.

11.3 Some words are both conjunctions and adverbs.

12 PARTICLES

12.1 Estonian has a large number of words, which its grammars class as particles, such as **küll**, *indeed*, or **kas**, which introduces a question. Those which are separate words are no problem, though sometimes they combine with other words to form distinct units of meaning, e.g. **kes ka ei tuleks**, *whoever comes*.

12.2 There is one, however, viz. **-ki/-gi**, which is suffixed to words, -gi being used after vowels, **l, m, n, r, v, z** and **ž**. Sometimes it forms new words, such as **keegi**, *somebody* (7.2.2) but more often emphasises similarity or contrast. Examples will be found in 8.6.3 and 8.12.4.

Y

13 WORD-FORMATION

13.1 Though it borrows more from other languages than Finnish does, Estonian still forms a great many words from native roots by the use of recurrent suffixes and pre-fixes, e.g. **keel**, *tongue*; **keeleline**, *linguistic*. The resulting words are mostly in the dictionary and only the most prolific suffixes are given here.

13.2 SUFFIXES

> **-ja** is universal and is given under the verb (8.11.5).
>
> **-tama** often makes transitive verbs from intransitive ones, e.g. **hajuma** (intr.), **hajutama** (tr.) *to disperse*. A few forms of these -ta- verbs are ambiguous; they could equally be impersonal forms of the simple verb, viz. **hajutama** itself, **ei hajuta, hajutatud, hajutaks** and **hajutav**.
>
> **-eerima** naturalises foreign verbs, e.g. **organiseerima**.
>
> **-uma** makes intransitive, reflexive or passive verbs, e.g. **koondama** (tr.), **koonduma** (intr.), *to assemble*.
>
> **-ne, -ane, -(l)ine** makes adjectives, e.g. **tugevaastmeline** from **tugev**, *strong*, and **aste**, *grade*.
>
> **-lik** also makes adjectives, e.g. **laadivahelduslik**, *involving a qualitative change*.
>
> **-us** forms abstact nouns from adjectives and nouns of action from verbs, e.g. **korrektsus**, *correctness* from **korrektne**.
>
> **-tu** forms negative adjectives. In the form **-matu** it makes adjectives of the form *un——able* and the like from verbs, e.g. **parandamatu**, *incorrigible*.

13.3 Compounds are freely made. The great majority can be found in a dictionary of the size of Silvet, but there will always be some which have to be constructed from their elements, e.g. **lava|teekond**, *stage career*. If so, one needs to remember that the first element may be in the genitive, as in **pinnamõõtmine** from **pind**, *surface*, and **mõõtmine**, *mensuration*.

GLOSSARY

aasta, *year* (1.8.6)
aastakäik, *volume* (1.8.4)
aastane, *annual*
aastaraamat, *yearbook*
ajakiri, *periodical* (1.8.1)
ajalugu, *history*
alandus, *discount*
anne, *number* (1.7.2)
autoriõigus, *copyright*

biblioteek, *library*
brošüür, *pamphlet*

eessõna, *preface*
eksemplaar, *copy*
esindaja, *agent* (1.8.1)

faktuur, *bill, invoice*

hinnaalandus, *reduction*
hind, *price* (1.8.6)

ilma, *free*
ilmua, *to come out* (1.8.5)

järgneb, *to be continued*

kaasanne, *supplement* (1.7.3)
kiri, *letter*
kirjanik, *writer*
kirjastamisõigus, *copyright*
kirjastus, *publishing house*
kogu, *collection* (1.4.1)
kogutud, *collected*
kokku võetud, *compiled*
koostanud, *compiled* (1.2.2)
kuu, *month* (1.8.5)

käsikiri, *manuscript*
köide, *volume* (1.4.1, 1.7.2, 1.8.4)

lehekülg, *page*
liige, *member*
lisa, *appendix, supplement* (1.8.4)
lugu, *story*
luule, *poetry*
lühendatud, *shortened*

märge, *note*
müüa, *for sale*

nädal, *week*
näidend, *play*

paberköites, *paper-covered*
parandatud, *improved* (1.5.2)
pilt, *illustration, picture*
poolaasta, *half-year* (1.8.6)
proov, *sample*
prooviks, *on approval*

raamat, *book* (1.3.3)
raamatukogu, *library*
raamatukoguhoida, *librarian*
redaktsiooni kolleegium, *editorial board*
register, *index*
revideerima, *to revise*
romaan, *novel*

saatma, *to send*
sama, *same*
sari, *series*
seesama, *the same*
seletus, *commentary*
sissejuhatus, *introduction*
suri, *died*

surnud, *dead*
sõnaraamat, *dictionary*
sündinud, *born*
sündis, *was born*

tabeli, *plate*
tellemishind, *subscription* (1.8.6)
teos, *work*
toimetaja, *editor* (1.2.3, 1.8.3)
toimetanud, *edited* (1.2.2)
toimetised, *transactions*
toimetus, *editing, publication* (1.6.1)
toimetuskolleegium, *editorial board*
trükikoda, *printing shop*
trükk, *impression, edition* (1.5.1)
trükkal, trükkija, *printer*
trükkima, *to print*
tõlkinud, *translated*
täiendatud, *enlarged, completed* (1.5.2)

uus, *new*
uustrükk, *reprint* (1.5.3)

vahetus, *exchange*
valismaa, *foreign country*
valitud, *selected*
veerandaasta, *quarter*
vih(i)k, *part* (1.4.1, 1.7.2)
väljaandja, *publisher*
väljaandmata, *unpublished*
väljaanne, *edition, publication* (1.5.1, 1.6.2)

äratrükk, *offprint* (1.5.3)

üksiknumber, *single number* (1.8.6)
ülevaade, *summary*
ümbertöötatud, *revised* (1.5.2)

GRAMMATICAL INDEX: WORDS

ehk, 11.1
ei, 8.22.1
emmakumma, 7.1.5
end(a), endi(d),
  enes(t)e, enna, 7.3.4
et, 11.2

ja, 11.1

kahe, 6.1.1
ke(lle)-, 7.2
kõige, 5.3.1, 7.1.6

lähen, läinud, läksin,
8.19.2
ma, me, meid, meie, min-,
  mu, 7.3.1

need, neid, 7.1.1, 7.3.1

GRAMMATICAL INDEX: ENDINGS

FINNISH

SPECIMEN

«Aikamme kulttuuri»-kirjasarja on suunniteltu poistamaan ajankohtaisen kansantajuisen tieteellisen kirjallisuuden puutetta. Sen toimittamisesta huolehtii Suomen Kulttuurirahaston asettama, eri alojen asiantuntijoista kokoonpantu «Aikamme kulttuuri»-toimikunta. Teosten kirjoittajiksi on saatu maamme tunnetuimpia tiedemiehiä sekä näiden ohjauksen alaisina työskenteleviä nuorempia tutkijoita.

The series 'Culture of our time' is designed to remove some of the deficiencies of current popular scientific literature. The achievement of this is ensured by the 'Culture of our time' Committee, composed of experts in various fields, appointed by the Finnish Culture Fund. As authors of the works have been got some of the best known scientists of our country and younger research-workers operating under their direction.

References to sections

1. 4.5.2	17. 8.11.3	35. 4.4.3(2); from **alainen,**
6. 8.11.3	20. 4.4.3(5)	*subordinate*
11. 4.6.4(1)	26. 4.4.3(9)	36. 2.5.1; from **työskennellä**
13. 8.11.4; 4.4.3(5)	30. 5.3.1	37. 5.3.1

0 GENERAL CHARACTERISTICS

0.1 DEGREE OF INFLEXION

Finnish is a highly synthetic language: the different persons and tenses of the verb are adequately distinguished by different forms, so that subject-pronouns can be omitted, and a great many more of the relations between nouns are expressed by terminations than is possible in most European languages. Apart from this there are a greater number of verbal nouns and participles than usual, which in combination with the above-mentioned terminations and possessive suffixes express concisely a variety of circumstances which might well require a clause in other languages. Add to this a large number of compounds, and the result is that a passage of Finnish gives the impression of consisting of comparatively few very long words.

0.2 ORDER OF WORDS

The sentence order SVO may be reversed for stylistic reasons, for instance to bring a list of names to the end of the sentence, and adverbial phrases are often put at the beginning. The second sentence of the specimen illustrates this, the translation following the order and substituting passive for active. Adjectives and dependent genitives always precede the noun.

0.4 RELATION TO OTHER LANGUAGES

Finnish belongs to the Uralic family of languages and is more narrowly classed along with Estonian and Hungarian as Finno-Ugrian. Finnish and Estonian are closely related but Hungarian belongs to another sub-group: resemblances between them are of the order Su **kolmant-** Ee **kolmand-** Hu **harmad-** (*third*); Su **pää** Ee **pea** Hu **fő** (*head*).

1 BIBLIOLINGUISTICS

1.1 NAMES

1.1.1 Modern Finnish names consist of Christian name and surname, in that order. Both are nouns (even if originally adjectives) and can take all the appropriate endings, but a Christian name in combination with a surname or epithet is invariable, e.g. **Juhon,** *Juho's,* but **Juho Mäkelän,** *of Juho Mäkelä*; **Mikael Efesolaisen,** *of Michael Ephesius.* Finnish names in **-lainen,** e.g. **Jaakko Suomalainen** (or Jacobus Finno) are treated as surnames but names like **Pertteli Iivarinpoika** (Bertel Ivarsson) are indexed under the Christian names. Most Christian names now are distinctively Finnish, but names like **August** occur which add any necessary endings with the aid of the auxiliary vowel **-i-.** Names in **-a** are slightly more likely to be feminine. Earlier names which are Swedish in form may have Finnish alternatives, at any rate in reference books, e.g. **Gustaf Mauritz (Kustaa Mauri) Armfelt.**

1.1.2 Endings are added to those surnames which are Finnish in form in accordance with the rules set out under nouns, e.g. **K. N. Rauhalan,** *of K. N. Rauhala*; **T. K. Kantelen,** *of T. K. Kannel*; **Emil Aaltosen Säätiö,** *the Emil Aaltonen Foundation.* The fairly numerous names which have Swedish or other foreign forms insert **-i-** before the ending, and may make matters clearer by marking off the ending with an apostrophe or by printing it in italics.

The names of foreigners follow Finnish patterns as far as possible, many of them having the auxiliary **-i-,** e.g. **Grotiuksella, Hobbesilla, Spinozalla, Pufendorfilla, Humella,** *in Grotius,* etc.

1.1.3 Names can be used in the plural, e.g. **Pääkköset,** *the Pääkkönens,* but if two Christian names are coupled with one surname, the latter is in the singular, e.g. **maistereita Irmeli ja Matti Pääkköstä,** *not* **Pääkköseitä.**

1.2 NAMES OF AUTHORS, EDITORS, ETC.

1.2.1 The names of authors are frequently put at the head of the title-page. Being grammatically isolated they are in the nominative and need no alterations as author headings.

1.2.2 Alternatively, the particular activity—authorship, editorship—is indicated by the past participle active and the name follows in the nominative, e.g. **laatinut M. E. Koskimies** (*M. E. K. having composed*). If there are two authors the participle will be plural, e.g. **toimittaneet** (*having edited*) **V. A. M. Karikoski ja K. A. Lavonius,** so if the phrase is quoted both names must be included. In prefaces the related past tense is found, e.g. **Toimitustyön on suorittanut Greta Littonen,** *G. L. has performed the editorial work.*

1.2.3 The agent may be indicated by a noun and the name is in apposition in the nominative, e.g. **Toimittaja: Juho Mäkelä** or with greater elaboration, **Eri osastojen ja lukujen kirjoittajina ovat olleet seuraavat henkilöt,** (*As*) *writers of separate sections and chapters have been the following persons,* followed by a list of names.

1.2.4 If the activity is expressed by a noun, the author's name is in the genitive. Sometimes the noun is a common one, but more often an infinitive in **-mA** is involved, e.g. **Israel Nesseliuksen mietinnöt,** *The reflexions of Israel Nesselius;* **K. N. Rauhalan toimittama hakuteos,** which is equivalent to *the reference work edited by K. N. Rauhala;* **K. F. Mennanderin lähettämiä ja saamia kirjeitä,** i.e. *letters sent and received by K. F. Mennander.* (For the grammar of the last two see 8.11.3, for **-mA** see 2.6.)

1.2.5 Corporate bodies as authors are given in the same way as personal authors. The names of departments, branches and subordinate institutions usually follow the name of the main body, which is put in the genitive and will need to be turned into the nominative before being used as a heading, e.g. **Suomen Pankin Taloustieteellinen Tutkimuslaitos (Suomen Pankki. Taloustieteellinen Tutkimuslaitos).** Sometimes both are already in the nominative, and in any case not every sequence of genitives betokens a subordinate body, e.g. **Suomen Ammattiyhdistysten Keskusliitto,** *Central Federation of Finnish Trade-Unions.*

1.3 TITLES

1.3.1 Most titles consist of nouns and adjectives with various suffixes indicating their relations to each other, e.g. **Suomen poliittisen työväenliikkeen historia,** *History of the political labour-movement of Finland;* **Hallintokoneistomme,** *Our administrative machinery;* **Katsaus Suomen valtiollisen järjestysmuodon historialliseen kehitykseen,** *Survey of the historical development of the state organisation-form of Finland.* (Though most of the endings have been translated *of,* that in **-een,** which goes with **katsaus,** is usually translated *into.*) In **Muuttoliikkeestä ja sen syistä** (*On-the-migration-movement and its causes*) the ending **-stA,** which literally means *out of,* defines the subject-matter, as *of* once did in English.

Belles-lettres and the literature of persuasion produce grammatically more varied titles, e.g. **Mitä SAK nyt tahtoo?,** *What does SAK want now?;* **Tuleeko kolmas maailmansota?,** *Is a third world war coming?* (For **-ko** see 12.2.)

1.3.2 Title entries of the Anglo-American type should cause no difficulty, but with British Museum rules one is up against the fact that the first noun in a title is quite apt to be in the genitive (0.2), and it is a question whether one should treat **Suomen** at times as an indeclinable adjective (=*Finnish*) or meticulously translate *of Finland.*

1.3.3 When a title occurs in the body of a sentence the principal noun may be affected by the grammatical relationship, e.g. **Leviathanin esipuheessa,** *in the preface of 'Leviathan';* **Gulliverin retkissään,** *in his 'Gulliver's travels'* and even « **Hiltun ja Ragnarin** » **alkusanoista,** *from the opening lines of 'Hiltu ja Ragnar'.* But often some such word as **teos** (*work*) is inserted and the title itself is unaffected. This must be done if the principal word is not in fact in the nominative, e.g. **Tilastollisia tiedonantojasarjan julkaisussa « Suomen kansantalouden tilinpito »,** *in the publication 'Suomen kansantalouden tilinpito' of the series 'Tilastollisia tiedonantoja'.* Here tilinpito is nominative and might, though somewhat awkwardly, have taken a suffix, but tiedonantoja is already in the partitive.

1.4 VOLUMES AND PARTS

1.4.1 There seems almost to be a conspiracy of silence about the words for *volume* and *part,* except in relation to series and periodicals. More often than not the several volumes of a work bear simply the different numerals, and the same is found in bibliographies. However, diligent search will unearth instances both of **osa** (cf. 1.7.2) and **nidos**.

1.4.2 Numeration not expressed simply by a numeral takes the form of an ordinal number, e.g. **kolmas osa**, *third volume*; **II nidos**. When there are only two volumes they may be numbered **edellinen** (*former*) and **jälkimmäinen** (*latter*) **osa** respectively.

1.5 EDITIONS

1.5.1 The word for *edition*, **painos**, is connected with words for printing, and is ambiguous as between *edition* and *impression*. It is not very likely for instance that **seitsemäskolmatta painos** means *27th edition* in the full sense of the term. The number, whether in word or figure, precedes. In bibliographies such abbreviations as **2.p.** are often found.

1.5.2 Revised editions are indicated by such adjectives as **korjattu** (*amended*), **uudistettu** (*renewed*), or there may be a statement such as: **Toiseen painokseen on tehty joukko lisäyksiä**, *A number of additions have been made to the second edition*.

1.5.3 An *offprint* is **eripainos**; *reprint*, **lisäpainos**; *reprinted*, **painettu uudelleen**.

1.6 IMPRINTS

1.6.1 Usually both publisher and place are stated, in either order, the printer's imprint if any being given on the back of the title-page. Sometimes only the place is given, especially if the publisher's name occurs in the series title. The publisher's name is in the nominative and may be preceded by **kustantaja** or **jakaja**: the former ('the one who pays') indicates the publisher in the full sense, the latter ('distributor') more an agent, as in **Jakaja: Akateeminen Kirjakauppa**, *For sale at the Academic Book Shop*. The term should not be pressed too far, however, for it is found where two bodies are responsible for a series, but the mechanics of publishing are in the hands of one of them. Occasionally the publisher is in the genitive preceding **Kustantama** (cf. 1.2.4), e.g. **Amerikan Suom. Sos. Kustannusliikkeiden Liiton kustantama**. Here only **liiton** is affected by the change to the nominative (**liitto**).

1.6.2 The place may be in the nominative or have the suffix **-ssA** (*at*), e.g. **Helsinki** or **Helsingissä**. Note the phonetic change caused by the termination (2.5.1).

1.6.3 The names of publishers may be commercial or institutional, and the commercial names may be based on personal names or arbitrary ones, e.g. **Werner Söderström Osakeyhtiö** (often abbreviated **WSOY**), **Kustannusosakeyhtiö Otava**, *Great Bear Publishing Co. Ltd*; **Suomen Ammattiyhdistysten Keskusliitto (S.A.K.) r.y.**, *Federation of Finnish Trade-Unions* (**r.y.** is short for **rekisteröity yhdistys**, *registered society*); **Turun Yliopisto**, *University of Turku*.

1.7 SERIES

1.7.1 The titles of series are most often found on the page facing the title-page, but they may also occur at the head or on the back of the title-page, or on the half-title or on the cover. They may be descriptive of the series as a whole, e.g. **Suomen Lakimiesliiton Kirjasarja**, *Book-series of the Finnish Association of Lawyers*, or of the several items, e.g. **Tiedonantoja Suomen Sosiaaliministeriön Julkaisemia**, *Bulletins published by the Finnish Social Ministry*, or they may be allusive, e.g. **Aikamme Kulttuuri**, *Culture of our Time*. The bald sort of title in the first example is not uncommon, but the same sort of sequence may be a mere description, as in **Valtiotieteellisen Yhdistyksen julkaisusarja Politiikan Tutkimuksia**, *Series of publications of the Political Science Institute: Studies in Politics*, where only **Politiikan Tutkimuksia** is the title.

In the examples given above **tiedonantoja** and **tutkimuksia** are both partitive, which is usual when the title is in the plural. On the rare occasions when one meets a form such as **Lastensuojelun Keskusliiton julkaisu n:o 8** (*Publication no. 8 of L.K.*), those libraries which prefer to have all series names in the plural should use the partitive **julkaisuja**.

Institutional series almost always have the name of the institution at the beginning of the title, in the genitive. Most libraries will no doubt prefer to separate the elements, e.g. **Lastensuojelun Keskusliitto. Julkaisuja.**

1.7.2 Individual items in a series are usually described as **osa** (*part*) or **numero** (abbr. **n:o**), sometimes **nide**, but often they are simply numbered. Despite the literal meaning of **osa** it corresponds in bilingual titles to Swedish **band** and Latin **tomus**. The word **sarja** is used equally of the series as a whole (1.7.1) and of sub-series, e.g. **sarja B, osa 87**.

1.7.3 Like book titles, series titles may be affected by the grammatical construction in which they occur, but they are more likely to be supported by the word **sarja** and left unaltered, e.g. «**Aikamme Kulttuuri**»-**sarjassa**, *in the series 'Aikamme Kulttuuri'*.

1.8 PERIODICALS

1.8.1 The titles of periodicals tend to be simple, not to say laconic, e.g. **Virke**, *The sentence*; **Virittäjä**, *The stimulator*; **Aika**, *The Age*; **Historiallinen aikakauskirja**, *Historical Journal*. If they occur in a sentence they are subject to the grammar of the sentence, e.g. **Ajan 66. vuosikerta, Suomalaisen Suomen 40. vuosikerta**, *vol. 66 of Aika*, *vol. 40 of Suomalainen Suomi*.

1.8.2 The body responsible may simply be put in the nominative at the head of the title-page, or it may be part of the title or sub-title in the genitive, e.g. **Kalevalaseuran vuosikirja**, *Year-book of Kalevalaseura*; **Äidinkielen Opettajain Liiton jäsenlehti**, *organ of the Äidinkielen Opettajain Liitto* (*Union of Teachers of the Mother Tongue*). Sometimes it follows **julkaisija(t)**, *publisher(s)*, or **julkaisevat**, *they publish*, and may be distinguished from **kustantaja**, who is concerned with the business side of publication.

1.8.3 Indications of editorship involve the term **toimit-**. There is usually a **toimitus-neuvosto**, *editorial committee* (**toimituskolleegio** in Karelia) but **toimitus** alone is found. At the head is the **päätoimittaja** with his deputy **varapäätoimittaja** and the assistance of a **toimitussihteeri**. Distinct from these is the **taloudenhoitaja** or manager. None of the names are grammatically affected.

1.8.4 Numeration is primarily by **vuosikerta**, *annual volume*, preceded by an ordinal number, e.g. **22.** (in words **kahdeskymmenestoinen**) **vuosikerta**. Subdivisions are **numero** (**n:o**), **nide** or **vihko**.

1.8.5 Periodicity is expressed straightforwardly by **ilmestyy** (*comes out*), e.g. **neljänä vihkona vuodessa**, *in four parts in the year*; **kahdeksan kertaa vuodessa**, *eight times a year*.

1.8.6 Subscription is **tilaushinta**, quoted by the year (**vuosikerta** again, abbreviated **1/1 vsk**), and a price may be given for single numbers, **irtonumerot**. Subscriptions may vary by region, e.g. **kotimaassa**, *internal*; **pohjoismaihin**, *to Scandinavia*; **muihin maihin**, *to other countries*, or **ulkomaille**, *for abroad*. Sometimes subscriptions to society publications are included in membership, e.g. **Historian Ystäväin Liiton jäsenmaksuun sisältyy** (*is included*) **aikakauskirjan tilaushinta**.

Back numbers are sometimes quoted. Some Finnish periodicals have strict ideas on what constitutes a back number, and statements like **vanhoja irtonumeroja v:n 1968 loppuun saatavana**; **hinta 1 mk kpl** (i.e. **kappale**) (**ilman lvv.**) mean *single back numbers*

are available to the end of 1968, price 1 mk per copy (without trading tax). (1969 onwards
are current and more expensive.)

1.8.7   Addresses distinguish between **toimitus** (1.8.3), **tilaukset ja osoitteenmuutokset,**
subscriptions (orders) and changes of address; **ilmoitukset,** *advertisements,* and **taloudenhoitaja,** *manager.*

2   ALPHABET, PHONETICS, SPELLING

2.1   ALPHABET

2.1.1   The order of the Finnish alphabet is as follows:

a b c d e f g h i j k l m n o p q r s š t u v
x y z å ä ö

Q, x, z and **å** occur only in foreign words. **C** and **š** are very rare, and though the words
in which they occur are Finnish in form, e.g. **chileläinen,** *Chilean*; **tšekki,** *Czech*, their
foreign origin is very near the surface and **sh** is found for **š**, especially in typing. **B, f**
and **g** are a little commoner and the words, such as **filosofia**, a little more acclimatised;
ng occurs in purely Finnish words. **W,** indexed as **v**, occurs in some names, having been
regularly used for **v** in the Germanised alphabet (2.7) and sometimes in the Latin one.

Double vowels are almost always simply long vowels, but for alphabetical order they
are two letters.

2.2   CAPITALISATION

2.2.1   The principle that proper names are spelt with a capital letter requires some
detailed explanation. The names of seasons, months, days of the week and even festivals
are not treated as proper names, nor are capitals extended to national and local adjectives. Words denoting status, such as **herra, neiti, ministeri, piispa**, are not treated as
names, and the common part of a geographical name, if it does not form one word
with the name, has a small initial letter, e.g. **Reinin joki,** *River Rhine.* On the other hand
Pohjoinen Jäämeri, *Arctic Ocean*, has capitals for both words. (**Jäämeri**, however, does
not mean simply *sea* but *polar sea*.)

2.2.2   The names of societies, institutions and such like bodies are usually capitalised
throughout, but one does meet instances such as **Suomen asiain komitea,** *Committee
for Finnish Affairs*, **Helsingin yliopiston kirjasto,** *Helsinki University Library*, where
the phrase has been treated as simply descriptive.

2.2.3   In the titles of books the first word and any proper names the title may
contain have capitals.

2.3   DIVISION OF WORDS

2.3.1   Rules 1, 4, 5a, 6a, 7a and 8 (p. xiii) apply. Prefixes are quite often followed by
doubled letters and cannot then be kept separate, but a word like **esi-isä** (*forefather*) is
always written with a hyphen because otherwise the two i's would be read as a long
vowel.

2.3.2   Diphthongs (rule 7a) are formed by any vowel followed by **i**, which may occur
anywhere in the word, and these other combinations: au, eu, iu, ou; ey, äy, öy; ie; uo;
yö, when they occur in the first syllable. Hence **pienien** may be divided after the first
e or the second **i**, but not after the first **i**.

2.4 PUNCTUATION AND ABBREVIATIONS

2.4.1 A hyphen is found at the end of a word which shares the last component of a following compound, e.g. **puolustus-, sosiaali- ja kokonaismenot,** *defence, social and total expenditure.* Similarly, though less frequently, at the beginning, as in **1860- ja -70 luvulla,** instead of the more usual **1860- ja 1870-luvulla** (*in the 1860's and 70's*).

2.4.2 Abbreviations can be expressed simply by the initial letter with a full stop, e.g. **2.p.** for **toinen painos** but may include the last letter, e.g. **no** or **n:o** for **numero.** When this is a case-ending, the colon is usual, e.g. **v:n** for **vuoden.** (Such abbreviations without the colon, e.g. **tri** for **tohtori,** can be trying.) The colon is also used when an ending is added to an abbreviation made up of initials or to a symbol, e.g. **SSL:n** for **Suomen Sanomalehtimiesten Liiton,** **14%:sta 19%:iin** for **neljästätoista prosentista yhdeksääntoista prosenttiin.** In **Leo XIII:n (kolmannentoista)** the appended **n** actually occurs in the middle of the word.

2.5 VARIATION OF CONSONANT: GRADATION AND ALTERNATIVE STEMS

2.5.1 A characteristic of Finnish is the alternation of strong and weak consonants in different forms of a word according as the immediately following syllable is open or closed, e.g. **muoto, muodon.** With the exception of the i-diphthongs of the plural and the imperfect, syllables containing long vowels and diphthongs are treated as open (**muotoon, muodoissa**).

There are some exceptions, or apparent exceptions, to this phonetic rule, which will be noted under the appropriate part of speech.

The forms correspond as follows:

| S | pp tt kk | mp nt lt rt nk | p t k |
| W | p t k | mm nn ll rr ng | v d - (see below) |

In certain contexts exceptional correspondences occur, e.g.

| S | uku yky | hke lke rke |
| W | uvu yvy | hje lje rje |

Alanne's dictionaries, *Suomalais–englantilainen sanakirja/suursanakirja* mark with an asterisk those words that change grade.

2.5.2 Apart from the changes of grade just mentioned, most words have the same stem throughout, but in some types both of nouns and verbs the stem may end in a vowel before most suffixes and in a consonant before certain others, e.g. those of partitive singular of nouns and of the first infinitive. The consonant stems of nouns are given in 4.7.2; those of verbs are usually obtained by cutting off the vowel of the vowel stem, but the corresponding consonant stem to **-kse-** is **-s-**, and to **-(k)e-, -h-**, e.g. **tekee,** *does*; **tehdä,** *to do.* These types include a good many common words.

2.6 VOWEL HARMONY

The vowels in an uncompounded word must harmonise. For the purpose of vowel harmony the vowels fall into three groups:

1 **a o u**
2 **ä ö y**
3 **e i**

Sets 1 and 2 are mutually exclusive, while 3 may go with either, e.g. **yöpyä** (all 2), **yhtiö** (2 and 3), **muutosta** (all 1), **osake** (1 and 3), **pelätä** (3 and 2), **perata** (3 and 1). In a compound word like **osakeyhtiö** each part follows its own rule. In terminations and suffixes -a-, -o- and -u- alternate with -ä-, -ö- and -y-, and the variable vowels are represented in these notes by **A, O** and **U** respectively. (Foreign words with mixed and neutral vowels cause confusion even to Finns.)

2.7 SPELLING
The present spelling rules are twentieth-century, but changes have been slight. In the 19th century one finds Gothic type and **w** for **v** as well as hesitation between **x** and **ks**. (**W** is found alongside **v** as late as 1909.) Earlier **x** is the rule, **c** is found for **k** except before forward vowels (**ca, ck,** but **kä, ki**) and **tz** is found for **ts**. In the 16th century one also finds **w** for **uu** and **sz** as an alternative to **ss** (or **s**).

3 ARTICLES

There are no articles, definite or indefinite, but the demonstratives **se** and **ne** (7.1) are sometimes almost equivalent to a definite article.

In a great many instances Finnish is indifferent to the distinction between definite and indefinite, but variation in word order or in the case used can indicate one or the other. For instance a definite subject or object tends to come early in the sentence, an indefinite one late, and in some constructions the accusative will indicate a definite object while the partitive indicates an indefinite one. But the matter is too complicated to do more than indicate that these devices exist.

4 NOUNS

4.1 GENDER AND ENDINGS
   4.1.1 There is no gender, and although nouns take a great variety of suffixes there is no need to arrange them in elaborate declensions. A few fundamental cases need to be noted, the behaviour of stems analysed, and the relational and possessive suffixes listed. Thus in the word **ankaruudessaan**, *in their severity*, **ankaruude-** is the stem (N **ankaruus**), **-ssa** a suffix roughly corresponding to the preposition *in*, while the lengthening of the vowel and the addition of **-n** is one of the ways of indicating *his, her, its, their*.
   4.1.2 Of the three sorts of endings—basic case endings, relational suffixes and possessive suffixes—the first two are usually treated together as cases, but there are differences in behaviour between them which make it worth while to treat them separately.

4.3 CASES
   4.3.1 The endings treated here as case endings are those of the nominative, accusative, genitive and partitive. The letter A stands for **a** or **ä** (2.6).

   4.3.2 *Singular*

     AG   **-n** added to the vowel stem. A strong consonant is weakened (2.5.1).
     P   **-A** added to the vowel stem; **-tA** added to vowel or consonant stem (4.7).

4.3.3 *Plural*

> *NA*   -t added to V.S. A strong consonant is weakened (2.5.1).
>
> *G*   -en, -den, -tten added to plural stem (4.7.4); -ten added to C.S.; -in added to V.S.
>
> *P*   -A, -tA added to plural stem (4.7.4), giving -iA, -jA or -itA.

4.4 RELATIONAL SUFFIXES

4.4.1 The addition of relational suffixes and their usage is less complicated than that of the basic cases. They are added to the vowel stem or the plural stem as the case may be. They correspond roughly in meaning to the simpler English prepositions. Only the basic meanings are given in the next paragraph, with some more detailed comments in 4.4.3.

4.4.2 The forms and basic meanings are as follows. They are arranged in order of the last letter, **A** standing for **a** or **ä** (2.6). The letters (S) and (W), where applicable, indicate strong and weak stem consonants (2.5).

(1)	-llA	(W)	*on, at* (rest)
(2)	-nA	(S)	*as* (state, function); *in, at*
(3)	-ssA	(W)	*in, at*
(4)	-ltA	(W)	*of, off, from*
(5)	-stA	(W)	(*out*) *of, from, about*
(6)	-ttA	(W)	*without*
(7)	-lle	(W)	*on, to* (motion)
(8)	-ne	(S)	See 4.4.3
(9)	-ksi (-kse-)	(W)	*as, to, into, for* (state)
(10)	-n	(W)	See 4.4.3
(11)	-an, -en, etc.;		
	-han, -hen, etc.;	(S)	*into, to, on, at* (motion)
	-seen, -siin		

> The vowel of the -an and -han series is a repetition of that of the stem, e.g. **kirjaan, työhön**. Not to be confused with the possessive *his, her,* etc. (4.5.1).

4.4.3 As with prepositions in other languages the range of meaning of these suffixes is wide and the equivalents given above are only approximate.

(1) indicates rest upon; proximity (*on, by, at*); means (*by, with*); indefinite time (*in those days*). Note the idiom **minulla on**, *I have*.

(2) indicates state or function; time at which; position, e.g. **Eri osastojen tarkastajina ovat olleet seuraavat henkilöt**, *The following persons have served* (lit. *been*) *as revisors of the various sections*; **sarjana**, *in the series*; **vuonna 1929**, *in the year 1929*. (Note the contracted form **vuonna** from **vuosi**, stem **vuote-**.) For a further example see (9).

(3) like *in* is extended to nonspatial relations; time within which; and with infinitives simultaneity or means (*while, on, by —ing*). For its use with the present participle passive see 8.16.4.

(5) by extension covers origin, subject matter (*about*) material, price, time and adverbial uses. Some verbs require it whose English equivalents govern direct objects.

(7) also indicates the indirect object.

(8) which is always used with the plural, whether the sense is plural or singular, indicates close accompaniment (*with*). When used with a noun it is followed by the possessive suffix -nsa or -en.

(9) indicates change of state or status; belief; purpose; time in the future; language: e.g. **hän pyysi Sofiaa seuralaisekseen** *she requested S. as her companion* **illaksi** *for the evening* **voidakseen** *so that she might be able* (8.11.1) **käydä kirkolla** *to go to the village*; **Se on suomeksi sanottuna . . .** , *As expressed in Finnish this is . . . .* As in the above examples it is frequently combined with, and modified by the personal suffixes (4.5).

(10) indicates means or manner (*by*, *with*); recurrence (*on* Fridays) and is used to form adverbs from adjectives and adverbial phrases from infinitives (8.11.2). Except for fossils, like **kerran**, *once upon a time*, from **kerta**, *time*, it is used only with the plural stem, for in the singular it is indistinguishable from the genitive.

(11) in negative and quasi-negative phrases indicates time extending from the past to the present (*for*).

4.5 PERSONAL SUFFIXES

4.5.1 The forms correspond to different persons as follows:

	S			P	
1	2	3	1	2	3
-ni	-si	-nsA/-Vn	-mme	-tte	-nsA/-Vn
my	*your*	*his, her*	*our*	*your*	*their*

4.5.2 The suffixes are added either to the stem or to an existing ending or suffix, the final consonant, if any, being omitted, e.g. **aikamme**, *our time(s)*, *of our time*. Note that the stem consonant is always strong before a personal suffix, even if this begins with two consonants (2.5.1), so that we have the paradoxical situation that the stem may be weak without the personal suffix and strong with it, e.g. **ajat**, *times*, but **aikamme**, *our times*.

4.5.3 The alternative form of the third person may be used when the form to which it is added ends in a single vowel. This vowel is doubled and **-n** added.

4.5.4 The suffixes denote relation to a person, that is, they correspond to the genitive of a noun (4.6.3). The most usual relation is possession, but see under the participle (8.12) and the infinitive (8.11) for other possibilities. The suffix of the third person by itself refers to the subject; if someone else is referred to, **hänen**, *of him*, or **heidän**, *of them*, must be inserted before the noun.

4.6 USE OF CASES

4.6.1 The nominative is principally used:
(1) as total subject (4.6.5);
(2) as predicate, expressing a casual attribute or matter of fact;
(3) as total object (4.6.5) of a passive verb (8.16.1);
(4) adverbially, e.g. **tämä päivä**, *today*.

4.6.2 The accusative is used:
(1) as total object (4.6.5);
(2) adverbially, e.g. **kolmannen kerran**, *the third time*.

4.6.3 The genitive is used:
(1) to qualify what follows. With ordinary nouns or verbal nouns in **-minen** it will usually be translated by a phrase with *of*, e.g. **isänmaan kirja**, *book of the fatherland*; **tämän saavuttamiseksi**, *towards the achievement of this*; occasionally *for*, *by* or some other preposition; with participles or infinitives it expresses the agent and may require *by* or a complete re-casting of the sentence, e.g. **jonkin ajan kuluttua**, *after a short time had passed*; hän **luulee minun kirjoittavan**, *he thinks I am writing*; **sotavuosien**

aiheuttamat olosuhteet, *circumstances due to years of war*; with adjectives it is equivalent to an adverb, e.g. **kummallisen vieras**, *wonderfully strange*;

(2) before many postpositions and after some prepositions, e.g. **talon edessä**, *in front of the house.*

4.6.4 The partitive is used:

(1) to indicate some or part of a larger group or whole, e.g. **on Suomen historian eniten tutkittuja ajanjaksoja**, *it is one of the best explored periods of Finnish history* (cf. 1.7);

(2) as partial subject (4.6.5), always with a singular verb;

(3) as predicate expressing a permanent attribute or general statement;

(4) as partial object (4.6.5);

(5) with prepositions and some postpositions. See also 8.16.4.

4.6.5 A subject or object is partial:

(1) if it is part of a larger whole;

(2) if it only partially participates in the action of the verb:

    (a) because of the nature of the verb;

    (b) because of the circumstances;

    (c) because the action is incomplete;

    (d) because the action is negated.

Otherwise it is total.

Examples: **Pahoja poliitikkoja voidaan vihata, mutta ei itse politiikkaa**, *One can hate bad politicians, but not politics itself* (1 and 2d); **He vahingoittavat häntä**, *They injure him* (2a); **Hän kirjoitti elämäkertaa**, *He was writing the biography* (but with **-kerran** it means *He wrote ...*) (2c).

4.7 STEMS

4.7.1 Some Finnish nouns have two stems, the vowel stem and the plural stem, others have in addition a consonant stem (2.5.2).

4.7.2 *The vowel and consonant stems* have the following relation to the nominative singular:

	1	2	3	4	5	6	7
V.S	vowel	-Ce-	-de-	-hde-	-ude-	-le-	-lle-
C.S	-	-C-	-t-	-h-	-ut-	-l-	-lt-
N	no change	-Ci	-si	-ksi	-us	-l	-lsi

	8	9	10	11	12	13
V.S	-me-/-ma-	-mmA-	-nne-	-rre-	-se-	-kse-
C.S	-n-	-n-	-nt-	-rt-	-s-	-s-
N	-n	-mpi/-n	-nsi/-s	-rsi	-nen	-s

	14	15	16	17	18
V.S	-aa-	-ee-	-ee-	-ii-	-ue-
C.S	-as-	-et-	-ut-/-yt-	-is-	-ut-
N	-as	-e	-ut/-yt	-is	-ut

mies has V.S. **miehe-**.

The vowel of type 1 may be any vowel except short **e**; C indicates a consonant other than those specified under other types.

4.7.3 The consonant in types 3–7 and 9–11 is given in the weak grade (2.5.1), for most suffixes form a closed syllable, e.g. **vuoden** GS of **vuosi**; but *for a year* is **vuoteen**, *in* *the year*, **vuotena** (or contracted **vuonna**) with open syllables and a strong consonant.

On the other hand types 14, 17 and 18 for obvious reasons and type 15 through loss of a final aspirate have a strong consonant in the vowel stem and a weak one in the nominative singular, e.g. **liikkeen** GS of **liike**, *movement*.

4.7.4 *The plural stem* ends in **-i-**, which becomes **-j-** between two vowels. Short **-e-** or **-ä-** disappears, diphthongs are simplified and **-a-** may be changed to **-o-** and **-i-** to **-e-**; plural stems in **-si** correspond to a nominative singular in **-si** (stem **-te-/-de**), e.g.

P.S.	**mai-**	**järvi-**	**tei-**	**töi-**	**soi-**	**kirjoi-**	**vuosi-**
V.S.	**maa-**	**järve-**	**tie-**	**työ-**	**suo-**	**kirja-**	**vuode-**
N	**maa**	**järvi**	**tie**	**työ**	**suo**	**kirja**	**vuosi**

5 ADJECTIVES

5.1 GENERAL

5.1.1 There being no gender, adjectives have only one set of forms, which are the same as those of nouns, e.g. **rikas** GS **rikkaan** (type 14), *rich*; **laaja** (type 1), *wide*; **poliittinen** (type 12), *political*.

5.1.2 Adjectives agree with nouns, that is they take the same suffixes, when they are strictly attributive, e.g. **kirjallisessa muodossa**, *in written form*. When predicative they agree in number but the case or suffix is determined by the construction (4.6.4). For an intermediate construction see word 35 in the specimen.

5.1.3 Although there are national adjectives such as **suomalainen**, *Finnish*, their use is restricted, and the normal equivalent of *Finnish* is **Suomen**, the genitive of **Suomi**, *Finland*. Similarly with other countries.

5.3 COMPARISON

5.3.1 *Comparative* **-mpi**; *Superlative* **-in**, both type 9 (4.7.2), added to the vowel stem (but see 5.3.2).

5.3.2 Disyllabic adjectives in **-A** (2.6) make their comparative in **-empi**, e.g. **vanha**, **vanhempi**, *old-er*.

The **-i-** of the superlative behaves like the **-i-** of the plural stem (4.7.4) except that **-a-** too disappears, e.g. **vanhin**, *oldest;* **uusin**, *newest*.

5.3.3 Some of the commonest adjectives have irregular comparisons. The more extreme, such as **parempi**, *better*; **paras** (vowel stem **parhaa-**), *best*, are given separately in the dictionary, but C **pitempi** (or **pidempi**) S **pisin** from **pitkä**, *long*, are not.

6 NUMERALS

6.1 CARDINAL

6.1.1

1 **yksi**	11 **yksitoista**	21 **kaksikymmentä yksi/**
2 **kaksi**	12 **kaksitoista**	**yksikolmatta**
3 **kolme**	and so on	30 **kolmekymmentä**
4 **neljä**		31 **kolmekymmentä yksi/**
5 **viisi**		**yksineljättä**
6 **kuusi**		100 **sata**
7 **seitsemän**		101 **sata yksi**
8 **kahdeksan**		200 **kaksisataa**
9 **yhdeksän**	19 **yhdeksäntoista**	1000 **tuhat/tuhannen**
10 **kymmenen**	20 **kaksikymmentä**	2000 **kaksituhatta**

6.1.2 All the numerals take case endings and suffixes with stems as given in 4.7.2: 1, 2 are type 4; 3, 4 type 1; 5, 6 type 3; the stems of 7–10 are got by removing the -n.

Despite their similarity, **yksitoista** and the other numerals up to 19, **yksikolmatta**, **yksineljättä** and the other alternatives for 21–29, 31–39 etc. on the one hand, and **kaksikymmentä, kolmekymmentä** and the other multiples of 10 on the other are differently formed and behave differently. The first set mean *one* (etc.) *of the second* (*third*, etc.), the second element being the partitive of the ordinal number for the decade. The first element takes the necessary endings, but the second element is invariable: *of twelve* is **kahdentoista**. The second set mean simply *two* (*three*, etc.) *tens*, and the second element is the partitive of **kymmenen**, *ten*. Both parts take endings: *of twenty* is **kahdenkymmenen**. Similarly with **kaksisataa** and the other hundreds (cf. 6.1.3).

Long compound numerals may be declined throughout, or all elements except the last may be invariable.

6.1.3 Numerals in the nominative and accusative are followed by nouns in the partitive singular, otherwise they take the same terminations as the noun, e.g. **kaksi eri asiaa**, *two different things*; **poliitikon «kahdesta minästä»**, *of the politician's* '*two egos*'.

6.2 ORDINAL
6.2.1

1 ensimmäinen	5 viides	9 yhdeksäs
2 toinen	6 kuudes	10 kymmenes
3 kolmas	7 seitsemäs	11 yhdestoista
4 neljäs	8 kahdeksas	12 kahdestoista

All other ordinals are formed in the same way by adding **-s** to the vowel stem of the cardinal.

All parts of a compound have the ordinal form **kahdeskymmenestoinen**, *22nd*.

6.2.2 Apart from **ensimmäinen** and **toinen** (type 12) all the ordinals have type 10 stems, but with the consonant stem in **-t-** not **-nt-** (4.7.2). **Yhdestoista**, etc. behave like **yksitoista**, etc. (6.1.2).

6.2.3 Ordinal numbers are adjectives (5.1.2).

6.3 FIGURES
Simple arabic figures represent the basic form of cardinals; with a full stop, any form of the ordinal; with a colon and a termination, the appropriate form of cardinal or ordinal as the case may be. Roman figures stand for ordinals, e.g.

5 = viisi; 5:s = viides; 5:ä = viidettä; 5:nnen = viidennen
5. = any form of viides; V = viides; V:n = viidennen; 15:n = viidentoista

6.4 DATES
6.4.1 All the months end in **-kuu** (month), viz.

tammikuu, helmi-, maalis-, huhti-, touko-, kesä-,
heinä-, elo-, syys-, loka-, marras-, joulukuu

6.4.2 Dates are expressed as follows:

on 10 May 1953, **toukokuun kymmenentenä päivänä (vuonna) yhdeksäntoista-sataa viisikymmentä kolme**. In figures: **toukokuun 10. päivänä 1953**

The month comes first in the genitive, the day has the ending -nA, **päivänä** (*on the day*) is obligatory, **vuonna** (*in the year*) optional and the year is expressed by cardinal numbers without any suffix. Alternatively the month may follow the day, in the partitive, viz. **10. p:nä toukokuuta.**

Where a suffix would be required the year must be preceded by the appropriate form of **vuosi**, e.g.

> *from 1815 to 1860*, **vuodesta 1815 vuoteen 1860**
> *of 1848*, **vuoden 1848**
> *in the 1890's*, **1890-luvulla**

Similarly the various forms of **1800-luku** are used for *the 19th century* much more often than **19. vuosisata.** Note the abbreviations **v.** = **vuonna**, **vv.** = **vuosina**, **v:n** = **vuoden**.

7 PRONOUNS

7.1 DEMONSTRATIVE

7.1.1 The endings of these pronouns are the same as those of nouns. The stems are as follows:

tämä	*this*	**tä-/tämä**
nämä(t)	*these*	**näi-**
se	*this, that, it*	**se-/si-/sii-**
ne	*these, they*	**nii-**
tuo	*that*	**tuo-**
nuo(t)	*those*	**noi-**

Note that **se** has some unusual forms: **siitä** (4.4.2, suffix 5; the partitive is **sitä**); **siihen** (4.4.2, suffix 11).

7.1.2 **Se** and **ne** are most often used for *it* and *they* or as antecedents to clauses, e.g. **se, joka on pahempi**, *the one which is worse*; **siitä että**, *because*. With nouns they are often hardly stronger than an article, e.g. **sen kerran**, *of the time*.

7.2 RELATIVE, INTERROGATIVE, INDEFINITE, ETC.

7.2.1 The endings are the same as nouns, but these pronouns have invariable suffixes in some or all of their forms.

Pronoun	*Stem*
joka, *who*	**jo-**
ken ⎫ *who?*	**ke-/kene-/pl. kei-**
kuka ⎭	
kumpi, *which?* (of two)	**kumma-/kumpa-**
mikä, *what?*	**mi-**

The suffix -kA is obligatory with monosyllabic forms, optional and infrequent with longer ones.

> **jokin,** *some(thing), any(thing)*
> **kukin,** *everybody*
> **kumpikin,** *each*

The **-kin** is added after other endings, e.g. **yksi kumpaakin**, *one of each*.

> **joku,** *somebody, anybody*
> **jompikumpi,** *either*

Both parts vary, and the pronouns are recognisable from their symmetry, e.g. **jommankumman**, *of either.*

7.2.2 Toinen, *other*, with a personal suffix means *each other*, e.g. **toisistaan**, *from each other* (and see 12.2:-**hAn**).

7.3 PERSONAL

7.3.1 The forms are:

	S			P		
	1	2	3	1	2	3
N	minä	sinä	hän	me	te	he
A	minut	sinut	hänet	meidät	teidät	heidät
G	minun	sinun	hänen	meidän	teidän	heidän
P	minua	sinua	häntä	meitä	teitä	heitä
Stem	minu-	sinu-	häne-	mei-	tei-	hei-

7.3.2 The third person pronouns refer to persons; for things see 7.1. The genitive form can be used instead of the accusative.

7.4 POSSESSIVE

7.4.1 The function of possessive pronouns is performed by **oma** with personal suffixes (4.5), e.g. **omani**, *mine*; **Sanani on tullut omaksesi**, *My speech has become yours.* For -**kse**- see 4.4.2 (9).

8 VERBS

8.1 STRUCTURE

8.1.1 The various parts of the verb are constructed by the addition of suffixes indicating:
(1) person and number;
(2) mood or tense.
This simple agglutinative structure is modified by the alternation of:
(1) strong and weak stems (2.5.1) e.g. **kirjoittaa, kirjoitan**;
(2) consonant and vowel stems (2.5.2) e.g. **juoksen, juosta; olen, olla**.
The relations between the stems are dealt with under the tenses. Verbs are usually given in the dictionary under the infinitive, but the first person singular of the present is sometimes used instead.

8.1.2 The personal endings are:

	S	P
1	-n	-mme
2	-t	-tte
3	see tenses	-vAt

8.2 PRESENT/FUTURE

8.2.1 The endings are added directly to the vowel stem.
3PS: lengthened (i.e. double) vowel; no change if the stem ends in a long vowel or diphthong.

8.2.2 The relation between the stem and the infinitive is as follows:
(1) The stem of most verbs ends in a consonant plus a short vowel, commonly **A** or

U: the infinitive is got by adding -A, e.g. **joutu-a, anta-a, eritty-ä**. In the first and second persons the consonant if variable (2.5.1) is weak: **joudun, annatte**.

(2) In verbs in which the stem ends in a long vowel or diphthong, the infinitive is got by adding -dA, e.g. **voi-da, jää-dä**. The latter type cannot be distinguished in the 3PS from type (1), so far as the ending goes (8.2.1), but though it includes some common verbs, they are not numerous and they have monosyllabic stems.

(3) Verbs with a stem ending: consonant, short vowel, -A drop the -A- and add -tA for the infinitive, and the consonant which is strong throughout the present tense changes to a weak one in the infinitive, e.g. **laukea-, laueta**. (The reasons for the apparent departure from the phonetic principle stated in 2.5.1 are historical.) If the first vowel is -A- the 3PS ends in -AA, e.g. **lepää** from **levätä**. There is thus some possibility of confusion with type (1), e.g. **vertaa** (*compares*) has I **verrata** but **murtaa** (*breaks*) has **murtaa**. The other persons are unambiguous, e.g. **vertaan, murran**.

(4) Some stems in -e- belong to type (1), but most of them belong to one or other of the following types:

Stem	Infinitive
-le-	-llA
-ne-	-nnA
-ene-	-etA

The preceding consonant is strong in the present and weak in the infinitive, e.g. **kuuntelen**, *I listen*; infinitive **kuunnella**.

-re-	-rrA
-(k)se-	-stA
-itse-	-itA

There is no change of consonant.

8.2.3 Whether this tense is present or future depends partly on the context and partly on the verb itself, e.g. **Jos kaksi poliitikkoa päättää pitää asian jonkin aikaa salassa, niin kolmas tietää sen jo seuraavana päivänä**, *If two politicians* decide *to keep something secret for a time, then a third* will know *it next day*.

With some verbs a partial object (4.6.5) indicates present action, but others, those which denote a momentary action or the beginning or end of one, are much more likely to be future. Others, expressing mental states are naturally incomplete and indicate present action unless the context makes it clear that the future is intended. Sometimes it may have to be translated by *would* or a past tense.

8.3 PAST
8.3.1 The tense suffix is -i- or -si-. The 3PS has no ending.
8.3.2 The stem to which the suffix is added is that of the present (8.2.2) but the -i- causes changes like those produced by the -i- of the plural (4.7.4).

The occurrence of -si- is ambiguous. As a tense suffix it corresponds to an infinitive in -tA, the stem being strong in the past and weak in the infinitive. But the -s- may be part of the stem (8.2.2, type 4), or it may be a modification of -t: **tunsi**, *he knew*, has infinitive **tuntea** (cf. also 8.6.1).

8.3.3 The tense functions both as an imperfect and as a simple past (cf. 4.6.5).

8.6 CONDITIONAL
8.6.1 The modal suffix is -isi-. The 3PS has no ending.

8.6.2 The stem to which the suffix is added is that of the present, but long vowels and diphthongs are reduced, -e- and -i- are omitted, and in type 3 stems (8.2.2) the final -a-, e.g. **saisi (saa-), söisi (syö-); olisi (ole-), lauke(a)isi (laukea-).**

8.6.3 The tense indicates an event which is hypothetical, uncertain or dependent, e.g. **Kuka kehtaisi?**, *Who would be unashamed ?* ; **Hän ei siedä sitä, että jonkin pensaan oksa olisi muita oksia pitempi**, *He does not permit the branch of any bush* to be *longer than the other branches.*

8.10 COMPOUND TENSES

8.10.1 The present, past and conditional of **olla**, *to be*, with the past participle active, in the singular or plural as the case may be, form the perfect, pluperfect and conditional perfect respectively, e.g. **ihmiskunta on niin nöyrästi siihen alistunut**, *humanity has so meekly acquiesced*; **olisivat tarkoittaneet**, *they would have meant.*

8.10.2 The present of **tulla**, *to come*, with the third infinitive in **-maan** (8.11.3), can be used if necessary to express the future.

8.11 VERBAL NOUNS

8.11.1 The first infinitive (*the* infinitive to English ideas), ends in **-A, -dA** or **-tA** (or by assimilation **-lA, -nA, -rA**) and is the usual entry in the dictionary. It is most commonly used as it stands, roughly in the same way in the English infinitive, e.g. **Parempi on kuolla kuin vihata ja pelätä**, *It is better to die than to hate and fear*; **kehtaisi väittää**, *would not be ashamed to declare.*

The only suffix it takes is **-kse-** and a personal suffix, to express purpose: see 4.4.3, suffix (9).

8.11.2 The second infinitive is a modification of the first, got by substituting **-e-** or the **-i-** of the plural for **-A**. It is used with the suffixes **-ssA** and **-n**, e.g. **maamme ilmastoa tarkastellessamme ...**, *on examining (if we examine) the climate of our country we ...*; **Erottaen toisistaan luonnonoikeuden ja kansojen oikeuden Grotius toteaa ...**, *In distinguishing from each other natural law and the law of nations Grotius asserts ....* This type of sentence, with the agent of both actions the same, is the commonest, but they may be different, in which case the infinitive is preceded by a noun or pronoun in the genitive. Or the infinitive may stand on its own, as in **tarvittaessa**, *if necessary* (passive of **tarvita**, *to need*).

8.11.3 The third infinitive ends in **-mA**, with or without suffixes (plural stem **-mi-**), added to the verb stem (8.2.2). With suffixes it corresponds partly to the English gerund with prepositions, e.g. **kirjoittamatta**, *without writing*; **kirjoittamalla**, *by writing*; partly to the infinitive, e.g. **on suunniteltu poistamaan**, *is designed to remove*; **kieltäytyä noudattamasta**, *to refuse to obey*. See also 8.10.2.

Without suffixes it functions adjectivally, corresponding in meaning, though not in construction to the English passive participle, e.g. **sotavuosien aiheuttamat olosuhteet**, *circumstances produced by war years*. It agrees in number and case with the noun it qualifies, but since it is itself a noun, the agent precedes it in the genitive or is appended in the form of a personal suffix (4.5). For its use in indicating authorship see 1.2.4. Some words that are technically infinitives in **-mA**, such as **elämä**, *life*, are entered independently in the dictionary, having long ceased to be thought of as such.

8.11.4 The fourth infinitive ends in **-minen**, added to the stem. It is a verbal noun (4.7.2, type 12) and takes an objective genitive, as in English, e.g. **tämän menetyksen korvaaminen**, *the making good of this loss*. Like any other noun it can take appropriate suffixes. It is sometimes entered separately in the dictionary.

8.11.5 A form sometimes known as the fifth infinitive ends in **-maisilla-** plus a personal suffix. It may be regarded as a derivative of the third infinitive, but could be confused with the fourth with the suffix **-lla**, viz. **-misella**. It is translated *about to*, e.g. **Olin kirjoittamaisillani**, *I was about to write*.

8.11.6 The suffix **-jA** added to the vowel stem (8.2.2) denotes the agent. If the stem ends in **-e-** this is changed to **-i-**, e.g. **lukijalle**, *to the reader* (**lukea**, *to read*).

8.12 PARTICIPLES

8.12.1 Passive participles are dealt with in 8.16.5; the active participles are:

Present	-vA	(Present stem: 8.2.2)
Past	-nUt	(Inf. -A, -dA)
	-nnUt	(Inf. -nnA, -tA)
	-llUt	(Inf. -llA)
	-rrUt	(Inf. -rrA)
	-ssUt	(Inf. -stA)

8.12.2 Participles are declined like nouns (4.7.2, types 1 and 16).

8.12.3 The present (or future) participle is used as an adjective as in English, e.g. **seuraava**, *following*, but much more freely, where English would have a relative clause, and as a substitute for a noun clause:

(1) After verbs of saying, thinking and the like, e.g. **Toivon kirjan käyttäjien saavan paremman yleiskäsityksen aiheesta**, *I hope the users of the book will get a better idea of the subject*; **Onneton on se nainen, joka huomaa tulevansa vanhaksi**, *Unhappy is the woman who discovers that she is growing old*. The logical subject of the noun clause is in the genitive (usually indistinguishable from the accusative) and so is the participle, but the participle is always in the singular. When the subject of both clauses is the same a personal suffix is used.

(2) With **olla**, *to be*, with the plural of the participle, the suffix **-na** and a personal suffix (4.4.2; 4.5); e.g. **Olin kirjoittavinani**, *I pretended to write (I was as if I . . .)*; **Oli kuulevinaan askeleita**, *He imagined he heard steps*.

8.12.4 The past participle is used in the same way as the present as an adjective and after verbs of thinking and the like, the construction and use of personal suffixes being the same. Thus the substitution of **saaneen** and **tulleensa** in the examples in 8.12.3 would change the sense to *have got* and *has grown*.

With the verb **tulla** *to come* and the suffix **-ksi** it expresses *to happen to*, e.g. **tulin ajatelleeksi**, *I happened to think of it*.

8.12.5 For the past participle as a component of the perfect and pluperfect tenses see 8.10.1. For its use on title-pages see 1.2.2.

8.16 IMPERSONAL OR PASSIVE

8.16.1 Finnish verbs do not have a passive in the same way as English ones. There is only one form to each tense, it can be formed from intransitive as well as transitive verbs, e.g. **voidaan**, *one can*, and it is not used where the agent is expressed. Its history is complex, but nowadays it is usually regarded as impersonal and has a pronoun object in the accusative, though a noun object, if total (4.6.5) is in the nominative, e.g. **Tämä julkaisu omistetaan kaikille huollon työntekijöille**, *This publication is dedicated to all welfare workers*. Usually, as here, the natural translation is the passive. (Quite often a derivative in **-UA** serves as a passive, but this is a matter of lexicon not morphology, verbs in **-UA** being just like any other verb.)

8.16.2   *The present* ends in **-tAAn, -dAAn** or by assimilation **-lAAn, -nAAn, -rAAn**, according to the type of verb, viz.

Passive	Infinitive
-VtAAn	-VA, -VtA
-etAAn	-eA/-AA
-stAAn	-stA
-dAAn	-dA
-lAAn	-lA
-nAAn	-nA
-rAAn	-rA

The stem is weak e.g. **kerrotaan** from **kertoa** (but **kerrataan** is from **kerrata**, verb in **-tA** having a weak stem in the infinitive).

8.16.3   *The past* ends in **-ttiin** and corresponds to the infinitive as follows:

Passive	Infinitive
-ttiin	-A, -tA
-ettiin	-eA/-AA
-stiin	-stA
-Vtiin	-VtA
-ltiin	-llA
-ntiin	-nnA
-rtiin	-rrA

8.16.4   *The conditional* ends in **-(t)tAisiin** and corresponds to the infinitive in the same way as the past.

8.16.5   *The participles* are:

Present	-(t)tAvA
Past	-(t)tU

They correspond to infinitives in the same way as the past, verbs in **-AA** having participles in **-ettAvA** and **-ettU**. As adjectives they take all the usual suffixes (4.4). The present participle indicates what can be or is to be done and commonly answers to the English *-able*, e.g. **Oli valitettavaa**, *It was regrettable*; **Kirjoja ei ollut saatavissa**, *Some books were not obtainable*.

The past participle is used as adjective, much more freely than in English, and enters into the formation of the perfect tenses, e.g. **oli siirrytty**, *there had been a movement*, from the intransitive verb **siirtyä**, *to move* (cf. 8.12.1). It is also used absolutely in the partitive as the equivalent of an adverbial clause, e.g. **Tuon vaikean ajan sivuutettuamme**, *If we disregard that difficult period*; **Hobbes toteaa, leuteltuaan luonnonoikeuden säännöt** ..., *Hobbes asserts, after enumerating the rules of natural law* .... In the first example **ajan** is an accusative (4.3.2) like **säännöt** in the second, and the agent is expressed in both cases by a personal suffix (4.5.). But if the agent is expressed by a noun, this will appear before the participle, in the genitive. e.g. **Tuon ajan kuluttua**, *When that time had gone by*.

8.16.6   The passive infinitive is found only in the forms **-essA** (second infinitive) **-mAn** (third infinitive). For the stem see 8.16.3.

8.19 IRREGULARITIES

8.19.1   Olla, *to be*, has present **olen, olet, on**; **olemme, olette, ovat.**

8.19.2   Tekee, *he does*; näkee, *he sees*, correspond to infinitive **tehdä** and **nähdä.** The other stems correspond normally, e.g. **teki, tehnyt, tehtävä.**

8.22 NEGATIVE

8.22.1   The negative is not expressed by an adverb coupled with the positive form but by a special negative verb coupled with the stem of the appropriate tense of the principal verb (complete with tense suffix), except in the past, when the past participle alone is used.

8.22.2   The forms of the negative verb are **en, et, ei**; **emme, ette, eivät.**

8.22.3   For the stems see 8.2.2, 8.3.2, 8.6.2. The present stem is weak, the passive stem is got by removing -Vn from the positive, e.g. **En väitä sitä, ettei oikeutta voitaisi määritellä muullakin tavalla,** *I do not claim* (**väittää**) *that justice could not be* (conditional passive from **voida**) *defined in some other way.* Note how **ei** combines with **että** (that) to form **ettei.** Any part of the negative verb may do this with conjunctions ending in a vowel, e.g. **jollen,** *if I . . . not.*

9   ADVERBS

9.1 FORMATION

Various relational suffixes (4.4) can be used for form adverbs, e.g. **samalla,** *at the same* (*time*), but **-n** (in practice **-in**) (suffix 10) and **-sti** added to the vowel stem (4.7.2) are the commonest, e.g. **hyvin,** *well*; **moraalisesti,** *morally*, from **hyvä** and **moraalinen.**

9.2 COMPARISON

The comparative and superlative are got by adding the **-in** suffix to the stem of the adjectival forms (5.3.1), e.g. **jyrkemmin,** *more sharply* (**jyrkkä,** *sharp*); **selvimmin,** *most clearly* (**selvä,** *clear*).

10   PREPOSITIONS AND POSTPOSITIONS

10.1 POSITION

Finnish has comparatively few prepositions. Instead of simple prepositions like *on, in*, etc. it uses suffixes (4.4). Corresponding to English compound prepositions such as *behind, on top of*, it has some prepositions but more postpositions, which differ from prepositions only in that they follow the noun.

10.2 FORMS AND SYNTAX

10.2.1   English compound prepositions are formed of simple preposition and noun, with or without a connecting *of*, and *in front of the house* corresponds formally to *on the roof of the house*. The latter in Finnish is **talon katolla,** with the genitive in its normal position. Similarly *in front of the house* is **talon edessä** : **edessä** is formed from the obsolete noun **esi** by means of the suffix **-ssA** and being preceded by the genitive becomes a postposition. Naturally enough postpositions with the genitive are the commonest type, but there are also some which can be either prepositions or postpositions. With the partitive prepositions are commoner than postpositions, and again some may be either.

10.2.2   A few prepositions or postpositions are used in conjunction with relational suffixes, e.g. **Mihin päin?,** *In what direction?*; **Mistä päin?,** *From what direction?*

10.2.3 Päin is used as a preposition with the partitive, but in the examples above might be classed as an adverb. Such flexibility is common and, seeing that both parts of speech have the same sort of origin, is not unexpected.

10.3 DERIVATIVES

Postpositions with the genitive take personal suffixes (4.5) instead of or in addition to the genitive of a personal pronoun, e.g. (meidän) kanssamme, *with us.*

11 CONJUNCTIONS

11.1 Conjunctions are less common in Finnish owing to the use of phrases with participles or infinitives. Their constructions are uncomplicated, but some distinctions between near-synonyms need watching: eli, tai, vai, are all translated *or*, but while eli expresses indifference, tai and vai in different ways indicate contrast.

11.2 For conjunctions ending in -ei and the like see 8.22.3.

12 PARTICLES

12.1 By particles are here meant certain suffixes which sometimes alter the meaning of words, sometimes emphasise it in some way or link sentences together.

12.2 The principal particles are these:

-kA is an essential part of some forms of the relative and interrogative pronouns (7.2.1) and is optional with other forms. When added to the negative verb (8.22.2) it means *and* (in combination *nor*).

-pA indicates a connexion, often a rejoinder. For instance niin means *so, as*; niinpä is used in answers, meaning *quite so*, and as a connective: *thus.*

-kAAn see -kin.

-hAn strengthens the emotional tone or suggests an excuse, explanation or deprecation, e.g. **Ei suomalaisten tarvitse koko elämäänsä vihata toinen toistaan pienten asioiden vuoksi. Sitähän ei vaadi edes kuuluisa suomalainen sisu, joka on pikemminkin myönteistä kuin kielteistä,** *Finns need not hate each other on account of small things their whole lives through. Even the famous Finnish doggedness, which after all is positive rather than negative, does not demand that.*

-kin (in negative sentences -kAAn) is an essential part of some pronouns (7.2.1), the meaning of which can be found from the dictionary. As an optional addition to any word it gives a simple emphasis and is found in the most technical of prose. Some words, like pikemmin in the example under -hAn, seem to attract it, and in such a phrase as **puhumattakaan niistä vaikeuksista, joita . . . ,** *not to mention those difficulties, which . . . ,* it adds nothing to the meaning which could be brought out in translation.

-ko indicates a question (example at the end of 1.3.1).

13 WORD-FORMATION

13.1 GENERAL

Borrowing as it does comparatively little from other languages, Finnish is correspondingly rich in suffixes which enable one to form derivatives. A glance at a dictionary under **tied-/tiet-** will reveal a score of words (excluding compounds) all connected with idea of knowing. However, they are in fact all in the dictionary, and there is no need therefore to give a long list of formative suffixes. A few are given which are liable to produce words not listed in the dictionary.

13.2 SUFFIXES

-**jA** is so universal that it is dealt with as a part of the verb (8.11.6).

-**UA** makes intransitive, reflexive or passive verbs, e.g. **perustua**, *to be founded* (*on*), (**perustaa**, *to found*).

-**lAinen** denotes a native of country or place, e.g. **Tuomas Akvinolainen**, *Thomas Aquinas*.

-**tOn** makes negative adjectives, especially from the 3rd infinitive, giving -**mAtOn**, e.g. **tietämätön**, *ignorant*, from **tietää**, *to know*.

-**o** is a common noun ending. Most of these nouns express action or its results and hence are closely related to the corresponding verbs. The great majority are adequately dealt with in dictionaries, but at times it pays to refer back to the verb. Thus **kesto** is given in Wuolle's *Finnish–English Dictionary* as *quantity* (of a vowel), but the word **kestokulutushyödykkeet** means *consumer durables* (**kulutus**, *consumption*; **hyödyke**, *commodity*). The verb **kestää** means among other things *to last*.

-**tar** makes feminines, e.g. **myyjätär**, *salesgirl*.

13.3 COMPOUNDS

Compounds are freely made and in a technical text one may expect about half of them not to be in the smaller general dictionaries. But like the example in 13.2 their meaning can usually be deduced from those of the component parts.

GLOSSARY

aikakauskirja, aikakauslehti, *periodical*
alennus, *discount, rebate*
alkusanat, *preface*

eripainos, *offprint* (1.5.3)
esipuhe, *preface*

faktuura, *invoice*

hakemisto, *index*
hakuteos, *reference work*
hinta, *price*
huomautus, *note*

ilmaiseksi, *free*
ilmestyä, *to come out* (1.8.5)
irtonumero, *single number* (1.8.6)

jakaja, *publisher* (1.6.1)
jatko(a) seuraa, jatkuu, *to be continued*
johdanto, *introduction*
julkaisematon, *unpublished*
julkaisija, *publisher* (1.8.2)
julkaisu, *publication* (1.7.1)
jäsen, *member*

kappale, *copy, item*
kertomus, *story, report*
kirja, *book*
kirjakauppa, *bookseller* (1.6.1)
kirjanen, *booklet, pamphlet*
kirjapaino, *printing shop*
kirjasarja, *series*
kirjasto, *library*
kirjastonhoitaja, *librarian*

kirje, *letter*
kirjoitelma, *essay, monograph*
kirjoittaja, *writer*
kokoelma, *collection*
kokous, *meeting*
kootut, *collected*
korjattu, *corrected* (1.5.2)
kuoli, *died*
kuollut, *dead*
kustannusoikeus, *copyright*
kustannusosakeyhtiö, *publishing company*
kustantaa, *to publish*
kustantaja, *publisher* (1.6.1, 1.8.2)
kuu, *month*
kuva, *illustration*
kuvaliite, *appendix of plates*
kääntää, *to translate*

laatinut, *compiled, composed* (1.2.2)
lasku, *bill, invoice*
liite, *appendix, supplement*
liitekuva, *plate*
liitto, *union, federation*
lisäpainos, *reprint*
lisätty, *enlarged*
lisäys, *addition*
loppuunmyyty, *out of print*
luettelo, *index, list*
lähettää, *to send*

monistaa, *to duplicate*
muotokuva, *portrait*
myytävänä, *on sale*

neljännes-, *quarterly*
neuvosto, *board*
nide, *part, volume* (1.7.2)
nidos, *volume* (1.4.1)
nidottu, *paperback* ('sewn')
novelli, *short story*
numero, *number* (1.7.2)
nähtäväksi, *on approval*
näyte, *sample*
näytelmä, *play*

osa, *part, volume* (1.4.1, 1.7.2)
osoite, *address* (1.8.7)

painaa, *to print*
painamatta, *not printed*

painos, *edition, impression* (1.5.1)
parantaa, *to improve*
pikkukirjanen, *pamphlet*
puhe, *speech*
puolivuotinen, *half-yearly*

romaani, *novel*
runo, *poem*

sama, *same*
sanakirja, *dictionary*
sarja, *(sub)series*
selitys, *commentary, explanation*
seura, *society*
sidottu, *bound*
sivu, *page*
suomentaa, *to translate into Finnish*
syntyi, *was born*
syntynyt, *born*

tarkastaa, *to revise*
taulu, *table*
tekijänoikeus, *copyright*
teos, *work* (1.3.3)
tiedonanto, *bulletin* (1.7.1)
tiivistelmä, *summary*
tilaus, *order* (1.8.7)
tilaushinta, *subscription* (1.8.6)
toimittaja, *editor* (1.2.3)
toimittanut, *edited*
toimitus, *editing, editorial staff*
toimitusneuvosto, *editorial board* (1.8.3)
tutkielma, tutkimus, *study* (1.7.1)

ulkomaat, *foreign countries* (1.8.6)
uudelleen, *anew*
uudistettu, *revised* (1.5.2)
uusi, *new*
uusintapainos, *reprint*

vaihto, *exchange*
valitut, *selected*
vanhoja numeroja, *back numbers*
vihko, *issue* (1.8.4)
vuosijulkaisu, *year-book*
vuosikerta, *year, volume* (1.8.4)
vuosikirja, *year-book*

yhdistys, *association*

GRAMMATICAL INDEX: WORDS

GRAMMATICAL INDEX: ENDINGS

Endings involving y, ä, or ö should be sought under u, a and o respectively.

HUNGARIAN

SPECIMEN

¹ ² ³ ⁴ ⁵ ⁶ ⁷ ⁸ ⁹ ¹⁰ ¹¹

E célkitüzések minden magyar dolgozót érintő nagy jelentősége arra ösztönöz bennünket,

könyvtárosokat is, hogy fokozottabb részt vállaljunk valóra váltásukban.

A szakirodalom felkutatása, a könyvek, egyéb források összegyűjtése és a munka

legcélszerűbb módszereinek és eszközeinek ismerete a legszorosabban összefügg az új

oktatási módszerek eredményességével. Mindez azonban sajátosan könyvtárosi feladat.

The great importance of these objectives, which concern every Hungarian worker, stimu-
lates us librarians also to play a more increased part in-their-conversion to-the-truth.
The searching out of technical literature, the collection of books [and] other sources,
and the knowledge of the most suitable methods and instruments for the work is most
intimately connected with the success of the new educational methods. All this however
[is] peculiarly a librarian's task.

References to sections

0 GENERAL CHARACTERISTICS

0.1 DEGREE OF INFLEXION

Hungarian is a markedly synthetic language, the verb having sufficiently distinct forms to make subject pronouns unnecessary, and the relations of the noun and even possessives being indicated by suffixes. There is an economy in the use of suffixes, exemplified by such a phrase as **negyed, fél, háromnegyed és évenkénti gyűjtőkötetek,** *quarter(ly),* *half(-yearly), nine-month(ly) and yearly cumulations,* in which only **évenkénti** has the suffix. One should also note that although suffixes are as it were selfcontained, so that they can be peeled off one by one, they are not unique. The personal suffixes (4.5) are the same as some verb endings, while among the usually distinctive relational suffixes (4.4) **-nak/-nek** is also the ending of the 3PP of the present.

0.2 ORDER OF WORDS

All qualifying expressions precede the noun, even if they are of considerable length. The following Solonian example is not untypical:

1 2 3 4 5 6 7 8 9 10
a tervszerű devizagazdálkodással kapcsolatos szabályokról szóló 1950. évi 30. számú

11 12 13 13 11 12 10 9 8
törvényerejű rendelet magyarázata, *explanation of statutory order no. 30 of the year*

7 6 5 4 1 2 3
1950 dealing with regulations relating to the planned management of foreign exchange.

0.3 RELATION TO OTHER LANGUAGES

The general connexions of Hungarian are stated under Finnish. There are some borrowings from Slavonic languages, some from Turkish and a few from German, and there are a number of 'international' words like **statisztika**. But they are not frequent enough to mitigate the generally exotic look of the page.

1 BIBLIOLINGUISTICS

1.1 NAMES

1.1.1 Modern Hungarian names consist of surname and personal name, in that order. Combinations of three elements may consist of (1) a surname and two Christian names, as in **Biró Lajos Pál**; (2) a compound surname followed by a Christian name, e.g. **Surányi-Unger Tivadar**; **Szent Istványi József**; (3) a married name followed by maiden name and Christian name, e.g. **Fenyőné Acsády Edith**, i.e. Edith (née) Acsády, wife of Fenyő; (4) a territorial epithet, surname and Christian name, as in **Kisleghi Nagy Dénes**; (5) a title, surname and Christian name, e.g. **gróf Teleki János**. Where the names are not printed entirely in capitals, both **Kisleghi** and **gróf** begin with a small letter. Possibilities involving initials are: **Cs. Szabó László**, in which **Cs.** is simply a distinguishing initial (main entry under **Szabó**); and **E. Abaffy Erzsébet**, a variant of (3) in which the husband's surname is represented by an initial. Older names, consisting of an epithet and a Christian name, such as **Temesvári Pelbárt**, *Pelbárt of Temesvár*, look no different from any others, and are treated no differently in encyclopaedias. Fortunately they are uncommon.

A number of names, e.g. **Lajos, Miklós, Sándor, Zoltán** may be either a Christian name or a surname.

1.1.2 Christian names do not undergo any modification on account of their grammatical relations, but as the last element in a name they may bear a suffix, e.g. **Petőfi Sándorig**, *up to Sándor Petőfi*. A man's name may also carry the suffix **-né**, meaning *wife of*, e.g. **Tordai Györgyné**, *Mrs. G. T.*

1.1.3 The names of Hungarian authors, in translations of their works, or when referred to in some other language, used often to be turned into the form usual in that language. Indeed the practice is not unknown even today. As equivalents are not always self-evident, some of the trickier are given here.

Adorján: *Hadrian*	Győző: *Victor*
Béla: *Adalbert*	Ilona: *Helen*
Ferenc: *Francis*	Imre: *Emerich*
Fülöp: *Philip*	István: *Stephen*
Gábor: *Gabriel*	Jenő: *Eugene*
Gergely: *Gregory*	Lajos: *Louis, Ludwig*

László: *Ladislaus*   Rezső: *Rudolph*
Loránd: *Roland*   Sándor: *Alexander*
Miklós: *Nicholas*   Tivadar: *Theodore*
Nándor: *Ferdinand*

As will be seen, -a is not a typically feminine ending.

1.1.4 Surnames not followed by a Christian name may have a suffix attached, e.g. **Leninnek és Sztálinnak megállapításai**, *the statements of Lenin and Stalin*, but this has no further effect on the form of the name. An example of the suffix **-né**, equivalent to *Mrs* is given in 1.1.1. Surnames may have plural forms, incorporating a possessive suffix, e.g. **Szentesék**, *the Szentes family*, or without, e.g. **Szentesek** (all people named *Szentes*). These forms are not used when there are Christian names.

1.1.5 The names of foreigners are now usually left unaltered, though one may well meet names like **Verne Gyula** or **Marx Károly** and bibliographies citing Russian translations of Marx have been known to transliterate the name as **Marksz**, as if it had been Russian. (Russian is transliterated according to Hungarian phonetics, not by the international standard.)

1.2 NAMES OF AUTHORS, EDITORS, ETC.

1.2.1 Names of authors are often put at the head of the title-page without grammatical connexion with the title. The name is in its basic form, but in some cases the title is affected. (See 1.3.2.)

1.2.2 Equally possible for authors and very common for editors, translators and the like is the position after the title, preceded by an active verb in the past objective (8.3.1), e.g. **összeállította Weger Imre**, *I. W. compiled it*; **szerkesztették Mészárovits Tibor és Szemenyei János**, *T. M. and J. S. edited it*. Note that the verb agrees in number with the subject in the last example. It need not; but if it does, one must beware how one shortens the title. (Such phrases as **összeállításért felel**, *is responsible for compilation*, usually denote legal responsibility and are of little bibliographical importance.) In many-volumed works the verb may be in the present (cf. 1.8.3).

1.2.3 Instead of a finite verb a present participle (8.12.1) may be found, functioning as it often does as an agent-noun, e.g. **szerkesztők Baróti Dezső és Vajda György**, *editors D. B. and G. V.* Once again the names are unaffected but the participle is singular or plural according as there is one name or more.

1.2.4 The activity may be expressed by a noun, e.g. **Szappanos Balázs és Vidor Pálné munkája**, *the work of B. S. and Mrs Pál Vidor*. The type is not common. The form of the name is unaffected.

1.2.5 There are various ways of expressing collaboration, from the simple use of **(fő)munkatárs(ak)**, *(chief) collaborator(s)* to phrases like **Bársony István, Bodnár Gyula [é.m.] közreműködésével szerkesztette Kain Albert**, i.e. *edited by A. K. with the collaboration of I. B. and G. B. [and others]*. The form of the name is not affected.

1.2.6 Statements of corporate authorship follow the same lines as those of personal authorship. Sometimes one finds only a statement of responsibility such as **Összeállításért felel: Pénzügyminisztérium számviteli tanulmányi ügyosztályának vezetője**, *Is responsible for compilation: The director of the accounting research department of the Ministry of Finance*. One hardly needs **vezetője**, but omission begins a chain of alterations, leaving **Pénzügyminisztérium. Számviteli Tanulmányi Ügyosztály** (4.4.4; 4.5.3). Similarly the Budapest Statistical Office, which invariably appears on the title-page as **Budapest Statisztikai Hivatala**, is cited in the bibliographies of the Budapest municipal library as **Budapest. Statisztikai Hivatal**.

1.3 TITLES

1.3.1 Most titles consist of nouns and adjectives, with suffixes, e.g. **A magyar jobbágyság története**, *The history of Hungarian serfdom*; **A nőnevelés Eötvös gondolat-világában**, *The education of women in the intellectual system of Eötvös*. Belles-lettres and the literature of persuasion produce greater grammatical variety, such as **Hogyan olvassunk?**, *How are we to read?*; **Meg kell oldani a magyar királykérdést!**, *The question of the Hungarian king must be settled.*

1.3.2 Title entries should not cause much trouble. Those operating with British Museum rules will find that the first noun in the title is usually in its basic form, though titles like **A szándéktól a következményig** (*From intention to result*: heading SZÁNDÉK) are occasionally met with. When ignoring articles it should be remembered that **az** may be the pronoun *that* (7.1.3) and **egy** the numeral *one*.

1.3.3 Titles which are an item in a sentence will have the appropriate grammatical ending added to the principal noun, whether they are Hungarian or foreign, e.g. **I. V. Sztálin műveinek magyar bibliográfiájá-tól**, *from 'I. V. Sztálin m. m. bibliográfiája'*; **forduljunk a Bolsaja Szovjetszkaja Énciklopédija-hoz**, *we must turn to the Bol'shaya Sovetskaya Entsiklopediya*. Where this is impossible a formula such as **A dialektikus és történelmi materializmusról c(ímű) műtől**, *From the work entitled 'A dialektikus'*, etc. where **mű** takes the suffix. It should be noted that the addition of the suffix has necessitated the lengthening of the final -a of **bibliográfiája** (2.6.2).

1.3.4 Some titles, such as those of collected works, correspondence and the like, may be grammatically connected with the name of the author, e.g. **Arany János összes költői művei**, *Complete poetical works of J. A.* A noun thus dependent has a possessive termination: **művei** not **művek**. Hungarians frequently cite such titles as they stand with no separate statement of the author, but one also finds such entries as **Berzsenyi Dániel, Ódái**, or notes such as **Művei. köt. 33.** So there is no need religiously to include the author's name in the title in order to justify the dependent form. (See also 1.5.4, 1.7.1.)

1.3.5 What we should regard as title and sub-title are often grammatically connected, e.g. **A büntetőtörvénykönyv általános része**, i.e. *Penal code: general part*, but grammatically *General part of the penal code* (4.5.3). It is better to leave well alone, though the two parts could be catalogued together as **A büntetőtörvénykönyv**, since this half of the title is not affected.

1.4 VOLUMES AND PARTS

1.4.1 The usual words are **kötet** and **rész** respectively. Like corresponding words in other languages **rész** can equally well mean a division of the subject matter, such as might occupy physically a whole volume or more than one volume. Other words occasionally used are: **pótkötet**, *supplementary volume*; **fél**, *half*; **füzet**, *fascicule* (of a work published in parts).

1.4.2 Numeration is by preceding ordinal number, expressed in words or figures, e.g. **I. rész; második kötet**. (Distinguish **3 kötet** in bibliographical citations, meaning 3 *volumes*.)

1.4.3 The numeration may be connected grammatically with the title, giving the forms **kötete** and **része** (4.5.3).

1.5 EDITIONS

1.5.1 The word for *edition*, **kiadás**, is the noun of action corresponding to **kiadni**, which means among other things *to publish*. In the appropriate context it means *edition*, but it can simply mean *publication* (1.6.1).

1.5.2 The number of the edition may be in words or figures e.g. **harmadik (3.)**
kiadás, or some suitable adjectives such as **átdolgozott**, *revised*; **teljes**, *complete*;
bővített, *enlarged*; **javított**, *improved*, may be substituted. On the other hand it may be
változatlan, *unchanged*, or **olcsó**, *cheap*.

1.5.3 An *impression* is expressed by **lenyomat**, an *offprint* by some such phrase
as **különlenyomat a** *Budapest* **1946. augusztusi számából**, *separate printing from the*
August 1946 number of 'Budapest'.

1.5.4 Indications of special editions may be grammatically linked to the title, e.g.
Surányi Miklós műveinek emlékkiadása, *Memorial edition of the works of M. S.* (1.3.4).

1.6 IMPRINTS

1.6.1 However the publisher is stated, the form of the name is unaffected. Usually
the name is set out without more ado at the foot of the title-page, but sometimes it has
been followed by **kiadása** or **kiadványa** (*his/its publication*) or preceded by **kiadja** (*is*
publishing) or **felelős kiadó** (*responsible publisher*). The last usually appears on the back
of the title-page, often in addition to the usual imprint. Among special imprints may
be noted **Szerző (saját) kiadása**, *Author's (own) publishing*.

Printers' imprints usually include some form of the root **nyom-**, e.g. **nyomás**, *printing*;
nyomda, *press*. But there is nothing to prevent a printer from publishing.

1.6.2 The place of publication is usually given in the basic form: **Budapest, Kolozs-**
vár (*Cluj*), but it occasionally has some locative suffix (4.4.2): **Budapesten, Kolozsvárt**.

1.6.3 Modern Hungarian imprints are institutional, the names being those of
learned bodies, state publishing houses or periodicals, e.g. **Magyar Tudományos**
Akadémia (*Hungarian Academy of Sciences*), **Közgazdasági és Jogi Könyvkiadó** (*Eco-*
nomics and Law Publishing House) **Szikra** (*Spark*). Of recent years state publishing
houses have dropped their long descriptive names and adopted short, symbolic ones
like **Kossuth Könyvkiadó, Magvető Kiadó** (*Sower Press*).

1.6.4 Older imprints include, besides a fair number of institutional and symbolic
names, firm names of a personal type such as **Kunossy, Szilágyi és társa** (*and Co.*) or
simply **Révai**, in full **Révai Testvérek irodalmi intézet részvénytársaság**. In **Pinger M.**
Bizománya, remembering the order of Hungarian names, one would check **bizomány**
and discover that it means *commission*.

1.7 SERIES

1.7.1 The titles of series usually appear opposite the title-page or at the head of it.
As in English they may be either in the singular, being directly or indirectly descriptive
of the series as a whole, e.g. **A propagandista Könyvtára** (*The Propagandist's Library*),
Tudomány és haladás (*Science and Progress*), or in the plural, descriptive of the individual items, e.g. **Értekezések a magyar művelődés-történelem köréből** (*Dissertations*
from the Field of Hungarian Culture History), **A Fővárosi Könyvtár Közleményei**
(*Publications of the Municipal Library*). The last type, in which the name of the institution and the word descriptive of the series are grammatically connected (4.5.3), can
cause trouble. If one omits the first three words (some may feel that one should not),
is one to leave **közleményei** as it is, leaving the grammatical connexion to be understood,
or should one change it to **közlemények**, the basic plural form? The Library of Congress
has the entry **Magyar Szociográfiai Intézet. Közleményei**, while the Fővárosi Könyvtár
itself uses the form **Közlemények**.

1.7.2 Numeration is by **szám** (*number*), **kötet** (*volume*) or **füzet** (*fascicule*), or may
stand by itself without specification. The numeral precedes, in the ordinal form.

z

Occasionally numeration is run together with the title, causing grammatical complications, e.g. A Magyar Pedagógusok Szakszervezete magyar irodalmi tankönyveinek XI. kötete, *11th volume of Hungarian Literature Textbooks of the Hungarian Union of Teachers.* Here the series entry, in its usual form, would be: Magyar Pedagógusok Szakszervezete. Magyar Irodalmi Tankönyvek. XI. kötet. As stated in 1.7.1, Tankönyvei would be equally possible, but the suffix -nek (4.4.4) must be omitted, as well as the -e of kötete. A different sort of complication occurs in a Magyar Gazdaságkutató Intézet 17. számú különkiadványa (*special publication No. 17 of the Hungarian Economic Research Institute*) which implies a series entry Magyar Gazdaságkutató Intézet. Különkiadványok. 17. szám. Here the adjectival számú (*numbered*) has to yield szám (*no.*) and the dependent singular különkiadványa the absolute plural in -ok. (Füzet needs care. It can be part of the title of the series, like the French cahier.)

1.8 PERIODICALS

1.8.1 The titles of periodicals do not differ grammatically from those of books, whether they are penny plain like Társadalmi Szemle (*Social Review*) or twopence coloured like Tartós békéért, népi demokráciáért (*For a lasting peace, for a people's democracy*) or Bolond gomba (*The mad mushroom*).

When a title is part of a sentence, a suffix may be added to it, even if it is in a foreign language, e.g. Magyar Folyóiratok Repertóriumá-t, Voproszü Filoszofii-ben (a Russian periodical). The only complication is the lengthening of the final vowel (2.6.3), but the first example was actually printed, misleadingly, Repertórium-át. As with book titles (1.3.3) this suffixation can be avoided.

1.8.2 In institutional periodicals the name of the institution and the title may form one grammatical whole, e.g. A Magyar Tudományos Akadémia Társadalmi Történeti Tudományok Osztályának Közleményei (*Transactions of the Section of Socio-historical Sciences of the Hungarian Academy of Sciences*). There is much to be said for simply cataloguing under the title, for split up the entry would read: Magyar Tudományos Akadémia. Társadalmi Történeti Tudományok Osztálya. Közlemények (4.4.4, 4.5.1, 4.5.3).

1.8.3 Editorship may be expressed by szerkeszti (*edits*) and a name, but more often there is a szerkesztő bizottság (*editorial board*) with a felelős szerkesztő (*responsible editor*) or főszerkesztő (*chief editor*) or with elnök (*chairman*) and tagjai (tag: *member*). A joint editor could be described as munkatárs (*collaborator*) but normally a phrase like e kötet munkatársai would mean *contributors of this volume.*

The publisher is indicated by some form of the root kiad-, e.g. kiadja a Statisztikai Kiadó Vállalat, or one may find terjeszti, *distributes.*

1.8.4 Numeration is usually by évfolyam (annual run, i.e. *volume*) and szám (*number*), e.g. XXV. új évfolyam 4.-5. szám, i.e. *New (series) vol. 25, no. 4-5.* Note the full stops; the numerals are ordinals. The numbers are occasionally spelt out: tizenhetedik évfolyam. A volume may also be referred to as kötet, a physical volume, and a part as füzet, a fascicule.

1.8.5 Periodicity is variously expressed. Representative expressions are: megjelenik havonta (egyszer), *appears (once) monthly*; megjelenik negyedévenként, évi 1 kötetben, *appears quarterly, in one volume a year*; or implicitly két kettősfüzet alkot egy kötetet, *two double fascicules make one volume*, i.e. publication is half-yearly. The presence of supplements may be indicated by mellékletekkel (*with supplements*) the title of the supplement itself being preceded by mellékelve, the gerund (8.13.3) of mellékelni, *to add.*

1.8.6 Subscriptions (előfizetési díj or ár) are payable (előfizethető) for varying periods: they may be annual (évi), for one year (egy évre), or for half a year or a quarter (félévre, egy negyedévre) or prices may be quoted per volume (kötetenként). They will be different for home (belföldre) and abroad (külföldre). Occasionally periodicals are stated to be *buyable in single copies* (példányonként megvásárolható).

1.8.7 Addresses distinguish the editorial side (szerkesztőség) from the business side (kiadóhivatal, *publishing office*), the latter being alluded to in such expressions as beszerezhető (*obtainable*) and megrendelhető (*may be ordered*). Sometimes both offices are the same: **Ugyanerre a címre küldendő minden szerkesztőségi és kiadóhivatali levelezés,** *All correspondence for the editor and the publishing office is to be sent* (8.12.3) *to the same address.*

2 ALPHABET, PHONETICS, SPELLING

2.1 ALPHABET

2.1.1 The present-day alphabet runs as follows:

a á b c cs d dz dzs e é f g gy h i í j k l ly m n

ny o ó ö ő p r s sz t ty u ú ü ű v z zs

Letters which are bracketed are treated as one and the same, otherwise each letter or cluster has a separate alphabetical position. When the digraphs are doubled only the first letter is repeated, viz. **ccs, ggy, lly, nny, ssz, tty, zzs,** but the resulting cluster is alphabetised as if it were **cscs, gygy** etc. so that **össze** does not follow **ősrégi** but **őszi**. For catalogue order see 2.1.3.

2.1.2 Departures from standard practice are found, especially in older works. For instance short **a** may be distinguished from long **á** and so on, so that every element in the alphabet in 2.1.1 has a separate place; or this may be done at the beginning of a word, but not in the middle.

2.1.3 For Hungarian alphabetical catalogues which include foreign authors there is a standard cataloguing alphabet a a ä b c d e f g h i j k l m n o ö p q r s t u ü v w x y z. Digraphs are analysed into their component letters, so that **cs** for instance is filed between **cr** and **ct** and not after **cz**.

2.2 CAPITALISATION

2.2.1 All names are spelt with an initial capital, but the words for months are not treated as names, and adjectives derived from place-names, such as **budapesti**, have small letters.

2.2.2 In complex names such as those of institutions, all parts have capitals, e.g. **Eötvös Lóránt Tudományegyetem Könyvtára,** *Lóránt Eötvös University Library*. The names of subdepartments are sometimes treated simply as descriptive expressions and not written with capitals, e.g. **számviteli tanulmányi ügyosztály,** *Accounting Research Department*. Similarly the generic parts of geographical and topographical names, if separate words, are spelt with small letters, e.g. **Váci utca,** *Váci Street*. But more often than not the word is a compound and the question does not arise, e.g. **Gellérthegy,** *Gellért Hill.*

2.2.3 Titles such as **úr**, *Mr*; **gróf**, *Count* are spelt small, e.g. **V. Kelemen pápa,** *Pope Clement V.*

2.3 DIVISION OF WORDS

2.3.1 Rules 1, 2, 4, 5a, 6a, 7a and 8 (p. xiii) apply.

2.3.2 **dz** and **dzs** are split if preceded by a vowel but not if preceded by **n**.

2.3.3 The digraphs **cs, cz** (still used for **c** in some names), **gy, ly, ny, sz, ty, zs** must not be divided, but **csz** and **szs** are ambiguous. The double digraphs such as **ccs** (see 2.1.1), when divided, are written in full, **cs-cs**, and may have to be converted in transcription, one way or the other.

2.4 PUNCTUATION AND ABBREVIATIONS

2.4.1 When successive compound words have the last element in common, it is omitted from the first word, which ends in a hyphen, e.g. **lap- és könyvkiadó,** *newspaper and book publishers.*

2.4.2 Abbreviations are usually followed by a full stop, whether, like **pl.** (**például,** *for example*) they include the last letter, or, like **stb.** (**és a többi,** *etc.*) and **kb.** (**körülbelül,** *about*) they do not. If, however, they have grammatical terminations, these are attached by a hyphen and there is no full stop, e.g. **jkv-ek** for **jelentéskönyvek.** In special cases one will find books that never use full stops or hyphens, e.g. dictionaries, where one will regularly find **vmnek** for **valaminek.** There is, however, a tendency nowadays to use acronyms on the Russian pattern, read as letters: hence **az SZT** (read: esz té), though in another work we find **a MNOSZ,** presumably read in full. Where there are suffixes they harmonize with the abbreviation as read, and are not derived from the original word, e.g. **az üb-je** (read übéje) for **üzemi bizottsága.**

2.4.3 The use of the full stop, denoting an abbreviation, as the sole indication of an ordinal number can have disconcerting effects, especially in dates. See 6.4.3.

2.5 VARIATION OF CONSONANT

Assimilation often takes place in pronunciation which is not reflected in spelling. There are also a few instances of assimilation which do affect the spelling. For instance, **-v-** is assimilated to the preceding consonant in the suffix **-val/-vel,** e.g. **arab számokkal,** *with arabic numerals,* for **számokval;** and blends with the vowel in words like **szó,** some parts of which have the stem **szav-.** See also 7.1.2, 8.7.2.

2.6 VOWEL HARMONY AND CHANGE OF VOWEL

2.6.1 The vowels in an uncompounded word must harmonise. For this purpose vowels are divided into four sets:

> *Front:* **e**
> *Rounded:* **ö, ő, ü, ű**
> *Back:* **a, á, o, ó, u, ú**
> *Neutral:* **é, i, í**

Within the stem of a word back vowels are compatible with back or neutral vowels; all other vowels are mutually compatible, e.g. **ablak, acél, fordít, likőr, legyőz.** The vowel **e,** always classed as a front vowel, is also found with back vowels, e.g. **puder, reform,** but it is not neutral in the same way as **i** and **í; é,** classed as neutral, is nearly always a front vowel.

2.6.2 Most vowels in terminations and suffixes are variable, unless they are neutral, and in this connexion **é** is definitely a front vowel. In most cases there are two variants, back and front, e.g. **-ban/-ben, -alom/-elem, -tás/-tés;** or back and rounded, e.g. **-ó/-ő, -unk/-ünk.** Back goes with back, front with front or rounded, and rounded with front or rounded, e.g. with the ending **-a/-e** we have **szám-a, szerep-e, könyv-e;** with **-ó/-ő** we have **igazgat-ó, vezet-ő, küld-ő.** When **-e-** occurs before back vowels it is the last syllable that counts, e.g. **reform-a**, but neutral vowels are simply by-passed, e.g. **kenyér-e, tányér-ja**, and by themselves are ambiguous, e.g. **rész-e, cél-ja, film-je, nyit-ott**. With some noun suffixes, and more frequently with verbs, the suffix has three forms, back, front and rounded, indicated by (3), e.g. **kiadás-hoz, eh-hez** (7.1.2), **könyv-höz; fordít-otta, készít-ette, küld-ötte**. These variable vowels will be represented by capitals, i.e. -A stands for -a- or -e-.

2.6.3 Final **-a** and **-e**, whether part of the stem or themselves endings, are usually lengthened to **-á-** and **-é-** when suffixes are added, e.g. **pártja** + **nak** > **pártjának; szükségessége** + **t** > **szükségességét**.

2.6.4 In some words the vowel of the last syllable is shortened before various endings; e.g. **-Vt** (object), **-Vk** (plural) and the possessive suffixes, e.g. **úr, urat; nyár, nyarak; szív, szivem; kevés, keveset**. In others the last vowel is omitted, e.g. **irodalom, irodalma**.

2.7 SPELLING

2.7.1 Hungarian spelling has been stable for some time. The principal differences between current spelling and that of the early periods, still preserved in some surnames, are:

Vowels	**aa** or **aá** for **á**
	eö for **ö**
	oó for **ó**
	y for **i**
Consonants	**ch** for **cs**
	cz for **c**
	th for **t**
	ts for **cs**
	w for **v**

2.7.2 Of these **ts** is still found in ordinary words in the early nineteenth century, while **cz** competes with **c** until well into the twentieth. That being so, **c** persisted in words like **critica**, which are now spelt with **k**. The regular simplification of double digraphs (2.1.1) is recent: some nineteenth-century texts have forms like **melylyet**. Earlier one finds **eggy** for **egy**. Among miscellaneous changes we may note **-kint** for present day **-ként**.

3 ARTICLES

3.1 DEFINITE

3.1.1 The definite article has the forms **a** before a consonant, **az** before a vowel. Apart from this it is invariable. For **az a(z)** and for **az** before a consonant see 7.1.3.

3.1.2 The Hungarian definite article corresponds only roughly to the English *the*. It is used with abstract nouns, e.g. **a tudomány**, *science*; while in phrases of the type **a szerző neve** (*the name of the author*) the second noun has no article (cf. *the author's name*).

3.2 INDEFINITE

The indefinite article is **egy**, which also means *one*. The sense *one* is never far away, and where the meaning is less emphatic the article is often omitted.

4 NOUNS

4.1 GENDER AND ENDINGS

4.1.1 There is no grammatical gender, and the notion of case is inappropriate. A large number of suffixes can be attached to the noun to denote the plural or the direct object or some other grammatical relationship or possession by this or that person, but (vowel harmony apart) they are the same whatever noun they are attached to.

4.1.2 If we look at some noun complexes in order of complexity, we can see how these various suffixes are added:

> részben: rész, *part* + -bAn, *in*
> munkában: similar, but the final -a of munka is lengthened (2.6.3)
> címe: cím, *title* + personal suffix -A, *its*
> okok: ok, *cause* + plural -k
> műveket: művek, pl. of mű, *work*, + -t, indicating the direct object
> pártunknak: párt, *party* + -unk, *our* + -nak, *to*; *to our party*
> bevezetésében: *in his introduction*; like the preceding but with vowel lengthening (2.6.3)
> egyetemeinket: egyetem, *university*, + pl. stem -ei- + -nk + -t: *our universities* (object)

One must strip off the suffixes one by one. The plural suffixes are dealt with in 4.2, the personal suffixes in 4.5 and the relational suffixes in 4.4.

4.2 PLURAL

4.2.1 The suffixes are:

> -k when no personal suffix follows
> -i when a personal suffix follows

They are added directly to words ending in a vowel, and by means of auxiliary to those that end in a consonant, viz.

kiadó	kiadók	kiadói
nyomda	nyomdák	nyomdái (2.6.3)
kiadvány	kiadványok	kiadványai
irodalom	irodalmak	irodalmai (2.6.4)
közlemény	közlemények	közleményei
kör	körök	körei
mű	művek	művei

The words in the third column also have the third-person suffix, which in this case is zero.

4.2.2 The laws of vowel harmony (2.6.2) apply. As between -ak and -ok there is no easy way of distinguishing. Mostly, however, one will need to find the plural of such words as **kiadvány** (*publication*), which occur in the names of series. Such derived words (13.3) all have plurals in -ok except those in -alom (-almak). Only if one follows British Museum rules, would one be faced with the necessity of producing the heading **városok** for a book with the morphologically ambiguous title Városaink (*Our towns*). Most words with rounded vowels have plurals in -ök; the only important exception apart from **mű** is **könyv**.

4.4 RELATIONAL SUFFIXES

4.4.1 The suffixes express the simpler relations which in English are expressed by such words as *in, for, as*. They have been treated in the past as case endings, making a fine array of cases, but see 4.1.1. Most of the suffixes have corresponding stems to which personal endings (4.5) are attached to express such ideas as *in me*, etc.

4.4.2 The suffixes, in alphabetical order of the last letter, with the corresponding stem, if any, and a rough translation, are as follows. The capitals indicate variations due to vowel harmony (2.6.2).

Suffix	Stem	Translation
-bA	**belé-**	*into*
-rA	**rá-/reá-**	*on to*; by (time) *for* (time, purpose)
-vÁ (-CCÁ)		*into* (transformation)
-lAg		makes adverbs (9.1)
-ig		*as far as, until*
-nAk	**nek-**	See 4.4.4
-nÁl	**nál-**	*at the house of, with; than*
-vAl (-CCAl)	**vel-**	*with*
-bÓl	**belől-**	*out of*
-rÓl	**ról-**	(*down*) *from, off; about*
-tÓl	**től-**	*from*
-Ul		See 4.4.4
-n	**rajt-**	*on, at*
-bAn	**benn-**	*in*(*side*)
-kor		*at* (time) See 4.4.4
-t		direct object
-t(t)		*at*
-ként		See 4.4.4
-nként		*at a time, per*
-ért	**ért-**	*for, because of*
hOz(3)	**hozzá-**	*to*(*wards*)

4.4.3 The **-CCÁ** and **-CCAl** under **-vÁ** and **-vAl** refer to the fact that the **-v-** is assimilated to the preceding consonant, producing a double consonant (2.5). The stems which end in a vowel, viz **rá-/reá-** and **hozzá-** have a long vowel when the personal ending is added, e.g. **hozzám, hozzá**, *to me, to him* (*her, it*). The suffix **-n** takes the auxiliary vowels **-o-, -e-, -ö-** when it means *on* or *at*; and **-a-** (commonly), **-o-** or **-e-** when it forms adverbs. The **-t** of the direct object can be added direct to some words, as is that meaning *at*, but **-tt** requires a vowel.

4.4.4 The suffix **-nAk** indicates the indirect object and may be translated *to* or *for*, as in **engedni fellángolásnak**, *to give way to enthusiasm*; but one of its commonest uses is to indicate possession. Where there are only two nouns it is unusual to find **-nAk**, the personal suffix is enough (4.5.3), but where there are three, the middle one has **-nAk**, e.g. **a fogalom meghatározásának jelentősége**, *the importance of the definition of the concept*. It is also used where the first element is a pronoun or if the two nouns are separated: **brosuránknak nem ez a célja**, *the aim of our brochure is not this*, or more naturally, *our brochure has not this aim*. Note, however, the use of a personal suffix in

Hungarian. The logical subject of an impersonal expression also takes -nAk, e.g. **nekem kell,** *I must.*

The suffix **-Ul** has a variety of uses: it expresses a temporary state, being either omitted in translation or rendered *as,* e.g. **például,** *as an example, (e.g.);* with languages it means *in;* and it makes adverbs from adjectives.

-kor, besides being attached to such obvious words as **óra** (*hour, time*) and numerals, is used with nouns of action and the suffix of the third person as the equivalent of a clause, e.g. **építésekor,** *when it was being built.* It does not lengthen the preceding vowel.

-ként, insofar as the words formed with it are not in the dictionary, may often be translated *as,* e.g. **a harc eredményeként,** *as a result of the struggle.* For **-nként** cf. 1.8.5, 1.8.6.

4.5 PERSONAL SUFFIXES

4.5.1 The suffixes are added directly to words or stems ending in a vowel, and by means of a connecting vowel to those which end in a consonant, viz.

$$
\begin{array}{rll}
 & 1 & \text{-(A)m, -(O)m} \\
S & 2 & \text{-(A)d, -(O)d} \\
 & 3 & \text{-(j)A} \quad \text{(See 4.2.1)}
\end{array}
$$

$$
\begin{array}{rll}
 & 1 & \text{-(U)nk} \\
P & 2 & \text{-(a)tok, -(e)tek, -otok, -(e)tök} \\
 & 3 & \text{-(j)Uk, -k}
\end{array}
$$

(The 3rd-person suffix may be used for the 2nd: cf. 7.3.2.)

Examples: **egyeteme,** *its university;* **egyetemünk,** *our university;* **egyetemei,** *its universities;* **egyetemeink,** *our universities;* **nyomdája,** *his (her, its) press;* **nyomdánk, nyomdái, nyomdáink** (from **nyomda,** 2.6.3); **nevem** (from **név,** 2.6.4); vowel harmony as in 4.2.1, e.g. **könyvem** not **-öm.**

4.5.2 The suffix **-jA** is used after a vowel, and may be found after **b, d, f, g, k, l, m, n, p, r, t.** It is obligatory after two consonants, but otherwise the rules are very complicated.

4.5.3 The possessive meaning of the suffixes is common, especially the use of the third person suffix where English uses *of,* e.g. **a könyv címe,** *the title of the book* (*the book its title*); **Magyar Dolgozók Pártja,** *Hungarian Workers' Party.* (Note the use of the singular suffix with a plural noun. This is usual.) It is not, however, the only meaning. The suffixes can be added to stems indicating relations (4.4) and to postpositions (10.3.1), e.g. **vele,** *with him (her, it);* **mögöttem,** *behind me,* to numerals and the like, e.g. **hármunk,** *the three of us;* **többük,** *several of them,* and to the infinitive (8.11.3). **Neki,** *to him, her, it,* **nektek,** *to you,* **nekik,** *to them,* are irregular.

4.5.4 There is a further suffix **-é** (after both front and back vowels) which means *that of,* though it will often be represented by a simple *'s.* It can be added to a noun which already has a possessive suffix, e.g. **apám,** *my father;* **az apámé,** *my father's,* and can receive in addition the plural and relational suffixes.

5 ADJECTIVES

5.1 GENERAL

5.1.1 Adjectives used attributively precede the noun and are invariable, e.g. **a felelős kiadók,** *the responsible publishers.*

5.1.2 When used alone or as predicates or in apposition, they are treated exactly like nouns, e.g. **a kiadók felelősek**, *the publishers are responsible*. The auxiliary vowels are -a-, -o- or -e-

5.3 COMPARISON

The comparative is formed by adding -bb, with auxiliary vowel if necessary, to the positive. The superlative is formed by prefixing **leg-** to the comparative. Changes of stem of the types mentioned in 2.5 and 2.6 occur, and a good many adjectives in -ú/-ű drop this vowel and add -abb/-ebb. There are also a few of the type **jómódú** > **jobb módú** (*well off, better off*). Natural enough, but **módú** alone is not in the dictionary (cf. 13.3: -U). Even nouns can take the comparative and superlative affixes.

6 NUMERALS

6.1 CARDINAL

6.1.1

1 egy	11, etc. **tizenegy**, etc.	101, etc. **százegy**, etc.
2 **kettő/két**	20 **húsz**	1000 **ezer**
3 **három**	21 **huszonegy**	2000 **kétezer**
4 **négy**	30 **harminc**	
5 **öt**	31 **harmincegy**	
6 **hat**	40 **negyven**	
7 **hét**	50 **ötven**	
8 **nyolc**	60 **hatvan**	
9 **kilenc**	90 **kilencven**	
10 **tíz**	100 **száz**	

6.1.2 Cardinal number behave as adjectives, taking suffixes or not according to the way they are used (5.1).

6.1.3 Numerals are followed by nouns in the singular, and this combination takes a singular verb, e.g. **Háromnál több szerző írta**, *More than three authors wrote it*. The plural verb, however, is used in such constructions as **öten jöttek**, *five of them came*. See also 4.5.3.

6.2 OTHER

6.2.1 *Ordinal*

1 **első**	4 **negyedik**	7 **hetedik**
2 **második**	5 **ötödik**	8 **nyolcadik**
3 **harmadik**	6 **hatodik**	9 **kilencedik**

and so on, adding -dik, with auxiliary vowel, to the stem of the cardinal. For the numerals 10–1,000 the vowel is -a- or -e-. In *21st, 22nd* and the like the endings are **-egyedik** and **-kettedik**.

6.2.2 Ordinals are adjectives and behave as such.

6.2.3 The ending -szOr can be added to cardinals to express the meaning *twice, three times*, etc. No auxiliary vowel is used.

6.3 FIGURES

6.3.1 Cardinal numbers are represented by simple arabic numerals.

6.3.2 Ordinals are represented by arabic numerals followed by a full stop, unless a termination is suffixed. As ordinals precede the noun, as in **39. lapon** (*on page 39*), and are used among other things for the year in a date, the effect of the stop can be unexpected. (See also 6.4.4.) Alternatively, roman numerals may be used, again with a full stop. Earlier, ordinals suffixed **-ik**; and **6-i** (see 6.4.2) was written less ambiguously, **6-iki**. *Francis I* is **I. Ferenc**.

6.4 DATES

6.4.1 The months are:

> **január, február, március, április, május, június,**
> **július, augusztus, szeptember, október, november, december**

6.4.2 Dates are given in the order year, month, day, e.g. *23 March 1953* = **ezer-kilencszázötvenharmadik (évi) március (hó) huszonharmadika (-dik napja)** as if it were *23rd* (*day*) *of the 1953rd* (*year's*) *March* (*month*). *On* is expressed by adding **-n** at the end, viz. **harmadikán** (or **napján** as the case may be). Some grammars prescribe cardinal numbers for the year.

This may be abbreviated in varying degrees, viz. **1953. (évi) március (hó) 23. (23-án** or **23. napján**); or the month may be abbreviated to **már.** or **III.**

In May 1945, however, is **1945 (ezerkilencszáznegyvenöt) májusában**, i.e. *in May of 1945*.

An entire date can be made into an adjective by adding **-i**, e.g. **1945. január 6-i ülésén**, *at the 6 January 1945 session.*

6.4.3 In expressions involving dates one would expect the year to have a full stop if it is an adjective and none if it is a noun, and this is usually so; but even Hungarian printers sometimes become confused, printing **1951. első negyedévében**, *in the first quarter of 1951*; and **az 1945–1952. közötti időszak**, *the period between 1945 and 1952.* In the latter it is **között** (*between*) that is made into an adjective, not the date, and elsewhere we find, correctly, **az 1960 és 1964 közötti ötéves periódus**, *the five-year period between 1960 and 1964.* When reading proof, therefore, one must not correct quotations by the light of theory. (What one must look for is the typist or printer who has taken the full stop for the end of a sentence and given the next word an unwarranted capital.)

6.4.4 As well as **-i** (6.4.2), **-s** with the appropriate vowel is used to make adjectives from cardinal numbers, e.g. **a Gazdasági Főtanács 1946-os januári rendelete**, *the decree of the Supreme Economic Council of January 1946*; **10 ezres főnyi munkástömeg**, *a crowd of workers ten thousand strong*; **az (19)50-es évek**, *the (19)50's.*

7 PRONOUNS

7.1/7.2 DEMONSTRATIVE, INTERROGATIVE, ETC.

7.1.1 There is little to note grammatically about any of these pronouns. When used adjectivally they all behave like adjectives, except **az** and **ez**, otherwise they take suffixes in the same way as nouns, e.g. **amelyekben** = **amely** (*which*) + **-ek** (plural) + **-ben** (*in*). The reflexive pronoun is simply **mag** (*self*) plus a personal ending: **magam**, *myself.*

7.1.2 **Az**, *that*, **e(z)**, *this*, share the peculiarity that they take suffixes even when used as adjectives, and assimilate the **-z** to the consonant of the suffix, except for **azt**, **ezt**, **azzal**, **ezzel** (**avval** and **evval** are also possible). So we find **ezzel a kérdéssel**, *with this problem*, as it were *with this, with the problem*, the article being indispensable. Similarly with postpositions (cf. 10), e.g. **ezek után a művek után**, *after these works.*

By itself, however, e(z) does not require the article, e.g. e **kötet szerzői**, *authors of this volume*.

7.1.3 **Az** may occasionally be ambiguous, since it has the same form as the definite article, but adjectivally it is either followed by the article, so that **az a(z)** the demonstrative contrasts with **a(z)** the article, or it has a suffix, or is followed by a postposition. As a pronoun it is always **az**, whereas the article has the form **az** only before vowels: **az ember** could therefore mean either *the man* or *that (is) a man*; **az a ház**, *that house* or *that (is) the house*; but **az ház** could only mean *that (is) a house*.

7.1.4 It may sometimes be more appropriate to translate **az** by *it* than *that*.

7.1.5 Compounds of **az** and **ez**, such as **ugyanaz (-ez)**, *the same*, share their peculiarities, e.g. **ugyanerre a címre**, *to the same address*.

7.2 RELATIVE AND INTERROGATIVE
See 7.1/7.2.

7.3 PERSONAL

7.3.1 The forms are:

	S			P		
	1	2	3	1	2	3
N	én	te/ön/maga	ő	mi	ti/önök/maguk	ők
A	engem(et)	téged(et)/önt/magát	őt	minket, bennünket	titeket, benneteket, önöket, magukat	őket

7.3.2 **Ön** and **maga**, the 'polite' forms, are both nouns and are grammatically third person. They are sometimes omitted, the third person then doing duty for the second. They take the usual range of relational suffixes, but not of course, personal ones: in fact **maga** and **maguk** already have personal suffixes and mean literally *himself* and *themselves*. The others do not take suffixes, personalised forms of the corresponding stems being used instead (4.4).

7.3.3 The third person pronouns apply to all genders, but as **az** (7.1.4) is available for *it*, **ő** is more likely to mean *he* or *she*.

7.3.4 Generally speaking the nominative forms are used for emphasis, and can emphasise a personal suffix as well as being used as subject, e.g. **az én könyvem**, *MY book*.

7.3.5 *Possessive*

In form these consist of the stem of the personal pronoun, the vowel **-e-** and the appropriate personal suffix, viz.

S		P
enyém	*mine*	enyéim
tied	*thine*	tieid
övé	*his, hers*	övéi
mienk	*ours*	mieink
tietek	*yours*	tieitek
övék	*theirs*	övéik

The **-é** of **övé** is identical with that mentioned in **4.5.4**. It is also added to **ön** and **maga**, which as already mentioned, are nouns.

8 VERBS

8.1 STRUCTURE

8.1.1 Basically the verb is made up of a stem, various suffixes, and auxiliary vowels. The suffixes indicate tense or mood, and person; but though some of the personal endings always indicate the same person, this is not true of all of them, and it is less tedious to set out the paradigms than to analyse each form in turn.

8.1.2 In transitive verbs every tense has two forms: subjective when there is no specific object, and objective when there is one. Intransitive verbs may simply have subjective forms, or, in the singular of certain tenses, peculiar forms sometimes known as middle. (More often these are treated as subjective and the verbs themselves called **-ik**-verbs from the ending of the 3PS of the present.) There is growing confusion between the forms. (See also 8.15.2.)

8.1.3 Verbs are entered in the dictionary either under the 3PS subjective of the present (8.2.1, 8.2.2), or less commonly nowadays, under the infinitive (8.11).

8.2 PRESENT

8.2.1 *Endings*

		Objective	*Subjective*	**-ik** *forms* (8.1.2)
	1	-Om(3)	-Ok(3)	-Om(3)
S	2	-Od(3)	-sz/-Ol(3)	-Ol(3)/-sz
	3	-ja/-i	-	-ik
	1	-jUk	-Unk	-Unk
P	2	-jatok/-itek	-tOk(3)	-tOk(3)
	3	-ják/-ik	-nAk	-nAk

The **-Ol** of the subjective is used if the stem ends in **-s, -sz** or **-z**; conversely the **-ik** form is **-sz** after **-l-**.

The capital letters refer to vowel harmony (2.6.2).

8.2.2 In some verbs the last vowel of the stem is fugitive, e.g. **érez**, **érzek** (2.6.4). In some verbs with stems in **-v-** it alternates with a doubled consonant, e.g. **jövök**, **jönnek**, (and 3PS **jön**) from **jönni**, *to come*; a few omit the **-v-** and lengthen the vowel; others have **-sz-** throughout the present, e.g. **veszek**, *I take*, *buy* from **venni**, but other verbs with **-sz-** have infinitives in **-Udni**, **-Odni** or **-Ozni**, e.g. **alszik**, *he sleeps*, from **aludni**. After **-s-**, **-sz-** and **-z-** the **-j-** of the ending is assimilated, producing **-ss-**, **-ssz-** and **-zz-**.

8.2.3 The present tense may have a future meaning, or refer to events going on up to the present (in English, perfect tense).

8.3 PAST

8.3.1 The characteristic of the tense is the insertion of **-t(t)-**, producing the following endings:

		Objective	*Subjective*
	1	-(Ot)tAm	-(Ot)tAm
S	2	-(Ot)tAd	-(Ot)tÁl
	3	-(Ot)tA	-(Ot)t
	1	-(Ot)tUk	-(Ot)tUnk
P	2	-(Ot)tÁtOk	-(Ot)tAtOk
	3	-(Ot)tÁk	-(Ot)tAk

The -Ot- is subject to triple harmony, viz. -ottam, -ettem, -öttem; -tok alternates with -tek.

8.3.2 Important classes of verbs which take the long endings are those with stems ending in two consonants e.g. szerkeszt|ette, those in -ít, e.g. fordít|otta and a number of monosyllable stems, e.g. fut|ottak. Conversely verbs with stems in -j, -l, -ly, -n, -ny, or -r have short endings and plain -t in the 3 p.s. subjective. Hence szerette must come from szeretni not szerni. Forms like vette correspond to infinitive venni, etc. (cf. 8.2.2).

8.3.3 The tense corresponds to the English imperfect, past, perfect, pluperfect and future perfect, being the only past tense in current use. Statistically, it is most likely to be simple past. See also 8.10.1.

8.3.4 In the nineteenth century another past tense still survives, usually functioning as a perfect, which has the forms of the conditional (8.6.1) without the conditional characteristic -n-.

8.5 FUTURE

8.5.1 The simple future has the characteristic -and-/-end- plus the same endings as the present, except that it has -jétek and -jék instead of -itek and -ik.

8.5.2 It is interchangeable with the periphrastic future (8.10.2), e.g. mely felölelendi a statisztika minden ágát s tartalmazni fogja..., *which will comprise every branch of statistics and will contain* .... It is almost obsolete, but see 8.12.3.

8.6 CONDITIONAL

8.6.1 The tense-suffix is -n-, producing:

		Objective	Subjective	-ik forms
	1	-nÁm	-nék	-nÁm
S	2	-nÁd	-nÁl	-nÁl
	3	-nÁ	-nA	-nék
	1	-nÁnk/-nÓk	-nÁnk	
P	2	-nÁtOk	-nÁtOk	
	3	-nÁk	-nÁnAk	

Capital letters indicate vowel harmony (2.6.2), viz. a/e, á/é, o/e, ó/ő.

8.6.2 The conditional, as its name implies, is used in conditional sentences, in both halves, and in some other subordinate clauses, e.g. mielőtt hozzáfognánk, *before we begin*.

8.7 SUBJUNCTIVE/IMPERATIVE

8.7.1 The characteristic suffix is -j-, producing:

		Objective	Subjective	-ik forms
	1	-jAm	-jAk	-jAm
S	2	-jAd	-jÁl	-jÁl
	3	-jA	-jOn (3)	-jék
	1	-jUk	-jUnk	
P	2	-jÁtOk	-jAtOk	
	3	-jÁk	-jAnAk	

Capital letters indicate vowel harmony (2.6.2).

8.7.2   Assimilation of -j- occurs in verbs whose stems involve a sibilant or -t-, viz.

Stem consonant	s	st	sz	szt	tsz	z	ít	űt	Ct	Vt
Subj. stem	ss	ss	ssz	ssz	ss/tssz	zz	íts	űts	Cts	Vss

e.g. **megkönnyítse** (8.7.4) from **megkönnyíteni**.

8.7.3   Verbs with stems in -v- and infinitives in -nni mostly have subjunctives in -gy-, e.g. **tegyünk**, *let us make*; but **jönni**, *to come* has **jöjj-**.

8.7.4   The forms can be used in independent sentences to express wishes or commands, and are common after certain subordinating conjunctions such as **hogy**, *that*, e.g. **Bibliográfiánknak az a célja, hogy a munkát megkönnyítse**, *It is the aim of our bibliography to make the work easier.*

8.10   COMPOUND TENSES

8.10.1   *The perfect and pluperfect* can be formed by adding **volt** (invariable: 8.17.2) to the present and past respectively, but both tenses are now obsolete.

8.10.2   *The future* is formed by combining the present of the auxiliary verb **fogni** with the infinitive. For example see 8.5.2.

8.10.3   *The conditional perfect* is formed by adding **volna** (8.17.5) to the past, e.g. **megjelent volna**, *would have been published.*

8.11   INFINITIVE

8.11.1   The infinitive ends in -ni. If the dictionary is not one which enters verbs under the infinitive see 8.2.2 for peculiarities of the present stem.

8.11.2   The infinitive is used, as in English, after other verbs, e.g. **Kiadványunk ezt a célt kívánja szolgálni**, *Our publication aims to serve this end.*

8.11.3   In an impersonal expression the infinitive may take personal suffixes making

	1 -nOm(3)		1 -nUnk
S	2 -nOd(3)	P	2 -nOtOk(3)
	3 -niA		3 -niUk or -niOk(2)

e.g. **tudnunk kell**, *we must know.*

8.12   PARTICIPLES

8.12.1   The present participle ends in -Ó. The stem may be assimilated or modified in the infinitive e.g. **jövő, jönni**; **alvó, aludni**; and modified in the present (8.2.2), but generally finding the dictionary form is straightforward.

The participle can be used as an adjective or a noun, and the nouns have a wide range of meaning. For instance **kiadó** from **kiadni**, *to publish* can mean *publishing* or *publisher*. (See 1.6.1.)

8.12.2   The present participle of potential verbs (8.23.5), ending in -hAtÓ, is passive in meaning and equivalent to *-able*, e.g. **beszerezhető**, *obtainable* from **beszerezni**, *to obtain.*

8.12.3   The future participle has the same ending as the present, with the insertion of the future characteristic -(A)nd-. Except for survivals like **állandó**, *permanent* (from **állni**, *to stand*) it is now rare. The 'future participle' of a transitive verb is passive in meaning and implies that something is to be done; for example see 1.8.7.

8.12.4   The past participle is the same as the 3PS of the past subjective (8.3.1). It is passive in meaning, like the past participle in English, e.g. **bővített kiadás**, *enlarged edition.*

8.13 GERUNDS

8.13.1 *Present:* -vA
Past: -vAn

Stems in -v- are simplified, e.g. **téve** from **tenni**, **alva** from **aludni** (cf. 8.2.2).

8.13.2 The gerunds, which are adverbial, are nearer in use to English participles than are the participles, but they cannot be simply equated with them, nor are the terms 'present' and 'past' wholly appropriate.

8.13.3 The principal uses of the gerund in -va are:

(a) Where English uses a present participle or equivalent clause, e.g. **Az iparosítást vizsgálva, tudnunk kell...**, *When examining industrialisation, we must know...*; **összefoglalva**, *to sum up.* (Note **kézbevéve**, one word, *taking up*, from **kézbe venni**, *to take into the hand*.)

(b) As a predicate, equivalent to an English passive participle, e.g. **külön feltételekhez van kötve**, *is subject to special conditions* (**kötni**, *to bind*); **nincsen korlátozva**, *is not restricted.*

8.13.4 The less common gerund in -vAn can usually be translated by an English perfect participle active: **hallván**, *having heard.* Some are specialised as adverbs, e.g. **nyilván**, *obviously*, and have separate entries in the dictionary.

8.15 PASSIVE

8.15.1 The passive only survives in very formal writing such as the texts of laws and official instructions, e.g. **általános népszámlálás rendeltetik el**, *a general census is decreed.*

8.15.2 The passive consists of the causative suffix -(t)At (8.23.6) with -ik endings (8.2.2). The characteristic -atik/-etik, as in the example above, is easily recognised, but some of the other forms (fortunately even rarer) are indistinguishable from the causative, e.g. **mellyel viseltetem**, *with which I am clothed.* Actually this form is both causative and passive, since **viselni** means *to wear.*

8.15.3 In most prose the passive is avoided, *I am encouraged*, for instance, appearing as **felbátorít engem** (*it encourages me*).

8.17 THE VERB **lenni**, *to be*

8.17.1 *Present:* **vagyok, vagy, van; vagyunk, vagytok, vannak**

8.17.2 *Past:* **voltam/lettem**, etc.

8.17.3 *Perfect:* **valék**, etc.

8.17.4 *Future:* **leszek**, etc. (present of **lenni**)

8.17.5 *Conditional:* **volnék/lennék**, etc.

8.17.6 *Subjunctive:* **legyek**, etc.

8.17.7 *Participles:*
Present: **való, levő**
Future: **leendő**
Past passive: **volt/lett**

8.17.8 *Gerunds:* **léve, lévén**

8.17.9 Except in sentences where the gerund in -va is used as a predicate (8.13.3), **van** is usually omitted. On the other hand **való** will often appear otiose to an English reader, as in **a velük való beszélgetés**, *the conversation with them*, or with a predicate may be equivalent to *is.*

8.21 INTERROGATIVE

In an interrogative sentence -e is suffixed to the verb. Consequently **hogy** (11.1) **akarunk-e írni** means *whether we wish to write*.

8.23 DERIVED VERBS: PREFIXES AND INFIXES

8.23.1 There are a large number of prefixes which alter the meaning of verbs to a greater or less degree, and as some dictionaries group words beginning with these prefixes together instead of putting them in their strict alphabetical position, a list of the common short ones is given here, viz. **át-, be-, el-, fel-, ide-, ki-, le-, meg-, rá-**.

8.23.2 The position of these prefixes is variable. They may be separated or may come last, e.g. **megjelenik havonta**, *comes out monthly*; **félévenként jelenik meg**, *comes out half yearly*; **meg kell említenünk** (8.11.3), *we must mention*. (See also 8.15.1.) To some extent their position is a matter of emphasis and style.

8.23.3 There are a number of syllables which can be inserted between the stem and the ending, making a new verb or deverbative of related meaning. Some of these are used with a few verbs only and the derived verb is given in most dictionaries but some are so universal that this would be impracticable.

8.23.4 The syllable **-gat-/-get-** makes frequentative verbs. Some like **hallgatni**, *to listen* (**hallni**, *to hear*) have achieved independence, but not all of them. Thus **ismétlés**, *repetition*, is given but not **ismételgetés**, *repeated repetition*!

8.23.5 The syllable **-hat-/-het-** makes potential verbs, e.g. **nem elégedhetnek meg**, *they cannot be satisfied*. Here the dictionary will simply give **megelégedni**, *to be satisfied*, or **megelégszik**, *is satisfied*, as the case may be. The ending **-ható/-hető** (*-able*) is particularly common.

8.23.6 The syllable **-(t)At** makes causative verbs, e.g. **dolgozni**, *to work*; **dolgoztatni**, *to make someone work*. As the insertion of *make* is often not appropriate, a great many causatives are given separately in the dictionary. The infix can be combined with the potential **-hat-** as in **nem változtathatunk**, *we cannot make any change* (**változni** *to change*). (See also 8.15.2.)

8.23.7 The syllables **-Ód-, -Óz-, -(Óz)kOd-, -(k)Oz-, -Ódz-** and **-Ul-** (2.6.2), are characteristic of intransitive (reflexive) verbs. The important verbs in this class are entered separately in the dictionary. They all have **-ik** forms (8.1.2).

8.23.8 The syllable **-ít-** is characteristic of transitive verbs.

9 ADVERBS

9.1 FORMATION

As in other languages, some adverbs are independent words, but most of them are formed from adjectives and nouns by adding **-(A)n, -Ul** or **-lAg**, e.g. **szép|en**, *beautifully*; **önálló|an**, *independently*; **rossz|ul**, *badly*; **jogi|lag**, *legally*.

9.2 COMPARISON

The comparative and superlative are got by adding the suffix to the comparative or superlative of the adjective or by putting **inkább** (*more*) before the positive.

10 POSTPOSITIONS

10.1 POSITION

As their name implies these words function as prepositions but follow the noun. They correspond to the more complex prepositions such as *instead of* and are analogous to them, being old nouns with relational suffixes (4.4), and just as *into the hands of youth* is **ifjúság kezébe** so *into the middle of the crowd* is **a tömeg közé**, with a postposition.

10.2 FORMS

Most of the postpositions go in threes, ending in -tt, -l and a vowel respectively, and indicating rest at, motion from, and motion towards, e.g. **között,** *among, between*; **közül,** *from among*; **közé,** *into the middle of, in among*.

10.3 DERIVATIVES

10.3.1 Postpositions are not used after pronouns, personal suffixes (4.5.1) are added instead, e.g. **közöttünk,** *among us*.

10.3.2 If a phrase ending with a postposition qualifies a noun, the suffix -i is added, e.g. **az 1946-os választások előtti állapot,** *the state of affairs before the 1946 elections*. (Cf. also 6.4.3.)

10.4 COMPOUND POSTPOSITIONS

A postposition does not as such affect the noun that it follows, but there are a number of words often regarded as postpositions but perhaps better regarded as adverbs, such as **együtt,** *together*, which, when they follow a noun, need to be combined with a relational suffix, e.g. **politikusokkal együtt,** *with politicians*.

11 CONJUNCTIONS

11.1 These should not cause much difficulty. Some are followed by the subjunctive, and **hogy,** *that*, with the subjunctive is frequently the equivalent of an English infinitive. For **hogy. . . -e** see 8.21.1.

11.2 Note also the very frequent combination of **az** with **hogy**, sometimes meaning *the fact that*, but often to be translated by a gerund, as in **hadakozott az ellen, hogy megmaradjon,** *fought against its remaining*, or ignored.

13 WORD-FORMATION

13.1 Hungarian makes derivatives and compounds freely, and on a typical page of technical writing over half the words may well be one or other or both. One may expect to find about 80% of these in a dictionary of 20,000 entries; the rest one must reconstruct.

13.2 COMPOUNDS

Compounds of noun and noun are most frequent, but noun and verb, adverb and verb, adjective and noun are also quite common. Analysis is usually easy: **élelmiszerhiány** splits into *food* + *shortage*; **hosszantartó** into **hossz** (*length*), **-an** (adverbial suffix), **tartó** (participle from **tartani,** *to last*) *long-lasting*. A word like **romeltakarítás** (still at the same dictionary level) presents more difficulty: **rom,** *ruins;* but **eltakarítás** is not there. However, **eltakarodni,** *to get out of the way*, and **takarítani,** *to tidy up*, are (cf. 8.23). The whole means *clearing away of ruins*. For **-ás** see 13.3.

13.3 DERIVATIVES

The principal suffixes with which derivatives are formed are:

-sÁg: nouns from adjectives (and nouns), either abstract nouns such as ostobaság, *stupidity*, or collectives such as küldöttség, *deputation* (küldött, *sent*).

-i: adjectives, meaning *of* or *pertaining to*, from nouns. One of the most prolific suffixes, frequently used instead of -nAk and a personal suffix, e.g. Népjóléti és Munkaügyi Minisztériumi Miniszteri Segédtitkár, *Assistant-Secretary to the Minister of the Ministry of Public Welfare and Labour.* More simply, elméleti, *theoretical.* Other examples will be found in 6.4.2, 6.4.3 and 10.3.2.

-(d)AlOm: nouns from verbs, expressing the result of the action, e.g. irodalom, *literature*, from írni, *to write.*

-t(A)lAn: negative adjectives, from nouns, e.g. határtalan, *boundless* (határ, *boundary*); from verbs, e.g. változatlan, *unchanged* (változni, *to change*); leküzdhetetlen, *unsurmountable* (leküzdeni, *to surmount*, -het- see 8.23.5); from adjectives, e.g. hűtlen, *unfaithful* (hű, *faithful*).

-mány, -vÁny: nouns from verbs, expressing the result of the action. Very few of any importance are missing from a reasonable-sized dictionary.

-s (-as, -os, -es, -ös after consonants): adjectives from nouns, adverbs and numerals, e.g. jelentős, *significant* (jelenteni, *to signify*, participle jelentő); tíz oldalas, 10-*page*; futólagos, *casual* (futólag, *casually*). See also 6.4.4. The more straightforward instances of this very common suffix, such as számos, *numerous*, have entries in the dictionary.

-Ás: nouns from verbs, expressing the action of the verb, e.g. szerzés, *acquisition* (szerezni, *to acquire*). Some have specialised meanings, e.g. kiadás, *edition* (kiadni, *to publish*), so it is as well to look them up separately first.

-Ász: nouns from nouns, indicating a person engaged in some task or occupation, e.g. kert|ész, *garden|er.*

-Ú: adjectives from nouns, either compound, like jóképű, *goodlooking*, or adjectives which though not formally compound have to be taken in connexion with what precedes, as in változó terjedelmű füzetek, *parts of varying size*; a MNOSZ 3497. számú „ Bibliográfiai hivatkozás" című szabvány, *MNOSZ standard no. 3497 entitled 'Bibliográfiai hivatkozás'.* The compounds tend to be in the dictionary, the others not.

GLOSSARY

ábra, *figure*
ár, *price*
arckép, *portrait*
átdolgozott, *revised* (1.5.2)

beszéd, *speech*
beszerezhető, *obtainable*
bevezetés, *introduction*
bizomány, *commission*
bizottság, *committee*
bővített, *enlarged*
brosúra, *pamphlet*

cím, *title, address*

csere, *exchange*

darab, *fragment, piece; play*

eddig megjelent, *already published*
egyes, *single*
egyesület, *society*
eladó, *on sale*
elbeszélés, *short story*
előfizetési ár (dij), *subscription* (1.8.6)

engedmény, *discount*
értekezlet, *conference*
év, *year*
évenként, évente, *annually*
évfolyam, *volume* (1.8.4)
évi, *of the year*
évkönyv, *yearbook*

faktúra, *invoice*
félévenként(i), *half-yearly*
folyóirat, *periodical*
folytatása következik, folytatjuk, *to be continued*
fordítás, *translation*
fordított, *translated*
főszerkesztő, *chief editor* (1.8.3)
függelék, *appendix*
füzet, *number, part* (1.7.2, 1.8.4)
fűzött, f(üz)ve, *paperback*

gyűjtés, *collection*
gyűjtőkötet, *cumulation*

halt meg, *died*
havonta, *monthly* (1.8.5)
hét, *week*

javított, *improved* (1.5.2)
jegyzet, *note*
jelentés, *bulletin*

kartonált, *in stiff covers*
kép, *illustration, portrait*
kéthetenként(i), *fortnightly*
kiadás, *edition* (1.5.1), *publication* (1.6.1)
kiadatlan, *unpublished*
kiadja, *publishes* (1.6.1)
kiadó, *publisher, press* (1.6.1)
kiadvány, *publication*
kijavítás, *correction*
kivonat, *summary, abstract*
költői, *poetical*
könyv, *book*
könyvkiadó, *publishing house* (1.6.3)
könyvtár, *library* (1.7.1)
könyvtáros, *librarian*
kötet, *volume* (1.4.1, 1.7.2, 1.8.4)
k(öt)ve, *hardback*
közlemény, *communication, publication* (1.7.1)

közreműködés, *collaboration* (1.2.5)
kutatás, *research, investigation*
küld, *sends*
külföld, *abroad* (1.8.6)
különlenyomat, *offprint* (1.5.3)

lap, *page*
lenyomat, *impression* (1.5.3)
levél, *letter*
levelezés, *correspondence*

magyarázat, *explanation, commentary*
megjelenik, *comes out* (1.8.5, 8.23.2)
megtekintésre, *on approval*
megrendelni, *to order* (1.8.7)
melléklet, *supplement* (1.8.5)
minden jog fenntartva, *all rights reserved*
minta(példány), *specimen (copy)*
munka, *work*
munkatárs, *collaborator, contributor* (1.2.5, 1.8.3)
mutató, *index*
mű(vek), *work(s)*

negyedévenként(i), *quarterly*
novella, *short story*
nyomás, *printing*
nyomda, *press*

oldal, *page*

összeállít, *compiles* (1.2.2)
összefoglalás, *summary*
összegyűjtött, *collected*
összes, *collected, complete*

példány, *copy*

regény, *novel*
régi példány, *back number*
rész, *part* (1.4.1)

sokszorosított, *duplicated*
sorozat, *series*
szám, *number* (1.7.2, 1.8.4)
számla, *invoice*
szemle, *review*
szerkeszti, *edits* (1.2.2)
szerkesztő, *editor* (1.2.3)
szerkesztőség, *editorial office* (1.8.7)

szerző, *author*
szerzői jog, *copyright*
színdarab, *play*
szótár, *dictionary*
született, *born*

tábla, *plate*
táblázat, *table*
tag, *member*
társaság, *society*
teljes, *complete*

térkép, *map*
tiszteletpéldány, *complimentary copy*
történelem, történet, *history*

ugyanaz, -ez, *same*
új, *new*
új lenyomat, *reprint*

válogatott, *selected*
változatlan, *unaltered* (1.5.2)
vizsgálat, *research, investigation*

GRAMMATICAL INDEX: WORDS, STEMS AND PREFIXES

át-, 8.23.1
az, az-, 3.1.1, 7.1

be-, 8.23.1
belé-, belől-, benn-, 4.4.2
benneteket, bennünket,
    2.3.1

el-, 8.23.1
engem(et), 7.3.1
ért-, 4.4.2
ez, ez-, 7.1

fel-, 8.23.1
fog-, 8.10.2

hozzá-, 4.4.2

ide-, 8.23.1

ki-, 8.23.1

le-, 8.23.1
leendő, 8.17.7
leg-, 5.3
legy-, 8.17.6
lenn-, 8.17.5
lesz-, 8.17.4
lett, 8.17.2, 8.17.7
lett-, 8.17.2
léve, lévén, 8.17.8
levő, 8.17.7

maguk(at), 7.3.1
meg-, 8.23.1
minket, 7.3.1

nál-, nek-, 4.4.2

rá-, 4.4.2, 8.2.3
rajt-, reá-, ról-, 4.4.2

téged(et), 7.3.1
titeket, 7.3.1
től-, 4.4.2

ugyanaz, -ez, etc., 7.1.5

vagy, 8.17.1
való, 8.17.7
van-, 8.17.1
var-, 8.17.3
vel-, 4.4.2
volna, etc., 8.10.3, 8.17.5
volt, 8.10.1, 8.17.2

GRAMMATICAL INDEX: INFIXES

-gat-, -get-, 8.23.4
-hat-, -het-, 8.23.5

-od-, -ód-, -oz-, -óz-,
    8.23.7

-(t)tat-, -(t)tet-, 8.15.2,
    8.23.6

GRAMMATICAL INDEX: ENDINGS

In this index the alternatives o/ö, ó/ő, u/ü, ú/ű (2.6.2) are mostly indexed as o, ó, u,
ú only and in any case interfiled.

-a, 4.5.1, 8.3.4, 8.6.1, 8.7.1
-á, 8.3.4, 8.6.1
-ba, 4.4.2
-nia, 8.11.3
-ja, 4.5.1, 8.2.1
-andja, 8.5.1

-ra, 4.4.2
-(ot)ta, 8.3.1
-va, 8.13.1
-vá, 4.4.2

-bb, 5.3, 9.2

-(a)d, 4.5.1
-ád, 8.3.4, 8.6.1, 8.7.1
-(ot)tad, 8.3.1
-ed, 4.5.1, 8.2.1
-éd, 8.3.4, 8.6.1, 8.7.1
-ended, 8.5.1
-(et)ted, -(öt)ted, 8.3.1
-and, -end, 8.5.1
-od, 4.5.1, 8.2.1
-andod, -endöd, 8.5.1
-nod, 8.11.3

-e, 4.5.1, 8.2.1, 8.3.4, 8.6.1, 8.7.1
-é, 4.4.2, 4.5.4, 8.3.4, 8.6.1
-be, 4.4.2
-nie, 8.11.3
-je, 4.5.1
-re, 4.4.2
-(et)te, -(öt)te, 8.3.1
-ve, 8.13.1
-vé, 4.4.2

-lag, 4.4.2, 9.1
-ság, 13.3
-leg, 4.4.2, 9.1
-ség, 13.3
-ig, 4.4.2

-i, 4.2.1, 8.2.1
-endi, 8.5.1

-k, 4.2.1, 4.5.1
-ák, 8.3.4, 8.6.1, 8.7.1
-ják, 8.2.1, 8.7.1
-andják, 8.5.1
-nak, 4.4.2, 8.2.1
-ának, 8.3.4, 8.6.1
-andnak, 8.5.1
-(ot)tak, -(ot)ták, 8.3.1
-ek, 8.2.1
-ék, 8.3.4, 8.6.1, 8.7.1
-endek, -endjék, 8.5.1
-nek, 4.4.2, 8.2.1
-endnek, 8.5.1
-ének, 8.3.4, 8.6.1
-tek, 4.5.1, 8.2.1, 8.3.1
-endtek, 8.5.1
-etek, 4.5.1, 8.2.1, 8.7.1
-étek, 8.3.4, 8.6.1, 8.7.1
-endjétek, 8.5.1

-netek, 8.11.3
-(et)tetek, -(öt)tetek, -(et)tétek, -(öt)tétek, 8.3.1
-itek, 8.2.1
-(et)tek, -(öt)ték, -(et)ték, -(öt)ték, 8.3.1
-ik, 8.2.1
-atik, -etik, 8.15.2
-nk, 4.5.1
-ánk, -énk, 8.3.4, 8.6.1
-unk, 4.5.1, 8.2.1, 8.7.1
-andunk, -endünk, 8.5.1
-nunk, 8.11.3
-(ot)tunk, -(et)tünk, -(öt)tünk, 8.3.1
-ok, 8.2.1
-andok, -endök, 8.5.1
-niok, 8.11.3
-(a)tok, -(e)tök, 4.5.1
-átok, 8.3.4, 8.6.1, 8.7.1
-andatok, 8.5.1
-jatok, 8.2.1
-(ot)tatok, -(ot)tátok, 8.3.1
-andtok, -endtök, 8.5.1
-otok, 4.5.1
-notok, 8.11.3
-(j)uk, 4.5.1, 8.2.1, 8.7.1
-niuk, 8.11.3
-andjuk, -endjük, 8.5.1
-(ot)tuk, -(et)tük, -(öt)tük, 8.3.1

-al, 4.4.2
-ál, 8.3.4, 8.7.1
-nál, 4.4.2, 8.6.1
-(ot)tál, 8.3.1
-val, 4.4.2
-el, 4.4.2, 8.2.1
-él, 8.3.4, 8.7.1
-nél, 4.4.2, 8.6.1
-(et)tél, -(öt)tél, 8.3.1
-vel, 4.4.2
-ol, 8.2.1
-ból, -ról, -tól, 4.4.2
-ul, 4.4.2, 9.1

-m, 4.5.1
-am, 4.5.1, 8.7.1
-ám, 8.3.4, 8.6.1
-(ot)tam, 8.3.1
-em, 4.5.1, 8.2.1, 8.7.1
-ém, 8.3.4, 8.6.1

-endem, 8.5.1
-delem, 13.3
-(et)tem, -(öt)tem, 8.3.1
-om, 4.5.1, 8.2.1
-andom, -endöm, 8.5.1
-nom, 8.11.3

-an, 9.1
-ban, 4.4.2
-t(a)lan, 13.3
-van, 8.13.1
-en, 9.1
-ben, 4.4.2
-t(e)len, 13.3
-ven, 8.13.1
-on, 8.7.1

-mány, -vány, -mény, -vény, 13.3

-ó, 8.12.1
-ható, -hető, 8.12.2
-andó, -endő, 8.12.3

-szer, 6.2.3
-kor, 4.4.2
-szor, 6.2.3

-s, 13.3
-ás, -és, 13.3

-sz, 8.2.1
-asz, 13.3
-andsz, -endsz, 8.5.1
-esz, 13.3

-t, 4.4.2, 8.3.1
-(n)ként, 4.4.2
-ért, 4.4.2
-tt, 4.4.2
-ett, -ott, 8.3.1, 8.12.4

-ú, 13.3

-hez, -hoz, -höz, 4.4.2

OTHER
LANGUAGES
Maltese
Turkish
Basque
Esperanto: a note

MALTESE

SPECIMEN

Il-għan li għalih twaqqfet ix-Xirka tagħna qiegħed jitwettaq qajla-qajla, iżda b'rieda qawwija li ma tafx tnikkir. Ma' l-ewwel tliet kotba li ħriġna sallum: "Ċensu Barbara", "Minn xtut in-Nil" u "L-akbar imħabba" sa nżidu r-raba' wieħed: "Ċejlu Tonna", rumanz storiku ta' Ġuże Muscat-Azzopardi. Lil dan il-kittieb issa tafuh tajjeb, għaliex qrajtu żgur xi kotba minn tiegħu jew smajtu b'kull ma għamel għall-ħolqien tal-letteratura maltija moderna.

The purpose for which our Society was set up is being confirmed gradually, but with steadfast, indefatigable will. To the first three books which we have published to date: 'Ċensu Barbara', 'From the banks (of) the Nile' and 'The greatest love', we shall add the fourth one: 'Ċejlu Tonna', a historical novel by Ġuże Muscat-Azzopardi. This writer by now you know well, for you have certainly read some books of his or heard of all that he has done for the creation of modern Maltese literature.

References to sections

3. 7.2.1	20. 4.2.2(9)	43. 10.2.4
4. 8.4.7	22. 8.4.2	44. 7.1.1
5. 3.1.2	27. 4.2.2(14)	47. 8.4.6, 7.4.6
6. 10.3	30. 5.3	48. 9.1.1
7. 8.17.3; 8.5.8	32. 8.17.5	50. 8.4.4
12. 5.2.1	33. 8.5.7	55. 10.3
14, 15. 8.22.1	34. 6.2.1	57. 8.4.3

0 GENERAL CHARACTERISTICS

0.1 DEGREE OF INFLEXION

Maltese is a moderately synthetic language, with one tendency balanced against another. The verb has a number of derivatives which are capable of expressing complex ideas by single words, and can usually dispense with subject pronouns, while object pronouns take the form of suffixes, e.g. isibulu, *they will find for him*. On the other hand there are only two tenses, making various auxiliaries necessary, and most relations between nouns necessitate the use of prepositions.

715

0.2 ORDER OF WORDS

The order of words is much the same as in English, though the standard SVO is sometimes changed to SOV or OSV for reasons of style or emphasis, or, as in the following example, O_1VO_2S: **Kemm ser jieħu żmien il-ktieb,** *How much time the book is going to take.*

0.4 RELATION TO OTHER LANGUAGES

Basically Maltese is an Arabic dialect, modified in vocabulary and to some extent in grammar by extensive borrowings from Sicilian, Italian, and to a lesser extent from English, e.g. **gvern,** *government;* **ittajpja,** *he typed;* **xeltrijiet,** *shelters.* The Semitic base shows clearly in the characteristic series of related words, each with the skeleton of the same three consonants but with different vowels and prefixes, e.g. **kiteb,** *he wrote;* **kittieb,** *writer;* **kitba,** *(way of) writing;* **kotba,** *books;* **ktieb,** *book;* **mikteb,** *school;* **miktub,** *written;* **nktib,** *registration;* **tikteb,** *she writes.*

0.5 PATTERNS

0.5.1 Grammatical endings thus play a smaller part in Maltese than they do in some inflected languages, and it is useful to know some of the typical patterns that are found both in the basic and in the secondary forms of inflected words. In the tables that follow separable endings are ignored, being dealt with elsewhere, as indicated in the index. V represents any vowel, C any consonant. Where a doubled consonant necessarily occurs in a pattern, C^2 is used. The patterns given are those which are found in inflected words of Arabic origin, patterns which are shared by many foreign borrowings. The patterns which occur only in words of foreign origin are too numerous to be listed exhaustively. Special patterns involving prefixes, infixes or suffixes are given in brackets. Native words containing more than three consonants will usually be found to be special patterns.

The parts of speech represented by the patterns are indicated thus:

fn   noun of foreign origin
fv   verb of foreign origin, basic form, i.e. 3PS masculine, past
fvf some other part of such a verb
pl   plural as listed in 4.2.2
n   native noun
v   native verb, basic form
vf   some other part of such a verb

Adjectives, unless specially mentioned, are included in nouns.

0.5.2 The principal patterns ending in a vowel (excluding inflexional endings) are:

VCCa: comparative; a few n
VCCVCa: fv; (inCaCa) v
VCCVCCa: (iC²VCCa) v; fv
VCCCa: pl 2 and 3
VCCCVCa: fv (usually iC -); (inCtaCa) v

(In many such patterns beginning with **i** the **i-** is euphonic: see 2.6.1.)

CVCa: n; fn; v; (j/n/tVCa) vf
CVCVCa: fn; (tuCija) n
CVCVCCa: fn; (mVCVCCa) n

CVCCa: n; pl; v; fv; (j/n/tiCCa) vf
CVCCVCa: fn; (tVCCVCa) n; (j/n/tinCVCa) vf
CVCCVCCa: fn; (j/n/tiC²VCCa) vf, fvf
CVCCVCCija: (mistoCCija) n
CVCCCa: fn; (mVCCCa) n
CVCCCVCa: fn; (mVCCCija) n; (j/n/tinCtVCa) vf
CCVCa: n; fn; pl 15, 16, 18; v
CCVCVCa: fn; (CCVCija, tCaCiCa, CtaCiCa) n
CCVCCa: n; fn; v; fv; (CCajCa) diminutives
CCVCCVCa: fn; (tCaC²iCa, staCCiCa) n
CCCVCCVCa: (stCVC²iCa) n

Many of these patterns are common to native and foreign words, but the latter have other patterns also, e.g. **idea, assemblea, legislatura, inkonvenjenza, industrija, università** and many others.

Words in -a' (mostly verbs) should be counted as ending in a consonant (2.1.5).

A few native nouns and many more of foreign origin end in **-i** or **-u**, and there are native and foreign adjectives in **-i** as well as some past participles, also pl. 17 and 30. The present tense of a number of verbs, mostly with past in **-a**, ends in **-i**.

The endings **-e** and **-o** are found in foreign words such as **kafe, burò**.

0.5.3   The principal patterns ending in a consonant are:

VCVC: n (rare); pl 1; (i-) vf
VCVCVC: (i-) vf
VCVC²: (i-) vf
VCVCCVC: (i-) vf
VCC: n (not common); fn
VCCVC: adjectives; pl 1; comparative; fn; (inCVC, iC²VC) vf
VCCVCVC: fvf; (inC-, iC²-) v; vf
VCCVCC: fn; fadj; inCVC², iCtVC²) v; (inCVC², iC²VC²) vf
VCCVCCVC: fn; fvf; (iC²VC²VC) v; (imC-, inC-, iC²-, int-) vf
VCCCVC: (inCtVC, intCVC) v
VCCCVCVC: (inCt-, intC-) v
VCCCVCC: (inCtVC², intCVC²) v
CVC: n; fn; v; (j/n/tVC) vf
CVCVC: n; fn; pl 4–8, 30; v; (miCieC) n; (j/n/tVCVC, CieCVC, miCuC) vf
CVCVCCVC: (gh-) pl 30
CVCC: n; fn; (CVC²) v
CVCCVC: n (CVC²VC, otherwise uncommon); fn; pl 10; v (CVC²VC, otherwise uncommon); (CejjeC, j/n/tVCCVC, maCCuC) vf; (mVCCVC, tVCCiC) n
CVCCVCVC: fn; (j/n/t-inCVCVC, -itCVCVC, i-C²VCVC) vf
CVCCVCC: fn; (j/n/t-inCVC², -iCtVC²) vf
CVCCVCCVC: fn; (j/m/n/titCVC²VC, j/n/tiC²VC²VC, j/m/n/tistaCCVC) vf
CVCCCVC: fn; (j/n/t-inCtVC, -intCVC) vf
CVCCCVCVC: fn; (j/n/t-inCtVCVC, -intCVCVC) vf
CCVC: n; fn; pl 11–14; v; (tCVC) vf

CCVCVC: fn; pl 19–25; (CtVCVC, tCVCVC) v; (CtVCiC, tCVCiC) n
CCVCC: fn; (mCVC²) n; (tCVC²) vf
CCVCCVC (commonly CCVC²VC):   (CCVjjVC) diminutives; pl 26–29;
   (staCCVC, tCVCCVC) v; (staCCiC, tCVCCiC) n
CCCVC: fn; (nCCiC) n
CCCVC²VC: (stCVC²VC) v; (Ci-) n

A good many words of foreign origin coincide with native patterns, but they exhibit others also, such as **agent, kampanjol, djakonat, skritt,** which are purely foreign.

1 BIBLIOLINGUISTICS

1.1 NAMES

1.1.1 Owing to the late appearance of Maltese as a literary language, Maltese authors' names are all of the modern Western type of Christian name and surname. The Christian names, as might be expected, are varied: beside those which are characteristically Maltese, such as **Ġorġ, Ġużè, Manwel,** we find others that are Italian or nearly so, such as **Carmelo, Rosario, Emanuel,** and not a few which are English. What is basically the same may appear in all forms—**Ġużè, Ġużi, Ġużeppi, Joseph,** and an author who writes in all three languages may well translate his name if it is international.

1.1.2 Some authors, of the late 19th century especially, who have Italianate Christian names have since adopted or are known by more Maltese forms, as **Emanuel/Leli; Anton/Ninu; Mario/Marju; Rosario/Ružar.** There are also variants such as **Gio. Antonio, Ġan Anton, Ġalanton.**

1.1.3 A few authors have used, regularly or occasionally, their Christian name only. The most famous is **Dun Karm** (**Dun** is commonly prefixed to the names of secular priests) whose full name was **Carmelo Psaila,** but we also find **is-sur Fons** for **Alfonżo Marija Galea.**

1.1.4 Surnames tend to be conservative in spelling, and in a language where a standard alphabet is a recent creation this results in half the names diverging from the standard. Diacritical marks are often omitted (**Buttigieg, Zammit** not **Buttiġieġ, Żammit**); C, Ch, and Q are found for K; Sci not X; Y not J. Occasionally the spelling is altered, perhaps only in a single publication: thus **Karuana** is found, though the traditional **Caruana** is usual.

1.1.5 There are a number of compound surnames in which the second name is the surname of the mother.

1.1.6 Plural forms are occasionally found, e.g. **Vassallijiet,** *Vassallis.*

1.2 NAMES OF AUTHORS, EDITORS, ETC.

1.2.1 None of the ways of giving the names of authors and such like has any effect on the names themselves. This is obvious when, as often happens, the name is put alone at the head of the title-page, but it applies equally when it follows the title and is itself preceded by a preposition or a noun such as **xogħol** (*work*), for there are no case endings in Maltese.

1.2.2 When the name is preceded by a noun which requires the article, care has to be taken when abbreviating the title if a preposition is combined with the article, as in **mill-Patri Ġorġ Xerri, mis-sur Fons, tas-Saċ. E. Federici.** The prepositions by themselves are **minn** and **ta',** so one cannot omit the nouns. (In any case **is-sur Fons** cannot be abridged since it is a set expression: see 1.1.3.) The abbreviation **P.** does not take the article, nor does **Dun.**

1.2.3 The relation of the writer to the work is commonly indicated by a passive participle, e.g. **miktub**, *written*; **miġbur**, *collected*; **annotat**, *annotated*; **miġjub, mfisser, maqlub**, *translated*, or in the feminine or plural, **miktuba, miktubin**, etc. Of the words for *translated* it should be noted that **miġjub** merely means *brought* and **maqlub**, *turned*; the language should be stated. The original author of an adaptation or abridgement may be indicated by **minn fuq ta'**, *from (the work) of*, or **meħud(a) mill-ktieb ta'**, *taken from the book of.*

1.3 TITLES

1.3.1 Most titles are made up of nouns and adjectives, with or without suffixes, and prepositions: e.g. **Ġrajjet Malta u n-nies tagħha**, *The story of Malta* (4.3.2) *and her people*; **L-ewwel safra tiegħi: tifkirijiet**, *My first journey: reminiscences.* In belles-lettres and in popular and instructional literature one is more likely to meet with verbs, e.g. **L-ewwel għajnuna lil min ikorri fi żmien ta' gwerra**, *First aid to the injured* (one who meets with an accident) *in time of war*; **X'nitgħallmu fil ġjografija**, *What we learn in geography*; **Ejjew nidħku ftit!**, *Let's laugh a little!*

1.3.2 Title entries do not for the most part cause any trouble, unless there are changes of spelling in the first word, say from **chelmtejn** to **kelmtejn** (*a few words*, 4.2.4). In applying British Museum rules, apart from the necessity at times of translating, one needs to watch out for construct forms of the feminine (4.3.2).

1.3.3 As there are no case endings, titles are not affected by their context, and as in English, one finds examples like **f' "Mill-Ġnejna Maltija"**, *in 'From the Maltese Garden'*; but if this strikes a writer as too harsh he can substitute **fl-antoloġija "Mill-Ġnejna Maltija"**. If a title begins with the article, a preposition does not combine with it, e.g. **ta' "Il-Muża Maltija"**.

1.4 VOLUMES AND PARTS

1.4.1 The nomenclature of divisions of a work is not very precise: the all-purpose **ktieb**, *book*, is very common. In addition one finds **parti** and **taqsima**. The latter means simply *a division* and is found not only for *chapter* but also for a part of work issued in separate covers though not necessarily with independent pagination. Where set publication in parts takes place, the word used is **faxxiklu.**

1.4.4 Occasionally the total number of volumes is stated, followed by a bare numeral, e.g. **Il-għana ta' Dun Karm fi tliet kotba. I.**, *The poems of Dun Karm in three books. I.*

1.5 EDITIONS

1.5.1 There are two words for *edition*: **ħarġa** (one special meaning of the verbal noun corresponding to **ħareġ**, *came out*) and **edizzjoni**. Or the indication of an edition may be by implication, e.g. **stampat (mitbugħ) it-tieni darba**, *printed for the second time.*

1.5.2 The specification of the edition is by a preceding numeral, e.g. **l-ewwel ħarġa**, *first edition*; **it-tieni edizzjoni**, *second edition.* Various past participles may be added to indicate particular changes, viz. **imqassra**, *abridged*; **mirquma**, *arranged*; **miżjuda**, *enlarged*; **annotata**, *annotated*; **msewwija**, *corrected* (or **maħruġa b'xi tiswijiet**, *furnished with some corrections*).

1.5.3 Offprints have no set form of words: **meħud minn** (*taken from*) **Il-Malti, 1939**; and even **maħruġ mis-Science Magazine** (*published*, i.e. originally, *by Science Magazine*).

1.6 IMPRINTS

1.6.1 The name of the publisher or printer may stand alone or be preceded by **minn** or **għand** (rarely **mingħand**). These prepositions have no effect on the form of the name. References to printing (**stamperija, tipografija; stampat, mitbugħ**) are more frequent than to publishers: often they are the only imprint there is. Publishers may be indicated simply by **jinbiegħ,** *is sold.*

1.6.2 The place of publication is rarely preceded by a preposition. Sometimes, however, the name of the town itself may begin with one, or with the article, e.g. **tas-Sliema** (in English, and sometimes in Maltese, **Sliema**), **il-Belt,** *Valetta.*

1.6.3 The actual names of the publishers or printers are of all sorts, Maltese and English: firms like **The New Art Press**; **A. C. Aquilina & Co.**; **Tonna Bianchi u sħabu** (*his partners*); periodicals like **Messaġier ta' Qalb ta' Ġesù**; institutions like **Università Rjali ta' Malta**. In a phrase like **Stampat fl-Empire Press mill-Kumitat tal-Festi** one must presumably take **stampat** as *caused to be printed* rather than *printed*, with the Festival Committee as publishers.

1.7 SERIES

1.7.1 Series titles, usually to be found at the head of the wrapper or title-page, sometimes on the opposite page, sometimes in place of the imprint, are mostly soberly descriptive, e.g. **Ġabra ta' poeżija (ta' kitba Maltija, ta' tagħlim) magħruġa mit-tabib Ġużè Bonnici)**, *Collection of poetry (of Maltese writing, of instruction) published by Dr Ġ. B.*; **Kollezzjoni "Żminijietna"**, '*Our Times' collection*; **Librerija popolari ta' " It-Torċa"**, '*It-Torċa' popular library*; **Kotba tal-mogħdija taż-żmien**, *Books for leisure.* (On **ta' It-Torċa**, not **tat-Torċa** see 1.8.1. *It-Torċa* is a newspaper.)

1.7.2 The numeration of series shares the general vagueness of nomenclature. **Għadd** (*number*) is the commonest word, but **No.** (short for **numru), volum** and **ktieb** are also found without any apparent difference of meaning. Very occasionally, where the publishing programme is regular, one finds expressions like **it-tieni sena** (*second year*).

1.8 PERIODICALS

1.8.1 The titles of periodicals are grammatically much like those of books, e.g. **Problemi ta' llum,** *Problems of today*; **Lil-ħutna,** *For our brothers*; **Dawl ġdid,** *New light.* As will be observed, however, they are not always self-explanatory.

The behaviour of a periodical title in the context of a sentence is the same as that of a book (1.3.3.) e.g. **ta' Il-Malti, f'Il-Malti**; or **fil-perjodiku L-angġlu tal-paċi.**

1.8.2 The body concerned with publication is indicated in various ways. It may appear in the form of a sub-title, e.g. **magazine ta' l-Għaqda Zgħazagħ Laburisti,** *magazine of the League of Labour Youth*; **leħen il-Kunsill Ċentrali ta' l'Opri Missjunarji Pontifiċji,** *Organ of the Central Council of Opera della Propagazione della Fede.* Alternatively a verb may be used, most often the past participle, e.g. **perjodiku maħruġ mill-Kommissjoni Emigranti,** *periodical published by the Emigrants Commission*; occasionally a relative clause, e.g. **qari li toħroġ l'Akkademja tal-Malti,** *reading-matter which the Maltese Academy publishes.*

1.8.3 Editorial indications are mostly straightforward: there is usually a **bord editorjali** with an **editur (responsabbli)**. Distinct from the editor there may be some sort of administrator—**segretarju amministrativ, amministratur ġenerali, prefett amministratur** or **direttur responsabbli**. At times, however, there is only a **direttur** or **direttur proprietarju,** or one of these with a **segretarju**. In such cases the **direttur**, whatever else he is, must be the editor.

1.8.4 In most cases numeration is primarily by **sena** (*year*), an occasional synonym being **volum**. The separate issues are designated **n(um)ru** or **għadd**, less often **ktieb** and sometimes in the case of continuous numeration **ħarġa** (1.5.1). The volume no. is frequently given in words, e.g. **għadd 6, is-sitta u għoxrin sena** (*vol. 26, no. 6*), occasionally both, e.g. **it-tielet u r-raba' ktieb tas-sitta u erbgħin sena** (*vol. 46, nos. 3 and 4*). References to foundation dates, with **sena** meaning *year* and not *annual volume*, e.g. **beda joħroġ f'Jannar tas-sena 1970** (*began to come out in January 1970*), are not unknown.

1.8.5 Periodicity nearly always involves the use of the word **kull** (*every*), e.g. **rivista (perjodiku, ktejjeb, folju) ta' kull xahar (kull tliet xhur)**, *monthly* (*quarterly*) *review*, etc. With a verb we have such expressions as M **joħroġ** F **toħroġ** (**maħruġ**) **darbtejn fix-xahar (kull xahar barra Lulju u Awissu)**, *comes out* (*published*) *twice a month* (*every month except July and August*).

1.8.6 Subscription (**abbonament** or **ħlas**, *payment*; **tabbona**, *you subscribe*) is usually quoted **fis-sena** (literally *in the year*) less often **għal sena** or **kull sena** (*for the year, each year*). Many periodicals are cheap, so it is not unreasonable to find **kull 4 snin**, which does not mean what we mean by *every four years*. The rates are usually quoted as **bil-posta** (**mħallsa**), *by post* (*post paid*), or may specify **bl-ajru**, *by air*; **bil-baħar**, *by sea*, and distinguish **Malta** and **barra** (*abroad*), direct sale (**bl-idejn**, *in the hands*) not being usually specified. Besides ordinary subscriptions religious and charitable periodicals may invite an **abbonament sostenitur** (patronage). A price may be quoted for a single number (**numru** or **ktieb wieħed**; **kull kopja**; **fix-xahar**) or this may simply bear a price, preceded by **prezz**, or by **jinbiegħ** (*it is sold*).

1.8.7 Addresses may simply designate the office (**uffiċċju**) or the editor, or **direzzjoni u amministrazzjoni**, but the directions are often more complicated. Typical are: **il-korrispondenza kollha u l-mistoqsiet għandhom jintbagħtu lill-Editur** (*all correspondence and questions are to be sent to the editor*), **kull korrispondenza għandha tintbagħat lil-Segretarju** (*all correspondence is to be sent to the secretary*). More directly: **ibagħtu xogħlijiet tagħkom għall-Forum lil . . .** (*send your works for Forum to . . .*); more delicately: **min irid jissieħeb f'dan il-qari jirrikorri għand id-Direttur** (*whoever wishes to be associated with this periodical will apply to the director*).

2 ALPHABET, PHONETICS, SPELLING

2.1 ALPHABET

2.1.1 The present alphabet, proposed in 1921 and officially recognised in 1934, is as follows:

a b ċ d e f ġ g h ħ(Ħ) i j k l m n għ o p q
r s t u v w x ż z

Note the position of the dotted letters and of the digraph **għ**. In Busuttil's dictionary, *Kalepin* (*dizjunarju*) *Malti/Ingliz* (the only one easily obtainable in the U.K.), **għ** follows g.

għ is always a digraph, since g is never followed by **ħ**.

2.1.2 Earlier alphabets, which continued in use after 1934, exhibit a bewildering array of minor variations and propose various solutions for such problem letters as ċ, ġ, ħ, għ, q, x, ż, z, but the majority of them tend to be Italianate. Thus A. Cremona, though he had collaborated in devising the present alphabet, used one in his grammar, published in 1929, with the following differences:

c	before a, o, u	= k
c	before e, i	= ċ
ch	before e, i	= k
g	before e, i	= ġ
gh	before e, i	= g
k		= q
qu		= kw

He used ċ and ġ before **a**, **o**, **u** and consonants, but many of the alphabets adopt the Italian convention, using **gia** for **ġa** and so on and also **scia** for **xa**. Before consonants some kept the **i** to indicate the soft sound, other inserted an apostrophe. A surprising number make no distinction between **ż** and **z**, and some of those that do use **z** for **ż**, representing **z** by **ts** or by special founts. Some mix Arabic letters with Roman ones.

2.1.3 The only accent in general use is the grave accent, which may be used in words borrowed from Italian or French which end in a stressed vowel, e.g. **diġà**, **lokalità**, **bidè**, **però**. (Without the accent the stress would naturally be taken to fall on the last syllable but one.)

2.1.4 Very occasionally a circumflex accent is used to distinguish one of a pair of homonyms.

2.1.5 An apostrophe replaces a missing letter at the end of a word, e.g. **f'**, **x'** for **fi**, **xi**. The most important case is that of **ta'** and numerous verbs ending in -**a'**, where the apostrophe stands for silent **għ**, for **għ** appears in other forms of the word, e.g. **ta'** *of*; **tagħha**, *hers*; **jista'**, **jistgħu**, *he can*, *they can*.

2.2 CAPITALISATION

The use of capitals varies: in some writers it is much the same as in English, in others more after the Italian manner. Note, however, **it-tlieta**, *the third*; **it-Tlieta**, *Tuesday*. In references to God even suffixes (7.4) have a capital; e.g. **Alla nnifsU**, *God Himself*. Adjectives of nationality and names of languages now usually have a small initial letter.

2.3 DIVISION OF WORDS

2.3.1 Rules 4, 5a, 6d, 8a (p. xiii) apply, but the more usual division of three consonants is $1 + 2$. This can result in examples like **jer-ġgħu**, which some would regard as undesirable, for though phonetically unexceptionable (2.7.1), it looks odd; so they would divide **jerġ-għu**. A word like **għandhom**, where -**hom** is a pronoun-suffix, would always be divided after the **d**.

2.3.2 A word such as **jemigraw** would be divided, Italian fashion, before the **g**, but the native **jidrob** before the **r**.

2.3.3 It is permissible for the article **l**- or its assimilated forms to stand at the end of the line, e.g. **x-|xogħol**, but divisions like **i-kun** should be avoided.

2.4 PUNCTUATION

2.4.1 A hyphen occurs at the end of a word in such instances as **għall- u mill- Uffiċċju tal-Posta**, *to and from the Post Office*.

2.4.2 Abbreviations may end in a full stop, whether or not they include the last letter of the full word, e.g. **cap.**, **nru.**; but forms like **ediz.t** for **edizzjonijiet** are also found.

2.5 VARIATION OF CONSONANT

2.5.1 The consonant structure is very stable and minor changes in pronunciation, e.g. of **nbid** (*wine*) as [mbit] are not reflected in spelling. The spelling is, however, affected in two types of complete assimilation.

2.5.2 The definite article (i)l- is assimilated to certain initial consonants, e.g. is-sena. Details are given at 3.1.2.

2.5.3 The t- of the present tense (8.5.2) is assimilated to ċ, d, ġ, s, x, ż, z, producing iċċ-, etc. (see also 2.6.1). Thus we have ikun *he will be*, tkun *she will be*, but isir, issir, *he, she, becomes*. Similarly, with the t of the reflexive passive, we have jitħallsu but jiċċaqlaq. But most instances of CiC²- will be from foreign verbs like jissuġġerixxu (*suggests*), which will have a double consonant in any case (8.18.1), and will not, indeed in words like jipprepara could not, imply the assimilation of -t-. See also 2.5.4.

2.5.4 In contrast to the n- of the noun nbid, the n- of the first person singular present is assimilated to l, m and r, giving il-, im-, ir-, so that irrid is for nrid, *I want*. Here again one should note that in verbs like irranġa, *he arranged*, the iC²- is original.

2.6 VARIATION OF VOWEL

2.6.1 The initial i of the article (3.1) and that before two consonants disappear if the preceding word ends in a vowel, e.g. jagħmlu x-xogħol, sejra ssir. Conversely an i- may be inserted for euphony's sake.

2.6.2 In other cases i- changes to j- and u- to w- after a vowel, e.g. li jkunu jsiru, issa wkoll.

2.6.3 Maltese words are in a sort of dynamic equilibrium: if anything is added they tend to change their shape by eliminating a syllable. The basic stress (before any reconstruction) goes back, if possible, as far as the second syllable from the end, but is trapped, as it were, by the combinations -V̄C- and -VCC-. (A vowel at the end of a word is treated as long.)

If we take the verb qasam, *he divided*, and add the endings of the other persons we get the unreconstructed forms:

	S	P
1	qa'samt	qa'samna
2		qa'samtu
3*f*	'qasamet	'qasamu

But an unstressed short vowel followed by CV is eliminated, giving:

qsamt	qsamna
	qsamtu
qasmet	qasmu

as in 8.2.2.

Similarly, with the addition of personal or plural suffixes or the negative -x, short vowels may be eliminated and long vowels shortened, while originally final vowels may become stressed and change their quality, e.g. tajjeb, tajbin; wieħed, waħda; nixtieq, nixtiqilhom; kellna, kellniex. Further details are given in the relevant sections, especially 4.2.1, 4.2.4, 5.2.1, 7.4 and 8.

2.6.4 Stressed -i- alternates with unstressed -e-, e.g. kiteb, ktibt.

2.6.5 Auxiliary vowels are inserted on occasion before or after għ, l, q and r. For details see 7.3.5.; 8.4.2., 4.2.2(30).

2.7 SPELLING

2.7.1 Since the adoption of the present alphabet there has been little change in spelling. But spelling is not altogether phonetic and this results in a certain amount of variation. Thus għ is silent in most contexts, merely modifying the vowel which precedes or follows: some words are spelt either Vgħ -or għV-. Other combinations

2A

with **għ** result in diphthongs: **igħid** is pronounced approximately like the English *Yate* and sometimes mis-spelt **igħejd**, but **igħid** reflects the structure better (8.5.7). Similarly there is variation between **-nb-** and **-mb-**.

2.7.2 Besides the change of alphabet there have been minor changes such as **perfez-joni** > **perfezzjoni**.

3 ARTICLES

3.1 DEFINITE

3.1.1 The basic form of the article is:

l-   before vowels, **h**, **għ**
il-   before consonants

3.1.2 Before **ċ, d, n, r, s, t, x, ż, z** the **l** is assimilated to the following consonant, e.g. **ir-raġuni**.

3.1.3 Before **sC-** in foreign words an **i-** is inserted (2.6.1) and the article is **l-**, e.g. **l-isptar**. The same is the case before **mC-, nC-, xC-** in native words, e.g. **l-imħallef**.

3.1.4 The article may be reduced to a simple consonant (2.6.1).

3.1.5 The article is often used where English has none.

3.2 INDEFINITE

3.2.1 There is no indefinite article. **Wieħed** (6.1.1) means *a certain*, or is a pronoun, *one*.

4 NOUNS

4.1 PATTERNS

4.1.1 The variety of patterns in nouns is so great (0.5) that it is not particularly easy to recognise them as nouns from their form, though there are some patterns which are especially likely to be nouns or again, plural forms. Except for the plural (4.2) and the construct form (4.3) nouns do not vary.

4.1.2 A variation of pattern not always reflected in the dictionary is that exemplified by **ħobż**, *bread*; **ħobża**, *a loaf*, **taqsim**, *division*; **taqsima**, *a part*. Usually the collective noun, or the noun denoting activity rather than an action or its result, simply lacks the **-a**; but **KaTBa** may correspond *inter alia* to **KaTaB** and **KaTeB** as well as to **KaTB**, and **KeTBa** and **KiTBa** to **KeTaB** and **KiTeB**. (K, T, B represent any consonants.) Not every noun with the pattern **KVTBa** belongs to a pair of this sort. For example, **hakma**, *rule, mastery*, corresponds to **ħâkem**, *governor*. This and similar changes take place between singular and plural, e.g. **ward**, *roses, flowers*; **warda**, *a rose*. See further 4.2.2.

4.2 PLURAL AND DUAL

4.2.1 The plural may be formed by the addition of an ending, by change of ending, or by internal change. The addition of suffixes may produce changes of vowel (2.6.3). The plural suffixes are:

-in (stressed)

ħalliel	**ħallilin**
tajjeb	**tajbin**
wieqaf	**weqfin, wiqfin**
biered	**berdin**
hieni	**henjin**
mħmli	**mimlijin**

-n added to nouns and adjectives in -i

malti	maltin

-an, -ien (both stressed) added to words of one syllable

qiegh	qighan
hajt	hitan
ġar	ġirien
bieb	bibien
sid	sidien

   exceptionally

sabi	subien
għatu	għotjien

-a (alternative to -in)

haddiem	haddiema
tajjeb	tajba

-at, -iet (both stressed)

werqa	werqat, werqiet

   and similarly all nouns in -a, including **alla,** *god*
   exceptionally

dnub	dnubiet

-ijiet added to native and foreign words

ahbar	ahbarijiet
isem	ismijiet
xoghol	xoghlijiet
radju	radjijiet
ċekk	ċekkijiet
kondizzjoni	kondizzjonijiet

-i added to words of foreign origin

travu	travi
raġġ	raġġi
suldat	suldati
kritiku	kritiċi (kritiki)
grammatika	grammatiki

4.2.2 'Broken' plurals are formed by a change of pattern. There may be endings, but they are part of the general change. Originally they were independent collective forms and the correspondence between them and the singular is not a simple one: one plural pattern may correspond to several singular patterns and vice versa. Later the change of pattern was extended even to some foreign nouns, e.g. **vers:** P **vrus, vrejjes,** or **versi** (4.2.1). In the list that follows the plural pattern is put first; following the colon are the possible singular patterns, **K, T,** and **B** standing for any three consonants, **V** for any vowel.

(1) VK(T)VB occurs in the following common words: **ijiem/ejiem: jum; erwieh: ruh; ulied: wild; eluf: elf; uċuh: wiċċ**

(2) **iKTBa: KaTaB, KeTeb, KiTeB, KTieB**

(3) **oKTBa: KaTaB, KaTiB, KaTBa**

(4) **KaTaB: KaTBa, KaTBi, KoTBa**

(5)   KaTeT: KaTTa

(6)   KiTeT: KiTTa

(7)   KoToB: aKTaB, aKTeB, iKTaB, aKTBa, KaTBa, KoTBa, KTi(e)B. Note also foloz from falz(a), *false*

(8)   KuTeB: iKTeB

(9)   KoTBa: KaTiB (KoTja: KaTi), KTiB, KTieB

(10)   KoTTieB: KaTeB

(11)   KTaB: (nouns) KaTₐB, KiTeB, KaTB(a), KoTB; (adjectives) KaTiB, KTiB. Note also bjar: bir; djar: dar

(12)   KTiB: only snin from sena, *year*, is common

(13)   KTieB: KaTeB, KaTiB, KaTuB, KeTeB, KiTeB, KeTB, KiTB, KoTB, KeTBa, KoTBa; (adjectives) KTiB. Note also: bwiet: but; rjieħ: riħ

(14)   KTuB: most commonly KaTB(a), KeTB(a); also KaTaB, KieTeB, KiTB, KoTB(a), KTuBi

(15)   KTaBa: KaTiB. Note also nsara: nisrani

(16)   KTieBa: KeTuB, KiTBi, KoTBi, KTiB. Note also ħżiena: ħażin

(17)   KTieBi: KaTBa, KeTBa, KeTBi, KiTBa, KiTBija. Note also bwieqi: bieqja and others of this type

(18)   KTuBa: KaTaB, KaTeB, KiTB, KaTBa

(19)   KTaTaB: KaTaB, KaTBa. Note also swaba': saba'

(20)   KTaTeB: KaTiB, KaTTaB, KaTTuB, KuTTaB. Note also slaten: sultan; xjaten: xitan; ġranet: ġurnata

(21a)   KwieTeB occurs in the following: żwiemel: żiemel; kwiekeb: kewkba

(21b)   KTieBeB: KeTBuB(a), KuTBieB. Also sniesel: sensiela or sinsla

(22)   mKaTaB: maKTaB

(23)   mKaTeB: maKTeB, moKTeB

(24)   mKaTeT: mKaTT

(25)   mwieTeB: miTieB

(26)   KTajjaB: KTaBa

(27)   KTajjeB: KaTBa, KeTBa. Note also rħajjel: raħal

(28)   KTejja(B): KeTa, KTi(e)Ba

(29)   KTejjeB: KTiB(a), KTaBa. Note also vrejjes: vers; mwejjed: mejda

(30)   Peculiar patterns occur when the first radical is għ (2.6.5), viz. għaTuB, għeTuB for (14); egħTieBi or għeTieBi for (17); għammajjar: għamara; għarajjes: għarus(a); għemejjel: għamil; għelejjel: għalla

4.2.3   Broken plurals not referring to persons are mostly construed as if they were singular.

4.2.4   Some nouns, especially those denoting things that go in pairs, have also a dual form, got by adding -ejn, or ajn (cf. tnejn, *two*). Feminine nouns in -a drop the -a and add -tejn (4.3.2), e.g. id-ejn, *hand(s)*; sieq, saqajn, *foot, feet*; xaħar, xaħrejn, *month, two months*; driegħ, dirgħajn, *arm(s)*; sena, sentejn, *year, two years*; kelma, kelmtejn, *a word (or two)*.

4.3   CONSTRUCT FORM

4.3.1   Though the usual way of joining two nouns one of which depends on the other is by means of the preposition ta' (*of*), it is possible in traditional style to dispense with it, e.g. mart il-Gvernatur, *the wife of the Governor*; but it is not common in colloquial Maltese outside set expressions like Ras ir-**Randan** (*head of Lent*), *Ash Wednesday*.

4.3.2 Masculine nouns are not affected by this construction but feminine nouns in -a of Arabic origin change the -a to -et, e.g. **suret in-nies**, *proper behaviour*. **Mara** (*woman, wife*) becomes **mart**. (The -a of the plural is not affected.)

4.3.3 A similar construction is found where we say *a piece of bread*, but here the feminine is unchanged, e.g. **qoffa lariṅ**, *a basketful of oranges*.

5 ADJECTIVES

5.1 GENERAL

5.1.1 Positive adjectives have a feminine form and a common plural; comparatives (5.3) are invariable.

5.1.2 Adjectives agree with the noun both when they are attributive (5.2.2) and when they are predicates, e.g. **il-kondizzjonijiet huma ħżiena**, *the conditions are bad*.

5.1.3 Without **huma** (7.3.1) the above could still mean the same, but is quite likely to mean *the bad conditions*. If, however, ambiguity is likely, the latter is rendered by **il-kondizzjonijiet il-ħżiena**.

5.2 ENDINGS

5.2.1 The feminine is got by adding -a. Unaccented vowels are omitted (2.6.3); adjectives in -i become -ja or -ija, those of foreign origin in -u change to -a, e.g. **bravu, brava**, those of native origin to -wa. Adjectives of the form aKTaB, iKTaB, iKTeB, mostly adjectives of colour, have feminines of the form KaTBa, KeTBa. When therefore one meets a form of this sort one cannot be sure of the masculine: e.g. **bajda : abjad; għarfa : għaref; falza : falz** (foreign).

5.2.2 The plural uses the suffixes -(i)n or -i with changes as in 4.2.1, or is the same as the feminine or may be 'broken' (4.2.2), e.g. **idjomi maltin**, *Maltese idioms*; **kondizzjonijiet tajbin, gravi, meħtieġa, ġodda** (4.2.2:9; S **ġdid**), **ħżiena** (4.2.2:16), *good, serious, necessary, new, bad conditions*.

5.3 COMPARISON

5.3.1 Some comparatives are made by changing the pattern to one beginning with a vowel, viz.

Comparative	*Positive*
aKTa	**KaTTi**
oKTa	e.g. **oħla : ħelu; ogħla : għoli**
aKTaB	**KieTeB, KTiB**
aKTeB	**KaTiB**
eKTeB	**aKTaB, oKToB, KaTeB, KaTiB**
iKTaB	**aKTaB, iKTiB, KaTiB, KeTTaB, KTiB**
iKTeB	**KieTeB, KaTTeB, KTiB, KTejTeB**

5.3.2 Alternatively, the comparative may be formed by putting **aktar** or **iżjed** (*more*) before the positive, and for a large number of adjectives, particularly ones of foreign origin, this is the only way.

5.3.3 The addition of the article turns the comparative into a superlative, e.g. **itjeb**, *better*; **l-itjeb**, *the best*.

6 NUMERALS

6.1 CARDINAL

6.1.1

1 wieħed, waħda	14 erbatax	70 sebgħin
2 zewġ; tnejn	15 ħmistax	80 tmenin
3 tliet/tlitt; tlieta	16 sittax	90 disgħin
4 erba'/erbat; erbgħa	17 sbatax	100 mitt; mija
5 ħames(t); ħamsa	18 tmintax	101 mitt . . . u wieħed;
6 sitt; sitta	19 dsatax	mija u wieħed
7 seba'/sebat; sebgħa	20 għoxrin	121 mija u wieħed u
8 tmien/tmint; tmienja	21 wieħed u għoxrin	għoxrin
9 disa'/disat; disgħa	22 tnejn u għoxrin	200 mitejn
10 għaxar(t); għaxra	30 tletin	300–900 tliet(–disa') mija
11 ħdax(-il)	40 erbgħin	1000 elf
12 tnax	50 ħamsin	2000 elfejn
13 tlettax	60 sittin	3000 tlitt elf

6.1.2 The forms after the semi-colon are used when not followed by a noun; the forms with an additional **-t** are used before vowels. All the teens may take **-il**. Note the difference in order between **21**, etc. and **101**, etc. In the latter case the second half of the number may follow the noun.

6.1.3 The numbers **2–10, 102–110** and so on have nouns in the plural, e.g. **disgħa u tletin elf tmien mija u għaxar liri**, £39,810, unless **2–10** are put after the noun, viz. . . . **tmien mitt lira u għaxra**. (Note **mitt** and **għaxar** before the noun, otherwise **mija** and **għaxra**.) All other numbers are followed by the singular.

6.2 ORDINAL

6.2.1

1 **ewwel**
2 **tieni**
3 **tielet**
4 **raba'**
5 **ħames**

Otherwise the same as cardinals e.g. **is-sitt skieda**, *the sixth schedule*; **ġie s-sitta**, *he came sixth*.

In practice a frequent mark of the ordinal is the presence of the definite article, though **is-sitta**, for instance, could mean both *the sixth* and *the six of them*.

6.2.2 Ordinals have no separate feminine.

6.3 FIGURES

6.3.1 As ordinals have no distinctive ending there is little point in using different symbols, so one finds **62 versi**, *62 verses*, and **it-62 wieħed**, *the 62nd one*.

6.3.2 The numbers from **11** to **19** are sometimes written **11-il** etc., presumably to show the form used.

6.4 DATES

6.4.1 The months are:

**Jannar, Frar, Marzu, April, Mejju, Ġunju,
Lulju, Awwissu, Settembru, Ottubru, Novembru, Diċembru**

6.4.2 Except for *1st*, dates are represented by cardinal numbers, in so far as they are different, viz.

> (*On*) *4 July 1971*, (f)l-erbgħa ta' Lulju, (ta' l-)elf disa' mija wieħed u sebgħin
> (fl-4 ta' Lulju ta' l-1971)
> *In 1964*, fl-1964

Dates are unaffected by prepositions.

6.4.3 *Monday–Thursday* have names meaning *second–fifth*, viz. it-Tnejn, it-Tlieta, l'Erbgħa, il-Ħamis. This can be confusing.

7 PRONOUNS

7.1 DEMONSTRATIVE, INDEFINITE, ETC.

7.1.1 The demonstratives are:

M	F	P	
dan	din	dawn	*this, these*
dak	dik	dawk	*that, those*

They are usually followed by the article, e.g. **dan l-Att**, *this Act*, since **dan Att** could mean, *this is an Act*. Both **dan** and **dawn** may combine with the various forms of the article to make **dal-, daċ,- dad-**, etc. (3.1.2).

7.1.2 **Kull** is given in the dictionary as meaning *every, all, whatsoever*; but in practice the simple **kull** tends to mean *any, every* (**kull wieħed**, *each*), while the meaning *all, the whole* is conveyed by the forms with pronoun suffixes: M **kollu**, F & P **kollha**, e.g. **f'kull żmien**, *at any time*; **kull Direttur**, *every Director*; **kull korrispondenza** or **il-korrispondenza kollha**, *all correspondence*; **dak l-għajjat kollu**, *all that noise*. As the basic meaning of **kollu, kollha** is *all of it, all of them*, they can be used without nouns, e.g. **dak kollu li hu malti**, *all that is Maltese*; **b'dak kollu**, *notwithstanding (for all that)*. (For other forms such as **kollni** see 7.4.9.)

7.2 RELATIVE, INTERROGATIVE

7.2.1 The relative **(il)li**, *who, which, what*, may be subject or object and is followed by prepositions with pronoun-suffixes (10.3), e.g. **li għalih**, *to whom* (lit. *who to-him*), **li ... tiegħu** M, **li ... tagħha** F, etc., *whose*. The latter can also be expressed by the addition of a simple personal suffix (7.4.2) to the noun, e.g. **raġel li missieru ...** , *a man whose father ...* .

7.2.2 The interrogative-relative **min** means *who?* or *he who. Whose?* is usually **ta' min**, but this also occurs idiomatically in phrases like **ta' min isemmi**, *worth mentioning* (**isemmi**, *he mentions*). *Whose son is he?* is **Bin min hu?** (4.3).

7.3 PERSONAL

7.3.1 The pronouns **jien(a), int(i), hu(wa), hi; aħna, intom, huma** are mostly used for clarity or emphasis or as equivalents of the verb *to be*, which Maltese lacks. After **kif** and **xi** the forms **inhu, inhi** and **inhuma** are used instead of **hu**, etc.:

> **Ir-reżultat huwa pessimu**, *The result is very bad*
> **X'inhi r-raġuni?**, *What is the reason?*
> **Jien infurmat**, *I (am) informed*
> (also **Jien ġejt infurmat, Ninsab infurmat,** 8.14.2)

7.3.2 When used as equivalents of *to be* the pronouns are negated like a verb (8.22.1), the forms being:

m'iniex, m'intix, m'hu(wie)x, m'hix; m'aħniex, m'intomx, m'humiex

e.g. **Mhux ċar li . . .?**, *Is it not clear that. . .?*

7.4 PERSONAL SUFFIXES

7.4.1 A good many grammatical relationships are expressed by personal suffixes, which can be attached to nouns as possessives, to some pronouns, to verbs as direct or indirect object, to adverbs and to prepositions (10.3).

7.4.2 The forms of these suffixes on the one hand as possessives or direct objects and on the other as indirect objects, are:

		S				P	
	1	2	3*m*	3*f*	1	2	3
P & D	-ni, *me*;	-ek/-(o)k	-u, -h, -hu	-ha	-na	-kom	-hom
	-i/-ja, *my*			-hie-			
I	-li	-lek/-lok	-lu	-lha	-(i)lna	-(i)lkom	-lhom

The suffix -ha, besides standing for any feminine noun, can be a vague neuter.

Both nouns (7.4.3) and verbs (7.4.4) are affected phonetically by the addition of the suffixes.

7.4.3 *Nouns*

(1) Unstressed vowels in the second syllable disappear before suffixes beginning with a vowel, e.g. ismu, *his name* (isem); għadmi, *my bones* (għadam); xogħlu, *his work* (xogħol). The most likely vowel is -e-.

(2) Before suffixes beginning with a consonant -e- changes to -i-, e.g. isimhom, *their name* (isem).

(3) -a in feminine nouns of Arabic origin changes to -t-, or -it-, e.g. martu, *his wife* (mara) (cf. 4.3.2).

(4) Auxiliary vowels are inserted where the original pattern is CVC|għa, -la, -ma, -na, -ra, CVqCa, CVgħCa, giving CVCVgħt-, etc., e.g. setegħtu (not setgħtu), *his strength* (setgħa).

7.4.4 *Verbs*

The changes in verbs are more extensive, viz.

    -ni: the stress shifts:
        'CeCa + ni may > 'CCieni
        'CVCeC + ni > CV'CiCni
        'CieCeC + ni > Ce'CiCni
    -k: The stress shifts; final -a and -i may become -ie- and the first vowel vanishes
    -ok: the second vowel may disappear or change position, viz. CoCCoC + ok > CoCCCok or CoCoCCok
    -ek: the second vowel disappears
    -h: the stress shifts; final -a and -i may become -ie-
    -u: the second vowel disappears
    -ha, -na, -kom, -hom: the stress shifts, with changes as for -ni

-li, -lek, -lu: the same

-lha, -lna, -lkom, -lhom: become -'ilha, etc. after a consonant, with weakening or elimination of the preceding vowel

Thus nixtieq + lhom > nixtiqilhom; CVCVC + lha > CVCCilha.

7.4.5 A verb may have both direct and indirect suffixes and the form of the direct suffix, which comes first, may be affected accordingly, e.g. **jagħtihielna**, *he gives it to us* (jagħti + ha + lna).

7.4.6 A verb may take a suffix even though the object is also expressed by a noun or a separate pronoun, e.g. **Lil dan il-kittieb issa tafuh tajjeb**, *This author by now you know (him) well.*

7.4.7 Maltese sometimes uses a direct suffix where we should expect an indirect one, e.g. **tana tnax-il poeżija**, *he has given us twelve poems.*

7.4.8 Some parts of verbs combine with personal suffixes to give special meanings:

> **kien**, *was*; **ikun**, *will be*, with the indirect object suffixes make **kelli, ikolli**, etc., *I had (to), I shall have (to)*
>
> **għodd**, *count*, given in the dictionaries as meaning *nearly*, requires the corresponding suffix, e.g. **għoddu wasal**, *he nearly arrived*; but **għoddni tiegħek** means *yours truly (count me yours)*
>
> **mess, imiss**, *it touched, touches*, produce **messni** etc., *I ought*, e.g. **ma messniex għamilna dan**, *we ought not to have done that*

7.4.9 Kollu, kollha have already been mentioned (7.1.2) The whole range of suffixes occurs, e.g. **kollna**, *all of us.*

Waħdi, weħidha, whidna, etc. mean *I [etc.] alone.*

7.4.10 In combination with the nouns **nifs**, *breath, soul* (P **nfus**) and **ruħ**, *spirit*, the suffixes make reflexive and emphatic pronouns.

(I)nnifsi . . . (i)nfusna, etc. are emphatic, or sometimes emphatic reflexive, e.g. **aqraw il-versi nfushom**, *read the verses themselves*; **bixra għaliha n-nifsha**, *its peculiar quality*; **huwa biżżejjed fih innifsu**, *is enough in itself.*

Ruħi, etc. are reflexive, e.g. **utilizza ruħu**, *availed himself, made himself useful*; **biex ikunu jistgħu jirregolaw ruħhom**, *so that they may be able to adjust themselves.*

7.4.11 For adverbs and prepositions with personal suffixes, e.g. **għaliha, fih** in 7.4.10, see 9.3; 10.3.

8 VERBS

8.1 STRUCTURE

8.1.1 Paradoxically, the Maltese verb occupies about half of most Maltese grammars, though any given verb has very few forms, and all verbs form their parts in essentially the same way. There are only two tenses: the past, the basic form to which all others are referred, and the present/future (traditionally called the imperfect); and besides these we find only the imperative and at most two participles.

8.1.2 Grammars cite verbs by the 3PSM of the past, a form which gives the bare verbal base. Dictionaries use either this or the 2PS of the present, the latter being to some extent equivalent in function to the infinitive in other languages (8.24.2). Busuttil's dictionary is unpredictable: most verbs are entered only under the 2PS of the present, a fair number under both forms (though rarely with the same entry) and a few only under the past.

8.1.3 The standard verb has the pattern **KVTVB** where K,T,B (the radicals) may be any three consonants, usually different, and **V** may be a variety of vowels.

If **B** is **għ** the pattern becomes **KVTa'**
If **B** is **j**   **KVTa**
If **B** is **T**   **KVTT**
If **T** is **j** or **w**   **KVB**

All these patterns include common verbs. There is also a pattern **KVTBVL** with four consonants, which may be all different. This pattern includes a certain number of old verbs of Italian origin, but most borrowed verbs are subsumed under **KVTa**.

8.1.4 Besides the primitive forms given above verbs may have a number of derived forms. Eight of these are current, but no verb seems to have more than four. As compared with **KVTVB** the forms are **KVTTVB** (to which a number of borrowed verbs have been adapted), **KieTeB, tKVTTVB, tKieTeB, n(t)KVTVB/nKtVTVB, KtVTVB, KTVB, staKTVB/stKVTTVB**.

8.1.5 The meanings of these derived verbs need not detain us: in so far as they are not given separate entries in the dictionary, they will be dealt with elsewhere. But the multiplicity of patterns means that even the application of the same formula produces a great variety of forms. Maltese words being as it were phonetically in a state of dynamic equilibrium, the addition of elements at the beginning or end causes them to assume a new shape, and the solutions, as will be seen, are varied. It will not always be necessary to give complete paradigms, but one must indicate the sort of patterns that arise.

8.2 PRESENT
See 8.5.

8.4 PAST
8.4.1 The endings of the past are:

	S	P
1	-t	-na
2	-t	-tu
3*f*	-Vt ⎱	
3*m*	- ⎰	-u

Unless otherwise stated P1 and 2 have the same stem as S1, 2 and P3 as S3f.

8.4.2 With base **KVTVB** we have these possibililies:

	1, 2	**KTaBt**	**KTiBt**	**KToBt**
S	3*f*	**KVTBet**	**KVTBet**	**KoTBot**
	3*m*	**KVTaB**	**KVTeB**	**KoToB**

If the first consonant is the silent **għ**, the first vowel is not omitted: **għaraft**, *I recognised*, not **għraft**. If the first consonant is **w**, we may have **wVT-** or **uT-**, e.g. **wasalna/usalna**, *we arrived*.

8.4.3 With base **KVTa'** we have:

	1, 2	**KTajt**
S	3*f*	**KVTgħet**
	3*m*	**KVTa'**

For the effect of gh and w as first consonant see 8.4.2.

8.4.4   With base **KVTa** we have:

		T = w	T = j		
	1, 2	**KTajt/KTejt**			
S	3f	**KTat/KTiet**	P		
	3m	**KVTa**		3	**KTaw/KTew**

For the effect of gh and w as first consonant see 8.4.2.

8.4.5   With base **KVTT** we have:

	1, 2	**KVTTejt**			
S	3f	**KVTTet**	P		
	3m	**KVTT**		3	**KVTTu/KVTTew**

8.4.6   With base **KVB** we have the following types:

		(T = w)		**(T = j)**	
	1, 2	mort	kont	sirt	ridt
S	3f	maret	kienet	saret	riedet
	3m	mar	kien	sar	ried

8.4.7   The quadriliterals and the derived verbs produce only minor variations, viz.

KVTBVLt, KVTBLet: 3m KVTBVL
(s)(t)KVTTVBt, (s)(t)KVTTBet: (s)(t)KVTTVB

but if **T = j** or **w** we have **KVjBet, KVwBet**

(t)KeTiBt/KiTiBt, KieTBet: KieTeB
n(t)KVTVB like KVTVB
KtVTVBt, KtVTBet: KtVTVB
KTaBt, KTaBet: KTaB
KTiBt, KTieBet: KTieB

Note the ambiguity of **KTaBt** and **KTiBt** (8.4.2).

staKTVBt, staKTBet: staKTVB

For other details see 8.4.2.

Verbs derived from **KVTa', KVTa, KVTT** and **KVB** produce no significant variations.

8.5   PRESENT/FUTURE TENSE

8.5.1   Though traditionally known as the imperfect it does not have the meaning usually attached to that tense, which is got by auxiliaries. Auxiliaries or particles may also be used to specify the future tense (8.17), though they are not indispensable.

8.5.2   The distinguishing mark of this tense is the personal prefix, viz. (i)n, t, j/i, e.g. from **KVTVB**:

	S		P	
1	n		n	
2, 3f	t	VKTVB	t	VKTBu
3m	j		j	

If **K = w** it vanishes, e.g. **wasal**, *he arrived*; **nasal** (not **nawsal**), *I arrive*.

If **T = l, m, n, r** or **gh** the plural is **nVKVTBu**, etc.

8.5.3 The vowels are not necessarily the same as in the past tense, but correspond as follows:

Present	Past
jaKTaB	KaTaB
jaKTeB	KaTeB
jeKTaB	KeTaB
jeKTeB	KeTeB
jiKTaB	KaTaB, KeTaB
jiKTeB	KeTeB, KiTeB
jiKToB	KaTaB, KeTaB, KiTeB, KoToB (K = d, ġ, s, t, x, ż)
joKToB	KaTaB, KaTeB, KeTaB, KoToB (K = any other consonant)

Past	Present			
KaTaB	jaKTaB	jiKTaB	jiKToB	joKToB
KaTeB	jaKTeB	joKToB		
KeTaB	jeKTaB	jiKTaB	jiKToB	joKToB
KeTeB	jeKTeB	jiKTeB		
KiTeB	jiKTeB	jiKToB		
KoToB	jiKToB	joKToB		

8.5.4 Corresponding to KVTa' we have:

jaKTa'/jiKTa'   **jaKTgħu/jiKTgħu**

8.5.5 Corresponding to KVTa we have:

jaKTa/jiKTa   **jaKT|aw, -ew, -u/jiKTaw, etc.**
jaKTi/jiKTi

8.5.6 Corresponding to KVTT we have:

$$\left.\begin{matrix}(i)n\\t\\i\end{matrix}\right|KVTT \qquad \left.\begin{matrix}n\\t\\i\end{matrix}\right|KVTTu \text{ or } \textbf{-ew}$$

The vowels correspond thus:

iKeTT: KaTT or KeTT
iKiTT: KeTT
iKoTT: KaTT

n- and t- may be assimilated (2.5.4, 2.5.3).

8.5.7 Corresponding to KVB we have:

iKuB: KaB/KieB (i.e. KVwVB)
iKiB: KaB/KieB (i.e. KVjVB)

n- and t- may be assimilated (2.5.4., 2.5.3); **imur** has plural **imorru**, etc. not **imuru**.

8.5.8 From the quadriliteral and the derived verbs we have, in the order of 8.1.4: **iKVTBL, iKVTTVB, iKieTeB, jitKVTTVB, jitKieTeB, jin(t)KVTVB/jinKtVTVB, jiKtVTVB, jiKTVB, jistaKTVB/jistKVTTVB.**

Those in **i-** show assimilation of **n-** and **t-** (2.5.4, 2.5.3).

Derivatives of KVTa' etc. do not differ essentially, but one should note the ambiguity of **jiCCAC** and **jinCieC**:

jiKTaB: KVTVB or **KTVB**
jinCaC: nVTVB, nTaB (K = n); nKVB (derived)
jinCieC: nTieB, nKieB

Thus **jinsab** means in fact *he is found* (**nsab**, *he was found*; **sab**, *he found*); there is a verb **nasab**, *he trapped*, but it makes **jonsob**.

8.9 IMPERATIVE

The imperative is the same as the present without the **j-, i-** or **ji**, e.g. **VKTVB, KVTT, tKieTeB**.

8.10 COMPOUND TENSES

See 8.17.

8.12 PARTICIPLES

8.12.1 *Present participle*

The basic form is:

	S		P
M	F		
KieTaB/KieTeB	**KieTBa**		**KeTBin**

Note **KieTgħa** from **KieTa'**; **KejBa** from **KejjeB** (past **KVB**); **KieTi-ja**, past **KVTa**. None of the other types of verb has a present participle.

8.12.2 *Past participle*

The basic forms are:

maKTuB, meKTuB or **miKTuB**

If **K = w** the form is **miTuB**:

KVTa' verbs make **maKTugħ** or **miKTugħ**
KVTa   **meKTi, miKTi** or **moKTi**
KVTT   **miKTuT**
KVB   **miKjuB**

The quadriliterals and the derived verbs listed in 8.1.4 have participles as follows:
(i)mKVTBVL; (i)mKVTTVB; (i)mKieTeB; mitKVTTVB; mitKieTeB; none; none; none; **mistaKTVB/mistKVTTVB.**

8.12.3 For the past participles of verbs of foreign origin see 8.18.3.

8.14/8.15 REFLEXIVE AND PASSIVE

8.14.1 The reflexive and the passive are expressed sometimes by derived verbs (8.1.4) sometimes by special constructions. Thus if **kiteb** means *he wrote*; **(i)nkiteb** can mean *it was written* (passive) or *he registered* (reflexive). These **n-** forms, which are more likely to be passive, and the **t-** forms, which are more likely to be reflexive, are not always given in the dictionary.

8.14.2 For various reasons a construction with a participle may be preferred for the passive. Thus we have **ninsab infurmat**, *I am informed*, in which **nsab**, itself the passive of **sab**, is used as a substitute for the verb *to be*. Another synonym is **ġie**, *came*, e.g. **ġiet magħmula**, *it was made*. **Kien** itself (8.17.2) is also used and so is **safa**, *became*.

8.14.3   The reflexive is expressed by **ruħu, innifsu**, etc. (7.4.10), the reciprocal by **xulxin** or **wieħed ieħor**.

8.17   AUXILIARIES

8.17.1   As there are only two tenses, the more exact indication of temporal relations has to be achieved by means of combinations of verbs or by the addition of particles, by which are here meant all invariable words of whatever origin.

8.17.2   One of the most frequent auxiliary verbs is **kien**, etc. *he* (etc.) *was* (8.4.6) of which the present-future **ikun**, etc. has a future meaning. They can be combined with either past or the present to give the following nuances:

Kien puts a past verb still further in the past. The translation is usually the pluperfect, but may be the simple past: **ħsibt li kienet mietet**, *I thought it had died*; **B'referenza għall-mistoqsija tiegħi nru 1353 fejn kont staqsejt ...**, *With reference to my question no. 1353, in which I asked ....*

Kien with the present expresses continuous action or state in the past: **Kif jixtri l-pubbliku, kont nixtri jien**, *As the public buys, so I was buying*; **ma kontx naf**, *I did not know*.

Ikun with the past usually expresses an action which is past in relation to a future event or to a timeless present: **It-triq tiġi msewwija wara li toroq oħra jkunu tlestew**, *The street will be repaired after other streets have been seen to.*

(Note that English is content with a simple perfect.)

Ikun with the present theoretically gives a continuous future, but has the same ambiguity: **jiġi maħdum fi ħbula kif ikunu jriduh is-sajjieda**, *it is worked into ropes as the fishermen want it*; **biex din il-Kamra tkun tista' tiddiskuti l'estimi**, *so that this Chamber will be able to discuss the estimates.*

8.17.3   The participle **qiegħed, qiegħda, qegħdin** (*standing*), often shortened to **qed**, indicates continuous action, e.g. **il-kwistjoni għadha qiegħda tiġi mistħarrġa**, *the question is still being investigated*; **kien qiegħed jaħdem**, *it was working*.

8.17.4   **Sejjer, sejra, sejrin**, abridged to **se(r)**, the present participle of **sar**, *he became*, indicates the immediate future, e.g. **x'passi sejjer jieħu**, *what steps he is going to take*; **kien ser joħroġ**, *it was about to appear.*

(The past tense also is found in combination with other verbs, e.g. **sirt naf**, *I became aware*; **naf**, *I know*.)

8.17.5   The particles **għad, ħa** and **sa** indicate various types of futurity: **għad**, distant; **ħa**, intention, **sa**, near; e.g. **dawk li għad iridu jiġu warajna**, *those who are to come after us* (posterity); **ħa ngħidlu**, *I will tell him* (**kont ħa ngħidlu**, *I intended to tell him*). **Sa** is not very common in this sense: it is more likely to be a preposition meaning *until* (**sa ma** is the corresponding conjunction) or occur in the expression **ilu (ilha) sa min**, e.g. **tgħid ilha sa mill-bidu tagħha**, *has been saying ever since its beginning.* Likewise **għad** is also an adverb meaning *still*, **għad li** a conjunction; **ħa** both means *he took* and is short for **ħalli**, *so that*.

8.17.6   Various other combinations of verbs have special meanings. Some take personal suffixes and are mentioned in 7.4.8; in other cases both verbs have the same tense, e.g. **jarġa' jitkellem wara**, *he will speak again afterwards* (**jarġa'** *he will repeat*); **reġgħu ntalbu**, *they have been asked for again*; **nibqa' ninsisti**, *I shall go on insisting*; **nittama li jkun laħaq tlesta**, *I hope it will at last have been prepared* (**laħaq**, *he arrived*).

8.18 VERBS OF FOREIGN ORIGIN

8.18.1 The great mass of verbs borrowed from Italian and English are modelled so far as their endings are concerned on verbs of the **KVTa** type (8.4.4, 8.5.5). The great majority begin with a vowel even when the original does not, e.g. **ordna**, *he ordered*; **studja**, *he studied*; **ittajpja**, *he typed*; **irċieva**, *he received*.

8.18.2 All types of -a verbs are represented: we find **iservu**, *they serve*; **jakkwistaw**, *they acquire*; **ottenew**, *they obtained*. The prefixes of the present tense, viz. **i-, j-** or **ji-** in the third person depend on the initial letter and do not affect the remainder of the word: thus, **jordna, jistudja, iservu**. Some verbs have **-ixxa** in the past and **-ixxi** in the present instead of **-a** and **-i**: **jipprojbixxi**, *he prohibits*, but **ipprojbejt**, *I prohibited*.

8.18.3 The past participles are quite different from those of native verbs, being modelled on Italian ones, e.g. **spezzjonat, trasferit, ottenut, deċiż**; and, English in origin but with an Italianate participle, **ittajpjat**.

8.18.4 There are no derived verbs.

8.19 IRREGULARITIES

8.19.1 **emmen**, *he believed*, has pr. **jemmen**, past participle **mwemmen** and derived verb **twemmen**, *it was believed*.

8.19.2 **ġie**, *he came*, behaves like a KVTa verb, e.g. **ġejt**, *I, you, came*; **jiġi**, *he comes*; **ġej**, *coming*.

8.19.3 **ħa**, *he took*, shows occasional signs of its original final **-d**.

> *Past:* **ħadt, ħadet, ħa; ħadna, ħadtu, ħadu**
> *Present:* **jieħu**, P **jieħdu**
> *Past participle:* **meħud**
> *Derived verb:* **ittieħed**, *it was taken*

8.19.4 **jaf**, *he knows*, has **naf**, *I know*; **nafu**, *we know*, etc. There is no past, **kien jaf** (8.17.2) being used instead.

8.19.5 **qal**, *he said*, is defective. The complete set of forms runs:

> *Past:* **għidt/għedt, qalet, qal**; with plural to match (8.2.1)
> *Present:* **ngħid, tgħid, jgħid/igħid**, etc.
> *Derived verbs:* **intqal, ingħad**, *it was said*

8.19.6 **ra**, *he saw*; **jara**, *he sees*, as 8.4.4 and 8.5.5.

8.19.7 **ta**, *he gave*, is short for **għata** (KVTa type). Hence:

> *Past:* **tajt**, etc. as 8.4.4
> *Present:* **jagħti** (8.5.5)
> *Past participle:* **mogħti**
> *Derived verb:* **in(t)għata**, *was given*

8.19.8 **waqaf**, *he stopped* has present **jieqaf**.

8.19.9 **wera**, *he showed* (cf. **ra**), has **u-** elsewhere.

> *Present:* **juri**, etc.,
> *Past participle:* **muri**

8.22 NEGATIVE

8.22.1 Verbs, and some other words that are equivalent to verbs, are negatived by putting ma in front and attaching **-x** (short for **xej**, *thing*). The **-x** attracts the stress and consequently may affect the quality of the vowels: e.g. **ma nqastx,** *I did not fail* (**nqast**); **ma jistax,** *he cannot* (**jista'**); **ma bediex,** *did not begin* (**beda**); **ma togħgobniex,** *it does not please us* (**togħgobna**); (quasi-verb) **m'għandix,** *I have not* (10.5.3). See also 7.3.2.

8.22.2 No **-x** is used when the negative is specified by some other word, e.g. **ma . . . xejn,** *nothing*; **ma . . . hadd,** *no-one*; **ma . . . qatt,** *never* (or **qatt ma,** etc.). Similarly with (l)**anqas,** *nor*, e.g. **u lanqas ma għażilt,** *nor have I chosen.*

8.22.3 The termination **-x** in itself may or may not be negative. It is found in indirect questions and in pointed or mocking direct questions, e.g. **jekk kienx sabiħ jew le, tistgħu tgħidu intom,** *whether it was fine or not, you can say*; **Huwiex il-ħsieb tal-Gvern . . . ?,** *Is it the intention of the Government . . . ?*

8.23 DERIVED VERBS
See 8.1.4.

8.24 SYNTAX

8.24.1 There is no infinitive or gerund in Maltese. Clauses beginning with a conjunction may be substituted or even without one, e.g. **flok jibnu,** *instead of building, they* . . . ; but the common practice is to use two finite verbs, e.g. **nixtieq naf,** *I want to know*; **ejjew naraw,** *let us see.*

8.24.2 One substitute for the infinitive, viz. the 2PS of the present, is accidentally important in that it provides entry words in dictionaries, e.g. **kif tikteb għall-palk,** *how to write* (lit. *you write*) *for the stage.* Hence entries like '**tista**', *to be able*'. (See also 10.5.2.)

8.24.3 In the absence of subordinating conjunctions the arrangement of words can be important, e.g. **kotba minn uħud li, jien u nikteb il-bijografija tagħhom, kienu għadhom ma ippubblikawhomx,** *books by some who, when I was writing their biographies, had not yet published them.*

The collocation subject + **u** (*and*) + verb indicates simultaneous action.

9 ADVERBS

9.1 FORMATION

9.1.1 While there are a number of adverbs of time, place, etc. such as **qatt,** *never*, **hawn,** *here*, which are underived, the bulk of native adverbs of manner are either formally indistinguishable from adjectives, e.g. **ktieb tajjeb,** *a good book*; **tafuh tajjeb,** *you know him well*; or are formed by prefixing **bil-(bid-** etc.), e.g. **biżżejjed,** *sufficiently.*

9.1.2 Adverbs borrowed from Italian very often have the characteristic ending **-ment,** e.g. **temporane(j)ament.**

9.1.3 The simple repetition of a noun may have adverbial force, e.g. **temmejtu biċċa biċċa,** *I finished it bit by bit*; or a noun alone such as **l-lum** (**illum**), (*to*)*day.*

9.2 COMPARISON

9.2.1 Comparison is the same as for adjectives.

9.3 ADVERBS WITH SUFFIXES

9.3.1 A number of adverbs normally incorporate a personal suffix (7.4), e.g. **għad,** *still*: **għadna nitkelma** *we still proclaim*; **għadhom ma,** see 8.24.3. Negativing the adverb, **m'għadhomx,** gives the sense *they no longer.*

9.3.2 The commonest equivalent of *ago* is **ilu**, which incorporates the 3rd person suffix, but **ili/ilni** etc. (7.4.2) agreeing with the subject are also found. (Note **revista ilha tohroġ 7 snin,** *the review has been coming out for 7 years*.)

9.3.3 **Daqs,** *as much as*, takes suffixes: **daqsi,** *as big (tall, old) as me*, and so on.

10 PREPOSITIONS

10.2 FORMS

10.2.1 Many prepositions combine with the definite article, viz.

> **bi (b')** makes **bil-(bid-** etc.), **bl'**; similarly **fi**
> **ma'** makes **mal-** (**mad-** etc.) but **ma' l-**; similarly **sa, ta'**
> **bhal** makes **bhall-** (**bhad-** etc.), but **bhal-** before a word beginning with l; similarly **ghal, lil, minn**

10.2.2 Similar combinations occur with the conjunction **li**, *that*; e.g. **billi**, *whereas*; **malli**, *as soon as*.

10.3 DERIVATIVES

Prepositions are not followed by pronouns but take suffixes (7.4.2) instead. The stem to which the suffix is attached may differ slightly, viz.

Stem	Preposition
għali-	għal
ħdej-	ħdejn
magħ-, miegħ-	ma'
qabl-	qabel
tagħ-, tiegħ-	ta'
waraj-	wara

The series **tiegħi**, etc. will usually be translated *my*, etc.

10.4 COMPOUND PREPOSITIONS

Double prepositions are not uncommon, especially with **minn** as the first element, e.g. **minn fost,** *from among*; **minn fuq,** *from above, on top of* (cf. 1.2.3).

10.5 USE

10.5.1 The usual caution should be employed when translating; standard equivalents are only a rough guide.

10.5.2 Fi with third-person suffixes means *contain(s)*, as well as *in it*, e.g. **la l-wiehed u anqas l-iehor ma fih xi tfahhar,** *neither the one nor the other contains anything to praise* (8.24.2).

In combination with **lok,** *place*, it makes the preposition **flok,** *instead of*.

10.5.3 **Ghand,** *with*, with suffixes expresses *I have*, etc. Like other verb equivalents the combinations can be negatived, and like **kelli**, etc. (7.4.8) can be used as auxiliaries (cf. 1.8.7).

They can also mean *at my* (etc.) *house*.

10.5.4 Besides the natural meaning *to*, **lil** may simply indicate the direct object (7.4.6).

10.5.5 **Minnu** is used in the sense *true*.

10.5.6 Some uses of ta' need watching: e.g. ħinijiet ħielsa ta' wara x-xogħol, *spare time after work*; minn fuq ta' Montalembert, *based on (the work) of Montalembert*; and cf. 7.2.2.

11 CONJUNCTIONS

11.1 FORMATION

11.1.1 Apart from primary conjunctions there are a fair number, which may not be given in the dictionary, which are formed from prepositions or adverbs by adding li or ma, e.g. waqt li, *while*; għad li, *although*; qabel ma, *before*; bħalma, *as*. Bla ma, a conjunction in Maltese, corresponds to a preposition and gerund in English, e.g. bla ma jqegħduh, *without putting him*.

11.2 USE

11.2.1 Biex, with ħalli, covers many uses of the English infinitive, e.g. ordnati biex, *ordered to*; mhux biżżejjed biex, *is not enough to*. (For ħalli see 8.17.6.) Li biex seems to be simply a variant of li, e.g. jiena nħoss li biex, *I feel that* . . . .

11.2.2 Both jekk and kieku mean *if*. Besides the fact that jekk also means *whether*, they differ in their implications: kieku kont means *if I had been*, while jekk kont means *if I was*; kieku nkun means *if I were*, while jekk nkun means *if I am*, either in reference to the present or the future. (A future reference is made clear by using sa in the main cause.)

GLOSSARY

abbonament, *subscription* (1.8.6)
aġġurnat, *brought up to date*
anwali, *annual*
atti, *proceedings*
awtur, *author*

barra, *abroad* (1.8.6)
għall-bejgħ, *for sale*
bibljoteka, *library*
bibljotekarju, *librarian*
bidla, *exchange*

daħla, *preface, introduction*
dalwaqt joħroġ, *forthcoming*
darbtejn fix-xahar, *twice a month*
direzzjoni, *administration, editorial office*
   (1.8.7)
diskors, *speech*
dramm, *play*

editjat, *edited*
eżawrit, *out of print*

faxxiklu, *part, instalment*

ġabra, *collection* (1.7.1)
ġdid, *new*
ġimagħtejn, *two weeks*
ġimgħa, *week*
ġrajja, *(hi)story*
ġurnal, *newspaper*

gazzetta, *newspaper*

ħanut, *shop*
ħareġ, *came out; published*
ħarġa, *edition* (1.5.1); *issue* (1.8.4)
ħlas, *payment, subscription*
bla ħlas, *free*

ibgħatu, *send*
im-, see m-
indirizz, *address*
ittra, *letter*

jinbagħat, *is sent*
jinbiegħ, *is sold*
jissokta, *(to be) continued*
joħroġ, *comes out* (1.8.5)

kelmtejn ta' qabel, *preface*
kittieb, *writer*
kollezzjoni, *collection* (1.7.1)
kont, *bill*
ktejjeb, *booklet, magazine*
ktieb, *book* (1.4.1, 1.7.2)
ta' kull ħmistax, *fortnightly* (and similar expressions with xahar, sena, etc.)
kumitat, *committee*

legat, *bound*
legatura, *binding*
librar, *bookseller*
librerija, *bookshop; library* (1.7.1)
lista, *list, table*

maħruġ, *published; furnished*
magħżul, *selected*
maqlub, *turned, translated* (from) (1.2.3)
meħud, *taken* (1.2.3, 1.5.3)
mfisser, *interpreted, translated* (into) (1.2.3)
mhux ippublikat, *unpublished*
miet, *died*
miġbur, *collected, compiled* (1.2.3)
miġjub, *brought, translated* (from) (1.2.3)
miktub, *written* (1.2.3)
mitbugħ, *printed* (1.6.1)
miżjud, *enlarged* (1.5.2)
mqassar, *abridged* (1.5.2)
msewwi, *corrected* (1.5.2)

novella, *short story*
numru, *number* (1.7.2, 1.8.4)

għadd, *number* (1.7.2, 1.8.4)
għana, *poems*
għaqda, *society, league*

b'omaġġi, *complimentary*
ordni, *order*

paġna, *page*
poeżija, *poem*
prezz, *price* (1.8.6)

rapport, *report*
riċerka, *research*
ritratt, *portrait, photograph*
rivedut, *revised*
rivista, *review*
rumanz, *novel*

sena, *year* (1.8.4)
sensiela, *series*
silta, *extract*
soċieta, *society*
stampat, *printed* (1.5.1)
stampat mill-ġdid, *reprinted*
stampatur, *printer*
stamperija, *printing-shop*
stess, *same*
storja, *(hi)story*

taħdit(a), *speech*
taqsima, *part* (1.4.1)
tegħmiża, *appendix*
tifkirijiet, *reminiscences*
tipografija, *printing-shop* (1.6.1)
tiswija, *correction*
toħroġ, *comes out*
tradott, *translated*
twieled, *born*

werrej, *index*
wieħed, *one, single* (1.8.6)

xahar, *month* (1.8.4, 1.8.6)
b'xejn, *for nothing*
xelti, *selected*
xogħol, *work*

żieda, *addition*

GRAMMATICAL INDEX: WORDS

bħall-, etc., 10.2.1
biex, 11.2.1
bil-, etc., bl', 10.2.1

ċ- (with hyphen), 2.6.1, 3.1.2

d- (with hyphen), 2.6.1, 3.1.2
dal- (daC-C-), 7.1.1
daqs-, 9.3.3
dawl-, dil-, 7.1.1
disa', disat, 6.1.1, 6.2.1

erba', erbat, 6.1.1
Erbgħa, 6.4.3

f', 2.1.5
fih(a), 10.5.2
fil-, etc., 10.2.1

GRAMMATICAL INDEX: ENDINGS

A good many grammatical differences are indicated by internal change and not by the addition of endings: see 0.5, 4.1, 4.2.2, 5.3.1, 8.1.4, 8.4, 8.5, 8.9, 8.12.

TURKISH

(For specimens see 0.5.1, 0.5.2)

0 GENERAL CHARACTERISTICS

0.1 DEGREE OF INFLEXION

Turkish is a highly synthetic language: the relations of nouns are largely expressed by terminations and complicated notions that would require several words to express in English can be expressed in Turkish by a single verb. Especially is this true of the large number of verbal nouns and adjectives. The different persons and tenses of the verbs are adequately distinguished by different forms, no pronouns or auxiliaries being necessary.

0.2 ORDER OF WORDS

As far as order goes, the golden rule is 'look to the end'. Not only do all adjectival expressions and what would in English be prepositional phrases precede nouns, and adverbs verbs, but the object precedes the verb, and what in English is expressed by prepositions is expressed in Turkish by endings or postpositions. Long phrases equivalent to subordinate clauses are placed before the words they qualify, so that there results one long sentence which grammatical analysis would describe as 'simple' but most foreign readers find difficult. So the foreign reader must acquire the habit of skipping from the beginning to the end and then reading a good part of the sentence backwards, as in the example in 0.5.1. As in English, grammatical categories are often fluid and not always obvious from the form: see, for instance, the uses of the ending **-DIk** (2.5.4, 2.6.1) in 8.12.3. Sometimes, however, Turkish will take pains to make the function of a word or phrase clear by a termination, distinguishing the adjective **içindeki** from the adverb **içinde**, where English would be content with *in it* in both cases, or inserting an almost empty marker like **da** (*also, indeed*), **olarak** (*being*), **olmak üzere** (*on the basis of being*), **suretiyle** (*by way of*), etc.

0.4 RELATION TO OTHER LANGUAGES

Turkish resembles the Finno-Ugrian languages in many points of structure but not in vocabulary, which apart from borrowings from Arabic, Persian, French and latterly English, is peculiar to the Turkic family of languages.

0.5 STRUCTURE

0.5.1 The following is an example of Turkish written with deliberate clarity, keeping the sentences reasonably short:

Bibliyotek kelimesi eski   Yunancadan alinmıştır.   Bibliyotek kitapların
Bibliyotek its-word ancient from-Greek has-been-taken. A library of-books
The word 'bibliyotek' is taken from ancient Greek. A library means a place

744

konulduğu,   **muhafaza edildiği**   **yer anlamına**   **gelir.**
their-being-placed, keeping their-being-done place to-its-meaning comes.
where books are placed and preserved.

Bu kelime, kitapların muhafaza edildiği   **bina**   **ile**   **beraber bu**
This word of-books keeping   their-being-done building with together this
Besides a building where books are preserved, the word later acquired a

binada   **vücuda**   **getirilen tesislerin**   **ve**   **organizasyonun**
in-building to-existence brought of-establishments and of-organisation
wider meaning, expressing the carrying on of the institutions and organisation

tamamını   **da** **ifade**   **etmek**   **suretiyle** **sonradan** **daha geniş**
their-fulfilment (obj.) also expression to make by way of afterwards more wide
brought into existence in this building.

bir anlam   **almıştır.**
a   meaning took.

Among the endings one may note -si, -u, -i, -ı (2, 8, 10, 12, 18, 29, 33), the suffix of the 3PS (4.5); -ın, -in, -un (7, 16, 26, 28) expressing *of* with singular and plural words alike (4.4); -lar, -ler expressing the plural; -a in 12 and 24 expressing *to*. (For the varying vowels see 2.6.1.) Words 8, 18 and 25 contain -il-, -ul- expressing the passive (8.23.2); -dik and its variants is a verbal adjective/noun (8.12.3). In 5 and 39 -mış- is the sign of the past, -tır (or -dır) of the verb *to be* (8.1.2).

0.5.2 In official language much longer sentences are found, so much so that I have inserted bar lines, e.g.

Her   **sayım memuru¹ binalar cetvelinde yazılı**   **ve**   **mıntakasına dahil**
Every census its agent houses in-their-list written and to-his-section included
After visiting all the houses recorded in the list of houses and included

bulunan   **binaların kâffesini**   **ziyaret¹ ve**   **içindeki**
being-found of houses their-totality (obj.) visit   and the in-its-interior (adj.)
in his section, and registering the population there,

nüfusu   **kaydettikten**   **sonra| yazdıklarını**   **birer birer gözden**
populations (obj.) from-registering after   his-writings (obj.) one by one from-eye
every enumerator shall review in detail what he has written, and after

geçirecek,‖   **eksik**   **bir nokta kalmadığına¹**   **ve mıntaka binalar**
will-make-to-pass deficient a   point at-its-not-remaining and section   houses
satisfying himself that there is nothing left out

cetvelindeki   **bütün binaları**   **ziyaret ettiğine¹ kanaat**   **hâsıl eyledikten¹**
in-their-list (adj.) all the houses (obj.) at-his-visiting   satisfaction from-producing
and that he has visited all the houses in the list of houses of the section,

ve   **binalar cetvelinin**   **altını**   **imza ettikten sonra| sayım defterini**
and houses of-their-list its-bottom (obj.) from-signing after   census its-register (obj.)
and signing the bottom of the list of houses, shall place the census

ve   **binalar cetvelini**   **hususi zarfına**   **koyarak¹ kapatmaksızın¹**
and houses their-list (obj.) special to-its-envelope putting   without-sealing
register and the list of houses in its special envelope, unsealed,

sayım gününün   akşamına   kadar kontrol memuruna;[1] kontrol memuru olmıyan
census of-its-day to-its-evening until   check   to-its-agent check   its-agent not-being
and shall deliver them by the evening of the day of the census to the census officer,

yerlerde[1] mahallin   en   büyük mülkiye   âmirine   teslim edecektir.
in-places of-the-place most great civil-service to-its-chief will-deliver.
or in places where there is no census officer, to the head of the local civil service.

Here again the subject, **her sayım memuru**, stands at the beginning of the sentence and is followed by two coordinate clauses, a comparatively short one ending with **geçirecek**, and the other with **edecektir** at the end of the sentence. Of these parallel main verbs only the last has the full form: the **-tir** of **edecektir** serves them both. Similarly in line 3 **ettikten**, abstracted from **kaydettikten**, is understood with **ziyaret**, making *visiting*, and in lines 5 and 6 both **eyledikten** and **ettikten** are construed with **sonra**.

In each half of the sentence there are inserted before the main verb long phrases ending in a verbal noun (ending **-DIk**) followed by **-DAn sonra**, corresponding here to English phrases beginning with *after*, though sometimes such phrases require to be translated by subordinate clauses. (For the capital letters see 2.5.4 and 2.6.1.) Within the phrases long sequences of words such as **binalar–bulunan** qualify the following word, and single words are equivalent to clauses. Thus **içindeki** (line 2), built-up from **iç** (*interior*) through **içi** (*interior of it*), **içinde** (*in the interior of it*), means *which is in the interior of it* and qualifies **nüfus**, just as **cetvelindeki** means *which are on the list of*. **Yazdıkları** (line 3) a verbal noun with a possessive suffix, means *what he has written*, and **olmıyan** (line 8) a negative present participle means *where there is not*. That-clauses are represented by the verbal nouns **kalmadık** (line 4) and **ettik** (line 5) with possessive suffixes and the further suffix **-A** (*at*) required by **kanaat**, *satisfaction*. In line 7 the ending **-ArAk** expresses the first of two successive actions, where as often as not English will use two coordinate verbs.

0.5.3 To construe modern, technical Turkish one needs a knowledge of the few basic phonetic rules, patience to disentangle the endings, and imagination to grasp the meaning of unfamiliar modes of expression. On the whole it is easier to make out the meaning of a Turkish sentence without having learnt the language than a Latin one. (The older Turkish is best left to experts.)

1 BIBLIOLINGUISTICS

1.1 NAMES

1.1.1 Since 1935 every Turk has had a surname (**soyadı**) as the last component of his name, but authors who have not written since then, and those who do not choose to use their surnames are still entered in *Türkiye bibliyografyası* under the first component of the name, even if it is an initial. For those who have written both before and after one can use the Roberts College index.*

1.1.2 Some transitional forms are found, as when the name now given as **İsmail Hakkı Uzunçarşılı**, formerly entered under **İsmail** and now under **Uzunçarşılı**, appears as **Uzunçarşılıoğlu İsmail Hakkı** (*Uzunçarşılı's son I. H.*) in typically Turkish order. (The surname is adjectival and precedes the word it qualifies.) This order is also found in the Turkish forms of medieval names such as *Thomas Aquinas*, viz. **Akino'lu St. Thomas, Güzel Philippe** (*Philippe le Bel*).

* Harry W. Chapman, *compiler. A first-name index to the Türkiye bibliyografyası 1939–1948.* İstanbul, Roberts College Research Center, 1968. (Bulletin series no. 501)

1.1.3 Difficulty is also caused by the fact that older writers who used the Arabic alphabet may appear in original works, reprints, translations and reference books in several different forms. The pronunciation of Arabic words was greatly modified in Turkish and the Arabic alphabet was an unsuitable one for representing Turkish (2.1.2). So the name now written **Celâlettin** might appear *inter alia* in an English catalogue as **Jalal-al-din** or **Jalalu'd-din**, in German as **Dschalaluddin**, in French as **Djalaleddin**. But it would be unwise to plump for **-ettin** every time; **-addin**, **-attin**, **-eddin**, **-üddin** are all found in modern Turkish. If one has no access to an encyclopaedia, it is better to refer older names to an expert. Even modern Turkish names are sometimes modified in foreign books. **Cafar** may appear as **Jafar**, **Djafar**, **Giafar** and so on. A knowledge of the respective phonetic values will enable one to restore such names to their correct Turkish form.

1.1.4 Conversely, Turkish pronunciation and spelling also affect Persian and Arabic names, for which Western catalogues will be using a different transliteration. Thus, the name which appears in the British Museum catalogue as **Muhammad ibn Muhammad (Jalāl al-Din) *Rūmī*** is indexed in *Türkiye bibliyografyası* under **Mevlâna Celâleddin Rumi**. This applies to some extent to any language that involves transliteration, for though *TB* uses the international standard transliteration of Cyrillic, it does not follow that every book will do so, and one even finds spellings like **Mişel Zevako** for **Michel Zévaco**, where there is no transliteration. (Not to mention **Lemmi Kovşun**.)

1.2 NAMES OF AUTHORS, EDITORS, ETC.

1.2.1 The name of the author often stands by itself at the head of the title-page or after the title. In neither case is its form affected.

1.2.2 The name may follow the title but be preceded by either an active participle (8.12.2) or by a noun with the third-person suffix (4.5) indicating the agent, e.g. **yazan**, *writing, writer*; **hazırlıyan**, *preparing*; **nakili**, *its narrator*. This will naturally be the case where a person has some special relation to the work, such as editor (**tertip eden**, *compiling, arranging*; **çıkaran**, *extracting*; **seçen**, **intihap eden**, *selecting*; **şerheden**, *commenting*) or translator (**çeviren**, *turning*; **nakleden**, *transporting*; **tercüme eden**, *translating*; **mütercim**, *translator*). The name is unaffected but in cases like **Hazırlıyanlar: Sabiha Taşçıoglu, Fahrettin Kıyak, Sadi Kazancı** the participle is in the plural and needs to be followed by at least two of the names.

1.2.3 Less commonly, the work done is expressed by a noun like **tercüme(si)**, *(its) translation*, and the name simply follows, again unaltered.

1.2.4 The author's name may be in the genitive in such instances as **İsmet Paşanın | Siyasi ve Içtimai | Nutukları 1920–1933**, *Ismet Paşa's Political and social speeches, 1920–1933*. But it is not obligatory, e.g. **Nâzım Hikmet | Bütün eserleri** and even **Ahmet Vefik Paşa Külliyatı**, without a break. Both expressions mean *Complete works*.

1.2.5 Societies and institutions and bodies generally, as authors and editors, may be indicated in any of the ways given above, though the relationship between the body and the book may be not so much literary authorship as sponsorship or responsibility.

In the names of such bodies the town, institution and department may all be given in one grammatically connected phrase, e.g. **Ankara Üniversitesi Dil ve Tarih-Coğrafya Fakültesi Kütüphanecilik Kursu**, *Ankara University Language History and Geography Faculty Librarianship Course*. *Türkiye bibliyografyası* divides this at **Üniversitesi** and **Fakültesi** but not after **Ankara**. As explained in 4.5.4–4.5.7 the suffixes **-si** and **-u** link the noun to which they are attached to what goes before. If the connexion is broken the suffix is not needed, but Turkish often uses it if a connexion is so much as implied.

Thus in a guide book the heading *Buildings* under any town would be **binaları** rather that **-lar**. Secondly, the **-si** of **Fakültesi** and the **-u** of **kursu** not merely link these to **Üniversitesi** and **Fakültesi** respectively but also to the immediately preceding words, so they cannot be omitted. As therefore one always can and sometimes must retain the suffix, it is safer to make it a rule to do so.

Naturally not every such concatenation of nouns is to be split up so. **Ticaret ve Sanayi Odaları Birliği**, like the equivalent *Federation of Chambers of Commerce and Industry*, is left as it is.

1.3 TITLES

1.3.1   These usually consist, like English ones, of nouns and adjectives and indications of relation, but nouns are frequently used where, jargon apart, we should have adjectives, and the relations are expressed by suffixes or postpositions not prepositions, e.g. **Kaniş Kārum'unun kronoloji problemleri hakkında müşahedeler**, *Observations on the chronological problems of the Kārum Kaniş*. Belles-lettres, popular books and propaganda are grammatically more varied, e.g. **Sana inandım sevgilim**, *I believed you my love*; **Uçaklar havada nasıl kalır?**, *How do aeroplanes stay in the air?*

1.3.2   Titles entries should not cause much trouble. There is no definite article, and it is standard Turkish practice not to ignore **bir**, the 'indefinite article' (3.2). Both **Bir çocuğun romanı** (*The story of a child*) and **Bir dakika** (*One minute*) are entered under **bir**. In translating a title like **Türk dili tarihi** for a British Museum type heading it is better to translate *ad sensum* and make the heading TURKISH LANGUAGE, even though **Türk** is a noun.

1.3.3   If the title of a book or periodical occurs in a sentence, the principal noun will take such suffixes as are appropriate, e.g. ***Türkiye bibliyografyası*'ndaki hatalar**, *errors in 'TB'*. The use of the apostrophe keeps the title separate. But *in our 'TB'* would be ***Türkiye bibliyografya*'mızda**, since a word can have only one personal suffix; having removed the **-mız** one has to restore the **-sı** (4.5.5). Difficulties of this sort can be avoided by using expressions of the form **Leman Güre'nin "Su üstünde gölgeler" adlı eseriyle biraradadır**, *together with Leman Güre's work entitled 'Su üstünde gölgeler'*, in which the title is unaffected.

1.3.4   Owing to the peculiarities of Turkish order titles are sometimes difficult to shorten. In **teoride ve pratikte paramızın iç ve dış değeri**, *the internal and external value of our money in theory and practice*, the obvious words to omit are **teoride ve pratikte**, as is done on the half-title. The book is liable to be cited without them and one is advised* to make a reference from the shorter form, especially if the subsidiary qualifying phrase is long. On the other hand **Sigorta bilgisi**, *Science of insurance*, could be shortened to **Sigorta** without offence, since **sigorta** is unaffected by the grammatical relationship.

1.3.5   When the name of the author and the title form one whole, e.g. **Türkiye Cumhuriyeti Merkez Bankası Kanunu**, *Constitution of the Central Bank of Turkey*, the operative word, in this case **kanun**, has the personal suffix. If the first four words are not treated as part of the title, one is left with **kanunu**. For the reasons given in 1.2.5 this would not be a solecism, but in such cases *TB* includes the name of the body in the title.

---

* In *Bibliyotekçinin elkitabı* by Adnan Öteken, 1947. *TB* title index has entries in both places.

1.4 VOLUMES AND PARTS

1.4.1 The word for *volume* is **cilt** (also *binding*); *part* is either **cüz** or **kısım**. Other words that are found are **kitap** (*book*) and **fasikül**. As usual, it is hard to differentiate between the various words. Hierarchically **cilt** is superior and can be subdivided by **cüz** or less frequently **kısım**; but it is not necessarily a separate physical volume, for one may find a work described as **2 cilt (birarada)**, *2 volumes in one*. Conversely physically separate volumes are not infrequently described as **kısım**. Both **kitap** and **fasikül** are used in connexion with books published in parts.

1.4.2 Numeration may be in words or figures, usually preceding the word for volume or part. Even if it follows it is read as a preceding ordinal, e.g. **Birinci cilt, 2. kısım; 2. cilt, VII. fasikül; cilt III** (read **üçüncü cilt**).

1.4.3 Occasionally the numeration is connected syntactically with the title and will have to be transcribed with it, e.g. **Anadolu Türk tarihi vesikalarından birinci (ikinci,** etc.) **kitap**, *First (second, etc.) book of documents of Anatolian Turkish history*. Here **vesikalarından** makes no sense without the following words.

1.5 EDITIONS

1.5.1 There is the same trouble with Turkish words for *edition* as in other languages. The words commonly used all refer to printing, viz. **basım, tabı,** *printing*; **bası,** *thing printed*; **basılış,** *fact of being printed*. Thus **tıpkı basım** (*identical printing*) indicates that the existing edition has been reprinted from stereotypes or by some sort of facsimile reproduction; **ayrı basım** means *offprint*, **tekrar basım** *reprint*. On the other hand if **basım** is preceded by such words as **düzeltilmiş, tashih edilmiş** (*corrected*), **ilâveli** (*supplemented*), **genişletilmiş** (*enlarged*), **gözden geçirilmiş** (*revised*) or the simple **yeni** (*new*), it obviously means *edition*. There is also a word **baskı** as in **Eserin ilk baskısı 1952 yılında yapılmıştır**, *The first edition of the work was published in 1952*.

1.5.2 Numeration is by preceding ordinal, e.g. **İkinci (2., 2 nci) bası**. One cannot be certain with simple statements of this kind whether the meaning is *2nd edition* or *2nd impression*. Nor is **ikinci defa basılmıştır** (*printed the second time*) unambiguous. Words for *revised* are given in the preceding paragraph.

1.5.3 See 1.5.1.

1.6 IMPRINTS

1.6.1 Present-day imprints are nearly always those of firms, with a good many firm names which are not personal names, such as **Yenilik Basımevi** (*Novelty Press*). The names nearly all end with one or other of the words **matbaa** (*printing, press*), usually in the form **matbaası; basımevi; kitabevi, yayınevi**, the last two meaning *publishing-house*. *Bibliyotekçinin elkitabı* recommends that the publisher's name should only be given in cataloguing if the printer is not stated and cannot be ascertained; but it seems wiser for Western librarians to take the imprint on the title-page, whatever it is. Detailed information about printing is usually given on the verso of the title-page or in the colophon.

1.6.2 The imprint is normally given in the order: place, press, the place name being without suffix. Sometimes it is preceded by some such word as **naşiri** (*its publisher*).

1.7 SERIES

1.7.1 About a third of all Turkish books are published in numbered series. It is perhaps not surprising therefore that a good many of the series titles are of the form: **Özyürek Yayınları** (*O. Publications*), the publisher being **Özyürek Yayınevi**. Other plurals such as **Neşriyat** (4.2.2), **Kitaplar** and so on also figure largely, e.g. **Öğretmen**

Kitapları (*Teacher's Books*). Somewhat disconcertingly one finds the same series now with Yayınları and now with Neşriyatı. In the singular one tends to find seri and kütüphane (*library*), e.g. Şirin Çocuk Kitapları Serisi (*Nice Child Book Series*), Okul ve Aile Kütüphanesi (*School and Family Library*). After these matter-of-fact titles it is almost a shock to meet Tarih Konuşuyor (*History Speaks*).

1.7.2 Numeration is quite often given by simply putting a numeral after the series title, but sayı or n(ümer)o may be inserted. (The form sayısı, grammatically connected with the series title, is also found.) Sometimes the numeration is grammatically connected with the title in another way, as in Türk Tarih Kurumu Yayınlarından XI seri, No. 21 (*Series XI, No. 21 from the Publications of the Turkish Historical Institute*). There is no objection to omitting -dan in giving the title: it is not an integral part of the title, which is found without it in other books. The series title in the last example is followed in the book by another series title: Istanbul Fethini Kutlama Kurulu Yayınları (*Publications Instituted to Celebrate the Capture of Constantinople*), without a number. This is not uncommon: indeed instances occur where three series are given in each of which the work has a different number.

1.7.3 In most of the titles quoted above the last word has the 3rd-person suffix (4.5.1), but the first part is descriptive and there is no question of splitting the title up. In İstanbul Üniversitesi Yayınları (*Publications of the University of Istanbul*) one should use the form Yayınları even if the name of the issuing body is omitted from the title. (See 1.2.7 and 1.7.2.)

1.8 PERIODICALS

1.8.1 The titles of periodicals are grammatically similar to those of books, e.g. Ticari Politika, *Commercial Policy*, though naturally one often meets less transparent titles such as Çatı, *The Roof*. In a sentence the title may have relational or personal suffixes, as explained in 1.3.3.

1.8.2 When a periodical is published by an institution or society, the name of the body may appear in various ways. Quite often it is simply put separately at the head of the page, e.g. Türk Tarih Kurumu. Belleten. Here belleten being grammatically unconnected does not have the 3rd-person suffix. As with series, however, all the information may be given in one grammatically linked phrase, Ankara Üniversitesi Yıllığı (*Ankara University Annual*), a title which is best left as it is.

1.8.3 The term which most nearly corresponds to *editor*, hazırlıyan, the present participle of hazırlamak, *to arrange*, is not common. More often one has phrases indicating some sort of legal responsibility: sahibi, *its proprietor* (glossed as *editor* in one bilingual periodical); yazı işlerini fiilen idare eden mesul müdür (glossed as '*directeur responsable*', which is a translation of the last two words), or similar phrases. Sometimes responsibility is limited by the words bu sayıda or bu nüshada, *in this issue*. Editorial committees are common: yazı kurulu (üyeleri), neşir heyeti and permutations of these, and danışma kurulu, *advisory committee*.

1.8.4 Numeration is commonly by yıl, *year* or cilt, *volume* (occasionally by both), subdivided by sayı, n(ümer)o or nu(mara).

1.8.5 Periodicity is expressed in two principal ways: by the use of the appropriate adjective or adverb in -lık, or by stating the period within which each number appears, e.g. haftalık siyasi dergi, *weekly political review*; dergimiz yıllık olarak çıkacaktır, *our review will come out annually*; yılda bir çıkarılır, *one is published in a year*; her üç ayda bir çıkar, *one appears every three months*. Occasionally a periodical may be described as gayrı mevkut, *irregular*.

1.8.6 Subscriptions are stated in terms similar to periodicity. Under the head **abone(si)**—most of the terms have the 3rd-person suffix—the various rates are given against the terms **yıllığı, altı aylığı, üç aylığı, sayısı.** Yıllık, etc. are nouns like **sayı,** meaning *a year's, six month's, etc. issues,* just as one can quote for **on iki tanesi,** *twelve of it* (for **tane** see 6.1.3). In other instances they are found as qualifiers, e.g. **yıllık abonesi,** *annual subscription.* Back numbers, **eski sayılar,** are occasionally quoted for.

A fair number give special rates for foreign countries—**yabancı** (or **dış**) **memleketler** (or **ülkeler**) **için;** or **yurd dışı senelik abone,** *annual subscription outside the country.*

1.8.7 Addresses given may specify **yönetim adresi,** *administration address;* **yazışma adresi,** *address for correspondence;* **mektup ve havale için adres,** *address for letters and remittances;* **(dizilip) basıldığı yer,** *place of (composition and) printing.*

2 ALPHABET, PHONETICS, SPELLING

2.1 ALPHABET

2.1.1 The present alphabet dates from 1928 and has the following letters, each with its own position in the alphabet:

a   b   c   ç   d   e   f   g   ğ   h   ı   i   j   k   l   m   n   o   ö   p   r   s   ş t   u   ü   v   y   z

(Foreign letters like **w** have their usual place.)

Note that **I** is the capital form of **ı,** capital **i** being dotted. The order of these two letters is reversed in some dictionaries, including Hony's. In view of what is said in 1.1.3 and 1.1.4 the pronunciation of the following letters should be noted: **c** = En j; **ç** = ch; **g** before **â, e, i, ö, û, ü** = gy; **ğ** is silent after **a, o, u** in most words and sounds like y after **e, i, ö, ü; j** is as in French (En s in pleasure); **ö** as in German (Fr **eu**); **s** = sh; **ü** as in German (Fr **u**).

2.1.2 Before 1928 the Arabic alphabet was used, usually in its Persian form, which was slightly less unsuitable for writing Turkish. It has too many consonants and not enough vowels; and though the ambiguities of the vowels are to some extent redressed by the use of a different consonant, nevertheless one cannot deduce the modern spelling simply from the Arabic letters. If an expert is available, it is better to consult one.

2.1.3 The apostrophe may be:

(a) the representation (usually silent) of the Arabic letters **elif** and **ain;**

(b) a device for separating a suffix from a proper name, book title, quotation or foreign word, e.g. **renvoi'lar** (cf 1.3.3);

(c) a device for distinguishing synonyms: **kar'ın** from **kar** (*snow*), **karı'n** from **karı** (*wife*) as distinct from **karın** (*belly*).

Some of these uses depend on personal preference, so one must not expect consistency.

2.1.4 The circumflex accent has two uses:

(a) to indicate that a preceding **g, k** or **l** is palatalised. The English *cure* would be represented by **kûr,** Byron's *Giaour* represents **gâvur.** This is obligatory in Arabic words and customary with Western borrowings like **plân** and **plâk** (*gramophone record*);

(b) to indicate an Arabic long vowel. Very often, as in **âlem** (*world*), **alem** (*banner*), it distinguishes one word from another.

2.2 CAPITALISATION

2.2.1 The use of initial capitals in Turkish is much the same as in English, though some words counted as proper names in English are not in Turkish. The names of months had capitals, but not as a rule the days of the week. Words like **Türkçe**, *Turkish language*, vary. Derived words such as **İslâmiyet**, *Mohammedanism*, have capitals.

2.2.2   Personal and institutional names are capitalised throughout, except for words like **ve** (*and*), e.g. **Sıvaslı Topal Hasan**, *Lame Hasan from Sıvas*; **Türk Tarih Kurumu Basımevi**, *Turkish Historical Society Press*; but if the name is considered as simply descriptive the rule in 2.2.3 is followed, e.g. **Galatasaray spor klübü**.

2.2.3   In geographical and topographical names the non-specific part has a small letter, e.g. **Ankara caddesi**, *Ankara Street*, **Ege denizi**, *Aegean Sea*. Some historical events follow the same pattern, e.g. **Fransız ihtilâli**, *French Revolution*, but wars usually have capitals throughout, e.g. **1918–1923 İstiktâl Savaşı**, *War of Independence*; **Büyük Harp**, *Great War*.

2.2.4   The titles of books are frequently cited with capitals throughout, except for conjunctions and postpositions; but bibliographical works follow the international standard practice.

2.2.5   Titles of rank, profession or status, whether in full or abbreviated, begin with a capital, e.g. **Profesör Dr. Z. F. Fındıkoğlu, Cumhur Reisi Millî Şef İsmet İnönü, Bay Çemberleyn**.

2.3   DIVISION OF WORDS

2.3.1   Rules 1, 4, 5a, 6a, 7a, 8a (p. xiii) apply.

2.3.2   Compounds, as distinct from derivatives, are comparatively rare. No attempt is made to divide the basic word from the endings: thus one has **yöneti-mini** from **yönetim**. There are no exceptions to division between two consonants: **sos-yalist, tek-rar** not so-syalist, te-krar.

2.4   PUNCTUATION AND ABBREVIATIONS

2.4.1   Turkish punctuation is sometimes helpful and sometimes disconcerting. Very often the subject, or the logical subject, is followed by a comma, which is a help: if a comma occurs near the beginning of a sentence this is probably what it indicates. On the other hand you will sometimes find a comma after a conjunction such as **ama**, *but*, or **ki**, *that*. No doubt that is hov̇ ̇e sentence is spoken, and **ki** is no ordinary conjunction (11.2.2).

2.4.2   A full stop may be used in the middle of a word to indicate an abbreviation, e.g. **Hz.ni** for **Hazretlerini** (*His Excellency*).

2.4.3   Quotation marks can occur in the middle of a word e.g. **"ben"in**, *of the* '*ego*'.

2.5   VARIATION OF CONSONANT

2.5.1   In present-day Turkish stems which end in **b, c, d, g** (**ğ**) change this to **p, ç, t, k** at the end of a word or before a suffix beginning with a consonant, e.g. **yıllığı/yıllık**; **ediyor/etmek**. If the following word begins with a vowel and is closely connected in sense the voiced consonant may be retained. This is especially true of expressions with **etmek**, so much so that they are usually written as one word: **icap etmek** (*to be necessary*) is usually **icabetmek**. (Hony's dictionary of 1957 and texts of the same period would have **icab** in all contexts.) The converse affects the suffixes **-AcAk** and **-DIk** (8.12.4).

In words borrowed from other languages the unvoiced consonant may be the original one, e.g. **grup** (G **grubun** or **grupun**) or the change may not take place, e.g. **miting, katalog**. There are also some pure Turkish words which do not change, e.g. **ad**, *name* (**at**, *horse* has G **atın**).

The converse change does not necessarily take place: we find **top**, *a ball*; **topu topu,** *all in all*; **neşriyat-ı,** *its publications.*

2.5.2 There are some words, borrowed from Arabic where the above alternations take the form of **p/bb, t/dd,** e.g. **ret,** *refusal*; **reddetmek,** *to refuse*. Here again there are exceptions, e.g. **had/haddi,** etc., *limit*, as opposed to **hat/hattı,** etc., *line.*

2.5.3 With other consonants alternations of single and double forms are found, e.g. **zan,** *belief*; **zannetmek,** *to believe*; **hak/hakkı,** etc., *right*; **af/affetmek,** *pardon.*

2.5.4 Suffixes and enclitics beginning with **c, d** or **g** change this to **ç, t, k** after an unvoiced consonant, e.g. **Türkçe-ingilizce, toplumdan, baştan, on da, ve yahut ta.** Whenever such suffixes are referred to here, the variable letter will be spelt with a capital, i.e. **D** means **d** or **t** as the case may be.

2.5.5 Two vowels together are not particularly common in Turkish: words of foreign origin involving **-ia-** and some other combinations are modified by the insertion or substitution of the related consonant, e.g. **biyoloji, sosyal, burjuva.** Similarly the word **fiat,** *price* (ultimately of Arabic origin) is sometimes spelt **fiyat,** and **y** is regularly inserted before vowel suffixes.

2.6 VARIATION OF VOWEL

2.6.1 One of the characteristic features of Turkish is vowel harmony. It applies to all the vowels in the great majority of native words, though so many quite common words are taken from Arabic that this aspect is best left aside, and to the majority of suffixes and the enclitics, which harmonize with the last syllable of the word they are attached to, and therefore have alternative vowels.

The vowels are classified as follows:

	Unrounded	Rounded
Back	a ı	o u
Front	e i	ö ü

and the alternations are **a/e** and **ı/i/u/ü.** Thus **a** and **e** are used after any of the vowels in the same line but **ı, i, u** and **ü** only after those in the same box, e.g. **bankalar, yazılar, yollar, bunlar; müesseseler, ginler, gözler, günler; bankacı, yazıcı; yolcu, sucu; dilenci, dinci; gözcü, büyücü; er mi; bina mı; okudunuz mu.**

Like the consonants (2.5.4) these variable vowels are represented here by capitals so that **-DIr** stands for any of the eight forms: **-dır, -dir, -dur, -dür, -tır, -tir, -tur, -tür.**

2.6.2 A number of foreign words with a back vowel in the last syllable may have a front vowel in the suffix under the influence of the final consonant, though common words tend more to keep the harmony. The consonants involved are **-d, -f, -k, -l, -m, -p/-b-, -r, -s, -t,** and except for those ending in **-l,** which may be French, the words are all of Arabic origin. It is only the ending **-i** where one would expect **-ı** that is likely to cause much trouble, for **harbi, kavmi, dikkati** suggest the very common Arabic adjectival ending **-i** (not subject to harmony) rather than the grammatical suffix **-I.**

2.6.3 To avoid clusters of consonants at the beginning or end of a syllable borrowed words used to be modified by the insertion of a vowel, e.g. **istasyon, tiren, külüp; kısım, bahis, terim.** Many words in the first group now dispense with the inserted vowel, e.g. **spor** (not **sıpor**), **tren, klüp.** Those in the second group usually omit it when a syllable beginning with a vowel is added, e.g. **kısmı, bahsi** (2.6.2), **termi.** There are a few native Turkish words which behave in this way, e.g. **oğul, oğlu.**

2.6.4   Intervocalic -y- in verbs usually changes the preceding -A- to -I-, e.g. **olmamak, olmıyan,** *not being.*

2.7 SPELLING

2.7.1   Not many changes have taken place in the short time that Turkish has been written in Latin characters. The most important variations, apart from those mentioned in 2.5.1 and 2.6.3, are these:

> **aa** has been used to indicate a long **a** after **g** and **k**, since **gâ** and **kâ** would indicate palatalisation (2.1.4a).
>
> **iy** has been used instead of **i** to represent Arabic long **i**, and **kıy** to represent Arabic **qı.**
>
> **ov** and **öv** have been used instead of **oğ** and **öğ.**

3 ARTICLES

3.1 DEFINITE

There is no definite article. There is a form of the noun which indicates the definite direct object (4.4.3) but it does not follow that the English translation will have the definite article, or vice versa.

3.2 INDEFINITE

3.2.1   The word translated by the indefinite article is the same as the numeral *one.* Turkish bibliographical practice makes no distinction (1.3.2). It is usually omitted with predicates.

3.2.2   It can be followed by a noun in the plural, e.g. **bir şeyler,** *something or other,* as opposed to **bir şey,** *a thing.*

3.2.3   **Bir** comes between an adjective and its noun, unless they make one idea, e.g. **başka bir bibliyografyacı,** *another bibliographer;* but **bir ilk adım,** *a first step.*

4 NOUNS

4.1 GENDER AND FORM

4.1.1   There is no gender in Turkish, though some writers when using an Arabic adjective with an Arabic feminine noun have given the adjective its feminine form in -ye. A number of these feminines appear, as nouns, in the older names of ministries, e.g. **Dahiliye Vekâleti,** *Ministry of the Interior.*

4.1.2   The Turkish noun, as it occurs in speech, consists of the basic form (the dictionary entry) with or without various suffixes. The basic form is used as subject, as indefinite object, as simple predicate, when qualifying what follows (4.5.5); and in absolute expressions it may be doubled to form adverbial phrases, e.g. **cilt cilt çıkarılan kitaplar,** *books published volume by volume.*

The suffixes are added in the following order:

(1) The plural **(4.2)**
(2) Personal **(4.5)**
(3) Relational or **case-endings (4.4)**

4.2 PLURAL

4.2.1   The plural suffix is **-lAr,** e.g. **kitaplar,** *books;* **şeyler,** *things.*

4.2.2 There are also Arabic plurals, e.g. **neşriyat**, *publications*, from **neşir**; **kütüp** from **kitap**; **evkaf**, *charitable foundations*, from **vakıf**; **şerait**, *conditions*, from **şart**. Those still current (and many of these are merely alternatives) are usually given separately in the dictionary. They may have the Turkish plural suffix as well, e.g. **evlât(lar)**, *one's children*.

4.2.3 Singular and plural are not used in quite the same way as in English. In particular the Turkish singular must sometimes be translated by a plural, e.g. **Aşk mektubu**, *Love letters*. Hence the common use of **Türk** to mean *Turkish*, i.e. *of the Turk* as a class. The plural denotes several individual objects. Conversely, abstract nouns can have plurals, like the English *kindnesses* but more freely. See also 3.2.2 and 6.1.2.

4.4 RELATIONAL SUFFIXES

4.4.1 These suffixes are five in number and correspond fairly closely to the cases found in other languages. The cases make convenient names, but the suffixes are added indifferently to the basic form of the noun, to the plural, and to forms which already have personal suffixes, e.g. **yayından**, *from the publication*; **yayınlardan**, *from the publications*; **yayınlarından**, *from its publications*. Except for vowel harmony (2.6.1) and consonant variation (2.5.4) they are invariable. They have not therefore been set out in declensions. Two other suffixes fall partly into this class but are dealt with fully elsewhere.

4.4.2 The forms of the suffixes are:

-(y)A; -nA	'dative'
-CA; -nCA	See 9.1.1
-DA; -nDA	'locative'
-lA	See 10.1.1
-(y)I; -nI	'accusative'
-DAn; -nDAn	'ablative'
-(n)In	'genitive'

The forms beginning with a consonant are used after vowels: where there are two, the second is used after the third-person suffix. Note that words like **elkitabı**, *handbook*, end with this suffix, being in fact compounds (cf. 4.5.4).

4.4.3 The uses of the suffixes are as follows:

-A: motion towards, indirect object, goal, cost. The preposition used in translation depends on the context, e.g. **konferansa iştirak ediyordu**, *took part in the conference*; **mülkiye âmirine teslim edecektir**, *will deliver to the head of the civil service*. (For postpositions in -nA see 10.4.)

-DA: location in space, time or metaphorically, e.g. **evde**, *in the house*; **saat kaçta**, *at what time*; **konuşmalarda**, *in conversations*. (For -mAktA see 8.11.2; for postpositions in -ndA see 10.4.)

-I: definite object, usually indicated in English by *the*, *this*, *my* and the like. For examples see 0.3.2. The accusative may be governed by a noun of action as well as by a verb (cf. 8.11.3).

-DAn: separation, distance, origin, cause (*from*); *by* (the hand), *by* (the door); (to talk) *about*; (better) *than*, e.g. **Tuna'dan Basra körfezine**, *from the Danube to the Persian Gulf*, **zelzeleden**, *as a result of the earthquake*. Note also **merkez heyeti azasından Besim Atalay, B. A.**, *a member* (from the members) *of the central committee*. (For postpositions in -ndAn see 10.4.)

2B

-In: possession (by a defined object) and analogous relationships (*of*). See 4.5.4, 4.5.5; for the genitive with verbal nouns see 8.11.4, 8.11.5; and for its use before postpositions, 10.1.

4.4.4   A number of suffixes are coupled with postpositions (10.1.2).

4.5 PERSONAL SUFFIXES

4.5.1   The forms for the different persons, singular and plural are:

-(I)m, -(I)n, -(s)I; -(I)mIz, -(I)nIz, -lArI

The vowels in brackets are used when the basic form ends in a consonant, -s- when it ends in a vowel. For changes of stem see 2.5 and 2.6.

4.5.2   The suffixes frequently indicate possession or analogous relationships (*of*), and for this reason are sometimes called possessive suffixes; but they have also a wider range of uses.

They are added to the noun denoting the thing 'possessed', and the 'possessor' may have the genitive ending (4.4.3, 7.3.1).

4.5.3   The suffixes on their own produce expressions of the types **çocukları**, *his children, their child(ren)*; **biriniz**, *one of you*; **aramızda**, *in between us*; **tuttuğu iş**, *the work he has undertaken*. Expressions of the last two types are quite common and are dealt with under the postposition (10.4) and the verb (8.11.4, 8.12.4) respectively.

4.5.4   The commonest use of the third person suffix is where one noun qualifies another, e.g. **müellifin adı**, *the name of the author*; **soy adı**, *family name*; "**Ahmet**" **adı**, *the name 'Ahmet'*; **Azerbaycan ordusunun temeli**, *the foundation of the army of Azerbaijan*; **Istanbul Mıntaka Liman Reisliği**, *Istanbul Sector Harbour Authority*; **binaların arasında**, *between the buildings*; **halkın tuttuğu iş**, *the work the people has undertaken*.

4.5.5   Note that in some cases the first noun has the genitive suffix **-In** (4.4.3) and in others not, but that the second (or last) always has the personal suffix. The genitive suffix is used, as above, where there is a definite 'possessor' which is not a place, or where the 'possessor' is separated from the 'possessed' by other words. Many of the indefinite groups have English equivalents of the same form, in others, such as **Merkez bankası**, English would use an adjective, viz. *Central Bank*. There is a difference also in the two chains **Azerbaycan**, etc. and **Istanbul**, etc. which can be expressed graphically thus:

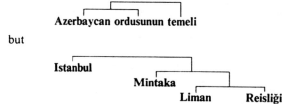

Azerbaycan ordusunun temeli

but

If an expression like **Liman Reisliği** has a suffix of the first or second person, this ousts that of the third (cf. 1.3.3). So does the adjectival suffix **-lI** (ibid. **adlı**).

4.5.6   In expressions like **depoların bakımı**, *the care of the stacks*, the singular suffix is used instead of the plural, which is ambiguous (4.5.3). Note also that **-lArI** is not always a personal suffix. It may simply be the plural **-lAr** plus the **-I** of the definite object.

4.5.7   Sometimes the third-person suffix is to be ignored in translation. To the examples in 1.2.5, 1.3.5, 1.7.3 we may add such expressions as **geceleri**, *evenings*, i.e.

every evening, and its use to make nouns or pronouns of adjectives, e.g. **doğrusu**, *in fact* (**doğru**, *true*); **hepsi**, *all* (*of it*); **bundan sonrası**, *the sequel* (**bundan sonra**, *after this*); also **harp sonrası**, *post-war*; and pronouns mentioned in 7.1.1.

4.5.8 The third-person suffix **-I**, which is added to the second (or last) noun, must not be confused with that derived from the Persian i found in words like **Koh-i-nur**, which works the other way round. In Turkish it is a survival, and most of the phrases which are still commonly used have been run into one word. It will be met with in the former names of ministries and in the titles of older books such as **İlm-i ahval-i kütüp**, *knowledge-of-the-state-of books*. The final vowel, which in some writers has the four-fold harmony (2.6.1) and in others varies only between i and ı, is often written without a hyphen. (See also 4.4.2 and 5.2.2.)

4.7 MISCELLANEOUS

Both the personal and the relational suffixes tend to be added to the last noun only of a series, e.g. **her forma, cüz veya cildin nushaları**, *copies of every fascicule, part or volume.*

5 ADJECTIVES

5.1 GENERAL

5.1.1 Adjectives are invariable and precede the noun and more often than not the indefinite article also (3.2.3). (See also 5.2.2.)

5.1.2 A great many adjectives may function as nouns or adverbs. A good many of the more elaborate adjectives are taken from Arabic and end in **-i**.

5.2 ENDINGS

5.2.1 Arabic adjectives have feminine forms in **-(y)e** which were taken over into older Turkish and survive as fossils or as nouns (cf. 4.1.1, 5.2.2).

5.2.2 Much less commonly nowadays, the adjective may follow the noun, which ends with the Persian-derived **-I** (4.5.8), e.g. **ulûmu diniye**, *theological sciences*. To what extent such constructions survive depends on the subject matter and the style of the writer, but forms such as **cenubu şarkî**, *south-eastern* (**cenup**, *south*) are universal.

5.3 COMPARISON

5.3.1 Comparison is frequently implied, but for precision **daha**, *more*, and **en**, *the most*, are used, e.g. **bu şeraitten daha elim**, *more tragic than these conditions*; **En iyi devlet, en az karışan devlettir**, *The best government is the government that interferes least.*

5.3.2 The absolute superlative (*most, very*) is expressed by **çok** or in some words by a modified repetition of the first syllable, e.g. **dolu**, *full*; **dopdolu**, *full up*.

6 NUMERALS

6.1 CARDINAL

6.1.1

1 **bir**	6 **altı**	11, etc. **on bir**, etc.	70 **yetmiş**
2 **iki**	7 **yedi**	20 **yirmi**	80 **seksen**
3 **üç**	8 **sekiz**	30 **otuz**	90 **doksan**
4 **dört**	9 **dokuz**	40 **kırk**	100 **yüz**
5 **beş**	10 **on**	50 **elli**	200 **iki yüz**
		60 **altmış**	1000 **bin**

(**Yüz** also means *face*, and **iki yüzlü**, *two-faced*.)

In compound numerals the elements are simply put together and are nowadays usually written separately, e.g. **on beş**, *fifteen*. But note that **beş on** means *five or ten* (or as we should say, *half a dozen*).

6.1.2   The cardinal numerals are usually adjectives and precede the noun, which is in the singular, e.g. **beş yıl**, *five years*. Well-known groups like **kırk haramiler**, *the Forty Thieves*, have a plural.

6.1.3   When not used before a noun numerals usually take a personal suffix, e.g. **her üçümüz**, *all three of us*; **iki canavardan biri**, *one of two brutes* (cf. 7.1.1). Sometimes where English has no noun, Turkish uses classifiers like **tane** (*a grain*). Cf. 1.8.6.

6.2   ORDINALS

6.2.1   Ordinals are formed by adding -(I)ncI to the cardinal, viz. **birinci, üçüncü, on altıncı, kırk dokuzuncu**, etc. *First* may also be **ilk**.

6.2.2   Some Arabic ordinals occur in fossil situations, e.g. in the names of sultans. As they are not all given in the smaller dictionaries they are listed here, viz.

> **evvel   sani   salis   rabi   hamis   sadis**
> *1st   2nd   3rd   4th   5th   6th*

They follow the name (5.2.2). They should not be used in expanding a modern title.

6.3   FIGURES

6.3.1   Plain arabic figures stand for cardinals, ordinals having a full stop or the ordinal ending, e.g. **1 inci, 2 nci**. As ordinals precede, one must be careful to distinguish **2 cilt** (**iki cilt**, *2 volumes*) from **2. cilt** (**ikinci cilt**, *vol. 2*). Roman figures, with or without a full stop, are used for ordinals in a few contexts and may either precede or follow names, e.g. **Papa XXIII. John, Mehmet II**. But note that the latter is now read **ikinci Mehmet** (6.2.2), though filed under **M**.

6.3.2   Numbered objects may appear as **No. 1**, in which case the number is read as a cardinal, or as **1. No.** with an ordinal. If, however, **sayılı** (*numbered*) is used as in **2527 sayılı Kanun**, *Law no. 2527*, the number is a cardinal. A similar reversal occurs with percentages, e.g. **%20 lik**, this being read as **yüzde yirmi(lik)**.

6.4   DATES

6.4.1   The current names of the months are:

> **ocak, şubat, mart, nisan, mayıs, haziran,**
> **temmuz, ağustos, eylül, ekim, kasım, aralık**

Earlier alternatives for some months are:

> October: **teşrinievvel, ilkteşrin, birinciteşrin**
> November: **teşrinisani, sonteşrin, ikinciteşrin**
> December: **kânunuevvel, ilkkânun, birincikânun**
> January: **kânunusani, sonkânun, ikincikânun**

They were also written as two words. All the forms mean the same, viz. *1st Teşrin, 2nd (last) Teşrin*, etc. The first form is the earliest (5.2.2), but there is some overlap. The official line may be deduced from *Türkiye Bibliyografyası* which used the **Teşrinievvel** type in 1939, while the last two issues of **1944** are dated **Ikinciteşrin** and **Aralık** respectively. The new names are specialised uses of ordinary words: indeed **bir aralık** is more likely to mean *for a time* than *one December*.

6.4.2 Dates are usually expressed in cardinals, with the appropriate suffix added to the last element, either to the number, leaving a space, or to the name, or to the words **yıl(ı)**, **sene(si)**, (*its*) *year*, **ayı**, *its month*, e.g.

> **1950 den**, **1950 yılından**, *since 1950*
> **1945 ile 1946 yıllarında**, *in* (*the years of*) *1945 and 1946*
> **28 nisanda**, *on 28 April*
> **1937 senesinin şubatı**, *February of 1937*
> **31 ocak 1953 te** (**otuz bir ocak bin dokuz yüz elli üçte**), *on 31 January 1953*
> **1920 nci yılda**, *in 1920*
> **bu ayın 23 ünde**, *on the 23rd of this month*

1853–1953 is read simply as two successive dates, though one naturally also finds expressions like **29 birinciteşrin 1923 ten 29 birinciteşrin 1933 e**, *from 29 November 1923 to 29 November 1933*.

7 PRONOUNS

7.1/7.2 DEMONSTRATIVE, RELATIVE, ETC.

7.1.1 Many of these are formed by adding the third-person suffix to the corresponding adjectives, e.g. **hangi?**, *which?*; **hangisi?**, *which one?*; **böyle**, *such*, **böyleleri**, *persons like this*; **biri** (*some*)*one*; or in the case of **hepsi**, *all of it*, *everyone*, to the adverb **hep**. **Hep** and some other words can take the suffixes of other persons, e.g. **çoğumuz**, *most of us*, from **çok**, *very*. Some words are indifferently adjective or pronoun.

7.1.2 The addition of relational suffixes (4.4) is straightforward, pronouns which incorporate the third-person suffix inserting the usual **-n-**, e.g. **öylesinden**, *from such a one*. The same insertion is found with **kendi**, *self*, after the adjectival suffix **-ki** (13) and even before **-lar** with **bu**, **o** and **şu**.

7.1.3 The pronoun **ne?**, *what?*, *which?*, has some difficult forms: the accusative may or may not take the definite **-I** (i.e. **neyi**) according to the context; the genitive may be either **neyin** or **nenin**; the dative **neye** has an alternative **niye**, which usually means *what for?* There are also forms with personal suffixes, **ne(yi)m**, etc. some uses of which, such as **neme lâzım?**, *what use is it to me?*, are idiomatic.

7.2 RELATIVE

See 7.1.

7.3 PERSONAL

7.3.1 The pronouns of the first and second persons take some of the suffixes with a difference and are therefore set out as a declension, viz.

	S		P	
	1	2	1	2
N	ben	sen	biz	siz
A	beni	seni	biz	sizi
G	benim	senin	bizim	sizin
D	bana	sana	bize	size
L	bende	sende	bizde	sizde
Ab	benden	senden	bizden	sizden

The third-person pronoun is the demonstrative **o**.

7.3.2 The suffix **-ki** added to the genitive makes a possessive pronoun, or something analogous. It can be added to any genitive and can itself take the plural suffix.

8 VERBS

8.1 STRUCTURE

8.1.1 The Turkish verb has a very large number of forms and is the head of a large family of related verbs. Person, tense, mood and even more complicated nuances are expressed by suffixes. But though complex, it is relatively easy to analyse, for all verbs, active and passive, have the same endings, and the same elements recur throughout the system. Verbs are entered in most dictionaries under the infinitive, ending in **-mAk**, but by Redhouse under the stem alone. The elements that are or may be found are:

(a) the stem

(b) one or more extensions of the stem, making the verb passive, causative, reciprocal, etc. (8.23)

(c) the negative, if any (8.22)

(d) the base (8.2.2), which may be nil

(e) the ending (8.1.2), frequently absent in the third person

for example: **bit-ecek-ler** (stem, future base, plural ending), *they will come to an end*; **bit-ir-il-mi-yecek-ler** (stem, causative extension, passive extension, negative, future base, plural ending), *they will not be completed*.

8.1.2 The endings are identical with the forms of the verb *to be*, viz.

$$Present:\text{ (y)Im, -(y)sIn, -(y)(DIr); -(y)Iz, -(y)sInIz, }\begin{cases} \text{-(y)DIrlAr} \\ \text{-lAr(dIr)} \end{cases}$$

$$Past:\begin{cases} \text{idim, idin, idi; idik, idiniz, idiler} \\ \text{-(y)DIm} \ldots \ldots \ldots \ldots \text{-lArdI} \end{cases}$$

Inferential (cf. 8.7): **imişim/-(y)mIşIm**, etc. as Present; 3PP **imişler, -(y)mIşlAr (dIr)** or **-lArmIş**

Hypothetical (cf. 8.8): **isem/-(y)sAm**, etc. as Past; 3PP **iseler/-(y)sAlAr**

The forms with hyphens, with their variable consonant and vowels (2.5.4, 2.6.1) are appended to the predicate, e.g. **Londralıyım (Londralıydım)**, *I am (was) a Londoner*, or are used to form the parts of other verbs, e.g. **satardık**, *we used to sell*. The **-DIr** of the third person is commonly omitted. A plural subject frequently has a singular verb.

8.2 COMBINATION OF BASES AND ENDINGS

8.2.1 The table in 8.2.2 shows for the very common verb **etmek**, *to do, make*, the various moods and tenses which result from combining the above endings with various bases, but does not show the imperative or the various verbal nouns, participles, etc., which are dealt with separately. In the second half of the table elements which appear elsewhere as endings are used as bases with other endings. This is important in the case of **-mİş**, which as an ending implies inference, but as a base does not.

In some cases the ending may appear as a separate word, and even the forms which are shown as one word are split up by the interrogative particle **mI**, e.g. **ediyorum**, *I am doing*; **ediyor muyum?**, *Am I doing?* (8.21). There are also some forms in which synonyms of the verb *to be* are used, e.g. **edilecek olursa** (8.3.4). The English equivalents are the merest indications and the notes should be consulted in all cases.

8.2.2

ENDING	Present -(y)Im	Past -(y)DIm	Inferential -(y)mIşIm/ imişim	Hypothetical -(y)SAm/ isem	Notes on stems
BASE None (et-/ed-)		ettim, *I (have) made*	etmişim, '*I have made*'	etsem, *If I made, were to make*	
-(I)yor- *actuality*	ediyorum, *I am making, I make*	ediyordum, *I was making*	ediyormuşum, '*I am (was) making*'	ediyorsam, *if I am making*	See 8.3
-r-/-Ar-/-Ir- *generality, habit*	ederim, *I make, intend to make*	ederdim, *I used to make, I should make*	edermişim, '*I (used to) make*'	edersem, *if I make*	See 8.3
-(y)AcAk- *future*	edeceğim, *I am going to make, shall make*	edecektim, *I should make, I should have made, I was about to make*	edecekmişim, '*I am (was) about to make*'	edeceksem, *if I am about to make*	See 8.4
-mAlI- *obligation*	etmeliyim, *I ought to make*	etmeliydim, etmeli idim, *I ought to have made*	etmeliymişim, '*I ought to have made*'	—	See 8.5
-Ay(A)- *subjunctive*	edeyim, *let me make, shall I make?, (that) I may make*	edeydim, *(that) I might make, if only I had made*	edeymişim, '*if only I had made*'		See 8.7
-dI- *past*	—	ettiydim, ettimdi, *I had made*	—	-DIysAm, -DImsA, idiysem	See 8.6
-mIş *past*	etmiştir, etmişlerdir, *he (they) made, have made*	etmiştim, *I had made*	etmiş imişim, '*I had made*'	-mIşsAm, imişsem	See 8.6
-sa- *hypothetical*		etseydim, *if (only) I had made*	etseymişim, etse imişim, '*If (only) I were to make*'		
Notes on endings		See 8.6.	See 8.6	See 8.8	

761

8.3 FORMATION AND USE OF -yor- AND -r- FORMS (8.2.2)

8.3.1   The -yor- base always has the form -Iyor- for if it follows -a- or -e- these are changed to -ı- and -i-: so **yazıyor** corresponds to **yazmak**, **anlıyor** to **anlamak**, and **taşıyor** to **taşımak**. Forms without an ending are usually third person, but if another form follows which has an ending, the ending goes with both (0.5.2).

8.3.2   There is a similar ambiguity about the -r- forms: after a vowel the base is -r-, after a consonant it is -Ir- if the stem has more than one syllable or is extended, and -Ar- otherwise. But thirteen common monosyllabic verbs, all except one ending in -l- or -r-, take -Ir-. So we have **taşir** from **taşımak**, **gerekir** from **gerekmek**, **denir** from **de-n-mek**, and exceptionally **sanır** from **san-mak**; **anlar** from **anlamak**, **taşar** from **taşmak**. Forms with no ending may be third person or due to economy, as with -yor, but they may also be participles (8.12.2).

8.3.3   The -yor- forms express not so much continuous action as what is actually happening. In the present they translate the English continuous present, both in reference to present time and to the immediate future, but there are very many cases, especially with verbs expressing states of mind, where the appropriate English equivalent is the simple present. The -r- forms, on the other hand, characteristically express general statements or, in the past especially, statements of habit. The present in -r-, like that in -yor-, can refer to the future, but expresses intention. In that case the appropriate translation is the future. With some verbs the contrast between -r- and -yor- forms is not so obvious, especially in the past, where the English simple past does for either. For examples see 8.3.4.

8.3.4   Examples of:

-yor- forms	-r- forms	-mAktAdIr (8.11.2)
hiç bir eşya celbedemiyor, *is not obtaining any goods*	**Parayı kim verirse düdüğü o çalar**, *He who pays the piper calls the tune*	**Times şöyle yazmaktadır**, *The Times writes as follows*
en son senelerde yazılıyor, *in the last (few) years people have been writing*	**yarın gelirim**, *I'll come tomorrow*	**zannedilmektedir**, *it is believed*
ben şimdi gidiyorum, *I am going now*	**Proudhon ... gerektiğini kabul eder**, *P. accepts the necessity of ...*	**aynı şekilde düşünmemekteydiler**, *they did not think alike*
şimdi anlaşılıyor, *it is now (becoming) understood*	**sorarlardı**, *they were in the habit of enquiring*	**bu fasiküller de hazırlanmakta olduğundan**, *now that these parts too are being prepared*
sanıyoruz, *we consider*	**gerekirdi**, *it was necessary*	**neşredilmiş bulunmaktadır**, *have been published*
Gambetta genel seçimi kabul ediyordu, *G. accepted the (idea of a) general election*	**yazmamış olmanızı dilerdim**, *I could wish you had not written it*	**tatbik edilmekte olan enstrüksiyon**, *the rule which is applied*
merdivenleri iniyordu, *she was going downstairs*	**mukayese edilecek olursa**, *if a comparison is made*	
piyasalar kapanmış oluyor, *the markets are closed*		
istiyorlarmış gibi, *as if they had been wanting*		

8.4 FUTURE BASE (8.2.2)

8.4.1 The addition of vowel endings causes the final **-k** to change to **-ğ-**, e.g. **edeceğiz**. The plain base may be third person, though most formal prose now seems to add **-tIr**; alternatively it may share an ending with a later form, or be a participle (8.12.3).

8.4.2 Apart from such obvious extensions as threats or commands, the Turkish future may express what is about to happen or alternatively, a probability, e.g. **ağabeyim evlenecekti**, *my brother was going to marry (her)*; but **zarfı düşürmüş olacaktı**, *she must have dropped the envelope*.

8.5 OBLIGATION

8.5.1 The **-mAlIydIm** forms (8.2.2) have a variety of possible meanings. The one given is the commonest, but when the whole sentence refers to the past, we have examples such as the following: **Federalistlere göre oy hakkı "kaymak tabakasına" hasredilmeliydi**, *According to the Federalists the right to vote ought to be confined to an élite* (not *ought to have been confined*).

8.6 FORMS IN -DI AND -mIş

8.6.1 There is little to note about the forms given in 8.2.2 except that in forms like **ettimdi** and **-DImsA**, the 'endings' are in the middle. The past hypotheticals have been given in generalised form since they can be added to the plain stem and to various bases to make the past equivalents of the forms in the last column, e.g. **ettiysem** or **ettimse**, *If I (have) made*; **ediyorduysam**, *if I was making*, and so on.

8.6.2 With the exception of the first two forms in the **-mIş** line all the **-mIş** forms express what is not known from direct experience (or even what is alleged, but known not to be true), e.g. *A.* **Ağabeyim evlenecekti; söz kesilmişti. Fakat, sonra vazgeçildi.** *B.* **Evlenecekmiş, vazgeçmişler**, A. *My brother was going to marry (her); it was settled. But afterwards it was called off.* B. *They were going to get married, you say, but called it off.*

8.6.3 The word **kesilmişti** in the last example has no inferential connotation; it is a straight pluperfect. Nor have the innumerable instances of **-mIştIr** and **-mIşlArdIr** that occur instead of **-DI** and **-lArdI** in the plain prose of news reports, official publications and technical writing. In sense **-mIş** here is a past participle (8.12.2).

8.7 SUBJUNCTIVE

8.7.1 For possible forms see 8.2.2. Some of the endings of the present subjunctive are peculiar, viz. the third person cannot take **-dIr** and the 1PP is **-yAlIm** not **-yAyIz**. (Considering the nature of the subjunctive this is not surprising.)

8.7.2 As the translations indicate, the subjunctive can be used in independent sentences, for wishes, requests and commands, and in dependent ones, e.g. **bakayım**, *let me look*; **dur bakayım**, *wait till I've had a look*.

8.8 HYPOTHETICAL FORMS

8.8.1 For the forms see 8.2.2. By themselves they include the element *if*; the conjunction **eğer** can be used but is not necessary (see example in 8.3.4).

8.8.2 A pair of forms, each followed by **DA**, expresses the idea *whether . . . or*, e.g. **o istese de istemese de**, *whether he wants to or not*.

8.8.3 With **kim** (*who*) and **ne** (*what*) the hypothetical form expresses the ideas *whoever, whatever*, e.g. **yaşımız ne olursa olsun**, *whatever our age may be* (cf. also 8.3.4, col. 2). Hence the idioms **ne ise** and **ne de olsa**, meaning *be that as it may, in any case*.

8.8.4 Some forms, such as **ise** (*if it is*), **yoksa** (*if not*) are used as conjunctions.

8.9 IMPERATIVE

8.9.1 The endings of the second and third persons (there is no first person) are:

-, -sIn; -(y)In(Iz), -sIn(lAr)

8.9.2 The meaning of the imperative is the usual one. In the third person it overlaps with the subjunctive, and is used as a substitute for the hypothetical, e.g. **bilenleriniz bilmeyenlerinize öğretsin,** *let those of you who know teach those of you who don't*; **yazılar yayımlansın yayımlanmasın geri verilmez,** *manuscripts whether published or not are not returned.*

8.11 VERBAL NOUNS

8.11.1 The infinitive in -mAk corresponds both to the English infinitive and to the gerund. It may be subject, predicate, object, qualifier or may have relational suffixes, e.g. **bu propagandayı yapmak bir hak olabilir,** *to put out this propaganda may be a right*; **demektir,** *is to say, means*; **sıyrılmak istiyordu,** *she wished to escape*; **muhafaza etmek hakkı,** *the right to retain*; **yapmağa mecbur,** *is obliged to make*; **adları bulmakta güçlük,** *difficulty in finding the names.*

8.11.2 One of the commonest occurrences of -mAktA is with the copula (8.1.2) or various forms of **olmak** (*to be, become*) to make yet another set of tenses. Despite their form (*I am, was,* etc. *a-doing*) these tenses are now to a great extent simply prosaic variants of other tenses, with no particular significance. As the examples in 8.3.4 show, the English equivalent more often than not is a simple tense. The -mAktA present does not refer to the future.

8.11.3 The form -mAksIzIn means *without,* e.g. **kapatmaksızın,** *without sealing it.*

8.11.4 The verbal noun in -mA shares many uses with the form in -mAk, e.g. **iyi bir eğitim görme hakkı,** *the right to receive a good education.* In concrete expressions like **yazışma adresi,** *mailing address,* however, only the -mA form is found. Many nouns in -mA have now special meanings, which should be sought in the dictionary.

Besides relational suffixes the -mA form takes personal suffixes, e.g. **defter bulunmaması,** *the absence of a form* (the first -ma- is negative); **Bolşevizmin yıkılmasından sonra,** *after the destruction of Bolshevism.* (In this expression the event is stated as an idea rather than as an actual happening: contrast -DIktAn sonra, 8.12.5.)

In **basma yazı,** *printed writing,* the -ı is not a personal suffix, for **basma** is used as an adjective. This is common.

For -mAdAn see 8.22.4.

8.11.5 The suffix -(y)Iş, denotes either the way or act of doing something. It is purely a noun, distinguished from the often synonymous forms in -I and -Im (13) by its universality, being found with all verbs including passive and negative, e.g. **yeni bir görüşle,** *with a new vision* (way of looking), **mütemadi bir gidiş geliş,** *a continual coming and going*; **istemeyiş,** *unwillingness* (**istememek,** *not to wish*). (Cf. 1.5.1.)

8.12 VERBAL ADJECTIVE/NOUNS (PARTICIPLES)

8.12.1 There are participles active and passive (8.23.2) corresponding to every tense. The present active and the past passive can often be translated directly into English, the others not, but all are equally natural in Turkish.

8.12.2 The following are most like English participles:

Present (*actual*): -(y)An, e.g. **basılmıyan yazılar,** *MSS which are not being printed*; **kontrol memuru olmıyan yerlerde** (0.5.2)

Present (general): -r/-Ar/-Ir, e.g. **okur yazar her şahıs,** *every person who reads or writes*; **görünür,** *visible*

Past: -mIş, e.g. **yamalı bir çarşaf giymiş ihtiyar bir kadın,** *an old woman who had put on a patched wrap*; **numerası bozulmuş binalar,** *houses with damaged numbers*

Like all adjectives they can be used as nouns, e.g. **olanlar,** *happenings,* and examples in 1.2.2, 1.8.3 and 8.9.2.

8.12.3 The remaining verbal adjectives are:

Past/Present: -DIk

Future: -(y)AcAk (Cf. 8.4.1.)

They differ from the preceding in that their meaning is rather 'characterised by past/ future doing', and this affects their usage. They may be passive in meaning even when derived from active verbs; and the simple adjectival use is not their characteristic one (8.12.4, 8.12.5).

The -DIk form has produced a number of adjectives and nouns such as **bildik,** *acquaintance* (**bilmek,** *to know*); **oku(n)madık,** *unread* (**okumak,** *to read*; **okunmak,** *to be read*).

The future participle also can be used as a simple adjective, e.g. **kalacak kısım,** *part to be retained* (**kalmak,** *to remain*); **gösterilecek usuller,** *methods which will be indicated*; **utanacak bir iş,** *a thing to be ashamed of* (**utanmak,** *to be ashamed*).

8.12.4 Both these participles, but especially -DIk, are commoner with personal endings. Here they are equivalent:

(a) to relative clauses in which the relative is not the subject or to phrases with a passive participle and a preposition, e.g. **bu kitabın incelediği konu,** *the subject which this book discusses* (*discussed in this book*);

(b) to subordinate clauses introduced by conjunctions, e.g. **bu vazifeyi yapacağımı beyan eylerim,** *I declare that I will carry out this duty*; **vesikalar gönderildiği zaman,** *when the documents are sent.* (See also 8.3.4. column 3.)

The subject of the relative or other subordinate clause is indicated by the personal suffix, e.g. **yapacağımı,** or by the preceding noun (**kitabın, vesikalar**).

8.12.5 The equivalent of a participial phrase or subordinate clause is also produced by -DIkçA and -DIktAn sonra, e.g. **bu vesaiki aldıkça,** *whenever he receives these documents*; **cetveli imza ettikten sonra,** *after signing the list.* (See also 8.11.4.)

8.12.6 Those participles which can also be finite tenses, viz. -r, -mIş, -(y)AcAk are often strengthened as participles by **olan** (*being*) or **bulunan** (*being found*), e.g. **bunları yapacak olan da devlettir,** *it is the state which will do these things.*

8.13 ADVERBIAL FORMS OF THE VERB

8.13.1 -(y)A is equivalent to our participle, e.g. **diye,** *saying* (from **demek,** 2.6.4); **güle güle,** *laughing(ly).* In the very common doubled form it suggests continuous or repeated action.

8.13.2 -(y)IncA: *as soon as, when,* e.g. **sayım bitince,** *when the census is over.*

8.13.3 -(y)IncAyA kadar: *until,* e.g. **sayımın bittiği ilân edilinceye kadar,** *until it is announced that the census is over.*

8.13.4 -(y)AlI, (y)AlI(dAn) beri: *since,* e.g. **bu kitabi (okudum) okuyalı,** *since I read this book.* The insertion of the past tense makes no difference to the meaning but may help to make the person clear.

8.13.5 -(y)ArAk expresses the earlier of a series of actions. It may correspond to our participle, e.g. **yeni basım, fotograf teksir usullerinden istifade edilerek ortaya konur,**

a new edition will be issued, taking advantage of photographic methods of reproduction; but more often we should use two coordinate verbs, e.g. **yenilenerek genişletilmiş**, *revised and enlarged*. (See also 0.5.2.) **Olarak** (*being*) is very common both with the meaning *as*, e.g. **bir disiplin olarak**, *as a discipline*, and to show that a preceding adjective is used as an adverb (9.1.2)

8.13.6 -(y)ken, or separately **iken**, is part of the copula meaning *while being*. Like other parts it can be appended to predicates or used with verb bases (8.2.2). By far the commonest base is that in -r-, even where -yor- might have been expected, e.g. **bir eserin ikinci basımı yapılırken**, *while the second edition of a work is being prepared*; **cevelân yapmakta iken**, *while cruising* (8.11.2).

8.13.7 -(y)Ip joins two verbs very closely together and takes its precise meaning from the following form. The verbs may be different, e.g.

(a) **bir günde başlayıp bir günde bitirilecektir**, *it will be begun and finished in one day*;

(b) **yazı yazıp 1939–1948 devresine girmeyen yazarlar**, *writers who do not write-and-enter-the-period 1939–1948* (i.e. who have not written on into 1939–1948). The negative -me- applies to both verbs;

(c) **evlenip te boşanmış ve tekrar evlenmemiş olan**, *being married, divorced and not re-married*. Here the negative is sealed off as it were by **te** (11.1.3) and applies only to its own verb;

(d) the verb may be the same, e.g. **yerlerine bulunup bulunmadıklarını tesbit etmişlerdir**, *they ascertained whether they were in their places or not*.

This type, in which the positive form in -(y)Ip is followed by the negative of the verbal noun in -mA or of the verbal adjectives in -DIk or -(y)AcAk, is one of the regular ways of expressing indirect questions, doubt or hesitation.

8.21 INTERROGATIVE

8.21.1 Besides interrogative pronouns, adjectives and adverbs, there is an interrogative particle **mI** which follows the emphatic word, e.g. **Bu baş yazıyı okudunuz mu?**, *Have you read this leader?*; **Harbiye mi bu işe bakacaktı?**, *Was it the War Office that would attend to this work?* It combines with the copula, resulting in forms like **bilir misiniz?**, *do you know?* (affirmative **bilirsiniz**).

8.21.2 The repetition of **mI** expresses *or* or *whether*, e.g. **binanın ev mi, otel mi, resmi bina mı? ilâ . . . ne olduğu yazılacaktır**, *it shall be stated what that building is, whether house, hotel or public building, etc.*

8.22 NEGATIVE

8.22.1 Verbs are negatived for the most part by the insertion of -mA- (usually -mI-before -y-) immediately after the stem and any extensions of it, e.g.

P	ettim	ediyorum	yazacağım	yazılacak
N	etmedim	etmiyorum	yazmıyacağım	yazılmıyacak

8.22.2 The -r- forms are negatived by turning -r-, -Ar- or -Ir into -mAz-, the present running thus:

-mAm, -mAzsIn, -mAz; -mAyIz, -mAzsInIz, -mAzlAr

The positive and negative participles coupled together express immediacy, e.g. **vapurdan çıkar çıkmaz**, *the moment I (etc.) got off the steamer*.

8.22.3 The use of -AmA- in place of -mA- denotes impossibility.

8.22.4 The ending -mAdAn may be -mA + dAn (8.11.4), but is more likely to mean *without* or *before*, e.g. **kızarmadan**, *unblushingly*; **basılmadan önce**, *before publication*.

8.22.5 The negative of the copula is **değilim**, etc., past **değil idim** or **değildim**. By itself **değil** may mean either *is not* or *not* negativing a single word. The negative of **var**, *existent*, which expresses *there is*, is **yok**.

8.23 EXTENSIONS OF THE STEM (PASSIVE, CAUSATIVE, ETC.)

8.23.1 Various syllables can be inserted after the stem (or after another such extension) to produce new verbs of related meaning. Most of these are given in the dictionary but they are made so freely that it is certain that at some point the dictionary will give up. They are added, in the order reflexive, reciprocal, causative, passive, but for convenience sake will be dealt with here in reverse order.

8.23.2 The passive infix is commonly -**Il**-, -**n**- and (after -l-) -**In**-, e.g. **yapılmak**, *to be made*; **denmek**, *to be said*; **alınmak**, *to be taken* (**yapmak**, **demek**, **almak**). Some verbs have slightly different forms, e.g. **anla|şıl|mak**, *to be understood*; **ko|nul|mak**, *to be placed*. Intransitive verbs can have impersonal passives.

8.23.3 The causative is -**DIr**- or (after vowels, -r- and -l-) -t, e.g. **dolmak**, *to be full*, **doldurmak**, *to fill*; **anlamak**, *to understand*, **anlatmak**, *to explain, tell*.

In *to cause X to do Y*, the word for *X* takes the dative suffix (4.4.2) and *Y*, if appropriate, that of the definite object.

Causative and passive infixes are often combined, as in **doldurulmak**, *to be filled*.

8.23.4 The reciprocal infix is -(**I**)**ş**-, e.g. **anlaşmak**, *to understand one another*. With the causative and passive infixes we get forms like **sıkıştırılmak**, *to be inserted*, via **sıkışmak**, *to press one another, to be crowded*. (Forms in -**leş**- are often not reciprocal.) Impersonal passives are found.

8.23.5 The reflexive is indicated by -(**I**)**n**, e.g. **hazırlanmak**, *to prepare (oneself)*. Apart from the fact that some forms can be passive, -n- forms often have special meanings not strictly reflexive, e.g. **görünmek**, *to appear* (**görmek**, *to see*; **görülmek**, *to be seen*). In combination with other infixes we get e.g. **bulundurulmak**, *to be procured* (**bulmak**, *to find*).

8.23.6 Formally very similar but differing in origin are the verbs which result from running two together. Thus -**bilmek** can be tacked on to the -**A** gerund (8.13.1) to convey the notion *to be able to*, e.g. **sayabiliriz**, *we can count*. The negative of this form is not used: *it cannot be published* is **neşredilemez** (8.22.3).

But the first part of the verb can be negatived, e.g. **neşredilmiyebilir**, which means *it may not be published*, expressing uncertainty.

9 ADVERBS

9.1 FORMATION

9.1.1 There is no single way of forming adverbs corresponding to the English -*ly*. The nearest equivalent is -**CA**, e.g. **sade**, *simple*, **sadece**, *simply*; **dostça**, *in a friendly way*. But the use of the suffix is much wider: sometimes it is equivalent to *by*, as in **zabıtaca takip olunan Topal Hasan**, *Lame Hasan who has been pursued by the police*, sometimes to *for*, e.g. **asırlarca**, *for centuries*; and words in -**CA** often come to be used adjectivally.

9.1.2 Another way of making adverbs is to append **olarak** (8.13.5) to the adjective. e.g. **teorik olarak savaşı desteklemek istemiyorlardı**, *theoretically they did not want to support the war*.

9.1.3 Even without these appendages an adjective, less frequently a noun, can be used adverbially, and if it is doubled the probability that it is so used is high, e.g. **bütün**, *complete*, **bütün bütün**, *completely*; **top**, *ball*, **topu topu**, *altogether*. Repeated nouns may however indicate multiplicity, as in **çeşit, çeşit**, *of all sorts*; **cilt cilt**, *volume by volume*.

9.1.4 Some adverbial expressions incorporate **ile** (10.2.1), e.g. **elektrikle**, *electrically*; **bu itibarla**, *therefore*. But both **elektrik** and **itibar** are nouns and **ile** has its normal meaning of *by* or *with*.

10 POSTPOSITIONS

10.1 POSITION
As their name implies they follow the noun.

10.2 SIMPLE POSTPOSITIONS AND THEIR SYNTAX
10.2.1 A few postpositions have one form only and the noun that they follow is unaffected. Pronouns are in the genitive except in the plural, e.g. **tunç gibi**, *like bronze*; **onun gibi**, *like him*; **onlar gibi**, *like them*. Of these **ile** may be attached to the noun in the form **-(y)lA**, e.g. **kısa bir cümle ile**, *in a short phrase*; **trenle**, *by train*; **suretiyle** (0.5.1). (See also 9.1.4.)

10.2.2 Some postpositions require to be helped out with a relational suffix, e.g. **-(y)A göre**, *according to*; **-(y)A doğru**, *towards*; **-DAn sonra**, *after*; **-DAn aleyhte**, *against*; **-DAn lehte**, *for*.

10.4 SECONDARY POSTPOSITIONS
10.4.1 A large number of postpositions are made up of nouns (some obsolete) or words treated as nouns, with a personal and a relational suffix, e.g. **kitapların ara|sın|da**, *between, among* (in the interval of) *the books*. The preceding noun has the genitive suffix **-In** if it is definite.

10.4.2 Dictionaries enter these postpositions under the basic noun, marked off here by a vertical line, in so far as they deal with them at all. Some of them can be translated literally on this basis, but their meanings are not always easy to deduce, so they are listed here. Those marked with an asterisk are peculiarly remote, and the preceding noun is not in the genitive. Those followed by etc. have three forms, after the pattern of **altına**, the first indicating motion towards, the second rest at, the third motion from.

aleyhinde: *against*
alt|ına, -ında, -ından: *below, under*
ara|sına, etc.: *between, among*
ard|ına, etc.: ⎫ *behind*
arka|sına, etc.: ⎭
baş|ına, etc.: *close by, at, on*
boy|unca: *along, throughout*
dış|ına, etc.: *outside*
etraf|ına, etc.: *around*
***hak|kında**: *concerning*
iç|ine, etc.: *in(side), within*
karşı|sına, etc.: *opposite*

lehinde: *for*
orta|sına, etc.: *in (etc.) the middle of*
ön|üne, etc.: *in front of*
saye|sinde: *thanks to*
***taraf|ından**: *by (agency)*
uğr|una, -unda: *for the sake of* (**uğur**)
üst|üne, etc.: ⎫
üzer|ine, etc.: ⎭ *on, over, above*
yan|ına, etc.: *beside*
yer|ine: *instead of*
***yüz|ünden**: *because of*
zarf|ında: *during*

10.5 USE

10.5.1 As their name implies, they have the same function as prepositions or prepositional phrases but differ in their position.

10.5.2 When used with verbal adjectives and nouns, postpositions are equivalent to conjunctions, e.g. **Marx'in söylediği gibi**, *as Marx said*; and see 8.3.4, col. 1; 8.12.4, 8.12.5.

11 CONJUNCTIONS

11.1 COORDINATING

11.1.1 Turkish has a large number of coordinating conjunctions to choose from, but often contrives to do without any of them, simply juxtaposing the words or phrases or using constructions with **-(y)Ip** (8.13.7) or **ile** (10.2.1). As **ile** is a postposition one is tempted to translate **A ile B** as *B and A*; but one should not.

11.1.2 Paired conjunctions are not dealt with very well by the small dictionaries. The commonest are:

> **gerek ... (ve) gerek(se)**, *both ... and*
> **hem ... (ve) hem (de)**, *both ... and (also)*
> **ne ... ne**, *neither ... nor*
> **ya ... (ve)ya**, *either ... or*

11.1.3 **DA** may sometimes be translated *and*, e.g. **Onlar da derler**, *And they said*; but it is not a straightforward conjunction. While connecting or contrasting it at the same time emphasises the word it follows. Besides *and* it may be translated *also, even, indeed, then, on the other hand, but*, as in **sözüme inanmıyor da eşeğin sözüne inanıyor**, *he does not believe my word but he believes the word of an ass*; or it may not be translated at all, as in **Müessese adları hariç, "kütüphane" kelimesi yerine niçin "bibliyotek" kelimesini kullandığımı da ilk sayfalarda izah ettim**, *Why, apart from institutional names, I have used the word 'bibliyotek' instead of the word 'kütüphane', I have explained in the opening pages*. The equivalent of **da** here is the order of the English sentence. See also 8.12.7(c).

11.2 SUBORDINATING

11.2.1 Subordinate clauses are rare in Turkish (see 0.5.2 and 8.11–8.13), so subordinating conjunctions are few. The principal are **eğer** and **şayet**, meaning *if*, which may stand at the beginning of a conditional clause, but are not needed, and **ki**.

11.2.2 **Ki** has no invariable translation. The usual equivalent is *that*, sometimes a parenthetical *who* or *which* or even *and*; or the phrases may have to be turned round, e.g. **Şimdi anlaşılıyor ki miknatıslı mayn imiş**, *It is now known that it was a magnetic mine*; **Bir muallim vardı ki aşırı derecede açıl fikirli idi**, *There was a teacher who was exceedingly free-thinking*; **Copyright kelimesi kullanılıyor ki bu terim, milletler arası mahiyet almıştır**, *The word 'copyright' is used—a term which is internationally accepted*. Not infrequently the sequel is left unstated, and the sentence ends with **ki**, e.g. **Mevlâna diyor ki**, *The master says* (book title).

13 WORD-FORMATION

Owing to the regularity of the structure of Turkish, there are a number of suffixes which recur in the formation of words. The most universal, which are liable to produce words not in the dictionary, are given here, in order of the last letter.

-CA tones down adjectives, e.g. **güzelce**, *quite nice* (but cf. 9.1.1).

-lA- makes verbs from nouns and adjectives, mostly with the meaning *to make X*.

-I makes nouns from verbs, denoting the action or its result, e.g. **yazı**, *writing, composition*.

-CI makes nouns from other nouns (occasionally from adjectives) and corresponds to *-er, -ist, -or*, etc., e.g. **kitapçı**, *bookseller*; **milliyetçi**, *nationalist*; **neci?**, *of what occupation?*; **kılcı**, *long-haired*.

-IcI, a combination of the preceding two, makes nouns and adjectives from verbs, e.g. **yazıcı**, *clerk*.

-ki makes adjectives from adverbs and adverbial phrases, especially from nouns with relational suffixes, e.g. **bibliyografya ile katalog arasındaki fark**, *the difference between a bibliography and a catalogue*; **önümüzdeki**, *next* (of dates; literally, *which is in front of us*); **içindekiler**, *contents*. See also 7.3.2 and for more examples 0.5.2.

-lI forms adjectives, indicating locality or possession (*of, with, -ed*) from nouns or phrases, e.g. **Ankaralı**, *of Ankara*; **üçten fazla müellifli eser**, *a work with more than three authors*. In the form **-lII** (cf. **-IcI**) it is derived from verbs, e.g. **bağlı listede isimleri yazılı memurlar**, *the officials whose names are written on the attached list*.

-sI makes adjectives from nouns or other adjectives and corresponds to *-ish*, e.g. **çocuksu**, *childish*. (Unlike the personal suffix it is attached only to words ending in a consonant.)

-Ik makes adjectives from verbs, corresponding roughly to *-ed* in its adjectival use, e.g. **birleşik**, *united*.

-lIk makes (1) abstract or collective nouns, e.g. **birlik**, *union, unit*; (2) adjectives (which may be used as nouns) indicating what a thing is for, e.g. **gözlük**, *glasses* (**göz**, *eye*), or its periodicity, e.g. **yıllık**, *annual*.

-sAl makes adjectives from nouns, e.g. **bilimsel**, *scientific*.

-Im makes nouns, denoting (a single) action, from verbs, e.g. **yayım**, *publication* (action or result).

-mAn denotes an agent, e.g. **öğretmen**, *teacher*.

-In makes concrete nouns from verbs, e.g. **yayın**, *a publication*.

-lAş- may be simply **-lA-** + **-ş-** (8.23.4) but may form independent verbs from adjectives and nouns, with the meaning *to become X*, e.g. **katılaşmak**, *to become hard*.

-sIz forms adjectives and adverbs indicating the absence of something, from nouns and pronouns, e.g. **tarihsiz**, *undated*. In the sense *without*, e.g. **onsuz**, *without him*, it might almost be considered a relational suffix.

GLOSSARY

abone, *subscription*
alınmıştır, *is taken*
araştırma, *investigation, research*
arka, *sequel*
arkası var, *to be continued*
aylık, *monthly*
aynı, *same*
ayrı basım, *offprint* (1.5.1)

âza, *member(s)*

b(a)k(ınız), *see*
basılan, *being printed*
basılış, *edition, impression* (1.5.1)
basılmakta olan, *being printed*
basım, *edition, impression* (1.5.1)
basımevi, *press* (1.6.1)

baskı, *edition, impression* (1.5.1)
baskısı tükenmiş, *out of print*
başlangıç, *introduction*
bibliyotek, *library*
bibliyotekçi, *librarian*
broşür, *pamphlet*

cemiyet, *society*
cetvel, *table*
cilt, *volume* (1.4.1, 1.8.5)
ciltli, *hardback*
ciltsiz, *paperback*
cüz, *part*

çevirmek, *to translate*
çıkarılmak, *to be published*
çıkarmak, *to extract*
çıkmak, *to come out*

dergi, *periodical*
derlemek, *to collect, compile*
dernek, *society, meeting*
devam, *continuation*
devamı var, *to be continued*
dış, *outside, foreign* (1.8.6)
doğmuş, *born*
düzelten, *editor, arranger*
düzeltilmiş, *corrected* (1.5.1), *arranged*

ek, *addition, appendix, supplement*
eser, *work*
eski sayı, *back number* (1.8.6)

fasikül, *part* (1.4.1)
fatura, *bill*
fiat, *price*
fihrist, *index*
forma, *fascicule*

gelecek, *forthcoming*
genişletilmiş, *enlarged* (1.5.1)
giriş, *introduction*
göndermek, *to send, dispatch*
gözden geçirilmiş, *revised* (1.5.1)

haftalık, *weekly*
hazır, *ready*
hazırlıyan, *arranging* (*editor*), *preparing*
  (1.2.2)

her hakkı mahfuzdur, *all rights reserved*
heyet, *committee*
hikâye, *short story*

ısmarlamak, *to order*

ilâve, *addition, supplement* (1.5.1)
intihap etmek, *to select* (1.2.2)
izah, *explanation*

kısım, *part* (1.4.1)
kitabevi, *publishing house* (1.6.1)
kitap, *book*
kitapçı, *bookseller*
konferans, *conference, lecture, speech*
konuşma, *speech*
kütüphane, *library*

levha, *plate*
lûgat, *dictionary*

makale, *article*
matbaa, *press* (1.6.1)
mecmua, *review*, *journal*
mektup, *letter*
mevcudu bitmiş (or kalmamış), *out of
  stock*
muhayyer olarak, *on approval*
mukaddime, *introduction, preface*
müdür, *director* (*editor*)
müellif, *author*
müstensih, *duplicator*
mütercim, *translator*

nakil, *narrator*
nakletmek, *to translate*
naşir, *publisher* (1.6.2)
neşir heyeti, *editorial committee* (1.8.3)
neşredilmemiş, *unpublished*
neşredilmiş, *published*
neşriyat, *publications* (1.7.1)
numune, *sample, specimen*
nüsha, *copy, issue*

onbeş günlük, *fortnightly*

ölmüş, *dead, died*
önsöz, *preface*
örnek, *sample, specimen*
özet, *summary*

parasız, *free*
piyes, *play*
plânş, *plate*

roman, *novel*

satılık, *on sale*
sayfa, *page*
sayı, *number* (1.7.3, 1.8.4)
seçmek, *to select*
senelik, *annual*
seri, *series*
sipariş, *order*
süreli yayım, *periodical*

şerh, *note*
şerhetmek, *to explain*
şiir, *poetry*

tabı, *edition, impression* (1.5.1)
tamamlamak, *to complete*
tarih, *history*
tashih, *correction*

tekrar basım, *reprint* (1.5.1)
telif hakkı, *copyright*
tenzilât, *discount, reduction*
tercüme, *translation*
tertip, *series*
tertip etmek, *to compile, arrange*
tiyatro, *plays*
toplamak, *to collect*

üye, *member*

yabancı, *foreign*
yayılmamış, *unpublished*
yayım, *publication* (1.7.1)
yayımlıyan, *editing (editor), publishing*
yayın, *publication* (1.7.1)
yayınevi, *publishing house* (1.6.1)
yazan, *writer* (1.2.2)
yazı, *manuscript, writing*
yazı kurulu, *editorial committee*
yeni, *new*
yenilenmek, *to be made new*
yıllık, *annual, yearbook* (1.8.2, 1.8.5,
   1.8.6)

GRAMMATICAL INDEX: WORDS

bana, ben-, 7.3.1
beri, 8.13.4
beş on, 6.1.1
bir, 3.2
birincikânun, birinciteşrin,
   6.4.1
biz-, 7.3.1

da, de, 8.8.2, 11.1.3
değil, 8.22.5

evvel, 6.2.2

gerek . . . gerek, 11.1.2

hamis, 6.2.2
hem, 11.1.2

idi, etc., 8.1.2
iken, 8.13.6
ikincikânun, ikinciteşrin,
   6.4.1

ile, 9.1.4, 10.2.1
ilk, 6.2.1
ilkkânun, ilkteşrin, 6.4.1
imiş, etc., 8.1.2
ise, etc., 8.1.2, 8.8.4

kadar, 8.13.3
kânunuevvel, kânunusani,
   6.4.1
ki, 11.2.2

mı, mi, mu, mü, 8.21

ne, 7.1.3, 8.8.3
ne . . . ne, 11.1.2
nem, nenin, neyi, etc.,
   niye, 7.1.3

olarak, 9.1.2

rabi, 6.2.2

sadis, salis, 6.2.2
sana, 7.3.1
sani, 6.2.2
sen-, 7.3.1
siz-, 7.3.1
sonkânun, 6.4.1
sonra, 8.12.5
sonteşrin, 6.4.1

ta, 8.8.2, 11.1.3
tane, 6.1.3
te, 8.8.2, 11.1.3
teşrinievvel, teşrinisani,
   6.4.1

var, 8.22.5

ya . . . ya, 11.1.2
yok, 8.22.5
yoksa, 8.8.4
yüz, 6.1.1

GRAMMATICAL INDEX: MIDDLES

Capital letters indicate alternative possibilities, e.g. **A** stands for **a** or **e**. Consult 2.5.4, 2.6.1 before using the index.

As ending may be piled on ending, elements which occur in the middle of a word may be indexed as endings. For possible phonetic changes see 2.5.1.

GRAMMATICAL INDEX: ENDINGS

See notes to Grammatical index: Middles.

BASQUE

SPECIMENS

Guipuzcoan

Kondarairen filosofia bat egiteari ekiten dio orri auetan García Venturini irakasleak.
Espainian lan-sail onetan ekin dioten apurretako bat da bera. Gaurko gizonak bere
buruari ezartzen dizkion galdekizunei erantzun billa dator egillea; ortarako antziñako
zibilizazio zarretatik asi eta Idazteuna eta Kristau-garaiko filosofiko sistema klasikoetatik
zear abiatzen da.

*In these pages Professor Garcia Venturini undertakes to form a philosophy of history. He
is one of the few who have undertaken this task in Spain. The author seeks to answer the
questions which men of today take into their heads; he starts from the old civilisations
previous to that and moves through Scripture and the classic philosophical systems based
on Christianity.*

References to sections

4: 8.8.9, 4.3.1
5, 6, 14, 15: 8.1.2, 8.1.3, 8.2.2
7, 8: 7.1.1, 7.1.2, 4.3.1
10: 4.6.1
15, 25: 8.5.2

16, 20, 31, 32, 39, 40: 4.6.2
31: 7.1.1
34: 4.3.1
44: 8.1.2, 8.3.1

Labourdin

Etor etxeak abiatu du sail berri bat «Kimu saila» eskoletako gazteeri euskal herriko
berri jakin arazi nahiz. Lehen liburu hunek XVI eta XVII-garren mendeetako euskal
literatura aipatzen ditu. Idazle eta irakurgai gehienak Ipar aldekoak dira: Etxepare . . .
Tartas eta beste. Hego aldetik: Garibay, Beriain, Otxoa.

*The house of Etor has set in motion a new enterprise 'Kimu saila' with the aim of providing
new information about the Basque country to school children. This first book tells them
(about) Basque literature of the 16th and 17th centuries. The principal authors and books*

of the North are: Etxepare . . . Tartas and others. From the South: Garibay, Beriain,

Otxoa.

References

> 3, 4, 27, 28: 8.1.2, 8.2.1
> 17: 0.5, 4.3.1
> 23: 6.2

Mixed

Liburu honek egundainoko arrakasta izan du nonbait. Lehen liburukitik 7.000 aletako edizioa egin zen, eta urtebeteren buruan ahitu. Bigarren ediziotik, berriz, 8.000 ale atera ziren salmentara, eta agortzer daude dagoeneko. Bigarren liburukiaren argitaraldiekin berdintsu ari da gertatzen, eta orobat liburu horren lagungarri den *Lecturas-1* delako-arekin.

This book has had a continuous success it seems. Of the first volume an edition of 7,000 copies was produced, and by the end of the year (it was) out-of-print. Of the second edition, again, 8,000 copies were put on sale, and by now are almost-sold-out. There has been an almost-equal success with-the-publication of the second volume and likewise with-the-(work)-entitled Lecturas-1, which-is a companion to that book.

References

> 2: 7.1.1
> 5, 6, 13, 14: 8.1.2, 8.3.5
> 11: 4.6.2
> 29: 8.11.1
>
> 41: 7.1.1
> 43: 8.5.2
> 45: 8.6.2

0 GENERAL CHARACTERISTICS

0.1 DEGREE OF INFLEXION

Basque is a highly synthetic language, dispensing very largely with prepositions and conjunctions and incorporating the subject and object pronouns in the verb, e.g. *because we have said it to you*, **esan baitizuegu**. But nearly all verbs are conjugated throughout by means of auxiliaries such as **baitizuegu** above.

0.2 ORDER OF WORDS

Though adjectives follow the noun, most other qualifiers precede, even if they are whole clauses. Such prepositions as there are follow their nouns, becoming post-positions, and many conjunctions are found at the end of the clause. The neutral sentence order S C O_i O_d V. V. can be varied for emphasis, the most emphatic position being immediately before the auxiliary; but the substantive verb is in practice rarely deposed, and the emphasised word precedes the verb complex. In negative sentences the neutral order is S Neg V. V. and the emphatic position is after the auxiliary.

2c

0.4 RELATION TO OTHER LANGUAGES

Basque is completely isolated among the languages of Europe, and attempts to link it with languages elsewhere (in the Caucasus for instance) have not commanded general assent. It naturally includes quite a number of words borrowed from French, Catalan or Spanish, as the specimens show, and some directly from Latin such as **gorputz**, *body*; **errege**, *king*.

0.5 STRUCTURE

The assignment of words to grammatical categories is sometimes fluid: **esan du** means *he (has) said* but **esan nahi du** means *he wishes to say*; and **esan** can also be a noun meaning *a saying*. **Nahi**, *wish*, can be an adjective, *wished for*. **Atxiki** may be a verb (*to hold*) or an adjective (*constant*). Other words are both adjective and adverb.

0.6 DIALECTS

There are five or six main dialects: Labourdin, Low Navarrese, High Navarrese, Souletin, Guipuzcoan, Biscayan. They differ principally in vocabulary and idiom, though there are some regular differences of pronunciation or spelling and a number of differences of morphology. But they all have much in common, especially Labourdin and Guipuzcoan, and 'interpenetrate each other inextricably'. Of recent years they have grown together, and unified Basque has become more generally accepted. Only Labourdin and Guipuzcoan, the principal sources of unified Basque, are dealt with here. The acceptability of forms in unified Basque has been checked against Larresoro's *Euskara Batua zertan den* (Jakin, 1974).

1   BIBLIOLINGUISTICS

1.1 NAMES

1.1.1   As Basques live partly in France and partly in Spain (or Spanish America), personal names tend to be subject to varied influences and may have alternative forms. Peculiarly Basque names are less likely to give trouble than those that are common to Basque and French or Spanish. The following are some of the less obvious Basque/Spanish equivalents:

Deunoro, *Santos*	**Gurutz**, *Cruz*	**Eskarne**, *Mercedes*
Gaizka, *Salvador*	**Kepa**, *Pedro*	**Iasone**, *Asunción*
Gorka, *Jorge*	**Koldo**, *Luis*	**Nekane**, *Dolores*
Gotzon, *Angel*	**Patxi**, *Francisco*	**Sorkunde**, *Concepción*

Synonyms for **Mari** (cf. Spanish 1.1.4) are numerous and as the four examples show, involve sheer translation. But even if the Basque forms are obvious, such as **Piarres**, **Joanes**, **Joseba**, one is quite likely in a purely Basque book to meet **Pedro** or **Pierre**, **Juan** or **Jean**, **Jose** or **Joseph**, or spelling may vary between Spanish and Basque norms, e.g. **Victoriano/Biktoriano**. Short of positive evidence it is unwise to alter the form found. In this unfamiliar language beware of the non-name **Aita** (*Father*), shortened to A., e.g. **Aita Onaindia** (i.e. **Santiago Onaindia Baseta**).

1.1.2   Surnames also appear in a variety of ways. Nowadays the name usually follows the French or Spanish pattern with the surname at the end, e.g. **Jean Etchepare**, **Domingo Agirre**, in which case the Spanish y may be represented by eta, as in **Lopez eta Mendizabal**, but the use of two surnames is not at all common. More typically Basque is the position before the Christian name, the surname taking the adjectival **-ko** (4.6.2) or the suffix **-tar/-tiar** (earlier **-tar**) which denotes a person belonging to some group, e.g. **Azkue-ko Resurrección Maria**, *R. M. Azkue*; **J. L. Arrizabalaga'tar K. M.**, *K. M. Arrizabalaga, S. J.* More rarely one finds expressions like **Lopez eta Mendizabalen seme Isaac**, *Isaac son of Lopez and Mendizabal*. Most names end in a vowel, or in l, n, s, or z.

1.1.3 The suffix **-ko** does not necessarily indicate a family name. In **Loiolako Iñigo, Paduako Antonio Santua, Bartolome Santa Teresaco** it is simply translated *of*. Nor does **-tar/-dar**, e.g. **Karmeldarra**, *the Carmelite*.

1.2 NAMES OF AUTHORS, EDITORS, ETC.

1.2.1 It is common nowadays for names to appear at the head of the title-page or after the title, without any grammatical connexion with it. If so they will usually be in the basic form.

1.2.2 It is possible, even in such cases, or in bibliographies, for the name to have the termination **-k** (4.3.1), e.g. **Zaitegi eta Plazaola'tar Iokin'ek Ph.D.**, and this is all the more likely if there is a transitive verb in the statement of authorship, e.g. **Agustin Cardaverazec emana**, *given by A. Cardaveraz*. Not that the **-k** need be attached to the name: e.g. **Domingo Agirre Abadeak egindako irakurgeia**, *novel composed by the Rev. D. A.* In earlier books the author's name may precede the title, forming one long grammatically linked phrase, e.g. **Jesus-en Compañiaco A. Sebastian Mendiburuc Euscaraz eracusten duen Jesus-en Bihotza-ren devocioa**, *Devotion to the Sacred Heart of Jesus which Fr. S. Mendiburu of the Society of Jesus is producing in Basque.*

1.2.3 Well-known works, collections of correspondence and the like may have the author's name in the genitive (suffix **-ren**) before the title, e.g. **Mitxelenaren lan hauta-tuak**, *Selected works of Mitxelena*; **Pio Baroja'ren Itxasoa laño dago**. The genitive is also found before nouns denoting activity, **Aita Villasanteren zuzendaritzaren pean**, *under the editorship of Fr. Villasante.*

1.2.4 Translations are indicated in a variety of ways, e.g. **Erdaraz escribitua, eta orai Escuaraz publicatzen duena** (8.5), *written in Spanish and now being published in Basque*; **Yon Etxaidetarrak euskerara emana**, *given into Basque by Yon Etxaide*; **Larresorok euskaratua**, *Basqued by Larresoro*; **Xabier Kintanak itzulirik**, *translated by X. Kintana* (Xavier Quintana).

1.2.5 Beware of announcements that give the author's name as **Elkar Lanean**: the words mean *in collaboration.*

1.3 TITLES

1.3.1 As most relations between nouns are expressed by suffixes, titles consist very largely of nouns, including verbal nouns, and adjectives, e.g. **Euskeraz irakuŕteko irakaspidea**, *Textbook of reading in Basque*; **Orhiotzapen eta gogoeta**, *Memories and reflections*. (Both nouns are grammatically singular.) In novels and popular works more varied titles are met with, e.g. **Nora naramazue?**, *Where are you taking me?* (8.9.2); **Haurtxoa zigoinak Paristik ekarria ote?**, *Is the baby really brought from Paris by the stork?*

1.3.2 The abridging of titles need not be pedantic, e.g. **Euskara Batua zertan den** (*Where Unified Basque stands*) is cited as **Euskara Batua**. The chief difficulty with older titles, as the example in 1.2.2 shows, is to find where they begin.

1.3.3 Titles in a grammatical context can take suffixes, but they are marked off by some sort of punctuation and cause no difficulty, e.g. **Uscaldunaren laguna'ren edizione berria**, *the new edition of 'Uscaldunaren laguna'*. Sometimes suffixation is avoided by using a prop like **liburu**, e.g. **«Omenaldi» liburuan**, *in the book 'Omenaldi'*.

1.4 VOLUMES AND PARTS

1.4.1 The standard word for *volume* is **liburuki**, but the vague **liburu**, *book*, occurs fairly often, sometimes glossed by **tomo**, e.g. **lenengo liburua edo tomoa**, *the first book or volume*. Sometimes one finds **zati**, e.g. **bigarren zati(j)a**, *the second portion*. **Part(h)e** is also found for *part*.

1.4.2 The numeration may be grammatically connected with the title, e.g. **Egercicioen IIen partea**, *2nd part of the Exercises*.

1.4.3 In announcements of many-volumed works we may meet phrases like **hiru tomotatik lehenbizikoa**, *the first of three volumes*; **hiru tomoetan**, *in three volumes*.

1.5 EDITIONS

1.5.1/1.5.2 Besides the straightforward **edizione berria**, *new edition*; **bigarren argitaralpena**, *second edition*, we find such expressions as **bigarren aldian**, *for the second time*; **2-garren agerraldia**, *2nd appearance*. In earlier books more discursive statements are found, e.g. **cembait gauza aumentaturic**, *somewhat enlarged*; **orain bostgarrenez imprimidu da**, *has now been printed for the fifth time*.

1.5.3 **Separata**, borrowed from the Spanish, translates *offprint*.

1.6 IMPRINTS

1.6.1 The name of the printer or publisher may be unchanged, standing alone or being followed by **bait(h)an** (Fr **chez**); or with the suffix **-(r)en** followed by **etxean**, *at the house*, or by a word denoting a printing shop. Less commonly one may find the suffix **-k** of the agent or the adjectival genitive **-ko** (4.6.2). Of recent years firm names such as **Euskal Izendegia** or **Etor liburu-etxea** (Etor '*book-house*') have become much more common. Such names are often symbolic.

1.6.2 In older books, before the establishment of the present publishing system, one usually finds an explicit reference either to printing or to bookselling, e.g. **Fauvet-Duhart Erregueren Liburu eguille eta Saltçaille baithan**, *By F-D Printer and Bookseller to the King*; **imprimaçaillearenean**, *at the printer's*; **saltzen da Bayonan, C. Cluzeau baithan**, *sold at Bayonne by C. Cluzeau*; **F. Pech & Cie baithan imprimatua**, *printed by F. Pech & Co.*; **Lalama-ren alargunaren moldezteguian**, *At the press of Lalama's widow*.

1.6.3 The place of publication frequently ends in **-n**, meaning *at*, e.g. **Tolosan, Bayonan, Bordelen, Bilbo(a)n**. These names are easy enough to recognise as imprints, though **Tolosa** can mean *Toulouse*. Other place-names are trickier: **Bergara** and **Errotxapea** for *Vergara* and *Rochapea* exhibit regular correspondences, but **Iru(i)ñea** is not *Irun* (unchanged in Basque) but *Pamplona*. Other names which are markedly different (a selection only) are:

Akize, *Dax*	**Gasteiz**, *Vitoria*
Arrasate, *Mondragón*	**Lizarra**, *Estella*
Biaizteri, *Laguardia*	**Miarritze**, *Biarritz*
Donemiliaga Kukulako, *San Millan de la Cogolla*	**Muskeria**, *Tudela*
	Orreaga, *Roncesvalles*
Doneztebe, *St Etienne*	**Saldua**, *Zaragoza*
Donibane (Lohitzune), *St Jean de Luz*	**Tutera**, *Tudela*
Donibane Garazi, *St Jean Pied de Port*	**Zaldua**, *Zaragoza*
Donostia, *San Sebastian*	**Zuraide**, *Souraide*

Occasionally in older books the place is linked grammatically with the rest of the imprint by the use of **-ko** (4.6.2), e.g. **Tolosako liburuguille Eusebio Lopez-en echean,** *at the house of E. Lopez, bookseller of Tolosa.*

1.7 SERIES

1.7.1 Basque books are found from time to time in Spanish series. Basque series usually include the word **sorta**, e.g. **Kuliska Sorta** (*Curlew Series*), **Jakin Sorta**, less often **bilduma** (*collection*). The series may be named only on the cover.

1.7.2 The numeration may be in the form **29 garren zenbaki** (*no. 29*); **6. alea** (*6th issue*).

1.8 PERIODICALS

1.8.1 The titles of Basque periodicals are for the most part laconic and evocative, e.g. **Anaitasuna** (*Brotherhood*), **Gure herria** (*Our country*), **Jaunaren deia** (*The message of the Lord*), **Zeruko argia** (*Heavenly light*). The structure of Basque makes it easy to add relational suffixes, e.g. **Zeruko argia'n** (or **ZERUKO ARGIAn**), *in 'Zeruko argia'*, but they are usually typographically distinct.

1.8.2 The body responsible may appear with the possessive suffix in the sub-title, e.g. **Euzko-Alderdi-Jetzalia'ren deia,** *Bulletin of the Basque Nationalist Party*, or there may be a separate statement of the form **Nafarroa-Kantauri eta Aragoiko Kaputxinoak argitaratua,** *Published by the Capuchins of Navarre-Cantabria and Aragon.*

1.8.3 Details of editorship, like all other formal details, are often given in French or Spanish. Where they are in Basque, the usual word for *editor* is **zuzendari, zuzendari ordezko** being his deputy. In addition we may meet **idazkola eta banakolaren buru**; **-ren buru** means *head of* and the other words are dealt with in 1.8.7.

1.8.4 Numeration is effectively by **zenbaki** (*number*). The year (**urtea**) is usually given as well, but the other numeration is nearly always independent, e.g. **XXXIII-garren urtea 500 zenbakia**; **berrogoi-ta-laugarren urtea—2**. (For **garren** see 6.2.)

1.8.5 Periodicity may be expressed by an adjective in **-eroko** (4.6.2), which can be used as a noun, e.g. **(h)illeroko argitalpena,** *monthly publication*; **(h)amabosteroko(a),** *fortnightly*. Alternatively there may be such a statement as **urtean lau zenbaki ateratzen dira,** *four numbers come out in the year.*

1.8.6 Subscription is expressed by **(h)arpide(tza), (h)arpide saria** (*subscription price*) or **abonamendu**. The period is specified by an adjective in **-ko**, e.g. **urteko** (*annual*), and distinctions may be made between internal rates (**barruan**), rates for countries in the Postal Union (**korreo batasunako errietan**) and other foreign countries (**atzerrietako beste errietan**). The date for renewal may be specified, viz. **urtero martxoan berritzen da arpidetza** (*subscription is renewed annually in March*). A single copy may be referred to as such (**ale bakoitza**) or may be implied by the word **salmetan** (*on sale*) or **prezioa** (*price*).

1.8.7 Address may specify **idazkola** and **banakola**. **Banakola** is *administration*; **idazkola** is sometimes glossed as **redacción**, but could apply to any secretarial activity. Also mentioned may be **imprimatzaile** (*printer*) and **moldatzaile** or **irarle** (*typesetter*) and offices in **general (bulegoak)**. The usual word for *address* is **zuzenbide**.

2 ALPHABET, PHONETICS, SPELLING

2.1 ALPHABET

2.1.1 The standard alphabet is:

a b d e f g h i j k l m n ñ o p r s t u x z

but departures from it are found and French and Spanish Basque often have slight differences. Words beginning with ll may follow those beginning with l; similarly tt. Until recently Guipuzcoan and Labourdin had different alphabets, Guipuzcoan omitting h, Labourdin inserting ch and y and omitting x, to which ch is equivalent. Older books may use c and q, and these are still required, along with v, w, and y, for borrowed words and Spanish names.

2.1.2 It is to be noted that Lhande's dictionary of the French dialects gives the short-lived Academy alphabet **a b d d̄ e f g h i j k l l̃ m n ñ o p r ŕ s t tx ĩ u ü x y z**, but in practice he puts **tx** between **tu** and **tz**, not as a separate character, equates **i** and **j**, and does not use **y**. The letters with a tilde are palatalised: **l̃** and **ĩ** are written **ll** and **tt** in the current alphabet, **d̄** either **dd** or **j**; **ñ** is sometimes used even in Labourdin, but the words in which it occurs often have alternatives with **-in-** or plain **-n-**. The 'strong r' (**ŕ**) is now written **-rr-** between vowels, but as both **r** and **ŕ** are pronounced the same before consonants and the weak **r** is rare at the end of a word, no doubling occurs in these positions. Bera and López Mendizábal in the third edition of their dictionary adopted the modern spelling but preserved the historical distinction, producing sequences like **ara ... arba ... arpegi ... arsa ... arza ... ar ... arra ... arba ... arre**, etc. (Order is restored in the 4th edition.) In the 1960 facsimile reprint of Azkue's dictionary **š** is used for **x**, and **h**, though printed, is ignored for the purpose of order.

2.1.3 An accent is sometimes used to distinguish homonyms, e.g. **amá** (**ama** + **a**), *the mother*; **zen**, *he was*, but **zèn** (**zen** + **n**), *which was*.

2.2 CAPITALISATION
Basque uses the same principles as French or Spanish.

2.3 DIVISION OF WORDS
Rules 4 and 5a (p. xiii) apply, but **ch ll rr ts tt tx tz** should be taken over whole. Division between vowels tends to be avoided, e.g. **tipia-gorik**, even though **-ago** is a suffix. Obvious compounds are divided according to sense.

2.4 PUNCTUATION AND ABBREVIATIONS
2.4.1 A hyphen may be found at the end of the first of two compounds that have the same final component.

2.4.2 A hyphen or apostrophe separates the ending if it is desired to show the form of the main word (cf. 1.2.2). An apostrophe is sometimes found after **ba-** meaning *if*, e.g. **eskatzen ba'duzu**, *if you order it*. The hyphen is standard practice.

2.4.3 A full stop is used at the end of an abbreviation, e.g. **etab.**, *etc.*, and sometimes between the year and the suffix **-eko**, e.g. **1973.eko**, *of 1973*. (See also 6.3.) Abbreviations consisting of capital letters without stops are also found, which take suffixes, e.g. **PNBren**, *of the GNP*.

2.5/2.6 PHONETIC CHANGES
2.5.1 Very little change take place in vowels in the course of inflexion. A vowel may be dropped as in **andere**, *lady*; **andrea**, *the lady*. On the other hand in borrowed words like **giristino**, *Christian*, we find a vowel inserted. In the conjugation of verbs **-a-** sometimes changes to **-e-**, e.g. **da** + **a** > **dea**; **da** + **n** > **den**.

2.5.2 P, t, k are changed to b, d, g after l, m or n. Hence borrowed words like **dembora**, *time, weather*; and variation between **-ko** and **-go** (4.3.1). Conversely **bai(t)-** (8.7.3) and **ez** (8.12) have the opposite effect.

2.5.3 Simplification of consonant clusters takes place, e.g. **ikusten** corresponds to **ikusi**, but **erakusten** is for **erakutsten** and corresponds to **erakutsi**.

2.7 SPELLING AND DIALECT VARIATION

2.7.1 Until comparatively recently spelling conventions were nearer to those of French and Spanish. The present-day **k** was represented by **c** before **a**, **o** and **u** and by **qu** before **e** and **i**, and likewise **g** before **e** and **i** was written **gu**, e.g. **eguiteco** for **egiteko**. **Z** occurs at the end of a word and before consonants, but before vowels it is written **c** or **ç** as the case may be. There is also some variation between **z** and **s**, e.g. **Euskaras** for **Euskaraz**. The Spanish-Basque practice of inserting **b** between **u** and a following vowel led to spellings like **liburuba** for **liburua**, and a phonetic **y** (or even **ll**) follows **i** in the same circumstances, e.g. **egoquiyac** for **egokiak**.

2.7.2 Apart from this, variation in spelling, which persists today, may well represent differences between dialects. That between **n** and **m** before **b** or **p** is mere spelling, but one still finds variation between **s** and **z** or **s** and **rz**, between **z** and **tz**, between **b**, **f** and **p**, between **a** and **au**; and one finds **h** omitted in Guipuzcoan, before vowels, between vowels, and after consonants, e.g. **(h)ama**, **za(ha)r**, **urt(h)e**. Sometimes Guipuzcoan has **g** for **h** and often **y** for **ih**. Unified Basque (0.6) retains **h** except after consonants.

3 ARTICLES

3.1 DEFINITE

3.1.1 The definite article takes the form of a suffix **-a**, e.g. **etxe**, *house*; **etxea**, *the house*. If the noun already ends in **-a**, most writers make no change (2.1.3). The article is added to singular nouns only. Further suffixes are added after the article (4.3). But see also 3.1.3.

3.1.2 The definite article is frequently used where English omits it, e.g. **fedea**, *faith*. What is more unexpected, the definite form is used for predicates, e.g. **aien herra neurri gabea izan da**, *their resentment has been unbounded*, where **gabe** is a postposition (10) meaning *without*.

3.1.3 Adjectives, and nouns with suffixes, may take the article and function as fresh nouns, e.g. **on**, *good*; **ona**, *the good*; **Zein politika? Alemanena**, *Which policy? The Germans'*.

3.2 INDEFINITE

Bat (*one*) also functions as an indefinite article: e.g. **poxiño bat**, *a little bit;* **andi bat**, *a great deal*. But Basque often omits it, e.g. **Euskaldun naiz**, *I am a Basque*.

4 NOUNS

4.1 FORM, GENDER AND ENDINGS

4.1.1 The dictionary form of most nouns (and adjectives) ends in a vowel. Other possible endings are **r**, **n**, **l**, **s**, **tx**, **z**. The basic form, with or without the article, is used as the subject of intransitive verbs and the object of transitive ones.

4.1.2 There is no grammatical gender.

4.1.3 The relations of nouns are expressed by suffixes, which have different but closely related forms in the singular and plural.

4.3 SUFFIXES

4.3.1 The usual forms of the principal suffixes, indeterminate, definite singular and plural, are:

I	DS	P	Meaning
-	-a	-ak	(basic)
-tara	-ra	-etara	to (motion)
-(r)i	-ari	-ai, -ei, -er(i)	to
-k	-ak	(-ek)	(agent)
-(r)ik			(some) of
-tatik/-tarik	-tik	-etatik/-etarik	from, by
-tan	-an	-etan	in, on, at
-(r)en	-aren	-en	of
-(r)ekin	-arekin	-ekin	with
-tako	-go/-ko	-etako	of, from
-taraino	-raino (-raño)	-etaraino	as far as
-tarat	-rat	-etarat	as far as
-tzat			as
-kotzat			for
-(r)entzat	-arentzat	-entzat	for
-z	-az	-ez	by, with

The typically Guipuzcoan -o- for -e- in the plural is found also in unified Basque, e.g. **Euskaldunok**, *we Basques*; **liburuok**, *the books*; **hiru hilabeteotan**, *in the(se) three months*. It suggests what is close at hand.

4.3.2 An -e- is inserted before some endings when the noun ends in -l, -n, -r, -s, -au, -x or -z. This causes some ambiguity, e.g. etxe, *house*; etxeren, *of a house*; etxearen, *of the house*; but **egunen**, *of a day, of the days*; **egunaren**, *of the day*; **egunean**, *on the day* (**egun**). Nouns that end in -r mostly add the suffixes that begin with **r** direct. Names like **Parise** make **Parisi, Paristik**.

4.3.3 A set of suffixes beginning with -gan- is used in connexion with living creatures instead of those listed above, viz. **-gana**, *to*; **-gandik**, *from*; **-gan**, *in, at*; **-ganaino**, *as far as*. In the singular they are added either to the stem or to the -(r)en suffix; in the plural to the -en suffix.

The suffix -gatik, *for*, may also be added to -(r)en, e.g. **lanarengatik**, *for the work*.

4.3.4 The indeterminate forms are used when the noun is indefinite or simply quantified: *a day, how many days, two days*.

4.6 USE OF SUFFIXES

4.6.1 The meanings are only a rough and ready guide. The -k of the agent is used not only where English has *by* (cf. 1.2.4) but also for what we should interpret as the subject of transitive verbs: **Mutikoak erraten du**, *The boy says*; but **Mutikoa goan zen**, *The boy went off*. In the plural G makes no distinction, but L and U use -ek for the agent. The plural -ak is also liable to confusion with the singular agent, and some suggest that the agent should be written -ák (cf. 2.1.3).

4.6.2 The suffixes -(r)en, -ko/-go and -(r)ik may all be translated *of*: -ren indicates possession and analogous relationships, e.g. **Rusiaren historia**, *the history of Russia*; **erlisionearen galtzea**, *damage to religion*; -ko is vaguer and can be added after other suffixes and to adverbs, making the word adjectival, e.g. **Espainiako Gobernua**, *the Spanish Government*; **22 × 28 zentimetrozko**, *measuring 22 × 28 cm*; **18 urtez gerokoak**, *those over 18.* Sometimes the result is a new noun like **eskualdungoa,** *the Basque spirit.* The suffix **-rik** is partitive, e.g. **herririk giristinoena,** *the most Christian of countries;* but adjectives in apposition to the subject or object often take this suffix, e.g. **alegerarik heldu zen,** *he had arrived joyful.*

All three suffixes are attached to parts of verbs: see 8.5, 8.6, 8.8.

5 ADJECTIVES

5.1 FORMS

5.1.1 There is no formal difference between adjectives and nouns, and since there is no gender, there can be no question of agreement. Either the noun or the adjective may carry the suffixes, e.g. **etxeak,** *houses;* **etxe zaharrak,** *old houses.* Only in such expressions as **begiak ertsiak ditu,** *has his eyes closed,* do both have the suffix.

5.1.2 When used as a predicate an adjective takes the article, e.g. **gauza errecha da,** *the thing is easy.*

5.3 COMPARISON

5.3.1 The comparative ends in **-ago,** *than* being expressed by **baino (baño),** e.g. **katoliko baino eskualdunago,** *more Basque than Catholic,* or by the suffix **-z.**

5.3.2 The superlative ends in **-en** and is construed with **-(r)ik, -etarik, -(e)tan** and **-ko** (4.3).

5.3.3 There is also a suffix **-egi** which means *too.*

6 NUMERALS

6.1 CARDINAL

6.1.1

1 bat	11 (h)ameka	21 hogei (e)ta bat
2 bi(ga)	12 (h)amabi	39 hogei ta hemeretzi
3 (h)iru(r)	13 (h)ama(h)iru(r)	40 berrogei, bi hogei
4 lau(r)	and so on	60 hiruetan hogei
5 bost, bortz		80 lauetan hogei
6 sei		100 e(h)un
7 zazpi		200 berrehun
8 zortzi	18 (h)amazortzi, hemezortzi	300, etc. hiruehun, etc.
9 bederatzi	19 (h)emeretzi	1000 mila
10 (h)amar	20 (h)ogei, hogoi	

The forms without **h-** are Guipuzcoan; **hogoi,** etc. are Labourdin.

Biga is used when standing alone. For 60 and 80 **hirurhogoi,** etc. are also found. In G **lauetan** may be found spelt **labetan.** Forms with hyphens may be used for the teens, e.g. **hama-bi,** and for higher numbers, e.g. **hogei-ta-hemeretzi.**

6.1.2 Numerals are followed (or in the case of **bat** preceded) by the indeterminate or plural of the noun as appropriate. e.g. **hiru mailatan,** *in three stages;* **hiru tomoetan,** *in the three volumes.* They can take the article and/or suffixes.

6.2 ORDINALS

6.2.1 Apart from **lehen (leheneko, lenengo),** *first,* the ordinals add **-garren,** e.g. **iruetan ogeigarren atalean,** *in the 60th verse;* **zazpigarrenean,** *on the 7th.* G and U have **boskarren** for *fifth.*

6.3 FIGURES

6.3.1 Plain figures indicate cardinals, figures with stops ordinals, e.g. **14 urthetan** (**urtez**), *14 years old*; **2. horrialde**, *2nd page*; **5ean** (**bostean**), *in the five*; **5.ean** (**boskarrenean**), *in the fifth*. But **Henri IV** is read **Henri laugarrena** with an ordinal just as much as **6-garren Paul Aita Santua**, *the Holy Father Paul VI*.

The standard representation of percentages is **%10**, read **ehuneko hamar**, but the more familiar **10%** is also found.

6.4 DATES

6.4.1 The names of the months are as follows:

	Standard	Variants
1	**urtarrila**	**ilbeltza, urthatsila**
2	**otsaila**	
3	**martxoa**	**epail(l)a**
4	**apirila**	**jorrail(l)a**
5	**maiatza**	**or(r)illa, ostaroa, ostoila**
6	**ekaina**	**garagarilla, er(r)earoa, udaila**
7	**uztaila**	**uzta, uztarilla**
8	**abuztua**	**dagonilla, agorril(l)a**
9	**iraila**	**agorra, buruila**
10	**urria**	**urrieta, uril(l)a**
11	**(h)azaroa**	**hazila**
12	**abendua**	**lotazilla, neguila, beltzil(l)a, otzaroa**

The final **-a** is the article, which is not always present. The standardisation is that of the Basque Academy, dating from October 1971. A glance at the variants shows how necessary it was. Standardisation is not complete, for even writers of unified Basque will be found using **agorrila** and **hazila**. The forms in **-lla** are G, the forms with **h** are L and U.

6.4.2 In G all parts of a date may be expressed in ordinals or cardinals, e.g. **1839** (**garren**) (**Mila zortzi-eun ogeitaemeretzigarren**) **urteko urriaren ogeitabostea**, *on the 25th of October of the year 1839*; **1937ko urtarrilaren lenengotik** (**lenengo egunean**), *from the 1st (on the 1st day) of January 1937*; **1972.eko abenduaren 15ekoa**, (issue) *of the 15th of December*.

In L cardinals are often preferred. *The first*, however, is **lehena**.

In periodicals the months may appear with a final **-k**, or if the issue covers several months, as **Ilbeltz–Jorrailak**, for example.

7 PRONOUNS

7.1 DEMONSTRATIVE, ETC.

7.1.1 The demonstrative and other pronouns take suffixes in the same way as nouns, but the relation between the basic form and the stem is often peculiar, viz.

	(h)au(r), *this*	**(h)ori**, *that*	**(h)ura**, *that yonder*	
Stem	**hun-/(h)on-**	**(h)or(r)-**	**(h)ar-**	
	hunta-/(h)on(e)ta-	**(h)or(re)ta-**	**(h)arta-**	
e.g.	**hunen, (h)onen**	**(h)orren**	**(h)aren**	(*of*)
	huntan, (h)onetan	**(h)ortan, horretan**	**(h)artan**	(*in*)

When subjects of transitive verbs they take the usual -**k**, e.g. **honek**, etc. The plural stems are:

hau(i)-/ho-	(h)o(r)-i-	hei-/(h)ai-
(G au-/abi-)		
hau(i)(e)ta-/hota-	(h)o(r)ieta-	heieta-/(h)aieta-

Labourdin and Unified Basque have transitive plural forms in -**ek** as opposed to **hauk, hoik, haik/hek** for the simple plural.

7.1.2 Demonstratives used adjectivally follow the noun, e.g. **herri hau**, *this country*. They alone take the necessary suffixes.

7.1.3 Demonstrative pronouns do duty as personal pronouns of the third person.

7.1.4 **Guzti**, *all*, has forms in -**o**- as well as -**e**- (cf. 4.3.1), e.g. **hauk guztiok**, *all these* (**hau guztiau**, *all this*). Similarly, **bion familiei**, *to the families of both of these*.

7.2 INTERROGATIVE AND RELATIVE

7.2.1 Interrogatives, which precede the noun, call for no comment as regards their form. **Zein**, *which?*, serves as a relative, but relative clauses are usually expressed by modifying the verb (8.5). Indirect interrogative clauses have the relative form of the verb (cf. 8.9.1).

7.3 PERSONAL

7.3.1 The personal pronouns are:

	S		P	
1	2	1	2	
ni	zu	gu	zuek, zui(e)k	

They take the usual suffixes and have more than one stem, e.g. **nik, nitaz**. The genitive suffix, which produces the possessives, is -**re**, e.g. **nere/nire**, except for **zuek**, which makes **zuen**. An alternative to **nere** is **ene**.

7.3.2 The demonstratives (7.1.1) serve for the third person, but there is a special word for *his, her* when it refers to the subject (or in certain circumstances to the object) of the sentence: **bere**, e.g. **amak erraten dio bere semeari**, *the mother says to her son*.

Their is usually **beren**, but some L writers still use **bere** for both singular and plural.

7.3.3 As subject and object pronouns are incorporated in the verb, separate personal pronouns are relatively uncommon.

8 VERBS

8.1 STRUCTURE

8.1.1 The Basque verb in its full deployment is complicated, for the transitive verbs incorporate the agent at the end in some tenses and at the beginning in others. (It is disputed whether such verbs are active or passive in Basque (4.6.1): I shall treat them as active, so that the agent is the subject.) Intransitive verbs always incorporate the subject at the beginning. At the other end of the transitive verb is the direct object, with the indirect object, if any, following it. These objects are always expressed as part of the verb, even if there is a noun object in the sentence. However, the familiar forms of the second person can be ignored, while many of the remaining combinations of objects are very rare. In addition, there are only two simple tenses in the indicative, and the vast majority of verbs have no forms of their own but are conjugated by means of verbal nouns with past, present and future reference and one of two auxiliaries. Thus in practice a limited number of forms occur frequently, made up of recurrent formative elements. I shall concentrate on this periphrastic pattern. In the tables below forms are to be built up by combining the appropriate subject and object with the stem.

8.1.2 The auxiliaries are **uk(h)an** or **euki**, *to have*, for transitive verbs and **izan**, *to be*, for intransitive ones. Three tenses are formed with the same auxiliary, viz. **egin du**, *he has done it*; **egiten du**, *he has it a-doing* (*is doing it*); **eginen** (L), **egingo** (G) **du**, *he has it to do* (*will do it*). Intransitive: **et(h)orri da**, *he is* (*has*) *come*; **et(h)ortzen da**, *he is coming*; **et(h)orriren** (**etorriko**) **da**, *he is to come* (*will come*). (See 8.8.3, 8.8.4, 8.8.8.) It is best to forget the literal meaning of the auxiliaries and to regard them as indicators of the subject and object and as distinguishing between transitive and intransitive. (Some verbs can be both.)

8.1.3 Some parts of **ukan** and **izan** are very similar, especially those forms, ignored here, which incorporate a reference to persons interested (ethic dative). One such convergence must be noted: **dugu** can mean either *we have* or *it is for us*.

8.2 TRANSITIVE AUXILIARY: uk(h)an, *to have*

8.2.1 *Present with direct object*

		O	Stem		S
	1	n(a)			t
S	2	zait			(t)zu
	3	d			-
			u/e		
	1	gait			gu
P	2	zait		zte	(t)zu(t)e
	3	dit			(z)te

The -zte in the third column distinguishes the true plural from the polite singular zait-, -it- being normally a pluraliser.

The options are to some extent a matter of dialect: L has **dut, duzu, -(t)zue**; G **det, dezu, -zute**. Both have **dute** but **dituzte** (3 P). The L forms **-tzu** and **-tzue** are used with a plural object.

> Examples: **ikusten dut (det),** *I see it*
> **ikusten nau,** *he sees me*
> **ikusten zaituztegu,** *we see you* (P)

When not used as an auxiliary it may have longer forms, e.g. **daukat, dauzkat** instead of **dut, ditut**; for which cf. 8.9.2.

8.2.2 *Present with 3rd-person direct object and indirect objects*

Labourdin

Direct object and stem:

> **dau-** (**+z** for plural object)

Indirect objects:

>after **dau-**: -t(a), -tzu, *; -ku, -tzue, *
>after **dauz-**: -kit, -kitzu, *; -k(ig)u, -kitzue, *

Subjects as in 8.2.1.

* With 3rd-person indirect object the stem is **-i-**, giving:

DO	IO	
S	S	**dio**
S	P	**diote**
P	S	**diozka, diozki, diotza, diotzi**
P	P	**diozkate, diozkite, diotzate**

followed by the subject.

Guipuzcoan

		DO	Stem	OP	IO	S
	1				t/da	t
S	2				zu	zu
	3	d			o	-
			i/au			
	1				gu	gu
P	2				zute	zute
	3	d		zki	(ot)e	te

Examples: **eman diot,** *I gave it to him*
daut (dit), *he gave it to me*
dautazu (didazu), *you gave it to me*
dauzkitzuegu (dizkizutegu), *we gave them to you*
diozkate (dizkiete), *they gave them to them*

The indirect object is combined with 3rd-person objects only.
(For another **dio** see 8.10.4.)

8.2.3 *Past with 3rd-person direct object*

Guipuzcoan

		S	OP	Stem	SP
	1	n			
S	2	zen			
	3	z			
				u	en
	1	gen			
P	2	zen			(z)t
	3	z	it		(z)t

Examples: **ikusten nuen,** *I saw it/him/her*
nituen, *I saw them*
zenuzten, *you* (P) *saw it*

Labourdin differs only in having **zin-** and **gin-** instead of **zen-**, **gen-**. When not used as an auxiliary the past may be **neuken,** etc. (cf. 8.9.3).

8.2.4 *Past with 3rd-person direct object and indirect objects*

Guipuzcoan

		S	Stem	OP	IO	SP
	1	n			da	
S	2	zen			zu	
	3	z			o	
			i			n
	1	gen			gu	
P	2	zen			zu(t)e	te
	3	z		zki	(ot)e	te

Examples: **eman nion,** *I had given it to him*
           eman genizkizuten, *we had given them to you*

L differs in having subjects **zin-, gin-**; stem **-au-**; IO **-ta, -ku** after **-au-**; **-tzu** and **-tzue** in all contexts. When the indirect object is in the 3rd person, the stem and pluralisers are the same as in 8.2.2. Hence **eman ginauzkitzuen,** *we had given them to you*; **eman giniozkan,** *we had given them to him.*

8.2.5 *Past with direct object in 1st and 2nd persons*

			G					L
		DO	Stem	OP	S			
	1	nind			da			**gint-, zint-** for **gind-, zind-**
S	2	zind			zu			
	3							**-(t)zu, -(t)zue** for **-zu, -zute**
			u			(e)n		
	1	gind			gu			
P	2	zind		zte	zute			
	3				(t)e			

Examples: **ikusiko zinduztedan (zint-),** *I shall have seen you* (P)
           ikusi ninduten, *they had seen me*
           ikusten ginduzun (gintutzun), *you saw us*

Note that the subject is once more at the end.

8.3 COPULA AND INTRANSITIVE AUXILIARY: **izan,** *to be*

8.3.1 The subject pronoun is invariably at the beginning. The present runs thus:

G **naiz, zera, da; gera, zerate, dira**
L **naiz, zare, da; gare, zarete, dire/dira**

e.g. **hasten dire,** *they begin.*

When followed by a suffix **dira** is changed to **dire-.** There is also an interrogative form **dea,** *is it?*

8.3.2 *Present with indirect object*

		S	Stem	SP	IO	SP
	1	na	tzai		t	
S	2	za	tzai		zu	
	3	-	zai		o	
	1	ga	tzai	zki	gu	
P	2	za	tzai	zki	zu(t)e	te
	3	-	zai	zki	(ot)e	

Examples: **joanen (goanen) natzaio,** *I am going to him*
et(h)orri zait, *he came to me*
hurbildu zaizkigu, *they approached us*

8.3.3 *Past*

G   **nitzan, ziñan, zan; giñan, ziñaten, ziran**
L & U   **nintzen, zinen, zen; ginen, zineten, ziren**

Examples: **mutikoa goan zen (mutilla joan zan),** *the boy set off*
pobreak ziren, *they were poor*

8.3.4 *Past with indirect object*

		S	Stem	SP	IO	SP
	1	nin			da	
S	2	zin			zu	
	3	zi			o	
			tzai			n
	1	gin		zki	gu	
P	2	zin		zki	zu(t)e	te
	3	zi(za)		zki	(ot)e	

Example: **hurbildu zintzaikidaten,** *you* (P) *had approached me*

8.3.5 **Izan** itself is ambiguous: **izan da,** *he has been*; **izan du,** *he has had.* So is **izanen** (8.8.4).

8.4 OTHER MOODS

8.4.1 The syllable -**ke**- has various related senses, viz. future, conditional, possibility, probability, depending on the stem used. The forms translated *would* below may also express conjecture, e.g. **ez zukeen espero,** *he could hardly have expected it.* The various tenses, which have much the same basic patterns as those of the indicative (8.2, 8.3), are set out in 8.4.2 and 8.4.3 under the form beginning with the 1st-person prefix, whatever the function of that prefix, all the other indications of person being 3rd-person, e.g. **ikus nazake,** *he can see me*; **eman nioke,** *I would give it to him.* The remaining forms are then specified by reference to the permutation patterns of the indicative.

8.4.2 The forms of the transitive auxiliary in Unified Basque, with their meanings are:

(a) **nazake,** etc.: *can.* Stem -**(e)za**; O and S as 8.2.1.

(b) **nauke,** etc.: *it is possible that.* O and S as 8.2.1.

(c) **dieza(zk)ioke,** etc.: *can,* with 3rd-person object and IO. IO and S as 8.2.2; -**ke**- follows IO.

(d) **nezake, nitzake,** etc.: *could*, with 3rd-person object. Singular object **-eza-**, plural object **-itza-**; S as 8.2.3, except 3 **l-** not **z-**.

(e) **nuke,** etc.: *would*, with 3rd-person object. S as 8.2.3, except 3 **l-** not **z-**.

(f) **nieza(zk)ioke,** etc.: *could*, with 3rd-person object and IO. S and IO as 8.2.4, except 3 **l-** not **z-**.

(g) **nioke,** etc.: *would*, with 3rd-person object and IO. S and IO as 8.2.4, except 3 **l-** not **z-**.

(h) **nintzake,** etc.: *could*, with 1st and 2nd-person objects. S and O as 8.2.5, except **-t** for **-da-**.

(i) **ninduke,** etc.: *could*, with 1st and 2nd-person objects. O and S as 8.2.5, except **-t** for **-da-**.

The past tenses may add **-en,** e.g. **nezakeen,** etc., *could have*.

8.4.3   The forms of the intransitive auxiliary in Unified Basque, with their meanings, are:

(a) **naizateke,** etc.: *it is possible that*. The forms of 8.3.1 + **(a)teke**; 2PP **zaratekete**.

(b) **naiteke,** etc.: *can*. S as 8.3.2, except 3 **da-**; SP **-z-** and **-te**.

(c) **nakioke,** etc.: *can*, with IO. S as preceding, SP and IO as 8.3.2.

(d) **nintzateke,** etc.: *would*. Follows pattern of 8.3.3; 3S **litzateke**; 3P **lirateke**.

(e) **ninteke,** etc.: *could*. S as 8.3.4, except 3 **li-** not **zi**.

(f) **nintzaioke,** etc.: *would*, with IO. The forms of 8.3.4 + **ke**.

(g) **nenkioke,** etc.: *could*, with IO. S **nen-, zen-, le-**; **gen-, zen-, le-**.

As with the transitive auxiliary, the past tenses may be made more remote by adding **-en.**

8.4.4   The subjunctive is characterised by **-n** (cf. 8.5) or in some circumstances by **-la.** Its typical use is in clauses dependent on verbs of wishing, commanding, fearing and the like (8.6.1). The forms of the transitive auxiliary correspond to **-ke** forms (8.4.2a, c, d, f, h), viz. **nazan, dieza(zk)ion, nezan, nieza(zk)ion, nintzan,** etc., a final **-n** (or **-la**) replacing the final or medial **-ke.** The only differences of detail are that in the past tenses both **l-** and **z-** are found, in different contexts, and the 1st-person object is always **-da-.**

8.4.5   For the most part the subjunctives of the intransitive auxiliary follow the pattern of 8.4.3b, c, e and g respectively, with 3rd person **z-** not **l-**, except that in the singular **nadin** (3 **dadin**) corresponds to **naiteke**; **nendin** (3 **zedin**) to **ninteke.**

8.4.6   The imperatives are:

Transitive: **(e)zazu, (e)zazu(t)e**
Intransitive: **zaitez, zaitezte**

8.5   THE DEPENDENT -n

8.5.1   Verbs become equivalent to clauses by the addition of certain suffixes or prefixes. One of the commonest of these is **-n,** which is an integral part of the subjunctive (8.4.4). Attached to the indicative it occurs in indirect questions, e.g. **ez dakit ethorriko den,** *I do not know if he is coming*, with verbs of believing and after (or before) certain conjunctions, e.g. **zeren gurea den,** *because it is ours*. (Further example in 11.2.)

8.5.2   The commonst use of **-n,** however, is to make the verb relative. Thus if **eman diete** means *they gave it to them*, **eman dieten gizonak** means either *the men who gave it to them* or *the men to whom they gave it*; **eman dieten liburu,** *the book which they gave to them*. Only the context shows how the relative is to be taken. Nor should the forms be slavishly translated by a relative: **joan den maiatza** is simply *last May* (and cf. 1.2.4: **duena**).

8.5.3   Some forms undergo further modification: **du** gives G **duan,** L **duen**; **dut/det**

gives **dudan/dedan**; **da** gives L **den**. Forms which already end in **-n** are unchanged and therefore to avoid ambiguity some put an accent on the relative form (2.1.3).

8.5.4   The **-n** forms do not always qualify a noun and may have suffixes of their own, e.g. **ikusten eztuenak**, *one who does not see* (**eztu** for **ez du**, *has not*); **iskribatu duanaren**, *of what he has written*. Certain suffixes give the relative form the value of an adverbial clause, **-nean** being equivalent to *when, at the moment that*; **-netik** to *from the time that*; **-neko** to *after, by the time that*; **-nez** to *as*.

8.6   OTHER DEPENDENT FORMS

8.6.1   The addition of **-la** makes a noun clause, e.g. **dire**, *they are*; **direla erraitean**, *saying that they are*. The natural translation is not always *that*, e.g. **eskatu aantzi dezatela**, *to ask them to forget* (8.4.4). It can also make a gerund.

8.6.2   Further suffixes can be added to **-la**, making principally **-larik**, *when, because, although*, and **-lako**. The latter is simply **-la** plus **-ko** (4.3.3), so that **ikusi duetelako gizona** (*the that-they-have-seen man*) naturally means *the man that they say they have seen*, and **delako** equals *entitled*; but the suffix can also mean *because*.

8.6.3   The phrase **d(ir)ela eta** means *about* or *for the purpose of*, e.g. **mitoak direla eta**, *about myths*.

8.7   SUBORDINATING PREFIXES

8.7.1   The prefix **ba-** usually means *if*, with different nuances according to the form of the verb, e.g. **bada**, *if he is*; **bazuen**, *if he was*; **balitz**, *if he were* (or with past participle *if he had . . .*); **baledi**, *if he should be*; **badut** (referring to the present), **badezat** (referring to the future), *if I have*; **balu**, *if he had*; **badezakezu**, *if you can*; **baleki**, *if he knew* (8.9). For the forms cf. 8.4 and note the shortening as compared with the past.

8.7.2   A different **ba-**, added to synthetic verbs (8.9) but not as a rule to auxiliaries, is simply affirmative, e.g. **Ongi bizi baziren**, *They lived happily ever after*. (**Ziren** is not an auxiliary here.)

8.7.3   **Bai(t)-** is not very precise. Its function is to indicate that the verb to which it is prefixed is in some way subordinate. It usually turns initial **b-, d-, g-,** to **p-, t-, k-,** e.g. **baitira**, *because they are*, and **z-** to **tz-**. Its commonest equivalents are *because, although, so that*, but like **-la** it may simply mean *the fact that*. Sometimes it makes relative clauses, e.g. **gizon bat ikusi baiginuen**, *a man whom we saw*, or with some interrogatives, adverbial clauses, **nola . . . bai-** means *as* (**nola**, *how?*); **zeren . . . bai-**, *for, because*; **non . . . bai-**, *so that*. Sometimes it is practically equivalent to *and* or *however*.

8.8   VERBAL NOUNS OR ADJECTIVES

8.8.1   There are four such: the past participle, which also answers in some contexts to the infinitive and under which verbs are entered in the dictionary (8.8.2 – 8.8.5); the short infinitive, which has the bare stem of the verb (8.8.6); the verbal noun, which is roughly equivalent to our infinitive or gerund (8.8.7 – 8.8.10); the gerundive (8.8.11). Between them the first and third provide periphrases for the past, present and future tense systems.

8.8.2   The commonest ending for the past participle is **-tu/-du**, this being the ending of the newer verbs. A number of common verbs end in **-n** or **-i** and there are one or two in **-o**.

8.8.3   By itself or with the article it refers, as one might expect, to the past, e.g. **Larresorok euskaratua**, *translated into Basque by Larresoro*; **ikusi du**, *he saw* (*has seen*); **joan da**, *he went*. It takes the article, as above, and if necessary a plural ending, when used as a predicate or in apposition, e.g. **egina da**, *it is done*; **egina zuen**, *he had finished it* (had it in a done state), as opposed to **egin zuen**, *he had done it*. With a word like **nahi** (0.5) or postpositions such as **gabe**, *without*, or **arte**, *until*, it will be translated by an infinitive or gerund or a clause. It can also denote an abstraction, e.g. **izana**, *the reality*.

8.8.4 With the addition of **-go/-ko** or **-(r)en** (4.3.1) it makes the future, e.g. **ikusiren (ikusiko) zuen**, *he will have seen it*; **joanen (joango) da**, *he will go*.

8.8.5 With other suffixes one mostly gets the equivalent of phrases with participles, but one must remember that in so far as it is an adjective, it can take any suffix in its normal sense.

-ta/-da (G) sometimes produces an active perfect participle, e.g. **eiztaria ikusita bildur naiz**, *having seen the hunter I am afraid*; but often it is hard to see any difference from the forms with the article, e.g. **zeŕbait geiŕuta aŕgitaratuten da**, *is being published somewhat enlarged*.

-tako/-dako (4.6.2) is the corresponding attributive adjective (cf. 1.2.1: **egindako**).

-(r)ik, by an understandable extension of its use with adjectives in apposition (4.6.2), forms absolute phrases that correspond to English participles, e.g. **batzar nagusienean bildurik**, *meeting (met) in sovereign assembly*; **lagunak joanik**, *his companions having gone*. Followed by **ere** it means *although*.

-aren should be distinguished from **-(r)en** (8.8.4). The ending has its normal meaning *of*, e.g. **ibiliaren ibiliaz**, *by dint of walking*.

-z may indicate time or cause and is equivalent to a present participle, e.g. **eri izanez**, *being ill*. Preceded by **ezin** it means *being unable to*, e.g. **ezin ikusiz**, *being unable to see*; but **ezin ikusizko** means *invisible*.

-z gero(z) means *since* or *if*.

8.8.6 The short infinitive lacks the endings **-tu/-du** or **-i**. If the participle ends in **-n**, there is generally no difference, though the **-n** may be lost before a suffix. A number of verbs ending in a vowel also have the same form for both.

It is used with the various forms of **deza** and **dedi** (8.4), e.g. **ikus dezake**, *he can see*, and in phrases like **zer egin?**, *what to do?*; **sar-athera**, *en passant*. The same form also serves as an imperative, e.g. **ikus**, *see*.

With the suffix **-ka** it means *by doing* something.

Some verbs take the suffix **-ki**, producing the idea of continuous action, e.g. **goaki zelarik**, *as he was going*.

8.8.7 The verbal noun ends in **-t(z)e**, corresponding as follows to the past participle:

-i	-lli	-rri	-(t)si	-(t)zi	-n	-o		-du/-tu
-itze	-lt(z)e	-rt(z)e	-ste	-zte	-(i)te	-otze/-oite	-tze	

In older books one sometimes finds **-dute/-tute** instead of **-tze**.

8.8.8 A very common occurrence of the verbal noun is with the suffix **-n**, making the present and imperfect tenses, e.g. **ikusten du (zuen)**, *he sees (saw)*; **joaten da (zen)**, *he is (was) going*. See also 8.8.9.

8.8.9 As it is a noun, it can take the article and the various suffixes in their usual meaning, e.g. **egi hoien jarraikitzeaz**, *by (the) following (of) these truths*. But with some suffixes it has also specialised meanings, viz.

-t(z)eari may indicate the beginning of an action;

-t(z)ean is equivalent to a present participle or a clause beginning with *as* or *when*, e.g. **irakurtzean**, *as I (he, etc.) was reading*;

-t(z)en, besides the use mentioned in 8.8.8, is used with verbs of perception, e.g. **joaten ikusi dut**, *I saw him going*;

-t(z)earekin means *while*;

-t(z)eko shows the adjectivalising function of **-ko**, e.g. **irakusteko ordua**, *time to read*, but is also found in phrases like **obeki erraiteko**, *to put it better*; **jarraitzeko**, *to be continued*;

-t(z)ez has much the same meaning as **-z** with the past participle.

8.8.10 As a noun the verbal noun may have its logical subject and object in the genitive; as a verb it will have its object in the basic form, while the subject will take **-k** or not according as the verb is transitive or intransitive. As this results in ambiguity, careful writers prefer to keep the genitive for the object (cf. 8.8.9), except in the case of **-t(z)ean**, which is always construed with the basic form.

8.8.11 The gerundive, ending in **-kizun**, has the meaning *which will, can* or *ought to be done*, e.g. **galdekizun**, *which can be asked*, i.e. *a question, query*; **etorkizun**, *future*.

8.9 SYNTHETIC VERBS

8.9.1 A few verbs are also conjugated directly, more of them in writing than in speech, e.g. as well as **zer ekartzen dizudan**, *what I am bringing you*, we can have **zer dakarzudan**, with the same elements attached to the root **-kar-** instead of to the auxiliary. Sometimes the synthetic and periphrastic forms have different senses, e.g. **dakit**, *I know*; **jakiten dut**, *I learn*.

8.9.2 *Transitive verb, present, with direct and indirect objects*

			G and L				L (DO only)			
		DO	Stem	OP	IO	S	DO	Stem	OP	S
	1	na			(ki)da/t	t	na			t
S 2		za			(kit)zu	zu	za			(t)zu
	3	da			(k)o	-	da			-
			kar					kar		
	1	ga			(ki)gu	gu	ga		tza	gu
P 2		za		z(ki)	(kit)zu(t)e	zu(t)e	za		tzate	(t)zue
	3	da			(ki)(ot)e	te	da		tza	(z)te

Examples: **dakart**, *I bring it*; **dakar(ki)t**, *he brings it to me*; **dakarzkizu**, *you bring them* (L **dakartzatzu**); *he brings them to you* (L **dakarzkitzu**); **dakarzkida(t)zu**, *you bring them to me*.

8.9.3 The past with third-person object follows the same lines, with subjects **n-**, **zen-/zin-**, **z-**; **gen-/gin-**, **zen-/zin-**, **z-** at the beginning, and **-n** at the end (8.2.3), e.g. **nekarren**, *I brought it*; **zekartzan** (L), *he brought them*; **zenekarzkidan** (G), *you brought them to me*.

With the object in the first or second person we have the objects **nind-**, **zind-**, **gind-** at the beginning and the subjects **-da-**, etc. before the final **-n**, as in 8.2.5, e.g. **nindekarzun**, *you carried me*.

8.9.4 *Intransitive verb, present, with or without indirect object*

		S	Stem	P	IO
	1	na			kit
S 2		za	tor		kizu
	3	da			kio
	1	ga			kigu
P 2		za	to(r)	z	kizute
	3	da			ki(ot)e

The forms given are G. The few forms that are still used in L are the same, but the stem is often spelt **-thor-**.

> Examples: **nat(h)or**, *I come*
> **datorkit**, *he comes to me*
> **dato(r)zkigu**, *they come to us*

8.9.5 *Past*

		S	Stem	PS	IO
	1	**nuen**			**kida**
S	2	**zen**	**etor(r)**		**kizu**
	3	**z**			**kio**
					(e)n
	1	**gen**			**kigu**
P	2	**zen**	**eto(r)**	**z**	**kizute**
	3	**z**		**z**	**ki(ot)e**

> Examples: **nuenetorren**, *I came*
> **zeto(r)zkigun**, *they came to us*

8.9.6 The past participle usually has an initial **e-** and the stem is usually obvious; but **-ki-** is the stem of **jakin**.

8.10 IRREGULAR VERBS

8.10.1 **egon**, *stay, stand, be*
Guipuzcoan
> *Present:* **nago, zaude, dago; gaude, zaudezte, dagoz/daude**
> *Imperfect:* **negon, zeunden, zegon; geunden, zeundeten, zeuden**
> *Conditional* (8.7.1): **banengo, bazeunde, balego**, etc.

Labourdin
> *Imperfect:* **nindagon, zinauden, zagon; ginauden, zinaudezten, zauden**
> *Conditional:* **banindago**, etc.

8.10.2 **ibil(l)i**, *go, walk, move*
Guipuzcoan
> *Present:* **nabil, zabiltz(a), dabil; gabiltza, zabiltzate, dabiltz(a)**
> *Imperfect:* **nebillen, zenbiltzan, zebillen; genbiltzan, zenbiltzaten, zebiltzan**

Labourdin
> *Present:* **nabila**, etc.
> *Imperfect:* **nindabilan, zinabiltzan, zabilan**, etc.

8.10.3 **juan (joan, goan)**, *go*
> *Present:* (G) **nua, zuaz, dijua; guaz, zuazte, dijuaz** (or **noa**, etc.)
> (L) **noa, zoatzi, doa; goatzi, zoazte, doatzi**
> *Imperfect:* (G) **ninjuan, zinjuazen, zijuan; ginjuazen, zinjuazten, zijuazen**
> (L) **nindoan, zinoatzin, zoan; ginoatzin, zinoazten, zoatzin**

8.10.4 **dio**, *he says*, etc., as 8.2.2.
> *Past:* **nion, zenion/zinion . . . zioten**

8.11 INTERROGATIVE

8.11.1 Special interrogative forms exist but are not obligatory. They have the suffix **-(i)a**, which may cause vowel changes, e.g. **dea?**, *is it?* (**da**, *is*); **ikusi duzuia?**, *did you see it?* There is also a separate particle **ot(h)e**, which suggests the answer *No*.

8.11.2 The suffix is not required with interrogative pronouns, adjectives or adverbs, e.g. **zer ikusi duzu?**, *what did you see?*

8.12 NEGATIVE

The negative **ez** is sometimes attached to the verb, affecting the spelling, e.g.

enuen	ez nuen
etzen	ez zen
ezkinen	ez ginen
ezpaldin	ez baldin
ezta	ez da
eztaki	ez daki
eztu	ez du

9 ADVERBS

9.1 FORMATION

9.1.1 Some adverbs are not formally distinct. A good many which denote locality end in **-(ea)n**, being formed from nouns, e.g. **gainean**, *above* (**gain**, *top*). Similarly with the suffix **-z** denoting manner or means. (Cf. 4.3.1.)

9.1.2 The suffix which converts adjectives into adverbs is **-ki/-gi**, e.g. **ongi**, *well*; **berriki**, *recently* (whereas **berrez** means *anew*).

9.2 COMPARISON

The endings **-ago**, **-egi**, and **-en** (5.3) are added after **-ki**.

10 POSTPOSITIONS

Most English prepositions are represented in Basque by suffixes (4.3.1). More complex notions may be expressed by postpositions, which are often a further noun with a suffix, following the main noun, which usually has the suffix **-(r)en**, e.g. **askatasun-aritzaren pean**, *beneath the freedom-oak* (**pe**, *bottom*); but it may have no suffix or one of the other ones, e.g. **elizari hurbil**, *near the church*. Most locative prepositions go in threes, e.g. **pean**, **pera**, **petik**, expressing rest, motion towards and motion from.

11 CONJUNCTIONS

11.1 There are the usual coordinating conjunctions such as **(e)ta** (sometimes **da**), *and*; **edo**, *or*. They have no syntactical effect. Note, however, that **eta** at the end of a clause is a subordinating conjunction meaning *because*.

11.2 Subordinating conjunctions are rarer. The verb forms which to a great extent replace them are given in 8.5–8.7. Where greater precision is needed, a noun with a suffix is used in a specialised sense, qualified by the relative form of the verb, e.g. **Euzkadiko gaztedia aurreneko gudatokietan gudakatzen dan bitartean**, *while the youth of Euzkadi is fighting in the front lines*. (Cf. 9.1.1 and 10.1.) Other words functioning as conjunctions are preceded by the past participle or short infinitive, e.g. **hori erran orduko**, *as soon as he said this*. (Note the typical position at the end of the sentence.)

GLOSSARY

agerraldi, *edition* (1.5.1)
agertu gabe, *unpublished*
agertzeko, *forthcoming*
agortu, ahitu, *out of print*
ai(n)tzin-solas, *preface*
aldizkari, *review*
ale, *issue, copy* (1.8.6)
antolatu, *revised*
antzerki, *play*
argazki, *illustration*
argipen, *commentary; edition* (1.5.1)
argitaletxe, *publishing-house*
argitalpen, *publication*
argitaralpen, *edition* (1.5.1)
argitaratu, *publish(ed)*
argitara(t)z(ai)le, *publisher*
aste, *week*
astekari, *weekly*
ateratzen da, *comes out* (1.8.5)
atzerri, *foreign country*

bakoitz, *single* (1.8.5)
banakola, *administration* (1.8.7)
banatzaile bakarra, *sole distributor*
barruan, *at home* (1.8.6)
batasun, *society, union*
batzar, *meeting*
batzorde, *commission*
batzorkide, *member*
ber, *same*
berregin, *duplicated*
berri, *new*
bibliotek(ari), *library* (-rian)
bigarren agerpen, *reprint*
bilduma, *collection, summary*
biltzar, *conference, congress*
bulego, *office* (1.8.7)
buru biltzar, *committee*

dohainik, doharik, *free*

editorial, *publishing house*
egile, *author*
egin, *compose(d)*
elaberri, *novel*
elkar-lan, *collaboration* (1.2.5)
erakusgai, *sample, specimen*

errebista, *review*
eskaintza, *complimentary*
eskatu, *order* (2.4.2)
eskubide zainduak, *all rights reserved*

gainerateko, *supplement(ary)*
geit(t)u, *enlarged* (1.5.1)
gutun, *letter*

hamabostero(ko), *fortnightly* (1.8.5)
harpide(tza), *subscription* (1.8.6)
hautatu, *selected*
helbide, *address*
hil, *die(d), dead*
hilabete, *month*
hillero(ko), *monthly* (1.8.5)
hitzaurre, *preface*
hiztegi, *dictionary*
horrialde, *page*

idazjabetasun, *copyright*
idazlan, *written work*
idazle, *writer*
imprimatzaile, *printer*
inprimategian, *in the press*
inprimategirako, *(ready) for the press*
ipui(n), *story*
iragan zenbaki, *back number*
irakurgei, *novel, writing*
irarpen, *impression*
irteteko, *forthcoming*
itzuli, *translate(d)*
itzulketa, itzulpen, *translation*
itzultzaile, *translator*
izenpean, *entitled*
izkribatu, *writ(t)e(n)*

jarraitzeko, *to be continued*
josi, *sewn*

kartonatu, *bound*
kondaira, *history*
kondu, *bill, invoice*

laburtu, *reduced*
lan, *work* (1.2.2), *article*
libereri, *bookshop*

liburu, *book, volume* (1.4.1)
liburu-etxe, *publishing-house*
liburugille, *printer*
liburuki, *volume*
liburutegi, *bookshop*
liburuxka, *pamphlet*
luzagarri, *appendix*

mintzaldi, *speech, talk*
moldatu, *compile(d), print(ed)*
moldatzaile, *compositor, typesetter*
moldiztegi, *press*
multikopiaz argitaratu, *duplicated*

nobela, *novel*

oharpen, *note*
oihalezko (oya-), *in cloth*
orraikotu, *brought up to date*
orraztatu, *correct(ed)*

pai, *page*
prezio, *price*

saiakera, *essay*
salgai, salmetan, *on sale*
sari, *prize, price*
sarrera, *introduction*
seña, *order*
separata, *offprint*
solas ondo, *appendix, epilogue*
sorta, *collection, series* (1.7.1)
sortu, *born*

urririk, *free*
urt(h)e, *year, volume* (1.8.4)
urt(h)ekari, *yearbook*

zati, *part* (1.4.1)
zenbaki, *number, copy* (1.7.2, 1.8.4)
zuzenbide, *address*
zuzendari(tza), *editor(ship)* (1.2.2, 1.8.3)
zuzendu, *corrected*

GRAMMATICAL INDEX: WORDS AND PREFIXES

GRAMMATICAL INDEX: MIDDLES

As ending may be piled on ending, elements which occur in the middle of a word may be indexed as endings.

GRAMMATICAL INDEX: ENDINGS

-kiote, 8.9.4

-zute, 8.2.1, 8.2.2, 8.3.2,
8.9.2

-kizute, 8.9.4

-zte, 8.2.1, 8.2.2, 8.8.7

-zue, 8.2.1, 8.2.2, 8.3.2,
8.9.2

-tze, 8.8.7

-i, -ai, -ei, 4.3.1

-gi, 9.1.2

-egi, 4.3.3

-ki, 9.1.2

-zki, 8.2.2

-ri, 4.3.1

-t(z)eari, 8.8.9

-eri, 4.3.1

-tzi, 8.2.2

-(e)k, 1.2.2, 4.3.1, 4.6.1.,
6.4.2

-ik, -dik, -gandik, 4.3.1,
4.6.1

-rik, 4.3.1, 4.6.1, 8.8.5

-larik, 8.6.2

-tarik, 4.3.1

-tik, -gatik, -etatik, 4.3.1

-ok, 4.3.1

-n, 4.3.1, 8.4.4, 8.5

-dan, 8.2.4, 8.2.5, 8.3.4,
8.9.3

-kidan, 8.9.5

-ean, 4.3.2, 9.1.1

-t(z)ean, 8.8.9

-gan, 4.3.1

-tan, 4.3.1

-tzan, 9.9.3

-en, 1.2.3, 4.3.1, 4.6.1,
5.3.2, 8.2.3, 8.2.5, 8.3.4,
8.8.4, 8.9.3, 9.2

-kien, 8.9.5

-ren, 1.2.3, 4.3.1, 8.8.4

-garren, 6.2

-ten, 8.2.3, 8.8.8, 8.8.9

-eten, -zueten, 8.2.4, 8.2.5

-oten, 8.2.4, 8.2.5, 8.3.4,
8.9.3

-kioten, 8.9.5

-zuten, 8.2.4, 8.2.5, 8.3.4,
8.9.3

-kizuten, 8.9.5

-zten, 8.2.3, 8.8.8., 8.8.9

-zuen, 8.2.4, 8.2.5, 8.9.3

-kizuen, 8.9.5

-tzen, 8.8.8, 8.8.9

-ekin/-okin, 4.3.1

-t(z)earekin, 8.8.9

-on, 4.3.1, 8.2.4, 8.3.4

-zun, -gun, 8.2.4, 8.2.5,
8.3.4, 8.9.3

-kizun, 8.8.11, 8.9.5

-o, 8.2.2, 8.3.2

-go, 4.3.1, 8.8.4

-ago, 5.3.1, 9.2

-kio, 8.9.4

-ko, 1.1.2, 4.3.1, 4.6.1,
8.8.4

-dako, 8.8.5

-lako, 8.6.2

-tako, 8.8.5

-etako/-otako, 4.3.1

-t(z)ko, 8.8.9

-raino, -raño, 4.3.1

-tar, 1.1.2

-t, 8.2.1, 8.2.2, 8.3.2, 8.9.2

-rat, 4.3.1

-tzat, -kotzat, -rentzat,
4.3.1

-kit, 8.9.4

-du, 8.8.2

-gu, 8.2.1, 8.2.2, 8.3.2,
8.9.2

-kigu, 8.9.4

-tu, 8.8.2

-zu, 8.2.1, 8.2.2, 8.3.2,
8.9.2

-kizu, 8.9.4

-tzu, 8.2.1, 8.2.2, 8.3.2,
8.9.2

-z, 4.3.1, 5.3.1, 8.8.5, 9.1.1

-ez, 4.3.1

-t(z)ez, 8.8.9

-rantz, 4.3.1

ESPERANTO: A NOTE

SPECIMEN

Necesis reviziigi
Estas nekredeble, ke la kompilinto-tradukinto de ĉi tiu antologieto de skandinaviaj poemoj kaj rakontoj kapablis mem fari tiom da eraroj gramatikaj, sintaksaj kaj eĉ ortografiaj. Povus ŝajni, ke li konfidis la transtajpon de sia verko al iu nekompetentulo, kies ambicio estis "plibonigi" ĝian lingvaĵon. Troviĝas ja en ĝi apenaŭ kelkaj paĝoj tute liberaj de iaj lingvaj misaĵoj.
  Mendu ĉe UEA.

He should have had it revised
It is unbelievable that the compiler-translator of this little anthology of Scandinavian poems and stories should himself have been capable of making such a quantity of grammatical, syntactical and even orthographical errors. It would seem that he entrusted the typing of his work to some incompetent whose ambition it was to 'improve' its language. Only a few pages are to be found in it which are quite free from some sort of linguistic mistakes.
  Order from UEA.

GENERAL

Although it would be improper to class Esperanto as a European language, its European origin and the number of periodicals in particular which are current in Europe make it desirable to provide some notes on the language; but as it is markedly regular not much needs to be said. It is moderately synthetic, inasmuch as it distinguishes subject and object by termination and has six different participles; but it makes great use of prepositions and the verb requires subject pronouns. Word order is free, and as OSV is almost as common as SVO, one needs to watch for the -n of the object. Words are formed from a number of roots by the use of some thirty suffixes, the most important of which are listed below, and a few prefixes. The source of most of the vocabulary is the Greek-Latin-Romance stock, but there are a number of common words of Germanic origin, e.g. **jaro, tago** (*year, day*), **helpi, ŝajn-** (*appear*), and some, e.g. **klopod-** (*endeavour*), which are Slavonic.

BIBLIOLINGUISTICS

The use of the language in books calls for little comment. Authors' names are usually left in their native form, though some authors have from time to time adopted Esperanto forms, e.g. **Vilêjo Verda** for *Will Green*. The name, whatever it is, is not modified in statements of authorship. More disconcerting is the occasional phonetic transcription of a title such as **Wiener Zeitung** as **Viner Cajtung**. Titles may also receive the **-n** of the object, as in **Ili verkis la Kudran kaj trikan terminaron,** *They wrote the* '*Kudra kaj trika terminaro*' (*Sewing and knitting glossary*).

Information about periodicals is given in a variety of ways, for stylistically Esperanto is hospitable and native phraseology tends to influence the choice of expression; but there are no grammatical complications.

ALPHABET, PHONETICS, ORTHOGRAPHY

The alphabet is as follows:

a b c ĉ d e f g ĝ h ĥ i j ĵ k l m n o p r
s ŝ t u ŭ v z

Each letter has a separate alphabetical position. A knowledge of the pronunciation of some of the letters will help to make words more recognisable. The corresponding English values are given, viz.

c	ĉ	ĝ	ĥ	j	ĵ	ŝ	ŭ
ts	ch	j	ch in *loch*	y	s in *pleasure*	sh	w

The evidence of a wide range of Esperanto periodicals suggests that there are no universally accepted rules of capitalisation or word division. Capitals are somewhat sparingly used, not for instance for months or days of the week, nor need they be for the titles of books. Institutions for the most part have capitals throughout. In word division rules 4 and 5a with a not too pedantic application of 1 and 2 will keep one close to the consensus; but the fact that the Universala Esperanto-Asocio can divide **mer-itus** suggests a fair degree of tolerance. (For the rules see p. xiii.)

GRAMMAR

Grammatical notions are expressed by differences of ending. These are arranged here by the last letter.

- **-a**: adjectival. Esperanto adjectives often correspond to nouns used attributively in English; cf. **kudra kaj trika** above. **La** is the definite article.
- **-ia**: possessives, from pronouns in **-i**, also **ia, kia**, etc., *sort of* (see under **-u**). **Tria,** *third*.
- **-anta, -inta, -onta**: active participles, present, past and future. They are adjectives and usually correspond to relative clauses; with **esti** they form compound tenses, e.g. **mi estas leganta**, *I am reading*; **mi estis leginta**, *I had read*.
- **-ata, -ita, -ota**: passive participles; cf. **-anta**, etc. They may be used with **esti** to form the passive.
- **-e**: adverbs and indefinite predicates, e.g. **bone**, *well*; **ŝajne**, *apparently*; **jare**, *annually*; **estas komprenable**, *it is understandable*. For **-ante**, see **-anta**. For **kie, tie**, etc., see under **-u**. **De** is a preposition.
- **-i**: infinitives; the numeral **tri**; and the personal pronouns **mi, vi, li, ŝi, ĝi** (*it*); **ni, vi, ili**, the indefinite **oni** (*one*), and the reflexive **si**.
- **-j**: plural of nouns, pronouns and adjectives.
- **-al**: adverbs of reason; **-el**: adverbs of manner. For details see **-u**.
- **-am**: adverbs of time; **-om**: adverbs of quantity. For details see **-u**.

-n: the accusative, mostly object (or objective), added to nouns, adjectives and pronouns, singular and plural (i.e. **-jn**) and to adverbs of place, e.g. **iri hejmen, tien**, *to go home, somewhere*. It is also used for length of time, measure and in dates.

-o: nouns and some pronouns, e.g. **tio**, *that*, for which see **-u**.

-anto, -into, -onto: nouns corresponding to active participles (see **-anta**). The **-anto** and **-into** forms commonly denote agents (cf. **eldonanto, verkinto**).

-s: tenses; **-as**, present; **-is**, past; **-os**, future, **-us**, conditional.

-es: possessive. For details see **-u**.

-u: imperative/subjunctive, e.g. **(oni) sendu**, (*you are to*) *send*; **ke ĝi klopodu**, *that it should endeavour*. There is also an important set of pronouns: **iu**, *some*(*one*), at times almost an indefinite article; **kiu**, *who, which*; **tiu**, *that* (**ĉi tiu**, *this*); **ĉiu**, *every, all*; **neniu**, *no*(*one*). The prefixes are applied to the other endings noted above, making similar sets. **Unu, du** are numerals, **ĉu** an interrogative particle (**ĉu . . . ĉu**, *whether . . . or*).

The numerals **unu, du, tri, kvar, kvin, ses, sep, ok, nau, dek, cent, mil** combine to form the remaining ones, e.g. **dekdu**, *12*; **dudek** (beware!) *20*. Dates have ordinals, which add **-a**, for day and year. The formatives **-obl-, -on-, -foje** denote multiples, fractions and repetitions respectively.

There is a preference for the active voice, e.g. **redaktis, eldonas** X rather than **redaktita, eldonata de X.**

WORD-FORMATION

Word-formation lies at the heart of Esperanto. Of the prefixes **el-**, *out* (not to be confused with **al-**, *to*), **ge-** and **mal-** may cause some initial difficulty. **Elangligis**, for instance, means the same as **tradukis el la angla**, *translated from the English*. **Ge-** denotes both sexes together: sometimes the meaning scarcely differs from that of the original word, e.g. **geamikoj**, sometimes the change is important, e.g. **patro**, *father*; **gepatroj**, *parents*. **Mal-** makes opposites, and what are primary words in English may be **mal-** forms in Esperanto, e.g. **malfermi**, *to open*; **maldekstra**, *left*; **malantaŭ**, *behind*.

The principal suffixes are **-ado**, activity, e.g. **agado**, *action*; **-aĵo**, thing done, e.g. **eldonaĵo** (see below); **-ano**, member, e.g. **senatano**; **-aro** collectivity, e.g. **registaro**, *government*; **-ebla**, possible, e.g. **havigebla**; **-eco**, quality, e.g. **facileco**; **-ejo**, place of activity, e.g. **presejo**; **-enda**, that should be done, e.g. **pagenda**, *payable*; **-ig-**, causative, e.g. **starigi**, *to set up* (**stari**, *to stand*); **-iĝ-**, intransitive, becoming, e.g. **interesiĝi**, *to be interested*, **fondiĝo**, *foundation*; **-ilo**, instrument, e.g. **informilo**; **-inda**, worthy, e.g. **laŭdinda**; **-ino**, female, e.g. **patrino**, *mother*; **-isto**, profession, e.g. **eldonisto**; **-ujo**, container, country. (Some writers prefer **-io** in the names of countries, e.g. **Anglio**, not **Anglujo**.) The suffixes are given in their commonest form, but other grammatical endings are possible.

GLOSSARY

abon(ad)o, and compounds of **abon-**, *subscription*
aĉeti, *to buy*
akirebla, *obtainable*

aldono, *addition, appendix*
antaŭparolo, *preface*
baldaŭ aperos, *will appear shortly*
laste aperis, *recently published*

bibliotekisto, *librarian*
bildo, *illustration*
bindita, *bound*
broŝita, *paper-covered*
broŝuro, *pamphlet, paperback*

ĉefredaktoro, *chief editor*
ĉiuj rajtoj rezervitaj, *all rights reserved*

daŭrig|o, -ita, *continu|ation, -ed*
demando, *enquiry*
dumonata, *bi-monthly*
duoblaĵo, *duplicate*
duonmonata, *semi-monthly*
dusemajno, *fortnight*

eksterlando, *foreign country*
ekzemplero, *copy*
elĉerpita, *out of print*
eldonaĵo, *publication*
eldonanto, *publisher* (of this work)
eldonejo, *publishing house*
eldonisto, *publisher* (by profession)
eldono, *edition*
elektita, *selected*
eltiraĵo, *offprint*
enhavo, *contents*
enkonduko, *introduction*

fakturo, *bill*
favorpreze, *at a discount*

havigebla, *obtainable*

informilo, *report*
interŝanĝi, *exchange*

jare, *annually*
jarkolekto, *annual volume*
jarlibro, *yearbook*
jaro, *year*

kolekto, *collection*
koncizigita, *abridged*
kondiĉe, *on approval*
kunlaborantoj, *assistant editors*
kvaronjar|a, -e, *quarterly*

laste, *recently*
leganto, *reader*

mallongigi, *to abridge*
mendo, *order*
monat|a, -e, *monthly*

naskita, *born*
novelo, *short story*

okazi, *to take place*

pagi, *to pay*
paĝo, *page*
parolado, *speech*
periodaĵo, *periodical*
plibonigi, *to improve*
pojare, *per year*
presejo, *press*
provnumero, *specimen copy*

rabato, *discount*
redakcio, *editorial office* or *board*
redakti, *to edit*
redaktoro, *editor*
re-eldono, *reprint*
renkontiĝo, *meeting*
repres(aĵ)o, *reprint*
resendi, *to return*
respondeca, *responsible*
romano, *novel*

sama, *same*
sekvas daŭrigo, fino, *to be continued, concluded*
senpage, *free*
serio, *series*
sidejo, *seat*

teatraĵo, *play*
temi, *to deal with*
tradu|ki, -ko, *translate, -tion*

unuafoje, *for the first time*
unuopa, *single*

verkaro, (*collected*) *works*
verki, *to write*
verkint(in)o, *author* (of this work)
verkist(in)o, *author* (professional)
vortaro, *dictionary*